lonely planet

New Z____ (Aotearoa)

**Bay of Islands
& Northland**
(p123)

Auckland
(p62)

**Waikato &
Coromandel
Peninsula**
(p166)

**Rotorua &
the Bay of Plenty**
(p278)

**Taupo & the
Central Plateau** (p250)

**Taranaki &
Whanganui**
(p216)

The East Coast
(p319)

**Marlborough
& Nelson**
(p382)

**Wellington
Region**
(p351)

The West Coast
(p425)

**Christchurch
& Canterbury**
(p457)

**Queenstown
& Wanaka**
(p540)

**Dunedin
& Otago**
(p508)

**Fiordland &
Southland**
(p575)

THIS EDITION WRITTEN AND RESEARCHED BY
Charles Rawlings-Way,
Brett Atkinson, Sarah Bennett, Peter Dragicevich, Lee Slater

Contents

PLAN YOUR TRIP

MATTEO COLOMBO/GETTY IMAGES ©

AUCKLAND P63

DOUG PEARSON/GETTY IMAGES ©

MT TARANAKI P226

ON THE ROAD

Contents

Welcome to New Zealand

As the planet heats up environmentally and politically, it's good to know that New Zealand exists. This uncrowded, green, peaceful and accepting country is the ultimate escape.

Walk on the Wild Side

There are just 4.6 million New Zealanders, scattered across 268,021 sq km: bigger than the UK with one-fourteenth the population. Filling in the gaps are the sublime forests, mountains, lakes, beaches and fiords that have made NZ one of the best hiking (locals call it 'tramping') destinations on earth. Tackle one of nine epic 'Great Walks' – you've probably heard of the Heaphy and Milford Tracks – or just spend a few hours wandering along a beach, paddling a canoe or mountain biking through some easily accessible wilderness.

The Real 'Big Easy'

Forget New Orleans... NZ can rightly claim the 'Big Easy' crown for the sheer ease of travel here. This isn't a place where you encounter many on-the-road frustrations: buses and trains run on time; roads are in good nick; ATMs proliferate; pickpockets, scam merchants and bedbug-ridden hostels are few and far between; and the food is unlikely to send you running for the nearest public toilets (usually clean and stocked with the requisite paper). And there are no snakes, and only one poisonous spider – the rare katipo, sightings of which are considered lucky. This decent nation is a place where you can relax and enjoy (rather than endure) your holiday.

Māori Culture

If you're even remotely interested in rugby, you'll have heard of NZ's all-conquering All Blacks, who would never have become back-to-back world champions without their unstoppable Māori players. But this is just one example of how Māori culture impresses itself on contemporary Kiwi life: across NZ you can hear Māori language, watch Māori TV, see main-street *marae* (meeting houses), join in a *hangi* (Māori feast) or catch a cultural performance with traditional Māori song, dance and usually a blood-curdling *haka* (war dance). You might draw the line at contemplating *ta moko*, traditional Māori tattooing (often applied to the face).

Food, Wine & Beer

Kiwi food was once a bland echo of a boiled British Sunday roast – but these days NZ chefs find inspiration in new-world culinary oceans, especially the South Pacific with its abundant seafood and encircling cuisines. And don't go home without seeking out some local faves: paua (abalone), kina (sea urchin) and kumara (sweet potato). For picnic fodder, head to NZ's fab farmers markets. Thirsty? NZ's cool-climate wineries have been filling trophy cabinets for decades (sublime pinot noir and sauvignon blanc), and the country's craft-beer scene is exploding. Contemporary coffee culture is also firmly entrenched.

Why I Love New Zealand

By Charles Rawlings-Way, Writer

As an English-born Australian, every trip to New Zealand presents a mix of landscapes and cultures that's at once familiar to me, and yet quirkily different. The rolling hills and hedgerows collude with the irreverent, easygoing locals to disarm, distract and delight. Māori culture is potent, the surf is world class, and the craft beer is awesome. NZ presents the best of old and new worlds with social and environmental sensibilities: a template for a new world order, perhaps? I love NZ!

For more about our writers, see page 672

Above: Aoraki/Mt Cook (p503)

New Zealand

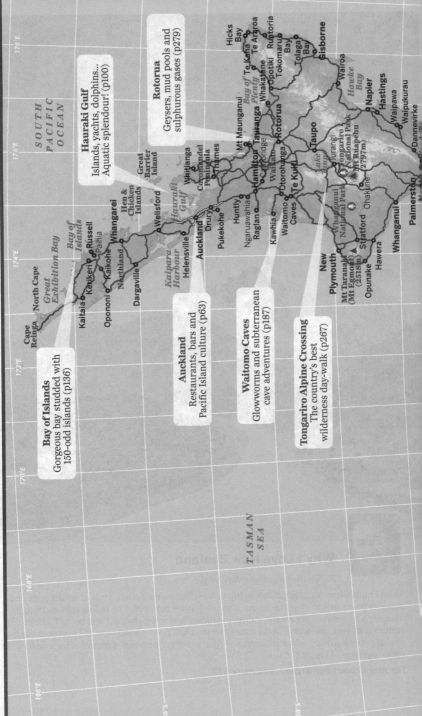

Bay of Islands
Gorgeous bay studded with
150-odd islands (p136)

Hauraki Gulf
Islands, yachts, dolphins...
Aquatic splendour! (p100)

Rotorua
Geysers, mud pools and
sulphurous gases (p279)

Auckland
Restaurants, bars and
Pacific Island culture (p63)

Waitomo Caves
Glowworms and subterranean
cave adventures (p187)

Tongariro Alpine Crossing
The country's best
wilderness day-walk (p267)

SOUTH
PACIFIC
OCEAN

TASMAN
SEA

0   200 km
0   100 miles

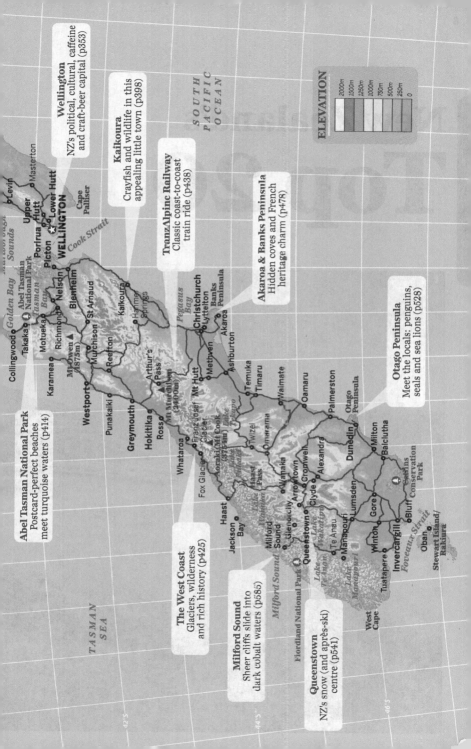

Wellington
NZ's political, cultural, caffeine and craft-beer capital (p353)

Kaikoura
Crayfish and wildlife in this appealing little town (p398)

TranzAlpine Railway
Classic coast-to-coast train ride (p438)

Akaroa & Banks Peninsula
Hidden coves and French heritage charm (p478)

Otago Peninsula
Meet the locals: penguins, seals and sea lions (p528)

Abel Tasman National Park
Postcard-perfect beaches meet turquoise waters (p414)

The West Coast
Glaciers, wilderness and rich history (p425)

Milford Sound
Sheer cliffs slide into dark cobalt waters (p585)

Queenstown
NZ's snow (and après-ski) centre (p541)

SOUTH
PACIFIC
OCEAN

TASMAN
SEA

Cook Strait

ELEVATION

2000m
1500m
1250m
1000m
750m
500m
250m
0

New Zealand's
Top 20

1

Waiheke Island & the Hauraki Gulf

1 A yachty's paradise, the island-studded Hauraki Gulf (p100) is Auckland's aquatic playground, sheltering its harbour and east-coast bays and providing ample excuse for the City of Sails' pleasure fleet to breeze into action. Despite the busy maritime traffic, the gulf has its own resident pods of whales and dolphins. Rangitoto Island is an icon of the city, its near-perfect volcanic cone providing the backdrop for many a tourist snapshot. Yet it's Waiheke, with its beautiful beaches, acclaimed wineries and upmarket eateries, that is Auckland's most popular island escape. Bottom left: Matiatia wharf, Waiheke Island (p102)

Urban Auckland

2 Held in the embrace of two harbours and built on the remnants of long-extinct volcanoes, Auckland (p62) isn't your average metropolis. It's regularly rated one of the world's most liveable cities, and while it's never going to challenge NYC or London in the excitement stakes, it's blessed with good beaches, is flanked by wine regions and has a large enough population to support a thriving dining, drinking and live-music scene. Cultural festivals are celebrated with gusto in this ethnically diverse city, which has the distinction of having the world's largest Pacific Islander population.

TROY WEGMAN / SHUTTERSTOCK ©

AMOS CHAPPLE / GETTY IMAGES ©

2

Wellington

3 One of the coolest little capitals in the world, windy Wellington (p353) lives up to the hype by keeping things hip, diverse and rootsy. It's long famed for a vibrant arts-and-music scene, fuelled by excellent espresso and more restaurants per head than New York...but a host of craft-beer bars have now elbowed in on the action. Edgy yet sociable, colourful yet often dressed in black, Wellington is big on the unexpected and unconventional. Erratic weather only adds zest to the experience. Below: *The Albatross* sculpture by Tanya Ashken on Wellington's waterfront

Bay of Islands

4 Turquoise waters lapping in pretty bays, dolphins frolicking at the bows of boats, pods of orcas gliding gracefully by: chances are these are the kinds of images that drew you to NZ in the first place, and these are exactly the kinds of experiences that the Bay of Islands (p136) delivers so well. Whether you're a hardened sea dog or a confirmed landlubber, there are myriad options to tempt you out on the water to explore the 150-odd islands that dot this beautiful bay. Top right: Urupukapuka Island (p147)

Kaikoura

5 First settled by Māori with their taste for seafood, Kaikoura (p398) (meaning 'to eat crayfish') is now NZ's best spot for both consuming and communing with marine life. Crayfish is still king, but on fishing tours you can hook into other edible wonders of the deep. Whales, dolphins and seals are definitely off the menu – but it's big business here to take a boat tour or flight to see them. Such tours attract controversy around the globe, but NZ's operators adhere to strict guidelines developed and monitored by the country's Department of Conservation. Left: Dolphin off the Kaikoura coast

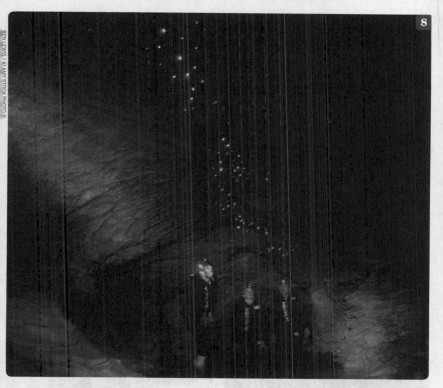

BEN LEWIS / A1 AMY STOCK PHOTO ©

The West Coast

6 Hemmed in by the wild Tasman Sea and the Southern Alps, the West Coast (p425) is like nowhere else in New Zealand. The far extremities of the coast have a remote, end-of-the-road vibe, from sleepy Karamea butting up against Kahurangi National Park, to the southern end of SH6, gateway to New Zealand's World Heritage Areas. In between is an alluring combination of wild coastline, rich wilderness, 'must see' sights like Punakaiki Rocks and Franz Josef and Fox Glaciers, and history in spades. Top left: Franz Josef Glacier (p447)

Geothermal Rotorua

7 The first thing you'll notice about Rotorua (p279) is the sulphur smell – this geothermal hotspot whiffs like old socks. But as the locals point out, volcanic by-products are what everyone is here to see: geysers, bubbling mud steaming cracks in the ground, boiling pools of mineral-rich water... Rotorua is unique: a fact exploited by some fairly commercial local businesses. But you don't have to spend a fortune while here – there are plenty of affordable (and free) volcanic encounters to be had in parks, Māori villages or just along the roadside. Bottom left: Champagne Pool (p295)

Waitomo Caves

8 Waitomo (p187) is a must-see: an astonishing maze of subterranean caves, canyons and rivers perforating the northern King Country limestone. Black-water rafting is the big lure here (like whitewater rafting but through a dark cave), plus glowworm grottoes, underground abseiling and more stalactites and stalagmites than you'll ever see in one place again. Above ground, Waitomo township is a quaint collaboration of businesses: a craft brewery, a cafe, a holiday park and some decent B&Bs. But don't linger in the sunlight – it's party time downstairs!

23PICTURES/ SHUTTERSTOCK ©

GLYN KIRK / GETTY IMAGES ©

Tongariro Alpine Crossing

9 At the centre of the North Island, Tongariro National Park (p266) presents an alien landscape of alpine desert punctuated by three smoking and smouldering volcanoes. This track offers the perfect taste of what the park has to offer, skirting the base of two of the mountains and providing views of craters, brightly coloured lakes and the vast Central Plateau stretching out beyond. It's for these reasons that it's often rated as one of the world's best single-day wilderness walks. Top left: Emerald Lakes (p268), Tongariro National Park

Rugby

10 Rugby Union is NZ's national game and governing preoccupation. If your timing's good you might catch the revered national team (and reigning back-to-back world champions), the All Blacks, in action. The 'ABs' are resident gods: drop any of their names into a conversation and you'll win friends for life. Visit the New Zealand Rugby Museum (p244) in Palmerston North, watch some kids running around a suburban field on a Saturday morning, or yell along with the locals in a small-town pub as the big men collide on the big screen. Top centre: All Blacks celebrating their 2015 World Cup win

Abel Tasman National Park

11 Here's nature at its most seductive: lush green hills fringed with golden sandy coves, slipping gently into warm shallows before meeting a crystal-clear cerulean sea. Abel Tasman National Park (p414) is the quintessential postcard paradise, where you can put yourself in the picture assuming an endless number of poses: tramping, kayaking, swimming, sunbathing, or even makin' whoopee in the woods. This sweet-as corner of NZ raises the bar and keeps it there.

THOMAS PICKARD / GETTY IMAGES ©

Māori Culture

12 NZ's indigenous Māori culture (p626) is accessible and engaging: join in a *haka* (war dance); chow down at a traditional *hangi* (Māori feast cooked in the ground); carve a pendant from bone or *pounamu* (jade); learn some Māori language; or check out an authentic cultural performance with song, dance, legends, arts and crafts. Big-city and regional museums around NZ are crammed with Māori artefacts and historical items, but this is truly a living culture: vibrant, potent and contemporary. Bottom right: Māori woman and man greet with a traditional *hongi*

BLAINE HARRINGTON III / ALAMY STOCK PHOTO ©

Otago Peninsula

13 The Otago Peninsula (p528) is proof that there's more to the South Island's natural thrills than alpine and lake scenery. Along with a constant backdrop of coastal vistas, the peninsula offers some of the best opportunities for wildlife spotting in the country. Dozens of little penguins achieve peak cuteness in their nightly beachside waddle, while their much rarer yellow-eyed cousin, the hoiho, can be glimpsed standing sentinel on deserted coves. Sea lions and seals laze around on the rocks while albatross from the world's only mainland colony soar above. Bottom left: Hangglider above the Otago Peninsula

Heaphy Track

14 Beloved of NZ trampers, and now mountain bikers in winter, the four-to six-day Heaphy Track (p422) is the jewel of Kahurangi National Park, the great wilderness spanning the South Island's northwest corner. Highlights include the mystical Gouland Downs and surreal nikau palm coast, while the townships at either end – at Golden Bay and Karamea – will bring you back down to earth with the most laid-back of landings.

DAVID WALL PHOTO / GETTY IMAGES ©

Central Otago

15 Here's your chance to balance virtue and vice. Take to two wheels to negotiate the easygoing Otago Central Rail Trail, cycling through some of NZ's most starkly beautiful landscapes (p531) and the heritage streetscapes of former gold-mining towns. All the while, snack on the summer stone-fruit for which the region is famous. Balance the ledger with well-earned beers at one of the numerous historic pubs. Alternatively, taste your way to viticultural ecstasy in the vineyards of one of the country's most acclaimed wine regions. Top: Otago Central Rail Trail (p536), near Omakau

Skiing & Snowboarding

16 New Zealand is studded with some massive mountains, and you're guaranteed to find decent snow right through the winter season (June to October). Most of the famous slopes are on the South Island: hip Queenstown (p541) and hippie Wanaka (p566) are where you want to be, with iconic ski runs like Coronet Peak, the Remarkables and Treble Cone close at hand. There are also dedicated snowboarding and cross-country (Nordic) snow parks here. And on the North Island, Mt Ruapehu offers the chance to ski down a volcano. Above: Snowboarder, Coronet Peak (p547)

Milford Sound

17 Fingers crossed you'll be lucky enough to see Milford Sound (p585) on a clear, sunny day. That's definitely when the world-beating collage of waterfalls, verdant cliffs and peaks, and dark cobalt waters is at its best. More likely, though, is the classic Fiordland combination of mist and drizzle, with the iconic profile of Mitre Peak revealed slowly through shimmering sheets of precipitation. Either way, keep your eyes peeled for seals and dolphins, especially if you're exploring NZ's most famous fiord by kayak.

Queenstown

18 Queenstown (p541) may be world-renowned as the birthplace of bungy jumping, but there's more to NZ's adventure hub than leaping off a bridge attached to a giant rubber band. Against the scenic backdrop of the jagged indigo profile of the Remarkables mountain range, travellers can spend days skiing, hiking or mountain biking, before dining in cosmopolitan restaurants or partying in some of NZ's best bars. Next-day options include hang gliding, kayaking or river rafting, or easing into your NZ holiday with sleepier detours to Arrowtown or Glenorchy.

17

AGE FOTOSTOCK / ALAMY STOCK PHOTO ©

WILLGA9LI / GETTY IMAGES ©

TranzAlpine Railway

19 One of the world's most scenic train journeys, the TranzAlpine (p438) cuts clear across the country from the Pacific Ocean to the Tasman Sea in less than five hours. Yes, there's a dirty great mountain range in the way – that's where the scenic part comes in. Leaving the Canterbury Plains, a cavalcade of tunnels and viaducts takes you up through the Southern Alps to Arthur's Pass, where the 8.5km Otira tunnel burrows right through the bedrock of NZ's alpine spine. Then it's all downhill (but only literally) to sleepy Greymouth.

Akaroa & Banks Peninsula

20 Infused with Gallic ambience, French-themed Akaroa (p480) bends languidly around one of the prettiest harbours on Banks Peninsula. The world's rarest dolphin inhabits clear waters perfect for kayaking and sailing. Elsewhere on the peninsula, the Summit Rd snakes around the rim of an ancient volcano while winding side roads descend off to hidden bays and coves. Spend your days discovering the peninsula's many surprises on land and sea, then relax at night in some of the country's most atmospheric accommodation. Bottom right: Lighthouse, Akaroa (p480)

Need to Know

For more information, see Survival Guide (p639)

Currency
New Zealand dollar ($)

Language
English, Māori and New
Zealand Sign Language

Visas
Citizens of Australia, the
UK and 58 other coun-
tries don't need visas
for New Zealand (length-
of-stay allowances vary).
See www.immigration.
govt.nz.

Money
ATMs are widely avail-
able in cities and larger
towns. Credit cards
accepted in most hotels
and restaurants.

Mobile Phones
European phones will
work on NZ's network,
but most American or
Japanese phones will
not. Use global roaming
or a local SIM card and
pre-paid account.

Time
New Zealand time is
GMT/UTC plus 12 hours
(two hours ahead of
Australian Eastern
Standard Time).

When to Go

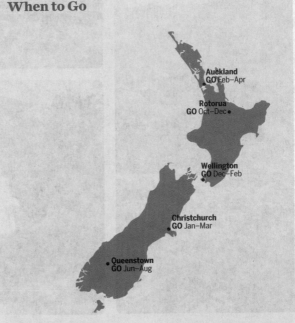

Auckland
GO Feb–Apr

Rotorua
GO Oct–Dec

Wellington
GO Dec–Feb

Christchurch
GO Jan–Mar

Queenstown
GO Jun–Aug

High Season
(Dec–Feb)

➡ Summer: busy
beaches, outdoor
explorations,
festivals and sporting
events.

➡ Big-city
accommodation
prices rise.

➡ High season in the
ski towns is winter
(Jun–Aug).

Shoulder Season
(Mar–Apr)

➡ Prime travelling
time: fine weather,
short queues, kids in
school and warm(ish)
ocean.

➡ Long evenings
sipping Kiwi wines
and craft beers.

➡ Spring (Sep–Nov)
is shoulder season,
too.

Low Season
(May–Aug)

➡ Head for
the slopes of
the Southern
Alps for some
brilliant southern-
hemisphere skiing.

➡ No crowds, good
accommodation
deals and a seat in
any restaurant.

➡ Warm-weather
beach towns may be
half asleep.

Useful Websites

100% Pure New Zealand (www.newzealand.com) Official tourism site.

Department of Conservation (www.doc.govt.nz) DOC parks and camping info.

Lonely Planet (www.lonelyplanet.com/new-zealand) Destination information, hotel bookings, traveller forum and more.

Destination New Zealand (www.destination-nz.com) Resource-packed tourism site.

DineOut (www.dineout.co.nz) Restaurant reviews.

Te Ara (www.teara.govt.nz) Online encyclopedia of NZ.

Important Numbers

Regular NZ phone numbers have a two-digit area code followed by a seven-digit number. When dialling within a region, the area code is still required. Drop the initial 0 if dialling from abroad.

NZ country code	✆64
International access code from NZ	✆00
Emergency (Ambulance, Fire, Police)	✆111
Directory Assistance	✆018
International Directory	✆0172

Exchange Rates

Australia	A$1	NZ$1.10
Canada	C$1	NZ$1.15
China	Y10	NZ$2.40
Euro zone	€1	NZ$1.62
Japan	¥100	NZ$1.25
Singapore	S$1	NZ$1.08
UK	UK£1	NZ$2.31
US	US$1	NZ$1.53

For current exchange rates see www.xe.com.

Daily Costs

Budget:
Less than $150

➡ Dorm beds or campsites: $25–38 per night

➡ Main course in a budget eatery: less than $15

➡ Explore NZ with a Naked Bus or InterCity bus pass: five trips from $151

Midrange: $150–250

➡ Double room in a midrange hotel/motel: $120–200

➡ Main course in a midrange restaurant: $15–32

➡ Hire a car and explore further: from $30 per day

Top End:
More than $250

➡ Double room in a top-end hotel: from $200

➡ Three-course meal in a classy restaurant: $80

➡ Domestic flight Auckland to Christchurch: from $100

Opening Hours

Opening hours vary seasonally (eg Dunedin is quiet during winter), but use the following as a general guide. Note that most places close on Christmas Day and Good Friday.

Banks 9.30am–4.30pm Monday to Friday, some also 9am–noon Saturday

Cafes 7am–4pm

Post Offices 8.30am–5pm Monday to Friday; larger branches also 9.30am–1pm Saturday

Pubs & Bars noon–late ('late' varies by region, and day)

Restaurants noon–2.30pm and 6.30–9pm

Shops & Businesses 9am–5.30pm Monday to Friday and 9am to noon or 5pm Saturday

Supermarkets 8am–7pm, often 9pm or later in cities

Arriving in New Zealand

Auckland Airport (p652) Airbus Express buses run into the city every 10 to 30 minutes, 24 hours. Door-to-door shuttle buses run 24 hours. A taxi into the city costs $75 to $90 (45 minutes).

Wellington Airport (p652) Airport Flyer buses run into the city every 10 to 20 minutes from 6.30am to 9.30pm. Door-to-door shuttle buses run 24 hours. A taxi into the city costs around $30 (20 minutes).

Christchurch Airport (p652) Christchurch Metro Purple Line runs into the city regularly from 6.45am to 11pm. Door-to-door shuttles run 24 hours. A taxi into the city costs around $50 (20 minutes).

Getting Around

New Zealand is long and skinny, and many roads are two-lane country byways: getting from A to B requires some thought.

Car Travel at your own tempo, explore remote areas and visit regions with no public transport. Hire cars in major towns. Drive on the left; the steering wheel is on the right (...in case you can't find it).

Bus Reliable, frequent services around the country (usually cheaper than flying).

Plane Fast-track your holiday with affordable, frequent, fast internal flights. Carbon-offset your flights if you're feeling guilty.

Train Reliable, regular services (if not fast or cheap) along specific routes on both islands.

For much more on **getting around,** see p653

For much more on getting around, see p653

What's New

Old Ghost Road

One of the most ambitious of New Zealand's new cycle trails, the 85km Old Ghost Road is a true backcountry experience retracing two historic gold-mining routes through untouched mountain landscapes. (p430)

Christchurch Art Gallery

The city's premier art institution, closed since the 2011 earthquake, has finally reopened better and brighter, and displays some of NZ's finest works. (p462)

Auckland City Limits

A replacement for the long-running Big Day Out rock festival and loosely based on the famous Austin City Limits, ACL brings big-name international artists to Western Springs Park in March. (p79)

Christchurch CBD

In the midst of its major rebuild, downtown Christchurch is cranking out new bars, restaurants and accommodation at a rapid rate of knots. (p460)

Hydro Attack

What's that leaping out of the waters of placid Lake Wakatipu? Yep, it's a giant shark. Or at least a jet-propelled, torpedo-like vessel painted to look like one. (p545)

Bill Richardson Transport World

This vast new automotive museum in Invercargill is home to an astonishing collection of beautifully restored historic trucks. (p590)

Museum of Waitangi

The heritage and ongoing impact in contemporary times of modern NZ's founding document, the 1840 Treaty of Waitangi, is showcased in this spectacular new museum in the Bay of Islands. (p143)

Skyline MTB Gravity Park

Rotorua's ongoing development into one of the planet's best places to ride a mountain bike is further enhanced by more than 10km of exciting downhill trails, all accessed by a gondola. (p286)

My Kiwi Adventure

This new outfit at Tongariro National Park can take you on NZ's highest-altitude guided stand-up-paddleboard adventure, or send you careening along the central North Island's finest mountain-bike tracks. (p272)

Len Lye Centre

Esteemed NZ artist Len Lye (1901–80) sure knew how to arouse people's curiosity with his challenging artworks. Check some of them out at New Plymouth's superb new gallery. (p217)

Sunshine Brewery

Gisborne's own craft-beer brewery has a fab new tasting room down near Waikanae Beach. Swing by for a tasting paddle, some takeaways or something to eat. (p327)

Pukeahu National War Memorial Park

Wellington's newest park is a poignant place – a wide, sensitively designed space below the old art-deco National War Memorial tower (1932), honouring NZ's servicemen and women. (p358)

For more recommendations and reviews, see lonelyplanet.com/new-zealand

If You Like...

Cities

Auckland Sydney for beginners? We prefer 'Seattle minus the rain', infused with vibrant Pacific Islander culture. (p62)

Wellington All the lures you'd expect in a capital city, packed into a compact CBD and hillsides dotted with Victorian architecture. (p353)

Christchurch Re-emerging post-earthquakes with energy and verve, largely due to the determination and resilience of proud locals. (p460)

Dunedin Exuding artsy, boozy ambience (so many students!) and close to superb wildlife-viewing opportunities on the Otago Peninsula. (p518)

Hamilton It doesn't raise much of a blip on the radar, but Hamilton's bars, restaurants, museum and river deserve a second look. (p169)

New Plymouth The perfect urban hub, with fab galleries, cool cafes and bars, and accessible wilderness. (p217)

Extreme Activities

Queenstown bungy Strap yourself into the astonishing Shotover Canyon Swing or Nevis Bungy, and propel yourself into the void. (p543)

Abel Tasman Canyons Swim, slide, abseil and leap down the Torrent River torrents. (p417)

Waitomo black-water rafting Don a wetsuit, a life vest and a helmet with a torch attached and rampage along an underground river – wild times! (p190)

Extreme Auckland Check out SkyWalk and SkyJump at the Sky Tower, and EcoZip Adventures – adventurous thrills with views. (p77)

Canyonz Negotiate cliffs, waterfalls and streams as you climb and abseil through pristine NZ bush near Thames. (p198)

Rafting the Buller River Widely regarded as NZ's classic rafting experience. There are two excellent operators based in Murchison. (p427)

Skydive Franz Get an eyeful of glacier from way up above one (you'll see Aoraki/Mt Cook too). (p450)

History

Waitangi Treaty Grounds In the Bay of Islands, where Māori chiefs and the British Crown signed the contentious Treaty of Waitangi. (p142)

Arrowtown This gold-rush era town is crammed with heritage buildings and the remains of one of NZ's earliest Chinese settlements. (p562)

Oamaru Victorian Precinct Beautifully restored whitestone buildings and warehouses, now housing eclectic galleries, restaurants and artisan workshops. (p513)

Denniston Plateau Explore the ghostly former coal-mining town of Denniston near Westport, once home to 1500 sooty locals. (p430)

Te Papa Wellington's vibrant treasure-trove museum, where history – both Māori and Pākehā (European New Zealanders) – speaks, sparkles and shakes. (p357)

Dunedin Railway Station More than 100 years old, with mosaic tiles and stained-glass windows; one of NZ's most photographed buildings. (p518)

Shantytown South of Greymouth, on the West Coast, is this authentic recreation of an 1860s gold-mining town. (p438)

Māori Culture

Rotorua Catch a cultural performance featuring a *haka* (war dance) and a *hangi* (Māori feast), with traditional song, dance and storytelling. (p287)

Footprints Waipoua Explore the staggeringly beautiful Waipoua Kauri Forest on Northland's west coast with a Māori guide. (p161)

Te Ana Māori Rock Art Centre
Learn about traditional Māori rock art in Timaru before exploring remote sites around South Canterbury. (p494)

Hokitika The primary source of NZ *pounamu*; home to master carvers of stone, bone and paua in traditional Māori designs. (p443)

Toi Hauāuru Studio Visit this Raglan studio for contemporary Māori carving, visual arts and *Ta Moko* (tattooing). (p178)

Pacific Coast Hwy Life rolls along at a traditional pace in this long-lost corner of NZ. (p322)

Off-The-Beaten-Track Experiences

Stewart Island The end of the line! Catch the ferry to Oban and get lost for a few days. (p599)

Northern West Coast Some of the best spectacles on the coast are in the northwest, including the eye-popping Oparara Basin. (p434)

East Cape Take a few days to detour around this very un-touristy corner of NZ. (p322)

Whanganui River Road Drive alongside the Whanganui River past Māori towns and stands of trees, remnants of failed Pākehā farms. (p239)

Forgotten World Highway A lonesome, forested 155km between Taumaranui and Stratford (or the other way around). (p229)

Northwest North Island coast This part of NZ is seriously understaffed – just how we like it. (p161)

Molesworth NZ's largest cattle farm traverses some seriously remote terrain – take a Molesworth tour. (p486)

PHILLIP LEE HARVEY / LONELY PLANET ©

Top: Hiker on the Routeburn Track (p559) above Lake Mackenzie.
Bottom: Wither Hills winery (p397), Marlborough

Tramping

Milford Track A justifiably famous 'Great Walk', Milford features 53.5km of gorgeous fiords, sounds, peaks and raindrops. (p582)

Routeburn Track Those with plenty of 'Great Walk' kilometres in their boots rate the Routeburn as the best of the bunch. (p559)

Banks Peninsula Track The rolling hills and picturesque bays might not look like the eroded remains of twin volcanoes. Geology lesson, anyone? (p479)

Mt Taranaki short walks You can loop around the mountain or bag the summit, but strolling its photogenic flanks is equally rewarding. (p227)

Lake Angelus Track Yes, the zigzag up Pinchgut Track is a bit of a rude awakening, but the views along Mt Robert Ridge last all day. (p423)

Whanganui Journey This 'Great Walk' is actually a 145km paddle down NZ's longest navigable river, through Whanganui National Park. (p241)

Queen Charlotte Track The joys of camping (sea breezes, lapping waves, starry nights) or luxurious lodges. Either way, you win. (p390)

Old Ghost Road Bike it or hike it, this engaging West Coast trail oozes history. (p430)

Pubs, Bars & Beer

Wellington craft beer Garage Project and Golding's Free Dive, just two of 20-something craft-beer dens in the capital (thirsty politicians?). (p368)

Queenstown The only place in NZ where you can head out for a big Monday or Tuesday night and not be the only one there. (p556)

Auckland The country's biggest city is developing as a hoppy hub: head to Galbraith's Alehouse, Hallertau or Brothers Beer. (p92)

Nelson craft beer Home of NZ hops, Nelson boasts its own craft-beer trail featuring a host of breweries and legendary inns. (p408)

Invercargill Brewery Not only produces its own range but also brews on behalf of some of NZ's best small producers. (p590)

Dunedin There are plenty of great bars to keep you off the streets in NZ's best university town. (p525)

Mike's Taranaki's finest craft brews are wobbling distance from New Plymouth. (p225)

Pomeroy's Old Brewery Inn The best pub in Christchurch. (p474)

Foodie Experiences

Eating in Auckland New restaurants, ethnic culinary enclaves and a growing food-truck scene all make Auckland New Zealand's eating capital. (p85)

Central Otago vineyard restaurants Eye-popping scenery combined with the best of NZ food and wine. (p538)

Bay of Plenty kiwifruit Pick up a dozen fuzzy, ripe and delicious kiwifruit from roadside stalls for as little as $1 per dozen. (p310)

Christchurch city scene The big southern CBD restaurant and bar scene is burgeoning (again). (p472)

Stewart Island Good cod! Is everyone on this island a fisherman? (Answer: yes. Bring lemons). (p599)

Wellington Night Market Foodie fun after work on Friday, then again after your lazy Saturday. (p370)

Wine Regions

Marlborough The country's biggest wine region just keeps on turning out superb sauvignon blanc (and other varieties): drink some. (p396)

Martinborough A small-but-sweet wine region a day trip from Wellington: easy cycling and easy-drinking pinot noir. (p377)

Waiheke Island Auckland's favourite weekend playground has a hot, dry microclimate: perfect for Bordeaux-style reds and rosés. (p102)

Central Otago Central Otago is responsible for much of the country's best pinot noir and riesling. (p531)

Waipara Valley A short hop north of Christchurch are some spectacular vineyards producing equally spectacular riesling. (p487)

Hawke's Bay Warm days shift into chardonnay nights on the sunstroked East Coast. (p346)

Markets

Otago Farmers Market Organic fruit and veg, robust coffee and homemade pies in Dunedin; stock up for life on the road. (p524)

Nelson Market A big, busy weekly market featuring everything from Doris' traditional bratwursts to new-age clothing. (p408)

River Traders Market Whanganui's riverside market is a Saturday-morning fixture: up to 100 stalls, with a particularly good farmers market section. (p238)

MICHAEL / GETTY IMAGES ©

Wharariki Beach (p421)

Harbourside Market The ulterior motive for visiting this weekly fruit-and-veg market is the multi-ethnic food stalls and adjacent artisan City Market. (p365)

Otara Flea Market A taste of the South Pacific in Auckland. (p97)

Rotorua Night Market Thursday night hoedown in downtown Rotorua. Food, drink, buskers... it's all good. (p293)

Hasting Farmers Market One of the original, and still one of the best, farmers markets in NZ. (p345)

Beaches

Karekare Classic black-sand beach west of Auckland, with wild surf (Eddie Vedder nearly drowned here!). (p114)

Hahei Iconic Kiwi beach experience on the Coromandel Peninsula, with mandatory side trip to Cathedral Cove. (p208)

Wainui On the North Island's East Coast: surfing, sandcastles, sunshine... The quintessential beach-bum beach. (p328)

Wharariki Beach No car park, no ice-cream vans... This

isolated stretch near Farewell Spit is for wanderers and ponderers. (p421)

Hillary Trail For sheer drama you can't beat a wild West Coast beach. Unless you tag on another, and another... (p113)

Manu Bay NZ's most famous surf break (seen *Endless Summer*?); there's not much sand, but the point break is what you're here for. (p179)

Abel Tasman Coast Track No need to Photoshop this postcard paradise – these golden beaches, blue bays and verdant hills are for real. (p414)

Month by Month

January

New Zealand peels its eyes open after New Year's Eve, gathers its wits and gets set for another year. Great weather, cricket season in full swing and happy holidays for the locals.

✨ Festival of Lights

New Plymouth's Pukekura Park is regularly plastered with adjectives like 'jewel' and 'gem', but the gardens really sparkle during this festival (www.festivalof lights.co.nz). It's a magical scene: pathways glow and trees shine with thousands of lights. Live music, dance and kids' performances, too.

☆ World Buskers Festival

Christchurch hosts a gaggle of jugglers, musos, tricksters, puppeteers, mime artists and dancers throughout this 10-day summertime festival (www. worldbuskersfestival.com). Shoulder into the crowd, see who's making a scene in the middle and maybe leave a few dollars. Avoid this if you're scared of audience participation...

February

The sun is shining, the kids are back at school, and the sav blanc is chillin' in the fridge: this is prime party time across NZ. Book your festival tickets (and beds) in advance.

☆ Wellington Sevens

It's not rugby season, but early February/late January sees the world's seven-a-side rugby teams crack heads in Wellington as part of the HSBC Sevens World Series (www.sevens.co.nz): everyone from stalwarts Australia, NZ and South Africa to minnows like the Cook Islands, Kenya and Canada. A great excuse for a party.

✨ Waitangi Day

On 6 February 1840 the Treaty of Waitangi (www. nzhistory.net.nz) was first signed between Māori and the British Crown. The day remains a public holiday across NZ, but in Waitangi itself (the Bay of Islands) there's a lot happening: guided tours, concerts, market stalls and family entertainment.

🍷 Marlborough Wine & Food Festival

NZ's biggest and best wine festival (www.wine-marlborough-festival.co.nz) features tastings from around 50 Marlborough wineries, plus fine food and entertainment. The mandatory over-indulgence usually happens on a Saturday early in the month. Keep quiet if you don't like sauvignon blanc...

☆ New Zealand Festival

Feeling artsy? This month-long spectacular (www. festival.co.nz) happens in Wellington in February to March every even-numbered year, and is sure to spark your imagination. NZ's cultural capital exudes artistic enthusiasm with theatre, dance, music, writing and visual arts. International acts aplenty.

☆ Fringe NZ

Wellington simmers with music, theatre, comedy, dance, visual arts...but not the mainstream stuff that makes it into the New

Zealand Festival. These are the fringe-dwelling, unusual, emerging, controversial, low-budget and/or downright weird acts that don't seem to fit in anywhere else (www.fringe.co.nz). Great stuff!

✳✳ Art Deco Weekend

In the third week of February, Napier, levelled by an earthquake in 1931 and rebuilt in high art-deco style, celebrates its architectural heritage with this high-steppin' fiesta (www.artdeconapier.com), featuring music, food, wine, vintage cars and costumes.

✳✳ Splore

Explore Splore (www.splore.net), a cutting-edge, three-day outdoor summer fest in Tapapakanga Regional Park on the coast east of Auckland. Contemporary live music, performance, visual arts, safe swimming, pohutukawa trees... If we were feeling parental, we'd tell you to take sunscreen, a hat and a water bottle.

March

March brings a hint of autumn, harvest time in the vineyards and orchards (great if you're looking for work), long dusky evenings and plenty of festivals plumping out the calendar. Locals unwind post–tourist season.

✳✳ Te Matatini National Kapa Haka Festival

This engrossing Māori *haka* (war dance) competition (www.tematatini.co.nz) happens in early March (or late February) in odd-numbered years: much

gesticulation, eye-bulging and tongue extension. Venues vary: 2017 will be at Kahungunu in Hawke's Bay. And it's not just the *haka*: expect traditional song, dance, storytelling and other performing arts.

✗ Wildfoods Festival

Eat some worms, hare testicles or crabs at Hokitika's comfort-zone-challenging food fest (www.wildfoods.co.nz). Not for the mild-mannered or weak-stomached... But even if you are, it's still fun to watch! There are usually plenty of quality NZ brews available, too, which help subdue any difficult tastes.

☆ WOMAD

Local and international music, arts and dance performances fill New Plymouth's Bowl of Brooklands to overflowing (www.womad.co.nz). An evolution of the original world-music festival dreamed up by Peter Gabriel, who launched the inaugural UK concert in 1990. Perfect for families (usually not too loud).

✳✳ Pasifika Festival

With upwards of 140,000 Māori and notable communities of Tongans, Samoans, Cook Islanders, Niueans, Fijians and other South Pacific Islanders, Auckland has the largest Polynesian community in the world. These vibrant island cultures come together at this annual fiesta (www.aucklandnz.com/pasifika) in the city's Western Springs Park.

☆ Auckland City Limits

Time to get yer rocks off! Auckland City Limits

(www.aucklandcitylimits.com) is a new international indie-rock festival loosely modelled on Austin City Limits in the US – the NZ version occupying four stages at Western Springs Stadium for a day in March.

April

April is when canny travellers hit NZ: the ocean is still swimmable and the weather still mild, with nary a tourist or queue in sight (...other than during Easter, when there's pricey accommodation everywhere).

☆ National Jazz Festival

Every Easter, Tauranga hosts the longest-running jazz fest (www.jazz.org.nz) in the southern hemisphere. The line up is invariably impressive (Kurt Elling, Keb Mo), and there's plenty of fine NZ food and wine to accompany the finger-snappin' za-bah-de-dah sonics.

✗ Clyde Wine & Food Festival

Easter is harvest time around Clyde in Central Otago, where the historic main street fills with tables and trestles hocking the best of regional food and wine (www.promotedunstan.org.nz).

May

The nostalgia of autumn runs deep: party nights are long gone and another chilly Kiwi winter beckons. Thank goodness for the Comedy Festival! Last chance to explore Fiordland and Southland in reasonable weather. Farmers markets overflow.

✗ Bluff Oyster & Food Festival

Bluff and oysters go together like, well, like a bivalve. Truck down to the deep south for some slippery, salty specimens (www.bluff oysterfest.co.nz). It's chilly down here in May, but the live music and oyster eating/opening competitions warm everybody up.

☆ New Zealand International Comedy Festival

Three-week laugh-fest (www.comedyfestival.co.nz) with venues across Auckland, Wellington and various regional centres: Whangarei to Invercargill with all the mid-sized cities in between. International gag-merchants (Arj Barker, Danny Bhoy) line up next to home-grown talent (anyone seen that Rhys Darby guy lately?).

June

Time to head south: it's ski season! Queenstown and Wanaka hit their stride. For everyone else, head north: the Bay of Plenty is always sunny, and is it just us, or is Northland underrated?

✷ Matariki

Māori New Year is heralded by the rise of Matariki (aka Pleiades star cluster) in May and the sighting of the new moon in June. Three days of remembrance, education, music, film, community days and tree planting take place, mainly around Auckland and Northland (www.teara.govt.nz/en/matariki-maori-new-year).

☆ New Zealand Gold Guitar Awards

We like both kinds of music: country and western! These awards (www.goldguitars.co.nz) in chilly Gore cap off a week of ever-lovin' country twang and booz-scootin' good times, with plenty of concerts and buskers.

July

Wellington's good citizens clutch collars, shiver and hang out in bookshops: Auckland doesn't seem so bad now, eh? Ski season slides on: hit Mt Ruapehu on the North Island if Queenstown is overcrowded.

✷ Queenstown Winter Festival

This southern snow-fest (www.winterfestival.co.nz) has been running since 1975, and now attracts around 45,000 snowbunnies. It's a 10-day party, studded with fireworks, jazz, street parades, comedy, a Mardi Gras, a masquerade ball and lots of snow-centric activities on the mountain slopes. Sometimes starts in late June.

☆ New Zealand International Film Festival

After separate film festivals (www.nzff.co.nz) in Wellington, Auckland, Dunedin and Christchurch, a selection of flicks hits the road for screenings in regional towns from July to November (film buffs in Gore and Masterton get positively orgasmic at the prospect).

✈ Russell Birdman

Birdman rallies are just so '80s...but they sure are funny! This one in Russell (www.russellbirdman.co.nz) features the usual cast of costumed contenders propelling themselves off a jetty in pursuit of weightlessness. Bonus points if your name is Russell.

August

Land a good deal on accommodation pretty much anywhere except the ski towns. Winter is almost spent, but there's still not much happening outside: music and art are your saviours...or watch some rugby!

🍷 Beervana

Attain beery nirvana at this annual craft-beer guzzle fest in Wellington (it's freezing outside – what else is there to do?). But seriously, the NZ craft-beer scene is booming – here's your chance to sample the best of it (www.beervana.co.nz).

✷ Taranaki International Arts Festival

Beneath the snowy slopes of Mt Taranaki, August used to be a time of quiet repose and reconstitution. Not anymore: this whizz-bang arts festival (www.taft.co.nz) now shakes the winter from the city (New Plymouth) with music, theatre, dance, visual arts and parades.

☆ Bay of Islands Jazz & Blues Festival

You might think that the Bay of Islands is all about sunning yourself on a yacht while dolphins splash saltwater on your stomach. And you'd be right. But in the depths of winter, this jazzy little festival (www.jazz-blues.co.nz) will give you something else to do.

September

Spring is sprung. The amazing and surprising World of WearableArt Award Show is always a hit. And will someone please beat Canterbury in the annual ITM rugby cup final?

✂️ Artists Open Studios & Festival of Glass

Whanganui has earned its artistic stripes as a centre for gorgeous glass, myriad local artists and workshops gearing up for this classy glassy fest in September (www.openstudios.co.nz, www.wanganuiglass.co.nz). Expect lots of 'how-to' demonstrations, exhibitions and open studios.

✂️ World of WearableArt Awards Show

A bizarre (in the best possible way) two-week Wellington event (www.worldofwearableart.com) featuring amazing hand-crafted garments. Entries from the show are displayed at the World of WearableArt & Classic Cars Museum in Nelson after the event (Cadillacs and corsetry?). Sometimes spills over into October.

October

Post-rugby and pre-cricket, sports fans twiddle their thumbs: a trip to Kaikoura,

perhaps? Around the rest of NZ October is 'shoulder season' – reasonable accommodation rates, minimal crowds and no competition for the good campsites.

✂️ Nelson Arts Festival

Sure, Nelson is distractingly sunny, but that doesn't mean the artsy good stuff isn't happening inside and out. Get a taste of the local output over two weeks in October (www.nelsonartsfestival.co.nz).

🍴 Kaikoura Seafest

Kaikoura is a town built on crayfish. Well, not literally, but there sure are plenty of crustaceans in the sea here, many of which find themselves on plates during Seafest (www.seafest.co.nz). Also a great excuse to drink a lot and dance around.

November

Across Northland, the Coromandel Peninsula, the Bay of Plenty and the East Coast, NZ's iconic pohutukawa trees erupt with brilliant crimson blooms. The weather is picking up, and a few tourists are starting to arrive.

✂️ NZ Tattoo & Art Festival

The biggest tattoo culture festival in Australasia (www.nztattooart.com) attracts thousands of tatt-fans to New Plymouth every November. It's quirky, edgy, sexy and hugely popular (not necessarily family viewing...).

🍷 Toast Martinborough

Bound for a day of boozy indulgence, wine-swilling Wellingtonians head over Rimutaka Hill and roll into upmarket Martinborough (www.toastmartinborough.co.nz). The Wairarapa region produces some seriously good pinot noir: don't go home without trying some (...as if you'd be so silly).

✂️ Oamaru Victorian Heritage Week

Ahhh, the good old days... When Queen Vic sat dourly on the throne, when hems were low, collars were high, and civic decency was a matter of course. Old Oamaru thoroughly enjoys this tongue-in-cheek historic homage in November (www.historicoamaru.co.nz): dress-ups, penny-farthing races, choirs, guided tours etc.

December

Summertime! The crack of leather on willow resounds across the nation's cricket pitches, and office workers surge towards the finish line. Everyone gears up for Christmas: avoid shopping centres like the plague.

✂️ Rhythm & Vines

Wine, music and song (all the good things) in sunny east-coast Gisborne on New Year's Eve (www.rhythmandvines.co.nz). Top DJs, hip-hop acts, bands and singer-songwriters compete for your attention. Or maybe you'd rather just drink some chardonnay and kiss someone on the beach.

Itineraries

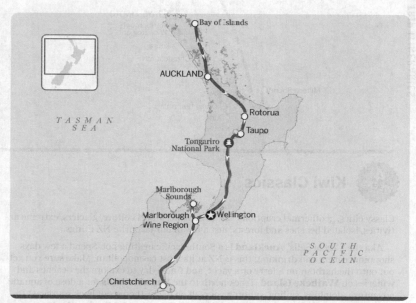

Bay of Islands

AUCKLAND

Rotorua

Taupo

Tongariro
National Park

Marlborough
Sounds

Marlborough
Wine Region

Wellington

Christchurch

*TASMAN
SEA*

*SOUTH
PACIFIC
OCEAN*

2 WEEKS · North & South

From the top of the north to halfway down the south, here's a quick-fire taste of New Zealand's best.

Kick things off in **Auckland**: it's NZ's biggest city, with awesome restaurants and bars, galleries and boutiques, beaches and bays. Not an urbanite? Hoof it a few hours north to the salt-licked **Bay of Islands** for a couple of days of R&R.

Set your bearings southwards to **Rotorua**, a unique geothermal hot spot: geysers, mud pools, volcanic vents and Māori culture make for an engaging experience. Further south, progressive **Taupo** has the staggeringly beautiful **Tongariro National Park** nearby. Get into some tramping, mountain biking or skydiving, then boot it down to **Wellington**, a hip little city with an irrepressible arts scene.

Across Cook Strait, see what all the fuss is about in the **Marlborough Wine Region**. If you're not a wine fan, the hypnotically hushed inlets, ranges and waterways of the **Marlborough Sounds** are nearby. Swinging further south, cruise into **Christchurch** for some southern culture and hospitality.

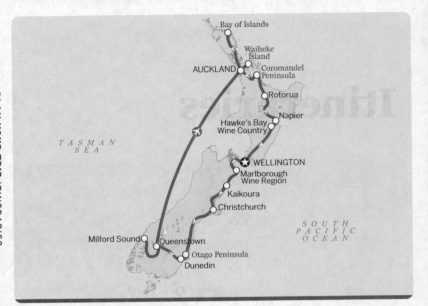

⁴WEEKS Kiwi Classics

Classy cities, geothermal eruptions, fantastic wine, Māori culture, glaciers, extreme activities, isolated beaches and forests: just a few of our favourite NZ things.

Aka the 'City of Sails', **Auckland** is a South Pacific melting pot. Spend a few days shopping, eating and drinking: this is NZ at its most cosmopolitan. Make sure you get out onto the harbour on a ferry or a yacht, and find a day to explore the beaches and wineries on **Waiheke Island**. Truck north to the **Bay of Islands** for a dose of aquatic adventure (dolphins, sailing, sunning yourself on deck), then scoot back southeast to check out the forests and holiday beaches on the **Coromandel Peninsula**. Further south in **Rotorua**, get a nose full of egg gas, confront a 30ft geyser, giggle at volcanic mud bubbles and experience a Māori cultural performance (work your *haka* into shape).

Cruise down to **Napier** on the East Coast, NZ's archetypal art-deco sun city. While you're here, don't miss the bottled offerings of the **Hawke's Bay Wine Country** (*...ohh*, the chardonnay). Down in **Wellington**, the coffee's hot, the beer's cold and wind from the politicians generates its own low-pressure system. This is NZ's arts capital: catch a live band, some buskers, a gallery opening or some theatre.

Swan over to the South Island for a couple of weeks to experience the best the south has to offer. Start with a tour through the sauvignon blanc heartland of the **Marlborough Wine Region**, then chill for a few days between the mountains and the whales offshore in laid-back **Kaikoura**. Next stop is the southern capital **Christchurch**, rapidly finding its feet again after the earthquakes. Follow the coast road south to the wildlife-rich **Otago Peninsula**, jutting abstractly away from the Victorian facades of Scottish-flavoured and student-filled **Dunedin**. Catch some live music while you're in town.

Head inland via SH8 to bungy- and ski-obsessed **Queenstown**. If you have time, detour over to Fiordland for an unforgettable encounter with **Milford Sound**, before returning to Queenstown for your flight back to Auckland.

Top: Hikers, Fox Glacier (p451)

Bottom: Kaikoura (p398) and the snowcapped Seaward Kaikoura Range

DOUG PEARSON / GETTY IMAGES ©

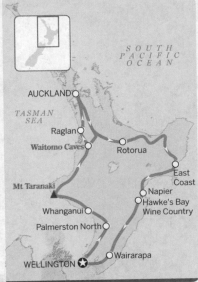

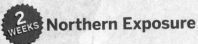

10 DAYS — Auckland Encounter

Is there another 1.4-million-strong city with access to *two* oceans and vibrant Polynesian culture?

Auckland also offers stellar bars and restaurants, museums, islands and beaches. Check out the Māori and South Pacific Islander exhibits at Auckland Museum, then wander across the Domain to K Rd for lunch. Pay a visit to the grand Auckland Art Gallery and the iconic Sky Tower, then Ponsonby for dinner and drinks.

Ferry over to **Rangitoto Island**, then chug into Devonport for a meal. Have a look at the tall timber in **Waitakere Ranges Regional Park**, or check out the wild surf at **Karekare** and **Piha**, then hit the Britomart restaurants. Have breakfast in Mt Eden, climb Maungawhau, then ferry-hop to **Waiheke Island** for wineries and beaches.

Take your pick of activities within easy reach of the big smoke: snorkelling at **Goat Island Marine Reserve**, sailing the **Bay of Islands**, ocean-gazing at **Cape Reinga**, ogling giant trees at **Waipoua Kauri Forest**, delving into **Waitomo Caves**, surfing at **Raglan** or beaching yourself at **Whitianga**.

2 WEEKS — Northern Exposure

Three-quarters of New Zealanders live on the North Island – time to find out why!

Begin in **Auckland**, NZ's biggest city. Eat streets abound: try Ponsonby Rd in Ponsonby, K Rd in Newton, and New North Rd in Kingsland. Hike up One Tree Hill (Maungakiekie) to burn off resultant calories, and don't miss the Auckland Art Gallery and Auckland Museum.

Venture south through geothermal **Rotorua** – home to some truly amazing volcanic sights – then cruise over to the sunny **East Coast**. By the seaside and encircled by the chardonnay vines of **Hawke's Bay Wine Country**, art-deco **Napier** is a hit with architecture buffs. Heading south, follow SH2 into the sheepy/winey region of **Wairarapa**, before driving over the Rimutaka Range into hip, art-obsessed **Wellington**.

Looping back northwest to Auckland, pick and choose your pit stops: the New Zealand Rugby Museum in **Palmerston North**, some crafty glass in **Whanganui**, or the epic **Mt Taranaki**, rising like Olympus behind New Plymouth. Go underground at **Waitomo Caves**, or surf the point breaks near **Raglan**.

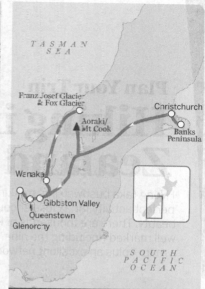

(3 WEEKS) Southern Circuit

Winging into **Christchurch** to launch this three-week escapade, you'll find a vibrant city rebuilding post-earthquakes. Grab a coffee at a cafe (try Addington Coffee Co-op or Supreme Supreme), then check out the excellent Canterbury Museum and the Avon River, cutting lazily through the Botanic Gardens.

City saturated? Visit the geologically/culturally eccentric **Banks Peninsula**, then head north for a wildlife encounter in **Kaikoura**. Continue through to the famous **Marlborough Wine Region**, and lose a day on the whisper-still waterways of the **Marlborough Sounds**.

Detour west through artsy **Nelson** to **Abel Tasman National Park** and eco-friendly **Golden Bay**. Southbound, dawdle down the dramatic West Coast with its wilderness and eye-popping **Franz Josef Glacier** and **Fox Glacier**. From here, track inland through to hip/hippie **Wanaka** and ski-central **Queenstown**. From here, desolate **Doubtful Sound** is mesmerising, while the overgrown deep-south **Catlins** are perfectly chilled out.

Back up the east coast, wheel through Dunedin to surprisingly hip **Oamaru**, before rolling back into Christchurch.

(10 DAYS) Winter Wanderer

Fly into **Christchurch** for a day or two to acclimatise, day-trip to the **Banks Peninsula**, then drive south to see snowy **Aoraki/Mt Cook**. Continuing south, internationalist **Queenstown** offers world-class skiing, great restaurants and a kickin' nocturnal scene. Coronet Peak is the area's oldest ski field, with treeless slopes, consistent gradients and excellent skiing for all levels (great for snowboarders, too). The visually remarkable Remarkables are more family-friendly.

Had enough snowy slopes? Take a drive around Lake Wakatipu to gorgeous **Glenorchy**, or lose an afternoon in the fab wineries of the **Gibbston Valley**. Alternatively, Queenstown's extreme activities keep the winter chills at bay.

As an alternative to Queenstown, head to **Wanaka** (Queenstown's little brother – all the benefits but none of the hype). Ski fields near here include Treble Cone, Cardrona and Snow Farm New Zealand, NZ's only commercial Nordic (cross-country) ski area.

From Wanaka, take an overnight trip to Westland Tai Poutini National Park on the West Coast to check out **Franz Josef Glacier** and **Fox Glacier**. Backtrack to Queenstown for your next flight.

Plan Your Trip

Hiking in New Zealand

Hiking (aka bushwalking, trekking or tramping, as Kiwis call it) is the perfect activity for a close encounter with New Zealand's natural beauty. There are thousands of kilometres of tracks here – some well marked (including the nine 'Great Walks'), some barely a line on a map – plus an excellent network of huts and campgrounds.

Top NZ Hikes

Top Five Multiday Hikes

Lake Waikaremoana Track, Te Urewera National Park

Abel Tasman Coast Track, Abel Tasman National Park

Heaphy Track, Kahurangi National Park

Routeburn Track, Fiordland/Mt Aspiring National Parks

Milford Track, Fiordland National Park

Top Five Day Hikes

Rangitoto Island Loop, Auckland

Tongariro Alpine Crossing, Tongariro National Park

Mt Robert Circuit, Nelson Lakes National Park

Avalanche Peak, Arthur's Park National Park

Key Summit, Fiordland National Park

Best Hikes for Beginners

Coromandel Coastal Walkway, Coromandel Peninsula

Mauao Summit Track, Mt Maunganui

Queen Charlotte Track, Marlborough Sounds

Abel Tasman Coast Track, Abel Tasman National Park

Rob Roy Glacier Track, Mt Aspiring National Park

Planning

When to Go

Mid-December–late January Tramping high season is during the school summer holidays, starting a couple of weeks before Christmas – avoid it if you can.

January–March The summer weather lingers into March: wait until February if possible, when tracks are (marginally) less crowded. Most non-alpine tracks can be walked enjoyably at any time from about October through to April.

June–August Winter is not the time to be out in the wild, especially at altitude – some paths close in winter because of avalanche danger and reduced facilities and services.

What to Bring

Primary considerations: your feet and your back. Make sure your footwear is tough and comfortable, and your pack fits well and isn't too heavy. Warm clothing and wet-weather gear are essential wherever you hike, as well as a hat to keep you warm and protect you from NZ's harsh sun. If you're camping or staying in huts without cooking facilities, bring a camping stove. Also pack insect repellent to keep sandflies away (although covering up is best), and don't forget your scroggin – a mixture of dried fruit and nuts (and sometimes chocolate) for munching en route.

TRACK SAFETY

Thousands of people tramp across NZ without incident but every year too many folks meet their maker in the mountains. Some trails are only for the experienced, fit and well equipped – don't attempt these if you don't fit the bill. Ensure you are healthy and used to walking for sustained periods.

New Zealand's volatile climate subjects high-altitude walks to snow and ice, even in summer, and rivers can rise rapidly: always check weather and track conditions before setting off, and be prepared to change your plans or sit out bad weather. Resources include the following:

www.doc.govt.nz DOC'S track info, alerts and a lot more.

www.adventuresmart.org.nz Log your walk intentions online (and tell a friend or local!).

www.mountainsafety.org.nz Tramping safety tips.

www.metservice.co.nz Weather forecasts.

Books & Resources

Before heading into the bush, get up-to-date information from the appropriate authority – usually the DOC (Department of Conservation; www.doc.govt.nz) or regional i-SITE visitor information centres. As well as current track condition and weather info, the DOC supplies detailed books on the flora, fauna, geology and history of NZ's national parks, plus leaflets (mostly $2 or less) detailing hundreds of NZ walking tracks.

➡ Lonely Planet's *Hiking & Tramping in New Zealand* describes over 50 walks of various lengths and degrees of difficulty.

➡ *101 Great Tramps* by Mark Pickering and Rodney Smith has suggestions for two- to six-day tramps around the country. The companion guide, *202 Great Walks: The Best Day Walks in New Zealand,* by Mark Pickering, is handy for shorter, family-friendly excursions.

➡ *A Walking Guide to New Zealand's Long Trail: Te Araroa* by Geoff Chapple is the definitive book for NZ's continuous trail that runs the length of the country.

➡ The Mountain Safety Council's *Bushcraft Manual* will help keep you safe on the trails and bring out your inner Bear Grylls.

➡ *Tramping* by Shaun Barnett and Chris Maclean is a meticulously researched history of NZ's favourite outdoor pastime.

➡ Bird's Eye Guides from Potton & Burton Publishing have fab topographical maps, and there are countless books covering tramps and short urban walks around NZ – scan the bookshops.

Maps

The NZ Topo50 topographical map series produced by Land Information New Zealand (LINZ; www.linz.govt.nz) is the most commonly used. Bookshops don't often have a good selection of these maps, but the LINZ website has a list of retailers, and DOC offices often sell the latest maps for local tracks. Outdoor stores also stock them. NZ Topo Map (www.topomap.co.nz) has an interactive topographic map, useful for planning.

Websites

www.doc.govt.nz Descriptions, alerts, and exhaustive flora and fauna information for all tracks in the conservation estate.

www.tramper.co.nz Articles, photos, forums and excellent track and hut information.

www.teararoa.org.nz The official website for NZ's 3000km trail from Cape Reinga to Bluff.

www.topomap.co.nz Online topographic map of the whole country.

www.mountainsafety.org.nz Safety tips, gear advice and courses.

www.freewalks.co.nz Descriptions, maps and photos of long and short tramps all over NZ.

www.trampingnz.com Region-by-region track info with readable trip reports.

Track Classifications

Tracks in NZ are classified according to various features, including level of difficulty. The widely used track classification system is as follows:

Short Walk (Easiest) Well formed; possibly allows for wheelchair access or is constructed to 'walking shoe' standard (ie walking boots not required). Suitable for people of all ages and fitness levels.

Walking Track (Easy) Well-formed longer walks; walking shoes or boots recommended. Suitable for people of most ages and fitness levels.

Great Walk or Easier Tramping Track (Intermediate) Well formed; major water crossings have bridges and track junctions have signs. Light hiking boots and average fitness required.

Tramping Track (Advanced) Requires skill and experience; hiking boots essential. Suitable for people of moderate physical fitness. Water crossings may not have bridges.

Route (Expert) Requires a high degree of skill, experience and navigation skills. Sturdy hiking boots essential. Well-equipped, fit trampers only.

The Great Walks

New Zealand's nine official 'Great Walks' (one of which is actually a canoe trip down a river!) are the country's most popular tracks. Natural beauty abounds, but prepare yourself for crowds, especially over summer.

All nine Great Walks are described in Lonely Planet's *Hiking & Tramping in New Zealand,* and are detailed in pamphlets

NZ'S NINE 'GREAT WALKS'

WALK	DISTANCE	DURATION	DIFFICULTY	DESCRIPTION
Abel Tasman Coast Track (p414)*	60km	3-5 days	Easy to intermediate	NZ's most popular walk (or sea kayak); beaches and bays in Abel Tasman National Park (South Island)
Heaphy Track (p422)*	78km	4-6 days	Intermediate	Forests, beaches and karst landscapes in Kahurangi National Park (South Island)
Kepler Track (p580)**	60km	3-4 days	Intermediate	Lakes, rivers, gorges, glacial valleys and beech forest in Fiordland National Park (South Island)
Lake Waikaremoana Track (p332)*	46km	3-4 days	Easy to intermediate	Lake views, bush-clad ridges and swimming in Te Urewera National Park (North Island)
Milford Track (p582)**	54km	4 days	Easy to intermediate	Rainforest, sheer valleys and peaks, and 580m-high Sutherland Falls in Fiordland National Park (South Island)
Rakiura Track (p602)*	39km	3 days	Intermediate	Bird life (kiwi!), beaches and lush bush on remote Stewart Island (Rakiura; off the South Island)
Routeburn Track (p559)**	32km	2-4 days	Intermediate	Eye-popping alpine scenery around Mt Aspiring and Fiordland National Parks (South Island)
Tongariro Northern Circuit (p269)**	43km	3-4 days	Intermediate to advanced	Through the active volcanic landscape of Tongariro National Park (North Island); see also Tongariro Alpine Crossing
Whanganui Journey (p241)**	145km	5 days	Intermediate	Canoe or kayak down a mysterious river in Whanganui National Park (North Island)

* Bookings required year-round

** Bookings required peak season only (October to April)

Great Walks

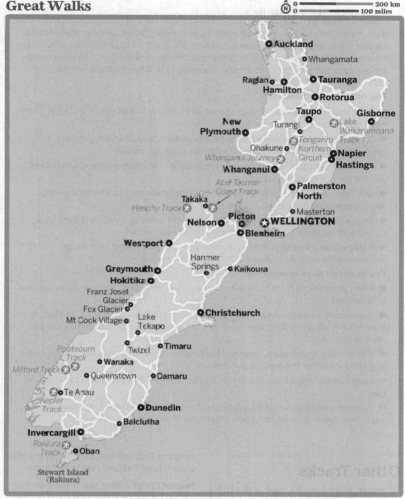

provided by DOC visitor centres and online at www.greatwalks.co.nz.

Tickets & Bookings

To tramp these tracks you'll need to book online or at DOC visitor centres and some i-SITES before setting out. These track-specific tickets cover you for hut accommodation (from $22 to $54 per adult per night, depending on the track) and/or camping ($6 to $18 per adult per night). You can camp only at designated camping grounds; note there's no camping on the Milford Track.

In the off-peak season (May to September) you can use Backcountry Hut Passes or pay-as-you-go Hut Tickets on all Great Walks except for the Lake Waikaremoana Track, Heaphy Track, Abel Tasman Coast Track and Rakiura Track (advance bookings required year-round). Kids under 17 stay in huts and camp for free on all Great Walks.

For bookings see www.greatwalks.co.nz, email greatwalksbookings@doc.govt.nz, phone ☏0800 694 732, or visit DOC visitor centres. Book as far in advance as possible, especially if you're planning on walking during summer.

RESPONSIBLE TRAMPING

If you went straight from the cradle into a pair of hiking boots, some of these tramping tips will seem ridiculously obvious; others you mightn't have considered. Online, www.lnt.org is a great resource for low-impact hiking, and the DOC site www.camping.org.nz has plenty more responsible camping tips. When in doubt, ask DOC or i-SITE staff.

The ridiculously obvious:

➡ Time your tramp to avoid peak season: less people = less stress on the environment and fewer snorers in the huts.

➡ Carry out *all* your rubbish. Burying rubbish disturbs soil and vegetation, encouraging erosion, and animals will probably dig it up anyway.

➡ Don't use detergents, shampoo or toothpaste in or near lakes and waterways (even if they're biodegradable).

➡ Use lightweight kerosene, alcohol or Shellite (white gas) stoves for cooking; avoid disposable butane gas canisters.

➡ Where there's a toilet, use it. Where there isn't one, dig a hole and bury your by-product (at least 15cm deep, 100m from any waterway).

➡ If tracks pass through muddy patches, just plough straight on through – skirting around the outside increases the size of the quagmire.

You mightn't have considered:

➡ Wash your dishes 50m from watercourses; use a scourer, sand or snow instead of detergent.

➡ If you *really* need to scrub your bod, use biodegradable soap and a bucket, at least 50m from any watercourse. Spread the waste water around widely to help the soil filter it.

➡ If open fires are allowed, use only dead, fallen wood in existing fireplaces. Leave any extra wood for the next happy camper.

➡ Keep food-storage bags out of reach of scavengers by tying them to rafters or trees.

➡ Feeding wildlife can lead to unbalanced populations, diseases and animals becoming dependent on handouts. Keep your dried apricots to yourself.

Other Tracks

Of course, there are a lot more walks in NZ than just the Great ones!

North Island

Te Paki Coastal Track A 48km, three- to four-day, easy beach tramp (camping only) along the rugged Northland coastline. A 132km six- to eight-day route is also possible.

Aotea Track This 25km, two- to three-day track follows routes laid down by loggers who came to Great Barrier Island in a quest for kauri trees, leaving historic relics in their wake. (p111)

Rangitoto Island Summit It's an easy boat trip from Auckland to the 600-year-old volcano of Rangitoto, best seen from its crater summit after a loop around the island (four to five hours).

Pouakai Circuit A 25km, two- to three-day loop passing lowland rainforest, cliffs and subalpine forest, tussock and swamp at the foot of Mt Taranaki in Egmont National Park. (p227)

Tongariro Alpine Crossing A brilliant 19km, one-day, moderate tramp through surreal Tongariro National Park. (p267)

Mt Holdsworth–Jumbo Circuit A 24km, medium-to-hard, classic three-day tramp along the alpine tops of Tararua Forest Park, close to Masterton.

South Island

Banks Peninsula Track A 35km, two-day (medium) or four-day (easy) walk over the hills and along the coast of Banks Peninsula. (p479)

Hollyford Track A typically hair-brained scheme of the era, the settlement of Jamestown was always a long shot. Cue: colourful characters and a dash of drama. A four- to five-day, 58km low-level tramping track in Fiordland. (p582)

Welcome Flat Follow the Karangarua River in the shadow of some of NZ's loftiest peaks, then reward yourself with a soak in natural hot pools. A two- to three-day moderate tramp over 50km in Westland Tai Poutini National Park.

Mueller Hut Route Yes, it involves a hardcore 1040m climb up the Sealy Range near Aoraki/Mt Cook, but this is a quintessential alpine experience: geological wonders, fascinating plant life and an amazing hut.

Lake Angelus Track A startling alpine ridge leads to a flash DOC hut beside a pristine cirque lake in Nelson Lakes National Park. A 22km-return, two-day moderate hike. (p423)

Queen Charlotte Track A 70km, three- to five-day moderate walk in the Marlborough Sounds, affording great watery views. Top-notch accommodation and water transport available. (p39C)

Rees-Dart Track A 70km, four- to five-day hard tramping track in Mt Aspiring National Park, through glacier-fed valleys and over an alpine pass.

St James Walkway This tramping track passes through a significant conservation area, home to some 43C species of flora from lowland grasses to mountain beech and alpine herbs. Five days over 66km around Lewis Pass. (p434)

Tuatapere Hump Ridge Track An excellent three-day, 58km alpine and coastal circuit beginning and ending at Te Waewae Bay, 20km from Tuatapere. (p588)

Backcountry Huts

In addition to Great Walk huts, DOC maintains more than 950 Backcountry Huts in NZ's national and forest parks. Hut categories are as follows:

Basic Huts Very basic enclosed shelters with little or no facilities. Free.

Standard Huts No cooking equipment and sometimes no heating, but mattresses, water supply and toilets. Fees are $5 per adult per night.

Serviced Huts Mattress-equipped bunks or sleeping platforms, water supply, heating, toilets

PLAN YOUR TRIP HIKING IN NEW ZEALAND

TE ARAROA

Epic! Te Araroa (www.teararoa.org.nz) is a 3000km tramping trail from Cape Reinga in NZ's north to Bluff in the south (or the other way around). The route links up existing tracks with new sections. Built over almost 20 years, mostly by volunteers, it's one of the longest hikes in the world: check the website for maps and track notes, plus blogs and videos from hardy types who have completed the end-to-end epic.

and sometimes cooking facilities. Fees are $15 per adult per night.

Note that bookings are required for some huts (see the website for listings): book online at https://booking.doc.govt.nz or at DOC visitor centres. Kids aged 11 to 17 stay for half-price; kids 10 and under stay free. For comprehensive hut details see www.doc.govt.nz/parks-and-recreation/places-to-stay.

If you do a lot of tramping, a six-month Backcountry Hut Pass ($92 per adult) might be a good idea; otherwise use pay-as-you-go Hut Tickets ($5; you'll need to use three of these for a Serviced Hut). Date your tickets and put them in the boxes provided at huts. Accommodation is on a first-come, first-served basis. In the low season (May to September), Backcountry Hut Tickets and Passes can also be used to procure a bunk or campsite on some Great Walks.

Backcountry Campsites are often nearby the huts, and usually have toilets and fresh water, and possibly picnic tables, fireplaces and/or cooking shelters. Prices vary from free to $8 per person per night.

Conservation Campsites

Aside from Great Walk campsites, DOC also manages 220-plus 'Conservation Campsites' (often vehicle-accessible), with categories as follows:

Basic Campsites Basic toilets and fresh water; free on a first-come, first-served basis.

Standard Campsites Toilets and water supply, and perhaps barbecues and picnic tables; from $6 on a first-come, first-served basis.

Scenic Campsites High-use sites with toilets and tap water, and sometimes barbecues, fireplaces, cooking shelters, cold showers, picnic tables and rubbish bins. Fees are $10 per night.

Serviced Campsites Full facilities: flush toilets, tap water, hot showers and picnic tables. They may also have barbecues, a kitchen and a laundry; around $15 per night.

Note that bookings are necessary for all Serviced Campsites, plus some Scenic and Standard Campsites in peak season (October to April). Book online – https://booking. doc.govt.nz – or at DOC visitor centres.

DOC publishes free brochures with descriptions, and instructions to find every campsite (even GPS coordinates). Pick up copies from DOC offices before you hit the road, or download them from their website.

Guided Walks

If you're new to tramping or just want a more comfortable experience than the DIY alternative, several companies can escort you through the wilds, usually staying in comfortable huts (showers!), with meals cooked and equipment carried for you.

Places on the North Island where you can sign up for a guided walk include Mt Taranaki, Lake Waikaremoana and Ton-

gariro National Park. On the South Island try the Abel Tasman Coast Track, Queen Charlotte Track, Heaphy Track, Routeburn Track, Milford Track or Hollyford Track. Prices for multiday guided walks start at around $1500, and rise towards $2200 for more deluxe experiences.

Getting To & From Trailheads

Getting to and from trailheads can be problematic, except for popular trails serviced by public and dedicated trampers' transport. Having a vehicle only helps with getting to one end of the track (you still have to collect your car afterwards). If the track starts or ends down a dead-end road, hitching will be difficult.

Of course, tracks accessible by public transport or shuttle bus services (eg Abel Tasman Coast Track) are also the most crowded. An alternative is to arrange private transport, either with a friend or by chartering a vehicle to drop you at one end then pick you up at the other. If you intend to leave a vehicle at a trailhead, don't leave anything valuable inside – theft from cars in isolated areas is a significant problem.

Plan Your Trip

Skiing & Snowboarding in New Zealand

New Zealand is an essential southern-hemisphere destination for snow bunnies, with downhill skiing, cross-country (Nordic) skiing and snowboarding all passionately pursued. The NZ ski season is generally June through September, though it varies considerably from one ski area to another, and can run as late as October.

Planning

Where to Go

The variety of locations and conditions makes it difficult to rate NZ's ski fields in any particular order. Some people like to be near Queenstown's party scene or Mt Ruapehu's volcanic landscapes; others prefer the quality high-altitude runs on Mt Hutt, uncrowded Rainbow or less-stressed club skiing areas. Club areas are publicly accessible and usually less crowded and cheaper than commercial fields, even though nonmembers pay a higher fee.

Practicalities

New Zealand's commercial ski areas aren't generally set up as 'resorts' with chalets, lodges or hotels. Rather, accommodation and après-ski carousing are often in surrounding towns, connected with the slopes via daily shuttles. Many club areas have lodges where you can stay, subject to availability.

Visitor information centres in NZ, and Tourism New Zealand (www.newzealand.com) internationally, have info on the various ski areas and can make bookings and organise packages. Lift passes usually cost between $70 and $110 per adult per

Best Skiing & Snowboarding

Best for Beginners or with Kids
Mt Hutt, Central Canterbury

Mt Dobson, South Canterbury

Roundhill, South Canterbury

Coronet Peak, Queenstown

The Remarkables, Queenstown

Best Snowboarding
Mt Hutt, Central Canterbury

Treble Cone, Wanaka

Cardrona, Wanaka

Ohau, South Canterbury

Whakapapa & Turoa, Tongariro National Park

Best Après-Ski Watering Holes
Powderhorn Chateau, Ohakune

Dubliner, Methven

Cardrona Hotel, Cardrona

Lalaland, Wanaka

Rhino's Ski Shack, Queenstown

day (half-price for kids). Lesson-and-lift packages are available at most areas. Ski and snowboard equipment rental starts at around $50 a day (cheaper for multiday hire). Private/group lessons start at around $120/60 per hour.

Websites

www.snow.co.nz Reports, cams and ski info across the country.

www.nzski.com Reports, employment, passes and webcams for Mt Hutt, Coronet Peak and the Remarkables.

www.newzealandski.co.nz Good all-round online portal for South Island ski areas.

www.chillout.co.nz Info on Mt Lyford, Awakino, Hanmer Springs, Cheeseman, Roundhill, Rainbow, Temple Basin, Treble Cone, Fox Peak, Mt Dobson, Mt Olympus, Porters, Craigieburn Valley and Broken River ski areas.

www.mtruapehu.com Reports, passes, courses and webcams for Mt Ruapehu's Whakapapa and Turoa ski areas.

North Island
Tongariro National Park

Whakapapa & Turoa (p270) On either side of Mt Ruapehu, these well-run twin resorts comprise

---

HELISKIING

New Zealand's remote heights are tailor-made for heliskiing, with operators covering a wide off-piste area along the pristine slopes of the Southern Alps, including extreme skiing for the hardcore. Costs range from around $825 to $1450 for three to eight runs. Heliskiing is available at Coronet Peak, Treble Cone, Cardrona, Mt Hutt, Mt Lyford, Ohau and Hanmer Springs; independent operators include the following:

Alpine Heliski (p548)

Harris Mountains Heli-Ski (p548)

Methven Heliski (p491)

Over The Top (p549)

Southern Lakes Heliski (p548)

NZ's largest ski area. Whakapapa has 65 trails spread across 1050 hectares, plus cross-country skiing, a terrain park and NZ's highest cafe! Drive from Whakapapa Village (6km; free parking) or shuttle-bus in from National Park Village, Taupo, Turangi or Whakapapa Village. Smaller Turoa has a beginners lift, snowboarding, downhill and cross-country skiing, and over 700m of vertical descent from the Highnoon Express chairlift. There's free parking or shuttle-bus transport from Ohakune, 17km away, which has the North Island's liveliest après-ski scene.

Tukino (p270) Club-operated Tukino is on Mt Ruapehu's east, 46km from Turangi. It's quite remote, 14km down a gravel road from the sealed Desert Rd (SH1), and you need a 4WD vehicle to get in. It's uncrowded, with mostly beginner and intermediate runs.

Taranaki

Manganui (p227) Offers volcano-slope, club-run skiing on the eastern slopes of spectacular Mt Taranaki in Egmont National Park, 22km from Stratford, 55km from New Plymouth (and a 25-minute walk from the car park). Taranaki is a surf-mad province so expect the slopes to be dominated by snowboarders. Limited lodge accommodation up the mountain.

South Island
Queenstown & Wanaka

Coronet Peak (p547) At the Queenstown region's oldest ski field, snow-making systems and treeless slopes provide excellent skiing and snowboarding for all levels. There's night skiing Friday and Saturday from July to September. Shuttles run from Queenstown, 16km away.

The Remarkables (p547) Visually remarkable, this ski field is also near Queenstown (24km away) – shuttle buses run during ski season. It has a good smattering of intermediate, advanced and beginner runs (kids under 10 ski free). Look for the sweeping 'Homeward Bound' run.

Treble Cone (p547) The highest and largest of the southern lakes ski areas is in a spectacular location 26km from Wanaka, with steep slopes suitable for intermediate to advanced skiers (a rather professional vibe). There are also half-pipes and a terrain park for boarders.

Cardrona (p573) Around 34km from Wanaka, with several high-capacity chairlifts, beginners

Ski Areas

tows and Parks 'n' Pipes for the freestylers. Buses run from Wanaka and Queenstown during ski season. A friendly scene with good services for skiers with disabilities, plus an on-mountain crèche.

Snow Farm New Zealand (p573) NZ's only commercial Nordic (cross-country) ski area is 33km from Wanaka on the Pisa Range, high above the Cardrona Valley. There are 55km of groomed trails, huts with facilities, and thousands of hectares of open snow.

South Canterbury

Ohau (p501) This commercial ski area is on Mt Sutton, 42km from Twizel. There are plenty of intermediate and advanced runs, excellent snowboarding, two terrain parks and Lake Ohau Lodge.

Mt Dobson (p498) The 3km-wide basin here, 26km from Fairlie, caters for learners and intermediates, and has a terrain park and famously dry powder. On a clear day you can see Aoraki/Mt Cook and the Pacific Ocean from the summit.

Fox Peak (p493) An affordable club ski area 40km from Fairlie in the Two Thumb Range. Expect rope tows, good cross-country skiing and dorm-style accommodation.

Roundhill (p499) A small field with wide, gentle slopes, perfect for beginners and intermediates. It's 32km from Lake Tekapo village.

Central Canterbury

Mt Hutt (p491) One of the highest ski areas in the southern hemisphere, as well as one of NZ's best. It's close to Methven; Christchurch is 118km to the west – ski shuttles service both towns. Road access is steep – be extremely cautious in lousy weather. Plenty of beginner, intermediate and advanced slopes, with chairlifts, heliskiing and wide-open faces that are good for learning to snowboard.

Porters (p488) The closest commercial ski area to Christchurch (96km away on the Arthur's Pass

DOUGLAS PEARSON / GETTY IMAGES ©

Top: Snowboarder, Cardrona Alpine Resort (p573)

Bottom: View over the ski field at Coronet Peak (p547)

road). 'Big Mama', at 620m, is one of the steepest runs in NZ, but there are wider, gentler slopes, too. There's also a terrain park, good cross-country runs along the ridge, and lodge accommodation.

Temple Basin (p488) A club field 4km from the Arthur's Pass township. It's a 50-minute walk uphill from the car park to the ski-area lodges. There's floodlit skiing at night and excellent backcountry runs for snowboarders.

Craigieburn Valley (p488) Centred on Hamilton Peak, Craigieburn Valley is 40km from Arthur's Pass. It's one of NZ's most challenging club areas, with intermediate and advanced runs (no beginners). Accommodation in please-do-a-chore lodges.

Broken River (p488) Not far from Craigieburn Valley, this club field is a 15- to 20-minute walk from the car park and has a real sense of isolation. Reliable snow, laid-back vibe. Catered or self-catered lodge accommodation available.

Cheeseman (p488) Another cool club area in the Craigieburn Range, this family-friendly operation is around 100km from Christchurch. Based on Mt Cockayne, it's a wide, sheltered basin with drive-to-the-snow road access. Lodge accommodation available.

Mt Olympus (p488) Difficult to find (but worth the search), 2096m Mt Olympus is 58km from Methven and 12km from Lake Ida. This club area has intermediate and advanced runs, and there are solid cross-country trails to other areas. Access is sometimes 4WD-only, depending on conditions. Lodge accommodation available.

Northern South Island

Hanmer Springs (p485) A commercial field based on Mt St Patrick, 17km from Hanmer Springs township, with mostly intermediate and advanced runs. The Adventure Centre provides shuttles during the season.

Mt Lyford (p485) Around 60km from both Hanmer Springs and Kaikoura, and 4km from Mt Lyford village, this is more of a 'resort' than most NZ ski fields, with accommodation and eating options. There's a good mix of runs and a terrain park.

Rainbow (p424) Borders Nelson Lakes National Park (100km from Nelson, a similar distance from Blenheim), with varied terrain, minimal crowds and good cross-country skiing. Chains are often required. St Arnaud is the closest town (32km).

Otago

Awakino (p512) A small player in North Otago, but worth a visit for intermediate skiers. Oamaru is 45km away; Omarama is 66km inland. Weekend lodge-and-ski packages available.

Plan Your Trip

Extreme New Zealand

An abundance of adventure activities tempt even the meekest and mildest to push their limits, but it's not all about the adrenaline buzz. Pants-wetting, often illogical escapades such as skydiving, bungy jumping mountain biking and jetboating may be thrilling, but they also immerse you in New Zealand's amazing landscapes in inspiring new ways.

Best Extreme New Zealand

Best Skydive Drop Zones
Queenstown

Motueka

Taupo

Fox & Franz Josef Glaciers

Top White-Water Rafting Trips
Buller Gorge, Murchison

Tongariro River, Taupo

Rangitata, Geraldine

Shotover Canyon, Queenstown

Top Mountain Biking Tracks
Queen Charlotte Track, Marlborough

Redwoods Whakarewarewa Forest, Rotorua

West Coast Wilderness Trail, Hokitika

Ohakune Old Coach Road, Central Plateau

Alps 2 Ocean, South Canterbury

On Land

Bungy Jumping

Bungy jumping was made famous by Kiwi AJ Hackett's 1986 plunge from the Eiffel Tower, after which he teamed up with champion NZ skier Henry van Asch to turn the endeavour into an accessible pursuit for anyone.

Today their original home base of Queenstown is a spiderweb of bungy cords, including the AJ Hackett's triad: the 134m Nevis Bungy (the highest); the 43m Kawarau Bungy (the original); and the Ledge Bungy (at the highest altitude – diving off a 400m-high platform). There's another scenic jump at Thrillseekers Canyon near Hanmer Springs. On the North Island, head to Taihape, Rotorua or Auckland, although the most scenic jump is over the Waikato River in Taupo. Huge rope swings offer variation on the theme; head to Queenstown's Shotover Canyon or Nevis Swings for that swooshy buzz.

Paragliding & Hang Gliding

A surprisingly gentle but still thrilling way to take to the skies, paragliding involves setting sail from a hillside or clifftop under a parachute-like wing. Hang gliding is similar but with a smaller, rigid wing.

Most flights are conducted in tandem with a master pilot, although it's also possible to get lessons to go it alone. To give it a whirl, try a tandem flight in Queenstown, Wanaka, Nelson, Motueka, Hawke's Bay or Auckland. The New Zealand Hang Gliding and Paragliding Association (www.nzhgpa.org.nz) rules the roost.

Mountain Biking & Cycle Touring

NZ has gone mountain bike mad. Referred to as 'the new golf' for its popularity among people of a certain age, it has actually emerged as an obsession for all ages. The New Zealand Cycle Trail has certainly propelled this off-road juggernaut, but there are a seemingly endless number of other trails all over the country.

Mountain bike parks – most with various trail grades and skills areas (and handy bike hire, usually) – are great for trying mountain biking NZ style. The most famous is Rotorua's Redwoods Whakarewarewa Forest, but among legions of others are Wellington's Makara Peak, Auckland's Woodhill Forest, and Queenstown's downhill park, fed by the Skyline Gondola.

Classic trails include the 42 Traverse around Tongariro National Park, the Rameka on Takaka Hill, and the trails around Christchurch's Port Hills – but this is just the tip of the iceberg. An increasing number of DOC hiking trails are being converted to dual use – such as the tricky but epic Heaphy Track – but mountain biking is often restricted to low season due to hiker numbers. Track damage is also an issue, so check with DOC before starting out.

Your clue that there's some great biking around is the presence of bike-hire outfits. Bowl on up and pick their brains. Most likely cycle-obsessed themselves, they'll soon point you in the direction of an appropriate ride. The go-to book is *Classic New Zealand Mountain Bike Rides* (from bookshops, bike shops and www.kennett.co.nz).

But what, you may ask, about cycle touring? Often perceived as uncomfortable and dangerous due to changeable weather and road conditions, there are some remarkable road journeys such as the Southern Scenic Route in the deep south. To find out more about this pursuit, check out the *Pedallers' Paradise* booklets by Nigel Rushton (www.paradise-press.co.nz).

Rock Climbing

Time to chalk-up your fingers and don some natty little rubber shoes. On the North Island, popular rock-climbing areas include Auckland's Mt Eden Quarry; Whanganui Bay, Kinloch, Kawakawa Bay and Motuoapa near Lake Taupo; Mangatepopo Valley and Whakapapa Gorge on the Central Plateau; Humphries Castle and Warwick Castle on Mt Taranaki; and Piarere and popular Wharepapa South in the Waikato.

On the South Island, try the Port Hills area above Christchurch or Castle Hill on the road to Arthur's Pass. West of Nelson, the marble and limestone mountains of Golden Bay and Takaka Hill provide prime climbing. Other options are Long Beach (north of Dunedin), and Mihiwaka and Lovers Leap on the Otago Peninsula.

Raining? You'll find indoor climbing walls all around the country, including at Rotorua, Whangarei, Auckland, Tauranga, Taupo, Wellington, Christchurch and Hamilton.

Climb New Zealand (www.climb.co.nz) has the low-down on the gnarliest overhangs around NZ, plus access and instruction info.

Skydiving

With some of the most scenic jump-zones in the world, New Zealand is a fantastic place to make the leap. First-time skydivers can knock off this bucket-list item with a tandem jump, strapped to a qualified instructor, experiencing up to 75 seconds of free fall before the chute opens. The thrill is worth every dollar (from $249 for a 9000ft jump to $559 from a whopping 19,000ft; extra for a DVD/photographs). Check out the New Zealand Parachute Federation (www.nzpf.org) for more info.

On the Water
Jetboating

The jetboat was invented in NZ by an engineer from Fairlie – Bill Hamilton – who wanted a boat that could navigate shallow, local rivers. He credited his eventual success to Archimedes, but as most jetboat drivers will inevitably tell you, Kiwi Bill is the hero of the jetboat story.

River jetboat tours can be found throughout NZ, and while much is made of the hair-raising 360-degree spins that see passengers drenched and grinning from ear to ear, they are really just a sideshow. Just as Bill would have it, jetboat journeys take you deep into wilderness you could otherwise never see, and as such they offer one of NZ's most rewarding tour experiences.

Big ticket trips such as Queenstown's Shotover, Kawarau and Dart all live up to the hype. But the quieter achievers will blow your skirt up just as high. Check out the Buller, Waiatoto (Haast) and Wilkin in Mt Aspiring National Park, and the Whanganui – one of the most magical A-to-B jetboat trips of them all.

Parasailing & Kiteboarding

Parasailing (dangling from a modified parachute over the water, while being pulled along by a speedboat) is perhaps the easiest way for humans to achieve assisted flight. There are operators in the Bay of Islands, Bay of Plenty, Taupo, Wanaka and Queenstown.

Kiteboarding (aka kitesurfing), where a mini parachute drags you across the ocean on a mini surfboard, can be attempted at Paihia, Tauranga, Mt Maunganui, Raglan, Wellington and Nelson. Karikari Peninsula near Cape Reinga on NZ's northern tip is a kiteboarding mecca.

You will also note that the stand-up paddleboard (SUP) is most definitely on the up, but this activity is less extreme and more knackering.

Scuba Diving

NZ has some rewarding scuba territory, with warm waters in the north, interesting sea life all over and the odd wreck for good measure. The flag-bearer is the Poor Knights Islands near Whangarei, where sub-tropical currents carry and encourage a vibrant mix of sea life. The wreck of the Greenpeace flagship *Rainbow Warrior* is nearby.

Other notable sites include the Bay of Islands, Hauraki Gulf, Goat Island and Gisborne's Te Tapuwae o Rongokako Marine Reserve. In the Marlborough Sounds, the *Mikhail Lermontov* is the largest diveable cruise-ship wreck in the world. In Fiordland head for Dusky Sound, Milford Sound and Doubtful Sound, which offer amazingly clear conditions.

Expect to pay anywhere from $180 for a short, introductory, pool-based scuba course, and around $600 for a four-day, PADI-approved, ocean-dive course. One-off organised boat- and land-based dives start at around $170. Resources include:

New Zealand Underwater Association (www. nzu.org.nz)

Dive New Zealand (www.divenewzealand.com)

Sea Kayaking

Sea kayaking offers a wonderful perspective of the coastline and gets you close to marine wildlife you may otherwise never see. It's also lots of fun and thrilling at times. There is a potential pitfall, and it's to do with tandem kayaks...let's just say that they don't call them 'divorce boats' for nothing!

As you'd expect for a seafaring nation, there are ample places to get paddling. Hotspots include Waiheke and Great Barrier Islands, the Bay of Islands and Coromandel Peninsula, Marlborough Sounds (from Picton) and Abel Tasman National Park. Kaikoura is exceptional for wildlife spotting, and Fiordland for jaw-dropping scenery. The Kiwi Association of Sea Kayakers (www.kask.org.nz) has useful information.

NGA HAERENGA

The New Zealand Cycle Trail (www.nzcycletrail.com) – known in Māori as Nga Haerenga, 'the journeys' – is a 23-strong series of off-road trails known as Great Rides. Spread from north to south they are of diverse length, terrain and difficulty, with many following history-rich old railway lines and pioneer trails, while others are freshly cut, flowing and big fun. Almost all penetrate remarkable landscapes.

There are plenty of options for beginner to intermediate cyclists, with several hardcore exceptions including the Old Ghost Road, which is set to be an internationally renowned classic. The majority are also well supported by handy bike hire, shuttles, and dining and accommodation options, making them a mighty desirable way to explore New Zealand. Most trails have their own websites with comprehensive details, but see the umbrella site listed above for an overview and links.

SURFING IN NZ

As a surfer I feel particularly guilty in letting the reader in on a local secret – NZ has a sensational mix of quality waves perfect for beginners and experienced surfers. As long as you're willing to travel off the beaten track, you can score some great, uncrowded waves. The islands of NZ are hit with swells from all points of the compass, so with a little weather knowledge and a little effort, numerous options present themselves. Point breaks, reefs, rocky shelves and hollow sandy beach breaks can all be found – take your pick!

Surfing New Zealand (www.surfingnz.co.nz) recommends a number of surf schools on its website. Most NZ beaches hold good rideable breaks. Some of the ones I particularly enjoy:

Waikato Raglan: NZ's most famous surf break and usually the first stop for overseas surfies

Coromandel Whangamata

Bay of Plenty Mt Maunganui, now with a 250m artificial reef that creates huge waves, and Matakana Island

Taranaki Fitzroy Beach, Stent Rd and Greenmeadows Point all lie along the 'Surf Highway'

East Coast Hicks Bay, Gisborne city beaches and Mahia Peninsula

Wellington Region Beaches such as Lyall Bay, Castlepoint and Tora

Marlborough & Nelson Kaikoura Peninsula, Mangamaunu and Meatworks

Canterbury Taylors Mistake and Sumner Bar

Otago Dunedin is a good base for surfing on the South Island, with access to a number of superb breaks, such as St Clair Beach

West Coast Punakaiki and Tauranga Bay

Southland Porridge and Centre Island

NZ water temperatures and climate vary greatly from north to south. For comfort while surfing, wear a wetsuit. In summer on the North Island you can get away with a spring suit and boardies; or the South Island, a 2mm–3mm steamer. In winter on the North Island use a 2mm–3mm steamer, and on the South Island a 3mm–5mm with all the extras.

Josh Kronfeld, surfer and former All Black

White-Water Rafting, Kayaking & Canoeing

Epic mountain ranges and associated rainfall mean there's no shortage of great rivers to raft, nor any shortage of operators ready to get you into the rapids. Rivers are graded from I to VI (VI meaning 'unraftable'), with operators often running a couple of different trips to suit ability and age (rougher stretches are usually limited to rafters aged 13 or above).

Queenstown's Shotover and Kawarau Rivers are deservedly popular, but the Rangitata (Geraldine), Buller (Murchison) and the Arnold and Waiho rate just as highly. For a multiday epic, check out the Landsborough. The central North Island dishes up plenty, including the popular Tongariro, Rangitikei, Mohaka and Wairoa. There are also the Kaituna Cascades near Rotorua, the highlight of which is the 7m drop at Okere Falls.

Kayaking and canoeing are rampant, particularly on friendly lake waters, although there are still plenty of places to paddle the rapids, including some relatively easy stuff on the Whanganui 'Great Walk'.

Resources include:

New Zealand Rafting Association (www.nz-rafting.co.nz)

Whitewater NZ (www.rivers.org.nz)

New Zealand Kayak (www.kayaknz.co.nz)

Plan Your Trip
Food & Drink

Top NZ Restaurants

Clooney (p89)
Auckland's best restaurant? Oh, how they argue... Unfortunately, no sign of George.

Blue Kanu (p555)
This surprising Queenstown eatery presents some of the best Māori, Pasifika and Asian flavours in NZ.

Gothenburg (p173)
Reason enough to visit Hamilton: super service, brilliant booze and marvellous mains (and tapas).

Ortega Fish Shack (p367)
New Zealand and the sea are inextricably intertwined. Super seafood in Wellington.

Roots (p477)
One of NZ's most stylish and lauded restaurants: local and seasonal degustation, in little Lyttelton.

Pegasus Bay (p487)
The pick of the Waipara Valley winery restaurants.

Travellers, start your appetites! Eating in New Zealand is a highlight of any visit. You can be utilitarian if money is tight, or embrace NZ's full culinary bounty, from fresh seafood and gourmet burgers to farmers market fruit-and-veg and crisp-linen fine dining. Eateries range from fish and chip shops and pub bistros to retro cafes and ritzy dining rooms. Drinking here, too, presents boundless opportunities to have a good time, with Kiwi coffee, craft beer and wine at the fore.

Modern NZ

Once upon a time in a decade not so far away, New Zealand subsisted on a modest diet of 'meat and three veg'. Fine fare was a Sunday roast boiled into submission, and lasagne was considered exotic. Fortunately, the country's culinary sophistication has evolved: kitchens now thrive on bending conventions and absorbing multicultural influences from around the planet. The resultant cuisine is dynamic and surprising.

Immigration has been key to this culinary rise – particularly the post-WWII influx of migrants from Europe, Asia and the Middle East – as has an adventurous breed of local restaurant-goers and the elevation of Māori and Pacific Islander flavours and ingredients to the mainstream.

In order to wow the socks off increasingly demanding diners, restaurants must now succeed in fusing contrasting ingredients and traditions into ever more innovative fare. The phrase 'Modern NZ' has been coined to classify this unclassifiable technique: a melange of East and West, a swirl

LOCAL DELICACIES

Touring the menus of NZ, keep an eye out for these local delights: kina (sea urchin), paua (abalone), kumara (sweet potato, often served as chips), whitebait (tiny fish, often cooked into fritters or omelettes), and the humble kiwifruit.

of Atlantic and Pacific Rim, and a dash of authentic French and Italian.

If this all sounds overwhelming, fear not. Traditional staples still hold sway (lamb, beef, venison, green-lipped mussels), but dishes are characterised by interesting flavours and fresh ingredients rather than fuss, clutter or snobbery. Spicing ranges from gentle to extreme, seafood is plentiful and meats are tender and full flavoured. Enjoy!

Vegetarians & Vegans

Most large urban centres have at least one dedicated vegetarian cafe or restaurant: see the Vegetarians New Zealand website (www.vegetarians.co.nz) for listings. Beyond this, almost all restaurants and cafes offer some vegetarian menu choices (although sometimes only one or two). Many eateries also provide gluten-free and vegan options. Always check that house-made stocks and sauces are vegetarian, too!

Lonely Planet uses a vegetarian icon in Eating listings to indicate either a good vegetarian selection, or an entirely vegetarian menu.

Cafes & Coffee

Somewhere between the early 2000s and now, New Zealand cottoned on to coffee culture in a big way. Caffeine has become a nationwide addiction: there are Italian-style espresso machines in virtually every cafe, boutique roasters are de rigueur and, in urban areas, the qualified barista (coffee maker) is the norm. Auckland, Christchurch and student-filled Dunedin have borne generations of coffee aficionados, but Wellington takes top billing as NZ's caffeine capital. The cafe and bean-roasting scene here rivals the most vibrant in the world, and is very inclusive and fam-

ily friendly. Join the arty local crew and dunk yourself into it over a late-night conversation or an early-morning recovery.

Pubs, Bars & Beer

Gone are the days when Kiwi pubs were male bastions with dim lighting, smoky air and sticky beer-soaked carpets – these days locals go to the pub with their kids for brunch or to meet friends for some tapas as much as anything else. Food has become integral to the NZ pub experience, along with the inexorable rise of craft beer in the national drinking consciousness.

Craft beer – small-batch beers brewed independently of big-label brewers with local ingredients, flavours and enthusiasm – is New Zealand's most recent obsession. Myriad small breweries have popped up around the country in the last several years, paralleled by a boom in small bars in which to sample the product. Wellington, in particular, offers dozens of dedicated craft-beer bars, with revolving beers on tap and passionate bar staff who know all there is to know about where the beers have come from, who made them and what's in them. A night on the tiles here has become less about volume and capacity, more about selectivity and virtue.

But aside from the food and the fancy beer, the NZ pub remains a place where all Kiwis can unite with a common purpose: to watch their beloved All Blacks play rugby on the big screen. Try to catch an AB's game at a pub or a bar while you're here – a raucous experience to say the least!

TO MARKET, TO MARKET

There are more than 50 farmers markets held around NZ. Most happen on weekends and are upbeat local affairs, where visitors can meet local producers and find fresh regional produce. Mobile coffee is usually present, and tastings are offered by enterprising and innovative stall holders. Bring a carry bag, and get there early for the best stuff! Check out www.farmersmarkets.org.nz for market locations, dates and times.

Grapevines at a vineyard, Marlborough (p396)

Wine Regions

Like the wine industry in neighbouring Australia, the New Zealand version has European migrants to thank for its status and success – visionary visitors who knew good soils and good climate when they saw it, and planted the first vines. NZ's oldest vineyard – Mission Estate Winery (p346) in Hawke's Bay – was established by French Catholic missionaries in 1851 and is still producing top-flight wines today.

But it wasn't until the 1970s that things really got going, with traditional agricultural exports dwindling, Kiwis travelling more and the introduction of BYO ('Bring Your Own' wine) restaurant licensing conspiring to raise interest and demand for local wines.

Since then, New Zealand cool-climate wines have conquered the world, a clutch of key regions producing the lion's share of bottles. Organised day tours via minivan or bicycle are a great way to visit a few select wineries.

Marlborough (p396) NZ's biggest and most widely known wine region sits at the top of the South Island, where a microclimate of warm days and cool nights is perfect for growing sauvignon blanc. You could spend many days touring the many cellar doors here (and why not?).

Hawke's Bay (p346) The North Island's sunny East Coast is the cradle of the NZ wine industry – chardonnay and syrah are the mainstays. The Gisborne region a bit further north also produces some terrific chardonnays.

The Wairarapa (p377) Just an hour or two over the hills from Wellington, the Wairarapa region – centred on boutiquey Martinborough – is prime naughty-weekender territory, and produces winning pinot noir.

Central Otago Reaching from Cromwell in the north to Alexandra in the south and Gibbston near Queenstown in the west, the South Island's Central Otago region produces sublime riesling and pinot noir.

Waipara Valley (p487) Not to be left out of proceedings, Christchurch has its own nearby wine region – the Waipara Valley just north of the city – where divine riesling and pinot gris comes to fruition.

Waiheke Island (p102) In the middle of the Hauraki Gulf a short ferry ride from Auckland, Waiheke has a hot, dry microclimate that just happens to be brilliant for growing reds and rosés.

Plan Your Trip
Travel with Children

New Zealand is a terrific place to travel with kids: safe and affordable, with loads of playgrounds, kid-centric activities, a moderate climate and chilli-free cuisine. And it never takes long to get from A to B here – helpful when the backseat drivers (or those in the front) are running thin on patience.

New Zealand for Kids

Fabulous wildlife parks, beaches, parks, snowy slopes, interactive museums and kids playgrounds (with slides, swings, see-saws etc) proliferate across NZ. This is a country where things happen on a comprehendable scale for kids.

Accommodation

Many motels and holiday parks have playgrounds, games rooms and kids' DVDs, and often fenced swimming pools, trampolines and acres of grass. Cots and high chairs aren't always available at budget and midrange accommodation, but top-end hotels supply them and often provide child-minding services. Many B&Bs promote themselves as blissfully kid-free, and hostels tend to focus on the backpacker demographic. But there are plenty of hostels (including YHA) that do allow kids.

For large families, book ahead if you all want to sleep in the same room: many motels and hotels have adjoining rooms that can be opened up to form large family suites.

Admission Fees & Discounts

Kids' and family rates are often available for accommodation, tours, attraction entry fees, and air, bus and train transport, with discounts of as much as 50% off the adult

Best Regions for Kids

Wellington Region

Little legs aren't very long – you need a compact city if you're walking around with kids. Wellington fits the bill, with a brilliant museum, a ratchety cable car, lots of cheery cafes and fab Kapiti Coast beaches less than an hour away.

Rotorua & the Bay of Plenty

Wow, bubbling volcanic mud, stinky gas, gushing geysers and Māori *haka* performances! Rotorua is hard to beat from a kid's perspective. And around the Bay of Plenty coast are beaut beaches and plenty of fish and chip shops.

Queenstown & Wanaka

The NZ snow scene can be very 'adult' if you want it to be. But it's just as easy to enjoy with kids (actually, it's more fun). Head for the kid-friendly resorts and go snow-crazy.

Christchurch & Canterbury

Nature parks, rowboats and botanic gardens in the big city, and the amazing Banks Peninsula not far away (wildlife aplenty).

rate. Note that the definition of 'child' can vary from under 12 to under 18 years; toddlers (under four years old) usually get free admission and transport.

Babysitting

For specialised child care, try www.rock mybaby.co.nz, or look under 'babysitters' and 'child care centres' in the Yellow Pages (www.yellow.co.nz).

Breastfeeding & Nappy Changing

Most Kiwis are relaxed about public breastfeeding and nappy changing: wrestling with a nappy (diaper) in the open boot of a car is a common sight! Alternatively, most major towns have public rooms where parents can go to feed their baby or change a nappy. Infant formula and disposable nappies are widely available.

Eating Out with Children

If you sidestep the flashier restaurants, children are generally welcome in NZ eateries. Cafes are kid-friendly, and you'll see families getting in early for dinner in pub dining rooms. Most places can supply high chairs. Dedicated kids menus are common, but selections are usually uninspiring (ham-and-pineapple pizza, fish fingers, chicken nuggets etc). If a restaurant doesn't have a kids' menu, find something on the regular menu and ask the kitchen to downsize it. It's usually fine to bring toddler food in with you. If the sun is shining, hit the farmers markets and find yourself a picnic spot.

Children's Highlights

Beaches

Hahei Beach (p208) The classic NZ summer beach. On the Coromandel Peninsula.

Mt Maunganui (p304) Sand and surf for the kids, cafes and bars for the oldies.

Hot Water Beach (p209) Dig your own hot pool in the Coromandel sand.

Ngarunui Beach (p179) Learn to surf on gentle Waikato waves.

St Kilda Beach (p521) It's a chilly swim in Dunedin, but the kids don't seem to mind.

Wildlife Encounters

Kiwi Birdlife Park (p542) Spot a Kiwi in Queenstown.

West Coast Wildlife Centre (p448) Meet a rowi – the rarest kiwi in the world. At Franz Josef.

Cape Palliser (p378) Sniff out the North Island's largest seal colony.

Auckland Zoo (p73) Check out NZ's pint-sized dinosaur, the tuatara.

Zealandia (p353) Twittering birds in the predator-free Wellington hills.

Amazing Museums

Te Papa (p357) Earthquakes, Māori culture and molten magma. In Wellington.

Auckland Museum (p68) The Auckland volcanic field and a 25m *waka taua* (war canoe).

New Zealand Rugby Museum (p244) Hands-on fun for mini–All Blacks in Palmerston North.

Canterbury Museum (p463) A mummy, dinosaur bones and a cool Discovery Centre in Christchurch.

Puke Ariki (p217) A mighty big shark in New Plymouth.

We're Hungry!

Hastings Farmers Market (p345) Fill a basket and have a picnic.

Mt Vic Chippery (p365) Wellington's best fish and (five kinds of!) chips.

Schoc Chocolates (p380) Otherworldly chocs in the Wairarapa.

Kiwifruit (p413) Pick up a ripe bag at harvest time around Motueka.

Planning

Lonely Planet's *Travel with Children* contains buckets of useful information for travel with little'uns. To aid your planning once you get to NZ, look for the free *Kidz Go!* (www.kidzgo.co.nz) and *LetsGoKids* (www.letsgokids.com.au) magazines at visitor information centres.

Handy family websites:

➡ www.kidspot.co.nz
➡ www.kidsnewzealand.com
➡ www.kidsfriendlytravel.com

Regions at a Glance

Auckland

Eating & Drinking
Geology
Coastline

Restaurants, Bars & Cafes

As well as having the lion's share of the nation's best restaurants, Auckland has excellent markets, a plethora of cheap Asian eateries, a hip cafe and bar scene, and wine regions on three of its flanks. And coffee culture is booming (don't tell anyone from Wellington...).

Volcanic Viewpoints

Auckland is, quite literally, a global hotspot: over 50 separate volcanoes have formed this unique topography – and the next one could pop up at any time. Take a hike up one of the dormant cones dotting the landscape for a high, wide and handsome city panorama.

Beaches

From the calm, child-friendly bays facing the Hauraki Gulf to the black-sand surf beaches of the west coast, to the breathtaking coastline of the offshore islands, beach-lovers are spoiled for choice around Auckland.

p62

Bay of Islands & Northland

Coastline
Wilderness
History

Beaches & Bays

Bay after beautiful bay lines Northland's east coast, making it a favourite destination for families, surfers and fishing fans. To the west, windswept beaches stretch for dozens of kilometres, forming towering sand dunes.

Ancient Forests

Kauri forests once blanketed NZ's entire north, and in the pockets where the giants remain, particularly in the Waipoua Forest, they're an imposing sight.

Kerikeri & Waitangi

New Zealand was settled top down by both Māori and Europeans, with missionaries erecting the country's oldest surviving buildings in Kerikeri. In nearby Waitangi, the treaty that founded the modern nation was first signed.

p123

Waikato & the Coromandel Peninsula

Coastline
Towns
Caves

Beaches & Surf

Around Raglan you'll find safe swimming and world-class surf at legendary Manu Bay. Beaches on the Coromandel are extremely popular in summer, but glorious isolation can still be yours.

That Small-Town Vibe

Te Aroha, Cambridge, Matamata and Raglan have great pubs, cafes, restaurants and friendly locals, while Thames and Coromandel Town display their historic gold-rush roots.

Waitomo Caves

Don't miss blackwater rafting (along underground rivers) at Waitomo Caves, NZ's most staggering cave site... or just float lazily through amazing grottoes of glowworms.

p166

Taranaki & Whanganui

Wilderness
Cities
Coastline

National Parks

Steeped in Māori lore, Whanganui National Park is one of NZ's most isolated and interesting parks. Lording over New Plymouth, Mt Taranaki (Egmont National Park) is a picture-perfect tramping peak.

Underrated Hubs

New Plymouth, Whanganui and Palmerston North are mid-sized cities usually overlooked by travellers. But stay a day: you'll find fantastic restaurants, hip bars, great coffee, wonderful museums and friendly folk.

Surf & Sand

Hit Surf Hwy 45 south of New Plymouth for black-sand beaches and gnarly breaks. Whanganui offers rugged beaches, while the Horowhenua District south of Palmerston North has acres of empty brown sand.

p216

Taupo & the Central Plateau

Wilderness
Scenery
Outdoor
Activities

Lake & Rivers

NZ's mightiest river (the Waikato) is born from NZ's greatest lake (Taupo): aquatic pursuits in picturesque settings abound. The water is famously chilly, but hot springs bubble up on the lakeside and riverbank.

Epic Landscapes

The three steaming, smoking, occasionally erupting volcanoes at the heart of the North Island – Ruapehu, Tongariro and Ngauruhoe – are an imposing sight, the focus of skiing in winter and tramping the rest of the year.

Extreme Taupo

Skydiving, bungy jumping, whitewater rafting, jetboating, mountain biking, wakeboarding, parasailing, skiing – you want thrills, you got 'em.

p250

Rotorua & the Bay of Plenty

Geothermal
Activity
Indigenous
Culture
Activities

Volcanic Hubbub

The Rotorua landscape is littered with geysers, steaming geothermal vents, hot mineral springs and boiling mud pools. NZ's only active volcano, Whakaari (White Island), is 48km off the coast of Whakatane.

Māori Cultural Experiences

Engage with Māori culture in Rotorua: cultural experiences for travellers include traditional dance and musical performances, *haka* (war dances) and *hangi* (Māori feasts).

Outdoor Sports

Paragliding, surfing, skydiving, zorbing, jetboating, blokarting, white-water rafting, mountain biking, kayaking... It's all here – or just have a swim at the beach.

p278

The East Coast

Coastline
Wine
Architecture

Coastal Scenery

Follow in the footsteps (or rather wake) of early Māori and James Cook along this stretch of coastline, home to the East Cape Lighthouse and Cape Kidnappers' gaggling gannet colony.

Gisborne & Hawke's Bay Wine Regions

Sip your way through Gisborne's bright chardonnays, then head to Hawke's Bay for seriously good Bordeaux-style reds and fine winery dining.

Art Deco Napier

Napier's art-deco town centre is a magnet for architecture lovers, the keenest of whom time their visit for the annual Art Deco Weekend, an extravaganza of music, wine, cars and costume.

p319

Wellington Region

Arts
Eating & Drinking
Nightlife

Museums & Galleries

Crowbarred into the city centre is a significant collation of quality display spaces, including the highly interactive Te Papa museum and internationally flavoured City Gallery Wellington.

Cafe Culture

With more than a dozen roasters and scores of hip cafes, Wellington remains the coffee capital of NZ. Get a hit from one of the best: Havana Coffee Works or Fidel's.

Bars

Between the boho bars around Cuba St and Courtenay Pl's glitzy drinking dens, you should find enough to keep you buzzed until sun-up.

p351

Marlborough & Nelson

Wilderness
Wine
Wildlife

National Parks

Not satisfied with just one national park, the Nelson region has three: Nelson Lakes, Kahurangi and Abel Tasman. You could tramp in all three over a week.

Marlborough Wine Region

Bobbing in Marlborough's sea of sauvignon blanc, riesling, pinot noir and bubbly are barrel-loads of quality cellar-door experiences and some fine regional food.

Kaikoura

The top of the South Island is home to a menagerie of creatures, both in the water and on the wing. Kaikoura offers myriad wildlife tours, but you might be just as content hanging out in this pretty little town.

p382

The West Coast

Wilderness
Outdoor Activities
History

Natural Wonders

With around 90% of its territory lying within the conservation estate, the West Coast is flush with natural wonders. Don't miss Oparara's famous arch and Punakaiki's Pancake Rocks.

Tramping

The West Coast offers tracks from an easy hour through to hardcore epics. Old mining and milling routes like Charming Creek Walkway and Mahinapua Walkway entice beginners and history buffs.

Pioneering Heritage

The West Coast's raffish pioneering heritage comes vividly to life at places like Denniston, Shantytown, Reefton and Jackson's Bay.

p425

Christchurch & Canterbury

History
Outdoor Activities
Scenery

Christchurch & Akaroa

Earthquakes have damaged Christchurch's architectural heritage, but key sights still showcase the city's history. Nearby, Akaroa proudly celebrates its French heritage.

Tramping & Kayaking

Explore alpine valleys around Arthur's Pass, kayak with dolphins on Akaroa Harbour, or visit Aoraki/Mt Cook National Park for tramping and kayaking amid glacial lakes.

Banks Peninsula & the Southern Alps

Descend from Banks Peninsula's Summit Rd to explore hidden bays and coves, and experience nature's grand scale: the river valleys, soaring peaks and glaciers of the Southern Alps.

p457

Dunedin & Otago

Wildlife
Wine
History

Birds, Seals & Sea Lions

Otago Peninsula's wild menagerie – seals, sea lions and penguins – patrol the rugged coastline, while rocky Taiaroa Head is the planet's only mainland breeding location for the magnificent royal albatross.

Bannockburn & Waitaki Valley

Barrel into the craggy valleys of Bannockburn for excellent vineyard restaurants and the world's best pinot noir, or delve into the up-and-coming Waitaki Valley wine scene for riesling and pinot gris.

Victoriana

Explore the arty and storied streets of Dunedin, or escape by foot or penny-farthing bicycle into the heritage ambience of Oamaru's Victorian Precinct.

p508

Queenstown & Wanaka

Outdoor Activities
Scenery
Wine

Extreme Queenstown

Nowhere else on earth offers so many adventurous activities: bungy jumping, river rafting and mountain biking only scratch Queenstown's adrenaline-fuelled surface.

Mountains & Lakes

Queenstown's photogenic combination of Lake Wakatipu and the soaring Remarkables is a real jaw-dropper. Or venture into prime NZ wilderness around Glenorchy and Mt Aspiring National Park.

Southern Wineries

Start with lunch at Amisfield Winery's excellent restaurant, then explore the Gibbston subregion and finish with a riesling tasting at Rippon, overlooking gorgeous Lake Wanaka.

p540

Fiordland & Southland

Scenery
Wilderness
Outdoor Activities

Epic Landscapes

The star of the deep-south show is remarkable Milford Sound, but take time to explore the rugged Catlins coast or experience the remote, end-of-the-world appeal of Stewart Island.

National Parks

Fiordland National Park comprises much of NZ's precious Te Wāhipounamu (Southwest New Zealand) World Heritage Area. Further south, Rakiura National Park showcases Stewart Island's isolated beauty.

Tramping & Sea Kayaking

Test yourself by tramping the Milford or Tuatapere Hump Ridge Tracks, or negotiate a sea kayak around glorious Doubtful Sound.

p575

On the Road

Auckland

Best Places to Eat

➡ Sidart (p90)

➡ Ortolana (p88)

➡ Depot (p87)

➡ Beirut (p87)

➡ Best Ugly Bagels (p86)

Best Places to Sleep

➡ Hotel DeBrett (p82)

➡ Enclosure Bay (p105)

➡ Ascot Parnell (p84)

➡ Fossil Bay Lodge (p105)

➡ Piha Beachstay – Jandal Palace (p114)

Why Go?

Paris may be the city of love, but Auckland is the city of many lovers, according to its Māori name, Tāmaki Makaurau. Those lovers so desired this place that they fought over it for centuries.

It's hard to imagine a more geographically blessed city. Its two harbours frame a narrow isthmus punctuated by volcanic cones and surrounded by fertile farmland. From any of its numerous vantage points you'll be surprised how close the Tasman Sea and Pacific Ocean come to kissing and forming a new island.

Whether it's the ruggedly beautiful west-coast beaches, or the glistening Hauraki Gulf with its myriad islands, the water's never far away. And within an hour's drive from the city's high-rise heart, there are dense tracts of rainforest, thermal springs, wineries and wildlife reserves. No wonder Auckland is regularly rated one of the world's top cities for quality of life and liveability.

When to Go

➡ Auckland has a mild climate, with the occasional chilly frost in winter and high humidity in summer.

➡ Summer months have an average of eight days of rain, but the weather is famously fickle, with 'four seasons in one day' possible at any time of the year.

➡ If you're after a big-city buzz, don't come between Christmas and New Year, when Aucklanders desert the city for the beach en masse; the sights remain open but many cafes and restaurants go into hibernation, some not surfacing again until well into January.

AUCKLAND

POP 1.5 MILLION

History

Māori occupation in the Auckland area dates back around 800 years. Initial settlements were concentrated on the Hauraki Gulf islands, but gradually the fertile isthmus beckoned and land was cleared for growing food.

Over hundreds of years Tamaki's many different tribes wrestled for control of the area, building *pa* (fortified villages) on the numerous volcanic cones. The Ngāti Whātua *iwi* (tribe) from the Kaipara Harbour took the upper hand in 1741, occupying the major *pa* sites. During the Musket Wars of the 1820s they were decimated by the northern tribe Ngāpuhi, leaving the land all but abandoned.

At the time the Treaty of Waitangi was signed in 1840, Governor Hobson had his base in the Bay of Islands. When Ngāti Whātua chief Te Kawau offered 3000 acres of land for sale on the northern edge of the Waitemata Harbour, Hobson decided to create a new capital, naming it after one of his patrons, George Eden (Earl of Auckland).

Beginning with just a few tents on a beach, the settlement grew quickly, and soon the port was busy exporting the region's produce, including kauri timber. However, it lost its capital status to centrally located Wellington after just 25 years.

Since the beginning of the 20th century Auckland has been New Zealand's fastest-growing city and its main industrial centre. Political deals may be done in Wellington, but Auckland is the big smoke in the land of the long white cloud.

In 2010 the municipalities and urban districts that made up the Auckland Region were merged into one 'super city', and in 2011 the newly minted metropolis was given a buff and shine to prepare it for hosting the Rugby World Cup. The waterfront was redeveloped, the art gallery and zoo were given a makeover, and a swag of new restaurants and bars popped up – leaving a more vibrant city in the cup's wake.

◎ Sights

Auckland is a city of volcanoes, with the ridges of lava flows forming its main thoroughfares and its many cones providing islands of green within the sea of suburbs. As well as being by far the largest, it's also the most multicultural of NZ's cities. A sizeable Asian community rubs shoulders with the biggest Polynesian population of any city in the world.

The traditional Kiwi aspiration for a freestanding house on a quarter-acre section has resulted in a vast, sprawling city. The CBD was long ago abandoned to commerce, and inner-city apartment living has only recently caught on. While geography has been kind, city planning has been less so. Unbridled and ill-conceived development has left the centre of the city with plenty of architectural embarrassments. To get under Auckland's skin you're best to head to the

---

AUCKLAND IN...

Two Days

Start by acquainting yourself with the inner city. Begin by walking from **Karangahape Rd** (K Rd) to the **Wynyard Quarter**, stopping along the way to have at least a quick whiz around the New Zealand section of the **Auckland Art Gallery**. Catch a ferry to **Devonport**, head up North Head and cool down at **Cheltenham Beach** (weather and tide permitting), before ferrying back to the city for dinner.

On day two, head up **One Tree Hill**, wander around **Cornwall Park** and then visit the **Auckland Museum** and **Domain**. Take a trip along **Tamaki Drive**, stopping at **Bastion** or **Achilles Point** to enjoy the harbour views. Spend the evening dining and bar hopping in **Ponsonby**.

Four Days

On the third day, get out on the **Hauraki Gulf**. Catch the ferry to **Waiheke Island** and divide your time between the beaches and the wineries.

For your final day, head west. Grab breakfast in **Titirangi** before exploring the **Waitakere Ranges Regional Park**, **Karekare** and **Piha**. Freshen up for a night on the town in **Britomart**.

Auckland Highlights

1 Hauraki Gulf (p100) Getting out on the water and visiting the island sanctuaries dotting this beautiful expanse.

2 Auckland Volcanic Field (p68) Going with the flows, exploring Auckland's fascinating volcanic mountains, lakes and islands.

3 West Coast Beaches (p114) Treading the mystical and treacherous black sands of Karekare and Piha.

4 Waiheke Island (p102) Schlepping around world-class wineries and beaches.

5 Ponsonby (p94) Buzzing around the cafes, restaurants and bars of Auckland's hippest inner-city suburb.

6 Auckland Museum (p68) Being awed by the Māori *taonga* (treasures) and moved, literally, in the eruption simulation and, figuratively, in the war memorial galleries.

7 Goat Island Marine Reserve (p121) Swimming with the fishes only a few steps from the beach at this pretty bay.

8 Pasifika Festival (p79) Soaking up the Polynesian vibe at this massive festival, held in March at Western Springs Park.

streets of Victorian and Edwardian villas in hip inner-city suburbs such as Ponsonby, Grey Lynn, Kingsland and Mt Eden.

City Centre

⭐ **Auckland Art Gallery** GALLERY
(Map p70; ☏09-379 1349; www.aucklandartgallery.com; cnr Kitchener & Wellesley Sts; ⊙10am-5pm) FREE Following a significant 2011 refurbishment, Auckland's premier art repository now has a striking glass-and-wood atrium grafted onto its 1887 French-chateau frame. It showcases the best of NZ art, along with important works by Pieter Bruegel the Younger, Guido Reni, Picasso, Cézanne, Gauguin and Matisse. Highlights include the intimate 19th-century portraits of tattooed Māori subjects by Charles Goldie, and the starkly dramatic text-scrawled canvasses of Colin McCahon.

Free tours depart from the foyer daily at 11.30am and 1.30pm.

Albert Park PARK
(Map p70; Princes St) Hugging the hill on the city's eastern flank, Albert Park is a charming Victorian formal garden overrun by students from the neighbouring University of Auckland during term time. The park was once part of the Albert Barracks (1847), a fortification that enclosed 9 hectares during the New Zealand Wars. A portion of the original barracks wall survives at the centre of the university campus.

Sky Tower TOWER
(Map p70; ☏09-363 6000; www.skycityauckland.co.nz; cnr Federal & Victoria Sts; adult/child $28/11; ⊙8.30am-10.30pm) The impossible-to-miss Sky Tower looks like a giant hypodermic giving a fix to the heavens. Spectacular lighting renders it space age at night and the colours change for special events. At 328m it is the southern hemisphere's tallest structure. A lift takes you up to the observation decks in 40 stomach-lurching seconds; look down through the glass floor panels if you're after an extra kick. Consider visiting at sunset and having a drink in the Sky Lounge Cafe & Bar.

The Sky Tower is also home to the SkyWalk (p77) and SkyJump (p77).

Civic Theatre THEATRE
(Map p70; ☏09-309 2677; www.civictheatre.co.nz; cnr Queen & Wellesley Sts) The 'mighty Civic' (1929) is one of only seven 'atmospheric theatres' remaining in the world and a

fine survivor from cinema's Golden Age. The auditorium has lavish Moorish decoration and a star-lit southern-hemisphere night sky in the ceiling, complete with cloud projections and shooting stars. It's mainly used for touring musicals, international concerts and film-festival screenings.

Even if nothing is scheduled, try and sneak a peek at the foyer, an Indian indulgence with elephants and monkeys hanging from every conceivable fixture. Buddhas were planned to decorate the street frontage but were considered too risqué at the time – neoclassical naked boys were chosen instead!

Old Government House HISTORIC BUILDING
(Map p70; Waterloo Quadrant) FREE Built in 1856, this stately building was the colony's seat of power until 1865 when Wellington became the capital. The construction is unusual in that it's actually wooden but made to look like stone. It's now used by the University of Auckland, but feel free to wander through the lush gardens.

University Clock Tower ARCHITECTURE
(Map p70; 22 Princes St) The University Clock Tower is Auckland's architectural triumph. This stately 'ivory' tower (1926) tips its hat towards art nouveau (the incorporation of NZ flora and fauna into the decoration) and the Chicago School (the way it's

Auckland

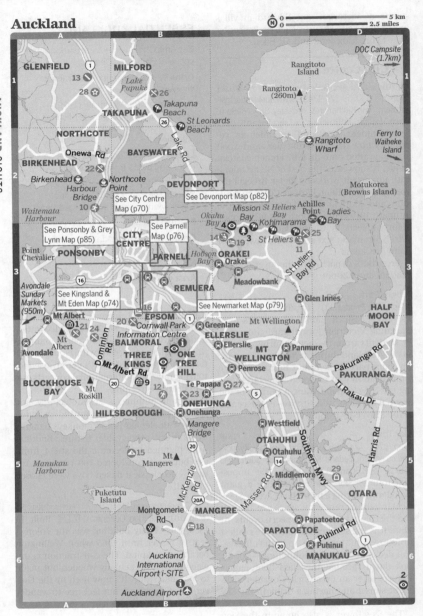

rooted into the earth). It's usually open, so wander inside.

St Patrick's Cathedral   CHURCH
(Map p70; ☑ 09-303 4509; www.stpatricks.org. nz; 43 Wyndham St; ☺ 7am-7pm) Auckland's Catholic cathedral (1907) is one of the city's loveliest buildings. Polished wood and Belgian stained glass lend warmth to the interior of the majestic Gothic Revival church. There's a historical display in the old confessional on the left-hand side.

Auckland

◉ Britomart, Viaduct Harbour & Wynyard Quarter

Stretching for only a small grid of blocks above the train station, Britomart is a compact enclave of historic buildings and new developments that has been transformed into one of the city's best eating, drinking and shopping precincts. Most of Auckland's top fashion designers have recently decamped to the Britomart area from further uptown in High St.

Once a busy commercial port, the Viaduct Harbour was given a major makeover for the 1999/2000 and 2003 America's Cup yachting events. It's now a fancy dining and boozing precinct, and guaranteed to have at least a slight buzz any night of the week. Historical plaques, public sculpture and the chance to gawk at millionaires' yachts make it a diverting place for a stroll.

Connected to the Viaduct by a bascule bridge, Wynyard Quarter opened in advance of another sporting tournament, 2011's Rugby World Cup. With its public plazas, waterfront eateries, events centre, fish market and children's playground, it has quickly become Auckland's favourite new place to promenade. At the Silo Park area, down the western end, free outdoor Friday night movies and weekend markets have become summertime institutions. Most of Wynyard's better restaurants are set back from the water, on Jellicoe St.

New Zealand Maritime Museum MUSEUM
(Map p70; ☏ 09-373 0800; www.maritime museum.co.nz; 149-159 Quay St; adult/child $20/10, incl harbour cruise $50/25; ◷ 9am-5pm, free tours 10.30am & 1pm Mon-Fri) This museum traces NZ's seafaring history, from Māori voyaging canoes to the America's Cup. Recreations include a tilting 19th-century steerage-class cabin and a 1950s beach store and bach (holiday home). *Blue Water Black Magic* is a tribute to Sir Peter Blake, the Whitbread-Round-the-World and America's Cup–winning yachtsman who was murdered in 2001 on an environmental monitoring trip in the Amazon. Packages including an optional one-hour harbour cruise on a heritage boat are also available.

Auckland Fish Market MARKET
(Map p70; ☏ 09-379 1490; www.auckland fishmarket.co.nz; 22-32 Jellicoe St; ◷ 6am-7pm) Early-morning auctions combine with fish shops, cafes and restaurants, and a seafood-cooking school.

◉ Mt Eden

Mt Eden VOLCANO
(Maungawhau; Map p74; 250 Mt Eden Rd) From the top of Auckland's highest volcanic cone (196m) the entire isthmus and both harbours are laid bare. The symmetrical crater (50m deep) is known as Te Ipu Kai a Mataaho (the Food Bowl of Mataaho, the god of things hidden in the ground) and is considered highly *tapu* (sacred). Do not enter it, but feel free to explore the remainder of the mountain. The remains of *pa* terraces and food storage pits are clearly visible.

AUCKLAND VOLCANIC FIELD

Some cities think they're tough just by living in the shadow of a volcano. Auckland's built on 50 of them and, no, they're not all extinct. The last one to erupt was Rangitoto about 600 years ago and no one can predict when the next eruption will occur. Auckland's quite literally a hot spot – with a reservoir of magma 100km below, waiting to bubble to the surface. But relax: this has only happened 19 times in the last 20,000 years.

Some of Auckland's volcanoes are cones, some are filled with water and some have been completely quarried away. Moves are afoot to register the field as a World Heritage Site and protect what remains. Most of the surviving cones show evidence of terracing from when they formed a formidable series of Māori *pa* (fortified villages). The most interesting to explore are Mt Eden (p67), One Tree Hill (p73), North Head (p69) and Rangitoto (p101), but Mt Victoria, Mt Wellington (Maungarei), Mt Albert (Owairaka), Mt Roskill (Puketāpapa), Lake Pupuke, Mt Mangere and Mt Hobson (Remuera) are all worth a visit.

Until recently it was possible to drive right up to the summit but concerns over erosion have led to restricted vehicle access. Paths lead up the mountain from six different directions and the walk only takes around 10 minutes, depending on your fitness.

Eden Garden　　　　　　　　　GARDENS
(Map p79; ☎09-638 8395; www.edengarden.co.nz; 24 Omana Ave; adult/child $8/6; ⊙9am-4pm) On Mt Eden's rocky eastern slopes, this mature garden is noted for its camellias, rhododendrons and azaleas.

👁 Parnell & Newmarket

Parnell is one of Auckland's oldest areas, and amid the cafes, restaurants and fancy retailers are several heritage buildings. Neighbouring Newmarket is a busy shopping precinct known for its boutiques.

★**Auckland Museum**　　　　　　MUSEUM
(Map p76; ☎09-309 0443; www.aucklandmuseum.com; Auckland Domain, Parnell; adult/child $25/10; ⊙10am-5pm) This imposing neoclassical temple (1929), capped with an impressive copper-and-glass dome (2007), dominates the Auckland Domain and is a prominent part of the Auckland skyline, especially when viewed from the harbour. Admission packages can be purchased, which incorporate a highlights tour and a Māori cultural performance ($45 to $55).

The displays of Pacific Island and Māori artefacts on the museum's ground floor are essential viewing. Highlights include a 25m war canoe and an extant carved meeting house (remove your shoes before entering). There's also a fascinating display on Auckland's volcanic field, including an eruption

simulation, and the upper floors showcase military displays, fulfilling the building's dual role as a war memorial. Auckland's main Anzac commemorations take place at dawn on 25 April at the cenotaph in the museum's forecourt.

Auckland Domain　　　　　　　PARK
(Map p76; Domain Dr, Parnell; ⊙24hr) Covering about 80 hectares, this green swathe contains the Auckland Museum (p68), sports fields, interesting sculpture, formal gardens, wild corners and the **Wintergarden** (Map p76; Wintergarden Rd, Parnell; ⊙9am-5.30pm Mon-Sat, to 7.30pm Sun Nov-Mar, 9am-4.30pm Apr-Oct) **FREE**, with its fernery, tropical house, cool house, cute cat statue, coffee kiosk and neighbouring cafe. The mound in the centre of the park is all that remains of Pukekaroa, one of Auckland's volcanoes. At its humble peak, a totara tree surrounded by a palisade honours the first Māori king.

Parnell Rose Garden　　　　　GARDENS
(Map p76; 85-87 Gladstone Rd, Parnell) These formal gardens are blooming excellent from November to March. A stroll through Dove-Myer Robinson Park leads to peaceful **Judges Bay** and tiny **St Stephen's Chapel** (Map p76; Judge St), built for the signing of the constitution of NZ's Anglican Church (1857).

Holy Trinity Cathedral　　　　CHURCH
(Map p76; ☎09-303 9500; www.holy-trinity.org.nz; cnr St Stephens Ave & Parnell Rd, Parnell; ⊙10am-3pm) Auckland's Anglican sathedral is a hodgepodge of architectural styles, especially compared to **St Mary's Church** (Map p76; Parnell Rd, Parnell; ⊙10am-3pm) next door, a wonderful wooden Gothic Revival

church with a burnished interior and interesting stained-glass windows (built 1886). Holy Trinity's windows are also notable, especially the rose window by English artist Carl Edwards, which is particularly striking above the simple kauri altar.

Kinder House
HISTORIC BUILDING

(Map p76; 09-379 4008; www.kinder.org.nz; 2 Ayr St, Parnell; entry by donation; noon-3pm Wed-Sun) Built of volcanic stone, this 1857 home displays the watercolours and memorabilia of the Reverend Dr John Kinder (1819–1903), headmaster of the Church of England Grammar School.

Highwic
HISTORIC BUILDING

(Map p79; 09-524 5729; www.historic.org.nz; 40 Gillies Ave; adult/child $10/free; 10.30am-4.30pm Wed-Sun) A marvellous Carpenter Gothic house (1862), sitting amid lush, landscaped grounds.

Ewelme Cottage
HISTORIC BUILDING

(Map p76; 09-524 5729; www.historic.org. nz; 14 Ayr St; adult/child $8.50/free; 10.30am-4.30pm Sun) Built in 1864 for a clergyman, this storybook cottage is an exceptionally well-preserved example of an early colonial house.

Tamaki Drive

This scenic, pohutukawa-lined road heads east from the city, hugging the waterfront. In summer it's a jogging/cycling/rollerblading blur.

A succession of child-friendly, peaceful swimming beaches starts at Ohaku Bay. Around the headland is **Mission Bay**, a popular beach with an electric-lit art-deco fountain, historic mission house, restaurants and bars. Safe swimming beaches **Kohimarama** and **St Heliers** follow. Further east along Cliff Rd, the **Achilles Point lookout** (Map p66; Cliff Rd, St Heliers) offers panoramic views and Māori carvings. At its base is **Ladies Bay**, popular with nudists.

Buses 767 and 769 from behind Britomart station follow this route, while buses 745 to 757 go as far as Mission Bay.

Kelly Tarlton's Sea Life Aquarium
AQUARIUM

(Map p66; 09-531 5065; www.kellytarltons. co.nz; 23 Tamaki Dr, Orakei; adult/child $39/22; 9.30am-5pm) In this topsy-turvy aquarium sharks and stingrays swim over and around you in transparent tunnels that were once stormwater tanks. You can also enter the tanks in a shark cage with a snorkel ($124), or dive straight into the tanks ($265). Other attractions include the Penguin Discovery tour (10.30am Tuesday to Sunday, $199 per person) where just four visitors per day can get up close with Antarctic penguins. For all tickets, there are significant discounts online.

A free shark-shaped shuttle bus departs from 172 Quay St (opposite the Ferry Building) hourly on the half-hour from 9.30am to 3.30pm.

Bastion Point
PARK

(Map p66; Hapimana St, Orakei) Politics, harbour views and lush lawns combine on this pretty headland with a chequered history. An elaborate cliff-top garden mausoleum honours Michael Joseph Savage (1872–1940), the country's first Labour prime minister, whose socialist reforms left him adored by the populace. Follow the lawn to a WWII gun embankment – one of many that line the harbour.

Devonport

With well-preserved Victorian and Edwardian buildings and loads of cafes, Devonport is an extremely pleasant place to visit and only a short ferry trip from the city. There are also two volcanic cones to climb and easy access to the first of the North Shore's beaches.

For a self-guided tour of historic buildings, pick up the *Old Devonport Walk* pamphlet from the i-SITE (p98). Bikes can be hired from the ferry terminal.

Ferries to Devonport (adult/child return $12/6.50, 12 minutes) depart from the Ferry Building at least every 30 minutes from 6.15am to 11.30pm (until 1am Friday and Saturday), and from 7.15am to 10pm on Sundays and public holidays. Some Waiheke Island and Rangitoto ferries also stop here.

Mt Victoria (Takarunga; Map p82; Victoria Rd, Devonport) and **North Head** (Maungauika; Map p82; Takarunga Rd, Devonport; 6am-10pm) were Māori *pa* and they remain fortresses of sorts, with the navy maintaining a presence. Both have gun embankments and North Head is riddled with tunnels, dug at the end of the 19th century in response to the Russian threat, and extended during WWI and WWII. The gates are locked at night, but that's never stopped teenagers from jumping the fence for scary subterranean explorations.

AUCKLAND

City Centre

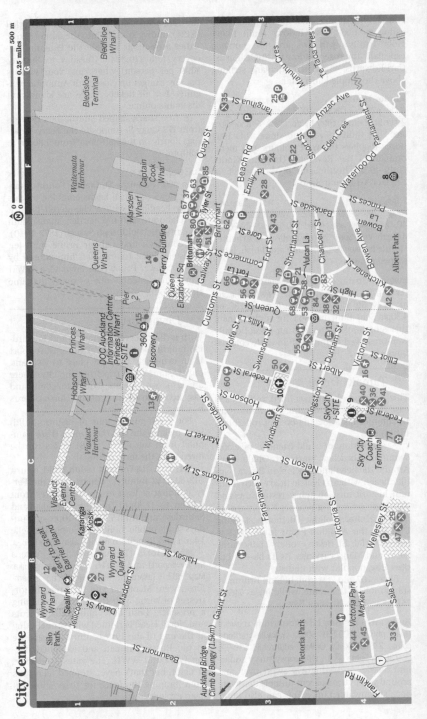

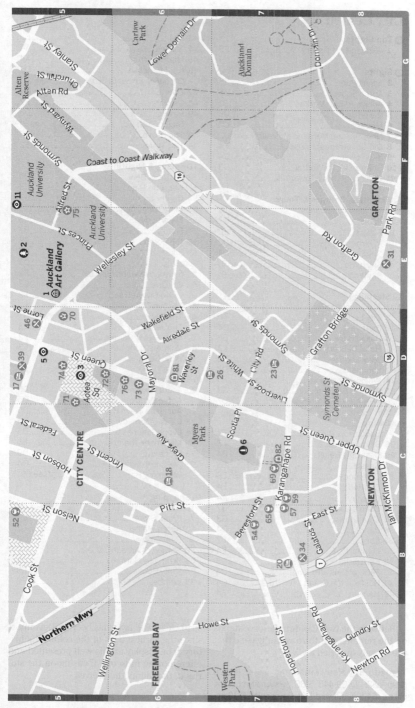

AUCKLAND

GRAFTON

Auckland Domain

Carlaw Park

Lower Domain Dr

Domain Dr

Park Rd

Grafton Rd

Coast to Coast Walkway

Stanley St

Churchill St

Alten Rd

Alten Reserve

Wynyard St

Symonds St

Auckland University

11

Alfred St

75

Princes St

Auckland University

Wellesley St

2

1 Auckland Art Gallery

Lorne St

46

70

Wakefield St

Airedale St

Symonds St

Grafton Bridge

17

39

5

74

Queen St

3

Aotea Sq

72

76

73

Mayoral Dr

81

Waverley St

26

White St

Liverpool St

City Rd

23

Symonds St Cemetery

Symonds St

31

16

CITY CENTRE

Federal St

Vincent St

Greys Ave

Myers Park

Scotia Pl

6

Upper Queen St

NEWTON

Hobson St

Nelson St

52

Pitt St

18

Beresford St

54

65

Karangahape Rd

69

82

57 59

East St

Galatos St

34

1

20

Ian McKinnon Dr

Cook St

Northern Mwy

Wellington St

FREEMANS BAY

Howe St

Western Park

Karangahape Rd

Hopetoun St

Gundry St

Newton Rd

City Centre

Between the two, Cambria Reserve stands on the remains of a third volcanic cone that was largely quarried away.

Torpedo Bay Navy Museum　　　MUSEUM
(Map p82; ☑ 09-445 5186; www.navymuseum. mil.nz; 64 King Edward Pde, Devonport; ⊙10am-

5pm) FREE The navy has been in Devonport since the earliest days of the colony. Its history is on display at this well-presented and often moving museum, focusing on the stories of the sailors themselves.

⊙ Kingsland & Western Springs

Auckland Zoo   ZOO
(Map p74; ☑ 09-360 3805; www.aucklandzoo.
co.nz; Motions Rd; adult/child $28/12; ⊙ 9.30am-
5pm, last entry 4.15pm) 🖉 At this modern, spacious zoo, the big foreigners tend to steal the
attention from the timid natives, but if you
can wrestle the kids away from the tigers
and orangutans, there's a well-presented NZ
section. Called Te Wao Nui, it's divided into
six ecological zones: Coast (seals, penguins),
Islands (mainly lizards, including NZ's
pint-sized dinosaur, the tuatara), Wetlands
(ducks, herons, eels), Night (kiwi, naturally,
along with frogs, native owls and weta), Forest (birds) and High Country (cheekier birds
and lizards).

Frequent buses (adult/child $4.50/2.50)
run from 99 Albert St in the city to bus stop
8124 on Great North Rd, where it is a 700m
walk to the zoo's entrance.

Western Springs   PARK
(Map p74; Great North Rd) Parents bring their
children to this picturesque park for the popular playground. It's a pleasant picnic spot
and a good place to get acquainted with playful pukeko (swamp hens), easygoing ducks
and pushy, bread-fattened geese. Formed by
a confluence of lava flows, more than 4 million litres of spring water bubble up into the
central lake daily. From the city, catch any bus
heading west via Great North Rd (adult/child
$4.50/2.50). By car, take the Western Springs
exit from the North Western Motorway.

Until 1902 this was Auckland's main water supply.

MOTAT   MUSEUM
(Museum of Transport & Technology; Map p74;
☑ 09-815 5800; www.motat.org.nz; 805 Great
North Rd, Western Springs; adult/child $16/8;
⊙ 10am-5pm) This technology boffin's paradise is spread over two sites and 19 hectares.
In the Great North Rd site look out for former Prime Minister Helen Clark's Honda 50
motorbike and the pioneer village. The Meo-
la Rd site features the Aviation Display Hall
with rare military and commercial planes.
The two are linked by a vintage tram (free
with admission, $1 otherwise), which passes
Western Springs Park and the zoo. It's a fun
kids' ride whether you visit MOTAT or not.

⊙ Other Areas

One Tree Hill   VOLCANO, PARK
(Maungakiekie; Map p66) This volcanic cone
was the isthmus' key *pa* and the greatest fortress in the country. At the top (182m) there
are 360-degree views and the grave of John
Logan Campbell, who gifted the land to the
city in 1901 and requested that a memorial
be built to the Māori people on the summit.
Nearby is the stump of the last 'one tree'. Allow time to explore surrounding **Cornwall
Park** with its mature trees and historic Acacia Cottage (1841).

The **Cornwall Park Information Centre**
(Map p66; ☑ 09-630 8485; www.cornwallpark.
co.nz; Huia Lodge; ⊙ 10am-4pm) has fascinating
interactive displays illustrating what the *pa*
would have looked like when 5000 people
lived here. Near the excellent children's playground, the **Stardome** (Map p66; ☑ 09-624
1246; www.stardome.org.nz; 670 Manukau Rd;
shows adult/child $15/12; ⊙ 10am-5pm Mon, to
9.30pm Tue-Thu, to 11pm Fri-Sun) **FREE** offers
regular stargazing and planetarium shows
that aren't dependent on Auckland's fickle
weather (usually 7pm and 8pm Wednesday
to Sunday, with extra shows on weekends).

To get to One Tree Hill from the city
take a train to Greenlane and walk 1km
along Green Lane West. By car, take the

ONE TREE TO RULE THEM ALL

Looking at One Tree Hill, your first thought will probably be 'Where's the bloody tree?'.
Good question. Up until 2000 a Monterey pine stood at the top of the hill. This was a replacement for a sacred totara that was chopped down by British settlers in 1852. Māori
activists first attacked the foreign usurper in 1994, finishing the job in 2000.

After much hand-wringing and consultation with local Māori and tree experts, it was
finally announced in late 2015 that a grove of pohutukawa, totara and other natives
would be planted on the summit. Then, in an arboreal version of the *X-Factor* the weaker
performing trees will be eliminated, leaving only one tree standing by 2026.

Auckland's most beloved landmark achieved international recognition in 1987 when
U2 released the song 'One Tree Hill' on their acclaimed *The Joshua Tree* album. It was
only released as a single in NZ, where it went to number one for six weeks.

Kingsland & Mt Eden

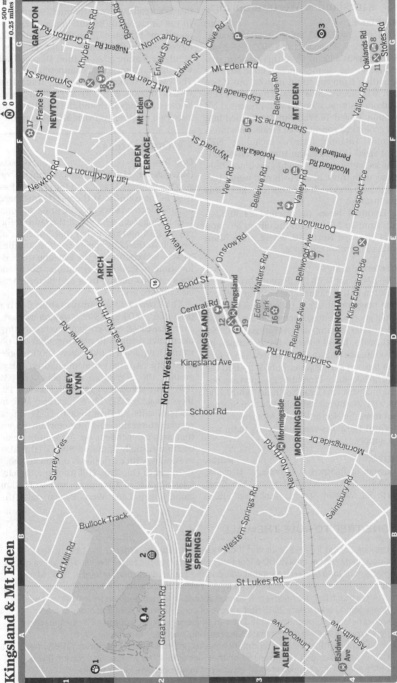

500 m
0.25 miles

GRAFTON

Grafton Rd

Bastion Rd

Khyber Pass Rd

Nugent Rd

Normanby Rd

Enfield St

Edwin St

Clive Rd

Mt Eden Rd

P

3

Oaklands Rd

Stokes Rd

8

11

Symonds St

France St

NEWTON

17

9

18 13

Mt Eden Rd

Esplanade Rd

Bellevue Rd

Sherbourne St

MT EDEN

5

Mt Eden

EDEN
TERRACE

Horoeka Ave

Wynyard St

Woodford Rd

Pentland Ave

Valley Rd

Prospect Tce

Ian McKinnon Dr

Newton Rd

View Rd

Bellevue Rd

Valley Rd

6

14

Dominion Rd

ARCH
HILL

Bond St

16

Onslow Rd

Walters Rd

Bellwood Ave

7

King Edward Pde

10

Crummer Rd

Great North Rd

New North Rd

North Western Mwy

Central Rd

Kingsland

KINGSLAND

12 15

19

Eden
Park

Reimers Ave

Sandringham Rd

SANDRINGHAM

16

GREY
LYNN

Kingsland Ave

School Rd

Morningside

New North Rd

MORNINGSIDE

Morningside Dr

Surrey Cres

Sainsbury Rd

Old Mill Rd

Bullock Track

WESTERN
SPRINGS

Western Springs Rd

St Lukes Rd

Great North Rd

Linwood Ave

MT
ALBERT

Asquith Ave

Baldwin Ave

1

2

4

Kingsland & Mt Eden

Greenlane exit off the Southern Motorway and turn right into Green Lane West.

Wallace Arts Centre GALLERY
(Map p66; ☎09-639 2010; www.tsbbankwallace artscentre.org.nz; Pah Homestead, 72 Hillsborough Rd, Hillsborough; ⊙10am-3pm Tue-Fri, to 5pm Sat & Sun) **FREE** Housed in a gorgeous 1879 mansion with views to One Tree Hill and the Manukau Harbour, the Wallace Arts Centre is endowed with contemporary New Zealand art from an extensive private collection, which is changed every four to six weeks. Have lunch on the veranda and wander among the magnificent trees in the surrounding park. The art is also very accessible, ranging from a life-size skeletal rugby ruck to a vibrant Ziggy Stardust painted on glass.

Bus 299 (Lynfield) departs every 15 minutes from Queen St (outside the Civic Theatre) and heads to Hillsborough Rd ($5, 40 minutes).

Auckland Botanic Gardens GARDENS
(Map p66; ☎09-267 1457; www.aucklandbotanicgardens.co.nz; 102 Hill Rd, Manurewa; ⊙8am-6pm Apr-Sep, to 8pm Oct-Mar) 🅿 **FREE** This 64-hectare park has over 10,000 plants (including threatened species), dozens of themed gardens and an infestation of wedding parties. By car, take the Southern Motorway, exit at Manurewa and follow the signs. Otherwise take the train to Manurewa ($8, 43 minutes) and then walk along Hill Rd (1.5km).

Alberton HISTORIC BUILDING
(Map p66; ☎09-846 7367; www.historic.org.nz; 100 Mt Albert Rd; adult/child $10/free; ⊙10.30am-4.30pm Wed-Sun) A classic colonial mansion (1863), Alberton featured as a backdrop for some scenes in *The Piano*. It's a 1km walk from Mt Albert train station.

Rainbow's End AMUSEMENT PARK
(Map p66; ☎09-262 2030; www.rainbowsend.co.nz; 2 Clist Cres, Manukau; unlimited rides adult/child $57/46; ⊙10am-5pm) It's a bit dull by international standards but Rainbow's End has enough rides (including a corkscrew roller coaster) to keep the kids happy all day.

🏃 Activities

Nothing gets you closer to the heart and soul of Auckland than sailing on the Hauraki Gulf. If you can't afford a yacht cruise, catch a ferry instead.

Visitor centres and public libraries stock the city council's *Auckland City's Walkways* pamphlet, which has a good selection of urban walks, including information on the Coast to Coast Walkway (p77).

Trading on the country's action-packed reputation, Auckland has sprouted its own set of thrill-inducing activities. Look around for backpacker reductions or special offers before booking anything.

Sailing & Kayaking

Auckland Sea Kayaks KAYAKING
(Map p66; ☎0800 999 089; www.aucklandseakayaks.co.nz; 384 Tamaki Dr, St Heliers) 🅿 Guided trips (including lunch) to Rangitoto ($175, 6½ hours) and Motukorea (Browns Island; $135, four hours). Multiday excursions and sunset paddles are also available.

Explore SAILING
(Map p70; ☎0800 397 567; www.explorenz.co.nz; Viaduct Harbour) 🅿 Shoot the breeze for two hours on a genuine America's Cup yacht (adult/child $170/120), take a 90-minute cruise on a glamorous large yacht (adult/child $75/55) or tuck into a 2½-hour Harbour Dinner Cruise ($120/85).

Fergs Kayaks KAYAKING
(Map p66; ☎09-529 2230; www.fergskayaks.co.nz; 12 Tamaki Dr, Orakei; ⊙9am-5pm) Hires

Parnell

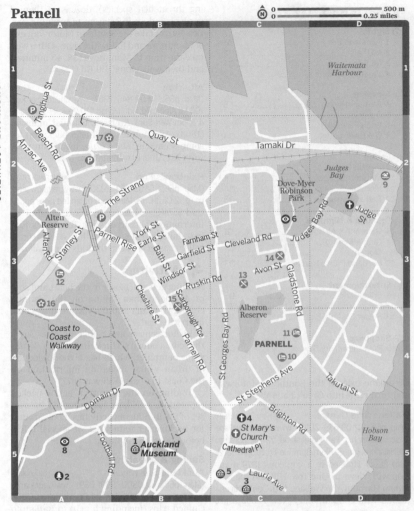

Parnell

kayaks (per hour/day from $20/80), paddle-boards ($25/70), bikes ($20/80) and inline skates ($15/45). Guided kayak trips head to Devonport ($100, 8km, three hours) or Rangitoto ($140, 13km, six hours).

Extreme Sports

Auckland Bridge Climb & Bungy
ADVENTURE SPORTS
(Map p66; ☑09-360 7748; www.bungy.co.nz; 105 Curran St, Westhaven; adult/child climb $125/85, bungy $160/130, both $230) ⟋ Climb up or jump off the Auckland Harbour Bridge.

SkyJump
ADVENTURE SPORTS
(Map p70; ☑0800 759 586; www.skyjump.co.nz; Sky Tower, cnr Federal & Victoria Sts; adult/child $225/175; ⊙10am-5.15pm) This thrilling 11-second, 85km/h base wire leap from the observation deck of the Sky Tower is more like a parachute jump than a bungy. Combine it with the SkyWalk (p77) in the Look & Leap package ($290).

SkyWalk
ADVENTURE SPORTS
(Map p70; ☑0800 759 925; www.skywalk.co.nz; Sky Tower, cnr Federal & Victoria Sts; adult/child $145/115; ⊙10am-4.30pm) The SkyWalk involves circling the 192m-high, 1.2m-wide outside halo of the Sky Tower without rails or a balcony. Don't worry, it's not completely crazy – there is a safety harness.

Sky Screamer
ADVENTURE SPORTS
(Map p70; ☑09-377 1328; www.skyscreamer.co.nz; cnr Albert & Victoria Sts; 2 people $100; ⊙9am-10pm Sun-Thu, 10am-2am Fri & Sat) Imagine a giant slingshot with yourself as the projectile as you're reverse-bungyed 60m into the air.

Other Activities

Parnell Baths
SWIMMING
(Map p76; ☑09-373 3561; www.parnellbaths.co.nz; Judges Bay Rd, Parnell; adult/child $6.40/free; ⊙6am-8pm Mon-Fri, 8am-8pm Sat & Sun Nov-Easter) Outdoor saltwater pools with an awesome 1950s mural.

Coast to Coast Walkway
WALKING
(Map p66; www.aucklandcity.govt.nz) Heading right across the country from the Tasman to the Pacific (which is actually only 16km), this walk encompasses One Tree Hill, Mt Eden, the Domain and the University, keeping mainly to reserves rather than city streets.

Do it in either direction: starting from the Viaduct Basin and heading south, it's marked by yellow markers and milestones; heading north from Onehunga there are blue markers. Our recommendation? Catch

---

NORTH SHORE BEACHES

Fine swimming beaches stretch from North Head to Long Bay. The gulf islands shelter them from strong surf, making them safe for supervised children. Aim for high tide unless you fancy a lengthy walk to waist-deep water. **Cheltenham Beach** is a short walk from Devonport. **Takapuna Beach**, closest to the Harbour Bridge, is Auckland's answer to Bondi and the most built up. Nearby **St Leonards Beach**, popular with gay men, requires clambering over rocks at high tide.

---

the train to Onehunga and finish up at the Viaduct's bars. From Onehunga station, take Onehunga Mall up to Princes St, turn left and pick up the track at the inauspicious park by the motorway.

Rapu NZ Surf'n'Snow Tours
SURFING
(☑09-828 0426; www.rapuadventures.com; 1-/2-/5-/7-/14-day tour $120/199/800/1160/2154) One- or two-day surfing courses include transport, gear and two two-hour lessons each day, usually at Piha (others can tag along for the ride only for $50). Tours of five days or longer include accommodation (October to May only). Snow packages include transport to Mt Ruapehu.

Dive Centre
DIVING
(Map p66; ☑09-444 7698; www.divecentre.co.nz; 97 Wairau Rd, Wairau Valley; PADI Open Water $599) PADI courses and diving charters.

⟋ Tours

Cultural Tours

Tāmaki Hikoi
CULTURAL TOUR
(☑021 146 9593; www.tamakihikoi.co.nz; 1-/3hr $40/95) Guides from the Ngāti Whātua *iwi* (tribe) lead various Māori cultural tours, including walking and interpretation of sites such as Mt Eden and the Auckland Domain.

TIME Unlimited
CULTURAL TOUR
(☑09-846 3469; www.newzealandtours.travel) ⟋ Cultural, walking and sightseeing tours from a Māori perspective.

Food & Wine

Big Foody Food Tour
TOUR
(☑021 481 177, 0800 366 386; www.thebigfoody.com; per person $125-185) Small-group city tours, including visits to markets and artisan producers, and lots of tastings.

MĀORI NEW ZEALAND: AUCKLAND

Evidence of Māori occupation is literally carved into Auckland's volcanic cones. The dominant *iwi* (tribe) of the isthmus was Ngāti Whātua, but these days there are Māori from almost all of NZ's *iwi* living here.

For an initial taste of Māori culture, start at **Auckland Museum** (p68), where there's a wonderful Māori collection and a culture show. For a more personalised experience, take a tour with **TIME Unlimited** (p77), **Potiki Adventures** (p103) or Ngāti Whātua's **Tāmaki Hikoi** (p77), or visit the *marae* and recreated village at **Te Hana** (p118).

Auckland Wine Trail Tours   TOUR
(☑ 09-630 1540; www.winetrailtours.co.nz) Small-group tours around west Auckland wineries and the Waitakere Ranges (half/full day $125/255); further afield to Matakana ($265); or a combo of the two ($265).

Fine Wine Tours   TOUR
(☑ 0800 023 111; www.insidertouring.co.nz) Tours of Kumeu, Matakana and Waiheke wineries, including a four-hour Kumeu tour ($199) and a six-hour tour including Muriwai Beach ($269).

Walking

Bush & Beach   WALKING TOUR
(☑ 09-837 4130; www.bushandbeach.co.nz) ⬤ Tours including guided walks in the Waitakere Ranges and along west-coast beaches ($150 to $235); three-hour city minibus tours ($78); and food and wine tours in either Kumeu or Matakana (half/full day $235/325).

Hiking New Zealand   TRAMPING
(☑ 0800 697 232; www.hikingnewzealand.com) Runs a wide range of 'hiking safaris' leaving from Auckland, including Far North ($1350, six days) and NZ Uncut ($7450, 13 days).

Auckland Ghost Tours   WALKING TOUR
(☑ 09-832 8047; www.aucklandghosttours.com; adult/child $50/25) Stories of Auckland's scary side on a two-hour walking tour of the central city.

Bus Tours

Auckland Hop On, Hop Off Explorer   BUS TOUR
(☑ 0800 439 756; www.explorerbus.co.nz; adult/child $45/20) This service departs from the Ferry Building every hour from 10am to 3pm (more frequently in summer), heading to 14 tourist sites around the city.

Toru Tours   BUS TOUR
(☑ 027 457 0011; www.torutours.com; per person $79) The three-hour Express Tour will depart with just one booking – ideal for solo travellers.

Boat Tours

Riverhead Ferry   CRUISE
(Map p70; ☑ 09-376 0819; www.riverheadferry.co.nz; Pier 3, Ferry Terminal; per cruise $35) Harbour and gulf cruises, including a 90-minute jaunt up the inner harbour to Riverhead, returning after two hours' pub time.

Fullers   CRUISE
(Map p70; ☑ 09-367 9111; www.fullers.co.nz; adult/child $42/21; ⊙10.30am & 1.30pm) Twice daily 1½-hour harbour cruises, including Rangitoto and a free return ticket to Devonport.

Other Tours

Auckland Seaplanes   SCENIC FLIGHTS
(Map p70; ☑ 09-390 1121; www.aucklandseaplanes.com; 11 Brigham St, Wynyard Quarter; per person from $200) Flights in a cool 1960s floatplane that explore Auckland's harbour and islands.

Red Carpet Tours   TOUR
(☑ 09-410 6561; www.redcarpet-tours.com) ⬤ Day trips to Hobbiton/Matamata ($275), or all around Middle Earth over 14 days ($6900).

✵ Festivals & Events

Auckland Tourism's website (www.auckland-nz.com) has a thorough events calendar.

ASB Classic   SPORTS
(www.asbclassic.co.nz; ⊙ Jan) Watch leading tennis players of both genders warm up for the Aussie Open; held early January at the ASB Tennis Centre.

Laneway Festival   MUSIC
(www.lanewayfestival.com.au; ⊙Jan) International indie bands in a one-day festival on Anniversary Day (the Monday following the last weekend in January).

Auckland Anniversary Day Regatta   SPORTS
(www.regatta.org.nz; ⊙ Jan) The 'City of Sails' lives up to its name; held Monday of the last weekend in January.

Movies in Parks   FILM
(www.moviesinparks.co.nz; ⊙ Jan-Mar) Free movies on Friday and Saturday nights in various locations.

Newmarket

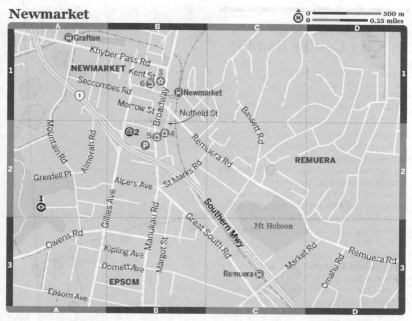

Music in Parks   MUSIC
(www.musicinparks.co.nz; ⊗Jan-Mar) Free gigs
in various locations.

Lantern Festival   CULTURAL
(www.aucklandnz.com/lantern; ⊗Feb) Three
days of Asian food, culture and elaborately
constructed lantern tableaux in a city park
to welcome the Lunar New Year (usually
held in February).

Auckland Pride Festival   GAY & LESBIAN
(www.aucklandpridefestival.org.nz; ⊗Feb) Two-
week festival of music, arts, sport and culture celebrating the LGBTI community.
Highlights include the Pride Parade, Pride
Party and the Big Gay Out (p79).

Big Gay Out   GAY & LESBIAN
(www.biggayout.co.nz; ⊗mid-Feb) Thousands
pack out Coyle Park, Pt Chevalier, on a Sunday in mid-February for a giant LGBTI fair
day with entertainment, food stalls and bars.

Auckland Cup Week   SPORTS
(www.ellerslie.co.nz; Ellerslie Racecourse; ⊗Mar)
The year's biggest horse races; early March.

Splore   MUSIC
(www.splore.net; Tapapakanga Regional Park;
⊗mid-Feb) Three days of camping and music

(generally of the dancey and soulful variety),
held by the beach. Headliners include big-
name international acts.

★ Pasifika Festival   CULTURAL
(www.aucklandnz.com/pasifika; ⊗Mar) Western
Springs Park hosts this giant Polynesian
party with cultural performances, food and
craft stalls; held over a weekend in early to
mid-March.

Auckland City Limits   MUSIC
(www.aucklandcitylimits.com; Western Springs
Park; ⊗Mar) One-day festival featuring big-
name international rock, indie and hip-hop
acts in mid-March.

🏃 City Walk
City Centre Ramble

START ST KEVIN'S ARCADE, KARANGAHAPE RD
END WYNYARD QUARTER
LENGTH 4.5KM; AROUND THREE HOURS

This walk aims to show you some hidden nooks and architectural treats in Auckland's somewhat scrappy city centre. Start among the second-hand boutiques of ❶ **St Kevin's Arcade** and take the stairs down to Myers Park. Look out for the reproduction of Michelangelo's ❷ **Moses** at the bottom of the stairs. Continue through the park, taking the stairs on the right just before the overpass to head up to street level.

Heading down Queen St, you'll pass the ❸ **Auckland Town Hall** (p96) and ❹ **Aotea Sq**, the civic heart of the city. On the next corner is the wonderful ❺ **Civic Theatre** (p65). Turn right on Wellesley St and then left onto Lorne St. Immediately to your right is ❻ **Khartoum Pl**, with tiling that celebrates NZ women's historic victory, becoming the first in the world to win the vote. Head up the stairs to the ❼ **Auckland Art Gallery** (p65).

Behind the gallery is ❽ **Albert Park** (p65). Cross through it and turn left into Princes St, where a row of ❾ **Victorian merchant's houses** faces the ❿ **University Clock Tower** (p65). Cut around behind the clock tower to ⓫ **Old Government House** (p65) and then follow the diagonal path back to Princes St. The attractive building on the corner of Princes St and Bowen Ave was once the city's main ⓬ **synagogue**.

Head down Bowen Ave and cut through the park past the ⓭ **Chancery precinct** to the ⓮ **High St** shopping strip. Take a left onto ⓯ **Vulcan Lane**, lined with historic pubs. Turn right onto Queen St and follow it down to the ⓰ **Britomart train station** (p100), housed in the former central post office. You're now standing on reclaimed land – the original shoreline was at Fort St. Detour to the nearby ⓱ **Britomart** precinct for good bars, restaurants and fashion boutiques.

From Britomart train station, turn left on Quay St and head to ⓲ **Viaduct Harbour**, bustling with bars and cafes, and then continue over the bridge to the rejuvenated ⓳ **Wynyard Quarter**.

Polyfest CULTURAL
(www.asbpolyfest.co.nz; Sports Bowl, Manukau; ☺mid-Mar) Massive Auckland secondary schools' Māori and Pacific Islands cultural festival.

**Auckland International
Cultural Festival** CULTURAL
(www.facebook.com/culturalfestival; Mt Roskill War Memorial Park; ☺Mar) One-day festival with ethnic food stalls and cultural displays and performances; late March.

Auckland Arts Festival PERFORMING ARTS
(www.aucklandfestival.co.nz; ☺Mar) Held over three weeks in March, this is Auckland's biggest celebration of the arts.

Royal Easter Show FAIR
(www.eastershow.co.nz; ASB Showgrounds, 217 Green Lane West; ☺Mar/Apr) It's supposedly agricultural but most people attend for the funfair rides.

NZ International Comedy Festival COMEDY
(www.comedyfestival.co.nz; ☺Apr-May) Three-week laughfest with local and international comedians; late April to mid-May.

NZ International Film Festival FILM
(www.nzff.co.nz; ☺Jul) Art-house films for two weeks from mid-July, many in the beautiful Civic theatre.

NZ Fashion Week FASHION
(www.nzfashionweek.com; ☺Aug) Held at the Viaduct Events Centre.

Auckland Heritage Festival CULTURAL
(www.heritagefestival.co.nz; ☺Sep) Two weeks of (mainly free) tours of Auckland's neighbourhoods and historic buildings; from late September.

Diwali Festival of Lights CULTURAL
(www.aucklandnz.com/diwali; Aotea Sq; ☺mid-Oct) Music, dance and food from Auckland's Indian community in Aotea Sq.

Grey Lynn Park Festival FAIR, MUSIC
(www.greylynnparkfestival.org; ☺Nov) Free festival of arts and crafts, food stalls and live music in one of Auckland's more interesting inner suburbs; third Saturday in November.

Christmas in the Park CHRISTMAS
(www.christmasinthepark.co.nz; ☺mid-Dec) A huge concert and party in Auckland Domain.

AUCKLAND FOR CHILDREN

All of the east-coast beaches (St Heliers, Kohimarama, Mission Bay, Okahu Bay, Cheltenham, Narrow Neck, Takapuna, Milford, Long Bay) are safe for supervised kids, while sights such as **Rainbow's End** (p75), **Kelly Tarlton's** (p69), **Auckland Museum** (p58) and **Auckland Zoo** (p73) are all firm favourites. **Parnell Baths** (p77) has a children's pool, but on wintry days head to the thermal pools at **Parakai** (p117) or **Waiwera** (p113)

Silo Cinema & Markets FILM
(www.silopark.co.nz; Silo Park, Wynyard Quarter; ☺Dec-Easter) Classic movies screened outdoors on Friday nights, and markets with food trucks, DJs and craft stalls on Friday nights and Saturday and Sunday afternoons.

🛏 Sleeping

Auckland's city centre has plenty of luxury hotels, with several international chains taking up inner-city real estate. At the other extreme, any backpackers who leave with a bad impression of Auckland have invariably stayed in crummy, noisy digs in the city centre. Not all of the cheap city accommodation is bad, but you'll find much better hostels in inner suburbs like Ponsonby, Parnell, Freemans Bay and Mt Eden. Devonport has beautiful Edwardian B&Bs within a relaxing ferry ride of the city.

🛏 City Centre

Attic Backpackers HOSTEL $
(Map p70; ☎09-973 5887; www.atticbackpackers.co.nz; 31 Wellesley St; dm $29-36, s/tw without bathroom $54/84; ☸🖥🛜) Centrally located Attic Backpackers features good facilities and an even better vibe. White walls and plenty of windows keep everything bright and fresh, and there's a rooftop area conducive to meeting other travellers.

YHA Auckland International HOSTEL $
(Map p70; ☎09-302 8200; www.yha.co.nz; 5 Turner St; dm $28-31,r $99, without bathroom $90; 🅿🛜) 🌿 Clean and brightly painted, this 170-bed YHA has a friendly vibe, good security, a games room and lots of lockers.

Devonport

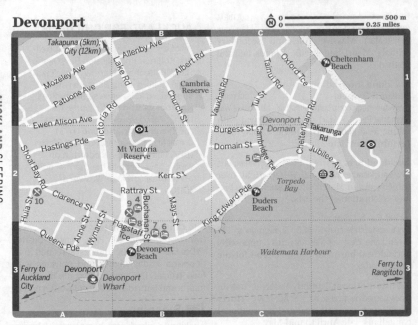

Devonport

◎ Sights
1 Mt Victoria	B2
2 North Head	D2
3 Torpedo Bay Navy Museum	D2

⌂ Sleeping
4 Devonport Motel	B2
5 Devonport Sea Cottage	C2
6 Hampton Beach House	B3
7 Parituhu	B3
8 Peace & Plenty Inn	B3

⊗ Eating
9 Bette's Bar & Eatery	B2
10 Calliope Road Cafe	A2

CityLife
HOTEL **$$**
(Map p70; ☑09-379 9222; www.heritageho-
tels.co.nz/citylife-auckland; 171 Queen St; apt from
$162; ⓟ☎✿) ✈ A worthy tower-block hotel
offering numerous apartments over dozens
of floors, ranging from studios to three-
bedroom suites. Facilities include a heated
lap pool, gym and valet parking. The loca-
tion couldn't be more central.

Waldorf Celestion
APARTMENT **$$**
(Map p70; ☑09-280 2200; www.celestion-wal-
dorf.co.nz; 19-23 Anzac Ave; apt from $191; ⓟ@☎)
A rash of Waldorfs have opened in recent
years, all presenting similar symptoms: affordable, modern apartments in city-fringe
locations. We prefer this one for its stylish
crimson and charcoal colour palate.

City Lodge
HOTEL **$$**
(Map p70; ☑09-379 6183; www.citylodge.co.nz;
150 Vincent St; s/d from $89/125; @☎) ✈ This
YMCA-run and purpose-built tower caters
well to the budget market. The tiny rooms
and stamp-sized bathrooms make for clean
and secure accommodation. There's also an
industrial-style kitchen and comfy lounge.

Jucy Snooze
HOTEL **$$**
(Map p70; ☑09-379 6633; www.jucyhotel.
com; 62 Emily Pl; hostel s/d $69/89, hotel r $129;
ⓟ@☎) This zippy budget hotel is brought
to you by the Jucy car-rental company, and
its lurid lime-green and plum corporate
colours are much in evidence throughout.
Rooms in the main section have en suites,
and there's a hostel wing with bunks and
rough-around-the-edges shared bathrooms.

★ Hotel DeBrett
BOUTIQUE HOTEL **$$$**
(Map p70; ☑09-925 9000; www.hoteldebrett.
com; 2 High St; r from $330; ☎) This hip his-
toric hotel has been zhooshed up with stripy
carpets and clever designer touches in every
nook of the 25 extremely comfortable rooms.

Prices include a continental breakfast, free unlimited wi-fi and a pre-dinner drink.

Waldorf Stadium
APARTMENT $$$

(Map p70; ☑ 09-337 5300; www.stadium-apartments-hotel.co.nz; 40 Beach Rd; apt from $204; ☎) This large newish block has spacious (if generic) family-friendly apartments with double-glazing to keep out the road noise.

Ponsonby & Grey Lynn

Ponsonby Backpackers
HOSTEL $

(Map p85; ☑ 09-360 1311; www.ponsonby-backpackers.co.nz; 2 Franklin Rd, Ponsonby; dm $29-32, s/d without bathroom $50/74; ▣@☎) This elegant two-storey turreted villa has a friendly vibe, sunny rooms and a nice garden area. Central Auckland is a pleasant 20-minute walk away, and the buzz of Ponsonby Rd is right on your doorstep.

Verandahs
HOSTEL $

(Map p85; ☑ 09-360 4180; www.verandahs.co.nz; 6 Hopetoun St; dm $31-35, s $39, d $100, without bathroom $80; ▣@☎) Ponsonby Rd, K Rd and the city are an easy walk from this grand hostel, housed in two neighbouring villas overlooking the mature trees of Western Park. It's definitely one of Auckland's best backpackers.

Brown Kiwi
HOSTEL $

(Map p85; ☑ 09-378 0191; www.brownkiwi.co.nz; 7 Prosford St, Ponsonby; dm $30-33, s/d without bathroom $61/78; @☎) This low-key hostel is tucked away in a busy-by-day commercial strip, a stone's throw from Ponsonby's shopping and grazing opportunities. The garden courtyard is made for mooching.

Abaco on Jervois
MOTEL $$

(Map p85; ☑ 09-360 6850; www.abaco.co.nz; 57 Jervois Rd, Ponsonby; r/ste from $145/193; ▣☎) Well positioned for cafes and buses, this contemporary, neutral-toned motel has stainless-steel kitchens with dishwashers in the fancier units, and fridges and microwaves in the studios. The darker rooms downstairs are cheaper.

Great Ponsonby Arthotel
B&B $$$

(Map p85; ☑ 09-376 5989; www.greatpons.co.nz; 30 Ponsonby Tce; r $250-400; ▣☎) ✦ In a quiet cul-de-sac near Ponsonby Rd, this deceptively spacious Victorian villa has gregarious hosts, impressive sustainability practices and great breakfasts. Studio apartments open onto an attractive rear courtyard. Rates include breakfast.

Newton

Haka Lodge
HOSTEL $

(Map p70; ☑ 09-379 4556; www.hakalodge.com; 373 Karangahape Rd, Newton; dm $25-32, r $99, without bathroom $89; ☎) ✦ The transformation of one of Auckland's dodgiest old pubs into a bright and shiny hostel is a modern miracle. Dorms have custom-made wooden bunks with privacy curtains, lockers and their own power points – making them perhaps the most comfortable bunkrooms in Auckland. Wi-fi is free and unlimited. And it couldn't be better located for the bustling K Rd scene.

Langham
HOTEL $$$

(Map p70; ☑ 09-379 5132; www.auckland.langhamhotels.co.nz; 83 Symonds St; r from $275; ▣@☎≋) ✦ The Langham's service is typically faultless, the beds are heavenly, and its day spa is one of Auckland's best.

Mt Eden

Bamber House
HOSTEL $

(Map p74; ☑ 09-623 4267; www.bamberhouse.co.nz; 22 View Rd, Mt Eden; dm $28-30, r $94, without bathroom $76; ▣@☎) ✦ The original house here is a mansion of sorts with some nicely maintained period trimmings and large grounds. The new prefab cabins have less character but come with en suites.

Oaklands Lodge
HOSTEL $

(Map p74; ☑ 09-638 6545; www.oaklandslodge.co.nz; 5a Oaklands Rd, Mt Eden; dm $28-32, s/d without bathroom $45/72; ▣@☎) In a leafy cul-de-sac, this bright, well-kept hostel is close to Mt Eden village and city buses.

Bavaria
B&B $$

(Map p74; ☑ 09-638 9641; www.bavaria-bandbhotel.co.nz; 83 Valley Rd, Mt Eden; s/d from $135/160; ▣@☎) This spacious villa offers large, airy, well-kept rooms, all of which have bathrooms, although some of them are closet sized. The communal TV lounge, dining room and deck all encourage mixing and mingling. A hot and cold buffet breakfast is included in the rates.

Eden Villa
B&B $$$

(Map p66; ☑ 09-630 1165; www.edenvilla.co.nz; 16 Poronui St, Mt Eden; r $250) These pretty wooden villas are what Auckland's leafy inner suburbs are all about. This one has three comfortable en-suite bedrooms, a pleasantly old-fashioned ambience and charming hosts who prepare a good cooked breakfast. We prefer the room at the rear, which has the original bathtub and views straight over the garden to Mt Eden itself.

Eden Park B&B B&B $$$
(Map p74; ☑09-630 5721; www.bedandbreakfastnz.com; 20 Bellwood Ave, Mt Eden; s/d $165/250; ☎) ✿ The hallowed turf of Auckland's legendary Eden Park rugby ground is only a block away and, while the rooms aren't overly large, they mirror the Edwardian elegance of this fine wooden villa.

Parnell & Newmarket

Quest Carlaw Park APARTMENT $$
(Map p76; ☑09-304 0521; www.questcarlawpark.co.nz; 15 Nicholls Lane; apt from $189; P@☎) ✿ It's in an odd spot but this set of smart, modern apartments is handy for Parnell, the city and the Domain, and if you've got a car, you're practically on the motorway.

Quality Hotel Parnell HOTEL $$
(Map p76; ☑09-303 3789; www.theparnell.co.nz; 10-20 Gladstone Rd; r from $138; P☎) More than 100 motel rooms and units are available in this renovated complex. The newer north wing has great harbour views.

★ Ascot Parnell B&B $$$
(Map p76; ☑09-309 9012; www.ascotparnell.com; 32 St Stephens Ave, Parnell; r $255-325; P@☎⛵) The Ascot's three luxurious bedrooms share a spacious apartment in a modern midrise block. You're in no danger of stumbling into the owners' private space; they have a completely separate apartment next door. The largest room grabs all of the harbour views but you can enjoy the same vista from the large terrace leading off the communal living area.

Devonport

Parituhu B&B $$
(Map p82; ☑09-445 6559; www.parituhu.co.nz; 3 King Edward Pde, Devonport; r $125-155; ☎) There's only one double bedroom (with its own adjoining bathroom) available in this relaxing and welcoming Edwardian waterfront bungalow.

Devonport Motel MOTEL $$
(Map p82; ☑09-445 1010; www.devonportmotel.co.nz; 11 Buchanan St, Devonport; r $160; P☎) This minimotel has two units in the tidy back garden. They're modern, clean,

self-contained and in a quiet location close to Devonport's attractions.

Devonport Sea Cottage COTTAGE $$
(Map p82; ☑09-445 7117; www.devonportseacottagenz.com; 3a Cambridge Tce, Devonport; cottage $150; ☎) Head up the garden path to your own cute and cosy self-contained cottage. Weekly rates are available.

Hampton Beach House B&B $$$
(Map p82; ☑09-445 1358; www.hamptonbeachhouse.co.nz; 4 King Edward Pde, Devonport; s/d from $195/245; @☎) This upmarket, waterside, Edwardian B&B has tasteful rooms that open onto a rear garden. Expect quality linen and gourmet breakfasts.

Peace & Plenty Inn B&B $$$
(Map p82; ☑09-445 2925; www.peaceandplenty.co.nz; 6 Flagstaff Tce, Devonport; s/d from $195/265; P☎) ✿ Stocked with antiques, this perfectly located, five-star Victorian house has romantic and luxurious en-suite rooms with TVs, flowers, free sherry/port and local chocolates.

Other Areas

Ambury Regional Park CAMPGROUND $
(Map p66; ☑09-366 2000; www.arc.govt.nz; 43 Ambury Rd, Mangere; sites per adult/child $15/6) A slice of country in suburbia, this regional park is also a working farm. Facilities are limited (a vault toilet, warm showers and not much shade) but it's handy to the airport, right on the water and dirt cheap.

Grange Lodge MOTEL $$
(Map p66; ☑09-277 8280; www.grangelodge.co.nz; cnr Grange & Great South Rds, Papatoetoe; units $125-190; ☎) ✿ If you've driven up from the south, consider staying at this friendly little suburban motel that's handy for the airport. From the Southern Motorway, take the East Tamaki Rd exit, turn right and right again onto Great South Rd.

Nautical Nook B&B $$
(Map p66; ☑09-521 2544; www.nauticalnook.com; 23b Watene Cres, Orakei; s/d $108/162; ☎) If you're a sailing buff you'll find a kindred spirit in Keith, who runs this cosy homestay with his wife, Trish. The lounge and terrace have views over the harbour, and the beach is close at hand.

Jet Park HOTEL $$
(Map p66; ☑09-275 4100; www.jetpark.co.nz; 63 Westney Rd, Mangere; r/ste from $189/289;

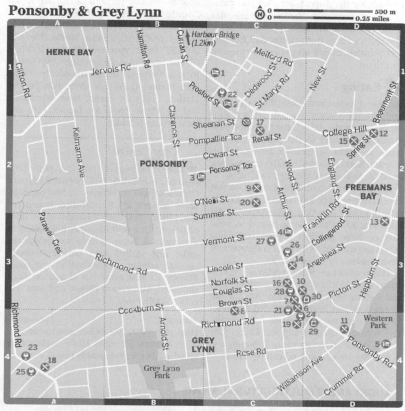

Ponsonby & Grey Lynn

🛏 Sleeping
1	Abaco on Jervois	C1
2	Brown Kiwi	C1
3	Great Ponsonby Arthotel	B2
4	Ponsonby Backpackers	C3
5	Verandahs	D4

🍴 Eating
6	Bird on a Wire	C3
7	Blue Breeze Inn	C3
8	Cocoro	C3
9	Dizengoff	C2
10	Il Buco	C3
11	MooChowChow	D4
12	New World	D2
13	Nishiki	D3
14	Ponsonby Road Bistro	C3
15	Queenie s	D2
16	Saan	C3
17	Sidart	C2
18	Siostra	A4
19	Street Food Collective	C4
20	The Unbakery	C2

🍷 Drinking & Nightlife
21	Bedford Soda & Liquor	C3
22	Dida's Wine Lounge & Tapas Bar	C1
23	Freida Margolis	A4
24	Golden Dawn	C4
25	Gypsy Tea Room	A4
26	Mea Culpa	C3
27	Shanghai Lil's	C3
28	SPQR	C3

🛍 Shopping
29	Karen Walker	D4
30	Women's Bookshop	D3
	Zambesi	(see 14)

@ 🛜 🖳) 🖉 Located within the industrial area edging the airport, Jet Park has comfortable rooms and a vibe that exceeds that of the average midrange airport hotel. With departure screens in the lobby and free airport shuttles, there's no excuse for missing your flight.

✕ Eating

Because of its size and ethnic diversity, Auckland tops the country when it comes to dining options and quality. Lively eateries have sprung up to cater to the many Asian students, and offer inexpensive Japanese, Chinese and Korean staples. If you're on a budget, you'll fall in love with the city's food halls.

Aucklanders demand good coffee, so you never have to walk too far to find a decent cafe, especially in suburbs like Ponsonby, Mt Eden and Kingsland. Some double as wine bars or have gourmet aspirations, while others are content to fill their counters with fresh, reasonably priced snacks.

The hippest new foodie enclaves are Britomart (the blocks above the train station) and Federal St (under the Sky Tower), and recent openings have resurrected and reinforced the culinary reputation of Ponsonby. The Wynyard Quarter and the former City Works Depot on the corner of Wellesley and Nelson Sts are also up-and-coming areas.

You'll find large supermarkets in most neighbourhoods: there's a particularly handy **Countdown** (Map p70; ☑09-275 2567; www.countdown.co.nz; 76 Quay St; ⊗24hr) at the bottom of town and a **New World** (Map p85; ☑09-307 8400; www.newworld.co.nz; 2 College Hill, Freemans Bay; ⊗7am-midnight) by Victoria Park. Self-caterers should consider the Otara Flea Market (p97) and Avondale Sunday Markets (p97) for cheap, fresh vegetables, and La Cigale (p91) for fancier fare and local artisan produce.

✕ City Centre

★ **Best Ugly Bagels**   BAKERY, CAFE $
(Map p70; ☑09-366 3926; www.bestugly.co.nz; City Works Depot, 90 Wellesley St; filled bagels $5-12; ⊗7am-3am; 🖉) Hand rolled, boiled and wood-fired, Best Ugly's bagels are a thing of beauty. Call into its super-hip bakery in a converted heavy vehicle workshop and order one stuffed with pastrami, bacon, smoked salmon or a variety of vegetarian fillings. Or just ask for a cinnamon bagel slathered with cream cheese and jam. The coffee is killer too.

Hansan   VIETNAMESE $
(Map p70; ☑09-379 8899; www.hansan.co.nz; 22-24 Kitchener St; mains $11-16; ⊗11am-10pm) Good, authentic, reasonably priced Vietnam-

---

AUCKLAND'S MULTICULTURAL MENU

Around 30% of New Zealanders live in Auckland, and the country's biggest city is also the most ethnically diverse. With immigration – especially from Asia – has come a cosmopolitan restaurant scene, and savvy Auckland foodies (and a few of the city's top chefs) keenly explore central fringe neighbourhoods for authentic tastes of the city's multicultural present and future.

Head to Dominion Rd in Balmoral (catch bus 267 from stop 7058 near the intersection of Queen and Wellesley Sts and get off at stop 8418) to be surrounded by Auckland's best Chinese food.

A few blocks west (catch bus 249 from stop 7022 in Victoria St East to stop 8316 on Sandringham Rd) are some of the city's best Indian and Sri Lankan restaurants. Our favourite is **Paradise** (Map p66; ☑09-845 1144; www.paradisetakeaway.co.nz; 591 Sandringham Rd, Sandringham; mains $12-18; ⊗11.30am-9.30pm; 🖉), specialising in the Mughlai cuisine you'd find on the streets of Hyderabad.

At the city's bustling night markets – held in a different suburban car park each night of the week – scores of stalls serve food from a diverse range of countries, from Argentina and Samoa, to Hungary and Turkey. Most convenient for travellers is the Monday **Onehunga Night Market** (Map p66; www.aucklandnightmarket.co.nz; 151 Arthur St, Onehunga; ⊗5.30-10pm Mon). Catch a train from Britomart to Onehunga and walk 550m to the car park below the Dress-Smart Outlet Shopping Centre.

If you're in town in late March, the **Auckland International Cultural Festival** (p81) offers a very tasty peek into the city's ethnically diverse future. Online, Cheap Eats (www.cheapeats.co.nz) scours Auckland for the city's best food for under $20.

ese eateries are in short supply in NZ, which makes this surprisingly upmarket-looking place a real find. There's free green tea and a large picture menu, and many of the mains come with a side serve of noodle soup. You may leave sloshing but you're unlikely to leave hungry.

Chuffed
CAFE $
(Map p70; ☑09-367 6801; www.chuffedcoffee. co.nz; 43 High St; mains $6.50-18; ☺7am-5pm Mon-Fri, 9am-5pm Sat & Sun) Tucked away in a lightwell at the rear of a building, this hip little place, liberally coated in street art, is a definite contender for the inner city's best cafe. Grab a seat on the indoor-outdoor terrace and tuck into cooked breakfasts, Wagyu burgers, lamb shanks or surprisingly flavour-packed toasted sandwiches.

Eighthirty
CAFE $
(Map p70; www.eighthirty.com; 35 High St; sandwiches $7.50-9; ☺7am-3.30pm Mon-Fri, 9am-2pm Sat) Primarily a coffee roaster, Eighthirty's High St branch serves the inner city's best coffee and a tasty array of fresh sandwiches, salads and sweet things. The dazzling white industrial decor is an interesting counterpoint to the wonderful heritage building in which it's housed.

No. 1 Pancake
KOREAN $
(Map p70; ☑09-302 0564; www.facebook.com/no1pancake; cnr Lorne & Wellesley Sts; pancakes $3.50-4.50; ☺10am-7pm Mon-Sat) The constant queue outside tells you all you need to know about this hole-in-the-wall eatery. It does only one thing and it does it well: delicious crispy Korean-style pancakes (*hotteok* or *ho dduk*, depending on who you ask), stuffed with savoury or sweet fillings and served piping hot in a paper bag.

Revive
VEGETARIAN $
(Map p70; ☑09-303 0420; www.revive.co.nz; 24 Wyndham St; mains $12-14; ☺10am-7pm Mon-Thu, 10am-3pm Fri; ✔) Vegetarian heaven with an enticing salad bar and economical daily meal deals.

★ Depot
MODERN NZ $$
(Map p70; www.eatatdepot.co.nz; 86 Federal St; dishes $16-34; ☺7am-late) TV chef Al Brown's popular eatery offers first-rate comfort food in informal surrounds (communal tables, butcher tiles and a constant buzz). Dishes are designed to be shared, and a pair of clever shuckers serve up the city's freshest clams and oysters. It doesn't take bookings, so get there early or expect to wait.

★ Beirut
LEBANESE $$
(Map p70; ☑09-367 6882; www.beirut.co.nz; 85 Fort St; mains $26-29; ☺7am-late Mon-Fri, 5pm-late Sat) Sacking curtains and industrial decor don't necessarily scream out Lebanese, but the sophisticated, punchy flavours bursting from the plates at this wonderful new restaurant certainly do. The cocktails are nearly as exciting as the food – and that's saying something.

Federal Delicatessen
AMERICAN $$
(Map p70; www.thefed.co.nz; 86 Federal St; mains $11-26; ☺7am-late) Celebrity chef Al Brown's take on a New York Jewish deli serves up simple stuff like bagels and sandwiches, matzo ball soup and lots of delicious comfort food to share (turkey meatloaf, spit-roasted chicken, New York strip steak). White butcher tiles, vinyl booth seating and waitstaff in 1950s uniforms add to the illusion.

Odette's
MODERN NZ $$
(Map p70; ☑09-309 0304; www.odettes. co.nz; Shed 5, City Works Depot, 90 Wellesley St; mains $17-25; ☺8am-3pm Sun & Mon, 7am-11pm Tue-Sat) Nothing about Odette's is run of the mill. Not the bubbly light fixtures or the quirky photography, and certainly not the menu. How about octopus or spicy short ribs for brunch? Or spongy wild mushrooms served with doughnuts and Persian feta? In the evening the more cafe-ish items are replaced with dishes for sharing. It gets hectic on weekends.

Ela Cuisine
INDIAN $$
(Map p70; ☑09-379 2710; www.elacuisine.co.nz; 41 Elliott St; mains $20-25; ☺11.45am-2.45pm & 5-9.30pm Mon-Sat, 5-8.30pm Sun) Tucked away at the rear of the Elliott Stables food court, this excellent Indian eatery serves up lip-smacking curries (Kerala beef, coconut lamb shank, 'butterless' chicken etc) and *masala dosa* (stuffed pancakes), each accompanied by a generous serve of rice and salad. It's great value too.

Ima
MIDDLE EASTERN $$
(Map p70; ☑09-377 5252; www.imacuisine. co.nz; 53 Fort St; breakfast & lunch $10-26, dinner shared dishes $17-27; ☺7am-11pm Mon-Fri, 9.30am-10pm Sat & Sun) Named after the Hebrew word for mother, Ima's menu features an array of Israeli, Palestinian, Yemeni and Lebanese comfort food, along with meat pies and sandwiches at lunchtime. Rustle up a group for Ima's excellent shared dinners and feast

on whole fish, chicken *meschan* (a whole bird slow-cooked with herbs and spices and then grilled) or slow-cooked lamb shoulder.

Gusto at the Grand ITALIAN $$
(Map p70; ☑09-363 7030; www.skycityauckland.co.nz; SkyCity Grand Hotel, 90 Federal St; mains $20-42; ☺noon-2.30pm & 5pm-late; ☑⊛) One of the more affordable eateries in the big, brash SkyCity casino complex, Gusto excels in delivering fresh pasta dishes, all of which are made from scratch when you order. The space feels like an extension of the hotel lobby, but you can sit at the marble counter and watch the action in the kitchen.

Cassia INDIAN $$
(Map p70; ☑09-379 9702; www.cassiarestaurant.co.nz; 5 Fort Lane; mains $28-34; ☺noon-3pm Wed-Fri, 5.30pm-late Tue-Sat) Occupying a moodily lit basement off an access lane, Cassia serves quality modern Indian food with plenty of punch and panache. Start with a *pani puri*, a bite-sized crispy shell bursting with flavour, before settling into a decadently rich curry. The Delhi duck is excellent, as is the piquant Goan fish curry.

★ Sugar Club MODERN NZ $$$
(Map p70; ☑09-363 6365; www.thesugarclub.co.nz; L53 Sky Tower, Federal St; 2-/3-/4-/5-course lunch $56/70/84/98, 3-/4-/5-/6-course dinner $90/108/118/128; ☺noon-2.30pm Wed-Sun & 5.30-9.30pm daily) It pays not to expect too much from restaurants stuck up towers, but when the executive chef is NZ's most famous culinary son, Peter Gordon, heralded in the UK as the 'godfather of fusion cuisine', you can comfortably raise your expectations. Gordon's meticulously constructed, flavour-filled dishes compete with the stupendous views and come out on top.

O'Connell Street Bistro EUROPEAN $$$
(Map p70; ☑09-377 1884; www.oconnellstbistro.com; 3 O'Connell St; mains lunch $32-38, dinner $40-42; ☺11.30am-3pm & 5.30-11pm Mon-Fri, 5.30-11pm Sat) O'Connell St is a grown-up treat, with smart decor and wonderful food and wine, satisfying lunchtime powerbrokers and dinnertime daters alike. If you're dining before 7.30pm, a fixed-price menu is available (two/three courses $40/45).

Grove MODERN NZ $$$
(Map p70; ☑09-368 4129; www.thegroverestaurant.co.nz; St Patrick's Sq, Wyndham St; 5-/9-course degustation $89/145; ☺noon-3pm Thu & Fri, 6pm-late Mon-Sat) Romantic fine dining: the room is moodily lit, the menu encourages sensual experimentation and the service is effortless. If you can't find anything to break the ice from the extensive wine list, give it up, mate – it's never going to happen.

✕ Britomart, Viaduct Harbour & Wynyard Quarter

★ Ortolana ITALIAN $$
(Map p70; www.ortolana.co.nz; 33 Tyler St, Britomart; mains $25-29; ☺7am-11pm) Mediterranean and regional Italian flavours are showcased at this stylish restaurant. Dishes are as artfully arranged as they are delicious, and much of the produce comes from the owners' small farm in rural west Auckland. Some of the sweets come from its sister patisserie, the very fabulous Milse, next door. It doesn't take bookings.

Baduzzi ITALIAN $$
(Map p70; ☑09-309 9339; www.baduzzi.co.nz; cnr Jellicoe St & Fish Lane, Wynyard Quarter; mains $16-40; ☺11.30am-late; ☑) This smart and sassy eatery does sophisticated spins on meatballs – try the crayfish ones – and other robust but elegant Italian dishes. Cosy up in the intimate booths, grab a seat at the bar, or soak up some Auckland sunshine outside.

Store CAFE $$
(Map p70; ☑09-366 1864; www.hipgroup.co.nz/thestore; 5b Gore St, Britomart; mains $18-25; ☺7am-3pm) With tables spilling into the fairylight- and flower-strewn space at the centre of Britomart, this chic cafe is as fresh and effervescent as the sparkling water that arrives unbidden when you're seated. Seasonal vegetables and fruits feature prominently on an interesting and enticing menu spanning cooked breakfasts, pasta dishes, market fish and salt-beef sandwiches.

Ebisu JAPANESE $$$
(Map p70; ☑09-300 5271; www.ebisu.co.nz; 116-118 Quay St, Britomart; large plates $34-39; ☺noon-3pm Mon-Fri, 5pm-late daily) Ebisu specialises in *izakaya,* a style of drinking and eating that eschews Japanese formality, yet doesn't involve food being flung around the room or chugging along on a conveyor belt. This large bar gets it exactly right, serving exquisite plates designed to be shared.

✕ Freemans Bay

Nishiki JAPANESE $
(Map p85; ☑09-376 7104; www.nishiki.co.nz; 100 Wellington St, Freemans Bay; dishes $5-17;

⊘6-10.30pm Tue-Sur; ⤴) Tucked away in an odd block of shops down the hill from Ponsonby Rd, Nishiki serves up a tasty array of dishes to a largely Japanese clientele. A picture menu makes it easier to select from the lengthy list of sushi, sashimi, salads, hot pots, skewers, tempura, robata, and rice and noodle dishes.

iVillage
INDIAN $$

(Map p70; ⤴09-309 4009; www.ivillageat-victoria.co.nz; 210-218 Victoria St, Freemans Bay; mains lunch $13-23, dinner $17-32; ⊘noon-3pm Tue-Fri, 6-11pm daily; ⤴) Specialising in delicious tandoori dishes and lamb curries, this top-flight Indian eatery has a wide-ranging menu with plenty of vegetarian selections and an Indochinese section. On a summer's night, enjoy your subcontinental feast in the courtyard of the historic Victoria Park Market.

Queenie's
CAFE $$

(Map p85; ⤴09-378 8977; www.queenies. co.nz; 24a Spring St, Freemans Bay breakfast $11-19, lunch $23-26; ⊘7am-3.30pm) Kiwiana reigns supreme at this eccentric corner cafe with one wall devoted to a 1950s paint-by-numbers Māori maiden mural. The food is a step up from standard cafe fare, with an adventurous menu (kedgeree Turkish eggs, Musabaha, cassoulet etc) justifying the prices.

★Clooney
MODERN NZ $$$

(Map p70; ⤴09-358 1702; www.clooney.co.nz; 33 Sale St, Freemans Bay; 2-/3-/7-course menu $80/100/150; ⊘6pm-late Tue-Sun, noon-3pm Fri) Like the Hollywood actor of the same name, Clooney is suave, stylish and extremely sophisticated, suited up in basic black. While the taste combinations are complex, the results are faultless – which, coupled with impeccable service, puts Clooney firmly in the pricey-but-worth-it category.

Matterhorn
MODERN NZ $$$

(Map p70; ⤴09-929 2790; www.matterhorn. co.nz; 37 Drake St, Freemans Bay; mains $35-36; ⊘3pm-late) It took over 50 years for this Wellington institution to open an Auckland branch, but this newcomer at the top end of Victoria Park Market is very welcome indeed. Expect robust dishes such as barbecue beef cheeks, wild red deer with black pudding, the legendary 'plate of pig' and a good-value Sunday roast.

✕ Ponsonby & Grey Lynn

Auckland's busiest restaurant-cafe-bar strip is so damn cool it has its own website (www. iloveponsonby.co.nz).

Street Food Collective
FAST FOOD $

(Map p85; ⤴021 206 4503; www.thestreetfood-collective.co.nz; Rear, 130 Ponsonby Rd, Grey Lynn; dishes $5-15; ⊘11am-3pm & 5-10pm) A great concept this: 14 different food trucks take turns to occupy four spots in a courtyard accessed from a narrow back lane running between Richmond Rd and Mackelvie St (look for the wrought-iron gates). The roster's posted online and there's a separate bar truck too.

Bird on a Wire
FAST FOOD $

(Map p85; ⤴09-378 6369; www.birdonawire. co.nz; 136-146 Ponsonby Rd; mains $10-16; ⊘11am-9.30pm) Tasty sandwiches and healthy burgers, seasonal salads and rotisserie chickens to take away. Select your baste of choice – Jamaican jerk or truffle butter, perhaps – and you're sorted.

Il Buco
PIZZA $

(Map p85; ⤴09-360 4414; www.ilbuco.co.nz; 113 Ponsonby Rd, Ponsonby; pizza per slice $6; ⊘7.30am-9pm; ⤴) Delicious pizza by the slice – including vegetarian options – and tasty Italian comfort food like lasagne, stuffed mushrooms, potato croquettes and cannoli.

Dizengoff
CAFE $

(Map p85; ⤴09-360 0108; www.facebook.com/ dizengoff.ponsonby; 256 Ponsonby Rd, Ponsonby; mains $6.50-20; ⊘6.45am-4.30pm) This stylish shoebox crams in a disparate crowd of corporate and fashion types, Ponsonby denizens and travellers. There's a Jewish influence to the food, with tasty Israeli platters, chopped liver, bagels and chicken salads, along with tempting baking, heart-starting coffee and a great stack of reading material.

★Saan
THAI $$

(Map p85; ⤴09-320 4237; www.saan.co.nz; 160 Ponsonby Rd, Ponsonby; dishes $14-28; ⊘5pm-late Mon & Tue, noon-late Wed-Sun) Hot in both senses of the word, this super-fashionable restaurant focusses on the fiery cuisine of the Isaan and Lanna regions of northern Thailand. The menu is conveniently sorted from least to most spicy and split into smaller and larger dishes for sharing. Be sure to order the soft-shell crab; it's truly exceptional.

Siostra

ITALIAN **$$**

(Map p85; ☑09-360 6207; www.siostra.co.nz; 472 Richmond Rd, Grey Lynn; mains brunch $17-20, dinner $28-36; ⊙4-11pm Tue-Thu, noon-11pm Fri, 9am-11pm Sat & Sun) Run by a charming pair of sisters, Siostra is the perfect little neighbourhood bistro, serving up hearty Italian fare with a modern sensibility. Their weekend brunches are substantial enough to placate even the meanest hangover.

Blue Breeze Inn

CHINESE **$$**

(Map p85; ☑09-360 0303; www.thebluebreezeinn.co.nz; Ponsonby Central, 146 Ponsonby Rd, Ponsonby; mains $26-32; ⊙noon-late) Regional Chinese flavours combine with a funky retro Pacific ambience at this so-hip-it-hurts eatery. The waitstaff are sassy, the rum cocktails are deliciously strong, and menu standouts include pork belly and pickled cucumber steamed buns, and cumin-spiced lamb.

MooChowChow

THAI **$$**

(Map p85; ☑09-360 6262; www.moochowchow. co.nz; 23 Ponsonby Rd, Ponsonby; dishes $20-34; ⊙noon-3pm Mon-Fri, 5.30pm-late Mon-Sat) It's Thai, Nahm Jim, but not as we know it. Bangkok's street food has been channelled into this supremely Ponsonby mooching spot without missing a piquant note. Killer Asian-inspired cocktails, too. Be ready to share a table with other diners.

Unbakery

CAFE **$$**

(Map p85; ☑09-555 3278; www.littlebirdorganics.co.nz; 1a Summer St, Ponsonby; mains $13-20; ⊙7am-4pm; ☑) ☑ Welcome to an 'unbakery', where virtually everything on the menu is prepared raw and uncooked, but still very tasty and healthy. Put on your best Gwyneth Paltrow visage and tuck into dishes studded with açai berries, chia seeds and organic fruit; there are even bagels, risotto, tacos and delicious cakes. The juices and smoothies are also great.

★ Sidart

MODERN NZ **$$$**

(Map p85; ☑09-360 2122; www.sidart.co.nz; Three Lamps Plaza, 283 Ponsonby Rd, Ponsonby; 8-course lunch $50, 5-9 course dinner $85-150; ⊙noon-2.30pm Fri, 6-11pm Tue-Sat) No one in Auckland produces creative degustations quite like Sid Sahrawat. It's food as art, food as science but, more importantly, food to fire up your taste buds, delight the brain, satisfy the stomach and put a smile on your face. The restaurant is a little hard to find, tucked away at the rear of what was once the Alhambra cinema.

Cocoro

JAPANESE **$$$**

(Map p85; ☑09-360 0927; www.cocoro.co.nz; 56a Brown St, Ponsonby; dishes $9-28, degustation menu $85-180; ⊙noon-2pm & 5.30-10pm Tue-Sat) Japanese elegance infuses everything about this excellent restaurant, from the soft lighting and chic decor, to the delicate flavours of the artistically arranged food. At lunchtime it offers an affordable *donburi* rice bowl ($20 to $24) and a three-course option ($49), while in the evening multicourse degustation menus showcase the chefs' skills.

Ponsonby Road Bistro

MODERN NZ **$$$**

(Map p85; ☑09-360 1611; www.ponsonbyroadbistro.co.nz; 165 Ponsonby Rd, Ponsonby; mains $34-36; ⊙noon-12.30am Mon-Fri, 4pm-12.30am Sat) The service is first-rate at this modern, upmarket restaurant, which introduces Asian flavours to predominantly French- and Italian-style bistro dishes. Imported cheese and wine are a highlight, and the crispy-based pizzas make a delicious shared snack.

⋇ Newton

Karangahape Rd (K Rd) is known for its late-night clubs, but cafes and plenty of inexpensive ethnic restaurants are mixed in with the vintage clothing stores, second-hand boutiques, tattooists and adult shops.

Coco's Cantina

ITALIAN **$$**

(Map p70; ☑09-300 7582; www.cocoscantina. co.nz; 376 Karangahape Rd, Newton; mains $28-33; ⊙5pm-late Tue-Sat) Rub shoulders with Auckland's hipsters and foodsters at this bustling cantina where the wait for a table is part of the experience. Propping up the bar is hardly a hardship: the ambience and drinks list see to that. The rustic menu is narrowly focused, seasonal and invariably delicious.

French Cafe

FRENCH **$$$**

(Map p74; ☑09-377 1911; www.thefrenchcafe. co.nz; 210 Symonds St, Newton; mains $46, tasting menu $145; ⊙noon-3pm Fri, 6pm-late Tue-Sat) The legendary French Cafe has been rated as one of Auckland's top restaurants for more than 20 years and it still continues to excel. The cuisine is nominally French-influenced, but chef Simon Wright sneaks in lots of tasty Asian and Pacific Rim touches. The service is impeccable.

⋇ Kingsland

Petra Shawarma

MIDDLE EASTERN **$$**

(Map p74; ☑09-815 8652; 482 New North Rd, Kingsland; mains $15-21; ⊙11am-late; ☑☑)

Owned by a friendly Jordanian family, Petra serves up light, healthy kebabs. The dips and salads are also worth the short train ride to Kingsland.

Mt Eden

Bolaven
CAFE $$

(Map p66; ☎09-631 7520; www.bolaven.co.nz; 597 Mt Eden Rd, Mt Eden; mains $11-26; ⊙8am-3pm Tue-Sun, 6-10pm Wed-Sat; ☑) Cafe fare with a heavy Lao accent is the big attraction at this stylish but informal eatery. Alongside the bagels and bircher muesli you'll find the likes of 'Grandpa's *pho*' (noodle soup), sticky rice with fried eggs and *mok pa* (steamed fish parcels). Come dinnertime the menu is more decidedly Lao, featuring vegetable curry, pork skewers and pan-fried squid.

Merediths
MODERN NZ $$$

(Map p74; ☎09-623 3140; www.merediths.co.nz; 365 Dominion Rd, Mt Eden; 5-/8-/9-course degustation $80/120/140; ⊙noon-3pm Fri, 6pm-late Tue-Sat) Dining at Merediths is the culinary equivalent of black-water rafting – tastes surprise you at every turn, you never know what's coming next and you're left with a sense of breathless exhilaration. There's no à la carte option and only the nine-course tasting is offered on Saturdays.

Molten
MODERN NZ $$$

(Map p74; ☎09-638 7236; www.molten.co.nz; 422 Mt Eden Rd, Mt Eden; mains $32-35; ⊙11.30am-3pm Wed-Fri, 6pm-late Mon-Sat) Under the volcano's shadow, Molten oozes neighbourhood charm and erupts with flavour. The consistently excellent menu takes advantage of seasonal produce to create innovative meals. The same lively modern menu is available at its wine bar next door, along with pizza, cheese and charcuterie.

Parnell & Newmarket

La Cigale
FRENCH, MARKET $

(Map p76; ☎09-366 9351; www.lacigale.co.nz; 69 St Georges Bay Rd, Parnell; cafe $8-18, bistro $12-22; ⊙market 9am-1.30pm Sat & Sun, cafe 9am-4pm Mon-Fri, to 2pm Sat & Sun, bistro 6pm-late Wed-Fri) Catering to Francophile foodies, this warehouse stocks French imports and has a patisserie-laden cafe. During the weekend farmers markets, this *cigale* (cicada) really chirps, with stalls laden with local artisan produce. On Wednesday evenings it becomes a food-truck stop, while on Thursdays and Fridays the space is converted into a quirky evening bistro serving simple rustic dishes.

Rosie
CAFE $$

(Map p76; www.hipgroup.co.nz/rosie; 82 Gladstone Rd, Parnell; mains $18-32; ⊙7am-late) Notorious as a hang-out for ponytail-tugging prime ministers (Google it), Rosie is nevertheless a swish spot for a cooked breakfast, an inventive bistro-style meal, or coffee and cake after a stroll around the rose gardens. Service is friendly and thoughtful, and there's always a little something for offal lovers on the menu.

Woodpecker Hill
ASIAN, FUSION $$$

(Map p76; ☎09-309 5055; www.woodpeckerhill.co.nz; 196 Parnell Rd, Parnell; large dishes $32-37; ⊙noon-late) Marrying the flavours and shared dining style of Southeast Asian cuisine with an American approach to meat (smoky slow-cooked brisket, sticky short ribs etc), this odd bird has pecked out a unique place on the Auckland dining scene. The decor is as eclectic as the food, a riotous mishmash of tartan, faux fur, copper bells and potted plants.

Devonport

Calliope Road Cafe
CAFE $$

(Map p82; ☎09-446 1209; www.callioperoadcafe.co.nz; 33 Calliope Rd, Devonport; mains $10-26; ⊙8am-3pm Wed-Mon; ☑) Devonport's best cafe is set a little back from the main tourist strip, and serves a tasty mix of cafe classics and Southeast Asian dishes to locals in the know.

Bette's Bar & Eatery
PUB FOOD $$

(Map p82; ☎09-446 6444; www.bettes.co.nz; 8 Victoria Rd, Devonport; mains $18-39; ⊙4pm-late Mon, 11am-late Tue-Sun) Decent wine, cocktails and beer, and good tapas and ethnically diverse mains make for a top spot to chill out after exploring Devonport.

Other Areas

Chinoiserie
CHINESE $

(Map p66; www.facebook.com/chinoiserieltd; 4 Owairaka Ave, Mt Albert; dishes $8-15; ⊙4-10pm Tue-Sun) Bringing hip decor and tasty Taiwanese street food to a nondescript strip of suburban shops, Chinoiserie specialises in *gua bao* – oversized steamed buns stuffed with the likes of pork, chicken, beef, squid or tofu. Combine one with a side of glass-noodle salad or sticky pork ribs for a lipsmackingly delicious meal. Don't bother with dessert.

Ceremony

CAFE $

(Map p70; www.ceremony.company; 7 Park Rd, Grafton; mains $12; ☺7am-3pm; 🐾) Don't expect any pomp or circumstance, as Ceremony keeps things simple: minimalist decor, heart-starting coffee, and a concise menu of delicious salads and sandwiches served in burger-like buns (try the pork-and-fennel sausage). The only extravagances on display are a bubbly profusion of lampshades, a turntable, a battered set of vinyl LPs and the beards on many of the clientele.

Jai Jalaram Khaman

INDIAN $

(☑09-845 5555; 570 Sandringham Rd, Sandringham; mains $10-13; ☺5-9pm Mon-Fri, 1-9pm Sat & Sun; 🖉) Excellent vegetarian Gujarati food.

Takapuna Beach Cafe

CAFE $$

(Map p66; ☑09-484 0002; www.takapunabeachcafe.co.nz; 22 The Promenade, Takapuna; mains $19-30; ☺7am-6pm) Sophisticated cafe fare combined with excellent views of Takapuna Beach ensure that this cafe constantly buzzes. If you can't snaffle a table, grab an award-winning ice cream – our favourite is the salted caramel – and take a lazy stroll along the beach.

L'oeuf

CAFE $$

(Map p66; ☑09-971 4155; www.facebook.com/LOeuf; 4a Owairaka Ave, Mt Albert; mains $10-20; ☺7am-3.30pm) It's an effort to get to, but this suburban cafe serves some of the prettiest and best breakfasts in Auckland, with dishes such as 'the Nest' (a filo nest housing a Scotch quail's egg on a bed of salad, feta and beetroot purée) and 'the Cambodian' (black rice and salted caramel cream topped with fruit and edible flowers).

St Heliers Bay Bistro

MODERN NZ $$

(Map p66; www.stheliersbaybistro.co.nz; 387 Tamaki Dr, St Heliers; brunch $16-27, dinner $25-27; ☺7am-11pm) Head along pretty Tamaki Dr to this classy eatery with harbour views. No bookings are taken, but the switched-on crew soon find space for diners. Look forward to upmarket takes on the classics (fish and chips, burgers, beef pie) along with cooked breakfasts, tasty salads and lots of Mediterranean influences.

Engine Room

MODERN NZ $$$

(Map p66; ☑09-480 9502; www.engineroom.net.nz; 115 Queen St, Northcote; mains $39-41; ☺noon-3pm Fri, 5-11pm Tue-Sat) One of Auckland's best restaurants, this informal eatery serves up lighter-than-air goat's cheese souf-

flés, inventive mains and oh-my-God chocolate truffles. It's worth booking ahead and catching the ferry to Northcote Point; the restaurant is a further 1km walk away.

🍷 Drinking & Nightlife

Auckland's nightlife is quiet during the week – for some vital signs, head to Ponsonby Rd, Britomart or the Viaduct. Karangahape Rd (K Rd) wakes up late on Friday and Saturday; don't even bother staggering this way before 11pm.

🍸 City Centre

★Brothers Beer

CRAFT BEER

(Map p70; ☑09-366 6100; www.brothersbeer.co.nz; City Works Depot, 90 Wellesley St; ☺noon-10pm) Our favourite Auckland beer bar combines industrial decor with 18 taps crammed with the Brothers' own brews and guest beers from NZ and further afield. Hundreds more bottled beers await chilling in the fridges, and bar food includes top-notch pizza. It also offers tasting flights (five small glasses for $25).

Gin Room

BAR

(Map p70; www.ginroom.co.nz; L1, 12 Vulcan Lane; ☺5pm-midnight Tue & Wed, 5pm-2am Thu, 4pm-4am Fri, 6pm-4am Sat) There's a slightly disheveled colonial charm to this bar, discreetly tucked away above Auckland's oldest pub, which is completely in keeping with its latest incarnation as a gin palace. There's at least 50 ways to ruin mother here – ask the bar staff for advice – and that's not even counting the juniper-sozzled cocktails.

Mo's

BAR

(Map p70; ☑09-366 6066; www.mosbar.co.nz; cnr Wolfe & Federal Sts; ☺3pm-late Mon-Fri, 6pm-late Sat; 🐾) There's something about this tiny corner bar that makes you want to invent problems just so the barperson can solve them with soothing words and an expertly poured martini.

Cassette Nine

CLUB

(Map p70; ☑09-366 0196; www.cassettenine.com; 9 Vulcan Lane; ☺4pm-late Tue-Fri, 6pm-late Sat) Hipsters gravitate to this eccentric bar-club for music ranging from live indie to international DJ sets.

Vultures' Lane

PUB

(Map p70; ☑09-300 7117; www.vultureslane.co.nz; 10 Vulcan Lane; ☺11:30am-late) With 22 taps, over 75 bottled beers and sports on

GAY & LESBIAN AUCKLAND

The Queen City (as it's known for completely coincidental reasons) has by far the country's biggest gay population, with the bright lights attracting gays and lesbians from all over the country. However, the even brighter lights of Sydney eventually steal many of the 30- to 40-somethings, leaving a gap in the demographic. There are very few gay venues and they only really kick off on the weekends. For the latest, see the monthly magazine *Express* (available from gay venues) or www.gaynz.com.

The big event on the calendar is the Auckland Pride Festival (p79). Also worth watching out for are the regular parties held by Urge Events (www.facebook.com/urgebar); the only reliably fun and sexy nights out for the over 30s, they book out quickly.

Venues change with alarming regularity, but these ones were the stayers at the time of writing:

Family (Map p70; ☑09-309 0213; 270 Karangahape Rd, Newton; ☺9am-4am) Trashy, brash and extremely young, Family gets crammed on weekends, with drag hosts and dancing into the wee hours, both at the back of the ground-level bar and in the club downstairs.

The Eagle (Map p70; ☑09-309 4979; www.facebook.com/the.eagle.bar; 259 Karangahape Rd, Newton; ☺4pm-midnight Tue, to 1.30am Wed, Thu & Sun, to 4am Fri & Sat) A cosy place for a quiet drink early in the evening, getting more raucous as the night progresses. Get in quick to put your picks on the video jukebox or prepare for an entire evening of Kylie and Taylor.

Centurian (Map p70; ☑09-377 5571; www.centuriansauna.co.nz; 18 Beresford St, Newton; admission before/after 3pm $24/29 ☺11am-2am Sun-Thu, to 6am Fri & Sat) Gay men's sauna.

the TV, this pleasantly grungy historic pub is popular with beard-stroking craft-beer cradlers.

Everybody's BAR
(Map p70; ☑09-929 2702; www.everybodys.co.nz; L1, 7 Fort Lane; ☺4pm-late Tue-Sat; ☏) Part of a transformation of a long-defunct cinema, Everybody's sprawls over two levels, with couches and banquettes on the mezzanine, and a plant-filled internal courtyard. The food's good too.

Jefferson BAR
(Map p70; www.thejefferson.co.nz; Easement, Imperial Bldg, Fort Lane; ☺4pm-1am Mon-Thu, to 3am Fri & Sat) Lit by the golden glow of close to 600 different whisky bottles, this subterranean den is a sophisticated spot for a nightcap. There's no list – talk to the knowledgeable bar staff about the kind of thing you're after (peaty, smooth, smoky, not-too-damaging-to-the-wallet) and they'll suggest something.

Ding Dong Lounge CLUB
(Map p70; ☑09-377 4712; www.dingdongloungenz.com; 26 Wyndham St; ☺5pm-4am Wed-Fri, 8pm-4am Sat) Rock, indie and alternative sounds from live bands and DJs, washed down with craft beer.

Britomart, Viaduct Harbour & Wynyard Quarter

Tyler Street Garage BAR
(Map p70; ☑09-300 5279; www.tylerstreetgarage.co.nz; 116-118 Quay St, Britomart; ☺11.30am-late) Just in case you were in any doubt that this was actually a garage, they've left the parking lines painted on the concrete floor. A compact roof terrace looks over the wharves. DJs get butts shaking on weekends.

Ostro City Terrace BAR
(Map p70; ☑09-302 9888; www.ostro.co.nz; L2, 52 Tyler St, Britomart; ☺noon-late) Ostro's bar may not gaze over the harbour like the highfalutin' restaurant it's attached to, but the view over the fairy-lit rear lane from its large 2nd-floor terrace is just as lovely. The cavernous interior wears traces of its industrial past but we prefer to quaff our cocktails around the firepit on the deck like overdressed urban campers.

Sixteen Tun CRAFT BEER
(Map p70; ☑09-368 7712; www.16tun.co.nz; 10-26 Jellicoe St, Wynyard Quarter; tasting 4/6/8 beers $12/18/24; ☺11.30am-late) The glister of burnished copper perfectly complements the liquid amber on offer here in the form

of dozens of NZ craft beers by the bottle and a score on tap. If you can't decide, go for a tasting 'crate' of 200mL serves.

Orleans
BAR

(Map p70; ☑09-309 5854; www.orleans.co.nz; 48 Customs St, Britomart; ⊙11.30am-late Sun-Thu, 4pm-late Fri & Sat) This South Pacific gumbo spin on a southern US jazz bar has wicked cocktails, and live jazz and blues most nights. Bar snacks include po'boy sandwiches.

Northern Steamship Co.
PUB

(Map p70; ☑09-374 3952; www.northernsteamship.co.nz; 122 Quay St, Britomart; ⊙11.30am-late) Standard lamps hang upside down from the ceiling while the mural behind the bar dreams of NZ summer holidays in this good-looking large pub near the train station.

⬤ Ponsonby & Grey Lynn

Along Ponsonby Rd, the line between cafe, restaurant, bar and club gets blurred. A lot of eateries also have live music or become clubs later on.

★ Gypsy Tea Room
BAR

(Map p85; ☑09-361 6970; www.gypsytearoom. co.nz; 455 Richmond Rd, Grey Lynn; ⊙4-11.30pm Sun-Thu, 3pm-2am Fri & Sat) This little neighbourhood cocktail-wine bar has dishevelled charm in bucketloads. Rest assured, no one comes here for tea.

★ Freida Margolis
BAR

(Map p85; ☑09-378 6625; www.facebook. com/freidamargolis; 440 Richmond Rd, Grey Lynn; ⊙4pm-late) Formerly a butchers – look for the Westlynn Organic Meats sign – this corner location is now a great little neighbourhood bar with a backstreets of Bogota ambience. Loyal locals sit outside with their well-behaved dogs, supping on sangria, wine and craft beer, and enjoying eclectic sounds from the owner's big vinyl collection.

★ Golden Dawn
BAR

(Map p85; ☑09-376 9929; www.goldendawn. co.nz; 134b Ponsonby Rd, Grey Lynn; ⊙4pm-midnight Tue-Fri, noon-midnight Sat & Sun) Occupying an old shopfront and an inviting stables yard, this hip drinking den regularly hosts happenings including DJs and live bands. There's also excellent food on offer, including pulled-pork rolls, and prawn buns with Japanese mayo and chilli. The entrance is via the unmarked door just around the corner on Richmond Rd.

Mea Culpa
COCKTAIL BAR

(Map p85; ☑09-376 4460; 3/175 Ponsonby Rd, Ponsonby; ⊙5pm-late Mon-Thu, 3pm-late Fri-Sun) If you can't find a cocktail to your taste in this small but perfectly formed bar, it's nobody's fault but your own.

SPQR
BAR

(Map p85; ☑09-360 1710; www.spqrnz.co.nz; 150 Ponsonby Rd, Ponsonby; ⊙noon-late) Quite the best place to see and be seen on the Ponsonby strip, SPQR is a magnet for local scenesters who are quick to nab the tables on the footpath. Head inside for a more discreet assignation lit by the flattering glow of candles reflected in the burnished copper bar. The food is excellent too, especially the Roman-style thin-crust pizza.

Shanghai Lil's
COCKTAIL BAR

(Map p85; ☑09-360 0396; www.facebook.com/lilsponsonby; 212 Ponsonby Rd, Ponsonby; ⊙5pm-late Tue-Sat) A louche old-world Shanghai vibe pervades this small bar, where the owner dispenses charm in a silk Mandarin jacket and octogenarian musicians tickle the ivories for satin-voiced jazz singers. It attracts a widely varied and eclectic crowd, with a healthy quotient of gay men in the mix.

Bedford Soda & Liquor
COCKTAIL BAR

(Map p85; ☑09-378 7362; www.bedfordsodaliquor.co.nz; Ponsonby Central, Richmond Rd, Ponsonby; ⊙noon-midnight) Candlelight and a semi-industrial fit-out set the scene for a New York–style bar devoted to the American drinking culture. The cocktails are pricey but worth it: some come wreathed in smoke, others in the alcoholic equivalent of a snow globe, while the 'salted caramel Malteaser whisky milkshake' is exactly as decadent as it sounds.

Dida's Wine Lounge & Tapas Bar
WINE BAR

(Map p85; ☑09-376 2813; www.didas.co.nz; 54 Jervois Rd, Ponsonby; ⊙noon-midnight) Great food and an even better wine list attract a grown-up crowd. There's an associated wine store, providore and cafe next door.

⬤ Newton

Wine Cellar
WINE BAR

(Map p70; www.facebook.com/winecellarstkevins; St Kevin's Arcade, 183 Karangahape Rd, Newton; ⊙5pm-1am) Secreted downstairs in an arcade, the Wine Cellar is dark, grungy and very cool, with regular live music in the neighbouring Whammy Bar (p95).

Galbraith's Alehouse
BREWERY, PUB

(Map p74; ☑ 09-379 3557; http://alehouse.
co.nz; 2 Mt Eden Rd, Newton; ☺ noon-11pm)
Brewing real ales and lagers on-site, this
cosy English-style pub in a grand heritage
building offers bliss on tap. There are always
more craft beers on the guest taps, and the
food's also very good.

Ink
CLUB

(Map p70; ☑ 09-358 5103; www.nkbar.co.nz;
268 Karangahape Rd, Newton; ☺ 9pm-4am Fri &
Sat) A long-running underground club for
serious dance aficionados, sometimes hosting big-name DJs.

Mt Eden

Molten
WINE BAR

(Map p74; ☑ 09-638 7263; www.molten.co.nz;
422 Mt Eden Rd, Mt Eden; ☺ 4.30pm-late Mon-Sat)
Grab a spot in the cosy leather banquettes
or venture out the back to the garden. Either
way enjoy a grown-up but relaxed ambience,
a great wine and beer list, and innovative food
courtesy of its sister restaurant next door.

Ginger Minx
BAR

(Map p74; ☑ 09-623 2121; www.facebook.com/
gingerminxnz; 117 Valley Rd, Mt Eden; ☺ 5pm-2am
Wed-Sat) Quirky decor, retro furniture and a
serious attitude to cocktails feature at this
hipsterish neighbourhood bar.

Kingsland

Portland Public House
BAR

(Map p74; ☑ 021 872 774; www.facebook.
com/theportlandpublichouse; 463 New North Rd,
Kingsland; ☺ 4pm-midnight Mon-Wed, 4pm-2am
Thu, noon-2am Fri & Sat, noon-midnight Sun) With
mismatched furniture, cartoon-themed art,
and lots of hidden nooks and crannies, the
Portland Public House is like spending a few
lazy hours at a hipster mate's place. It's also
an excellent location for live music.

☆ Entertainment

For listings, check the *New Zealand Herald's Time Out* magazine on Thursday and
again in its Saturday edition. Tickets for
most major events can be bought from Ticketek (☑ 0800 842 538; www.ticketek.co.nz), with
an outlet at SkyCity Theatre (Map p70;
☑ 09-363 6000; www.skycity.co.nz; cnr Wellesley
& Hobson Sts), and Ticketmaster (☑ 09-970
9700; www.ticketmaster.co.nz) at Vector Arena
(p95) and the Aotea Centre (Map p70;
☑ 09-309 2677; www.aucklandlive.co.nz; 50 May-

AUCKLAND TOP 10 PLAYLIST

Download these Auckland songs to your
MP3 player:

➡ *Me at the Museum, You in the
Wintergardens* – Tiny Ruins (2014)

➡ *400 Lux* – Lorde (2013)

➡ *Grey Lynn Park* – The Veils (2011)

➡ *Auckland CBD Part Two* – Lawrence
Arabia (2009)

➡ *Forever Thursday* – Tim Finn (2008)

➡ *Riverhead* – Goldenhorse (2004)

➡ *A Brief Reflection* – Nesian Mystik
(2002)

➡ *Dominion Road* – The Mutton Birds
(1992)

➡ *Andy* – The Front Lawn (1989)

➡ *One Tree Hill* – U2 (1987)

oral Dr). iTicket (☑ 0508 484 253; www.iticket.
co.nz) handles a lot of smaller gig and dance
party tickets.

Live Music

Kings Arms Tavern
LIVE MUSIC

(Map p74; ☑ 09-373 3240; www.kingsarms.
co.nz; 59 France St, Newton) This heritage pub
with a great beer garden is Auckland's leading small venue for local and up-and-coming
international bands.

Whammy Bar
LIVE MUSIC

(Map p70; www.facebook.com/thewhammybar;
183 Karangahape Rd, Newton; ☺ 8.30pm-4am Wed-
Sat) Small but a stalwart on the live indie
music scene nonetheless.

Power Station
LIVE MUSIC

(Map p74; www.powerstation.net.nz; 33 Mt Eden
Rd, Eden Terrace) Midrange venue popular
with up-and-coming overseas acts and established Kiwi bands.

Vector Arena
STADIUM

(Map p76; ☑ 09-358 1250; www.vectorarena.
co.nz; Mahuhu Cres) Auckland's top indoor
arena for major touring acts.

Cinema

Most cinemas offer cheaper rates on weekdays
before 5pm; Tuesday is usually bargain day.

Academy Cinemas
CINEMA

(Map p70; ☑ 09-373 2761; www.academy-
cinemas.co.nz; 44 Lorne St; adult/child $16/10)

Foreign and art-house films in the basement of the Central Library.

Rialto
CINEMA

(Map p79; ☑09-369 2417; www.rialto.co.nz; 167 Broadway, Newmarket) Mainly art-house and international films, plus better mainstream fare and regular specialist film festivals.

Event Cinemas
CINEMA

(Map p70; ☑09-369 2400; www.eventcinemas. co.nz; Level 3, 297 Queen St) Blockbusters, bowling alley and food court.

Theatre, Classical Music & Comedy

Auckland's main arts and entertainment complex is grouped around Aotea Sq. Branded Auckland Live (☑09-309 2677; www.aucklandlive.co.nz), it's comprised of the Town Hall, Civic Theatre and Aotea Centre, along with the Bruce Mason Centre in Takapuna.

Auckland Town Hall
CLASSICAL MUSIC

(Map p70; ☑09-309 2677; www.aucklandlive. co.nz; 305 Queen St) This elegant Edwardian venue (1911) hosts the NZ Symphony Orchestra (www.nzso.co.nz) and Auckland Philharmonia (www.apo.co.nz), among others.

Q Theatre
THEATRE

(Map p70; ☑09-309 9771; www.qtheatre.co.nz; 305 Queen St) Theatre by various companies and intimate live music. Silo Theatre (www.silotheatre.co.nz) often performs here.

Classic Comedy Club
COMEDY

(Map p70; ☑09-373 4321; www.comedy.co.nz; 321 Queen St; ☺6.30pm-late) Stand-up performances most nights, with legendary late-night shows during the annual Comedy Festival.

Maidment Theatre
THEATRE

(Map p70; ☑09-308 2383; www.maidment. auckland.ac.nz; 8 Alfred St) The University of Auckland's theatre often stages Auckland Theatre Company (www.atc.co.nz) productions.

Sport

Eden Park
SPECTATOR SPORT

(Map p74; ☑09-815 5551; www.edenpark.co.nz; Reimers Ave, Mt Eden) This stadium hosts top rugby (winter) and cricket (summer) tests by the All Blacks (www.allblacks.com) and the Black Caps (www.blackcaps.co.nz), respectively. It's also the home ground of Auckland Rugby (www.aucklandrugby.co.nz), the Blues Super Rugby team (www.theblues.co.nz) and Auckland Cricket (www.aucklandcricket. co.nz). Catch the train from Britomart to Kingsland and follow the crowds.

Mt Smart Stadium
SPECTATOR SPORT

(Map p66; ☑09-366 2048; www.mtsmart stadium.co.nz; 2 Beasley Ave, Penrose) Home ground for the Warriors rugby league team (www.warriors.kiwi), Auckland Football Federation (www.aucklandfootball.org.nz) and Athletics Auckland (www.athleticsauckland. co.nz). Also *really* big concerts.

North Shore Events Centre
SPECTATOR SPORT

(Map p66; ☑09-443 8199; www.nseventscentre.co.nz; Argus Pl, Wairau Valley) One of the two home courts of the NZ Breakers basketball team (www.nzbreakers.co.nz) and an occasional concert venue. The other home court is at Vector Arena (p95).

ASB Tennis Centre
SPECTATOR SPORT

(Map p76; www.tennisauckland.co.nz; 1 Tennis Lane, Parnell) In January the women's and men's ASB Classic (p78) is held here.

🔒 Shopping

Followers of fashion should head to the Britomart precinct, Newmarket's Teed and Nuffield Sts, and Ponsonby Rd. For vintage clothing and second-hand boutiques try Karangahape Rd (K Rd) or Ponsonby Rd.

🔒 City Centre

★ Real Groovy
MUSIC

(Map p70; ☑09-302 3940; www.realgroovy. co.nz; 369 Queen St; ☺9am-7pm Sat-Wed, to 9pm Thu & Fri) Masses of new, second-hand and rare releases in vinyl and CD format, as well as concert tickets, giant posters, DVDs, books, magazines and clothes.

★ Unity Books
BOOKS

(Map p70; ☑09-307 0731; www.unitybooks. co.nz; 19 High St; ☺8.30am-7pm Mon-Sat, 10am-6pm Sun) The inner city's best independent bookshop.

★ Zambesi
CLOTHING

(Map p70; ☑09-303 1701; www.zambesi.co.nz; 56 Tyler St; ☺9.30am-6pm Mon-Sat, 11am-4pm Sun) Iconic NZ label much sought after by local and international celebs. Also in Ponsonby (Map p85; ☑09-360 7391; www.zambesi. co.nz; 169 Ponsonby Rd, Ponsonby; ☺9.30am-6pm Mon-Sat, 11am-4pm Sun) and Newmarket (Map p79; ☑09-523 1000; www.zambesi.co.nz; 38 Osborne St, Newmarket; ☺9.30am-6pm Mon-Sat, 11am-4pm Sun).

Strangely Normal   CLOTHING

(Map p70; ☎09-309 0600; www.strangely normal.com; 19 O'Connell St; ☺10am-6pm Mon-Sat, 11am-4pm Sun) Quality, NZ-made, men's tailored shirts straight out of *Blue Hawaii* sit alongside hipster hats, sharp shoes and cufflinks.

Barkers'   CLOTHING

(Map p70; ☎09-303 2377; www.barkersonline. co.nz; 1 High St; ☺9am-7pm Mon-Sat, 10am-5pm Sun) This NZ menswear label has lifted its game and uncovered a cache of cool it never knew it had. Proof is this elegant concept store with its own café, upstairs 'groom room' and, of course, quality tailored clothes, artfully displayed.

Kapiti Store   FOOD

(Map p70; ☎09-358 3835; www.kapitistore. co.nz; 19 Shortland St; ☺9am-6pm Mon-Fri, 11.30am-4.30pm Sat) Equally famous in NZ for its cheese and its ice cream, you can stock up on both here.

🛍 Britomart

Karen Walker   CLOTHING

(Map p70; ☎09-309 6299; www.karenwalker. com; 18 Te Ara Tahuhu Walkway, Britomart; ☺10am-6pm) Join Madonna and Kirsten Dunst in wearing Walker's cool (but pricey) threads. Also in **Ponsonby Rd** (Map p85; ☎09-361 6723; 128a Ponsonby Rd, Grey Lynn ☺10am-5.30pm Mon-Sat, 11am-4pm Sun) and **Newmarket** (Map p79; ☎09-522 4286; 6 Balm St, Newmarket; ☺10am-6pm).

🛍 Ponsonby & Grey Lynn

Women's Bookshop   BOOKS

(Map p85; ☎09-376 4399; www.womensbook shop.co.nz; 105 Ponsonby Rd, Ponsonby; ☺10am-6pm) Excellent independent bookshop.

Texan Art Schools   ARTS, CRAFTS

(Map p79; ☎09-529 1021; www.texanart schools.co.nz; 366 Broadway; ☺9.30am-5.30pm) A collective of 100 local artists sell their wares here.

🛍 Kingsland

★**Royal Jewellery Studio**   JEWELLERY

(Map p74; ☎09-846 0200; www.royaljewellery studio.com; 436 New North Rd, Kingsland ☺10am-4pm Tue-Sun) Work by local artisans, including beautiful Māori designs and authentic *pounamu* (greenstone) jewellery.

PASIFIKA IN AUCKLAND

There are nearly 180,000 Pacific Islanders (PI) living in Auckland, making it the world's principal Polynesian city. Samoans are by far the largest group, followed by Cook Islanders, Tongans, Niueans, Fijians, Tokelauans and Tuvaluans. The biggest PI communities can be found in South Auckland and pockets of West and Central Auckland.

Like the Māori renaissance of recent decades, Pasifika has become a hot commodity for Auckland hipsters. You'll find PI motifs everywhere: in art, architecture, fashion, homewares, movies and especially in music.

🛍 Other Areas

★**Otara Flea Market**   MARKET

(Map p66; ☎09-274 0830; www.otarafleamarket. co.nz; Newbury St; ☺6am-noon Sat) Held in the car park between the Manukau Polytech and the Otara town centre, this market has a palpable Polynesian atmosphere and is good for South Pacific food, music and fashions. Take bus 472, 487 or 497 from 55 Customs St in the city ($6.50, 50 minutes).

Avondale Sunday Markets   MARKET

(www.avondalesundaymarkets.co.nz; Avondale Racecourse, Ash St; ☺5am-noon Sun) This large, popular market has a strong Asian and Polynesian atmosphere and is excellent for fresh produce. Take the train from Britomart station to Avondale.

ℹ Information

INTERNET ACCESS

Auckland Council offers free wi-fi in parts of the city centre, Newton, Ponsonby, Kingsland, Mt Eden and Parnell. All public libraries offer free wi-fi, and internet cafes catering to gaming junkies are scattered about the inner city.

MEDICAL SERVICES

Auckland City Hospital (☎09-367 0000; www.adhb.govt.nz; 2 Park Rd, Grafton; ☺24hr) The city's main hospital has a dedicated accident and emergency (A&E) service.

Auckland Travel Clinic (☎09-373 4621; www. aucklandmetrodoctors.co.nz; 17 Emily Pl; ☺9am-5.30pm Mon-Fri, 10am-2pm Sat) Health care for travellers, including vaccinations and travel consultations.

PLANE DELAYED? TIME FOR A TIPPLE!

Clearly the roar of jets doesn't bother grapes, as NZ's most awarded winery is just 4km from the airport. The parklike grounds of **Villa Maria** (Map p66; ☑09-255 0666; www.villamaria.co.nz; 118 Montgomerie Rd, Mangere; ⊙9am-6pm Mon-Fri, 9am-4pm Sat & Sun) are a green oasis in the encircling industrial zone. Short tours ($5) take place at 11am and 3pm. There's a charge for tastings ($5, refundable on purchase), but lingering over wine and antipasto (platters $40 to $50, lunch $33 to $36) on the terrace sure beats hanging around the departure lounge.

A series of concerts is held here every January and February featuring big international artists popular with the 40- to 50-something wine-swilling demographic.

Starship Children's Health (☑09-307 4949; www.adhb.govt.nz; Park Rd, Grafton; ⊙24hr) Has its own A&E department.

POST

Post Office (Map p70; ☑0800 501 501; www.nzpost.co.nz; 155 Queen St; ⊙9am-5.30pm Mon-Fri) There's also a branch in Ponsonby (Map p85; 314 Ponsonby Rd; ⊙9am-5.30pm Mon-Fri, to 1pm Sat) .

TOURIST INFORMATION

Auckland International Airport i-SITE (Map p66; ☑09-365 9925; www.aucklandnz.com; International Arrivals Hall; ⊙6.30am-10.30pm)

Devonport i-SITE (Map p82; ☑09-365 9906; www.aucklandnz.com; Devonport Wharf; ⊙8.30am-5pm; ☎)

Karanga Kiosk (Map p70; ☑09-365 1290; www.waterfrontauckland.co.nz; cnr Jellicoe & Halsey Sts, Wynyard Quarter; ⊙9.30am-4.30pm) Looking like a precariously stacked set of shipping containers, this volunteer-run centre dispenses information on goings-on around the waterfront.

Princes Wharf i-SITE (Map p70; ☑09-365 9914; www.aucklandnz.com; 139 Quay St; ⊙9am-5pm) Auckland's main official information centre, incorporating the DOC Auckland Visitor Centre (Map p70; ☑09-379 6476; www.doc.govt.nz; 137 Quay St, Princes Wharf; ⊙9am-5pm Mon-Fri, extended in summer).

SkyCity i-SITE (Map p70; ☑09-365 9918; www.aucklandnz.com; SkyCity Atrium, cnr Victoria & Federal Sts; ⊙9am-5pm)

❶ Getting There & Away

AIR

Auckland is the main international gateway to NZ, and a hub for domestic flights. **Auckland Airport** (AKL; Map p66; ☑09-275 0789; www.aucklandairport.co.nz; Ray Emery Dr, Mangere) is 21km south of the city centre. It has separate international and domestic terminals, a 10-minute walk apart from each other via a signposted footpath; a free shuttle service operates every 15 minutes (5am to 10.30pm). Both terminals have left-luggage facilities, eateries, ATMs and car-rental desks.

Air Chathams (☑09-257 0261; www.airchathams.co.nz) Flies to Whakatane and the Chatham Islands.

Air New Zealand (☑09-357 3000; www.airnewzealand.co.nz) Flies to Kerikeri, Whangarei, Hamilton, Tauranga, Rotorua, Taupo, Gisborne, New Plymouth, Napier, Whanganui, Palmerston North, Kapati Coast, Wellington, Nelson, Blenheim, Christchurch, Queenstown and Dunedin.

Jetstar (☑0800 800 995; www.jetstar.com) Flies to Wellington, Christchurch, Queenstown and Dunedin.

Virgin Australia (www.virginaustralia.com) Flies to Dunedin.

BUS

Coaches depart from 172 Quay St, opposite the Ferry Building, except for InterCity services, which depart from **SkyCity Coach Terminal** (Map p70; 102 Hobson St). Many southbound services also stop at the airport.

Go Kiwi (☑07-866 0336; www.go-kiwi.co.nz) Daily Auckland City–Auckland Airport–Thames–Tairua–Hot Water Beach–Whitianga shuttles.

InterCity (☑09-583 5780; www.intercity.co.nz) Direct services include Kerikeri (from $29, 4½ hours, three daily), Hamilton (from $18, two hours, 16 daily), New Plymouth (from $49, 6¼ hours, daily), Taupo (from $26, five hours, five daily) and Wellington (from $31, 11 hours, four daily).

Naked Bus (www.nakedbus.com; fares vary) Travels along SH1 as far north as Kerikeri (four hours) and as far south as Wellington (12 hours), as well as heading to Tauranga (3½ hours), Rotorua (3¾ hours) and Napier (12 hours).

CAR & CAMPERVAN

Hire

Auckland has many hire agencies around Beach Rd and Stanley St close to the city centre.

A2B (☑0800 545 000; www.a2b-car-rental.co.nz; 167 Beach Rd; ⊙7am-7pm Nov-Apr, 8am-5pm May-Oct) Cheap older cars with no visible hire-car branding.

Apex Car Rentals (☑09-307 1063; www.apexrentals.co.nz; 156 Beach Rd; ⊙8am-5pm)

Budget (☑09-976 2270; www.budget.co.nz; 163 Beach Rd; ☺8am-5pm)

Escape (☑0800 216 171; www.escaperentals. co.nz; 61 The Strand; ☺9am-3pm) Eccentrically painted campervans.

Gateway 2 NZ (☑0508 225 587; www. gateway2nz.co.nz; 50 Ascot Rd, Mangere ☺7am-7pm)

Gateway Motor Home Hire (☑09-296 1652; www.motorhomehire.co.nz; 33 Spartan Rd, Takanini)

Go Rentals (☑09-257 5142; www.gorentals. co.nz; Bay 4-10, Cargo Central, George Bolt Memorial Dr, Mangere; ☺6am-10pm)

Hertz (☑09-367 6350; www.hertz.co.nz 154 Victoria St; ☺7.30am-5.30pm)

Jucy (☑0800 399 736; www.jucy.co.nz; 2-16 The Strand; ☺8am-5pm)

Kea, Maui & Britz (☑09-255 3910; www.maui. co.nz; 36 Richard Pearse Dr, Mangere; ☺8am-6pm)

NZ Frontiers (☑09-299 6705; www.newzealand frontiers.com; 30 Laurie Ave, Papakura)

Omega (☑09-377 5573; www.omegarentals. com; 75 Beach Rd; ☺8am-5pm)

Quality (☑0800 680 123; www.qualityrental. co.nz; 8 Andrew Baxter Dr, Mangere; ☺8am-4pm)

Thrifty (☑09-309 0111; www.thrifty.co.nz; 150 Khyber Pass Rd; ☺8am-5pm)

Wilderness Motorhomes (☑09-255 5300; www.wilderness.co.nz; 11 Pavilion Dr Mangere; ☺8am-5pm)

Purchase

Mechanical inspection services are on hand at second-hand car fairs, where sellers pay to display their cars.

Auckland Car Fair (☑09-529 2233; www. carfair.co.nz; Ellerslie Racecourse, Green Lane East; display fee $35; ☺9am-noon Sun) Auckland's largest car fair.

Auckland City Car Fair (☑09-837 7817; www. aucklandcitycarfair.co.nz; 6 West St; display fee $30; ☺8am-3pm Sat)

MOTORCYCLE

NZ Motorcycle Rentals (☑09-486 2472; www. nzbike.com; 72 Barrys Point Rd, Takapuna; per day $140-290) Guided tours of NZ also available.

TRAIN

Northern Explorer (☑0800 872 467; www. kiwirailscenic.co.nz) trains leave from **Auckland Strand Station** (Ngaoho Pl) at 7.45am on Monday, Thursday and Saturday and arrive in Wellington at 6.25pm. Stops include Hamilton (2½ hours), Otorohanga (three hours), Tongariro National Park (5½ hours), Ohakune (six hours), Palmerston North (8½ hours) and

Paraparaumu (9¾ hours). Standard fares to Wellington range from $119 to $219, but some discounted seats are available at $99 (first in, first served).

ⓘ Getting Around

TO/FROM THE AIRPORT

Taxi Usually costs $75 to $90 to the city, more if you strike traffic.

SkyBus (☑09-222 0084; www.skybus.co.nz; one way/return adult $16/28, child $6/12) Runs red buses between the terminals and the city every 10 to 15 minutes from 5.15am to 7pm and at least half-hourly through the night. Buy a ticket from the driver, the airport kiosk or online. The trip usually takes less than an hour (longer during peak times).

Super Shuttle (☑09-522 5100; www.super shuttle.co.nz) Convenient door-to-door shuttle charging $37 for one person heading to a city hotel; price increases for outlying suburbs. Save money by sharing a shuttle.

380 Bus A lengthier alternative is to catch the 380 bus to Onehunga ($4.50, 30 minutes, at least hourly 7am to 7.30pm), where you can catch a train to Britomart in the city centre ($5, 27 minutes, half-hourly 6am to 10pm).

BICYCLE

Auckland Transport (p100) Publishes free cycle maps, available from public buildings such as stations, libraries and i-SITEs. Bikes can be taken on most ferries and trains for free (dependent on available space), but only folding bikes are allowed on buses.

Adventure Cycles (☑09-940 2453; www. adventure-auckland.co.nz; 9 Premier Ave, Western Springs; per day $30-40, per week $120-160, per month $260-350; ☺7.30am-7pm Thu-Mon) Hires road, mountain and touring bikes, runs a buy-back scheme, and does repairs.

CAR & MOTORCYCLE

Auckland's motorways jam badly at peak times, particularly the Northern and Southern Motorways. It's best to avoid them between 7am and 9am, and from 4pm to 7pm. Things also get tight around 3pm during term time, which is the end of the school day.

Expect to pay for parking in central Auckland from 8am to 10pm. Most parking meters are pay-and-display and take coins and credit cards; display tickets inside your windscreen. City fringe parking is free on Sundays.

Prices can be steep at parking buildings. Better value are the council-run open-air car parks near the old train station at 126 Beach Rd ($8 per day) and on Ngaoho Pl off the Strand ($7 per day).

PUBLIC TRANSPORT

The **Auckland Transport** (☏ 09-366 6400; www.at.govt.nz) information service covers buses, trains and ferries, and has an excellent trip-planning feature.

Auckland's public transport system is run by a hodgepodge of different operators, but there is now an integrated AT HOP smartcard (www.athop.co.nz), which provides discounts of at least 20% on most buses, trains and ferries. AT HOP cards cost $10 (nonrefundable), so are really only worthwhile if you're planning an extended stay in Auckland. An AT HOP day pass costs $16 and provides a day's transport on most trains and buses and on North Shore ferries.

Ferry

Auckland's Edwardian baroque **Ferry Building** (Map p70; 99 Quay St) sits grandly at the end of Queen St. Ferry services run by **Fullers** (☏ 09-367 9111; www.fullers.co.nz) (to Bayswater, Birkenhead (Map p66), Devonport (Map p82), Great Barrier Island, Half Moon Bay, Northcote Point (Map p66), Motuihe, Motutapu, Rangitoto and Waiheke), **360 Discovery** (Map p70; ☏ 09-307 8005; www.fullers.co.nz) (to Coromandel, Gulf Harbour, Motuihe, Rotoroa and Tiritiri Matangi) and **Explore** (☏ 0800 000 469; www.explorewaiheke.co.nz) (to Motutapu, Rangitoto and Waiheke) leave from adjacent piers.

Sealink (Map p70; ☏ 0800 732 546; www.sealink.co.nz) ferries to Great Barrier Island leave from Wynyard Wharf, along with some car ferries to Waiheke, but most of the Waiheke car ferries leave from Half Moon Bay in east Auckland.

Bus

Bus routes spread their tentacles throughout the city and you can purchase a ticket from the driver. Some bus stops have electronic displays giving an estimate of waiting times, but be warned, they are often inaccurate.

Single-ride fares in the inner city are $1/50c (adult/child). If you're travelling further afield, there are fare stages from $2.50/1.50 to $11/6.50.

The most useful services are the environmentally friendly Link Buses that loop in both directions around three routes (taking in many of the major sights) from 7am to 11pm:

City Link (adult/child 50c/30c, free for AT HOP cardholders, every seven to 10 minutes) Wynyard Quarter, Britomart, Queen St, Karangahape Rd.

Inner Link (adult/child $2.50/1.50, every 10 to 15 minutes) Queen St, SkyCity, Victoria Park, Ponsonby Rd, Karangahape Rd, Museum, Newmarket, Parnell and Britomart.

Outer Link (maximum $4.50, every 15 minutes) Art Gallery, Ponsonby, Herne Bay, Westmere, MOTAT 2, Pt Chevalier, Mt Albert, St Lukes Mall, Mt Eden, Newmarket, Museum, Parnell, University.

Train

Auckland's train services are limited and infrequent but the trains are generally clean, cheap and on time – although any hiccup on the lines can bring down the entire network.

Impressive **Britomart train station** (Queen St) has food retailers, foreign-exchange facilities and a ticket office. Downstairs there are left-luggage lockers.

There are just four train routes. One heads west to Swanson, while the other three head south, terminating in Onehunga, Manukau and Pukekohe. Services are at least hourly from around 6am to 10pm (later on the weekends). Buy a ticket from machines or ticket offices at train stations. All trains have wheelchair ramps.

TAXI

Auckland's many taxis usually operate from ranks, but they also cruise popular areas. **Auckland Co-op Taxis** (☏ 09-300 3000; www.cooptaxi.co.nz) is one of the biggest companies. Cab companies set their own fares, so there's some variance in rates. There's a surcharge for transport to and from the airport and cruise ships, and for phone orders. Uber also operates in Auckland.

HAURAKI GULF ISLANDS

The Hauraki Gulf, stretching between Auckland and the Coromandel Peninsula, is dotted with *motu* (islands) and gives the Bay of Islands stiff competition in the beauty stakes. Some islands are only minutes from the city and make excellent day trips. Wine-soaked Waiheke and volcanic Rangitoto really shouldn't be missed. Great Barrier requires more effort (and cash) to get to, but provides an idyllic escape from modern life.

There are more than 50 islands in the Hauraki Gulf Marine Park, many of which are administered by DOC. Some are good-sized islands, others are no more than rocks jutting out of the sea. They're loosely put into two categories: recreation and conservation. The recreation islands can easily be visited and their harbours are dotted with yachts in summer. The conservation islands, however, have restricted access. Permits are required to visit some, while others are closed refuges for the preservation of rare plants and animals, especially birds.

The gulf is a busy highway for marine mammals. Sei, minke and Bryde's whales are regularly seen in its outer reaches, along with orcas and bottlenose dolphins. You might even spy a passing humpback.

Rangitoto & Motutapu Islands

POP 75

Sloping elegantly from the waters of the gulf, 259m Rangitoto (www.rangitoto.org), the largest and youngest of Auckland's volcanic cones, provides a picturesque backdrop to all of the city's activities. As recently as 600 years ago it erupted from the sea and was probably active for several years before settling down. Māori living on Motutapu (Sacred Island; www.motutapu.org. nz), to which Rangitoto is now joined by a causeway, certainly witnessed the eruptions, as footprints have been found embedded in ash, and oral history details several generations living here before the eruption.

Rangitoto makes for a great day trip. Its harsh scoria slopes hold a surprising amount of flora (including the world's largest pohutukawa forest) and there are excellent walks, but you'll need sturdy shoes and plenty of water. Although it looks steep, up close it's shaped more like an egg sizzling in a pan. The walk to the summit only takes an hour and is rewarded with sublime views. At the top a loop walk goes around the crater's rim. A walk to lava caves branches off the summit walk and takes 30 minutes return. There's an information board with walk maps at the wharf.

Motutapu, in contrast to Rangitoto, is mainly covered in grassland, which is grazed by sheep and cattle. Archaeologically, this is a very significant island, with the traces of centuries of continuous human habitation etched into its landscape.

At Home Bay on Motutapu there's a **DOC campsite** (www.doc.govt.nz; sites per adult/child $6/3) with only basic facilities (running water and a flush toilet). Bring cooking equipment, as open fires are forbidden, and book online. It's a three-hour walk from Rangitoto wharf (Map p66); Explore runs direct ferries to Home Bay on weekends and public holidays.

In 2011 both islands were officially declared predator-free after an extensive eradication program. Endangered birds such as takahe and tieke (saddleback) have been re-leased and others such as kakariki and bellbirds have returned of their own volition.

ⓘ Getting There & Away

Explore (☑ 09-359 5987; www.exploregroup. co.nz; adult/child return $36/18) Runs two boats a day between Quay St's Pier 3D and Rangitoto (15 minutes) and a boat to Motutapu's Home Bay (30 minutes) on weekends and public holidays.

Fullers (☑ 09-367 9111; www.fullers.co.nz; adult/child return $30/15) Has ferry services to Rangitoto from Auckland's Ferry Building (25 minutes, three daily on weekdays, four on weekends) and Devonport (two daily). It also operates the Volcanic Explorer (☑ 09-367 9111; adult/child inc ferry $65/33; ⊗ departs Auckland 9.15am & 12.15pm), a guided tour around the island in a canopied 'road train'.

Motuihe Island

Between Rangitoto and Waiheke Islands, 176-hectare Motuihe (www.motuihe.org.nz) has a lovely white-sand beach and a fascinating history. There are three *pa* sites, last occupied by the Ngāti Pāoa tribe. The island was sold in 1840 (for a heifer, blankets, frocks, garden tools, pots and pans) and from 1872 to 1941 served as a quarantine station. During WWI the dashing swashbuckler Count von Luckner launched a daring escape from the island (where he was interned with other German and Austrian nationals), making it 1000km to the Kermadec Islands before being recaptured.

Motuihe has been rendered pest-free and is now subject to a vigorous reforestation project by enthusiastic volunteers. As a result, endangered birds have returned, including the loquacious tieke.

Apart from the trust's headquarters, the only accommodation on the island is a basic **DOC campsite** (☑ 09-379 6476; www.doc. govt.nz; sites per adult/child $6/3); only toilets and water are provided, and bookings are essential. There are no permanent residents or shops, except for a weekend kiosk in summer.

ⓘ Getting There & Away

Motuihe is a yachtie's paradise, and the easiest way to get here is on your own boat. **Fullers** (☑ 09-367 9111 www.fullers.co.nz; adult/child return $32/16) runs sporadic ferries on a seemingly random schedule.

Waiheke Island

POP 8300

Tantalisingly close to Auckland and blessed with its own warm, dry microclimate, blissful Waiheke Island has long been a favourite escape for city dwellers and visitors alike. On the island's landward side, emerald waters lap at rocky bays, while its ocean flank has some of the region's best sandy beaches.

While beaches are Waiheke's biggest drawcard, wine is a close second. There are around 30 boutique wineries scattered about, many with tasting rooms, swanky restaurants and breathtaking views. The island also boasts plenty of quirky galleries and craft stores, a lasting legacy of its hippyish past.

When you've had enough of supping, dining, lazing on the sand and splashing in the surf, there are plenty of other pursuits to engage in. A network of walking trails leads through nature reserves and past the clifftop holiday homes of the Auckland elite. The kayaking is excellent and there are ziplines to whizz along and clay pigeons to shoot. All in all, it's a magical place.

◉ Sights

Beaches

Waiheke's two best beaches are **Onetangi**, a long stretch of white sand at the centre of the island, and **Palm Beach**, a pretty little horseshoe bay between Oneroa and Onetangi. Both have nudist sections; head west just past some rocks in both cases. **Oneroa** and neighbouring **Little Oneroa** are also excellent, but you'll be sharing the waters with moored yachts in summer. Reached by an unsealed road through farmland, **Man O' War Bay** is a compact sheltered beach that's excellent for swimming.

Wineries

Goldie Wines   WINERY
(☑ 09-372 7493; www.goldiewines.co.nz; 18 Causeway Rd, Surfdale; tastings $10, refundable with purchase; ⊙noon-4pm) Founded as Goldwater Estate in 1978, this is Waiheke's pioneering vineyard. The attached delicatessen sells well-stocked baskets for a picnic among the vines ($55 for two people).

Man O' War   WINERY
(☑ 09-372 9678; www.manowarvineyards.co.nz; 725 Man O' War Bay Rd; ⊙11am-6pm Dec-Feb, to 4.30pm Mar-Nov) Settle in with a tapas platter and a glass of Man O' War's Valhalla Chardonnay at Waiheke's only beachfront tasting room. If the weather is good, go for a swim in beautiful Man O' War Bay.

Passage Rock Wines   WINERY
(☑ 09-372 7257; www.passagerockwines.co.nz; 438 Orapiu Rd; ⊙11am-4pm daily Jan, Wed-Sun Feb-Apr & Dec, Sat & Sun Aug-Nov) 'Waiheke's most awarded winery' serves excellent pizza among the vines.

Stonyridge   WINERY
(☑ 09-372 8822; www.stonyridge.com; 80 Onetangi Rd; tastings per wine $4-18; ⊙11.30am-5pm) 🖋 Waiheke's most famous vineyard is home to world-famous reds, an atmospheric cafe, tours ($10 including tastings of two wines, 30 minutes, 11.30am Saturday and Sunday) and the occasional dance party. Order a bottle of wine and a gigantic deli platter and retreat to one of the cabanas in the garden.

Wild On Waiheke   WINERY, BREWERY
(☑ 09-372 3434; www.wildonwaiheke.co.nz; 82 Onetangi Rd; tastings per beer or wine $2-3; ⊙11am-4pm Thu-Sun, daily in summer; 🖼) This winery and microbrewery offers tastings, archery, laser clay shooting, *pétanque,* a sandpit and a giant chessboard.

Art, History & Culture

The *Waiheke Art Map* brochure, free from the i-SITE, lists galleries and craft stores.

Dead Dog Bay   GARDENS
(☑ 09-372 6748; www.deaddogbay.co.nz; 100 Margaret Reeve Lane; adult/child $10/free; ⊙9am-5pm) Wander steep pathways through privately owned rainforest, wetlands and gardens scattered with sculpture.

Waiheke Island Artworks   ARTS CENTRE
(2 Korora Rd, Oneroa) The Artworks complex houses the **Artworks Theatre** (☑ 09-372 2941; www.artworkstheatre.org.nz), the **Waiheke Island Community Cinema** (☑ 09-372 4240; www.waihekecinema.net; adult/child $15/8), the attention-grabbing **Waiheke Community Art Gallery** (☑ 09-372 9907; www.waihekeartgallery.org.nz; ⊙10am-4pm) 𝗙𝗥𝗘𝗘 and **Whittaker's Musical Museum** (☑ 09-372 5573; www.musical-museum.org; suggested donation $5; ⊙1-4pm, live shows 1.30pm Sat), a collection of antique instruments. This is also the place for free internet access, either on a terminal at the **Waiheke Library** (☑ 09-374 1325; www.aucklandlibraries.govt.nz; ⊙9am-6pm Mon-Fri, 10.30am-4pm Sat; 🛜) or on its wi-fi network.

Waiheke Museum
& Historic Village
MUSEUM

(www.waihekemuseum.org.nz; 165 Onetangi Rd; admission by donation; ⊙noon-4pm Wed, Sat & Sun) Displays islander artefacts in six restored buildings.

🏃 Activities

Tramping

Ask at the i-SITE about the island's beautiful coastal walks (ranging from one to three hours) and the 3km Cross Island Walkway (from Onetangi to Rocky Bay). Other tracks traverse **Whakanewha Regional Park**, a haven for rare coastal birds and geckos, and the Royal Forest & Bird Protection Society's three reserves: **Onetangi** (Waiheke Rd), Te **Haahi-Goodwin** (Orapiu Rd) and **Atawhai Whenua** (Ocean View Rd).

Other Activities

EcoZip Adventures   ZIPLINING
(☑09-372 5646; www.ecozipadventures.co.nz; 150 Trig Hill Rd; adult/child/family $119/79/$317; ⊙9am-5pm) With vineyard, native bush and ocean views, EcoZip's three separate 200m lines make for an exciting ride, and there's a gentle 1.5km walk back up through the bush after the thrills. Costs include free transfers from Matiatia Wharf or Oneroa if you don't have your own transport. Bookings are essential.

Ross Adventures   KAYAKING
(☑09-372 5550; www.kayakwaiheke.co.nz; Matiatia Beach; half-/full-day trips $125/195, per 1/2/3/6hr $30/45/50/60) It's the fervently held opinion of Ross that Waiheke offers kayaking every bit as good as the legendary Abel Tasman National Park. He should know – he's been offering guided kayak trips for over 20 years. Experienced sea kayakers can comfortably circumnavigate the island in four days, exploring hidden coves and sand spits inaccessible by land.

👉 Tours

Ananda Tours   TOUR
(☑09-372 7530; www.ananda.co.nz) Wine tours ($110), gourmet wine and food tours ($170), and a wine connoisseurs' tour ($250) are among the options. Small-group, informal tours can be customised, including visits to artists' studios.

Waiheke Island Wine Tours   TOUR
(☑09-372 2140; www.waihekeislandwinetours.co.nz) Options include Views, Vines & Wines ($110 per person, six hours with a two-hour break for lunch at a restaurant of your choice), tailor-made Platinum Private Tours ($495 per couple) and Indulgence Two-Day Tours ($920 per person including two nights' accommodation).

Hike Bike Ako   WALKING, CYCLING
(☑021 465 373; www.hikebikeako.co.nz; tour 3/5hr $99/125) Explore the island with Māori guides on a walking or biking tour, or a combination of both. Tours include pick up from the ferry, and a large dose of Māori legend, history and culture.

Potiki Adventures   CULTURAL TOUR
(☑021 422 773; www.potikiadventures.co.nz; adult/child from $150/80) Day-long island tours from a Māori cultural perspective, including beaches, a bush walk, a vineyard visit and demonstrations of traditional musical instruments and weaving.

Fullers   TOUR
(☑09-367 9111; www.fullers.co.nz) Runs a Wine on Waiheke tour (adult $130, 4½ hours, departs Auckland 1pm) visiting three of the island's top wineries, and including a platter of nibbles; Taste of Waiheke (adult $140, 5½ hours, departs Auckland 11am) includes three wineries plus an olive grove and light lunch. There's also a 1½-hour Explorer Tour (adult/child $57/29, departs Auckland 10am, 11am and noon).

Other packages include EcoZip's zipline and car hire. All prices include the ferry and an all-day local bus pass.

🎊 Festivals & Events

Headland Sculpture on the Gulf   ART
(www.sculptureonthegulf.co.nz; ⊙Feb) A 2.5km cliff-top sculpture walk, held for a month in February in odd-numbered years.

Waiheke Island of
Wine Vintage Festival   WINE, FOOD
(www.waihekevintagefestival.co.nz; ⊙mid-Mar) Five days of wine, food and music events. Seventeen different vineyards are involved, and shuttle buses travel between the different ent locations.

Waiheke Island
International Jazz Festival   MUSIC
(www.waihekejazzfestival.co.nz; prices vary by event; ⊙Mar/Apr) Local and international acts across the island from Friday to Sunday during Easter.

Waiheke Island

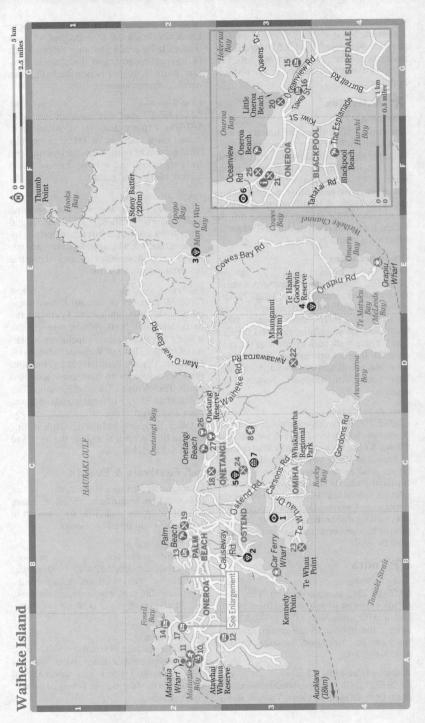

SURFDALE

Hekerua
Bay

Queens Dr

15

Oceanview Rd

16
Tawa St

Burrell Rd

Oneroa
Bay

Little
Oneroa
Beach

20

Oceanview
Rd

Oneroa
Beach

25

ONEROA

6

21

1

Kiwi St

The Esplanade

BLACKPOOL

Tahatai Rd

Blackpool
Beach

Hurrahi
Bay

Te Matuku
Bay
(McLeods
Bay)

0
0.5 miles
1 km

5 km
2.5 miles

Thumb
Point

Hooks
Bay

Stony Batter
(220m)

Opopo
Bay

Man O' War
Bay

3 Man O' War

Cowes
Bay

Coxes Bay Rd

Waiheke Channel

Omaru
Bay

Orapiu
Wharf

Orapiu Rd

Te Haahi-
Goodwin
Reserve

4

Maunganui
(231m)

Awaawaroa Rd

22

Waiheke Rd

Man O' War Bay Rd

Awaawaroa
Bay

HAURAKI GULF

Onetangi Bay

26

Onetangi
Reserve

27

Onetangi
Beach

ONETANGI

18

5 24

7

8

Carsons Rd

Whakanewha
Regional
Park

Gordons Rd

OMIHA

Rocky
Bay

Ostend Rd

OSTEND

Causeway
Rd

Nau Dr

Te Whau Dr

1

23

Te Whau
Point

Palm
Beach

13 19

PALM
BEACH

ONEROA

See Enlargement

12

2

Car Ferry
Wharf

Kennedy
Point

Tomaki Strait

Auckland
(18km)

Fossil
Bay

14

17

11

9

10

Mattatia
Wharf

Matiatia
Bay

Atawhai
Whenua
Reserve

Waiheke Island

Sleeping

Waiheke is so popular in the summer holidays that many locals rent out their houses and bugger off elsewhere. You'll need to book ahead and even then there are very few bargains. Prices drop considerably in winter, especially midweek. For midrange accommodation, a good option is to book a holiday home through www.bookabach.co.nz or www.holidayhouses.co.nz.

★Fossil Bay Lodge   CABIN $
(09-372 8371; www.fossilbay.net; 58 Korora Rd, Oneroa; s $60, d $85-90, tents $100-120, apt $130;) Three cutesy cabins open onto a courtyard facing the main building, which houses the communal toilets, kitchen and living area, and a compact self-contained upstairs apartment. Best of all are the four 'glamping' tents, each with a proper bed and its own toilet. Apart from the occasional squawking duck – or toddler from the adjacent Steiner kindergarten – it's a peaceful place.

Hekerua Lodge   HOSTEL $
(09-372 8990; www.hekerualodge.co.nz; 11 Hekerua Rd, Oneroa; sites $18, dm $31-33, s $55, d $90-120;) This secluded hostel is surrounded by native bush and has a barbecue, stone-tiled pool, spa pool, sunny deck, casual lounge area and its own walking track. It's far from luxurious, but it has a laid-back and social feel.

Tawa Lodge   GUESTHOUSE $$
(09-372 6675; www.pungalodge.co.nz; 15 Tawa St, Oneroa; r $110-120, apt $175-225;) Between the self-contained two-person cottage at the front (our pick of the lot, due to the sublimely romantic views) and the apartment and house at the rear are three reasonably priced loft rooms sharing a small kitchen and bathroom.

★Enclosure Bay   B&B $$$
(09-372 8882; www.enclosurebay.co.nz; 9 Great Barrier Rd; r/ste $390/495;) If you're going to shell out for a luxury B&B you expect it to be special, and that's certainly what's offered here. Each of the three guest rooms have sumptuous views and balconies, and the owners subscribe to the nothing's-too-much-trouble school of hospitality.

Waiheke Dreams   RENTAL HOUSE $$$
(09-818 7129; www.waihekedreams.co.nz; 43 Tiri Rd, Oneroa; 1-/2-bedroom house $200/300) Dream a little dream of a luxurious, modern, spacious, open-plan, two-bedroom house on the crest of a hill with unsurpassed views over Oneroa Bay and the Hauraki Gulf – then pinch yourself and wake up with a smug smile in View43. Tucked at the rear is the considerably smaller one-bedroom CityLights, which glimpses Auckland's glimmer over the back lawn.

Cable Bay Views
APARTMENT $$$

(☏09-372 2901; www.cablebayviews.co.nz; 103 Church Bay Rd; r $300; 🐾) These three modern, self-contained studio apartments have stellar vineyard views and are handy to a couple of Waiheke's best vineyard restaurants. Check the website for good midweek and off-peak discounts.

✖ Eating

Waiheke has some excellent eateries and, if you're lucky, the views will be enough to distract from the hole being bored into your hip pocket. There's a supermarket in Ostend.

Dragonfired
PIZZA $

(☏021 922 289; www.dragonfired.co.nz; Little Oneroa Beach, Oneroa; mains $10-18; ⊘10am-8pm daily Dec-Feb, 11am-7pm Fri-Sun Mar-Nov; 🍴) Specialising in 'artisan woodfired food', this caravan by the beach serves the three Ps: pizza, polenta plates and pocket bread. It's easily Waiheke's best place for cheap eats. It has another location by the shop in **Palm Beach** (☏0272 372 372; Matapana Reserve, Palm Beach; ⊘10am-8pm daily Dec-Feb, 11am-7pm Fri-Sun Mar-Nov).

Shed at Te Motu
MODERN NZ $$

(☏09-372 6884; www.temotu.co.nz/the-shed; 76 Onetangi Rd; shared plates small $12-18, large $22-36; ⊘noon-3pm daily, 6pm-late Fri & Sat Nov-Apr, reduced hours in winter) Secure a table shaded by umbrellas in the Shed's rustic courtyard for shared plates imbued with global culinary influences and served by the restaurant's savvy and equally international wait staff. Highlights include shiitake pancakes with kimchi and black garlic, or the wonderfully slow-cooked lamb shoulder partnered with a delicate biryani-spiced pilaf. Te Motu's standout wines are its stellar Bordeaux-style blends.

On Friday nights, the Shed offers a good value prix-fixe menu (two/three courses $45/55). Bookings are recommended for both lunch and dinner.

Oyster Inn
SEAFOOD $$

(☏09-372 2222; www.theoysterinn.co.nz; 124 Oceanview Rd, Oneroa; mains $28-35; ⊘noon-late) The Oyster Inn is a popular destination for Auckland's smart set. They're attracted by the excellent seafood-skewed bistro menu, oysters and champagne, and a buzzy but relaxed vibe that's part bar and part restaurant. In summer, brunch on the veranda is a great way to ease into another Waiheke day.

Casita Miro
SPANISH $$

(☏09-372 7854; www.casitamiro.co.nz; 3 Brown St, Onetangi; tapas $12-20, ración $26; ⊘noon-3pm Thu-Mon, 6-10pm Fri & Sat) A wrought-iron and glass pavilion backed with a Gaudí-esque mosaic garden is the stage for a very entertaining troupe of servers who will guide you through the menu of delectable tapas and *ración* (larger dishes), designed to be shared. In summer the sides open up, but otherwise, at busy times, it can get noisy.

Wai Kitchen
CAFE $$

(☏09-372 7505; www.waikitchen.co.nz; 1/149 Oceanview Rd, Oneroa; mains $17-26; ⊘8.30am-3.30pm, extended hours in summer; 🍴) Why? Well firstly there's the lively menu that abounds with Mediterranean and Asian flavours. Then there's the charming service and the breezy ambience of this glassed-in wedge, facing the *wai* (water).

Poderi Crisci
ITALIAN $$

(☏09-372 2148; www.podericrisci.co.nz; 205 Awaawaroa Rd; lunch mains $25-33, dinner degustation $85; ⊘noon-5pm Sun, Mon & Thu, to 10pm Fri & Sat May-Sep, extended hours Oct-Apr) 🍴 Poderi Crisci has quickly gained a sterling reputation for its food, particularly its legendary four-hour long lunches on Sundays ($70 per person). Italian varietals and olives have been planted alongside the existing vines, and tastings are offered in the atmospheric cellar ($10, refunded upon purchase). It's definitely worth the drive into the winery's isolated valley, but book first.

Cable Bay
MODERN NZ $$$

(☏09-372 5889; www.cablebay.co.nz; 12 Nick Johnstone Dr; mains $42-44; ⊘noon-3pm Tue-Sun, 6pm-late Tue-Sat; 🐾) Impressive ubermodern architecture, interesting sculpture and beautiful views set the scene for this acclaimed restaurant. The food is sublime, but if the budget won't stretch to a meal, stop in for a wine tasting ($10 for five wines, refundable with a purchase, 11am to 5pm daily) or platters and shared plates at the Verandah bar.

Te Whau
MODERN NZ $$$

(☏09-372 7191; www.tewhau.com; 218 Te Whau Dr; mains $40-42; ⊘11am-5pm daily & 6.30-11pm Thu-Sat Dec & Jan, 11am-5pm Wed-Mon & 6.30-11pm Sat Feb-Easter, 11am-4.30pm Fri-Sun & 6.30-11pm Sat Easter-Nov) 🍴 Perched on the end of Te Whau peninsula, this winery restaurant has exceptional views, food and service, and one of the finest wine lists you'll see in the country. The attached tasting room offers samples of its own impressive Bordeaux blends (11am to 5pm, four tastes for $12).

🍷 Drinking & Nightlife

Sand Shack
BAR, CAFE

(☑ 09-372 2565; www.fourthavenue.co.nz; 1 Fourth Ave, Onetangi; ⊗ 8am-11pm) Part bar and part beach cafe, all served up with cool decor and Onetangi Beach views from the sunny deck. There's a good selection of tap beers and a menu of uncomplicated stomach fillers such as cooked breakfasts, burgers and pizzas.

Charlie Farley's
BAR

(☑ 09-372 4106; www.charliefarleys.co.nz; 21 The Strand, Onetangi; ⊗ 8.30am-late) It's easy to see why the locals love this place when you're supping on a Waiheke wine or beer under the pohutukawa on the beach-gazing deck.

🛈 Information

Waiheke Island i-SITE (☑ 09-372 1234; www. aucklandnz.com; 116 Ocean View Rd; ⊗ 9am-4pm) As well as the very helpful main office, there's a (usually unstaffed) counter in the ferry terminal at Matiatia Wharf.

🛈 Getting There & Away

360 Discovery (☑ 09-307 8005; www.fullers. co.nz) You can pick up this tourist ferry at Orapiu on its limited voyages between Auckland and Coromandel Town. However, note that Orapiu is quite remote and not served by buses.

Explore (☑ 0800 000 469; www.explore-waiheke.co.nz; return adult/child $36/13; ⊗ 8.30am-8.15pm) At least a dozen sailings a day between Auckland's Ferry Building and Matiatia Wharf (40 minutes).

Fullers (☑ 09-367 9111; www.fullers.co.nz; return adult/child $36/18; ⊗ 5.20am-11.45pm Mon-Fri, 6.15am-11.45pm Sat, 7am-10.30pm Sun) Frequent passenger ferries from Auckland's Ferry Building to Matiatia Wharf (40 minutes), some via Devonport (adding an extra 10 minutes to the journey time).

Sealink (☑ 0800 732 546; www.sealink. co.nz; return adult/child/car/motorcycle $37/20/158/63; ⊗ 6am-6pm) Runs car ferries to Kennedy Point, mainly from Half Moon Bay, east Auckland (45 to 60 minutes, at least hourly), but some leave from Wynyard Wharf in the city (60 to 80 minutes, three per day).

🛈 Getting Around

BICYCLE
Various bicycle routes are outlined in the *Bike Waiheke!* brochure, available from the wharf and the i-SITE; be prepared for a few hills.

Waiheke Bike Hire (☑ 09-372 7937; www. waihekebikehire.co.nz; Matiatia; per day $35) hires mountain bikes from its base in the car park near the wharf.

Parts of Waiheke are quite hilly, so ease the load with a hybrid machine from **Onya Bikes** (☑ 022 050 2233; www.ecyclesnz.com; 124 Oceanview Rd; per hr/day $20/60) combining pedalling with electric motors.

BUS
The island has bus services, starting from Matiatia Wharf and heading through Oneroa (adult/child $2/1, three minutes) on their way to all the main settlements, as far west as Onetangi (adult/child $4.50/2.50, 35 minutes). A day pass (adult/child $10/6) is available from the Fullers counter at Matiatia Wharf. Some services in the middle of the day can be as much as an hour apart, so to avoid lengthy waits at bus stops, consult a timetable from Auckland Transport (p100).

CAR, MOTORCYCLE & SCOOTER
There are petrol stations in Oneroa and Onetangi.

Fun Rentals (☑ 09-372 8001; www.funrentals. co.nz; 14a Belgium St, Ostend; per day car/scooter/4WD from $59/49/59) Includes free pick-ups and drop-offs to the ferries.

Rent Me Waiheke (☑ 09-372 3339; www.rent mewaiheke.co.nz; 14 Oceanview Rd, Matiatia; per day car/scooter $69/59)

Waiheke Auto Rentals (☑ 09-372 8998; www. waihekerentals.co.nz; Matiatia Wharf; per day car/scooter from $79/69)

Waiheke Rental Cars (☑ 09-372 8635; www. waihekerentalcars.co.nz; Matiatia Wharf; per day car/4WD from $79/109)

TAXI
Island Taxis (☑ 09-372 4111; www.islandtaxis. co.nz)

Waiheke Express Taxis (☑ 0800 700 789; www.waihekeexpresstaxis.co.nz)

Waiheke Independent Taxis (☑ 0800 300 372; www.waihekeindependenttaxis.co.nz)

Rotoroa Island

From 1911 to 2005 the only people to have access to this blissful little island on the far side of Waiheke were the alcoholics and drug addicts who came (or were sentenced) here to dry out, and the Salvation Army staff who cared for them. In 2011, 82-hectare Rotoroa (☑ 0800 768 676; www.rotoroa.org.nz; access fee adult/child $5/3; ⊗ dusk-dawn) 🚣 opened to the public for the first time in a century, giving visitors access to three sandy swimming beaches and the social history and art displays in the restored buildings of the former treatment centre.

There are also three well-appointed, wildly retro holiday homes for rent, sleeping four ($375) to eight ($650) people, and excellent hostel accommodation in dorms (per person $35) in the former Superintendent's House.

❶ Getting There & Away

360 Discovery (☑ 09-307 8005; www.fullers. co.nz; adult/child from Auckland $52/30, from Orapiu $23/13) From Auckland the ferry takes 75 minutes, stopping at Orapiu on Waiheke Island en route. Services are infrequent and don't run every day. Prices include the island access fee.

Tiritiri Matangi Island

This magical, 220-hectare, predator-free island (www.tiritirimatangi.org.nz) is home to the tuatara (a prehistoric lizard) and lots of endangered native birds, including the very rare and colourful takahe. Other birds that can be seen here include the bellbird, stitchbird, saddleback, whitehead, kakariki, kokako, little spotted kiwi, brown teal, New Zealand robin, fernbird and penguins; 78 different species have been sighted in total. The saddleback was once close to extinction, with just 150 left, but there are now up to 1000 on Tiritiri alone. To experience the dawn chorus in full flight, stay overnight at the **DOC bunkhouse** (☑ 09-425 7812; www.doc.govt.nz; adult/child $30/20); book well ahead and ensure there's room on the ferry.

The island was sold to the Crown in 1841, deforested, and farmed until the 1970s. Since 1984 hundreds of volunteers have planted 250,000 native trees and the forest cover has regenerated. An 1864 **lighthouse** stands on the eastern end of the island.

Be sure to book a guided walk ($5) with your ferry ticket; the guides know where all the really cool birds hang out.

❶ Getting There & Away

360 Discovery (☑ 09-307 8005; www.fullers. co.nz; ⊙ Wed-Sun) Ferries depart for Tiritiri Matangi Island at 9am from Wednesday to Sunday, leaving the island at 3.30pm. The journey takes 70 minutes from Auckland's ferry terminal (adult/child return $70/40) or 20 minutes from Gulf Harbour ($55/32).

Motuora Island

Halfway between Tiritiri Matangi and Kawau, Motuora has 80 predator-free hectares and is used as a kiwi 'crèche'. There's a wharf on the west coast of the island, but you'll need your own boat to get here. The **DOC campsite** (☑ 09-379 6476; www.doc.govt. nz; sites per adult/child $6/3) requires bookings and provides toilets, cold showers and water. There's also a cottage that sleeps five ($60); bring your own linen and food.

Kawau Island

POP 300

Kawau Island lies 50km north of Auckland off the Mahurangi Peninsula. There are few proper roads through the island, the residents relying mainly on boats.

The main attraction is **Mansion House** (☑ 09-422 8882; www.doc.govt.nz; adult/child $4/2; ⊙ noon-2pm Mon-Fri, noon-3.30pm Sat & Sun), an impressive wooden manor extended from an 1845 structure by Governor George Grey, who purchased the island in 1862. It houses a fine collection of Victoriana, including some of Grey's effects, and is surrounded by the original exotic gardens. A set of short walks (10 minutes to two hours) are signposted from Mansion House, leading to beaches, the old copper mine, and a lookout; download DOC's *Kawau Island Historic Reserve* map (www.doc.govt.nz).

🛏 Sleeping & Eating

Beach House   BOUTIQUE HOTEL **$$$**
(☑ 09-422 8850; www.kawaubeachhouse.co.nz; Vivian Bay; r/ste from $345/620) In the north of the island, on Kawau's best sandy beach, this upmarket complex has luxurious rooms facing the beach, facing a large paved courtyard or in a cottage set back in the bush. It's a remote spot but it has its own restaurant, so there's no need to go anywhere.

Kawau Lodge   B&B **$$$**
(☑ 09-422 8831; www.kawaulodge.co.nz; North Cove; r $350; 🖥) 🍃 This eco-conscious property has its own jetty, wraparound decks and views. Meals ($6 to $75) can be arranged, as can excursions.

Mansion House Cafe   CAFE **$$**
(☑ 09-422 8903; www.facebook.com/mansionhousenz; lunch $16-18, dinner $18-28; ⊙ hours vary) If you haven't packed a picnic, this idyllically

situated eatery serves all-day breakfasts, salads, curries and hearty evening meals.

ℹ Getting There & Away

Kawau Cruises (☏ 0800 111 616; www.kawau-cruises.co.nz) Ferries from Sandspit to Kawau (adult/child return $55/31) at least four times daily and a water-taxi service (minimum charge $143). The Super Cruise (adult/child $63/34, including barbecue lunch $95/50) departs Sandspit at 10.30am and circles the island, delivering the post to 75 different wharves.

Great Barrier Island

POP 850

Great Barrier has unspoilt beaches, hot springs, old kauri dams, a forest sanctuary and a network of tramping tracks. Because there are no possums on the island, the native bush is lush.

Named Aotea (meaning cloud) by the Māori, and Great Barrier (due to its position at the edge of the Hauraki Gulf) by James Cook, this rugged and exceptionally beautiful place falls in behind South, North and Stewart as NZ's fourth-largest island (285 sq km). It closely resembles the Coromandel Peninsula to which it was once joined, and like the Coromandel it was once a mining, logging and whaling centre. Those industries have long gone and today two-thirds of the island is publicly owned and managed by DOC.

Although only 88km from Auckland, Great Barrier seems a world – and a good many years – away. The island has no supermarket, no electricity supply (only private solar, wind and diesel generators) and no main drainage (only septic tanks). Many roads are unsealed and petrol costs are high. Mobile-phone reception is very limited and there are no banks, ATMs or street lights.

From around mid-December to mid-January is the peak season, so make sure you book transport, accommodation and activities well in advance.

Tryphena is the main settlement, 4km from the ferry wharf at Shoal Bay. Strung out along several kilometres of coastal road, it consists of a few dozen houses and a handful of shops and accommodation places. From the wharf it's 3km to Mulberry Grove, and then another 1km over the headland to Pa Beach and the Stonewall Store (p112).

The airport is at **Claris**, 12km north of Tryphena, a small settlement with a general store, bottle shop, laundrette, garage, pharmacy and cafe.

Whangaparapara is an old timber town and the site of the island's 19th-century whaling activities. **Port Fitzroy** is the other main harbour on the west coast, a one-hour drive from Tryphena. These four main settlements have fuel available.

🏃 Activities

Water Sports
The beaches on the west coast are safe, but care needs to be taken on the surf-pounded eastern beaches. **Medlands Beach**, with its wide sweep of white sand, is one of the most beautiful and accessible beaches on the island. Remote **Whangapoua**, in the northeast, requires more effort to get to, while **Kaitoke**, **Awana Bay** and **Harataonga** on the east coast are also worth a visit.

Okiwi Bar has an excellent right-hand break, while Awana has both left- and right-hand breaks. Pohutukawa trees shelter the pretty bays around Tryphena.

Diving is excellent, with shipwrecks, pinnacles, lots of fish and more than 33m visibility at some times of the year.

Mountain Biking
With rugged scenery and relatively little traffic on the roads, mountain biking is a popular activity. There's a designated 25km ride beginning on Blind Bay Rd, Okupu, winding beneath the Ahumata cliffs before crossing Whangaparapara Rd and beginning the 15km Forest Rd ride through beautiful forest to Port Fitzroy. Cycling on other DOC walking tracks is prohibited.

Tramping
The island's very popular walking tracks are outlined in DOC's free *Great Barrier Island (Aotea Island)* booklet. Before setting out, make sure you're properly equipped with water and food, and be prepared for both sunny and wet weather.

The most popular easy walk is the 45-minute **Kaitoke Hot Springs Track**, starting from Whangaparapara Rd and leading to natural hot springs in a bush stream. Check the temperature before getting in and don't put your head under the water.

Windy Canyon, which is only a 15-minute walk from Aotea Rd, has spectacular rock outcrops and affords great views of the island. From Windy Canyon, an excellent trail continues for another two to three hours through scrubby forest to Hirakimata (Mt Hobson; 621m), the highest point on

Great Barrier Island

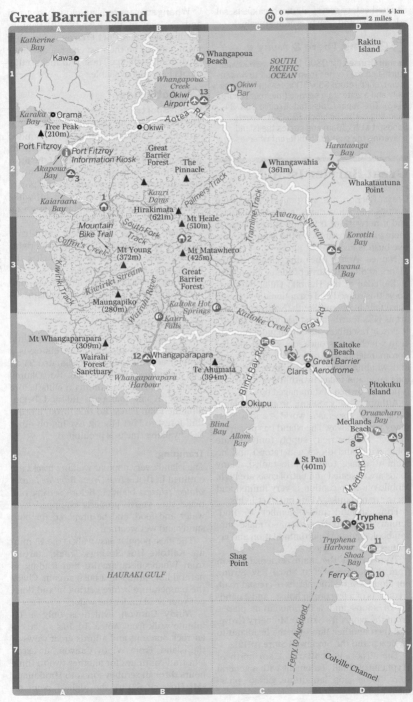

0 — 4 km
0 — 2 miles

Katherine Bay

Kawa

Whangapoua Beach

Whangapoua Creek

Okiwi Airport

13

Okiwi Bar

Okiwi

SOUTH PACIFIC OCEAN

Rakitu Island

Karaka Bay

Orama

Tree Peak (210m)

Port Fitzroy

Port Fitzroy Information Kiosk

Akapoua Bay

3

Great Barrier Forest

The Pinnacle

Whangawahia (361m)

Harataonga Bay

7

Whakatautuna Point

Kaiaraara Bay

1

Kauri Dams

Hirakimata (621m)

Mt Heale (510m)

Palmers Track

Awana Stream

Korotiti Bay

Mountain Bike Trail

South Fork Track

2

Mt Matawhero (425m)

Tramline Track

5

Awana Bay

Coffin's Creek

Mt Young (372m)

Kiwiriki Track

Kiwiriki Stream

Maungapiko (280m)

Wairahi River

Great Barrier Forest

Kaitoke Hot Springs

Kaitoke Creek

Gray Rd

Kauri Falls

Mt Whangaparapara (309m)

Wairahi Forest Sanctuary

12

Whangaparapara

Te Ahumata (394m)

6

14

Claris

Kaitoke Beach

Great Barrier Aerodrome

Pitokuku Island

Whangaparapara Harbour

Okupu

Blind Bay Rd

Blind Bay

Allom Bay

St Paul (401m)

Medlands Beach

Oruawharo Bay

8

9

Medland Rd

4

Tryphena

16

15

11

Tryphena Harbour

Shoal Bay

Shag Point

HAURAKI GULF

Ferry

10

Ferry to Auckland

Colville Channel

Great Barrier Island

the island, with views across the Hauraki Gulf and Coromandel. Near the top of the mountain are lush forests and a few mature kauri trees that survived the logging days. From Hirakimata it is 40 minutes south to Mt Heale Hut.

A more challenging tramp is the hilly **Tramline Track** (five hours), which starts on Aotea Rd and follows old logging tramlines to Whangaparapara Harbour. The initial stages of this track are not maintained and in some parts the clay becomes slippery after rain.

Of a similar length, but flatter and easier walking, is the 11km **Harataonga Coastal Walk** (five hours), which heads from Harataonga Bay to Whangapoua.

Many other trails traverse the forest, taking between 30 minutes and five hours. The **Aotea Track** combines bits of other paths into a three-day walk, overnighting in each of the huts.

🛏 Sleeping

Unless you're camping, Great Barrier isn't a cheap place to stay. At pretty much every price point you'll pay more than you would for a similar place elsewhere. In the low season, however, rates drop considerably.

Island Accommodation (☑ 021 138 7293; www.islandaccommodation.co.nz) offers a booking service, which is handy for finding self-contained houses for longer stays.

Check accommodation and island information websites for packages including flights and car rental. Note that accommodation rates soar for around two weeks following Christmas and the island also gets very busy during this time.

DOC has two huts in the Great Barrier Forest with bunk beds, cold running water, chemical toilets and a kitchen-dining area. Bring your own sleeping bag and cooking/eating equipment and book online. **Mt Heale Hut** (☑ 09-379 6476; www.doc.govt.nz; dm per adult/child $15/7.50) sleeps 20 people and has a gas cooker, but **Kaiaraara Hut** (☑ 09-379 6476; dm per adult/child $15/7.50), which sleeps 24, doesn't. Both must be booked in advance.

There are DOC campsites at **Harataonga Bay** (☑ 09-379 6476; www.doc.govt.nz; Harataonga Rd; sites per adult/child $10/5), **Medlands Beach** (Sandhills Rd; sites per adult/child $10/5), **Akapoua Bay** (Kaiaraara Bay Rd; sites per adult/child $10/5), **Whangapoua** (off Aotea Rd; sites per adult/child $10/5), **The Green** (Whangaparapara Harbour; sites per adult/child $10/5) and **Awana Bay** (off Aotea Rd; sites per adult/child $10/5). All have basic facilities, including water, cold showers (except for the Green), toilets and a food-preparation shelter. You need to bring your own gas cooking stove as open fires are prohibited. Book in advance online.

**Medlands Beach
Backpackers & Villas**   HOSTEL $
(☑ 09-429 0320; www.staymedlands.com; 9 Mason Rd; dm/d without bathroom $35/90, units from $250; 🐾) Chill out in the garden of this house or the hill, overlooking beautiful Medlands Beach. The backpackers area is simple, with a little double chalet for romantic budgeteers at a slight remove from the rest. The self-contained houses sleep up to seven.

Crossroads Lodge   HOSTEL $
(☑ 09-429 0889; www.xroadslodge.com; 1 Blind Bay Rd; dm/s/d $30/50/75; @🐾) This low-key backpackers is 2km from the airfield and close to forest walks and hot springs. Covered walkways connect the sleeping blocks to the main lodge, which has the kitchen, lounge and bathrooms.

Aotea Lodge   APARTMENT $$
(☑ 09-429 0623; www.aotealodge.com; 41 Medland Rd; units $120-220; 🐾) A well-tended, sunny garden surrounds these reasonably

priced units, perched on the hill just above Tryphena. They range from a two-bedroom house to an unusual mezzanine unit loaded with bunks, and each has its own cooking facilities.

Shoal Bay Lodge　　　　RENTAL HOUSE **$$**
(☑ 09-429 0890; www.shoalbaylodge.co.nz; 145 Shoal Bay Rd; house from $160) Hidden among the trees, this three-bedroom house offers sea views, birdsong and solar power. Arm yourself with a glass of wine and stake a place on the deck at sunset.

Sunset Waterfront Lodge　　　MOTEL **$$**
(☑ 09-429 0051; www.sunsetlodge.co.nz; 5 Mulberry Grove Rd; units from $195) Gaze across the lawn to the sea from the attractive studio units, or fight over who's going to get the pointy room in the two-bedroom A-frame villas. There's a small shop and cafe next door.

✖ Eating

In summer, most places are open daily but for the rest of the year the hours can be sporadic. A monthly guide to opening hours is on www.thebarrier.co.nz, but it pays to call ahead for an evening meal.

Self-caterers will find small stores in Tryphena, Claris, Whangaparapara and Port Fitzroy. The **Stonewall Store** (☑ 09-429 0451; 82 Blackwell Dr; ⊘ 8.30am-5.30pm) in Tryphena has a good selection of wine, beer and locally grown produce, and also operates a small alfresco market from 10am on Saturday mornings. The best place for takeaway burgers and hot chips is the **Hub**, operating out of a wooden shed by the harbour at Port Fitzroy.

Wild Rose　　　　　　　CAFE **$$**
(☑ 09-429 0905; 82 Blackwell Dr; mains $11-21; ⊘ 7.30am-3pm Wed-Sat, 9am-3pm Sun; ☑) ⌁ Wild Rose does the best impersonation of an Auckland cafe on the island, albeit with the addition of local crowd-pleasers such as toasted sandwiches and burgers. It uses freerange, organic and sustainable local produce whenever possible.

Currach Irish Pub　　　　PUB FOOD **$$**
(☑ 09-429 0211; www.currachirishpub.co.nz; 78 Blackwell Dr; mains $19-30; ⊘ 4pm-late daily Dec-Feb, Thu-Tue Mar-Nov; ☎⛽) This lively, child-friendly pub has a changing menu of seafood, steak and burgers, and is the island's main social centre. Rub shoulders with local musos on jam nights.

Tipi & Bob's　　　　　　PUB FOOD **$$$**
(☑ 09-429 0550; www.waterfrontlodge.co.nz; 38 Puriri Bay Rd; breakfast $16-20, dinner $34-40; ⊘ 7.30-10am & 5-10pm) Serving simple but satisfying meals in large portions, this popular haunt has an inviting deck overlooking the harbour. There's also a cheaper menu in the bar.

ⓘ Information

There's an information kiosk at the GBI Rent-A-Car office (p113) in Claris.

Port Fitzroy Information Kiosk (☑ 09-429 0848; www.thebarrier.co.nz; ⊘ 9am-3pm Mon-Sat) is a privately run kiosk that publishes the *Great Barrier Island Visitor Information Guide*.

Claris Texas (☑ 09-429 0811; 129 Hector Sanderson Rd; ⊘ 8am-4pm; ☎) cafe has internet access.

ⓘ Getting There & Away

AIR

Barrier Air (☑ 0800 900 600, 09-275 9120; www.barrierair.kiwi; adult/child from $114/96) Departs from both Auckland Domestic Airport and North Shore Aerodrome 42 times a week for the 30-minute flight to Claris. Flights from Auckland to Okiwi, and Claris to Whitianga or Tauranga are available on request.

FlyMySky (☑ 09-256 7025, 0800 222 123; www.flymysky.co.nz; adult/child from $118/91) Flies at least three times a day between Claris and Auckland. Cheaper flights are available if you travel to the island on a Sunday or leave on a Friday ($89), and there's a special return fare for flying one way and ferrying the other (adult/child $193/140).

Sunair (☑ 0800 786 247; www.sunair.co.nz; one way $150-190) Flies to Claris from Whitianga ($130), Tauranga ($190) and Hamilton ($190) daily, and from Ardmore Airport in Papakura, south Auckland, twice daily ($130).

BOAT

SeaLink (☑ 09-300 5900, 0800 732 546; www.sealink.co.nz; adult/child/car one way $79/58/275, return $100/79/340) Runs car ferries four days a week from Wynyard Wharf in Auckland to Tryphena's Shoal Bay (4½ hours) and once a week to Port Fitzroy (five hours).

ⓘ Getting Around

Most roads are narrow and windy but even small hire cars can handle the unsealed sections. Many of the accommodation places will pick you up from the airport or wharf if notified in advance.

Aotea Car Rentals (☑ 0800 426 832; www.aoteacarrentals.co.nz; Mulberry Grove) Rents cars (from $60), 4WDs (from $80) and vans (from $99). Rental clients can use Great Barrier Travel services for free.

GBI Rent-A-Car (☑ 09-429 0062; www.great barrierisland.co.nz; 67 Hector Sanderson Rd) Has a somewhat battered fleet of cars starting at $40 and 4WDs from $70. It also operates shuttle services from Claris to Tryphena ($20), Medlands ($15), Whangaparapara ($20) and Port Fitzroy ($30, minimum four passengers), as well as trampers' shuttles. There's a $5 flagfall for solo passengers; call ahead to book.

Great Barrier Travel (☑ 09-429 0474, 0800 426 832; www.greatbarriertravel.co.nz) Runs shuttles between Tryphena and Claris (timed to meet the planes and boats), and a daily bus from Tryphena to Port Fitzroy, stopping at various trailheads. Call ahead to confirm times and to book.

WEST AUCKLAND

West Auckland epitomises rugged: wild black-sand beaches, bush-shrouded ranges and mullet-haired, black-T-shirt-wearing 'Westies'. The latter is just one of several stereotypes of the area's denizens. Others include the back-to-nature hippie, the eccentric bohemian artist and the dope-smoking surfer dude, all attracted to a simple life at the edge of the bush.

Add to the mix Croatian immigrants, earning the fertile fields at the base of the Waitakere Ranges the nickname 'Dalie Valley' after the Dalmatian coast where most hailed from. These pioneering families planted grapes and made wine, founding one of NZ's major industries.

Titirangi

POP 3200

This little village marks the end of Auckland's suburban sprawl and is a good place to spot all manner of Westie stereotypes over a coffee, wine or cold beer. Once home to NZ's greatest modern painter, Colin McCahon, there remains an artsy feel to the place. Titirangi means 'Fringe of Heaven' – an apt name for the gateway to the Waitakere Ranges. This is the last stop for petrol and ATMs on your way west.

◎ Sights

**Te Uru Waitakere
Contemporary Gallery**   GALLERY
(☑ 09-817 8087; www.teeuru.org.nz; 420 Titirangi Rd; ⊙10am-4.30pm) FREE An excellent mod-

ern art gallery housed in the former Hotel Titirangi (1930), on the edge of the village. A significant restoration and contemporary extension have further enhanced the building's heritage glory.

McCahon House   MUSEUM
(☑ 09-817 7200; www.mccahonhouse.org.nz; 67 Otitori Bay Rd, French Bay; admission $5; ⊙1-4pm Wed-Sun) It's a mark of the esteem in which Colin McCahon is held that the house he lived and painted in during the 1950s has been opened to the public as a mini-museum. The swish pad next door is home to the artist lucky enough to win the McCahon Arts Residency. Look for the signposts pointing down Park Rd, just before you reach Titirangi village.

ⓘ Getting There & Away

Various buses connect Titirangi with central Auckland ($6.50, one hour).

Waitakere Ranges

This 160-sq-km wilderness was covered in kauri until the mid-19th century, when logging claimed most of the giant trees. A few stands of ancient kauri and other mature natives survive amid the dense bush of the regenerating rainforest, which is now protected inside the Waitakere Ranges Regional Park. Bordered to the west by wildly beautiful beaches on the Tasman Sea, the park's rugged terrain makes an excellent day trip from Auckland.

◎ Sights & Activities

Arataki   CULTURAL CENTRE
(☑ 09-817 0077; www.aucklandcouncil.govt.nz; 300 Scenic Dr; ⊙9am-5pm) 🅟 FREE As well as providing information on the 250km of trails within Waitakere Ranges Regional Park, this impressive centre also features Māori carvings and spectacular views. The carvings at the entrance depict the ancestors of the Kawerau *iwi*. You can also book here for several basic campsites (adult/child $8/4) within the park. A 1.6km nature trail opposite the centre leads visitors past labelled native species, including mature kauri.

Hillary Trail   TRAMPING
(www.aucklandcouncil.govt.nz) Arataki visitor centre is the starting point for this challenging 77km trail honouring Everest-conqueror Sir Edmund Hillary. It can be tackled in stages or in its four- to six-day entirety, staying at campsites along the way.

Walkers head to the coast at Huia, then continue past Whatipu, Karekare, Piha and Anawhata. From here continue up the coast to Te Henga and Muriwai, or head through bush to the Cascades Kauri to end at Swanson train station.

Other noted walks in Waitakere Ranges Regional Park include the **Kitekite Track** (1.8km, 30 minutes one way), the **Fairy Falls Track** (3.2km, 1½ hours one way) and the **Auckland City Walk** (1.5km, one-hour loop).

AWOL Canyoning   ADVENTURE SPORTS
(☑09-834 0501; www.awoladventures.co.nz; ☺half-/full day $165/195) Offers plenty of slippery, slidey, wet fun in Piha Canyon and the Blue Canyon, including glowworm-illuminated night trips ($185); transfers from Auckland are included.

ⓘ Getting There & Away

Auckland's Western train line terminates at Swanson, which is within a kilometre of the northwestern edge of the regional park. However, this is a long way away from the main park attractions. There are no bus services through the main part of the park.

Karekare

Few stretches of sand have more personality than Karekare. Those prone to metaphysical musings inevitably settle on descriptions such as 'spiritual' and 'brooding'. Perhaps history has left its imprint: in 1825 it was the site of a ruthless massacre of the local Kawerau *iwi* by Ngāpuhi invaders. Wild and gorgeously undeveloped, this famous beach has been the setting for on-screen moments both high- and lowbrow, from Oscar-winner *The Piano* to *Xena: Warrior Princess*.

From the car park the quickest route to the black-sand beach involves wading through a stream. Karekare rates as one of the most dangerous beaches in the country, with strong surf and ever-present rips, so don't even think about swimming unless the beach is being patrolled by lifeguards (usually only in summer). Pearl Jam singer Eddie Vedder nearly drowned here while visiting Neil Finn's Karekare pad.

Follow the road over the bridge and up along Lone Kauri Rd for 100m, where a short track leads to the pretty **Karekare Falls**. This leafy picnic spot is the start of several walking tracks.

Karekare has no shops of any description and no public transport. To get here take Scenic Dr and Piha Rd until you reach the well-signposted turn-off to Karekare Rd.

Piha
600

If you notice an Auckland surfer dude with a faraway look, chances are they're daydreaming about Piha. This beautifully rugged, iron-sand beach has long been a favourite for Aucklanders escaping from the city's stresses – whether for day trips, weekend teenage parties or family holidays.

Although Piha is popular, it's also incredibly dangerous, with wild surf and strong undercurrents, so much so that it's spawned its own popular reality TV show, *Piha Rescue*. If you don't want to inadvertently star in it, always swim between the flags, where lifeguards can provide help if you get into trouble.

Piha may be bigger and more populated than neighbouring Karekare, but there's still no supermarket, liquor shop, bank or petrol station, although there is a small general store that doubles as a cafe, takeaway shop and post office.

⊙ Sights & Activities

The view of the coast as you drive down Piha Rd is spectacular. Perched on its haunches near the centre of the beach is **Lion Rock** (101m), whose 'mane' glows golden in the evening light. It's actually the eroded core of an ancient volcano and a Māori *pa* site. A path at the south end of the beach takes you to some great lookouts. At low tide you can walk south along the beach and watch the surf shooting through a ravine in another large rock known as the **Camel**. A little further along, the waves crash through the **Gap** and form a safe swimming hole. A small colony of little penguins nests at the beach's north end.

For surfboard hire, try Piha Store (p115) or Piha Surf Shop (p115).

🛏 Sleeping & Eating

★**Piha Beachstay –
Jandal Palace**   HOSTEL $
(☑09-812 8381; www.pihabeachstay.co.nz; 38 Glenesk Rd; dm/s $35/70, d $120, without bathroom $80; @🛜) Attractive and ecofriendly, this wood-and-glass lodge has extremely smart facilities. It's 1km from the beach but there's

a little stream at the bottom of the property and bushwalks nearby. In winter an open fire warms the large communal lounge.

Piha Surf Accommodation
CABIN $

(☑ 09-812 8723; www.pihasurf.co.nz; 122 Seaview Rd; caravans & cabins $60-90) Each basic but charmingly tatty caravan has its own linen, TV, fridge, cooker and long-drop toilet, and they share a very simple shower. The private cabins have the same rudimentary bathroom arrangement but are a more comfortable option.

Black Sands Lodge
APARTMENT $$

(☑ 021 969 924; www.pihabeach.co.nz; Beach Valley Rd; cabin $160, apt $220-260; ☎) These two modern conjoined apartments with private decks match their prime location with appealing touches, such as stereos and DVD players. The cabin is kitted out in a 1950s Kiwiana bach style and shares a bathroom with the main house. Bikes and wi-fi are free for guests, and in-room massage and lavish dinners can be arranged on request.

Piha Store
EAKERY $

(☑ 09-812 8844; 26 Seaview Rd; snacks $2-10; ☺ 7.30am-5.30pm) Call in for pies and other baked goods, groceries and ice creams. The attached Lion Rock Surf Shop rents surfboards and body boards.

Piha Cafe
CAFE $$

(☑ 09-812 8808; www.pihacafe.com; 20 Seaview Rd; mains $14-27; ☺ 8.30am-3.30pm Mon-Wed, to 10pm Thu-Sat, to 5pm Sun) ✐ Big-city standards mesh seamlessly with sand-between-toes informality at this attractive ecofriendly cafe. Cooked breakfasts and crispy pizzas provide sustenance for a hard day's surfing. After the waves, head back for a cold beverage on the deck.

🛍 Shopping

Piha Surf Shop
OUTDOOR EQUIPMENT

(☑ 09-812 8723; www.pihasurf.co.nz; 122 Seaview Rd; ☺ 8am-5pm) A family-run venture, with well-known surfboard designer Mike Jolly selling his wares and wife Pam selling a small range of crafts. Surfboards (per three hours/day $25/35), wetsuits ($8/15) and body boards ($15/25) can be hired, and private surfing lessons can be arranged.

West Coast Gallery
ARTS, CRAFTS

(☑ 09-812 8029; www.westcoastgallery.co.nz; Seaview Rd; ☺ 10am-5pm) The work of more than 200 local artists is sold from this small not-for-profit gallery next to the Piha fire station.

❶ Getting There & Away

There's no public transport to Piha, but **Rapu** (☑ 09-828 0426; www.rapuadventures.com; return $50) provides shuttles when the surf's up. **Go Hitch** (☑ 0800 467 442; www.gohitch.co.nz; up to 3 people $300) also operates a Piha shuttle from central Auckland and Ponsonby on weekends.

Te Henga (Bethells Beach)

Breathtaking Bethells Beach is reached by taking Te Henga Rd at the northern end of Scenic Dr. It's a raw, black-sand beach with surf, windswept dunes and walks, such as the popular one over giant sand dunes to Lake Wainamu (starting near the bridge on the approach to the beach).

🍴 Eating

Bethells Cafe
BURGERS, PIZZA $

(☑ 09-810 9387; www.facebook.com/thebethellscafe; beach car park; mains $12-17; ☺ 5.30-9.30pm Fri, 10am-6pm Sat & Sun Nov-May, 10am-6pm Sun Jun-Oct) Less a cafe and more a food truck with an awning, the Bethells Cafe does a roaring trade in burgers (beef and vegetarian), pizza, cakes and coffee. On Friday nights it's pretty much the perfect Kiwi beach scene, with live musicians entertaining the adults while the kids surf the sand dunes. Enquire about glamping opportunities nearby.

Kumeu & Around

West Auckland's main wine-producing area still has some vineyards owned by the original Croatian families who kick-started NZ's wine industry. The fancy eateries that have mushroomed in recent years have done little to dint the relaxed farmland feel to the region, but everything to encourage an afternoon's indulgence on the way back from the beach or the hot pools. Most cellars offer free tastings.

🏃 Activities

Kumeu River
WINERY

(☑ 09-412 8415; www.kumeuriver.co.nz; 550 SH16; ☺ 9am-4.30pm Mon-Fri, 11am-4.30pm Sat) Owned by the Brajkovich family, this winery produces one of NZ's best chardonnays, among other varietals.

Coopers Creek
WINERY

(☑ 09-412 8560; www.cooperscreek.co.nz; 601 SH16, Huapai; ☺ 10.30am-5.30pm) Buy a bottle,

THE GREAT GANNET OE

After honing their flying skills, young gannets get the ultimate chance to test them – a 2000km journey to Australia. They usually hang out there for several years before returning home, never to attempt the journey again. Once back in the homeland they spend a few years waiting for a piece of waterfront property to become available in the colony, before settling down with a regular partner to nest – returning to the same patch of dirt every year. In other words, they're your typical young New Zealander on their right-of-passage Overseas Experience (OE).

spread out a picnic in the attractive gardens and, from January to Easter, enjoy Sunday afternoon jazz sessions.

 **Eating & Drinking**

Tasting Shed   TAPAS **$$**
(☑ 09-412 6454; www.thetastingshed.co.nz; 609 SH16, Huapai; dishes $14-26; ☺ 4-10pm Wed & Thu, noon-11pm Fri-Sun) Complementing its rural aspect with rustic chic decor, this slick eatery conjures up delicious dishes designed to be shared. It's not strictly tapas, as the menu strays from Spain, and appropriates flavours from Asia, the Middle East, Croatia, Serbia, Italy and France.

Hallertau   BREWERY
(☑ 09-412 5555; www.hallertau.co.nz; 1171 Coatesville-Riverhead Hwy, Riverhead; ☺ 11am-midnight) Hallertau offers tasting paddles ($14) of its craft beers served on a vine-covered terrace edging the restaurant. Regular guest beers, good food (shared plates $11 to $15, mains $24 to $31), and occasional weekend DJs and live music make it very popular with Auckland's hopheads.

Riverhead   PUB
(☑ 09-412 8902; www.theriverhead.co.nz; cnr Queen & York Sts, Riverhead; ☺ 11am-late) A blissful terrace, shaded by oak trees and overlooking the river, makes this 1857 hotel a memorable drink stop, even if the menu (mains $26 to $36) doesn't quite live up to its gastropub ambitions. Make a day of it, with a boat cruise (p78) from the city to the pub's own jetty.

🛈 Getting There & Away

From central Auckland, Kumeu is 25km up the Northwestern Motorway (SH16). Helensville-bound buses (route 60) head here from 105 Albert St (adult/child $8.50/5, one hour), but you'll need a car or bike to get around.

Muriwai Beach

A rugged black-sand surf beach, Muriwai Beach's main claim to fame is the **Takapu Refuge gannet colony**, spread over the southern headland and outlying rock stacks. Viewing platforms get you close enough to watch (and smell) these fascinating seabirds. Every August hundreds of adult birds return to this spot to hook up with their regular partners and get busy – expect lots of outrageously cute neck-rubbing, bill-touching and general snuggling. The net result is a single chick per season; December and January are the best times to see the little fellas testing their wings before embarking on an impressive odyssey.

Nearby, a couple of short tracks will take you through beautiful native bush to a lookout that offers views along the 60km length of the beach. Wild surf and treacherous rips mean that swimming is safe only when the beach is patrolled (swim between the flags). Apart from surfing, Muriwai Beach is a popular spot for hang gliding, parapunting, kiteboarding and horse riding. There are also tennis courts, a golf course and a cafe that doubles as a takeaway chippie.

Helensville

POP 2600

A smattering of heritage buildings, antique shops and cafes makes village-like Helensville a good whistle-stop for those taking SH16 north.

 Activities

Tree Adventures   OUTDOORS
(☑ 0800 827 926; www.treeadventures.co.nz; Restall Rd, Woodhill; ropes courses $17-42; ☺ 10am-5pm Sat & Sun) A set of high-ropes courses within Woodhill Forest, consisting of swinging logs, nets, balance beams, Tarzan swings and a flying fox.

Woodhill Mountain Bike Park   MOUNTAIN BIKING
(☑ 027 278 0969; www.bikepark.co.nz; Restall Rd, Woodhill; adult/child $8/6, bike hire from $30;

◷8am-5.30pm Thu-Tue, 8am-10pm Wed) Maintains many challenging tracks (including jumps and beams) within Woodhill Forest, 14km south of Helensville.

Parakai Springs SWIMMING, SPA
(☑09-420 8998; www.parakaisprings.co.nz; 150 Parkhurst Rd; adult/child $22/11; ◷10am-9pm) Aucklanders bring their bored children to Parakai, 2km northwest of Helensville, on wet wintry days as a cheaper alternative to Waiwera. It has large thermally heated swimming pools, private spas (per 30 minutes per person $5) and a couple of hydroslides.

❶ Information

Visitor Information Centre (☑09-420 8060; www.helensville.co.nz; 5 Commercial Rd; ◷10am-4pm Mon-Sat) Housed inside the Art Stop Cafe. Pick up free brochures detailing the *Helensville Heritage Trail* and *Helensville Riverside Walkway*.

❶ Getting There & Away

Bus 60 heads from 105 Albert St in central Auckland to Helensville ($11, 1½ hours).

NORTH AUCKLAND

The Auckland supercity sprawls 90km north of the CBD to just past the point where SH16 and SH1 converge at Wellsford. The semirural area north of Auckland's suburban sprawl encompasses beautiful beaches, regional parks, tramping trails, quaint villages and wineries. Plus there are excellent opportunities for kayaking, snorkelling and diving. Consider visiting on a day trip from Auckland or as a way to break up your trip on the journey north.

Long Bay Regional Park

The northernmost of Auckland's East Coast bays, Long Bay is a popular family picnic and swimming spot, attracting over a million visitors a year. A three-hour-return coastal walk heads north from the sandy beach to the Okura River, taking in secluded Grannys Bay and Pohutukawa Bay (which attracts nude bathers).

❶ Getting There & Away

Regular buses head to Long Bay from Mayoral Dr in the city (adult/child $8/4.50, one hour). If you're driving, leave the Northern Motorway at the Oteha Valley Rd exit, head towards Browns Bay and follow the signs.

---

❶ WHICH HIGHWAY?

From Auckland, the multilane Northern Motorway (SH1) bypasses Orewa and Waiwera or the Northern Gateway Toll Road. It will save you about 10 minutes, provided you pay the **NZ Transport Agency** (☑0800 40 20 20; www.tollroad. govt.nz; per car & motorbike $2.30) online (in advance or within five days of your journey) rather than stopping to queue at the toll booths.

Between Christmas and New Year SH1 can be terribly gridlocked heading north between the toll road and Wellsford; winding SH16 through Kumeu and Helensville is a sensible alternative. The same is true if heading south in the first few days of the new year.

Shakespear Regional Park

Shooting out eastward just before Orewa, the Whangaparaoa Peninsula is a heavily developed spit of land with a sizeable South African expat community. At its tip is this gorgeous 376 hectare regional park, its native wildlife protected by a 1.7km pest-proof fence.

Sheep, cows, peacocks and pukeko ramble over the grassy headland, while pohutukawa-lined **Te Haruhi Bay** provides great views of the gulf islands and the city. Walking tracks take between 40 minutes and two hours, exploring native forest, WWII gun embankments, Māori sites and lookouts. If you can't bear to leave, there's an idyllic beachfront camping ground (☑09-366 6400; www.aucklandcouncil.govt.nz; sites per adult/child $15/6) with flush toilets and cold showers.

❶ Getting There & Away

It's possible to get here via a tortuous 1½-hour bus trip from Albert St (adult/child $11/6.50). An alternative is to take the 50-minute **360 Discovery** (☑09-307 8005; www.fullers.co.nz; adult/child $14/8.40) ferry service to Gulf Harbour, a Noddy-town development of matching townhouses, a marina, country club and golf course. Enquire at the ferry office about picking up a bus or taxi from here. Alternatively, walk or cycle the remaining 3km to the park. The ferry is a good option for cyclists wanting to skip the boring road trip out of Auckland; carry-on bikes are free.

WORTH A TRIP

TE HANA TE AO MARAMA

You'll see the terraces of a lot of historic *pa* (fortified village) sites etched into hillsides all around NZ, but if you want to get an idea of how these Māori villages actually looked, take a one-hour guided tour of the recreated *pa* at **Te Hana Te Ao Marama** (☑09-423 8701; www.tehana.co.nz; 307-308 SH1, Te Hana; adult/child $28/17; ☺9am-5pm Wed-Sun). It's best to book ahead.

Orewa

POP 7400

Locals have fears that Orewa is turning into NZ's equivalent of Queensland's Gold Coast, but until they start exporting retirees and replacing them with bikini-clad parking wardens that's unlikely to happen. It is, however, very built-up and high-rise apartment towers have begun to sprout.

◉ Sights & Activities

Orewa Beach   BEACH
Orewa's 3km-long stretch of sand is its main drawcard. Being in the Hauraki Gulf, it's sheltered from the surf but it's still patrolled by lifeguards in the peak season.

Millennium Walkway   WALKING
Starting from South Bridge this 8km route loops through various parks before returning along the beach; follow the blue route markers.

Snowplanet   SNOW SPORTS
(☑09-427 0044; www.snowplanet.co.nz; 91 Small Rd, Silverdale; day pass adult/child $66/47; ☺10am-10pm Sun-Thu, 10am-midnight Fri & Sat) Snowplanet offers indoor skiing, snowboarding and tubing throughout the year. It's just off SH1, 8km south of Orewa.

⌨ Sleeping & Eating

Orewa Motor Lodge   MOTEL $$
(☑09-426 4027; www.orewamotorlodge.co.nz; 290 Hibicus Coast Hwy; units $160-210; ☎) One of the motels lining Orewa's main road, this complex has scrupulously clean wooden units prettied up with hanging flower baskets. There's also a spa pool.

Waves   MOTEL $$$
(☑09-427 0888; www.waves.co.nz; cnr Hibiscus Coast Hwy & Kohu St; units from $185; ☎) Like a motel only flasher, this complex offers spacious, self-contained apartments, and the downstairs units have gardens and spa baths. It's only a few metres from the beach.

Casablanca   MEDITERRANEAN $$
(☑09-426 6818; www.casablancacafenz.co.nz; 336 Hibiscus Coast Hwy; mains $18-32; ☺10am-late) Turkish, North African and Mediterranean flavours feature at this buzzy cafe. Try the hearty baked Moorish eggs and you'll be set for the next chapter of your Kiwi road trip.

ⓘ Getting There & Away

Direct buses head to Orewa from central Auckland (adult/child $12/7, 1¼ hours) and Waiwera (adult/child $2.50/1.50, 12 minutes).

Waiwera

POP 285

This pleasant river-mouth village has a great beach, but it's the *wai wera* (hot waters) that people come here for. Warm mineral water bubbles up from 1500m below the surface to fill the 19 pools of the **Waiwera Thermal Resort** (☑09-427 8800; www.waiwera.co.nz; 21 Waiwera Rd; adult/child $30/16; ☺9am-8pm, 10am-7pm public holidays). There are various big water slides, barbecues, private tubs ($40) and a health spa, or you can soak and stew while watching a flick in the movie pool. Despite the prices edging up year on year, the facilities are a little rough around the edges. Still, it's a lot of fun, especially for families.

Squeezed between the Waiwera and Puhoi Rivers, the exquisite 134-hectare **Wenderholm Regional Park** (☑09-366 2000; www.aucklandcouncil.govt.nz; 37 Schischka Rd) has a diverse ecology, abundant bird life, beaches and walks (30 minutes to 2½ hours). **Couldrey Homestead** (www.aucklandcouncil.govt.nz; adult/child $5/free; ☺1-4pm Sat & Sun, daily Jan-Easter), the original farmhouse dating from the 1860s, is now a museum. The camping ground provides only tap water and toilets, and the council also rents three comfortable self-contained houses.

ⓘ Getting There & Away

Bus 991X from Auckland's Albert St heads to Waiwera (adult/child $11/6.50, 1¼ hours) via Orewa.

Puhoi

POP 450

Forget dingy cafes and earnest poets – this quaint village is a slice of the real Bohemia. In 1863 around 200 German-speaking immigrants from the present-day Czech Republic settled in what was then dense bush.

◉ Sights & Activities

Bohemian Museum MUSEUM
(📞 09-422 0852; www.puhohistoricalsociety.org. nz; Puhoi Rd; adult/child $3.50/free; ☺ noon-3pm Sat & Sun, daily Jan-Easter) Tells the story of the hardship and perseverance of the original Bohemian pioneers.

Church of Sts Peter & Paul CHURCH
(www.holyname.org.nz; Puhoi Rd) The village's pretty Catholic church dates from 1881 and has an interesting tabernacle painting (a copy of one in Bohemia), stained glass and statues.

Puhoi River Canoe Hire CANOEING, KAYAKING
(📞 09-422 0891; www.puhoirivercances.co.nz; 84 Puhoi Rd) Hires kayaks and Canadian canoes, either by the hour (kayak/canoe $25/50) or for an excellent 8km downstream journey from the village to Wenderholm Regional Park (single/double kayak $50/100, including return transport). Bookings are essential.

✖ Eating & Drinking

Puhoi Valley CAFE $$
(📞 09-422 0670; www.puhoivalley.co.nz; 275 Ahuroa Rd; mains $15-22; ☺ 10am-4pm) Renowned across NZ, Puhoi Valley cheese features heavily on the menu of this upmarket cheese shop and cafe, set blissfully alongside a lake, fountain and children's playground. In the summer there's music on the lawn, perfect with a gourmet ice cream.

★ Puhoi Pub PUB
(📞 09-422 0812; www.puhoipub.com; 5 Saleyards Rd; ☺ 10am-10pm Mon-Sat, to 8pm Sun) There's character and then some in this 1879 pub, with walls completely covered in old photos, animal heads and vintage household goods.

❶ Getting There & Away

Puhoi is 1km west of SH1. The turn-off is 2km past the Johnstone Hills tunnel.

Mahurangi & Scandrett Regional Parks

Straddling the head of Mahurangi Harbour, **Mahurangi Regional Park** (📞 09-366 2000; www.aucklandcouncil.govt.nz; 190 Ngarewa Dr, Mahurangi West) is a boater's paradise incorporating areas of coastal forest, *pa* sites, and a historic homestead and cemetery. Its sheltered beaches offer prime sandy spots for a dip or picnic and there are loop walks ranging from 1½ to 2½ hours.

The park has three distinct fingers: Mahurangi West, accessed from a turn-off 3km north of Puhoi; Scott Point on the eastern side, with road access 16km southeast of Warkworth; and isolated Mahurangi East, which can only be reached by boat. Accommodation is available in four basic campsites and four baches sleeping six to eight. Campervans can also park for $6 per person.

On the way to Mahurangi West you'll pass **Zealandia Sculpture Garden** (📞 09-422 0099; www.zealandiasculpturegarden.co.nz; 138 Mahurangi West Rd; admission $10; ☺ by appointment Nov-Mar), where the work of well-known artist Terry Stringer is showcased within impressive architecture and grounds.

On the ocean side of the Mahurangi Peninsula, **Scandrett Regional Park** (📞 09-366 2000; www.aucklandcouncil.govt.nz; 114 Scandrett Rd, Mahurangi East) has a sandy beach, walking tracks, patches of regenerating forest, another historic homestead, more *pa* sites and great views towards Kawau Island. Three baches (sleeping six to eight) are available for rent and there's room for campervans (per adult/child $8/4).

Warkworth

POP 3300

River-hugging Warkworth makes a pleasant pit stop, its cutesy main street retaining a village atmosphere.

◉ Sights & Activities

Dome Forest FOREST
(SH1) Two kilometres north of Warkworth, a track leads through this regenerating forest to the Dome summit (336m). On a fine day you can see the Sky Tower from a lookout near the top. The summit walk takes about 1½ hours return, or you can continue for a gruelling seven-hour one-way tramp through the Totora Peak Scenic Reserve, exiting on Govan Wilson Rd.

Warkworth District's Museum MUSEUM
(☑09-425 7093; www.warkworthmuseum.co.nz; Tudor Collins Dr; adult/child $7/3; ☺10am-3pm) Pioneer-era detritus is displayed at this small local museum. Of more interest is the surrounding **Parry Kauri Park**, which harbours a couple of giant kauri trees, including the 800-year-old McKinney kauri (girth 7.6m).

Ransom Wines WINERY
(☑09-425 8862; www.ransomwines.co.nz; Valerie Close; tasting with purchase free, otherwise donation to Tawharanui Open Sanctuary $5; ☺10am-5pm Tue-Sun) Well signposted from SH1, about 3km south of Warkworth, Ransom produces great food wines and showcases them with good-value tasting platters (per person $20), crammed with smoked meats and local cheeses. A tasting flight of five wines is $15.

✖ Eating & Drinking

Chocolate Brown CAFE $$
(☑09-422 2677; www.chocolatebrown.co.nz; 6 Mill Lane; mains $10-22; ☺8am-4pm) Decked out with quirky NZ-themed art – mostly for sale – this cafe serves excellent coffee, robust eggy breakfasts and delicious home-style baking. Definitely leave room for a few cacao-infused goodies from the chocolate shop next door; there are also plenty of gift packs for the folks back home.

Tahi Bar CRAFT BEER
(☑09-422 3674; www.tahibar.com; 1 Neville St; ☺3.30pm-late Tue-Thu, noon-late Fri-Sun) Tucked down a quiet laneway, Tahi features nine ever-changing taps of New Zealand craft beer. It's an exceptionally friendly spot with decent platters and pub grub, and a rustic and sunny deck.

🛍 Shopping

Honey Centre FOOD
(☑09-425 8003; www.honeycentre.co.nz; 7 Perry Rd; ☺8.30am-5pm) About 5km south of Warkworth, the Honey Centre makes a diverting pit stop, with its cafe, free honey tasting and glass-fronted hives. The shop sells all sorts of bee-related products, from candles to mead.

ⓘ Getting There & Away

InterCity (☑09-583 5780; www.intercity.co.nz) and Naked Bus (www.nakedbus.com) services both pass through town, en route between Auckland and the Bay of Islands.

Matakana

POP 291

Around 15 years ago, Matakana was a nondescript rural village with a handful of heritage buildings and an old-fashioned country pub. Now the locals watch bemused as Auckland's chattering classes idle away the hours in stylish wine bars and cafes. The striking **Matakana Cinemas complex** (☑09-422 9833; www.matakanacinemas.co.nz; 2 Matakana Valley Rd) has a domed roof reminiscent of an Ottoman bathhouse, and an excellent **farmers market** (www.matakanavillage.co.nz; Matakana Sq, 2 Matakana Valley Rd; ☺8am-1pm Sat) is held in its shadow.

The reason for this transformation is the area's boutique wineries, which are developing a name for pinot gris, merlot, syrah and a host of obscure varietals. Local vineyards are detailed in the free *Matakana Coast Wine Country* (www.matakanacoast.com) and *Matakana Wine Trail* (www.matakanawine.com) brochures, available from the Matakana information centre.

⊙ Sights & Activities

Tawharanui Regional Park BEACH
(☑09-366 2000; www.aucklandcouncil.govt.nz; 1181 Takatu Rd) A partly unsealed road leads to this 588-hectare reserve at the end of a peninsula. This special place is an open sanctuary for native birds, protected by a pest-proof fence, while the northern coast is a marine park (bring a snorkel). There are plenty of walking tracks (1½ to four hours) but the main attraction is **Anchor Bay**, one of the region's finest white-sand beaches.

Camping is allowed at two basic sites near the beach (adult/child $15/6) and there's a six-person bach for hire ($168).

Omaha Beach BEACH
The nearest swimming beach to Matakana, Omaha has a long stretch of white sand, good surf and ritzy holiday homes.

Blue Adventures WATER SPORTS
(☑022 630 5705; www.blueadventures.co.nz; 331 Omaha Flats Rd, Omaha; lessons per hour $40-80) Offers kitesurfing, paddle boarding and wakeboarding lessons from Omaha and Orewa.

Matakana Bicycle Hire BICYCLE RENTAL
(☑09-423 0076; www.matakanabicyclehire.co.nz; 951 Matakana Rd; half-/full-day hire from $30/40, tours from $70) Hire a bike to explore local vineyards and beaches.

✖ Eating & Drinking

Mahurangi River
Winery & Restaurant MODERN NZ **$$**
(☑ 09-425 0306; www.mahurangiriver.co.nz; 162
Hamilton Rd; mains $28-34; ⊙11am-4pm Thu-
Mon) Expansive vineyard views partner with
a relaxed ambience and savvy food at this
rural spot off Sandspit Rd.

The Matakana PUB FOOD **$$**
(☑ 09-422 7518; www.matakana.co.nz; 11 Ma-
takana Valley Rd; mains $17-25; ⊙noon-12.30am)
Following a trendy makeover, Matakana's
heritage pub now features quirky decor,
Matakana wines and craft beers, and decent
bistro food including local Mahurangi oysters. Occasional DJs and live acts enliven the
cool outdoor space.

Vintry WINE BAR
(☑ 09-423 0251; www.thevintry.co.nz; 2 Matakana
Valley Rd; ⊙10am-10pm) In the Matakana Cinemas complex, this wine bar serves as a one-
stop cellar door for all the local producers.

ⓘ Information

Matakana Information Centre (☑ 09-422
7433; www.matakanainfo.org.nz; 2 Matakana
Valley Rd; ⊙10am-1pm) In the foyer of the
Matakana Cinemas complex.

ⓘ Getting There & Away

Matakana is a 10km drive northeast of Warkworth
along Matakana Rd; there's no public transport.
Ferries for Kawau Island leave from Sandspit,
8km east of Warkworth along Sandspit Rd.

Leigh
POP 390

Appealing little Leigh (www.leighbythesea.
co.nz) has a picturesque harbour dotted
with fishing boats, and a decent swimming
beach at **Matheson Bay**.

Apart from the extraordinary Goat Island
Marine Reserve on its doorstep, Leigh's other claim to fame is the legendary live-music
venue Leigh Sawmill Cafe (p122), which
sometimes sees surprisingly big names
drop in to play a set or two. If you imbibe
too much of the good stuff from the on-site
microbrewery, there's accommodation inside the old sawmill shed, including basic
backpacker rooms (from $25) and massive
doubles with en suites ($125). Alternatively,
you can rent the Cosy Sawmill Family Cottage (from $200, sleeps 10).

◉ Sights

★**Goat Island**
Marine Reserve WILDLIFE RESERVE
(www.doc.govt.nz; Goat Island Rd) Only 3km
from Leigh, this 547-hectare aquatic area
was established in 1975 as the country's first
marine reserve. In less than 40 years the sea
has reverted to a giant aquarium, giving an
impression of what the NZ coast must have
been like before humans arrived. You only
need step knee-deep into the water to see
snapper (the big fish with blue dots and
fins), blue maomao and stripy parore swimming around.

Excellent interpretive panels explain the
area's Māori significance (it was the landing
place of one of the ancestral canoes) and
provide pictures of the species you're likely
to encounter.

There are **dive areas** all around Goat
Island, which sits just offshore, or you can
snorkel or dive directly from the beach. Colourful sponges, forests of seaweed, boarfish,
crayfish and stingrays are common sights,
and if you're very lucky you may see orcas and bottle-nosed dolphins. Visibility is
claimed to be at least 10m, 75% of the time.

Goat Island
Marine Discovery Centre AQUARIUM
(☑ 09-923 3645; www.goatislandmarine.co.nz; 160
Goat Island Rd, Leigh; adult/child/family $9/7/20;
⊙10am-4pm daily Dec-Feb, Sat & Sun Mar-Nov)
Staffed by marine experts and graduate students from the University of Auckland, this
centre is packed with interesting exhibitions
on the ecosystem of the marine reserve, and
is worth visiting before venturing into Goat
Island's waters. The interactive displays and
the tide pool full of marine creatures are
great for children.

🏃 Activities

Octopus Hideaway SNORKELLING
(☑ 09-422 6212; www.theoctopushideaway.nz;
7 Goat Island Rd; ⊙10am-5pm) Up the road
from the beach, this crew hires snorkelling
gear (adult/child $25/18, including wet-
suit $38/26), and offers guided two-hour
day ($75/55) and night ($95/70) snorkel
expeditions.

Goat Island Dive & Snorkel DIVING
(☑ 09-422 6925; www.goatislanddive.co.nz; 142a
Pakiri Rd; snorkel set hire adult/child $25/18, incl
wetsuit $38/26) This long-standing operator
offers guided snorkelling, PADI courses and

AUCKLAND LEIGH

dive trips in the Goat Island Marine Reserve and other key sites throughout the year. It also hires snorkelling and diving gear.

Tours

Glass Bottom Boat Tours   BOAT TOUR
(☑09-422 6334; www.glassbottomboat.co.nz; Goat Island Rd; adult/child $28/15) A glass-bottomed boat provides an opportunity to see the underwater life while staying dry. Trips last 45 minutes and run from the beach year-round, weather permitting; go online or ring to check conditions and to book. It also hires snorkel sets (per two/four hours $28/36), kayaks (per hour $28) and offers guided snorkelling for beginners (adult/child $75/55).

⚑ Drinking & Nightlife

Leigh Sawmill Cafe   PUB
(☑09-422 6019; www.sawmillcafe.co.nz; 142 Pakiri Rd; ⊗10am-late daily Jan-Mar, 10am-late Thu-Sun Apr-Nov) This spunky little venue is a regular stop on the summer rock circuit, sometimes attracting surprisingly big names. The pizzas ($14 to $35) are thin and crunchy like they should be, and best enjoyed in the garden on a lazy summer's evening.

❶ Getting There & Away

You'll need your own wheels to get here.

Pakiri

Blissful Pakiri Beach, 12km past Goat Island (4km of the road is unsealed), is an unspoilt expanse of white sand and rolling surf – a large chunk of which is protected as a regional park.

Right by the water, **Pakiri Beach Holiday Park** (☑09-422 6199; www.pakiriholidaypark. co.nz; 261 Pakiri River Rd; sites from $70, units from $120, without bathroom from $100) 🏖 has a shop and tidy units of varying degrees of comfort in a secure setting under the shade of pohutukawa.

Just 6km on from Pakiri is **Pakiri Horse Riding** (☑09-422 6275; www.horseride-nz.co.nz; Rahuikiri Rd), which has 60 horses available for superb bush-and-beach rides, ranging from one hour ($65) to multiday 'safaris'. Accommodation is provided in basic but spectacularly situated beachside cabins (dorm/cabin $40/200) or in a comfortable four-bedroom house ($500), secluded among the dunes.

❶ Getting There & Away

There's no public transport to Pakiri; you'll need your own car to get here.

Bay of Islands & Northland

Best Places to Eat

➔ à Deco (p132)

➔ Wood Street Freehouse (p127)

➔ Gables (p142)

➔ Food at Wharepuke (p150)

➔ Little Kitchen on the Bay (p154)

Best Places to Sleep

➔ Endless Summer Lodge (p158)

➔ Waipoua Lodge (p163)

➔ Tree House (p160)

➔ Kahoe Farms Hostel (p153)

➔ Kokohuia Lodge (p161)

Why Go?

For many New Zealanders, the phrase 'up north' conjures up sepia-toned images of family fun in the sun, pohutukawa in bloom and dolphins frolicking in pretty bays. From school playgrounds to work cafeterias, owning a bach (holiday house) 'up north' is a passport to popularity.

Beaches are the main drawcard and they're here in profusion. Visitors from more crowded countries are flummoxed to wander onto beaches without a scrap of development or another human being in sight. The west coast shelters the most spectacular remnants of the ancient kauri forests that once blanketed the top of the country; the remaining giant trees are an awe-inspiring sight and one of the nation's treasures.

It's not just natural attractions that are on offer: history hangs heavily here. The site of the earliest settlements of both Māori and Europeans, Northland is unquestionably the birthplace of the nation.

When to Go

➔ Northland's beaches go crazy at New Year and remain busy throughout the January school holidays, with the long, lazy days of summer usually continuing into February and March.

➔ The 'winterless north' boasts a subtropical climate, most noticeable from Kerikeri upwards, which averages seven rainy days per month in summer, but 16 in winter.

➔ In winter the average highs hover around 16°C and the average lows around 7°C.

➔ Temperatures are often a degree or two warmer than Auckland, especially on the east coast.

Bay of Islands & Northland Highlights

1 Matauri Bay
(p151) Splashing about, body surfing, sunbathing and strolling.

2 Cape Reinga
(p155) Watching oceans collide while souls depart.

3 Waipoua Forest
(p162) Paying homage to the ancient kauri giants of this forest.

4 Poor Knights Islands (p135) Diving at one of the world's top spots.

5 Bay of Islands
(p136) Cruising northern waters and claiming your own island paradise among the many in this bay.

6 Ninety Mile Beach (p155) Surfing the sand dunes.

7 Waitangi Treaty Grounds (p142) Delving into history and culture.

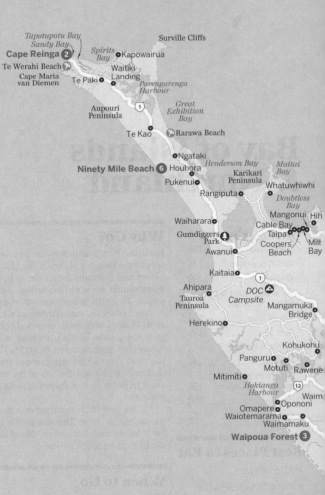

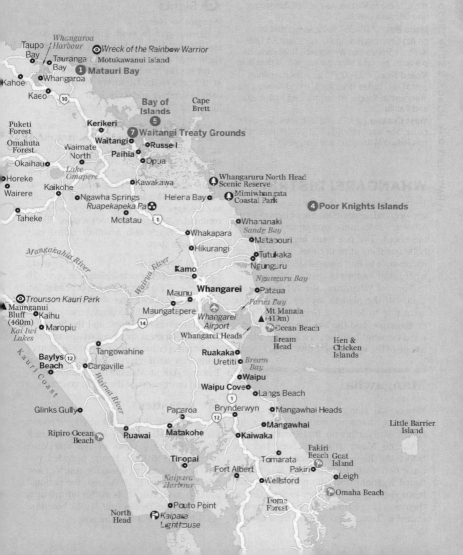

SOUTH PACIFIC OCEAN

50 km
25 miles

Whangaroa
Harbour
Taupo
Bay
Tauranga
Bay
Whangaroa
Kahoe
Kaeo
10

● Wreck of the Rainbow Warrior
Motukawanui Island
❶ Matauri Bay

Puketi
Forest
Omahuta
Forest
Okaihau
Horeke
Wairere
Taheke

Kerikeri
Bay of
Islands
Cape
Brett
❺
❼ Waitangi Treaty Grounds
Waitangi
● Russel
Waimate
North
Paihia
● Opua
Lake
Omapere
Kaikohe
Ngawha Springs
Ruapekapeka Pa
Motatau
1
● Kawakawa

Whangaruru North Head
Scenic Reserve
Helena Bay ● ● Mimiwhangata
Coastal Park
❹ Poor Knights Islands

Mangakahia River
Whakapara
Hikurangi
Kamo
Maunu
Whananaki
Sandy Bay
Matapouri
Tutukaka
Ngunguru
Ngunguru Bay
● Pataua
Pataua River

Whangarei
Whangarei
Airport
Whangarei Heads

Parua Bay
Mt Manaia
(419m)
● Ocean Beach
Bream
Head

Hen &
Chicken
Islands

Trounson Kauri Park
Maunganui
Bluff
(460m)
Kaihu
Maropiu
Kai Iwi
Lakes
Maungatapere
14

Waipoua River

Tangowahine
Baylys
Beach
Dargaville
12

Ruakaka
Uretiti
Bream
Bay

Waipu
Waipu Cove ●
● Langs Beach

Glinks Gully
Wairoa River
Ruawai
Paparoa
Matakohe
12
Brynderwyn
1
Mangawhai Heads

Little Barrier
Island

Ripiro Ocean
Beach
Tiropai
Fort Albert
Kaipara
Harbour
North
Head
Pouto Point
Kaipara
Lighthouse

Kaiwaka
Mangawhai

Tomarata
Pakiri
Wellsford
Dome
Forest

Fakiri
Beach
❼
Pakiri
Goat
Island
● Leigh

❼ Omaha Beach

ⓘ Getting There & Away

AIR

Air New Zealand (✆ 0800 737 000; www.air newzealand.co.nz) Daily flights from Auckland to Whangarei and Kerikeri.

Barrier Air (✆ 09-275 9120, 0800 900 600; www.barrierair.kiwi) Links Kaitaia to Whangarei and Auckland.

BUS

InterCity (✆ 09-583 5780; www.intercity. co.nz) Along with associated Northliner services, these buses head from Auckland to Kerikeri via Waipu, Whangarei and Paihia; and from Paihia to Kaitaia via Kerikeri, Mangonui and Coopers Beach.

Mana Bus (✆ 09-367 9140; www.manabus. co.nz) Services linking Auckland and Kaitaia via Kerikeri, Paihia and Whangarei. Note some departures are on a shared basis with Naked Bus.

Naked Bus (✆ 09-979 1616; www.nakedbus. com) Daily buses from Auckland to Kerikeri via Warkworth, Waipu, Whangarei and Kawakawa and Paihia.

West Coaster (✆ 021 380 187; www.dargaville. co.nz; one way/return $10/20) Weekday shuttles linking Whangarei and Dargaville.

WHANGAREI DISTRICT

To truly experience this area you'll need to get wet, and scores of beaches offer opportunities for swimming, surfing or just splashing about. The hot spots heave with Kiwi holidaymakers at peak times, but even then it's possible to find isolated stretches of sand where your footprints are the only ones.

North of Whangarei, the Tutukaka Coast is one of the planet's top three coastlines, according to *National Geographic Traveler* magazine, and the late Jacques Cousteau rated the neighbouring Poor Knights Islands as one of the world's best dive sites.

Mangawhai

POP 2400

Mangawhai village sits at the base of a horseshoe harbour, but it's Mangawhai Heads, 5km further on, that's really special.

Various Māori tribes inhabited the area before the 1660s, when Ngāti Whatua became dominant. In 1807 Ngāti Whatua defeated Ngāpuhi from the north in a major battle, letting the survivors escape. One of them was Hongi Hika, who in 1825 returned, armed with muskets obtained from Europe-ans. The ensuing bloodbath all but annihilated Ngāti Whatua and the district became *tapu* (sacred, taboo). British squatters moved in and were rewarded with land titles by the government in the 1850s. Ceremonies were only performed to lift the *tapu* in the 1990s.

In a new century, Mangawhai is benefiting from improved traffic links with Auckland, and new housing subdivisions are expanding the spread of the area. Down on the surf beach in summer though, it's still a quintessential and thoroughly laid-back New Zealand beach town.

⊙ Sights

Mangawhai Heads   BEACH
A narrow spit of sand stretches for kilometres to form the harbour's south head, sheltering a seabird sanctuary. Across the water sits the holiday town with a surf beach at its northern tip. Lifesavers patrol on weekends in summer and daily during school holidays, but it's not especially dangerous.

Mangawhai Museum   MUSEUM
(✆ 09-431 4645; www.mangawhai-museum.org. nz; Molesworth Dr; adult/child $12/3; ⊙ 10am-4pm) One of regional New Zealand's best museums, this spectacular building on the main road linking Mangawhai village to Mangawhai Heads is packed with interesting displays on the area's history and environment. Check out the roof shaped like a stingray. There's also a sun-drenched cafe worthy of a stop.

Te Whai Bay Wines   VINEYARD
(✆ 09-945 0580; www.tewhaibaywines.co.nz; 26 Bush Lane; ⊙ 10am-5pm daily late Oct-Easter, Sat, Sun & public holidays Easter-late Oct) Handcrafted wines include chardonnay, pinot gris and Bordeaux-style red wines, and the beautiful vineyard is a great spot for a shared antipasto platter to enhance the pleasant illusion of being in a southern hemisphere version of Tuscany. Ask at Mangawhai's visitor information centre about other local vineyards.

☆ Activities

Mangawhai Cliff Top Walkway   TRAMPING
Starting at Mangawhai Heads, this track affords extensive views of sea and land. It takes two to three hours, provided you time it with a return down the beach at low tide. This is part of Te Araroa, the national walking track. Ask at the visitor information centre for the *Tracks and Walks* brochure detailing other walks in the area.

Wined About Bike Tours
BICYCLE TOUR

(☑021 945 050, 09-945 0580; www.winedabout.
co.nz; per person $50) Three different self-
guided tour options include all the good things
in life. Art and chocolate, wine and olives, or
a freestyle exploration of Mangawhai village
and nearby beaches. Pick-ups are included in
the prices, both before and after riding

🛏 Sleeping

Mangawhai Heads
Holiday Park
HOLIDAY PARK $

(☑09-431 4675; www.mangawhaiheadsholiday-
park.co.nz; Mangawhai Heads Rd; sites $16-18,
units $105-135; 🐾) With an absolute water-
front location on the sandy expanse of Mangawhai's estuary, this laid-back combo of
campsites, units and cabins is a retro slice
of Kiwiana holiday style. Visit in summer
for a vibrant halo of red blooms from groves
of pohutukawa trees. Just note it's a family-
friendly place, with an expectation of no
noise after 10.30pm.

Sunhill Cottages
COTTAGE $$

(☑09-431 4393; www.sunhill.co.nz; 2306 Cove Rd;
cottages $185; 🐾🏊) In rural surroundings
just a short inland drive from Mangawhai,
Sunhill's two self-contained cottages are
spacious and airy, and include private decks
looking out to the nearby Brynderwyn rang-
es. A heated pool and shared outdoor bar
area is ideal for relaxing at the end of the
day. B&B accommodation (double $130) is
also available in the main house.

Mangawhai Lodge
B&B $$$

(☑09-431 5311; www.seaviewlodge.co.nz; 4
Heather St Mangawhai Heads; s $185 d $130, unit
$175-220; 🐾) Smartly furnished rooms have
access to a picture-perfect wraparound
veranda at this boutique B&B, which also
features great views.

🍴 Eating & Drinking

Mangawhai Market
MARKET $

(Moir St; ⊙9am-1pm Sat) Held in the library
hall in Mangawhai village, this is a good
place to stock up on organic produce (including wine and olive oil) and peruse local
crafts. Another market is held on Sunday
mornings in the Mangawhai Heads Domain
from mid-October to Easter.

★ Wood Street Freehouse
CAFE $$

(☑09-431 4051; www.facebook.com/woodst
freehouse; 12 Wood St, Mangawhai Heads; mains
$16-22, shared plates $11-14; ⊙noon late Mon-Fri,

from 10am Sat & Sun) Craft beer has arrived in
Mangawhai at this buzzing cafe, including
beers from local Northland brewers such as
Schippers and the Sawmill Brewery. Excel-
lent food includes burgers, gourmet pizzas
and shared plates – the truffle and parme-
san fries are addictive – and from Friday
to Sunday fresh local oysters from Wood
Street's raw bar are best devoured on the
sunny deck.

Harvest Blue
CAFE $$

(☑09-431 4111; www.facebook.com/harvestcafe
mangawhai; 198 Molesworth Dr; mains $18-28;
⊙8am-2pm Sun, Mon & Thu, to 9pm Fri & Sat)
Rustic wooden furniture and overflowing pots of flowers and fresh herbs fill the
deck of this relaxed cafe's sunny courtyard.
New owners have revitalised the menu, and
brunch classics such as Spanish omelette
and sweetcorn fritters now segue to Asian-
style salads crammed with calamari or tuna
for lunch. On Friday and Saturday Harvest
Blue is also open for dinner.

Evening meals are a good opportunity to
try wines from local Mangawhai vineyards
Lochiel Estate and Millars.

Mangawhai Tavern
PUB

(☑09-431 4505; www.mangawhaitavern.co.nz;
Moir St; ⊙11am-late) One of the country's
oldest pubs – built in 1865 – the tavern's

MĀORI NEW ZEALAND: BAY OF ISLANDS & NORTHLAND

Known to Māori as Te Tai Tokerau, this region has a long and proud Māori history and to-day has one of the country's highest percentages of Māori people. Along with East Cape, it's a place where you might hear Māori being spoken. In mythology the region is known as the tail of the fish of Maui.

Māori sites of particular significance include **Cape Reinga** (p155), the **Waitangi Treaty Grounds** (p142), **Ruapekapeka Pa Historic Reserve** (p143) and, in the Waipoua Forest, **Tane Mahuta** (p162).

Māori cultural experiences are offered by many local operators, including **Footprints Waipoua** (p161), **Motuti Marae** (p159), **Ahikaa Adventures** (p156), **Sand Safaris** (p156), **Terenga Paraoa** (p131) and **Rewa's Village** (p149). Many businesses catering to travellers are owned or run by Māori individuals or *hapu* (subtrib-al) groups. Tai Tokerau Tourism (www.taitokerau.co.nz) lists many of them on its website.

harbourside location is a top spot for an afternoon beer. There's live music most Saturday nights and Sunday afternoons, and across the Christmas–New Year period some of NZ's top bands rock the garden bar. The pub meals are deservedly world-famous-in-Northland.

ℹ️ Information

Visitor Information Centre (☏ 09-431 5090; www.mangawhai.co.nz) Staffed sporadically (mainly on weekends and in summer), but there are information boards outside. Ask about opportunities to visit local vineyards and olive groves.

Waipu & Bream Bay

POP 1854

The original 934 British settlers came to Waipu from Scotland via Nova Scotia (Canada) between 1853 and 1860. These dour Scots had the good sense to eschew frigid Otago, where so many of their kindred settled, for sunnier northern climes. Their story comes to life through holograms, a short film and interactive displays at the **Waipu Museum** (☏ 09-432 0746; www.waipumuseum.co.nz; 36 The Centre; adult/child $8/3; ⊙ 10am-4.30pm).

There are also excellent walks in the area, including the **Waipu Coastal Trail**, which heads south from Waipu Cove – around to Langs Beach, passing the **Pancake Rocks** on the way. The 2km **Waipu Caves Walking Track** starts at Ormiston Rd and passes through farmland and a scenic reserve en route to a large cave containing glowworms and limestone formations; bring a torch, a compass and sturdy footwear to delve the depths.

Just south of Waipu township, there's good swimming at **Waipu Cove** and **Langs Beach**.

Bream Bay has miles of blissfully deserted beach, blighted only slightly by a giant oil refinery at the north end. At **Uretiti**, a stretch of beach south of a **DOC campsite** (www.doc.govt.nz; SH1; sites per adult/child $10/5) is unofficially considered 'clothing optional'. Over New Year the crowd is evenly split between Kiwi families, serious European nudists and gay guys.

🎆 Festivals & Events

Highland Games   FESTIVAL
(www.waipugames.co.nz; adult/child $15/5; ⊙ 1 Jan) Only 10% of current residents are direct descendants of the original Scots, but there's a big get together every year, when the Highland Games, established in 1871, take place in Caledonian Park.

🛏️ Sleeping & Eating

Waipu Wanderers Backpackers   HOSTEL $
(☏ 09-432 0532; www.waipu-hostel.co.nz; 25 St Marys Rd; dm/s/d $33/50/70; ⚡) There are only three rooms at this friendly backpackers in Waipu township. Look forward to free fruit in season.

Waipu Cove Resort   RESORT, MOTEL $$
(☏ 09-432 0348; www.waipucoveresort.co.nz; 891 Cove Rd; units $120-220; ⚡⚡) Modern self-contained apartments with private courtyards pleasingly blur the line between resort and boutique hotel. Nestled behind sand dunes, the arcing sprawl of the beach is just metres away, and the complex also includes a spa pool and a swimming pool.

Little Red
CAFE $

(www.facebook.com/blackshedwaipu.co.nz.; 7 Cove Rd; snacks $4-7; ⊙8am-3pm late Oct-Easter) Waipu's best coffee, artisan icy treats, organic soft drinks and kombucha, and homestyle baking – all served from a funky red shipping container. Grab a spot on one of the colourful Cape Cod–style chairs out the front and tuck into brioche and brownies.

Cove Cafe
CAFE $$

(☑09-432 0234; 910 Cove Rd, Waipu Cove; breakfast $5-15, pizza $20-24, mains $20-23; ⊙7am-10.30pm) This heritage cottage near Waipu covers all the bases, from coffee and breakfast bagels to pizza, gourmet burgers and craft beer, and the deck is a very pleasant spot to celebrate exploring NZ. Healthy smoothies – try the Vita Berry Blast with banana, strawberries and blueberries – will provide a boost for the next stage of your Kiwi itinerary.

McLeod's Pizza Barn
ITALIAN $$

(☑09-432 1011; 2 Cove Rd; pizzas $13-28 mains $19-30; ⊙11.30am-late Wed-Sun Apr-Nov daily Dec-Mar) Popular platters, light fare and great pizzas go well with craft beer from Waipu's very own McLeod's Brewery. Partner the Wharfinger pizza with prawns, avocado and feta with the hoppy IPA.

ⓘ Information

Tourist brochures and internet access are available at the Waipu Museum.

ⓘ Getting There & Away

Waipu Cove can be reached by a particularly scenic route that heads from Mangawhai Heads through Langs Beach. Otherwise turn off SH1 38km south of Whangarei.

InterCity (p126) and Naked Bus (p126) both operate bus services.

Whangarei

POP 52,900

Northland's only city is surrounded by natural beauty, and its compact town centre offers plenty of rainy-day diversions. There's a thriving artistic community, some good walks, and interesting cafes and bars.

⦿ Sights

⦿ Town Basin

This attractive riverside marina is home to vintage car and clock museums, cafes, shops, public art and an information centre. It's a great place for a stroll, with a marked Art Walk and Sculpture & Heritage Trail. An artisans' market is held on Saturdays from October to April under the shade of the pedestrian bridge.

★ Whangarei Art Museum
GALLERY

(☑09-430 4240; www.whangareiartmuseum.co.nz; The Hub, Town Basin; admission by donation; ⊙10am-4pm) At the Te Manawa Hub information centre (p133), Whangarei's public gallery has an interesting permanent collection, the star of which is a 1904 Māori portrait by Goldie. Also planned is the Hundertwasser Arts Centre, based on architectural plans by the late Austrian artist Friedensreich Hundertwasser. See www.yeswhangarei.co.nz for details of the campaign to raise support and funding for the project. A model of the proposed design can be seen at Hundertwasser HQ (p129), a pop-up store designed to increase awareness of the project.

★ Clapham's Clocks
MUSEUM

(☑09-438 3993; www.claphamsclocks.com; Town Basin; adult/child $10/4; ⊙9am-5pm) This very interesting collection of 1400 ticking, gonging and cuckooing timepieces constitutes the National Clock Museum.

⦿ City Centre

Old Library Arts Centre
GALLERY

(☑09-430 6432; www.oldlibrary.org.nz; 7 Rust Ave; ⊙10am-4pm Tue-Thu) FREE The work of local artists is exhibited in this wonderful art-deco building. Check the website for occasional concerts. Set between the old and new libraries is Pou, an intriguing sculpture consisting of 10 large poles carved with Māori, Polynesian, Celtic, Croatian and Korean motifs. Grab an interpretive pamphlet from the library.

⦿ Surrounds

Hundertwasser HQ
ARTS CENTRE

(☑021 907 321; www.facebook.com/hundertwasserhq; 2 James St; ⊙10.30am-2.30pm Mon-Fri, 10am-1pm Sat) This pop-up information centre is dedicated to raising awareness (and funds) for the establishment of a Hundertwasser Arts Centre in Whangarei.

Abbey Caves
CAVE

(Abbey Caves Rd) FREE Abbey Caves is an undeveloped network of three caverns full of glow-worms and limestone formations, 6km

BAY OF ISLANDS & NORTHLAND WHANGAREI

Whangarei

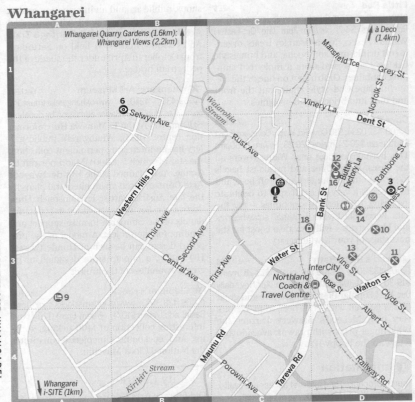

east of town. Grab a torch, strong shoes, a mate for safety and prepare to get wet. The surrounding reserve is a forest of crazily shaped rock extrusions. Ask at the i-SITE about an information sheet for the caves.

Kiwi North MUSEUM, WILDLIFE RESERVE
(☏ 09-438 9630; www.kiwinorth.co.nz; 500 SH14, Maunu; adult/child $15/5; ☉10am-4pm) ➢ Five kilometres west of Whangarei, this complex includes 19th-century buildings and a museum displaying Māori and colonial artefacts. A gecko and kiwi house offers a rare chance to see the country's feathery fave in a darkened nocturnal house.

Whangarei Falls WATERFALL
(Otuihau; Ngunguru Rd) Short walks around these 26m-high falls provide views of the water cascading over the edge of an old basalt lava flow. The falls can be reached on the Tikipunga bus ($3, no service on Sundays), leaving from Rose St in the city.

Whangarei Quarry Gardens GARDENS
(☏ 09-437 7210; www.whangareigardens.org.nz; Russell Rd; admission by donation; ☉9am-5pm) ➢ Green-fingered volunteers have transformed this old quarry into a blissful park with a lake, waterfalls, pungent floral aromas, wild bits, orderly bits and lots of positive energy. To get here, take Rust Ave, turn right into Western Hills Dr and then left into Russell Rd. A flash new visitor centre and cafe opened in late 2015.

Quarry Arts Centre ARTS CENTRE
(☏ 09-438 1215; www.quarryarts.org; 21 Selwyn Ave; ☉9.30am-4.30pm) **FREE** An eccentric village of artists' studios and co-operative galleries where you can often pick up well-priced art and craft.

🏃 Activities

The free *Whangarei Walks* brochure, available from the i-SITE, has maps and detailed

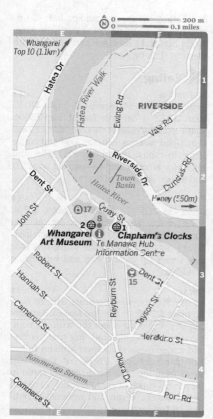

Whangarei

◎ Top Sights
1 Clapham's Clocks	F3
2 Whangarei Art Museum	E3

◎ Sights
3 Hundertwasser HQ	D2
4 Old Library Arts Centre	C2
5 Poi	C2
6 Quarry Arts Centre	B1

⊕ Activities, Courses & Tours
7 Pupurangi Hire & Tour	E2
8 Terenga Paraoa	E3

🛏 Sleeping
9 Lodge Bordeaux	A3

✦ Eating
10 Fresh	D3
11 La Familia	D3
12 Nectar	D2
13 Nomad	D3
14 Pimarn Thai	D3

⊙ Drinking & Nightlife
15 Brauhaus Frings	F3
16 The Old Stone Butter Factory	D2

⊕ Shopping
17 The Bach	E2
18 Tuatara	C3

descriptions of some excellent local tracks. The **Hatea River Walk** follows the river from the Town Basin to the falls (three hours return). Longer tracks head through **Parihaka Reserve**, which is just east of the Hatea River and encompasses the remnants of a volcanic cone (241m) and a major *pa* (fortified village) site. The city is spread out for inspection from the lookout at the top, which is accessible by car. Other tracks head through **Coronation Scenic Reserve**, an expanse of bush immediately west of the centre that includes two *pa* sites and abandoned quarries.

Skydive Ballistic Blondes ADVENTURE SPORTS (☏0800 695 867; www.skydiveballisticblondes. co.nz; per skydive $199-380) Not only is this the oddest-named skydiving outfit in the country, it's also the only one licensed to land on the beach (Ocean Beach Ruakaka or Paihia).

Pacific Coast Kayaks KAYAKING (☏09-436 1947; www.nzseakayaking.co.nz; hire 4/8hr $60/80, tours $40-140) Hires kayaks and offers guided paddles to various Whangarei region locations.

☞ Tours

Pupurangi Hire & Tour CULTURAL TOUR (☏0800 538 891, 09-438 8117; www.hirentour. co.nz; Jetty 1, Riverside Dr; ☺9.30am-5.30pm daily Oct-Apr, Sat & Sun May-Sep) Various hour-long tours of Whangarei, all with a Māori flavour, including *waka* (canoe) trips on the river ($35). Also hires kayaks (per hour $17), *waka* ($25), aquacycles ($17) and bikes ($15).

Terenga Paraoa CULTURAL TOUR (☏09-430 3083; departs Town Basin; adult/child morning $55/30, afternoon $32/20; ☺9.30am & 1pm) Guided Māori cultural tours taking in Whangarei Harbour, Mt Manaia, the Kauri Park and, in the mornings, Parihaka *pa*.

🛏 Sleeping

Little Earth Lodge HOSTEL $
(☑ 09-430 6562; www.littleearthlodge.co.nz; 85 Abbey Caves Rd; dm/s/d/tr from $32/62/72/96, cabin s/d $66/78; @🛜) Set on a farm 6km from town and right next to Abbey Caves, most other hostels look downright shabby compared to Little Earth. Forget dorm rooms crammed with nasty, spongy bunks: settle down in a proper cosy bed with nice linen and a maximum of two room-mates. Resident critters include miniature horses, and there's also a private cabin available.

Honey HOSTEL $
(☑ 027 355 7433, 09-430 8757; www.honeybnb. com; 52 Punga Grove; dm $22; 🛜) Friendly digs in a shared house across the Hatea River from the Town Basin. Look forward to a few hints of Asian design, free breakfast and good views of the city.

Whangarei Falls Holiday Park & Backpackers HOSTEL $
(☑ 09-437 0609; www.whangareifalls.co.nz; 12 Ngunguru Rd, Glenbervie; sites $19, dm $28-32, cabins $62-72; 🛜⛲) Located 5km from central Whangarei, but a short walk from Whangarei Falls, with good-value cabins and dorms, some with small kitchenettes. There's also room for tents and campervans. It's also part of the YHA network.

Whangarei Top 10 HOLIDAY PARK $
(☑ 09-437 6856; www.whangareitop10.co.nz; 24 Mair St; sites from $22, units $68-160; @🛜) This centrally located riverside holiday park has friendly owners, a better-than-average set of units, and super-shiny stainless-steel surfaces. Mair St is off Hatea Dr, north of the city centre.

Whangarei Views APARTMENT $$
(☑ 09-437 6238; www.whangareiviews.co.nz; 5 Kensington Heights Rise; apt $159; 🛜) Modern and peaceful, with a self-contained two-bedroom apartment and a friendly welcome from the well-travelled Swiss-British owners. To get here, take Rust Ave, turn right into Western Hills Dr and then left into Russell Rd. Kensington Heights Rise is off Russell Rd. There's a minimum two-night stay, and yes, the views are excellent.

Lodge Bordeaux MOTEL $$$
(☑ 09-438 0404; www.lodgebordeaux.co.nz; 361 Western Hills Dr; apt $390-460; @🛜) Lodge Bordeaux has tasteful units with stellar kitchens and bathrooms (most with spa baths), private balconies and access to excellent wine. To get here, take Rust Ave and turn left into Western Hills Dr.

🍴 Eating

La Familia CAFE $
(www.lafamilia.nz; 84 Cameron St; mains $10-16, pizza $13-21; ⏱7am-4pm Tue-Sat, 9am-2.30pm Sun) Versatility rules at this cosy corner location. Good pastries, counter food and coffee segue to robust Italian-themed mains and pizzas for lunch. There's a compact wine list and a good selection of beers.

Fresh CAFE $
(☑ 09-438 2921; 12 James St; mains $12-14; ⏱7.30am-4pm Mon-Fri, to 3pm Sat, to 2pm Sun) Fresh as a daisy, and with supersized-flower photography on the walls, this chic cafe serves up great coffee and interesting breakfasts.

Nectar CAFE $
(☑ 09-438 8084; www.nectarcafe.co.nz; 88 Bank St; mains $12-20; ⏱7am-3pm Mon-Fri, 8am-2pm Sat; 🍴) 🌿 Nectar offers the winning combination of friendly staff, fair-trade coffee, and generous servings from a menu full of Northland produce. Check out the urban views from the back windows, and settle in for a lazy brunch of eggs Benedict served on chewy bagels. Vegan and organic ingredients all feature.

Nomad MOROCCAN $$
(☑ 09-955 1146; www.nomadcafe.co.nz; Quality St Mall, 71 Cameron St; mains $24-28; ⏱5pm-late Tue-Sat) In a pedestrian laneway lined with cafes and restaurants, the menu standouts at this chic Moroccan-themed bar and eatery include spicy prawns, kofta and tagines. 'Dining & Vibe' is the claim on the window, and we can only agree.

Pimarn Thai THAI $$
(☑ 09-430 0718; www.pimarnthai.co.nz; 12 Rathbone St; mains $16-23; ⏱11am-2.30pm Mon-Sat, from 5pm daily; 🍴) As gaudy as every good Thai restaurant should be, Pimarn features all of Thailand's blockbuster dishes, including an excellent *yum talay* (spicy seafood salad).

★ à Deco MODERN NZ $$$
(☑ 09-459 4957; www.facebook.com/adeco.restaurant; 70 Kamo Rd; mains $37-42; ⏱noon-3pm Fri, 6pm-late Tue-Sat) Northland's best restaurant

offers an inventive menu that prominently features local produce, including plenty of seafood. Art-deco fans will adore the setting – a wonderfully curvaceous marine-style villa with original fixtures. To get here, head north on Bank St and veer left into Kamo Rd. Bookings recommended.

TopSail
MODERN NZ $$$

(☑ 09-436 2985; www.topsail.co.nz; Onerahi Yacht Club, 206 Beach Rd, Onerahi; mains $39-44; ☻ 6pm-late Wed-Sat) Located upstairs in the Onerahi Yacht Club, around 10km from central Whangarei, TopSail serves superlative bistro classics – think duck breast with manuka honey and lemon – and lots of fresh Northland seafood and NZ produce such as South Island Fiordland venison. Definitely a worthwhile destination, just a 15-minute taxi ride from town. Booking ahead is recommended.

 ## Drinking & Nightlife

Old Stone Butter Factory
BAR

(☑ 09-430 0044; www.thebutterfactory.co.nz; 84 Bank St; ☻ 10am-late) Occupying a converted bank building, this cool basement bar hosts live gigs from Thursday to Saturday. As the hours dissolve, DJs kick in. It's also popular for touring Kiwi bands and musos, and has local craft beers and wine. Burgers and pizza are good value, and the sunny courtyard is ideal for a coffee. Check Facebook for what's on.

Brauhaus Frings
PUB

(☑ 09-438 4664; www.frings.co.nz; 104 Dent St; ☻ 10am-10pm) This popular pub brews its own beers, and has a terrace, wood-fired pizzas, and live music on Wednesday (jam night) and from 7pm on Friday to Sunday. It's usually closed by 10pm on weekdays, but can push on to 3am on weekends.

 ## Shopping

You can often pick up well-priced art and craft at Quarry Arts Centre (p130).

Tuatara
ARTS, CRAFTS

(☑ 09-430 0121; www.tuataradesignstore.co.nz; 29 Bank St; ☻ 9.30am-4.30pm Mon-Fri 8am-2pm Sat) Māori and Pasifika design, art and craft.

Bach
ARTS, CRAFTS

(☑ 09-438 2787; www.thebach.gallery; Town Basin; ☻ 9.30am-4.30pm) Co-op store representing over 100 Northland artisans.

ⓘ Information

DOC Office
(☑ 09-470 3300; www.doc.govt.nz; 2 South End Ave, Raumanga; ☻ 8am-4pm Mon-Fri) Located on South End Ave; turn right off SH1 around 2km south of central Whangarei.

Post Office
(16-20 Rathbone St) Centrally located.

Te Manawa Hub Information Centre
(☑ 09-430 1188; Town Basin; ☻ 9am-5pm Mon-Fri, 9am-4.30pm Sat & Sun; ☎) Central branch of the i-SITE, in the foyer of the Whangarei Art Museum.

Whangarei i-SITE
(☑ 09-438 1079; www.whangarei nz.com; 92 Otaika Rd (SH1); ☻ 9am-5pm Mon-Fri, 9am-4.30pm Sat & Sun; ☎) Information, cafe, toilets and internet access.

ⓘ Getting There & Around

AIR

Whangarei Airport (WRE; ☑ 09-436 0047; www.whangareiairport.co.nz; Handforth St) is at Onerahi, 6km southeast of the city centre. Air New Zealand flies to/from Whangarei from Auckland, and Barrier Air links Whangarei to Kaitaia. Taxis into town cost around $35. A city bus stops 400m away on Church St ($3, 18 buses on weekdays, seven on Saturday). A shuttle operated by **Whangarei Bus Services** (☑ 09-438 6005; www.whangareibus.co.nz) also meets all flights.

BUS

Bus services to Whangarei are run by InterCity (p126), whose buses stop outside the **Northland Coach & Travel Centre** (☑ 09-438 3206; 3 Bank St; ☻ 8am-5pm Mon-Fri). Buses from Naked Bus (p126) and Mana Bus (p126) stop at the Hub, in the Town Basin. West Coaster (p126) shuttles linking Whangarei with Dargaville also depart from the Hub.

TAXI

A1 Cabs (☑ 09-438 3377; www.whangarei.bluebubbletaxi.co.nz) Whangarei's leading taxi company.

Whangarei Heads

Whangarei Heads Rd winds 35km along the northern reaches of the harbour to the Heads' entrance, passing mangroves and picturesque pohutukawa-lined bays. Holiday homes, B&Bs and galleries are dotted around the water-hugging small settlements. There are great views from the top of Mt Manaia (419m), a sheer rock outcrop above McLeod Bay, but prepare for a lung- and leg-busting 1½-hour climb.

Bream Head caps off the craggy finger of land. A five-hour one-way walking track from Urquharts Bay to Ocean Beach passes through the Bream Head Scenic Reserve and lovely Smugglers Bay and Peach Cove.

Magnificent Ocean Beach stretches for miles on the other side of the headland. There's decent surfing to be had and lifeguards patrol the beach in summer. A detour from Parua Bay takes you to glorious Pataua, a small settlement that lies on a shallow inlet linked to a surf beach by a footbridge.

🏃 Activities

Bream Head Coast Walks   TRAMPING
(☎09-434 0571; www.coastwalks.nz; 2/3 nights $415/515) Enjoyed across two or three days, this self-guided walking network traverses farmland, public walkways and stunning coastal scenery. Accommodation is in a luxury lodge and excellent food is included. The lodge is used as a base for each night after undertaking a variety of walks in the area. Track notes are included and pick-ups from Whangarei can be arranged.

🛏 Sleeping & Eating

Kauri Villas   B&B $$
(☎09-436 1797; www.kaurivillas.com; 73 Owhiwa Rd, Parua Bay; d $130-175; 🛜🐕) Perched on a hill with views back over the harbour to Whangarei, this pretty blue-trimmed villa has an old-world feel, due in part to some very chintzy wallpaper. The decor's more restrained in the self-contained lodge and annexe rooms.

Ara Roa   RENTAL HOUSE $$$
(☎09-436 5028; www.araroa.nz; Harambee Rd, Taiharuru; d $295-750; 🛜🐕) This collection of five different properties dotted around a coastal peninsula ranges from the two-bedroom Guest House – with sunset views and a bush track where kiwi are often heard after dark – to the stunning one-bedroom Glass House at the very end of the peninsula. Other accommodation dubbed the Cliff House and Aria also provide sublime privacy and luxury.

Parua Bay Tavern   PUB FOOD $$
(☎09-436 5856; www.paruabaytavern.co.nz; 1034 Whangarei Heads Rd; mains $15-28; ⏱11.30am-late Tue-Sun) A magical spot on a summer's day, this friendly pub is set on a thumb-shaped peninsula, with a sole pohutukawa blazing red against the green water. Grab a seat on the deck, a cold beverage and a decent pub meal, including good burgers and pizza.

Tutukaka Coast & the Poor Knights Islands

At the Poor Knights Islands, stunning underwater scenery combines with two decommissioned navy ships that have been sunk for divers to explore.

Following the road northeast of Whangarei for 26km, you'll first come to the sweet village of Ngunguru near the mouth of a broad river. Tutukaka is 1km further on, its marina bustling with yachts, dive crews and game-fishing boats.

From Tutukaka the road heads slightly inland, popping out 10km later at the golden sands of Matapouri. A blissful 20-minute coastal walk leads from here to Whale Bay, fringed with giant pohutukawa trees.

Continuing north from Matapouri, the wide expanse of Sandy Bay, one of Northland's premier surf beaches, comes into view. Long-boarding competitions are held here in summer. The road then loops back to join SH1 at Hikurangi. A branch leading off from this road doubles back north to the coast at Whananaki, where there are more glorious beaches and the Otamure Bay DOC campsite (☎09-433 8402; www.doc.govt. nz; sites per adult/child $10/5).

🏃 Activities

Dive trips leave from Tutukaka and cater for both first-timers and experts. There are some excellent walks along the coast. Pick up a copy of the *Tutukaka Coast Tracks & Walks* brochure from the Whangarei i-SITE (p133).

Dive! Tutukaka   DIVING
(☎0800 288 882; www.diving.co.nz; Marina Rd; 2 dives incl gear $269) 🤿 Dive courses including a five-day PADI open-water course. For non-divers, the Perfect Day Ocean Cruise ($169) includes lunch and snacks, snorkelling in the marine reserve, kayaking through caves and arches, paddleboarding, and sightings of dolphins (usually) and whales (occasionally). Cruises run from November to May, departing at 11am and returning at 4pm.

Check the website for upcoming initiatives, including a six-room dive lodge, and multiday dive trips on the RV *Acheron*, a live-aboard expedition-style research vessel.

MARINE RICHES AT THE POOR KNIGHTS

Established in 1981, the Poor Knights marine reserve is rated as one of the world's top-10 diving spots. The islands are bathed in a subtropical current from the Coral Sea, so varieties of tropical and subtropical fish not seen in other NZ waters can be observed here. The waters are clear, with no sediment or pollution problems. The 40m to 60m underwater cliffs drop steeply to the sandy bottom and are a labyrinth of archways, caves, tunnels and fissures that attract a wide variety of sponges and colourful underwater vegetation. Schooling fish, eels and rays are common (including manta rays in season).

The two main volcanic islands, Tawhiti Rahi and Aorangi, were home to the Ngāti Wai tribe, but since a raiding-party massacre of 1825 the islands have been *tapu* (forbidden). Even today the public is barred from the islands, in order to protect their pristine environment. Not only do tuatara and Butler's shearwater breed here, but there are unique species of flora, such as the Poor Knights lily.

Tutukaka Surf Experience SURFING
(021 227 0072; www.tutukakasurf.co.nz; Marina Rd; 2hr lesson $75) Runs surf lessons at 9.30am most days in summer and on the weekends otherwise, operating from whichever beach has the best beginner breaks that day. Sandy Bay is usually popular. Also hires surfboards (per day $45) and stand-up paddle boards (per day $20). Trips leave from Tutukaka in a cool retro-style surf van.

🛏 Sleeping & Eating

Lupton Lodge B&B $$
(09-437 2989; www.luptonlodge.co.nz; 555 Ngunguru Rd; s $125-155, d $150-260, apt $275-385; 🅿🌐) The rooms are spacious, luxurious and full of character in this historic homestead (1896), peacefully positioned in farmland halfway between Whangarei and Ngunguru. Wander the orchard, splash around the pool or shoot some snooker in the guest lounge. Also available is a stylish apartment – for up to four people – in a renovated barn.

Marina Pizzeria PIZZA $$
(09-434 3166; www.marinapizzeria.co.nz; Tutukaka Marina; pizzas $18-21, mains $25-30; 4pm-late Fri, 10am-late Sat & Sun) Everything is homemade at this excellent takeaway and restaurant – the bread, the pizza and the ice cream. Hearty breakfasts are served from 10am on weekends. Look forward to a concise but well-chosen selection of craft beer and cider. Longer hours during summer and on public holidays.

Schnappa Rock CAFE $$
(09-434 3774; www.schnapparock.co.nz; cnr Marina Rd & Marlin Pl; breakfast & lunch $13-29, dinner $27-35, bar snacks $8-19; 8am-late, closed Sun night Jun-Sep) Filled with expectant divers in the morning and those capping off their Perfect Days in the evening, this cafe-restaurant-bar is often buzzing. Top NZ bands sometimes play on summer weekends.

ℹ Getting There & Away

Whangarei Commuter Shuttles (0800 435 355; www.coastalcommuter.co.nz; one way/return per person $25/40) Whangarei Commuter Shuttles runs a daily shuttle for travellers on dive trips, leaving Whangarei in the morning and returning in the afternoon.

Coastal Route to Russell

The quickest route to Russell takes SH1 to Opua and then crosses by ferry. The old Russell Rd is a snaking scenic and coastal route that adds about half an hour to the trip.

The turn-off is easy to miss, located 6km north of Hikurangi at Whakapara (look for the sign to Oakura). Stop after 13km at the **Gallery & Cafe** (09-433 9616; www.gallery helenabay.co.nz; 1392 Old Russell Rd, Helena Bay; mains $14-18; 10am-5pm, closed Mon & Tue winter) high above Helena Bay for fair-trade coffee, scrummy cake, amazing views, and interesting Kiwiana art and craft. Look forward to being welcomed by Wolfie and Picasso, two burly but very gentle and friendly Newfoundland dogs.

At **Helena Bay** an unsealed detour leads 8km to **Mimiwhangata Coastal Park**, which features sand dunes, pohutukawa trees, jutting headlands and picturesque beaches DOC-managed accommodation includes a simple but comfortable cottage, and a beach house (per week S613), both of which sleep seven to eight people. Basic camping (per adult/child $10/5) is available at secluded Waikahoa Bay.

Back on Russell Rd, you'll find **The Farm** (☑ 09-433 6894; www.thefarm.co.nz; 3632 Russell Rd; sites from $13, dm/s $20/30, d $80), a rough-and-ready backpackers that rambles through various buildings, including an old woolshed fitted out with a mirror ball. The rooms are basic, and the Farm is popular with trail bikers during the summer holidays; off season it's a chilled-out rustic escape. On offer are horse treks ($50, two hours), and they can also arrange kayaking and fishing.

At an intersection shortly after the Farm, Russell Rd branches off to the left for an unsealed, winding section traversing the **Ngaiotonga Scenic Reserve**. Unless you're planning to explore the forest (there are two short walks: the 20-minute **Kauri Grove Nature Walk** and the 10-minute **Twin Bole Kauri Walk**), you're better off veering right onto the sealed Rawhiti Rd.

After 2.6km, a side road leads to the **Whangaruru North Head Scenic Reserve**, which has beaches, walking tracks and fine scenery. A loop route from DOC's **Puriri Bay Campsite** (☑ 09-433 6160; www.doc.govt.nz; sites per adult/child $10/5) leads up to a ridge, offering a remarkable coastal panorama.

If you want to head directly to Russell, continue along Rawhiti Rd for another 7km before veering left onto Manawaora Rd, which skirts a succession of tiny idyllic bays before reconnecting with Russell Rd.

Otherwise take a detour to isolated **Rawhiti**, a small Ngāpuhi settlement where life still revolves around the *marae* (temple). Rawhiti is the starting point for the tramp to Cape Brett, a tiring eight-hour, 16.3km walk to the top of the peninsula, where overnight stays are possible in DOC's **Cape Brett Hut** (dm $15). The hut must be booked in advance. An access fee is charged for crossing private land (adult/child $30/15), which you can pay at the

Bay of Islands i-SITE (p147). Another option is to take a water taxi to Cape Brett lighthouse from Russell or Paihia and walk back.

A shorter one-hour walk leads through Māori land and the **Whangamumu Scenic Reserve** to **Whangamumu Harbour**. There are more than 40 ancient Māori sites on the peninsula and the remains of an unusual whaling station.

BAY OF ISLANDS

The Bay of Islands ranks as one of NZ's top tourist drawcards, and the turquoise waters of the bay are punctuated by around 150 undeveloped islands. In particular, Paihia has excellent budget accommodation, and boat trips and water sports are very popular.

The Bay of Islands is also a place of enormous historical significance. Māori knew it as Pewhairangi and settled here early in their migrations. As the site of NZ's first permanent British settlement (at Russell), it is the birthplace of European colonisation in the country. It was here that the Treaty of Waitangi was drawn up and first signed in 1840; the treaty remains the linchpin of race relations in NZ today.

 Activities

The Bay of Islands offers some fine subtropical diving, made even better by the sinking of the 113m navy frigate HMNZS *Canterbury* in Deep Water Cove near Cape Brett. Local operators also head to the wreck of the *Rainbow Warrior* off the Cavalli Islands, about an hour north of Paihia by boat. Both offer a colourful feast of pink anemones, yellow sponges and abundant fish life.

There are plenty of opportunities for kayaking or sailing around the bay, either on a

---

ℹ SWIMMING WITH DOLPHINS

Cruises offering the opportunity to interact with wild dolphins operate year-round. They have a high success rate and you're generally offered a free trip if dolphins aren't sighted. Dolphin swims are subject to weather and sea conditions, with restrictions if calves are present.

It's totally up to the dolphins as to whether they choose to swim with you or not. You'll need to be a strong swimmer to keep abreast with them – even when they're humouring you by cruising along at half-speed. Those concerned with the welfare of dolphins should be aware that swimming with dolphins in the wild is considered by some to be disruptive to the habitat and behaviour of the animals.

Only three operators are licensed for dolphin swimming: Explore NZ (p145), Fullers Great Sights (p145) and the yacht Carino (p138). All pay a portion of the cost towards marine research, via DOC.

Bay of Islands

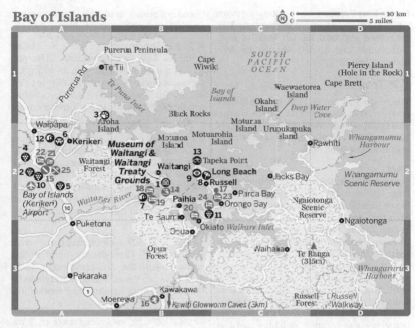

Bay of Islands

guided tour or by renting and going it alone. Cruises and dolphin swimming are also available. Note that some boat companies do not operate during the winter months.

Northland Paddleboarding WATER SPORTS
(📞 027 777 4135; www.northlandpaddleboarding. co.nz; beginner lessons per hour $60) Lessons and guided cruises.

Horse Trek'n HORSE RIDING
(📞 027 233 3490; www.horsetrekn.co.nz; 2hr ride $120) Through the Waitangi Forest.

Great Escape Yacht Charters SAILING
(📞 09-402 7143; www.greatescape.co.nz) Offers introductory sailing lessons (two-day course $445) and longer options.

Flying Kiwi Parasail ADVENTURE SPORTS

(✆ 0800 359 691; www.parasailnz.com; solo $115, per tandem adult/child $95/69) Departs from both Paihia and Russell wharves for NZ's highest parasail (1200ft).

☞ Tours

Where do you start? First by praying for good weather, as torrential rain or choppy seas could exclude some options. The Bay of Islands i-SITE (p147) and accommodation operators can book tours.

Boat

Options include sailing boats, jetboats and large launches. Boats leave from either Paihia or Russell, calling into the other town as their first stop.

One of the bay's most striking islands is **Piercy Island (Motukokako)** off Cape Brett, at the bay's eastern edge. This steep-walled rock fortress features a vast natural arch – the famous **Hole in the Rock**. Provided the conditions are right, most boat tours will pass right through the heart of the island. En route it's likely you'll encounter bottlenose and common dolphins, and you may see orcas, other whales and penguins.

The best way to explore the bay is under sail. Either help crew the boat (no experience required), or just spend the afternoon

---

POU HERENGA TAI TWIN COAST CYCLE TRAIL

Planned to be completed by late 2016, this cycle route stretches from the Bay of Islands clear across the country to the Hokianga Harbour. OK, so that's only 84km, but as far as we're concerned that still gives you boasting rights when you get home. The complete route will travel from Opua via Kawakawa, Ngawha Springs, Kaikohe and finish up in Horeke.

At the time of research, around half of the total distance had been completed, and most popular was a 20km section from **Kaikohe** to **Okaihau**, starting west of Kaikohe and passing through an abandoned rail tunnel before skirting **Lake Omapere**. For maps, tips and updates on the progress of the trail, see www.nzcycletrail.com. Visit www.toptrail.co.nz for details of bike hire and shuttle transport, including from Paihia if you're staying in the Bay of Islands.

---

island-hopping, sunbathing, swimming, snorkelling, kayaking and fishing.

R Tucker Thompson SAILING

(✆ 09-402 8430; www.tucker.co.nz; ☻ Nov-Apr) Run by a charitable trust with an education focus, the *Tucker* is a majestic tall ship offering day sails (adult/child $145/73, including a barbecue lunch) and late-afternoon cruises (adult/child $65/33).

Carino SAILING

(✆ 09-402 8040; www.sailingdolphins.co.nz; adult/child $119/74) ✎ This 50ft catamaran is licensed by NZ's Department of Conservation (DOC) for swimming with dolphins and it adheres to NZ's Marine Mammal Protection Act of 1978. A barbecue lunch is available for $6.

Ecocruz SAILING

(✆ 0800 432 627; www.ecocruz.co.nz; dm/d $650/1500) ✎ Three-day/two-night sailing cruise aboard the 72ft ocean-going yacht *Manawanui*. Prices include accommodation, food, fishing, kayaking and snorkelling.

Mack Attack BOAT TOUR

(✆ 0800 622 528; www.mackattack.co.nz; 9 Williams Rd, Paihia; adult/child $99/49) An exhilarating, high-speed 1½-hour jetboat trip to the Hole in the Rock. Another option is an Inner Bay of Islands tour (adult/child $85/49).

Rock OVERNIGHT CRUISE

(✆ 0800 762 527; www.rocktheboat.co.nz; dm/d/f from $238/440/772) ✎ A former vehicle ferry that's now a floating hostel, the *Rock* has dorms, private rooms and a bar. The cruise departs at 5pm and includes a barbecue and seafood dinner with live music, then time spent island-hopping, fishing, kayaking, snorkelling and swimming the following day. Day cruises only are $108 per person.

Phantom SAILING

(✆ 0800 224 421; www.yachtphantom.com; adult/child $110/55) A fast 50ft racing sloop, known for its wonderful food. BYO (bring your own) beer and wine is allowed.

Tango Jet Ski & Island Boat Tours BOAT TOUR

(✆ 0800 253 8754; www.tangojetskitours.co.nz; boat tours/jet ski tours from $65/180) Zip around the bay in a speedy inflatable boat or skipper your own jet ski. Jet skis can take two people.

Bus

It's cheaper and quicker to take trips to Cape Reinga from Ahipara, Kaitaia or Doubtless Bay, but if you're short on time, several long day trips (10 to 12 hours) leave from the Bay of Islands. They all drive one way along Ninety Mile Beach, stopping to sandboard on the dunes.

Fullers Great Sights (p145) runs regular bus tours and backpacker-oriented versions, both stopping at Puketi Forest. The standard, child-friendly version (adult/child $149/75) includes an optional lunch at Pukenui. It also runs Awesome NZ (09-0800 653 339; www.awesomenz.com; tour $129) tours, with louder music, more time sandboarding, and stops to chuck a frisbee around at Tapotupotu Bay and devour fish and chips at Mangonui.

Explore NZ's (p145) Dune Rider (adult/child $150/110) also samples Mangonui's feted fish and chips and includes a stop at Gumdiggers Park.

Transport options to the Hokianga and Waipoua Forest are limited, so a day trip makes sense if you don't have your own car or if you're time starved. Fullers' Discover Hokianga (adult/child $118/59) takes in Tane Mahuta and Wairere Boulders on an eight-hour tour with local Māori guides.

Other Tours

Salt Air SCENIC FLIGHTS
(09-402 8338; www.saltair.co.nz; Marsden Rd, Paihia) Scenic flights include a five-hour light aircraft and 4WD tour to Cape Reinga and Ninety Mile Beach ($425), and helicopter flights out to the Hole in the Rock ($250). Another tour even lands on the famed island (from $399) where visitors are welcomed by a local Māori guide.

✦ Festivals & Events

Country Rock Festival MUSIC
(09-404 1063; www.country-rock.co.nz; festival pass $50; ☺May) Second weekend in May.

Russell Birdman SPORTS
(www.russellbirdman.co.nz; ☺Jul) Lunatics with various flying contraptions jump off Russell wharf into frigid waters.

Jazz & Blues Festival MUSIC
(09-404 1063; www.jazz-blues.co.nz; festival pass $50; ☺Aug) Second weekend in August.

Weekend Coastal Classic SPORTS
(021 521 013; www.coastalclassic.co.nz; ☺Oct) NZ's largest yacht race, from Auckland to the Bay of Islands, held on Labour Weekend in October.

ℹ Getting There & Away

AIR

Air New Zealand (0800 737 000; www.air newzealand.co.nz) Daily flights from Auckland to Whangarei and Kerikeri.

Barrier Air (09-275 9120, 0800 900 600; www.barrierair.kiwi) Links Kaitaia to Whangarei and Auckland.

BUS

Bus companies including InterCity (p126), Naked Bus (p126) and Mana Bus (p126) all make stops in key Bay of Islands centres such as Paihia and Kerikeri.

ABC Shuttles & Tours (022 025 0800; www.abcshuttle.co.nz; tours from $40) Airport transfers to/from Kerikeri, sightseeing around the Bay of Islands, and trips from Paihia to Kawakawa for the Kawiti Glowworm Caves and the Hundertwasser toilets.

Russell

POP 816

Although it was once known as 'the hellhole of the Pacific', those coming to Russell for debauchery will be sadly disappointed: they've missed the orgies on the beach by 180 years. Instead they'll find a historic town with gift shops and B&Bs, and, in summer, you can rent kayaks and dinghies along the Strand.

Before it was known as a hellhole, or even as Russell, it was Kororareka (Sweet Penguin), a fortified Ngāpuhi village. In the early 19th century the tribe permitted it to become Aotearoa's first European settlement. It quickly became a magnet for rough elements, such as fleeing convicts, whalers and drunken sailors. By the 1830s dozens of whaling ships at a time were anchored in the harbour. Charles Darwin described it in 1835 as full of 'the refuse of society'.

In 1830 the settlement was the scene of the so-called Girls' War, when two pairs of Māori women were vying for the attention of a whaling captain called Brind. A chance meeting between the rivals on the beach led to verbal abuse and fighting. This minor conflict quickly escalated as family members rallied around to avenge the insult and harm done to their respective relatives. Hundreds were killed and injured over a two-week period before missionaries managed to broker a peace agreement.

After the signing of the Treaty of Waitangi in 1840, Okiato (where the car ferry now leaves from) was the residence of the

Russell

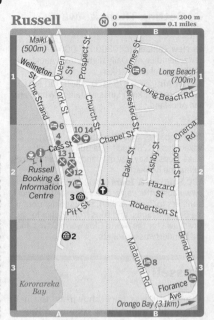

Russell

governor and the temporary capital. The capital was officially moved to Auckland in 1841 and Okiato, which was by then known as Russell, was eventually abandoned. The name Russell ultimately replaced Kororareka.

◉ Sights

Pompallier Mission HISTORIC BUILDING
(☑09-403 9015; www.pompallier.co.nz; The Strand; tours adult/child $10/free; ◷10am-4pm) Built in 1842 to house the Catholic mission's printing press, this rammed-earth building is the mission's last remaining building in the western Pacific. A staggering 40,000 books were printed here in Māori. In the 1870s it was converted into a private home, but it is now restored to its original state, complete with tannery and printing workshop.

Christ Church CHURCH
(Church St) English naturalist Charles Darwin made a donation towards the cost of building the country's oldest church (1836). The graveyard's biggest memorial commemorates Tamati Waka Nene, a powerful Ngāpuhi chief from the Hokianga who sided against Hone Heke in the Northland War. The church's exterior has musket and cannonball holes dating from the 1845 battle.

Maiki HILL
(Flagstaff Rd) Overlooking Russell, this is the hill where Hone Heke chopped down the flagpole four times. You can drive up, but the view justifies a climb. Take the track west from the boat ramp along the beach at low tide, or head up Wellington St.

Russell Museum MUSEUM
(☑09-403 7701; www.russellmuseum.org.nz; 2 York St; adult/child $10/3; ◷10am-4pm) This small, modern museum has a well-presented Māori section, a large 1:5-scale model of Captain Cook's *Endeavour*, and a 10-minute video on the town's history.

Omata Estate WINERY
(☑09-403 8007; www.omata.co.nz; Aucks Rd; ◷tastings & food 10am-5pm Nov-Mar, tastings only 11am-5pm Wed-Sun Apr-Oct) With a growing reputation for red wines – especially its old-growth syrah – Omata Estate is one of Northland's finest wineries. To complement the tastings and stunning sea views, shared platters ($40) are available. Phone ahead from April to October to confirm it's open. The winery is on the road from Russell to the car ferry at Okiato.

☞ Tours

Russell Nature Walks ECOTOUR
(☑027 908 2334; www.russellnaturewalks.co.nz; 6080 Russell Whakapara Rd; day walk adult/child $38/20, night walk $45/20; ◷day walk 10am, night walk varies depending on sunset) Located in pri-

vately owned native forest 2.5km south of Russell, guided day and night tours provide the opportunity to see native birds, including the weka and tui, and insects such as the weta. Glow-worms softly illuminate night tours, and after dark there's the opportunity to hear (and very occasionally see) NZ's national bird, the kiwi. Walks last 1½ to two hours.

Owners Eion and Lisette also run a kiwi nesting program.

Russell Mini Tours BUS TOUR
(☑ 09-403 7866; www.russellminitours.com; cnr The Strand & Cass St; adult/child $29/15; ☺ tours 11am, 1pm, 2pm & 3pm, also 10am & 4pm Oct-Apr) Minibus tour around historic Russell with commentary.

✦ Festivals & Events

Tall Ship Race SPORTS
(☺ Jan) Held in Russell on the first Saturday after New Year's Day.

🛏 Sleeping

Wainui HOSTEL $
(☑ 09-403 8278; www.wainuilodge-russell-nz.com; 92d Te Wahapu Rd; dm/s/d $28/53/65; 🖥) Hard to find but worth the effort, this modern bush retreat with direct beach access has only two rooms that share a pleasant communal space. It's 5km from Russell on the way to the car ferry. Take Te Wahapu Rd and then turn right into Waiaruhe Way.

Russell-Orongo Bay Holiday Park HOLIDAY PARK $
(☑ 09-403 7704; www.russellaccommodation. co.nz; 5960 Russell Rd; unpowered/powered sites $42/46, teepee $80-90, cabins & units $90-165; @ 🖥 ⛱) ✿ Surrounded by 14 acres studded with native forest and birdlife, this relaxed holiday park is around 3km from Russell after departing the ferry from Opua to Okiato. The wide range of accommodation includes a quirky teepee and comfortable self-contained units.

Ferry Landing Backpackers HOSTEL $
(☑ 09-403 7985; www.ferrylanding-russell.co.nz; 395 Aucks Rd, Okiato Pt; dm/s/d $30/60/80; @ 🖥) More like a homestay than a hostel, with only two rooms on offer within the owners' house. It sits on the hill directly above the ferry landing in Okiato – you'll need a car to get here.

Russell Top 10 HOLIDAY PARK $
(☑ 09-403 7826; www.russelltop10.co.nz; 1 James St; sites/cabins/units from $45/80/160; @ 🖥) ✿ This leafy park has a small store, good facilities, wonderful hydrangeas, tidy cabins and nice units. Showers are clean, but metered.

Duke of Marlborough HISTORIC HOTEL $$
(☑ 09-403 7829; www.theduke.co.nz; 35 The Strand; r $165-360; 🖥) Holding NZ's oldest pub licence, the Duke boasts about 'serving rascals and reprobates since 1827', although the building has burnt down twice since then. The upstairs accommodation ranges from small, bright rooms in a 1930s extension, to snazzy, spacious doubles facing the water.

Russell Motel MOTEL $$
(☑ 09-403 7854; www.motelrussell.co.nz; 16 Matauwhi Rd; units $135-210; 🖥 ⛱) Sitting amid well-tended gardens, this old-fashioned motel offers a good range of units and a kidney-shaped pool that the kids will love. The studios are a little dark, but you really can't quibble for this price in central Russell.

Arcadia Lodge B&B $$$
(☑ 09-403 7756; www.arcadialodge.co.nz; 10 Florance Ave; d $215-300; 🖥) ✿ The characterful rooms of this 1890 hillside house are decked out with interesting antiques and fine linen, while the breakfast is probably the best you'll eat in town – organic, delicious and complemented by spectacular views from the deck.

Hananui Lodge & Apartments MOTEL $$$
(☑ 09-403 7875; www.hananui.co.nz; 4 York St; units $150-270; 🖥) Choose between sparkling motel-style units in the trim waterside lodge or apartments in the newer block across the road. Pick of the bunch are the upstairs waterfront units with views straight over the beach.

🍴 Eating

Hell Hole CAFE $
(☑ 022 604 1374; www.facebook.com/hellholecoffee; 19 York St; snacks $6-12; ☺ 7am-5pm mid-Dec-Feb, 8am-3pm Mar, Apr & Oct–mid-Dec) Bagels, baguettes and croissants all feature with the best coffee in town at this compact spot one block back from the waterfront. Beans are locally roasted and organic soft drinks and artisan ice blocks all combine to make Hell Hole a hugely popular place, especially during Russell's peak season from mid-December to February.

★ **Gables** MODERN NZ **$$**
(☑ 09-403 7670; www.thegablesrestaurant.co.nz; 19 The Strand; lunch $23-29, dinner $27-34; ☺ noon-3pm Fri-Mon, from 6pm Thu-Mon) Serving an imaginative take on Kiwi classics (lamb, venison, seafood), the Gables occupies an 1847 building on the waterfront, built using whale vertebrae for foundations. Ask for a table by the windows for maritime views and look forward to local produce, including oysters and cheese. Cocktails are summery and there's a decent selection of NZ beer and wine.

Waterfront CAFE **$$**
(www.waterfrontcafe.co.nz; 23 The Strand; mains $11-20; ☺ 8am-4pm; 🐾) Your best bet for a big breakfast and the first coffee of the day is this spot with brilliant harbour views. Secure a seat at one of the absolute waterfront tables and keep an eye out for dolphins showing off around the nearby wharf.

Hone's Garden PIZZA **$$**
(☑ 022 466 3710; www.facebook.com/hones garden; York St; pizza $18-25, wraps & salads $14-16; ☺ noon-late summer only) Head out to Hone's pebbled courtyard for wood-fired pizza (with 11 different varieties), cold craft beer on tap and a thoroughly easygoing Kiwi vibe. An expanded menu now also features tasty wraps and healthy salads. Antipasto platters ($29 to $45) are good for groups and indecisive diners.

Duke PUB FOOD **$$**
(☑ 09-403 7829; www.theduke.co.nz; 35 The Strand; lunch $15-25, dinner $25-38; ☺ 11am-late) There's no better spot in Russell to while away a few hours, glass in hand, than the Duke's sunny deck. Thankfully the upmarket bistro food matches the views, plus there's an excellent wine list and a great selection of NZ craft beers.

🍷 Drinking & Nightlife

Duke of Marlborough Tavern PUB
(☑ 09-403 7831; www.duketavern.co.nz; 19 York St; ☺ noon-late) A cool, cosy tavern with pool tables and a local's vibe. Pub quiz on a Tuesday night (from 7pm) is always good fun, and there are well-priced burgers and fish and chips.

❶ Information

Russell Booking & Information Centre (☑ 09-403 8020, 0800 633 255; www.russell info.co.nz; Russell Pier; ☺ 8am-5pm, extended hours summer) Loads of ideas for how to explore the area.

❶ Getting There & Away

The quickest way to reach Russell by car is via the car ferry (car/motorcycle/passenger $11/5.50/1), which runs every 10 minutes from Opua (5km from Paihia) to Okiato (8km from Russell), between 6.40am and 10pm. Buy your tickets on board. Note that only cash is accepted for tickets. If you're travelling from the south, a scenic alternative is the coastal route via Russell Rd.

On foot, the easiest way to reach Russell is on a passenger ferry from Paihia (adult/child one way $7/3, return $12/6). They run from 7am to 7pm (until 10pm October to May), generally every 20 minutes, but hourly in the evenings. Buy your tickets on board or at the i-SITE (p147) in Paihia.

Paihia & Waitangi

POP 1800

The birthplace of NZ (as opposed to Aotearoa), Waitangi inhabits a special, somewhat complex place in the national psyche – aptly demonstrated by the mixture of celebration, commemoration, protest and apathy that accompanies the nation's birthday (Waitangi Day, 6 February).

It was here that the long-neglected and much-contested Treaty of Waitangi was first signed between Māori chiefs and the British Crown, establishing British sovereignty or something a bit like it, depending on whether you're reading the English or Māori version of the document. If you're interested in coming to grips with NZ's history and race relations, this is the place to start.

Joined to Waitangi by a bridge, Paihia would be a fairly nondescript coastal town if it wasn't the main entry point to the Bay of Islands. If you're not on a tight budget, catch a ferry to Russell, which is far nicer.

There are some good walks in the area, including an easy 5km track that follows the coast from Opua to Paihia.

◉ Sights

★ **Waitangi Treaty Grounds** HISTORIC SITE
(☑ 09-402 7437; www.waitangi.org.nz; 1 Tau Henare Dr; adult/child $40/20; ☺ 9am-5pm Mar-24 Dec, 9am-6pm 26 Dec-Feb) 🏛 Occupying a headland draped in lawns and bush, this is NZ's most significant historic site. Here, on 6 February 1840, the first 43 Māori chiefs, after much discussion, signed the Treaty of Waitangi with the British Crown; eventually, over 500 chiefs would sign it. Admission incorporates entry to the Treaty Grounds,

a guided tour and cultural performance, and also entry to the new Museum of Waitangi (p143). Admission for NZ residents is $20 upon presentation of a passport or driver's licence.

The importance of the treaty is well understood by a NZ audience, but visitors might find it surprising that there's not more information displayed here about the role it has played in the nation's history: the long litany of breaches by the Crown, the wars and land confiscations that followed, and the protest movement that led to the current process of redress for historic injustices.

The Treaty House was built in 1833 as the four-room home of British resident James Busby. It's preserved as a memorial and museum containing displays, including a copy of the treaty. Just across the lawn, the magnificently detailed *whare runanga* (meeting house) was completed in 1940 to mark the centenary of the treaty. The fine carvings represent the major Māori tribes. Near the cove is the 35m *waka taua* (war canoe), also built for the centenary. A photographic exhibit details how it was fashioned from gigantic kauri logs.

★ **Museum of Waitangi**   MUSEUM
(☑09-402 7437; www.waitangi.org.nz; 1 Tau Henare Dr; adult/child $40/20; ⊗9am-5pm Mar-24 Dec, 9am-6pm 26 Dec-Feb) The new Museum of Waitangi is a modern and comprehensive showcase of the role of the Treaty of Waitan-gi in the past, present and future of New Zealand. The second storey is comprised of the Ko Waitangi Tēnei (This is Waitangi) exhibition and the ground floor features special temporary exhibitions and an education centre. Many *taonga* (treasures) associated with Waitangi were previously scattered around NZ, and this excellent museum is now a safe haven for a number of key historical items.

Admission incorporates entry to the Waitangi Treaty Grounds (p142), a guided tour and a cultural performance.

Opua Forest   FOREST
Just behind Paihia, this regenerating forest has walking trails ranging from 10 minutes to five hours. A few large trees have escaped axe and fire, including some big kauri. Walk up from School Rd for about 30 minutes to good lookouts. Information on Opua Forest walks is available from the i-SITE. Drive into the forest by taking Oromahoe Rd west from Opua.

St Paul's Church   CHURCH
(Marsden Rd) The characterful St Paul's was constructed of Kawakawa stone in 1925, and stands on the site of NZ's first church, a simple *raupo* (bulrush) hut erected in 1823. Look for the native birds in the stained glass above the altar – the kotare (kingfisher) represents Jesus (the king plus 'fisher of men'), while the tui (parson bird) and kereru (wood

---

HONE HEKE & THE NORTHLAND WAR

Just five years after he had been the first signatory to the Treaty of Waitangi, Ngāpuhi chief Hone Heke was so disaffected that he planned to chop down Kororareka's flagstaff, a symbol of British authority, for the fourth time. Governor FitzRoy was determined not to let that happen and garrisoned the town with soldiers and marines.

On 11 March 1845 the Ngāpuhi staged a diversionary siege of the town. It was a great tactical success, with Chief Kawiti attacking from the south and another party attacking from Long Beach. While the troops rushed off to protect the township, Hone Heke felled the Union Jack on Maiki (Flagstaff Hill) for the fourth and final time. The British were forced to evacuate to ships lying at anchor. The captain of the HMS *Hazard* was wounded severely in the battle and his replacement ordered the ships' cannons to be fired on the town; most of the buildings were razed. The first of the New Zealand Wars had begun.

In the months that followed, British troops (united with Hokianga-based Ngāpuhi) fought Heke and Kawiti in several battles. During this time the modern *pa* (fortified village) was born, effectively the world's first sophisticated system of trench warfare. It's worth stopping at **Ruapekapeka Pa Historic Reserve** (Ruapekapeka Rd), off SH1 south of Kawakawa, to see how impressive these fortifications were. Here you can wander the site of the last battle of the Northland War, brought to life through detailed information boards. Eventually Heke, Kawiti and George Grey (the new governor) made their peace, with no side the clear winner.

Paihia

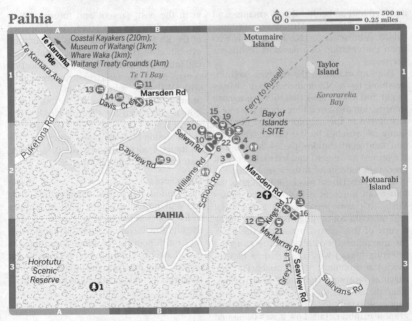

Paihia

◉ Sights
| 1 Opua Forest | A3 |
| 2 St Paul's Church | C2 |

➕ Activities, Courses & Tours
3 Explore NZ	C2
4 Fullers Great Sights	C2
5 Island Kayaks & Bay Beach Hire	C2
6 Mack Attack	C2
7 Paihia Dive	C2
8 Salt Air	C2

🛏 Sleeping
9 Allegra House	B2
10 Haka Lodge	C2
11 Paihia Beach Resort & Spa	B1

12 Peppertree Lodge	C3
13 Seabeds	A1
14 Seaspray Suites	B1

✴ Eating
15 35 Degrees South	C1
16 Alfresco's	C2
17 El Cafe	C2
Paihia Farmers Market	(see 3)
18 Provenir	B1

◉ Drinking & Nightlife
19 Alongside	C2
20 Bay of Islands Swordfish Club	B2
21 Pipi Patch Bar	C3
22 Sauce	C2

pigeon) portray the personalities of the Williams brothers (one scholarly, one forceful), who set up the mission station here.

Haruru Falls WATERFALL
(Haruru Falls Rd) A walking track (one way 1½ hours, 5km) leads from the Treaty Grounds along the Waitangi River to these attractive horseshoe falls. Part of the path follows a boardwalk through the mangroves. Otherwise you can drive here, turning right off Puketona Rd onto Haruru Falls Rd.

🏃 Activities

Coastal Kayakers KAYAKING
(☑ 0800 334 661; www.coastalkayakers.co.nz; Te Karuwha Pde, Paihia) Runs guided tours (half-/full day $89/139, minimum two people) and multiday adventures. Kayaks (half-/full day $40/50) can also be rented for independent exploration.

**Island Kayaks
& Bay Beach Hire** KAYAKING, BOATING
(☑ 09-402 6078; www.baybeachhire.co.nz; Marsden Rd, Paihia; half-day kayaking tour $79; ⊙ 9am-

5.30pm) Hires kayaks (from $15 per hour), sailing catamarans ($50 first hour, $40 per additional), motor boats ($85 first hour, $25 per additional), mountain bikes ($35 per day), boogie boards ($25 per day), fishing rods ($10 per day), wetsuits and snorkelling gear (both $20 per day).

Paihia Dive   DIVING
(☑ 0800 107 551, 09-402 7551; www.divenz.com; Williams Rd, Paihia; dives from $239) Combined reef and wreck trips to either the *Canterbury* or the *Rainbow Warrior*.

Tours

Fullers Great Sights   CRUISE
(☑ 0800 653 339; www.dolphincruises.co.nz; Paihia Wharf) The four-hour Dolphin Cruise (adult/child $105/53) departs Paihia daily at 9am and 1.30pm, offering the chance to see dolphins en route to the Hole in the Rock, and stopping at Urupukapuka Island on the way back. The four-hour Dolphin Eco Experience (adult/child $117/58, departs 8am and 12.30pm) is focused on finding dolphins to swim with.

The full-day Cream Trip (adult/child $127/64) follows the mail route around the bay and includes dolphin swimming, too. Boats stop at Russell wharf for pick-ups on all the above trips.

Explore NZ   CRUISE, SAILING
(☑ 09-402 8234; www.explorenz.co.nz cnr Marsden & Williams Rds, Paihia) The four-hour Swim with the Dolphins Cruise (adult/child $95/50, additional $15 to swim) departs Paihia at 8am and 12.30pm from November to April. The four-hour Discover the Bay Cruise (adult/child $115/65) departs at 9am and 1.30pm, heading to the Hole in the Rock and stopping at Urupukapuka Island. There are also combo options available including a bus trip along Ninety Mile Beach. Explore NZ is licensed by NZ's Department of Conservation to run dolphin tours.

Festivals & Events

Waitangi Day   CULTURAL
(☺ Feb) Various ceremonial events at Waitangi on 6 February.

Bay of Islands Food
& Wine Festival   FOOD, WINE
(www.paihianz.co.nz/it_festival; adult/child $45/15; ☺ 11am-6pm) Food, wine and local music in Paihia on the last Saturday of October.

Sleeping

If your budget is more flexible, Russell has more atmosphere, but Paihia is more convenient and has motels, apartments and B&Bs on the waterfront and around the surrounding hills. Paihia has an excellent range of hostels, and Kings Rd is the main 'backpackers' row'.

Haka Lodge   HOSTEL $
(☑ 09-402 5637; www.hakalodge.com; 76 Marsden Rd; dm $29-31 d & tw $89; ☞) Located above good restaurants and across the road from the wharf, it's impossible to be more central than Haka Lodge. Paihia's newest hostel also scores points for its modern and colourful decor, and excellent shared spaces with huge flat-screen TVs and unlimited wi-fi access. Accommodation ranges from excellent dorms to private rooms.

Seabeds   HOSTEL $
(☑ 09-402 5567; www.seabeds.co.nz; 46 Davis Cres; dm/s/d/apt $28/68/85/95; @ ☞) Offering comfortable, friendly, stylish budget digs in a converted motel, Seabeds is one of Paihia's best hostels. Little design touches give it a stylish ambience, and it's in a quieter location than most of Paihia's more social hostels along Kings Rd.

Bay of Islands Holiday Park   HOLIDAY PARK $
(☑ 09-402 7646; www.bayofislandsholidaypark. co.nz; 678 Puketona Rd; sites/units from $38/74; @ ☞ ☰) Under tall trees by a set of shallow rapids on the Waitangi River, 7km down Puketona Rd, this wonderful holiday park has excellent cabins, units and shady campsites.

Peppertree Lodge   HOSTEL $
(☑ 09-402 6122; www.peppertree.co.nz; 15 Kings Rd; dm $26-29, r $76-90, unit $113; @ ☞) Simple, clean rooms with high ceilings and good linen, plus bikes, racquets, kayaks and two barbecues for guests' use, making this a sociable choice. There's a separate self-contained studio unit.

Seaspray Suites   BOUTIQUE HOTEL $$
(☑ 09-402 0013; www.seaspray.co.nz; 138 Marsden Rd; d from $210; ☞) One of the best of the phalanx of motels and apartments lining the Paihia waterfront, Seaspray Suites has chic and modern self-contained one- and two-bedroom options, some with sea-view balconies or private courtyards.

Baystay B&B   B&B $$
(☑ 09-402 7511; www.baystay.co.nz; 93a Yorke Rd, Haruru Falls; r $140-175; @ ☞) Enjoy valley views

from the spa pool of this slick, gay-friendly establishment. Yorke Rd is off Puketona Rd, just before the falls. Minimum stay of two nights; no children under 12 years.

Cook's Lookout
MOTEL $$

(☑09-402 7409; www.cookslookout.co.nz; Causeway Rd; r $175, apt $295; ☜☒) Cook's Lookout is an old-fashioned motel with friendly owners, breathtaking views and a solar-heated swimming pool. Take Puketona Rd towards Haruru Falls, turn right into Yorke Rd and then take the second right.

Paihia Beach Resort & Spa
APARTMENT $$$

(☑0800 870 111; 130 Marsden Rd; d $555-664; ☜☒) Stylish and modern studio apartments feature at this recently renovated accommodation with all suites enjoying sea views. An elegant downstairs piazza includes a swimming pool, and luxury spa services are also available. The resort's Provenir restaurant is one of Paihia's best spots for fine dining. Check online for good-value packages and last-minute discounts.

Allegra House
B&B $$$

(☑09-402 7932; www.allegra.co.nz; 39 Bayview Rd; r $245-270, apt $285; ☜) Offering quite astonishing views of the bay from an eyrie high above the township, Allegra has three handsome B&B rooms and a spacious self-contained apartment.

✕ Eating

El Cafe
CAFE, SOUTH AMERICAN $

(☑09-402 7637; www.facebook.com/elcafepaihia; 2 Kings Rd; snacks & mains $5-15; ☺8am-4pm Tue-Thu, to 9.30pm Fri-Sun; ☜) Excellent Chilean-owned cafe with the best coffee in town and terrific breakfast burritos, tacos and baked egg dishes, such as spicy Huevos Rancheros. Say *hola* to owner Javier for us. His Cuban pulled-pork sandwich is truly a wonderful thing. The fruit smoothies are also great on a warm Bay of Islands day.

Paihia Farmers Market
MARKET $

(www.bayofislandsfarmersmarket.org.nz; Village Green; ☺2-5.30pm Thu) Stock up on local fruit, vegetables, pickles, preserves, honey, fish, smallgoods, eggs, cheese, bread, wine and oil, straight from the producer.

35 Degrees South
SEAFOOD $$

(☑09-402 6220; www.35south.co.nz; 69 Marsden Rd; shared plates $15-18, mains $28-26; ☺11.30am-late) Service can be a bit disorganised, but you can't beat the over-the-water location in central Paihia. The menu is at its best with local oysters from nearby Orongo Bay, local seafood and the shared small plates. Try the salt-and-pepper squid and pan-fried scallops, and maybe share a dessert of Dutch raisin doughnuts.

Alfresco's
PUB FOOD $$

(☑09-402 6797; www.alfrescosrestaurantpaihia. com; 6 Marsden Rd; breakfast & lunch $12-20, dinner $18-33; ☺8am-late) Locals flock to this casual restaurant-cafe-bar for great food – including lots of local seafood – and reasonable prices. Settle in for live music from 3pm to 6pm every Sunday afternoon. There's happy-hour bar prices from 3pm to 6pm every day, too.

Provenir
MODERN NZ $$$

(☑09-402 0111; www.paihiabeach.co.nz; 130 Marsden Rd, Paihia Beach Resort & Spa; mains $32-34; ☺8-10.30am & 6pm-late) A concise seasonal menu of main dishes showcases local seafood and regional NZ produce, and subtle Asian influences underpin smaller plates, including scallops and plump oysters from nearby Orongo Bay. The wine list is one of Northland's best, and during summer dining poolside is where you want to be.

Provenir is also open for 'Revive at Five' from 5pm to 7pm for a combination of classy bar snacks, beer and wine, all at a well-priced $8 each.

🍷 Drinking & Nightlife

God bless backpackers: they certainly keep the bars buzzing. There are plenty of places along Kings Rd and in the town centre to explore, so don't feel hemmed in by our list.

Alongside
BAR

(☑09-402 6220; www.alongside35.co.nz; 69 Marsden Rd; ☺8am-10pm) Quite possibly the biggest deck in all of Northland extends over the water, and a versatile approach to entertaining begins with coffee and bagels for breakfast before the inevitable transformation of Alongside into a very enjoyable bar. There's good bar snacks and meals on offer, and lots of comfy lounges are ready for conversations fuelled by cocktails or cold beer.

Or you could just look out at the great ocean vistas...

Sauce
CRAFT BEER

(☑09-402 7590; www.facebook.com/saucepizza andcraft; Marsden Rd; ☺11am-10pm) Design-your-own pizzas (pizza $12 to $22) plus the added attraction of excellent craft beer on

HOLD ON UNTIL KAWAKAWA

Kawakawa is just an ordinary Kiwi town, located on SH1 south of Paihia, but the public toilets (60 Gillies St) are anything but. They were designed by Austrian-born artist and eco-architect Friecensreich Hundertwasser, who lived near Kawakawa in an isolated house without electricity from 1973 until his death in 2000. The most photographed toilets in NZ are typical Hundertwasser – lots of organic wavy lines decorated with ceramic mosaics and brightly coloured bottles, and with grass and plants on the roof. Other examples of his work can be seen in Vienna and Osaka.

Kawakawa also has a railway line running down the main street. Take a 45-minute spin pulled by **Gabriel the Steam Engine** (☑09-404 0684; www.bayofislandsvintagerailway. org.nz; adult/child $20/5; ⊘10.45am, noon, 1.15pm, 2.30pm Fri-Sun, daily school holidays).

South of town, a signpost from SH1 points to **Kawiti Glowworm Caves** (☑09-404 0583; www.kawiticaves.co.nz; 49 Waiomio Rd; adult/child $20/10; ⊘8.30am-4.30pm). Explore the insect-illuminated caverns with a 30-minute subterranean tour. Guided tours only.

Minibus tours from Paihia to Kawakawa and the caves are offered by **ABC Shuttles & Tours** (p139).

tap from Hamilton's Good George Brewery, and a few well-chosen bottles from other smaller Kiwi breweries.

Pipi Patch Bar BAR
(☑09-402 7111; www.facebook.com/basebayofislands; 18 Kings Rd; ⊘5pm-late) The party hostel has the party bar: a popular spot with large video screens and a decent terrace. You'll be shuffled inside at midnight to keep the neighbours happy – although most of them are backpackers who'll be here anyway.

Bay of Islands Swordfish Club BAR
(Swordy; ☑09-403 7857; www.swordfish.co.nz; upstairs, 96 Marsden Rd; ⊘4.30pm-late) Great views, cold beer and tall tales abound at this brightly lit club-bar where creatures from the deep protrude from every available surface. Decent burgers, steaks and seafood ($15 to $28) are also served.

ⓘ Information

Bay of Islands i-SITE (☑09-402 7345; www. northlandnz.com; Marsden Rd; ⊘8am-5pm Mar–mid-Dec, 8am-7pm mid-Dec–Feb) Information and bookings.

ⓘ Getting There & Away

All buses serving Paihia, such as InterCity (p126), Mana Bus (p126) and Naked Eus (p126), stop at the Maritime Building by the wharf.

Ferries depart regularly for Russell.

ⓘ Getting Around

For bikes, visit **Island Kayaks & Bay Beach Hire** (p144).

Urupukapuka Island

The largest of the bay's islands, Urupukapuka is a tranquil place criss-crossed with walking trails and surrounded by aquamarine waters. Native birds are plentiful thanks to a conservation initiative that has rendered this and all of the neighbouring islands predator-free; check that there aren't any rats, mice or ants stowing away on your boat or in your gear before leaving the mainland.

Most of the regular boat tours moor at Otehei Bay for a little island time; if you want to stay over, you can usually arrange to split the trip up and return at a later date. There are **DOC campsites** (www.doc.govt.nz; sites per adult/child $10/5) at Cable, Sunset and Urupukapuka Bays, which have water supplies, cold showers (except Sunset Bay) and composting toilets; bring food, a stove and fuel.

Bay of Islands Kayaking (☑021 272 3353; www.bayofislandskayaking.co.nz; double kayak 2-day rental $170) can arrange kayaking trips and camping gear for the island. Note that it does not rent to solo kayakers so you'll need to find a friend.

Kerikeri

POP 5500

Kerikeri means 'dig dig', which is apt, as lots of digging goes on around the area's fertile farmland. Famous for its oranges, Kerikeri also produces kiwifruit, vegetables and wine. If you're looking for some back-breaking, poorly paid work that the locals aren't keen to do, your working holiday starts here.

Kerikeri

Kerikeri

A snapshot of early Māori and Pākehā (European New Zealander) interaction is offered by a cluster of historic sites centred on the picturesque river basin. In 1819 the powerful Ngāpuhi chief Hongi Hika allowed Reverend Samuel Marsden to start a mission under the shadow of his Kororipo Pa. There's an ongoing campaign to have the area recognised as a Unesco World Heritage Site.

Sights

★ Stone Store   HISTORIC BUILDING
(☎09-407 9236; www.historic.org.nz; 246 Kerikeri Rd; ◎10am-4pm) Dating from 1836, the Stone Store is NZ's oldest stone building. It sells interesting Kiwiana gifts as well as the type of goods that used to be sold in the store. Tours of the wooden **Mission House** (www.historic. org.nz; tours $10), NZ's oldest building (1822), depart from here and include entry to the Soul Trade exhibition on the 1st floor of the store.

Just up the hill is a marked historical walk, which leads to the site of Kororipo Pa. Huge war parties led by Hika once departed from here, terrorising much of the North Island and slaughtering thousands during the Musket Wars. The role of missionaries in arming Ngāpuhi remains controversial. The walk emerges near the cute wooden St James Anglican Church (1878).

Aroha Island   WILDLIFE RESERVE
(☎09-407 5243; www.arohaisland.co.nz; 177 Rangitane Rd; ◎9.30am-5.30pm) 🌿 **FREE** Reached via a permanent causeway through the mangroves, this 5-hectare island provides a haven for the North Island brown kiwi and other native birds, as well as a pleasant picnic spot for their nonfeathered admirers. It has a visitor centre, kayaks for rent, and after-dark walks to spy kiwi in the wild (per person $35) can also be arranged. You've got around a 50% chance of seeing a kiwi, and booking ahead is essential.

Ake Ake   WINERY
(☎09-407 8230; www.akeakevineyard.co.nz; 165 Waimate North Rd; tastings $5; ◎cellar door 10am-

4.30pm, restaurant noon-3pm & 6-9pm Mon-Sat, noon-3pm Sun, reduced hours outside summer) Wine tastings are free with lunch or purchase of wine. The restaurant (mains $28 to $34, lunch platters $25 to $43) is one of Northland's best, but phone ahead for opening hours outside of the summer months. Free overnight parking is available in the vineyard grounds for self-contained vehicles, and there's also a 1km self-guided walking trail exploring the vineyard.

Rewa's Village MUSEUM
(☑09-407 6454; www.rewasvillage.co.nz; Landing Rd; adult/child $10/5; ⊙10am-4pm) If you had a hard time imagining Kororipo Pa in its original state, take the footbridge across the river to this mock-up of a traditional Māori fishing village.

🏃 Activities

Kerikeri River Track WALKING
Starting from Kerikeri Basin, this 4km-long track leads past **Wharepuke Falls** and the **Fairy Pools** to the **Rainbow Falls** where the sheet of water encloses a moss-covered cavern. Alternatively, you can reach the Rainbow Falls from Rainbow Falls Rd, in which case it's only a 10-minute walk.

Dive North DIVING
(☑09-402 5359; www.divenorth.co.nz; 1512 Springbank Rd; reef & wreck $235) Based in Kerikeri but offering free pick-ups from Paihia.

☞ Tours

Total Tours FOOD
(☑0800 264 868; www.totaltours.co.nz) Explore around Kerikeri on a half-day Food, Wine and Craft tour ($70) or half-day wine tour ($80).

🛏 Sleeping

Aroha Island CAMPGROUND $
(☑09-407 5243; www.arohaisland.co.nz; 177 Rangitane Rd; sites/units from $20/160) 🍃 Kip among the kiwi on the eco island of love (aroha). There's a wide range of reasonably priced options, from the peaceful campsites with basic facilities by the shelly beach, to a whole house. The entire island, indoors and out, is nonsmoking.

Relax a Lodge HOMESTAY $
(☑09-407 6989; www.relaxalodge.co.nz; 1574 Springbank Rd (SH10); s $55, d & tw $70, cottages $110-145; @🅿🛜♨) Less a farm, more an orange grove, this quiet rural house 4km out of town sleeps just 12 people and is a cosy and

BAY OF ISLANDS & NORTHLAND KERIKERI

KERIKERI COTTAGE INDUSTRIES

You'd be forgiven for thinking that everyone in Kerikeri is involved in some small-scale artisanal enterprise, as the bombardment of craft shops on the way into town attests.

While Northland isn't known for its wine, a handful of vineyards are doing their best to change that. The little-known red grape chambourcin has proved particularly suited to the region's subtropical humidity, along with pinotage and syrah.

Look out for the *Art & Craft Trail* and *Wine Trail* brochures. Here are our tasty recommendations.

Kerikeri Farmers Market (www.boifm.org.nz; Hobson Ave; ⊙8.30am-noon Sun) From gourmet sausages to *limoncello*.

Old Packhouse Market (p150) Every Saturday morning.

Get Fudged & Keriblue (☑09-407 1111; www.keriblueceramics.co.nz; 560 Kerikeri Rd; ⊙9am-5pm) An unusual pairing of ceramics and big, decadent slabs of fudge.

Makana Confections (☑09-407 6800; www.makana.co.nz; 504 Kerikeri Rd; ⊙9am-5.30pm) Artisan chocolate factory with lots of sampling.

Marsden Estate (☑09-407 9398; www.marsdenestate.co.nz; 56 Wiroa Rd; ⊙10am-5pm) Excellent wine and lunch on the deck.

Ake Ake (p148) Wine tastings are free with lunch or purchase of wine, and the restaurant is one of Northland's best.

Cottle Hill (☑09-407 5203; www.cottlehill.co.nz; Cottle Hill Dr; tastings $5, free with purchase; ⊙10am-5.30pm Nov-Mar, 10am-5pm Wed-Sun Apr-Oct) Wine and port.

Byrne Northland Wines (Fat Pig Wine Cellar; ☑09-407 3113; www.byrnewine.com/wordpress; 177 Puketotara Rd; ⊙11am-7pm) Excellent viognier and rosé.

welcoming place. Some recently refurbished cottages dotted around the property are also very good value.

Kauri Park
MOTEL $$

(☑09-407 7629; www.kauripark.co.nz; 512 Kerikeri Rd; units $140-170; 🛜🍽) Hidden behind tall trees on the approach to Kerikeri, this well-priced motel has a mixture of units of varying layouts. The premium suites are extremely comfortable, but all options are good value and stylishly furnished.

Wharepuke Subtropical Accommodation
CABIN $$

(☑09-407 8933; www.accommodation-bay-of-islands.co.nz; 190 Kerikeri Rd; cabins $150; 🛜) 🅿
Best known for its food and lush gardens, Wharepuke also rents five self-contained one-bedroom cottages hidden among the palms. They have the prefabricated look of holiday-park cabins, but are a step up in terms of fixtures and space.

Pagoda Lodge
LODGE, CAMPGROUND $$

(☑09-407 8617; www.pagoda.co.nz; 81 Pa Rd; sites/safari tent/caravan from $40/120/130, apt $120-350; 🛜) Built in the 1930s by an oddball Scotsman with an Asian fetish, this lodge features pagoda-shaped roofs grafted onto wooden cottages. The property descends to the river and is dotted with Buddhas, gypsy caravans, and safari tents with proper beds, or you can pitch your own. To get here, take Cobham Rd, turn left into Kerikeri Inlet Rd and then left into Pa Rd.

Bed of Roses
B&B $$$

(☑09-407 4666; www.bedofroses.co.nz; 165 Kerikeri Rd; r $295-475; 🛜) It's all petals and no thorns at this stylish B&B, furnished with French antiques, luxe linens and comfy beds. The house has an art-deco ambience and awesome views.

✗ Eating

Village Cafe
CAFE $

(☑09-407 4062; www.facebook.com/thevillagecafe-kerikeri; Village Mall, 85 Kerikeri Rd; mains $10-18; ⊙8am-4pm Mon-Fri, 8am-2pm Sat & Sun) This chic and cosmopolitan spot is popular with locals for good coffee, freshly prepared counter food, and a relaxed menu of brunch and lunch dishes. Grab a table outside in the Northland sunshine, and order the hearty potato hash.

Old Packhouse Market
MARKET $

(☑09-401 9588; www.theoldpackhousemarket.co.nz; 505 Kerikeri Rd; ⊙8am-1.30pm Sat) Local artisans, produce growers and farmers crowd this market in an old fruit-packing shed on the outskirts of town. On a Saturday morning it's the best place in town to have a leisurely breakfast.

Cafe Jerusalem
MIDDLE EASTERN $

(☑09-407 1001; www.facebook.com/cafejerusalem; Village Mall, 85 Kerikeri Rd; snacks & mains $9-18; ⊙11am-late Mon-Sat) Northland's best falafels and lamb kebabs, all served with a smile and a social vibe. Good salads, and wine and beer are also available. Try the *shakshuka* (baked eggs in a spicy tomato sauce) for a hearty brunch.

Fishbone
CAFE $

(☑09-407 6065; www.fishbonecafe.co.nz; 88 Kerikeri Rd; mains $8-20; ⊙8am-4pm Mon-Wed, to 8pm Thu & Fri, 8.30am-3pm Sat & Sun) Kerikeri's best brekkie spot serves excellent coffee and food. Dr Seuss fans should try the green (pesto) eggs and ham. On Thursday and Friday nights Fishbone morphs into a cosy wine bar for a few hours from 4pm.

★ Food at Wharepuke
CAFE $$

(☑09-407 8936; www.foodatwharepuke.co.nz; 190 Kerikeri Rd; breakfast $14-22, lunch & dinner $24-39; ⊙10am-10.30pm Tue-Sun) 🅿 With one foot in Europe, the other in Thailand and its head in the lush vegetation of Wharepuke Subtropical Gardens, this is Kerikeri's most unusual and inspired eatery. On Friday nights it serves popular Thai banquets (three courses $47.50), while on Sunday afternoons it often hosts live jazz. Adjacent is the interesting Wharepuke Print Studio & Gallery.

Ziezo
BISTRO $$

(☑09-407 9511; 55 Kerikeri Rd; mains $19-28; ⊙3pm-late Thu-Sat, from 10am Sun) This stylish bistro with glam and colourful decor certainly brightens up Kerikeri's retail-focused main street, and the food is equally interesting. An international menu offers Dutch pancakes or eggs Benedict for Sunday brunch, before moving on to Greek-style fish or an Indonesian beef rendang curry for dinner.

Pear Tree
INTERNATIONAL $$

(☑09-407 8479; www.thepeartree.co.nz; 215 Kerikeri Rd; mains $18-31; ⊙10am-10pm Thu-Mon) Kerikeri's best located and most upmarket restaurant occupies an old homestead right on the basin (book ahead for a table on the veranda). Mains run the gamut of tasty meaty grills and lighter bistro favourites. Partner

PUKETI & OMAHUTA FORESTS

Inland from Kerikeri, the Puketi and Omahuta Forests form a continuous expanse of native rainforest. Logging in Puketi was stopped in 1951 to protect not only the remaining kauri but also the endangered kokako bird. Keep an eye out for this rare charmer (grey with a blue wattle) on your wanders.

The forests are reached by several entrances and contain a network of walking tracks varying in length from 15 minutes (the wheelchair-accessible Manginangina Kauri Walk) to two days (the challenging Waipapa River Track); see the DOC website for other walks.

You'll find a **DOC campsite** (☑ 09-407 0300; www.doc.govt.nz; Waiare Rd; sites per adult/child $6/3) and an 18-bunk hut ($18) at the Puketi Recreation Area on the forests' eastern fringe. The hut has hot showers, a kitchen and a flush toilet, while the campsite makes do with cold showers.

Adventure Puketi (www.forestwalks.com; 476 Puketi Rd; tours $55-155) leads guided ecowalks through the forest, including night-time tours to seek out the nocturnal wildlife. It also offers very comfortable B&B accommodation ($175 to $200) on the edge of the forest. Check the website for packages incorporating tours and accommodation.

the venison with one of the Pear Tree's excellent range of NZ craft beers.

🍸 Drinking & Nightlife

La Taza Del Diablo　　　　　BAR
(☑ 09-407 3912; www.facebook.com/eltazadeldiablo; 3 Homestead Rd; ⊗ 4-9pm Sun, Tue & Wed, 11am-midnight Thu-Sat) This Mexican-style bar is about as energetic and raffish as buttoned-down Kerikeri gets with a decent selection of tequila and mezcal, Mexican beers, and just maybe Northland's best margaritas. Tacos, enchiladas and chimichangas all feature on the bar snacks menu ($10 to $18), and occasional live gigs sometimes raise the roof in this genteel town.

ℹ️ Information

Procter Library (Cobham Rd; ⊗ 8am-5pm Mon-Fri, 9am-2pm Sat; 🛜) Tourist information and free internet access.

ℹ️ Getting There & Away

AIR

Bay of Islands (Kerikeri) Airport (☑ 09-407 7147; www.bayofislandsairport.co.nz; 218 Wiroa Rd) is 8km southwest of town. Air New Zealand flies from Auckland to Kerikeri. **Super Shuttle** (☑ 0800 748 885; www.supershuttle.co.nz; one way $25) operates a shuttle service from the airport to Kerikeri, Paihia, Opua and Kawakawa.

BUS

InterCity (p126) and partner buses leave from a stop at 9 Cobham Rd, opposite the library.

THE FAR NORTH

Here's your chance to get off the beaten track, even if that does mean onto unsealed roads. The far-flung Far North always plays second fiddle to the Bay of Islands for attention and funding, yet the subtropical tip of the North Island has more breathtaking coastline per square kilometre than anywhere but the offshore islands. While the 'winterless north' may be a popular misnomer, summers here are long and leisurely. Note that parts of the Far North are noticeably economically depressed and in places could best be described as gritty.

ℹ️ Getting There & Away

Busabout North (☑ 09-408 1092; www.busaboutnorth.co.nz) Busabout North has services linking Mangonui to Kaitaia ($5, one hour), Ahipara to Kaitaia ($3.50, 15 minutes) and Pukenui to Kaitaia ($5, 45 minutes).

Matauri & Tauranga Bays

It's a short detour from SH10, but the exceptionally scenic loop route leading inland to these awesome beaches is a world away from the glitzy face presented for tourists in the Bay of Islands.

Matauri Bay is a long, sandy surf beach, 18km off SH10, with the 17 Cavalli Islands scattered offshore. **Matauri Bay Holiday Park** (☑ 09-405 0525; www.matauribayholidaypark.co.nz; sites from $20, units $130-140) takes up the north end of the beach and has a shop selling groceries, booze and petrol. On top of the headland above the park is a monument to the *Rainbow Warrior;* the Greenpeace ship's underwater resting place among the Cavalli Islands is a popular dive site.

DOC maintains a 12-person hut (☎09-407 0300; www.doc.govt.nz; adult/child $15/7.50) on Motukawanui Island, but you'll need a boat or kayak to reach it and you'll need to book ahead. Only water, mattresses and a composting toilet are provided; bring everything else.

Back on the main road, the route heads west, passing through pleasant Te Ngaere village and a succession of little bays before the turn-off to Tauranga Bay, a smaller beach where the sand is a peachy pink colour. **Tauranga Bay Holiday Park** (☎09-405 0436; www.taurangabay.co.nz; sites from $20, cabins $97-170; ◎⑤) has campsites and log cabins on the picturesque beachfront, but it lacks trees and bears the brunt of the weather. A minimum $54 charge per night for campsites and a seven-night minimum stay applies from mid-December to the end of January.

Down a private road leading from Tauranga Bay, **Northland Sea Kayaking** (☎09-405 0381; www.northlandseakayaking.co.nz; half-/full day tours $90/115) leads kayak explorations of this magical coastline of coves, sea caves and islands. Accommodation is available in conjunction with tours for $35 extra per person.

There's no public transport to these parts or to neighbouring Whangaroa.

Whangaroa Harbour

Just around the headland from Tauranga Bay is the narrow entrance to Whangaroa Harbour. The small fishing village of Whangaroa is 6km from SH10 and calls itself the 'Marlin Capital of NZ'.

There are plenty of charter boats for game-fishing (December to April); prices start at around $1200 a day. If you're planning to hook a monster, insist on it being released once caught – striped marlin and swordfish are among NZ's least-sustainable fishing options.

An excellent 20-minute hike starts from the car park at the end of Old Hospital Rd and goes up **St Paul's Rock** (213m), which

THE BOMBING OF THE RAINBOW WARRIOR

On the morning of 10 July 1985, New Zealanders awoke to news reporting that a terrorist attack had killed a man in Auckland Harbour. The Greenpeace flagship *Rainbow Warrior* had been sunk at its anchorage at Marsden Wharf, where it was preparing to sail to Moruroa Atoll near Tahiti to protest against French nuclear testing.

A tip-off from a Neighbourhood Watch group eventually lead to the arrest of two French foreign intelligence service (DGSE) agents, posing as tourists. The agents had detonated two mines on the boat in staggered explosions – the first designed to cause the crew to evacuate and the second to sink her. However, after the initial evacuation, some of the crew returned to the vessel to investigate and document the attack. Greenpeace photographer Fernando Pereira was drowned below decks following the second explosion.

The arrested agents pleaded guilty to manslaughter and were sentenced to 10 years' imprisonment. In response, the French government threatened to embargo NZ goods from entering the European Economic Community – which would have crippled NZ's economy. A deal was struck whereby France paid $13 million to NZ and apologised, in return for the agents being delivered into French custody on a South Pacific atoll for three years. France eventually paid over $8 million to Greenpeace in reparation – and the bombers were quietly freed before their sentence was served.

Initially French President François Mitterrand denied any government involvement in the attack, but following an inquiry he eventually sacked his Defence Minister and the head of the DGSE, Admiral Pierre Lacoste. On the 20th anniversary of the attack, *Le Monde* newspaper published a report from Lacoste dating from 1986, declaring that the president had personally authorised the operation.

The bombing left a lasting impact on NZ, and French nuclear testing at Moruroa ceased for good in 1996. The wreck of the *Rainbow Warrior* was re-sunk near Northland's Cavalli Islands, where, today, it can be explored by divers. The masts were bought by the Dargaville Museum and overlook the town. The memory of Fernando Pereira endures in a peaceful bird hide in Thames, while a memorial to the boat sits atop a Māori *pa* site at Matauri Bay, north of the Bay of Islands.

dominates the village. At the top you have to use a wire cable to pull yourself up, but the views make it worth the effort.

The **Wairakau Stream Track**, heading north to Pekapeka Bay, begins near the church hall on Campbell Rd in Totara North on the other side of the bay. Its an extremely beautiful, undeveloped stretch and you can cool off in swimming holes along the way. The two-hour hike passes through forest, an abandoned farm and around a steep-walled estuary before arriving at DOC's **Lane Cove Hut** (☑09-407 0300; www.doc.govt.nz; adult/child $15/7.50), which has 16 beds plus composting toilets. Bring everything else and reserve well ahead; it's usually booked out by Kiwi families over summer.

Duke's Nose Track (1¼ hours return) starts behind the cottage and leads up Kairara Rocks; look for the Duke of Wellington's aquiline profile in the rock face. You'll need to haul yourself up a chain for the last 10m, but the views are worth it. If you don't fancy walking back – or if you don't fancy walking at all – **Bushmansfriend** (☑027 680 5588; www.bushmansfriend.co.nz) arranges water taxis from Lane Cove ($20) and 90-minute boat tours ($58).

On the other side of the harbour's north head is **Taupo Bay**, a surf beach that attracts a loyal Kiwi contingent in summer. On easterly swells, there are quality right-handers to surf at the southern end of the bay, by the rivermouth. It's reached by an 11km sealed road signposted from SH10.

🛏 Sleeping & Eating

★**Kahoe Farms Hostel** HOSTEL $
(☑09-405 1804; www.kahoefarms.co.nz; dm $32, r $86-112) On SH10, 10km north of the turn-off to Whangaroa, this hostel has a deservedly great reputation – for its comfortable accommodation, bucolic setting and home-cooked Italian food, but mostly for its welcoming owners. The backpackers' cottage is great, but slightly up the hill there's an even more impressive villa with excellent-value en-suite rooms.

Sunseeker Lodge HOSTEL $
(☑09-405 0496; www.sunseekerlodge.co.nz; Old Hospital Rd; dm/d $35/80, unit $130; @🕿) Up the hill in Whangaroa, this friendly lodge has a sublime spa with a jaw-dropping view, free use of kayaks and can arrange 90-minute harbour tours (adult/child $45/15). Staff can pick up travellers from the nearest bus stop (Kaeo on SH10).

Marlin PUB FOOD $$
(☑09-405 0347; www.marlinhotel.co.nz; Whangaroa Rd; mains $15-26; ☺noon-9pm) A friendly local pub with good honest tucker served from the attached cafe. Inside there are a few impressive wall-mounted game fish that definitely didn't get away.

ℹ Information

Boyd Gallery (☑09-405 0230; www.whangaroa.co.nz Whangaroa Rd; ☺8am-7pm) Boyd Gallery is the general store, but also acts as a tourist information office. The website lists self-contained and B&B accommodation around the area.

ℹ Getting There & Away

There is no public transport to Whangaroa Harbour. Buses usually drop off at SH10 in nearby Kahoe, around 15km further north.

Doubtless Bay
POP 6030

The bay gets its unusual name from an entry in Cook's logbook, where he wrote that the body of water was 'doubtless a bay'. No kidding, Cap'n. It's a bloody big bay at that, with a string of pretty swimming beaches heading towards the Karikari Peninsula.

The main centre, **Mangonui** (meaning 'Big Shark'), retains a fishing-port feel, despite cafes and gift shops now infesting its well-labelled line of historical waterfront buildings. They were constructed in the days when Mangonui was a centre of the whaling industry (1792-1850) and exported flax, kauri wood and gum.

The popular holiday settlements of **Coopers Beach**, **Cable Bay** and **Taipa** are restful pockets of beachside gentrification.

⊙ Sights & Activities

Grab the free *Heritage Trail* brochure from the visitor information centre for a 3km self-guided walk that takes in 22 historic sites. Other walks lead to attractive **Mill Bay**, west of Mangonui, and **Rangikapiti Pa Historic Reserve**, which has ancient Māori terracing and a spectacular view of Doubtless Bay – particularly at sunrise and sunset. A walkway runs from Mill Bay to the *pa,* but you can also drive nearly to the top.

Butler Point Whaling Museum MUSEUM
(☑0800 687 386; www.butlerpoint.co.nz; Marchant Rd, Hihi; adult/child $20/5; ☺by appointment)

At Hihi, 15km northeast of Mangonui, is this small private museum and Victorian homestead (1843) set in lovely gardens. Its first owner, Captain Butler, left Dorset when he was 14 and at 24 was captain of a whaling ship. He settled here in 1839, had 13 children and became a trader, farmer, magistrate and Member of Parliament.

🛏 Sleeping

Puketiti Lodge HOSTEL $
(☑09-406 0369; www.puketitilodge.co.nz; 10 Puketiti Dr; dm/s/d/tr $40/130/150/170; @🛜) If this is what they mean by flashpacking, bring it on. For $40 you get a comfy bunk in a spacious six-person dorm that opens onto a large deck with awesome views, a locker big enough for the burliest backpack and, perhaps most surprisingly, breakfast. Turn inland at Midgley Rd, 6km south of Mangonui village, just after the Hihi turn-off.

Reia Taipa Beach Resort RESORT $$
(☑0800 142 82472; www.taipabay.co.nz; 22 Taipa Point Rd, Taipa; d from $220; 🛜☀) Recently renovated accommodation and a warm welcome combine at this spot with the option of beachfront and poolside studio units and apartments. There's also a good on-site restaurant, a tennis court and a spa pool.

Mangonui Waterfront Apartments Motel APARTMENT $$
(☑09-406 0347; www.mangonuiwaterfront.co.nz; 88 Waterfront Dr; apt $125-225; @🛜) Sleeping two to eight people, these historic apartments on the Mangonui waterfront have loads of character, each one different but all with balconies, a sense of space and their own barbecue. Try to book 100-year-old Tahi.

Old Oak BOUTIQUE HOTEL $$$
(☑09-406 1250; www.theoldoak.co.nz; 66 Waterfront Dr, Mangonui; d $175-275, ste $275-325; 🛜) This atmospheric 1861 kauri inn is now an elegant boutique hotel with contemporary design and top-notch furnishings. It oozes character, not least because the building is reputedly haunted.

🍴 Eating

Mangonui Fish Shop FISH & CHIPS $
(☑09-406-0478; 137 Waterfront Dr; fish & chips around $13; ⊙10am-8pm; 🛜) Eat outdoors over the water at this famous chippie, which also sells smoked fish and seafood salads. Grab a crayfish salad and a cold beer, and you'll be sorted.

★**Little Kitchen on the Bay** CAFE $$
(☑09-406 1644; www.facebook.com/littlekitchennz; 1/78 Waterfront Dr, Mangonui; breakfast & lunch $8-14, shared plates $13-16; ⊙7.30am-3pm Mon-Wed, to 9.30pm Thu & Fri, 8am-3pm Sat & Sun) Our favourite Doubtless Bay eatery is this cute spot just across from the harbour. During the day the sun-drenched interior has Mangonui's best coffee, excellent counter food and good mains – try the terrific burger. On Thursday and Friday nights the emphasis shifts to wine, craft beer, and shared plates such as pork empanadas and Swiss cheese beef sliders.

Thai Chef THAI $$
(☑09-406 1220; www.thethaimangonui.co.nz; 80 Waterfront Dr, Mangonui; mains $18-26; ⊙5-11pm Tue-Sun) Northland's best Thai restaurant serves zingy dishes with intriguing names such as The 3 Alcoholics, Spice Girls and Bangkok Showtime, and there's also a good range of Isaan (northeastern Thai) dishes to go with a frosty Singha beer. Actually, make that one of New ZZ's best Thai restaurants.

🔒 Shopping

Exhibit A ARTS, CRAFTS
(☑09-406 2333; www.facebook.com/exhibita.mangonui; Old Courthouse, Waterfront Dr; ⊙10am-4.30pm) This co-op gallery showcases Far North artists.

Flax Bush ARTS, CRAFTS
(☑09-406 1510; www.flaxbush.co.nz; 50 Waterfront Dr, Mangonui; ⊙10am-5pm) Seashells, Pasifika and Māori crafts.

ℹ Information

Doubtless Bay Visitor Information Centre
(☑09-406 2046; www.doubtlessbay.co.nz; 118 Waterfront Dr, Mangonui; ⊙10am-5pm, reduced hours winter) Excellent source of local information.

ℹ Getting There & Away

InterCity buses depart near the Waterfront Cafe in Mangonui, outside the wholesalers in Coopers Beach, opposite the shop in Cable Bay and outside the Shell petrol station in Taipa. Busabout North (p151) has services to Kaitaia ($5, one hour).

Karikari Peninsula

The oddly shaped Karikari Peninsula bends into a near-perfect right angle. The result is beaches facing north, south, east and west in close proximity, so if the wind's annoying you or you want to catch some surf, a sunrise or a sunset, just swap beaches. Despite its natural assets, the sun-baked peninsula is blissfully undeveloped, with farmers well outnumbering tourist operators. There's no public transport and you won't find a lot of shops or eateries either. In late 2013 the resort and the holiday park were both purchased by overseas interests for eventual marketing to Chinese tourists, but it is envisaged any change in direction for the two properties will not begin for several years.

◉ Sights & Activities

Tokerau Beach is the long, sandy stretch forming the western edge of Doubtless Bay. Neighbouring **Whatuwhiwhi** is smaller and more built-up, facing back across the bay. **Maitai Bay**, with its tiny twin coves, is the loveliest of them all, at the lonely end of the peninsula down an unsealed road. It's a great spot for swimming – the water is sheltered enough for the kids, but with enough swell to body surf.

Rangiputa faces west at the elbow of the peninsula; the pure white sand and crystal-clear sheltered waters come straight from a Pacific Island daydream. A turn-off on the road to Rangiputa takes you to remote **Puheke Beach**, a long, windswept stretch of snow-white sand dunes forming Karikari's northern edge.

Karikari Estate WINERY
(☑ 09-408 7222; www.karikariestate.co.nz; Maitai Bay Rd; tastings $15; ⊗ 11am-4pm Oct-Apr, pizza evenings from 5pm late Dec-Feb) Impressive Karikari Estate produces acclaimed red wines and has a cafe attached (mains and platters $16 to $40), and while the wine tastings are shamelessly overpriced, at least the sublime views are free. During the peak of summer, good pizza is served from 5pm in the cafe.

⌊═⌋ Sleeping

Whatuwhiwhi Top 10
Holiday Park HOLIDAY PARK $
(☑ 09-408 7202; www.whatuwhiwhitop10.co.nz; 17 Whatuwhiwhi Rd; sites from $50, units $65-185; ☎) Sheltered by hills and overlooking the beach, this friendly complex has a great location, good facilities, free barbecues and kayaks for hire. It also offers dive fills and PADI diving instruction.

Maitai Bay DOC Campsite CAMPGROUND $
(www.doc.govt.nz; Maitai Bay Rd; sites per adult/child $10/5) ⌀ A large first-in, first-served

(no bookings) camping ground at the peninsula's most beautiful beach, with chemical toilets, drinking water and cold showers.

Pepper's Carrington Resort RESORT $$$
(☑ 09-408 7222; www.peppers.co.nz; 109 Matai Bay Rd; r/villa from $295/395; ☎ ☒) There's something very Australian-looking about this hilltop lodge, with its wide verandas and gum trees, tempered by Māori and Pacific design in the spacious rooms and villas. The view over the golf course to the dazzling white beach is exquisite. The resort's Carrington restaurant is open for dinner from 6.30pm. Expect a focus on seafood, including local scallops and oysters.

Cape Reinga & Ninety Mile Beach

Māori consider Cape Reinga (Te Rerenga-Wairua) the jumping-off point for souls as they depart on the journey to their spiritual homeland. That makes the Aupouri Peninsula a giant diving board, and it even resembles one – long and thin, it reaches 108km to form NZ's northern extremity. On its west coast Ninety Mile Beach (Ninety Kilometre Beach would be more accurate) is a continuous stretch lined with high sand dunes, flanked by the Aupouri Forest.

◉ Sights

Cape Reinga LANDMARK
Standing at windswept **Cape Reinga Lighthouse** (a rolling 1km walk from the car park) and looking out over the ocean engenders a real end-of-the-world feeling. This is where the waters of the Tasman Sea and Pacific Ocean meet, breaking together into waves up to 10m high in stormy weather. Little tufts of cloud often cling to the ridges, giving sudden spooky chills even on hot days.

Visible on a promontory slightly to the east is a spiritually significant 800-year-old pohutukawa tree; souls are believed to slide down its roots. Out of respect to the most sacred site in Māoridom, don't go near the tree and refrain from eating or drinking anywhere in the area.

Te Paki Recreation Reserve NATURE RESERVE
A large chunk of the land around Cape Reinga is part of the Te Paki Recreation Reserve managed by DOC. It's public land with free access; leave the gates as you found them

BAY OF ISLANDS & NORTHLAND CAPE REINGA & NINETY MILE BEACH

SEED FOR THE FUTURE

The local Ngati Kuri, guardians of the sacred spaces around the Cape, have come up with a unique way of funding reforestation. For $20 you can assuage your carbon guilt by planting a native tree or bush of your choice – or, if you don't want to break a nail, letting the staff plant it for you; contact **Natives** (☑ 09-409 8482; www.natives.co.nz).

and don't disturb the animals. There are 7 sq km of giant sand dunes on either side of the mouth of Te Paki Stream. Clamber up to toboggan down the dunes. During summer, Ahikaa Adventures (p156) are on hand to rent sandboards ($15).

Great Exhibition Bay
BEACH

On the east coast, Great Exhibition Bay has dazzling snow-white silica dunes. There's no public road access, but some tours pay a *koha* (donation) to cross Māori farmland or approach the sand by kayak from Parengarenga Harbour.

Nga-Tapuwae-o-te-Mangai
TEMPLE

(6576 Far North Rd) With its two domed towers (Arepa and Omeka, alpha and omega) and the Ratana emblem of the star and crescent moon, you could be forgiven for mistaking this temple for a mosque. Ratana is a Māori Christian sect with more than 50,000 adherents, formed in 1925 by Tahupotiki Wiremu Ratana, who was known as 'the mouthpiece of God'. The temple is built on land where Ratana once stood, and the name translates as 'the sacred steps of the mouthpiece'.

You'll pass it at Te Kao, 46km south of Cape Reinga.

Gumdiggers Park
MUSEUM

(www.gumdiggerspark.co.nz; 171 Heath Rd, Waiharara; adult/child $12/6; ⊙ 9am-4.30pm) Kauri forests covered this area for 100,000 years, leaving ancient logs and the much-prized gum (used for making varnish and linoleum) buried beneath. Digging it out was the region's main industry from the 1870s to the 1920s. In 1900 around 7000 gumdiggers were digging holes all over Northland, including at this site. Start with the 15-minute video, and then walk on the bush tracks, leading past gumdiggers' huts, ancient kauri stumps, huge preserved logs and holes left by the diggers.

🏃 Activities

Cape Reinga Coastal Walkway
TRAMPING

Contrary to expectation, Cape Reinga isn't actually the northernmost point of the country; that honour belongs to **Surville Cliffs** further to the east. A walk along **Te Werahi Beach** to **Cape Maria van Diemen** (a five-hour loop) takes you to the westernmost point. This is one of many sections of the three- to four-day, 53km Cape Reinga Coastal Walkway (from Kapowairua to Te Paki Stream) that can be tackled individually.

Beautiful Tapotupotu Bay is a two-hour walk east of Cape Reinga, via Sandy Bay and the cliffs. From Tapotupotu Bay it's an eight-hour walk to Spirits Bay, one of NZ's most beautiful beaches. Both bays are also accessible by road.

☞ Tours

Bus tours go to Cape Reinga from Kaitaia, Ahipara, Doubtless Bay and the Bay of Islands, but there's no scheduled public transport up here.

**Far North
Outback Adventures**
ADVENTURE TOUR

(☑ 09-409 4586; www.farnorthtours.co.nz; price on application) Flexible, day-long, 4WD tours from Kaitaia/Ahipara, including morning tea and lunch. Options include visits to remote areas such as Great Exhibition Bay.

Harrisons Cape Runner
ADVENTURE TOUR

(☑ 0800 227 373; www.harrisonscapereingatours.co.nz; adult/child $50/25) Day trips from Kaitaia along Ninety Mile Beach that include sandboarding and a picnic lunch.

Sand Safaris
ADVENTURE TOUR

(☑ 0800 869 090, 09-408 1778; www.sandsafaris.co.nz; adult/child $50/30) Coach trips from Ahipara and Kaitaia, including sandboarding and a picnic lunch.

Ahikaa Adventures
CULTURAL TOUR

(☑ 09-409 8228; www.ahikaa-adventures.co.nz; tours $50-190) Māori culture permeates these tours, which can include sandboarding, kayaking, fishing and pigging out on traditional *kai* (food).

🛏 Sleeping

There's limited hostel and motel accommodation and a good array of DOC campsites.

DOC Campsites
CAMPGROUND $

(www.doc.govt.nz; sites per adult/child $10/5) There are spectacularly positioned sites at Kapowairua. Tapotupotu Bay and Rarawa Beach. Only water, composting toilets and cold showers are provided. Bring a cooker, as fires are not allowed, and plenty of repellent to ward off mosquitoes and sandflies. 'Freedom/Leave No Trace' camping is allowed along the Cape Reinga Coastal Walkway.

North Wind Lodge Backpackers HOSTEL $
(☑09-409 8515; www.northwind.co.nz; 88 Otaipango Rd, Henderson Bay; dm/s/tw/d $30/60/66/80) Six kilometres down an unsealed road on the Aupouri Peninsula's east side, this unusual turreted house offers a homey environment and plenty of quiet spots on the lawn to sit with a beer and a book.

Pukenui Lodge Motel MOTEL $$
(☑09-409 8837; www.pukenuilodge.co.nz; 3 Pukenui Wharf Rd; motel d $99-125, hostel dm/d $27/70; ☎☒) Decent motel accommodation and the bonus of backpacker-friendly dorms and rooms in nearby Thomas House, a 1925 heritage building that was home to the first Pukenui Post Office.

ℹ Getting There & Away

Apart from numerous tours, there's no public transport past Pukenui, which is linked to Kaitaia ($5, 45 minutes) by Busabout North (p151).

As well as Far North Rd (SH1), rugged vehicles can travel along Ninety Mile Beach itself. However, cars have been known to hit soft sand and be swallowed by the tides – look out for unfortunate vehicles poking through the sands. Check tide times before setting out; avoid it 2½ hours either side of high tide. Watch out for 'quicksand' at Te Paki Stream – keep moving. Many car-rental companies prohibit driving on the sands; if you get stuck, your insurance won't cover you.

Fill up with petrol before hitting the Aupouri Peninsula.

Kaitaia

POP 4900

Nobody comes to the Far North to hang out in this provincial town, but it's a handy stop if you're after a supermarket, a post office or an ATM. It's also a jumping-off point for tours to Cape Reinga and Ninety Mile Beach.

◉ Sights

Te Ahu Centre ARTS CENTRE
(☑09-401 5200; www.teahu.org.nz; Matthews Ave) This civic and community centre features a cinema, the Te Ahu Heritage (☑09-408 9454; www.teahuheritage.co.nz; adult/child

$7/3; ☉10am-4pm Mon-Fri) FREE exhibits of the Far North Regional Museum, and the local i-SITE information centre. There's also a cafe and free wi-fi at the library. The centre's foyer is circled by a series of *pou* (carved Māori memorial posts) featuring the different cultures – Māori, Croatian etc – making up the unique backgrounds of the area's residents.

Okahu Estate Winery WINERY
(☑09-408 2066; www.okahuestate.co.nz; 520 Okahu Rd; ☉10am-5pm daily 26 Dec-Feb, noon-5pm Thu-Sat Mar-Jun & Oct-24 Dec) Just south of town, off the road to Ahipara, Kaitaia's only winery offers free tastings and sells local produce, including the famous Kaitaia Fire chilli sauce.

🛏 Sleeping & Eating

Loredo Motel MOTEL $$
(☑09-408 3200 www.loredomotel.co.nz; 25 North Rd; units $120-155; ☎☒) Opting for a breezy Spanish style, this tidy motel has well-kept units set among palm trees and lawns, with a swimming pool.

Gecko Cafe CAFE $
(☑09-408 1160; 80 Commerce St; mains $9-15; ☉7am-4pm Mon & Tue, to 8.30pm Wed-Fri, 8am-4pm Sat) Morning queues of locals attest to the Gecko Cafe having the best coffee in town, and the food's pretty good, too. Kick off another day on the road with mushrooms and chorizo, or grab a Moroccan chicken wrap later in the day for lunch.

Beachcomber SEAFOOD $$
(☑09-408 2010; www.beachcomber.net.nz; 222 Commerce St; lunch $19-33, dinner $22-37; ☉11am-3pm Mon-Fri, 5pm-late Mon-Sat) Easily the best place to eat in town, with a wide range of seafood and meaty fare, and a well-stocked salad bar. We're still thinking about the crumbed scallops we enjoyed on our last visit.

ℹ Information

DOC Kaitaia Area Office (☑09-408 6014; www.doc.govt.nz; 25 Matthews Ave; ☉8.30am-4.30pm Mon-Fri) Track information, especially good for getting to grips with the Cape Reinga Coastal Walkway.

Far North i-SITE (☑03-408 9450; www.nortlandnz.com; Te Ahu Community Centre, cnr Matthews Ave & South Rd; ☉8.30am-5pm) An excellent information centre with advice for all of Northland.

BAY OF ISLANDS & NORTHLAND KAITAIA

❶ Getting There & Away

AIR

Kaitaia Airport (☑ 021 818 314; www.bayof islandsairport.co.nz; Quarry Rd) is 6km north of town. Both **Air New Zealand** (p139) and **Barrier Air** (☑ 0800 900 600, 09-275 9120; www.barrierair.kiwi; one way from $99) link the town to Auckland.

BUS

Busabout North (p151) has services to Doubtless Bay ($5, one hour), Pukenui ($5, 45 minutes) and Ahipara ($3.50, 15 minutes). **InterCity** (☑ 09-623 1503; www.intercity coach.co.nz) buses stop in Kaitaia.

Ahipara

POP 1130

All good things must come to an end, and Ninety Mile Beach does at this spunky beach town. A few holiday mansions have snuck in, but mostly it's just the locals keeping it real, rubbing shoulders with visiting surfers.

The area is known for its huge sand dunes and massive gum field, where 2000 people once worked. Sandboarding and quad-bike rides are popular activities on the dunes above Ahipara and further around the Tauroa Peninsula.

◉ Sights

Shipwreck Bay   BEACH
(Wreck Bay Rd) The best surfing is at this small cove at Ahipara's western edge, so named for shipwrecks still visible at low tide.

Ahipara Viewpoint   VIEWPOINT
(Gumfields Rd) This spectacular lookout on the bluff behind Ahipara is reached by an extremely rough road leading off the unsealed Gumfields Rd, which starts at the western end of Foreshore Dr.

⚐ Activities

Ahipara Adventure Centre   ADVENTURE SPORTS
(☑ 09-409 2055; www.ahiparaadventure.co.nz; 15 Takahe St) Hires sand toboggans ($10 per half day), surfboards ($30 per half day), mountain bikes ($50 per day), kayaks ($25 per hour), blokarts for sand yachting ($65 per hour) and quad-bikes ($95 per hour).

NZ Surf Bros   SURFING
(☑ 09-945 7276, 021 252 7078; www.nzsurfbros. com; c/o 90 Mile Beach Ahipara Holiday Park; surf lessons $60-120) NZ Surf Bros offers surfing lessons, plus day excursions and multiday trips that take in beaches on both the west and east coasts of Northland.

Ahipara Treks   HORSE RIDING
(☑ 09-409 4122; http://taitokerauhoney.co.nz/ ahipara-horse-treks; 1/2hr $65/80) Offers beach canters, including some farm and ocean riding (when the surf permits).

🛏 Sleeping & Eating

★ Endless Summer Lodge   HOSTEL $
(☑ 09-409 4181; www.endlesssummer.co.nz; 245 Foreshore Rd; dm $34, d $78-92; @🖙) Across from the beach, this superb kauri villa (1880) has been beautifully restored and converted into an exceptional hostel. There's no TV, which encourages bonding around the long table and wood-fired pizza oven on the vine-covered back terrace. Body boards and sandboards can be borrowed and surfboards can be hired.

**90 Mile Beach
Ahipara Holiday Park**   HOLIDAY PARK $
(☑ 0800 888 988; www.ahiparaholidaypark.co.nz; 168 Takahe St; sites from $40, dm/r $28/75, units $75-135; @🖙) There's a large range of accommodation on offer at this holiday park, including cabins, motel units and a worn but perfectly presentable YHA-affiliated backpackers' lodge. The communal hall has an open fire and colourful murals.

Beachfront   APARTMENT $$
(☑ 09-409 4007; www.beachfront.net.nz; 14 Kotare St; apt $175; 🖙) Who cares if it's a bit bourgeois for Ahipara? These two upmarket, self-contained apartments have watery views and there's direct access to the beach.

Bidz Takeaways   FISH & CHIPS $
(Takahe St; meals $7-15; ⊙ 9am-8pm) Fresh fish for sale, and the best fish, chips and burgers in town. There's also a small grocery store attached.

North Drift Cafe   CAFE $$
(☑ 09-409 4093; www.facebook.com/northdrift cafe; 3 Ahipara Rd; mains $12-29; ⊙ 7am-3pm Mon-Wed, 7am-3pm & 5pm-late Thu-Sun) Ahipara's best coffee and a hip relaxed atmosphere both feature at this cafe with a spacious and sunny deck. Brunch and lunch standouts include the zucchini and corn fritters and the giant green-lipped mussels in a green curry sauce, and over summer it's a top spot for a few beers and dinner specials, such as NZ lamb crusted with Mediterranean-style dukkah.

NGĀTI TARARA

As you're travelling around the north you might notice the preponderance of road names ending in '-ich'. As the sign leading into Kaitaia proclaims, '*haere mai, dobro došli* and welcome' – and thus, welcome to one of the more peculiar ethnic conjunctions in the country.

From the end of the 19th century, men from the Dalmatian coast of what is now Croatia started arriving in NZ looking for work. Many ended up in Northland's gum fields. Pākehā (European New Zealander) society wasn't particularly welcoming to the new immigrants, particularly during WWI, as they were on Austrian passports. Not so the small Māori communities of the north. Here they found an echo of Dalmatian village life with its emphasis on extended family and hospitality, not to mention a shared history of injustice at the hands of colonial powers.

The Māori jokingly named them Tarara, as their rapid conversation in their native tongue sounded like 'ta-ra-ra-ra-ra' to Māori ears. Many Croatian men married local *wahine* (women), founding clans that have left several of today's famous Māori with Croatian surnames, such as singer Margaret Urlich and former All Black Frano Botica. You'll find large Tarara communities in the Far North, Dargaville and West Auckland.

ℹ Getting There & Around

Busabout North (p151) runs services from Kaitaia ($3.50, 15 minutes).

HOKIANGA

The Hokianga Harbour stretches out its skinny tentacles to become the fourth-biggest in the country. Its ruggedly beautiful landscape is painted in every shade of green and brown. The water itself is rendered the colour of ginger ale by the bush streams that feed it.

Of all the remote parts of Northland, this is the pocket that feels the most removed from the mainstream. Pretension has no place here. Isolated, predominantly Māori communities nestle around the harbour's many inlets, as they have done for centuries. Discovered by legendary explorer Kupe, it's been settled by Ngāpuhi since the 14th century. Hippies arrived in the late 1960s and their legacy is a thriving little artistic scene.

Many of the roads remain unsealed, and, while tourism dollars are channelled eastward to the Bay of Islands, this truly fascinating corner of the country remains remarkably undeveloped, just how many of the locals like it.

ℹ Getting There & Away

There is no public transport on these sleepy secondary roads. An option is to visit on a Discover Hokianga tour with Fullers Great Sights (p145) from the Bay of Islands.

Motuti

From Kohukohu, it's worth taking a short detour on winding roads – 25km or 40 minutes – to the sleepy settlement of Motuti. The nearby **Motuti Marae** (☑09-409 5545; www.motuti.co.nz; 318 Motuti Rd; tours 90min/day $36/60, stay $216; ☺Sun-Fri) offers *marae* tours and stays, including a traditional Māori welcome and, on the longer tours, the opportunity to take part in flax-weaving, carving and stick games. Booking ahead is essential.

◉ Sights

St Mary's Church   CHURCH
(Hata Maria; ☑09-405 2527; www.hokiangapompallier.org.nz; Motuti Rd) About halfway along the 40km drive from Kohukohu via Panguru, it's worth a short detour to visit St Mary's Church, where NZ's first Catholic bishop was buried beneath the altar. Jean Baptiste Pompallier arrived in the Hokianga in 1838, celebrating NZ's first Mass at Totara Point. He was interred here in 2002 after an emotional 14-week pilgrimage full of Māori ceremony brought his remains back from France.

Kohukohu

POP 190

Quick, someone slap a preservation order on Kohukohu before it's too late. There can be few places in NZ where a Victorian village full of interesting kauri buildings has been so completely preserved with hardly a modern monstrosity to be seen. During the height of the kauri industry it was a busy town with a sawmill, shipyard, two newspapers and banks. These days it's a very quiet backwater on the north side of Hokianga Harbour, 4km from the Rawene car ferry (p161). There are no regular bus services, but there's good eating at the local pub and on the cosy deck of the adjacent **Koke Cafe** (☑09-405 5808; www.kohukohu.co.nz; Kohukohu Rd; mains $10-14; ☻8am-4pm Sun-Wed, to 6pm Thu-Sat).

Village Arts (☑09-405 5827; www.villagearts.co.nz; 1376 Kohukohu Rd; ☻10am-4pm daily, reduced hours winter) is an excellent little gallery exhibiting works by mainly Hokianga artists.

Tree House (☑09-405 5855; www.treehouse. co.nz; 168 West Coast Rd; sites/dm $20/32, s $64-70, tw & d $88; ☎) ✹ is the best place to stay in the Hokianga, with helpful hosts and brightly painted little cottages set among exotic fruit and nut trees. This quiet retreat is 2km from the ferry terminus (turn sharp left as you come off the ferry).

Horeke & Around

Tiny Horeke was NZ's second European settlement after Russell. A Wesleyan mission operated here from 1828 to 1855, while in 1840, 3000 Ngāpuhi gathered here for what was the single biggest signing of the Treaty of Waitangi. The rustic **Horeke Tavern** (☑09-401 9133; www.horeketavern.co.nz; 2118 Horeke Rd; ☻1pm-late Wed-Sun, bistro 5.30-8pm Thu-Sun) is reputedly New Zealand's oldest pub – the first cold one was poured back in 1826 – and the garden bar rocks with live music on occasional weekends during summer.

Horeke is also the western end point of the Pou Herenga Tai Twin Coast Cycle Trail (p138).

◉ Sights

Wairere Boulders Nature Park PARK
(☑09-401 9935; www.wairereboulders.co.nz; McDonnell Rd; adult/child/family $15/5/35, cash only; ☻to 5pm/7pm winter/summer) ✹ At Wairere, massive basalt rock formations have been eroded into odd fluted shapes by the acidity of ancient kauri forests. Allow an hour for the main loop track; expect a few dips and climbs. An additional track leads through rainforest to a platform at the end of the boulder valley (1½ hours). The park is sign-

posted from SH1 and Horeke; the last 3km are unsealed. Without your own transport, get here on a Fullers' Discover Hokianga tour departing from Paihia.

Mangungu Mission House HISTORIC BUILDING
(www.historic.org.nz; Motukiore Rd; adult/child $10/free; ☻noon-4pm Sat & Sun Nov-Apr) Completed in 1839, this sweet wooden cottage contains relics of the missionaries who once inhabited it, and of Horeke's shipbuilding past. In the grounds there's a large stone cross and a simple wooden church. Mangungu is 1km down the unsealed road leading along the harbour from Horeke village.

🛏 Sleeping

Horeke Tavern PUB $$
(☑09-401 9133; www.horeketavern.co.nz; 2118 Horeke Rd; d/f $85/135) Simple but clean accommodation in the local pub.

Rawene

POP 440

Founded shortly after Horeke, Rawene was NZ's third European settlement. A surprising number of historic buildings (including six churches!) remain from a time when the harbour was considerably busier than it is now. Information boards outline a heritage trail of the main sights.

There's an ATM in the 4 Square grocery store, and you can get petrol here.

◉ Sights

Clendon House HISTORIC BUILDING
(☑09-405 7874; www.historic.org.nz; Clendon Esplanade; adult/child $10/free; ☻10am-4pm Sun May-Oct, Sat & Sun Nov-Apr) Clendon House was built in the bustling 1860s by James Clendon, a trader, shipowner and magistrate. After his death, his 34-year-old half-Māori widow Jane was left with a brood of kids and a whopping £5000 debt. She managed to clear the debt and her descendants remained in the house until 1972, when it passed to the Historic Places Trust.

🛏 Sleeping & Eating

Rawene Holiday Park HOLIDAY PARK $
(☑09-405 7720; www.raweneholidaypark.co.nz; 1 Marmon St; dm $20, sites/units from $32/65; ☎✹) Tent sites shelter in the bush at this nicely managed park. The cabins are simple, with one converted into a bunkroom for backpackers (linen costs extra).

Boatshed Cafe
CAFE $

(☑ 09-405 7728; 8 Clendon Esplanade; mains $10-22; ☺ 8.30am-4pm) Eat overlooking the water at this cafe, a cute place with excellent food and a gift shop that sells local art and crafts. The cafe sometimes opens for dinner at the weekend.

❶ Getting There & Away

There are no regular bus services to Rawene. A **car ferry** (☑ 09-405 2602; car/campervan/motorcycle $20/40/5, passenger $2; ☺ 7.30am-8pm) heads to the northern side of the Hokianga, docking 4km south of Kohukohu at least hourly. You can buy your ticket for this 15-minute ride on board. It usually leaves Rawene on the half-hour and the north Kohukohu side on the hour.

Opononi & Omapere

POP 480

These tranquil settlements near the south head of Hokianga Harbour run into one another. The water's much clearer here and good for swimming, and views are dominated by the mountainous sand dunes across the water at North Head. If you're approaching Omapere from the south, the view of the harbour is nothing short of spectacular.

🏃 Activities

Arai te Uru Heritage Walk
WALKING

Starting at the car park at the end of Signal Station Rd, this walk (30 minutes return) follows the cliffs and passes through a tall stand of manuka before continuing to the grassy southern headland of the Hokianga. At the headland are the remains of an old signal station built to assist ships making the treacherous passage into the harbour.

The station was closed in 1951 due to the decline in shipping in the harbour.

Jim Taranaki's Bone Carving Studio
COURSE

(☑ 09-405 8061; hokiangabonecarvingstudio@gmail.com; 15 Akiha St, Omapere; class incl lunch $60) Create your own Māori-inspired bone-carving in a studio with ocean views.

👉 Tours

Footprints Waipoua
CULTURAL TOUR

(☑ 09-405 8207; www.footprintswaipoua.co.nz; adult/child $95/35; ☺ from 5pm Apr-Oct, 6pm Nov-Mar) 🌿 Led by Māori guides, this four-hour twilight tour into Waipoua Forest is a fantastic introduction to both the culture and the forest giants. Tribal history and stories are shared, and mesmerising *karakia* (prayers, incantations) are recited before the gargantuan trees. Daytime tours ($80) are also available, but the twilight tours amplify the sense of spirituality.

Hokianga Express
ADVENTURE SPORTS

(☑ 021 405 872, 09-405 8872; per tour $27; ☺ 10am-2pm summer) A boat departs from Opononi Jetty and takes you across the harbour to the large golden sand dunes, where you can spend an hour sandboarding down a 30m slope or skimming over the water. Boogie boards are provided and bookings are essential. Outside of the peak season, the service is not always available.

🛏 Sleeping

GlobeTrekkers Lodge
HOSTEL $

(☑ 09-405 8183; www.globetrekkerslodge.com; SH12, Omapere; dm/s/d $28/50/60; @ 🐾) Unwind in casual style at this home-style hostel with harbour views and bright dorms. Private rooms have plenty of thoughtful touches, such as writing desks, mirrors, art and fluffy towels. There's a stereo, but no TV, encouraging plenty of schmoozing in the grapevine-draped barbecue area.

Copthorne Hotel & Resort
HOTEL $$

(☑ 09-405 8737; www.milleniumhotels.co.nz; 336 SH12, Omapere; r $140-200; 🐾 ✱) Despite the original Victorian villa having been hijacked by aluminium windows, this waterside complex remains an attractive spot for a summer's drink or bistro meal ($25 to $32). The more expensive rooms in the newer accommodation block have terraces and water views. Even if you're not staying here, it's definitely worth dropping in for a drink at the cosy bar.

Check online for worthwhile midweek and off-peak specials.

★ Kokohuia Lodge
B&B $$$

(☑ 021 779 927; www.kokchuialodge.co.nz; 101 Kokohuia Rd, Omapere; d $295-320; 🐾) 🌿 Luxury and sustainable, ecofriendly practices combine at this B&B, nestled in regenerating native bush high above the silvery dune-fringed expanse of the Hokianga Harbour. Solar energy and organic and free-range produce all feature, but there's no trade-off for luxury in the modern and stylish accommodation.

Hokianga Haven
B&B $$$

(☑ 09-405 8285; www.hokiangahaven.co.nz; 226 SH12, Omapere; r $220-240; 🐾) This modern house with original Kiwi art on the walls offers spacious accommodation on the harbour's edge and glorious views of the sand dunes. Alternative healing therapies can be arranged, and there are accommodation discounts for stays longer than one night.

✖ Eating

Landing CAFE $$
(☑09-405 8169; www.thelandingcafe.co.nz; 29 SH12; snacks & mains $6-19; ☺8.30am-3pm) Stylish Kiwiana decor combines with good cafe fare at this new opening with an expansive view-friendly deck. Try one of the hearty butter-chicken pies, or combine the mussel fritters with a dollop of locally produced relish. Salad fans will enjoy options including Israeli couscous, or a roast beetroot and feta cheese combo.

Opononi Hotel PUB FOOD $$
(☑09-405 8858; www.opononihotel.com; 19 SH12; mains $18-30; ☺11am-late) Options at the friendly local pub include decent pizza in the main bar, or flasher bistro meals in the attached Boar and Marlin restaurant. Either way, try and score an outside table so you can take in the improbable views of Opononi's massive sand dunes just across the harbour.

❶ Information

Opononi i-SITE (☑09-405 8869; 29 SH12; ☺8.30am-5pm) Excellent information office with a good range of local souvenirs.

❶ Getting There & Away

There's no regular public transport to these parts, so you'll need to rent a car from Kerikeri or Paihia for independent exploration. Another option is a Discover Hokianga day trip from Paihia with Fullers Great Sights (p145), taking in Opononi, Omapere and the Waiere Boulders.

Waiotemarama & Waimamaku

The neighbouring Waiotemarama and Waimamaku villages, nestled between the Hokianga Harbour and the Waipoua Forest, are the first of many tiny rural communities scattered along this underpopulated stretch of SH12.

🏃 Activities

Labyrinth Woodworks OUTDOORS
(☑09-405 4581; www.nzanity.co.nz; 647 Waiotemarama Gorge Rd; maze adult/child $4/3; ☺9am-5pm) Crack the code in the outdoor maze by collecting letters to form a word. The puzzle museum and lots of retro board games are also interesting. Nearby walks lead to a waterfall and magnificent kauri trees.

✖ Eating

Morrell's Cafe CAFE $$
(☑09-405 4545; 7235 SH12, Waimamaku; mains $11-24; ☺9am-4pm) This cafe and craft shop occupies a former cheese factory. It's the last good eatery before Baylys Beach, so drop in for coffee or an eggy breakfast.

KAURI COAST

Apart from the odd bluff and river, this coast is basically unbroken and undeveloped for the 110km between the Hokianga and Kaipara Harbours. The main reason for coming here is to marvel at the kauri forests, one of the great natural highlights of NZ. You'd need 8m arms to get them around some of the big boys here.

There are few stores or eateries and no ATMs north of Dargaville, so stock up beforehand. Trampers should check DOC's website (www.doc.govt.nz) for walks in the area.

Waipoua Forest

The highlight of Northland's west coast, this superb forest sanctuary – proclaimed in 1952 after much public pressure – is the largest remnant of the once-extensive kauri forests of northern NZ. The forest road (SH12) stretches for 18km and passes some huge trees – a kauri can reach 60m in height and have a trunk more than 5m in diameter.

Control of the forest has been returned to Te Roroa, the local *iwi* (tribe), as part of a settlement for Crown breaches of the Treaty of Waitangi. Te Roroa runs the Waipoua Forest Visitor Centre (p163), near the south end of the park.

Another option to visit the forest is on a twilight tour, departing from Omapere with Footprints Waipoua (p161).

◉ Sights

Tane Mahuta TREE
Near the north end of the park, not far from the road, stands mighty Tane Mahuta, named for the Māori forest god. At 51.5m,

with a 13.8m girth and wood mass of 244.5 cu metres, he's the largest kauri alive, and has been holding court here for somewhere between 1200 and 2000 years.

Te Matua Ngahere
TREE

From the Kauri Walks car park, a 20-minute (each way) walk leads past the **Four Sisters**, a graceful stand of four tall trees fused together at the base, to Te Matua Ngahere (the Father of the Forest). At 30m, he has a significant presence. Reinforced by a substantial girth – he's the fattest living kauri (16.4m) – the tree presides over a clearing surrounded by mature trees resembling mere matchsticks in comparison.

A 30-minute (one way) path leads from near the Four Sisters to **Yakas**, the seventh-largest kauri.

Waipoua Forest Visitor Centre
ARTS CENTRE

(☑ 09-439 6445; www.teroroa.iwi.nz/visit-waipoua; 1 Waipoua River Rd; ☺ 9am-4pm Oct-Apr, 10am-4pm Tue-Sun May-Sep) Interesting exhibition on the kauri forests, guided tours ($25), flax-weaving lessons ($5) and a good cafe. You can also plant your own kauri tree – complete with GPS coordinates – for $180.

🛏 Sleeping

Waipoua Forest Campground
CAMPGROUND $

(☑ 09-439 6445; www.teroroa.iwi.nz/visit-waipoua; 1 Waipoua River Rd; sites/units/house from $15/20/175) Situated next to the Waipoua River and the visitor centre, this peaceful camping ground offers hot showers, flush toilets and a kitchen. The cabins are extremely spartan, with unmade squab beds (bring your own linen or hire it). There are also whole houses for rent, sleeping 10.

★ Waipoua Lodge
B&B $$$

(☑ 09-439 0422; www.waipoualodge.co.nz; SH12; d incl breakfast $585; ☏) This fine old villa at the southern edge of the forest has four luxurious, spacious suites, which were originally the stables, the woolshed and the calf-rearing pen. Decadent dinners ($80) are available.

ℹ Information

Waipoua Forest Visitor Centre (☑ 09-439 6445; www.teroroa.iwi.nz/visit-waipoua; 1 Waipoua River Rd; ☺ 9am-6.30pm summer, 9am-4pm winter) Waipoua Forest Visitor Centre, run by Te Roroa, is a cafe and camping ground near the south end of Waipoua Forest.

Trounson Kauri Park

The 450-hectare Trounson Kauri Park has an easy half-hour loop walk that leads from the picnic area by the road. It passes through beautiful forest with streams, some fine kauri stands, a couple of fallen trees, and two pairs of trees with conjoined trunks known as the Four Sisters. DOC operates a **campsite** (www.doc.govt.nz; sites per adult/child $10/5) at the edge of the park with a communal kitchen and hot showers.

Just 2km from SH12, **Kauri Coast Top 10 Holiday Park** (☑ 09-439 0621, 0800 807 200; www.kauricoasttop10.co.nz; Trounson Park Rd; sites/units from $42/125; @ ☏) is an attractive riverside camping ground with good facilities and a small shop. It also organises nighttime **nature walks** (adult/child $25/15), which explain the flora and nocturnal wildlife that thrives here. This is a rare chance to see a kiwi in the wild. Trounson has a predator-eradication program and has become a mainland refuge for threatened native bird species, so you should at least hear a morepork (a native owl) or a brown kiwi.

If you're approaching from the north, it's easier to take the second turn-off to the park, near Kaihu, which avoids a rough unsealed road.

Kai Iwi Lakes

These three trout-filled freshwater lakes nestle together near the coast, 12km off SH12. The largest, **Taharoa**, has blue water fringed with sandy patches. **Lake Waikere** is popular with water-skiers, while **Lake Kai Iwi** is relatively untouched. A half-hour walk leads from the lakes to the coast and it's another two hours to reach the base of volcanic **Maunganui Bluff** (460m); the hike up and down it takes five hours.

Camping (☑ 09-439 0986; www.kaipara.govt.nz; adult/child $10/5) is permitted at the side of Lake Taharoa; cold showers, drinking water and flush toilets are provided.

Baylys Beach

A village of brightly coloured baches and a few new holiday mansions, Baylys Beach is 12km from Dargaville, off SH12. It lies on 100km-long Ripiro Ocean Beach, a surf-pounded stretch of coast that has been the site of many shipwrecks. The beach is a gazetted highway:

you can drive along its hard sand at low tide, although it is primarily for 4WDs. Despite being NZ's longest drivable beach, it's less well known and hence less travelled than Ninety Mile Beach. Ask locals about conditions and check your car-rental agreement before venturing onto the sand. Quad bikes can be hired at the holiday park; ask there also about an equine outing along the sand with **Baylys Beach Horse Treks** (☑ 027 697 9610; www. baylysbeachhorsetreks.webs.com; 24 Seaview Rd; 1/2/3hr $50/70/90; ☺ late Oct-Easter).

🛏 Sleeping

Baylys Beach Holiday Park   HOLIDAY PARK **$**
(☑ 09-439 6349; www.baylysbeach.co.nz; 24 Seaview Rd; sites/units from $18/65; @ 🛜) Circled by pohutukawa trees, this midsized camping ground has tidy facilities and attractive cream and green units, some with funky Kiwiana decor. Options range from basic cabins to a cottage sleeping six.

Sunset View Lodge   B&B **$$**
(☑ 09-439 4342; www.sunsetviewlodge.co.nz; 7 Alcmene Lane; r $175-195; 🛜 ▦) If gin-in-hand sunset gazing is your thing, this large, modern B&B fits the bill. The upstairs rooms have terrific sea views and there's a self-service bar with an honesty box in the guest lounge.

Dargaville

POP 4500

When a town proclaims itself the 'kumara capital of NZ' (it produces two-thirds of the country's sweet potatoes), you should know not to expect too much. Founded in 1872 by timber merchant Joseph Dargaville, this once-important river port thrived on the export of kauri timber and gum. As the forests were decimated, it declined, and today it's a quiet backwater servicing the agricultural Northern Wairoa area.

👁 Sights

Dargaville Museum   MUSEUM
(☑ 09-439 7555; www.dargavillemuseum.co.nz; Harding Rd; adult/child $15/5; ☺ 9am-4pm, to 5pm summer) The hilltop Dargaville Museum is more interesting than most regional museums. There's a large gumdigging display, plus maritime, Māori and musical-instrument sections, and a neat model railway. Outside, the masts of the *Rainbow Warrior* are mounted at a lookout near a *pa* site, and there's a recreation of a gumdiggers' camp.

Kumara Box   FARM
(☑ 09-439 7018; www.kumarabox.co.nz; 503 Pouto Rd; kumara show $20, train ride $10; ☺ by prior booking) To learn all about kumara, book ahead for Kumara Ernie's show. It's surprisingly entertaining, usually involving a journey by home-built tractor-train through the fields to 'NZ's smallest church'.

🛏 Sleeping & Eating

Campervans can stay at the Dargaville Museum car park for $15 per night, and there are decent motels and a backpackers hostel.

Greenhouse Backpackers   HOSTEL **$**
(☑ 09-439 6342; greenhousebackpackers@ihug. co.nz; 15 Gordon St; dm/d $29/70; @ 🛜) This converted 1921 schoolhouse has classrooms partitioned into a large dorm and a communal lounge, both painted with colourful murals. Better still are the cosy units in the back garden.

Blah, Blah, Blah...   CAFE **$$**
(☑ 09-439 6300; 101 Victoria St; breakfast $10-19, lunch $10-20, dinner $22-35; ☺ 9am-4pm Sun & Mon, 9am-late Tue-Sat) The number-one eatery in Dargaville has a garden area, hip music, deli-style snacks, a global menu, including dukkah, pizza and steak, and beer, wine and cocktails.

Aratapu Tavern   TEX-MEX, PUB FOOD **$$**
(☑ 09-439 5923; www.aratapu.com; 701 Pouto Rd; mains $10-30; ☺ kitchen 11am-10pm, bar 11am-late) This welcoming country pub around 7km from Dargaville on the road to Poutu Point is deservedly famous for its lamb shanks, but also of flavour-packed interest is the Tex-Mex food, including tacos and burritos, prepared by the bubbly Texan co-owner. There's also occasional live music in the garden bar on Saturdays.

ℹ Information

DOC Kauri Coast Area Office (☑ 09-439 3450; www.doc.govt.nz; 150 Colville Rd; ☺ 8am-4.30pm Mon-Fri) Good selection of Northland tramping and camping information.

Visitor Information Centre (☑ 09-439 4975; www.kauriinfocentre.co.nz; 4 Murdoch St; ☺ 9am-5.30pm; 🛜) Operates out of the Woodturners Kauri Gallery & Studio. Books accommodation and tours.

ℹ Getting There & Away

Weekday shuttle buses run by West Coaster (p126) link Dargaville with Whangarei. **Te Wai-**

roa Coachlines (☑027 482 2950; www.tewaio-racoachlines.co.nz; one way adult/child $50/40) leaves Auckland on a Friday night and returns from Dargaville on Sunday evening.

Poutu Point

A narrow spit descends south of Dargaville, bordered by the Tasman Sea and Wairoa River, and comes to an abrupt halt at the entrance of NZ's biggest harbour, the Kaipara. It's an incredibly remote headland, punctuated by dozens of petite dune lakes and the lonely Kaipara Lighthouse (built from kauri in 1884). Less than 10km separates Kaipara Harbour's north and south heads, but if you were to drive between the two you'd cover 267km.

A 4WD can be put to its proper use on the ocean-hugging 71km stretch of beach from Dargaville. DOC's *Pouto Hidden Treasures* is a helpful guide for motorists, with tips for protecting both your car and the fragile ecosystem. It can be downloaded at www.doc.govt.nz.

To explore the huge expanse of sand dunes on an organised tour, contact Jock at **Poutu Sand Safaris** (☑09-439 6678; www.pouto.co.nz/activities.html; per person from $35). For somewhere to stay, go to **Poutu Point Accommodation** (☑09-439 0199; www.pouto.co.nz/accommodation.html; sites & dm $15, apt $150).

Matakohe

POP 400

Apart from the rural charms of this village, the key reason for visiting is the superb **Kauri Museum** (☑09-431 7417; www.kaurimuseum.com; 5 Church Rd; adult/child $25/8;

⊗9am-5pm). The giant cross-sections of trees are astounding, but the entire industry is brought to life through video kiosks, artefacts, fabulous furniture and marquetry, and reproductions of a pioneer sawmill, boarding house, gumdigger's hut and Victorian home. The Gum Room holds a weird and wonderful collection of kauri gum, the amber substance that can be carved, sculpted and polished to a jewel-like quality. The museum shop stocks mementoes crafted from kauri wood and gum.

Facing the museum is the tiny kauri-built **Matakohe Pioneer Church** (1867), which served both Methodists and Anglicans, and acted as the community's hall and school. Nearby, you can wander through a historic school house (1878) and post office/telephone exchange (1909).

🛏 Sleeping

Matakohe Holiday Park   HOLIDAY PARK **$**
(☑09-431 6431; www.matakoheholidaypark.co.nz; 66 Church Rd; sites/units from $38/65; ⊛🢣🢥) This little park has modern amenities, plenty of space and good views of Kaipara Harbour.

Matakohe House   B&B **$$**
(☑09-431 7091; www.matakohehouse.co.nz; 24 Church Rd; d $160; 🢣) This B&B occupies a pretty villa with a cafe attached. The simply furnished rooms open out onto a veranda and offer winning touches such as complimentary port and chocolates.

ℹ Getting There & Away

Te Wairoa Coachlines (p164) runs a bus to Dargaville leaving Auckland on Friday night and returning on Sunday night. This service stops at Matakohe's Kauri Museum on request.

Waikato & the Coromandel Peninsula

Best Beaches & Outdoors

➔ New Chum's Beach (p204)

➔ Cathedral Cove (p208)

➔ Opito (p204)

➔ Manu Bay (p179)

➔ Waitomo Caves (p187)

Best Places to Sleep

➔ Earthstead (p182)

➔ Hush Boutique Accommodation (p201)

➔ Purangi Garden Accommodation (p208)

➔ Hidden Valley (p176)

➔ Aroha Mountain Lodge (p185)

Why Go?

Verdant rolling hills line New Zealand's mighty Waikato River, and adrenaline junkies can surf at Raglan, or undertake extreme underground pursuits in the extraordinary Waitomo Caves.

But this is also Tainui country. In the 1850s this powerful Māori tribal coalition elected a king to resist the loss of land and sovereignty. The fertile Waikato was forcibly taken from them, but they retained control of the rugged King Country to within a whisper of the 20th century.

To the northeast, the Coromandel Peninsula juts into the Pacific, forming the Hauraki Gulf's eastern boundary. The peninsula's east coast has some of the North Island's best white-sand beaches, and the muddy wetlands and picturesque stony bays of the west coast have long been a refuge for alternative lifestylers. Down the middle, the mountains are crisscrossed with walking tracks, allowing trampers to explore large tracts of isolated bush studded with kauri trees.

When to Go

➔ Beachy accommodation in Waihi, Whitianga, Whangamata and Raglan peaks during the summer holidays from Christmas until the end of January. New Year's Eve in particular can be very busy.

➔ Balmy February and March are much quieter around the Coromandel Peninsula with settled weather and smaller crowds. Rainfall peaks in the mountainous Coromandel region from May to September.

➔ The Waikato region can see summer droughts, but the southern area around Taumarunui is often wetter and colder.

➔ If you avoid the height of summer school holidays (Christmas to January), accommodation is plentiful in the Waikato region.

➔ Raglan's surf breaks are popular year-round.

❶ Getting There & Away

Hamilton is the region's transport hub, with its airport servicing extensive domestic routes. Buses link the city to everywhere in the North Island. Most inland towns are also well connected on bus routes, but the remote coastal communities (apart from Mokau on SH3) are less well served.

Transport options on the Coromandel Peninsula are more limited, and the beaches and coastline of the area are most rewarding with independent transport.

WAIKATO

History

By the time Europeans started to arrive, this region – stretching as far north as Auckland's Manukau Harbour – had long been the homeland of the Waikato tribes, descended from the Tainui migration. In settling this land, the Waikato tribes displaced or absorbed tribes from earlier migrations.

Initially European contact was on Māori terms and to the advantage of the local people. Their fertile land, which was already cultivated with kumara and other crops, was well suited to the introduction of new fruits and vegetables. By the 1840s the Waikato economy was booming, with bulk quantities of produce exported to the settlers in Auckland and beyond.

Relations between the two cultures soured during the 1850s, largely due to the colonists' pressure to purchase Māori land. In response, a confederation of tribes united to elect a king to safeguard their interests, forming what became known as the Kingitanga (King Movement).

In July 1863 Governor Grey sent a huge force to invade the Waikato and exert colonial control. After almost a year of fighting, known as the Waikato War, the Kingites retreated south to what became branded the King Country.

The war resulted in the confiscation of 3600 sq km of land, much of which was given to colonial soldiers to farm and defend. In 1995 the Waikato tribes received a full Crown apology for the wrongful invasion and confiscation of their lands, as well as a $170 million package, including the return of land that the Crown still held.

Rangiriri

Following SH1 south from Auckland you're retracing the route of the colonial army in the spectacular land grab that was the Waikato War. On 20 November 1863 around

1500 British troops, backed by gunboats and artillery, attacked the substantial fortifications erected by the Māori king's warriors at Rangiriri. They were repulsed a number of times and lost 49 men, but overnight many of the 500 Māori defenders retreated; the remaining 183 were taken prisoner the next day after the British gained entry to the *pa* (fortified village) by conveniently misunderstanding a flag of truce.

◉ Sights

Māori War & Early Settlers Cemetery CEMETERY
(Rangiriri Rd ⊙24hr) The Māori War & Early Settlers Cemetery houses the soldiers' graves and a mound covering the mass grave of 36 Māori warriors.

Rangiriri Heritage Centre MUSEUM
(☑07-826 3667; www.nzmuseums.co.nz; 12 Rangiriri Rd; admission $3, free with cafe purchase; ⊙9am-3pm) The Rangiriri Heritage Centre screens a short documentary about the battle. There's also a small museum and cafe here.

✖ Eating

Rangiriri Hotel PUB FOOD $$
(☑07-826 3667; 8 Talbot St; mains lunch $12-20, dinner $17-33; ⊙11am-11pm) Next to the Rangiriri Heritage Centre is the historic Rangiriri Hotel, a cheery spot for lunch or a beer.

Waikato & the Coromandel Peninsula Highlights

1 **Far North Coromandel** (p202) Travelling remote gravel roads under a crimson canopy of ancient pohutukawa trees.

2 **Te Whanganui-A-Hei Marine Reserve** (p205) Kayaking around hidden islands, caves and bays.

3 **Karangahake Gorge** (p214) Penetrating the mystical depths of the dense bush.

4 **Hahei Beach** (p208) Watching the offshore islands glow in the dying haze of a summer sunset.

5 **Waitomo Caves** (p187) Seeking subterranean stimulation and trying black-water rafting.

6 **Raglan** (p175) Hitting the surf (and then the pub) at this unhurried surf town.

7 **Sanctuary Mountain Maungatautari** (p181) Tramping through an inland island paradise.

8 **Hobbiton Movie Set Tours** (p183) Channelling your inner Bilbo or Frodo at this fascinating film set.

Hamilton

POP 206,400

Landlocked cities in an island nation are never going to have the glamorous appeal of their coastal cousins. Rotorua compensates with boiling mud and Taupo has its lake, but Hamilton, despite the majestic Waikato River, is more prosaic.

The city definitely has an appeal, with vibrant bars and excellent restaurants and cafes around Hood and Victoria Sts. You're guaranteed to eat really well after visiting highlights like the Hamilton Gardens.

Oddly, the great grey-green greasy Waikato River rolls right through town, but the city's layout largely ignores its presence: unless you're driving across a bridge you'll hardly know it's there.

Most people blast along SH1 between Auckland and Hamilton in about 1½ hours, but if you're in the mood to meander, the upper Waikato has some interesting diversions including Ngaruawahia, where you will find Turangawaewae Marae.

◉ Sights

★ **Hamilton Gardens** GARDENS
(☏ 07-838 6782; www.hamiltongardens.co.nz; Cobham Dr; guided tour adult/child $15/8; ☺ enclosed gardens 7.30am-5pm, info centre 9am-5pm, guided tours 11am Sep-Apr) FREE Spread over 50 hectares southeast of the city centre, Hamilton Gardens incorporates a large park, cafe, restaurant and extravagant themed enclosed gardens. There are separate Italian Renaissance, Chinese, Japanese, English, American and Indian gardens complete with colonnades, pagodas and a mini Taj Mahal. Equally interesting are the sustainable Productive Garden Collection, fragrant herb garden and precolorisation Māori Te Parapara garden. Look for the impressive *Nga Uri O Hinetuparimaunga* (Earth Blanket) sculpture at the main gates.

Recent additions include a Tudor-style garden and a tropical garden with more than 200 different warm climate species. Booking ahead for the guided tours is recommended.

★ **Waikato Museum** MUSEUM
(www.waikatomuseum.co.nz; 1 Grantham St; admission by donation; ☺ 10am-4.30pm) FREE The excellent Waikato Museum has five main areas: an art gallery; interactive science galleries; Tainui galleries housing Māori treasures, including the magnificently carved *waka taua* (war canoe), *Te Winikawaka;* a WWI exhibition entitled 'For Us They Fell'; and a Waikato River exhibition. The museum also runs a rigorous program of public events. Admission is charged for some exhibits.

Waikato River RIVER, PARK
Bush-covered walkways run along both sides of the river and provide the city's green

---

MĀORI NZ: WAIKATO & THE COROMANDEL PENINSULA

The Waikato and King Country region remains one of the strongest pockets of Māori influence in New Zealand. This is the heartland of the Tainui tribes, descended from those who disembarked from the Tainui *waka* (canoe) in Kawhia in the 14th century. Split into four main tribal divisions (Waikato, Hauraki, Ngāti Maniapoto and Ngāti Raukawa), Tainui are inextricably linked with the Kingitanga (King Movement), which has its base in Ngaruawahia.

The best opportunities to interact with Māori culture is Ngaruawahia's Regatta Day and Koroneihana celebrations. Interesting *taonga* (treasures) are displayed at museums in Hamilton and Te Awamutu.

Reminders of the Waikato Land War can be found at Rangiriri, Rangiaowhia and Orakau. See www.waikatowar.co.nz to download maps, audio files and a smartphone app covering various locations of the fighting from 1863 to 1864.

Dozens of *marae* (meeting house) complexes are dotted around the countryside – including at Awakino, and at Kawhia, where the Tainui *waka* is buried. You won't be able to visit these without permission, but you can get decent views from the gates. Some regional tours include an element of Māori culture, including Ruakuri Cave at Waitomo.

Although it has a long and rich Māori history, the nearby Coromandel Peninsula doesn't offer many opportunities to engage with the culture. Historic *pa* (fortified village) sites are dotted around, with the most accessible being Paaku. There are others at Opito Beach, Hahei and Hot Water Beach.

belt. Jogging paths continue to the board-walk circling Lake Rotoroa, west of the centre. Memorial Park is closer to town and has the remains of PS *Rangiriri* – an iron-clad, steam-powered gunboat from the Waikato War – embedded in the river bank.

Zealong Tea Estate TEA ESTATE
(📞0800 932 566; www.zealong.com; 495 Gordonton Rd, Gordonton; tea experience adult/child $25/13; ⏰10am-5pm Tue-Sun, tours 9.30am & 2.30pm) Interesting tours learning about the only tea plantation in NZ, located around 10km north-east of Hamilton. For an extra $35, partner the tea experience with a tiffin-style high tea spread of sweet and savoury snacks. There's also a good on-site cafe serving high tea without the tour ($42) and offering tea tastings ($9 per person) and main dishes.

Riff Raff MONUMENT
(www.riffraffstatue.org; Victoria St) One of Hamilton's more unusual public artworks is a life-sized statue of *Rocky Horror Picture Show* writer Richard O'Brien aka Riff Raff, the time-warping alien from the planet Transsexual. It looks over a small park on the site of the former Embassy Theatre where O'Brien worked as a hairdresser, though it's hard to imagine 1960s Hamilton inspired the tale of bisexual alien decadence. Free wi-fi emanates from Riff Raff's three-pronged stun gun.

Hamilton Zoo ZOO
(📞07-838 6720; www.hamiltonzoo.co.nz; 183 Brymer Rd; adult/child/family $22/10/60; tours extra; ⏰9am-5pm, last entry 3.30pm) Hamilton Zoo houses 500-plus species including wily and curious chimpanzees. Guided-tour options include Eye2Eye and Face2Face opportunities to go behind the scenes to meet various animals, plus daily Meet the Keeper talks from the critters' caregivers. The zoo is 8km northwest of Hamilton city centre.

Classics Museum MUSEUM
(www.classicsmuseum.co.nz; 11 Railside Pl, Frankton; adult/child $20/8; ⏰9am-4pm) Travel in time amid this collection of over 100 classic cars from the first half of the 20th century. Even if you're not a motorhead, you'll still be dazzled by the crazy Amphicar and the cool Maserati and Corvette sports cars. The museum is just off SH1, northwest of central Hamilton.

🏃 Activities

Waikato River Explorer CRUISE
(📞0800 139 756; www.waikatoexplorer.co.nz; Hamilton Gardens Jetty; adult/child $29/15; ⏰Wed-Sun, daily 26 Dec-6 Feb) Scenic 1½-hour cruises along the Waikato River depart from the Hamilton Gardens jetty. On Sunday at 11am, the boat cruises (adult/child $79/40) to the Vilagrad Winery for wine tasting and a Mediterranean-style spit roast lunch. On Saturday from 2pm, there's more wine tasting and a cheese platter at the nearby Mystery Creek area ($79/35).

Extreme Edge ROCK CLIMBING
(📞07-847 5858; www.extremeedge.co.nz; 90 Greenwood St; day pass incl harness adult/child $18.50/14; ⏰noon-9.30pm Mon-Fri, 9am-7pm Sat & Sun) Near the Frankton train station, west of town, Extreme Edge has hyper-coloured climbing walls, 14m of which is overhanging. There's a kids' climbing zone and free safety lessons.

Kiwi Balloon Company BALLOONING
(📞07-843 8538, 021 912 679; www.kiwiballooncompany.co.nz; per person $350) Floating above lush Waikato countryside, the whole experience takes about four hours and includes a champagne breakfast and an hour's flying time.

⭐ Festivals & Events

Hamilton Gardens Arts Festival PERFORMING ARTS
(📞07-859 1317; www.hgaf.co.nz; ⏰Feb) Music, comedy, theatre, dance and movies, all served up alfresco in the Hamilton Gardens during the last two weeks of February.

Balloons over Waikato SPORTS
(📞07-856 7215; www.balloonsoverwaikato.co.nz; ⏰Mar) A colourful hot-air-balloon fest.

🛏 Sleeping

The road into town from Auckland (Ulster St) is lined with dozens of unremarkable, traffic-noisy motels, which are passable for short stays. Hotels in the city centre have regular online discounts and provide good access to cafes, restaurants and bars.

Backpackers Central HOSTEL $
(📞07-839 1928; www.backpackerscentral.co.nz; 846 Victoria St; dm $30, s $50, r $80-125; @🖥) Well-run hostel with dorms and singles on one floor, doubles and family rooms on another – some with en suite bathrooms and all with access to a shared kitchen and lounge. Worth considering as an alternative to a motel room if you're travelling as a couple or in a group.

Hamilton City Holiday Park HOLIDAY PARK $
(📞07-855 8255; www.hamiltoncityholidaypark.co.nz; 14 Ruakura Rd; campsites/cabins/units from

$35/50/80; @ 🤖) Simple cabins and leafy sites are the rule at this shady park. It's reasonably close to town (2km east of the centre) and very affordable.

City Centre B&B
B&B $$

(📞 07-838 1671; www.citycentrebnb.co.nz; 3 Anglesea St; r $90-125; @ 🤖 ✻) At the quiet river-side end of a central city street (five minutes' walk to the Victoria and Hood Sts action), this sparkling self-contained apartment opens onto a swimming pool. There's also a bedroom available in a wing of the main house. Self-catering breakfast is provided.

Anglesea Motel
MOTEL $$

(📞 0800 426 453, 07-834 0010; www.angleseamotel.co.nz; 36 Liverpool St; units $140-300; @ 🤖 ✻) Getting great feedback from travellers and a preferred option to anything on Ulster St's 'motel row', the Anglesea has plenty of space, friendly managers, pool, squash and tennis courts, and not un-stylish decor.

Ibis Hotel
HOTEL $$

(📞 07-859 9200; www.ibis.com; 18 Alma St; r $110-130; ✻ 🤖) The riverfront Ibis is a good option if you're looking for quiet, centrally located digs just a short walk from the best of Hamilton's bars and restaurants. Rooms

Waikato & King Country

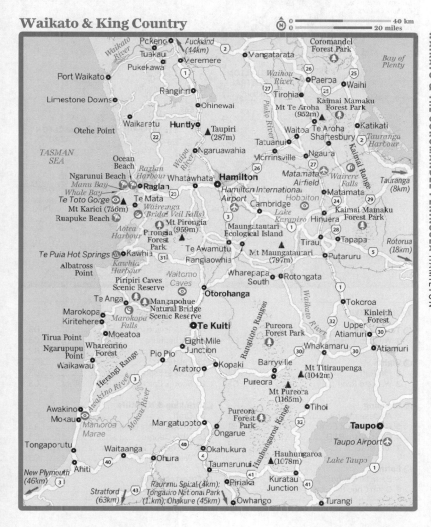

are compact but clean and well designed. The shared public areas are spacious and colourful.

✕ Eating

★ **Duck Island Ice Cream** ICE CREAM $
(☎ 07-856 5948; 300 Grey St; ice cream from $4; ⊙ 11am-6pm Tue-Thu & Sun, to 8pm Fri & Sat) A

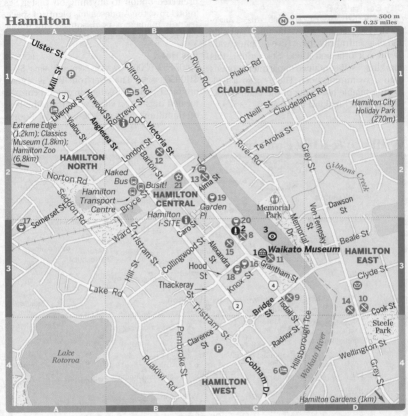

Hamilton

dazzling array of ever-changing flavours – how does crab-apple crumble or coconut and kaffir lime sound – make Duck Island quite probably NZ's best ice-cream parlour. The sunny corner location is infused with a hip retro vibe, and the refreshing house-made sodas and ice cream floats are other worthy reasons to cross the river to Hamilton East.

Banh Mi Caphe
VIETNAMESE $

(☑ 07-839 1141; www.facebook.com/banhmicaphe; 198/2 Victoria St; snacks & mains $10-17; ⊗11am-4pm Tue-Wed, to 9pm Thu-Sat) Fresh spring rolls, Vietnamese *banh mi* (sandwiches) and steaming bowls of *pho* (noodle soup) all feature at this hip spot channelling the backstreets of Hanoi.

Hamilton Farmers Market
MARKET $

(☑ 022 639 1995; www.waikatofarmersmarkets.co.nz; Te Rapa Racecourse; ⊗8am-noon Sun) Relocated around 4km north of central Hamilton to the Te Rapa Racecourse, this farmers market is a veritable Sunday-morning feast of local cheeses, baked goods and produce. A coffee from the Rocket caravan and a flash hot dog from Bangin Bangaz is our recommended breakfast combo.

Scott's Epicurean
INTERNATIONAL $

(☑ 07-839 6680; www.scottsepicurean.co.nz; 181 Victoria St; mains $11-20; ⊗7am-5pm Mon-Fri, 8.30am-4pm Sat & Sun) This gorgeous joint features swanky leather banquettes, pressed-tin ceilings, great coffee and an interesting and affordable menu: try the *pytti panna* (Swedish bubble-and-squeak) for breakfast or the ever-popular *spaghetti aglio e olio* (spaghetti with garlic and oil) for a quick lunch. Friendly service and fully licensed.

Rocket Espresso
CAFE $$

(☑ 07-856 5616; www.facebook.com/rocketespressobar; 385 Grey St; mains $12-22; ⊗7am-4pm Mon-Fri, 8.30am-3pm Sat & Sun) Part of the emerging dining scene across the river in Hamilton East, Rocket Espresso lures caffeine fiends to gather at communal tables strewn with foodie magazines and newspapers. The concise menu ranges from excellent counter food through to robust mains including a Mexican breakfast omelette and a terrific smoked fish pie for lunch.

★ Gothenburg
TAPAS $$

(☑ 07-834 3562; www.gothenburg.co.nz; ANZ Centre, 21 Grantham St; shared plates $7-24; ⊗9am-11pm Mon-Fri, 11.30am-late Sat) Relocated to a scenic river-side spot with high ceilings and a summer-friendly deck, Gothenburg has morphed from a bar into our favourite Hamilton restaurant. The menu of shared plates effortlessly spans the globe – try the pork and kimchi dumplings or the beef and chorizo meatballs – and the beer list features rotating taps from local Waikato craft brewers.

The range of wine and cocktails is equally stellar – especially the pomegranate mojito – and the dessert of coconut and lime panna cotta is fast becoming a Gothenburg classic.

Hazel Hayes
CAFE $$

(☑ 07-839 1953; www.hazelhayes.co.nz; 587 Victoria St; mains $10-23; ⊗7am-4pm Mon-Fri, 8am-2pm Sat) This mash-up of country kitchen decor showcases inventive cafe fare. Free-range and organic options punctuate the short, focused menu, and both the service and coffee are very good. Try the homemade hash browns with salmon and a rich hollandaise sauce and you'll definitely be set for the day.

Chim Choo Ree
MODERN NZ $$$

(☑ 07-839 4329; www.chimchooree.co.nz; 14 Bridge St; mains $36-37; ⊗11.30am-2pm & 5pm-late Mon-Sat) In an airy heritage building beside the river, Chim Choo Ree focuses on small plates like Thai fish and papaya salad, gin-cured salmon and confit pork belly, plus larger, equally inventive mains using duck, lamb venison and snapper. Local foodies wash it all down with a great wine list and flavourful NZ craft beers.

Palate
MODERN NZ, FUSION $$$

(☑ 07-834 2921; www.palaterestaurant.co.nz; 20 Alma St; mains $34-38; ⊗11.30am-2pm Tue-Fri, 5.30pm-late Mon-Sat) Simple, sophisticated Palate has a well-deserved reputation for lifting the culinary bar across regional NZ. The innovative menu features highlights like red roasted duck with yams, scallops, shiitake and a chilli broth. The wine selection is Hamilton's finest.

🍷 Drinking & Nightlife

The blocks around Victoria and Hood Sts make for a boozy bar-hop, with weekend live music and DJs. The city also has a good craft beer scene worth exploring. Friday is the big night of the week.

Craft
CRAFT BEER

(☑ 07-839 4531; www.facebook.com/craftbeerhamilton; 15 Hood St; ⊗3pm-late Wed-Thu, 11.30am-late Fri-Sun) Fifteen rotating taps of amber goodness flow at Craft, which is plenty to keep the city's craft beer buffs coming back. Brews from around NZ make a regular appearance, with occasional surprising additions from international cult breweries. Quiz night kicks off most Wednesdays at 7.30pm, and decent sliders and wood-fired pizza could well see you making a night of it.

Local Taphouse
BAR

(☑ 07-834 4923; www.facebook.com/thelocaltaphouse; 346 Victoria St, City Co-Op; ☺ 11am-late) Part of Hamilton's new City Co-Op eating and drinking precinct, the Local Taphouse features locally sourced beers from the nearby regions of Waikato, Bay of Plenty and Coromandel. Food is served, including hearty pots of mussels and gourmet burgers. Other recently opened and adjacent City Co-Op options include a Spanish tapas and grill restaurant and an after-dark cocktail bar.

Little George
CRAFT BEER

(☑ 07-834 4345; www.facebook.com/littlegeorgepopupbar; 15 Hood St; ☺ 4-11pm Tue-Thu, 2pm-1am Fri-Sun) The more compact and central sibling to Good George, Little George is another excellent bar along Hood St's nightlife strip. Beers from Good George are regularly featured, but guest taps often showcase other Kiwi craft breweries. Good bar snacks – check out $3 Taco Tuesdays – and a concise wine list are other diverting attractions.

Good George Brewing
BREWERY

(☑ 07-847 3223; www.goodgeorge.co.nz; 32a Somerset St, Frankton; tours incl beer & food $19; ☺ 11am-late, tours from 6pm Tue-Thu) Channelling a cool industrial vibe, the former Church of St George is now a shrine to craft beer. Order a flight of five beers ($16), and partner the hoppy heaven with wood-fired pizzas ($20 to $23) or main meals ($18 to $33). Our favourite brews are the citrusy American Pale Ale and the zingy Drop Hop Cider. Tours must be booked ahead.

Check online for lots of weekly beer and food specials, and look forward to tasty seasonal brews from Good George's sour beer program.

Wonderhorse
COCKTAIL BAR, CRAFT BEER

(☑ 07-839 2281; www.facebook.com/wonderhorsebar; 232 Victoria St; ☺ 5pm-3am Wed-Sat) Tucked away around 20m off Victoria St, Wonderhorse regularly features craft beers from niche local brewers like Shunters Yard and

Brewaucracy. Vintage vinyl is often spinning on the turntable, and sliders and Asian street eats combine with killer cocktails at one of Hamilton's best bars.

☆ Entertainment

Lido Cinema
CINEMA

(☑ 07-838 9010; www.lidocinema.co.nz; Level 1, Centre Place, 501 Victoria St; adult/child $16/10; ☺ 10am-late) Art-house movies with $10.50 Tuesday tickets.

ℹ Information

Anglesea Clinic (☑ 07-858 0800; www.angleseamedical.co.nz; cnr Anglesea & Thackeray Sts; ☺ 24hr) For accidents and urgent medical assistance.

DOC (Department of Conservation; ☑ 07-858 1000; www.doc.govt.nz; Level 5, 73 Rostrevor St; ☺ 8am-4.30pm Mon-Fri) Maps and brochures on walking tracks, campsites and DOC huts.

Hamilton i-SITE (☑ 07-958 5960, 0800 242 645; www.visithamilton.co.nz; cnr Caro & Alexandra Sts; ☺ 9am-5pm Mon-Fri, 9.30am-3.30pm Sat & Sun; ☏) Accommodation, activities and transport bookings, plus free wi-fi right across Garden Pl.

Post Office (☑ 0800 501 501; 1b/20 Clyde St, Hamilton East; ☺ 9am-5pm Mon-Fri, to noon Sat) Across the river in Hamilton East but the nearest branch to central Hamilton.

Waikato Hospital (☑ 07-839 8899; www.waikatodhb.govt.nz; Pembroke St; ☺ 24hr) Main hospital for the Waikato region; around 3km south of central Hamilton.

ℹ Getting There & Away

AIR

Air New Zealand (☑ 0800 737 000; www.airnewzealand.co.nz) has regular direct flights from Hamilton to Auckland, Christchurch, Palmerston North and Wellington. **Kiwi Regional Airlines** (☑ 07-444 5020; www.flykiwiair.co.nz) flies to/from Hamilton to Nelson, linking from there to Dunedin.

BUS

All buses arrive and depart from the **Hamilton Transport Centre** (☑ 07-834 3457; www.hamilton.co.nz; cnr Anglesea & Bryce Sts; ☏).

Waikato Regional Council's **Busit!** (☑ 0800 4287 5463; www.busit.co.nz) coaches serve the region, including Ngaruawahia, Cambridge, Te Awamutu and Raglan.

InterCity (☑ 09-583 5780; www.intercity.co.nz) services numerous destinations including the following:

DESTINATION	PRICE	TIME	FREQUENCY (DAILY)
Auckland	$12-35	2hr	11
Cambridge	$10-20	25min	9
Matamata	$10-25	50min	4
Ngaruawahia	$10-21	20min	9
Rotorua	$14-35	1½hr	5
Te Aroha	$10	1hr	2
Te Awamutu	$10-22	35min	3
Wellington	$27-70	5hr	3

Naked Bus (www.nakedbus.com) services run to the following destinations (among many others):

DESTINATION	PRICE	TIME	FREQUENCY (DAILY)
Auckland	$17-19	2hr	5
Cambridge	$15	30min	5-7
Matamata	$20	1hr	1
Ngaruawahia	$15	30min	5
Rotorua	$10	1½hr	4-5
Wellington	$20-30	9½hr	1-2

SHUTTLE BUS

Aerolink Shuttles (☎0800 151 551; www.aerolink.nz; one-way $80) On-demand shuttle buses between Hamilton and Auckland airport.
Raglan Scenic Tours (☎021 0274 7014, 07-825 0507; www.raglanscenictours.co.nz) Shuttle linking Raglan with Hamilton International Airport (one-way $42.50) and the Hamilton Transport Centre or Frankton train station ($35).

TRAIN

Hamilton is on the **Northern Explorer** (☎0800 872 467; www.kiwiscenic.co.nz) route between Auckland ($49, 2½ hours) and Wellington ($179, 9½ hours) via Otorohanga ($49, 45 minutes). Trains depart Auckland on Monday, Thursday and Saturday and stop at Hamilton's **Frankton train station** (Fraser St), 1km west of the city centre: there are no ticket sales here – see the website for ticketing details.

ⓘ Getting Around

TO/FROM THE AIRPORT

Hamilton International Airport (HIA; ☎07-848 9027; www.hamiltonairport.co.nz; Airport Rd) Hamilton airport is 12km south of the city.
Super Shuttle (☎0800 748 885, 07-843 7778; www.supershuttle.co.nz; one-way $30) Book online prior to departure.

BUS

Busit! (☎0800 4287 5463; www.busit.co.nz; city routes adult/child $3.30/2.20) Hamilton's Busit! network services the city centre and suburbs daily from around 7am to 7.30pm (later on Friday). It also runs a free CBD shuttle looping around Victoria, Liverpool, Anglesea and Bridge Sts every 10 minutes (7am to 6pm weekdays).

CAR

Rent-a-Dent (☎07-839 1049; www.rentadent.co.nz; 383 Anglesea St; ⊙7.30am-5pm Mon-Fri, 8am-noon Sat) Car hire.

TAXI

Hamilton Taxis (☎07-8477 477, 0800 477 477; www.hamiltontaxis.co.nz) Local taxi company.

Raglan
POP 2740

Laid-back Raglan may well be NZ's perfect surfing town. It's small enough to have escaped mass development, but it's big enough to exhibit signs of life including good eateries and a bar that attracts big-name bands in summer. Along with the famous surf spots to the south, the harbour just begs to be kayaked upon. There's also an excellent arts scene, with several galleries and shops worthy of perusal.

⊙ Sights

Old School Arts Centre ARTS CENTRE, GALLERY
(☎07-825 0023; www.raglanartscentre.co.nz; Stewart St; ⊙10am-2pm Mon & Wed, exhibition hours vary) FREE A community hub, the Old School Arts Centre has changing exhibitions and workshops, including weaving, carving, yoga and storytelling. Movies screen here regularly during summer ($11): grab a snack and a beer to complete the experience. The hippie/artsy **Raglan Creative Market** happens out the front on the second Sunday (10am to 2pm) of the month.

🏃 Activities

Raglan Rock ROCK CLIMBING, CAVING
(☎0800 724 7625; www.raglanrock.com; climbing half/full day $100/180, caving $100-120, minimum 2 people) Full instruction and all equipment for climbing on the limestone cliffs of nearby Stone Valley, or the exciting Stupid Fat Hobbit climb and abseil above Raglan Harbour. Caving options include Stone Valley and the more challenging Rattlesnake.

Raglan Kayak
KAYAKING

(☑ 07-825 8862; www.raglaneco.co.nz; Bow St Jetty; single/double kayaks per half day $40/60, 3hr guided harbour paddle per person $75; ☺ Nov-May) Raglan Harbour is great for kayaking. This outfit rents kayaks and runs guided tours. Learn the basics on the gentle Opotoru River, or paddle out to investigate the nooks and crannies of the pancake rocks on the harbour's northern edge.

Raglan Watersports
WATER SPORTS

(☑ 07-825 0507; www.raglanwatersports.co.nz; 5a Bankart St; group/private paddle-boarding lessons per person $45/65) A well-run, one-stop spot for paddle-boarding lessons, hire and guided tours; kayak rental and tours; kiteboarding and surfing lessons; and board hire. Bikes can also hired – see the website for recommendations on local rides.

Solscape
SURFING

(☑ 07-825 8268; www.solscape.co.nz; 611 Wainui Rd; board & wetsuit hire per half day $35) Super Solscape offers 2½-hour surfing lessons ($85).

👉 Tours

Waihine Moe Sunset Harbour Cruise
CRUISE

(☑ 07-825 7873; www.raglanboatcharters.co.nz; Raglan Wharf; adult/child $50/30; ☺ Thu-Sun late Dec-Mar) Two-hour sunset cruises, including a few drinks, around Raglan Harbour on the *Wahine Moe*. Ninety-minute morning harbour cruises ($30/15 per adult/child) leaving from Raglan's Bow St jetty are also available on the smaller *Harmony* vessel. Complimentary pick-ups are included.

Raglan Scenic Tours
GUIDED TOUR

(☑ 07-825 0507; www.raglanscenictours.co.nz; 5a Bankart St; 2½hr Raglan sightseeing tour adult/child $55/20) Sightseeing tours, including around the Raglan area and departures (adult/child $48/15) to Bridal Veil Falls or Te Toto Gorge. Treks up Mt Karioi can be arranged (adult from $60).

🛏 Sleeping

Solscape
HOSTEL, CABIN $

(☑ 07-825 8268; www.solscape.co.nz; 611 Wainui Rd; campsites per person $20, caboose dm/d $30/80, teepees per person $40, cottage d $100-220; @ 🛜) 🏊 With a hill-top location fringed by native bush, Solscape's ecofriendly accommodation includes teepees, rammed-earth domes, railway carriages and stylish eco-baches. There's room for tents and campervans, and simpler cottages are also available. Environmental impact is minimised with solar energy, and organic produce from the permaculture garden is used for guest meals in the Conscious Kitchen cafe.

Yoga, massage and surfing lessons are all available. Solscape is also YHA-affiliated.

Raglan West Accommodation
MOTEL $

(☑ 07-282 0248; www.raglanwestaccommodation. com; 45 Wainui Rd; d $90; 🛜) Good-value accommodation with self-contained kitchenettes just a short walk – via a handy footbridge – to the cafes, restaurants and shops of Raglan. There's also a good cafe close by for a leisurely breakfast.

Raglan Backpackers
HOSTEL $

(☑ 07-825 0515; www.raglanbackpackers.co.nz; 6 Wi Neera St; vehicle sites per person $19, dm $28-30, s $60, tw & d $74-84; @) This laid-back hostel is right on the water, with sea views from some rooms. Other rooms are arranged around a garden courtyard or in a separate building. There are free bikes and kayaks for use, and surfboards for hire, or take a yoga class, strum a guitar or drip in the sauna. No wi-fi – it 'ruins the vibe'.

Raglan Kopua Holiday Park
HOLIDAY PARK $

(☑ 07-825 8283; www.raglanholidaypark.co.nz; Marine Pde; campsites $36-40, units $85-135; @ 🛜) A neatly maintained outfit with lots of sleeping options, on the spit across the inlet from town (there's a footbridge, or drive the long way around). No shade, but there's beach swimming and plenty of room to run amok.

★ Hidden Valley
COTTAGE $$

(☑ 07-825 5813; www.hiddenvalleyraglan.com; SH23, Te Uku; d $175-245) Located on 12 hectares of native forest 3km from Raglan, Hidden Valley features two individual chalets, both with private spa pools. The Tree Tops chalet is nestled beside a stand of kahikatea (NZ white pine), while the Mountain View chalet looks out towards Mt Kariori. Decor is stylish and modern with fully self-contained kitchens. Check online for good midweek discounts.

Bow St Studios
APARTMENT $$

(☑ 07-825 0551; www.bowstreet.co.nz; 1 Bow St; studios $170-195, cottages $170-235; 🛜) With a waterfront location right in town, Bow St has self-contained studios and a historic cottage. The cool and chic decor is stylish and relaxing. The property is surrounded by a subtropical garden and shaded by well-established pohutukawa trees.

Raglan

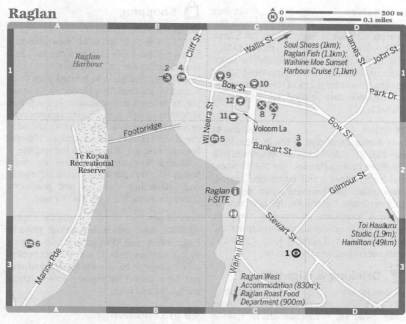

Raglan

◉ Sights
1 Old School Arts Centre C3

◉ Activities, Courses & Tours
2 Raglan Kayak B1
3 Raglan Scenic Tours C2
Raglan
Watersports .... (see 3)

◉ Sleeping
4 Bow St Studios B1
5 Raglan Backpackers C2

6 Raglan Kopua Holiday
Park A3

◉ Eating
7 Raglan Social Club C1
8 The Shack C1

◉ Drinking & Nightlife
9 Bow St Depot C1
10 Harbour View Hotel C1
11 Raglan Roast C1
12 Yot Club C1

✖ Eating

Raglan Social Club CAFE, BURGERS $
(RSC; ☏ 07-825 8405; 23 Bow St; shared plates
& burgers $15-18; ⊙ 8am-4pm Sun-Wed, until late
Thu-Sat) Shared tables and a kids playground
definitely put the social into the Raglan Social Club, and light meals – including salt
and pepper squid with lime mayonnaise –
partner with healthy salads that can also be
purchased to take away. On Thursday to Saturday evenings, the RSC is even more social
as it becomes a haven of grilled goodness as
Ragburger. There are also plenty of vegetarian and vegan options.

Raglan Roast Food Department CAFE $
(☏ 07-282 0248; www.facebook.com/food
departmentraglanroast; 45 Wainui Rd; pizza slices
$6, mains $10-14; ⊙ 8.30am-9pm) Pizza by the
slice and interesting gelato flavours – our favourite is the cinnamon and rice – reinforce
the authentic Italian credentials of Raglan
Roast Food Department. The scattering of
mismatched retro furniture is good for the
first coffee of the day, and hearty comfort
food like lasagna and gnocchi can be purchased to eat in or take away.

Raglan Fish   FISH & CHIPS $

(☑ 07-825 7544; www.facebook.com/raglan-fishshop; 92 Wallis St, Raglan Wharf; fish & chips $7-10; ☺ 9am-7pm) Super-fresh fish and chips and funky decor at this locals' favourite right on Raglan's recently restored wharf about a kilometre north of town. Fresh oysters, mussels and seafood salads are also available.

★**Shack**   CAFE, INTERNATIONAL $$

(www.theshackraglan.com; 19 Bow St; tapas $6-14, mains $12-21; ☺ 8am-5pm Sun-Thu, until late Fri & Sat; 🛜🍴) Brunch classics – try the chickpea-and-corn fritters – and interesting shared-plate mains like tempura squid and star-anise chicken feature at the best cafe in town. A longboard strapped to the wall, wobbly old floorboards, up-tempo tunes and international staff serving Kiwi wines and craft beers complete the picture.

🍷 Drinking & Nightlife

Raglan Roast   CAFE, COFFEE

(☑ 07-825 8702; www.raglanroast.co.nz; Volcom Lane; coffee $4; ☺ 7am-5pm, shorter hours in winter) Hole-in-the-wall coffee roaster with the best brew in town. Stop by for a cup, a cookie and a conversation. If this location is busy, pop around the corner to Electric Ave, which is normally quieter. Don't leave town without buying a few fragrant bags of coffee for life on the road.

Bow St Depot   BAR, CAFE

(☑ 07-825 0976; www.bowstreetdepot.co.nz; 2 Bow St; ☺ 11am-1am) On a warm summer's night, the best place to be in town is at Bow St Depot's spacious garden bar. Kick back with a few craft beers from Hamilton's Good George, relax into the beats of the occasional DJs, or graze on shared plates including prawn and lemongrass dumplings or pulled pork sliders.

Yot Club   BAR, LIVE MUSIC

(☑ 07-825 8968; wwww.facebook.com/YOTClub Raglan; 9 Bow St; admission free-$25; ☺ 8pm-late Wed-Sat, 4pm-late Sun) Raucous, nocturnal bar with DJs and touring bands.

Harbour View Hotel   PUB

(☑ 07-825 8010; www.harbourviewhotel.co.nz; 14 Bow St; ☺ 11am-late) Classic old pub with main-street drinks on the shaded veranda. Decent pizza too and occasional live music on weekends and during summer.

🛍 Shopping

★**Toi Hauāuru Studio**   ARTS

(☑ 021 174 4629, 07-825 0244; www.toihauauru. com; 4338 Main Rd; ☺ 10am-5pm Wed-Sun) Run by local artist Simon Te Wheoro, this excellent gallery and shop is located 2km from Raglan on the road from Hamilton. Contemporary artwork and sculpture with a Māori influence as well as *pounamu* (greenstone) carvings are for sale. Simon is also skilled in the Māori art of *ta moko* (tattoo) – if you're keen for one, get in touch via the website.

Quirky local surfwear and colourful Māori *hei tiki* (pendants) make affordable and interesting souvenirs and *pounamu* (greenstone) carvings are also for sale.

Soul Shoes   SHOES, ACCESSORIES

(☑ 07-825 8765; www.soulshoes.co.nz; Wallis St, Raglan Wharf; ☺ 9.30am-5pm) World famous in Raglan since 1973. In a new century, Soul Shoes' range of handmade leather footwear has been joined by equally cool satchels, backpacks and bags.

ⓘ Information

Raglan i-SITE (☑ 07-825 0556; www.raglan. org.nz; 13 Wainui Rd; ☺ 9am-7pm Mon-Fri, 9.30am-6pm Sat & Sun) Department of Conservation (DOC) brochures, plus information about accommodation and activities including kitesurfing and paddle boarding. Check out the attached museum, especially the exhibition on the history of Raglan's surfing scene.

West Coast Health Centre (☑ 07-825 0114; wchc@wave.co.nz; 12 Wallis St; ☺ 9am-5pm Mon-Fri) General medical assistance.

ⓘ Getting There & Around

Raglan is 48km west of Hamilton along SH23. Unsealed back roads connect Raglan to Kawhia, 50km south; they're slow, winding and prone to rockslides, but scenic and certainly off the beaten track. Head back towards Hamilton for 7km and take the Te Mata/Kawhia turn-off and follow the signs; allow at least an hour.

Waikato District Council's **Busit!** (☑ 0800 4287 5463; www.busit.co.nz; adult/child $9/5.60) heads between Hamilton and Raglan (one hour) three times daily on weekdays and twice daily on weekends.

Raglan Scenic Tours (p176) runs a Raglan–Hamilton shuttle bus (one-way $42.50) and direct transfers to/from Auckland International Airport.

For a cab, call **Raglan Taxi** (☑ 027 525 0506, 07-825 0506).

South of Raglan

South of Raglan, the North Island's west coast unfurls with a series of excellent surf beaches. Whale Bay and Manu Bay draw board riders from around the world, and for non-surfers, there are scenic walking opportunities around Mt Karioi and Mt Pirongia.

◉ Sights

Mt Karioi   MOUNTAIN
(Sleeping Lady) In legend, Mt Karioi (756m), the Sleeping Lady (check out that profile), is the sister to Mt Pirongia. At its base (8km south of Whale Bay), **Te Toto Gorge** is a steep cleft in the mountainside, with a vertigo-inducing lookout perched high over the chasm. Starting from the Te Toto Gorge car park, a strenuous but scenic track goes up the western slope. It takes 2½ hours to reach a lookout point, followed by an easier hour up to the summit.

From the eastern side, the **Wairake Track** is a steeper 2½-hour climb to the summit, where it meets the Te Toto Track.

Waireinga   WATERFALL
(Bridal Veil Falls) Just past Te Mata (a short drive south of the main Raglan–Hamilton road) is the turn-off to the 55m-high Waireinga, 4km from the main road. From the car park, it's an easy 10-minute walk through mossy native bush to the top of the falls (not suitable for swimming). A further 10-minute walk leads down to the bottom. Lock your car: theft is a problem here.

Mt Pirongia   MOUNTAIN, FOREST
(www.mtpirongia.org.nz) The main attraction of the 170-sq-km **Pirongia Forest Park** is Mt Pirongia, its 959m summit clearly visible from much of the Waikato. The mountain is usually climbed from Corcoran Rd (three to five hours, one way) with tracks to other lookout points. Interestingly, NZ's tallest known kahikatea tree (66.5m) grows on the mountainside. There's a six-bunk DOC hut near the summit if you need to spend the night; maps and information are available from Hamilton DOC (p174).

🏃 Activities

The surf spots near Raglan – Indicators, Whale Bay and Manu Bay – are internationally famous for their point breaks. Bruce Brown's classic 1964 wave-chaser film *The Endless Summer* features Manu Bay.

Ocean Beach   WINDSURFING, KITESURFING
Ocean Beach sits at the mouth of the harbour, 4km southwest of Raglan down Riria Kereopa Memorial Dr. It's popular for windsurfing and kitesurfing, but strong currents make it extremely treacherous for swimmers.

Ngarunui Beach   SURFING, SWIMMING
Less than 1km south of Ocean Beach, Ngarunui Beach is great for grommets learning to surf. On the cliff top is a clubhouse for the volunteer lifeguards who patrol part of the black-sand beach from late October until April. This is the only beach with lifeguards, and is the best ocean beach for swimming.

Manu Bay   SURFING
A 2.5km journey from Ngarunui Beach will bring you to Manu Bay, a legendary surf spot said to have the longest left-hand break in the world. The elongated uniform waves are created by the angle at which the Tasman Sea swell meets the coastline (it works best in a southwesterly swell).

Whale Bay   SURFING
Whale Bay is a renowned surf spot 1km west of Manu Bay. It's usually less crowded than Manu Bay, but from the bottom of Calvert Rd you have to clamber 600m over the rocks to get to the break.

Raglan Surf School   SURFING
(☑07-825 7873; www.raglansurfingschool.co.nz; 5b Whaanga Rd, Whale Bay; rental per hour surfboards from $20, body boards $5, wet suits $5, 3hr lesson incl transport from Raglan $90) Raglan Surf School prides itself on getting 95% of first-timers standing during their first lesson. It's based at Karioi Lodge in Whale Bay. It also operates Surfdames (www.surfdames. co.nz; surfing lessons per person $100), which offers women-only surfing experiences incorporating lessons with yoga, massage and beauty treatments.

🛏 Sleeping

Karioi Lodge   HOSTEL $
(☑07-825 7873; www.karioilodge.co.nz; 5b Whaanga Rd, Whale Bay; dm/d $30/80; @ 🛜) Deep in native bush, Karioi Lodge offers a sauna, mountain bikes, bush and beach walks, sustainable gardening, tree planting and the Raglan Surf School. There are no en suites, but the rooms are clean and cosy. Campervan travellers can stay for $15 per person in forested surroundings with access to Karioi's bathroom and kitchen facilities.

Sleeping Lady Lodging
LODGE $$

(☎07-825 7873; www.sleepinglady.co.nz; 5b Whaanga Rd; lodges $175-260) Sleeping Lady Lodges is a collection of very comfortable self-contained houses all with ocean views.

ℹ️ Getting There & Around

There is no public transport. Tours are available with **Raglan Scenic Tours** (p176).

Te Awamutu
POP 9800

Deep into dairy-farming country, Te Awamutu (which means 'The River Cut Short'; the Waikato beyond this point was unsuitable for large canoes) is a pleasant rural service centre. With a blossom-tree-lined main street and a good museum, TA (aka Rose Town) makes a decent overnighter.

◉ Sights & Activities

★ Te Awamutu Museum
MUSEUM

(☎07-872 0085; www.tamuseum.org.nz; 135 Roche St; admission by donation; ⊙10am-4pm Mon-Fri, to 2pm Sat) Te Awamutu Museum has a superb collection of Māori *taonga* (treasures) and an excellent display on the Waikato War. The highlight is the revered *Te Uenuku* ('The Rainbow'), an ancient Māori carving estimated to be up to 600 years old. If you're a fan of the Finn brothers from Crowded House, videos, memorabilia and a scrapbook are available on request – Te Awamutu is their home town.

TE AWAMUTU'S SACRED SOUND

In the opening lines of Crowded House's first single 'Mean to Me', Neil Finn single-handedly raised his sleepy home town, Te Awamutu, to international attention. It wasn't the first time it had provided inspiration – Split Enz songs 'Haul Away' and 'Kia Kaha', with big bro Tim, include similar references.

Despite New Zealand's brilliant song-writing brothers being far from the height of their fame, Finn devotees continue to make the pilgrimage to Te Awamutu. Ask at the i-SITE (p181) about Finn postage stamps and the interesting scrapbook focused on the brothers' achievements. For Finn completists, there's more to see at the Te Awamutu Museum by request.

St Paul's Church
CHURCH

(☎07-871 5568; Rangiaowhia Rd, Rangiaowhia; ⊙services 9am 1st & 3rd Sun of month) All that remains of Rangiaowhia is the cute 1854 Anglican St Paul's Church and the Catholic mission's cemetery, standing in the midst of rich farming land – confiscated from the Māori and distributed to colonial soldiers. Rangiaowhia (5km east of Te Awamutu on Rangiaowhia Rd; ask at the i-SITE for directions) was once a thriving Māori farming town, exporting wheat, maize, potatoes and fruit to as far afield as Australia.

Bryce's Rockclimbing
ROCK CLIMBING

(☎07-872 2533; www.rockclimb.co.nz; 1424 Owairaka Valley Rd; 1-day instruction for 1-2 people $440) Bryce's Rockclimbing is situated in a rural area 25km southeast of Te Awamutu, near hundreds of climbs at various crags (many of which are within walking distance). The surreal landscape provides some of the best rock climbing in the North Island, but it's an area best suited to those with at least basic climbing skills.

On-site is NZ's largest retail climbing store, selling and hiring a full range of gear. There's also comfortable accommodation, and all rooms have private en suite bathrooms (dorm/double $30/76). Breakfast is available to guests on request. Accommodation is also open to hikers, cyclists, anglers and general travellers. Your own transport is required to get here.

🛏️ Sleeping & Eating

Rosetown Motel
MOTEL $$

(☎0800 767 386, 07-871 5779; www.rosetownmotel.co.nz; 844 Kihikihi Rd; d $125-140; 🌐🐾) The older-style units at Rosetown have kitchens, new linen and TVs, and share a spa. A solid choice if you're hankering for straight-up, small-town sleeps.

Walton St Coffee
CAFE $

(☎022 070 6411; www.facebook.com/waltonstreetcollective; 3 Walton St; snacks & meals $6-12; ⊙6.30am-3pm Tue-Fri, to 1pm Sat) 🌿 In a rustic building with exposed beams and retro furniture, this combo of cafe, gallery and performance space is Te Awamutu's top spot for a coffee. The menu has a strong focus on organic and gluten-free options. Try the Buddha Bowl, a changing concoction of fresh seasonal vegies and the grain of the day, topped with a cashew and herb dressing.

SANCTUARY MOUNTAIN MAUNGATAUTARI

A community trust has erected 47km of pest-proof fencing around the triple peaks of Maungatautari (797m) to create the impressive **Sanctuary Mountain Maungatautari** (www.sanctuarymountain.co.nz; adult/child $18/8) This atoll of rainforest dominates the skyline between Te Awamutu and Karapiro and is now home to its first kiwi chicks in 100 years. There is also a 'tuatarium', where New Zealand's iconic reptile the tuatara can be seen. The main entrance is at the visitor centre at the sanctuary's southern side.

Guided tours (adult/child $35/15) leaving from the visitor centre from Tuesday to Sunday include an afternoon wetlands tour, and morning and afternoon departures exploring the bird and insect life of the sanctuary's Southern Enclosure. Online or phone bookings for guided tours must be made at least 24 hours in advance.

Accommodation option **Out in the Styx** (07-872 4505; www.styx.co.nz; 2117 Arapuni Rd, Pukeatua; dm/s/d $95/155/260) is near the southern end of the Maungatautari guided day- and night-walk options. The three stylishly furnished themed rooms (Polynesian, African or Māori) are especially nice, plus there are bunk rooms and a spa for soothing weary legs. Prices include a four-course dinner and breakfast. Guided night walks are also available.

They also provide a drop-off service ($10 per person, minimum $40) if you wish to walk across the mountain from north to south (around six hours).

Red Kitchen
CAFE $$

(07-871 8715; www.redkitchen.co nz; 51 Mahoe St; mains $14-20; 7am-5.30pm Mon-Fri, 7.30am-2.30pm Sat) Excellent coffee, counter food, cosmopolitan brunches and lunches, and food store all feature at this sunny spot. Try the macadamia and cranberry muesli or the creamy mushrooms on ciabatta. Pick up gourmet TV dinners from Monday to Friday – actually really good – and fire up the motel microwave for your evening meal.

Redoubt Bar & Eatery
PUB FOOD $$

(07-871 4768; www.redoubtbarandeatery.co.nz; cnr Rewi & Alexandra Sts; mains $15-26; 11am-9pm Mon-Fri, 10am-9pm Sat & Sun) A relaxed place to eat or drink, with cheap but potent cocktails, classic old photos of Te Awamutu sports teams on the walls, and a decent menu stretching from pasta and pizza to hearty burgers and chowder.

☆ Entertainment

Regent Theatre
CINEMA

(07-871 6678; www.facebook.com/Regent Teawamutu; 235 Alexandra St; adult/child $16/10; 10am-late) Art-deco cinema with movie memorabilia.

ℹ Information

Te Awamutu i-SITE (07-871 3259; www. teawamutuinfo.co.nz; 1 Gorst Ave; 9am-5pm Mon-Fri, to 2.30pm Sat & Sun) Has plenty of local information.

ℹ Getting There & Away

Te Awamutu is on SH3, halfway between Hamilton and Otorohanga (29km either way). The regional bus service **Busit!** (0800 4287 5463; www.busit.co.nz) is the cheapest option for Hamilton (adult/child $7.88/5, 50 minutes, eight daily weekdays, three daily weekends).

Three daily **InterCity** (09-583 5780; www. intercity.co.nz) services connect Te Awamutu with Auck and (2½ hours, $23) and Hamilton (30 minutes, $11).

Cambridge

POP 15,200

The name says it all. Despite the rambunctious Waikato River looking nothing like the Cam, the good people of Cambridge have done all they can to assume an air of English gentility with village greens and tree-lined avenues.

Cambridge is famous for the breeding and training of thoroughbred horses. Equine references are rife in public sculpture, and plaques boast of past Melbourne Cup winners.

◎ Sights

Cambridge Museum
MUSEUM

(07-827 3319; www.cambridgemuseum.org.nz; 24 Victoria St; admission by donation; 10am-4pm Mon-Fri, to 2pm Sun) In a former courthouse, the quirky Cambridge Museum has plenty of pioneer relics, a military history room and a small display on the local Te Totara Pa before it was wiped out.

Jubilee Gardens　　GARDEN, MONUMENT

(Victoria St) Apart from its Spanish Mission town clock, Jubilee Gardens is a whole-hearted tribute to the 'mother country'. A British lion guards the cenotaph, with a plaque that reads, 'Tell Britain ye who mark this monument faithful to her we fell and rest content.'

Lake Karapiro　　LAKE

(☑ 07-827 4178; www.waipadc.govt.nz; Maungatautari Rd) Eight kilometres southeast of Cambridge, Lake Karapiro is the furthest downstream of a chain of eight hydroelectric power stations on the Waikato River. It's an impressive sight, especially when driving across the top of the 1947 dam. The 21km-long lake is also a world-class rowing venue.

🏃 Activities

Te Awa　　CYCLING, WALKING

(The Great New Zealand River Ride; www.te-awa.org.nz) Upon completion in 2017, the Te Awa cycling and walking path will meander 70km along the Waikato River, from Ngaruawahia north of Hamilton to Horahora south of the city. At the time of research, an 18km stretch from Cambridge's Avantidrome – the home of NZ's Olympic cyclists – followed a scenic route south to the Mighty River Domain at Lake Karapiro.

Boatshed Kayaks　　KAYAKING

(☑ 07-827 8286; www.theboatshed.net.nz; 21 Amber Lane; single/double kayak for 3hr $25/50, paddle board per 2hr $20; ☺9am-5pm Wed-Sun) Boatshed Kayaks has basic kayaks and paddle boards for hire. You can paddle to a couple of waterfalls in around an hour. There are also guided kayak trips (adult/child $110/75) at twilight to see a glowworm canyon up the nearby Pokewhaenua stream. Bookings are essential for these trips. It's located at the Boatshed Cafe, on the edge of Lake Karapiro.

Waikato River Trails　　CYCLING, WALKING

(www.waikatorivertrails.com) The 100km Waikato River Trails track is part of the Nga Haerenga, New Zealand Cycle Trail (www.nzcycle trail.com) project. Winding south and east from near Cambridge, the trails pass Lake Karapiro and into the South Waikato area to end at the Atiamuri Dam. You can either walk or cycle the five combined trails (or parts thereof), with lots of history and local landscapes en route. Download the free map showing five stages from the website.

🛌 Sleeping

Cambridge Motor Park　　HOLIDAY PARK $

(☑ 07-827 5649; www.cambridgemotorpark.co.nz; 32 Scott St; campsites from $36, units $70-115; ☺) A quiet, well-maintained camping ground with lots of green, green grass. The emphasis is on tents and vans here, but the cabins and units are fine. It's a 2km drive over the skinny Victoria Bridge from Cambridge town centre.

Cambridge Coach House　　B&B, CABIN $$

(☑ 07-823 7922; www.cambridgecoachhouse.co.nz; 3796 Cambridge Rd, Leamington; d $165, cottages $175; ☺⊠) This farmhouse accommodation is a beaut spot to relax amid Waikato's rural splendour. There are two stylish doubles and a self-contained cottage. Flat-screen TVs and heat pumps are new additions, and guests are welcome to fire up the barbecue in the leafy grounds. It's a couple of kilometres south of town, en route to Te Awamutu.

Earthstead　　B&B $$$

(☑ 07-827 3771; www.earthstead.co.nz; 3635 Cambridge Rd, Monvale; d $220-350; ☺) 🖉 In a rural setting a short drive south of Cambridge, Earthstead has three units constructed using ecofriendly and sustainable adobe-style architecture – such as the Earth House and Cob Cottage – and two other options with an elegant European vibe. Fresh and organic produce from Earthstead's compact farm is used for breakfast, including eggs, honey and freshly baked sourdough bread.

🍴 Eating

Paddock　　CAFE $

(☑ 07-827 4232; www.facebook.com/paddockreal goodfuel; 46a Victoria St; snacks & mains $8-14; ☺8am-5pm Mon-Thu, to 8pm Fri & Sat, to 4pm Sun) Free-range this and organic that punctuate the menu at the cool slice of culinary style that looks like it's dropped in from Auckland or Melbourne. Distressed timber furniture and a vibrant and colourful mural enliven Paddock's corner location, and artisan sodas and healthy smoothies – try the banana, date and cinnamon – partner well with gourmet bagels and burgers.

Boatshed Cafe　　CAFE $

(☑ 0800 743 321; www.theboatshedkarapiro.co.nz; 21 Amber Lane, off Gorton Rd; mains $10-19; ☺10am-3pm Thu-Sun) This stylish cafe on the edge of Lake Karapiro is a top place for a leisurely brunch or lunch. Order the eggs Benedict or the corn-and-coriander fritters, and grab an outside table for lake views and Waikato birdsong. To get here, head south from Cambridge on SH1 and then turn right onto Gorton Rd.

★ **Alpino cucina e vino** ITALIAN $$

(☑ 07-827 5595; www.alpino.co.nz; 43 Victoria St; pizzas $18-25, mains $27-36; ⊙ 11.30am-2.30pm & 5pm-late Tue-Thu, 9am-late Fri-Sun) In a heritage former post office, the stylish and elegant yet informal and approachable Alpino cucina e vino is one of the best restaurants in the Waikato region. The main menu focuses on excellent pasta and hearty Italian-style mains – try the slow-roasted pork belly with polenta and asparagus – and top-notch wood-fired pizza that is also available for takeaway.

Red Cherry CAFE $$

(☑ 07-823 1515; www.redcherrycoffee.co.nz; cnr SH1 & Forrest Rd; meals $11-23; ⊙ 7.30am-4.30pm; ☑) With a cherry-red espresso machine working overtime, barn-like Red Cherry offers coffee roasted on-site, delicious counter food and impressive cooked breakfasts. For lunch, the gourmet beef burger is hard to beat. Cambridge's best cafe is 4km from town, en route to Hamilton.

ⓘ Information

Cambridge i-SITE (☑ 07-823 3456; www.cambridge.co.nz; cnr Victoria & Queen Sts; ⊙ 9am-5pm Mon-Fri, 10am-4pm Sat & Sun; ☎) Free *Heritage & Tree Trail* and town maps, plus internet access.

ⓘ Getting There & Away

Being on SH1, 22km southeast of Hamilton, Cambridge is well connected by bus. Waikato Regional Council's **Busit!** (☑ 0800 4287 5463; www.busit.co.nz) heads to Hamilton ($6.70, 40 minutes, seven daily weekdays, three daily weekends).

InterCity (☑ 09-583 5780; www.intercity.co.nz) services numerous destinations including the following:

DESTINATION	PRICE	TIME	FREQUENCY (DAILY)
Auckland	$25-59	2½hr	12
Hamilton	$17	30min	8
Matamata	$22	30min	2
Rotorua	$15-31	1¼hr	5
Wellington	$24-66	8½hr	3

Naked Bus (www.nakedbus.com) runs services to the same destinations:

DESTINATION	PRICE	TIME	FREQUENCY (DAILY)
Auckland	$22	2½hr	6
Hamilton	$15	30min	5
Matamata	$28	2¼hr	1
Rotorua	$12	1¼hr	4
Wellington	$70	9½hr	1

Matamata

POP 7800

Matamata was just one of those pleasant, horsey county towns you drove through until Peter Jackson's epic film trilogy *The Lord of the Rings* put it on the map. During filming, 300 locals got work as extras (hairy feet weren't a prerequisite).

Following the subsequent filming of *The Hobbit,* the town has now ardently embraced its Middle-earth credentials, including a spooky statue of Gollum, and given the local information centre an appropriate extreme makeover.

Most tourists who come to Matamata are dedicated Hobbit-botherers. For everyone else there's a great cafe, avenues of mature trees and undulating green hills.

◉ Sights & Activities

Hobbiton Movie Set Tours FILM LOCATION

(☑ 0508 446 224 866, 07-888 1505; www.hobbitontours.com; 501 Buckland Rd, Hinuera; adult/child tours $79/39.50, dinner tours $190/100; ⊙ tours 10am-4.30pm) Due to copyright, all the movie sets around NZ were dismantled after the filming of *The Lord of the Rings,* but Hobbiton's owners negotiated to keep their hobbit holes, which were then rebuilt for the filming of *The Hobbit.* Tours include a drink at the wonderful Green Dragon Inn. Free transfers leave from the Matamata i-SITE – check timings on the Hobbiton website. Booking ahead is strongly recommended. The popular Evening Dinner Tours on Sunday and Wednesday include a banquet dinner.

To get to Hobbiton with your own transport, head towards Cambridge from Matamata, turn right into Puketutu Rd and then left into Buckland Rd, stopping at the Shire's Rest Cafe.

Wairere Falls   WATERFALL
About 15km northeast of Matamata are the spectacular 153m Wairere Falls, the highest on the North Island. From the car park it's a 45-minute walk through native bush to the lookout or a steep 1½-hour climb to the summit.

Firth Tower   MUSEUM, HISTORIC BUILDING
(☑07-888 8369; www.firthtower.co.nz; Tower Rd; grounds free, tours adult/child $5/1; ⊙grounds 10am-4pm daily, buildings 10am-4pm Thu-Mon) Firth Tower was built by Auckland businessman Josiah Firth in 1882. The 18m concrete tower was then a fashionable status symbol; now it's filled with Māori and pioneer artefacts. Ten other historic buildings are set around the tower, including a school room, church and jail. It's 3km east of town.

Opal Hot Springs   HOT SPRING
(☑0800 800 198; www.opalhotsprings.co.nz; 257 Okauia Springs Rd; adult/child $8/4, 30min private spas $10/5; ⊙9am-9pm) Opal Hot Springs isn't nearly as glamorous as it sounds, but it does have three large thermal pools. Turn off just north of Firth Tower and follow the road for 2km. There's a holiday park here, too.

🛌 Sleeping

**Broadway Motel
& Miro Court Villas**   MOTEL $$
(☑07-888 8482; www.broadwaymatamata.co.nz; 128 Broadway; d $110-175, 2-bedroom apt $265; @🐾) This sprawling family-run motel complex has spread from a well-maintained older-style block to progressively newer and flasher blocks set back from the street. The nicest are the chic apartment-style Miro Court villas.

🍴 Eating & Drinking

Workman's Cafe Bar   CAFE $$
(☑07-888 5498; 52 Broadway; mains $12-30; ⊙7.30am-late) Truly eccentric (old transistor radios dangling from the ceiling; a wall-full of art-deco mirrors; Johnny Cash on the stereo), this funky eatery has built itself a reputation that extends beyond Matamata. It's also a decent bar later at night.

Redoubt Bar & Eatery   PUB
(☑07-888 8585; www.redoubtbarandeatery.co.nz; 48 Broadway; ⊙11am-2pm & 5-9pm Mon-Fri, 11am-9pm Sat & Sun) Look forward to thin-crust pizzas named after *LOTR* characters, a winning salmon and hash stack, occasional movie

nights in the adjacent laneway, and live music most weekends. It's also a mini-shrine to all things sporty and Matamata-related, and a few interesting tap beers definitely hit the spot. Say gidday to the always-cool Clifford Williams, the only Jamaican in Matamata apparently.

ℹ Information

Matamata i-SITE (☑07-888 7260; www.matamatanz.co.nz; 45 Broadway; ⊙9am-5pm) Housed in a wonderful Hobbit gatehouse. Hobbiton tours leave from here.

ℹ Getting There & Away

InterCity (☑09-583 5780; www.intercity.co.nz) Runs to Cambridge ($22, 40 minutes, two daily), Hamilton ($27, one hour, three daily), Rotorua ($25, one hour, one daily) and Tauranga ($26, one hour, two daily).

Naked Bus (www.nakedbus.com) Runs to Auckland ($20, 3½ hours, two daily), Cambridge ($28, two hours, one daily), Hamilton ($20, 3½ hours, two daily) and Tauranga ($14, one hour, one daily).

Te Aroha

POP 3800

Te Aroha has a great vibe. You could even say that it's got 'the love', which is the literal meaning of the name. Tucked under the elbow of the bush-clad Mt Te Aroha (952m), it's a good base for tramping or 'taking the waters' in the town's therapeutic thermal springs. It's also the southern trailhead on the Hauraki Rail Trail. The sleepy main street is good for trawling for quirky antiques and vintage clothing and accessories.

⊙ Sights & Activities

Te Aroha Museum   MUSEUM
(☑07-884 4427; www.tearoha-museum.com; Te Aroha Domain; adult/child $5/2; ⊙11am-4pm Nov-Mar, noon-3pm Apr-Oct) In the town's ornate former thermal sanatorium (aka the 'Treasure of Te Aroha'). Displays include quirky ceramics, old spa-water bottles, historical photos and an old printing press.

Mt Te Aroha   TRAMPING, MOUNTAIN BIKING
Trails up Mt Te Aroha start at the top of the domain. It's a 45-minute climb to Bald Spur/Whakapipi Lookout (350m), then another 2.7km (two hours) to the summit. Ask at the i-SITE about mountain-bike trails.

Te Aroha Mineral Spas   SPA

(☑07-884 8717; www.tearohamineralspas.co.nz;
Boundary St, Te Aroha Domain; 30min session
adult/child $18/11; ⏰10.30am-9pm Mon-Fri,
to 10pm Sat & Sun) In the Edwardian Hot
Springs Domain, this spa offers private tubs,
massage, beauty therapies and aromathera-
py. Also here is the temperamental **Moke-
na Geyser** – the world's only known soda
geyser – which blows its top around every
40 minutes, shooting water 3m into the air
(the most ardent eruptions are between
noon and 2pm). Book ahead for spas and
treatments.

🛌 Sleeping & Eating

Te Aroha Holiday Park   HOLIDAY PARK $

(☑07-884 9567; www.tearohaholidaypark.co.nz;
217 Stanley Rd; campsites from $18, on-site vans s/d
$30/40, cabins & units $53-110; @ 🛜 🏊) Wake
up to a bird orchestra among the oaks at this
site equipped with a grass tennis court, gym
and hot pool, 2km southwest of town.

★ Aroha Mountain Lodge   LODGE, B&B $$

(☑07-884 8134; www.arohamountainlodge.co.nz; 5
Boundary St; s/d/cottages $125/145/320) Spread
over two *aroha*-ly Edwardian villas on the
hillside above town, the plush Mountain
Lodge offers affordable luxury (*sooo* much
nicer than a regulation motel) and optional breakfast ($20 per person). The self-
contained Chocolate Box sleeps six to eight.

Domain Cottage Cafe   CAFE $

(☑07-884 9222; Whittaker St, Te Aroha Domain;
snacks & mains $8-21; ⏰9am-3pm Tue-Sun) Very
pleasant daytime cafe in the heritage surroundings of the Te Aroha Domain. Definitely worthy of a stop for coffee and cake even if
you're only passing through town.

Ironique   CAFE $$

(☑07-884 8439; www.ironique.co.nz; 159 Whitaker
St; mains $10-35; ⏰8am-4pm Sun-Wed, until late
Thu-Sat) Come for a coffee and a restorative
breakfast of eggs Benedict after tackling the
Hauraki Rail Trail, or grilled salmon or confit duck for dinner. Don't overlook venturing
to the quiet courtyard out the back for a few
drinks.

ℹ Information

Te Aroha i-SITE (☑07-884 8052; www.tearoha
nz.co.nz; 102 Whitaker St; ⏰9.30am-5pm Mon-
Fri, to 4pm Sat & Sun) Ask about walking trails
on Mt Te Aroha and other local sights.

ℹ Getting There & Away

Busit! (☑0800 4287 5463; www.busit.co.nz)
Waikato Regional Council's Busit! runs to/from
Hamilton (adult/child $6/3, one hour, two daily
weekdays).

THE KING COUNTRY

Holding good claim to the title of NZ's rural
heartland, this is the kind of no-nonsense
place that raises cattle and All Blacks. A
bastion of independent Māoridom, it was
never conquered in the war against the King
Movement. The story goes that King Tawhi-
ao placed his hat on a large map of NZ and
declared that all the land it covered would
remain under his *mana* (authority), and the
region was effectively off limits to Europeans until 1883.

The Waitomo Caves are the area's major
drawcard. An incredible natural phenomenon in themselves, they also feature lots of
adrenaline-inducing activities.

Kawhia

POP 670

Along with resisting cultural annihilation,
low-key Kawhia (think mafia with a K) has
avoided large-scale development, retaining
its sleepy fishing-village vibe. There's not
much here except for the general store, a
couple of takeaways and a petrol station.
Even Captain Cook blinked and missed the
narrow entrance to the large harbour when
he sailed past in 1770.

👁 Sights

Ocean Beach   BEACH, HOT SPRING

(Te Puia Rd) Four kilometres west of Kawhia is
Ocean Beach and its high, black-sand dunes.
Swimming can be dangerous, but one to two
hours either side of low tide you can find
the **Te Puia Hot Springs** in the sand – dig a
hole for your own natural hot pool.

Maketu Marae   HISTORIC SITE

(www.kawhia.maori.nz; Kaora St) From Kawhia
Wharf, a track extends along the coast to Maketu Marae, which has an impressively carved
meeting house, Auaukiterangi. Two stones
here – Hani and Puna – mark the burial place
of the **Tainui waka** (a 14th-century ancestral
canoe). You can't see a lot from the road, but
the *marae* is private property and shouldn't
be entered without permission. Email the Maketu Marae Committee for access.

KINGITANGA

The concept of a Māori people is a relatively new one. Until the mid-19th century, New Zealand was effectively comprised of many independent tribal nations, operating in tandem with the British from 1840.

In 1856, faced with a flood of Brits, the Kingitanga King Movement formed to unite the tribes to better resist further loss of land and culture. A gathering of leaders elected Waikato chief Potatau Te Wherowhero as the first Māori king, hoping that his increased *mana* (prestige) could achieve the cohesion that the British had under their queen.

Despite the huge losses of the Waikato War and the eventual opening up of the King Country, the Kingitanga survived – although it has no formal constitutional role. A measure of the strength of the movement was the huge outpouring of grief when Te Arikinui Dame Atairangikaahu, Potatau's great-great-great-granddaughter, died in 2006 after 40 years at the helm. Although it's not a hereditary monarchy (leaders of various tribes vote on a successor), Potatau's line continues to the present day with King Tuheitia Paki.

The Tainui *waka* made its final landing at Kawhia. The expedition leaders – Hoturoa, the chief/captain, and Rakataura, the *tohunga* (priest) – searched the west coast until they recognised their prophesised landing place. Pulling into shore, they tied the *waka* to a pohutukawa tree, naming it Tangi te Korowhiti. This unlabelled tree still stands on the shoreline between the wharf and Maketu Marae. The waka was then dragged up onto a hill and buried: sacred stones were placed at either end to mark its resting place, now part of the *marae*.

Kawhia Regional Museum & Gallery　MUSEUM, GALLERY
(☑07-871 0161; www.kawhiaharbour.co.nz; Omimiti Reserve, Kawhia Wharf; admission by gold coin donation; ◷noon-3pm Wed-Sun) Kawhia's modest waterside museum has local history, nautical and Māori artefacts, and regular art exhibitions. It doubles as the visitor information centre.

 Activities

Kayaks can be hired from Kawhia Beachside S-Cape and Kawhia Motel.

Dove Charters　FISHING
(☑07-871 5854; www.westcoastfishing.co.nz; full day per person $115) Full-day fishing trips catching snapper, kingfish, gurnard and kahawai.

Sleeping

Kawhia Beachside S-Cape　HOLIDAY PARK $
(☑07-871 0727; www.kawhiabeachsidescape.co.nz; 225 Pouewe St; campsites from $30, cabin dm/d from $30/60, cottages $120-160) This water's edge campground looks shabby from the road but has comfortable cottages, plus cabins and camping with shared bathrooms. Two-hour kayak hire is $10 per person.

Kawhia Motel　MOTEL $$
(☑07-871 0865; www.kawhiamotel.co.nz; cnr Jervois & Tainui Sts; d $130-160; ☜) These six perkily painted, well-kept, old-school motel units are right next to the shops. Kayaks and bikes for hire.

Eating & Drinking

Annie's Cafe & Restaurant　CAFE, RESTAURANT $
(☑07-871 0198; 146 Jervois St; mains $10-22; ◷9.30am-3.45pm) An old-fashioned licensed eatery on the main street, serving espresso, sandwiches and local specialities such as flounder and whitebait with kumara chips.

Blue Chook Inn　PUB
(☑07-871 0778; 136 Jervois St; mains $15-25; ◷4pm-midnight Wed-Sun) Kawhia's friendly pub combines decent eating with occasional live music.

Getting There & Away

Kawhia doesn't have a bus service. Take SH31 from Otorohanga (58km) or explore the scenic but rough road to Raglan (50km, 22km unsealed).

Otorohanga

POP 2700

Otorohanga's main street is festooned with images of cherished Kiwiana icons: sheep, gumboots, jandals, No 8 wire, All Blacks, pavlova and the beloved Buzzy Bee children's toy. The town's Kiwi House is also well worth a visit.

◉ Sights

Otorohanga Kiwi House & Native Bird Park
ZOO

(☎ 07-873 7391; www.kiwihouse.org.nz; 20 Alex Telfer Dr; adult/child $24/8; ⊙ 9am-5pm, kiwi feedings 10am,1.30pm & 3.30pm daily) This bird barn has a nocturnal enclosure where you can see active kiwi energetically digging with their long beaks, searching for food. This is one of the only places where you can see a great spotted kiwi, the biggest of the three kiwi species. Brown kiwi are also on display, and there's a brown kiwi breeding program. Other native birds on show include kaka, kea, morepork and weka.

Ed Hillary Walkway
MEMORIAL

As well as the Kiwiana decorating the main street, the Ed Hillary Walkway (running off Maniapoto St) has information panels on the All Blacks, Marmite and, of course, Sir Ed.

⊨ Sleeping

Otorohanga Holiday Park
HOLIDAY PARK $

(☎ 07-873 7253; www.kiwiholidaypark.co.nz; 20 Huiputea Dr; campsites from $30, cabins & units $70-120; @ ⓢ) It's not the most attractive locale, but this friendly park's tidy facilities include a fitness centre and sauna.

♀ Drinking & Nightlife

Origin Coffee Station
CAFE, COFFEE

(☎ 07-873 8550; www.origincoffee.co.nz; 7 Wahanui Cres; coffee $4-5; ⊙ 8.30am-4.30pm Mon-Fri) The folks at Origin are dead serious about coffee – sourcing, importing and roasting it themselves. They're at the railway station, so if you time it right you could see the Northern Explorer pull up to the platform. Roast and ground coffee can also be bought to take away.

Thirsty Weta
PUB, CRAFT BEER

(☎ 07-873 6699; www.theweta.co.nz; 57 Maniapoto St; ⊙ 10am-2am) Hearty meals including pizza, steak, burgers and quesadillas (mains $12 to $38). Later on a pub-meets-wine-bar ambience kicks off as the local musos plug in. It's one of just a handful of places you'll find craft beers on tap from the local King Country Brewing Co. Our favourite is the well-balanced pale ale.

❶ Information

Otorohanga i-SITE (☎ 07-873 8951; www. otorohanga.co.nz; 27 Turongo St; ⊙ 9am-5pm Mon-Fri year-round, plus 10am-2pm Sat Oct-Apr; ⓢ) Free wi-fi and local information.

❶ Getting There & Away

BUS

InterCity (☎ 09-583 5780; www.intercity. co.nz) Buses run from Otorohanga to Auckland ($20 to $42, 3¾ hours, three daily), Te Awamutu ($10 to $21, 30 minutes, three daily), Te Kuiti ($10 to $21, one hour, three daily) and Rotorua ($25 to $53, 3½ hours, two daily).

Naked Bus (☎ 0900 625 33; www.nakedbus. com) Runs one bus daily to Waitomo Caves at 10.35am ($20, 30 minutes). Other departures include Hamilton ($25, one hour) and New Plymouth ($30, 3¼ hours).

Waitomo Shuttle (☎ 07-873 8279, 0800 808 279; www.waitomo.org.nz/transport-to-waitomo; one-way adult/child $12/7) Heads to the Waitomo Caves five times daily, coordinating with bus and train arrivals. Bookings recommended

TRAIN

Northern Explorer (☎ 0800 872 467; www. kiwirailscenic.co.nz) Otorohanga is on the Northern Explorer train route between Auckland (from $49, 3¼ hours) and Wellington (from $139, nine hours) via Hamilton (from $49, 50 minutes); it also stops at Palmerston North, Ohakune and National Park. Southbound trains run on Monday, Thursday and Saturday, and northbound trains return from Wellington to Auckland on Tuesday, Friday and Sunday.

Waitomo Caves

POP 500

Even if damp, dark tunnels are your idea of hell, head to Waitomo anyway. The limestone caves and glowing bugs here are one of the North Island's premier attractions.

The name Waitomo comes from *wai* (water) and *tomo* (hole or shaft): dotted across this region are numerous shafts dropping into underground cave systems and streams. There are 300-plus mapped caves in the area: the three main caves – Glowworm, Ruakuri and Aranui – have been bewitching visitors for over 100 years.

Your Waitomo experience needn't be claustrophobic: the electrically lit, cathedral-like Glowworm Cave is far from squeezy. But if it's tight, gut-wrenching, soaking-wet, pitch-black excitement you're after, Waitomo can oblige.

⊙ Sights

Waitomo Caves Visitor Centre VISITOR CENTRE
(☑0800 456 922; www.waitomo.com; Waitomo Caves Rd; ☺9am-5pm) The big-three Waitomo Caves are all operated by the same company, based at the spectacular Waitomo Caves Visitor Centre (behind the Glowworm Cave). Various combo deals are available, including a Triple Cave Combo (adult/child $95/42), and other deals incorporate exciting underground thrills with the Legendary Black Water Rafting Company. Check the website. For the cave tours, try to avoid the large tour groups, most of which arrive between 10.30am and 2.30pm.

★ **Glowworm Cave** CAVE
(☑0800 456 922; www.waitomo.com/waitomo-glowworm-caves; adult/child $49/22; ☺45min tours half-hourly 9am-5pm) The guided tour of the Glowworm Cave, which is behind the visitor centre, leads past impressive stalactites and stalagmites into a large cavern known as the Cathedral. The highlight comes at the tour's end when you board a boat and swing off onto the river. As your eyes grow accustomed to the dark you'll see a Milky Way of little lights surrounding you – these are the glowworms. Book your tour at the visitor centre.

The acoustics are so good that Dame Kiri Te Kanawa and the Vienna Boys Choir have given concerts here.

Aranui Cave CAVE
(☑0800 456 922; www.waitomo.com/aranui-cave; adult/child $49/22; ☺1hr tours depart 9am-4pm) Three kilometres west from the Glowworm Cave is Aranui Cave. This cave is dry (hence no glowworms) but compensates with an incredible array of limestone formations. Thousands of tiny 'straw' stalactites hang from the ceiling. Book tours at the visitor centre, from where there is transport to the cave entrance. A 15-minute bush walk is also included.

Ruakuri Cave CAVE
(☑0800 782 587, 07-878 6219; www.waitomo.com/ruakuri-cave; adult/child $71/27; ☺2hr tours 9am, 10am, 11am, 12.30pm, 1.30pm, 2.30pm & 3.30pm) Ruakuri Cave has an impressive 15m-high spiral staircase, bypassing a Māori burial site at the cave entrance. Tours lead through 1.6km of the 7.5km system, taking in caverns with glowworms, subterranean streams and waterfalls, and intricate limestone structures. Visitors have described it as spiritual – some claim it's haunted – and it's customary to wash your hands when leaving to remove the *tapu* (taboo). Book tours at the visitor centre, or at the departure point, the Legendary Black Water Rafting Company (p189).

Waitomo Caves Discovery Centre MUSEUM
(☑0800 474 839, 07-878 7640; www.waitomo-caves.com; 21 Waitomo Caves Rd; ☺9am-5.30pm, longer hours in summer) **FREE** Adjoining the Waitomo i-SITE, the Waitomo Caves Discov-

---

GLOWWORM MAGIC

Glowworms are the larvae of the fungus gnat. The larva glowworm has luminescent organs that produce a soft, greenish light. Living in a sort of hammock suspended from an overhang, it weaves sticky threads that trail down and catch unwary insects attracted by its light. When an insect flies towards the light it gets stuck in the threads – the glowworm just has to reel it in for a feed.

The larval stage lasts from six to nine months, depending on how much food the glowworm gets. When it has grown to about the size of a matchstick, it goes into a pupa stage, much like a cocoon. The adult fungus gnat emerges about two weeks later.

The adult insect doesn't live very long because it doesn't have a mouth. It emerges, mates, lays eggs and dies, all within about two or three days. The sticky eggs, laid in groups of 40 or 50, hatch in about three weeks to become larval glowworms.

Glowworms thrive in moist, dark caves but they can survive anywhere if they have the requisites of moisture, an overhang to suspend from and insects to eat. Waitomo is famous for its glowworms but you can see them in many other places around New Zealand, both in caves and outdoors.

When you come upon glowworms, don't touch their hammocks or hanging threads, try not to make loud noises and don't shine a light right on them. All of these things will cause them to dim their lights. It takes them a few hours to become bright again, during which time the grub will go hungry. The glowworms that shine most brightly are the hungriest.

Waitomo Caves

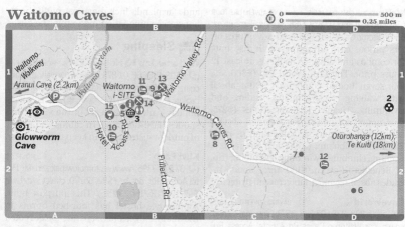

Waitomo Caves

ery Centre has excellent exhibits explaining how caves are formed, the flora and fauna that thrive in them, and the history of Waitomo's caves and cave exploration.

🏃 Activities

Underground

Legendary Black Water Rafting Company CAVING, ADVENTURE TOUR
(☑ 0800 782 5874; www.waitomo.com/black -water-rafting; 585 Waitomo Caves Rd; ⊘ Black Labyrinth tour 9am, 10.30am, noon, 1.30pm & 3pm, Black Abyss tour 9am & 2pm, Black Odyssey tour 10am & 3pm) The Black Labyrinth tour (three hours, $135) involves floating in a wetsuit on an inner tube down a river that flows through Ruakuri Cave. The highlight is leaping off a small waterfall and then floating through a long, glowworm-covered passage. The trip ends with showers, soup and bagels in the cafe. The more adventurous Black Abyss tour (five hours, $235) includes a 35m

abseil into Ruakuri Cave, a flying fox and more glowworms and tubing.

Also available is the Black Odyssey tour (four hours, $175), a challenging dry caving adventure including flying foxes and negotiating high wires. Minimum ages apply for all tours, and there are 10% discounts if you prebook online. Check the website for combo deals also incorporating entry to the other Waitomo Caves.

Spellbound CAVING, GUIDED TOUR
(☑ 07-878 7622, 0800 773 552; www.glowworm. co.nz; 10 Waitomo Caves Rd; adult/child $75/26; ⊘ 3hr tours 10am, 11am, 2pm & 3pm) Spellbound is a good option if you don't want to get wet, are more interested in glowworms than an 'action' experience, and want to avoid the big groups in the main caves. Small-group tours access parts of the heavily glowworm-dappled Mangawhitikau cave system, 12km south of Waitomo (and you still get to ride in a raft!).

Waitomo Adventures
CAVING, ADVENTURE TOUR

(☑ 0800 924 866, 07-878 7788; www.waitomo.co.nz; 654 Waitomo Caves Rd) Waitomo Adventures offers various cave adventures, with discounts for combos and advance bookings at least 12 hours prior. The Lost World trip ($360/515, four/seven hours) combines a 100m abseil with walking, rock climbing, wading and swimming. Haggas Honking Holes ($275, four hours) includes three waterfall abseils, rock climbing and a subterranean river. TumuTumu Toobing ($190, four hours) is a walking, climbing, swimming and tubing trip. St Benedict's Cavern ($190, three hours) includes abseiling and a subterranean flying fox.

CaveWorld
CAVING, ADVENTURE TOUR

(☑ 0800 228 338, 07-878 6577; www.caveworld.co.nz; cnr Waitomo Caves Rd & Hotel Access Rd) CaveWorld runs the Tube It black-water rafting trip ($140, two hours) through glowworm-filled Te Anaroa. Also available is the Footwhistle Glowworm Cave Tour ($60, one hour), incorporating a stop in a forest shelter for a mug of restorative *kawakawa* tea, a natural tonic made with leaves from an indigenous bush plant. Twilight Footwhistle tours are $65.

Kiwi Cave Rafting
CAVING, ADVENTURE TOUR

(☑ 07-873 9149, 0800 228 372; www.blackwaterraftingwaitomo.co.nz; 95 Waitomo Caves Rd) These small-group expeditions ($250, five hours) start with abseil training, followed by a 27m descent into a natural cave, and then a float along a subterranean river on an inner tube. After some caving, a belayed rock climb up a 20m cliff brings you to the surface. A three-hour dry tour ($125) without the inner tube adventure is also available.

Walking

The Waitomo i-SITE has free pamphlets on walks in the area. The walk from **Aranui Cave** to **Ruakuri Cave** is an excellent short path. From the Waitomo Caves Visitor Centre, the 5km, three-hour-return **Waitomo Walkway** takes off through farmland, following Waitomo Stream to the **Ruakuri Scenic Reserve**, where a 30-minute return walk passes by a natural limestone tunnel. There are glowworms here at night – drive to the car park and bring a torch to find your way.

Dundle Hill Walk
TRAMPING

(☑ 07-878 7640; www.dundlehillwalk.com; adult/child $75/35) The self-guided privately run Dundle Hill Walk is a 27km, two-day/one-night loop walk through Waitomo's bush and farmland, including overnight bunkhouse accommodation high up in the bush.

🛏 Sleeping

Waitomo Top 10 Holiday Park
HOLIDAY PARK $

(☑ 0508 498 666, 07-878 7639; www.waitomopark.co.nz; 12 Waitomo Caves Rd; campsites from $22, cabins & units $95-170; @ 🛜 🏊) This lovely holiday park in the heart of the village has spotless facilities, modern cabins and plenty of outdoor distractions to keep the kids busy.

Kiwi Paka
HOSTEL $

(☑ 07-878 3395; www.waitomokiwipaka.co.nz; Hotel Access Rd; dm/s/d $32/65/70, chalet s/d/tw/q $95/100/110/160; @ 🛜) This purpose-built, Alpine-style hostel has four-bed dorms in the main lodge, plus separate peak-roofed chalets, on-site Morepork Cafe and super-tidy facilities. Popular with big groups.

YHA Juno Hall Waitomo
HOSTEL $

(☑ 07-878 7649; www.junowaitomo.co.nz; 600 Waitomo Caves Rd; campsites from $17, dm $30, d with/without bathroom $84/74; @ 🛜 🏊) A slick purpose-built hostel 1km from the village with a warm welcome, a warmer wood fire in the woody lounge area, and an outdoor pool and tennis court.

Abseil Inn
B&B $$

(☑ 07-878 7815; www.abseilinn.co.nz; 709 Waitomo Caves Rd; d from $150; 🛜) A *veeery* steep driveway takes you to this delightful B&B with four themed rooms, great breakfasts and witty hosts. The biggest room has a double bath and valley views.

Huhu Chalet
RENTAL HOUSE $$

(www.airbnb.com; 10 Waitomo Caves Rd; d $140) Concealed in a quirky pyramid structure that was once part of an advertising sign, Huhu Chalet has a cosy mezzanine bedroom upstairs, and a vibrant (red!) and modern bathroom and living space downstairs. With its simple wooden walls and a scattering of retro furniture, there's a warm Kiwiana vibe to the chalet, and Waitomo's best restaurant is literally metres away.

🍴 Eating & Drinking

★ Huhu
MODERN NZ $$

(☑ 07-878 6674; www.huhucafe.co.nz; 10 Waitomo Caves Rd; small plates $8-15, mains $19-34; ⊙ noon-late; 🛜) Huhu has views from the terrace and sublime contemporary NZ food. Sip a Kiwi wine or craft beer – including brews from the local King Country Brewing

Co – or graze through a seasonal tapas-style menu of delights like slow-cooked lamb, teriyaki salmon and organic rib-eye steak. Downstairs is a small King Country Brewing beer bar that's open mainly in summer.

Waitomo General Store   CAFE **$$**
(☏07-878 8613; www.facebook.com/waitomo generalstore; 15 Waitomo Caves Rd; snacks & mains $8-18; ☺8.30am-7pm Sun-Thu, to 9pm Fri & Sat; ☏) The Waitomo General Store cafe has pre- and post-caving sustenance including hearty burgers, good coffee and tap beer. Fire up the free wi-fi on the sunny deck.

Curly's Bar   PUB
(☏07-878 8448; www.curlysbar.co.nz; Hotel Access Rd; ☺11am-late) Resurrected after a devastating 2012 fire, Curly's Bar is Waitomo's pub and home turf for the King Country Brewing Co. Friendly owners Curly and Crusty are usually up for a chat, and a frosty pale ale and the massive pork ribs could be just the thing after a busy day underground. Served on Curly's sunny deck of course.

ℹ️ Information

Waitomo i-SITE (☏07-878 7640, 0800 474 839; www.waitomocaves.com; 21 Waitomo Caves Rd; ☺9am-5.30pm) Internet access, post office and booking agent.

ℹ️ Getting There & Around

Naked Bus (☏0900 625 33; www.nakedbus. com) Runs once daily to Otorohanga ($20, 20 minutes), Hamilton ($25, 1¼ hours) and New Plymouth ($30, three hours).

Waitomo Shuttle (☏07-873 8279, 0800 808 279; www.waitomo.org.nz/transport-to-waitomo; one-way adult/child $12/7) Heads to the caves five times daily from Otorohanga (15 minutes away), coordinating with bus and train arrivals.

Waitomo Wanderer (☏03-477 9083, 0800 000 4321; www.travelheadfirst.com) Operates a daily return service from Rotorua or Auckland, with optional caving, glowworm and tubing add-ons. It will even integrate Hobbiton into the mix if you're a JRR Tolkien or Sir Peter Jackson fan.

South from Waitomo to Taranaki

This obscure route heading west of Waitomo on Te Anga Rd is a slow but fascinating alternative to SH3 if Taranaki's your goal. Only 12km of the 111km route remains unsealed,

but it's nearly all winding and narrow. Allow around two hours (not including stops) and fill up with petrol.

Walks in the **Tawarau Forest**, 20km west of the Waitomo Caves, are outlined in DOC's *Waitomo & King Country Tracks* booklet ($1, available from DOC in Hamilton or Te Kuiti), including a one-hour track to the Tawarau Falls from the end of Appletree Rd.

The **Mangapohue Natural Bridge Scenic Reserve**, 26km west of Waitomo, is a 5.5-hectare reserve with a giant natural limestone arch. It's a five-minute walk to the arch on a wheelchair-accessible pathway. On the far side, big rocks full of 35-million-year-old oyster fossils jut up from the grass, and at night you'll see glowworms.

About 4km further west is **Piripiri Caves Scenic Reserve**, where a five-minute walk leads to a large cave containing fossils of giant oysters. Bring a torch and be prepared to get muddy after heavy rain. Steps wind down into the gloom...

The impressively tiered, 30m **Marokopa Falls** are 32km west of Waitomo. A short track (15 minutes return) from the road leads to the bottom of the falls.

Just past Te Anga you can turn north to Kawhia, 59km away, or continue southwest to **Marokopa** (population 1560), a small black-sand village on the coast with some scarily big new mansions starting to appear. The whole Te Anga/Marokopa area is riddled with caves.

Marokopa Campground (☏07-876 7444; marokopacampground@xtra.co.nz; Rauparaha St; campsites from $24, dm $20, van d $50) ain't flash but it's in a nice spot, close to the coast. There's a small shop for grocery basics.

The road heads south to **Kiritehere**, through idyllic farmland to **Moeatoa** then turning right (south) into Mangatoa Rd. Now you're in serious backcountry, heading into the dense **Whareorino Forest**. For trampers, the 16-bunk DOC-run **Leitch's Hut** (☏07-878 1050 www.doc.govt.nz; per adult $5) has a toilet, water and a wood stove.

At **Waikawau** take the 5km detour along the unsealed road to the coast near **Ngarupupu Point**, where a 100m walk through a dank tunnel opens out on an exquisitely isolated stretch of black-sand beach. Think twice about swimming here as there are often dangerous rips in the surf.

The road then continues through another twisty 28km, passing lush forest and the occasional farm before joining SH3 east of Awakino.

Te Kuiti

POP 4380

Cute Te Kuiti sits in a valley between picturesque hills. Welcome to the shearing capital of the world, especially if you visit for the annual Great New Zealand Muster.

◉ Sights

Big Shearer   LANDMARK

(Rora St) This 7m-high, 7½-tonne Big Shearer statue is at the southern end of town.

✯ Festivals & Events

Great New Zealand Muster   CULTURAL, FOOD

(www.waitomo.govt.nz/events/the-great-nz-muster; ⊘ late Mar/early Apr) The highlight of the Great New Zealand Muster is the legendary Running of the Sheep: when 2000 woolly demons stampede down Te Kuiti's main street. The festival includes sheep-shearing championships, a parade, Māori cultural performances, live music, barbecues, *hangi* and market stalls.

🛏 Sleeping & Eating

Waitomo Lodge Motel   MOTEL $$

(☑ 07-878 0003; www.waitomo-lodge.co.nz; 62 Te Kumi Rd; units $130-165; 🐾) At the Waitomo end of Te Kuiti, this motel's modern rooms feature contemporary art, flat-screen TVs and little decks overlooking Mangaokewa Stream from the units at the back.

Simply the Best B&B   B&B $$

(☑ 07-878 8191; www.simplythebestbnb.co.nz; 129 Gadsby Rd; s/d incl breakfast $70/110) It's hard to argue with the immodest name when the prices are this reasonable, the breakfast this generous, and the hosts this charming.

Bosco Cafe   CAFE $

(☑ 07-878 3633; www.boscocafe.me; 57 Te Kumi Rd; mains $10-21; ⊘ 8am-4pm; 🐾) This excellent industrial-chic cafe offers great coffee and tempting food – try the bacon-wrapped meatloaf with greens. Free wi-fi with purchase.

Stoked Eatery   CAFE $$

(☑ 07-878 8758; www.facebook.com/stoked eatery; Te Kuiti Railway Station, 2 Rora St; mains $17-38; ⊘ 10am-late) This recent opening in the railway station celebrates a great location on the station platform with a relaxed ambience and a menu handily divided into Paddock, Ocean and Garden. Meals are hearty and generous; standouts include a crispy pork hock and smoked fish pie.

ℹ Information

DOC (Department of Conservation; ☑ 07-878 1050; www.doc.govt.nz; 78 Taupiri St; ⊘ 8am-4.30pm Mon-Fri) Area office for the surrounding Maniapoto region.

Te Kuiti i-SITE (☑ 07-878 8077; www.waitomo. govt.nz; Rora St; ⊘ 9am-5pm Mon-Fri, 10am-2pm Sat & Sun, closed weekends May-Oct; 🐾) Internet access and visitor information.

ℹ Getting There & Away

InterCity (☑ 09-583 5780; www.intercity. co.nz) buses run daily to the following destinations (among others):

DESTINATION	PRICE	TIME (HR)	FREQUENCY (DAILY)
Auckland	$24-58	3½	3
Mokau	$14-30	2	2
New Plymouth	$15-31	2½	2
Otorohanga	$10-21	¾	3
Taumarunui	$16-34	1¼	1

Naked Bus (☑ 09-979 1616; www.nakedbus. com) runs once daily to Auckland ($25 to $30, four hours), Hamilton ($25 to $27, 1½ hours), New Plymouth ($30, 2¼ hours) and Otorohanga ($20, 30 minutes).

Pio Pio, Awakino & Mokau

From Te Kuiti, SH3 runs southwest to the coast before following the rugged shoreline to New Plymouth. Detour at Pio Pio northwest to the Mangaotaki valley and **Hairy Feet Waitomo** (☑ 07-877 8003; www.hairyfeet waitomo.co.nz; 1411 Mangaotaki Rd; tours adult/child $50/25; ⊘ tours 10am & 1pm), one of NZ's newest Middle-earth–themed film location attractions. Scenes from *The Hobbit* were shot here with a background of towering limestone cliffs. At Pio Pio, the **Fat Pigeon Cafe** (☑ 07-877 8822; www.theowlsnest.co.nz/ fat-pigeon-cafe.html; 41 Moa St; mains $13-22; ⊘ 8am-5pm Mon-Sat, 9am-5pm Sun) combines good-value mains like a chicken and mushroom quesadilla, with huge freshly baked muffins and bagels crammed with salmon and cream cheese.

Along this scenic route the sheep stations sprout peculiar limestone formations before giving way to lush native bush as the highway winds along the course of the Awakino River.

The Awakino River spills into the Tasman at Awakino (population 60), a small settlement where boats shelter in the estuary while locals find refuge at the rustic **Awakino Hotel** (☑06-752 9815; www.awakinohotel. co.nz; SH3 meals $11-20; ☺7am-11pm).

A little further south the impressive **Maniaroa Marae** dominates the cliff above the highway. This important complex houses the anchor stone of the *Tainui waka* which brought this region's original people from their Polynesian homeland. You can get a good view of the intimidatingly carved meeting house, Te Kohaarua, from outside the fence – don't cross into the *marae* unless someone invites you.

Five kilometres further south, as Mt Taranaki starts to emerge on the horizon, is the village of Mokau (population 400). It offers a fine black-sand beach and good surfing and fishing. From August to November the Mokau River (the second-longest on the North Island) spawns whitebait and subsequent swarms of territorial whitebaiters. The town's interesting **Tainui Historical Society Museum** (☑06-752 9072; mokaumuseum@vodafone.co.nz SH3; admission by donation; ☺10am-4pm) has old photographs and artefacts from when this once-isolated outpost was a coal and lumber shipping port for settlements along the river. **Mokau River Tours** (☑0800 665 282; www.mokauriver.co.nz; adult/child $60/10) operate a three-hour river cruise on the MV *GlenRoyal* including a stop upriver in an old campsite in the forest.

Just north of Mokau, **Seaview Holiday Park** (☑0800 478 786; seaviewhp@xtra.co.nz; SH3; campsites from $14, d cabin/unit from $65/90) is rustic, but it's right on an expansive beach. Above the village the **Mokau Motel** (☑06-752 9725; www.mokaumotels.co.nz; SH3; s/d/ste from $100/115/130; ☎) offers fishing advice, self-contained units and three luxury suites.

Taumarunui

POP 5140

Taumarunui on a cold day can feel a bit miserable, but this town in the heart of the King Country has potential. The main reason to stay here is to kayak on the Whanganui River or as a cheaper base for skiing in Tongariro National Park. There are also some beaut walks and cycling tracks around town.

For details on the Forgotten World Hwy between Taumarunui and Stratford, see Taranaki (p258). For details on canoeing and kayaking on the Whanganui River, see Whanganui National Park (p241).

◉ Sights

Raurimu Spiral   RAILWAY
The Raurimu Spiral, 30km south of town, is a unique feat of railway engineering that was completed in 1908 after 10 years of work. Rail buffs can experience the spiral by catching the Northern Explorer train linking Auckland and Wellington to National Park township. Unfortunately as of 2012 this train no longer stops in Taumarunui.

⚡ Activities

The 3km **Riverbank Walk** along the Whanganui River runs from Cherry Grove Domain 1km south of town, to Taumarunui Holiday Park. **Te Peka Lookout**, across the Ongarue River on the western edge of town, is a good vantage point.

Epic Cycle Adventures   MOUNTAIN BIKING
(☑022 023 7958; www.thetimbertrail.nz; 9 Rata St; bike & shuttle $100) Arranges bike hire and convenient shuttles if you're keen to tackle the Timber Trail. Check the website for more details on this interesting ride.

☞ Tours

Forgotten World Adventures   TOUR
(☑0800 7245 2278; www.forgottenworldadventures.co.nz; 1 Hakiaha St; 1/2 days from $210/495; ☺booking office 9am-2pm) Ride the rails on quirky converted former golf carts along the railway line linking Taumarunui to the tiny hamlet of Whangamomona in the Taranaki region. The most spectacular trip takes in 20 tunnels. Other options include a rail and jet-boat combo and a longer two-day excursion covering the full 140km from Taumarunui to Stratford (including an overnight stay in Whangamomona).

Taumarunui Jet Tours   ADVENTURE TOUR
(☑0800 853 386, 07-895 6055; www.taumarunuijettours.co.nz; Cherry Grove Domain; 30/60min tours from $60/100) High-octane jetboat trips on the Whanganui River.

🛏 Sleeping & Eating

Taumarunui Holiday Park   HOLIDAY PARK $
(☑07-835 9345; www.taumarunuiholidaypark. co.nz; SH4; campsites from $18, cabins & cottages

PUREORA FOREST PARK

Fringing the western edge of Lake Taupo, the 780-sq-km Pureora Forest is home to New Zealand's tallest totara tree. Logging was stopped in the 1980s after a long campaign by conservationists, and the subsequent regeneration is impressive. Tramping routes through the park include tracks to the summits of **Mt Pureora** (1165m) and the rock pinnacle of **Mt Titiraupenga** (1042m). A 12m-high tower, a short walk from the Bismarck Rd car park, provides a canopy-level view of the forest for birdwatchers.

To stay overnight in one of three standard **DOC huts** (www.doc.govt.nz; adult/child $5/2.50) you'll need to buy hut tickets in advance, unless you have a Backcountry Hut Pass. The three **campsites** (www.doc.govt.nz; adult/child $6/3) have self-registration boxes. Hut tickets, maps and information are available from DOC.

Awhina Wilderness Experience (☏027 329 0996; www.awhinatours.co.nz; per person $100) offers five-hour walking tours with local Māori guides through virgin bush to the summit of Titiraupenga, their sacred mountain.

Another option is to ride the spectacular **Timber Trail** from Pureora village in the north of the forest southwest for 85km to Ongarue. Two days is recommended. Accommodation and shuttle transport is available at **Pa Harakeke** (☏07-929 8708; www.paharakeke.co.nz; 138 Maraeroa Rd; d $150), an interesting Māori-operated initiative near Pureora village, and **Black Fern Lodge** (☏07-894 7677; www.blackfernlodge.co.nz; Ongarue Stream Rd; per person $40-58) at Waimiha gets rave reviews for its home cooking. For shuttles and bike hire, contact **Epic Cycle Adventures** (p193) in Taumarunui.

See www.thetimbertrail.com and www.thetimbertrail.nz for maps, shuttle and bike hire information and route planning.

$55-90; @) On the banks of the Whanganui River, 4km east of town, this shady camping ground offers safe river swimming and clean facilities. The friendly owners have lots of ideas on what to see and do.

Twin Rivers Motel　　　　　　MOTEL $$
(☏07-895 8063; www.twinrivers.co.nz; 23 Marae St; units $90-215;) The 12 units at Twin Rivers are spick and span. Bigger units sleep up to seven.

Anna's Cafe　　　　　　　　　　CAFE $$
(☏07-896 7442; 75 Hakiaha St; mains $13-20; ⊙7am-4pm Mon-Fri, to 10pm Sat & Sun) Anna's country kitchen style is brightened up by big-format photos of food, and luckily the menu fulfils this culinary promise. Wine, beer and Taumarunui's coffee is all available along with well-prepared versions of cafe classics like hotcakes with mixed berries.

ℹ Information

Taumarunui i-SITE (☏07-895 7494; www.visitruapehu.com; 116 Hakiaha St; ⊙8.30am-5.30pm) Visitor information and internet access.

ℹ Getting There & Away

InterCity (☏0508 353 947; www.intercity.co.nz) InterCity buses head to Auckland ($42, 4½ hours) via Te Kuiti and to Palmerston North ($31, 4½ hours) via National Park.

Owhango

POP 210

A pint-sized village where all the street names start with 'O', Owhango makes a cosy base for walkers, mountain bikers (the **42 Traverse** ends here) and skiers who don't want to fork out to stay closer to the slopes in Tongariro National Park. Take Omaki Rd for a two-hour loop walk through virgin forest in **Ohinetonga Scenic Reserve**.

🛏 Sleeping & Eating

Forest Lodge　　　　　　　　　LODGE $
(☏07-895 4854; www.forest-lodge.co.nz; 12 Omaki Rd; dm/d from $25/60, motel d $80; @) A snug backpackers with comfortable, clean rooms and good communal spaces. For privacy junkies there's a separate self-contained motel next door. Mountain-bike rental and bike-shuttle services for the 42 Traverse are also available.

Blue Duck Station　　　　LODGE, HOSTEL $$
(☏07-895 6276; www.blueduckstation.co.nz; RD2, Whakahoro; dm/d $45/195) ✍ Overlooking the Retaruke River 36km southwest of Owhango (take the Kaitieke turn-off 1km south of town), this ecosavvy place is actually various lodges, offering accommodation from dorms in an old shearers quarters to a

self-contained family cottage sleeping eight. The owners are mad-keen conservationists, restoring native bird habitats and historic buildings. Activities include bush tours, horseriding, kayaking and mountain biking.

Cafe 39 South CAFE $
(☑ 07-895 4800; www.cafe39south.co.nz; SH4; mains $13-21; ☺ 8am-4pm daily & 5.30-9pm Fri) The food is delicious (try the sweetcorn fritters), the coffee is excellent, and the electric fire and daily soup specials will make you want to linger on cold days. The 39° South latitude marker is just across the road.

❶ Getting There & Away

InterCity (☑ 0508 353 947; www.intercity. co.nz) All the InterCity buses that stop in Taumarunui also stop here.

COROMANDEL PENINSULA

The Coromandel Peninsula juts into the Pacific east of Auckland, forming the eastern boundary of the Hauraki Gulf. Although relatively close to the metropolis, the Coromandel offers easy access to splendid isolation. Its dramatic, mountainous spine bisects it into two very distinct parts.

The east coast has some of the North Island's best white-sand beaches. When Auckland shuts up shop for Christmas and New Year, this is where it heads. The cutesy historic gold-mining towns on the western side escape the worst of the influx, their muddy wetlands and picturesque stony bays holding less appeal for the masses. This coast has long been a refuge for alternative lifestylers. Down the middle, the mountains are crisscrossed with walking tracks, allowing trampers to explore large tracts of untamed bush where kauri trees once towered and are starting to do so again.

History

This whole area – including the peninsula, the islands and both sides of the gulf – was known to the Māori as Hauraki. Various *iwi* (tribes) held claim to pockets of it, including the Pare Hauraki branch of the Tainui *iwi* and others descended from Te Arawa and earlier migrations. Polynesian artefacts and evidence of moa-hunting have been found, pointing to around 1000 years of continuous occupation.

The Hauraki *iwi* were some of the first to be exposed to European traders. The region's proximity to Auckland, safe anchorages and ready supply of valuable timber initially lead to a booming economy. Kauri logging was big business on the peninsula. Allied to the timber trade was shipbuilding, which took off in 1832 when a mill was established at Mercury Bay. Things got tougher once the kauri around the coast became scarce and the loggers had to penetrate deeper into the bush for timber. Kauri dams, which used water power to propel the huge logs to the coast, were built. By the 1930s virtually no kauri remained and the industry died.

Gold was first discovered in NZ near Coromandel Town in 1852. Although this first rush was short-lived, more gold was discovered around Thames in 1867 and later in other places. The peninsula is also rich in semiprecious gemstones, such as quartz, agate, amethyst and jasper. A fossick on any west-coast beach can be rewarding.

Despite successful interactions with Europeans for decades, the Hauraki *iwi* were some of the hardest hit by colonisation. Unscrupulous dealings by settlers and government to gain access to valuable resources resulted in the Māori losing most of their lands by the 1880s. Even today there is a much lower Māori presence on the peninsula than in neighbouring districts.

❶ Getting There & Away

Daily buses on the Auckland–Tauranga route pass through Thames and Waihi, while others loop through Coromandel Town, Whitianga and Tairua.

It's definitely worth considering the beautiful **360 Discovery** (p202) ferry ride from Auckland via Waiheke Island to Coromandel Town.

Miranda

It's a pretty name for a settlement on the swampy Firth of Thames, just an hour's drive from Auckland. The two reasons to come here are splashing around in the thermal pools and birdwatching.

This is one of the most accessible spots for studying waders or shorebirds all year round. The vast mudflat is teeming with aquatic worms and crustaceans, which attract thousands of Arctic-nesting shorebirds over the winter – 43 species of wader have been spotted here. The two main species are the bar-tailed godwit and the lesser or red

Coromandel Peninsula

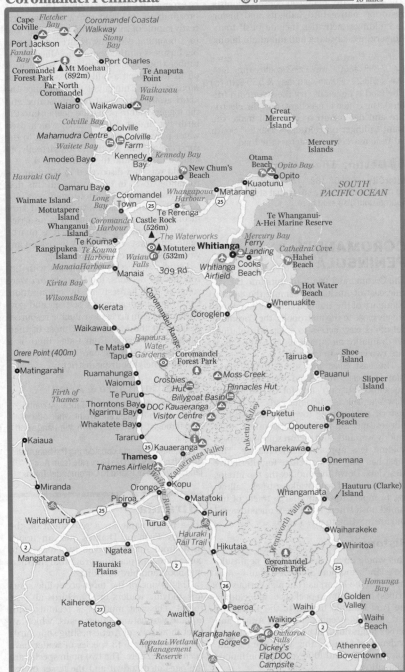

knot, but it isn't unusual to see turnstones, sandpipers and the odd vagrant red-necked stint. One godwit tagged here was tracked making an 11,570km nonstop flight from Alaska. Short-haul travellers include the pied oystercatcher and the threatened wrybill from the South Island, and banded dotterels and pied stilts.

◉ Sights & Activities

Miranda Shorebird Centre WILDLIFE
(☑ 09-232 2781; www.miranda-shorebird.org.nz; 283 East Coast Rd; birdwatching pamphlet $2; ☺ 9am-5pm) The Miranda Shorebird Centre has bird-life displays, hires out binoculars and sells useful birdwatching pamphlets. Nearby is a hide and several walks (30 minutes to two hours). The centre offers clean bunk-style accommodation (dorm beds/rooms $25/95) with a kitchen.

Miranda Hot Springs HOT SPRING
(☑ 07-867 3055; www.mirandahotsprings.co.nz; Front Miranda Rd; adult/child $14/7, private spa extra $15; ☺ 9am-9.30pm) Miranda Hot Springs has a large thermal swimming pool (reputedly the largest in the southern hemisphere), a toasty sauna pool and private spas.

⌕ Sleeping

Miranda Holiday Park HOLIDAY PARK $
(☑ 07-867 3205; www.mirandaholidaypark.co.nz; 595 Front Miranda Rd; campsites per person $25, units $85-190; @ �) ❧ Next door to the Miranda Hot Springs, Miranda Holiday Park has excellent sparkling-clean units and facilities, its own hot-spring pool and a floodlit tennis court.

Thames

POP 6800

Dinky wooden buildings from the 19th-century gold rush still dominate Thames, but grizzly prospectors have long been replaced by alternative lifestylers. It's a good base for tramping or canyoning in the nearby Kauaeranga Valley.

Captain Cook arrived here in 1769, naming the Waihou River the 'Thames' 'on account of its bearing some resemblance to that river in England'; you may well think otherwise. This area belonged to Ngāti Maru, a tribe of Tainui descent. Their spectacular meeting house, Hotunui (1878), holds pride of place in the Auckland Museum.

THE HAURAKI RAIL TRAIL

The cycle trail running from Thames south to Paeroa, and then further south to Te Aroha, or east to Waihi, the Hauraki Rail Trail, is growing in popularity due to its proximity to the bigger cities of Auckland and Hamilton. Two- and three-day itineraries are most popular, but shorter sections of the trail can be very rewarding too. The spur from Paeroa east through the Karangahake Gorge via Waikino to Waihi is spectacular as it skirts a picturesque river valley. The key centres of Thames, Paeroa, Te Aroha and Waihi have an expanding range of related services including bike hire, shuttles and accommodation.

See www.haurakirailtrail.co.nz for detailed information including trail maps and recommendations for day rides. At the time of writing, planning was underway to extend the trail west from Kopu around the Firth of Thames via Miranda to Kaiaua. Check the website for the latest.

After opening Thames to gold-miners in 1867, Ngāti Maru were swamped by 10,000 European settlers within a year. When the initial boom turned to bust, a dubious system of government advances resulted in Māori debt and forced land sales.

◉ Sights

★ **Goldmine Experience** MINE
(☑ 07-868 8514; www.goldmine-experience.co.nz; cnr Moanataiari Rd & Pollen St; adult/child $15/5; ☺ 10am-4pm daily Jan-Mar, to 1pm Sat & Sun Apr, May & Sep-Dec) Walk through a mine tunnel, watch a stamper battery crush rock, learn about the history of the Cornish miners and try your hand at panning for gold ($2 extra).

**School of Mines
& Mineralogical Museum** MUSEUM
(☑ 07-863 6227; www.historicplaces.org.nz; 101 Cochrane St; adult/child $10/free; ☺ 11am-3pm Wed-Sun Mar-Dec, daily Jan & Feb) The Historic Places Trust runs tours of these buildings, which house an extensive collection of NZ rocks, minerals and fossils. The oldest section (1868) was part of a Methodist Sunday School, situated on a Māori burial ground. The Trust has a free self-guided tour pamphlet taking in Thames' significant buildings.

Thames

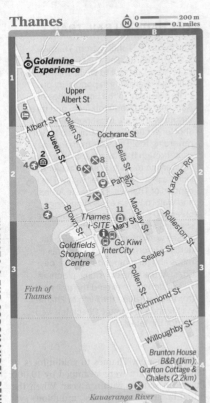

Thames Small Gauge Railway   RAILWAY
(www.facebook.com/www.thamesrailway; Brown St; tickets $2; ⊙11am-3pm Sun) Young ones will enjoy the 900m loop ride on this cute-as-a-button train.

Karaka Bird Hide   BIRDWATCHING
✐ **FREE** Built with compensation funds from the *Rainbow Warrior* bombing, this hide can be reached by a boardwalk through the mangroves just off Brown St.

⛏ Sleeping

Sunkist Backpackers   B&B $
(☎07-868 8808; www.sunkistbackpackers.com; 506 Brown St; dm $30-35, s/d $65/85; @🐾) This character-filled 1860s heritage building has shared rooms, private singles and doubles, and a sunny garden. Breakfast is included and all rooms share bathrooms. Also on offer are shuttle services to the Pinnacles and various points along the Hauraki Rail Trail; bikes can be hired. Cars can also be rented for exploring more remote areas of the Coromandel Peninsula.

Cotswold Cottage   B&B $$
(☎07-868 6306; www.cotswoldcottage.co.nz; 46 Maramarahi Rd; r $180-210; 🐾) ✐ Looking over the river and racecourse, 3km southeast of town, this pretty villa features luxuriant linen and an outdoor spa pool. The comfy rooms all open onto a deck.

Butterfly & Orchid Garden   GARDENS
(☎07-868 8080; www.butterfly.co.nz; Victoria St; adult/child $12/6; ⊙9.30am-4.30pm Sep-May) Around 3km north of town within the Dickson Holiday Park is this enclosed jungle full of hundreds of exotic flappers.

🏃 Activities

Canyonz   CANYONING
(☎0800 422 696; www.canyonz.co.nz; trips $360) ✐ All-day canyoning trips to the Sleeping God Canyon in the Kauaeranga Valley. Expect a vertical descent of over 300m, requiring abseiling, water-sliding and jumping. Trips leave from Thames at 8.30am; 7am pick-ups from Hamilton are also available. Note that Thames is only a 1½-hour drive from central Auckland, so with your own transport a day trip from Auckland is possible.

Coastal Motor Lodge

MOTEL $$

(☑ 07-868 6843; www.stayatcoastal.co.nz; 608 Tararu Rd; units $150-179; ☎) Motel and chalet-style accommodation is provided at this smart, welcoming place, 2km north of Thames. It overlooks the sea, making it a popular choice, especially in the summer months.

Grafton Cottage & Chalets

CHALET $$

(☑ 07-868 9971; www.graftoncottage.co.nz; 304 Grafton Rd; units $140-220; ☎☎☎) Most of these attractive wooden chalets perched on a hill have decks with awesome views. The hospitable hosts provide free internet access and breakfast, as well as use of the pool, spa and barbecue areas.

✗ Eating

Cafe Melbourne

CAFE $

(☑ 07-8683159;www.facebook.com/cafemelbourne grahamstown; 715 Pollen St; mains $13-18; ☺8am-5pm Mon-Thu, to 9pm Fri, 9am-4pm Sat & Sun) Stylish and spacious, this cafe definitely channels the cosmopolitan vibe of a certain Australian city. Shared tables promote a convivial ambience, and the menu travels from ricotta pancakes to beef sliders and fish curry for lunch. It's in a repurposed building called The Depot where you'll also find a juice bar and a deli with artisanal bread and takeaway salads.

Wharf Coffee House & Bar

CAFE $

(☑ 07-868 6828; www.facebook.com/thewharf coffeehouseandbar; Queen St, Shortland Wharf; snacks & mains $10-18; ☺9am-3pm Mon, to 7pm Tue, Wed & Sun, to 9pm Thu-Sat) Perched beside the water, this rustic wood-lined pavilion does great fish and chips. Grab a table outside with a beer or a wine to understand why the Wharf is a firm local favourite.

Coco Espresso

CAFE $

(☑ 07-868 8616; 661 Pollen St; snacks from $5; ☺7.30am-2pm Mon-Fri, 8.30am-12.30pm Sat) Occupying a corner of an old villa, this chic little cafe serves excellent coffee and enticing pastries and cakes.

Nakontong

THAI $$

(☑ 07-868 6821; www.nakontong.com; 728 Pollen St; mains $16-21; ☺11am-2.30pm Mon-Fri & 5-10pm daily; ☎) This is the most popular restaurant in Thames by a country mile. Although the bright lighting may not induce romance, the tangy Thai dishes will provide a warm glow.

☺ Drinking & Nightlife

Junction Hotel

PUB

(☑ 07-868 6008; www.thejunction.net.nz; 700 Pollen St; ☺10am-late) Serving thirsty gold-diggers since 1869, the Junction is the archetypal slightly rough-around-the-edges, historic, small-town pub. Live music attracts a younger crowd on the weekends, while families head to the corner-facing Grahamstown Bar & Diner for hearty pub grub (mains $15 to $30).

🔒 Shopping

Thames Market

MARKET

(☑ 07-868 9841; Pollen St, Grahamstown; ☺8am-noon Sat) ✿ On Saturday mornings the Grahamstown market fills the street with organic produce and handicrafts.

ℹ Information

Thames i-SITE (☑ 07-868 7284; www.thecoromandel.com/thames; 200 Mary St; ☺9am-5pm Mon-Fri, to 2pm Sat, 10am-4pm Sun) Excellent source of information for the entire Coromandel Peninsula.

ℹ Getting There & Away

Go Kiwi (☑ 0800 446 549; www.go-kiwi.co.nz) Handy services to Auckland ($44, 2¼ hours), Coromandel Town ($34, 1¾ hours) and Whitianga ($34, 1¾ hours).

InterCity (☑ 09-583 5780; www.intercity.co.nz) Services to Auckland ($30, 1½ hours) and Hamilton ($24, 1¾ hours).

Coastal Route from Thames to Coromandel Town

Narrow SH25 snakes along the coast past pretty little bays and rocky beaches. Sea birds are plentiful, and you can fish, dig for shellfish and fossick for quartz, jasper and even gold-bearing rocks. The landscape turns crimson when the pohutukawa (often referred to as the 'New Zealand Christmas tree') blooms in December.

A handful of stores, motels, B&Bs and camping grounds are scattered around the picturesque bays. Just north of Te Puru, stop at the colourful **Waiomu Beach Cafe** (☑ 07-868 2554; 62 Thames Coast Rd, Waiomu Bay; mains $10-23; ☺7am-5pm, to 8pm Fri in summer) for gourmet pizza, freshly squeezed juices and healthy salads. Locally brewed craft beer from around the peninsula is also available.

On Friday nights in summer, hours are extended for occasional burger specials.

At **Tapu** turn inland for a mainly sealed 6km drive to the **Rapaura Water Gardens** (☑07-868 4821; www.rapaurawatergardens. co.nz; 586 Tapu-Coroglen Rd; adult/child $15/6; ☺9am-5pm), combining water, greenery and sculpture. There's on-site accommodation (cottage/lodge $165/285) and a well-regarded cafe (mains $14 to $29).

From **Wilsons Bay** the road heads away from the coast and climbs over several hills and valleys before dropping down to Coromandel Town, 55km from Thames. The view looking towards the island-studded Coromandel Harbour is exquisite.

Coromandel Town

POP 1480

Crammed with heritage buildings, Coromandel Town is a thoroughly quaint little place. Its natty cafes, interesting art stores, excellent sleeping options and delicious smoked mussels could keep you here longer than you expected.

Gold was discovered at Driving Creek in 1852. Initially the local Patukirikiri *iwi* (tribe) kept control of the land and received money from digging licences. After initial financial success the same fate befell them as the Ngāti Maru in Thames. By 1871, debt had forced them to sell all but 778 mountainous acres of their land. Today fewer than 100 people remain who identify as part of this *iwi*.

Note that Coromandel Town is just one part of the entire Coromandel Peninsula, and its location on the peninsula's west coast means it is not a good base for visiting Cathedral Cove and Hot Water Beach on the peninsula's east coast.

◉ Sights

Many historic sites are featured in the Historic Places Trust's *Coromandel Town* pamphlet, available at the Coromandel Town Information Centre.

Coromandel Goldfield
Centre & Stamper Battery   HISTORIC BUILDING
(☑021 0232 8262; www.coromandelstamper battery.weebly.com; 360 Buffalo Rd; adult/child $10/5; ☺10am-4pm, tours hourly 10am-3pm, closed Fri in winter) The rock-crushing machine clatters into life during the informative tours of this 1899 plant. You can also try panning for gold ($5) and stop to see NZ's largest

working waterwheel. Ask about the special summertime tours by lamplight at 5pm daily.

Coromandel Mining
& Historic Museum   MUSEUM
(☑07-866 8987; 841 Rings Rd; adult/child $5/ free; ☺10am-1pm Sat & Sun Feb–mid-Dec, 10am-4pm daily mid-Dec–Jan) Small museum with glimpses of pioneer life.

☲ Activities

★**Driving Creek**
Railway & Potteries   RAILWAY
(☑07-866 8703; www.drivingcreekrailway. co.nz; 380 Driving Creek Rd; adult/child $35/13; ☺10.15am & 2pm, additional times in summer) ✐ A lifelong labour of love for its conservationist owner, this unique train runs up steep grades, across four trestle bridges, along two spirals and a double switchback, and through two tunnels, finishing at the 'Eye-full Tower'. The one-hour trip passes artworks and regenerating native forest – more than 17,000 natives have been planted, including 9000 kauri. Booking ahead is recommended in summer.

It's worth lingering for the video about the extraordinary guy behind it all, well-known potter, the late Barry Brickell.

Mussel Barge Snapper Safaris   FISHING
(☑07-866 7667; www.musselbargesafaris.co.nz; adult/child $55/30) Fishing trips with a local flavour and lots of laughs. Pick-up available.

ⵐ Tours

Coromandel Adventures   DRIVING TOUR
(☑07-866 7014; www.coromandeladventures. co.nz; 480 Driving Creek Rd; 1-day tour adult/child $80/50) Various tours around Coromandel Town and the peninsula, plus shuttles to Whitianga and Auckland.

⍢ Sleeping

Lion's Den   HOSTEL $
(☑07-866 8157; www.lionsdenhostel.co.nz; 126 Te Tiki St; dm/r $30/70; ☏) Chill out to the hippie boho vibe at this magical place. A tranquil garden with fish pond, fairy lights and wisteria, an on-site massage therapist, and a relaxed collection of comfy rooms make for a soothing stay.

Anchor Lodge   MOTEL, HOSTEL $
(☑07-866 7992; www.anchorlodgecoromandel. co.nz; 448 Wharf Rd; dm $31, d $73, units $135-320; ◉☏✈) This upmarket backpacker-motel combo has its own gold mine, glowworm

COROMANDEL FOREST PARK

More than 30 walks crisscross the Coromandel Forest Park, spread over several major blocks throughout the centre of the Coromandel Peninsula. The most popular hike is the challenging six- to eight-hour return journey up to the **Pinnacles** (759m) in the Kauaeranga Valley behind Thames. Other outstanding tramps include the Coromandel Coastal Walkway in Far North Coromandel, from Fletcher Bay to Stony Bay, and the Puketui Valley walk to abandoned gold mines.

The **DOC Kauaeranga Visitor Centre** (Department of Conservation; ☑ 07-867 9080; www.doc.govt.nz; Kauaeranga Valley Rd; ⊗ 8.30am-4pm) has interesting displays about the kauri forest and its history. Maps and conservation resources are available for purchase and staff dispense advice. The centre is 14km off SH25; it's a further 9km along a gravel road to the start of the trails. Enquire at the Thames hostels about shuttles.

The DOC **Pinnacles Hut** (adult/child $15/7) has 80 beds, gas cookers, heating, toilets and cold showers. The 10-bunk **Crosbies Hut** (adult/child $15/7.50) is a four- to six-hour tramp from Thames or the Kauaeranga Valley. There are also four basic **backcountry campsites** (adult/child $6/3) in this part of the park: one near each hut and others at Moss Creek and Billygoat Basin; expect only a toilet. A further eight **conservation campsites** (adult/child $10/5) are accessible from Kauaeranga Valley Rd. Bookings must be made online for the huts and some of the campsites.

For a guided walking adventure in the Coromandel, contact **Walking Legends.** (☑ 07-312 5297, 0800 925 569; www.walkinglegends.com; 4-day trip from $1550)

cave, small heated swimming pool and spa. The 2nd-floor units have harbour views.

Coromandel Motel & Holiday Park HOLIDAY PARK $
(☑ 07-866 8830; www.coromandeltop10.co.nz; 636 Rings Rd; campsites from $46, units $80-185; @ 🛜 ☒) Well-kept and welcoming, with nicely painted cabins and manicured lawns, this large park includes the semi-separate Coromandel Town Backpackers. It gets busy in summer, so book ahead. Also hires bikes ($20 per day).

★**Hush Boutique Accommodation** STUDIO $$
(☑ 07-866 7771; www.hushaccommodation.co.nz; 425 Driving Creek Rd; campervans $45, cabins & studios $145-175) Rustic but stylish studios are scattered throughout native bush at this easygoing spot. Lots of honey-coloured natural wood creates a warm ambience, and the shared Hush alfresco area with kitchen facilities and a barbecue is a top spot to catch up with fellow travellers. Hush Petite ($145) is a very cosy stand-alone one-bedroom cottage that was originally a potter's cottage.

Jacaranda Lodge B&B $$
(☑ 07-866 8002; www.jacarandalodge.co.nz; 3195 Tiki Rd; s $90, d $155-185; 🛜) 🚲 Located among 6 hectares of farmland and rose gardens, this two-storey cottage is a relaxing retreat. Look forward to excellent breakfasts from the friendly new owners, Judy and Gerard, often using produce – plums, almonds, macadamia nuts and citrus fruit – from the property's spray-free orchard. Some rooms share bathrooms.

Green House B&B $$
(☑ 07-866 7303; www.greenhousebandb.co.nz; 505 Tiki Rd; r $180; @ 🛜) Good old-fashioned hospitality with three smartly furnished rooms on offer. The pretty downstairs Garden Room has recently been refurbished, and guests enjoy sea views and a rural outlook.

Little Farm APARTMENT $$
(☑ 07-866 8427; www.thelittlefarmcoromandel. co.nz; 750 Tiki Rd; r $90-130; 🛜) Overlooking a private wetland reserve at the rear of a fair-dinkum farm, these three comfortable units offer plenty of peace and quiet. The largest has a full kitchen and superb sunset views.

Coromandel Accommodation Solutions ACCOMMODATION SERVICE $$
(☑ 07-866 8803; www.accommodationccromandel.co.nz; 265 Kapanga Rd; units & apt $120-250; 🛜) Booking service for cottages and rental houses around the Coromandel region; an excellent opportunity for coastal scenery. It also has two stylish apartments centrally located in Coromandel Town.

Driving Creek Villas
COTTAGE $$$

(☑07-866 7755; www.drivingcreekvillas.com; 21a Colville Rd; villas $325; ☎) This is the posh, grown-up's choice – three spacious, self-contained, modern, wooden villas with plenty of privacy. The Polynesian-influenced interior design is slick and the bush setting, complete with bubbling creek, sublime.

✗ Eating

Driving Creek Cafe
VEGETARIAN, VEGAN $

(☑07-866 7066; www.drivingcreekcafe.com; 180 Driving Creek Rd; mains $9-18; ⊙9.30am-5pm; ☎☑) ✐ Vegetarian, vegan, gluten-free, organic and fair-trade delights await at this funky mudbrick cafe. The food is beautifully presented, fresh and healthy. Once sated, the kids can play in the sandpit while the adults check their email on the free wi-fi. Don't miss ordering a terrific juice or smoothie.

Coromandel Oyster Company
SEAFOOD $

(☑07-866 8028; 1611 Tiki Rd; snacks & meals $5-25; ⊙10am-5.30pm Sat-Thu, to 6.30pm Fri) Briny-fresh mussels, scallops, oysters and cooked fish and chips and flounder. Coming from Thames you'll find them on the hill around 7km before you reach Coromandel Town.

★ Coromandel Mussel Kitchen
SEAFOOD $$

(☑07-866 7245; www.musselkitchen.co.nz; cnr SH25 & 309 Rd; mains $18-21; ⊙9am-3.30pm, plus dinner late Dec-Feb) This cool cafe-bar sits among fields 3km south of town. Mussels are served with Thai- and Mediterranean-tinged sauces or grilled on the half-shell. In summer the garden bar is perfect for a mussel-fritter stack and a frosty craft beer from MK Brewing Co, the on-site microbrewery. Smoked and chilli mussels and bottles of the beers are all available for takeaway.

Pepper Tree
MODERN NZ $$

(☑07-866 8211; www.peppertreerestaurant.co.nz; 31 Kapanga Rd; mains lunch $16-28, dinner $25-39; ⊙10am-9pm; ☎) Coromandel Town's most upmarket option dishes up generously proportioned meals with an emphasis on local seafood. On a summer's evening, the courtyard tables under the shady tree are the place to be.

🍷 Drinking & Nightlife

Star & Garter Hotel
PUB

(☑07-866 8503; www.starandgarter.co.nz; 5 Kapanga Rd; ⊙11am-late) Making the most of the simple kauri interior of an 1873 building, this smart pub has pool tables, decent sounds and a roster of live music and DJs on the weekends. The beer garden is smartly clad in corrugated iron.

ⓘ Information

Coromandel Town Information Centre (☑07-866 8598; www.coromandeltown.co.nz; 85 Kapanga Rd; ⊙10am-4pm; ☎) Good maps and local information. Pick up the Historic Places Trust's *Coromandel Town* pamphlet here.

ⓘ Getting There & Away

The best way to Coromandel Town from Auckland is on a **360 Discovery** (☑0800 360 3472; www.360discovery.co.nz) ferry (one-way/return $55/90, two hours, five times weekly, daily in summer), which makes a stop at Orapiu on Waiheke Island en route. The ferry docks at Hannafords Wharf, Te Kouma, from where free buses shuttle passengers the 10km into Coromandel Town.

There's no charge for carrying your bike on a 360 Discovery ferry. Touring cyclists can avoid Auckland's traffic fumes and treacherous roads completely by catching the ferry at Gulf Harbour to Auckland's ferry terminal and then leapfrogging directly to Coromandel Town.

InterCity (☑09-583 5780; www.intercity.co.nz) has buses linking Coromandel Town to Hamilton ($40, 3½ hours) and **Go Kiwi** (☑0800 446 549; www.go-kiwi.co.nz) heads to Thames and Auckland ($59, 4½ hours).

Far North Coromandel

Supremely isolated and gobsmackingly beautiful, the rugged tip of the Coromandel Peninsula is well worth the effort required to reach it. The best time to visit is summer, when the gravel roads are dry, the pohutukawa trees are in their crimson glory and camping's an option (there isn't much accommodation up here).

The 1260-hectare **Colville Farm** (☑07-866 6820; www.colvillefarmholidays.co.nz; 2140 Colville Rd; d $75-130; @☎) has accommodation including bare-basics bush lodges and self-contained houses. Guests can try their hands at farm work (including milking) or go on horse treks ($40 to $150, one to five hours).

The nearby **Mahamudra Centre** (☑07-866 6851; www.mahamudra.org.nz; RD4, Main Rd, Colville; campsite/dm/s/tw $18/28/50/80) is a serene Tibetan Buddhist retreat with a stupa, meditation hall and regular meditation courses. It offers simple accommodation in a parklike setting.

Another kilometre on is the tiny settlement of **Colville** (25km north of Coromandel Town). It's a remote rural community by a muddy bay and a magnet for alternative lifestylers. There's not much here except for the quaint **Colville General Store** (☏07-866 6805; Colville Rd; ⊗8.30am-5pm), selling everything from organic food to petrol (warning: this is your last option for either). Another essential stop as you continue north is **Hereford 'n' a Pickle** (☏021 136 8952; www.facebook.com/hereford.n.a.pickle; pies $4-6; ⊗9am-4pm; 🖘). Good coffee, fresh fruit ice cream, and pies made from meat from local Hereford cattle are the standouts at this rustic self-described 'farm shop' that also boasts free wi-fi and sunny outdoor seating. Sausages and smoked meats are available to take away, along with other local produce including fresh juices, jams and pickles.

Three kilometres north of Colville the sealed road turns to gravel and splits to straddle each side of the peninsula. Following the west coast, ancient pohutukawa spread overhead as you pass turquoise waters and stony beaches. The small DOC-run **Fantail Bay campsite** (☏07-866 6685; www.doc.govt.nz; Port Jackson Rd; adult/child $10/5), 23km north of Colville, has running water and a couple of long-drop toilets under the shade of puriri trees. Another 7km brings you to the **Port Jackson campsite** (☏07-866 6932; www.doc.govt.nz; Port Jackson Rd; adult/child $10/5), a larger DOC site right on the beach.

There's a spectacular lookout about 4km further on, where a metal dish identifies the various islands on the horizon. Great Barrier Island is only 20km away, looking every part the extension of the Coromandel Peninsula that it once was.

The road stops at **Fletcher Bay** – a magical land's end. Although it's only 37km from Colville, allow an hour for the drive. There's another **DOC campsite** (☏07-866 6685; www.doc.govt.nz; adult/child $10/5) here, as well as **Fletcher Bay Backpackers** (☏07-866 6685; www.doc.govt.nz; dm $26) – a simple affair with four rooms with four bunks in each. Bring sheets and food.

The **Coromandel Coastal Walkway** is a scenic, 3½-hour one-way hike between Fletcher Bay and **Stony Bay**. It's a relatively easy walk with great coastal views and an ambling section across farmland. If you're not keen on walking all the way back, **Coromandel Discovery** (☏07-866 8175; www.

coromandeldiscovery.co.nz; adult/child $130/75) will drive you from Coromandel Town up to Fletcher Bay and pick you up from Stony Bay four hours later.

At Stony Bay, where the east coast road terminates, there's another **DOC campsite** (☏07-866 6822; www.doc.govt.nz; adult/child $10/5, bach $77) and a small DOC-run bach (holiday home) that sleeps five. Heading south there are a couple of nice beaches peppered with baches on the way to the slightly larger settlement of **Port Charles**.

Here, **Tangiaro Kiwi Retreat** (☏07-866 6614; www.kiwiretreat.co.nz; 1299 Port Charles Rd, units $220-350; 🖘) offers eight very comfortable one- or two-bedroom self-contained wooden cottages. There's a bush-fringed spa, an in-house massage therapist ($75 per hour), and in summer, a cafe and licensed restaurant. The 20km road down to Port Charles from the intersection of Port Charles Rd and Waikawau Rd is winding and unsealed.

Another 8km brings you to the turn-off leading back to Colville, or you can continue south to **Waikawau Bay**, where there's a large **DOC campsite** (☏07-866 1106; www.doc.govt.nz; Waikawau Beach Rd; adult/child $10/5) which has a summer-only store. The road then winds its way south past **Kennedy Bay** before cutting back to come out near the Driving Creek Railway.

Coromandel Town to Whitianga

309 Road

There are two routes from Coromandel Town southeast to Whitianga. The main road is the slightly longer but quicker SH25, which enjoys sea views and has short detours to pristine sandy beaches. The other is the less-travelled but legendary 309 Rd, an unsealed, untamed route through deep bush. Starting 3km south of Coromandel Town, the 309 Rd cuts through the Coromandel Range for 21km (most of which is unsealed but well maintained), rejoining SH25 7km south of Whitianga. The wonderfully bizarre **Waterworks** (www.thewaterworks.co.nz; 471 309 Rd; adult/child $24/18; ⊗10am-6pm Nov-Apr, to 4pm May-Oct; 🖘) 🅿, 5km from SH25, is filled with whimsical water-powered amusements made from old kitchen knives, washing machines, bikes and toilets.

Two kilometres on there's a two-minute walk through bush to the 10m-high **Waiau Falls**. A further 500m on, an easy 10-minute bush walk leads to an amazing **kauri grove**. This stand of 600-year-old giants escaped the carnage of the 19th century, giving a majestic reminder of what the peninsula once looked like. The biggest tree has a 6m circumference.

If you enjoy the remoteness and decide to linger, **Wairua Lodge** (07-866 0304; www.wairualodge.co.nz; 251 Old Coach Rd; r $170-250) is a peaceful B&B with charming hosts, nestled in the bush towards the Whitianga end of the 309. There's a river-side swimming hole on the property, barbecue, spa and romantic outdoor bathtub.

State Highway 25

SH25 starts by climbing sharply to an incredible lookout before heading steeply down. The turn-off at Te Rerenga follows the harbour to **Whangapoua**. There's not much at this beach except for holiday homes and the pleasant **Whangapoua Holiday Park** (07-866 5215; www.whangapouaholidaypark.co.nz; 1266 Whangapoua Rd, Whangapoua; campsites from $20, cabins $75-90), but you can walk along the rocky foreshore for 30 minutes to the remote, beautiful and often-deserted and undeveloped **New Chum's Beach**, regarded as one of the most beautiful in the country. Back in Te Rerenga on SH25, the **Castle Rock Cafe** (07-866 4542; www.castlerockcafe.co.nz; 1242 Whangapoua Rd, Te Rerenga; mains $12-22; 10am-4pm Wed, Thu & Sun, to 8.30pm Fri, 9am-8.30pm Sat) offers cafe dining, good takeaway pizzas and gourmet burgers, plus its own range of jams, dressings and sauces.

Continuing east on SH25 you soon reach **Kuaotunu**, a more interesting holiday village on a beautiful stretch of white-sand beach, with a cafe-gallery, a store and an ancient petrol pump. In Kuaotunu village, **Luke's Kitchen & Cafe** (07 866 4420; www.lukeskitchen.co.nz; 20 Blackjack Rd, Kuaotunu; mains & pizza $15-28; cafe & gallery 8.30am-3.30pm, restaurant & bar 11am-10pm, shorter hours in winter) has a rustic surf-shack ambience, cold brews (including craft beers from around NZ) and excellent wood-fired pizza. Occasional live music, local seafood and creamy fruit smoothies make Luke's an essential stop. Adjacent is Luke's new daytime cafe and gallery with very good coffee, home-baked goodies and eclectic local art for sale. Try the Spanish eggs or a bacon-and-egg roll in Kuaotunu sunshine and you'll be a happy traveller.

For more luxury, head back along the beach to **Kuaotunu Bay Lodge** (07-866 4396; www.kuaotunubay.co.nz; SH25; s/d $270/295;), an elegant B&B set among manicured gardens, offering a small set of spacious sea-gazing rooms.

Heading off the highway at Kuaotunu takes you (via an unsealed road) to one of Coromandel's best-kept secrets. First the long stretch of **Otama Beach** comes into view – deserted but for a few houses and farms. Continue along the narrowing road, the sealed road finally starts again and you reach **Opito**, a hidden-away enclave of 250 flash properties (too smart to be called baches), of which only 16 have permanent residents. From this magical beach, you can walk to the Ngāti Hei *pa* (fortified village) site at the far end.

At Opito, **Leighton Lodge** (07-866 0756; www.leightonlodge.co.nz; 17 Stewart Pl; s $160-190, d $200-220;) is a smart B&B with friendly owners, a self-contained flat downstairs, and an upstairs room with a view-hungry balcony.

Whitianga

POP 3800

Whitianga's big attractions are the sandy beaches of Mercury Bay and the diving, boating and kayaking opportunities afforded by the craggy coast and nearby Te Whanganui-A-Hei Marine Reserve. The pretty harbour is a renowned base for game fishing (especially marlin and tuna between January and March).

The legendary Polynesian explorer and seafarer Kupe is believed to have landed near here sometime around AD 950. The name Whitianga is a contraction of Te Whitianga a Kupe (Crossing Place of Kupe).

⊙ Sights

Buffalo Beach stretches along Mercury Bay, north of Whitianga Harbour. A five-minute passenger ferry ride (p207) will take you across the harbour to **Ferry Landing**. From here you can walk to local sights like Whitianga Rock Scenic & Historical Reserve, a park with great views over the ocean, and the **Shakespeare Cliff Lookout**. Further afield are Hahei Beach (13km), Cathedral Cove (15km) and Hot Water Beach (18km, one hour by bike). Look forward to relatively flat terrain if you're keen on riding from Ferry Landing to these other destinations. Cathedral Cove Shuttles (p207) runs a handy service from Ferry Landing to these destinations, and in summer from late December to March, Go Kiwi (p207) shuttles also run the convenient Beach Bus starting from Ferry Landing.

Lost Spring   SPRING
(07-866 0456; www.thelostspring.co.nz; 121a Cook Dr; per 90min/day $38/68; 10.30am-6pm Sun-Fri, to 8pm Sat) This expensive but intriguing Disney-meets-Polynesia thermal complex comprises a series of hot pools in a lush jungle-like setting complete with an erupting volcano. It's the ideal spot to relax in tropical tranquillity, with a cocktail in hand. There's also a day spa and cafe. Children under 14 must be accompanied by an adult in the pools.

Mercury Bay Museum   MUSEUM
(07-866 0730; www.mercurybaymuseum.co.nz; 11a The Esplanade; adult/child $7.50/50¢; 10am-4pm) A small but interesting museum focusing on local history – especially Whitianga's most famous visitors, Kupe and Cook.

🏃 Activities

Bike Man   BICYCLE RENTAL
(07-866 0745; thebikeman@xtra.co.nz; 16 Coghill St; per day $25; 9am-5pm Mon-Fri, to 1pm Sat) Rent a bike to take across on the ferry and journey to Hahei and Hot Water Beach.

Windborne   SAILING
(027 475 2411; www.windborne.co.nz; day sail $95; Dec-Apr) Day sails in a 19m 1928 schooner from December to April, and also departures to the Mercury Islands ($150) in February and March.

👉 Tours

There are a baffling number of tours to Te Whanganui-A-Hei Marine Reserve, where you'll see interesting rock formations and, if you're lucky, dolphins, fur seals, penguins and orcas. Some are straight-out cruises while others offer optional swims and snorkels.

Ocean Leopard   BOAT TOUR
(0800 843 8687; www.oceanleopardtours.co.nz; adult/child $80/45; 10.30pm, 1.30pm & 4pm) Two-hour trips taking in coastal scenery, naturally including Cathedral Cove. The

Whitianga

boat has a handy canopy for sun protection. A one-hour Whirlwind Tour (adult/child $60/35) is also on offer.

Whitianga Adventures   BOAT TOUR
(0800 806 060; www.whitianga-adventures.co.nz; adult/child $75/45) A two-hour Sea Cave Adventure in an inflatable.

WAIKATO & THE COROMANDEL PENINSULA WHITIANGA

Glass Bottom Boat
BOAT TOUR

(☑ 07-867 1962; www.glassbottomboatwhitianga.
co.nz; adult/child $95/50) Two-hour
bottom-gazing tours exploring the Te
Whanganui-A-Hei Marine Reserve.

Cave Cruzer
BOAT TOUR

(☑ 07-866 0611; www.cavecruzer.co.nz; adult/child
1hr $50/30, 2hr $75/40) Tours on a rigid-hull
inflatable.

🎉 Festivals & Events

Scallop Festival
FOOD

(☑ 07-867 1510; www.scallopfestival.co.nz; ⊙ early
Sep) One-day showcase of food, entertainment, and more than a few people's favourite bivalves.

🛏 Sleeping

On the Beach Backpackers Lodge
HOSTEL $

(☑ 07-866 5380; www.coromandelbackpackers.
com; 46 Buffalo Beach Rd; dm/s/d $27/42/82; @)
Brightly painted and beachside, this large
YHA-affiliate has a wide range of rooms, including some with sea views and en suites.
It provides free kayaks, boogie boards and
spades (for Hot Water Beach). Bikes ($20)
are also available if you're keen to catch the
ferry and cycle to Hahei.

Turtle Cove
HOSTEL $

(☑ 07-867 1517; www.turtlecove.co.nz; 14 Bryce St;
dm $28-32, d $75-85; @🐾) Colourful shared
areas and a spacious modern kitchen make
Turtle Cove one of the best hostels in the
Coromandel Peninsula and Waikato area.
The largest dormitories have only six beds,
making Turtle Cove more like a friendly
homestay than a rip-roaring party palace.
The team at reception is unfailingly helpful
with plenty of ideas on how to maximise
your time.

Mercury Bay Holiday Park
HOLIDAY PARK $

(☑ 07-866 5579; www.mercurybayholidaypark.
co.nz; 121 Albert St; campsites from $23, units $85-
160; @🐾🏊) Strangely planted in a subur-
ban neighbourhood, this small holiday park
is comfortable and clean, with playgrounds,
trampoline, swimming pool and pool table.

Beachside Resort
MOTEL $$

(☑ 07-867 1356; www.beachsideresort.co.nz; 20
Eyre St; units $195-225; 🐾🏊) Attached to the
sprawling Oceans Resort, this modern motel
has tidy units with kitchenettes and balco-
nies on the upper level. Despite the name,
it's set back from the beach but it does have
a heated pool.

Within the Bays
B&B $$$

(☑ 07-866 2848; www.withinthebays.co.nz; 49
Tarapatiki Dr; r $275-325; @🐾) It's the com-
bination of charming hosts and incredible
views that make this B&B set on a hill overlooking Mercury Bay really worth considering. It's extremely well set up for guests
with restricted mobility – there's even a
wheelchair-accessible bush track on the
property. Find it 5km from Whitianga town.

🍴 Eating

Cafe Nina
CAFE $

(☑ 07-866 5440; www.facebook.com/cafenina
whitianga; 20 Victoria St; mains $8-20; ⊙ 8am-
3pm) Barbecue for breakfast? Why the hell
not. Too cool to be constricted to four walls,
the kitchen grills bacon and eggs on an outdoor hotplate while the punters spill out
onto tables in the park. Other dishes include
robust Greek salads and tasty quesadillas.

Blue Ginger
SOUTHEAST ASIAN $$

(☑ 07-867 1777; www.blueginger.co.nz; 1/10 Black-
smith Lane; shared plates $9-14, mains $22-28;
⊙ 11am-2pm Tue-Fri & 5pm-late Tue-Sat) South-
east Asian flavours infuse the menu at this
relaxed spot with shared tables. Highlights
include Indonesian-style beef rendang, pad
thai noodles and a great roast duck red curry.

Mercury Bay Estate
WINERY $$

(☑ 07-866 4066; www.mercurybayestate.co.nz;
761a Purangi Rd, Cooks Beach; platters $18-48, wine
tasting $8-15; ⊙ 10am-5pm Mon-Fri, 9am-6pm Sat
& Sun) Repurposed timber and corrugated
iron feature at this rustic but chic vineyard en route from Ferry Landing to Cooks
Beach. Seafood, cheese and charcuterie platters team well with wines like the excellent
Lonely Bay chardonnay. Local artwork is
also for sale. It's 35km from Whitianga town.

Squids
SEAFOOD $$

(☑ 07-867 1710; www.squids.co.nz; 15/1 Blacksmith
Lane; mains $15-32; ⊙ 11am-2.30pm & 5.30pm-
late) On a corner facing the harbour, this in-
formal restaurant offers good-value seafood
meals in a prime location. Steamed mussels,
smoked seafood platters, and chowder com-
bine with occasional Asian touches. The
steaks are also good.

Poivre & Sel
MODERN NZ $$$

(☑ 07-866 0053; www.poivresel.co.nz; 2 Mill
Rd; mains $35-40; ⊙ 6pm-late Tue-Sat) This
Mediterranean-style villa – complete with a
garden shaded by palm trees – is the most
stylish eatery in town. Begin with crab and

black garlic in an avocado and grapefruit parfait before moving on to delicate porcini-stuffed quail with asparagus. Happy-hour $5 drinks from 5pm to 6pm are a good way to kick things off. Booking for dinner is recommended.

Drinking & Nightlife

Whitianga Hotel PUB
(☑ 07-866 5818; www.whitiangahotel.co.nz; 1 Blacksmith Lane; ⊙ 11am-late) Good value pub food, lots of frosty beers on tap and a relaxed garden bar equal a classic Kiwi pub experience. Challenge the locals on the pool table and return on weekend nights for DJs and cover bands playing songs you'll probably know all the words to.

❶ Information

Whitianga i-SITE (☑ 07-866 5555; www. whitianga.co.nz; 66 Albert St; ⊙ 9am-5pm Mon-Fri, to 4pm Sat & Sun) Information and internet access. Hours are extended in summer.

❶ Getting There & Around

AIR
Sunair (☑ 0800 786 247; www.sunair.co.nz) Operates flights linking Whitianga to Auckland, Great Barrier Island and Tauranga.

BUS
Cathedral Cove Shuttles (☑ 027 422 5899; www.catheralcoveshuttles.co.nz; per person $40; ❸) Convenient transport services from Ferry Landing to nearby beaches and attractions. Service is on request via phone or text.
Go Kiwi (☑ 07-866 0336; www.go-kiwi.co.nz) Links Whitianga to Thames and Auckland. From late December to March it also runs the convenient summertime-only **Beach Bus** (p209), starting from Ferry Landing and heading to Hahei, Cathedral Cove and Hot Water Beach.
InterCity (☑ 07-348 0366; www.intercity. co.nz) Has two routes to/from the Coromandel Peninsula: Auckland–Thames–Paeroa–Waihi–Tauranga and Hamilton–Te Aroha–Paeroa–Thames–Coromandel Town. Local routes include Thames–Coromandel Town–Whitianga and Whitianga–Tairua–Thames.
Naked Bus (www.nakedbus.com) Buses on the Auckland–Tauranga–Mt Maunganui–Rotorua–Gisborne route stop at Ngatea and on to Whitianga.

FERRY
Passenger Ferry Ride (☑ 021 025 10169; www.whitiangaferry.co.nz; adult/child/bicycle $4/2/1.50; ⊙ 7.30am-7.30pm & 8.30-10.30pm) A five-minute passenger ferry ride will take you across the harbour to Whitianga Rock Scenic & Historical Reserve, Flaxmill Bay, Shakespeare's Lookout, Captain Cook's Memorial, Lonely Bay and Cooks Bay.

Coroglen & Whenuakite

The blink-and-you'll-miss-them villages of Coroglen and Whenuakite are on SH25, south of Whitianga and west of Hot Water Beach.

Running from Labour Day to Queen's Birthday, **Coroglen Farmers Market** (☑ 07-866 3315; www.facebook.com/coroglenfarmers market; SH25; ⊙ 9am-1pm Sun late Oct-early Jun) sells a bit of everything local from vegetables to compost. Nearby, the folks at **Rangihau Ranch** (☑ 07-866 3875; www.rangihauranch. co.nz; Rangihau Rd; rides per hour $50) will lead you on horseback up a historic packhorse track through beautiful bush to spectacular views.

Located at the friendly **Seabreeze Holiday Park** (☑ 07-866 3050; www.seabreeze holidaypark.co.nz; 1043 SH25; campsite per person from $22, dm $29, unit $72-145; ☎) in Whenuakite, **Hot Water Brewing Co** (☑ 07-866 3830; www.hotwaterbrewingco.com; ⊙ 11am-late) is a modern craft brewery with lots of outdoor seating. Standout brews include the hoppy Kauri Falls Pale Ale and the robust Walkers Porter. Platters and pizzas all make it easy to order another beer, and the lamb burger is deservedly famous around these parts. Ask if the superb Barley Wine is available.

For the archetypal middle-of-nowhere country pub, stop by the legendary **Coroglen Tavern** (☑ 07-866 3809; www.coroglen tavern.co.nz; 1937 SH25; ⊙ 10am-late), which attracts big-name Kiwi bands in summer.

Better than your average highway stop, **Colenso** (☑ 07-866 3725; www.colensocafe. co.nz; SH25, Whenuakite; mains $10-18; ⊙ 10am-4pm) has excellent fair-trade coffee, scones, cakes and light snacks, as well as a shop selling homewares and gifts. Try the delicious macadamia nut brittle.

❶ Getting There & Away

InterCity (p199) buses linking Thames to Whitianga stop at Whenuakite and Coroglen.

Hahei

POP 27C (7000 IN SUMMER)

A legendary Kiwi beach town, little Hahei balloons to bursting in summer but is nearly abandoned otherwise – apart from the busloads of tourists doing the obligatory stop-off at Cathedral Cove. It's a charming spot and a great place to unwind for a few days, especially in the quieter months. It takes its name from Hei, the eponymous ancestor of the Ngāti Hei people, who arrived in the 14th century on the Te Arawa canoe. Online, see www.hahei.co.nz.

◎ Sights

Cathedral Cove   BEACH
Beautiful Cathedral Cove, with its famous gigantic stone arch and natural waterfall shower, is best enjoyed early or late in the day – avoiding the worst of the hordes. From the car park, a kilometre north of Hahei, it's a rolling walk of around 30 to 40 minutes. On the way there's rocky Gemstone Bay, which has a snorkelling trail where you're likely to see big snapper, crayfish and stingrays, and sandy Stingray Bay.

If you walk from Hahei Beach to Cathedral Cove, it will take about 70 minutes. Other options are to take the 10-minute Cathedral Cove Water Taxi (p209) or the Beach Bus (p209) from Go Kiwi Shuttles. Note that over the peak summer months, both the car park and the cove itself can be exceptionally busy.

Hahei Beach   BEACH
Long, lovely Hahei Beach is made more magical by the view to the craggy islands in the distance. From the southern end of Hahei Beach, it's a 15-minute walk up to Te Pare, a *pa* (fortified village) site with splendid coastal views.

🏃 Activities

Cathedral Cove Sea Kayaking   KAYAKING
(☏ 07-866 3877; www.seakayaktours.co.nz; 88 Hahei Beach Rd; half-/full day $105/170; ⊗ 8.45am & 1.30pm) This outfit runs guided kayaking trips around the rock arches, caves and islands in the Cathedral Cove and Mercury Bay area. The Remote Coast Tour heads the other way when conditions permit, visiting caves, blowholes and a long tunnel.

Hahei Beach Bikes   BICYCLE RENTAL
(☏ 021 701 093; www.haheibeachbikes.co.nz; 2 Margot Pl; bike hire half-/full day $35/45) Friendly owner Jonny also provides local maps with key points of interest and a spade for digging a personal spa pool at Hot Water Beach. By arrangement, bikes can be delivered to Ferry Landing to meet travellers arriving off the ferry from Whitianga.

☞ Tours

Hahei Explorer   ADVENTURE TOUR
(☏ 07-866 3910; www.haheiexplorer.co.nz; adult/child $85/50) Hour-long jetboat rides touring the coast.

🛏 Sleeping

Tatahi Lodge   HOSTEL, MOTEL $
(☏ 07-866 3992; www.tatahilodge.co.nz; Grange Rd; dm $33, r $90-130, units $140-225; @ 🤙) A wonderful place where backpackers are treated with at least as much care and respect as the lush, bromeliad-filled garden. The dorm rooms and excellent communal facilities are just as attractive as the pricier motel units.

Purangi Garden Accommodation   COTTAGE $$
(☏ 07-866 4036; www.purangigarden.co.nz; Lees Rd; d $180-200) On a quiet cove on the Purangi River, this relaxing spot has accommodation ranging from comfortable chalets through to larger houses and a spacious, self-contained yurt. Well-established gardens and rolling lawns lead to the water – perfect for swimming and kayaking – and don't be surprised if the friendly owners drop off some organic fruit or freshly baked bread.

Hahei and Hot Water Beach are both a short drive away.

The Church   COTTAGE $$
(☏ 07-866 3533; www.thechurchhahei.co.nz; 87 Hahei Beach Rd; cottages $140-215; 🤙) ✎ Set within a subtropical garden, these beautifully kitted-out, rustic timber cottages have plenty of character. The switched-on new owners are really welcoming and have loads of ideas on what to do and see around the area.

🍴 Eating & Drinking

The Church   MEDITERRANEAN $$
(☏ 07-866 3797; www.thechurchhahei.co.nz; 87 Hahei Beach Rd; shared plates $10-28; ⊗ 5.30pm-late Mon-Sat, shorter hours outside summer) This ultra-charming wooden church is Hahei's swankiest eatery with excellent Spanish- and North African–inspired dishes made to be shared, as well as a stellar, if pricey, selection of Kiwi craft beers. Try the lamb tagine with yoghurt and couscous or the Moroccan-style steamed mussels. Booking ahead is recommended as the dining room is cosy and compact.

★ Pour House   PUB
(www.coromandelbrewingcompany.co.nz; 7 Grange Rd; ⊗ 11am-11pm) Home base for the Coromandel Brewing Company, this pub and bis-

tro regularly features around five of its beers in a modern ambience. Platters of meat, cheese and local seafood combine with decent pizzas in the beer garden. Our favourite brew is the Code Red Irish Ale.

Purangi Winery WINERY, BEER GARDEN
(07-866 3724; www.facebook.com/purangi estateltd; 450 Purangi Rd; 11am-8pm) Rustic and laid-back – almost to the point of being pleasantly ramshackle – this slightly eccentric combination of winery, beer garden and wood-fired pizza restaurant (pizzas $18 to $25) is in a rural setting 6km from Hahei on the road from Ferry Landing. Try the feijoa fruit wine, liqueur and cider, and say gidday to the friendly posse of cats usually mooching around.

Getting There & Around

In the absolute height of summer school holidays the council runs a bus service from the Cooks Beach side of Ferry Landing to Hot Water Beach, stopping at Hahei. Ask at the **Whitianga i-SITE** (p207).

Another option is the **Beach Bus** (0800 446 549; www.go-kiwi.co.nz; adult/child/family $10/5/22, adult/family day pass $28/50; 9.15am-5.15pm late Dec-Easter). This handy summertime-only service shuttles five times daily between Ferry Landing and Hahei, Cathedral Cove and Hot Water Beach. Try and book online in advance, as seating is limited and priority is given to those with prepurchased tickets.

Cathedral Cove Shuttles (p207) offers a convenient transport service from Ferry Landing to nearby beaches and attractions. Service is on request via phone or text.

From Ferry Landing to Hahei is around 10km. Bikes can be rented from **Hahei Beach Bikes** (p208).

Cathedral Cove Water Taxi (027 919 0563; www.cathedralcovewatertaxi.co.nz; return/one-way adult $25/15, child $15/10; every 30min) runs water taxis from Hahei to Cathedral Cove.

Hot Water Beach

Justifiably famous, Hot Water Beach is quite extraordinary. For two hours either side of low tide, you can access an area of sand in front of a rocky outcrop at the middle of the beach where hot water oozes up from beneath the surface. Bring a spade, dig a hole and, voila, you've got a personal spa pool. Surfers stop off before the main beach to access some decent breaks. The headland between the two beaches still has traces of a Ngāti Hei *pa* (fortified village).

BEACH SAFETY

Hot Water Beach has dangerous rips, especially directly in front of the main thermal section. It's one of the four most dangerous beaches in New Zealand in terms of drowning numbers, although this may be skewed by the huge number of tourists that flock here. Regardless, swimming here is *not* safe if the lifeguards aren't on patrol.

Activities

Hot Water Beach Store OUTDOORS
(07-866 3006; Pye Pl; 9am-5pm) Spades ($5) can be hired from the Hot Water Beach Store, which has a cafe attached.

Sleeping & Eating

Hot Water Beach
Top 10 Holiday Park HOLIDAY PARK $
(07-866 3116; www.hotwaterbeachholidaypark. com; 790 Hot Water Beach Rd; campsites from $23, dm $30, units $90-180;) Bordered by tall bamboo and gum trees, this is a very well-run holiday park with everything from grassy campsites through to a spacious and spotless backpackers lodge and stylish villas with arched ceilings crafted from NZ timber.

Hot Waves CAFE $$
(07-866 3887; 8 Pye Pl; mains $12-26; 8.30am-4pm Mon-Thu & Sun, to 8.30pm Fri & Sat) In summer everyone wants a garden table at this excellent cafe. For a lazy brunch, try the eggs Benedict with smoked salmon or a breakfast burrito. It also hires spades for the beach ($5). Ask about occasional Friday-night music sessions.

Getting There & Away

The **Cathedral Cove Shuttle** (027 422 5899; www.cathedralcoveshuttles.co.nz; per person $4-40, depending on destination; summer 9am-late, winter to 10.30pm) and the summertime **Beach Bus** (p209) both stop here. It's also a popular destination for cyclists leaving from Ferry Landing across the water from Whitianga. Look forward to a rolling ride of around 18km from Ferry Landing to Hot Water Beach.

Tairua & Pauanui
POP 1270

Tairua and its twin town Pauanui sit either side of a river estuary that's perfect for windsurfing or for little kids to splash about in.

Both have excellent surf beaches (Pauanui's is probably a shade better) and both are ridiculously popular in the summertime, but that's where the similarity stops. While Tairua is a functioning residential town (with shops, ATMs and a choice of eateries), Pauanui is an upmarket refuge for Aucklanders. Friendly Tairua knows how to keep it real.

◉ Sights & Activities

Paaku
MOUNTAIN

Around seven million years ago Paaku was a volcanic island, but now it forms the northern head of Tairua's harbour. Ngāti Hei had a *pa* here before being invaded by Ngāti Maru in the 17th century. It's a steep 15-minute walk to the summit from the top of Paku Dr, with the pay-off being amazing views over Tairua, Pauanui and the Alderman Islands. Plaques along the way detail Tairua's colonial history; only one is devoted to its long Māori occupation.

Tairua Dive & Marine
DIVING

(☑07-864 8800; www.tairuadiveandmarine.co.nz; 7 The Esplanade; boat dives from $150; ⊙7.30am-5pm) A solid operator with reliable service. Also hires snorkelling gear, kayaks and paddle boards, and runs snorkelling and sightseeing trips ($75 per person).

🛏 Sleeping & Eating

Tairua Beach Villa Backpackers
HOSTEL $

(☑07-864 8345; www.tairuabackpackers.co.nz; 200 Main Rd; dm $25-30, s $65-75, d $70-90; @🖙) Rooms are homely and casual at this estuary-edge hostel in a converted house, and the dorm scores great views. Guests can help themselves to fishing rods, kayaks, sailboards and bikes.

Pacific Harbour Lodge
HOTEL $$

(☑07-864 8581; www.pacificharbour.co.nz; 223 Main Rd; chalets $170-200; @🖙) This 'island-style' resort in the town centre has spacious self-contained chalets, with natural wood and Gauguin decor inside and a South Seas garden outside. Discount packages are usually available online.

Sunlover Retreat
B&B $$$

(☑07-864 9024; www.sunlover.co.nz; 20 Ridge Rd; d $260-350; 🖙) Enjoy stunning views of Paaku and Tairua at this stylish B&B high above the harbour. Two of the three suites have private outdoor balconies and huge picture windows provide plenty of light and space. Decor is chic, modern and dotted with quirky NZ art, and guests receive a warm welcome from Rover, the Sunlover Retreat labradoodle.

Check the website for packages incorporating diving, fishing and cycling.

Manaia Kitchen & Bar
CAFE $$

(☑07-864 9050; www.manaiakitchenbar.co.nz; 228 Main Rd; mains breakfast $12-19, lunch $17-24, dinner $24-29; ⊙8.30am-late; 🐾) With courtyard seating for lazy summer brunches and a burnished-copper bar to prop up later in the night, Manaia is the most cosmopolitan spot on the Tairua strip. Interesting menu options include dukkah-crusted chicken and a great corn fritter stack for a lazy breakfast. There's live music and the occasional DJ most Friday nights.

Old Mill Cafe
CAFE $$

(☑07-864 9390; www.theoldmillcafetairua.com; 1 The Esplanade; mains $15-25; ⊙8am-10pm Wed-Sun) Zooshed up with bright-pink feature walls and elegant veranda furniture, the Old Mill Cafe serves interesting cafe fare for breakfast and lunch, as well as bigger mains for dinner. Look forward to lots of seafood – including scallop mornay or salt and pepper squid – and outdoor seating with harbour views. Quite possibly the Coromandel's best muffins too.

ℹ Information

Tairua Information Centre (☑07-864 7575; www.thecoromandel.com/tairua; 223 Main Rd; ⊙9am-5pm) Information, maps, and accommodation and transport bookings.

ℹ Getting There & Away

InterCity, Naked Bus and Go Kiwi all run bus services to Tairua.

Tairua and Pauanui are connected by a **passenger ferry** (☑027-497 0316; one-way/return $3/5; ⊙daily Dec & Jan), which departs every two hours from 9am to 5pm (until 11pm in January). In other months the ferry offers a water taxi service.

Puketui Valley

Located 12km south of Tairua is the turn-off to Puketui Valley and the historic **Broken Hills Gold-Mine Workings** (www.doc.govt.nz), which are 8km from the main road along a mainly gravel road. There are short walks up to the sites of stamper batteries, but the best hike is through the 500m-long Collins Drive mine tunnel. After the tunnel, keep an eye out for the short 'lookout' side trail which affords panoramic views. It takes about three hours return; remember to take a torch and a jacket with you. Look for the DOC brochure in information centres in Tairua and Whangamata.

There's a basic **DOC campsite** (www.doc. govt.nz; adult/child $10/5) located in a pretty spot by the river. This is a wilderness area so take care and be properly prepared. Water from the river should be boiled before drinking.

Opoutere

File this one under Coromandel's best-kept secrets. Apart from a cluster of houses there's nothing for miles around. Swimming can be dangerous, especially near Hikinui Islet, which is close to the beach. On the sand spit is the **Wharekawa Wildlife Refuge**, a breeding ground for the endangered New Zealand dotterel.

🛏 Sleeping

YHA Opoutere HOSTEL $
(☑ 07-865 9072, 0800 278 299; www.yha.co.nz; 389 Opoutere Rd; dm $28-32, r $90-130) 🖉 Housed partly in the historic Opoutere Native School, this wonderful get-away-from-it-all hostel resounds with birdsong. Kayaks, hot-water bottles, alarm clocks, stilts and hula hoops can all be borrowed. In winter (April to October), the hostel is only open from Friday to Saturday.

Copsefield B&B $$
(☑ 07-865 9555; www.copsefield.co.nz; 1055 SH25; r $100-200; 🖳) On SH25 but closer to Opoutere than it is to Whangamata, Copsefield is a peaceful country-style villa set in attractive, lush gardens with a spa and a river-side swimming hole. The main house has three attractive B&B rooms, while cheaper accommodation is offered in a separate bach-style cottage.

ⓘ Getting There & Away

Go Kiwi (☑ 0800 446 549; www.go-kiwi.co.nz) With a change in Hikuai, it's possible to catch the Go Kiwi Auckland–Whitianga to Opoutere.

Whangamata

POP 3560

When Auckland's socially ambitious flock to Pauanui, the city's young and free head to Whangamata to surf, party and hook up. It can be a raucous spot over New Year, when the population swells to more than 40,000. It's a true summer-holiday town, but in the off-season there may as well be tumbleweeds rolling down the main street.

🏃 Activities

Besides fishing (game-fishing runs from January to April), snorkelling near Hauturu (Clarke) Island, surfing, kayaking, orienteering and mountain biking, there are excellent walks. A popular destination for kayaking and paddle boarding is Whenuakura (Donut Island), around 1km from the beach. Note that in an effort to boost the islands' status as wildlife sanctuaries, it's not permitted to land on them. Boating around the islands is allowed.

The **Wentworth Falls walk** takes 2½ hours (return); it starts 3km south of the town and 4km down the unsealed Wentworth Valley Rd. A further 3km south of Wentworth Valley Rd is Parakiwai Quarry Rd, at the end of which is the **Wharekirauponga walk**, a sometimes muddy 10km return track (allow 3½ to four hours) to a mining camp, battery and waterfall that passes unusual hexagonal lava columns and loquacious bird life.

SurfSup BICYCLE RENTAL, PADDLE BOARDING
(☑ 021 217 1201; www.surfsupwhangamata.com; 101b Winifred Ave; hire half-/full-day surfboard $30/50, kayak from $40/60, 1/2hr paddle board $20/30) Paddle-boarding and surfing lessons are available, and kayaking and paddle-boarding tours to Whenuakura (Donut Island) run daily from December to March.

Kiwi Dundee Adventures TRAMPING
(☑ 07-865 8809; www.kiwidundee.co.nz) 🖉 Styling himself as a local version of Crocodile Dundee, Doug Johansen offers informative one- to 16-day wilderness walks and guided tours in the Coromandel Peninsula and countrywide.

🎉 Festivals & Events

Whangamata Beach Hop CULTURAL
(www.beachhop.co.nz; ⊙late Mar-early Apr) This annual celebration of retro American culture – expect hot rods, classic cars, motorbikes and rock and roll music – is a great time to be in town. Dust off the classic white T-shirt and leather jacket combo, pile high the beehive hairdo, but definitely book accommodation if you're planning on attending.

🛏 Sleeping

Surf n Stay NZ
HOSTEL $

(☎ 07-865 8323; www.whangamata-backpackers. co.nz; 227 Beverly Tce; dm $33-36, s $45, d $110; ☜) Run by a friendly Kiwi-Brazilian couple, the rebooted Whangamata Backpackers also offers surf and paddle-boarding lessons (from $70), gear hire including paddle boards and kayaks (from $30), and multisport packages where you can mix and match marine-based activities. In a quiet street a block from the waves, dorms and private rooms are clean and comfortable. Cooked breakfast is included.

Wentworth Valley Campsite
CAMPGROUND $

(☎ 07-865 7032; www.doc.govt.nz; 474 Wentworth Valley Rd; adult/child $10/5) ✦ More upmarket than most DOC camping grounds, this campsite is accessed from the Wentworth Falls walk and has toilets, showers and gas barbecues.

Breakers
MOTEL $$

(☎ 07-865 8464; www.breakersmotel.co.nz; 324 Hetherington Rd; units $165-240; ☜☒) Facing the marina on the Tairua approach to Whangamata, this newish motel features an enticing swimming pool and spa pools on the decks of the upstairs units.

🍴 Eating & Drinking

Soul Burger
BURGERS $

(☎ 07-865 8194; www.soulburger.co.nz; 441 Port Rd; burgers $11-16; ☺ 5pm-late Wed-Sun) Serving audacious burgers with names like Soul Blues Brother and Vegan Vibe, this hip corner joint is also licensed so you can have an ice-cold beer with your burger.

Argo Restaurant
MODERN NZ $$

(☎ 07-865 7157; www.argorestaurant.co.nz; 328 Ocean Rd; mains $28-33; ☺ 5.30-9.30pm Thu-Sun & 9am-2.30pm Sat & Sun, daily from late Dec-early Feb; ☜) Whangamata's most stylish restaurant offers a concise menu of innovative bistro classics including garlic-infused linguine with Coromandel mussels and fish with a black rice risotto and a curry coconut sauce. The starter of pork belly croquettes go really well with a hoppy IPA, and the airy deck is perfect for a few lazy afternoon drinks.

SixfortySix
CAFE $$

(☎ 07-865 6117; www.facebook.com/sixfortysixwhangamata; 646 Port Rd; mains $10-26; ☺ 7.30am-11pm) Rightly lauded as one of regional NZ's better cafes, SixfortySix does tasty counter food like baguettes crammed with hoisin pulled pork, as well as more substantial mains including spicy fish tacos and a great scallop and bacon burger. New Zealand wine, local craft beer from Coromandel's Hot Water Brewing Co and freshly squeezed juices and smoothies join good coffee on the drinks menu.

Lincoln
PUB

(☎ 07-865 6338; www.facebook.com/thelincolnwhangamata; 501 Port Rd; ☺ 5pm-late Tue-late, 9am-late Sat) Part pub, part bistro, part cafe and all-round good times feature at this versatile spot on Whangamata's main drag. DJs kick in on summer weekends.

ℹ Information

Whangamata Info Plus (☎ 07-865 8340; www.thecoromandel.com/whangamata; 616 Port Rd; ☺ 9am-5pm Mon-Fri, 9.30am-3.30pm Sat & Sun) Staffed by a friendly and well-informed team.

ℹ Getting There & Away

Go Kiwi (☎ 0800 446 549; www.go-kiwi.co.nz) Go Kiwi has a shuttle bus service to Auckland and other parts of the Coromandel region.

Waihi & Waihi Beach

POP 4500 & 1800

Gold and silver have been dragged out of Waihi's Martha Mine, NZ's richest, since 1878. The town formed quickly thereafter and blinged itself up with grand buildings and a show-offy avenue of phoenix palms, now magnificently mature.

After closing down in 1952, open-cast mining restarted in 1988, and current proposals to harness the potential of other nearby mines forecast mining to continue to around 2020. Another more low-key bonanza is also taking place, with Waihi an integral part of the excellent Hauraki Rail Trail (p197).

While Waihi is interesting for a brief visit, it's Waihi Beach where you'll want to linger. The two places are as dissimilar as surfing is from mining, separated by 11km of farmland. The long sandy beach stretches 9km to Bowentown, on the northern limits of Tauranga Harbour, where you'll find sheltered harbour beaches such as beautiful Anzac Bay. There's a very popular 45-minute walk north through bush to pristine Orokawa Bay, which has no road access.

◉ Sights

Waihi's main drag, Seddon St, has interesting sculptures, information panels about Waihi's golden past and roundabouts that look like squashed daleks. Opposite the visitor centre, the skeleton of a derelict **Cornish Pumphouse** (1904) is the town's main landmark, atmospherically lit at night. From here the **Pit Rim Walkway** has fascinating views into the 250m-deep **Martha Mine**.

The *Historic Hauraki Gold Towns* pamphlet (free from the Waihi i-SITE) outlines walking tours of both Waihi and Paeroa.

Gold Discovery Centre
MUSEUM

(☑07-863 9015; www.golddiscoverycentre.co.nz; 126 Seddon St, Waihi; adult/child $25/12; ☉9am-5pm, to 4pm in winter) Waihi's superb new Gold Discovery Centre tells the area's gold-mining past, present and future through interactive displays, focusing on the personal and poignant to tell interesting stories. Holograms and short movies both feature, drawing visitors in and informing them through entertainment. Good luck in taking on the grizzled miner at 'virtual' Two-Up (a gambling game using coins).

Athenree Hot Springs
SPRING

(☑07-863 5600; www.athenreehotsprings.co.nz; 1 Athenree Rd, Athenree; adult/child $7/4.50; ☉10am-7pm) ✿ In cooler months, retreat to these two small but blissful outdoor hot pools, hidden within a holiday park.

Waihi Arts Centre & Museum
MUSEUM

(☑07-863 8386; www.waihimuseum.co.nz; 54 Kenny St, Waihi; adult/child $5/3; ☉10am-3pm Thu & Fri, noon-3pm Sat-Mon) The Waihi Arts Centre & Musuem has an art gallery and displays focusing on the region's gold-mining history. Prepare to squirm before the collection of miners' chopped-off thumbs preserved in glass jars.

🏃 Activities

Goldfields Railway
RAILWAY

(☑07-863 8251; www.waihirail.co.nz; 30 Wrigley St, Waihi; adult/child return $18/10, bikes $2 extra per route; ☉departs Waihi 10am, 11.45am & 1.45pm Sat, Sun & public holidays) Vintage trains depart Waihi for a 7km, 30-minute scenic journey to Waikino. It's possible to take bikes on the train so they can be used to further explore the Karangahake Gorge section of the Hauraki Rail Trail. The timetable varies seasonally so check the website.

Waihi Bicycle Hire
BICYCLE RENTAL

(☑07-863 8418; www.waihibicyclehire.co.nz; 25 Seddon St, Waihi; bike hire half-/full day from $30/40; ☉8am-5pm) Bike hire and loads of information on the Waihi end of the Hauraki Rail Trail.

🎫 Tours

Waihi Gold Mine Tours
TOUR

(☑07-863 9015; www.golddiscoverycentre.co.nz/tours; 126 Seddon St, Gold Discovery Centre, Waihi; adult/child $34/17; ☉10am & 12.30pm daily, additional tours in summer) To get down into the spectacular Martha Mine, join a 1½-hour Waihi Gold Mine Tour departing from the Gold Discovery Centre.

🛏 Sleeping

Bowentown Beach Holiday Park
HOLIDAY PARK $

(☑07-863 5381; www.bowentown.co.nz; 510 Seaforth Rd, Waihi Beach; campsites from $46, units $85-195; @ 🛜) Having nabbed a stunning stretch of sand, this impressively maintained holiday park makes the most of it with first-rate motel units and camping facilities.

Waihi Beach Top 10 Holiday Resort
HOLIDAY PARK $

(☑0800 924 448; www.waihibeachtop10.co.nz; 15 Beach Rd, Waihi Beach; campsites from $29, units $120-214; @ 🛜 🏊) This massive, resort-style holiday park is pretty darn flash, with a pool, gym, spa, beautiful kitchen and a smorgasbord of sleeping options.

Westwind B&B
B&B $

(☑07-863 7208; westwindgarden@xtra.co.nz; 58 Adams St, Waihi; s/d $50/90) Run by a charming couple who are inveterate travellers themselves, this old-fashioned homestay B&B has two comfortable rooms with a shared bathroom.

Waihi Beach Lodge
B&B $$$

(☑07-863 5818; www.waihibeachlodge.co.nz; 170 Seaforth Ave, Waihi Beach; d $295) A short stroll from the beach, this boutique accommodation features colourful, spacious and modern rooms as well as a studio apartment with its own kitchenette. Legendary breakfasts are often served on a sunny deck. Ask the friendly owners Greg and Ali how they're going with their homemade honey and limoncello, and hopefully look forward to sampling both.

Manawa Ridge
LODGE $$$

(☑07-863 9400; www.manawaridge.co.nz; 267 Ngatitangata Rd, Waihi; r $950) ✿ The views from this castle-like ecoretreat, perched on a 310m ridge 6km northeast of Waihi, take in the entire Bay of Plenty. Made of recycled railway timber, mudbrick and lime-plastered straw walls, the rooms marry earthiness with sheer luxury.

✗ Eating

Boy Oh Boy　　　　　　　　　CAFE $
(www.facebook.com/boyohboy; 28 Wilson Rd, Waihi Beach; snacks $6-8; ⊙6am-4pm) Caffeine-infused cosmopolitan style comes to Waihi Beach at this sunny rustic cottage with loads of outdoor seating. Other tasty diversions include top fruit smoothies, and wholemeal pies and calzones. Vegan and organic influences also abound in Waihi Beach's smallest and friendliest cafe.

Waihi Beach Hotel　　　　　　BISTRO $$
(☑07-863 5402; www.waihibeachhotel.co.nz; 60 Wilson Rd, Waihi Beach; mains $20-32) Auckland restaurateurs the Hip Group helped to inspire the excellent local dining scene when they took over this classic Kiwi hotel in 2014. The versatile menu runs from ricotta hotcakes with lemon curd and mascarpone for brunch to a terrific beef burger with hand-cut chips for dinner. Relaxed sophistication inspires the service and an excellent wine and craft beer selection.

Don't miss the adjacent store dispensing great coffee, the North Island's best gourmet sausage rolls and excellent ice cream (try the salted caramel).

Flatwhite　　　　　　　　　　CAFE $$
(☑07-863 1346; www.flatwhitecafe.co.nz; 21 Shaw Rd, Waihi Beach; mains brunch $14-20, dinner $20-35; ⊙8am-late; 🐾) Funky, licensed and right by Waihi Beach, Flatwhite has a lively brunch menu, decent pizzas and flash burgers. A recent makeover has added huge decks with brilliant ocean views. Our favourite off the new dinner menu is the blackened salmon with a chargrilled corn and saffron salsa.

Porch Kitchen & Bar　　　　　CAFE $$
(www.theporchwaihibeach.co.nz; 23 Wilson Rd, Waihi Beach; mains brunch $14-35, dinner $28-35; ⊙8am-late) Resurrected as an even better restaurant after a fire, Waihi Beach's buzziest combo of cafe and bar serves sophisticated and substantial mains. Kick off with macadamia crumbed scallops for lunch, or return at night for grilled chicken with a spicy chipotle harissa and garlicky gourmet potatoes.

❶ Information

Waihi i-SITE (☑07-863 9015; www.waihi.org.nz; 126 Seddon St, Waihi; ⊙9am-5pm, to 4pm winter) Local information and the interesting **Gold Discovery Centre** (p213), a modern and interactive showcase of the gold-flecked past, present and future of the Waihi region.

❶ Getting There & Away

Waihi is serviced by **InterCity** (p174) buses, which head to Hamilton ($36, 2½ hours), Tauranga ($19, one hour) and Thames ($17, 50 minutes).

Karangahake Gorge

The road between Waihi and Paeroa, through the bush-lined ramparts of the Karangahake Gorge, is one of the best short drives in the country. Walking and biking tracks take in old Māori trails, historic mining and rail detritus, and dense bush. In Māori legend the area is said to be protected by a *taniwha* (supernatural creature). The local *iwi* managed to keep this area closed to miners until 1875, aligning themselves with the militant Te Kooti.

The very worthwhile 4.5km **Karangahake Gorge Historic Walkway** (www.doc.govt.nz) takes 1½ hours (each way) and starts from the car park 14km west of Waihi. It follows the disused railway line and the Ohinemuri River to Waikino station, where you can pick up the vintage train to Waihi, stopping in at **Waikino Station Cafe** (☑07-863 8640; www.waikinostationcafe.co.nz; SH2; mains $10-18; ⊙9.30am-3pm) while you wait. The eastern spur of the Hauraki Rail Trail also passes through, and it's possible to combine a ride on the train from Waihi with a spin on the trail through the most spectacular stage of the gorge. Bikes can be rented from the Waikino Station Cafe ($45 per day). Across the river from the cafe, the **Victoria Battery Tramway & Museum** (☑027 351 8980; www.vbts.org.nz; Waikino; ⊙10am-3pm Wed, Sun & public holidays) is the former site of the biggest quartz-ore processing plant in Australasia. There's a dinky tram ride and guided tours of the underground kilns.

A few kilometres further west, Waitawheta Rd leads across the river from SH2 to **Owharoa Falls**. Opposite the falls, the **Bistro at the Falls Retreat** (☑07-863 8770; www.fallsretreat.co.nz; 25 Waitawheta Rd; pizzas $20-24, mains $25-28; ⊙10am-10pm) is located in a wooden cottage under a shaded canopy of trees. Gourmet pizzas and rustic meat dishes emerge from the wood-fired oven on a regular basis, and there's an excellent wine and craft beer list and a great little playground for the kids. Adjacent **Rose Cottage** (☑07-212 8087; www.fallsretreat.co.nz/accommodation; d $150) offers self-contained and charming, country-style accommodation.

There is a range of shorter walks and loop tracks leading from the main car park at Karangahake Gorge; bring a torch as some pass through tunnels. A two-hour tramp will bring you to **Dickey's Flat**, where there's a free **DOC campsite** (www.doc.govt.nz; Dickey's Flat Rd; adult/child $6/3) and a decent swimming hole. River water will need to be boiled for drinking. You'll find DOC information boards about the walks and the area's history at both the station and the main car park.

Further up the same road, **Ohinemuri Estate Winery** (☑07-862 8874; www.ohinemuri.co.nz; Moresby St; mains $16-33, shared platters $45; ☉10am-4pm Wed-Sun) has Latvian-influenced architecture and serves excellent lunches. You'd be right if you thought it was an unusual site for growing grapes – the fruit is imported from other regions. Tastings are $5, refundable with purchase. If you imbibe too much, snaffle the chalet-style hut ($135 per night) and revel in the charming atmosphere of this secluded place.

Paeroa

POP 3980

Paeroa is the birthplace of Lemon & Paeroa (L&P), an icon of Kiwiana that markets itself as 'world famous in NZ'. Ironically, the fizzy drink is now owned by global monster Coca-Cola Amatil and produced in Auckland. Still, generations of Kiwi kids have pestered their parents to take this route just to catch a glimpse of the giant L&P bottles. See www.paeroa.org.nz for the full story of this iconic Kiwi tipple.

◉ Sights

Paeroa Museum   MUSEUM
(☑07-862 8942; 37 Belmont Rd; adult/child $2/1; ☉noon-3pm Tue-Fri) This small museum has a grand selection of Royal Albert porcelain and other pioneer and Māori artefacts – look in the drawers.

🛏 Sleeping & Eating

Refinery   COTTAGE $$
(☑07-862 7678; www.the-refinery.co.nz; 5 Willoughby St; d $120-145; 🐾) Choose from either the Refinery Guard's Cottage or the Miner's Cabin – both options feature rustic but chic decor, dotted with savvy design touches.

Refinery   CAFE $
(☑07-862 7678; www.the-refinery.co.nz; 5 Willoughby St; snacks $8-14; ☉8.30am-4pm Wed-Fri, from 9am Sat-Sun) Be ready to get pleasantly lost in the Refinery, a spacious showcase of 1960s and 1970s Kiwiana style including a turntable where customers are encouraged to play overflowing bins of vinyl records. Good coffee and food (especially the grilled sandwiches) are best enjoyed on the retro collection of old sofas and dining room furniture filling this heritage building. There's stylish accommodation here too.

L&P Cafe, Bar & Brasserie   CAFE $$
(☑07-862 6753; www.lpcafe.co.nz; SH2; mains $11-20; ☉9am-late) The L&P Cafe, Bar & Brasserie has had a stylish makeover, and you can order everything from L&P battered onion rings and fish and chips through to L&P and bourbon barbecue slow-cooked pork ribs. There's loads of L&P memorabilia, of course lashings of the town's eponymous lemon-flavoured lolly water. Leave room for dessert of L&P ice-cream. Of course.

ⓘ Information

Paeroa Information Centre (☑07-862 6999; www.paeroa.org.nz; Old Post Office Bldg, 101 Normanby Rd; ☉9am-5pm Mon-Fri) Information and brochures including on how to tackle the Hauraki Rail Trail.

ⓘ Getting There & Away

InterCity (☑09-583 5780; www.intercity.co.nz) runs buses to Paeroa linking to Thames and Hamilton.

Taranaki & Whanganui

Best Places to Eat

➡ Tomato Cafe (p247)

➡ Yellow House Café (p236)

➡ Cafe Lahar (p231)

➡ Federal Store (p223)

➡ Arborio (p224)

Best Places to Sleep

➡ One Burgess Hill (p223)

➡ Ahu Ahu Beach Villas (p230)

➡ Anndion Lodge (p235)

➡ King & Queen Hotel Suites (p223)

➡ 151 on London (p236)

Why Go?

Halfway between Auckland and Wellington, Taranaki (aka 'the 'Naki') is the Texas of New Zealand: oil and gas stream in from offshore rigs, plumping the region with enviable affluence. New Plymouth is the regional hub, home to two excellent art galleries, a provincial museum, and enough decent espresso joints to keep you humming.

Behind the city, the moody volcanic cone of Mt Taranaki demands to be visited. Taranaki also has a glut of black-sand beaches: surfers and holidaymakers swell summer numbers.

Further east the history-rich Whanganui River curls its way through Whanganui National Park down to Whanganui city, a 19th-century river port that's ageing with artful grace.

Palmerston North, the Manawatu region's main city, is a town of two peoples: tough-talkin' country fast-foodies in hotted-up cars, and caffeinated Massey University literati. Beyond the city the region blends rural grace with yesterday's pace: you might even find time for a little laziness!

When to Go

➡ Mt Taranaki is one of NZ's wettest spots, and frequently cops snowfalls, even in summer: weather on the mountain can be extremely changeable.

➡ Conversely, just below Mt Taranaki, New Plymouth frequently tops the North Island's most-sunshine-hours list. Expect warm summers and cool winters.

➡ Over in Whanganui the winters are milder, but they're chillier on the Palmerston North plains. Sunshine is also abundant hereabouts – around 2000 hours per year!

❶ Getting There & Away

In Taranaki, Air New Zealand (p225) has domestic flights to/from New Plymouth. Naked Bus (www.nakedbus.com) and InterCity (www.intercity.co.nz) buses also service New Plymouth. Shuttle services run between Mt Taranaki itself and New Plymouth.

Whanganui and Palmerston North airports are also serviced by Air New Zealand, and both cities are on the radar for InterCity and Naked Bus services. KiwiRail Scenic Journeys (p248) trains stop in Palmerston North, too, travelling between Auckland and Wellington.

New Plymouth

POP 56,300

Dominated (in the best possible way) by Mt Taranaki and surrounded by lush farmland, New Plymouth is the only international deep-water port in this part of NZ. Like all port towns, the world washes in and out on the tide, leaving the locals buzzing with a global outlook. The city has a bubbling arts scene (with two superb galleries), some fab cafes and a rootsy, outdoorsy focus. Surf beaches and Mt Taranaki (Egmont National Park) are just a short hop away.

History

Local Māori *iwi* (tribes) have long contested Taranaki lands. In the 1820s they fled to the Cook Strait region to escape Waikato tribes, who eventually took hold of the area in 1832. Only a small group remained, at Okoki Pa (in today's New Plymouth). When European settlers arrived in 1841, the coast of Taranaki seemed deserted and there was little opposition to land claims. The New Zealand Company bought extensive tracts from the remaining Māori.

When other members of local tribes returned after years of exile, they fiercely objected to the land sale. Their claims were upheld by Governor FitzRoy, but the Crown gradually acquired more land from Māori, and European settlers sought these fertile lands. The settlers forced the government to abandon negotiations with Māori, and war erupted in 1860. By 1870 over 500 hectares of Māori land had been confiscated.

Ensuing economic growth was largely founded on dairy farming. The 1959 discoveries of natural gas and oil in the South Taranaki Bight have kept the province economically healthy in recent times.

ESSENTIAL TARANAKI & WHANGANUI

Eat In one of Palmerston North's hip George St eateries.

Drink A bottle of Mike's Pale Ale from Mike's organic brewery (p225).

Read The *Wanganui Chronicle*, NZ's oldest newspaper.

Listen to The rockin' album *Back to the Burning Wreck* by Whanganui riff-monsters the Have.

Watch *The Last Samurai*, co-starring Tom Cruise (Mt Taranaki gets top billing).

Go Green Paddle a stretch of the Whanganui River, an awe-inspiring slice of NZ wilderness.

Online www.visit.taranaki.info, www.whanganuinz.com, www.manawatunz.co.nz

Area code ✆06

◎ Sights

★ **Len Lye Centre**   GALLERY
(☎06-759 6060; www.lenlyefoundation.com; 42 Queen St; ⊙10am-6pm Mon, Wed & Fri-Sun, to 9pm Thu; 🅿) **FREE** 'Great art goes 50-50 with great architecture'. So said Len Lye, the world-beating NZ artist (1901–80) to whom this super new art gallery is dedicated. And indeed, the architecture is amazing: an interlocking facade of tall, mirror-clad concrete flutes, inside of which is a series of galleries linked by ramps, housing Lye's works – kinetic, noisy and surprising. There's also a cinema, kids' art sessions and the broader Govett-Brewster Art Gallery (p220) next door. Don't miss it!

★ **Puke Ariki**   MUSEUM
(☎06-759 6060; www.pukeariki.com; 1 Ariki St; ⊙9am-6pm Mon, Tue, Thu & Fri, to 9pm Wed, to 5pm Sat & Sun) **FREE** Translating as 'Hill of Chiefs', Puke Ariki is home to the i-SITE (p225), a museum, a library, a cafe and the fabulous Arborio (p224) restaurant. The excellent museum has an extensive collection of Māori artefacts, plus colonial, mountain geology and wildlife exhibits (...we hope the shark suspended above the lobby isn't life-size).

Taranaki & Whanganui Highlights

1 Mt Taranaki (p228) Hiking up or around this massive cone.

2 Len Lye Centre (p217) Getting experimental at New Plymouth's dazzling new art gallery.

3 New Zealand Rugby Museum (p244) Flexing your All Blacks spirit in Palmerston North.

4 Surf Highway 45 (p230) Riding the big breaks along this surf-battered coast.

5 New Plymouth's cafes (p223) Bouncing from bean to bean.

6 Chronicle Glass Studio (p233) Watching a glass-blowing demonstration in Whanganui.

7 Whanganui National Park (p238) Redefining serenity on a Whanganui River canoe or kayak trip.

8 Whanganui River Road (p238) Traversing the rainy River Rd by car or bike – it's all about the journey, not how fast you get there.

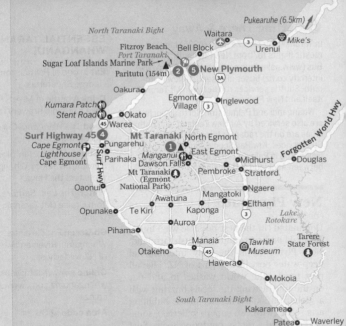

Pukearuhe (6.5km)

North Taranaki Bight

Waitara
Mike's
Bell Block
Urenui
Fitzroy Beach
Port Taranaki
Sugar Loaf Islands Marine Park
5 New Plymouth
Paritutu (154m)
Oakura

Egmont Village
Inglewood

Kumara Patch
Stent Road
Okato
Warea

Surf Highway 45 4
Cape Egmont
Lighthouse
Cape Egmont
Pungarehu
Parihaka
Manganui
Dawson Falls
Mt Taranaki
North Egmont
East Egmont
Midhurst
Douglas
Pembroke
Stratford

Mt Taranaki (Egmont) National Park

Oaonui
Awatuna
Mangatoki
Ngaere
Eltham

Opunake
Te Kiri
Kaponga
Lake Rotokare

Pihama
Auroa
Tarere State Forest

Otakeho
Manaia
Tawhiti Museum

Hawera

Mokoia

Forgotten World Hwy

South Taranaki Bight

Kakaramea

Patea
Waverley

TASMAN SEA

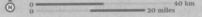

N

0 _____ 40 km
0 _____ 20 miles

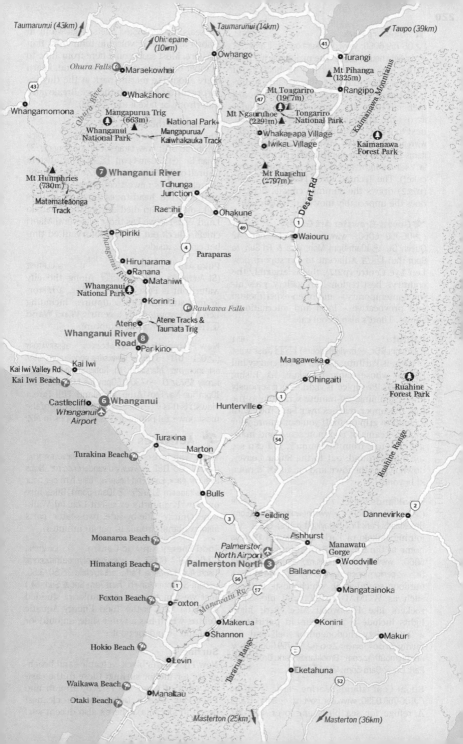

★ **Pukekura Park** GARDENS
(☑ 06-759 6060; www.pukekura.org.nz; Liardet St; ⊙ daylight hours) FREE The pick of New Plymouth's parks, Pukekura has 49 hectares of gardens, playgrounds, trails, streams, waterfalls, ponds and display houses. **Rowboats** (per half-hour $12, summer only) meander across the main lake (full of arm-size eels), next to which the **Tea House** (☑ 06-758 7205; www.pukekura.org.nz; Pukekura Park, Liardet St; items $6-11; ⊙ 9am-4pm, extended summer hours; ☑) serves light meals (and awesome carrot cake!). The Technicolored Festival of Lights (p222) draws the summer crowds here, as does the impeccably mowed **cricket oval**.

★ **Govett-Brewster Art Gallery** GALLERY
(☑ 06-759 6060; www.govettbrewster.com; 42 Queen St; ⊙ 10am-6pm Mon, Wed & Fri-Sun, to 9pm Thu) FREE Adjacent to the superb new Len Lye Centre (p217), this is arguably the country's best regional art gallery, presenting contemporary – and often experimental and provocative – local and international shows. There's also a cool cafe.

Paritutu HILL
(Centennial Dr; ⊙ daylight hours) FREE Just west of town is Paritutu, a steep-sided, craggy hill (154m) whose name translates as 'Rising Precipice'. 'Precipice' is right – it's a seriously knee-trembling, 20-minute scramble to the top, the upper reaches over bare rock with a chain to grip on to. If you can ignore your inner screams of common sense and make it to the top, from the summit you can see for miles around: out to the Sugar Loaves, down across the town and out to Mt Taranaki beyond.

Brooklands Park PARK
(☑ 06-759 6060; www.newplymouthnz.com; Brooklands Park Dr; ⊙ daylight hours) FREE Adjoining Pukekura Park, Brooklands Park is home to the **Bowl of Brooklands** (☑ 06-759 6060; www.npeventvenues.nz; Brooklands Park Dr; ⊙ performance days only), a world-class outdoor sound-shell, which hosts festivals such as WOMAD (p222), and old-school rockers like Fleetwood Mac. Park highlights include a 2000-year-old puriri tree, a 300-variety rhododendron dell and the farmy **Brooklands Zoo** (☑ 06-759 6060; www.newplymouthnz.com; Brooklands Park, Brooklands Park Dr; ⊙ 9am-5pm; ☑) FREE.

Sugar Loaf Islands Marine Park ISLAND
(☑ 06-759 0350; www.doc.govt.nz; ⊙ 24hr) FREE A refuge for sea birds and over 400 NZ fur seals, these rugged islets (Ngā Motu in Māori) are eroded volcanic remnants, 1km offshore. Most seals come here from June to October but some stay all year round. Learn more about the marine park at the tiny **interpretation booth** on the Lee Breakwater waterfront, or take a tour (p222).

Taranaki Cathedral Church of St Mary CHURCH
(☑ 06-758 3111; www.taranakicathedral.org.nz; 37 Vivian St; ⊙ 8.30am-6pm) FREE The austere Church of St Mary (1846) is NZ's oldest stone church and its newest cathedral! Its graveyard has the headstones of early settlers and soldiers who died during the Taranaki Land Wars, as well as those of several Māori chiefs. Check out the fabulous vaulted timber ceiling inside.

Puke Ariki Landing SCULPTURE
(St Aubyn St; ⊙ 24hr) FREE Along the city waterfront is Puke Ariki Landing, a historic area studded with sculptures, including Len Lye's wonderfully eccentric **Wind Wand** FREE, a kooky kinetic sculpture.

New Plymouth Observatory OBSERVATORY
(☑ 021 071 3315; www.sites.google.com/site/astronomynp; Marsland Hill, Robe St; adult/child/family $5/3/10; ⊙ 7.30-9.30pm Tue Mar-Oct, 8.30-10pm Tue Nov-Feb) Atop Marsland Hill (great views!) is this wee observatory, with one of the most powerful public-access telescopes in NZ.

🏃 **Activities**

Wind Wanderers BICYCLE RENTAL
(☑ 027 358 1182; www.windwanderer.co.nz; Nobs Line car park, East End Reserve; bike hire per hour single/tandem $15/25; ⊙ 10am-5pm) Bike hire on New Plymouth's excellent Coastal Walkway. Quirky side-by-side two-seater carts also available (from $10 per 10 minutes).

Todd Energy Aquatic Centre SWIMMING
(☑ 06-759 6060; www.newplymouthnz.com; Tisch Ave, Kawaroa Park; adult/child $5.50/3.50; ⊙ 6am-8.30pm Mon-Fri, 7am-7pm Sat & Sun; ☑) Just west of town in pohutukawa-studded Kawaroa Park is the Todd Energy Aquatic Centre, which has a water slide, an outdoor pool and an indoor pool.

Surfing
New Plymouth's black, volcanic-sand beaches are terrific for surfing! Close to the eastern edge of town are **Fitzroy Beach** and **East End Beach** (allegedly the cleanest beach in Oceania). There's also decent surf

New Plymouth

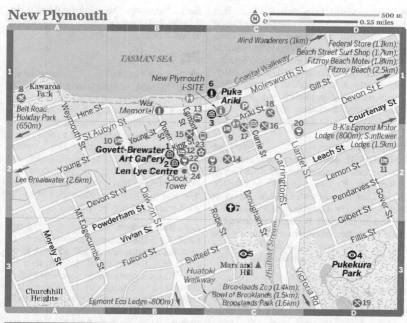

N ☉ 0 ————————— 500 m
0 ————————— 0.25 miles

New Plymouth

◎ Top Sights

◎ Sights

◎ Activities, Courses & Tours

🛏 Sleeping

🍴 Eating

🍷 Drinking & Nightlife

◎ Entertainment

🛍 Shopping

at **Back Beach**, near Paritutu, at the western end of the city. Otherwise, head south along Surf Hwy 45.

Beach Street Surf Shop SURFING
(☏ 06-758 0400; www.lostinthe60s.com; 39 Beach St; 90min lessons per person $75; ☉ 10am-5pm Mon-Fri, to 3pm Sat & Sun) Close to Fitzroy Beach, this surf shop offers lessons, gear hire

(surfboard/wet suit per hour $10/5) and surf advice (see the website for the low-down on local breaks).

Walking

The New Plymouth i-SITE (p225) stocks the *Taranaki: A Walker's Guide* booklet, which includes coastal, local reserve and park walks. The excellent **Coastal**

TARANAKI & WHANGANUI NEW PLYMOUTH

Walkway (11km) from Bell Block to Port Taranaki gives you a surf-side perspective on New Plymouth and crosses the sexily engineered **Te Rewa Rewa Bridge**. The **Huatoki Walkway** (5km), following Huatoki Stream, is a rambling walk into the city centre. Alternatively, the *New Plymouth Heritage Trail* brochure, taking in historic hot spots, is a real blast from the past.

Tours

Chaddy's Charters   BOAT TOUR

(☑ 06-758 9133; www.chaddyscharters.co.nz; Ocean View Pde, Lee Breakwater; trips adult/child $40/10; ⊙9am-4pm; ⓘ) Take a trip out to visit the Sugar Loaf Islands with Chaddy: expect at least four laughs a minute on a one-hour bob around on the swell. Departs daily from Lee Breakwater, tide and weather permitting. You can also hire kayaks (single/double per hour $15/30) and bikes ($10 per hour) here.

Canoe & Kayak Taranaki   KAYAKING

(☑ 06-751 2340; www.canoeandkayak.co.nz; 3hr tours $95) Paddle out to the Sugar Loaf Islands Marine Park (p220) and see the seals, or over the gentle Waitara River rapids a short drive east of New Plymouth.

Festivals & Events

WOMAD   MUSIC, CULTURAL

(World of Music, Arts & Dance; www.womad.co.nz; ⊙Mar) A diverse array of local and international artists perform at the Bowl of Brooklands each March. Hugely popular, with music fans trucking in from across NZ.

Taranaki International Arts Festival   ART

(www.taft.co.nz; ⊙Aug) The regional big-ticket arts fest: theatre, dance, music, visual arts, parades, and plenty of food and wine.

NZ Tattoo & Art Festival   CULTURAL

(www.nztattooart.com; ⊙Nov) This saucy skin fest attracts thousands of ink fans over a busy weekend in November. Get yourself a new 'badge', or check out the BMX stunt riders or the burlesque gyrators.

Taranaki Garden Spectacular   CULTURAL

(www.gardenfestnz.co.nz; ⊙Nov) A long-running NZ flower fest, held in early November each year: more rhododendrons than you'll ever see in one place again.

Festival of Lights   CULTURAL

(www.festivaloflights.co.nz; ⊙late Dec–late Jan) Complete with live music, 1000 light installations and costumed characters roaming

the undergrowth, this colourful display illuminates Pukekura Park from late December to late January.

Sleeping

★ Ducks & Drakes   HOSTEL, HOTEL $

(☑06-758 0404; www.ducksanddrakes.co.nz; 48 Lemon St; hostel dm/s/d from $32/68/90, hotel r from $130; ⓐ) The hostel here occupies a labyrinthine 1920s heritage building with striped wallpaper and fancy timber work, brimming with character. The upstairs rooms are the pick: secluded, quiet and catching the morning sun. Next door is a pricier (newer) hotel wing with snazzy studios and one-bedroom suites. Say hi to the good-mannered Border collies.

Ariki Backpackers   HOSTEL $

(☑06-769 5020; www.arikibackpackers.com; L1, cnr Ariki & Brougham Sts; dm $30, d $70-90; @ⓐ) Upstairs at the old Royal Hotel (Queen Liz stayed here once!), welcoming Ariki offers downtown hostelling with funky carpets, a roomy lounge area with retro couches, and a fantastic roof terrace looking across the park to Puke Ariki. Most rooms have their own shower and toilet. Bikes and surfboards for hire (per day $10 and $25 respectively).

Belt Road Holiday Park   HOLIDAY PARK $

(☑06-758 0228, 0800 804 204; www.beltroad.co.nz; 2 Belt Rd; camp sites from $22, cabins $70-140; ⓐ) ✔ This environmentally attuned, pohutukawa-covered holiday park sits atop a bluff overlooking the increasingly interesting Lee Breakwater area, about a 10-minute walk from town. The half-dozen best cabins have million-dollar views. 'Recycle – that's what Kiwis do!', says the manager. Bikes $25 per day.

Sunflower Lodge   HOSTEL $

(☑06-759 0050, 0800 422 257; www.sunflowerlodge.co.nz; 33 Timandra St; dm/s/tw/d/tr from $31/55/75/75/99; @ⓐ) Down a steep driveway, a few minutes' drive south of town, the YHA Sunflower does its best to transcend its rest-home origins, and (with the exception of some relentless timber ceilings) succeeds. Bonuses such as quality mattresses, a herb garden, a BBQ pavilion, a sun lounge, and a heavy-duty kitchen and laundry help the cause.

Egmont Eco Lodge   HOSTEL $

(☑06-753 5720; www.mttaranaki.co.nz; 12 Clawton St; unpowered sites $20, dm/s/d/f from $28/75/75/120; @ⓐ) A tidy BBH hostel in a glade with chirping birds, a couple of sheep and a chuckling creek (with eels!). Mixed dorms in the main lodge; smaller pinewood cabins down below (sleeping four). It's a hike uphill from town, but the prospect of free nightly Egmont cake will put a spring in your step. Grassy campsites, too.

★ **One Burgess Hill** MOTEL, APARTMENTS $$
(☑ 06-757 2056; www.oneburgesshill.co.nz 1 Burgess Hill Rd; d from $145, 1-bedroom ste from $175; ⊛) Doing the motel thing a bit differently, One Burgess Hill is a complex of 15 very sassy units on a green suburban hillside about 5km south of New Plymouth (en route to Mt Taranaki). Slick interior design, nifty kitchens, wood heaters and private valley views offer a real departure from the usual drive-in motel affairs. Just lovely!

Dawson Motel MOTEL $$
(☑ 06-758 1177; www.thedawsonmotel.co.nz; 16 Dawson St; d from $150, 1-/2-bedroom units from $200/250; ⊛) Just a handful of years old, the handsome, corporate Dawson is a sharp-looking, two-storey number – all white, red and black inside – with sea and mountain views from the top-floor rooms. The location is primo: a five-minute walk into town and 100m to the Coastal Walkway.

Fitzroy Beach Motel MOTEL $$
(☑ 06-757 2925; www.fitzroybeachmotel.co.nz; 25 Beach St; 1-/2-bedroom units d from $155/200, extra person $20; ⊛) This quiet, old-time motel (just 160m from Fitzroy Beach) has been thoroughly redeemed with a major overhaul and extension. Highlights include quality carpets, double glazing, lovely bathrooms, big TVs, and an absence of poky studio-style units (all are one- or two-bedroom). Free bikes, too.

BK's Egmont Motor Lodge MOTEL $$
(☑ 0800 115 033, 06-758 5216; www.bksegmont motorlodge.co.nz; 115 Coronation Ave; d from $140, 1-/2-/3-bedroom units from $165/210/220; ⊛) Opposite the racecourse and a short roll downhill into town, low-slung BK's has 18 ground-floor units and oceans of parking. Rooms are smart, comfortable and clean, and the managers (and travellers) readily share a laugh with the cleaners (a good sign). Free wi-fi and DVDs.

★ **King & Queen Hotel Suites** BOUTIQUE HOTEL $$$
(☑ 06-757 2999; www.kingandqueen.co.nz; cnr King & Queen Sts; ste from $205; @ ⊛) A relatively new kid on the NP accommodation block, this regal hotel occupies the corner of King and Queen Sts (get it?). Run by unerringly professional staff, it's an interesting 17-room affair over two levels. Each suite features antique Moroccan and Euro furnishings, plush carpets, lustrous black tiles, hip art, retro leather couches and *real* flowers. Cafe/bean roastery onsite.

Waterfront HOTEL $$$
(☑ 06-769 5301, 0508 843 928; www.waterfront. co.nz; 1 Egmont St; d/f from $200/310; @ ⊛) Sleek and snazzy, Waterfront is the place to stay if the boss is paying. The minimalist studios are pretty flash, while the penthouses steal the show with big TVs and little balconies. It's got terrific views from some – but not all – rooms, and certainly from the curvy-fronted bar-restaurant Salt.

✗ Eating

Chaos CAFE $
(☑ 06-759 8030; www.chaoscafe.co.nz; 36 Brougham St; mains $8-18; ⊙ 7.30am-3.30pm Mon-Fri, 8.30am-3pm Sat, 9am-2pm Sun; ☑ ⊛) Not so much chaotic as endearingly boho, Chaos is a dependable spot for a coffee and a zingy brunch. Spicy beans with avocado and cheese, background jazz, smiley staff and artful interior design – hard to beat! Plenty of vegetarian and gluten-free options, too. Love the graffiti-covered side wall.

Petit Paris CAFE $
(☑ 06-759 0398; www.petitparis.co.nz; 34 Currie St; mains $8-15; ⊙ 7.30am-4pm Mon-Fri, 8am-3pm Sat & Sun; *Ooh-la-la!* Buttery French treats! Flying the *tricolore* with pride, Petit Paris is a boulangerie and patisserie turning out crispy baguettes and *tartes au citron* (lemon tarts), plus omelettes and croque-monsieurs for lunch. Good coffee is best sipped at the cheery street-side counter.

★ **Federal Store** CAFE $$
(☑ 06-757 8147; www.thefederalstore.com; 440 Devon St E; mains $10-20; ⊙ 7am-5pm Mon-Fri, 8am-5pm Sat, 9am-5pm Sun; ☑ ⊛) Superpopular and crammed with retro furniture, Federal conjures up a 1950s corner-store vibe. Switched-on staff in dinky head scarves take your coffee requests as you queue to order food at the counter, keeping you buoyant until your hot cakes, New Yorker sandwich or pulled-pork bun arrive. Terrific cakes, tarts and pre-made counter food (love the veggie frittata). Kid-friendly.

Bach on Breakwater CAFE, RESTAURANT $$

(☑06-769 6967; www.bachonbreakwater.co.nz; Ocean View Pde, Lee Breakwater; mains $11-24; ☺9.30am-4pm Thu & Fri, to 5pm Sat & Sun; ⚥) Constructed from weighty recycled timbers, this cool cafe-bistro in the emerging Lee Breakwater precinct looks like an old sea chest washed up after a storm. Expect plenty of seafood and steak, sunny outdoor tables and killer coffee. The seafood chowder is a real winter warmer. Lots of gluten-free and vegetarian options.

Kathakali SOUTH INDIAN $$

(☑06-758 8848; www.kathakali.co.nz; 39a Devon St E; mains $14-25; ☺noon-2pm & 5-10pm Tue-Sun; ⚥) Wander up the stairs from Devon St into this atmospheric and very un-Devonian diner. The menu delivers all sorts of South Indian delights, from *dosa* (savoury pancakes) with coconut chutney and *sambar* (lentil soup), to a mixed vegetable korma with coconut and ground cashews. With all the coconut and the balmy vibes, somehow Kerala doesn't seem so far away.

Frederic's PUB FOOD $$

(☑06-759 1227; www.frederics.co.nz; 34 Egmont St; plates $13-21, mains $19-26; ☺noon-late) Freddy's is a fab gastro-bar with quirky interior design (rusty medieval chandeliers, peacock-feather wallpaper, religious icon paintings), serving generous share plates. Order some Peking duck pancakes, or some green-lipped mussels with coconut cream, chilli and coriander, to go with your Monteith's pale ale.

Portofino ITALIAN $$

(☑06-757 8686; www.portofino.co.nz; 14 Gill St; mains $20-49; ☺5pm-late Tue-Sun) This discreet little family-run eatery has been here for years, serving old-fashioned Italian pasta and pizza just like nonna used to make. The rigatoni Portofino is a knockout (spinach, feta, garlic and sun-dried tomatoes).

★Arborio MEDITERRANEAN $$$

(☑06-759 1241; www.arborio.co.nz; Puke Ariki, 1 Ariki St; breakfast & lunch mains $12-26, dinner $31-55; ☺9am-late) Despite its resemblance to a cheese grater, Arborio, in the Puke Ariki building, is the star of New Plymouth's food show. It's airy, arty and modern, with sea views and faultless service. The Med-influenced menu ranges from an awesome tandoori chicken pizza to steaks, risottos, and tempura battered fish and chips. Cocktails and NZ wines seal the deal.

🍷 Drinking & Nightlife

★Hour Glass BAR

(☑06-758 2299; www.facebook.com/the hourglass49; 49 Liardet St; ☺4pm-late Tue-Sat) On an unremarkable rise of Liardet St is this late-night tapas and craft-beer bar, with richly brocaded crimson drapes, straight-backed wooden chairs and interesting timber panelling. Upwards of 80 craft beers in a big fridge, killer cocktails and zingy tapas: New Plymouth can't get enough! Informal jam sessions Friday nights; conversation the rest of the time.

Snug Lounge COCKTAIL BAR

(☑06-757 9130; www.snuglounge.co.nz; cnr Devon St W & Queen St; ☺4pm-late Mon-Sat) This savvy new bar on the downtown fringe is the classiest place in town for a drink. Dress to the nines, order a Lychee Long Time (sake, vodka, apple juice and rosewater) and act like you own this town. A few excellent Japanese share plates will ensure you stay vertical.

Mayfair BAR

(☑06-759 2088; www.themayfair.co.nz; 69 Devon St W; ☺11am-late) This old theatre has expanded into the adjoining shopfronts to become the Mayfair, a fairly mainstream but always busy bar-restaurant and live-music space. Everyone from rock bands to jazz trios, stand-up comedy acts, DJs and chamber orchestras play the main room out the back; the front bar offers pizzas, burgers, platters and a decent wine list.

☆ Entertainment

Basement LIVE MUSIC, COMEDY

(☑06-758 8561; www.facebook.com/thebasementnightclub; cnr Devon St W & Egmont St) Underneath a regulation Irish pub, the grungy Basement is the best place in town to catch up-and-coming live bands, broadly sheltering under a rock, metal and punk umbrella, as well as comedy. Opening hours vary with gigs.

🔒 Shopping

★Kina ARTS, JEWELLERY

(☑06-759 1201; www.kina.co.nz; 101 Devon St W; ☺9am-5.30pm Mon-Fri, 9.30am-4pm Sat, 11am-4pm Sun) Fabulous Kiwi crafts, jewellery, art and design, plus regular gallery exhibitions, in a lovely shopfront on the main drag. It's the perfect spot to pick up an authentic NZ souvenir.

ℹ️ Information

DOC (Department of Conservation; ☑ 06-759 0350; www.doc.govt.nz; 55a Rimu St; ☺8am-4.30pm Mon-Fri) Info on regional national parks, tramping and camping.

New Plymouth i-SITE (☑ 06-759 6060; www.taranaki.co.nz; Puke Ariki, 1 Ariki St; ☺9am-6pm Mon, Tue, Thu & Fri, to 9pm Wed, to 5pm Sat & Sun) In the Puke Ariki building, with a fantastic interactive tourist-info database.

Phoenix Urgent Doctors (☑ 06-759 4295; www.phoenixdoctors.co.nz; 95 Vivian St; ☺8.30am-8pm) Doctors by appointment and urgent medical help. Pharmacy onsite.

Post Office (☑ 0800 501 501; www.nzpost.co.nz; 21 Currie St; ☺9am-5pm Mon-Fri, to 1pm Sat) Ditch Facebook and write someone a letter.

Taranaki Base Hospital (☑ 06-753 6139; www.tdhb.org.nz; David St, Westown; ☺24hr) Accident and emergency.

ℹ️ Getting There & Away

AIR

New Plymouth Airport (☑ 06-759 6060; www.newplymouthairport.com; Airport Dr) is 11km east of the centre off SH3. **Scott's Airport Shuttle** (☑ 06-769 5974, 0800 373 001; www.npairportshuttle.co.nz; per person $18-28, per 2 people $22-32) operates a door-to-door shuttle to/from the airport.

Airlines include the following:

Air New Zealand (☑ 06-757 3300; www.airnewzealand.co.nz; 12-14 Devon St E; ☺9am-5pm Mon-Fri) Daily direct flights to/from Auckland, Wellington and Christchurch, with onward connections.

Virgin Australia (www.virginaustralia.com) Flies the same routes as Air New Zealand.

Singapore Airlines (www.singaporeair.com) Flies between New Plymouth, Christchurch and Auckland.

BUS

Services run from the **Bus Centre** (cnr Egmont & Ariki Sts) in central New Plymouth.

InterCity (www.intercity.co.nz) services include the following:

DESTINATION	FARE	TIME (HR)	FREQUENCY
Auckland	$73	6	2 daily
Hamilton	$49	4	2 daily
Palmerston North	$35	4	1 daily
Wellington	$45	7	1 daily
Whanganui	$29	2¼	1 daily

Naked Bus (www.nakedbus.com) services ply similar routes:

DESTINATION	FARE	TIME (HR)	FREQUENCY
Auckland	$40	8½	1 daily
Hamilton	$40	4¼	1 daily
Palmerston North	$28	4½	1 daily
Wellington	$40	6¼	1 daily
Whanganui	$23	2½	1 daily

ℹ️ Getting Around

BICYCLE

Cycle Inn (☑ 06-758 7418; www.cycleinn.co.nz; 133 Devon St E; per 2hr/day $10/20; ☺8.30am-5pm Mon-Fri, 9am-4.30pm Sat, 10am-2pm Sun) rents out bicycles, as does Wind Wanderers (p220) on the Coastal Walkway, and Chaddy's Charters (p222) at Lee Breakwater.

BUS

Citylink (☑ 0800 872 287; www.taranakibus.info; tickets adult/child $3.50/2.10) services run Monday to Friday around New Plymouth, as well as north to Waitara and south to Oakura. Buses depart from the Bus Centre (p225).

CAR

Rent-a-Dent (☑ 06-757 5362, 0800 736 823; www.rentadent.co.nz; 592 Devon St E; ☺8am-5pm Mon-Fri, to noon Sat) For cheap car hire, try Rent-a-Dent.

TAXI

Energy City Cabs (☑ 06-757 5580; www.energycabs.co.nz) Taxis in New Plymouth.

Around New Plymouth

There are a few interesting places to visit heading north from New Plymouth along SH3, with various seaward turn-offs to high sand dunes and surf beaches. Urenui, 16km past Waitara, is a summer hot spot. There is also a scattering of worthwhile sights south of New Plymouth, between the city and Mt Taranaki.

◉ Sights

About 5km past riverside Urenui, you'll find arguably the highlight of North Taranaki – Mike's **Brewery** (☑ 06-752 3676; www.mikesbeer.co.nz; 487 Mokau Rd, Urenui; tastings/tours $15/25; ☺10am-6pm). A little further on is the turn-off to **Pukearuhe** and **White**

Cliffs, huge precipices resembling their Dover namesakes. From Pukearuhe boat ramp you can tackle the **White Cliffs Walkway**, a three-hour loop walk with mesmerising views of the coast and mountains (Taranaki and Ruapehu). The tide can make things dicey along the beach: walk between two hours either side of low tide.

Continuing north towards **Mokau**, stop at the **Three Sisters** rock formation signposted just south of the Tongaporutu Bridge – you can traverse the shore at low tide. Two sisters stand somewhat forlornly off the coast: their other sister collapsed in a heap last decade, but check the progress of a new sis emerging from the eroding cliffs.

Pukeiti GARDENS
(📞0800 736 222; www.pukeiti.org.nz; 2290 Carrington Rd, New Plymouth; ⏱9am-5pm) **FREE**
This 4-sq-km garden, 20km south of New Plymouth, is home to masses of rhododendrons and azaleas. The flowers bloom between September and November, but it's worth a visit any time. The drive here passes between the Pouakai and Kaitake Ranges, both part of Egmont National Park. There's a cafe here, too.

Tupare HISTORIC BUILDING, GARDENS
(📞0800 736 222; www.tupare.info; 487 Mangorei Rd, New Plymouth; ⏱9am-5pm Apr-Oct, to 8pm Nov-Mar, tours 11am Fri-Mon Oct-Mar) **FREE** Tupare is a Tudor-style house designed by the renowned architect James Chapman-Taylor. It's as pretty as a picture, but the highlight of this 7km trip south of New Plymouth will likely be the rambling 3.6-hectare garden surrounding it. Bluebells and birdsong under the boughs...picnic paradise.

Taranaki Aviation, Transport & Technology Museum MUSEUM
(TATATM; 📞06-752 2845; http://tatatm.tripod.com/museum; cnr SH3 & Kent Rd, New Plymouth; adult/child/family $7/2/16; ⏱10.30am-4.30pm Sat & Sun) Around 9km south of New Plymouth is this roadside museum, with ramshackle displays of old planes, trains, automobiles and general household miscellany. Ask to see the stuff made by the amazing bee guy (hexagons ahoy!).

Mt Taranaki (Egmont National Park)

A classic 2518m volcanic cone dominating the landscape, Mt Taranaki is a magnet to all who catch his eye. Geologically, Taranaki is the youngest of three large volcanoes – Kaitake and Pouakai are the others – which stand along the same fault line. With the last eruption over 350 years ago, experts say that the mountain is overdue for another go. But don't let that put you off – this mountain is an absolute beauty and the highlight of any visit to the region.

Access points for the mountain are North Egmont, Dawson Falls and East Egmont. There are DOC info centres at North Egmont (p228) and Dawson Falls (p228); for accommodation and supplies head to Stratford or Inglewood.

History

According to Māori legend, Mt Taranaki belonged to a tribe of volcanoes in the middle of the North Island. However, he was forced to depart rather hurriedly when he was caught with Pihanga, the beautiful volcano near Lake Taupo and the lover of Mt

---

MĀORI NEW ZEALAND: TARANAKI & WHANGANUI

Ever since Mt Taranaki fled here to escape romantic difficulties, the Taranaki region has had a turbulent history. Conflicts between local *iwi* (tribes) and invaders from the Waikato were followed by two wars with the government – first in 1860–61, and then again in 1865–69. Following the wars there were massive land confiscations and an extraordinary passive-resistance campaign at Parihaka.

Further east, a drive up the Whanganui River Rd takes you into traditional Māori territory, passing the Māori villages of Atene, Koriniti, Ranana and Hiruharama along the way. In Whanganui itself, run your eyes over amazing indigenous exhibits at the **Whanganui Regional Museum** (p233), and check out the superb Māori carvings in **Putiki Church** (p233).

Over in Palmerston North, **Te Manawa** (p245) museum has a strong Māori focus, while the **New Zealand Rugby Museum** (p244) pays homage to Māori All Blacks, without whom the team would never have become back-to-back Rugby World Cup Winners.

Tongariro. As he fled south (some say in disgrace; others say to keep the peace), Taranaki gouged out a wide scar in the earth (now the Whanganui River) and finally settled in the west in his current position. He remains here in majestic isolation, hiding his face behind a cloud of tears.

🏃 Activities

Hiking

Due to its accessibility, Mt Taranaki ranks as the 'most climbed' mountain in NZ. Nevertheless, tramping on this mountain is dangerous and should not be undertaken lightly. It's crucial to get advice before departing and to leave your intentions with a Department of Conservation (DOC) visitor centre or i-SITE.

Most walks are accessible from North Egmont, Dawson Falls or East Egmont. Check out DOC's collection of detailed walk pamphlets ($1 each) or the free *Taranaki: A Walker's Guide* booklet for more info.

From North Egmont, the main walk is the scenic **Pouakai Circuit**, a two- to three-day, 25km loop through alpine, swamp and tussock areas with awesome mountain views. Short, easy walks from here include the **Ngatoro Loop Track** (one hour), **Veronica Loop** (two hours) and **Nature Walk** (15-minute loop). The **Mt Taranaki Summit Climb** also starts from North Egmont. It's a 14km poled route taking eight to 10 hours return, and should not be attempted by inexperienced people, especially in icy conditions or snow.

East Egmont has the **Potaema Track** (wheelchair accessible; 30 minutes return) and **Stratford Plateau Lookout** (10 minutes return). A longer walk is the steep **Enchanted Track** (two to three hours return).

At Dawson Falls you can do several short walks including **Wilkies Pools Loop** (1¼ hours return) or the excellent but challenging hike to **Fanthams Peak** (five hours return), which is snowed-in during winter. The **Kapuni Loop Track** (one-hour loop) runs to the impressive 18m **Dawson Falls** themselves. You can also see the falls from the visitor centre via a 10-minute walk to a viewpoint.

The difficult 55km **Around-the-Mountain Circuit** takes three to five days and is for experienced trampers only. There are a number of huts en route, tickets for which should be purchased in advance.

The **York Road Loop Track** (three hours), accessible from York Rd north of Stratford, is a fascinating walk following part of a disused railway line.

ℹ️ DECEPTIVE MOUNTAIN

Mt Taranaki might look like an easy peak to bag, but this cute cone has claimed more than 60 lives. The mountain microclimate changes fast: from summery to white-out conditions almost in an instant. There are also precipitous bluffs and steep icy slopes.

There are plenty of short walks here, safe for much of the year, but for adventurous trampers January to March is the best time to go. Take a detailed topographic map (the Topo50 1:50,000 Mt Taranaki or Mt Egmont map is good) and consult a DOC officer for current conditions. You must register your tramping intentions with DOC visitor centres or the mountain – **Dawson Falls** (p223) or **North Egmont** (p228), **New Plymouth i-SITE** (p225) or online via www.adventuresmart.org.nz.

You can tramp without a guide from February to March when snowfalls are low, but at other times inexperienced climbers can check with DOC for details of local clubs and guides. It costs around $300 per day to hire a guide.

Skiing

Manganui Ski Area SKIING
(🎿 ski lodge 05-765 5493, snow phone 06-759 1119; www.skitaranaki.co.nz off Pembroke Rd, East Egmont daily lift passes adult/child $45/30) From Stratford take Pembroke Rd up to Stratford Plateau, from where it's a 1.5km (20-minute) walk to the small Manganui Ski Area. The Stratford i-SITE (p230) has daily weather and snow reports; otherwise ring the snow phone or check the webcam online. There's also shared-facilities ski lodge accommodation here (adult/child/family $45/15/100).

👉 Tours

Top Guides Taranaki TRAMPING
(🎿 0800 448 433; www.topguides.co.nz; half-/full-day tramps per person from $99/199) Guided Mt Taranaki tramps, from a half- to full-day – two trampers minimum. Shuttles between New Plymouth and the mountain are also available.

Taranaki Tours TOUR
(🎿 06-757 9888, 0800 886 877; www.taranaki tours.com; per person from $145) Runs an

TARANAKI & WHANGANUI MT TARANAKI (EGMONT NATIONAL PARK)

around-the-mountain day tour, strong on Māori culture and natural history. Forgotten World Hwy tours and mountain shuttle runs also available.

Beck Helicopters
SCENIC FLIGHTS

(✆0800 336 644, 06-764 7073; www.heli.co.nz; flights per person from $265) Buzz around the big mountain on a scenic helicopter flight (and you thought it looked good from ground level!). Maximum four passengers.

🛏 Sleeping

Several DOC huts are scattered about the mountain wilderness, and are accessible via tramping tracks. Most cost $15 per night (Syme and Kahui cost $5); purchase hut tickets in advance from DOC. BYO cooking, eating and sleeping gear. Bookings are not accepted – it's first come, first served.

On the road-accessible slopes of the mountain you'll find a hostel, two DOC-managed bunkhouses and some interesting lodges.

EcoInn
HOSTEL, COTTAGE $

(✆06-752 2765; www.ecoinnovation.co.nz; 671 Kent Rd, Korito; s/tw/d $35/70/70, cottage $140; @ 🛜) 🅿 About 6.5km up the road from the turn-off at the Taranaki Aviation, Transport & Technology Museum, this ecofriendly place is made from recycled timber and runs on solar, wind and hydropower. There's also a spa and pool table. Book the little bach (sleeps four), or the hostel (sleeps eight). Good group rates.

Camphouse
HOSTEL $

(✆06-756 0990; www.doc.govt.nz; Egmont Rd, North Egmont; per adult/child $25/15, exclusive use $600) Bunkhouse-style accommodation behind the North Egmont Visitor Centre in a historic 1850 corrugated-iron building, complete with gun slots in the walls (through which settlers fired at local Māori during the Taranaki Land Wars). Enjoy endless horizon views from the porch. Sleeps 32 in four rooms, with communal facilities.

★ Ngāti Ruanui
Stratford Mountain House
LODGE $$

(✆06-765 6100; www.stratfordmountainhouse. co.nz; 998 Pembroke Rd, East Egmont; d/f from $155/195) This snappily run lodge on the Stratford side of the big hill (15km from the SH3 turn-off and 3km to the Manganui Ski Area) has a wing of recently renovated, motel-style rooms and a mod, European-style restaurant (breakfast and lunch mains $12 to $21, dinner $31 to $42). DB&B packages also available (from $345).

ℹ Information

Dawson Falls Visitor Centre (✆06-443 0248; www.doc.govt.nz; Manaia Rd, Dawson Falls; ⊗9am-4pm Thu-Sun, daily school holidays) On the southeastern side of the mountain, fronted by an awesome totem pole.

MetPhone (✆0900 999 06) Mountain weather updates.

North Egmont Visitor Centre (✆06-756 0990; www.doc.govt.nz; Egmont Rd, North Egmont; ⊗8am-4.30pm, reduced winter hours) Current and comprehensive national park info, and definitive details on tramping and huts.

ℹ Getting There & Away

There are three main entrance roads to Egmont National Park, all of which are well signposted. Closest to New Plymouth is North Egmont: turn off SH3 at Egmont Village, 12km south of New Plymouth, and follow Egmont Rd for 14km. From Stratford, turn off at Pembroke Rd and continue for 15km to East Egmont and the Manganui Ski Area. From the southeast, Manaia Rd leads up to Dawson Falls, 23km from Stratford.

There are no public buses to the national park, but there are a few shuttle/tour operators who will take you there for around $40/60 one-way/return (usually cheaper for groups).

Eastern Taranaki Experience (✆027 246 6383, 06-765 7482; www.eastern-taranaki. co.nz; day trips per person from $60) Mountain shuttle services as well as tours and accommodation. Based in Stratford.

Taranaki Tours (p227) New Plymouth to North Egmont return – good for day walks.

Top Guides Taranaki (p227) Mountain shuttle services, with pick-up points around New Plymouth. Usually departs around 7.30am. Mountain guides also available.

Around Mt Taranaki

Mt Taranaki rises like a god above the fertile plains below – an improbably good-looking peak that has inspired awe, wonder and camera-clicks for millennia. Take a hike around this mesmerising mount, wander through the surrounding towns of Inglewood and Stratford, or go exploring along the Forgotten World Hwy, an untouristed 155km backcountry route between Stratford and Taumarunui.

ℹ Getting There & Away

Drive yourself up and down Mt Taranaki, or there are shuttle services running from New Plymouth up the national park's main access roads. InterCity (www.intercity.co.nz) and Naked Bus (www.naked

FORGOTTEN WORLD HIGHWAY

The remote 155km road between Stratford and Taumarunui (SH43) has become known as the Forgotten World Hwy. The drive winds through hilly bush country, passing Māori *pa* (fortified villages), abandoned coal mines and memorials to those long gone. Just a short section (around 12km) is unsealed road. Allow four hours and plenty of stops, and fill up with petrol at either end (there's no petrol along the route itself). Pick up the *Forgotten World Highway* pamphlet from i-SITEs or DOC visitor centres in the area.

Sights

The town of **Whangamomona** (population 30) is a highlight. This quirky village declared itself an independent republic in 1989 after disagreements with local councils. The town celebrates Republic Day in January every odd-numbered year, with a military-themed extravaganza. In the middle of town is the unmissable grand old **Whangamomona Hotel** (☑ 06-762 5823; www.whangamomonahotel.co.nz; 6018 Forgotten World Hwy, Whangamomona; r per person incl breakfast $75; ☺ 11am- ate), a pub offering simple accommodation and big country meals. There's also a self-contained cottage here – **Whanga Bridge House** (☑ 06-762 5552; www.facebook.com/whanga.bridgehouse; Ohura Rd, Whangamomona; per person $75) – sleeping eight.

Tours

If you're not driving, try a tour through the area by Eastern Taranaki Experience (p228) or Taranaki Tours (p227). See also Forgotten World Adventures (p193) in Taumarunui.

bus.com) services run through Stratford and Inglewood on their Whanganui–New Plymouth route. The Forgotten World Hwy is a DIY road trip, or there are a couple of tour companies that can scoot you through here and show you the sights.

Inglewood
POP 3250

Handy to Mt Taranaki on SH3, the little main-street town of Inglewood is a handy stop for supermarket supplies or a bite to eat.

Sights

Fun Ho! National Toy Museum MUSEUM
(☑ 06-756 7030; www.funhotoys.co.nz; 25 Rata St, Inglewood; adult/child $7/3.50; ☺ 10am-4pm; 🅿) Inglewood's shining light is the cute Fun Ho! National Toy Museum, which exhibits (and sells) old-fashioned sand-cast toys. It doubles as the local visitor information centre. Everybody shout, 'Fun Ho!'.

Sleeping & Eating

White Eagle Motel MOTEL $$
(☑ 06-756 8252; www.whiteeaglemotel.co.nz; 87b Rata St, Inglewood; s/d from $90/105, extra person $20; 🅿) On the road into Inglewood from New Plymouth, White Eagle Motel is an old-school motel, but very tidy and quiet with blooming flower boxes. The two-bedroom units feel bigger than they are. Quiet, quaint, quick.

Funkfish Grill PIZZA, SEAFOOD $$
(☑ 06-756 7287; 32 Matai St, Inglewood; takeaways $8-19, mains $13-32; ☺ 4-9pm) Funky Funkfish is a hip pizzeria and fish-and-chippery doing eat-in and takeaway meals; try the tempura scallops. Doubles as a bar at night.

Stratford
POP 5610

Forty kilometres southeast of New Plymouth on SH3, Stratford plays up its connection to namesake Stratford-upon-Avon, Shakespeare's birthplace, by naming its streets after bardic characters. Stratford is also home to NZ's first (and last) **glockenspiel clock**. Four times daily (10am, 1pm, 3pm and 7pm) this tall, mock-Tudor clock on the main street doth chime out Shakespeare's greatest hits, with some fairly wooden performances.

Sights

Percy Thomson Gallery GALLERY
(☑ 06-765 0917; www.percythomsongallery.org.nz; Prospero Pl, Broadway S, Stratford; ☺ 10.30am-4pm Mon-Fri, to 3pm Sat & Sun) FREE Right next door to Stratford i-SITE, this progressive community gallery (named after the former mayor) displays eclectic local and touring art shows.

Taranaki Pioneer Village MUSEUM
(☑ 06-765 5399; www.pioneervillage.co.nz; SH3, Stratford; adult/child $12/5; ◷ 10am-4pm; ⛟) About 1km south of Stratford on SH3, the Taranaki Pioneer Village is a 4-hectare outdoor museum housing 40 historic buildings. It's very bygone-era (...and more than a little spooky). There's a cafe here, too.

🛏 Sleeping

**Stratford Top Town
Holiday Park** HOLIDAY PARK $
(☑ 0508 478 728, 06-765 6440; www.stratfordtop-townholidaypark.co.nz; 10 Page St, Stratford; camp sites/dm/cabins/units from $20/25/50/100; ☎) Seemingly embalmed in calamine lotion, the old-fashioned Stratford Top Town Holiday Park is a trim caravan park offering one-room cabins, motel-style units and backpackers' bunks. Love the neat little hedges between the campervan sites.

Amity Court Motel MOTEL $$
(☑ 06-765 4496; www.amitycourtmotel.co.nz; 35 Broadway N, Stratford; d/apt from $120/224; ☎) All stone-clad columns, jaunty roof angles, timber louvres and muted cave-colours, newish Amity Court Motel has upped the town's accommodation standings 100%. The two-bedroom apartments are a good set-up for families.

❶ Information

Stratford i-SITE (☑ 0800 765 6708, 06-765 6708; www.stratford.govt.nz; Prospero Pl, Broadway S, Stratford; ◷ 8.30am-5pm Mon-Fri, 10am-3pm Sat & Sun) All the local low-down, plus good advice on walks on Mt Taranaki. Down an arcade off the main street.

Surf Highway 45

Sweeping south from New Plymouth around the coastline to Hawera, the 105km-long SH45 is known as Surf Highway 45. There are plenty of black-sand beaches dotted along the route, but don't expect to see waves crashing ashore the whole way. The drive generally undulates through farmland – be ready to swerve for random tractors and cows. Pick up the *Surf Highway 45* brochure at visitor centres.

❶ Getting There & Away

This part of NZ is delightfully untouristed and off the main bus routes. You'll need your own wheels to get around (cycling is a good option – the terrain is level most of the way).

Alternatively, local SouthLink (www.taranaki bus.info) buses depart New Plymouth once on Fridays to Oakura, Okato and Opunake on SH45, before detouring inland to Hawera via Eltham. SouthLink also runs from New Plymouth to Hawera once daily Monday to Friday via Stratford on the inland route.

Oakura

POP 1380

From south New Plymouth, the first cab off the rank is laid-back Oakura, 15km southwest on SH45. Its broad sweep of beach is hailed by waxheads for its right-hander breaks, but it's also great for families (take sandals – that black sand gets scorching hot!). Sharpen your wave skills with some lessons from **Vertigo Surf** (☑ 06-752 7363; www.vertigosurf.com; 1135 SH45; lessons from $80; ◷ 9am-5pm Mon-Fri, 10am-4pm Sat) or **Tarawave Surf School** (☑ 021 119 6218, 06-752 7474; www.taranakisurfschool.com; 90min lessons per person from $50).

🛏 Sleeping & Eating

Oakura Beach Holiday Park HOLIDAY PARK $
(☑ 06-752 7861; www.oakurabeach.com; 2 Jans Tce; campsites from $20, cabins $75-140; @☎) Squeezed between the cliffs and the sea, this classic beachside park caters best to caravans, but also has simple cabins and well-placed spots to pitch a tent (absolute beachfront!).

Wave Haven HOSTEL $
(☑ 027 694 1069, 06-752 7800; www.thewave haven.co.nz; cnr Lower Ahu Ahu Rd & SH45; dm/s/d from $25/50/60; ☎) A sandy backpackers close to the big breaks, this colonial charmer has a coffee machine, a large deck to chill out on, outdoor chairs made out of old surfboards, and empty wine bottles strewn about the place. Look for the longboard sign on the highway.

Oakura Beach Motel MOTEL $$
(☑ 06-752 7680; www.oakurabeachmotel.co.nz; 53 Wairau Rd; d/f $115/160; ☎) A very quiet, seven-unit motel set back from the main road, just three-minutes' walk to the beach. It's a '70s number; all units have kitchenettes and are utterly shipshape. There are 300 DVDs to watch – the sleepy black cat doesn't seem to mind which one you choose.

⭐ **Ahu Ahu Beach Villas** BOUTIQUE HOTEL $$$
(☑ 06-752 7370; www.ahu.co.nz; 321 Lower Ahu Ahu Rd; d/q from $295/650; ☎) Pricey,

but pretty amazing. Set on a knoll overlooking the big wide ocean, these luxury, architect-designed villas are superbly eccentric, with huge recycled timbers, bottles cast into walls, lichen-covered French tile roofs and polished-concrete floors with inlaid paua. A lodge addition sleeps four. Rock stars stay here!

Carriage Café
CAFE $

(☑06-752 7226; 1143 SH45; meals S10-20; ⏰8.30am-3pm; ▣) Housed in a very slow-moving 1917 railway carriage set back from the main street, this is an unusual stop for good-value breakfast stacks, bacon-and-egg pies and cheese scones. Good coffee, smoothies and milkshakes, too.

Okato & Around

Between Oakura and Opunake, SH45 veers inland through Okato, with detours to sundry beaches along the way. There are legendary surf spots at **Stent Rd** (Stent Rd, Warea), just south of Warea, and **Kumara Patch** (Komene Rd, Okato; ⏰24hr), west of Okato. Near Pungarehu, Cape Egmont is home to a historic **lighthouse** (Cape Rd, Pungarehu; ⏰24hr) FREE and associated **museum** (☑06-763 8499; www.southtaranaki.com; Bayly Rd, Warea; by donation; ⏰11am-3pm Sat-Mon).

🛏 Sleeping & Eating

Stony River Hotel
PUB $$

(☑06-752 4454; www.stonyriverhotel.co.nz; 2502 SH45, Okato; tw/d/tr incl breakfast $110/120/170; ☎) On the highway near Okato the lemon-yellow, 136-year-old Stony River Hotel has Austrian vibes. There are bright, super-tidy, country-style en-suite rooms upstairs, and a restaurant downstairs (mains $18 to $38) serving lunch Friday to Sunday and dinner Wednesday to Sunday. And yes, the river has rather a lot of stones in it.

★ Cafe Lahar
CAFE $

(☑06-752 4865; 64 Carthew St, Okato; mains $10-22; ⏰8am-4pm Wed & Thu, 8am-late Fri, 8.30am-late Sat & Sun) Excellent new Lahar occupies an angular, black-trimmed timber box in the middle of Okato (hard to miss – there's not much else here). It's a lofty space with spinning fans, a couple of tempting couches out the front and a menu ranging from pork sausages and beans, to tandoori chicken salad and pizzas on Friday, Saturday and Sunday nights. Good coffee.

Opunake

POP 1370

A summer town and the surfie epicentre of the 'Naki, Opunake has a sheltered family beach and plenty of challenging waves further out.

🏃 Activities

Dreamtime Surf Shop
SURFING

(☑06-761 7570; www.dreamtimesurf.co.nz; cnr Tasman & Havelock Sts; surfboards/body boards/wet suits per half-day $30/20/10; ⏰9am-5pm, closed Sun Jun-Aug) Dreamtime Surf Shop has wi-fi, coffee, surf-gear hire and advice on the best local breaks; hours can be patchy if the surf is up – call in advance.

Opunake Walkway
WALKING

(Layard St; ⏰daylight hours) FREE Feel like stretching your pins? The Opunake Walkway is a signposted 7km, three-hour ramble around the Opunake waterfront, starting (or finishing) at Opunake Lake on Layard St.

🛏 Sleeping & Eating

Opunake Beach Holiday Park
HOLIDAY PARK $

(☑0800 758 009, 06-761 7525; www.opunake beachnz.co.nz; 3 Beach Rd; d campsites/cabins/cottages $38/70/105; @☎) Opunake Beach Holiday Park is a mellow spot behind the surf beach. Sites are grassy, the camp kitchen is big, the amenities block is cavernous and the waves are just a few metres away. The black-sand beach is great for beach combing when the surf is blown out.

Headlands
HOTEL $$

(☑06-761 8358; www.headlands.co.nz; 4 Havelock St; r $120-250; ☎) Just 100m back from the beach, Headlands is a newish operation encompassing a mod, airy bistro (mains $14 to $32; open 8.30am till late) and an upmarket, three-storey accommodation tower. The best rooms snare brilliant sunsets. B&B and DB&B packages available, plus a four-bedroom family villa (sleeps 12!), which can be configured to suit the mood of your brood.

★ Sugar Juice Café   CAFE $$

(☏ 06-761 7062; 42 Tasman St; snacks $4-10, mains $11-35; ◷ 9am-4pm Sun-Wed, 9am-late Thu-Sat, closed Mon Jun-Aug; ✎) Happy, hippie and wholesome, Sugar Juice Café has some of the best food on SH45. It's brimming with delicious, homemade, filling things (try the crayfish-and-prawn ravioli or cranberry lamb shanks). Terrific coffee, salads, wraps, tarts, cakes and big brekkies – don't pass it by.

❶ Information

Opunake Library (☏ 0800 111 323; www.opunakenz.co.nz; 43 Tasman St; ◷ 9am-5pm Mon-Fri, 9.30am-1pm Sat; ☎) Doubles as the local visitor information centre, with a couple of internet terminals and free 24-hour wi-fi in the forecourt.

Hawera

POP 11,750

Don't expect much urban virtue from agricultural Hawera, the largest town in South Taranaki. Still, it's a good pit stop to pick up supplies, visit the info centre, stretch your legs or bed down for a night. And don't miss Elvis!

◉ Sights

★ KD's Elvis Presley Museum   MUSEUM

(☏ 06-278 7624; www.elvismuseum.co.nz; 51 Argyle St; admission by donation; ◷ by appointment) Elvis lives! At least he does at Kevin D Wasley's astonishing museum, which houses over 10,000 of the King's records and a mind-blowing collection of Elvis memorabilia collected over 50 years. 'Passion is an understatement', says KD. Just don't ask him about the chubby Vegas-era Elvis: his focus is squarely on the rock 'n' roll King from the '50s and '60s. Admission is by appointment – phone ahead.

Hawera Water Tower   TOWER, VIEWPOINT

(☏ 06-278 8599; www.southtaranaki.com; 55 High St; adult/child/family $2.50/1/6; ◷ 10am-2pm) The austere, 54.21m Hawera Water Tower is one of the coolest things in Hawera. Grab the key from the neighbouring i-SITE (p233), ascend the 215 steps, then scan the horizon for signs of life (you can see the coast and Mt Taranaki on a clear day). The tower was closed for earthquake-proofing at the time

of writing, but should be open again by the time you read this.

Tawhiti Museum   MUSEUM

(☏ 06-278 6837; www.tawhitimuseum.co.nz; 401 Ohangai Rd; adult/child $15/5; ◷ 10am-4pm Fri-Sun, daily Jan, Sun only Jun-Aug) The excellent Tawhiti Museum houses a collection of exhibits, dioramas and creepily lifelike human figures modelled on people from the region. A large collection of tractors pays homage to the area's rural heritage; there's also a bush railway and a 'Traders & Whalers' boat ride (extra charges for both). It's near the corner of Tawhiti Rd, 4km north of town.

🛏 Sleeping & Eating

Wheatly Downs Farmstay   FARMSTAY $

(☏ 06-278 6523; www.mttaranaki.co.nz; 484 Ararata Rd; campsites from $20, dm/s/tw $33/75/83, d with/without bathroom $115/83) Set in a rural idyll, this heritage building is a classic, with its clunky wooden floors and no-nonsense fittings. Host Gary is an affable bloke, and might show you his special pigs. To get there, head past the turn-off to Tawhiti Museum and continue on Ararata Rd for 5.5km. Pick-ups by arrangement.

Tairoa Lodge   B&B $$

(☏ 027 243 5782, 06-278 8603; www.tairoa-lodge. co.nz; 3 Puawai St; s/d $165/195, cottage d $245, extra adult/child $50/30, all incl breakfast ; ☎) Gorgeous old Tairoa is a photogenic 1875 Victorian manor house on the eastern outskirts of Hawera, with three guest rooms and two outlying cottages (two and three bedrooms). Lashings of heritage style, bird-filled gardens (often full of wedding parties, too) and big cooked breakfasts await.

Hawera Central Motor Lodge   MOTEL $$

(☏ 0800 668 353, 06-278 8831; www.hawera centralmotorlodge.co.nz; 53 Princes St; d $140-170; ☎) The pick of the town's motels (quieter and fancier than any of those along South Rd), shiny, two-tier Hawera Central does things with style: grey-and-eucalyptus colour scheme, frameless glass showers, big TVs, good security, DVD players, free movie library and free wi-fi.

Indian Zaika   INDIAN $$

(☏ 06-278 3198; 91 Princes St; mains $17-20; ◷ 11am-2pm Tue-Sat, 5pm-late daily; ✎) For a fine lunch or dinner, try this spicy-smelling, black-and-white diner, serving decent curries in upbeat surrounds. Love the lurid murals and the 'India 12,550km' street sign.

ⓘ Information

South Taranaki i-SITE (☑ 06-278 8599; www.
southtaranaki.com; 55 High St; ⊗ 8.30am-5pm
Mon-Fri, 10am-3pm Sat & Sun; 🔊) Get the
South Taranaki low-down. Extended summer
weekend hours.

Whanganui

POP 43,600

With rafts of casual Huck Finn sensibility,
Whanganui is a raggedy historic town on the
banks of the wide Whanganui River. Despite
the occasional flood (much of the city centre
was underwater in June 2015), the local arts
community is thriving: old port buildings
are being turned into glass-art studios, and
the town centre has been rejuvenated. There
are few more appealing places to while away
a sunny afternoon than the dog-free zone
beneath Victoria Ave's leafy canopy.

History

Māori settlement at Whanganui dates
from around 1100. The first European on
the river was Andrew Powers in 1831, but
Whanganui's European settlement didn't
take off until 1840 when the New Zealand
Co could no longer satisfy Wellington's land
demands – settlers moved here instead.

When Māori understood that the gifts the
Pākehā settlers had given them were in permanent exchange for their land, they were
understandably irate, and seven years of
conflict ensued. Thousands of government
troops occupied the Rutland Stockade in
Queens Park. Ultimately, the struggle was
settled by arbitration; during the Taranaki
Land Wars the Whanganui Māori assisted
the Pākehā.

⊙ Sights

★ **Whanganui Regional Museum** MUSEUM
(☑ 06-349 1110; www.wanganui-museum.org.nz;
Watt St, Queens Park; ⊗ 10am-4.30pm) FREE
One of NZ's better natural-history museums.
Māori exhibits include the carved Te Mata o
Houroa war canoe and some vicious-look-
ing *mere* (greenstone clubs). The colonial
and wildlife installations are first rate, and
there's plenty of button-pushing and drawer-
opening to keep the kids engaged.

★ **Waimarie Centre** MUSEUM
(☑ 06-347 1863, 0800 783 2637; www.waimarie.
co.nz; 1a Taupo Quay; admission free, cruises adult/
child/family $45/15/90; ⊗ 10am-2pm Tue-Sun Oct-

Apr; 🚢) The historical displays are interesting, but everyone's here for the PS *Waimarie*, the last of the Whanganui River paddle
steamers. In 1900 she was shipped out from
England and paddled the Whanganui until she sank ingloriously at her mooring in
1952. Submerged for 41 years, she was finally
raised restored, then relaunched on the first
day of the 21st century. She now offers two-
hour tours up the river, boarding 10.30am.
Book in advance.

★ **Sarjeant on the Quay** GALLERY
(☑ 06-349 0506; www.sarjeant.org.nz; 38 Taupo
Quay; ⊗ 10.30am-4.30pm) FREE The elegant
old neoclassical Sarjeant Gallery building in
Queens Park is closed for earthquake proof-
ing. Until that work is finished, this estima-
ble art collection is housed on Taupo Quay.
There's not as much room here as up on the
hill, so exhibits are limited (but revolving).
There's more on show above the Whanganui i-SITE (p238) across the road. Fab gift
shop, too, with lots of Whanganui glass.

★ **Chronicle Glass Studio** GALLERY
(☑ 06-347 1921; www.chronicleglass.co.nz; 2 Rutland St ⊗ 9am-5pm Mon-Fri, 10am-3pm Sat &
Sun, closed Sun & Mon Jun-Sep) FREE The pick
of Whanganui's many glass studios. Watch
glass-blowers working, check out the gallery,
take a weekend glass-blowing course ($390)
or a one-hour 'Make a Paperweight' lesson
($100), or just hang out and warm up on a
chilly afternoon.

Durie Hill Elevator TOWER, VIEWPOINT
(☑ 06-345 8525; www.wanganui.govt.nz; Anzac
Pde; adult/child one-way $2/1; ⊗ 8am-6pm Mon-
Fri, 10am-5pm Sat & Sun) Across City Bridge
from downtown Whanganui, this elevator
was built with grand visions for Durie Hill's
residential future. A tunnel burrows 213m
into the hillside, from where a 1919 elevator rattles 65.8m to the top. At the summit
you can climb the 176 steps of the **War
Memorial Tower** (www.whanganuinz.com; off
Durie St; ⊗ daylight hours) FREE and scan the
horizon for Mt Taranaki and Mt Ruapehu.
There's another **lookout** (⊗ daylight hours)
FREE atop the lift machinery housing (just
41 steps).

Putiki Church CHURCH
(☑ 06-349 0508; 20 Anaua St; per person $2, plus
key deposit $20; ⊗ service 9am Sun) Across the
City Bridge from town and 1km towards
the sea is the Putiki Church (aka St Paul's
Memorial Church). It's unremarkable

Whanganui

Whanganui

externally but, just like the faithful pew-fillers, it's what's inside that counts: the interior is magnificent, completely covered in Māori carvings and *tukutuku* (wall panels). Show up for Sunday service, or borrow a key from the i-SITE (p238).

Kai Iwi Beach BEACH
(Mowhanau Dr, off Rapanui Rd; ⊙24hr) Kai Iwi Beach is a wild ocean frontier, strewn with black sand and masses of broken driftwood. To get here follow Great North Rd 4km north of town, then turn left onto Rapanui Rd and head seawards for 10km.

🏃 Activities

Wanganui Horse Treks
HORSE RIDING

(📞021 930 950, 06-345 3285; www.facebook.
com/wanganuihorsetreks; Manuka St, Castlecliff;
1½/2/3/4hr rides $80/100/140/200) Climb
onto an agreeable horse and ride around
the beaches and dunes at Castlecliff, a short
drive west of downtown Whanganui. Cheaper per person if you can lasso a group of
friends together. Call for times, directions
and bookings. Giddy-up!

Splash Centre
SWIMMING

(📞06-349 0113; www.splashcentre.co.nz; Springvale Park, London St; adult/child $5/3.50, water
slide $3; ⊙6am-8pm Mon-Fri, 8am-6pm Sat & Sun)
If the sea is angry, try the Splash Centre for
a safe swim and a convoluted tubular water
slide or two.

👉 Tours

Wanganui City
Guided Walking Tours
WALKING TOUR

(📞06-349 3258; www.mainstreetwanganui.co.nz/
tours; per person $10; ⊙10am & 2pm Sat & Sun
Oct-Apr) Sign up for a 90-minute guided tour
through old Whanganui, giving your legs a
workout as you pass historic sights. Tours
depart from the i-SITE (p238); book tickets inside.

🎊 Festivals & Events

Vintage Weekend
CULTURAL

(www.vintageweekend.co.nz; ⊙Jan) Timetravelling cars, clothes, music, markets, architecture and good times over three January days by the Whanganui River.

Artists Open Studios
& Festival of Glass
ARTS

(www.openstudios.cc.nz; ⊙Mar) Classy glass
fest. Plenty of open studios, demonstrations
and workshops.

Whanganui Literary Festival
CULTURAL

(www.writersfest.co.nz; ⊙Sep) Thoughts, words,
and thoughts about words. Every second
September (odd-numbered years).

Whanganui River Week
CULTURAL

(⊙Nov) The wide Whanganui River got a bit
too wide in 2015 – the flood aftermath took
months to clean up. But locals still love their
river, and celebrate it over a week in November with all kinds of events.

Cemetery Circuit Motorcycle Race
SPORTS

(www.cemeterycircuit.co.nz; ⊙26 Dec) Pandemoniac Boxing Day motorcycle race around
Whanganui's city streets. The southern hemisphere's version of the Isle of Man TT?

🛏 Sleeping

★ Anndion Lodge
HOSTEL $

(📞0800 343 056, 06-343 3593; www.anndion
lodge.co.nz; 143 Anzac Pde; s/d/f/ste from
$75/88/105/135; @ 🛜 🏊) Hell-bent on constantly improving and expanding their
fabulous hyperhostel, hosts Ann and Dion
(Anndion, get it?) go to enormous lengths to
make things homey: stereo systems, big TVs,
spa, sauna, swimming pool, barbecue area,
restaurant, bar, courtesy van etc. 'No is not
in our vocabulary', says super-helpful Ann.

Tamara Backpackers Lodge
HOSTEL $

(📞06-347 6300; www.tamaralodge.com; 24
Somme Pde; dm/s/tr/q from $29/44/93/116, d
& tw with/without bathroom from $86/62; @ 🛜)
Tamara is a photogenic, mazelike, twostorey heritage house with a wide balcony,
lofty ceilings (people weren't taller in 1904
were they?), a kitchen, a TV lounge, free
bikes, a leafy back garden and Phil Collins
playing on the stereo (party dampener or
starter, it's up to you). Ask for one of the
beaut doubles overlooking the river.

Braemar House YHA
HOSTEL $

(📞06-348 2301; www.braemarhouse.co.nz; 2
Plymouth St; dm/s/tw/d/f $30/50/75/75/130,
guesthouse incl breakfast s & d $130; @ 🛜) Riverside Braemar brings together an 1895 Victorian B&B guesthouse and a reliable YHA
backpackers. Centrally heated guesthouse
rooms are floral and fancy; airy dorms conjure up a bit more fun out the back. Chooks
patrol the lawns out in the yard.

Astral Motel
MOTEL $

(📞0800 509 063, 06-347 9063; www.astralmotel.
co.nz; 46 Somme Pde; d/f from $85/110; 🛜 🏊)
Astrally aligned with the very terrestrial
Dublin Bridge nearby, rooms here are dated
and a tad noisy but are well serviced, roomy,
have big TVs and are good bang for your
buck. There's also a pool and 24-hour checkin if you're rolling in off the midnight highway. Free *Wanganui Chronicle* newspaper
on your doorstep daily.

Whanganui River
Top 10 Holiday Park
HOLIDAY PARK $

(📞06-343 8402, 0800 272 664; www.wrivertop10.co.nz; 460 Somme Pde, Aramoho; unpowered/powered sites $39/46, cabins/units from
$68/119; 🛜 🏊) This tidy Top 10 park sits on
the Whanganui's west bank 6km north of

Dublin Bridge. Facilities (pool, games room, jumping pillow) are prodigious. Kayak hire is also available: the owners shuttle you up river then you paddle back to camp. Budget cabins by the river have big-dollar views. Local buses trundle past here.

★151 on London MOTEL **$$**
(☎06-345 8668, 0800 151 566; www.151onlondon.co.nz; 151 London St; d $115-160, apt $200-280; 📶) This six-year-old, snappy-looking spaceship of a motel wins plenty of fans with its architectural angles, quality carpets and linen, natty lime/silver/black colour scheme and big TVs. At the top of the price tree are some excellent upstairs/downstairs apartment-style units sleeping six: about as ritzy as Whanganui accommodation gets. Cafe across the car park.

Aotea Motor Lodge MOTEL **$$**
(☎06-345 0303; www.aoteamotorlodge.co.nz; 390 Victoria Ave; d from $160, 1-bedroom ste from $195; 📶) It gladdens the heart to see a job done well, and the owners of one of Whanganui's newest motels have done just that. On the upper reaches of Victoria Ave, this flashy, two-storey contemporary motel features roomy suites, lavish linen, leather chairs, dark timbers and plenty of marble and stone – classy stuff.

Grand Hotel HOTEL **$$**
(☎0800 843 472, 06-345 0955; www.thegrandhotel.co.nz; cnr St Hill & Guyton Sts; s/d/ste incl breakfast from $79/99/130; 📶) If you can't face another soulless motel room, rooms at this stately old-school Whanganui survivor (built 1927) have a bit more personality. Singles and doubles are basic but good value, suites are spacious; all have bathrooms. The Grand Irish Pub (p237) and a restaurant are downstairs.

Hipango Haven RENTAL HOUSE **$$**
(☎021 664 599, 027 329 4654; www.whanganuinz.com; 49 Hipango Tce, Durie Hill; d $140, extra person $10; 📶) Wow, what a time warp! Step back into the 1960s at Hipango, a retro rental house high on Durie Hill, sleeping up to four. Two bedrooms, two bathrooms, two decks and one wide, handsome panorama across Whanganui. To get here, turn up Taylor St next to the Red Lion pub.

Eating

★Yellow House Café CAFE **$**
(☎06-345 0083; cnr Pitt & Dublin Sts; meals $10-19; ⏲8am-4pm Mon-Fri, 8.30am-4pm Sat & Sun; 🖉) Take a walk away from the main drag for funky tunes, buttermilk pancakes, local art and courtyard tables beneath a chunky-trunk cherry blossom tree. Ooh look – lemon coconut slice! Super-friendly staff bend over backwards to help (well, not literally, but you know what we mean). There's a sunny terrace out the front, too. Beer-and-ale pie for lunch.

★Mischief on Guyton CAFE **$**
(☎06-347 1227; 96 Guyton St; mains $10-25; ⏲7.30am-3pm Mon-Fri) 'I believe in reality every now and then' says the little sign in the window. How mischievous. Step inside for cafe classics (eggs Benedict, savoury mince) and globally inspired lunch mains (Thai green prawn curry, Moroccan beef sirloin, chicken and bean tortillas). Excellent counter cakes and salads; little courtyard out back. Good stuff!

Ambrosia CAFE, DELI **$**
(☎06-348 5524; www.facebook.com/ambrosiadelicatessenlabolsanegra; 63a Ridgway St; mains $10-22; ⏲8.30am-4pm Mon, to 5pm Tue-Fri, 9am-2pm Sat; 📶) The counter at Ambrosia is full of fab pies and quiches, or you can order something from the kitchen – perhaps a ploughman's lunch, some quesadillas, a chunky sandwich, a BLT or just a Havana coffee (beans from Wellington). The shelves are stocked with NZ produce to go, from curry powder to pasta. Neil Finn on the stereo (*sooo* NZ).

WA Japanese Kitchen JAPANESE **$**
(☎06-345 1143; www.facebook.com/wa.whanganui; Victoria Court, Victoria Ave; sushi $2.50-3.50, mains $8-15; ⏲11.30am-2.30pm Tue-Fri, 5-8.30pm Tue-Sat) Duck into the quiet Victoria Court minimall on the main street and discover this sweet little Japanese restaurant serving great-value sushi, ramen noodle soups and *donburi* rice bowls. There never seems to be anyone else here – what a find!

Jolt Coffee House CAFE **$**
(☎06-345 8840; 19 Victoria Ave; items $3-8; ⏲7am-4.30pm Mon-Fri, 7.30am-1pm Sat, 8am-1pm Sun) Give your morning a jolt at this hip coffee house inside a 107-year-old former pharmacy. There's not much on the menu (muffins, caramel slice, chocolate croissants): the focus is squarely on fair-trade caffeine. Pretend you're Bob Dylan at acoustic music nights on the second Friday of each month.

Big Orange CAFE **$$**
(☎06-348 4449; www.facebook.com/bigorangecafe; 51 Victoria Ave; meals $14-22; ⏲7am-5pm Mon-Fri, 8am-5pm Sat & Sun; 📶) Inside a gorgeous old Whanganui red-brick building, Big Orange is a babbling espresso bar serving gourmet

WHANGANUI OR WANGANUI?

Yeah, yeah, we know, it's confusing. Is there a 'h' or isn't there? Either way, the pronunciation is identical: 'wong-ga', not 'as in the rest of the country', 'fong-ga'.

Everything was originally spelled Wanganui, because in the local dialect *whanga* (harbour) is pronounced 'wong-ga'. However, in 1991 the New Zealand Geographic Board officially adopted the correct Māori spelling (with an 'h') for the Whanganui River and Whanganui National Park. This was a culturally deferential decision: the Pākehā-dominated town and region retained the old spelling, while the river area – Māori territory – adopted the new.

In 2009 the board assented that the town and region should also adopt the 'h'. This caused much community consternation; opinions on the decision split almost evenly (outspoken Mayor Michael Laws was particularly anti-'h'). Ultimately, NZ Minister for Land Information Maurice Williamson decreed that either spelling was acceptable, and that adopting the querulous 'h' is up to individual businesses or entities. A good old Kiwi compromise!

This middle-ground held shakily until 2014, when the Wanganui District Council voted to ask the New Zealand Geographic Board to formalise the change to Whanganui. A public consultation process began, culminating in an announcement in late 2015 by Land Information Minister Louise Upston that the district's name would be officially changed to Whanganui. Whanderful!

burgers, big breakfasts, muffins, cakes and sandwiches (try the BLT). The outdoor tables go berserk during summer. Ceramic Lounge, next door, takes over after dark.

Ceramic Lounge MODERN NZ $$
(06-348 4449; www.facebook.com/ceramic loungebar; 51 Victoria Ave; mains $23-35; 5pm-late Wed-Sat;) In a split-business arrangement with adjacent Big Orange, Ceramic takes over for the dinner shift, serving upmarket food (including killer tortellini) in a low-lit, rust-coloured interior. Occasional DJs flow tunes across the tables to cocktail-sipping seducers.

Spice Guru INDIAN $$
(06-348 4851; www.spiceguru.co.nz; 23a Victoria Ave; mains $17-25; 11am-2pm Tue-Sat, 4.30pm-late Tue-Sun;) There are a few Indian joints in the River City (an affinity with the Ganges, perhaps?), but the Guru takes the cake for its charismatic black-and-chocolate-coloured interior, attentive service and flavoursome dishes (the chicken tikka masala is great). Plenty of veggie options.

Stellar CAFE $$
(06-345 7278; www.stellarwanganui.co.nz; 2 Victoria Ave; mains $14-36; 11am-late) Stellar is a buzzy bar-cum-restaurant in a stellar location on the corner of the main street and Taupo Quay. Inside, tuck into pizzas, steaks, pastas, lamb shanks, big salads and cold beers as the All Blacks collide on the big screens. Kids' menu, too.

🍷 Drinking & Nightlife

Grand Irish Pub IRISH PUB
(06-345 0955; www.thegrandhotel.co.nz; cnr St Hill & Guyton Sts; 11am-late) Still tapping into NZ's waning passion for Irish pubs, the Grand Hotel's version is as good a spot as any to elbow down a few pints of Guinness on a misty river afternoon. Good pub meals (mains $10 to $29).

Shotz BAR
(06-348 1922; www.facebook.com/shotz wanganui; 75 Guyton St; noon-1.30am Mon & Tue, noon-2am Wed-Sat, 5pm-midnight Sun) Pool tables, happy hours, Jack Daniel's, Metallica on the jukebox and local young bucks trying to out-strut each other – it's just like 1989 minus the cigarettes.

☆ Entertainment

Riverside Bar LIVE MUSIC
(021 259 0071; www.riversidebar.co.nz; 49 Taupo Quay; 6pm-late Fri & Sat) Hunker down by the moody river in this rockin' room, where touring metal, rock and blues outfits grace the stage and assuage your ears.

Embassy 3 Cinemas CINEMA
(06-345 7958; www.embassy3.co.nz; 34 Victoria Ave; adult/child from $12.50/9; 11am-midnight) Nightly new-release blockbusters selling out faster than you can say 'bored Whanganui teenagers'. Cheap tickets on Tuesdays.

🛍 Shopping

**River Traders Market
& Whanganui Farmers Market** MARKET
(📞027 229 9616; www.therivertraders.co.nz;
Moutoa Quay; ⊙9am-1pm Sat) The Saturday-
morning River Traders Market, next to the
Waimarie Centre, is crammed with local arts
and crafts. The Whanganui Farmers Market
runs concurrently alongside, with loads of
organic produce.

ℹ Information

DOC (Department of Conservation; ☑06-349
2100; www.doc.govt.nz; 34-36 Taupo Quay;
⊙8.30am-4.30pm Mon-Fri) For national park
and regional camping info.

Post Office (☑0800 501 501; www.nzpost.
co.nz; 115 Victoria Ave; ⊙9am-5pm Mon-Fri,
to 1pm Sat)

Whanganui Hospital (☑06-348 1234; www.
wdhb.org.nz; 100 Heads Rd; ⊙24hr) Accident
and emergency.

Whanganui i-SITE (☑06-349 0508; www.
whanganuinz.com; 31 Taupo Quay; ⊙8.30am-
5pm Mon-Fri, 9am-3pm Sat & Sun; 🛜) Tourist
and DOC information (if DOC across the street
is closed) in an impressive renovated riverside
building (check out the old floorboards!).
Sarjeant Gallery (p233) exhibition space
upstairs; internet access downstairs.

ℹ Getting There & Away

AIR
Whanganui Airport (☑06-349 0001; www.
wanganuiairport.co.nz; Airport Rd) is 4km
south of town, across the river towards the
sea. **Air New Zealand** (☑06-348 3500; www.
airnewzealand.co.nz; 133 Victoria Ave; ⊙9am-
4.30pm Mon-Wed & Fri, to 6pm Thu) has daily
direct flights to/from Auckland, with onward
connections.

BUS
InterCity buses operate from the **Whanganui
Travel Centre** (☑06-345 7100; 156 Ridgway St;
⊙8.15am-5.15pm Mon-Fri).

DESTINATION	FARE	TIME (HR)	FREQUENCY
Auckland	$65	8	1 daily
Hamilton	$58	5½	1 daily
New Plymouth	$29	2½	1 daily
Palmerston North	$26	1½	3 daily
Wellington	$39	4½	2 daily

Naked Bus departs from Whanganui i-SITE to
most North Island centres, including the
following:

DESTINATION	FARE	TIME (HR)	FREQUENCY
Auckland	$44	9	1 daily
Hamilton	$37	7	1 daily
New Plymouth	$23	2½	1 daily
Palmerston North	$20	1½	1 daily
Wellington	$25	4	1 daily

ℹ Getting Around

BICYCLE
Bike Shed (☑06-345 5500; www.bikeshed.
co.nz; cnr Ridgway & St Hill Sts; ⊙8am-5.30pm
Mon-Fri, 9am-2pm Sat) Hires out city bikes
from $35 per day, including helmet and lock. Also
a good spot for info on the **Mountains to Sea**
bike trail from Mt Ruapehu to Whanganui, which
is part of the Nga Haerenga, New Zealand Cycle
Trail (www.nzcycletrail.com).

BUS
Trafalgar Square Bus Stop (www.horizons.
govt.nz; tickets adult/child $2.50/1.50) Ho-
rizons operates four looped council-run bus
routes departing Trafalgar Sq shopping centre
on Taupo Quay, including orange and purple
routes past the Whanganui River Top 10 Holiday
Park in Aramoho.

TAXI
Rivercity Cabs (☑0800 345 3333, 06-345
3333; www.wanganui.bluebubbletaxi.co.nz)

Whanganui National Park

The Whanganui River – the lifeblood of
Whanganui National Park – curls 290km from
its source on Mt Tongariro to the Tasman Sea.
It's the longest navigable river in NZ, and today conveys canoes, kayaks and jetboats, its
waters shifting from deep mirror greens in
summer to turbulent winter browns.

The native bush here is thick podocarp
broad-leaved forest interspersed with ferns.
Occasionally you'll see poplars and other introduced trees along the river, remnants of
long-vanished settlements. Traces of Māori
settlements also appear, with old *pa* (fortified village) and *kainga* (village) sites, and
Hauhau *niu* (war and peace) poles at the
convergence of the Whanganui and Ohura
Rivers at Maraekowhai.

The impossibly scenic Whanganui River Rd, a river-hugging route from Whanganui to Pipiriki, makes a fabulous alternative to the faster but less magical SH4.

History

In Māori legend the Whanganui River was formed when Mt Taranaki, after brawling with Mt Tongariro over the lovely Mt Pihanga, fled the central North Island for the sea, leaving a long gouge behind him. He turned west at the coast, finally stopping at his current address. Mt Tongariro sent cool water to heal the gouge – thus the Whanganui River was born.

Kupe, the great Polynesian explorer, is believed to have travelled 20km up the Whanganui around AD 800; Māori lived here by 1100. By the time Europeans put down roots in the late 1830s, Māori settlements lined the river valley. Missionaries sailed upstream and their settlements – at Hiruharama, Ranana, Koriniti and Atene – have survived to this day.

Steamers first tackled the river in the mid-1860s. In 1886 a Whanganui company established the first commercial steamer transport service. Others soon followed, utilising the river between Whanganui and Taumarunui.

New Zealand's contemporary tourism leviathan was seeded here. Internationally advertised trips on the 'Rhine of Māoriland' became so popular that by 1905, 12,000 tourists a year were making the trip up river from Whanganui to Pipiriki or downriver from Taumarunui. The engineering feats and skippering ability required on the river became legendary.

From 1918 land upstream of Pipiriki was granted to returning WWI soldiers. Farming here was a major challenge, with many families struggling for years to make the rugged land productive. Only a few endured into the early 1940s.

The completion of the railway from Auckland to Wellington and improving roads ultimately signed river transport's death warrant; 1959 saw the last commercial riverboat voyage. Today, just one old-fleet vessel cruises the river – the PS *Waimarie* (p233).

◉ Sights

The scenery along the **Whanganui River Road** en route to Pipiriki from Whanganui is camera conducive – stark, wet mountain slopes plunge into lazy jade stretches of the Whanganui River.

The Māori villages of **Atene**, **Koriniti**, **Ranana** and **Hiruharama** crop up as you travel upstream – ask a local before you go sniffing around. Along the road you'll spot some relics of earlier settlements, such as the 1854 **Kawana Flour Mill** (☑ 04-472 4341; www.nzhistory.net.nz/media/photo/kawana-flourmill; Whanganui River Rd; ⊙ dawn-dusk) FREE near Matahiwi, **Operiki Pa** (Whanganui River Rd) FREE, and other *pa* sites.

Pipiriki is beside the river at the north end of Whanganui River Rd. It's a rainy river town without much going on (no shops or petrol), but was once a humming holiday hot spot serviced by river steamers and paddle boats. Seemingly cursed, the old **Pipiriki Hotel**, formerly a glamorous resort full of international tourists, burned to the ground twice. Recent attempts to rebuild it have stalled due to funding issues; it's been vandalised and stripped of anything of value, leaving a hollow brick husk riddled with potential. Pipiriki is the end point for canoe trips coming down the river and the launching pad for jetboat rides.

Bridge to Nowhere BRIDGE

(Whanganui River) FREE Standing in mute testimony to the optimism of the early settlers is the Bridge to Nowhere, built in 1936. The lonesome bridge – once part of a long-lost 4.5m-wide roadway from Raetihi to the river – is on the Mangapurua Track. Alternatively, it's a 40-minute walk from Mangapurua Landing, upstream from Pipiriki, accessible by jetboat.

St Joseph's Church CHURCH

(☑ 06-342 8190; www.compassion.org.nz; Whanganui River Rd; ⊙ 9am-5pm) FREE Around a corner in the Whanganui River Rd in Jerusalem, the picture-perfect, red-and-mustard spire of St Joseph's Church stands tall on a spur of land above a deep river bend. A French Catholic mission led by Suzanne Aubert established the Daughters of Our Lady of Compassion here in 1892. **Moutoa Island**, site of a historic 1864 battle, is just downriver.

The sisters take in bedraggled travellers, offering 20 dorm-style beds (adults S25, children S5, linen $10 extra) and a simple kitchen – book ahead for the privilege.

Aramoana Hill VIEWPOINT

(Whanganui River Rd) FREE From Aramoana Hill, near the southern end of the Whanganui River Rd, there's a terrific view: peaks, paddocks, poplars and the curling river.

Whanganui National Park Area

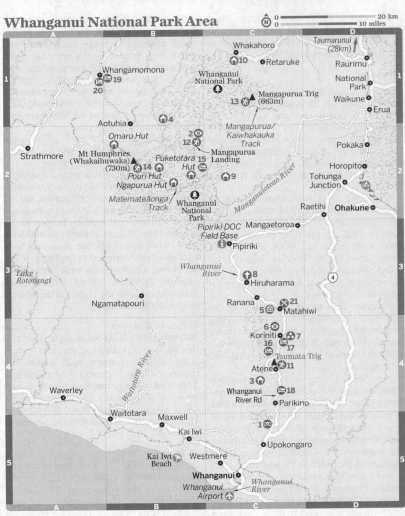

Whanganui National Park Area

⚓ Activities

Canoeing & Kayaking

The most popular stretch of river for canoeing and kayaking is the 145km downstream run from Taumarunui to Pipiriki. This has been added to the NZ Great Walks system as the **Whanganui Journey**. It's a Grade II river – easy enough for the inexperienced, with enough roiling rapids to keep things interesting. If you need a Great Walks Ticket you must arrange one before you start paddling.

Taumarunui to Pipiriki is a five-day/four-night trip, **Ohinepane to Pipiriki** is a four-day/three-night trip, and **Whakahoro to Pipiriki** is a three-day/two-night trip. **Taumarunui to Whakahoro** is a popular overnight trip, especially for weekenders, or you can do a one-day trip from **Taumarunui to Ohinepane** or **Ohinepane to Whakahoro**. From Whakahoro to Pipiriki, 87km downstream, there's no road access so you're wed to the river for a few days. Most canoeists stop at Pipiriki.

The season for canoe trips is usually from September to Easter. Up to 5000 people make the river trip each year, mostly between Christmas and the end of January. During winter the river is almost deserted – cold currents run swift and deep as wet weather and short days deter potential paddlers.

To hire a two-person Canadian canoe for one/three/five days costs around $100/200/250 per person not including transport (around $50 per person). A single-person kayak costs about $70 per day. Operators provide you with everything you need, including life jackets and waterproof drums (essential if you go bottom-up).

You can also take guided canoe or kayak trips – prices start at around $350/850 per person for a two-/five-day guided trip.

Adrift Guided
Outdoor Adventures
CANOEING
(☑ 0800 462 374, 07-892 2751; www.adriftnz.co.nz; trips 1/3 days adult $245/850, ch ld $215/600) Paddle downstream with the experts on these guided multiday canoe trips on the wide Whanganui River. River guide only $100 per day.

Canoe Safaris
CANOEING, KAYAKING
(☑ 06-385 9237, 0800 272 335; www.canoesafaris.co.nz; canoe hire 3/4/5 days $190/195/205) Three- to five-day DIY river trips with all the requisite supports, ex-Ohakune. River guides and Rangitikei and Mohaka river trips also available.

Taumarunui Canoe Hire
CANOEING, KAYAKING
(☑ 0300 226 6348, 07-895 7483; www.taumarunuicanoehire.co.nz; trips per person from $65) Based in Taumarunui, these guys offer freedom-hire river trips with plenty of background support (maps, DOC tickets, jetboats etc). Paddles from two hours to eight days.

Unique Whanganui
River Experience
CANOEING, KAYAKING
(☑ 06-323 9842, 027 245 2567; www.uniquewhanganuiriver.co.nz; 5-day trips $910) All-inclusive guided five-day river trips with a knowledgeable and experienced local. Based in Feilding.

Wades Landing Outdoors
CANOEING, KAYAKING
(☑ 07-895 4854, 027 678 6461; www.whanganui.co.nz; trips 1/2/3/4/5 days per person from $100/160/170/180/190, river guides per day $225) Myriad multiday options down the big river, with or without a river guide to point out the sights. Book your own DOC accommodation.

Whanganui River Canoes
CANOEING, KAYAKING
(☑ 06-385 4176, 0800 408 888; www.whanganuirivercanoes.co.nz; hire per person 3/4/5 days from $160/170/180, guided trips per person 3/4/5 days from $665/785/885) Freedom kayak and canoe hire, plus all-inclusive guided trips. The one-day trip – jetboat to Bridge to Nowhere then canoe down to Pipiriki – is a good option if you're short on time.

Yeti Tours
CANOEING, KAYAKING
(☑ 0800 322 388, 06-385 8197; www.canoe.co.nz; hire 2-3 days $175-260, 2/3/5-day tours $420/620/850) Freedom canoe and kayak hire, plus guided Whanganui River trips.

Jetboating

Hold onto your hats – jetboat trips give you the chance to see parts of the river that would otherwise take you days to paddle through. Jetboats depart from Pipiriki and Whanganui; four-hour tours start at around $125 per person. Most operators can also provide transport to the river ends of the Matemateāonga and Mangapurua Tracks.

Bridge to Nowhere Tours
OUTDOORS
(☑ 0800 480 308, 06-385 4622; www.bridgetonowhere.co.nz; jetboating adult/child $130/75, 2-day canoeing adult/child from $235/165) Jetboat tours, canoeing, mountain biking, tramping... The folks at Bridge to Nowhere Lodge (p243) coordinate it all, with accommodation in the middle of nowhere afterwards.

Whanganui River Adventures

BOATING, CANOEING

(☏ 0800 862 743; www.whanganuiriveradventures.co.nz; trips from $80) Jetboat rides up river from Pipiriki, with camping, cabins and a cottage at Pipiriki also available. Its one-day jetboat-and-canoe combos ($95 to $150) give you a good taste of the national park if you're in a hurry.

Whanganui Scenic Experience Jet

BOATING, CANOEING

(☏ 06-342 5599, 0800 945 335; www.whanganuiscenicjet.com; 2-8hr trips adult $80-195, child $60-145) Jetboat tours up river from Whanganui (adult/child from $65/30), plus longer expeditions (two to eight hours) into the national park with tramping detours. Canoe and canoe/jetboat combo trips also available.

Tramping

Bridge to Nowhere Track

TRAMPING

(☏ 06-349 2100; www.doc.govt.nz; Whanganui National Park; ⊙ daylight hours) FREE The most popular track in Whanganui National Park is the 40-minute walk from Mangapurua Landing (30km upstream from Pipiriki by jetboat) to the long-lost Bridge to Nowhere (p239). Contact jetboat operators for transport (around $100 per person one way).

Atene Viewpoint Walk & Atene Skyline Track

TRAMPING

(☏ 06-349 2100; www.doc.govt.nz; Whanganui River Rd; ⊙ daylight hours) FREE At Atene, on the Whanganui River Rd about 22km north of the SH4 junction, tackle the short Atene Viewpoint Walk – about a one-hour ascent. The track travels through native bush and farmland along a 1959 roadway built by the former Ministry of Works and Development during investigations for a Whanganui River hydroelectric scheme (a dam was proposed

at Atene that would have flooded the river valley almost as far as Taumarunui). Expect great views across the national park.

From the viewpoint walk you can continue along the circular 18km Atene Skyline Track. The track takes six to eight hours, showcasing native forest, sandstone bluffs and the Taumata Trig (523m), with its broad views as far as Mt Ruapehu, Mt Taranaki and the Tasman Sea. The track ends back on the Whanganui River Rd, 2km downstream from the starting point.

Matemateāonga Track

TRAMPING

(☏ 06-349 2100; www.doc.govt.nz; Whanganui National Park) FREE Three to four days from end to end, the 42km Matemateāonga Track gets kudos as one of NZ's best walks. Probably due to its remoteness, it doesn't attract the hordes of trampers that amass on NZ's more famous tracks. Penetrating deep into wild bush and hill country, it follows the crest of the Matemateāonga Range along the route of the Whakaihuwaka Rd. Work on the road began in 1911 to create a more direct link from Stratford to the railway at Raetihi. WWI interrupted progress and the road was never finished.

On a clear day, a 1½-hour side trip to the top of **Mt Humphries** (730m) rewards you with sigh-inducing views all the way to Mt Taranaki and the volcanoes of Tongariro. There's a steep section between the Whanganui River (75m above sea level) and the Puketotara Hut (427m above sea level), but mostly it's easy walking. There are four DOC backcountry huts (☏ 06-349 2100; www.doc.govt.nz; Whanganui National Park; adult/child $15/7.50) along the way: **Omaru** (eight bunks), **Pouri** (12 bunks), **Ngapurua** (10 bunks) and **Puketotara**; hut tickets cost $15/7.50 per adult/child per night. There's road access at the track's western end.

Mangapurua/Kaiwhakauka Track

TRAMPING

(☏ 06-349 2100; www.doc.govt.nz; Whanganui National Park) FREE The Mangapurua/Kaiwhakauka Track is a 40km trail between Whakahoro and the Mangapurua Landing, both on the Whanganui River. The track runs along the Mangapurua and Kaiwhakauka Streams (both Whanganui River tributaries). Between these valleys a side track leads to the 663m **Mangapurua Trig**, the area's highest point, from which cloudless views extend to the Tongariro and Egmont National Park volcanoes. The route also passes the amazing Bridge to Nowhere

---

ℹ REMOTE TRACK ACCESS

The Matemateāonga and Mangapurua/Kaiwhakauka Tracks are brilliant longer tramps (DOC booklets $1, or downloadable from www.doc.govt.nz). Both are one-way tracks beginning (or ending) at remote spots on the river, so you have to organise jetboat transport to or from the river trailheads – ask any jetboat operator. Between Pipiriki and the Matemateāonga Track is around $50 per person; for the Mangapurua Track it's around $100.

(p239). Walking the track takes 20 hours (three to four days).

The **Whakahoro Bunkroom** (☑06-349 2100; www.doc.govt.nz; Whanganui National Park; per adult $10) at the Whakahoro end of the track is the only hut, but there's plenty of good camping (free to $14). There's road access to the track both at the Whakahoro end, and from a side track from the end of the Ruatiti Valley–Ohura Rd (from Raetihi).

Mountain Biking

The Whanganui River Rd and Mangapurua/Kaiwhakauka Track have been incorporated into the 317km **Mountains to Sea** Mt Ruapehu–Whanganui bike track (www.mountainstosea.co.nz), itself part of the Nga Haerenga, New Zealand Cycle Trail project (www.nzcycletrail.com). As part of the experience, from Mangapurua Landing on the Whanganui River near the Bridge to Nowhere, you catch a (prebooked) jetboat downstream to Pipiriki, then continue riding down the Whanganui River Rd. For repairs and info try Bike Shed (p238) in Whanganui.

☞ Tours

Whanganui River Road Tours   TOUR
(☑0800 201 234; www.whanganuiriverroad.com; per person from $80) Take a five-hour minibus ride up the River Rd with lots of stops and commentary. Or, you can take a truncated tour up to Pipiriki then cycle back to Whanganui ($100 per person; bikes supplied). Minimum four people on both tours.

Whanganui Tours   TOUR
(☑027 201 2472, 06-345 3475; www.whanganuitours.co.nz; per person $75) Join the mail carrier on the Whanganui River Rd to Pipiriki (departs 7am), with lots of social and historical commentary. Returns midafternoon. Ask about transport/cycling options from Jerusalem back down the road to Whanganui.

Eastern Taranaki Experience   TOUR
(☑06-765 7482; www.eastern-taranaki.co.nz; per person incl lunch $230) Departing Stratford in neighbouring Taranaki (with pick-ups in Whanganui), these day trips take you up the Whanganui River Rd to Pipiriki, from where you jetboat upstream to tramp to the Bridge to Nowhere, then make the return journey. Minimum six people.

🛏 Sleeping

🛏 Whanganui National Park

Whanganui National Park has a sprinkling of huts, a lodge and numerous camping grounds (free to $14). Along the Taumarunui-Pipiriki section are two huts classified as Great Walk Huts during summer and Backcountry Huts in the off-season: **John Coull Hut** (☑06-349 2100; www.doc.govt.nz; Whanganui National Park; per adult $32) and **Tieke Kainga Hut** (per person $32), which has been revived as a *marae* (you can stay here, but full *marae* protocol must be observed – eg no alcohol). The Whakahoro Bunkroom (p243) is also on this stretch of river. On the lower part of the river, **Downes Hut** (☑06-349 2100; www.doc.govt.nz; Whanganui National Park; per adult $15) is on the west bank, opposite Atene.

Bridge to Nowhere Lodge   LODGE $
(☑0800 480 308, 06-385 4622; www.bridgetonowhere.co.nz; Whanganui National Park; dm/d from $50/100) This remote lodge lies deep in the national park, 21km up river from Pipiriki near the Matemateāonga Track. The only way to get here is by jetboat from Pipiriki or on foot. It has a licensed bar, and meals are quality home-cooked affairs. The lodge also runs jetboat, canoe and mountain-bike trips. Transport/accommodation/meals packages available.

🛏 Whanganui River Road

Along the River Rd there are a couple of lodges for travellers to bunk down in. There's also a free informal campsite with toilets and cold water at Pipiriki, and another one (even less formal) just north of Atene. Also at Pipiriki are a campsite, some cabins and a cottage run by Whanganui River Adventures (p242).

Kohu Cottage   RENTAL HOUSE **$**

(📞 06-342 8178; www.whanganuiriver.co.nz/accommodation1/kohu-cottage; 3154 Whanganui River Rd; d from $70) A snug little cream-coloured weatherboard cottage (100 years old!) above the road in Koriniti, sleeping up to four bods. There's a basic kitchen and a wood fire for chilly riverside nights.

Flying Fox   LODGE, B&B **$$**

(📞 06-342 8160; www.theflyingfox.co.nz; Whanganui River Rd; campsites $20, d $100-200) 🍃 This eco-attuned getaway is on the river bank across from Koriniti. You can self-cater in the Brewers Cottage, James K or Glory Cart; opt for B&B ($120 per person); or pitch a tent in a bush clearing. Access is by jetboat; otherwise you can park across the river from the accommodation then soar over the river on the eponymous flying fox.

Rivertime Lodge   LODGE **$$**

(📞 06-342 5599; www.rivertimelodge.co.nz; 1569 Whanganui River Rd; d $170, extra person $35) A rural idyll: grassy hills folding down towards the river and the intermittent bleating of sheep. Rivertime is a simple riverside farmhouse with two bedrooms, a laundry, a wood heater, a lovely deck and no TV! Sleeps five; meals available.

🍴 Eating

There are a couple of takeaway food vans in Pipiriki open during summer, plus the casual cafe **Matahiwi Gallery** (📞 06-342 8112; 3925 Whanganui River Rd, Matahiwi; snacks $4-8; ⊙ 9am-4pm Wed-Sun Oct-May) – call ahead to ensure it's open. Otherwise, pack a sandwich.

ℹ Information

For national park information, try the affable Whanganui (p238) or Taumarunui (p194) i-SITEs, or check out www.doc.govt.nz and www.whanganuiriver.co.nz. Otherwise, a more tangible resource is the NZ Recreational Canoeing Association's *Guide to the Whanganui River* ($10; see http://rivers.org.nz/whanganui-guide). The

Wanganui Tramping Club (📞 06-348 9149; www.wanganuitrampingclub.org.nz) puts out the quarterly *Wanganui Tramper* magazine.

DOC's **Pipiriki** (📞 06-385 5022; www.doc.govt.nz; Owairua Rd, Pipiriki; ⊙ irregular) and **Taumarunui** (📞 07-895 8201; www.doc.govt.nz; Cherry Grove Domain, Taumarunui; ⊙ irregular) centres are field bases rather than tourist offices, and aren't always staffed. Mobile-phone coverage along the River Rd is patchy at best.

ℹ Getting There & Away

From the north, there's road access to the Whanganui River at Taumarunui, Ohinepane and Whakahoro, though the latter is a long, remote drive on mostly unsealed roads. Roads to Whakahoro lead off from Owhango and Raurimu, both on SH4. There isn't any further road access to the river until Pipiriki.

From the south, the Whanganui River Rd veers off SH4 14km north of Whanganui, rejoining it at Raetihi, 91km north of Whanganui. It takes about two hours to drive the 79km between Whanganui and Pipiriki. The full circle from Whanganui through Pipiriki and Raetihi and back along SH4 takes four hours minimum (longer if you want to stop and look at some things!). Alternatively, take a River Rd tour from Whanganui.

Note that the River Rd was badly damaged by floods in 2015 – reconstruction work is ongoing. Ask the Whanganui i-SITE (p238) for an update.

There are no petrol stations or shops along the River Rd.

Palmerston North

POP 80,080

The rich sheep- and dairy-farming Manawatu region embraces the districts of Rangitikei to the north and Horowhenua to the south. The hub of it all, on the banks of the Manawatu River, is Palmerston North, with its moderate high-rise attempts reaching up from the plains. Massey University, NZ's largest, informs the town's cultural and social structures. As a result 'Palmy' has an open-minded, rurally bookish vibe.

None of this impressed a visiting John Cleese who scoffed, 'If you wish to kill yourself but lack the courage to, I think a visit to Palmerston North will do the trick'. The city exacted revenge by naming a rubbish dump after him.

◉ Sights

⭐ **New Zealand Rugby Museum**   MUSEUM
(📞 06-358 6947; www.rugbymuseum.co.nz; Te Manawa Complex, 326 Main St; adult/child/family $12.50/5/30; ⊙ 10am-5pm) Fans of the oval ball

Palmerston North

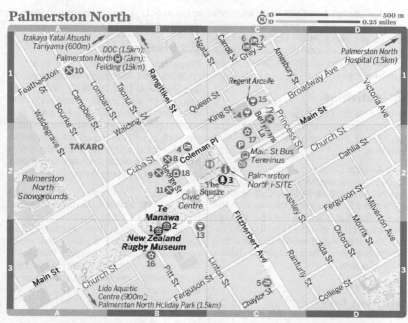

holler about the New Zealand Rugby Museum, an amazing space overflowing with rugby paraphernalia, from a 1905 All Blacks jumper to a scrum machine and the actual whistle used to start the first game of every Rugby World Cup. Of course, NZ won back-to-back Rugby World Cups in 2011 and 2015; quiz the staff about the All Blacks' 2019 prospects.

★ **Te Manawa** MUSEUM
(📞 06-355 5000; www.temanawa.co.nz; 326 Main St; ⊗10am-5pm; 🅿) **FREE** Te Manawa merges

a museum and art gallery into one experience, with vast collections joining the dots between art, science and history. The museum has a strong Māori focus, while the gallery's exhibits change frequently. Kids will get a kick out of the hands-on exhibits and interactive play area. The New Zealand Rugby Museum is in the same complex.

The Square PARK
(⊗24hr) **FREE** Taking the English village green concept to a whole new level, the

Square is Palmy's heart and soul. Seventeen spacey acres, with a clock tower, a duck pond, giant chess, Māori carvings, statues and trees of all seasonal dispositions. Locals eat lunch on the manicured lawns in the sunshine. Free wi-fi!

🏃 Activities

Swing into the i-SITE (p248) and pick up the *Discover City Walkways* booklet and the *Cycling the Country Road Manawatu* brochure.

Lido Aquatic Centre   SWIMMING
(☑06-357 2684; www.lidoaquaticcentre.co.nz; 50 Park Rd; adult/child/family $5/4/13.50, hydroslide day passes $12; ⊙6am-8pm Mon-Thu, 6am-9pm Fri, 8am-8pm Sat & Sun) When the summer plains bake, dive into the Lido Aquatic Centre. It's a long way from the Lido Beach in Venice, but it has a 50m pool, water slides, a cafe and a gym.

👉 Tours

Tui Brewery Tours   TOUR
(☑06-376 0815; www.tuibrewery.co.nz; SH2, Mangatainoka; 35min tours per person $25; ⊙11am & 2pm) Even if you're more of a craft-beer fan than a drinker of the ubiquitous Tui, this boozy tour is a doldrum-beating outing. Check out the interesting old brewery and museum, and taste a Tui or three. About 30 minutes east of Palmerston North; bookings essential.

Feilding Saleyard Tours   TOUR
(☑06-3233318; www.feilding.co.nz/sale-yard-tours.html; 10 Manchester Sq, Feilding; tours $10; ⊙11am Fri) Local farmers instruct you in the gentle art of selling livestock at this small town north of the city centre. Before or after the tour, check out the **Feilding Farmers Market** (9am to 1.30pm every Friday).

✴️ Festivals & Events

Festival of Cultures   CULTURAL
(www.foc.co.nz; ⊙late Mar) A massive one-day arts/culture/lifestyle festival, with a food-and-craft market in the Square.

Manawatu International Jazz & Blues Festival   MUSIC
(www.mjc.org.nz; ⊙late May–early Jun) All things jazzy, bluesy and swingin', including plenty of workshops.

Manawatu Beerfest   BEER
(www.facebook.com/manawatubeerfest; ⊙Oct) One day in October, the bars along Regent Arcade, including Fish (p247) and the Celtic Inn (p247), get all Germanic and beery, with live music and good times.

🛏️ Sleeping

Peppertree Hostel   HOSTEL $
(☑06-355 4054; www.peppertreehostel.co.nz; 121 Grey St; dm/s/d/f $31/65/78/124; 🐾) Inexplicably strewn with green-painted boots, this endearing 100-year-old house is the best budget option in town. Mattresses are thick, the kitchen will never run out of spatulas, and the piano and wood fire make things feel downright homey. Unisex bathrooms, but there is a gals-only dorm.

@ the Hub   HOTEL $
(☑06-356 8880; www.atthehub.co.nz; 25 Rangitikei St; r $75-170; 🐾) There are lots of students in Palmy, and lots of them stay here during the term. But there are usually also plenty of rooms available for travellers. Book a serviced en-suite double unit with kitchenette, a simple student shoebox, or a three-bedroom family apartment. Great location, great value! Reception at 10 King St (where there's also long-term accommodation).

Palmerston North Holiday Park   HOLIDAY PARK $
(☑06-358 0349; www.palmerstonnorthholidaypark.co.nz; 133 Dittmer Dr; campsites/cabins from $35/50, d/f units $85/109; 🐾) About 2km from the Square, off Ruha St, this shady park with daisy-speckled lawns has a bit of a boot-camp feel to it, but it's quiet, affordable and right beside Victoria Esplanade gardens. Great for kids.

Primrose Manor   GUESTHOUSE $$
(☑06-355 4213; www.primrosemanor.co.nz; 123 Grey St; d $145) Managed by Peppertree Hostel (p246) next door, Primrose Manor takes things more upmarket – it's an endearing guesthouse done up in snappy new-century style. There's a fancy central communal kitchen and lounge area, with five guest rooms beyond, most with en suites and all with TVs. A sociable alternative to a motel.

Fitzherbert Castle Motel   MOTEL $$
(☑0800 115 262, 06-358 3888; www.fitzcastlemotel.co.nz; 124 Fitzherbert Ave; d $120-195; 🐾) It looks unapologetically like a Tudor castle from outside, but inside it's more like an intimate hotel. Offers fourteen immaculate rooms with cork-tiled bathroom floors and quality carpets, plenty of trees, friendly staff and small kitchens in some units. Free wi-fi and laundry.

✗ Eating

★ Tomato Cafe
CAFE BISTRO $

(☑ 06-357 6663; www.tomatocafe.cc.nz; 72 George St; mains $11-23; ⊙ 7am-2.30pm Mon-Sat, 8am-3pm Sun) This buzzy cafe is a yellow box plastered with Kiwiana: retro NZ album covers, photos, prints and canvases. Infused with entrepreneurial spirit, the boss gets up at 5am to make the daily dough. His enthusiasm is infectious: happy staff deliver beaut salads, pizzas and croissant BLTs, plus an astounding breakfast gumbo with spicy sausage. Winner!

Yeda
ASIAN $$

(☑ 06-358 3978; www.yeda.co.nz; 78 Broadway Ave; mains $16-19; ⊙ 11am-9pm) A hit with the student crowd, Yeda sweeps a culinary broom across Asia, from Vietnamese pho to sizzling spicy Thai chicken and Japanese teriyaki salmon. Inside it's a long, minimalist room with polished concrete floors, blonde-timber tables and strategically placed pots of black chopsticks. Sip a Japanese Slipper or an Asahi while you wait (which won't be long).

Izakaya Yatai Atsushi Taniyama
JAPANESE $$

(☑ 06-356 1316; www.yatai.co.nz; 316 Featherston St; mains $11-22; ⊙ noon-2pm Tue-Fri, 6-9pm Tue-Sat; ☑) ☞ Simple, fresh, authentic Japanese food cooked by Atsushi Taniyama in an unpretentious suburban house with empty sake bottles lining the window sills. All the chicken, pork, beef and eggs on the menu are NZ free range. Good vegetarian and set-menu options available as well.

Café Cuba
CAFE $$

(☑ 06-356 5750; www.cafecuba.co.nz; cnr George & Cuba Sts; mains brunch $10-26, dinner $25-32; ⊙ 7am-late Mon-Sat; ☑☑) Need a sugar shot? Proceed to day-turns-to-night Café Cuba – the cakes here are for professional chocoholics only. Supreme coffees and cafe fare (risottos, salads, curries, corn fritters) also draw the crowds. The halloumi and eggplant stack is bodacious. Kid-friendly, too.

Indian2nite
IND AN $$

(☑ 06-353 7400; www.indian2nite.com; 22 George St; mains $14-18; ⊙ 10.30am-2pm & 5pm-late; ☑) With just the right touch of Bollywood schmaltz (ie not much at all), this reasonably upmarket place smells enticing and certainly won't break the bank. Behind George St picture windows and tucked under a curved wall-cum-ceiling, northern Indian curries are served by super-polite waiting staff. Try the *dal makhani,* slow-stewed overnight.

Table One E ght Eight
BISTRO $$$

(☑ 06-353 0076; www.facebook.com/table183kitchenandbar; 188 Featherston St; mains $30-36; ⊙ 5pm-late Tue & Wed, 10am-late Thu-Sun) No 188 Featherston St has worn many different guises over the decades: dairy, gift shop, fish-and-chipper, furniture store... These days it's a classy bistro, and the top branch on Palmy's dining tree. The seasonal menu is a bit French, a bit Italian and a lot NZ. Try the Waikanae crab and kumara cakes. Nice wines, too.

🍷 Drinking & Nightlife

Fish
COCKTAIL BAR

(☑ 06-354 9559; Regent Arcade; ⊙ 4-11pm Wed, to 1am Thu to 3am Fri & Sat) A progressive, stylish, vaguely South Seas cocktail bar, the Fish has got its finger firmly on the Palmy pulse. DJs smooth over your problems on Thursday and Friday nights as a sexy, urbane crew sips Manhattans and Tamarillo Mules (yes, they kick).

Brewer's Apprentice
PUB

(☑ 06-358 8888; www.brewersapprentice.co.nz; 334 Church St; ⊙ 4pm-late Mon-Wed, 11am-late Thu-Sun) What was once a grungy student pub is now a slick Monteith's-sponsored bar. Business crowds flock for meals (lunch mains $17 to $22, dinner $25 to $34), and drinkers 25 years and over fill the beer terrace after dark. Live music Friday nights. 'Keep Palmy Beered', pleads the sign. No objections here.

Celtic Inn
IRISH PUB

(☑ 06-357 5571; Regent Arcade; ⊙ 11am-midnight Mon-Thu, 11am-2am Fri & Sat, 4pm-midnight Sun; ☑) Expect good old-fashioned pub stuff. Labourers, travellers and students bend elbows with a few tasty pints of the black stuff. Friendly staff, live music, red velvet chairs, kids darting around parents' legs – it's all here.

☆ Entertainment

CinemaGold
CINEMA

(☑ 06-353-1902; www.cinemagold.co.nz; Downtown Shopping Arcade, Broadway Ave; tickets adult/child $17/12; ⊙ 10am-late) In the same complex as the more mainstream Downtown Cinemas (☑ 06-355 5335; www.dtcinemas.co.nz; 70 Broadway Ave; tickets adult/child $17/10; ⊙ 10am-late), CinemaGold ups the ante. Plush seats and a booze licence enhance art-house classics and limited-release screenings.

TARANAKI & WHANGANUI PALMERSTON NORTH

Centrepoint Theatre
THEATRE

(06-354 5740; www.centrepoint.co.nz; 280 Church St; ⊗ box office 9am-5pm Mon-Fri) A mainstay of the simmering Palmerston North theatre scene, Centrepoint serves up big-name professional shows, theatre sports and seasonal plays. Dinner and a show, anyone?

Shopping

Bruce McKenzie Booksellers
BOOKS

(06-356 9922; www.bmbooks.co.nz; 37 George St; ⊗ 9am-5.30pm Mon-Fri, to 5pm Sat, 10am-4pm Sun) An excellent independent bookshop. Pick up that guide to NZ craft beer you've been looking for.

❶ Information

DOC (Department of Conservation; ☑ 06-350 9700; www.doc.govt.nz; 28 North St; ⊗ 8am-4.30pm Mon-Fri) DOC information, 2km north of the Square.

Palmerston North Hospital (☑ 06-356 9169; www.midcentraldhb.govt.nz; 50 Ruahine St; ⊗ 24hr) Accident and emergency assistance.

Palmerston North i-SITE (☑ 0800 626 292, 06-350 1922; www.manawatunz.co.nz; The Square; ⊗ 9am-5.30pm Mon-Thu, to 7.30pm Fri & Sun, to 3pm Sat; 🛜) A super-helpful source of tourist information.

Post Office (☑ 0800 501 501; www.nzpost. co.nz; 480 Main St; ⊗ 8am-5.30pm Mon-Fri, 9am-5.30pm Sat)

Radius Medical, The Palms (☑ 06-354 7737; www.careforyou.co.nz/the-palms; 445 Ferguson St; ⊗ 8am-7pm Mon-Fri, 9am-6pm Sat & Sun) Urgent medical help, plus doctors by appointment and a pharmacy.

❶ Getting There & Away

AIR

Palmerston North Airport (☑ 06-351 4415; www.pnairport.co.nz; Airport Dr) is 4km north of the town centre.

Air New Zealand (☑ 06-351 8800; www.air newzealand.co.nz; 382 Church St; ⊗ 9am-5pm Mon-Fri) runs daily direct flights to Auckland, Christchurch and Wellington. Jetstar (www. jetstar.com) has flights to/from Auckland and Wellington.Originair (www.originair.nz) flies between Palmy and Nelson, down south.

BUS

InterCity buses operate from the Main St bus terminus on the east side of the Square; destinations include the following:

DESTINATION	FARE	TIME (HR)	FREQUENCY
Auckland	$72	9½	2 daily
Napier	$29	3½	2 daily
Taupo	$35	4	2 daily
Wellington	$39	2¼	7 daily
Whanganui	$26	1½	3 daily

Naked Bus services also depart the Main St bus terminus to most North Island hubs:

DESTINATION	FARE	TIME (HR)	FREQUENCY
Auckland	$35	10	1-2 daily
Napier	$25	2½	2 daily
Taupo	$25	4	1 daily
Wellington	$24	2½	2-4 daily
Whanganui	$20	1½	1 daily

TRAIN

KiwiRail Scenic Journeys (☑ 0800 872 467, 04-495 0775; www.kiwirailscenic.co.nz) runs long-distance trains between Wellington and Auckland, stopping at the retro-derelict **Palmerston North Train Station** (Mathews Ave), off Tremaine Ave about 2.5km north of the Square. From Palmy to Wellington, take the *Northern Explorer* ($49, 2½ hours) departing at 4.20pm Monday, Thursday and Saturday; or the *Capital Connection* ($35, two hours) departing Palmy at 6.15am Monday to Friday. To Auckland, the *Northern Explorer* ($219, nine hours) departs at 10am on Tuesday, Friday and Sunday. Buy tickets from KiwiRail Scenic Journeys directly, or on the train for the *Capital Connection* (no ticket sales at the station).

❶ Getting Around

TO/FROM THE AIRPORT

There's no public transport between the city and airport, but taxis abound, and **Super Shuttle** (☑ 0800 748 885, 09-522 5100; www.super shuttle.co.nz; tickets $19) can whizz you into town in a minivan (prebooking required). A city-to-airport taxi costs around $20.

BICYCLE

Crank It Cycles (☑ 06-358 9810; www.crankit cycles.co.nz; 244 Cuba St; ⊗ 8am-5.30pm Mon-Fri, 9.30am-3pm Sat, 10am-2pm Sun) Hires out city bikes from $20/30 per half/full day, including helmet and lock (deposit $50).

Daisy's Bikes (☑ 0800 626 292; www.daisys bikes.co.nz; Palmerston North i-SITE, The Square; ⊗ 9am-5pm Mon-Fri, to 3pm Sat & Sun) Tandems for hire from the Palmerston North i-SITE ($30 per hour; $60 for four hours).

BUS

Horizons (www.horizons.govt.nz; tickets adult/child $2.50/1.50) Runs daytime buses departing from the Main St bus terminus on the east side of the Square. Bus 12 goes to Massey University; none go to the airport.

TAXI

Gold & Black Taxis (☑ 06-351 2345, 0800 351 2345; www.taxisgb.co.nz) Family-run local taxi outfit.

Around Palmerston North

About 15km northeast of Palmerston North (aka 'Student City'), SH2 dips into **Manawatu Gorge** – one of the few places in NZ where a river flows across a mountain range. Māori named the gorge Te Apiti (the Narrow Passage), believing the big reddish rock near the centre of the gorge was its guardian spirit. The rock's colour is said to change intensity when a prominent Rangitane tribe member dies or sheds blood. It takes around four hours to walk through the gorge from either end.

Heading south of Palmerston North into the underrated Horowhenua district, **Shannon** (population 1240) and **Foxton** (population 2650) are sedentary country towns en route to Wellington.

Foxton Beach is one of a string of broad, shallow Tasman Sea beaches along this stretch of coast – brown sand, driftwood and holiday houses proliferate. Other worthy beaches include **Himatangi, Hokio** and **Waikawa**.

The town of Levin (population 20,300) is more sizeable, but is too close to both Wellington and Palmerston North to warrant the through-traffic making an extended stop.

◉ Sights & Activities

Owlcatraz   ZOO
(☑ 06-362 7872; www.owlcatraz.co.nz; 44 Margaret St, Shannon; adult/child incl 2hr tour $30/10; ⊙9am-5pm, reduced winter hours) Our fine feathered friends at Owlcatraz have obligingly adopted oh-so-droll names such as Owlvis Presley and Owl Capone. It's a 30-minute drive south of Palmerston North in Shannon.

Tararua Wind Farm   FARM
(☑ 0800 878 787; www.windenergy.org.nz/tararua-wind-farm; Hall Block Rd, Ballance; ⊙24hr) On the southwestern edge of Manawatu Gorge, about 40-minutes' drive from Palmerston North, is the Tararua Wind Farm, allegedly the largest wind farm in the southern hemisphere. It's on private land, but there are awesome views of the turbines from Hall Block Rd.

Timeless Horse Treks   HORSE RIDING
(☑ 06-376 6157, 027 446 8536; www.timelesshorsetreks.co.nz; Gorge Rd, Ballance; 1/2hr rides from $50/80; ⓓ) Flee Palmerston North and visit Timeless Horse Treks. Gentle trail rides take in the Manawatu River and surrounding hills, or saddle up for an overnight summertime trek ($225). Palmy pick-up/drop-off available.

Taupo & the Central Plateau

Best Places to Eat

➡ Lakeland House (p265)

➡ Storehouse (p261)

➡ The Bistro (p261)

➡ Spoon & Paddle (p261)

➡ Eat (p276)

Best Places to Sleep

➡ Station Lodge (p275)

➡ Braxmere (p265)

➡ Creel Lodge (p265)

➡ The Lake (p260)

➡ Ruapehu Country Lodge (p276)

Why Go?

From river deep to mountain high, New Zealand's geology takes centre stage in this diverse region – and boy, does it shoot for the moon. Much of the drama happens along the Taupo Volcanic Zone – a line of geothermal activity that stretches via Rotorua to Whakaari (White Island) in the Bay of Plenty. It's the commotion below the surface that has gifted the region with some of the North Island's star attractions, including the country's largest lake and the three hot-headed peaks of Tongariro National Park.

And the thrills don't stop there, for this area rivals Queenstown for outdoor escapades. How about hooning on a jetboat up to a waterfall, bouncing on a bungy over a river, skydiving or skiing fresh powder? Or maybe you'd rather take it easy, soaking in thermal baths or frittering away a day or two with some fly-fishing. If so, mark Taupo and the Central Plateau as a must-do on your North Island itinerary.

When to Go

➡ Equally popular in winter and summer, there's not really a bad time to visit the centre of NZ.

➡ The ski season runs roughly from July to October, but storms and freezing temperatures can occur at any time on the mountains, and above 2500m there is a small permanent cap of snow.

➡ Due to its altitude, the Central Plateau has a generally cool climate, with average high temperatures ranging from around 3°C in winter up to around 24°C in summer.

➡ Lake Taupo is swamped with Kiwi holidaymakers from Christmas to late January, so it pays to book ahead for accommodation during this time.

ℹ️ Getting There & Away

AIR

Air New Zealand (p262) has daily flights to Taupo from Auckland and **Sounds Air** (p262) links Taupo and Wellington.

BUS

Taupo is a hub for **InterCity** (📞 07-348 0366; www.intercitycoach.co.nz) coach services, with regular services running through on direct routes to Auckland (via Rotorua and Hamilton), Tauranga (via Rotorua), Napier and Hastings, and Wellington via Turangi, Waiouru, Taihape, Palmerston North and Kapiti Coast towns. The Palmerston North–Auckland service passes through Whanganui before skirting the western edge of Tongariro National Park via Ohakune and National Park Village before heading north via Taumaranui, Te Awamutu and Hamilton.

Naked Bus (www.nakedbus.com) services extend from Taupo to Auckland via Hamilton, as well as Rotorua and Tauranga, Gisborne via Rotorua, Napier and Hastings, and Wellington via Turangi, Waiouru, Taihape, Palmerston North and Kapiti Coast towns.

Mana Bus (www.manabus.com) runs Auckland to Wellington services stopping at Hamilton, Rotorua and Taupo en route.

TRAIN

KiwiRail Scenic (📞 04-495 0775, 0800 872 467; www.kiwirailscenic.co.nz) The Northern Explorer services stop at National Park Village, Ohakune and Taihape on the Auckland–Hamilton–Palmerston North–Wellington route

LAKE TAUPO REGION

New Zealand's largest lake, Lake Taupo, sits in the caldera of a volcano that began erupting about 300,000 years ago. The caldera was formed by a collapse during the Oruanui eruption about 26,500 years ago, which threw out 750 cu km of ash and pumice, making Krakatoa (8 cu km) look like a pimple.

The last major cataclysm was in AD 180, shooting up enough ash into the atmosphere for the red skies to be noted by the ancient Romans and Chinese. The area is still volcanically active and, like Rotorua, has fascinating thermal hot spots.

Today the 622-sq-km lake and its surrounding waterways are serene enough to attract fishing enthusiasts from all around the world. Well positioned by the lake, both Taupo and Turangi are popular tourist centres. Taupo, in particular, has plenty of activities and facilities catering to families and independent travellers alike.

ESSENTIAL TAUPO & THE CENTRAL PLATEAU

Eat Trout – but you'll have to catch it first!

Drink Lakeman Brewing's Taupo Pale Ale.

Read *Awesome Forces* by Hamish Campbell and Geoff Hicks – the geological story of NZ in explosive detail.

Listen to The sonorous chirruping of tui along the Tongariro River Trail.

Watch *The Lord of the Rings* and *The Hobbit* movies, and spot Tongariro's movie-star mountains.

Pedal Taupo's Craters of the Moon MTB Park.

Explore Tongariro National Park's alpine flora and geological oddities.

Online www.greatlaketaupo.com, www.visitruapehu.com, www.nationalpark.cc.nz www.visitohakune.co.nz

Area code 📞 07, 📞 06

Taupo

POP 26,100

With a postcard-perfect setting on the northeastern shores of the lake, Taupo now rivals Rotorua as the North Island's premier resort town. There's an abundance of adrenaline-pumping activities on offer but for those with no appetite for white knuckles and churned stomachs, there's plenty of enjoyment to be had simply strolling by the lake and enjoying the views, which on clear days encompass the snowy peaks of Tongariro National Park. It's also a magnet for outdoor athletes and is emerging as one of NZ's greatest cycling destinations, both on- and off-road.

New Zealand's longest river, the Waikato, originates from Lake Taupo at the township, before crashing its way through the Huka Falls and Aratiatia Rapids and then settling down for a sedate ramble to the west coast, just south of Auckland.

History

When Māori chief Tamatea-arikinui first visited this area, his footsteps reverberated, making him think the ground was hollow; he therefore dubbed the area Tapuaeharuru (Resounding Footsteps). The modern name,

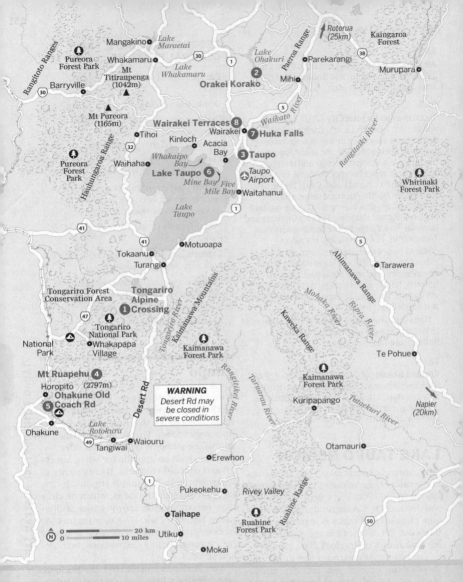

Taupo & the Central Plateau Highlights

1 Tongariro Alpine Crossing (p267) Exploring fascinating volcanic terrain while tackling this iconic walk.

2 Orakei Korako (p258) Rediscovering this volcanic 'lost valley'.

3 Taupo (p251) Hurtling to earth strapped to a complete stranger above the world's skydiving capital.

4 Mt Ruapehu (p266) Carving fresh powder at Turoa or Whakapapa.

5 Ohakune Old Coach Road (p274) Mountain biking over the 284m Hapuawhenua Viaduct.

6 Lake Taupo (p253) Paddling kayaks to check out the modern Māori rock carvings.

7 Huka Falls (p253) Rocketing up the Waikato River to the base of these falls in a jetboat.

8 Wairakei Terraces (p253) Soaking in the healing geothermal waters of these hot pools.

however, originates from the story of Tia. After Tia discovered the lake and slept beside it draped in his cloak, the area became known as Taupo Nui a Tia (Great Cloak of Tia).

Europeans settled here in force during the East Coast Land War (1868–72), when it was a strategic military base. A redoubt was built in 1869 and a garrison of mounted police remained until the defeat of Te Kooti later that year.

In the 20th century the mass ownership of the motorcar saw Taupo grow from a lakeside village of about 750 people to a large resort town, easily accessible from most points on the North Island. Today the population increases considerably at peak holiday times, when New Zealanders and international visitors alike flock to the 'Great Lake'.

⊙ Sights

Many of Taupo's attractions are outside the town, with a high concentration around Wairakei Park to the north. Taupo's main attraction is the lake and all the things you can do in, on and around it.

★ Taupo Museum MUSEUM
(Map p257; ☑ 07-376 0414; www.taupodc.govt.nz; Story Pl; adult/child $5/free; ⊙ 10am-4.30pm) With an excellent Māori gallery and quirky displays, which include a 1960s caravan set up as if the occupants have just popped down to the lake, this little museum makes an interesting rainy-day diversion. The centrepiece is an elaborately carved Māori meeting house, Te Aroha o Rongoheikume. Historical displays cover local industries, a mock-up of a 19th-century shop and a moa skeleton, and there's also a gallery devoted to local and visiting exhibitions. Don't miss the rose garden alongside.

Set up in a courtyard, the 'Ora Garden of Wellbeing' is a recreation of NZ's gold-medal-winning entry into the 2004 Chelsea Flower Show.

★ Huka Falls WATERFALL
(Map p254; Huka Falls Rd) Clearly signposted and with a car park and kiosk, these falls mark where NZ's longest river, the Waikato, is slammed into a narrow chasm, making a dramatic 10m drop into a surging pool. From the footbridge you can see the full force of this torrent that the Māori called Hukanui (Great Body of Spray). Take one of the short walks around the area, or walk the Huka Falls Walkway (p255) back to town or the Aratiatia Rapids Walking/Cycling Track to the rapids.

On sunny days the water is crystal clear and you can take great photographs from the lookout (Map p254) on the other side of the footbridge.

Māori Rock Carvings CARVINGS
Accessible only by boat, these 10m-high carvings were etched into the cliffs near Mine Bay by master carver Matahi Whakataka-Brightwell in the late 1970s. They depict Ngatoro-i-rangi, the visionary Māori navigator who guided the Tuwharetoa and Te Arawa tribes to the Taupo area a thousand years ago.

Aratiatia Rapids WATERFALL
(Map p254) Two kilometres off SH5, this was a spectacular part of the Waikato River until the government plonked a hydroelectric dam across the waterway, shutting off the flow. The spectacle hasn't disappeared completely, with the floodgates opening from October to March at 10am, noon, 2pm and 4pm and April to September at 10am, noon and 2pm. You can see the water surge through the dam from two good vantage points (Map p254). Drive here or leisurely cycle along the river from town (four-hour return; 30km).

⊙ Geothermal Area

★ Wairakei Terraces & Thermal Health Spa HOT SPRING
(Map p254; ☑ 07-378 0913; www.wairakeiterraces.co.nz; Wairakei Rd; thermal walk adult/child $18/9, pools $25, massage from $85; ⊙ 8.30am-8.30pm Fri-Wed, to 7pm Thu) Mineral-laden waters from the Wairakei geothermal steamfield cascade over silica terraces into pools (open to those 14 years and older) nestled in native gardens. Take a therapeutic soak and a self-guided tour on the Terraces Walkway featuring a recreated Māori village, carvings depicting the history of NZ, Māori and local iwi (tribe) Ngāti Tuwharetoa, and artificially made geysers and silica terraces echoing – on a smaller scale – the famous Pink and White Terraces that were destroyed by the Tarawera eruption in 1886.

The night-time Māori Cultural Experience (adult/child $104/52) – which includes a traditional challenge, welcome, concert, tour and hangi meal – gives an insight into Māori life in the geothermal areas.

Volcanic Activity Centre MUSEUM
(Map p254; ☑ 07-374 8375; www.volcanoes.co.nz; Karetoto Rd; adult/child $12/7; ⊙ 9am-5pm Mon-Fri, 10am-4pm Sat & Sun) What's with all the

Taupo & Wairakei

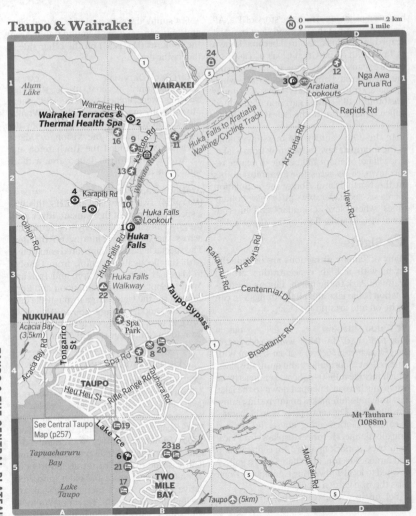

geothermal activity around Taupo? This centre has the answers, with excellent, if text-heavy, displays on the region's geothermal and volcanic activity, including a live seismograph keeping a watch on what's currently going on. A favourite exhibit with kids is the Earthquake Simulator, a little booth complete with teeth-chattering shudders and jarring wobbles. You can also configure your own tornado then watch it wreak havoc, or see a simulated geyser above and below ground.

A small theatre screens footage of local eruptions and a 10-minute film of the 2011 Christchurch earthquake.

Craters of the Moon   THERMAL AREA
(Map p254; ☏ 027 6564 684; www.cratersof themoon.co.nz; Karapiti Rd; adult/child $8/4; ☉ 8.30am-5pm) This geothermal area sprang to life as a result of the hydroelectric tinkering that created the power station. When underground water levels fell and pressure shifted, new steam vents and bubbling mud pools sprang up. The perimeter loop walk takes about 45 minutes and affords great views down to the lake and mountains beyond. There's a kiosk at the entrance, staffed by volunteers who keep an eye on the car park. It's signposted from SH1 about 5km north of Taupo.

Taupo & Wairakei

🏃 Activities

Walking & Cycling

Obtain trail maps and hire bikes from **Pack & Pedal** (Map p257; ☑ 07-377 4346; www.pack andpedaltaupo.com; 5 Tamamutu St; full-day rental $35; ☺ 8am-6pm Mon-Fri, 8am-5pm Sat, 9am-4pm Sun), **Bike Barn** (Map p257; ☑ 07-377 6060; www.bikebarn.co.nz; cnr Horomatang & Ruapehu Sts; half-/full day $35/50; ☺ 8.30am-5pm Mon-Fri, 9am-4.30pm Sat & Sun) or **Top Gear Cycles** (Map p257; ☑ 07-377 0552; www.tcpgearcycles. co.nz; Suncourt Plaza, 19 Tamamutu St; rental full day $35; ☺ 8.30am-5pm Mon-Fri, 9am-2pm Sat). You'll need to become a temporary member of Bike Taupo ($10 for seven days) to ride on local tracks. The bike shops in town can sort out a temporary membership. Pick up the *10 Great Rides* map at the Taupo i-SITE.

Craters of the Moon
MTB Park   MOUNTAIN BIKING
(Map p254; www.biketaupo.org.nz; Craters Rd) For a good selection of exciting off-road mountain-biking options, head to the Craters of the Moon MTB Park, around 10 minutes' drive north of Taupo in the Wairakei Forest. Don't forget to arrange a temporary membership with Bike Taupo before heading up there. The bike shops in town can sort out a temporary membership.

Great Lake Trail   WALKING, CYCLING
(www.greatlaketrail.com) A purpose-built 71km track from Whakaipo Bay to Waihaha in the remote northwestern reaches of the lake. The W2K section between Whakaipo and Kinloch has splendid views across the lake to Tongariro National Park.

Huka Falls Walkway   WALKING, CYCLING
Starting from the Spa Park car park at the end of County Ave (off Spa Rd), this scenic, easy walk takes just over an hour to reach Huka Falls, following the east bank of the Waikato River. Continuing on from the falls is the 7km **Huka Falls to Aratiatia Rapids Walking Track** (another two-plus hours). The Taupo–Huka Falls–Aratiatia loop bike ride will take around four hours in total.

Great Lake Walkway   WALKING, CYCLING
(Lion's Walk; Map p257; www.greatlaketaupo. com/things-to-do/biking/trails/lions-walk/) This pleasant path follows the Taupo lakefront south from the Taupo Boat Harbour to Five Mile Bay (10km). It's flat, easy walking or cycling along public-access beaches.

Hot Springs

Combine a soak in the hot pools with a walk around a fascinating thermal area at Wairakei Terraces (p253).

Spa Park Hot Spring   HOT SPRING
(Map p254) **FREE** The hot thermal waters of the Otumuheke Stream meet the bracing Waikato River at this pleasant and well-worn spot under a bridge, creating a free natural spa bath. Take care: people have been known to drown while trying to cool off in the fast-moving river. It's near the beginning of the Huka Falls Walkway, about 20 minutes from the centre of town.

Taupo DeBretts Hot Springs   HOT SPRING
(Map p254; ☑ 07-378 8559; www.taupodebretts. co.nz; 76 Napier Taupo Rd; adult/child $22/11; ☺ 8.30am-9.30pm) 🖉 A variety of therapeutic

mineral-rich indoor and outdoor thermal pools and freshwater chlorinated pools are on offer. The kids will love the heated dragon slide, two curved racing hydroslides and the interactive 'Warm Water Playground' with a tipping bucket, while the adults can enjoy a great selection of treatments, such as relaxation massages and body treatments.

Water Sports

Lake Taupo is famously chilly, but in several places – such as **Hot Water Beach** (Map p254), immediately south of the town centre – there are thermal springs just below the surface. You can swim right in front of the township, but **Acacia Bay**, 5km west, is a particularly pleasant spot. Even better and quieter is **Whakaipo Bay**, another 7km further on, an undeveloped waterfront reserve perfect for a lazy day.

Taupo Kayaking Adventures KAYAKING
(☑0274 801 231, 07-376 8981; www.tka.co.nz; Acacia Bay) Runs guided kayaking trips from its base in Acacia Bay to the Māori rock carvings, with the return trip taking around four hours ($100, including refreshments). Longer trips and walk/bike combos also available.

Canoe & Kayak CANOEING, KAYAKING
(Map p257; ☑0800 529 256, 07-378 1003; www.canoeandkayak.co.nz/taupo; 54 Spa Rd) Instruction and boat hire, as well as guided tours, including a two-hour trip on the Waikato River ($59) or a half-day to the Māori rock carvings for $95.

Lake Fun Taupo BOATING
(Map p257; ☑0800 876 882; www.lakefuntaupo.co.nz; Taupo Marina, Ferry Rd) Located five minutes' walk from the town centre at the marina, this outfit hires out single/double kayaks ($25/35 per hour), paddle boards ($30 per hour), self-drive motor boats (from $11 per hour) and jet skis ($150 per hour).

Anarchy Boarding Park WATER SPORTS
(Map p254; ☑07-378 7666; www.anarchyboardingpark.com; 210 Karetoto Rd; per lesson $80; ⊙10am-late Nov-Apr, Sat & Sun only May-Oct) Using an overhead cable, NZ's only wakeboarding park offers the opportunity to learn this exciting sport. All safety gear and tuition is provided.

AC Baths SWIMMING, CLIMBING
(Map p254; ☑07-376 0350; www.taupodc.govt.nz; 26 AC Baths Ave; adult/child $8/4, slides $5, climbing wall adult/child $12/10; ⊙6am-9pm, climbing wall hours vary) At the Taupo Events Centre, about 2km east of town, this large complex has three heated pools, two waterslides, private mineral pools and a sauna. There's also a climbing wall and gym.

Adventure & Adrenaline

More than 30,000 jumps a year are made over Taupo, which makes it the skydiving capital of the world. It's certainly a terrific spot to do it with the deep blue lake and snowcapped volcanic peaks of Tongariro National Park providing epic, dizzying views. Just remember to keep your eyes open. Taupo Airport is 8km south of town (free pick-ups available).

Skydive Taupo SKYDIVING
(☑0800 586 766, 07-378 4662; www.skydivetaupo.co.nz; Anzac Memorial Dr; 12,000ft/15,000ft jump from $249/339) Packages available (from $439), including a reduced-price second jump for altitude junkies.

Taupo Bungy BUNGY JUMPING
(Map p254; ☑0800 888 408, 07-377 1135; www.taupobungy.co.nz; 202 Spa Rd; solo/tandem jump

MĀORI NZ: TAUPO & THE CENTRAL PLATEAU

The North Island's central region is home to a group of mountains that feature in several Māori legends of lust and betrayal, which end with a few mountains fleeing to other parts of the island (refer to Mt Taranaki's sad tale).

Long after all that action was over, the *tohunga* (priest) Ngatoro-i-rangi, fresh off the boat from Hawaiki, explored this region and named the mountains that remained. The most sacred was Tongariro, consisting of at least 12 volcanic cones, seen as the leader of all the other mountains.

The major *iwi* (tribe) of the region is Ngāti Tuwharetoa (www.tuwharetoa.co.nz), one of the few *iwi* in New Zealand that has retained an undisputed *ariki* (high chief). The current *ariki* is Sir Tumu Te Heuheu Tukino VIII, whose great-great-grandfather, Te Heuheu Tukino IV (a descendent of Ngatoro-i-rangi), gifted the mountains of Tongariro to NZ in 1887.

To discover the stories of local Māori and their ancestors, visit **Taupo Museum** (p253), the carved cliff faces at **Mine Bay** (p253) or **Wairakei Terraces** (p253).

Central Taupo

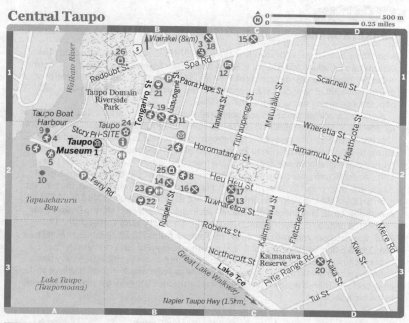

$169/338 ⊗9am-5pm, extended hours summer)
On a cliff high above the Waikato River, this
picturesque bungy site is the North Island's
most popular, with plenty of vantage points
for the chickens. The courageous can throw
themselves off the edge of a platform, jutting
20m out over the cliff, for a heart-stopping
47m plunge. Tandem leaps are available,

as they are for the Cliffhanger giant swing
(solo/tandem $119/238).

**Rafting NZ
Adventure Centre**   ADVENTURE SPORTS
(Map p257; ☑0800 238 3688; www.rafting-
newzealand.com; 47 Ruapehu St; ⊗8.30am-5pm)
With a handy location in central Taupo, this

ORAKEI KORAKO

A bit off the beaten track, **Orakei Korako** (☎07-378 3131; www.orakeikorako.co.nz; 494 Orakeikorako Rd; adult/child $36/15; ☺8am-4.30pm) gets fewer visitors than other thermal areas. Yet, since the destruction of the Pink and White Terraces, it is arguably the best thermal area left in New Zealand, even though two-thirds of the original site now lies beneath a dammed section of the Waikato River.

A walking track follows stairs and boardwalks around the colourful **silica terraces** for which the park is famous, and passes **geysers** and **Ruatapu Cave** (allow 1½ hours). This impressive natural cave has a jade-green pool, thought to have been used as a mirror by Māori women preparing for rituals (Orakei Korako means 'Place of Adorning'). Entry includes the boat ride across the lake from the pleasant visitor centre and cafe.

It's about 30 minutes to Orakei Korako from Taupo. Take SH1 towards Hamilton for 23km, and then travel for 14km from the signposted turn-off. From Rotorua the turn-off is on SH5, via Mihi. You can also arrive via the **NZ River Jet** (☎0800 748 375, 07-333 7111; www.riverjet.co.nz; Mihi Bridge, SH5; 1½hr ride adult/child $169/89, incl entry to Orakei Korako).

Located halfway between Rotorua and Taupo, the nearby **Mihi Cafe** (☎07-333 8909; www.facebook.com/mihicafe; 4089 SH5, Reporoa; mains $10-22; ☺8am-3pm Mon-Thu, 8am-3pm & 6-8pm Fri, 9am-3pm Sat & Sun) is both a quirky and colourful retro homage to classic Kiwiana style from the 1950s and 1960s, but also a terrific little eatery that's definitely worth breaking your journey for. Try the delicate peach friands or upsize to the chilli beef pie. There's a cute little playground for the kids if they're getting a bit restless in the back seat.

---

well-run operation can hook you up with everything from rafting on the Tongariro River through to skydiving, jetboating and bungy jumping, and more leisurely pursuits such as lake cruises and fishing.

Hukafalls Jet   JETBOATING
(Map p254; ☎0800 485 253, 07-374 8572; www.hukafallsjet.com; 200 Karetoto Rd; adult/child $115/69) ✎ This 30-minute thrill ride takes you up the river to the spray-filled foot of the Huka Falls and down to the Aratiatia Dam, all the while dodging daringly and doing acrobatic 360-degree turns. Trips run all day (prices include shuttle transport from Taupo).

Rapids Jet   JETBOATING
(Map p254; ☎0800 727 437, 07-374 8066; www.rapidsjet.com; Nga Awa Purua Rd; adult/child $105/60; ☺9am-5pm summer, 10am-4pm winter) This sensational 35-minute ride shoots along the lower part of the Aratiatia Rapids – rivalling boat trips to Huka Falls for thrills. The boat departs from the end of the access road to the Aratiatia lookouts. Go down Rapids Rd and then turn into Nga Awa Purua Rd.

Taupo Tandem Skydiving   SKYDIVING
(☎0800 826 336, 07-377 0428; www.taupotandemskydiving.com; Anzac Memorial Dr; 12,000ft/15,000ft jump $249/339) Various packages that include DVDs, photos, T-shirts etc ($388 to $679); bungy combo available.

Rock'n Ropes   ROPE CLIMBING
(Map p254; ☎0800 244 508, 07-374 8111; www.rocknropes.co.nz; 65 Karetoto Rd; per person $30-70) A vertiginous and challenging high-ropes course that includes balancing in teetering 'tree-tops', negotiating a tricky two-wire bridge and scaling ropes. The combo includes the swing, high beam and trapeze.

Fishing

Fish Cruise Taupo   FISHING
(Launch Office; Map p257; ☎07-378 3444; www.fishcruisetaupo.co.nz; Taupo Boat Harbour, Redoubt St; ☺9am-5pm Oct-Mar, 9.30am-3pm Apr-Sep) Representing a collective of 13 local boats, this booking office can hook you up with private charters whether you're looking for fishing on a small runabout, or a leisurely cruise on a yacht.

Taupo Troutcatcher   FISHING
(Map p257; ☎0800 376 882; www.taupotroutcatcher.co.nz; Taupo Marina, Ferry Rd; per hour from $110) Two decades of fishing experience on Lake Taupo adds up to a good choice of operators if you're looking to get lucky on the lake. Boats accommodating up to five or 10 people are both available.

Huka Prawn Park   FISHING
(Map p254; www.hukaprawnpark.co.nz; Karetoto Rd; adult/child $28/16; ☺9am-4pm) One of the world's only geothermally heated freshwater

prawn farms, this place offers a surprising cocktail of activities, including prawn 'fishing', Killer Prawn Golf and an interactive walk around the prawn ponds. And, of course, there's a restaurant.

Other Activities

Wairakei Golf & Sanctuary GOLF
(Map p254; ☑ 07-374 8152; www.wairakeigolf course.co.nz; SH1; 18 holes $200) 🍴 Surrounded by a 2m-high, 5km-long pest-proof fence, this challenging, beautiful golf course doubles as a native bird sanctuary.

👉 Tours

Sail Barbary ECAT TOUR
(Map p257; ☑ 07-378 5879; www.sailbarbary. com; Taupo Boat Harbour, Redoubt St; adult/child $44/25; ⊙10.30am & 2pm year-round, plus 5pm Dec-Feb) 🍴 A classic 1926 yacht offering 2½-hour cruises to the Maori rock carvings daily.

Ernest Kemp Cruises BOAT TOUR
(Map p257; ☑ 07-378 3444; www.ernestkemp.co.nz; Taupo Boat Harbour, Redoubt St; adult/child $40/10; ⊙10.30am & 2pm year-round, additional 5pm departure Oct-Apr) Board the *Ernest Kemp* replica steamboat for a two-hour cruise to view the Maori rock carvings, Hot Water Beach, lakefront and Acacia Bay. Lively commentary and complimentary tea and coffee. Book at Fish Cruise Taupo (p258). A special 90-minute cruise sometimes departs at 12.30pm.

Sail Fearless SAILING
(Map p257; ☑ 022 189 1847; www.sailfearless. co.nz; Taupo Marina; adult/child $39/15; ⊙10.30am, 1.30pm, additional 4pm sailing in summer) Leisurely sailing trips taking around two to 2½ hours – including visiting the Maori rock carvings – on a ketch with striking brick-red sails.

Taupo's Floatplane SCENIC FLIGHTS
(Map p257; ☑ 07-378 7500; www.tauposfloat plane.co.nz; Taupo Boat Harbour, Ferry Rd; flights $105-790) Located near the marina, the floatplane offers a variety of trips, including quick flights over the lake and longer forays over Mt Ruapehu or White Island. The three-hour 'Taupo Trifecta' combines a scenic flight, visit to Orakei Korako (p258) and jetboat ride ($505).

Chris Jolly Outdoors BOAT TOUR, FISHING
(Map p257; ☑ 07-378 0623, 0800 252 628; www. chrisjolly.co.nz; Taupo Boat Harbour, Ferry Rd; ⊙ adult/child $44/16) Operates the *Cruise*

Cat, a large, modern launch that offers fishing trips and daily cruises to the Maori rock carvings (10.30am, 1.30pm and 5pm). Sunday brunch trips (adult/child $62/34) are also worthwhile. Charters, and guided tramping and mountain-biking trips also available.

Heli Adventure Flights SCENIC FLIGHTS
(Map p254; ☑ 0508 435 474, 07-374 8680; www. helicoptertours.co.nz; 415 Huka Falls Rd; flights $99-740) Offers a variety of scenic helicopter flights, from 10 minutes to 1½ hours. Combine a flight with the Hukafalls Jet (p258) in the Helijet combo (S189). Heli-biking and hunting adventures also available.

🎊 Festivals & Events

Taupo Summer Concert MUSIC
(www.greatlaketaupo.com/events/iconic-events/ summer-concert; ⊙ Jan/Feb) Annual summertime gig from touring international acts who had their last hits back in the 1970s and 1980s. The 2016 vintage included Melissa Etheridge and Huey Lewis & the News.

Wanderlust MUSIC, CULTURAL
(www.wanderlust.com/festivals/great-lake-taupo; ⊙ early Feb) A self-described 'all out celebration of mindful living', the four-day Wanderlust combines relaxing and recharging music with yoga, meditation, and a focus on alternative therapies and natural health.

Ironman New Zealand SPORTS
(www.ironman.com; ⊙ early Mar) Bring a magnet, as buns of steel are plentiful during this pimped-up triathlon, which attracts some of the world's finest athletes. There's a shorter 70.3km event in early December.

Lake Taupo Cycle Challenge SPORTS
(www.cyclechallenge.com; ⊙ Nov) One of NZ's biggest annual cycling events, the 160km Lake Taupo Cycle Challenge sees some 10,000 people pedalling around the lake on the last Saturday in November.

🛏 Sleeping

Taupo has plenty of accommodation, all of which is in hot demand during late December and January and during major sporting events. Book ahead at these times. Self-contained campervan travellers can camp for free at 'Freedom Camp' between 5pm and 10am in a car park along Ferry Rd; non-self-contained vans have the option of **Reid's Farm Recreation Reserve** (Map p254; Huka Falls Rd), a scruffy spot beside the Waikato River.

Lake Taupo Top 10 Holiday Resort
HOLIDAY PARK $

(Map p254; ☑07-378 6860, 0800 332 121; www.taupotop10.co.nz; 41 Centennial Dr; sites from $44, units $113-324; @🛜🏊) 🏊 This slick 8-hectare park about 2.5km from the i-SITE has all mod-cons, including a huge new heated swimming pool – we're talking mini-lagoon-sized here – pétanque, basketball, volleyball and tennis courts, and an on-site shop. Manicured grounds, swish accommodation options and spotless facilities help make it a contender for camp of the year.

Finlay Jacks
HOSTEL $

(Map p257; ☑07-378 9292; www.finlayjacks.co.nz; 20 Taniwha St; dm $28, s & d $84; @🛜) Fashioned from an ageing motel, our favourite Taupo hostel has private rooms with en suites and super-comfy beds. It's just a short walk to the bars and restaurants on the waterfront, and there's some outdoor tables that are great for catching up with fellow guests at the end of the day.

Taupo DeBretts Spa Resort
HOLIDAY PARK $

(Map p254; ☑07-378 8559; www.taupodebretts.co.nz; 76 Napier Taupo Rd; sites from $24, units $85-255; @🛜) 🏊 More a trim holiday park than a flashy resort, DeBretts offers everything from hedged tent sites to motel units. The five-minute drive from central Taupo is well worth the hop for the indulgent thermal pools on-site (half-price entry for guests). Three different hydroslides should keep the kids busy.

Tiki Lodge
HOSTEL $

(Map p257; ☑0800 845 456, 07-377 4545; www.tikilodge.co.nz; 104 Tuwharetoa St; dm $27-29, d $80; @🛜) This hostel has lake and mountain views from the balcony, a spacious kitchen, comfy lounges, Māori artwork and a spa pool out the back. Scooters and bikes for hire.

★ Waitahanui Lodge
MOTEL $$

(☑07-378 7183, 0800 104 321; www.waitahanuilodge.co.nz; 116 SH1, Waitahanui; d $119-179; 🛜) Ten kilometres south of Taupo, this enclave of genuine retro bach-style units is ideally positioned for swimming, fishing and superb sunsets. Pick of the bunch are the two absolute-lakefront units, but all have lake access, sociable communal areas plus free use of rowboats and kayaks. The units are all self-contained with kitchenettes, or you can fire up the shared barbecue.

★ The Lake
MOTEL $$

(Map p254; ☑07-378 4222; www.thelakeonline.co.nz; 63 Mere Rd; d $155-185; @🛜) A reminder that 1960s and '70s design wasn't all Austin Powers–style groovaliciousness, this boutique motel is crammed with furniture from the era's signature designers. The four one-bedroom units have kitchenettes and dining and living areas, and everyone has use of the pleasant garden at the back. Some of the units are enlivened with stunning paintings of well-known musos by the owners' son.

Reef Resort
APARTMENT $$

(Map p254; ☑0800 733 378, 07-378 5115; www.accommodationtaupo.com; 219 Lake Tce; d $150-250; 🛜🏊) This smart complex stands out among Taupo's waterfront apartment complexes for its classy, well-priced one- to three-bedroom apartments, centred on an appealing pool patio.

Cottage Mews
MOTEL $$

(Map p254; ☑0800 555 586, 07-378 3004; www.cottagemews.co.nz; 311 Lake Tce, Two Mile Bay; d $125-150, q $160; 🛜) Few motels muster much charm, but this cute gable-roofed block, festooned with hanging flowers, manages to seem almost rustic. Some units have lake views, most have spa baths and all have a small private garden. Bikes and kayaks for hire.

Acacia Cliffs Lodge
B&B $$$

(☑07-378 1551; www.acaciacliffslodge.co.nz; 133 Mapara Rd, Acacia Bay; d $700; @🛜) 🏊 This luxurious B&B, high above Acacia Bay, offers four contemporarily and artfully designed suites, three with grand lake views and one that compensates for the lack of them with a curvy bath and a private garden ($595). The chef-owner dishes up high-quality fare, with dinner available. Tariff includes breakfast, pre-dinner drinks, canapes and Taupo Airport transfer.

Hilton Lake Taupo
HOTEL $$$

(Map p254; ☑07-378 7080; www.hilton.com/laketaupo; 80-100 Napier Rd; r from $225; @🛜🏊) Occupying the historic Terraces Hotel (1889) and a modern extension, this large complex offers the expected Hilton standard of luxury, including swish suites, an outdoor heated pool, and Bistro Lago, the decent in-house restaurant. It's a little out of town but is handy for the DeBretts thermal complex.

✖ Eating

Merchant
DELI $

(Map p257; www.themerchant.co.nz; 114 Spa Rd; ⊙9am-6pm Mon-Thu, 9am-7pm Fri-Sat, 10am-6pm Sun) Championing NZ artisan producers and importing specialities from abroad, this grocery on the town fringe is a fruitful stop for those looking to stock up on supplies ranging from cheese to chocolate to craft beer. Pick up some local brews from Taupo-based Lakeman Brewing. Our favourite is the Hairy Hop IPA.

L'Arté
CAFE $

(☑07-378 2962; www.larte.co.nz; 255 Mapara Rd, Acacia Bay; snacks $4-9, mains $10-19; ⊙8am-4pm Wed-Sun, daily Jan) Lots of mouth-watering treats are made from scratch at this fantastically artful cafe on the hill that backs Acacia Bay. Brunch in the sunshine, then check out the sculpture garden and gallery.

Spoon & Paddle
CAFE $$

(Map p257; ☑07-378 9664; www.facebook.com/spoonandpaddle; 101 Heu Heu St; mains $12-19; ⊙8am-4pm) Filling a spacious and airy 1950s house with colourful decor, Spoon & Paddle is more evidence you'll find great cafes pretty well anywhere in NZ. Excellent coffee partners with a concise beer and wine list, and the energetic and youthful owners focus on delivering dishes like tasty lamb shoulder tortillas, and just maybe the country's best eggs Benedict.

A mini-fort in the garden will get the kids exploring, while Mum and Dad tuck into mid-afternoon treats such as macarons or lemon meringue pie.

Storehouse
CAFE $$

(Map p257; ☑07-378 8820; www.facebook.com/storehousenz; 14 Runanga St; shared plates $7-14; ⊙7am-4pm Mon-Wed, 7am-10pm Thu-Fri, 8am-10pm Sat, 8am-3.30pm Sun) Hands-down Taupo's coolest eatery, Storehouse does tasty double duty as a cool daytime cafe serving a hipsters' holy trinity of bagels, sliders and coffee, before morphing into a night-time bar with craft beer on tap, cocktails, wine, and shared plates including tacos, empanadas, and garlic and chilli prawns. Leave room for dessert of the salted caramel and macadamia ice-cream sundae.

On Friday nights there's often live music. Check Facebook for details.

The Bistro
MODERN NZ $$

(Map p257; ☑07-377 3111; www.thebistro.co.nz; 17 Tamamutu St; mains $24-36; ⊙5pm-late) Popular with locals – bookings are recommended – the Bistro focuses on doing the basics very, very well. That means harnessing local seasonal produce for dishes such as confit duck with truffle potatoes or crab and pork belly tortellini, and channelling an intimate but unpretentious ambience. A small but perfectly formed beer and wine list makes it a very reliable choice.

Indian Affair
INDIAN $$

(Map p257; ☑07-378 2295; www.indianaffair.co.nz; cnr Ruapehu & Tuwharetoa Sts; mains $16-29; ⊙11.30am-2pm & 5pm-late; 🐾) Eschewing the staid, traditional curry house vibe in favour of bold, floral feature walls and high-back leather chairs, this thoroughly modern Indian restaurant serves up spicy classics (try the tikka lamb chops and chicken *jalfrezi*) with warm service. Alfresco tables bask in late sun; good whiskies.

Plateau
PUB FOOD $$

(Map p257; ☑07-377 2425; www.plateautaupo.co.nz; 64 Tuwharetoa St; mains $19-33; ⊙noon-10pm; 🐾) An ambient place for a handle or two of the Monteith's range, popular Plateau delivers in the food department, too. Its menu of modern pub classics features the likes of confit duck, pork belly and an artful steak sandwich.

Brantry
MODERN NZ $$$

(Map p257; ☑07-378 0484; www.thebrantry.co.nz; 45 Rifle Range Rd; 2-/3-course set menu $45/55; ⊙from 5.30pm Tue-Sat) Operating out of an unobtrusive 1950s house, the Brantry continues its reign as one of the best in the region for its well-executed, good-value offerings centred on meaty mains turned out in classical style. Book-ending with entrée and dessert is highly recommended.

🍷 Drinking & Nightlife

Lakehouse Taupo
CRAFT BEER

(Map p257; ☑07-377 1545; www.lakehousetaupo.co.nz; 10 Roberts St; ⊙7.30am-midnight) Craft beer central is the Lakehouse with a fridge full of interesting bottled offerings, and five taps serving a rotating selection of brews from around NZ. Order a tasting box of four beers ($15), partner them with a pizza or stone-grilled steak, and sit outside for lake views – and, if the clouds lift – glimpses of the mountains.

Crafty Trout Brewing
BREWERY

(Map p257; ☑07-989 8570; www.craftytrout.co.nz; 135 Tongariro St; ⊙10am-late Wed-Mon)

With slightly mad decor combining Austrian Alpine style and a cosy fishing lodge, Crafty Trout's comfy leather sofas or sunny veranda are great places to be at the end of the day. Robust meals including good wood-fired pizza go well with around eight different beers and ciders. We're partial to the refreshing Hefeweizen wheat beer tinged with coriander and grapefruit.

Vine Eatery & Bar
WINE BAR

(Map p257; ☑07-378 5704; www.vineeatery.co.nz; 37 Tuwharetoa St; ⊙11am-late) The clue's in the name at this wine bar sharing its barn-like home with the Scenic Cellars wine store. Share traditional tapas ($9 to $18) alongside larger divisible dishes (mains $32 to $35), accompanied by your choice of an expansive array of wines at keen prices. This is Taupo's best bet for a sophisticated nibble and natter among the town's well-heeled.

☆ Entertainment

Great Lake Centre
CONCERT VENUE

(Map p257; ☑07-376 0340; www.taupodc.govt.nz; Tongariro St) Hosts performances, exhibitions and conventions. Ask at the Taupo i-SITE for the current program.

🔒 Shopping

Lava Glass
CRAFTS

(Map p254; ☑07-374 8400; www.lavaglass.co.nz; 165 SH5; ⊙10am-5pm) More than 500 unique glass sculptures fill the garden and surroundings of this gallery around 10km north of Taupo on SH5. Glass-blowing displays and an excellent cafe provide great reasons to linger while you're considering what to purchase in the Lava Glass shop. All items can be (very carefully) shipped anywhere in the world.

Taupo Riverside Market
FOOD, CRAFTS

(Map p257; ☑027 306 6167; www.riverside market.co.nz; Redoubt St; ⊙9am-1pm Sat) Handmade souvenirs, arts and crafts and a scattering of tasty food stalls are all good reasons to make your first coffee of the day an alfresco espresso at this popular weekend market.

Kura Gallery
ARTS

(Map p257; ☑07-377 4068; www.kura.co.nz; 47a Heu Heu St; ⊙10am-4pm) This compact gallery represents more than 70 artists from around NZ. Works for sale include weaving, carving, painting and jewellery, and many items are imbued with a Māori or Pasifika influence.

ⓘ Information

Post Office (Map p257; 46 Horomatangi St; ⊙ 9am-5pm Mon-Fri, 9am-12.30pm Sat) Centrally located.

Taupo i-SITE (Map p257; ☑07-376 0027, 0800 525 382; www.greatlaketaupo.com; Tongariro St; ⊙8.30am-5pm) Handles bookings for accommodation, transport and activities; dispenses cheerful advice; and stocks Department of Conservation (DOC) maps and town maps.

ⓘ Getting There & Away

Taupo Airport (☑07-378 7771; www.taupo airport.co.nz; Anzac Memorial Dr) is 8km south of town. Expect to pay about $25 for a cab from the airport to the centre of town. **Air New Zealand** (☑0800 737 000; www.airnz.co.nz) offers flights linking Auckland and Taupo. **Sounds Air** (☑0800 505 005; www.soundsair. com) runs flights to/from Wellington three times a day Monday to Friday, and twice daily Saturday and Sunday.

InterCity (☑07-348 0366; www.intercity. co.nz), Mana Bus (www.manabus.com) and Naked Bus (www.nakedbus.com) services stop outside the Taupo i-SITE, where bookings can be made.

Tongariro Expeditions (☑0800 828 763; www.tongariroexpeditions.com) runs shuttles from Taupo ($65, 1½ hours), Turangi ($45, 45 minutes) and Whakapapa ($35, 15 minutes) to the Crossing and the Northern Circuit.

ⓘ Getting Around

Local Connector buses are run by **Busit!** (☑0800 4287 5463; www.busit.co.nz), including the Taupo North service running as far as Huka Falls and Wairakei, twice daily Monday to Friday.

Great Lake Shuttles (☑021 656 424; www. greatlakeshuttles.co.nz) offers charter services around the area, and can hook you up with bike hire.

Taxi companies include **Blue Bubble Taxis** (☑07-378 5100; www.taupo.bluebubbletaxi. co.nz) and **Top Cabs** (☑07-378 9250).

There are plenty of shuttle services operating year-round to Turangi and Tongariro National Park. Ask at the Taupo i-SITE who will best suit your needs as services vary according to season (ski or hike).

Turangi & Around

POP 3000

Once a service town for the nearby hydro-electric power station, sleepy Turangi's claim to fame nowadays is as the 'Trout Fishing Capital of the World' and as one of the country's premier white-water-rafting destinations. Set on the Tongariro River, the town is a shortish hop for snow bunnies from the ski fields and walking tracks of Tongariro National Park.

◉ Sights

Tongariro National Trout Centre AQUARIUM
(☏ 07-386 8085; www.troutcentre.com; SH1; adult/child $12/free; ☺ 10am-4pm Dec-Apr, 10am-3pm May-Nov) Around 4km south of Turangi, this DOC-managed trout hatchery has polished educational displays, a collection of rods and reels dating back to the 1880s and freshwater aquariums displaying river life, both nasty and nice. A gentle stroll along the landscaped walkway leads to the hatchery, keeping ponds, an underwater viewing chamber, the Tongariro River and a picnic area.

🏃 Activities

The Tongariro River Trail offers enjoyable walks from the centre of town. Further afield, good leg-stretchers include **Hinemihi's Track**, near the top of Te Ponanga Saddle, 8km west of Turangi on SH47 (15 minutes return); **Maunganamu Track**, 4km west of Turangi on SH41 (40 minutes return); and **Tauranga–Taupo River Walk** (30 minutes), which starts at Te Rangiita, 12km north of Turangi on SH1.

The Tongariro River has some superb Grade III rapids for **river rafting**, as well as Grade I stretches suitable for beginners in the lower reaches during summer.

It's also a likely spot for **trout fishing**, as evident by anglers stationed on every bend of the river.

⭐ **Tongariro River Trail** WALKING, CYCLING
(www.tongarirorivertrail.co.nz) The Tongariro River Trail is a 16km dual-use walking and cycling track starting from town and taking in the National Trout Centre en route upriver to the Red Hut suspension bridge. Walk the loop (four hours) or bike (two hours) it on easy terrain. Hire bikes from Tongariro River Rafting, which offers a $35 bike-hire and Trout Centre entry package.

Shorten your outing by crossing at Major Jones Bridge – a circuit known as the Tongariro River Lookout Track, which is a 1½-hour riverside amble passing lookout points to Mt Pihanga.

Rafting NZ RAFTING
(☏ 07-386 0352, 0800 865 226; www.rafting newzealand.com; 41 Ngawaka Pl) The main trips offered by this slick outfit are a four-hour,

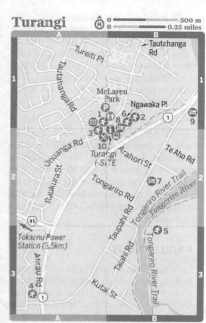

Turangi

Grade III trip on the Tongariro River with an optional waterfall jump (adult/child $129/119) and a family fun run over more relaxed rapids (Grade II, $90/70, three hours). Groups of four or more can tackle a two-day trip overnighting at a riverside camp (Grade III+, $375 per person).

Tongariro River Rafting RAFTING
(☏ 07-386 6409, 0800 101 024; www.trr.co.nz; Atirau Rd) 🏃 Test the white waters with a Gentle Family Float (adult/child $85/70) or splash

straight into the Grade III rapids ($125/109). Raft fishing is available in summer (price on enquiry). Turangi's original rafting company also hires out mountain bikes and runs guided trips around local rides, including the 42 Traverse, Tongariro River Trail, Tree Trunk Gorge and Fishers Track. Ask about multi-activity combos.

Vertical Assault CLIMBING
(☏ 07-386 6558; www.verticalassault.co.nz; 26 Ngawaka Pl; climbing adult/child $20/15; ⊙10am-5pm Mon-Sat, 10am-4pm Sun) With a climbing wall, a more sedate bouldering area, and a trampoline for the under fives. Bikes, including tandems, are also available for hire (adult/child per day $40/35). Climbing shoes are an additional $5.

Tokaanu Thermal Pools HOT SPRING
(☏ 07-386 8575; www.nzhotpools.co.nz; Mangaroa St, Tokaanu; adult/child $6/4, private pools per 20min $10/6; ⊙10am-9pm) Soak in thermally heated water at this unpretentious, family-orientated facility, 5km northwest of Turangi. A 10-minute stroll along the boardwalk (wheelchair accessible) showcases boiling mud pools, thermal springs and a trout-filled stream.

🛏 Sleeping

Motutere Bay Holiday Park HOLIDAY PARK $
(☏ 07-386 8963; www.motuterebay.co.nz; 2819 SH1, Motutere Bay; sites from $38, cabins & units $75-115; @🛜) Around 8km north of Turangi, this cute holiday park boasts a beautiful lakeside location and assorted accommodation,

---

ABOUT TROUT

Early European settlers, wishing to improve New Zealand's farming, hunting and fishing opportunities, were responsible for the introduction of such ghastly wreckers as possums and rabbits. One of their more benign introductions was that of trout – brown and rainbow – released into NZ rivers in the second half of the 19th century.

Today they are much prized by sports anglers, whom you may stumble across flicking their flies, thigh-deep in limpid rivers or on the edge of deep green pools. While this pastime, nay obsession, remains a mystery to us, it is apparent that it brings much unbridled joy and satisfaction to the lives of its patrons. To quote NZ author and poet Kevin Ireland in his illuminating book *How to Catch a Fish*, 'It has as much to do with simple stubbornness and personal compulsion as it does with any complex notions of happiness and mystical fulfilment. The last thing to which it has any reasonable relationship is success.'

The Tongariro River is the largest and most important spawning river in the Taupo district, and well known all over the world for its fish. Tall tales boast of Taupo trout weighing more than a sack of spuds and measuring the length of a surfboard. Truth be told, more than 28,000 legal trout are bagged annually, by both domestic and international fishing enthusiasts.

Trout fishing is highly regulated, with plenty of rules regarding where and how, and licences most certainly required. Read more at Fish & Game New Zealand (www.fishandgame.org.nz), but our best advice is to seek out a guide. Most offer flexible trips, with $250 for a half-day a ballpark figure.

Creel Tackle House & Cafe (☏ 07-386 7929; www.creeltackle.com; 183 Taupahi Rd; ⊙cafe 8am-4pm, tackle shop 7.30am-5pm) Fishing equipment, tips, guiding and coffee.

Bryce Curle Fly Fishing (☏ 07-386 6813; www.brycecurleflyfishing.com) Turangi-based guide.

Flyfishtaupo (☏ 07-377 8054; www.flyfishtaupo.com) Guide Brent Pirie offers a range of fishing excursions, including seniors-focused 'Old Farts & Tarts' trips.

Greig's Sporting World (☏ 07-386 6911; www.greigsports.co.nz; 59 Town Centre; ⊙7.30am-5pm Mon-Sat) Hires and sells gear and handles bookings for guides and charters.

Sporting Life (☏ 07-386 8996; www.sportinglife-turangi.co.nz; The Mall, Town Centre; ⊙8.30am-5.30pm Mon-Sat, 9.15am-5pm Sun) Sports store laden with fishing paraphernalia. Its website details the latest fishing conditions.

Ian & Andrew Jenkins (☏ 07-386 0840; www.tui-lodge.co.nz) Father and son fly-fishing guides.

Central Plateau Fishing (☏ 027 681 4134, 07-378 8192; www.cpf.net.nz) Turangi-based guide Brett Cameron.

including colourful VW Kombi vans and quirky wooden cabins shaped like the bow of a boat. Swans paddling about on a very quiet cove of the lake are just metres away.

Extreme Backpackers
HOSTEL $

(☏07-386 8949; www.extremebackpackers.co.nz; 22 Ngawaka Pl; dm $26-28, s $50-60, d $64-74; @🛜) Crafted from native timber and corrugated iron, this modern backpackers has the bonus of a climbing wall and cafe, a lounge with an open fire and a sunny courtyard with hammocks. Dorms range from four to eight beds and the pricier private rooms have en suites. Staff will happily help with arrangements for the Alpine Crossing and other activities.

Sportmans Lodge
LODGE $

(☏07-386 8150, 0800 366 208; www.sportsmanslodge.co.nz; 15 Taupahi Rd; r $85-90, cottages $115; 🛜) Backing on to the river, this lodge is a hidden bargain for trout-fishing folk unbothered by punctuation. Tidy, compact rooms share a lounge with an open fire and a well-equipped kitchen. The self-contained cottage sleeps four.

★ Braxmere
MOTEL $$

(☏07-386 6449; www.braxmere.co.nz; 88 Waihi Rd, Tokaanu; apt from $180) Near Tokaanu on the southern fringes of Lake Taupo, Braxmere is a collection of stylish self-contained apartments arrayed on a grassy lawn with absolute lakefront views. The spacious one-bedroom units all have decks and private courtyards, the decor is chic and modern, and also on-site is the excellent Lakeland House restaurant. Turangi is around 8km away.

Creel Lodge
LODGE $$

(☏0800 273 355, 07-386 8081; www.creel.co.nz; 183 Taupahi Rd; units $140-155; 🛜 ⊘ Set in green and peaceful grounds, this heavenly hideaway backs onto a fine stretch of the Tongariro River. Spacious units have separate lounges, kitchens, soothing patios for sundowners and free use of barbecues. Creel Tackle House & Cafe (p264) on-site.

Oreti Village
APARTMENT $$$

(☏07-386 7070; www.oretivillage.com; Mission House Dr, Pukawa; apt $220-350; 🛜) This enclave of smart self-contained apartments sits high over the lake surrounded by bird-filled native bush and landscaped with colourful rhododendrons. Gaze at blissful lake views from the balcony, undertake a spot of tennis or go for a dip in the indoor pool. Take SH41 for 15km, heading northwest of Turangi, and turn right into Pukawa Rd.

Eating

Hydro Eatery
CAFE $

(☏07-386 6612; www.facebook.com/Hydroeatery; cnr Ohuanga Rd & Pihanga St; mains $9-18; ☺6.30am-4pm) This recently added adjunct to the popular Turangi Tavern is a spacious and modern spot delivering traveller-friendly meals in colourful surroundings. There's a brilliant outdoor deck with the promise of sunshine, and the menu wanders deliciously from homemade corn fritters for brunch to tasty lunch options including calamari and chorizo salad and a chicken and pesto wrap.

Peruse the rustic Kiwiana art that's up for sale as you make plans to return to the adjacent tavern for a few drinks later in the day.

River Vineyard & Restaurant
MODERN NZ $$

(☏07-386 6704; www.riverwines.co.nz; 2/134 Old Mill Lane, off Grace Rd; mains $14-34; ☺10am-late Tue-Sun) Wines crafted from grapes hand-picked on-site and excellent dinner mains in the vineyard restaurant are essential reasons to visit this welcoming spot. Partner the pinot gris with the baked salmon with gourmet potatoes, green beans and a lemon *beurre blanc* dressing. Brunch items include eggs Benedict and a tasty ciabatta sandwich with local Taupo beef.

Lakeland House
INTERNATIONAL $$

(☏07-386 6442; www.braxmere.co.nz; 88 Waihi Rd, Waihi; mains lunch $16-25, dinner $38-40; ☺10am-3pm & 6pm-late) Destination dining at the southern end of Lake Taupo, with generous pastas, salads and chowder dominating the daytime menu. Craft beer from Tuatara Brewing is on tap, and come evening diners can salivate over duck breast with a star anise and honey glaze rounded off with a slice of New York baked cheesecake. Six kilometres from Turangi, just off SH41.

There's excellent accommodation on-site at Braxmere too.

ℹ Information

Turangi i-SITE (☏07-386 8999, 0800 288 726; www.greatlaketaupo.com; Ngawaka Pl; ☺8.30am-5pm; 🛜) A good stop for information on Tongariro National Park, Kaimanawa Forest Park, trout fishing, and snow and road conditions. It issues DOC hut tickets, ski passes and fishing licences, and makes bookings for transport, accommodation and activities.

ⓘ Getting There & Away

InterCity (☏ 07-348 0366; www.intercity.co.nz), Mana Bus (www.manabus.com) and Naked Bus (www.nakedbus.com) coaches stop outside the Turangi i-SITE. **Backyard Tours** (☏ 022 314 2656, 07-386 5322; www.backyardtours.com) and **Turangi Alpine Shuttles** (☏ 0272 322 135, 0508 427 677; www.alpineshuttles.co.nz) can both arrange transfers for the Tongariro Alpine Crossing.

RUAPEHU REGION

Highlights of the Ruapehu region include tramping and snow sports in Tongariro National Park, and taking mountain-biking and kayaking trips from Ohakune and National Park Village. The Tongariro Alpine Crossing is rightly regarded as one of the best one-day hikes in the world.

Tongariro National Park

Tongariro National Park (797 sq km) lies in the heart of the North Island. Its major landmarks are three active volcanoes – Ruapehu, Ngauruhoe and Tongariro. These form the southern end of a chain that extends northwest through the heart of the North Island, past Taupo and Rotorua, to finally reach Whakaari (White Island). The volcanic nature of the region is responsible for Tongariro's hot springs, boiling mud pools, fumaroles and craters. Tongariro National Park has dual Unesco World Heritage status, recognising this spectacular volcanic landscape, and also the area's important Māori cultural and spiritual heritage.

Geologically speaking, the Tongariro volcanoes are relatively young. Both Ruapehu and Tongariro are less than 300,000 years old. They were shaped by a mixture of eruptions and glacial action, especially in the last Ice Age. At one time, glaciers extended down Ruapehu to lower than 1300m, leaving polished rock far below their present snouts.

Today the park is the most popular in NZ, receiving around 200,000 visitors each year. Many visitors come to ski – Ruapehu's snowfields being the only legitimate ski area north of Wellington – but more people arrive each summer to tramp up, down and around the mountains. The park can get busy, most noticeably on the popular day walks, but most visitors consider this a small price to pay for the chance to experience its magic.

The most popular tramps in the park are the Tongariro Alpine Crossing and the Tongariro Northern Circuit, but there are plenty more besides. These range from short ambles to excellent day walks such as the Whakapapa Valley and Tama Lakes Tracks, both of which begin from the Tongariro National Park Visitor Centre at Whakapapa. There are also various challenging routes that should only be attempted by the fit, experienced and well equipped. One of these is the Round the Mountain Track, a remote 71km, four- to six-day tramp, circuiting Mt Ruapehu.

History

Tongariro was NZ's first national park, established in 1887. The previous year, in the aftermath of the New Zealand Wars (Land Wars), the Native Land Court met to determine the ownership of the land around Tongariro. Ngāti Tuwharetoa chief Horonuku Te Heuheu Tukino IV pleaded passionately for the area to be left intact, mindful of Pakeha eyeing it up for grazing. 'If our mountains of Tongariro are included in the blocks passed through the court in the ordinary way,' said the chief, 'what will become of them? They will be cut up and sold, a piece going to one Pakeha and a piece to another.'

In 1887 chief Horonuku ensured the land's everlasting preservation when he presented the area to the Crown for the purpose of a national park, the first in NZ and only the fourth in the world. With incredible vision for a man of his time, the chief realised that Tongariro's value lay in its priceless beauty and heritage, not as another sheep paddock.

Development of the national park was slow, and it was only after the main trunk railroad reached the region in 1909 that visitors arrived in significant numbers. Development mushroomed in the 1950s and 1960s as roads were sealed, tracks cut and more huts built.

◎ Sights

Mt Ruapehu   VOLCANO
(www.mtruapehu.com) Mt Ruapehu (2797m) is the North Island's highest mountain and one of the world's most active volcanoes. One year-long eruption began in March 1945, spreading lava over Crater Lake and sending clouds of ash as far as Wellington. On Christmas Eve 1953, the crater-lake lip collapsed and an enormous lahar (volcanic mudflow) swept away everything in its path, including a railway bridge. Moments later a crowded

TAUPO & THE CENTRAL PLATEAU TONGARIRO NATIONAL PARK

train plunged into the river killing 151 people, making it one of NZ's worst tragedies.

Ruapehu also rumbled in 1969 and 1973, and significant eruptions occur with suspicious frequency. In 2007 a primary school teacher had a lucky shave when a rock was propelled through the roof of a trampers' shelter, crushing his leg. No wonder, then, that the mountain's name translates as 'pit of sound'.

Mt Tongariro
VOLCANO

(www.visitruapehu.com/new-zea and/Mt-Tongariro) Ongoing rumbles are reminders that all the volcanoes in the area are very much in the land of the living. The last major event was in 2012 when Mt Tongariro – the northernmost and lowest peak in the park (1967m) – gave a couple of good blasts from its northern craters, causing a nine-month partial closure of the famous Alpine Crossing Track. (To see video of recent eruptions, visit www.doc.govt.nz/eruption.)

Mt Ngauruhoe
VOLCANO

(www.visitruapehu.com/new-zealand/Mt-Ngauruhoe) Northeast of Ruapehu, Mt Ngauruhoe (2287m) is the North Island's youngest volcano. Its first eruptions are thought to have occurred 2500 years ago. Until 1975 Ngauruhoe had erupted at least every nine years, including a 1954 eruption that lasted 11 months and disgorged 6 million cu metres of lava. Ngauruhoe is a conical, single-vent volcano with perfectly symmetrical slopes – which is the reason that it was chosen to star as Mt Doom in Peter Jackson's *The Lord of the Rings*.

Activities

Tramping

The DOC and i-SITE visitor centres at Whakapapa (p271), Ohakune (p276) and Turangi (p265) have maps and information on walks in the park, as well as current track and weather conditions. Each January, DOC offers an excellent guided-walks program in and around the park; ask at DOC centres for information or book online.

The safest and most popular time to tramp in the national park is December to March, when the tracks are normally clear of snow and the weather is more settled. In winter many of the tracks become full alpine adventures, requiring mountaineering experience, an ice axe and crampons. Guided winter tramps are available with Adrift Outdoor Guided Adventures (p273).

Scattered around the park's tramping tracks are 10 huts, most of which are $15 per

person. However, as the Tongariro Northern Circuit is a Great Walk, Mangatepopo, Oturere and Waihohonu huts are designated Great Walk huts ($32) during the Great Walk season (mid-October to April). Each hut has gas cookers, heating, cold running water and good old long-drop toilets, along with communal bunk rooms with mattresses. Campsites are located next to the huts; the $15 fee allows campers use of the hut facilities.

Great Walk hut tickets must be obtained in advance, either from the Tongariro National Park Visitor Centre (p271), **Great Walks Bookings** (📞0800 694 732; www.greatwalks.co.nz) or DOC visitor centres nationwide. It will pay to book early during the Great Walk season. In the low season, the huts become Standard huts ($5), the gas cookers are removed, and fees can be paid with Backcountry Hut Passes and tickets.

⭐ Tongariro Alpine Crossing
TRAMPING

(www.tongarirocrossing.org.nz) This popular crossing is often lauded as NZ's finest one-day walk, and around 10,000 trampers complete it yearly. Amid the thrilling scenery are steaming vents and springs, crazy rock formations and peculiar moonscape basins, impossible scree slopes and vast views. Diverse vegetation zones range from alpine scrub and tussock to higher zones with no plant life at all.

This is a fair-weather tramp. In poor conditions it is little more than an arduous up-and-down, with only orange-tipped poles to mark the passing of the day. Should strong winds be blowing on top, you'll be practically crawling along the ridge of Red Crater, the high point of the trek.

Tongariro National Park & Around

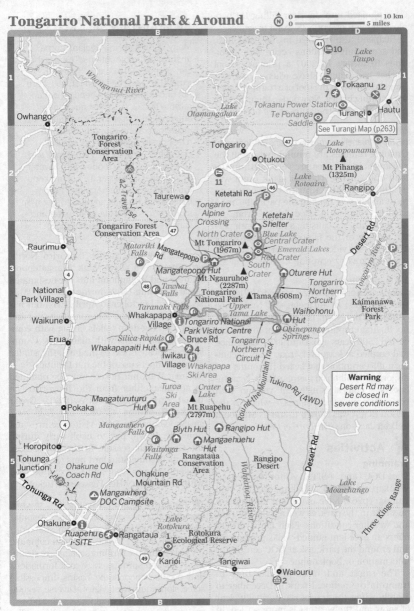

This is an alpine crossing, and it needs to be treated with respect. You need a reasonable level of fitness and you should be prepared for all types of weather. Shockingly ill-equipped trampers are legendary on this route – stupid shoes, no rain jackets, blue jeans soaked to the skin – we've seen it all.

As well as proper gear, you'll need plenty of water, as there is none available between Mangatepopo and Ketetahi. If you're keen to undertake a guided tramp, contact Adrift Guided Outdoor Adventures (p273) or Adventure Outdoors (p272).

Tongariro National Park & Around

◎ **Sights**
1 Lake Rotokura B6
2 National Army Museum C6
3 Tongariro National Trout Centre D2

◉ **Activities, Courses & Tours**
4 Crater Lake Guided Walk B4
5 Mountain Air B3
6 Ruapehu Homestead A6
7 Tokaanu Thermal Pools D1

8 Tukino Ski Area C4

🛏 **Sleeping**
9 Braxmere D1
10 Oreti Village D1
11 Tongariro Family Holiday Park C2

✕ **Eating**
Lakeland House .... (see 9)
12 River Vineyard & Restaurant D1

The most crowded times on the track are the first nice days after Christmas and Easter, when there can easily be more than 1000 people strung out between the two road ends. The upside of this popularity is excellent shuttle connections, with plenty of operators offering round-trip transport. Be sure to book your ride in advance, and keep an eye on your progress so you don't miss your ride. Shuttles operate from Whakapapa Village, National Park Village, Ohakune and Taumarunui, making them all possible overnight bases for the tramp.

The Crossing starts at Mangatepopo Rd car park, off SH47, and finishes at Ketetahi Rd, off SH46. It takes seven to eight hours to make the 19.4km journey, although this will vary significantly if you decide to take side trips up to the summits of Ngauruhoe or Tongariro – both very worthwhile and taking around two and three hours respectively. A word of warning: if you summit Ngauruhoe, keep an eagle-eye out for dislodged boulders careening down the slopes. Injuries do occur.

ROUTE	ESTIMATED SUMMER WALK TIME (HR)
Mangatepopo Rd end to Mangatepopo Hut	¼
Mangatepopo Hut to South Crater	1½-2
South Crater to Mt Ngauruhoe summit (side trip)	2-3 (return)
Red Crater to Mt Tongariro summit (side trip)	1½ (return)
South Crater to Emerald Lakes	1-1½
Emerald Lakes to Ketetahi Shelter	1½
Ketetahi Shelter to road end	1½

Tongariro Northern Circuit   TRAMPING
(www.doc.govt.nz/tongarironortherncircuit) Circumnavigating Ngauruhoe, this 43km track can be easily walked in four days from Whakapapa Village, Mangatepopo Rd or Ketetahi Rd, all regularly serviced by shuttles. Although there is some moderate climbing, the track is well marked and maintained, making it achievable by people with medium fitness and tramping experience.

Optional side trips include the summits of Ngauruhoe and Tongariro, both of which lie along the Tongariro Alpine Crossing, part of which makes up a leg of this circuit.

The Northern Circuit passes plenty of the spectacular and colourful volcanic features that have earned the park its Unesco World Heritage Area status. Highlights include craters, including the South Crater, Central Crater and Red Crater; brilliantly colourful lakes, including the Emerald Lakes, Blue Lake, and the Upper and Lower Tama Lakes; the cold Soda Springs; and various other formations, including cones, lava flows and glacial valleys.

The traditional place to start and finish the tramp is Whakapapa Village, the site of the park's visitor information centre. However, many trampers begin at Mangatepopo Rd to ensure they have good weather for the tramp's most dramatic day. This reduces it to a three-day tramp, with stays at Oturere and Waihohonu Huts, ending at Whakapapa Village.

ROUTE	ESTIMATED SUMMER WALK TIME (HR)
Whakapapa Village to Mangatepopo Hut	3-5
Mangatepopo Hut to Oturere Hut	5-6
Oturere Hut to Waihohonu Hut	3
Waihohonu Hut to Whakapapa Village	5-6

TAUPO & THE CENTRAL PLATEAU TONGARIRO NATIONAL PARK

Round the Mountain Track   TRAMPING

(www.doc.govt.nz) This off-the-beaten-track hike is a quieter alternative to the busy Tongariro Northern Circuit, but it's particularly tough, has some potentially tricky river crossings, and is not recommended for beginners or the unprepared. Looping around Mt Ruapehu, the trail takes in diverse country from glacial rivers to tussocky moors to majestic mountain views. You should allow at least four days to complete the hike.

Six days is a realistic estimate for this hike if you're including side trips to the Blyth Hut or Tama Lakes.

You can get to the Round the Mountain trail from Whakapapa Village, the junction near Waihohonu Hut, Ohakune Mountain Rd or Whakapapaiti Hut. Most trampers start at Whakapapa Village and return there to finish the loop.

The track is safest from December to March when there is little or no snow, and less chance of avalanche. At other times of year, navigation and walking is made difficult by snow, and full alpine gear (ice axe, crampons and specialised clothing) is a requirement. To attempt the track you should prepare thoroughly. Take sufficiently detailed maps, check on the latest conditions, and carry clothing for all climes and more-than-adequate food supplies. Be sure to leave your plans and intended return date with a responsible person, and check-in when you get back.

This track is served by Waihohonu, Rangipo, Mangaehuehu, Mangaturuturu and Whakapapaiti Huts, and a side trip can be made to Blyth Hut.

Crater Lake Guided Walk   TRAMPING

(☎0508 782 734; www.mtruapehu.com; adult/child incl chairlift $99/75; ⏲Dec-Apr) The unmarked rugged route up to Ruapehu's Crater Lake (seven hours return) allows you to see the acidic lake up close. This moderate-to-difficult walk begins at Iwikau Village at the top of Bruce Rd. You can cut three hours off it by catching the chairlift from Whakapapa Ski Area.

Guided walks to Crater Lake are hosted by Safety & Mountaineering Guides along with local Ngāti Hikairo cultural guides, and run from mid-December to May, weather dependent.

Walking Legends   TRAMPING

(☎0800 925 569, 07-312 5297; www.walkinglegends.com) Guided tramps tackling the Tongariro Alpine Crossing and the Tongariro Northern Circuit.

Skiing & Snowboarding

The linked Whakapapa and Turoa resorts straddle either side of Mt Ruapehu and are NZ's two largest ski areas. Each offers similar skiing at an analogous altitude (around 2300m), with areas to suit each level of experience – from beginners' slopes to black-diamond runs for the pros. The same lift passes cover both ski areas.

The only accommodation at the Whakapapa ski field is in private lodges (mainly owned by ski clubs), so most visitors stay at Whakapaka or National Park Village. Turoa is only 16km from Ohakune, which has the best après-ski scene.

The Turoa and Whakapapa Ski Areas are both managed by the same company and passes cover both sides of the mountain.

Whakapapa Ski Area   SKIING

(☑07-892 3738; www.mtruapehu.com/winter/whakapapa; daily lift pass adult/child $95/57) Whakapapa Ski Area, on the northwestern slopes of Mt Ruapehu, is NZ's largest ski area, with more than 65 trails across 1050 hectares and a maximum altitude of 2300m. It's a good location for beginners with some easy runs. The only accommodation is in private ski club lodges and most visitors stay at Whakapapa or National Park Villages.

Turoa Ski Area   SKIING

(☑06-385 8456; www.mtruapehu.com/winter/Turoa; daily lift pass adult/child $95/57) Turoa Ski Area on the southwestern slopes of Mt Ruapehu has Australasia's longest vertical descent and NZ's highest lift, the Highnoon Express. Beginners are catered for, with gear hire, ski school, good learner areas and nice easy runs. The town of Ohakune is around 16km from Turoa, and is the most happening hub for après-ski good times.

Tukino Ski Area   SKIING, SNOWBOARDING

(☑0800 885 466, 06-387 6294; www.tukino.co.nz; day pass adult/child $60/30) Club-operated Tukino is on Mt Ruapehu's east, 46km from Turangi. It's quite remote, 14km down a gravel road from the sealed Desert Rd (SH1), and you need a 4WD vehicle to get in. It offers uncrowded, backcountry runs, mostly beginner and intermediate.

☞ Tours

Mountain Air   SCENIC FLIGHTS

(☑0800 922 812; www.mountainair.co.nz; junction SH47 & SH48; flights 15/25/35min $120/195/245) Offers scenic flights from its base halfway between Whakapapa Village and National Park. Turangi and Taupo departures also available.

Whakapapa Village

POP 100 (SUMMER), 300 (WINTER)

Located within the bounds of Tongariro National Park on the lower slopes of Mt Ruapehu, Whakapapa Village (pronounced 'fa-ka-pa-pa'; altitude 1140m) is the gateway to the park, home of the park's visitor centre, and the starting point for numerous walking tracks.

🏃 Activities

Tama Lakes Track
TRAMPING

Part of the Tongariro Northern Circuit, starting at Whakapapa Village, this 17km return track leads to the Tama Lakes on the Tama Saddle between Ruapehu and Ngauruhoe (five to six hours return). The upper lake affords fine views of Ngauruhoe and Tongariro.

Ridge Track
TRAMPING

A 30-minute return walk from the village that climbs through beech forest to alpine-shrub areas for views of Ruapehu and Ngauruhoe.

Taranaki Falls Track
TRAMPING

A two-hour, 6km loop track heads from the village to Taranaki Falls, which plunge 20m over an old lava flow into a boulder-ringed pool.

🛏 Sleeping

Whakapapa Village has limited accommodation, and during ski season prices hit their peak. A greater range of options can be found in National Park Village and Ohakune, with the latter offering the most in the way of eating and shopping. The peak of summer over Christmas/New Year and around Easter also sees accommodation prices rise.

Tongariro Family Holiday Park
HOLIDAY PARK $

(📞 07-386 8062; www.thp.co.nz; SH47; sites per person from $22, cabins $65-100 ; 🛜) Conveniently situated for Alpine Crossing trampers, halfway along the highway between the start and finish points, this wee gem is in the middle of nowhere and everywhere at the same time. It's a welcoming camp – simple, sunny and surrounded by forest, with plenty of grass, trees and a playground. Communal facilities, cabins and self-contained units are unflashy but well tended.

It's 24km to both Whakapapa Village and Turangi.

Skotel Alpine Resort
HOSTEL $

(📞 07-892 3719, 0800 756 835; www.skotel.co.nz; Ngauruhoe Pl; s/tw/tr without bathroom $40/65/80, r $140-185, cabins $185; 🛜) If you think of it more as a hostel than a hotel, you'll excuse the odd bit of stained carpet or cheap lino, and enjoy the timber-lined alpine ambience and decidedly non-hostel-like facilities: free sauna, spa pool and gym, and ski hire, restaurant and bar.

Whakapapa Holiday Park
HOLIDAY PARK $

(📞 07-892 3897; www.whakapapa.net.nz; sites $21, dm $28, cabins $76-119; 🛜) This popular DOC-associated park beside Whakapapanui Stream has a wide range of accommodation options, including campervan sites perched on the edge of beautiful beech forest, a 32-bed backpackers lodge (linen required), cabins (linen required) and a self-contained unit. The camp store stocks basic groceries.

Chateau Tongariro Hotel
HOTEL $$$

(📞 0800 242 832, 07-892 3809; www.chateau.co.nz; Whakapapa Village; d from $245; @🛜🏊) With its sublime setting and grandeur, this iconic hotel was quite the location when it first opened in 1929, but now its grandeur is just a tad faded. But the Chateau is still one of NZ's most romantic hotels, complete with high tea in the library, aperitifs in the foyer bar and evening dining in the grand Ruapehu Room.

Other facilities include two cafes, indoor pool, cinema and nine-hole golf course. Choose from rooms in either the historic hotel (with greater charm) or the adjacent modern wing. Check online for package discounts.

🍴 Eating

Ruapehu Room
INTERNATIONAL $$$

(📞 0800 242 832; www.chateau.co.nz/ruapehu-restaurant; Whakapapa Village; mains $32-38; ⏱ from 6.30pm) The Chateau Tongariro Hotel's elegant à la carte option. Bookings are recommended and note that gentlemen dining must wear a collared shirt and long trousers.

ℹ Information

Tongariro National Park Visitor Centre

(📞 07-892 3729; www.doc.govt.nz; Whakapapa Village; ⏱ 8am-5pm) has maps and info on all corners of the park, including walks, huts and current skiing, track and weather conditions. Its exhibits on the geological and human history of the area should keep you busy for a couple of hours on a rainy day. The *Walks in*

TAUPO & THE CENTRAL PLATEAU WHAKAPAPA VILLAGE

and around Tongariro National Park brochure provides a helpful overview of 30 walks and tramps in the park ($3).

Further national park information is available from the i-SITEs in **Ohakune** (p276), **Turangi** (p265) and **Taupo** (p262).

ⓘ Getting There & Away

BUS

Tongariro National Park is well serviced by shuttle operators, which service Whakapapa Village, National Park Village, Ohakune, Taupo and Turangi, as well as popular trailheads. In summer tramping trips are their focus, but in winter most offer ski-field shuttles. Book your bus in advance to avoid unexpected strandings.

Many shuttle operators are offshoots or affiliates of accommodation providers, so ask about transport when you book your stay. **Roam** (☑ 0800 762 612, 021 588 734; www.roam. net.nz) is a local Whakapapa Village–based company

Otherwise, try Taupo-based **Tongariro Expeditions** (p262) or Turangi-based **Turangi Alpine Shuttles** (p266).

CAR & MOTORCYCLE

Tongariro National Park is bounded by roads: SH1 (called the Desert Rd) to the east, SH4 to the west, SH46 and SH47 to the north and SH49 to the south. The main road up into the park is SH48, which leads to Whakapapa Village and continues further up the mountain as Bruce Rd leading to the Whakapapa Ski Area. Ohakune Mountain Rd leads up to the Turoa Ski Area from Ohakune. The Desert Rd is regularly closed when the weather is bad; detours will be in force. Likewise, Ohakune Mountain Rd and Bruce Rd are subject to closures, and access beyond certain points may be restricted to 4WDs or cars with snow chains.

National Park Village

POP 200

This small sprawl of a town lies at the junction of SH4 and SH47 at 825m above sea level, 15km from the hub of Whakapapa Village. In ski season the township is packed, but in summer it's sleepy despite being a handy base for activities in and around the park.

As you'll discover, it's railway country around here. About 20km south on SH4 at **Horopito** is a monument to the Last Spike, the spike that marked the completion of the Main Trunk Railway Line between Auckland and Wellington in 1908 (although Horopito is better known for Smash Palace, NZ's most famous car graveyard). Five kilometres north from National Park Village, at **Raurimu**, is evidence of the engineering masterpiece that is the 'spiral'. Trainspotters will marvel, while non-trainspotters will probably wonder what the hell they're looking at it (there's not much to see).

✦ Activities

There's little to do in the village itself, its major enticement being its proximity to national-park tramps, mountain-bike trails, canoe trips on the Whanganui River, and winter skiing. Most accommodation in town offers packages for lift passes and ski hire, sparing you the steeper prices further up the mountain. Ski gear can be hired from **Eivins** (☑ 07-892 2843; www.eivins.co.nz; Carroll St), **Snow Zone** (☑ 07-892 2757; www.snowzone. co.nz; 25-27 Buddo St) and **Ski Biz** (☑ 07-892 2717; www.skibiz.co.nz; 10 Carroll St; ⏲ 4-7pm summer, 7.30am-7pm winter).

Daily shuttles leave from here to the Tongariro Alpine Crossing and Whakapapa Village in summer, and the ski area in winter.

My Kiwi Adventure   MOUNTAIN BIKING
(☑ 021 784 202, 0800 784 202; www.mykiwi adventure.co.nz; 15 Findlay St; paddle boarding $50, mountain biking $45-95) Offers the unique, only-in-National-Park activity of stand-up paddle boarding on Lake Otamangakau. Look forward to alpine mountain vistas as you negotiate the lake's silken surface. Trips include gear and shuttle transport. Also available is mountain biking, including bikes and shuttles, on standout local tracks including the Ohakune Old Coach Rd, Fishers Track and the 42 Traverse.

A great-value Tongariro Adventure Package ($99) combines the Tongariro Alpine Crossing with paddle boarding and biking the Old Coach Road across two days.

Standalone bike rental (half-/full day $35/55) is also available.

Adventure Outdoors   TRAMPING, KAYAKING
(☑ 0800 386 925, 027 242 7209; www.adventure outdoors.co.nz) Guided trips on the Tongariro Alpine Crossing – in summer ($225) or winter ($185) – and negotiating the Whanganui or Whakapapa Rivers on inflatable two-person kayaks (half-/full day $119/189). Wetsuits and lifejackets are all provided so you're good to go.

Kiwi Mountain Bikes   MOUNTAIN BIKING
(☑ 0800 562 4537, 07-892 2911; www.kiwi mountainbikes.com; Macrocarpa Cafe, 3 Waimarino–

Tokaanu Rd) Rents mountain bikes (half-/full day from $35/60) and provides information and bike transport ($35) for Fishers Track, the Ohakune Old Coach Road, the 42 Traverse and the Bridge to Nowhere. It can also provide transport for the Tongariro Crossing. Pop in to see them at the Macrocarpa Cafe.

Fishers Track — MOUNTAIN BIKING
Starting from National Park Village, this track is a 17km (mainly) downhill blast, and now forms part of the Ruapehu Whanganui Trails.

42 Traverse — MOUNTAIN BIKING
This four- to six-hour, 46km mountain-bike trail through the Tongariro Forest is one of the most popular one-dayers on the North Island. The Traverse follows old logging tracks, making for relatively dependable going, although there are plenty of ups and downs – more downs as long as you start from Kapoors Rd (off SH47) and head down to Owhango.

Adrift Guided
Outdoor Adventures — CANOEING, TRAMPING
(☑ 07-892 2751; www.adriftnz.co.nz; 3 Waimarino–Tokaanu Rd) Runs guided canoe trips on the Whanganui River (one/three days $245/859), and lots of different guided tramps in Tongariro National Park (two hours to three days, $95 to $950) including the Tongariro Alpine Crossing ($225 to $279) and tramps to Crater Lake on Mt Ruapehu ($225). Half-day mountain-bike excursions ($17) are also available.

🛏 Sleeping

National Park Village is a town of budget and midrange accommodation. This makes sense, as you'll probably spend most of your time in the great outdoors.

Our listings give summer prices; be warned that when the ski season is in full swing, accommodation is tight and bookings are essential.

Note that summer is definitely becoming busier, especially with visitors undertaking the Tongariro Alpine Crossing.

National Park Backpackers — HOSTEL $
(☑ 07-892 2870; www.npbp.co.nz; 4 Findlay St; sites $15, dm $26-29, c $62-86; ◉ 🛜) This big, old board and batten YHA hostel has a large garden for lounging, a well-equipped kitchen and standard rooms. It's a good one-stop

shop for booking activities in the area, and is home to the **Climbing Wall** (☑ 07-892 2870; www.npbp.co.nz; 4 Findlay St; adult/child $15/10; ⊙ 9am-8pm) for when the weather turns to custard. Small shop on-site.

Plateau Lodge — LODGE, HOSTEL $
(☑ 07-892 2993; www.plateaulodge.co.nz; 17 Carroll St; dm $30, d $75-115, apt from $160; ◉ 🛜) Family-friendly Plateau has cosy rooms, some with en suite and TV, as well as an attractive communal lounge, kitchen and hot tub. The dorms don't get bigger than two sets of bunks and there are two-bedroom apartments sleeping up to six. Local shuttle services available and campervans can park for $38.

Wood Pigeon Lodge — LODGE $$
(☑ 07-892 2933; www.woodpigeonlodge.com; 130 Top Mill Rd, Raurimu; d $200-250) Three separate accommodation options make up this very comfortable place in a rural setting in Raurimu, around 5km north of National Park Village. Sleeping up to five, the Tree House is self-sufficient for electricity harnessing wind and solar energy. More cosy and compact is the Hut with a wonderfully warm wooden interior and an outdoor bathtub. Note there is a two-night minimum stay.

For groups up to eight, the Barn is a spacious and rustic option.

Tongariro Crossing Lodge — LODGE $$
(☑ 07-892 2688; www.tongarirocrossinglodge.com; 27 Carroll St; d $140-180; ◉ 🛜) This pretty white weatherboard cottage is decorated with a baby-blue trim and rambling blooms in summer. Cosy accommodation ranges from standard doubles to larger self-contained apartments, and is dotted with period furniture. Rates shown include breakfast, but it is optional. There's a sunny deck and barbecue area, and a friendly black cat who definitely thinks he owns the place.

Parkview Apartments — APARTMENT $$$
(☑ 0800 727 588; www.parkviewnationalpark.com; 24 Waimarino–Tokaanu Rd; d $280; 🛜) Stylish and thoroughly modern accommodation comes to National Park Village at these recently built apartments. Both two-bedroom apartments sleep up to four people, and expansive picture windows make it easy to take in the beautiful alpine scenery outside. Indoor distractions such as big-screen TVs, gas fireplaces and contemporary kitchens could well delay your eventual enjoyment of the surrounding area.

Eating & Drinking

Station Cafe
CAFE $$

(☎ 07-892 2881; www.stationcafe.co.nz; cnr Findlay St & Station Rd; mains lunch $15-20, dinner $28-34; ⏱ 9am-4pm Mon-Tue, to 9pm Wed-Sun) Count your blessings ye who find this little railway station along the line, a lovely old dear, restored with care and now serving eggy brunches, sandwiches, coffee and yummy cakes, plus an impressive à la carte evening menu. Try the grilled pork tenderloin with a creamy blue cheese sauce. Three-course Sunday night roasts ($40) are world famous around these parts.

Schnapps
PUB

(☎ 07-892 2788; www.schnappsbarruapehu.com; Findlay St; ⏱ noon-late) This popular pub has a meat-fest menu (meals $14 to $28), open fire, big-screen TV, pool table and a handy ATM. Things crank up on wintry weekends, and it's recently added a mini-golf course out the front to entice kids of all ages (adult/child $11/6). Just look for the giant kiwi made of driftwood out the front.

ℹ Information

There's no i-SITE in the village, so visit www.nationalpark.co.nz and www.visitruapehu.com for info. The nearest i-SITEs are in **Taumarunui** (p194) and **Ohakune** (p276).

ℹ Getting There & Away

Passing through are buses run by **InterCity** (☎ 09-583 5780; www.intercity.co.nz) and Naked Bus (www.nakedbus.com), as well as the Northern Explorer train run by **KiwiRail Scenic** (p251).

Ohakune

POP 1000

Expect to see carrots crop up all over Ohakune, for this is indisputably the country's carrot capital. Carrots were first grown in the area during the 1920s by Chinese settlers, who cleared the land by hand and explosives. Today the venerable vegetable is celebrated during the annual **Carrot Carnival** (www.carrotcarnival.org.nz; ⏱ early Jun), and immortalised in a roadside tribute – the impossible-to-miss **Big Carrot** (Rangataua Rd), erected in 1984.

A pretty retreat in summer, Ohakune offers many outdoor adventures, including the excellent Old Coach Road mountain-bike trail and also easy access to the Whanganui National Park to the south. Ohakune gets even busier in winter when the snow drifts down on Turoa Ski Area and the snow bunnies invade.

There are two distinct parts to the town: the commercial hub is strung along the highway, but in winter the northern end around the train station, known as the Junction, is the epicentre of the action. The two are linked by the **Mangawhero River Walkway**, a leafy amble taking around 25 minutes on foot.

🏃 Activities

There are several scenic walks near the town, many starting from the Ohakune Mountain Rd, which stretches 17km from Ohakune to the Turoa Ski Area (p270) on Mt Ruapehu. The handy DOC brochure *Walks in and Around Tongariro National Park* ($3), available from the Ruapehu i-SITE, is a good starting point.

The Tongariro Alpine Crossing (p267) is readily accessible via regular shuttle services from Ohakune, while the Round the Mountain track (p270) can be accessed by continuing on the Waitonga Falls track.

Ohakune Old Coach Road
MOUNTAIN BIKING

(www.ohakunecoachroad.co.nz) One of NZ's best half-day (three to four hours) cycle rides, this gently graded route passes engineering features including the historic Hapuawhenua and Toanui viaducts – the only two remaining curved viaducts in the southern hemisphere. It also passes through ancient forests of giant rimu and totara that survived the Taupo blast of AD 180, being in the lea of Ruapehu.

Waitonga Falls Track
TRAMPING

The path to Waitonga Falls (1½ hours return, 4km), Tongariro's highest waterfall (39m), offers magnificent views of Mt Ruapehu. The track starts from Ohakune Mountain Rd.

Ruapehu Homestead
HORSE RIDING

(☎ 027 267 7057; www.ruapehuhomestead.co.nz; cnr Piwara St & SH49, Rangataua; 30min-3hr adult $30-120, child $15-90) Four kilometres east of Ohakune (near Rangataua), Ruapehu Homestead offers guided treks around its paddocks, as well as longer rides along the river and on backcountry trails with views of the mountain.

Canoe Safaris
CANOEING, RAFTING

(☎ 06-385 9237, 0800 272 3353; www.canoesafaris.co.nz; 6 Tay St) Offers guided canoeing trips on the Whanganui River (one to five days, $135 to $1095) and Rangitikei River (one to four days, $195 to $905), plus guided rafting trips on the Mohaka River (two to four days, $505 to $1075). Also offers canoe and kayak hire (two to five days $170 to $205).

Yeti Tours
CANOEING, KAYAKING

(☑0800 322 388, 06-385 8197; www.yetitours.co.nz; 61 Clyde St; guided tours 2-6 days $420-895, hire 2-6-days $175-210) Leads guided canoeing safaris on the Whanganui and Mokau Rivers, and hires canoes and kayaks.

Mountain Bike Station
MOUNTAIN BIKING

(☑06-385 8797; www.mountainbikestation.co.nz; 60 Thames St) Rents mountain bikes (half-/full day from $35/50) and provides transfers to biking routes, including the Ohakune Old Coach Road for $20; bike and transport packages are available. It can also arrange transfers and rentals for the Bridge to Nowhere and Mangapurua tracks on the Whanganui River, and the 17km Turoa Downhill Madness ride down the Mt Ruapehu ski-field access road.

Vertigo Climbing Centre
CLIMBING

(☑06-385 9018; www.slr.co.nz; Goldfinch St; per day adult/child $20/10; ⊙7.30am-8pm Mon-Thu, to midnight Fri, 7am-6pm Sat & Sun winter, limited hours in summer) Vertigo's climbing wall is 12m long and 10m high with over 40 different possible routes. Shoe hire is an additional $4. Summer opening hours are very flexible, so phone ahead to check.

🛏 Sleeping

The prices listed are for summer; expect to pay around 50% more in winter and book well ahead. Savings can be made on winter rates by booking midweek. Booking ahead is also recommended during summer weekends and holidays.

Station Lodge
HOSTEL $

(☑06-385 8797; www.stationlodge.co.nz; 60 Thames St; dm $28, r $70, apt $130-160; @🛜) Housed in a lovely old villa with wooden floors and high ceilings, this excellent YHA hostel has a well-equipped kitchen, comfortable lounge, spa pool, and tidy garden with a pizza oven. If you're after privacy, separate chalets and apartments are available. The clued-up owners also run Mountain Bike Station and Ski & Board Station.

Ohakune Top 10 Holiday Park
HOLIDAY PARK $

(☑0800 825 825, 06-385 8561; www.ohakune.net.nz; 5 Moore St; sites $42, units $66-136; @🛜)

LAKE ROTOKURA

Rotokura Ecological Reserve (www.doc.govt.nz) is 14km southeast of Ohakune, at Karioi (karioi means 'places to linger'), just off SH49. There are two lakes here: the first is Dry Lake, actually quite wet and perfect for picnicking; the furthest is Rotokura, tapu (sacred) to Māori, so eating, fishing and swimming are prohibited. The return-trip walk will take you 45 minutes – longer if you linger to admire the ancient beech trees and waterfowl, such as dabchicks and paradise ducks.

A bubbling stream borders this holiday park, which has a wide range of accommodation, including tidy motel units. Extras include a playground, barbecue area and private spa bath.

Rocky Mountain Chalets
MOTEL $$

(☑06-385 9545; www.rockymountainchalets.com; 20 Rangataua Rd; apt from $190; 🛜) Just out of town in a rural setting, these two- and three-bedroom apartments and chalets are a very good option for families and groups. Each of the chalets is individually owned, so they all feature slightly different style and decor. Many have been refurbished recently, and what's consistent across all the accommodation is spacious and modern design, and self-contained kitchens.

Good discounts for stays of two nights or more.

Snowhaven
APARTMENT, B&B $$

(☑06-385 9498; www.snowhaven.co.nz; 92 Clyde St; apt $95, r $195, townhouse from $195; 🛜) A tasty trio is on offer here: modern studio apartments in a slate-fronted block on the main drag; three self-contained, three-bedroom townhouses by the Junction; or luxury B&B rooms somewhere between the other two. All are top, well-priced options.

Peaks Motor Inn
MOTEL $$

(☑0508 343 732, 06-385 9144; www.thepeaks.co.nz; cnr Mangawhero Tce & Shannon St; units $120-139; 🛜) This well-kept motel offers spacious rooms with good bathrooms and full kitchens. Communal facilities include grassy lawns, a basic gym, large outdoor spa, and sauna. Check the website for good-value packages incorporating transport for the Tongariro Alpine Crossing. The friendly owners definitely have the good oil on things to do and local restaurants.

Powderhorn Chateau
HOTEL **$$**

(☑06-385 8888; www.powderhorn.co.nz; cnr Thames St & Mangawhero Tce; r from $220; @ 🛜 🖳) Enjoying a long-standing reputation as the hub of activity during the ski season, the Powderhorn has a Swiss-chalet feel with woody interiors, slate floors and exposed rafters. The spa-temperature indoor pool is a relaxing way to recover from the slopes before enjoying revelry in the popular in-house establishments.

★ Ruapehu Country Lodge
B&B **$$$**

(☑06-385 9594; www.ruapehucountrylodge.co.nz; 630 Raetihi–Ohakune Rd; d $287; 🛜) Around 4km south of Ohakune on the road to Raetihi, Ruapehu Country Lodge is a perfect combination of elegant and classy decor, and you'll get a friendly welcome from Heather and Peter, the well-travelled and thoroughly unpretentious hosts. Framed by expansive gardens and situated on 2 hectares, the lodge is separated from the local golf course by a meandering river.

Cooked breakfasts are included, and when we dropped by, an outdoor pizza oven was being installed for lazy conversation-fuelled evening meals on spring and summer nights.

✖ Eating

★ Eat
CAFE **$**

(☑027 443 1426; 49 Clyde St; snacks & mains $9-14; ⊙9am-4pm) Bagels, innovative salads, and tasty American and Tex Mex–influenced dishes combine with the best coffee in town at this modern spot on Ohakune's main drag. There's a strong focus on organic ingredients and sustainable practices, and dishes such as the breakfast burrito or the chicken tacos with carrot and cumin slaw really hit the spot after a busy day's adventuring.

Cyprus Tree
ITALIAN **$$**

(☑06-385 8857; www.cyprustree.co.nz; cnr Clyde & Miro Sts; mains $16-34; ⊙9am-late) Open year-round, this restaurant and bar serves up Italian and Kiwi-influenced dishes: think pizza, pasta, risotto and sumac-spiced lamb. The high-season chaos is tempered by a friendly team, and we're pleased to see Ohakune's best range of NZ craft beers join the comprehensive drinks menu, which also features cocktails and wine. Bar snacks are served from 3pm to 5pm.

Bearing Point
INTERNATIONAL **$$**

(☑06-385 9006; Clyde St; mains $26-36; ⊙6pm-late Tue-Sat) Hearty, accomplished fare is offered at this surprisingly chic establishment. Warm your cockles with a venison hot pot, maple-glazed salmon, aged steaks or spicy Thai curry.

Powderkeg
RESTAURANT **$$**

(☑06-385 8888; www.powderhorn.co.nz; cnr Thames St & Mangawhero Tce; bar menu $11-22, mains $22-42; ⊙4pm-late) The Powderkeg is the party bar of the Powderhorn Chateau, with DJs in winter and occasional dancing on the tables. Food-wise, it's also no slouch year-round, with top-notch burgers and pizza, meaty mains such as lamb rump, and another good selection of NZ craft beers that are just the thing after negotiating the Old Coach Road on two wheels.

❶ Information

Ruapehu i-SITE (☑06-385 8427; www.visit ruapehu.com; 54 Clyde St; ⊙8am-5.30pm) Can make bookings for activities, transport and accommodation; DOC officers are usually on hand from 10am to 4.30pm most days.

❶ Getting There & Around

Passing through are buses run by **InterCity** (p251) and Naked Bus (www.nakedbus.com), as well as the Northern Explorer train run by **KiwiRail Scenic** (p251).

Ruapehu Connexions (☑021 045 6665, 06-385 3122; www.ruapehuconnexions.co.nz) is based in Ohakune, offering services around the Ruapehu region, including to biking and walking tracks, the Tongariro Alpine Crossing, and a handy ski-season shuttle around Ohakune's nightlife hot spots.

Waiouru

POP 740

At the junction of SH1 and SH49, 27km east of Ohakune, Waiouru (altitude 792m) is primarily an army base and a refuelling stop for the 56km-long Desert Rd leading to Turangi. A barren landscape of reddish sand with small clumps of tussock, Rangipo Desert isn't actually a desert. This unique landscape is in fact the result of two million years of volcanic eruptions – especially the Taupo eruption about 2000 years ago that coated the land with thick deposits of pumice and destroyed all vegetation. In winter, the road occasionally closes due to snow.

Housed in a large, concrete bunker at the south end of the township, the **National Army Museum** (📞 06-387 6911; www.armymuseum.co.nz; adult/child $15/5; ⊙ 9am-4.30pm) 🏷 preserves the history of the NZ army and its various campaigns, from colonial times to the present. Moving stories are told through displays of arms, uniforms, medals and memorabilia. Until mid-2018, the museum will be hosting a series of special exhibitions marking the centenary of WWI.

Taihape & Around

POP 1500

Taihape, 20km south of Waiouru, enjoys the dubious distinction of being the Gumboot Capital of the World, celebrated with – you guessed it – a giant corrugated gumboot on the main road. It is also the access point for Mokai **Gravity Canyon** (📞 0800 802 864, 06-388 9109; www.gravitycanyon.co.nz; 332 Mokai Rd; ⊙ 9am-5pm), 20km southeast of Taihape, where adrenaline junkies can take a 1km, 170m-high flying-fox ride at speeds of up to 160km/h ($155); dive from the North Island's highest bridge bungy (80m, $179); or swing on the world's highest tandem swing ($159). Multi-thrill packages are available. Slightly less nerve-wracking, but equally spectacular, is a gentle ride on the Hydrolift ($40), a unique in NZ water-powered chairlift.

Taihape is also the nearest town to **River Valley** (📞 06-388 1444; www.rivervalley.co.nz), an adventure centre and lodge 32km to the northeast (follow the signs from Taihape's Gretna Hotel). Its popular half-day white-water rafting trip takes in the thrilling Grade V rapids of the Rangitikei River ($175). Free-style horse treks are also offered, which take in views of Mt Ruapehu, the Ruahine Range and the Rangitikei River (two hours $109, half-day $175). Lodge accommodation (from $31) and camping ($18 per person) are also offered, as are meals in the on-site restaurant, featuring fresh ingredients from the lodge's gardens.

Rotorua & the Bay of Plenty

Best Places to Eat

➜ Macau (p302)

➜ Elizabeth Cafe & Larder (p302)

➜ Post Bank (p307)

➜ Abracadabra Cafe Bar (p291)

➜ Sabroso (p292)

Best Places to Sleep

➜ Koura Lodge (p290)

➜ Warm Earth Cottage (p309)

➜ Moanarua Beach Cottage (p316)

➜ Opotiki Beach House (p317)

➜ Tauranga on the Waterfront (p301)

Why Go?

Captain Cook christened the Bay of Plenty when he cruised past in 1769, and plentiful it remains. Blessed with sunshine and sand, the bay stretches from Waihi Beach in the west to Opotiki in the east, with the holiday hubs of Tauranga, Mt Maunganui and Whakatane in between.

Offshore from Whakatane is New Zealand's most active volcano, Whakaari (White Island). Volcanic activity defines this region, and nowhere is this subterranean spectacle more obvious than in Rotorua. Here the daily business of life goes on among steaming hot springs, explosive geysers, bubbling mud pools and the billows of sulphurous gas responsible for the town's 'unique' eggy smell.

Rotorua and the Bay of Plenty are also strongholds of Māori tradition, presenting numerous opportunities to engage with NZ's rich indigenous culture: check out a power-packed concert performance, chow down at a *hangi* (Māori feast) or skill-up with some Māori arts-and-crafts techniques.

When to Go

➜ The Bay of Plenty is one of NZ's sunniest regions: Whakatane records a brilliant 2350 average hours of sunshine per year! In summer (December to February) maximums hover between 20°C and 27°C. Everyone else is here, too, but the holiday vibe is heady.

➜ Visit Rotorua any time: the geothermal activity never sleeps, and there are enough beds in any season.

➜ The mercury can slide below 5°C overnight here in winter, although it's usually warmer on the coast (and you'll have the beach all to yourself).

❶ Getting There & Around

Air New Zealand (☑ 0800 737 000; www. airnewzealand.co.nz) has direct flights from Tauranga and Rotorua to Auckland, Wellington and Christchurch.

InterCity and ManaBus services connect Tauranga, Rotorua and Whakatane with most other main cities in NZ. Bay Hopper bus services run between Tauranga, Whakatane and Opotiki. Twin City Express buses link Tauranga and Rotorua.

ROTORUA

POP 65,280

Catch a whiff of Rotorua's sulphur-rich, asthmatic airs and you've already got a taste of NZ's most dynamic thermal area, home to spurting geysers, steaming hot springs and exploding mud pools. The Māori revered this place, naming one of the most spectacular springs Wai-O-Tapu (Sacred Waters). Today 35% of the population is Māori, with their cultural performances and traditional *hangi* as big an attraction as the landscape itself.

Despite the pervasive eggy odour, 'Sulphur City' is one of the most touristed spots on the North Island, with nearly three million visitors annually. Some locals say this steady trade has seduced the town into resting on its laurels, and that socially Rotorua lags behind more progressive towns such as Tauranga and Taupo. And with more motels than nights in November, the urban fabric of 'RotoVegas' isn't particularly appealing... but still, where else can you see a 30m geothermal geyser!

History

The Rotorua area was first settled in the 14th century when the canoe *Te Arawa*, captained by Tamatekapua, arrived from Hawaiki at Maketu in the central Bay of Plenty. Settlers took the tribal name Te Arawa to commemorate the vessel that had brought them here.

In the next few hundred years, subtribes spread and divided through the area, with conflicts breaking out over limited territory. A flashpoint occurred in 1823 when the Arawa lands were invaded by tribes from the Northland in the so-called Musket Wars. After heavy losses on both sides, the Northlanders eventually withdrew.

During the Waikato Land War (1863–64) Te Arawa threw in its lot with the government against its traditional Waikato enemies, gaining troop support and preventing East Coast reinforcements getting through to support the Kingitanga (King Movement).

With peace in the early 1870s, word spread of scenic wonders, miraculous landscapes and watery cures for all manner of diseases. Rotorua boomed. Its main attraction was the fabulous Pink and White Terraces, formed by volcanic silica deposits. Touted at the time as the eighth natural wonder of the world, they were destroyed in the 1886 Mt Tarawera eruption.

◉ Sights

◉ City Centre

★ Rotorua Museum   MUSEUM, GALLERY
(Map p284; ☑ 07-350 1814; www.rotoruamuseum. co.nz; Queens Dr, Government Gardens; adult/ child $20/8; ⏰ 9am-5pm Mar-Nov, to 6pm Dec-Feb, tours hourly 10am-4pm, plus 5pm Dec-Feb) This outstanding museum occupies a grand Tudor-style edifice. A 20-minute film on the history of Rotorua, including the Tarawera eruption, runs every 20 minutes from 9am. The **Don Stafford Wing**, dedicated to Rotorua's Te Arawa people, features woodcarving, flax weaving, jade and the stories of the revered WWII 28th Māori Battalion. Also here are two **art galleries** and a cool cafe with garden views (although the best view in town is from the **viewing platform** on the roof).

The museum was originally an elegant spa retreat called the Bath House (1908):

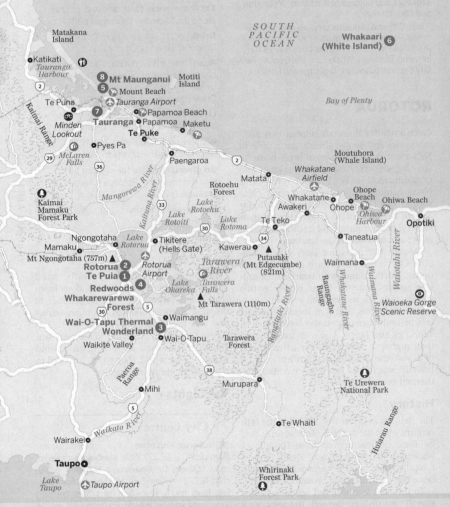

Rotorua & the Bay of Plenty Highlights

1 **Rotorua geysers**
(p279) Watching geysers
blow their tops at Te Puia or
Whakarewarewa.

2 **Rotorua** (p286)
Experiencing one of the
world's best destinations for
mountain biking.

3 **Wai-O-Tapu Thermal
Wonderland** (p295) Ogling
kaleidoscopic colours and
bubbling mud pools.

4 **Redwoods
Whakarewarewa Forest**
(p283) Negotiating shaded
walking tracks and the new
Redwoods Treewalk.

5 **Mt Maunganui** (p304)
Carving up the surf over
NZ's first artificial reef, then
relaxing over a well-earned
local craft beer.

6 **Whakaari (White Island)**
(p315) Flying over or taking
a boat trip out to NZ's only
active marine volcano.

7 **Tauranga** (p298) Dining
in the Strand's excellent
restaurants and cafes.

8 **Mauao** (p304)
Circumnavigating Mt
Maunganui's spectacular
walking track.

MĀORI NZ: ROTORUA & THE BAY OF PLENTY

The Bay of Plenty's traditional name, Te Rohe o Mataatua, recalls the ancestral *Mataatua* canoe, which arrived here from Hawaiki to make an eventful landfall at Whakatane. The region's history stretches back further than that, though, with the Polynesian settler Toi setting up what's claimed to be Aotearoa's first settlement in about AD 800.

Major tribal groups in the region are the **Ngāti Awa** (www.ngatiawa.iwi.nz) of the Whakatane area, **Whakatohea** (www.whakatohea.co.nz) of Opotiki, **Ngāi Te Rangi** (www.ngaiterangi.org.nz) of Tauranga, and **Te Arawa** (www.tearawa.iwi.nz) of Rotorua. Tribes in this region were involved on both sides of the Land Wars of the late 19th century, with those fighting against the government suffering considerable land confiscations that have caused legal problems right up to the present day.

There's a significant Māori population around the region, and many ways for travellers to engage with Māori culture. Opotiki has **Hiona St Stephen's Church** (p317) – the death here of government spy Reverend Carl Volkner in 1865 inspired the charming eyeball-eating scene in *Utu*. Whakatane has a visitor-friendly main-street **marae** (p311; meeting house complex) and **Toi's Pa** (p312), perhaps New Zealand's oldest *pa* (fortified village) site. Rotorua has traditional Māori villages, *hangi* (Māori feasts) and cultural performances aplenty.

displays in the former shower rooms give a fascinating insight into some of the eccentric therapies once administered here, including 'electric baths' and the Bergonie Chair.

Government Gardens
GARDENS

(Map p284; Hinemaru St) The manicured English-style Government Gardens surrounding the Rotorua Museum are pretty as a picture, with roses aplenty, steaming thermal pools dotted about and civilised amenities such as croquet lawns and bowling greens.

Blue Baths
HISTORIC BUILDING

(Map p284; ☑07-350 2119; www.bluebaths.co.nz; Government Gardens; adult/child/family $11/6/30; ◷10am-6pm Nov-Mar) The gorgeous Spanish Mission-style Blue Baths opened in 1933 (and, amazingly, were closed from 1982 to 1999). If you feel like taking a dip, the heated pool awaits.

Lake Rotorua
LAKE

Lake Rotorua is the largest of the district's 16 lakes and is – underneath all that water – a spent volcano. Sitting in the lake is Mokoia Island, which has for centuries been occupied by various subtribes of the area. The lake can be explored by boat, with several operators situated at the lakefront.

Ohinemutu
HISTORIC SITE

(Map p284; FREE) Ohinemutu is a lakeside Māori village (access via Kiharoa, Haukotuku or Korokai Sts off Lake Rd, north of Rotorua Hospital) that traces the fusing of European and Māori cultures. Highlights include the sacred 1905 **Tama-te-kapua Meeting House** (not open to visitors), many steaming volcanic vents, and the historic timber St Faith's Anglican Church, which features intricate Māori carvings, *tukutuku* (woven panels) and a stained-glass window of Christ wearing a Māori cloak as he walks on the waters of Lake Rotorua.

Be respectful if you're visiting the village: this is private land, and locals don't appreciate loud, nosy tourists wandering around taking photos.

St Faith's Anglican Church
CHURCH

(Map p284; ☑07-348 2393; cnr Mataiawhea & Korokai Sts, Ohinemutu; admission by donation; ◷8am-5pm, services 9am Sun & 10am Wed) The historic timber church in the lakeside Māori village of Ohinemutu is intricately decorated with Māori carvings, *tukutuku* (woven panels), painted scrollwork and stained-glass windows. One window features an etched image of Christ wearing a Māori cloak as he appears to walk on the waters of Lake Rotorua.

Kuirau Park
PARK

(Map p284 cnr Ranolf & Pukuatua Sts) FREE Want some affordable geothermal thrills? Just west of central Rotorua is Kuirau Park, a volcanic area you can explore for free. In 2003 an eruption covered much of the park (including the trees) in mud, drawing crowds of spectators. It has a crater lake, pools of boiling mud and plenty of huffing steam. Take care – the pools here are boiling, and accidents have happened.

◉ Thermal Reserve

Te Whakarewarewa
VOLCANIC AREA

(Map p296) Rotorua's main drawcard is Te Whakarewarewa (pronounced 'fa-ka-re-wa-re-wa'), a thermal reserve 3km south of the city centre. This area's full name is Te Whakarewarewatanga o te Ope Taua a Wahiao, meaning 'The Gathering Together of the War Party of Wahiao', although many people just call it 'Whaka'. Either way, the reserve is as famous for its Māori cultural significance as for its steam and bubbling mud. There are more than 500 springs here, including a couple of famed geysers.

Highlights of this volcanically active area include Te Puia and Whakarewarewa Village.

Te Puia
GEYSER, CULTURAL CENTRE

(Map p296; ☑ 0800 837 842, 07-348 9047; www. tepuia.com; Hemo Rd; adult/child tours $49.50/23, daytime tour & performance combos $58/29, evening tour, performance & hangi combos $140/70; ⊙ 8am-6pm Oct-Apr, to 5pm May-Sep) This thermal reserve is 3km south of the city centre, and features more than 500 springs. The most famous is **Pohutu** ('Big Splash' or 'Explosion'), a geyser which erupts up to 20 times a day, spurting hot water up to 30m skyward. You'll know when it's about to blow because the adjacent **Prince of Wales' Feathers** geyser will start up shortly before. Tours (90 minutes) depart hourly from 9am, and daytime 45-minute cultural performances start at 10.15am, 12.15pm and 3.15pm.

Nightly three-hour Te Po indigenous concerts and *hangi* feasts start at 6pm (following on from a 4.30pm tour in a combo package).

Also here is the **National Carving School** and the **National Weaving School**, where you can discover the work and methods of traditional Māori woodcarvers and weavers, plus a carved meeting house, a cafe, galleries, a kiwi reserve and a gift shop.

Whakarewarewa Village
VILLAGE

(Map p296; ☑ 07-349 3463; www.whakarewarewa. com; 17 Tryon St; tour & cultural performance adult/child $35/15; ⊙ 8.30am-5pm, tours hourly 9am-4pm & cultural performances 11.15am & 2pm) Whakarewarewa Thermal Village is a living village where *tangata whenua* (the locals) still reside, as they have for centuries. The villagers show you around and tell you the stories of their way of life and the significance of the steamy bubbling pools, silica terraces and geysers which, although inaccessible from the village, are easily viewed from vantage points (the view of Pohutu is just as good from here as it is from Te Puia, and considerably cheaper).

The village shops sell authentic arts and crafts, and you can learn more about Māori traditions such as flax weaving, carving and *ta moko* (tattooing). Nearby you can eat tasty, buttery sweetcorn ($2) pulled straight out of the hot mineral pool – the only genuine geothermal *hangi* in town. Other bigger *hangi* meal options range from $18.50 to $21 per person.

ROTORUA IN...

Two Days
Have breakfast with lake views at **Third Place Cafe** (p292), then stroll back into town via steamy **Kuirau Park** (p281). Next stop is the fabulous **Rotorua Museum** (p279), followed by a soak at the **Blue Baths** (p281). In the evening, catch a *hangi* and concert at **Tamaki Maori Village** (p293) or **Mitai Maori Village** (p293).

Start the second day with a tour of **Whakarewarewa Village** (p282) and watch Pohutu geyser blow its top. From here, it's a quick hop to the **Redwoods Whakarewarewa Forest** (p283) for a couple of hours exploring and checking out the new **Redwoods Treewalk** (p285).

Four Days
Too much geothermal excitement is barely enough! Explore the hot spots to the south: **Waimangu Volcanic Valley** (p294) and **Wai-O-Tapu Thermal Wonderland** (p295). The nearby **Waikite Valley Thermal Pools** (p297) are perfect for an end-of-day plunge.

On your last day, head southeast and visit the **Buried Village** (p297), swim in **Lake Tarawera** (p295), or take a long walk on one of the tracks at nearby **Lake Okataina** (p286). Back in town, cruise the restaurants and bars on **Tutanekai St** (p291; aka 'Eat Street'), and toast your efforts with a few cold beers at **Brew** (p292).

Surrounds

Redwoods Whakarewarewa Forest FOREST
(Map p296; ☑07-350 0110; www.redwoods.co.nz;
Long Mile Rd, off Tarawera Rd; ☺8.30am-5pm)
FREE This magical forest park is 3km southeast of town on Tarawera Rd. It was originally home to over 170 tree species planted
from 1899 to see which could be grown
successfully for timber. Mighty Californian
redwoods give the park its grandeur today.
Walking tracks range from a half-hour wander through the Redwood Grove to a whole-
day route to the Blue and Green Lakes.
Most walks start from the Redwoods i-SITE
(p294). A recent addition is the spectacular
Redwoods Treewalk (p285).

Aside from walking, the park is great for
picnics, and is acclaimed for its accessible
mountain biking. Mountain Bike Rotorua
(p286) and Planet Bike (p286) offer bike
hire, across the park off Waipa State Mill Rd.

Rainbow Springs WILDLIFE RESERVE
(Map p296; ☑0800 724 626; www.rainbow
springs.co.nz; 192 Fairy Springs Rd; 24hr passes adult/child/family $40/20/99; ☺8.30am-
late) The natural springs here are home to
wild trout and eels, which you can peer at
through an underwater viewer. There are
interpretive walkways, a new 'Big Splash'
water ride, and plenty of animals including
tuatara (a native lizard) and native birds
(kea, kaka and pukeko). A highlight is the
Kiwi Encounter, offering a rare peek into
the lives of these endangered birds: excellent 30-minute tours (an extra $10 per per-
son) have you tiptoeing through incubator
and hatchery areas.

Rainbow Springs is around 3km north of
central Rotorua.

Wingspan National
Bird of Prey Centre BIRD SANCTUARY
(Map p296; ☑07-357 4469; www.wingspan.co.nz;
1164 Paradise Valley Rd, Ngongotaha; adult/child
$25/10; ☺9am-3pm) Wingspan is dedicated
to conserving three threatened NZ birds: the
falcon, the hawk and the owl. Learn about
the birds in the museum display, then take
a sneaky peek into the incubation area before walking through the all-weather aviary.
Don't miss the 2pm flying display.

Paradise Valley Springs WILDLIFE RESERVE
(☑07-348 9667; www.paradisevalleysprings.co.nz;
467 Paradise Valley Rd; adult/child $30/15; ☺8am-
dusk, last entry 5pm) In Paradise Valley at the
foot of Mt Ngongotaha, 8km from Rotorua,

is Paradise Valley Springs, a 6-hectare park
with trout springs, big slippery eels and
various land-dwelling animals such as deer,
alpacas, possums and a pride of lions (fed at
2.30pm). There's also a coffee shop and an
elevated treetop walkway.

Volcanic Hills Winery WINERY
(Map p296; ☑07-282 2018; www.volcanichills.
co.nz; 176 Fairy Springs Rd; tastings three/five wines
$7.50/12.50; ☺11am-7pm Oct-Apr, to 6pm May-Sep)
Excellent wines sourced from iconic NZ viti-
culture areas including Marlborough, Central
Otago and Hawkes Bay; the stupendous views
of the lake and the city definitely add to the
occasion. It can only be reached by the gondola – additional fees apply – but if you purchase
the five-wine tasting option before you go up,
you'll save $2 on the whole experience.

Agrodome AGRICULTURAL
(Map p296; ☑07-357 1050; www.agrodome.co.nz;
141 Western Rd, Ngongotaha; 1hr tours adult/child/
family $47/24/118; 1hr shows $33.50/17/87.50,
tour & show $65/32/154; ☺8.30am-5pm, shows
9.30am, 11am & 2.30pm, tours 10.40am, 12.10pm,
1.30pm & 3.40pm) Learn everything you need
to know about sheep at the Agrodome.
Shows include a parade of champion rams,
a livestock auction, and shearing and doggy
displays. The tour lets you check out farm animals including, among others, sheep. Other
agro-attractions include a shearing-shed
museum and cafe. Yes, some of the jokes are
corny, but it's still a very entertaining show,

Activities

Adventure Sports

Rotorua Canopy Tours ADVENTURE SPORTS
(Map p296; ☑07-343 1001, 0800 226 679; www.
canopytours.co.nz; 173 Old Taupo Rd; 3hr tours per
adult/child/family $139/95/419; ☺8am-8pm Oct-
Apr, to 6pm May-Sep) Explore a 1.2km web of
bridges, flying foxes, zip lines and platforms,
22m high in a lush native forest canopy 10
minutes out of town (...they say that rimu
tree is 1000 years old!). Plenty of native birds
to keep you company. Free pick-ups available.

Agroventures ADVENTURE SPORTS
(Map p296; ☑0800 949 888, 07-357 4747; www.
agroventures.co.nz; Western Rd, off Paradise Valley
Rd, Ngongotaha; 1/2/4/5 rides $49/79/109/189;
☺9am-5pm) Agroventures is a hive of action, 9km north of Rotorua on SH5 (shuttles
available). Start off with the 43m **bungy** and
the **Swoop**, a 130km/h swing. The **Freefall**
Xtreme simulates skydiving, and also here
is the **Shweeb**, a monorail velodrome from

Rotorua

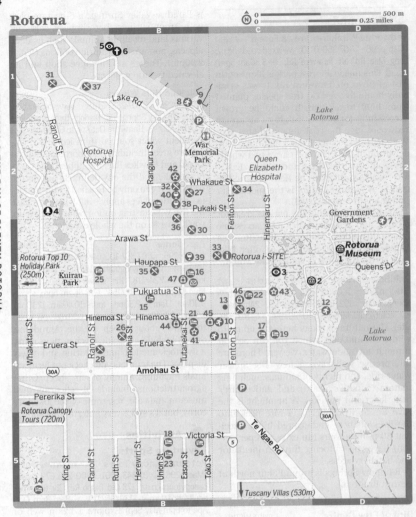

which you hang in a clear capsule and pedal yourself along at speeds of up to 60km/h.

Alongside is the Agrojet, allegedly NZ's fastest jetboat, splashing and weaving around a very tight 1km course.

Zorb ADVENTURE SPORTS
(Map p296; ☑ 07-357 5100, 0800 227 474; www.zorb.com; cnr Western Rd & SH5, Ngongotaha; rides from $39; ☺ 9am-5pm, to 7pm Dec-Mar) The Zorb is 9km north of Rotorua on SH5 – look for the grassy hillside with large, clear, people-filled spheres rolling down it. Your eyes do not deceive you! There are three

courses: 150m straight, 180m zigzag or 250m 'Drop'. Do your zorb strapped in and dry, or freestyle with water thrown in. A recent addition is 'zurfing' where you can ride a boogie board inside one of the giant spheres.

Ogo ADVENTURE SPORTS
(Map p296; ☑ 0800 646 768, 07-343 7676; www.ogo.co.nz; 525 Ngongotaha Rd; rides from $45; ☺ 9am-5pm, to 6.30pm Dec-Feb) The Ogo (about 5km north of town) involves careening down a grassy hillside in a big bubble, with water or without. Silly? Fun? Terrifying? All of the above...

Rotorua

Skyline Rotorua ADVENTURE SPORTS
(Map p296; ☎07-347 0027; www.skyline.co.nz; Fairy Springs Rd; adult/child gondola $28/14; ☺9am-11pm) This gondola ascends Mt Ngongotaha, about 3km northwest of town. There are great lake views, and you can ride a speedy luge back down on three different tracks (three rides adult/child $28/14). For even speedier antics, try the exciting Sky Swing (adult/child $80/67) or the Zoom Zipline ($95/85).

The summit also features a restaurant and cafe, wine-tasting at the Volcanic Hills Winery (p283), and walking tracks and nature trails.

Note the Sky Swing and Zipline prices include the gondola and five luge rides. If you're into fun on two wheels, the new Skyline MTB Gravity Park (p286) combines downhill thrills with gondola access to the summit.

Redwoods Treewalk WALKING
(Map p296; ☎07-350 0110; www.treewalk.co.nz; Redwoods Whakarewarewa Forest; adult/child $25/15; ☺8.30am-6pm) More than 500m is traversed on this suspended walkway combining 21 wooden bridges between century-old redwood trees. Most of the pathway is around 6m off the forest floor, but it ascends to 12m in some parts. The Treewalk opened in January 2016; plans for stage two of the project include raising the height to 20m.

Kawarau Jet BOATING
(Map p284; ☎0800 538 7746, 07-343 7600; www.kjetrotorua.co.nz; Lakefront; 30min adult/child $85/54; ☺9am-6pm) Speed things up on a jetboat ride with Kawarau Jet, which tears around the lake. Parasailing (30 minutes tandem/solo $80/115) is also available.

Adventure Playground ADVENTURE SPORTS
(Map p296; ☎0800 782 396; www.adventureplaygrounc.co.nz; 451 Ngongtaha Rd; from $75) Quad bikes, horse trekking and clay-bird shooting all feature at this versatile adrenaline-fuelled spot. More-leisurely scenic buggy tours through a nearby stand of native forest are also available.

Wall   ROCK CLIMBING

(Map p284; ☑ 07-350 1400; www.basement cinema.co.nz; 1140 Hinemoa St; adult/child incl harness $16/12, shoe hire $5; ⊙ noon-10pm Mon-Fri, 10am-9.30pm Sat & Sun) Get limbered up at the Wall, a three-storey indoor climbing wall with overhangs aplenty.

Mountain Biking

On the edge of town is the Redwoods Whakarewarewa Forest (p283), home to some of the best mountain-bike trails in the country. There are close to 100km of tracks to keep bikers of all skill levels happy for days on end. Note that not all tracks in the forest are designated for bikers, so adhere to the signposts. Pick up a trail map at the forest visitor centre. Another essential destination for mountain bikers is the new Skyline MTB Gravity Park where access up Mt Ngongotaha is provided by a gondola.

Also nearby is the **Te Ara Ahi** ride, one of the New Zealand Cycle Trail's 'Great Rides' (www.nzcycletrail.com). It's an intermediate, two-day, 66km ride heading south of town to Wai-O-Tapu Thermal Wonderland and beyond.

For more information, the Rotorua i-SITE has a special display area dedicated to the growing mountain-biking scene. Online, see www.riderotorua.com.

Skyline MTB Gravity Park   MOUNTAIN BIKING

(☑ 07-347 0027; www.skyline.co.nz/rotorua; Fairy Springs Rd; 1/15 gondola rides with bike $28/55; ⊙ 9am-5pm) More evidence of Rotorua's continued emergence as a world-class mountain-biking destination is the new network of 11 MTB tracks coursing down Mt Ngongotaha. There are options for riders of all experience, and access to the top of the peak is provided by the Skyline gondola (p285). Bike rental (two hours/half day from $60/90) is available on-site from Mountain Bike Rotorua.

Mountain Bike Rotorua   MOUNTAIN BIKING

(Map p296; ☑ 0800 682 768; www.mtbrotorua. co.nz; Waipa State Mill Rd; mountain bikes per 2hr/ day from $35/45, guided half-/full-day rides from $130/275; ⊙ 9am-5pm) This outfit hires out bikes at the Waipa Mill car park entrance to the Redwoods Whakarewarewa Forest (p283), the starting point for the bike trails. You can also stop by their new central Rotorua **adventure hub** (Map p284; ☑ 07-348 4290; www.mtbrotorua.co.nz; 1128 Hinemoa St; ⊙ 9am-5pm) for rentals, mountain-biking information, and a cool little cafe, and they can fit you out with a bike at the Skyline MTB Gravity Park, too.

Planet Bike   BICYCLE RENTAL

(Map p296; ☑ 027 280 2817; www.planetbike. co.nz; Waipa Bypass Rd; mountain bikes per 2hr/day from $35/60) Bike hire and guided mountain-bike rides (three hours/half-day $150/199) in the Redwoods Whakarewarewa Forest (p283).

Tramping

There are plenty of opportunities to stretch your legs around Rotorua, with day walks a speciality. The booklet *Walks in the Rotorua Lakes Area* ($2.50), available from the i-SITE, showcases town walks, including the popular lakefront stroll (20 minutes). See also www.doc.govt.nz.

The **Eastern Okataina Walkway** (three hours one way) goes along the eastern shoreline of Lake Okataina to Lake Tarawera and passes the Soundshell, a natural amphitheatre that has *pa* (fortified village) remains and several swimming spots. The **Western Okataina Walkway** (five hours one way) mimics this route on the western side of the lake.

The **Northern Tarawera Track** (three hours one way) connects to the Eastern Okataina Walkway, creating a two-day walk from either Ruato or Lake Okataina to Lake Tarawera with an overnight camp at either Humphries Bay (sites free) or Tarawera Outlet (sites $6/3 per adult/child). From Tarawera Outlet you can walk on to the 65m **Tarawera Falls** (four hours return). There's a forestry road into Tarawera Outlet from Kawerau, a grim timber town in the shadow of Putauaki (Mt Edgecumbe), off the road to Whakatane; access costs $5, with permits available from the Kawerau Information Centre (p298).

The **Okere Falls** are about 21km northeast of Rotorua on SH33, with an easy track (30 minutes return) past the 7m falls (popular for rafting), through native podocarp (conifer) forest and along the Kaituna River. Along the way is a lookout over the river at Hinemoa's Steps.

Just north of Wai-O-Tapu on SH5, the **Rainbow Mountain Track** (1½ hours one way) is a strenuous walk up the peak known to Māori as Maungakakaramea (Mountain of coloured earth). There are spectacular views from the top towards Lake Taupo and Tongariro National Park. **Hamurana Springs** (Map p296) offers a short walk on the northern edge of Lake Rotorua.

There are also a couple of good walks at Mt Ngongotaha, 10km northwest of Rotorua: the easy 3.2km **Nature Walk** loop through native forest, and the steep 5km return **Jubilee Track** to the (viewless) summit. See www.ngongotaha.org.

Mt Tarawera Volcanic Experience TRAMPING
(Katikati Adventures; ☑0800 338 736; www.mt-tarawera.com; per person $149) Get up close and personal with the massive volcanic landscapes of Mt Tarawera on this guided adventure combining an exciting 4WD drive with a walk around the crater's edge. There's even the opportunity to make a run down the volcanic scree into the crater. Combo deals feature a helicopter ride above the mountain and nearby lakes.

White-Water Rafting, Sledging & Kayaking

There's plenty of kayaking and white-water action around Rotorua with the chance to take on the Grade V **Kaituna River**, complete with a startling 7m drop at Okere Falls. Most of these trips take a day. Some companies head further out to the **Rangitaiki River** (Grade III–VI) and **Wairoa River** (Grade V), raftable only when the dam is opened every second Sunday. Sledging (in case you didn't know) is zooming downriver on a body board. Most operators can arrange transport.

River Rats RAFTING
(☑07-345 6543, 0800 333 900; www.riverrats.co.nz) Takes on the Wairoa ($129), Kaituna ($105) and Rangitaiki ($139), and runs a scenic trip on the lower Rangitaiki (Grade II) that is good for youngsters (adult/child $139/110). Kayaking options include freedom hire ($59/39) and there's also exciting river sledging on the Kaituna ($129).

Wet 'n' Wild RAFTING
(☑0800 462 7238, 07-348 3191; www.wetnwildrafting.co.nz) Runs trips on the Kaituna ($99), Wairoa ($110) and Mokau ($160), as well as easy-going Rangitaiki trips (adult/child $130/100) and longer trips to remote parts of the Motu and Mohaka (two to five days, $650 to $1095).

Raftabout RAFTING
(☑0800 723 822, 07-343 9500; www.raftabout.co.nz) Rafting trips on the Kaituna ($105), Rangitaiki ($139) and Wairoa ($129), plus sledging on the Kaituna ($129). The Kaituna rafting option features the exciting highlight of going over the 7m-high Tutea Falls.

Kaituna Cascades RAFTING, KAYAKING
(☑0800 524 8862, 07-345 4199; www.kaitunacascades.co.nz) Rafting on the Kaituna ($89),

MĀORI CONCERTS & HANGI

Māori culture is a big-ticket item in Rotorua and, although it is commercialised, it's a great opportunity to learn about the indigenous culture of New Zealand. The two big activities are concerts and *hangi* feasts, often packaged together in an evening's entertainment featuring the famous *hongi* (Māori greeting; the pressing of foreheads and noses, and sharing of life breath) and *haka* and *poi* dances.

Tamaki Maori Village (p293) and family-run **Mitai Maori Village** (p293) are established favourites. **Te Puia** (p282) and **Whakarewarewa Village** (p282) also put on shows, and many of the big hotels offer mainstream Māori concerts and *hangi*.

Rangitaiki ($125) and Wairoa ($115), plus kayaking options and combos.

Kaitiaki Adventures RAFTING
(☑0800 338 736, 07-357 2236; www.kaitiaki.co.nz) Offers white-water rafting trips on the Kaituna ($95) and Wairoa ($125) rivers, plus sledging on a Grade III section of the Kaituna ($109).

Kaituna Kayaks KAYAKING
(☑07-362 4486; www.kaitunakayaks.co.nz; guided tours $160, lessons per half-/full day from $199/299) Guided tandem trips and kayaking lessons (cheaper for groups) on the Kaituna River.

Thermal Pools & Massage

Spa/pool complexes in the area include Hells Gate & Wai Ora Spa (p295), 16km northeast of Rotorua, and Waikite Valley Thermal Pools (p297), around 35km south.

Polynesian Spa SPA
(Map p284; ☑07-348 1328; www.polynesianspa.co.nz; 1000 Hinemoa St; private pools per 30min adult/child from $18/7, family pools adult/child/family $22/9/45; ⊗8am-11pm) A bathhouse opened at these Government Gardens springs in 1882, and people have been swearing by the waters ever since. There is mineral bathing (36°C to 42°C) in several pools at the lake's edge, in marble-lined terraced pools and in a larger, main pool. Also here are luxury therapies (massage, mud and beauty treatments; from $89; 10am to 7pm) and a cafe.

Fishing

There's always good trout fishing to be had somewhere around Rotorua. Hire a guide or go solo: either way a licence ($20/45/87 per one/three/nine days) is essential, and available from **O'Keefe's Fishing Specialists** (Map p284; ☑07-346 0178; www.okeefesfishing.co.nz; 1113 Eruera St; ☉8.30am-5pm Mon-Fri, 9am-2pm Sat). You can fish Rotorua's lakefront with a licence, though not all lakes can be fished year-round; check with O'Keefe's or the i-SITE.

Trout Man   FISHING
(☑0800 876 881, 07-357 5255; www.waiteti.com; 2hr/day trips from $40/140) Learn to fish with experienced angler Harvey Clark, from a couple of hours to multiday trips.

Gordon Randle   FISHING
(☑07-349 2555; www.rotoruatrout.co.nz; half-/full-day charters $420/860) Reasonable hourly rates also available.

Other Activities

Ballbusters   GOLF
(Map p284; ☑07-348 9126; www.ballbusters.co.nz; Queens Dr, Government Gardens; ☉9am-7.30pm) Ballbusters has a nine-hole course (adult/child $16/12), minigolf ($12/9) and a driving range (80 balls $11). There's also a baseball batting cage (bucket of balls $10) and the quirky thrills of Bubble Soccer ($35), where participants wearing inflatable plastic domes run around bouncing into each other. Paintball and target shooting complete the action-packed menu.

aMAZEme   MAZE
(Map p296; ☑07-357 5759; www.amazeme.co.nz; 1335 Paradise Valley Rd, Ngongotaha; adult/child/family $16/9/45; ☉9am-5pm) This amazing 1.4km maze is constructed from immaculately pruned, head-high escallonia hedge. Lose yourself (or the kids) in the endless spirals.

Farmhouse   HORSE RIDING
(Map p296; ☑07-332 3771; www.thefarmhouse.co.nz; 55 Sunnex Rd, off Central Rd; 30min/1hr/2hr $26/42/74) North of Lake Rotorua at the Farmhouse you can saddle-up for a short beginners horse-riding trip, or take a longer trek for experienced riders.

☞ Tours

Rotorua Duck Tours   TOUR
(Map p284; ☑07-345 6522; www.rotoruaducktours.co.nz; 1241 Fenton St; adult/child/family $68/38/175; ☉tours 11am, 1pm & 3.30pm Oct-Apr, 11am & 2.15pm May-Sep) Ninety-minute trips in an amphibi-

ous biofuelled vehicle taking in the major sites around town and heading out on to three lakes (Rotorua, Okareka and Tikitapu/Blue). Longer Lake Tarawera trips also available.

Rotorua Paddle Tours   WATER SPORTS
(☑0800 787 768; www.rotoruapaddletours.co.nz; tours from $90; ☉10am & 3pm) Keen to try stand-up paddle boarding without any waves to contend with? This outfit runs 90-minute trips on Lake Rotorua, Lake Rotoiti and the Blue Lake with boundless beautiful scenery and the occasional diversion into relaxing in hot pools. No experience required.

Foris Eco Tours   ECOTOUR
(☑0800 367 471; www.foris.co.nz; adult/child $249/99) ✿ Check out some ancient rainforest on a one-hour walk in Whirinaki Forest Park then raft along the easy-going Rangitaiki River on this full-day trip. Full-day walks also available. Includes lunch, pick-up/drop-off and lots of wildlife-spotting.

Thermal Land Shuttle   TOUR
(☑0800 894 287; www.thermalshuttle.co.nz; adult/child from $70/35) Daily scheduled morning, afternoon and night tours around a selection of key sights, including Waimangu, Wai-O-Tapu, Te Puia and Rainbow Mountain. Transport-only options also available.

Geyser Link Shuttle   TOUR
(☑03-477 9083, 0800 304 333; www.travelheadfirst.com/local-legends/geyser-link-shuttle) Tours of some of the major sights, including Wai-O-Tapu (half-day adult/child $75/35), Waimangu (half-day $75/35), or both (full day $125/65). Trips incorporating Hobbiton and Whakarewarewa are also available.

Volcanic Air   SCENIC FLIGHTS
(Map p284; ☑0800 800 848, 07-348 9984; www.volcanicair.co.nz; Rotorua City Lakefront, Memorial Dr; trips $195-995) A variety of floatplane and helicopter flights taking in Mt Tarawera and surrounding geothermal sites including Hell's Gate, the Buried Village and Waimangu Volcanic Valley. A 3¼-hour Whakaari (White Island)/Mt Tarawera trip tops the price list.

Happy Ewe Tours   BICYCLE TOUR
(☑022 622 9252; www.happyewetours.com; adult/child $55/35; ☉10am & 2pm) Saddle-up for a three-hour, small-group bike tour of Rotorua, wheeling past 20 sights around the city. It's all flat and slow-paced, so you don't need to be at your physical peak (you're on holiday after all).

Mana Adventures
CRUISE, KAYAKING

(Map p284; 📞07-348 4186, 0800 333 660; www.
manaadventures.co.nz; Lakefront; ⏰9am-5pm
Wed-Mon) Down at the lake, Mana Adventures offers (weather permitting) rental pedal
boats (adult/child $10/8 per 20 minutes) and
kayaks ($16/28 per half-hour/hour). A new
addition is walking on water inside a giant
inflatable Mana Ball ($11 per five minutes).

🛏 Sleeping

Rotorua has plenty of holiday parks and an
ever-changing backpacker scene. Generic
motels crowd Fenton St: better and more interesting rooms are away from the main drag.

★ Funky Green Voyager
HOSTEL $

(Map p284; 📞07-346 1754; www.funkygreen
voyager.co.nz; 4 Union St; dm from $27, d with/with-
out bathroom $72/64; @🛜) 🌿 Green on the
outside and the inside – due to several cans
of paint and a dedicated environmental policy – the shoe-free Funky GV features laid-
back tunes and plenty of sociable chat among
a spunky bunch of guests and worldly-
wise owners, who know what you want
when you travel. The best doubles have
bathrooms; dorms are roomy with quality
mattresses and solid timber beds.

Rotorua Thermal Holiday Park
HOLIDAY PARK $

(Map p296; 📞07-346 3140; www.rotoruathermal.
co.nz; 463 Old Taupo Rd; sites from $40, d cabins/
units from $60/95; @🛜⛱) This super-friendly
holiday park on the edge of town sits deep
in the leisure groove, with barbecues, a playground, campsites galore, a shop and a cafe.
There's plenty of room and lots of trees and
open grassy areas, plus hot mineral pools to
soak the day away. Bike hire is available, and
we're big fans of the rustic log cabins.

Rotorua Top 10 Holiday Park
HOLIDAY PARK $

(Map p296; 📞0800 223 267, 07-348 1886; www.
rotoruatop10.co.nz; 1495 Pukuatua St; sites/cabin/
motel from $46/100/150; @🛜⛱) A small but
perfectly formed holiday park with a great
children's playground. The amenities blocks
and mineral hot pools are all kept spick
and span. Cabins are in good nick and have
small fridges and microwaves. Shrubberies
and picnic tables aplenty.

YHA Rotorua
HOSTEL $

(Map p284; 📞07-349 4088; www.yha.co.nz; 1278
Haupapa St; dm $26-29, s $75, d with/without bathroom from $94/80; @🛜) Bright and sparkling
clean, this classy, purpose-built hostel is great
for those wanting to get outdoors, with staff

eager to assist with trip bookings, and storage
for bikes and kayaks. Pricier rooms come with
bathroom, and there's a barbecue area and
deck for hanging out on (though this ain't a
party pad). Off-street parking is a bonus.

Waiteti Trout Stream Holiday Park
HOLIDAY PARK $

(Map p296; 📞07-357 5255, 0800 876 881; www.
waiteti.com; 14 Okona Cres, Ngongotaha; sites $40,
dm/cabin/motel from $30/65/115; @🛜) This
keenly maintained park is a great option if
you don't mind the 8km drive into town. Set
in two tidy garden acres abutting a trout-filled
stream, it's a cute classic with character-filled
motel units, compact cabins, a tidy backpackers lodge and beaut campsites by the stream.
Free kayaks and dinghies; fly-fishing lessons
from $30. And no sulphur smell!

Rock Solid Backpackers
HOSTEL $

(Map p284; 📞07-282 2053; www.rocksolid
rotorua.co.nz; 1140 Hinemoa St; dm $19-27, d with/
without bathroom $90/70; @🛜) Cavernous,
locally owned Rock Solid occupies a former
shopping mall: you might be bunking down
in a florist or a delicatessen. Dorms over the
street are sunny, and there's a big, bright
kitchen. Downstairs is the Wall (p286)
rock-climbing facility, and the hostel's spacious lounge looks right out at the action.
Free wi-fi and a pool table seal the deal.

Rotorua Central Backpackers
HOSTEL $

(Map p284; 📞07-349 3285; www.rotoruacentral
backpackers.co.nz; 1076 Pukuatua St; dm $26-29,
tw & d $64; @🛜) This heritage hostel was
built in 1936 and retains original features
including dark-wood skirting boards and
door frames, deep bathtubs and geothermal-
ly powered radiators. Dorms have no more
than six beds (and no bunks), plus there's a
spa pool and barbecue. Perfect if you're not
looking to party.

Blarney's Rock
HOSTEL $

(Map p284; 📞07-343 7904; www.blarneysrock.
com; 1210 Tutanekai St; dm $23-27, d $60; @🛜)
You might expect a backpackers above an
Irish pub to be effervescing with drunken
antics. Sorry to disappoint: this one's quiet,
clean and comfy, with live-in managers who
ensure the party stays downstairs. It's a small,
homey affair, with a little sunny deck, free wi-
fi, free apple pie twice weekly and hot-water
bottles in your bed on chilly nights.

Astray
MOTEL, HOSTEL $

(Map p284; 📞07-348 1200, 0800 481 200;
www.astray.co.nz; 1202 Pukuatua St; dm/s/d from

$25/45/65, f $105-150; @ wi-fi) Even if you are 6ft 3in, Astray – a 'micro motel' that would probably be more at home in Tokyo than Rotorua – is a decent bet. Clean, tidy, quiet, friendly and central: just don't expect acres of space. Free wi-fi is a bonus.

Crash Palace HOSTEL $

(Map p284; ☎07-348 8842, 0800 892 727; www.crashpalace.co.nz; 1271 Hinemaru St; dm/s/d from $22/45/65; @ wi-fi) Crash occupies a big, blue 1930s hotel near Government Gardens. The atmosphere strikes a balance between party and pristine, without too much of either. The nicest rooms have floorboards, and there's lots of art on the walls, a pool table and DJ console in the lobby, and a beaut terrace out the back. Limited off-street parking.

Tuscany Villas MOTEL $$

(Map p296; ☎07-348 3500, 0800 802 050; www.tuscanyvillasrotorua.co.nz; 280 Fenton St; d from $165; wi-fi) With its Italian-inspired architecture and pointy conifers, this family-owned eye-catcher is the pick of the Fenton St motels. It pitches itself at both corporate and leisure travellers, all of whom appreciate the plush furnishings, multiple TVs, DVD players and deep spa baths. Free wi-fi.

Six on Union MOTEL $$

(Map p284; ☎07-347 8062, 0800 100 062; www.sixonunion.co.nz; 6 Union St; d/f $130/180; wi-fi pool) Hanging baskets ahoy! This modest place is an affordable bonanza with pool and spa, and small kitchenettes in all units. Rooms are functional, and the friendly expat owners (from Yorkshire) keep the swimming-pool area in good nick. It's away from traffic noise, but still an easy walk into town.

Victoria Lodge MOTEL $$

(Map p284; ☎07-348 4039, 0800 100 039; www.victorialodge.co.nz; 10 Victoria St; d/apt from $118/169; wi-fi) The friendly Vic has seen a lot of competitors come and go, maintaining its foothold in the market with individual-feeling apartments and studios with thermally heated plunge pools. Fully equipped, recently renovated apartments can squeeze in seven, though four would be comfortable.

Sandi's Bed & Breakfast B&B $$

(Map p296; ☎0800 726 3422, 07-348 0884; www.sandisbedandbreakfast.co.nz; 103 Fairy Springs Rd; s/d incl breakfast $85/130; wi-fi pool) A friendly family B&B run by the well-humoured Sandi who offers local advice with a ready smile. It's on a busy road a couple of kilometres north of town, so the best bets are the two bohemian chalets out the back with a TV and plenty of room to move.

Ann's Volcanic Motel MOTEL $$

(Map p284; ☎07-347 1007, 0800 768 683; www.rotoruamotel.co.nz; 107 Malfroy Rd; units $119-139; wi-fi) Ann's is an affordable motel with friendly hosts offering loads of local advice. Larger rooms feature courtyard spas and facilities for travellers with disabilities, and a house next door is available for big groups (sleeps nine). Rooms close to the street can be a tad noisy.

★ **Koura Lodge** B&B $$$

(Map p296; ☎07-348 5868; www.kouralodge.co.nz; 209 Kawaha Point Rd; r/ste/apt $465/545/645; wi-fi) Secluded on the lake's western shore, this 10-bedroom lodge features spacious doubles, luxury suites and a two-bedroom apartment. Decks and balconies segue to lake views, and kayaking right from the property is possible. Shared spaces include warm wooden floors, Oriental rugs and a cosy fireplace. Gourmet breakfasts around the huge wooden table are perfect for meeting other travellers.

A spa, sauna and tennis court are all essential diversions.

Mokoia Downs Estate B&B B&B $$$

(Map p296; ☎07-332 2930; www.mokoiadowns.com; 64 Mokoia Rd; s/d $200/250; wi-fi pool) The B&B accommodation here is very comfortable, but the real appeal is the warm welcome from the English-Irish owners Mick and Teresa, plus the other attractions at this great semirural retreat. Say hi to the sheep, donkeys and miniature horses, kick back in the private cinema and library, or sample Mick's liqueurs made from local organic fruit in his microdistillery.

Organic produce also features for breakfast, and there's a solar-heated swimming pool from mid-November to mid-April. Mokoia Downs is around 11km north of central Rotorua.

Regent of Rotorua BOUTIQUE HOTEL $$$

(Map p284; ☎07-348 4079, 0508 734 368; www.regentrotorua.co.nz; 1191 Pukaki St; d/ste from $200/325; wi-fi pool) A renovated 1960s motel, the Regent really delivers. 'The '60s was a glamorous time to travel', say the owners: the decor follows suit, with hip black-and-white tones, funky mirrors, retro wallpaper and colourful splashes. There's a pool and restaurant, the Tutanekai St eateries are an amble away, and there's a whole new wing of rooms next door.

Millennium Hotel Rotorua
HOTEL $$$

(Map p284; ☑ 07-347 1234; www.millennium rotorua.co.nz; cnr Eruera & Hinemaru Sts; d from $200; ⊗ ⊙ ⊛) The slick Māori-inspired lobby sets the scene for this elegant five-storey hotel. Lakefront rooms afford excellent views as does the club lounge, popular with the suits and internationalists swanning about. The poolside *hangi* is fab, as is the in-house restaurant Nikau. Advance booking rates slip into midrange territory.

✖ Eating

The lake end of Tutanekai St – known as 'Eat Streat' – has a strip of eateries beneath a roof, but there are plenty of other options around town.

Mistress of Cakes
BAKERY $

(Map p296; ☑ 07-345 6521 www.mistressof cakes.co.nz; Shop 2, 26 Lynmore Ave; snacks $4-8; ⊙ 8.30am-5.30pm Tue-Fri, 9am-3pm Sat & Sun) Fab muffins, slices, biscuits, scones and quiches, too, all homemade with local ingredients. Mistress of Cakes is now in a new location handily close to the Redwoods Whakarewarewa Forest. A coffee and a stonking sausage roll could be just the thing when you've been walking or mountain biking. Pop in also to see what takeaway ready-made meals are available.

Gold Star Bakery
BAKERY $

(Map p296; ☑ 07-349 1959; 89 Old Taupo Rd; pies $4-5; ⊙ 6am-3pm Mon-Sat) As you head into Rotorua from the north, it's essential that you stop at this award-winning bakery with a stellar reputation for turning out some of NZ's best pies. Great-value savoury treats to devour include chicken and mushroom, or the classic steak 'n' cheese. Good luck choosing from the huge selection.

Coconut Cafe & Restaurant
SOUTH INDIAN $

(Map p284; ☑ 07-343 6556; www.coconutcafe. co.nz; 1240 Fenton St; mains $9-17; ⊙ 11am-3pm & 5-11pm; ☑) Owned by a friendly southern Indian family from Kerala, this riot of yellow and lime-green decor also serves up authentic dishes from nearby Sri Lanka. Try the fish *moilee* (a hearty Keralan-style curry laced with coconut milk), and wash it down with a Kingfisher beer or a refreshing mango lassi. There's also an excellent range of vegetarian options.

Fish & Chip Shop
FISH & CHIPS $

(Map p284; ☑ 07-343 7400; 47 Lake Rd; meals $5-15; ⊙ 11am-8pm Mon-Thu, 11am-8.30pm Fri-Sun) What you see is what you get: top-notch takeaway fish and chips from a little sky-blue shopfront out near Ohinemutu.

Library Store
CAFE $

(Map p284; ☑ 07-346 0018; www.okerefallsstore. co.nz 1127 Haupapa St, Rotorua Public Library; snacks & mains $8-12; ⊙ 7.30am-5pm Mon-Fri, 9am-4pm Sat) Close to the departure point for buses, the Library Store has great coffee, bags of style – secure a sunny spot on the retro furniture out front – and loads of organic, vegetarian and gluten-free options. Slightly less healthy is the tasty option of 'Bratwurst in a Bun', a good choice between sightseeing stops or if you're waiting on a bus.

★ Abracadabra Cafe Bar
MIDDLE EASTERN $$

(Map p284; ☑ 07-348 3883; www.abracadabra cafe.com; 1363 Amohia St; mains $15-30, tapas $10-15; ⊙ 10.30am-11pm Tue-Sat, to 3pm Sun) Channelling Spain, Mexico and Morocco, Abracadabra is a magical cave of spicy delights, from beef-and-apricot tagine to king-prawn fajitas and Tijuana pork chilli. There's a great beer terrace out the back – perfect for combining a few local craft brews and shared tapas. We can highly recommend the breakfast burrito and a revitalising bottle of kombucha for the morning after.

Atticus Finch
BISTRO $$

(Map p284; ☑ 07-460 0400; www.atticusfinch. co.nz; 1106 Tutanekai St, Eat Street; shared plates $15-32; ⊙ noon-3pm & 5pm-late) With a Harper Lee cocktail, the iconic novel *To Kill a Mockingbird* certainly features at this relaxed spot along Eat Streat. Beyond the literary references, the menu of shared plates channels Asian and Mediterranean flavours – try the chilli and ginger prawns or the mozzarella balls – and a concise menu of NZ beer and wine imparts a local flavour.

The cheese or charcuterie platters ($17 to $34) are good value for snacking couples or grazing groups.

Thai Restaurant
THAI $$

(Map p284; ☑ 07-348-6677; www.thethai restaurant.co.nz; 1141 Tutanekai St; mains $20-28; ⊙ noon-2.30pm & 5pm-late) Our pick of the global selection of ethnic eateries along Tutanekai St, the Thai Restaurant overcomes an unimaginative name with excellent service and top-notch renditions of classics you previously enjoyed on Koh Samui or Khao San Rd. Seafood is particularly good – try the squid with basil or the scallops with garlic and black pepper.

Leonardo's Pure Italian ITALIAN $$

(Map p284; ☑ 07-347 7084; www.facebook.com/
LeonardosPureItalian; 1099 Tutanekai St, Eat Streat;
mains $22-34; ⏲ 5-9.30pm Sun-Wed, 11.30am-
2.30pm & 5-9.30pm Thu-Sat) Now relocated to
Rotorua's 'Eat Streat', Leonardo's goes heavy
on the hokey 'just like mama used to make'
marketing, but what comes out of the kitch-
en is far from kitsch. Try the simple but perfect gnocchi with tomato, mozzarella and
pesto, or the angel-hair pasta with mussels
and anchovies.

Third Place Cafe CAFE $$

(Map p284; ☑ 07-349 4852; www.thirdplacecafe.
co.nz; 36 Lake Rd; mains $14-19; ⏲ 7.30am-4pm
Mon-Fri, to 3.30pm Sat & Sun) This interesting
cafe is away from the hubbub and has awesome lake views. All-day breakfast/brunch
sidesteps neatly between fish and chips, and
an awesome 'mumble jumble' of crushed
kumara (sweet potato), green tomatoes and
spicy chorizo topped with bacon, a poached
egg and hollandaise sauce. Hangover? What
hangover? Slide into a red-leather couch or
score a window seat overlooking Ohinemutu.

Fat Dog Cafe & Bar CAFE $$

(Map p284; ☑ 07-347 7586; www.fatdogcafe.
co.nz; 1161 Arawa St; mains breakfast & lunch $12-
26, dinner $28-32; ⏲ 7am-9pm; ☑ 🖘 🌸) With
paw prints and silly poems painted on the
walls, this is the town's friskiest and most
child-friendly cafe. During the day it dishes
up burgers (try the Dogs Bollox version), nachos, salads and massive sandwiches; in the
evening it's candlelit lamb and venison. Fine
craft brews from Kawerau's Mata Beer are
also served. Try the hoppy Tumeke NZ IPA.

Sabroso LATIN AMERICAN $$

(Map p284; ☑ 07-349 0591; www.sabroso.co.nz;
1184 Haupapa St; mains $19-30; ⏲ 5-9pm Wed-
Sun) This modest Latin American cantina –
adorned with sombreros, guitars and salt-
and-pepper shakers made from Corona bottles – serves zingy south-of-the-border fare.
The black-bean chilli and the calamari tacos
are excellent, as are the zesty margaritas.
Booking ahead is highly recommended as
Sabroso is *muy popular*. Buy a bottle of the
owners' hot sauce to enliven your next Kiwi
barbecue.

Urbano Bistro MODERN NZ $$

(Map p296; ☑ 07-349 3770; www.urbanobistro.
co.nz; cnr Fenton & Grey Sts; mains breakfast &
lunch $14-21, dinner $24-43; ⏲ 9am-11pm Mon-
Sat, to 3pm Sun) This hip suburban diner,
with mega-checkerboard carpet and curvy
wallpaper, is a bold move by reputable local restaurateurs. Try the beef, pineapple
and kumara curry – rich in flavour and well
executed. Fine wines and five-star service to
boot. During the day it's a more casual and
good-value cafe.

Lime Caffeteria CAFE $$

(Map p284; ☑ 07-350 2033; cnr Fenton &
Whakaue Sts; mains $13-24; ⏲ 7.30am-4.30pm;
☑) Occupying a quiet corner near the lake,
this zesty cafe offers alfresco breakfasts and
dishes with a welcome twist: try the chicken-
and-chorizo salad or prawn-and-salmon risotto in lime sauce. Classy counter snacks
and excellent coffee.

Bistro 1284 MODERN NZ $$$

(Map p284; ☑ 07-346 1284; www.bistro1284.
co.nz; 1284 Eruera St; mains $36-42; ⏲ 6pm-late)
A fine-dining hot spot on an unremarkable
stretch of Eruera St, this intimate place (all
chocolate and mushroom colours) serves
stylish NZ cuisine with Asian and European influences. Try the pecan-crusted lamb,
and definitely leave room for a dessert of the
peach and mango crumble.

🍷 Drinking & Nightlife

Brew CRAFT BEER

(Map p284; ☑ 07-346 0976; www.brewpub.co.nz;
1103 Tutanekai St, Eat Streat; ⏲ 11am-late Mon-
Fri, 9am-late Sat & Sun) Run by the lads from
Croucher Brewing Co, Rotorua's best micro-
brewers, Brew sits in a sunny spot on Rotorua's 'Eat Streat'. Thirteen taps showcase
the best of Croucher's brews as well as guest
beers from NZ and overseas. Try the hoppy
Croucher Pilsner with the pulled pork and
prawn pizza. Good coffee, too, plus occasional Friday night bands and DJs.

Ponsonby Rd COCKTAIL BAR

(Map p284; ☑ 021 640 292; www.ponsonbyrd.
co.nz; 1109 Tutanekai St, Eat Streat; ⏲ 5pm-late)
Former TV weatherman Tamati Coffey has
introduced flash big-city style to Rotorua –
the bar is named after Auckland's pre-
eminent eating and drinking strip. Drenched
in red light and trimmed with velvet, the decor is certainly vibrant, and cosy booths are
perfect for sipping on cocktails named after
local Māori legends. Look forward to live
music from 9pm most weekends.

Pig & Whistle PUB

(Map p284; ☑ 07-347 3025; www.pigandwhistle.
co.nz; cnr Haupapa & Tutanekai Sts; ⏲ 11am-late)

Inside a former police station, this busy pub serves up frosty lager, big-screen TVs, a beer garden and live music Thursday to Saturday, plus solid grub (mains $19 to $32). The menu runs the gamut from harissa-spiced chicken salad to hearty burgers and vegetarian nachos.

☆ Entertainment

Mitai Maori Village MĀORI CONCERT
(Map p296; ✆07-343 9132; www.mitai.cc.nz; 196 Fairy Springs Rd; adult/family $116/315, child $23-58; ⊙6.30pm) This family-run outfit offers a popular three-hour evening event with a concert, *hangi* and glowworm bushwalk. The experience can be combined with a tour of Rainbow Springs Kiwi Wildlife Park next door, with coloured nightlights and a walk through the kiwi enclosure (four hours total, adult/child five to nine years/child 10 to 15 years $148/43/80). Pick-ups available. A concert-only option is also available.

Tamaki Maori Village MĀORI CONCERT
(Map p284; ✆0508 826 254, 07-349 2999; www.tamakimaorivillage.co.nz; booking office 1220 Hinemaru St; adult/family $115/310, child $25-65; ⊙tours depart 5pm, 6.15pm & 7.30pm Nov-Apr, 6.15pm May-Oct) Tamaki does a twilight tour to a *marae* (meeting house) and Māori village 15km south of Rotorua. Buses collect from the Hinemaru St booking office and local accommodation. The experience is very hands-on, taking you on an interactive journey through Māori history, arts, traditions and customs from pre-European times to the present day. The concert is followed by a *hangi*.

Basement Cinema CINEMA
(Map p284; ✆07-350 1400; www.basementcinema.co.nz; 1140 Hinemoa St; tickets $15; ⊙noon-10pm Mon-Fri, 10am-10pm Sat & Sun) The Basement offers up offbeat, foreign-language and art-house flicks. Tickets are just $10 on Tuesdays.

Novotel Rotorua MĀORI CONCERT
(Map p284; ✆07-346 3888; www.novotelrotorua.co.nz; 11 Tutanekai St; concerts adult/child $39/18, incl hangi $69/19) Entertaining shows include a live performance from local Māori performers and a *hangi*. Held near the lake in the Matariki Cultural Centre.

Millennium Hotel Rotorua MĀORI CONCERT
(Map p284; ✆07-347 1234; www.millennium-rotorua.co.nz; cnr Eruera & Hinemaru Sts; adult/child incl hangi $70/35) Entertaining shows include a live performance from local Māori

performers and a *hangi*. Held poolside for excellent photo opportunities.

🔒 Shopping

Maori Made CLOTHING, CRAFTS
(Map p284; ✆022 047 5327, 021 065 9611; maorimade.rotorua@gmail.com; 1180 Hinemoa St; ⊙10am-5pm Mon-Fri, to 2pm Sat) Traditional and contemporary Māori design merge at this excellent shop showcasing work from several local designers. Apparel, homewares, weaving and jewellery are all represented, and much of the work is uniquely available at this shop. Check out the quirky Kiwiana T-shirts from Paua Frita, stylish women's fashion from Mereana Ngatai, or Mahi Toi's vibrant paintings.

Rākai Jade CRAFTS
(Map p284; ✆027 443 9295; www.rakaijade.co.nz; 1234 Fenton St) In addition to purchasing off-the-shelf *pounamu* (jade) pieces, you can work with Rākai's on-site team of local Māori carvers to design and carve your own pendant or jewellery. A day's notice for 'Carve Your Own' experiences ($150 to $180) is preferred if possible. Look forward to spending a full day creating your personal memento of Rotorua.

Rotorua Night Market MARKET
(Map p284; www.facebook.com/rotoruanightmarket; Tutanekai St; ⊙5pm-late Thu) Tutanekai St is closed off on Thursday nights between Haupapa and Pukuatua Sts to allow the Rotorua Night Market to spread its wings. Expect local arts and crafts, souvenirs, cheesy buskers, coffee, wine and plenty of deli-style food stalls for dinner.

Moko 101 ARTS
(Map p284; ✆022 129 2468; www.facebook.com/MOKO101; 1130a Hinemoa St; tattooing per hour $150; ⊙10am-5pm Mon-Fri) Traditional *ta moko* (Māori tattooing) is offered here. Painting and mixed-media work from local Māori artists is also displayed and for sale.

ℹ Information

Lakes Care Medical (✆07-348 1000; 1165 Tutanekai St; ⊙8am-8pm Mon-Fri) Urgent medical care.

Police (✆07-348 0099; www.police.govt.nz; 1190 Fenton St; ⊙24hr) Centrally located.

Post Office (Map p284; www.nzpost.co.nz; cnr Tutanekai & Pukuatua Sts; ⊙9am-5pm Mon-Fri, to 1pm Sat) Centrally located.

Redwoods i-SITE (Map p296; ☑ 07-350 0110; www.redwoods.co.nz; Long Mile Rd, off Tarawera Rd; ⊙ 8.30am-5.30pm Mon-Fri, 10am-5pm Sat & Sun Oct-Mar, 8.30am-4.30pm Mon-Fri, 10am-4pm Sat & Sun Apr-Sep) Information centre for the **Redwoods Whakarewarewa Forest** (p283).

Rotorua Hospital (☑ 07-348 1199; www.lakesdhb.govt.nz; Arawa St; ⊙ 24hr) Round-the-clock medical care.

Rotorua i-SITE (Map p284; ☑ 0800 768 678, 07-348 5179; www.rotoruanz.com; 1167 Fenton St; ⊙ 7.30am-6pm) The hub for travel information and bookings, including Department of Conservation (DOC) walks. Also has a cafe, showers and lockers, and plenty of information on Rotorua's world-class mountain-biking scene.

❶ Getting There & Away

AIR

Air New Zealand (☑ 0800 737 000; www.airnewzealand.co.nz) flies to/from Auckland, Wellington and Christchurch.

Sunair (www.sunair.co.nz) has flights to/from Gisborne and Auckland's smaller North Shore airport.

BUS

All the major bus companies stop outside the Rotorua i-SITE, where you can arrange bookings.

InterCity destinations include the following:

DESTINATION	PRICE	TIME (HR)	FREQUENCY
Auckland	$66	3½	7 daily
Gisborne	$60	4½	1 daily
Hamilton	$43	1½	5 daily
Napier	$66	4	1 daily
Taupo	$29	1	4 daily
Tauranga	$29	1½	2 daily
Wellington	$65	7	5 daily
Whakatane	$46	1½	1 daily

ManaBus services include the following:

DESTINATION	PRICE	TIME (HR)	FREQUENCY
Auckland	$15	4hr	3 daily
Gisborne	$19	4¾hr	1 daily
Hamilton	$10	1½hr	3 daily
Napier	$18	3hr	3 daily
Taupo	$8	1hr	3 daily
Tauranga	$10	1½hr	3 daily
Wellington	$19	8hr	1 daily
Whakatane	$14	1½hr	1 daily

Twin City Express (☑ 0800 422 928; www.baybus.co.nz) buses run twice daily Monday to Friday between Rotorua and Tauranga/Mt Maunganui via Te Puke ($11.60, 1½ hours).

❶ Getting Around

TO/FROM THE AIRPORT

Rotorua Regional Airport (ROT; Map p296; ☑ 07-345 8800; www.rotorua-airport.co.nz; SH30) is 10km northeast of town. **Super Shuttle** (☑ 09-522 5100, 0800 748 885; www.supershuttle.co.nz; 1st passenger/each additional passenger $21/5) offers a door-to-door airport service. Baybus (www.baybus.co.nz) runs an airport bus service (route 10, $2.60). A taxi to/from the city centre costs about $30.

BUS

Many local attractions offer free pick-up/drop-off shuttle services. Shuttle services are also available to/from outlying attractions.

Baybus (☑ 0800 422 928; www.baybus.co.nz) operates local bus services around town, and also to Ngongotaha (route 1, $2.60) for Rainbow Springs, Skyline Rotorua, Agroventures and Zorb, and to the airport (route 10, $2.60). Catch route 3 ($2.60) for the Redwoods Whakarewarewa Forest.

CAR

The big-name car-hire companies vie for your attention at Rotorua Airport. Otherwise, try **Rent a Dent** (☑ 07-349 3993; www.rentadent.co.nz; 39 Fairy Springs Rd; ⊙ 8am-5pm Mon-Fri, to noon Sat).

TAXI

Rotorua Taxis (☑ 07-348 1111; www.rotoruataxis.co.nz) Well-established Rotorua taxi company.

AROUND ROTORUA

Highlights of this area include Lake Tarawera, where visitors can explore the lake on a boat tour or hike the Tarawera Trail. The region's explosive volcanic past and present is on display at interesting sites including Wai-O-Tapu Thermal Wonderland, Waimangu Volcanic Valley and Hells Gate & Wai Ora Spa.

⊙ Sights

Waimangu Volcanic Valley

VOLCANIC AREA, SPRING

(Map p296; ☑ 07-366 6137; www.waimangu.co.nz; 587 Waimangu Rd; adult/child walking tours $37/12, boat cruises $42.50/12; ⊙ 8.30am-5pm, to 6pm Jan, last admission 3pm, 4pm Jan) This thermal area was created during the eruption of Mt Tarawera in 1886. The downhill stroll through the valley passes spectacular thermal and volcanic features, including **Inferno Crater Lake**, where overflowing water can reach 80°C, and **Frying Pan Lake**, the largest hot spring in the world. The walk continues down to Lake Rotomahana (Warm Lake), where options include a return shuttle or a 45-minute lake boat trip past steaming cliffs and the former site of the Pink and White Terraces.

Waimangu (Black Water) refers to the dark, muddy colour of much of the water here. The site is 20 minutes south of Rotorua, 14km along SH5 (towards Taupo) and then 6km from the marked turn-off.

Lake Tarawera   LAKE

(Tarawera Rd) Pretty Lake Tarawera offers swimming, fishing, cruises and walks. **Clearwater Cruises** (Map p296; ☑ 027 362 8590, 07-345 6688; www.clearwater.co.nz; per hour cruise vessels/self-drive runabouts $550/145) runs scenic cruises and self-drive boat options, while Lake Tarawera Water Taxi & Eco Tours (p298) offers boat trips and water taxi transfers (must be prebooked) to Hot Water Beach and for the Tarawera Trail (p297; 15km, five to six hours). The **Landing Café** (Map p296; ☑ 07-362 8502; www.thelanding laketarawera.co.nz; mains $15-40; ☑ 10am-late) offers fresh fruit ice creams and lake views. There's a privately run campsite (boat access only; prebooking required) at **Hot Water Beach** (Map p296; ☑ 07-349 3463; www.whakarewarewa.com/tarawera; adult/child $10/5), and a DOC-managed site at **Tarawera Outlet**. (Map p296; ☑ 07-323 6300; www.doc.govt.nz; adult/child $6/3). The Blue Lake Top 10 Holiday Park (p298) offers camping next to the Blue Lake.

Tarawera means 'Burnt Spear', named by a visiting hunter who left his bird spears in a hut and on returning the following season found both the spears and hut had been burnt.

Wai-O-Tapu Thermal
Wonderland   VOLCANIC AREA, GEYSER

(Map p296; ☑ 07-366 6333; www.waiotapu.co.nz; 201 Waiotapu Loop Rd, off SH5; adult/child/family $32.50/11/80; ☑ 8.30am-5pm, last admission 3.45pm) Wai-O-Tapu (Sacred Waters) has several interesting geothermal features packed into a small area, including the boiling, multihued **Champagne Pool**, bubbling **mud pool**, stunning **mineral terraces** and **Lady Knox Geyser**, which spouts off (with a little

---

WORTH A TRIP

WHIRINAKI FOREST PARK

This lush podocarp (conifer) forest park offers canyons, waterfalls, lookouts and streams, plus the **Oriuwaka Ecological Area** and **Arahaki Lagoon**. Walking tracks here vary in length and difficulty: the DOC booklet *Walks in Whirinaki Forest* ($2.50) details walking and camping options. Pick one up at DOC's **Murupara visitor centre** (☑ 07-366 1080; www.doc.govt.nz; SH38; ☑ 9am-5pm Mon-Fri).

A good short walk is the **Whirinaki Waterfalls Track** (four hours return), which follows the Whirinaki River. Longer walks include the **Whirinaki Track** (two days), which can be combined with **Te Hoe Track** (four days). There's also a rampaging 16km **mountain-bike track** here.

Whirinaki Forest Park is 90km southeast of Rotorua off SH38, en route to Te Urewera National Park (take the turn-off at Te Whaiti to Minginui). There are several accessible camping areas and 10 backcountry huts (free to $15) in the park; pay at the DOC office.

---

prompting from an organic soap) punctually at 10.15am and gushes up to 20m for about an hour (be here by 9.45am to see it). Wai-O-Tapu is 27km south of Rotorua along SH5 (towards Taupo), and a further 2km from the marked turn-off.

Hells Gate & Wai Ora Spa   VOLCANIC AREA

(Map p296; ☑ 07-345 3151; www.hellsgate. co.nz; SH30, Tikitere; admission adult/child/family $35/17.50/85, mud bath & spa $75/35/185; ☑ 8.30am-8.30pm) Known as Tikitere to the Māori, Hells Gate is an impressive geothermal reserve 16km northeast of Rotorua on the Whakatane road (SH30). The reserve covers 10 hectares, with a 2.5km walking track to the various attractions, including a hot thermal waterfall. You can see a master woodcarver at work, and learn about flax weaving and other Māori traditions.

Long regarded by Māori as a place of healing, Tikitere also houses Wai Ora Spa, where you can get muddy with a variety of treatments. A courtesy shuttle to/from Rotorua is available.

Tikitere is an abbreviation of *Taku tiki i tere nei* (My youngest daughter has floated

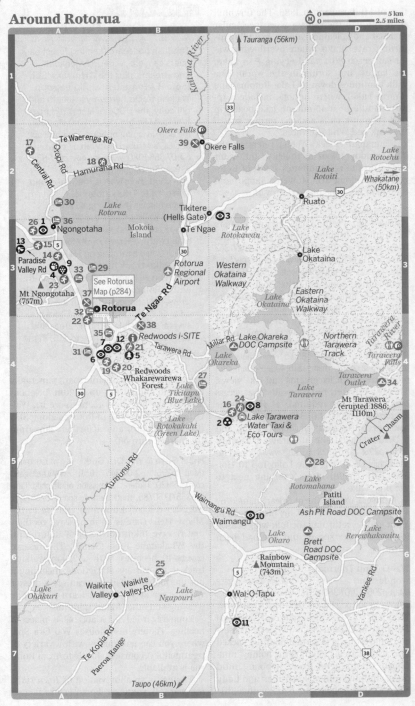

Around Rotorua

N

0   5 km
0   2.5 miles

Tauranga (56km)

Kaituna River

33

Okere Falls

39 Okere Falls

Te Waerenga Rd

17

Oropi Rd

Central Rd

18 Hamurana Rd

Lake
Rotoehu

Lake
Rotoiti

Whakatane
(50km)

30

30

Lake
Rotorua

Ruato

30

Tikitere
(Hells Gate)

3

26 1 36
Ngongotaha

Te Ngae

Mokoia
Island

Lake
Rotokawau

13 15
5

14

Paradise
Valley Rd

9

4

33 29

23

Lake
Okataina

Lake
Okataina

Lake
Okataina

Western
Okataina
Walkway

Eastern
Okataina
Walkway

Lake
Okataina

37

Mt Ngongotaha
(757m)

32

22

Rotorua

Te Ngae Rd

Rotorua
Regional
Airport

30

See Rotorua
Map (p284)

38

35 Redwoods i-SITE

7 12

31

6

21

5

Tarawera Rd

Millar Rd

Lake
Okareka
DOC Campsite

Northern
Tarawera
Track

Tarawera River

Tarawera
Falls

19 20

Redwoods
Whakarewarewa
Forest

27

Lake
Tikitapu
(Blue Lake)

Lake
Okareka

Lake
Tarawera

Tarawera
Outlet

34

Mt Tarawera
(erupted 1886;
1110m)

16 24

2

8

Lake Tarawera
Water Taxi &
Eco Tours

Lake
Rotokakahi
(Green Lake)

28

Crater

Chasm

30

5

Tumunui Rd

Lake
Rotomahana

Patiti
Island

Ash Pit Road DOC Campsite

Waimangu Rd

10

Waimangu

Lake
Okaro

Brett
Road DOC
Campsite

Lake
Rerewhakaaitu

Yankee Rd

Rainbow
Mountain
(743m)

5

25

Waikite
Valley

Waikite
Valley Rd

Lake
Ngapouri

Wai-O-Tapu

Lake
Ohakuri

11

Te Kopia Rd

Paeroa Range

38

Taupo (46km)

Around Rotorua

away), remembering the tragedy of a young girl jumping into a thermal pool. The English name originates from a 1934 visit by George Bernard Shaw.

Buried Village   ARCHAEOLOGICAL SITE
(Map p296; ☑07-362 8287; www.buriedvillage. co.nz; 1180 Tarawera Rd; adult/child/family $32.50/10/65; ⊙9am-5pm Nov-Mar, to 4.30pm Apr-Oct) Fifteen kilometres from Rotorua on Tarawera Rd, beyond the Blue and Green Lakes, is the buried village of Te Wairoa, interred by the 1886 eruption of Mt Tarawera. Te Wairoa was the staging post for travellers coming to see the Pink and White Terraces.

Today a museum houses objects dug from the ruins, and guides in period costume escort groups through the excavated sites. There's also a walk to the 30m **Te Wairoa Falls** and a teahouse for coffee and snacks.

Booking ahead online offers a good discount.

🏃 Activities

Tarawera Trail   TRAMPING
(Map p296) Starting at the Te Wairoa car park on Tarawera Rd, a 15-minute drive from Rotorua, this recently opened track

(five to six hours) meanders 15km along Lake Tarawera's edge and through forest to Hot Water Beach where there is camping (p295) available. Water taxis (p298) (must be prebooked) ferry passengers to and from Tarawera Landing and Hot Water Beach. Download the Tarawera Trail brochure from www.doc.govt.nz.

Waikite Valley Thermal Pools   HOT SPRING
(Map p296; ☑07-333 1861; www.hotpools. co.nz; 648 Waikite Valley Rd; public pools adult/ child/family $16.50/9/42, private pools 40min per person $20; ⊙10am-9pm) Around 35km south of Rotorua are these excellent open-air pools, formalised in the 1970s but utilised for centuries before then. There are four main pools: two more relaxing, smaller pools, and four private spas, all ranging from 35°C to 40°C. There's also a cafe and camping (adult/child unpowered sites $22/11, powered sites $25/13; pools free for campers).

To get here, turn right off SH5 opposite the Wai-O-Tapu turn-off, and continue 6km (worth the drive if only for the gorgeous valley view as you come over the hill).

⌕ Tours

Awhina Wilderness Experience   TRAMPING
(📞 027 329 0996; www.awhinatours.co.nz; per
person $100) Offers five-hour walking tours
with local Māori guides through virgin bush
to the summit of Titiraupenga, their sacred
mountain.

🛏 Sleeping & Eating

Blue Lake Top 10 Holiday Park HOLIDAY PARK $
(Map p296; 📞 07-362 8120, 0800 808 292;
www.bluelaketop10.co.nz; 723 Tarawera Rd; sites
from $45, units $80-185; @ 🛜) Offers camping next to the Blue Lake (good for swimming and kayaking), 6km before you get to
Lake Tarawera; well run, this holiday park
has spotless facilities and a handy range of
cabins.

Okere Falls Store   CAFE $
(Map p296; 📞 07-362 4944; www.okerefalls
store.co.nz; SH33, Okere Falls; snacks $5-15;
⊙ 7am-7pm, beer garden to 8.30pm Sat) Around
20km from Rotorua, Okere Falls Store is
definitely worth the short and very scenic
drive. Cool down on the raffish balcony
with fruit smoothies and great views of
Lake Rotoiti, or kick back in the beer garden with wine, local craft brews and delicious home-baked savoury pies. There's
also a very good deli with artisan produce
from around NZ.

If you time it right, you'll be at Okere
Falls Store for its annual beer festival in late
October.

ⓘ Information

Kawerau Information Centre (📞 07-323
6300; www.kawerauonline.com; Plunkett St
bus terminal; ⊙ 9am-4pm) The visitor centre at
Kawerau, on the road to Tarawera, has details
on local accommodation and sells permits to
access walks and camping at Tarawera Outlet
and Tarawera Falls.

ⓘ Getting There & Around

There's little public transport around Rotorua,
but **Rotorua Duck Tours** (p288) make trips to
Lake Tarawera.

Lake Tarawera Water Taxi & Eco Tours (Map
p296; 📞 07-362 8080; www.ecotoursrotorua.
co.nz; 1375 Tarawera Rd; adult/child $65/35;
⊙ departs at 2pm) Boat trips on Lake Tarawera
taking in the opportunity for a dip at Hot Water
Beach. Also run pick-ups from the Hot Water
Beach end of the Tarawera Trail.

BAY OF PLENTY

The Bay of Plenty stretches along the
pohutukawa-studded coast from Waihi Beach
to Opotiki and inland as far as the Kaimai
Range. This is where New Zealanders have
come on holiday for generations, lapping up
salt-licked activities and lashings of sunshine.

Tauranga

POP 117,600

Tauranga (pronounced 'toe-rung-ah') has
been booming since the 1990s, and remains
one of NZ's fastest-growing cities – especially popular with families and retirees cashing
up from Auckland's hyperkinetic real-estate
market. It's also NZ's busiest port – with
petrol refineries and mountains of coal and
lumber – but it's beach-seeking holidaymakers who have seen the old workhorse reborn
as a show pony. Restaurants and bars line the
vamped-up waterfront, fancy hotels rise high,
and the once-sleepy burbs of Mt Maunganui
and Papamoa have woken up to new prosper-
ity. This is about as Riviera as NZ gets.

ⓞ Sights

★ **Tauranga Art Gallery**   GALLERY
(📞 07-578 7933; www.artgallery.org.nz; cnr Wharf &
Willow Sts; ⊙ 10am-4.30pm) FREE The Tauranga
Art Gallery presents historic and contemporary art, and houses a permanent collection
along with frequently changing local and visiting exhibitions. The building itself is a former bank, although you'd hardly know it – it's
an altogether excellent space with no obvious
compromise. Touring the ground-floor and
mezzanine galleries will take an hour or so.

Minden Lookout   VIEWPOINT
(Minden Rd) From Minden Lookout, about
10km west of Tauranga towards Katikati,
there's a superb view back over the cranes
in Tauranga Harbour and across the Bay of
Plenty. To get there, take SH2 to Te Puna and
turn off south on Minden Rd; the lookout is
about 3km up the road.

Classic Flyers NZ   MUSEUM
(📞 07-572 4000; www.classicflyersnz.com; 8
Jean Batten Dr; adult/child/family $15/7.50/30;
⊙ 9.30am-4pm) Out near the airport, Classic
Flyers NZ is an interesting aviation museum
(biplanes, retired US Airforce jets, helicopters etc) with a buzzy on-site cafe.

Mills Reef Winery   WINERY
(📞 07-576 8800; www.millsreef.co.nz; 143 Moffat
Rd, Bethlehem; ⊙ 10am-5pm) Stately Mills Reef,

Tauranga

7km from the town centre at Bethlehem, has tastings of its award-winning wines (dig the chardonnay) and a refined restaurant (read: great food but not much fun) that's open for lunch daily and dinner by reservation (mains $25 to $39).

Monmouth Redoubt ARCHAEOLOGICAL SITE, PARK
(Monmouth St; ⊙24hr) **FREE** Shaded by huge pohutukawa trees, spooky Monmouth Redoubt was a fortified site during the Māori Wars. Next door is **Robbins Park** (Cliff Rd). At the foot of the Redoubt, on the end of the Strand, is **Te Awa nui Waka**, a replica Māori canoe, on display in an open-sided building.

Elms Mission House HISTORIC BUILDING
(⌨07-577 9772; www.theelms.org.nz; 15 Mission St; house adult/child $5/50c, gardens free; ⊙10am-4pm) Built in 1847, Elms Mission House is the oldest building in the Bay of Plenty. Furnished in period style, it sits among other well-preserved mission buildings in leafy gardens.

Mission Cemetery CEMETERY
(cnr Marsh St & Dive Cres) The spooky Mission Cemetery lies not far from the Elms Mission House, and is a shady tangle of trees and headstones.

Brain Watkins House HISTORIC BUILDING
(⌨07-578 1835; www.taurangahistorical. blogspot.co.nz; 233 Cameron Rd; adult/child/family $4/2/10; ⊙2-4pm Sun) A demure Victorian villa stranded on a hill as the roads around it grew, Brain Watkins House (no, not Brian) was built in 1881 from kauri (wood) and remains one of Tauranga's best-preserved colonial homes.

🏃 Activities

The free *Tauranga City Walkways* pamphlet (from the i-SITE) details walks around Tauranga and Mt Maunganui. History buffs should pick up the free *Historic Tauranga* brochure and stroll around the town's cache of historic sites.

Adrenalin Forest
ADVENTURE SPORTS

(☑07-929 8724; www.adrenalin-forest.co.nz; Upper Pyes Pa Rd, TECT All Terrain Park; adult/child $42/27; ☺10am-2.30pm daily, closed Mon & Tue Apr-Sep) About 26km from Tauranga en route to Rotorua is this heart-starter: a series of high wires, flying foxes, platforms and rope bridges strung through a grove of tall conifers. There are six different routes of increasing difficulty to test your nerve.

Waimarino Adventure Park
WATER SPORTS

(☑0800 456 996, 07-576 4233; www.waimarino.com; 36 Taniwha Pl; kayak tours from $99, kayak hire per hour/day $26/55, park day-passes adult/child $42/32; ☺10am-6pm Sep-Apr, to 5pm May-Aug) On the banks of the Wairoa River 8km west of town, Waimarino offers freedom kayak hire, self-guided kayak tours, sea-kayaking trips and a magical Glowworm Tour ($130 per person) at McLaren Falls Park. The adventure park here has all kinds of watery distractions: a kayak slide, diving board, ropes course, water-walking zorbs, warm pools, and a human catapult called 'The Blob' – intense!

Kaimai Mamaku Forest Park
TRAMPING

(www.doc.govt.nz; SH29) The backdrop to the Western Bay of Plenty is the rugged 70km-long Kaimai Mamaku Forest Park, 35km southwest of Tauranga, with tramps for the intrepid and huts (free to $15 per person per night) and campsites ($6). For more info see DOC's pamphlet *Kaimai to Coast* ($2.50), or contact **Kaimai New Zealand Tours** (☑07-552 5257; www.kaimai-new-zealand-tours.com) to arrange a guided tramp.

Elements Watersports
WATER SPORTS

(☑0800 486 729; www.elementsonline.co.nz; lessons from $80) If you're new to the sea and want to splash safely into the big blue, Elements Watersports runs sailing, windsurfing and paddle-boarding lessons, and has gear for hire.

Blue Ocean Charters
FISHING

(☑07-544 3072, 0800 224 278; www.blueocean.co.nz; trips from $100) Fishing, diving and sightseeing trips (including one to Tuhua Island) on the MV *Te Kuia* and MV *Ratahi*.

Tauranga Tandem Skydiving
ADVENTURE SPORTS

(☑07-574 8533; www.tandemskydive.co.nz; 2 Kittyhawk Way, Tauranga Airport; jumps 10,000/12,000ft $325/375) Tauranga Tandem Skydiving offers exhilarating jumps with views of Whakaari (White Island), Mt Ruapehu and across the Bay of Plenty on the way down.

Dive Zone
DIVING

(☑07-578 4050; www.divezone.co.nz; 213 Cameron Rd; trips/courses from $120/600; ☺8am-6pm Mon-Fri, 7.30am-4pm Sat, 7.30am-2pm Sun) PADI courses and trips to local wrecks and reefs, plus gear rental.

☞ Tours

Bay Explorer
BOAT TOUR

(☑021 605 968; www.bayexplorer.co.nz; adult/child $115/65) This popular cruise incorporates wildlife spotting – potentially including whales, dolphins and bird life – with the opportunity to go paddle boarding, kayaking and snorkelling around nearby Motiti Island.

Dolphin Blue
BOAT TOUR

(☑027 666 8047; www.dolphinblue.co.nz; day trips adult/child $150/100; ☺departs 8.30am) 🍃 Unhurried, small-group (15 people maximum) day trips across Tauranga Harbour and out on to the Bay of Plenty in pursuit of pods of dolphins. When you find them, you can jump in and splash around with them. Those concerned with the welfare of dolphins should be aware that swimming with dolphins in the wild is considered by some to be disruptive to the habitat and behaviour of the animals.

Tauranga Tasting Tours
TOUR

(☑07-544 1383; www.tastingtours.co.nz; tours $130) Whips around a local brewery, Mills Reef and Morton Estate wineries, and back to town for cocktails.

Dolphin Seafaris
BOAT TOUR

(☑0800 326 8747, 07-577 0105; www.nzdolphin.com; half-day trips adult/child $150/110) 🍃 Eco-attuned dolphin-spotting trips where you can get into the water and swim with them. Those concerned with the welfare of dolphins should be aware that swimming with dolphins in the wild is considered by some to be disruptive to the habitat and behaviour of the animals.

Aerius Helicopters
SCENIC FLIGHTS

(☑0800 864 354; www.aerius.co.nz; flights from $115) Local flights and aerial excursions as far away as Lake Tarawera, Rotorua and Whakaari (White Island), departing Tauranga.

✹ Festivals & Events

National Jazz Festival
JAZZ

(www.jazz.org.nz; ☺Easter) An extravaganza of big blowers and scoobee-doobee-doo, with concerts and food and wine galore.

Tauranga Arts Festival PERFORMING ARTS

(☑07-928 6213; www.taurangafestival.co.nz; ⊙Oct) Kicking off on Labour weekend (in odd-numbered years), showcasing dance, comedy, plays and other things arty.

🛏 Sleeping

Loft 109 HOSTEL $

(☑07-579 5638; www.loft109.co.nz; 109 Devonport Rd; dm/d from $31/80; @ 🛜) This small, central hostel feels like somebody's upstairs flat, with an intimate kitchen-lounge and a cute little balcony over Devonport St. It's bright, with plenty of skylights and a gas fire for colder days. Super-relaxed without being lax about things like security or boozy badness.

Harbourside City Backpackers HOSTEL $

(☑07-579 4066; www.backpacktauranga.co.nz; 105 The Strand; dm/tw/d from $28/78/78; @ 🛜) Soak up the sea air at this sociable hostel (a former hotel), conveniently handy to the Strand's bars and restaurants. Rooms are smallish but clean, and you'll spend more time on the awesome roof terrace anyway. There's no parking, but down the road is a public car park that empties out at the right time.

Tauranga Tourist Park HOLIDAY PARK $

(☑07-578 3323; www.taurangatouristpark.co.nz; 9 Mayfair St; campsites/cabins from $30/55; @ 🛜) The layout at this harbourside holiday park feels a bit tight (don't expect rolling acres), but it's well maintained, clean and tidy. Aim for a site down by the bay under the pohutukawa trees.

⭐ Tauranga on the Waterfront MOTEL $$

(☑07-578 7079; www.thetauranga.co.nz; 1 Second Ave; r/ste from $165/215; 🛜) A short stroll from central Tauranga, this well-established motel has recently renovated studios with compact private courtyards, and brilliant harbour suites with huge picture windows and outstanding views. Sunlight streams in to brighten the chic and stylish decor, modern bathrooms are equipped with premium toiletries, and compact self-contained kitchenettes come with Nespresso machines for the first coffee of the day.

Hotel on Devonport HOTEL $$

(☑07-578 2668; www.hotelondevonport.net.nz; 72 Devonport Rd; d/ste from $170/220; @ 🛜) City-centre Devonport is top of the town, with bay-view rooms, noise-reducing glass, slick interiors and sassy staff, all of which appeals to business travellers and upmarket weekenders. Help yourself to an apple from the bowl in the lobby.

Harbour City Motor Inn MOTEL $$

(☑0800 253 525, 07-571 1435; www.taurangaharbourcity.co.nz; 50 Wharf St; d/f from $165/210; 🛜) With a winning location right in the middle of town (and with plenty of parking), this lemon-yellow motor inn has all the mod cons. There are spa baths in each room, and friendly staff who can offer sound advice on your itinerary.

Roselands Motel MOTEL $$

(☑0800 363 093, 07-578 2294; www.roselands.co.nz; 21 Brown St; d from $139; 🛜) Tarted up with splashes of orange paint and new linen, this sweet, old-style motel is in a quiet but central location. Expect spacious units (all with kitchenette), friendly first-name-basis hosts and new TVs.

City Suites HOTEL $$

(☑07-577 1480; www.citysuites.co.nz; 32 Cameron Rd; apt/ste $155/199; 🛜🏊) The spacious rooms here (all with either terrace or balcony) have a rather regal feel, with king-sized beds and full kitchens. A swimming pool, free wi-fi and secure parking complete the list of essentials for wandering business bods.

Trinity Wharf HOTEL $$$

(☑07-577 8700, 0800 577 8700; www.trinitywharf.co.nz; 51 Dive Cres; d from $188; @ 🛜🏊) This blocky three-storey number near the harbour bridge has a slick, contemporary lobby – all white tiles and spiky pot plants – leading to the upmarket in-house restaurant Halo (mains $20 to $41). Rooms are supersized and luxurious in tones au naturel. Amenities include an underutilised gym, infinity-edge swimming pool and free wi-fi. Very flashy.

🍴 Eating

Me & You CAFE $

(☑07-577 0567; 48 First Ave; snacks & mains $8-21; ⊙7.30am-3.30pm; ☑) One of our favourite Tauranga cafes combines funky retro decor with an outdoor deck, and the hip baristas really know their way around the coffee machine. A huge array of counter food – including a forever-changing range of fresh salads – combines with eggy breakfasts, and there's usually a good selection of raw and gluten-free menu options.

Tauranga Farmers Market MARKET $

(☑07-552 5278; www.taurangafarmersmarket.co.nz; Arundel St, Tauranga Primary School; snacks $5-10; ⊙8am-noon Sat) Kick-start your Saturday morning with a breakfast burrito and an organic coffee, then explore this popular weekly market that usually features local dogs enjoying entertainment from an eclectic range of buskers. Check the website for your own foodie hit list, and be sure to stock up for on-the-road picnics.

Grindz Café
CAFE $

(☑ 07-579 0017; 50 First Ave; meals $11-18; ☺ 7am-4pm Mon-Fri, 8am-3.30pm Sat, 8am-3pm Sun; 🛜🚗) Along wide-open First Ave, Grindz is a hip cafe with scattered footpath tables. Inside it's a roomy, split-level affair, with funky wallpaper, antiques and retro relics. Bagels, vegie stacks, muffins, cakes and salads are the order of the day, plus creative coffee (try 'The Trough' if you're sleepy: a four-shot soup bowl of caffeine heaven). Free wi-fi.

Bobby's Fresh Fish Market
FISH & CHIPS $

(☑ 07-578 1789; 1 Dive Cres; meals from $7; ☺ 11am-8pm) A local legend serving up fresh fish and chips, with hexagonal outdoor tables on the water's edge and plenty of seagulls to keep you company.

★ Macau
ASIAN $$

(☑ 07-578 8717; www.dinemacau.co.nz; 59 The Strand; shared plates $14-31; ☺ 11am-late Mon-Fri, 10am-late Sat) Zingy Asian flavours take centre stage at this recent addition to the strip along the Strand. Plates – small and large – are all designed to be shared. Menu highlights include crispy Sichuan-spiced eggplant, and the moreish steamed buns with roasted pork belly. Stylish decor, Asian-inspired cocktails and a good craft beer list make this one of Tauranga's best.

★ Elizabeth Cafe & Larder
MODERN NZ $$

(☑ 07-579 0950; www.elizabethcafe.co.nz; 247 Cameron Rd; mains $12-25; ☺ 7am-4pm Mon-Fri, 8am-3pm Sat-Sun) 'Eat, drink, enjoy' at Elizabeth, a hip cafe-bar on the ground floor of a four-storey city-centre office block. Many of the customers drift down from upstairs, but you don't need a suit to enjoy a knockout eggs Benedict with potato rösti or the snapper taco with a zingy Mexican slaw. Interesting industrial aesthetics and Peroni on tap complete the picture.

Rye American
Kitchen & Spirits
AMERICAN $$

(☑ 07-571 4138; www.ryekitchen.co.nz; 19 Wharf St; mains $15-30; ☺ 4pm-late Tue-Sun) Southern American cuisine features at this spot with a rustic and relaxed ambience. Grab an outdoor table and combine a burger or hearty bowl of jambalaya with a craft brew from NZ, Australia or the US, or sample a few American bourbons and whiskeys. The surrounding Wharf St area is currently being developed as a pedestrian-friendly dining precinct.

Get exploring and look forward to a few more tasty new openings in the area.

Collar & Thai
THAI $$

(☑ 07-577 6655; www.collarandthai.co.nz; 21 Devonport Rd, Goddards Centre; mains lunch $14-17, dinner $24-32; ☺ 11.30am-2pm Mon-Sat, 5-10pm daily) No tie required at this upstairs eatery that artfully elaborates on Thai standards and uses plenty of fresh seafood. Perfect for a premovie meal (the Rialto Cinemas are right next door). Good-value lunch specials.

★ Harbourside
MODERN NZ $$$

(☑ 07-571 0520; www.harboursidetauranga.co.nz; Railway Bridge, The Strand; mains $22-40; ☺ 11.30am-2.30pm & 5.30pm-late) In a wonderfully atmospheric 100-year-old boathouse at the end of the Strand, Harbourside is the place for a romantic dinner, with lapping waves and the overhead railway bridge arching out over the harbour. The Asian-style roast duck with wontons and green tea soba noodles is hard to beat, or you can just swing by for a moody predinner drink.

Somerset Cottage
MODERN NZ $$$

(☑ 07-576 6889; www.somersetcottage.co.nz; 30 Bethlehem Rd, Bethlehem; mains $30-40; ☺ 11.30am-2.30pm Wed-Fri, 6-9pm Mon-Sat) The most awarded restaurant in the Bay, Somerset Cottage is a simple but elegant venue for that special treat. The food is highly seasonal, made from the best NZ ingredients, impressively executed without being too fussy. Standout dishes include baked cheese soufflé, duck with coconut kumara and the famous liquorice ice cream. Craft beers from Tauranga's Fitzpatrick's Brewing complement an excellent wine list.

🍷 Drinking & Nightlife

Brew
CRAFT BEER

(☑ 07-578 3543; www.brewpub.co.nz; 107 The Strand; ☺ 11.30am-late Mon-Fri, 10.30am-late Sat & Sun) The long concrete bar here has room for plenty of elbows, and for plenty of glasses of Croucher's crafty seasonal ales, Pilsners and stouts (pray the Ethiopian coffee stout is on tap). The vibe is social, with communal tables, and good pizza and plates of bar food designed to share (mains $15 to $31). Look forward to guest beers from around NZ, too.

Phoenix PUB
(☑07-578 8741; www.thephoenixtauranga.co.nz; 67 The Strand; ◷10.30am-late Mon-Fri, 8.30am-late Sat & Sun) At the northern end of the Strand, this sprawling gastropub pours Monteiths beers (once niche, now mainstream) and serves pizza and meaty pub meals (mains $20 to $36; try the pork tenderloin). Dressed-up drinkers, and Red Hot Chilli Peppers on the stereo. Craft-beer fans should ask if any of the more-flavoursome Black Dog brews are on tap.

☆ Entertainment

Rialto Cinemas CINEMA
(☑07-577 0445; www.rialtotauranga.co.nz; 21 Devonport Rd, Goddards Centre; adult/child $17/10.50; ◷opens 30min before screenings) Home to the Tauranga Film Society, the Rialto is the best spot in town to catch a flick – classic, offbeat, art-house or international. And you can sip a coffee or a glass of wine in the darkness. Tickets are discounted to $11.50 on Tuesdays.

❶ Information

NZ Post (www.nzpost.co.nz; 17 Grey St; ◷8.30am-5.30pm Mon-Fri, 9am-4pm Sat, 10am-3pm Sun) Inside the Paper Plus store.
Tauranga Hospital (☑07-579 8000; www.bopdhb.govt.nz; 375 Cameron Rd; ◷24hr) A couple of kilometres south of town.
Tauranga i-SITE (☑07-578 8103; www.bayofplentynz.com; 8 Wharf St; ◷8.30am-5.30pm, reduced hours winter; ☎) Local tourist information, bookings, InterCity bus tickets and DOC maps.

❶ Getting There & Away

AIR

Air New Zealand (☑0800 737 000; www.airnewzealand.co.nz) Has daily direct flights to Auckland, Wellington and Christchurch.
Sunair (☑0800 786 247; www.sunair.co.nz) Links Tauranga to Whitianga, Gisborne and Great Barrier Island.

BUS

Twin City Express (☑0800 422 928; www.baybus.co.nz) buses run twice daily Monday to Friday between Tauranga/Mt Maunganui and Rotorua via Te Puke ($11.60, 1½ hours).

InterCity tickets and timetables are available at the i-SITE. Destinations include the following:

DESTINATION	PRICE	TIME (HR)	FREQUENCY
Auckland	$46	4	3 daily
Hamilton	$33	2	2 daily
Rotorua	$29	1½	2 daily
Taupo	$51	3	2 daily
Wellington	$59	9	1 daily

ManaBus destinations include the following:

DESTINATION	PRICE	TIME (HR)	FREQUENCY
Auckland	$14	3¼	3 daily
Hamilton	$10	3	2 daily
Napier	$35	5	2 daily
Rotorua	$10	1	3 daily
Taupo	$12	3	2 daily

Shuttle Bus

A couple of companies can pick you up at Auckland or Rotorua airports and bus you to Tauranga (though you'll pay upwards of $100 for the privilege).
Aerolink Shuttles (☑0800 151 551; www.aerolink.nz) Shuttles from Tauranga to Auckland airport.
Luxury Airport Shuttles (☑07-547 4444; www.luxuryairportshuttles.co.nz) Also shunts travellers between Tauranga Airport and Tauranga (from $10).

CAR

If you're heading to Hamilton on route K, the toll road costs $1.80 per car. Heading east to Whakatane or south to Rotorua, there's also the new option of the Tauranga Eastern Link Toll Road ($2 per car) which begins near Papamoa. Tolls need to be paid online at www.nzta.govt.nz.

❶ Getting Around

BICYCLE

Cycle Tauranga (☑07-571 1435; www.cycletauranga.co.nz; 50 Wharf St, Harbour City Motor Inn; per half-/full day $29/49) Has road-trail hybrid bikes for hire, including helmets, locks, saddlebags and maps. Tours also available.

BUS

Tauranga's bright-yellow Bayhopper buses run to most locations around the area, including Mt Maunganui ($3.20, 15 minutes) and Papamoa ($3.20, 30 minutes). There's a central stop on Wharf St; timetables available from the i-SITE.

CAR

Numerous car-rental agencies have offices in Tauranga, including **Rent-a-Dent** (☑07-578 1772, 0800 736 823; www.rentadent.co.nz; 19 Fifteenth Ave; ◷8am-5pm Mon-Fri, to noon Sat).

TAXI

Tauranga Mount Taxis ([✆]07-578 6086; www.taurangataxis.co.nz) A taxi from the centre of Tauranga to the airport or Mt Maunganui costs around $25.

Mt Maunganui

POP 19,100

Named after the hulking 232m hill that punctuates the sandy peninsula occupied by the township, uptempo Mt Maunganui is often just called 'the Mount', or Mauao, which translates as 'caught by the light of day'. It's considered part of greater Tauranga, but really it's an enclave unto itself, with great cafes and restaurants, hip bars and fab beaches. Sunseekers flock to the Mount in summer, served by an increasing number of 10-storey apartment towers studding the spit.

◉ Sights

★ **Mauao**   MOUNTAIN, LOOKOUT
Explore Mauao (Mt Maunganui) itself on the walking trails winding around it and leading up to the summit. The steep **summit walk** takes about an hour return (with a rest at the top!). You can also clamber around the rocks on **Moturiki Island**, which adjoins the peninsula. The island and the base of Mauao comprise the **Mauao Base Track** (3½km, 45 minutes), wandering through magical groves of pohutukawa trees that bloom between November and January.

Pick up the Mauao map from the info desk at Beachside Holiday Park.

🏃 Activities

The Mount lays claim to being NZ's premier **surfing** city (they teach surfing at high school!). You can carve up the waves at **Mount Beach**, which has lovely beach breaks and a 100m artificial surf reef not far offshore. Learn-to-surf operators include **Hibiscus** ([✆]07-575 3792, 027 279 9687; www.surfschool.co.nz; 2hr/2-day lessons $75/165), **Discovery Surf School** ([✆]027 632 7873; www.discoverysurf.co.nz; 2hr lessons $90) and **Mount Surfshop** ([✆]07-575 9133; www.mountsurfshop.co.nz; 96 Maunganui Rd; 2hr lessons $80, board hire $30; ⊙9am-5pm Mon-Sat, 10am-5pm Sun).

Mount Hot Pools   HOT SPRING
(www.tcal.co.nz; 9 Adams Ave; adult/child/family $11/8/31; ⊙6am-10pm Mon-Sat, 8am-10pm Sun) If you've given your muscles a workout traipsing up and down Mauao, take a long relaxing soak at these hot-water pools at the foot of the hill.

Rock House   ROCK CLIMBING
(www.therockhouse.co.nz; 9 Triton Ave; adult/child $17.50/15.50, gear hire extra; ⊙noon-9pm Tue-Fri, 10am-6pm Sat & Sun) Try rock climbing at the Rock House, a huge blue steel shed with huge blue climbing walls inside.

Baywave   SWIMMING
([✆]07-575 0276; www.tcal.co.nz; cnr Girven & Gloucester Rds; adult/child $7.50/5, hydroslide $4.80; ⊙6am-9pm Mon-Fri, 7am-7pm Sat & Sun) For unsalted swimming-pool action plus NZ's biggest wave pool, a hydroslide and aqua aerobics, visit Baywave.

🛏 Sleeping

Seagulls Guesthouse B&B   B&B, HOSTEL $
([✆]07-574 2099; www.seagullsguesthouse.co.nz; 12 Hinau St; dm/s/d/f from $30/65/85/110; @ 🖎) Can't face another crowded, alcohol-soaked hostel? On a quiet street not far from town, Seagulls is a gem: an immaculate, upmarket backpackers where the emphasis is on peaceful enjoyment of one's surrounds rather than wallowing in the excesses of youth. The best rooms have bathrooms and TVs. Free wi-fi.

Beachside Holiday Park   HOLIDAY PARK $
([✆]07-575 4471; www.mountbeachside.co.nz; 1 Adams Ave; sites from $42, on-site vans $70-90, cabins $110-130; @) With three different camping areas nooked into the foot of Mt Maunganui itself, this community-run park has spectacular camping with all the requisite facilities, plus it's handy to the Mount Hot Pools (discounts for campers) and a strip of good eateries. Reception doubles as a local info centre.

Pacific Coast Lodge
& Backpackers   HOSTEL $
([✆]07-574 9601, 0800 666 622; www.pacificcoastlodge.co.nz; 432 Maunganui Rd; dm/d from $28/84; @ 🖎) Not far from the action, this efficiently run, sharp-looking hostel is sociable but not party-focused, with drinkers gently encouraged to migrate into town after 10pm. Purpose-built bunk rooms are roomy and adorned with beachy murals. Free bikes and surfboards.

Cosy Corner Holiday Park   HOLIDAY PARK $
([✆]07-575 5899, 0800 684 654; www.cosycorner.co.nz; 40 Ocean Beach Rd; sites from $44, cabins & units $75-125; ⊙mid Dec–Easter; @ 🖎 🖎) This compact, spartan camping ground has a sociable feel, with barbecues, trampolines and a games room. Handy to the beach, too (access via a little path just across the road). Note it's open to independent travellers from mid-December to Easter only.

Mt Maunganui

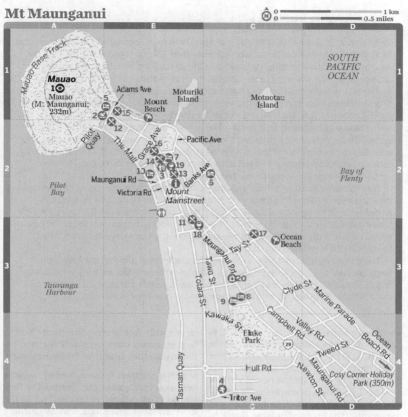

Mt Maunganui

◎ Top Sights
1 Mauao A1

✈ Activities, Courses & Tours
2 Mount Hot Pools A1
3 Mount Surfshop B2
4 Rock House C4

🛏 Sleeping
5 Beachside Holiday Park B1
6 Belle Mer C2
7 Mount Backpackers B2
8 Pacific Coast Lodge &
   Backpackers C3
9 Seagulls Guesthouse B&B C3
10 Westhaven Motel B2

🍴 Eating
11 Easy Go Thai B3
12 Mount Bistro B2
13 Mount Mainstreet Farmers
   Market B2
14 Post Bank B2
15 Pronto B1
16 Provdores Urban Food Store B2
17 Tay Street Beach Cafe C3

🍷 Drinking & Nightlife
Astrolabe Brew Bar ....(see 14)
18 Hop House B3
19 Mount Brewing Co B2

🛍 Shopping
20 Little Big Markets C3

Mount Backpackers HOSTEL $
(☎ 07-575 0860; www.mountbackpackers.co.nz;
87 Maunganui Rd; dm $27-31; @ 🖥) A tight, tidy
hostel on the main drag, bolstered by location – close to the beach and a mere stagger
from the Mount's best restaurants and bars –
plus extras such as cheap surfboard and bike
hire and discounted surf lessons.

THE WRECK OF THE RENA

On 5 October 2011 the 47,000-tonne cargo ship MV *Rena*, loaded with 1368 containers and 1900 tonnes of fuel oil, ran aground on Astrolabe Reef 22km off the coast of Mt Maunganui. The ship had been attempting to enter Tauranga Harbour, New Zealand's busiest port, but inexplicably hit one of the most consistently charted obstacles on the way. Pitched acutely on the reef with a rupturing hull, the *Rena* started spilling oil into the sea and shedding containers from its deck. Over subsequent days, disbelieving locals watched as oil slicks, containers, and dead fish and seabirds washed up on their glorious beaches.

The blame game began: the captain? The owners? The company that chartered the vessel? Thousands of volunteers pitched in to help with the clean-up. Salvors eventually managed to remove most of the oil from the ship, but on 8 January 2012 the *Rena* finally broke in two, spilling remnant oil and dozens more containers into the sea. The stern section subsequently slipped below the surface.

With the initial focus on preventing an oil spill, the elephant in the corner of the room – the *Rena* itself – seemed a problem too large. Now that refloating the ship is no longer an option, debate rages on about what to do: drag the bow section off the rocks, too? A future dive site for the Bay of Plenty? At the time of writing the plan was to cut the bow section down to 1m below the waterline, and remove the four-storey accommodation tower from the submerged stern.

The grounding has been an environmental and economic disaster, but long-term impacts are hard to gauge: local businesses suffered at the time but are back in full swing, and the beautiful beaches are clean again. See www.renaproject.co.nz for updates, or ask a local for their take on the situation (a sure-fire conversation starter!).

Westhaven Motel   MOTEL $$

(⏰ 07-575 4753; www.westhavenmotel.co.nz; 27a The Mall; units $130-150; 🔊) The 1969 architecture here is funky, but the owners are modernising things room by room (get in now if you're a retro fan!). Full kitchens are perfect for self-caterers, and it's an easy walk to the shops and restaurants. The most affordable motel in miles, and just metres from good swimming.

Belle Mer   APARTMENT $$$

(⏰ 07-575 0011, 0800 100 235; www.bellemer. co.nz; 53 Marine Pde; apt $285-450; 🔊🈂️) A flashy beachside complex of one-, two- and three-bedroom apartments, some with sea-view balconies and others opening on to private courtyards (though you'll more likely head for the resort-style pool terrace). Rooms are tastefully decorated in warm tones with soft edges, and have everything you need for longer stays, with full kitchens and laundries.

✖️ Eating

Pronto   BURGERS $

(⏰ 07-572 1109; www.facebook.com/pronto gourmetnz; 1 Marine Pde; burgers $10-14; ⏰ 9am-3pm Mon, to 8.30pm Tue-Fri, 8am-8.30pm Sat & Sun) Life's pretty simple sometimes. Combine endless views of the Pacific Ocean and Mauao's imposing profile with a super selection of gourmet burgers. The *peri peri* chick-

en one with chunky avocado is pretty hard to beat, especially when eaten with the sand between your toes, sitting on the nearby beach.

Mount Mainstreet Farmers Market   MARKET $

(www.mountmaunganui.org.nz; Phoenix Car Park, Maunganui Rd; ⏰ 9am-1pm Sun) Roll up to the local farmers market for a Sunday-morning fix-me-up: fresh fruit and vegies, coffee, pastries, honey, cheese, juices... Arts and crafts are banned!

Providores Urban Food Store   CAFE $

(⏰ 07-572 1300; 19a Pacific Ave; meals $7-22; ⏰ 7.30am-5pm, closed Mon & Tue Apr-Oct; 🍴) Mexican rugs and comfy couches set the mood here as your eyes peruse fresh-baked breads, buttery croissants, home-smoked meats and cheeses, organic jams and free-range eggs – perfect ingredients for a bang-up breakfast or a hamper-filling picnic on the beach.

Tay Street Beach Cafe   CAFE $$

(⏰ 07-572 0691; www.taystreetbeachcafe.co.nz; cnr Tay St & Marine Pde; mains $14-25; ⏰ 8am-9pm Mon-Sat, to 4pm Sun) Around 2km south of Mauao, the Tay Street Beach Cafe is removed from the central Mount's occasional bustle. Savvy locals crowd in for coffee in bright morning sunshine, linger over brunch classics like corn fritters, or dine on fish tacos or seared tuna salad for lunch. An outstanding wine selection and craft beer from around the North Island seals the deal.

Tapas and dinner from around 4pm are equally appealing. Try the Thai fishcakes or lamb kofta.

Easy Go Thai
THAI $$

(07-574 8500; www.thaitakeaways.co.nz; 277 Maunganui Rd; mains $15-19; 4.30pm-late) This low-key eatery sits on an unsexy part of the Mount's main street, but the Thai cuisine here is the zingy real deal. Try the *gaeng dang bhed* (red duck curry) or classic Thai fishcakes. If you order $25 worth of food, they'll even deliver it for free. How does alfresco dining beside the beach sound?

★ Post Bank
MODERN NZ $$$

(07-575 4782; www.postbank.co.nz; 82 Maunganui Rd; mains $24-34; noon-2.30pm Tue-Fri, 5pm-late nightly) Bookcases crammed with an eclectic range of tomes give Post Bank the ambience of a gentlemen's club, but there's nothing stuffy about the food on offer. Asian and Mediterranean influences combine in a menu playfully divided up into 'Chapter 1, 2 and 3'. Highlights have included the Vietnamese beef and prawn salad, and a great Thai chicken curry.

The smoothly professional team behind the bar concoct classy cocktails worthy of a 1920s speakeasy.

Mount Bistro
MODERN NZ $$$

(07-575 3872; www.mountbistro.nz; 6 Adams Ave; small plates $15, mains $26-36; 5.30-9pm Tue-Sun) The buttermilk-coloured Mount Bistro, an unpretentious fine-dining experience at the foot of Mauao, is on to a good thing: quality local meats (fish, lamb, beef, crayfish, chicken, duck) creatively worked into classic dishes (lamb shanks, seafood chowder) and served with flair. Makes for a classy night out.

🍷 Drinking & Nightlife

★ Hop House
BAR

(07-574 5880; www.thehophouse.co.nz; 297 Maunganui Rd; 4-11pm Tue-Fri, noon-late Sat & Sun) Formerly named after one of David Bowie's best songs, this quirky bar has been reborn as the best destination for craft-beer fans in the Tauranga and Mt Maunganui area. Multiple taps are kept fresh with a rotation of brews from around NZ, and the bottled selection is pretty stellar, too. Live music kicks off around 8pm most Fridays.

Mount Brewing Co
CRAFT BEER

(07-575 7792; www.mountbrewingco.co.nz; 109 Maunganui Rd; 11am-1am) With a relaxed beachy ambience, this main-street pub is perfect for whiling away a few Bay of Plenty hours. Try all the different beers in a tasting paddle – our favourite is the hoppy Mermaid's Mirth American Pale Ale – and linger for burgers, shared platters and occasional live music from local bands on Tuesday and Friday nights.

Brewer's Bar
PUB

(07-575 2739; www.facebook.com/BrewersBar; 107 Newton St; 11am-11pm) Home base for the Mount Brewing Co, and located in a light industrial area around 4km from central Mt Maunganui, Brewer's Bar hosts occasional live music. The adjacent Brewer's Field is used for outdoor gigs by some of NZ's biggest bands and DJs from late December to mid-January.

Astrolabe Brew Bar
PUB

(07-574 8155; www.astrolabe.co.nz; 82 Maunganui Rd; 10am-1am) Astrolabe conjures up a funky-retro bach vibe, with floral carpet, bookshelves jammed with old novels, beach umbrellas and battered suitcases. If all that doesn't float your holiday boat, a hoppy Green Beret IPA from NZ's well-known Mac's Brewery and a burger, pizza or steak might. The salads – try the Thai-style 'Jimmy the Cow' beef one – are also good.

🛍 Shopping

Little Big Markets
MARKET

(021 032 7823; www.facebook.com/thelittlebigmarkets; cnr Maru St & Maunganui Rd; 9am-1pm 1st Sat of the month Oct-Apr) Arts, crafts and tasty food all feature at this monthly morning market.

ℹ Information

The reception desk at **Beachside Holiday Park** (p304) doubles as an informal info centre for the Mount, open 8.30am to 7pm. **Mount Mainstreet** (07-575 9911; www.mountmaunganui.org.nz; 141 Maunganui Rd; 8.30am-5pm) also has information and maps.

ℹ Getting There & Away

BUS

InterCity, ManaBus and Naked Bus services visiting Tauranga also stop at Mt Maunganui, with fares similar to those to/from **Tauranga** (p303). Buses stop on Salisbury Ave.

CAR

Mt Maunganui is across the harbour bridge from Tauranga, or accessible from the south via Te

OFF THE BEATEN TRACK

TUHUA (MAYOR ISLAND)

Commonly known as Mayor Island, this dormant volcano is 35km north of Tauranga. It's a privately owned island noted for its black, glasslike obsidian rock and bird life, including a clutch of kiwi introduced to the predator-free isle in 2006. Walking tracks cut through the overgrown crater valley, and the northwest corner is a **marine reserve**.

You need permission to visit from the island's *kaitiaki* (guardians), via the **Tuhua Trust Board** (☑ 07-579 0580; tuhuakaitiaki@hotmail.com). There's a $5 landing fee, and visitors must observe strict quarantine regulations. Accommodation is limited to basic camping/cabins ($15/35); bring your own food and water (no fridges). The landing fee is included in accommodation costs. Tauranga-based boat-charter companies will take you to Tuhua. Contact the Tuhua Trust Board or the **DOC** (☑ 07-578 7677; www.doc.govt.nz; 253 Chadwick Rd, Greerton) in Tauranga for more info, and download the *Tuhua/Mayor Island – How to Get There* brochure from the DOC website.

Maunga on SH2. For car hire, try **Rite Price Rentals** (☑ 07-575 2726, 0800 250 251; www.ritepricerentals.co.nz; 63 Totara St; ⊗ 8am-5pm).

Papamoa

POP 20,100

Papamoa is a burgeoning 'burb next to Mt Maunganui, separated now by just an empty paddock or two, destined for subdivision. With big new houses on pristine streets, parts of Papamoa have the air of a gated community, but the beach beyond the sheltering dunes is awesome – you can't blame folks for moving in.

🏃 Activities

Blo-kart Heaven　　　　ADVENTURE SPORTS
(☑ 07-572 4256; www.blokartheaven.co.nz; 176 Parton Rd; blokarts 30/50min $30/50, driftkarts 15min $25; ⊗ 10am-5.30pm Oct-Mar, to 4.30pm Apr-Sep) Back a few kilometres from Papamoa Beach, Blo-kart Heaven is the place to attempt land-sailing around a custom-built speedway (blokarts are like seated windsurfers on wheels). They've recently added electric-powered driftkarts, so action is now possible even when there's no wind. Both activities are loads of fun, easily mastered, and highly recommended.

🛏 Sleeping & Eating

Papamoa Beach Resort　　　HOLIDAY PARK $
(☑ 07-572 0816, 0800 232 243; www.papamoabeach.co.nz; 535 Papamoa Beach Rd; sites from $48, villas & units $90-150; @ �) The sprawling Papamoa Beach Resort is a spotless, modern park, primed and priced beyond its caravan-park origins, with fab self-contained villas behind the dunes (shhhh, listen to the surf).

Rental bikes and pedal go-karts are great fun for families.

Beach House Motel　　　　　MOTEL $$
(☑ 0800 429 999, 07-572 1424; www.beachhousemotel.co.nz; 224 Papamoa Beach Rd; d from $140; �) With its angular corrugated-iron exterior and tasteful cane-ware furnishings, Beach House Motel offers an immaculate, upmarket version of the Kiwi bach holiday, relaxed and close to the beach. There's a pool for when the beach is too windy, and orange daisies poking up through rock gardens.

Bluebiyou　　　　　　　　SEAFOOD $$
(☑ 07-572 2099; www.bluebiyou.co.nz; 559 Papamoa Beach Rd; mains $16-40; ⊗ 11.30am-late Tue-Fri, 10.30am-late Sat & Sun) Bluebiyou is a casual, breezy restaurant riding high on the dunes, serving big brunches, Italian-influenced seafood specialities and shared tapas. The seafood risotto is a sure-fire winner, and fried anchovies or oysters are great bar snacks. Open seven days in summer.

ℹ Getting There & Away

Bayhopper bus 30 runs from Mt Maunganui to Papamoa.

Katikati

POP 4060

'Katikat' to the locals, this busy little town was the only planned Ulster settlement in the world, and it celebrates this history with a series of colourful **murals**. There are now more than 60 murals in the town, and occasional festivals mean the display is always being added to. The **Katikati Information Centre** (☑ 07-549 1658; www.katikati.org.nz; 36 Main Rd; ⊗ 9am-1pm Mon-Fri, extended hours in summer; ☎) sells a guide to the murals ($5), or you can take a small-group guided tour.

⊙ Sights

Katikati Bird Gardens
BIRD SANCTUARY

(☑07-549 0912; www.birdgardens.co.nz; 263 Walker Rd E; adult/child/family $9.50/5/25; ☺10am-4.30pm daily mid-Sep–May, Sat, Sun & public holidays only Jun–mid-Sep) About 7km south of town, the 4-hectare Katikati Bird Gardens is all aflap with native birdlife (ever seen a kawaupaka?). There's a cafe and gallery here, too, plus boutiquey cottage accommodation (double B&B $175).

Morton Estate
WINERY

(www.mortonestatewines.co.nz; 2389 SH2; ☺9.30am-5pm) Channelling Cape Dutch architecture from South Africa's wine country, Morton Estate is one of NZ's bigger wineries and sits on SH2 8km south of Katikati. It's open for tastings and stock-ups: try the smooth-as-cream chardonnay.

Western Bay Museum
MUSEUM

(☑07-549 0651; www.westernbaymuseum.com; Main Rd, The Old Fire Station; ☺9am-4pm Mon-Fri, 10am-4pm Sat & Sun) FREE Relocated in early 2016 to colourful new surroundings in a former fire station, this regional museum traces Katikati's heritage with an engaging mix of Māori artefacts and Ulster history. Don't miss the old Katikati Jail standing in the grounds, a compact hut with room for only two prisoners at a time.

🏃 Activities

Katikati Mural Tours
CULTURAL TOUR

(☑07-549 5250; www.muraltown.co.nz; per person $10; ☺11am Sat & Sun Oct-Mar by prior appointment other times) Guided tours featuring some of the 60-plus murals dotting the town.

Haiku Pathway
WALKING

(www.katikati.co.nz) Kicking off a few hundred metres past the information centre, Katikati's Haiku Pathway rambles along the Uretara River past boulders inscribed with haiku verses. A serene scene.

🛏 Sleeping

Kaimai View Motel
MOTEL $$

(☑07-549 0398; www.kaimaiview.co.nz; 84 Main Rd; d from $130; ☎⛱) Beyond a funky mural on the street-side wall, this jaunty, mod motel offers neat rooms (all named after NZ native trees) with CD player, kitchenette and,

in larger rooms, spa. The namesake views extend over the back fence.

★Warm Earth Cottage
COTTAGE $$$

(☑07-549 0962; www.warmearthcottage.co.nz; 202 Thompsons Track; d $250) Reignite your romance or simmer in simple pleasures at this rural idyll, 5km south of town then 2km west of SH2. Two pretty, electricity-less cottages sit by the swimmable Waitekohe River. Fire up the barbecue, melt into a wood-fired outdoor bath, or chew through a book in the lovely guest lounge/library. Big DIY breakfasts are included in the price.

🍴 Eating & Drinking

Ambria Restaurant & Bar
MODERN NZ $$

(☑07-549 2272; www.ambria.co.nz; 5/62 Main Rd; mains lunch $16-20, dinner $25-35; ☺5pm-late Tue & Wed, 11am-late Thu-Sat, 10am-late Sun) Surprisingly atmospheric, Ambria is a hip bar-eatery in a nondescript shopping strip on the eastern side of town. Order a glass of Kiwi wine to wash down your roasted confit duck with kumara mash. Gourmet pizzas ($24 to $26) straddle both the lunch and dinner menus. Try the tasty Ambria pizza with seared beef, caramelised onions and blue cheese.

Talisman Hotel & Landing Restaurant
PUB

(☑07-549 2218; www.facebook.com/talisman hotel; 7 Main Rd; ☺11am-late Mon-Fri, 10am-late Sat & Sun) The Talisman is the local boozer, with occasional live music, a great pub quiz on Thursday nights, and regular good-value specials at the Landing Restaurant. Wednesday is pizza-and-a-pint night, and the burgers and steaks are also well priced.

ℹ Getting There & Away

InterCity and Naked Bus both stop in Katikati.

Maketu
POP 1240

Take SH2 through Te Puke then turn left onto Maketu Rd and you'll find yourself deposited at this seaside town which, although historic, has seen better days.

Maketu played a significant role in NZ's history as the landing site of *Te Arawa* canoe in 1340, commemorated with a somewhat underwhelming 1940 monument on the foreshore. The town is now famous for Maketu Pies (p310).

✖ Eating

Maketu Pies   FAST FOOD $
(☑07-533 2358; www.maketupies.co.nz; 6 Little Waihi Rd; pies $4-6; ⊗9am-3.30pm Mon-Fri) The famous Maketu Pies are baked fresh daily here, employing a good proportion of the population. You can buy a pie, hot from the oven, at the factory shopfront, or from the shop next door if you're here on a weekend (go for the chilli, cheese and beef flavour).

Te Puke
POP 7500

Welcome to the 'Kiwifruit Capital of the World', a busy town during the picking season when there's plenty of work around.

◉ Sights

Kiwi360   FARM
(☑07-573 6340, 0800 549 4360; www.kiwi360. com; 35 Young Rd, off SH2; admission free, tours adult/child/family $20/6/46; ⊗9am-5pm) For the low-down on all things kiwifruit, swing into Kiwi360 at the turn-off for Maketu. Sitting among orchards of nashi pears, citrus, avocados and (you guessed it) kiwifruit, this visitor centre peels off a range of attractions including a 35-minute 'kiwicart' orchard tour, kiwifruit viewing tower (not much of a view) and a cafe serving kiwifruit delights.

⌷ Sleeping

Te Puke Backpackers   HOSTEL $
(☑07-573 8015; www.tepukebackpackers.com; 2 No 1 Rd; dm/tw/d from $25/60/60; @🖢🛜) For fruit-pickers and doyens of dorm-life there's basic hostel accommodation at Te Puke Backpackers, a sociable, barnlike affair on the Whakatane side of town with a roomy communal space and small, tidy bedrooms.

They can usually fix travellers up with seasonal work; see the website for details.

🔒 Shopping

Comvita   BEAUTY
(☑07-533 1987; www.experiencecomvita.com; 23 Wilson Rd S, Paengaroa; admission free, guided tours adult/child $18/9; ⊗8.30am-5pm Mon-Fri, 9.30am-4pm Sat & Sun) About 10km south of Te Puke in Paengaroa, Comvita is home to NZ's most famous honey- and bee-derived health-care products. The big new visitor centre offers 40-minute guided tours exploring how bee by-products and native NZ plants such as manuka are harvested for health products. Grab a pot of vitamin E cream with bee pollen and manuka honey on your way out.

We can also recommend the honey-flavoured ice cream – slightly less healthy, but delicious.

ⓘ Information

Te Puke Visitor Information Centre (☑07-573 9172; www.tepuke.co.nz; 130 Jellicoe St; ⊗8am-5pm Mon-Fri, 9am-noon Sat; 🛜) The Te Puke Visitor Information Centre is in the same building as the public library (staff will confirm that 'Puke' rhymes with cookie, not fluke).

ⓘ Getting There & Away

InterCity and Naked Bus both stop at Te Puke.

Whakatane
POP 18,950

A true pohutukawa paradise, Whakatane (pronounced 'fokka-*tar*-nay') sits on a natural harbour at the mouth of the river of the same name. It's the hub of the Rangitaiki agricultural district, but there's much more to Whakatane than farming – blissful beach-

---

HOT FUZZ: KIWIFRUIT

The humble kiwifruit earns New Zealand more than a billion dollars every year, and with the Bay of Plenty in the thick of the action, it's no wonder the locals are fond of them.

The fruit's origins are in China, where it was called the monkey peach (they were considered ripe when the monkeys munched them). As they migrated to NZ, they were renamed the Chinese gooseberry – they were a lot smaller then, but canny Kiwis engineered them to more generous sizes and began exporting them in the 1950s. The fruit was then sexily rebranded as the Zespri. Today the Zesprians grow two types of kiwifruit: the common fuzzy-skinned green fruit, and the gold fruit with its smooth complexion. To learn more about the kiwifruit, visit **Kiwi360**.

For visitors after a dollar or two, there's always kiwifruit-picking work around the area, most of it during harvest (May and June): don't expect to make much more than $15 an hour. Enquire at regional i-SITEs, or check online at www.picknz.co.nz.

Whakatane

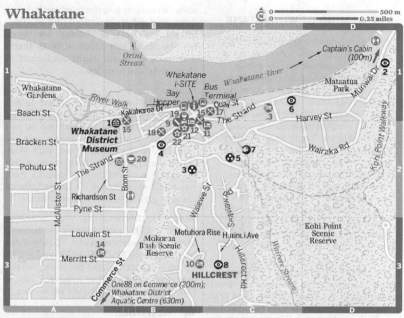

Whakatane

es, a sunny main-street vibe and volcanic Whakaari (White Island) for starters. And (despite Nelson's protestations) it's officially NZ's sunniest city. It's also the departure point for boat trips to nearby Moutuhora (Whale Island), just 9km off the coast.

◎ Sights

On the cliff tops behind the town are two ancient Ngāti Awa *pa* sites – Te Papaka

and Puketapu – both of which offer sensational (and very defendable) outlooks over Whakatane.

Te Manuka Tutahi Marae CULTURAL CENTRE
(☏ 07-308 4271; www.mataatua.com; 105 Muriwai Dr; 90min cultural tours adult/child $49/15; ⊙ 9am-4pm Dec-Feb, reduced hours Mar-Nov) FREE The centrepiece of this recently opened Ngāti Awa *marae* isn't new: Mataatua Wharenui (The House that Came Home) is a fantastically

THE NAMING OF WHAKATANE

Whakatane's name originated some eight centuries ago, 200 years after the original Māori settlers arrived here. The warrior Toroa and his family sailed into the estuary in a huge ocean-going *waka* (canoe), the *Mataatua*. As the men went ashore to greet local leaders, the tide turned, and the *waka* – with all the women on board – drifted out to sea. Toroa's daughter, Wairaka, cried out *'E! Kia whakatane au i ahau!'* (Let me act as a man!) and, breaking the traditional *tapu* (taboo) on women steering a *waka*, she took up the paddle and brought the boat safely ashore. A whimsical **statue of Wairaka** stands proudly atop a rock in Whakatane's harbour in commemoration of her brave deed.

carved 1875 meeting house. In 1879 it was dismantled and shipped to Sydney, before spending 71 years in the Otago Museum from 1925. It was returned to the Ngāti Awa in 1996. You can check out Mataatua Wharenui from the outside for free (behave respectfully), or book an excellent cultural tour.

★ **Whakatane**
District Museum MUSEUM, GALLERY
(☑ 07-306 0509; www.whakatanemuseum.org.nz; Esplanade Mall, Kakahoroa Dr; admission by donation; ⊙ 9am-5pm Mon-Fri, 10am-2pm Sat & Sun) This impressive museum-gallery in the library building has artfully presented displays on early Māori and European settlement in the area: Māori *taonga* (treasures) trace a lineage back to the *Mataatua* canoe. Other displays focus on Whakaari (White Island) and Moutuhora (Whale Island). The gallery section presents a varied program of NZ and international exhibitions.

Wairere Falls WATERFALL
(Te Wairere; Toroa St) Tumbling down the cliffs behind town, picture-perfect Te Wairere occupies a deliciously damp nook, and once powered flax and flour mills and supplied Whakatane's drinking water. It's a gorgeous spot, and goes almost completely unheralded: in any other country there'd be a ticket booth, interpretive audiovisual displays and a hot-dog van!

Pohaturoa LANDMARK
(cnr The Strand & Commerce St) Beside a roundabout on the Strand is Pohaturoa, a large

tapu (sacred) rock outcrop, where baptism, death, war and *moko* (tattoo) rites were performed. The Treaty of Waitangi was signed here by Ngāti Awa chiefs in 1840; there's a monument to the Ngāti Awa chief Te Hurinui Apanui here, too.

Muriwai's Cave CAVE
(Muriwai Dr) The partially collapsed Te Ana o Muriwai (Muriwai's Cave) once extended 122m into the hillside and sheltered 60 people, including Muriwai, a famous seer and aunt of Wairaka (p312). Along with Wairere Falls and a rock in the harbour-mouth, the cave was one of three landmarks Toroa was told to look for by his father Irakewa, when he arrived in the *Mataatua* canoe.

Whakatane Observatory OBSERVATORY
(☑ 07-308 6495; www.whakatane.info/business/whakatane-astronomical-society; 22 Hurinui Ave; adult/child/family $15/5/35; ⊙ 7.30pm Tue & Fri) Up on a hill top behind the town, Whakatane Observatory offers plentiful Bay of Plenty star-spotting when the sky is clear.

🏃 Activities

Feel like a stroll? The **Kohi Point Walkway** is highly recommended: a bushy four-hour, 5.5km track with panoramic cliff-top views and a genuine 'gasp' moment when you set eyes on Otarawairere Bay. A short detour rewards you with amazing views from **Toi's Pa** (Kapua te rangi), reputedly the oldest *pa* site in NZ. You can also get to Toi's Pa by a partly unsealed access road off the Whakatane–Ohope road. From Ohope, you can catch the bus back to Whakatane if there aren't any more kilometres in your legs. Ask the i-SITE for a walk map.

A flatter option is the **River Walk** (two to three hours), following the Whakatane River past the Botanical Gardens, Muriwai's Cave and on to Wairaka's statue.

Diveworks Dolphin
& Seal Encounters DIVING, WILDLIFE TOUR
(☑ 07-308 2001, 0800 354 7737; www.whaleislandtours.com; 96 The Strand; dolphin & seal swimming adult/child $160/130, diving incl gear from $215) This dive/ecotour company runs dolphin- and seal-swimming trips from Whakatane (cheaper if you're just watching from the boat), plus guided tours of Moutuhora (Whale Island; adult/child $120/85) and diving at Whakaari (White Island; two dives including gear $300). Fishing trips also available.

Those concerned with the welfare of dolphins and other marine mammals should be aware that swimming with them in the wild is considered by some to be disruptive to the habitat and behaviour of the animals.

Whakatane

District Aquatic Centre
SWIMMING
(☏ 07-308 4192; www.whakatane.govt.nz/aquatic; 28 Short St; adult/child/family $4/2.20/11.50; ⏰ 6am-8pm Mon-Fri, 7am-6pm Sat & Sun) Indoor and outdoor pools, spa pools and a tubular yellow worm of a water slide ($4).

🛏 Sleeping

Windsor Backpackers
HOSTEL $
(☏ 07-308 8040; www.windsorlodge-backpackers. co.nz; 10 Merritt St; dm/s/d from $26/49/68; @ 🛜) Whakatane's best backpackers occupies a converted funeral parlour...so expect a restful sleep! Excellent rooms range from serviceable dorms to a couple of motel-standard doubles out the front. The communal kitchen, lounge and barbecue courtyard are spacious and tidy.

Whakatane Hotel
HOTEL $
(☏ 07-307 1670; www.whakatanehotel.co.nz; 79 The Strand; dm $25, d from $70; 🛜) This lovely old art-deco classic has basic (but very decent) rooms upstairs in two wings. Clean shared bathrooms, high ceilings, communal kitchen... great value for money. Some rooms cop a bit of noise from the pub downstairs, but the owners try to shuffle people around to dodge the din.

Awakeri Hot Springs
HOLIDAY PARK $
(☏ 07-304 9117; www.awakerisprings.co.nz; SH30; sites $36, d cabins/flats/units $70/85/95; 🛜) About 16km from Whakatane on the road to Rotorua (SH30) you'll come to the immaculate Awakeri Hot Springs, an old-fashioned holiday park complete with (as the name suggests) hot springs (adult/child $7.50/5), picnic areas and a bed for every budget.

One88 on Commerce
MOTEL $$
(☏ 07-307 0915; www.one88commerce.co.nz; 188 Commerce St; d/ste from $160/200) This new motel features spacious rooms and extra-large super-king suites. Most options feature spa baths and private courtyards; together with classy kitchen appliances and huge flat-screen TVs, it all adds up to the best rooms in town. One88 is in a quiet location a 10-minute walk from central Whakatane. Welcome to one of the best new hotels in NZ.

Captain's Cabin
APARTMENT $$
(☏ 07-308 5719; www.captainscabin.co.nz; 23 Muriwai Dr; d $230) On the serene side of town with sparkling water views, this homely self-contained unit is perfect if you're hanging around for a few days (cheaper for two nights or more). A cosy living area cleverly combines bedroom, lounge, kitchen and dining room, with a second smaller room and bijou bathroom – all sweetly decorated along nautical lines. Sleeps three.

Tuscany Villas
MOTEL $$
(☏ 07-308 2244; www.tuscanyvillas.co.nz; 57 The Strand E; d $150-225; 🛜) This mod motel may be a long way from Florence, but it still offers a few rays of Italian sunshine with interesting architecture, wrought-iron balconies and floral plantings wherever there's room. Rooms are luxurious and comfy, with super-king beds and spa pools, and its new bistro should now be open.

White Island Rendezvous
HOTEL, B&B $$
(☏ 07-308 9588, 0800 242 299; www.whiteisland rendezvous.co.nz; 15 The Strand E; d $120-150, apt from $180, B&B $190; 🛜) An immaculate 28-room complex run by the on-the-ball White Island Tour people (cheaper rates for tour goers). Lots of balcony and deck space for inhaling the sea air, while interiors are decked out with timber floors for a nautical vibe. Deluxe rooms come with spas; disabled-access facilities available. The B&B next door includes cooked breakfast.

Motuhora Rise B&B
B&B $$$
(☏ 07-307 0224; www.motuhorarise.com; 2 Motuhora Rise; d $230; 🛜) At the top of the town in both senses (steep driveway!), this jaunty hill-top spot feels vaguely Rocky Mountains, and affords a distant glimpse of Moutuhora (Whale Island). Expect a gourmet cheeseboard on arrival, along with other extras such as a home theatre, an outdoor spa, and fishing rods and golf clubs. Kid-free zone.

🍴 Eating

L'Epicerie
CAFE $
(☏ 07-308 5981; www.lepicerie.co.nz; 73 The Strand; mains $10-16; ⏰ 7.30am-3.30pm Mon-Fri, 8.30am-2.30pm Sat, 9am-2pm Sun) Sacré bleu! This classic French cafe in central Whakatane is a real surprise, serving terrific omelettes, croissants, crepes and croques monsieur at communal tables. Fabulous coffee and deli shelves crammed with preserves, breads mustards and deliciously stinky French cheeses complete a very Gallic scene. Try an excellent galette (savoury pancake) for a leisurely breakfast.

Niko Niko
JAPANESE $

(☑07-307 7351; 43 Kakahoroa Dr; sushi $2-3; ☺9am-6.30pm) Quick-fire sushi joint tucked between the Strand and the waterfront. Order a couple of gorgeously presented chilli chicken rolls and hit the sunny outdoor tables. Priced from $11 to $14, the extra-long sushi rolls are really good value.

Soulsa
MODERN NZ $$$

(☑07-307 8689; www.whakatane.info/website/183; 126 The Strand; mains lunch $17-20, dinner $28-33; ☺5.30-9pm Tue-Sat & 11am-2pm Fri) Seasonal produce is transformed into excellent dishes at this cosy spot on Whakatane's main street. Begin with the duck and blueberry spring rolls before trying the venison with kumara (sweet potato), parsnip puree and roasted macadamias. There's a good wine list, and Friday lunch is a more relaxed affair with well-priced mains including a top beef burger with caramelised onions.

Roquette
MODERN NZ, MEDITERRANEAN $$$

(☑07-307 0722; www.roquette-restaurant.co.nz; 23 Quay St; mains lunch $20-34, dinner $30-37; ☺10am-late Mon-Sat) A modern waterside restaurant, ritzy Roquette serves up refreshing Mediterranean-influenced fare with lots of summery salads, risotto and fish dishes. Laid-back tunes, lots of glass and mosaics, good coffee and sexy staff to boot. Try the chargrilled lamb salad or the prawn and chorizo *arancini*. An early-bird menu (5pm to 6pm) Monday to Friday incorporates a glass of wine for $23.

🍺 Drinking & Nightlife

Straight Up Espresso
CAFE

(☑021 069 9637; 5 Boon St; ☺7.30am-4pm Mon-Fri) Does exactly what it is says on the tin with the best coffee in town. Colourful wall art, cool tunes and tasty snacks are all valid reasons to linger.

Detour Bar & Lounge
BAR

(☑07-308 0398; www.facebook.com/DetourBar Lounge; 84 The Strand; ☺noon-late) Detour is Whakatane's classiest lounge bar serving tapas ($12 to $20), platters ($25 to $36) and cocktails to an over-25s crowd. Meaty mains ($25 to $31) off the Stonegrill kick in at 4pm.

Office
BAR

(☑07-307 0123; www.whakatane.info/business/office-bar-grill; 82 The Strand; ☺10am-late) The sporty Office does what it does well: beer, big meals with chips and salad all over (mains $18 to $32), and live bands and/or DJs Thursday to Saturday nights.

☆ Entertainment

Boiler Room
LIVE MUSIC

(☑07-307 1670; www.whakatanehotel.co.nz; Whakatane Hotel, 79 The Strand; ☺10pm-2.30am Fri & Sat) Whakatane's only club is at the Whakatane Hotel. DJs, live bands and the occasional Kiwi stand-up comic raise the roof. Check the Whakatane Hotel on Facebook to see what's scheduled.

WhakaMax Movies
CINEMA

(☑07-308 7623; www.whakamax.co.nz; 99 The Strand; adult/child $14/9; ☺10am-late) Right in the middle of the Strand, WhakaMax screens new-release movies. Cheaper tickets before 5pm and on Tuesdays.

ℹ Information

Post Office (www.nzpost.co.nz; 197 The Strand; ☺8.30am-5pm Mon-Fri, 9am-noon Sat) Centrally located.

Whakatane Hospital (☑07-306 0999; www.bopdhb.govt.nz; cnr Stewart & Garaway Sts; ☺24hr) Emergency medical treatment.

Whakatane i-SITE (☑07-306 2030, 0800 924 528; www.whakatane.com; cnr Quay St & Kakahoroa Dr; ☺8.30am-5.30pm Mon-Fri, 9am-4pm Sat & Sun; 🛜) Free internet access (including 24-hour wi-fi on the terrace outside the building), tour bookings, accommodation and general DOC enquiries. Also bike hire for exploring nearby coastal pathways.

ℹ Getting There & Away

AIR

Air Chathams (☑0800 580 127; www.air chathams.co.nz) Links Whakatane to Auckland.

Sunair (☑0800 786 247; www.sunair.co.nz) Flies on weekdays from Whakatane to Gisborne and Hamilton.

BUS

InterCity buses stop outside the i-SITE. Destinations include the following, with onward connections:

DESTINATION	PRICE	TIME (HR)	FREQUENCY
Auckland	$36	6	1 daily
Gisborne via Opotiki	$16	3	1 daily
Rotorua	$23	1¼	1 daily
Tauranga via Rotorua	$25	8	1 daily

MOUTUHORA (WHALE ISLAND)

Nine kilometres off Whakatane is Moutuhora (Whale Island) – so-called because of its leviathan shape. It's one of the less active members of the Taupo Volcanic Zone, although there are hot springs along its shore. The summit is 353m high and the island has several historic sites, including an ancient *pa* (fortified village) site, a quarry and a camp.

Whale Island was originally home to a Māori settlement. In 1829, Māori massacred sailors from the trading vessel *Haweis* while it was anchored at Sulphur Bay. In 1867 the island passed into European ownership and remains privately owned, although since 1965 it has been a DOC-protected wildlife refuge for seabirds and shorebirds. New Zealand fur seals are also frequently spotted.

The island's protected status means landing is restricted. Operators departing from Whakatane include **White Island Tours** (☑0800 733 529; www.moutuhora.co.nz; 15 The Strand East, Whakatane; adult/child $90/60; ☼10am-1.30pm), **Diveworks Dolphin & Seal Encounters** (p312) and **KG Kayaks** (p315).

Naked Bus destinations include the following:

DESTINATION	PRICE	TIME (HR)	FREQUENCY
Auckland	$40	6	1 daily
Gisborne	$28	3¼	1 daily
Hamilton	$35	2½	1 daily
Rotorua	$25	1½	1 daily
Tauranga	$20	4	1 daily
Wellington	$80	10	1 daily

Bay Hopper (☑0800 422 928; www.baybus. co.nz) local buses run to Ohope ($3.20, 45 minutes, six daily), Opotiki ($9, one hour, two daily Monday and Wednesday) and Tauranga ($14.50, two hours, one daily Monday to Saturday).

Whakaari (White Island)

New Zealand's most active volcano (it last erupted in 2013) lies 49km off the Whakatane coast. The small island was originally formed by three separate volcanic cones of different ages. The two oldest have been eroded, while the younger cone has risen up between them. Mt Gisborne is the highest point on the island at 321m. Geologically, Whakaari is related to Moutuhora (Whale Island) and Putauaki (Mt Edgecumbe), as all lie along Taupo Volcanic Zone.

The island is dramatic, with hot water hissing and steaming from vents over most of the crater floor. Temperatures of 600°C to 800°C have been recorded.

The island is privately owned so you can only visit it with a licensed tour operator. Fixed-wing air operators run flyover tours only, while boat and helicopter tours will usually include a walking tour around the island including a visit to the ruins of the sulphur-mining factory – an interesting story in itself. Most tours depart Whakatane; scenic flights are also possible ex-Tauranga and Rotorua.

Activities

White Island Flights   SCENIC FLIGHTS
(☑0800 944 834; www.whiteislandflights.co.nz; Whakatane Airport; flights per person $249) Fixed-wing scenic flights over Whakaari, with lots of photo opportunities. A Whakaari/Mt Tarawera combo flight costs $339.

Frontier Helicopters   SCENIC FLIGHTS
(☑0800 804 354; www.whiteislandvolcano.co.nz; Whakatane Airport; flights per person from $650) A two-hour trip to Whakaari (departing from Whakatane) that includes a one-hour guided walk on the volcano.

White Island Tours   BOAT TOUR
(☑0800 733 529, 07-308 9588; www.whiteisland. co.nz; 15 The Strand, Whakatane; 6hr tours adult/ child $199/130; ☼departures 7am-12.30pm) The only official boat trip to Whakaari (on board the good ship *Pee Jay*), with dolphin-spotting en route and a two-hour tour of the island. Moutuhora (Whale Island) tours also available (adult/child $95/59).

Ohope

POP 2760

Just 7km over the hill from Whakatane, Ohope has great beaches, perfect for lazing or surfing, and is backed by sleepy **Ohiwa Harbour**.

Activities

KG Kayaks   KAYAKING
(☑07-315 4005, 027 272 4073; www.kgkayaks. co.nz; 93 Kuatere Wharf Rd, Kuatere; tours $85-155, 2hr hire s/d $45/70) Based on the shores

of Ohiwa Harbour, just 1km from Kutarere (18km southeast of Ohope), KG Kayaks offers guided tours and kayak hire around the eastern Bay of Plenty. Popular guided options include Ohiwa Harbour, four-hour boat trips to Moutuhora (Whale Island) – with two hours of kayaking around the island – and a coastal adventure between Whakatane and Ohope.

Moonlight kayaking trips are also available, and freedom kayak hires – including all safety gear and dry bags – allow travellers to explore compact islands in Ohiwa Harbour. In December and January, KG Kayaks also operates from Port Ohope.

Salt Spray Surf School   SURFING
(☑ 021 149 1972; www.facebook.com/bysaltspraysurf-school; 2hr lessons from $70) If you want to splash around in the Ohope Beach surf, get some lessons at Salt Spray Surf School, which provides all gear and offers discounts for groups.

↷ Tours

Moanarua Tours   BOAT TOUR
(☑ 07-312 5924; www.moanarua.co.nz; 2 Hoterini St; 3hr boat tours per person $80, bike/kayak rental from $10/15) Offers boat trips with a Māori cultural and historical focus, plus sunset tours and fishing trips. Also bike and kayak hire for those who wish to go exploring.

🛏 Sleeping

Aquarius Motel   MOTEL $
(☑ 07-312 4550; www.aquariusmotorlodge.co.nz; 103 Harbour Rd; d $100-150; 🐾) For a quiet, affordable motel-style option, roll into Aquarius, a basic complex with various room configurations, all with kitchens and just 100m from the beach (you don't need a swimming pool).

Ohope Beach Top 10
Holiday Park   HOLIDAY PARK $
(☑ 0800 264 673, 07-312 4460; www.ohopebeach.co.nz; 367 Harbour Rd; sites $46, cabins/units/apts from $95/144/250; @🐾🏊) The Ohope Beach Top 10 Holiday Park is the very model of a modern holiday park, with a raft of family-friendly facilities: sports courts, minigolf, pool... Plus some great apartments peeking over the dunes at the Bay of Plenty. Busy as a woodpecker in summer (with prices to match).

★ Moanarua Beach Cottage   B&B $$
(☑ 07-312 5924; www.moanarua.co.nz; 2 Hoterini St; d $155-165) Well-travelled owners Miria and Taroi trace their ancestry back to the North Island's Ngāti Awa and Tuhoe tribes, and they're adept at combining a warm welcome

with information on local Māori heritage, art and culture. Accommodation is either in the self-contained Moanarua Beach Cottage – trimmed with Māori design – or in the charming Pohutukawa room in the main house.

Taroi can hook visitors up with bike and kayak rental, and arrange fishing and boating trips.

🍴 Eating

Port Ohope General Store   CAFE $
(☑ 07-312 4707; www.portohope.co.nz; 311 Harbour Rd; mains $11-25; ⏱9am-6pm) This cute little cafe offers fresh juices, real fruit ice creams and gourmet burgers, and is a top spot for an alfresco wine or beer with pizza or fish and chips. During summer a retro caravan serves up coffee, and there's also paddle-board and bike rental available.

Ohiwa Oyster Farm   SEAFOOD $
(☑ 07 312 4565; www.whakatane.info/business/ohiwa-oyster-farm; 111 Wainui Rd; meals $7-15; ⏱8.30am-6.30pm) Poised over a swampy back-reach of Ohiwa Harbour (serious oyster territory), this classic roadside fish shack is perfect for a fish and chip (and oyster) picnic.

Fisherman's Wharf   CAFE $$
(☑ 07-312 4017; www.facebook.com/fishermanswharfcafe; 340 Harbour Rd; mains $18-32; ⏱6-10pm Wed-Sun & 10am-3pm Sun) Look forward to stellar harbour views at this new restaurant with spacious decks. A relaxed beachy vibe showcases meals including excellent steaks and seafood – try the fish tacos – and there's a decent beer and wine selection to ease you into another Ohope evening. Takeaway fish and chips are available from a handy window outside.

Hui Bar & Grill   MODERN NZ $$
(☑ 07-312 5623; www.huibarandgrill.com; 19 Pohutukawa Ave; mains $12-22; ⏱3-8pm Mon, 10am-10pm Tue-Fri, 8.30am-10pm Sat & Sun) With polished concrete floors, white leather banquettes and fold-back windows, Hui is a ritzy bar-grill making a splash in little Ohope's shopping strip. Try some chipotle mussels with garlic and herbs or the legendary big breakfast. Look forward to NZ wines, and occasional live music from 2pm on Sunday afternoons

❶ Getting There & Away

Bayhopper route 122 makes the short 30-minute journey across the hill from Whakatane to Ohope.

Opotiki

POP 8440

The Opotiki area was settled from at least 1150, some 200 years before the larger 14th-century Māori migration. Māori traditions are well preserved here, with the work of master carvers lining the main street and the occasional facial *moko* passing by. The town acts as a gateway to the East Coast, and has excellent beaches – Ohiwa and Waiotahi – and an engaging museum.

Sights

Pick up the *Historic Opotiki* brochure from the i-SITE (or download from www.opotikinz.com) for the low-down on the town's heritage buildings.

Hiona St Stephen's Church   CHURCH

(128 Church St; ⊙services 8am & 9.30am Sun, 10am Thu) White-weatherboard St Stephen's (1862) is an Anglican church with a perfectly proportioned timber-lined interior. Reverend Carl Volkner, known by the local Whakatohea tribe to have acted as a government spy, was murdered here in 1865. In 1992 the governor-general granted Mokomoko, the man who hanged for the crime, a full pardon, which hangs in the lobby.

Shalfoon & Francis Museum   MUSEUM

(☑07-315 5193; www.opotikimuseum.org.nz; 129 Church St; adult/child/family incl Opotiki Museum $10/5/25; ⊙10am-4pm Mon-Fri, to 2pm Sat) Opotiki's original general store has been born again, with shelves piled high with old grocery and hardware products. Handbags, sticky-tape dispensers, sets of scales, books – you name it, they had it. An amazing collection.

Opotiki Museum   MUSEUM

(☑07-315 5193; www.opotikimuseum.org.nz; 123 Church St; adult/child/family incl Shalfoon & Francis Museum $10/5/25; ⊙10am-4pm Mon-Fri, to 2pm Sat) Run by volunteers, Opotiki's excellent museum has interesting heritage displays including Māori *taonga* (treasures) militaria, re-created shopfronts (a barber, carpenter, printer...), and agricultural items including tractors and a horse-drawn wagon.

Hukutaia Domain   FOREST, ARCHAEOLOGICAL SITE

(Woodlands Rd; ⊙daylight hours) FREE Around 8km south of town is Hukutaia Domain, home to one of the finest collections of native plants in NZ. In the centre is Taketakerau, a 23m puriri tree estimated to be more than 2000 years old and a burial place for the distinguished dead of the Upokorehe *hapu* (subtribe) of Whakatohea. The remains have since been reinterred elsewhere.

Activities

Motu Trails   MOUNTAIN BIKING

(☑04-472 0080; www.motutrails.co.nz) One of the New Zealand Cycle Trail's 20 'Great Rides' Motu Trails comprises three trails around Opotiki – the easy 19km Dunes Trail, the intermediate 78km Motu Road Trail and the advanced 44km Pakihi Track – parts of which combine to form the 91km Loop Trail. See the website for details. For bike hire, camping and lodge accommodation, and shuttle services see www.motucycletrails.com or www.hireandshuttle.co.nz.

Wet 'n' Wild   RAFTING

(☑0800 462 7238, 07-348 3191; www.wetnwildrafting.co.nz; trips from $1095) Offers 100km multiday rafting and camping adventures on the Motu River (Grade III-IV rapids) near Opotiki. Wet 'n' Wild is based in Rotorua.

Motu Jet   BOATING

(☑027 470 7315, 07-325 2735; www.motujet.co.nz; SH35; trips from adult/child $95/65) Runs as many as three one-hour trips on the Motu River (which runs through the Raukumara Ranges near Opotiki) every day through summer. Winter trips by arrangement.

Festivals & Events

Opotiki Rodeo   RODEO

(☑07-322 3215 www.opotikirodeo.co.nz; adult/child $20/10; ⊙late Dec) Dust off your spurs and cowboy hat for the annual Opotiki Rodeo. Giddy-up.

Sleeping

★ Opotiki Beach House   HOSTEL $

(☑07-315 5117; www.opotikibeachhouse.co.nz; 7 Appleton Rd; dm/s/d from $30/48/66; �ⓢ) A cruisy shoe-free beachside pad with a sunny, hammock-hung deck, sea views and a *very* wide sandy backyard. Beyond the dorms and breezy lounge are decent doubles and a quirky caravan (sleeps two) for those who want a real taste of the Kiwi summer holiday. About 5km west of town; sleeps 14.

Central Oasis Backpackers   HOSTEL $

(☑07-315 5165; 30 King St; dm $22-25, s/d $35/50; �ⓢ) Inside a late-1800s kauri (timber) house, this central backpackers is a snug spot with spacious rooms, a crackling fire and a big front yard to hang out in. There's also a handy coffee caravan – open to the public – serving organic coffee, tea and fresh juices.

Capeview Cottage COTTAGE $$

(☑ 07-315 7877, 0800 227 384; www.capeview. co.nz; 167 Tablelands Rd; d $145, extra person $30; ☎) Surrounded by chirruping birds and kiwifruit orchards, this serene, self-contained cottage has two bedrooms, a barbecue and a brilliant outdoor spa from which you can soak up some rather astonishing coastal views. Weekly rates available. Say g'day from us to Jack, one of Capeview's very friendly canine hosts.

Eastland Pacific Motor Lodge MOTEL $$

(☑ 07-315 5524; www.eastlandpacific.co.nz; cnr Bridge & St John Sts; r $120-160; ☎) Bright, clean Eastland is a well-kept motel with recently modernised carpets and TVs, spa baths as standard, and a wing of five new units out the back. The two-bedroom units are top value (extra person $30).

✗ Eating

★ Two Fish CAFE $

(☑ 07-315 5448; 102 Church St; snacks $5-10, mains $7-21; ☺8am-3pm Mon-Fri, to 2pm Sat) Decent eating options are thin on the ground in Opotiki, but this cafe serves up robust homemade burgers, chowder, toasties, steak sandwiches, fab muffins and salads, plus a jumbo selection in the cabinet. Two Fish has happy staff, Cuban tunes and a retro-groovy interior and courtyard. And super coffee! Sorted.

☆ Entertainment

De Luxe Cinema CINEMA

(☑ 07-315 6110; www.facebook.com/Opotiki DeluxeTheatre; 127 Church St; adult/child $15/8) The beguiling old De Luxe shows recent movies and hosts the odd brass-band concert. Check the cinema's window or Facebook for upcoming events.

🛍 Shopping

Tangata Whenua Gallery ARTS, CRAFTS

(☑ 07-315 5558; 106 Church St; ☺9am-5pm Mon-Fri, to noon Sat & Sun) An interesting selection of arts and crafts from local Māori designers.

❶ Information

DOC (Department of Conservation; ☑ 07-315 1001; www.doc.govt.nz; 70 Bridge St; ☺8am-noon Mon-Fri) Information on tramping and mountain biking.

Opotiki i-SITE (☑ 07-315 3031; www.opotikinz. com; 70 Bridge St; ☺9am-4.30pm Mon-Fri, to 1pm Sat & Sun; ☎) Takes bookings for activities and transport and stocks the indispensable free East Coast booklet *Pacific Coast Highway*.

❶ Getting There & Away

Travelling east from Opotiki there are two routes: SH2, crossing the spectacular Waioeka Gorge, or SH35 around East Cape. The SH2 route offers some day walks in the Waioeka Gorge Scenic Reserve, with the gorge getting steeper and narrower as you travel inland, before the route crosses typically green, rolling hills, dotted with sheep, on the descent to Gisborne.

Buses stop at the Hot Bread Shop on the corner of Bridge and St John Sts, though tickets and bookings are made through the i-SITE or **Travel Shop** (☑ 07-315 8881; www.travelshop.co.nz; 104 Church St; ☺9am-4pm Mon-Thu, to 2pm Fri). The Travel Shop also rents out bikes and kayaks ($25/35 per half-/full day).

InterCity has daily buses connecting Opotiki with Whakatane (from $15, 45 minutes), Rotorua (from $15, 2½ hours) and Auckland (from $26, 7½ hours). Heading south, daily buses connect Opotiki with Gisborne (from $15, two hours).

Naked Bus runs daily services to destinations including the following:

DESTINATION	PRICE	TIME (HR)
Auckland	$45	6
Gisborne	$20	2½
Rotorua	$18	2½
Tauranga	$37	5
Wellington	$70	11

The local Bay Hopper (number 47) bus runs to Whakatane ($9, 1¼ hour, two daily Monday and Wednesday).

The East Coast

Best Places to Eat

➡ Mister D (p342)

➡ Opera Kitchen (p347)

➡ Three Doors Up (p342)

➡ Eastend Cafe (p335)

➡ Te Puka Tavern (p324)

Best Places to Sleep

➡ Stranded in Paradise (p324)

➡ Clive Colonial Cottages (p347)

➡ Millar Road (p347)

➡ Ahi Kaa Motel (p329)

➡ Pebble Beach Motor Inn (p341)

Why Go?

New Zealand is known for its mix of wildly divergent landscapes, but on the East Coast it's the sociological contours that are most pronounced. There's a full spectrum of NZ life here, from the earthy settlements on the East Cape to Havelock North's moneyed, wine-soaked streets.

Māori culture is never more visible than it is on the East Coast. Exquisitely carved *marae* (meeting house) complexes dot the landscape, and *te reo* and *tikanga* (the language and customs) are alive and well.

Intrepid types will have no trouble losing the tourist hordes – along the Pacific Coast Hwy, through rural back roads, on remote beaches, or in the mystical wilds of Te Urewera National Park. And when the call of the wild gives way to caffeine withdrawal, you can get a quick fix in Gisborne or Napier. You'll also find plenty of wine here: the Hawke's Bay region is striped with vine-rows.

When to Go

➡ The East Coast basks in a warm, mainly dry climate. Summer temperatures around Napier and sunny Gisborne nudge 25°C; in winter they rarely dip below 8°C.

➡ The Hawke's Bay region enjoys mild, dry, grape-growing conditions year-round with an average annual rainfall of just 800mm. Harvest time is autumn (March to May).

➡ In winter heavy downpours sometimes wash out sections of the Pacific Coast Hwy (SH35) around the East Cape: check road conditions at either end (Opotiki or Gisborne) before you hit the highway.

East Coast Highlights

1 Napier (p336)
Time-warping back to the 1930s, surrounded by art deco, in this mighty charming town.

2 Hawke's Bay Wine Region (p346) Sniffing and sipping your way around the local wineries.

3 Gisborne Wineries (p328)
Finding more fab NZ wine around Gisborne.

4 Te Urewera National Park (p332) Losing yourself in these mighty forests, rich in Māori culture.

5 Pacific Coast Hwy (p322)
Counting off landmarks as you cruise around the East Cape: Cape Kidnappers, Tolaga Bay, Tokomaru Bay

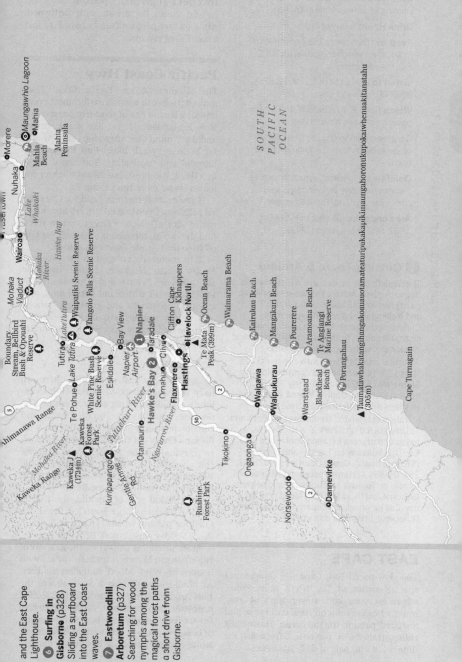

and the East Cape Lighthouse.

6 Surfing in Gisborne (p328)
Sliding a surfboard into the East Coast waves.

7 Eastwoodhill Arboretum (p327)
Searching for wood nymphs among the magical forest paths a short drive from Gisborne.

SOUTH PACIFIC OCEAN

Morere
Maungawhio Lagoon
Mahia
Nuhaka
Mahia Beach
Mahia Peninsula

Wairoa

Hawke Bay

Mohaka Viaduct
Mohaka River

Lake Whakaki

Boundary Stream, Bellbird Bush & Opouahi Reserve

Tutira
Lake Tutira
Te Pohue
Waipatiki Scenic Reserve
Tangoio Falls Scenic Reserve

White Pine Bush Scenic Reserve

Kaweka Forest Park
Kaweka J (1724m)

Kaweka Range

Mohaka River

Ahimanawa Range

Eskdale
Bay View

Napier
Napier Airport

Clifton
Cape Kidnappers

Havelock North
Ocean Beach

Waimarama Beach

Taradale
Omahu
Clive

Hastings
Flaxmere
Hawke's Bay

Te Mata Peak (399m)

Kairakau Beach
Mangakuri Beach

Kuripapango
Gentle Annie Rd

Otamauri

Ngaruroro River

Tutaekuri River

Waipawa
Waipukurau

Pourerere
Aramoana Beach

Te Angiangi Marine Reserve

Porangahau

Tikokino

Ongaonga

Wanstead

Blackhead Beach

Taumatawhakatangihangakoauauotamateaturipukakapikimaungahoronukupokaiwhenuakitanatahu (305m)

Cape Turnagain

Ruahine Forest Park

Norsewood

Dannevirke

ESSENTIAL EAST COAST

Eat Delicious fresh produce from the Hastings Farmers Market (p345).

Drink Hawke's Bay chardonnay.

Read Witi Ihimaera's 1987 novel *Whale Rider;* then watch the powerful 2002 movie adaptation.

Listen to Uawa FM (88.5FM, 88.8FM, 99.3FM) in Tolaga Bay.

Watch *Boy* (2010), Taika Waititi's hilarious film, shot at Waihau Bay.

Go green Millton (p328) vineyard – organic, biodynamic, and delicious to boot.

Online www.hawkesbaynz.com, www. gisbornenz.com, www.lonelyplanet. com/new-zealand/the-east-coast

Area code Opotiki east to Hicks Bay ☑07; rest of the region ☑06

ⓘ Getting There & Around

The region's only airports are in Gisborne and Napier. Air New Zealand (www.airnewzealand. co.nz) flies to both towns from Auckland and Wellington, and also to Napier from Christchurch. Sunair Aviation (www.sunair. co.nz) flies direct from Gisborne to Rotorua and Whakatane, with onward connections.

Regular InterCity (www.intercity.co.nz) and Naked Bus (www.nakedbus.com) services ply State Hwy 2 (SH2) and State Hwy 5 (SH5), connecting Gisborne, Opotiki, Wairoa, Napier and Hastings with all the main centres.

Transport is limited around the East Cape and Te Urewera National Park. Bay Hopper (www. baybus.co.nz) runs between Opotiki and Potaka/Cape Runaway on Tuesday and Thursday ($16, two hours). **Cooks Couriers** (☑021 371 364, 06-864 4711) runs between Te Araroa and Opotiki on Tuesday and Thursday, and between Gisborne and Hicks Bay daily Monday to Saturday. Call for prices and departure/arrival times. Otherwise, bring your own wheels.

EAST CAPE

The slow-paced East Cape is a unique and special corner of NZ. It's a quiet place, where everyone knows everyone and community ties are built on rural enterprise and a shared passion for the ocean. Horse-back riding, tractors on the beach, fresh fish for dinner – it's all part of daily life here.

Inland, the wild Raukumara Range forms the Cape's jagged spine. Tracing the fringe of the land, the 327km Pacific Coast Hwy (SH35) runs from Opotiki to Gisborne. Lonely shores lie strewn with driftwood, while picture-postcard sandy bays lure just a handful of visitors.

Pacific Coast Hwy

The winding 327km Pacific Coast Hwy around the North Island's easternmost point has long been a rite of road-trip passage for New Zealanders. If you like scenic drives and don't mind that attractions are few and far between, you'll likely find the journey intrepid and captivating. You can drive it in a day if you must, but an overnighter (or longer) is far more rewarding.

If you're short on time, head for Gisborne via SH2 from Opotiki: a 147km, 2½-hour alternative via the Waioeka Gorge, where you'll find the two- to three-hour loop walk leading off from the historic Tauranga Bridge.

Both routes are covered in the excellent *Pacific Coast Highway Guide,* available at Gisborne (p330) and Opotiki (p318) i-SITEs. Set off with a full petrol tank, and stock up on snacks and groceries – shops and petrol stations are in short supply. Sleeping and eating options are also pretty spread out: plan accordingly.

◉ Sights

Along the coast east of Opotiki, there are hazy views across to Whakaari (White Island), a chain-smoking active volcano. The desolate beaches at Torere, Hawai and Omaio are steeply shelved and littered with flotsam. Check out the magnificent *whakairo* (carving) on the Torere school gateway. Hawai marks the western boundary of the Whanau-a-Apanui tribe, whose *rohe* (traditional land) extends to Cape Runaway.

Some 67km east of Opotiki, the fishing town of Te Kaha once sounded the death knell for passing whales. Here you'll find a shop, holiday park, hostel, B&B and resort.

At Papatea Bay stop to see the gateway of Hinemahuru Marae, intricately carved with images of WWI Māori Battalion soldiers. At blink-and-you'll-miss-it Raukokore, the 1894 Anglican Christ Church (☑07-352 3979; ruakokore.church@gmail.com; SH35; ☺8am-8pm Oct-Apr, 9am-5pm May-Sep) is a sweet beacon of belief on a lonely promontory. The simple white and grey interior is suitably demure (look for the mouse on high). There are services at 11am on Sundays.

Some 17km east of **Waihau Bay**, where there's a petrol pump, pub and accommodation, **Whangaparaoa (Cape Runaway)** was where kumara was first introduced to NZ. It can only be reached on foot. East of Whangaparaoa the road tracks inland, crossing into hilly Ngāti Porou territory before hitting the coast at **Hicks Bay**, a real middle-of-nowhere settlement with a grand beach. There's safe sandy swimming at **Onepoto Bay** nearby.

Around 10km east of Hicks Bay is **Te Araroa**, a lone-dog village with shops, a petrol pump, a takeaway and beautifully carved *marae*. The geology changes here from igneous outcrops to sandstone cliffs: the dense bush backdrop doesn't seem to mind which it grows on. More than 350 years old, 20m high and 40m wide, **Te-Waha-O-Rerekohu**, allegedly NZ's largest pohutukawa tree, stands in the Te Araroa schoolyard.

From Te Araroa, drive out to see the **East Cape Lighthouse**, the easterly tip of mainland NZ. It's 21km (30 minutes) east of town along a mainly unsealed road, with a 25-minute climb (750 steps!) to the lighthouse. Set your alarm and get up there for sunrise.

Heading through farmland south of Te Araroa, the first town you come to is **Tikitiki**. If you haven't yet made it into a *marae*, you'll get a fair idea of what you're missing out on by visiting the extraordinary **St Mary's Church** (1889 SH35; by donation; ☺9am-5pm), built in 1924. It's nothing special from the outside, but step inside for a sensory overload. There are woven *tukutuku* (flax panels) on the walls, geometrically patterned stained-glass windows, painted beams and amazing carvings – check out the little guys holding up the pulpit. A stained-glass crucifixion scene behind the pulpit depicts WWI Māori Battalion soldiers in attendance.

Beyond Tikitiki, **Mt Hikurangi** (1752m) juts out of the Raukumara Range – it's the highest nonvolcanic peak on the North Island and the first spot on Earth to see the sun each day. According to local tradition it was the first piece of land dragged up when Maui snagged the North Island. The Ngāti Porou version of the Maui story has his canoe and earthly remains resting here on their sacred mountain. Pick up the Ngāti Porou-produced *Mt Hikurangi* brochure from regional visitor information centres for more info.

Continuing south, the road passes **Ruatoria** (shop, petrol and general desolation) and **Te Puia Springs** (ditto). Along this stretch a 14km loop road offers a rewarding detour to **Waipiro Bay**.

Eleven kilometres south of Te Puia Springs is **Tokomaru Bay**, perhaps the most interesting spot on the entire route, its broad beach framed by sweeping cliffs. The town has weathered hard times since the freezing works closed in the 1950s, but it still sports several attractions including good beginner surfing, swimming, and a good pub (p324). You'll also find a supermarket, takeaway and post office in the town (...and a B&B in the former post office), plus some crumbling surprises at the far end of the bay.

Heading south from Tokomaru Bay is a bucolic 22km stretch of highway to the turn-off to **Anaura Bay**, 6km away. It's a definite 'wow' moment when the bay springs into view far below. Captain Cook arrived here in 1769 and commented on the 'profound peace in which the people were living and their 'truly astonishing' cultivations.

Back on the highway it's 14km south to **Tolaga Bay**, East Cape's largest community (population 830) The Tolaga Bay Visitor Information Centre (p325) is in the foyer of the local radio station (Uawa FM; 88.5FM). Just off the main street, **Tolaga Bay Cashmere Company** (✆06-862 6746; www.cashmere.co.nz; 31 Solander St, Tolaga Bay; ☺10am-4pm Mon-Fri) inhabits the art-deco former council building. Watch the knitters knit, then perhaps purchase one of their delicate works: call to check it's open.

Tolaga is defined by its amazing **historic wharf**. Built in 1929 and commercially functional until 1968, it's the longest in the southern hemisphere (660m), and is caught somewhere between rusty decay and dedicated (expensive!) preservation efforts.

🏃 Activities

Cooks Cove Walkway   TRAMPING
(www.doc.govt.nz; Wharf Rd, Tolaga Bay; ☺closed Aug-Oct) Near the amazing old wharf at Tolaga Bay is Cooks Cove Walkway, an easy 5.8km, 2½-hour loop through farmland and native bush to a cove where the captain landed. At the northern end of the beach is the Tatarahake Cliffs Lookout, a sharp 10-minute walk to an excellent vantage point.

Eastender Horse Treks   HORSE RIDING
(✆021 025 8072; www.eastenderhorsetreks.co.nz; 836 Rangitukia Rd, Rangituka; 2/4hr treks $85/120) Amid the farming sprawl of Rangitukia, 8km down towards the coast from Tikitiki, Eastender Horse Treks runs horse rides along the beach or through the bush. Also offers

overnight camps ($290) and can hook you up with bone-carving lessons (from $60).

Wet 'n' Wild Rafting RAFTING
(07-348 3191, 0800 462 7238; www.wetnwild rafting.co.nz; 2-5 days $995-1095) Wet 'n' Wild Rafting offers multiday excursions on the Motu River, with the longest taking you 100km down the river. The two-day tour requires you to be helicoptered in, and therefore costs as much as the five-day trip.

🛏 Sleeping

★ Stranded in Paradise HOSTEL $
(06-864 5870; www.bbh.co.nz; 21 Potae St, Tokomaru Bay; campsites per person $15, dm/s/d $28/45/66; 🛜) Up on the hill behind town, 12-bed Stranded in Paradise scores points for views, eco-loos and free wi-fi. There are two tricky loft dorm rooms, a double downstairs and three wave-shaped cabins. Tenters have a panoramic knoll (astonishing bay views!) on which to pitch.

Tolaga Bay Holiday Park HOLIDAY PARK $
(06-862 6716; www.tolagabayholidaypark.co.nz; 167 Wharf Rd, Tolaga Bay; sites per adult/child from $16/10, cabins $60-100; 🛜) Tolaga Bay Holiday Park is right next to the wharf. The stiff ocean breeze tousles Norfolk Island pines as open lawns bask in the sunshine. It's a special spot.

Anaura Bay Motor Camp CAMPGROUND $
(06-862 6380; www.gisbornenz.com/accommodation/view/401; Anaura Bay Rd, Anaura Bay; sites per adult/child from $18/9; 🛜) Friendly Anaura Bay Motor Camp is all about the location – right on the beachfront by the little stream where Captain Cook once stocked up with water. There's a decent kitchen, showers and toilets.

There's also a standard Department of Conservation (DOC) campsite here for fully self-contained campers only (adult/child $6/3).

Te Kaha Homestead Lodge HOSTEL $
(07-325 2194; www.facebook.com/tekahahomesteadlodge; 6606 SH35, Te Kaha; dm $30, d with/without bathroom $100/60, f $120; @🛜) The raffishly charming Te Kaha Homestead Lodge is brilliantly positioned on the shore, with a hot tub by the water, rolling lawns and basic hostel rooms. The affable manager sings 'Welcome to the Homestead at Te Kaha' (to the tune of 'Hotel California') given the slightest provocation. Fishing trips by arrangement.

Te Araroa Backpackers HOSTEL $
(06-864 4896; 57 Waione Rd, Te Araroa; dm from $25) There's very basic but character-laden accommodation in an amazing 135-year-old house at Te Araroa Backpackers, surrounded by bird-filled gardens. Does the old saxophone on the wall still work?

Hicks Bay Motel Lodge MOTEL $
(06-864 4880; www.hicksbaymotel.co.nz; 5198 SH35, Hicks Bay; dm $23, d $85-135, 2-bedroom units $165; 🛜❄) Knock-out views distract from the mildly barracks-like ambience at this 50-year-old motel squatting high above the bay. The clean, old-fashioned rooms are nothing flash, although the restaurant (mains $21 to $35, open for breakfast and dinner), shop, pool and glowworm grotto compensate.

Tui Lodge B&B $$
(07-325 2922; www.tuilodge.co.nz; 200 Copenhagen Rd, Te Kaha; s/d/f incl breakfast from $135/150/160) Tui Lodge is a capacious, modern guesthouse that sits in groomed 3-acre gardens, irresistible to tui and many other birds. Delicious meals are available by arrangement, as are horse-trekking, fishing and diving trips.

Waikawa B&B B&B $$
(07-325 2070; www.waikawa.net; 7541 SH35, Te Kaha; d/units from $110/130, extra person $35; @) About 7km north of Te Kaha, magical Waikawa B&B sits in a private rocky cove with views of the sunset and Whakaari (White Island). The artful buildings blend weathered timber, corrugated iron and paua inlay to great effect. There are two B&B options here – a double room, and a two-bedroom self-contained bach (small house) sleeping up to six wanderers.

✗ Eating

Pacific Coast Macadamias ICE CREAM $
(07-325 2960; www.macanuts.co.nz; 8462 SH35, Whanarua Bay; snacks $4-10; ◷10am-3pm, closed Jun-Aug; 🖳) Heaven is a tub of homemade macadamia and honey ice cream at Pacific Coast Macadamias, accompanied by views along one of the most spectacular parts of the coast. Toasted sandwiches and nutty sweet treats make this a great lunch stop. Call ahead to check it's open – hours can be sketchy.

Te Puka Tavern PUB FOOD $$
(06-864 5465; www.tepukatavern.co.nz; 135 Beach Rd, Tokomaru Bay; mains $13-28; ◷11am-late; 🛜) The well-run pub with cracker ocean views is a cornerstone of the community, keeping everyone fed and watered, and offering visitors a place to stay.

Four natty split-level, self-contained units sleep up to six (doubles $150 to $190, extra

Page 325

MĀORI NZ: THE EAST COAST

The main *iwi* (tribes) in the region are Te Whanau-a-Apanui (www.apanui.co.nz; west side of East Cape), Ngāti Porou (www.ngatiporou.com; east side of East Cape), Ngāti Kahungunu (www.kahungunu.iwi.nz; the coast from Hawke's Bay down) and Ngāti Tuhoe (www.ngaituhoe.iwi.nz; inland in Te Urewera).

Ngāti Porou and Ngāti Kahungunu are the country's second- and third-biggest *iwi*, respectively. In the late 19th century they produced the great leaders James Carroll (the first Māori cabinet minister) and Apirana Ngata (who was briefly acting prime minister). Ngata whose face adorns New Zealand's $50 note, worked tirelessly in parliament to orchestrate a cultural revival within Māoridom. The region's magnificent carved *marae* (meeting houses) are part of his legacy.

Māori life is at the forefront around the East Cape, in sleepy villages centred upon the many *marae* that dot the landscape. Living in close communities, drawing much of their livelihoods from the sea and the land, the *tangata whenua* (local people) of the Cape offer a fascinating insight into what life might have been, had they not been so vigorously divested of their land in the 19th century.

You will meet Māori wherever you go. For accommodation with Māori flavour, consider **Te Kaha Homestead Lodge** (p324) or **Hikihiki's Inn** (p334). For an intimate introduction to *Māoritanga* (things Māori), take a guided tour with **Long Island Guides** (p346) or **Waimarama Tours** (p346).

For a more passive brush with the culture, visit Gisborne's **Tairawhiti Museum** (p327), **Otatara Pā** (p339) in Napier, and Tikitiki's **St Mary's Church** (p323).

---

person $30) and there's room for a couple of campervans (powered sites $21, unpowered sites free).

Waihau Bay Lodge PUB FOOD $$
(07-325 3805; www.thewaihaubaylodge.co.nz; Orete Point Rd, Waihau Bay; mains $25-35; 4pm-late Sun-Wed, 2pm-late Thu-Sat) A two-storey timber pub by the pier, serving hefty meals and with accommodation ranging from campsites ($15) to four-bed dorms (from $23 per person), en suite doubles ($135) and roomy en suite units sleeping eight (double $185, extra person $25).

🛍 Shopping

East Cape Manuka Company FOOD
(06-864 4824; www.eastcapemanuka.co.nz; 4464 Te Araroa Rd, Te Araroa; 8.30am-4.30pm daily Nov-Apr, Mon-Fri only May-Oct) The progressive East Cape Manuka Company sells soaps, oils, creams and honey made from potent East Cape manuka. It's a good stop for a coffee, a feta-and-spinach muffin or a smoothie (meals and snacks $6 to $13). Check out the busy bees at work in the wall display.

ℹ Information

Tolaga Bay Visitor Information Centre
(06-862 6826; uawafm@xtra.co.nz; 55 Cook St, Tolaga Bay; 9am-5pm Mon-Fri;) The information centre is in the foyer of the local radio station (Uawa FM; 88.5FM, 88.8FM, 99.3FM)

ℹ Getting Around

By far the most fun and free way to experience the Pacific Coast Hwy is with your own wheels (motorised or pedal-powered). Otherwise, Bay Hopper (www.baybus.co.nz) runs between Opotiki and Potaka/Cape Runaway on Tuesday and Thursday. **Cooks Couriers** (021 371 364, 06-864 4711) runs between Te Araroa and Opotiki on Tuesday and Thursday, and between Gisborne and Hicks Bay daily Monday to Saturday.

Gisborne

POP 35,700

'Gizzy' to her friends, Gisborne (pronounced *Gis-born* not *Gis-bun*) is a pretty place, squeezed between surf beaches and a sea of chardonnay, and it proudly claims to be the first city on Earth to see the sun. It's a good place to put your feet up for a few days, hit the beach and sip some wine.

History

The Gisborne region has been settled for over 700 years. A pact between two migratory *waka* (canoe) skippers, Paoa of the *Horouta* and Kiwa of the *Takitimu*, led to the founding of Turanganui a Kiwa (now Gisborne). Kumara flourished in the fertile soil and the settlement blossomed.

THE EAST COAST GISBORNE

Gisborne

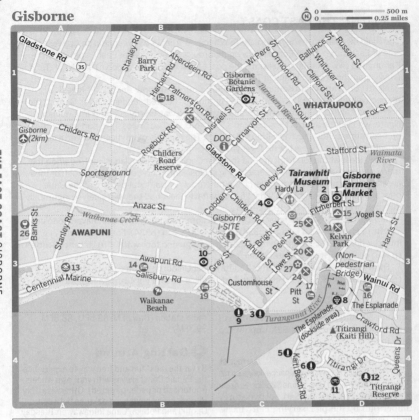

THE EAST COAST GISBORNE

Gisborne

In 1769 this was the first part of NZ sighted by Captain Cook's expedition. Eager to replenish supplies and explore, they set ashore, much to the amazement of the locals. Setting an unfortunate benchmark for intercultural relations, the crew opened fire when the Māori men performed their traditional blood-curdling challenge, killing six of them.

The *Endeavour* set sail without provisions. Cook, perhaps in a fit of petulance, named the area Poverty Bay as 'it did not afford a single item we wanted'.

European settlement began in 1831 with whaling and farming; missionaries followed. In the 1860s battles between settlers and Māori erupted. Beginning in Taranaki, the Hauhau insurrection spread to the East Coast, culminating in the battle of Waerenga a Hika in 1865.

To discover Gisborne's historical spots, pick up the *Historic Walk* pamphlet from Gisborne i-SITE (p330).

⊙ Sights

★ Tairawhiti Museum
MUSEUM
(www.tairawhitimuseum.org.nz; Kelvin Rise, Stout St; adult/child $5/free, Mon free; ◷10am-4pm Mon-Sat, 1.30-4pm Sun) The Tairawhiti Museum, with its fab gallery extension, focuses on East Coast Māori and colonial history. It is Gisborne's arts hub, with rotating exhibits and excellent historic photographic displays. There's also a maritime wing, with displays on *waka*, whaling and Cook's Poverty Bay, although these pale in comparison to the vintage surfboard collection. There's also a shop, and a cafe overlooking Kelvin Park. Outside is the reconstructed Wyllie Cottage (1872), Gisborne's oldest house.

Titirangi Reserve
PARK
(www.gdc.govt.nz; Titirangi Dr, off Queens Dr; ⓟ) High on a hill overlooking Gisborne, Titirangi was once a *pa* (fortified village). Reach it via Queens Dr, or join the sweaty joggers on the track from the Cook Monument (Kaiti Beach Rd). Near the lookout at the top is yet another Cook edifice, Cook's Plaza (Titirangi Dr). Due to a cock-up of historic proportions, the Cook statue here looks nothing like Cap'n Jim. A plaque proclaims, 'Who was he? We have no idea!'. Adjacent is a modest pohutukawa tree planted by Princess Di in 1983.

Eastwoodhill Arboretum
GARDENS
(☎06-863 9003; www.eastwoodhill.org.nz; 2392 Wharekopae Rd, Ngatapa; adult/child/family $15/2/34; ◷9am-5pm) Arboreal nirvana, Eastwoodhill Arboretum is the largest collection of northern hemisphere trees and shrubs in the southern hemisphere. It's staggeringly beautiful, and you could easily lose a day wandering around the 25km of themed tracks in this pine-scented paradise. It's well signposted, 35km northwest of Gisborne.

There's basic accommodation in bunks and private rooms (dorm bed $35, double room $120, both including garden admission). Meals are available by arrangement, or you can use the fully equipped kitchen (BYO food as there aren't any shops nearby).

Sunshine Brewery
BREWERY
(☎06-867 7777; www.sunshinebrewery.co.nz; 49 Awapuni Rd; ◷3pm-7pm Mon-Wed, noon-8pm Thu-Sat) Sunshine, Gisborne's own natural brewery, has a fab new tasting room near Waikanae Beach, bottling-up a clutch of quality craft beers including the flagship Gisborne Gold lager. Tasting paddles (five beers) are $15. You can also get a bite to eat here.

Gisborne Farmers Market
MARKET
(☎027 251 8608; www.gisbornefarmersmarket. co.nz; cnr Stout & Fitzherbert Sts; ◷9.30am-12.30pm Sat) Stock up on fresh fruit, macadamia nuts (and macadamia nut paste!), smallgoods, honey, herbs, coffee, wine, bread, pastries, fish, cheese and Gisborne oranges...all of it locally grown or procured.

Gisborne Botanic Gardens
GARDENS
(☎06-867 2049; www.gdc.govt.nz/botanical-gardens; Aberdeen Rd; ◷24hr; ⓟ) The town gardens are sitting pretty beside the Taruheru River – a beaut spot for a picnic and a romp around the big playground. Wiggle through the NZ native Bushland Walkway.

East Coast Museum of Technology
MUSEUM
(ECMOT; ☎027 221 5703; www.ecmot.org.nz; SH2, Makaraka; adult/child $5/2; ◷10am-4pm Sun-Fri, 1-4pm Sat) Think analogue rather than digital; old-age rather than space-age. About 5km west of the town centre, this improbable medley of farm equipment, fire engines and sundry appliances has found an appropriate home in a motley old milking barn and surrounding outhouses. Dig the millennium welcome sign!

Statue of Young Nick
MONUMENT
(Customhouse St) There's no let-up in Gisborne's *Endeavour* endeavours: in the riverside park is a dynamic statue of Nicholas Young, Cook's cabin boy, whose eagle eyes

THE EAST COAST GISBORNE

were the first to spot NZ (the white cliffs at Young Nick's Head). There's another **Captain Cook statue** nearby, erected on a globe etched with his roaming routes.

🏃 Activities

On the Water

Surfing is de rigueur in Gisborne, with the teenage population looking appropriately shaggy. **Waikanae Beach** and **Roberts Road** are good for learners; experienced surfers get tubed south of town at the **Pipe**, or east at **Sponge Bay** and **Tuamotu Island**. Further east along SH35, **Wainui** and **Makorori** also have quality breaks.

There's safe swimming between the flags at Waikanae and **Midway Beach**.

Rere Rockslide   SWIMMING
(Wharekopae Rd; ☉ daylight hours) This natural phenomenon occurs in a section of the Rere River 50km northwest of Gisborne along Wharekopae Rd. Grab a tyre tube or boogie board to cushion the bumps and slide down the 60m-long rocky run into the pool at the bottom. Three kilometres downriver, the **Rere Falls** send a 20m-wide curtain of water over a 5m drop; you can walk behind it if you don't mind getting wet.

Walking On Water Surf School   SURFING
(WOW; ☎06-863 2969, 022 313 0213; www.wow surfschool.com; 2hr/4hr/2-day/3-day lessons per person from $50/95/180/270; 🖐) Surfing is

just like walking on water, right? Wrong. It's much harder than that – but these guys know how to turn even the most naive novice into an upstanding surfer in no time. Kids' lessons and gear hire, too.

Olympic Pool   SWIMMING
(☎06-867 6220; www.gdc.govt.nz; 45 Centennial Marine Dr, Awapuni; adult/child $4/3; ☉6am-8pm daily Sep-Apr, 8am-8pm Sat & Sun May-Aug; 🖐) Gisborne's big pool is a tepid 50m indoor-outdoor affair with a 98m water slide and a deep diving pool.

On the Land

There are many miles of walks to tackle around Gisborne, starting with a gentle stroll along the river. The Gisborne i-SITE (p330) can provide you with brochures for the *Historic Walk* and the *Walking Trails of Gisborne City*.

Winding its way through farmland and forest with commanding views, the **Te Kuri Walkway** (two hours, 5.6km, closed August to October) starts 4km north of town at the end of Shelley Rd.

Haurata High Country Walks   TRAMPING
(☎06-867 8452; www.haurata.co.nz; walks guided/unguided per person from $15/25) Take a hike in the hills with Haurata, which offers guided or unguided short and long day walks through the gorgeous high country behind Gisborne. Meals, farmhouse accommodation and hot-tub soaks also available.

GISBORNE WINERIES

With hot summers and fertile loam soils, the Waipaoa River valley to the northwest of Gisborne is one of New Zealand's foremost grape-growing areas. The region is traditionally famous for its chardonnay, and is increasingly noted for gewürztraminer and pinot gris. See www.gisbornewine.co.nz for a cellar-door map. Opening hours scale back out of peak season. Four of the best:

Bushmere Estate (☎06-868 9317; www.bushmere.com; 166 Main Rd, Matawhero; ☉11am-3pm Wed-Sun) Great chardonnay, gewürztraminer and cafe lunches at the sassy restaurant Vines (lunch mains $26 to $30), and live music on summer Sundays. Reduced winter hours; longer summer hours.

Kirkpatrick Estate (☎06-862 7722; www.kew.co.nz; 569 Wharekopae Rd, Patutahi; ☉noon-4pm) Sustainable winery with lovely wines across the board, including a delicious malbec. Tuck into an antipasto platter in the sun.

Matawhero (☎06-867 6140; www.matawhero.co.nz; Riverpoint Rd, Matawhero; ☉noon-4pm Sat & Sun) Home of a particularly buttery chardy. Enjoy your picnic in bucolic splendour, accompanied by a flight of fine wines.

Millton (☎06-862 8680; www.millton.co.nz; 119 Papatu Rd, Manutuke; ☉10am-5pm Mon-Sun, reduced winter hours) Sustainable, organic and biodynamic to boot. Bring a picnic and kick back surrounded by sturdy-trunked vines.

🖙 Tours

Tairāwhiti Tours CULTURAL TOUR
(☑ 021 276 5484; www.tairawhititours.co.nz; tours per person from $225, cheaper for groups) Excellent 5½-hour guided tours around Gisborne, digging into history, wine, food and culture (all the interesting stuff).

Gisborne Cycle Tour Company CYCLING
(☑ 06-927 7021; www.gisbornecycletours.co.nz; half-/full-day tours from $100/200, bicycle hire per day from $50) Half-day to multiday guided cycle tours around local sights and further afield, including wineries and Eastwoodhill Arboretum. Bike hire also available (maps and advice on tap).

✲✩ Festivals & Events

Rhythm & Vines MUSIC, WINE
(R&V; www.rhythmandvines.co.nz; ❂ Dec) A huge event on Gizzy's music calendar, R&V is a three-day festival leading up to New Year's Eve, featuring big-time local and international bands and DJs. Local accommodation feels the squeeze.

Gisborne Wine & Food Festival WINE, FOOD
(www.gisbornewineandfoodfestival.co.nz; ❂ Oct) Cellar-door spectacular, with local winemakers and foodies pooling talents. Pick up a tasting glass, a map and a wristband at the **Gisborne Wine Centre** (☑ 06-867 4085; www.gisbornewine.co.nz; Shed 3, 50 The Esplanade; ❂ 10am-5pm Sun-Wed, to 7pm Thu-Sat) then drive the winery trail (actually – get someone else to do the driving).

🛏 Sleeping

Gisborne YHA HOSTEL $
(☑ 06-867 3269; www.yha.co.nz; 32 Harris St; dm/s/d/f $28/52/68/115; @❂) A short wander across the river from town, this rambling, mustard-coloured 1925 charmer houses a well-kept hostel. The rooms are large and comfy (even the 10-bed dorm in the attic), while outside the deck and lawns kindle conversation. Family en suite unit and surfboard and bike hire also available.

**Waikanae Beach
Top 10 Holiday Park** HOLIDAY PARK $
(☑ 0800 867 563, 06-867 5634; www.gisborneholidaypark.co.nz; 280 Grey St; sites per person from $20, cabins & units d $70-170; ❂) Right by the beach and an easy 10-minute walk to town, this grassy holiday park offers basic cabins, better units and grassy lanes for pitching tents and parking vans. Surfboards and bikes for hire.

SUMMER CAMPING

Gisborne District Council (GDC; ☑ 06-867 2049, 0800 653 800; www.gdc.govt.nz/summer-camping; 15 Fitzherbert St, Gisborne) Gisborne District Council operates a handful of designated 'summer camping' sites between Te Araroa and Gisborne from the end of September to early April. Apply for a permit online for two, 10 or 28 consecutive nights at a cost of $16, $31 and $66 respectively, for up to six people (or buy one at the Gisborne or Opotiki i-SITEs).

Your own gas cooker, chemical toilet and water supply are obligatory.

★ **Ahi Kaa Motel** MOTEL $$
(☑ 06-867 7107; www.ahikaa.co.nz; 61 Salisbury Rd; d $110-180; @❂) An uptown motel offering in a quiet backstreet, a short sandy-footed stroll across the road from Waikanae Beach. Fancy linen, tasteful bathrooms, double glazing, outdoor showers, recycled timbers, solar power and recycling savvy – nice one!

Teal Motor Lodge MOTEL $$
(☑ 0800 838 325, 06-868 4019; www.teal.co.nz; 479 Gladstone Rd; d from $140, f $205-235; ❂) With super street appeal on the main drag (500m into town), the vaguely alpine (and just a bit *Mad Men*) Teal boasts a solid offering of tidy, family-friendly units plus a saltwater swimming pool and immaculate lawns to run around on. Free wi-fi.

Portside Hotel HOTEL, APARTMENT $$
(☑ 0800 767 874, 06-869 1000; www.portsidegisborne.co.nz; 2 Reads Quay; d/2-bedroom apt from $175/220; @❂) The wandering business traveller's hotel of choice in Gisborne, Portside offers three levels of sassy apartments, right by the river mouth where the big ships come and go. Charcoal-and-cream colour scheme, with little glass-fronted balconies.

Knapdale Eco Lodge LODGE $$$
(☑ 06-862 5444; www.knapdale.co.nz; 114 Snowsill Rd, Waihirere; d incl breakfast from $420; ❂) Indulge yourself at this rural idyll, complete with lake, farm animals and home-grown produce. The mod lodge is filled with international artwork, its glassy frontage flowing out to an expansive patio with brazier, barbecue and pizza oven. Five-course dinner by arrangement ($95). To get here head 10km northwest of Gisborne, via Back Ormond Rd.

✕ Eating

Frank & Albie's
CAFE $

(☑06-867 7847; www.frankandalbie.co.nz; 24 Gladstone Rd; mains $6-10; ⊙ 7am-2.30pm Mon-Fri) 'We cut lunch, not corners' is the motto at Frank & Albie's, a neat little hipster nook on Gisborne's main drag (check out the old art-deco leadlighting above the door). Nifty plywood benches, recycled timber tables and dinky white stools set the scene for super sandwiches, coffee, teas and smoothies.

Muirs Bookshop & Café
CAFE $

(www.muirsbookshop.co.nz; 62 Gladstone Rd; meals $5-14; ⊙ 9am-3.30pm Mon-Fri, to 3pm Sat) Situated above Muirs Bookshop, a beloved, age-old independent bookseller in a lovely heritage building, this simple cafe offers a small but sweet selection of counter food and cakes. Fans of fine espresso coffee and literature may need to be forcibly removed. Over-street balcony for balmy days.

Morrell's Artisan Bakery
BAKERY $

(☑06-867 8266; www.facebook.com/morrellsartisanbakery; 437 Gladstone Rd; items $3-7; ⊙ 6.30am-2pm Mon-Sat, 9am-2pm Sun; 🖉) Artisan bakers with killer pies, wholesome bread, delicious pastries, soups, cookies and cute staff, all made on-site (except the staff). Overlooking the espresso cheesecake brownie would be a mistake.

PBC Cafe
CAFE $$

(☑06-863 3165; www.facebook.com/pbccafe; 38 Childers Rd; mains breakfast $15-25, lunch $20-30; ⊙ 7am-3pm Mon-Fri, 8am-3pm Sat & Sun; 🖉) The creaky old grandeur of the Poverty Bay Club for gentlemen (1874) is reason enough to visit. This cafe within it certainly adds impetus: appealing counter food, all-day brunch, pizza, blackboard specials and reasonable prices. Love the big pew along the outside wall. There's the Dome Cinema and a sweet little gift shop here, too.

Zest
CAFE $$

(☑06-867 5787; www.zestcafe.co.nz; 22 Peel St; mains $15-21; ⊙ 6am-4pm Mon-Sat, 8am-4pm Sun) Pop quiz: how many cafes are there in the Western world called 'Zest'? Plenty. But unoriginality aside, this is one of the East Coast's better cafes, offering pizzas, pastas, big breakfasts, salads, wraps, waffles, teas and smoothies. Again, nothing too original, but perfectly executed, affordable and super-fresh. Is the knitting group still taking up all the seats?

★ USSCO Bar & Bistro
MODERN NZ $$$

(☑06-868 3246; www.ussco.co.nz; 16 Childers Rd; mains $38-45; ⊙ 4.30pm-late) Housed in the restored Union Steam Ship Company building (USSCO – get it?), this place is all class. Silky kitchen skills shine in a highly seasonal menu featuring the likes of soy-glazed pork belly with caramelised yams, parsnip puree and toasted nut salad. Devilishly good desserts, plus plenty of local wines and NZ craft beers. Generous portions and multicourse deals.

Marina Restaurant
FRENCH $$$

(☑06-868 5919; www.marinarestaurant.co.nz; 2 Vogel St; mains lunch $20, dinner $37-39; ⊙ noon-2pm Thu-Sat, 6-9pm Tue-Sat) Oft touted as Gisborne's best restaurant, the Marina offers casual bistro-style lunches and formal fine-dining dinners, all with very Gallic vibes. The building itself is lovely – an old white weatherboard boathouse by the river, with lofty ceilings, white linen and balloon-like wine glasses. Divine duck breast with honey jus.

🍷 Drinking & Nightlife

★ Smash Palace
BAR

(☑06-867 7769; www.smashpalacebar.com; 24 Banks St; ⊙ 3pm-late Mon-Thu, 2pm-late Fri, noon-late Sat, 2-11pm Sun) Get juiced at the junkyard: an iconic drinking den in Gisborne's industrial wastelands (make as much noise as you like!), full to the gunwales with ephemera and its very own DC3 crash-landed in the beer garden. Occasional live music; vinyl sessions Sunday afternoons.

☆ Entertainment

★ Dome Cinema
CINEMA, BAR

(☑08-324 3005; www.domecinema.co.nz; 38 Childers Rd; tickets $14; ⊙ from 5.30pm Wed-Sun) The excellent Dome is inside the charming old Poverty Bay Club building (1874): beanbags and art-house flicks now occupy the glass-domed ballroom. There's a cool bar next door (occasional live music and pasta nights; constant classy drinkers and black-painted floorboards). PBC Cafe is also here.

ℹ Information

DOC (Department of Conservation; ☑06-869 0460; www.doc.govt.nz; 63 Carnarvon St; ⊙ 8am-4.30pm Mon-Fri)

Gisborne Hospital (☑06-869 0500; www.tdh.org.nz; 421 Ormond Rd, Riverdale; ⊙ 24hr)

Gisborne i-SITE (☑06-868 6139; www.gisbornenz.com; 209 Grey St; ⊙ 8.30am-5.30pm

MAHIA PENINSULA

In between Gisborne and Napier, the Mahia Peninsula's eroded hills, sandy beaches and vivid blue sea make it a mini-ringer for the Coromandel, without the tourist hordes and fancy subdivisions, and with the bonus of dramatic Dover-ish cliffs. It's an enduring holiday spot for East Coasters, who come largely for boaty, beachy stuff, and you can easily get in on the action if you have your own transport. A day or two could be spent exploring the scenic reserve and the bird-filled Maungawhio Lagoon, hanging out at the beach (Mahia Beach at sunset can be spectacular), or even playing a round of golf.

Mahia has several small settlements offering between them a few guesthouses, a holiday park, a bar-bistro and a couple of stores. See www.voyagemahia.co.nz for accommodation listings.

The peninsula is a short detour east of the road between Gisborne and Wairoa (SH2). Turn off at Nuhaka – the main settlements are about 20km away. No buses run here – you'll need your own vehicle.

Mon-Fri, 9am-5pm Sat, 10am-4pm Sun; 🕾)
Beside a doozy of a Canadian totem pole, this information centre has all and sundry, including a travel desk, internet access, bike hire, toilets and a bowl of Gisborne oranges on the counter.

Post Office (www.nzpost.co.nz; 127 Gladstone Rd; ⊗9am-5pm Mon-Fri, to noon Sat)

Three Rivers Medical (☑06-367 7411; www. 3rivers.co.nz; 75 Customhouse St; ⊗8am-8pm Mon-Fri, 9am-6pm Sat & Sun) Doctors and dentists available by appointment.

🛈 Getting There & Away

The **Gisborne i-SITE** (p330) handles bookings for local and national transport services.

AIR

Gisborne Airport (www.eastland.co.nz/ gisborne-airport; Aerodrome Rd, Awapuni) is 3km west of the city. Air New Zealand (www. airnewzealand.co.nz) flies to/from Auckland and Wellington. Sunair Aviation (www.sunair. co.nz) flies direct from Gisborne to Rotorua and Whakatane, with onward connections.

BUS

InterCity and Naked Bus services depart from Gisborne i-SITE, with daily buses to the following:

DESTINATION	COMPANY	PRICE	TIME (HR)
Auckland	InterCity	$85	9
Napier	InterCity	$45	4
Opotiki	InterCity	$31	2
Opotiki	Naked Bus	$22	2
Rotorua	InterCity	$60	5
Rotorua	Naked Bus	$28	4½
Taupo	Naked Bus	$25	6
Wairoa	InterCity	$29	1½

CAR

Gisborne Airport Car Rental (☑0800 144 129; www.gisborneairportcarhire.co.nz) Agent for nine car-hire companies including big brands and local outfits.

TAXI

A city–airport taxi fare costs about $20. Try **Gisborne Taxis** (☑0800 505 555, 06-867 2222).

South of Gisborne

From Gisborne heading south towards Napier, you can take the coast road or the inland road. The coastal route is a marginally better choice, being quicker and offering occasional views out to sea. However, SH36 (Tiniroto Rd) is also an interesting drive (or bike route) with several good stopping points en route.

👁 Sights

Doneraille Park, 49km from Gisborne, is a peaceful bush reserve with a frigid river to jump into and freedom camping for self-contained vehicles. **Hackfalls Arboretum** (☑06-863 7083; www.hackfalls.org.nz; 187 Berry Rd, Tiniroto; adult/child $10/free; ⊗9am-5pm) is a 3km detour from the turn-off at the Tiniroto Tavern. The snow-white cascades of **Te Reinga Falls**, 12km further south, are well worth a stop.

The busier SH2 route heads inland and soon enters the **Wharerata State Forest** (beware of logging trucks). Just out of the woods, 55km from Gisborne, **Morere Hot Springs** (☑06-837 8856; www.morerehotsprings. co.nz; SH2; adult/child $12/6, private pools $15/10, nonswimmers $3; ⊗10am-5pm, extended hours Dec-Feb) burble up from a fault line in the **Morere Springs Scenic Reserve**.

From Gisborne on SH2, keep an eye out for the brightly painted Taane-nui-a-Rangi Marae on the left. You can get a decent view from the road; don't enter unless invited.

Continuing south, SH2 leads to Nuhaka at the northern end of Hawke Bay. From here it's west to Wairoa or east to the sea-salty Mahia Peninsula (p331). Not far from the Nuhaka roundabout is Kahungunu Marae (www.wairoadc.govt.nz/pages/kahungunu_marae; cnr Ihaka & Mataira Sts, Nuhaka).

Sleeping

Morere Hot Springs
Lodge & Cabins   BUNGALOWS $
(☑06-837 8824; www.morerelodge.co.nz; SH2, Morere ; d $80-120, extra adult/child $20/10) Morere Hot Springs Lodge is a a farmy enclave where the lambs gambol and the dog wags her tail at you nonstop. Sleeping options include a classic 1917 farmhouse (sleeps 12) with kitchen and sweet sleep-out, another two-bedroom farmhouse (sleeps four), and two photogenic cabins. Great value.

Morere Tearooms
& Camping Ground   CAMPGROUND $
(☑06-837 8792; www.morereaccommodation.co.nz; SH2, Morere; campsites from $17, d $60-90; ☎) Opposite Morere Hot Springs are the Morere Tearooms & Camping Ground, where you can get a respectable toasted sandwich (meals $5 to $18), and avail yourself of campsites and snug cabins alongside the babbling Tunanui Stream.

Te Urewera National Park

Shrouded in mist and mysticism, Te Urewera National Park is the North Island's largest, encompassing 2127 sq km of virgin forest cut with lakes and rivers. The highlight is Lake Waikaremoana (Sea of Rippling Waters), a deep crucible of water encircled by the Lake Waikaremoana Track, one of NZ's Great Walks. Rugged bluffs drop away to reedy inlets, the lake's mirror surface disturbed only by mountain zephyrs and the occasional waterbird taking to the skies.

History

The name Te Urewera still has the capacity to make Pākehā New Zealanders feel slightly uneasy – and not just because it translates as 'The Burnt Penis'. There's something primal and untamed about this wild woodland, with its rich history of Māori resistance.

The local Tuhoe people – prosaically known as the 'Children of the Mist' – never signed the Treaty of Waitangi and fought with Rewi Maniapoto at Orakau during the Waikato Wars. The army of Te Kooti took refuge here during running battles with government troops. The claimant of Te Kooti's spiritual mantle, Rua Kenana, led a thriving community beneath the sacred mountain Maungapohatu (1366m) from 1905 until his politically motivated 1916 arrest. This effectively erased the last bastion of Māori independence in the country. Maungapohatu never recovered, and only a small settlement remains today. Nearby, Ruatahuna's extraordinary Mataatua Marae celebrates Te Kooti's exploits.

Tuhoe remain proud of their identity and traditions, with around 40% still speaking te reo (the language) on a regular basis.

Activities

There are dozens of walks within the park's vast boundaries, most of which are outlined in DOC's *Lake Waikaremoana Walks* pamphlet ($2). Plenty of short walks kick off from the visitor centre and Waikaremoana Holiday Park, or tackle the longer Lake Waikaremoana Track.

Lake Waikaremoana Track
This 46km, three- to four-day Great Walk scales the spectacular Panekire Bluff (1180m), with open panoramas interspersed with fern groves and forest. The walk is rated as moderate with the only difficult section being the Panekire ascent, and during summer it can get busy.

Although it's a year-round track, winter rain deters many people and makes conditions much more challenging. At this altitude (580m above sea level), temperatures can drop quickly, even in summer. Walkers should take portable stoves and fuel as there are no cooking facilities en route.

There are five huts (adult/child $32/free) and campsites (adult/child $14/free) spaced along the track, all of which must be prebooked through DOC, regardless of the season. Book at regional DOC offices, i-SITEs or online at www.greatwalks.co.nz.

If you have a car, it is safest to leave it at the Waikaremoana Holiday Park or Big Bush Holiday Park, and then take a water taxi to either trailhead. Alternatively, you can take the fully catered, three-night guided tour offered by the enthusiastic and experienced Walking Legends (p333) or Te Urewera Treks (p333).

TE KOOTI

Māori history is littered with mystics, prophets and warriors, one of whom is the legendary Te Kooti (rhymes with naughty, not booty).

In 1865 he fought with the government against the Hauhau (adherents of the Pai Marire faith, founded by another warrior-prophet) but was accused of being a spy and imprisoned on the Chatham Islands without trial.

While there, Te Kooti studied the Bible and claimed to receive visions from the archangel Michael. His charismatic preaching and 'miracles' – including producing flames from his hands (his captors claimed he used phosphorus from the head of matches) – helped win over the Pai Marire to his distinctly Māori take on Christianity.

In 1867 Te Kooti led an astounding escape from the Chathams, hijacking a supply ship and sailing to Poverty Bay with 200 followers. En route he threw a doubter overboard as a sacrifice. Upon their safe arrival, Te Kooti's disciples raised their right hands in homage to God rather than bowing submissively; *ringa tu* (upraised hand) became the name of his church.

Te Kooti requested a dialogue with the colonial government but was once again rebuffed, with magistrate Reginald Biggs demanding his immediate surrender. Unimpressed by Pākehā justice, Te Kooti commenced a particularly effective guerrilla campaign – starting with killing Biggs and around 50 others (including women and children, Māori and Pākehā) at Matawhero near Gisborne.

A four-year chase ensued. Eventually Te Kooti took refuge in the King Country, the Māori king's vast dominion where government troops feared to tread.

Proving the pointlessness of the government's approach to the whole affair, Te Kooti was officially pardoned in 1883. By this time his reputation as a prophet and healer had spread and his Ringatu Church was firmly established. Today it claims more than 16,000 adherents.

Propel yourself onto the trail either clockwise from just outside **Onepoto** in the south, or anticlockwise from **Hopuruahine Suspension Bridge** in the north.

Estimated walking times:

ROUTE	TIME (HR)
Onepoto to Panekire Hut	5
Panekire Hut to Waiopaoa Hut	3-4
Waiopaoa Hut to Marauiti Hut	4-5
Marauiti Hut to Waiharuru Hut	1½
Waiharuru Hut to Whanganui Hut	2
Whanganui Hut to Hopuruahine Suspension Bridge	2

Walking Legends TRAMPING
(☎07-312 5297, 0800 925 569; www.walking legends.com; per person $1450) This enthusiastic and experienced company offers fully catered, four-day guided tours around Lake Waikaremoana, ex-Rotorua.

Te Urewera Treks TRAMPING
(☎07-929 9669; www.teureweratreks.co.nz; per person $1390) ⚲ Small-group, guided four-day hikes along the Lake Waikaremoana Great Walk. One- and three-day Te Urewera walks are also available, sometimes with

tree-planting activities as part of the experience. Trips depart Rotorua.

Other Walks

With its untouched islands, **Lake Waikare-iti** is an enchanting place. Starting near the Te Urewera National Park Visitor Centre, it's an hour's walk to its shore.

Accessed from the track to Lake Waikareiti, the more challenging **Ruapani Circuit Track** (six-hour loop) passes through wetlands and dense, virgin forest. Also from Lake Waikare-iti it's a three-hour walk to the **Sandy Bay Hut** at the northern end of the lake.

🛏 Sleeping

There are more than 30 DOC huts and campsites within the park, most of which are very basic, plus the DOC-managed Waikaremoana Holiday Park. There are also a couple of B&Bs and another holiday park in the area.

Waikaremoana Holiday Park HOLIDAY PARK $
(☎06-837 3826; www.waikaremoana.info; 6249 Lake Rd/SH38; unpowered/powered sites from $30/36 cabins/chalets d from $65/100, extra adult/child $25/13) Right on the shore, this DOC-managed place has Swiss-looking

Lake Waikaremoana Track

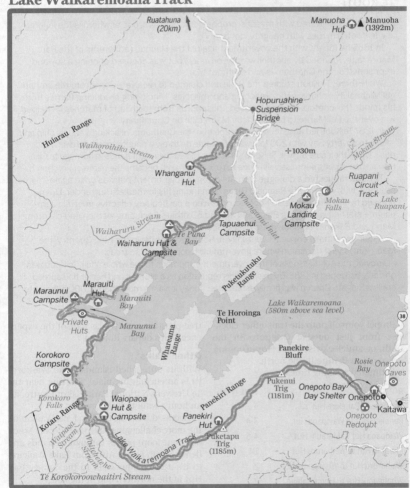

chalets, fisher's cabins and campsites, most with watery views, plus an on-site shop.

Big Bush Holiday Park HOLIDAY PARK $
(☑0800 525 392, 06-837 3777; www.lakewaikaremoana.co.nz; SH38; sites per person from $20, s/d from $35/70) About 4km from the Onepoto trailhead, Big Bush offers tent sites, trim cabins and backpacker rooms. Transfers to/from Wairoa, pick-ups/drop-offs around the lake, water taxis and storage also available.

Lake Road B&B B&B $$
(☑06-838 6890; www.staywitha.kiwi; 2311 Lake Rd/SH38, Ardkeen; s/d incl breakfast from

$140/150; ☏) About 24km up the road to Lake Waikaremoana from Wairoa is this newish little B&B, which is a handy pre- or posthike option if you've got your own wheels. There's a cool-running creek where you can soak before putting your feet up. Sleeps five. Picnic lunches and dinners (Thai!) also available.

Hikihiki's Inn B&B $$$
(☑06-8373 701; www.hikihiki.co.nz; 9 Rotten Row, Tuai; s/d $140/255) In the sweet settlement of Tuai, 6km from Onepoto, this little weatherboard gem serves as a B&B run by '100% Kiwi' hosts. Prices include continen-

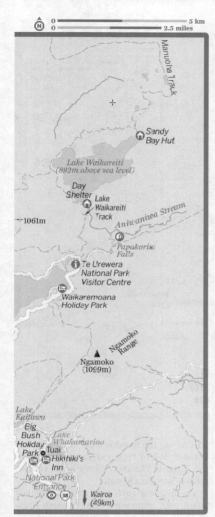

to Rotorua – the entire SH38 route is named the **Te Urewera Rainforest Route**. Around 95km of the entire 195km Wairoa–Rotorua route is unsealed: it's a four-hour, bone-rattling drive (but a great adventure!).

Big Bush Water Taxi (☑ 0800 525 392, 06-837 3777; www.lakewa karemoana.co.nz/water-taxi; per person one-way $50-60) will boat you to either Onepoto or Hopuruahine trailhead, with hut-to-hut pack transfers for the less gung-ho. It also runs minibus shuttles to and from Wairoa (from $50 per person one way).

HAWKE'S BAY

Hawke Bay, the name given to the body of water that stretches from the Mahia Peninsula to Cape Kidnappers, looks like it's been bitten out of the North Island's eastern flank. Add an apostrophe and an 's' and you've got a region that stretches south and inland to include fertile farmland, surf beaches, mountainous ranges and forests. With food, wine and architecture the prevailing obsessions, it's smugly comfortable but thoroughly appealing, and is best viewed through a rosé-tinted wine glass.

Wairoa & Around

The small river town of Wairoa (population 4260) is trying hard to shake its rough-edged rep. Not scintillating enough to warrant an extended stay, the town does have a couple of points of interest, including an exceptional (and exceptionally early-opening) pie shop called **Oslers** (☑ 06-838 8299; 116 Marine Pde; pies $4-5, meals $7-15; ☺ 8am-4pm Mon-Fri, to 2.30pm Sat & Sun). The arty **Eastend Cafe** (☑ 06-838 6070; eastendcafe@xtra.co.nz; 250 Marine Pde; meals $6-20; ☺ 7am-2.30pm) is part of the revamped **Gaiety Cinema & Theatre** (☑ 06-838 3104; www.gaietytheatre.co.nz; 252 Marine Pde; tickets $10; ☺ 10am-10pm Thu-Sun) complex – the town's cultural hub. Other diversions include the plaque-studded **River Walkway**, and the **Wairoa Museum** (☑ 06-838 3108; www.wairoamuseum.org.nz; 142 Marine Pde; ☺ 10am-4pm Tue-Fri, to noon Sat) **FREE** inside an old bank.

☉ Sights

The stretch of highway between Wairoa and Napier traipses through unphotogenic farmland and forestry blocks for much of its 117km. Most of it follows a railway line, currently only used for freight – you'll realise what a travesty this is when you pass under

(map labels:)

Manuoha Track

Sandy Bay Hut

Lake Waikareiti (892m above sea level)

Day Shelter

Lake Waikareiti Track

1061m

Aniwaniwa Stream

Papakorito Falls

Te Urewera National Park Visitor Centre

Waikaremoana Holiday Park

Ngamoko Range

Ngamoko (1099m)

Lake Kaiwawa

Big Bush Holiday Park

Lake Whakamarino

Tuai

Hikihiki's Inn

National Park Entrance

Wairoa (49km)

38

0 — 5 km
0 — 2.5 miles

tal breakfast; other meals at additional cost (24-hours' notice required). Sleeps six.

ℹ Information

Te Urewera National Park Visitor Centre (☑ 06-837 3803/900; www.doc.govt.nz; SH38, Aniwaniwa; ☺ 8am-4.45pm) Te Urewera National Park visitor centre has weather forecasts, accommodation information and hut/campsite passes for the Lake Waikaremoana Track.

ℹ Getting There & Away

Lake Waikaremoana is about an hour (64km) from Wairoa on SH38, which continues through

Hawke's Bay

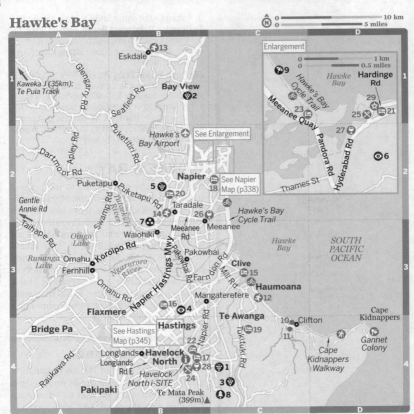

the **Mohaka Viaduct** (1937), the highest rail viaduct (97m) in Australasia.

Occupied by early Māori, **Lake Tutira** has walkways and a bird sanctuary. At Tutira village, just north of the lake, Pohokura Rd leads to the wonderful **Boundary Stream Scenic Reserve**, a major conservation area. Three loop tracks start from the road, ranging in length from 40 minutes to three hours. Also along this road you'll find the **Opouahi** and **Bellbird Bush Scenic Reserves**, which both offer rewarding walks. See www.doc. govt.nz for info on all of these reserves.

Off Waipatiki Rd, 34km outside Napier, Waipatiki Beach is a beaut spot boasting a low-key campsite and the 64-hectare **Waipatiki Scenic Reserve**. Further down the line, **White Pine Bush Scenic Reserve**, 29km from Napier on SH2, bristles with kahikatea and nikau palms. **Tangoio Falls Scenic Reserve**, 27km north of Napier, has Te Ana Falls, stands of wheki-ponga (tree ferns) and native orchids. Again, www.doc.

govt.nz has the low-down on these reserves. Between White Pine and Tangoio Reserves the **Tangoio Walkway** (three hours return) follows Kareaara Stream.

The highway surfs the coast for the last 20km, with impressive views towards Napier. Hawke's Bay wine country starts in earnest at the mouth of the Esk River.

ⓘ Information

Wairoa i-SITE (☎06-838 7440; www.visit wairoa.co.nz; cnr SH2 & Queen St; ☺8.30am-4.45pm Mon-Fri, 10am-4.45pm Sat & Sun) The spot for local info, including advice on Lake Waikaremoana and accommodation around town.

Napier

POP 57,240

The Napier of today – a charismatic, sunny, composed city with the air of an affluent English seaside resort – is the silver lining

Hawke's Bay

of the dark cloud that was the deadly 1931 earthquake. Rebuilt in the popular architectural styles of the time, the city retains a unique concentration of art-deco buildings. Don't expect the Chrysler Building – Napier is resolutely low-rise – but you will find amazingly intact 1930s facades and streetscapes, which can provoke a *Great Gatsby* swagger in the least romantic soul.

History

The Napier area has been settled since around the 12th century and was known to Māori as Ahuriri (now the name of a suburb of Napier). By the time James Cook eyeballed the scene in October 1769, Ngāti Kahungunu was the dominant tribe, controlling the whole coast down to Wellington.

In the 1830s whalers malingered around Ahuriri, establishing a trading base in 1839. By the 1850s the Crown had purchased – often by dubious means – 1.4 million acres of Hawke's Bay land, leaving Ngāti Kahungunu with less than 4000 acres. The town of Napier was planned in 1854 and obsequiously named after the British general and colonial administrator Charles Napier.

At 10.46am on 3 February 1931, the city was levelled by a catastrophic earthquake (7.9 on the Richter scale). Fatalities in Napier and nearby Hastings numbered 258. Napier suddenly found itself 40 sq km larger, as the earthquake heaved sections of what was once a lagoon 2m above sea level (Napier airport was once more 'port', less 'air'). A fevered rebuilding program ensued, resulting in one of the world's most uniformly art-deco cities.

⊙ Sights

Napier's claim to fame is undoubtedly its architecture, and a close study of these treasures could take several days (especially if you're stopping to eat). Beyond the edge of town, the Hawke's Bay wineries are a treat.

★ **Daily Telegraph Building**   ARCHITECTURE
(Map p338; ☏ 06-834 1911; www.heritage.org.nz/the-list/details/1129; 49 Tennyson St; ⊗9am-5pm Mon-Fri) The Daily Telegraph is one of the stars of Napier's art-deco show, with superb zigzags, fountain shapes and a ziggurat aesthetic. If the front doors are open, nip inside and ogle at the painstakingly restored foyer (it's a real-estate office these days).

★ **MTG Hawke's Bay**   MUSEUM, THEATRE
(Museum Theatre Gallery; Map p338; ☏06-835 7781; www.mtghawkesbay.com; 1 Tennyson St; adult/child $10/free; ⊗10am-5pm) The beating cultural heart of Napier is the smart-looking MTG. It's a gleaming-white museum-theatre-gallery space by the water, and it brings live performances, film screenings, and regularly changing gallery and

museum displays together with touring and local exhibitions.

National Tobacco Company Building ARCHITECTURE
(Map p336; ☏ 06-834 1911; www.heritage.org.nz/the-list/details/1170; cnr Bridge & Ossian Sts, Ahuri-ri; ◷ lobby 9am-5pm Mon-Fri) Around the shore at Ahuriri, the National Tobacco Company Building (1932) is arguably the region's deco masterpiece, combining art-deco forms with the natural motifs of art nouveau. Roses, raupo (bulrushes) and grapevines frame the elegantly curved entrance. During business

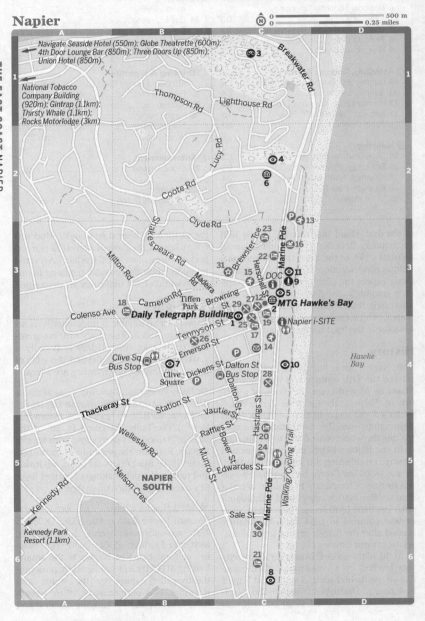

Napier

hours, pull on the leaf-shaped brass door handles and enter the first two rooms.

Marine Parade
STREET

(Map p338) Napier's elegant seaside avenue is lined with huge Norfolk Island pines, and dotted with motels and charming timber villas. Along its length are parks, quirky **sunken gardens**, a minigolf course, a skate park, a sound shell, a swim centre and an aquarium. Near the north end of the parade is the **Tom Parker Fountain**, best viewed at night when it's lavishly lit. Next to it is the **Pania of the Reef** sculpture, with dubious boobs.

National Aquarium of New Zealand
AQUARIUM

(Map p338; ☑06-834 1404; www.national aquarium.co.nz; 546 Marine Pde; adult/child/family $20/10/54; ⊙9am-5pm, feedings 10am & 2pm, last entry 4.30pm) Inside this mod complex with its stingray-inspired roof are piranhas, terrapins, eels, kiwi, tuatara and a whole lotta fish. Snorkellers can swim with sharks ($82), or sign up for a Little Penguin Close Encounter ($65).

Bluff Hill Lookout
VIEWPOINT

(Map p338; Lighthouse Rd) The convoluted route to the top of Bluff Hill (102m) goes up and down like an elevator on speed (best to drive), but rewards with expansive views across the port. Bring a picnic or some fish and chips.

Napier Urban Farmers Market
MARKET

(Map p338; ☑027 697 3737; www.hawkesbayfarm ersmarket.co.nz; Clive Sq, Lower Emerson St; ⊙9am-1pm Sat) Score some super-fresh local produce: fruit, veggies, bread, coffee, dairy products, honey, wine... Who needs supermarkets?

Centennial Gardens
GARDENS

(Map p338; www.napier.govt.nz; Coote Rd; ⊙24hr) Woah! A massive waterfall right in the middle of Napier! There may be an artificial pump system in play, but we don't mind – it's still an impressive sight. Ducks, rockeries and flower beds revolve around the ponds below.

Otatara Pā
Historic Reserve
ARCHAEOLOGICAL SITE

(Map p336; ☑06-834 3111; www.doc.govt.nz; off Springfield Rd; ⊙24hr) FREE Wooden palisades, carved *pou* (memorial posts) and a carved gate help bring this *pa* (fortified village) site to life. An hour-long loop walk across grassy hills passes barely discernible archaeological remains but affords terrific views of the surrounding countryside. From the city head southwest on Taradale Rd and Gloucester St. Turn right into Springfield Rd just before the river.

Napier Prison
HISTORIC BUILDING

(Map p338; ☑06-835 9933; www.napierprison. com; 55 Coote Rd; adult/child/family $20/10/50; ⊙9am-5pm) On the run from the law? Assuage your guilt with a tour of the grim 1906 Napier Prison on the hill behind the town.

There's a self-guided audio set-up, available in 16 languages.

🏃 Activities

Napier's pebbly ocean beach isn't safe for swimming. Instead, to cool off, locals head north of the city to **Westshore Beach** (Map p336; off Ferguson Ave, Westshore), or to the surf beaches south of Cape Kidnappers.

Ocean Spa   SWIMMING
(Map p338; ☑ 06-835 8553; www.oceanspanapier. co.nz; 42 Marine Pde; adult/child $11/8, private pools 30min adult/child $13/10; ☺ 6am-10pm Mon-Sat, 8am-10pm Sun) A spiffy waterfront pool complex that features a lane pool, hot pools, a beauty spa and a gym. Exhausting...

New Zealand Wine Centre   WINERY
(Map p338; ☑ 06-835 5326; www.nzwinecentre. co.nz; 1 Shakespeare Rd; tastings 3/6 wines $18/29; ☺ 10am-6pm daily, closed Sun Jun-Aug) No time for a full-blown Hawke's Bay winery tour? Swing by the NZ Wine Centre for a taste of the region's best drops on 'Wine Tasting Adventures'.

Mountain Valley   ADVENTURE SPORTS
(☑ 06-834 9756; www.mountainvalley.co.nz; 408 McVicar Rd, Te Pohue; horse treks/rafting/fishing per person from $70/80/250) About 60km north of Napier on SH5, Mountain Valley is a hub of outdoorsy action: horse trekking, white-water rafting, kayaking and fly fishing. There's also simple accommodation on-site (sites/dorms/doubles from $16/22/100).

👉 Tours

If you haven't got time for a guided or self-guided art-deco walking tour, just take to the streets – particularly Tennyson and Emerson. Remember to look up!

Deco Centre   CULTURAL TOUR
(Map p338; ☑ 06-835 0022; www.artdeconapier. com; 7 Tennyson St; ☺ 9am-5pm; 🚶) Start your explorations at the Deco Centre, which runs daily one-hour guided deco walks ($18) departing the Napier i-SITE at 10am; and daily two-hour tours ($20) leaving the Deco Centre at 2pm. There's also a little shop here, plus brochures for the self-guided *Art Deco Walk* ($8), *Art Deco Scenic Drive* ($3) and *Marewa Meander* ($3).

Other options include a minibus tour ($40, 1¼ hours), vintage car tour ($75, 1¼ hours) and the kids' *Art Deco Explorer* treasure hunt ($5).

Absolute de Tours   BUS TOUR
(☑ 06-844 8699; www.absolutedetours.co.nz; tours 90min/half-day from $40/60) Runs quick-fire bus tours of the city, Marewa and Bluff Hill in conjunction with the Deco Centre, as well as half-day tours of Napier and Hastings.

Ferg's Fantastic Tours   TOUR
(☑ 0800 428 687; www.fergstours.co.nz; tours half-/full day from $40/120) Tours from two to seven hours, exploring Napier and surrounding areas: wineries, Te Mata Peak, lookouts and foodie stops.

Bay Tours & Charters   TOUR
(☑ 06-845 2736; www.baytours.co.nz; tours 3/4hr $75/100; 🚗) Family-friendly tours, including a four-hour 'Napier Highlights' tour and a three-hour 'Best of the Bay' jaunt.

Hawke's Bay Scenic Tours   TOUR
(☑ 06-844 5693, 027 497 9231; www.hbscenic tours.co.nz; tours from $50) A grape-coloured bunch of tour options including the 2½-hour 'Napier Whirlwind' ($50), full-day Hawke's Bay scenic tour ($135), and a 4½-hour wine and brewery jaunt ($95).

🎊 Festivals & Events

Art Deco Weekend   CULTURAL
(www.artdeconapier.com; ☺ Feb) In the third week of February, Napier and Hastings co-host the sensational Art Deco Weekend. Around 125 events fill the week (dinners, picnics, dances, balls, bands, Gatsby-esque fancy dress), many of which are free. Expect around 40,000 art-deco fans!

🛏 Sleeping

Napier YHA   HOSTEL $
(Map p338; ☑ 06-835 7039; www.yha.co.nz; 277 Marine Pde; dm/s/d from $26/45/69; 📶) Napier's friendly YHA is housed in a lovely old timber beachfront villa with a seemingly endless ramble of rooms. There's a fabulous reading nook and a sunny rear courtyard. Staff can help with bookings and local info. It's the best of several backpackers along Marine Pde. Bike hire $20 per day.

Criterion Art Deco Backpackers   HOSTEL $
(Map p338; ☑ 06-835 2059; www.criterion artdeco.co.nz; 48 Emerson St; dm/s/d/f without bathroom from $29/53/66/112, d with bathroom from $85; 📶) The owners have spent a lot of money sprucing up this 1st-floor, ruby-red city-centre hostel – Napier's best Spanish Mission specimen – which has a beaut little balcony over Emerson St and an

CYCLE THE BAY

The 200km network of Hawke's Bay Trails (www.nzcycletrail.com/hawkes-bay-trails) – part of the national Nga Haerenga, New Zealand Cycle Trails project – offers cycling opportunities from short, city scoots to hilly, single-track shenanigans. Dedicated cycle trails encircle Napier, Hastings and the coastline, with landscape, water and wine themes. Pick up the *Hawke's Bay Trails* brochure from the **Napier i-SITE** (p344) or online.

Napier itself is very cycle-friendly, particularly along Marine Pde where you'll find **Fishbike** (Map p338; ☑ 06-833 6979, 0800 131 600; www.fishbike.nz; 22 Marine Pde, Pacific Surf Club; bike hire per half-/full day $30/40, tandems per hour $30; ☺ 9am-5pm) renting comfortable bikes – including tandems for those willing to risk divorce. **Napier City Bike Hire** (Map p338; ☑ 0800 245 344, 021 959 595; www.bikehirenapier.co.nz; 117 Marine Pde; kids/city/mountain bike per half-day from $20/25/30, full day from $25/35/40; ☺ 9am-5pm) is another option.

Mountain bikers head to **Pan Pac Eskdale MTB Park** (Map p336; ☑ 022 544 0069, 06-873 8793; www.hawkesbaymtb.co.nz; off SH5; 3-week permits $10) for a whole lot of fun in the forest: see the website or call for directions. You can hire mountain bikes from **Pedal Power** (Map p336; ☑ 06-344 9771; www.pedalpower.co.nz; 340 Gloucester St, Taradale; half-/full day from $30/50; ☺ 8am-5.30pm Mon-Fri, 9am-3pm Sat, 10am-3pm Sun), just out of the city centre, or from Napier City Bike Hire.

Given the conducive climate, terrain and multitudinous tracks, it's no surprise that numerous cycle companies pedal fully geared-up tours around the bay, with winery visits near mandatory. Operators include the following:

Bike About Tours (☑ 06-845 4836, 027 232 4355 www.bikeabouttours.co.nz; tours half-/full day from $35/45)

Coastal Wine Cycles (☑ 06-875 0302; www.winecycles.co.nz; tours per day $40)

On Yer Bike Winery Tours (☑ 06-650 4627; www.onyerbikehb.co.nz; full day with/without lunch $60/50)

Tākaro Trails (☑ 06-835 9030; www.takarotrails.co.nz; day rides from $40)

amazing old fireplace in the lounge area. A super-charming hostel in a top spot.

Kennedy Park Resort HOLIDAY PARK $
(Map p336; ☑ 0800 457 275, 06-343 9126; www.kennedypark.co.nz; 1 Storkey St; sites from $48, cabins & units $61-239; @ � ☝ ☀) Less a campground and more an entire suburb of holidaymakers, this complex is top dog on the Napier camping scene. It's the closest campsite to town (2.5km out, southwest of the centre) and has every facility imaginable, plus a swathe of cabin and unit configurations. And a karaoke machine!

Stables Lodge Backpackers HOSTEL $
(Map p338; ☑ 06-835 6242; www.stableslodge. co.nz; 370 Hastings St; dm/c/cottages from $21/69/135; ☝) Formerly an actual stables, this is an atmospheric, laid-back place to get off your horse, with hippie vibes, a barbecue courtyard, murals, saddles festooned around the place and free wi-fi. There's also a cottage for two in nearby Clive (sleeps five).

★ **Sea Breeze B&B** B&B $$
(Map p338; ☑ 06-835 8067; www.seabreezebnb. co.nz; 281 Marine Pde; r incl breakfast $100-135;

☝) Inside this Victorian seafront earthquake survivor (1906) are three richly coloured themed rooms (Chinese, Indian and Turkish), decorated with a cornucopia of artefacts. It's all tastefully done, avoiding the risk of being over the top. The price and location are right. Self-serve continental breakfast and free wi-fi included.

★ **Pebble Beach Motor Inn** MOTEL $$
(Map p338; ☑ 06-835 7496, 0800 723 224; www.pebblebeach.co.nz; 445 Marine Pde; r $145-295; ☝) Unlike the majority of NZ motels, this one is owner-operated (they own the building, rather than lease it from a higher power) – so maintenance and service top the list of staff priorities. There are 25 immaculate rooms over three levels, all with kitchens, spas, balconies and ocean views. Full to capacity most nights.

Seaview Lodge B&B B&B $$
(Map p338; ☑ 027 235 0202, 06-835 0202; www.aseaviewlodge.co.nz; 5 Seaview Tce; r $130-180; ☝) This grand Victorian villa (1890) is queen of all she surveys – which is most of the town and a fair bit of ocean. The elegant rooms

have tasteful period elements and either bathroom or en suite. It's hard to resist a sunset tipple on the veranda, which opens off the relaxing guest lounge. Free wi-fi and off-street parking are a bonus.

Mission B&B on the Avenue   B&B $$
(Map p336; ☑ 06-844 3988; www.missionbnb. co.nz; 140 Avenue Rd, Greenmeadows; d incl breakfast $150-250, whole house self-catering $200-400; ☎) Out in hushed Napier burbs near Mission Estate Winery (p346), this excellent B&B is an immaculate 1970s number with a 2008 makeover, fastidiously maintained and managed. Free bikes, a big guest lounge and breakfast on the deck. It's a fair hike from town (seven minutes' drive), but close to the Taradale shops and eateries. Book a room, or the whole house.

Rocks Motorlodge   MOTEL $$
(Map p336; ☑ 0800 835 9626, 06-835 9626; www.therocksmotel.co.nz; 27 Meeanee Quay, Westshore; units $100-180; ☎) Just 80m from Westshore Beach, the Rocks has corrugated and mosaic stylings that have raised the bar on motel row. Interiors are plush and roomy with colour-splashes: some have spa baths, others claw-foot baths. Free (and fast) wi-fi, free gym, and a laundry for grubby road warriors. Good one!

Scenic Hotel Te Pania   HOTEL $$
(Map p338; ☑ 06-833 7733; www.scenichotels. co.nz; 45 Marine Pde; d/1-bedroom/2-bedroom from $190/260/340; ☎☎) Looking like a mini UN HQ by the sea, the refurbished, curvalicious, six-storey Te Pania has instant retro appeal. Rooms are far from retro, however, with designer linen, leather lounges and floor-to-ceiling windows that slide open for lungfuls of sea air.

Navigate Seaside Hotel   HOTEL, APARTMENT $$
(Map p336; ☑ 06-831 0077; www.navigatenapier. co.nz; 18 Hardinge Rd, Ahuriri; d/f/2-bedroom apt from $170/245/305; ☎) Navigate yourself towards Navigate for 26 snazzy apartment-style units over three levels, with funky furnishings, nifty perforated-metal balconies and sea views from the best rooms. There's a big kids' playground across the street for the offspring. Just four years old – everything is still in good nick.

Green House on the Hill   B&B $$
(Map p338; ☑ 06-835 4475; www.the-greenhouse.co.nz; 18b Milton Rd; s $90-115, d $120-135; ☎) ☞ This meat-free, environmentally attuned B&B is up a steep hill and rewards

with leafy surrounds and magical city and sea views. The guest floor has two bedrooms, one with an en suite and one with a private (but separate) bathroom. Home-baked goodies and fine herbal teas are likely to make an appearance. Great value. Free wi-fi.

Masonic Hotel   HOTEL $$$
(Map p338; ☑ 06-835 8689; www.masonic.co.nz; cnr Tennyson St & Marine Pde; r $199-499; ☎) The art-deco Masonic is the heart of the old town, with its accommodation, restaurants and bars taking up most of a city block. A much-needed refurb has revived the old stager, with stripy carpets and quirky wallpaper adorning the original bones. All 42 rooms have bathrooms; the best have sea views and access to the roof terrace.

✖ Eating

Groove Kitchen Espresso   CAFE $
(Map p338; ☑ 06-835 8530; www.groovekitchen. co.nz; 112 Tennyson St; mains $9-19; ☺ 8am-2pm Mon-Fri, 8.30am-2pm Sat & Sun; ☎) A sophisticated cafe squeezed into an old Spanish Mission–style house, where the turntable spins and the kitchen cranks out A1 brunch along with interesting wraps, baps, salads and killer coffee. With a bit of luck you'll be around for one of the occasional DJ gigs.

★ Mister D   MODERN NZ $$
(Map p338; ☑ 06-835 5022; www.misterd.co.nz; 47 Tennyson St; mains $25-33; ☺ 7.30am-4pm Sun-Wed, to late Thu-Sat) This long, floorboarded room with its green-tiled bar is the pride of the Napier foodie scene. Hip and slick but not unaffordable, with quick-fire service delivering the likes of pulled pork with white polenta or roast duck risotto. Novelty of the Year award: doughnuts served with syringes full of chocolate, jam or custard (DIY injecting). Bookings essential.

★ Three Doors Up   MODERN NZ $$
(Map p336; ☑ 06-834 0835; www.threedoorsup.co.nz; 3 Waghorne St, Ahuriri; mains $24-38; ☺ 5.30pm-late) The fab old Union Hotel (p343) has ceded part of its territory to Three Doors Up, a hip new restaurant serving classic fare such as risotto, eye fillet steak, slow-cooked pork belly and seafood chowder, all done to perfection. Love the sheet-music wallpaper! The 4th Door Lounge Bar (p343) is next door for a pre-dinner drink (if the Union's not your bag).

Indigo   INDIAN $$
(Map p338; ☑ 06-834 4085; www.indigonapier. co.nz; 24a Hastings St; mains $14-22; ☺ noon-

2pm Thu-Sun, 5pm-late daily; 🎏) How long has it been since you had a really good curry? Too long... Get thee to Indigo, a stylish subcontinental outfit that feels like it should be charging more for its dishes than it does. There are also 200 whiskies to worry about, plus seasonal chef's specials with an NZ twist (lamb-chop masala!).

Café Ujazi
CAFE $$

(Map p338; 🕿 06-835 1490; www.facebook.com/ujazicafe; 28 Tennyson St; mains $10-22; ⏰ 8am-5pm; 🎏) The most bohemian of Napier's cafes, Ujazi folds back its windows and lets the alternative vibes spill out onto the pavement. It's a long-established, consistent performer offering blackboard meals and hearty counter food (vegetarian and vegan a speciality). Try the classic *rewena* special – a big breakfast on traditional Māori bread. Oooh – homemade limeade!

Restaurant Indonesia
INDONESIAN $$

(Map p338; 🕿 06-835 8303; www.restaurantindonesia.co.nz; 409 Marine Pde; mains $20-27; ⏰ 5.30-9pm Tue-Sun; 🎏) Crammed with Indonesian curios, this intimate space oozes authenticity. Lip-smacking Indo-Dutch *rijsttafel* smorgasbords are the house speciality (14 dishes, $30 to $36) – a romantic option if you're hungry with love.

MINT Restaurant
MODERN NZ $$$

(Map p338; 🕿 06-835 4050; www.mintrestaurant.co.nz; 189 Marine Pde; mains $29-34; ⏰ 6-10pm Mon-Sat) Fine dining on Marine Pde: a tightly edited menu features the likes of beef cheek braised in red wine with wild mushrooms, blue cheese and roast parsnip. Sensuously shaped glassware and snappy staff. Just ignore the raucous 'Super Cool Zone' skate park across the street...

🍷 Drinking & Nightlife

★ Emporium
BAR

(Map p338; 🕿 06-835 0013; www.emporiumbar.co.nz; Masonic Hotel, cnr Tennyson St & Marine Pde; ⏰ 7am-late; 🛜) Napier's most civilised bar, Emporium, with its marble-topped bar, fab art-deco details and old-fashioned relics strewn about, is super atmospheric. Brisk staff, creative cocktails, good coffee, NZ wines, bistro fare (plates $15 to $35) and a prime location seal the deal.

Thirsty Whale
BAR

(Map p336; 🕿 06-835 8815; www.thethirstywhale.co.nz; 62 West Quay, Ahuriri; ⏰ 11am-late Mon-Fri, 9am-late Sat & Sun; 🛜) Does a whale drink? Or just filter krill? Either way, this big dockside bar is a sporty spot to join some fellow mammals for a brew or a bite (mains $12 to $39). Beneath 'Hawke's Bay's biggest screen' is the place to watch the All Blacks.

4th Door Lounge Bar
COCKTAIL BAR

(Map p336; 🕿 06-834 0835; www.threedoorsup.co.nz/the-4th-door; 3 Waghorne St, Ahuriri; ⏰ 5pm-late Wed-Sat, 3pm-late Sun) Next to Three Doors Up (p342) is 4th Door, continuing the door-centric nomenclature and offering an alternative to Ahuriri's mainstream waterfront bars. It's a classy, moody little nook, perfect for a predinner drink, or a nightcap. Live piano guy Friday nights; Sunday afternoon jazz.

Gintrap
PUB

(Map p336; 🕿 06-835 0199; www.gintrap.co.nz; 64 West Quay, Ahuriri; ⏰ 11am-late Mon-Fri, 9.30am-late Sat & Sun) The pick of the big rambling restaurant-bars out on the Ahuriri waterfront, where the city council is endeavouring to isolate noisy after-dark crowds. Enjoy seafood in the sunshine (mains $14 to $33), lofty interiors and a sunny deck.

Union Hotel
PUB

(Map p336; 🕿 06-835 1274; 3 Waghorne St, Ahuriri; ⏰ 11am-late) Wow, what a classic! Before the advent of craft beer and ritzy bar-cafes, this is what all the watering holes in NZ were like: a tad underlit, with Tui on tap, crusty old dudes at the bar and '80s metal on the juke. Authentic! Interesting art-deco facade, too.

☆ Entertainment

Globe Theatrette
CINEMA

(Map p336; 🕿 06-833 6011; www.globenapier.co.nz; 15 Hardinge Rd, Ahuriri; tickets adult/child $16/14; ⏰ 1pm-late Tue-Sun) A vision in purple, this boutique 45-seat cinema screens art-house flicks in a sumptuous cinema lounge with ready access to upmarket snacks and drinks.

Cabana Bar
LIVE MUSIC

(Map p338; 🕿 06-835 1102; www.cabana.net.nz; 11 Shakespeare Rd; ⏰ 6pm-late Wed-Sat) This legendary music venue of the '70s, '80s and '90s died in 1997, but thanks to some forward-thinking rock fans, it's risen from the grave to save the day for Napier's gig lovers. Expect Led Zepp tribute acts, NZ original bands and karaoke nights.

ℹ Information

City Medical Napier (🕿 06-878 8109; www.hawkesbay.health.nz; 76 Wellesley Rd; ⏰ 24hr) Round-the-clock medical assistance.

DOC (Department of Conservation; Map p338; ☑ 06-834 3111; www.doc.govt.co.nz; 59 Marine Pde; ☺ 9am-4.15pm Mon-Fri) Maps, advice and passes.

Napier i-SITE (Map p338; ☑ 06-834 1911; www.napiernz.co.nz; 100 Marine Pde; ☺ 9am-5pm, extended hours Dec-Feb; ☎) Central, helpful and right by the bay.

Napier Post Office (Map p338; www.nzpost. co.nz; 1 Dickens St; ☺ 9am-5pm Mon-Fri, 9.30am-12.30pm Sat)

❶ Getting There & Away

AIR

Hawke's Bay Airport (Map p336; www. hawkesbay-airport.co.nz; SH2) is 8km north of the city.

Air New Zealand (☑ 06-833 5400; www.air newzealand.co.nz; cnr Hastings & Station Sts; ☺ 9am-5pm Mon-Wed & Fri, 9.30am-5pm Thu, 9am-noon Sat) flies direct to/from Auckland, Wellington and Christchurch. Sunair Aviation (www.sunair.co.nz) has direct weekday flights between Napier, Gisborne and Hamilton.

BUS

InterCity (www.intercity.co.nz) buses can be booked online or at the i-SITE. Naked Bus (www. nakedbus.com) tickets are best booked online.

Both companies depart from Clive Sq bus stop (Map p338), with daily services (several daily for Hastings) to the following:

DESTINATION	COMPANY	PRICE	TIME (HR)
Auckland	InterCity	$82	7½
Auckland	Naked Bus	$33	9
Gisborne	InterCity	$45	4
Hastings	InterCity	$19	½
Palmerston North	Naked Bus	$20	3
Taupo	InterCity	$33	2
Taupo	Naked Bus	$15	2
Wairoa	InterCity	$32	2¼
Wellington	InterCity	$39	5½
Wellington	Naked Bus	$28	5

❶ Getting Around

BICYCLE

Bikes (including tandems and children's) can be hired from **Fishbike** (p341) or **Napier City Bike Hire** (p341).

BUS

GoBay (www.hbrc.govt.nz) local buses (fitted with bike racks!) run many times daily between Napier, Hastings and Havelock North. Napier to Hastings (adult/child $4.30/2.20) takes 30 minutes (express) or 55 minutes (all stops). Buses depart Dalton St bus stop (Map p338).

CAR

See www.rentalcars.com for car-hire deals with companies at Hawke's Bay Airport, including the big brands and local outfits. **Rent-a-Dent** (☑ 06-834 0688, 0800 736 823; www.renta dent.co.nz; Hawke's Bay Airport, SH2; ☺ 8am-5pm Mon-Fri, to 1pm Sat) is also at the airport.

TAXI

A city–airport taxi costs around $25. Try **Hawke's Bay Combined Taxis** (☑ 06-835 7777; www. hawkes-bay.bluebubbletaxi.co.nz) or the door-to-door **Super Shuttle** (☑ 0800 748 885; www. supershuttle.co.nz; one way $20, extra person $5).

Hastings & Around

POP 77,900

Positioned at the centre of the Hawke's Bay fruit bowl, busy Hastings is the commercial hub of the region, 20km south of Napier. A few kilometres of orchards still separate it from Havelock North, with its prosperous village atmosphere and the towering backdrop of Te Mata Peak.

◉ Sights

Like Napier, Hastings was devastated by the 1931 earthquake and also boasts some fine art-deco and Spanish Mission buildings, built in the aftermath. Main-street highlights include the **Westerman's Building** (Map p345; cnr Russell St & Heretaunga St E), arguably the Bay's best example of the Spanish Mission style, although there are myriad architectural gems here. The i-SITE stocks the *Art Deco Hastings* brochure ($1), detailing two self-guided walks.

Te Mata Peak PARK
(Map p336; ☑ 06-873 0080; www.tematapark.co.nz; off Te Mata Rd, Havelock North) Rising melodramatically from the Heretaunga Plains 16km south of Havelock North, Te Mata Peak (399m) is part of the 1-sq-km **Te Mata Trust Park**. The summit road passes sheep trails, rickety fences and vertigo-inducing stone escarpments, cowled in a bleak, lunar-meets-Scottish-Highlands atmosphere. On a clear day, views from the lookout fall away to Hawke Bay, Mahia Peninsula and distant Mt Ruapehu.

The park's 30km of trails offer walks ranging from 30 minutes to two hours: pick up the *Te Mata Park's Top 5 Walking Tracks* brochure from local i-SITEs.

Hastings

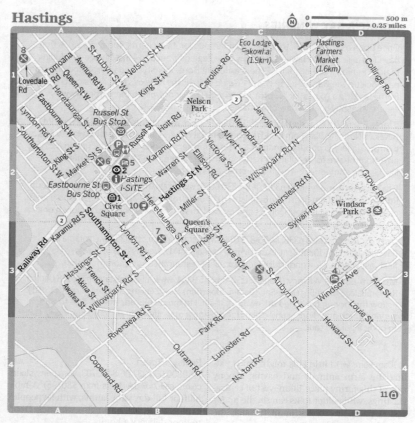

Hastings Farmers Market   MARKET
(Map p336; ☏ 027 697 3737; www.hawkesbay-farmersmarket.co.nz; Showgrounds, Kenilworth Rd; ☺ 8.30am-12.30pm Sun) If you're around on Sunday, the Hastings market is mandatory. Bring an empty stomach, some cash and a roomy shopping bag.

Hastings City Art Gallery   GALLERY
(HCAG; Map p345; ☏ 06-871 5095; www.hastingscityartgallery.co.nz; 201 Eastbourne St E; ☺ 10am-4.30pm) FREE The city's neat little gallery presents contemporary NZ (including Māori) and international art in a bright, purpose-built space. Expect some wacky stuff (much wackier than Hastings itself...).

🏃 Activities

Hawke's Bay Farmyard Zoo   HORSE RIDING
(Map p336; ☏ 06-875 0244; www.farmyardzoo.co.nz; 32 East Rd, Haumoana; farm admission adult/child/family $10/7/35, horse rides 1/2hr $70/100;

HAWKE'S BAY WINERIES

Once upon a time, this district was most famous for its orchards. Today it's vines that have top billing, with Hawke's Bay now New Zealand's second-largest wine-producing region (behind Marlborough). Expect excellent Bordeaux-style reds, syrah and chardonnay. Pick up the *Hawke's Bay Winery Guide* map or the *Hawke's Bay Trails* cycling map from **Hastings** (p348) or **Napier** (p344) i-SITEs, or download them from www. winehawkesbay.co.nz. A few of our faves:

Black Barn Vineyards (Map p336; ☑06-877 7985; www.blackbarn.com; Black Barn Rd, Havelock North; ⊙9am-5pm Mon-Fri, 10am-5pm Sat & Sun) This hip, inventive winery has a bistro, a gallery, a popular summer Saturday farmers market (one of the first in NZ) and an amphitheatre for regular concerts and movie screenings. The flagship chardonnay is like kissing someone pretty on a summer afternoon.

Crab Farm Winery (Map p336; ☑06-836 6678; www.crabfarmwinery.co.nz; 511 Main North Rd, Bay View; ⊙10am-5pm daily, 6pm-late Fri) Decent, reasonably priced wines, and a great cafe with regular live troubadours and relaxed, rustic vibes. A good stop for lunch or a glass of rosé (preferably both).

Craggy Range (Map p336; ☑06-873 0141; www.craggyrange.com; 253 Waimarama Rd, Havelock North; ⊙10am-6pm, closed Mon & Tue Apr-Oct) Definitely one of Hawke's Bay's flashiest wineries – wonderful wines, excellent restaurant and accommodation.

Mission Estate Winery (Map p336; ☑06-845 9354; www.missionestate.co.nz; 198 Church Rd, Taradale; ⊙9am-5pm Mon-Sat, 10am-4.30pm Sun) New Zealand's oldest winery (1851!). Follow the *looong* tree-lined driveway up the hill to the restaurant (mains $28 to $35, serving lunch and dinner) and cellar door, inside a magnificently restored seminary. Call to book a guided tour.

⊙10am-5pm; ⊛) Little kids might enjoy patting the farm animals and having a pony ride at this farmy place 13km west of central Hastings, while older folks can saddle up for a slow-paced horseback jaunt through the coastal countryside.

Airplay Paragliding PARAGLIDING
(☑06-845 1977; www.airplay.co.nz; 1-day courses $220) Te Mata Peak is a paragliding hot spot, with updraughts aplenty. Airplay offers full-day beginners' courses if you're keen to take the drop.

Splash Planet SWIMMING
(Map p345; ☑06-873 8033; www.splashplanet. co.nz; Grove Rd, Hastings; adult/child $28/18; ⊙10am-5.30pm Nov-Feb) A massive, watery wonderland with myriad pools, slides and aquatic distractions. Cheaper after 3pm.

👉 Tours

Long Island Guides GUIDED TOUR, CULTURAL
(☑06-874 7877; www.longislandtoursnz.com; half-day tours from $180) Customised Hawke's Bay tours across a wide range of interests including Māori culture, tramping, kayaking, horse riding, fishing and, inevitably, food and wine.

Prinsy's Tours WINE
(☑0800 004 237, 06-845 3703; www.prinsystours. co.nz; half-/full-day tours from $80/95) Affable half- or full-day wine jaunts, with laypeople's explanations, at four or five wineries. Door-to-door delivery a bonus.

Waimarama Tours CULTURAL
(☑021 057 0935; www.waimaramaori.com; 2-4hr tours from $80, transport from $40) Māori-run tours of Te Mata Peak, with plenty of cultural insights en route. Minimum numbers apply.

✪ Festivals & Events

Hastings Blossom Festival CULTURAL
(www.blossomfestival.co.nz; ⊙Sep) The Hastings Blossom Festival is a petalled spring fling, infamous for its 12-person 'riot' in 1960. The flowery insubordination happens in the second half of September: parades, arts, crafts and visiting artists.

🛏 Sleeping

Hastings Top 10 Holiday Park HOLIDAY PARK $
(Map p345; ☑06-878 6692; www.hastingstop10. co.nz; 610 Windsor Ave, Hastings; unpowered/powered sites from $44/46, units $78-160, apt $140-300; @🐾🛌) Hastings Top 10 puts the 'park' back into holiday park. Within its se-

rene confines are sycamore hedges, a topiary 'welcome' sign and a little stream all aflap with ducks. The heated pool, spa complex and tennis court satisfy the young, old and nimble respectively.

Rotten Apple HOSTEL $
(Map p345; ☎06-878 4363; www.rottenapple.co.nz; Upstairs, 114 Heretaunga St E, Hastings; dm/tw/d $26/70/70, weekly $125/140/140; @ 📶) This central-city, 1st-floor option is a fairly fruity affair, with orchard workers settled-in paying weekly rates. There's a bit of deck, a decent kitchen and sociable vibes, and staff can help you find work (sorting the rotten apples from the good ones). There's a dedicated 'quiet room' if you don't want to par-tay.

Eco Lodge Pakowhai HOSTEL $
(Map p336; ☎027 298 8910; www.ecolodge-pakowhai.co.nz; 1000 Pakowhai Rd, Hastings; sites/dm/s from $22/25/60, d with/without bathroom $75/60; 📶) The same family have tilled this land since 1885, but the attitude here is very forward-thinking. The talkative owner cuts carbon emissions with solar panels, rainwater collection systems, worm farms, double-glazing...and is expert at finding farm work for travellers. Accommodation comprises neat cabins or dorms in an old farmhouse. Good weekly rates; free wi-fi and laundry.

★ **Clive Colonial Cottages** COTTAGE $$
(Map p336; ☎06-870 1018; www.clivecolonialcottages.co.nz; 198 School Rd Clive; d from $145; 📶) A two-minute walk to the beach and almost equidistant from Hastings, Napier and Havelock, these three tasteful kitchen cottages encircle a courtyard garden on a 2-acre spread. Communal areas include barbecue, giant chess set and snooker room. Bikes onsite; trail on doorstep.

Havelock North Motor Lodge MOTEL $$
(Map p336; ☎06-877 8627; www.havelocknorthmotorlodge.co.nz; 7 Havelock Rd, Havelock North; units $140-195; 📶) Smack bang in the middle of Havelock North this modern motel does the job well. Tidy, clean and simple one- and two-bedroom units feature spa baths, nice art and kitchenettes. Hungry? Across the street there's Mexican, Italian, Chinese, Indian, burgers...

Off The Track COTTAGE $$
(Map p336; ☎06-877 0008; www.offthetrack.co.nz; 114 Havelock Rd, Havelock North; 1/2/3-bedroom cottages from $160/180/230; 📶) Not so much off the beaten track as just beside it, these three woody self-contained cottages are handy to Havelock North and a good option if you're trucking around with the family in tow. There's a busy cafe-restaurant here, too, but the cottages are privately positioned away from the hubbub.

Millar Road VILLA $$$
(Map p336; ☎06-875 1977; www.millarroad.co.nz; 83 Millar Rd, Hastings; villas/house from $400/650; 📶 🏊) Set in the Tuki Tuki Hills with vineyard and bay views, Millar Road is architecturally heaven-sent. Two plush villas (each sleep four) and a super-stylish house (sleeps eight) are filled with NZ-made furniture and local artworks. Explore the 20-hectare grounds or look cool by the pool.

Eating

Bay Espresso CAFE $
(Map p336; ☎06-877 9230; www.bayespresso.co.nz; 19 Middle Rd, Havelock North; mains $9-23; ⏲7.30am-4pm Mon-Sat, 8am-4pm Sun) On Middle Rd in the middle of Havelock, this enduringly popular cafe is far from middling, serving up house-roasted organic coffee and handsome counter food and brunch. Blaring Freddie Mercury and blueberry pancakes – a winning combo. Good smoothies, too.

Little Blackbird CAFE $
(Map p345; ☎06-870 7462; www.littleblackbird.co.nz; 108 Market St S, Hastings; mains $6-12; ⏲7.30am-3.30pm Mon-Fri, 8am-2.30pm Sat) At the bottom of an old art-deco office building, mostly full of lawyers, is this tidy little eatery with retro interior design, funky lighting, Nicaraguan beans (!) and smiling staff (always a good sign). Head for the row of little tables by the street for some savoury scones or a beaut salad bowl.

Rush Munro's ICE CREAM $
(Map p345; ☎06-878 9634; www.rushmunro.co.nz; 704 Heretaunga St W, Hastings; ice cream $4-7; ⏲noon-5pm Mon-Fri, 11am-5pm Sat & Sun, extended hours summer) Rush Munro's is a Hastings institution, serving locally made ice cream since 1926. Don't overlook the maple walnut.

★ **Opera Kitchen** CAFE $$
(Map p345; ☎06-870 6020; www.operakitchen.co.nz; 312 Eastbourne St E, Hastings; mains $9-26; ⏲7.30am-4pm Mon-Fri, 9am-3pm Sat & Sun 🖉) Set your rudder right with whisky porridge with cream and giant oats at this mod, stylish cafe abutting the Hawke's Bay Opera House (has the earthquake-proofing

construction finished?). For a more practical start to the day, the farmer's breakfast is also a winner. Heavenly pastries, great coffee and snappy staff.

Alessandro's
PIZZA $$

(Map p336; ☑06-877 8844; www.alessandros pizzeria.co.nz; 24 Havelock Rd, Havelock North; mains $20-24; ⊙5-9pm Tue-Thu, 4.30-9.30pm Fri-Sun) Excellent new Alessandro's does handmade wood-fired pizzas, thin and flavoursome, just like back in Napoli. Order the *Nico e Pere* (pear, Gorgonzola, mozzarella, walnuts and truffle honey) with a mean affogato for dessert. Snappy interior design; Peroni on tap.

Pipi
PIZZA $$

(Map p336; ☑06-877 8993; www.pipicafe.co.nz; 16 Joll Rd, Havelock North; mains $16-33; ⊙4-10pm) Shockingly pink with candy stripes, chandeliers and mismatched furniture, Pipi cheekily thumbs its nose at small-town conventionality. The food focus is on simple pasta dishes, Roman-style thin-crusted pizza, craft beer and local wines. **Pipi Truck** randomly turns up around the bay, taking the food to the streets (check Facebook for locations).

Deliciosa
TAPAS $$

(Map p336; ☑06-877 6031; www.deliciosa. co.nz; 21 Napier Rd, Havelock North; tapas $10-22; ⊙4pm-late Mon & Tue, 11am-late Wed-Sat) Great things come in small packages at this rosy little tapas bar. The kitchen delivers sassy, locally sourced edibles such as pork belly with pomegranate jus, and salt-and-pepper squid with orange and parsley. The wine list roams from Spain to Italy and back. Terrific beer list and breezy front terrace, too.

Vidal
MODERN NZ $$$

(Map p345; ☑06-872 7440; www.vidal.co.nz; 913 St Aubyn St E, Hastings; mains lunch $25-29, dinner $29-38; ⊙11.30am-3pm & 6pm-late Mon-Sat, 11.30am-3pm Sun) There's nothing suburban about this winery restaurant on the suburban backstreets of Hastings. The warm, wood-lined dining room is a worthy setting for such elegant food: order the eye fillet or the duck confit, sip some syrah and feel your holiday come to fruition. Classy stuff.

☕ Drinking & Nightlife

★ Common Room
BAR

(Map p345; ☑027 656 8959; www.common roombar.com; 227 Heretaunga St E, Hastings; ⊙3pm-late Wed-Sat) There's pretty much nothing wrong with this hip little bar in central Hastings: cheery staff, bar snacks, craft beer, local wines, creative retro interiors, garden bar, Persian rugs, live music and a tune-scape ranging form jazz to alt-country to indie. All the right stuff! Open Sundays as well in summer.

Filter Room
BREWERY

(Map p336; ☑06-834 3986; www.thefilterroom. co.nz; 20 Awatoto Rd, Meeanee; ⊙10am-5pm Tue-Sun, closed Tue May-Oct) Surrounded by orchards, these folks proffer impressive craft beers and ciders (try the Black Duck Porter or the passion-fruit cider), all brewed on-site, plus tasting trays and belly-filling food (mains $12 to $22 – burgers, salads, lamb shanks...). Hours extend on summer evenings.

Hugo Chang
COCKTAIL BAR

(Map p336; ☑06-877 3310; www.hugochang. com; 15b Joll Rd, Havelock North; ⊙4.30pm-late Tue-Sat) When the lights go down over Havelock North and a hush falls over the vine rows, over-25s with a yearning for some urban savvy head for Hugo Chang – a tucked-away, Asian-themed bar serving up cocktails, local wines and smooth beats.

🔒 Shopping

Strawberry Patch
FOOD

(Map p336; ☑06-877 1350; www.strawberry patch.co.nz; 76 Havelock Rd, Havelock North; ⊙9am-5.30pm) Pick your own berries in season (late November through summer), or visit year-round for fresh produce, picnic supplies, coffee and real fruit ice cream ($4).

Telegraph Hill
FOOD

(Map p345; ☑06-878 4460; www.telegraphhill. co.nz; 1279 Howard St, Hastings; ⊙9am-5pm Mon-Fri, plus 10am-3pm Sat Oct-Mar) A passionate producer of olives, oils and sundry Mediterranean-inspired gourmet treats, sourced from eight olive groves around Hawke's Bay (sunny, dry, not too cold – perfect olive weather). Free tastings.

ℹ Information

Hastings i-SITE (Map p345; ☑06-873 0080; www.visithastings.co.nz; Westermans Bldg, cnr Russell St & Heretaunga St E; ⊙9am-5pm Mon-Fri, to 3pm Sat, 10am-2pm Sun) The usual array of maps, brochures and bookings.

Hastings Memorial Hospital (☑06-878 8109; www.hawkesbay.health.nz; Omahu Rd, Camberley; ⊙24hr)

Havelock North i-SITE (Map p336; ☑06-877 9600; www.havelocknorthnz.com; cnr Te Aute & Middle Rds; ⊙10am-5pm Mon-Fri, to 4pm Sat, to 3pm Sun; 🛜) Local info in a cute little booth.

Post Office (Map p345; www.nzpost.co.nz; 200 Market St N, Hastings; ⏱8.30am-5pm Mon-Fri, 9am-noon Sat)

ⓘ Getting There & Away

Napier's **Hawke's Bay Airport** (p344) is a 20-minute drive from Hastings. **Air New Zealand** (⏱06-873 2200; www.airnewzealand. co.nz; 117 Heretaunga St W; ⏱9am-5pm Mon-Fri) has an office in central Hastings.

InterCity buses stop at the Russell St bus stop (Map p345). Book InterCity (www.intercity. co.nz) and Naked Bus (www.nakedbus.com) buses online or at the i-SITE.

ⓘ Getting Around

GoBay (www.hbrc.govt.nz) local buses (with bike racks) run between Hastings, Havelock North and Napier. Daily Hastings to Napier buses (adult/child $4.30/2.20) take 30 minutes (express) or 55 minutes (all stops). Hastings to Havelock North buses run Monday to Saturday (adult/child $2.90/1.50, 35 minutes). Buses depart from the **Eastbourne St bus stop** (Map p345).

Hastings Taxis (⏱0800 875 055, 06-878 5055; www.hastingstaxis.co.nz) is the local cab outfit.

Cape Kidnappers

From mid-September to late April, Cape Kidnappers (named when local Māori tried to kidnap Captain Cook's Tahitian servant boy) erupts with squawking gannets. These big ocean birds usually nest on remote islands but here they settle for the mainland, completely unfazed by human spectators.

The birds nest as soon as they arrive, and eggs take about six weeks to hatch, with chicks arriving in early November. In March the gannets start their migration; by May they're gone.

Early November to late February is the best time to visit. Take a tour or the walkway to the colony (Map p336; ⏱06-834 3111; www.doc.govt.nz; off Clifton Rd, Clifton; ⏱Nov-Jun; FREE): it's about five hours return from Clifton. En route are interesting cliff formations, rock pools, a sheltered picnic spot, and the gaggling gannets themselves. The walk is tide dependent: leave no earlier than three hours after high tide; start back no later than 1½ hours after low tide.

ⓕ Tours

Gannet Beach Adventures ECOTOUR (Map p336; ⏱06-875 0898, 0800 426 638; www. gannets.com; 475 Clifton Rd, Clifton; adult/child/

family $44/24/106; ⓓ) Ride along the beach on a tractor-pulled trailer before wandering out on the Cape for 90 minutes. This four-hour, guided return trip departs from the Clifton waterfront, and is good fun.

Gannet Safaris ECOTOUR (Map p336; ⏱06-875 0888; www.gannetsafaris. co.nz; 396 Clifton Rd, Te Awanga; adult/child $75/35; ⓓ) Overland 4WD trips across farmland into the gannet colony. Three-hour tours depart at 9.30am and 1.30pm. Pickups from Napier and Hastings cost extra (adult/child additional $30/15).

Central Hawke's Bay

Grassy farmland stretches south from Hastings, dotted with the grand homesteads of Victorian pastoralists. It's an untouristed area (aka 'Lamb Country'), rich in history and deserted beaches. The main regional town is Waipukurau (aka 'Wai-puk'; population 3750) – not exactly thrilling but a functional hub for petrol, motels, a supermarket and the Central Hawke's Bay Information Centre (p350) with adjunct coffee booth.

◉ Sights & Activities

There are no fewer than six windswept beaches along the coast here: Kairakau, Mangakuri, Pourerere, Aramoana, Blackhead and Porangahau. The first five are good for swimming, and between the lot they offer a range of sandy, salty activities including surfing, fishing, and driftwoody, rock-pooly adventures. Between Aramoana and Blackhead Beach lies the DOC-managed **Te Angiangi Marine Reserve** – bring your snorkel.

It's a nondescript hill in the middle of nowhere, but the place with the world's longest name is good for a photo op. Believe it or not, **Taumatawhakatangihangakoauauotamateaturipukakapikimaungahoronukupokaiwhenuakitanatahu** is the abbreviated form of 'The Brow of a Hill Where Tamatea, the Man with the Big Knees, Who Slid, Climbed, and Swallowed Mountains, Known as Land Eater, Played his Flute to his Brother'. To get there, fuel-up in Waipukurau and drive 40km to the Mangaorapa junction on route 52. Turn left and go 4km towards Porangahau. At the intersection with the signposts turn right and continue 4.3km to the sign.

Onga Onga, a historic village 16km west of Waipawa, has interesting Victorian and

Edwardian buildings. Pick up a pamphlet for a self-guided walking tour from the info centre in Waipukurau.

Central Hawke's Bay Settler's Museum
MUSEUM

(☑06-857 7288; www.chbsettlersmuseum.co.nz; 23 High St, Waipawa; adult/child $5/1; ☺10am-4pm) The Central Hawke's Bay Settler's Museum in Waipawa has pioneer artefacts, informative 'homestead' displays and a good specimen of a river *waka* (canoe). Look for the anchor of the ill-fated schooner *Maroro* out the front.

✖ Eating

★Paper Mulberry Café
CAFE $

(☑06-856 8688; www.papermulberrycafe.co.nz; 89 SH2, Pukehou; snacks $4-10, lunch mains $10-17; ☺7am-4pm) Halfway between Waipawa and Hastings, this retro cafe-gallery in a 100-year-old, aquamarine-coloured church serves excellent coffee, smoothies and home-spun food (unbeatable fudge). Well worth a stop for a chomp, a browse through the local crafts on the side tables and to warm your buns by the wood heater in winter.

❶ Information

Central Hawke's Bay Information Centre
(☑06-858 6488, 0800 429 537 229; www.lambcountry.co.nz; Railway Esplanade, Waipukurau; ☺9.30am-4pm Mon-Fri, to 1pm Sat) Helpful visitor centre in the old railway station (with coffee booth on one side).

❶ Getting There & Away

InterCity (www.intercity.co.nz) and Naked Bus (www.nakedbus.com) pass through Waipawa and Waipukurau on their Wellington–Napier routes.

Kaweka & Ruahine Ranges

The remote Kaweka and Ruahine Ranges separate Hawke's Bay from the Central Plateau. These forested wildernesses offer some of the North Island's best tramping. See www.doc.govt.nz for track/hut/campsite info on Ruahine Forest Park and the downloadable pamphlet *Kaweka Forest Park & Puketitiri Reserves*.

🏃 Activities

An ancient 136km Māori track, now know as the **Gentle Annie Road**, runs inland from Omahu near Hastings to Taihape, via Otamauri and Kuripapango (where there's a basic but charming DOC campsite, adult/child $6/3). This isolated route takes around three hours (or a couple of days by bike).

Kaweka J, the highest point of the range (1724m), can be reached by a three- to five-hour tramp from the end of Kaweka Rd; from Napier take Puketitiri Rd then Whittle Rd. The drive is worthwhile in itself; it's partly unsealed and takes three hours return.

Enjoy a soak in natural hot pools before or after the three-hour walk on **Te Puia Track**, which follows the picturesque **Mohaka River**. From Napier, take Puketitiri Rd, then Pakaututu Rd, then Makahu Rd to the road-end **Mangatutu Hot Pools** (☑06-834 3111; www.doc.govt.nz; ☺daylight hours) 𝐅𝐑𝐄𝐄. Parts of the road can be dicey – bring a 4WD if you've got one.

The Mohaka can be rafted with **Mohaka Rafting** (☑027 825 8539, 06-839 1808; www.mohakarafting.co.nz; day trips $115-185, 3 days per 2 people $3850).

Wellington Region

Best Places to Eat

➡ Ortega Fish Shack
(p367)

➡ Logan Brown (p367)

➡ Fidel's (p365)

➡ Gladstone Inn (p381)

➡ Beach Road Deli (p375)

Best Places to Sleep

➡ YHA Wellington City
(p363)

➡ City Cottages (p364)

➡ Museum Art Hotel
(p364)

➡ Ohtel (p364)

➡ Martinborough Top 10
Holiday Park (p378)

Why Go?

If your New Zealand travels thus far have been all about the great outdoors and sleepy rural towns, Wellington will blow the cobwebs away. Art-house cinemas, funky boutiques, hip bars, live bands and endless restaurants all await you in NZ's cultural capital.

Wellington is the crossing point between the North and South Islands, so travellers have long been passing through these parts. The likes of Te Papa and Zealandia now stop visitors in their tracks, and even a couple of days' pause will reveal myriad other attractions: a windswept harbour with a walkable waterfront, hillsides clad in pretty weatherboard houses, urban surprises and some of the freshest city air on the planet.

Less than an hour away to the north, the Kapiti Coast has a slower, beachy vibe, with Kapiti Island nature reserve a highlight. An hour away to the northeast over the Rimutaka Range, the Wairarapa plains are dotted with quiet towns, farms and hip wineries, hemmed in by rugged, wild coastline.

When to Go

➡ Wellington has a bad rep for blustery, cold, grey weather, but this isn't the whole story: 'Windy Welly' breaks out into blue skies and T-shirt temperatures at least several days a year, when you'll hear locals exclaim, 'You can't beat Wellington on a good day'

➡ November to April are the warmer months here, with average maximums hovering around 20°C. From May to August it's colder and wetter – daily temperatures lurk around 12°C.

➡ The Kapiti Coast and Wairarapa are a different story – both warmer and less windy, with more blue-sky days to bask in.

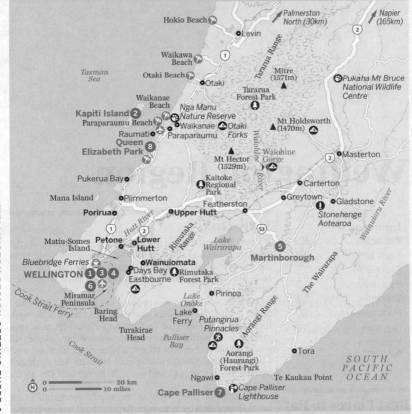

Wellington Region Highlights

1 Te Papa (p357)
Getting interactive at NZ's finest museum, followed by drinks on Cuba St.

2 Kapiti Island (p374)
Meeting a real live kiwi on a nocturnal walk.

3 Drinking in Wellington (p368) Seeing what kind of fun comes your way along Cuba St after dark.

4 Wellington Botanic Gardens (p353) Riding the cable car up from Lambton Quay, or getting an alternative view from Mt Victoria Lookout.

5 Wairarapa Wine Country (p377)
Maintaining a straight line on your bicycle as you tour the wineries around Martinborough.

6 Mt Victoria Lookout (p353) Getting an eye-full of Wellington below, and a lungful of hill-top air.

7 Cape Palliser (p378)
Scaling the lighthouse steps on this wild and remote headland.

8 Queen Elizabeth Park (p375) Rambling through the dunes near beachy Paekakariki.

ⓘ Getting There & Away

Wellington is a major transport hub, being the North Island port for the interisland **ferries** (p371). Long-distance KiwiRail Scenic Journey (www.kiwirailscenic.co.nz) trains run from Wellington to Auckland via Palmerston North. **Wellington Airport** (p371) is serviced by international and domestic airlines.

InterCity (www.intercity.co.nz) is the main North Island bus company, travelling just about everywhere. Approaching Wellington city from the north, you'll pass through either the Kapiti Coast to the west via SH1, or the Wairarapa and Hutt Valley to the east via SH2.

WELLINGTON

POP 204,000

A small city with a big rep, Wellington is famous for being NZ's constitutional and cultural capital. It is *infamous* for its weather, particularly the gale-force winds that barrels through. It lies on a major geologic fault line; negotiating the city's one-way traffic system can also leave you quaking with rage.

But don't be deterred – these are mere trifles on Welly's multilayered, jam-packed stand of sweet treats. For starters it's lovely to look at. Gorgeous Victorian timber architecture laces the bushy hillsides above the harbour. There are hill-top lookouts, waterfront promenades and craggy shorelines to the south. Downtown, the compact CBD vibrates with museums, theatres, galleries and boutiques. Everyone here looks arty and a tad depleted, like they've been up all night molesting canvases. These creative vibes are fuelled by kickin' caffeine and craft-beer scenes. Mandatory Wellington accessories: skateboards, beards and tatts...preferably all three.

⊙ Sights

★ **City Gallery Wellington**   GALLERY
(Map p360; ☑04-913 9032; www.citygallery.org.nz; Civic Sq, Wakefield St; ☉10am-5pm) FREE Housed in the monumental old library in Civic Sq, Wellington's much-loved City Gallery does a cracking job of securing acclaimed contemporary international exhibitions, as well as unearthing up-and-comers and supporting those at the forefront of the NZ scene. Charges may apply for major exhibits; the Nikau Cafe (p366) compensates.

★ **Zealandia**   WILDLIFE RESERVE
(☑04-920 9200; www.visitzealandia.com; 53 Waiapu Rd, Karori; adult/child/family exhibition only $9/5/21, exhibition & admission $18.50/10/46; ☉9am-5pm, last entry 4pm) ✈ This groundbreaking eco-sanctuary is hidden in the hills about 2km west of town; the Karori bus (No 3) passes nearby, or see the Zealandia website for info on the free shuttle. Living wild within the fenced valley are more than 30 native bird species, including rare takahe, saddleback, hihi and kaka, as well as tuatara and little spotted kiwi. An excellent exhibition relays NZ's natural history and world-renowned conservation story.

More than 30km of tracks can be explored independently, or on regular guided tours. The night tour provides an opportunity to spot nocturnal creatures including kiwi, frogs and glowworms (adult/child $75/36). Cafe and shop on-site.

★ **Mt Victoria Lookout**   VIEWPOINT
(Map p354 Lookout Rd) The city's most accessible view point is atop 196m-high Mt Victoria, east of the city centre. You can take the No 20 bus most of the way up, but the rite of passage is to sweat it out on the walk (ask a local for directions or just follow your nose). If you've got wheels, take Oriental Pde along the waterfront and then scoot up Carlton Gore Rd. Awesome views and actually rather interesting info panels.

★ **Wellington Botanic Gardens**   GARDENS
(Map p354; ☑04-499 4444; www.wellington.govt.nz; 101 Glenmore St, Thorndon; ☉daylight hours) FREE These hilly, 25-hectare botanic gardens can be *almost* effortlessly visited via the Wellington Cable Car (p356) (nice bit of planning, eh?), although there are several other entrances hidden in the hillsides. The gardens boast a tract of original native forest, the beaut Lady Norwood Rose Garden, 25,000 spring tulips and various international plant collections. Add in fountains, a playground, sculptures, a duck pond, a cafe and city skyline views, and you've got a grand day out indeed.

Greater Wellington

500 m
0.25 miles

Wellington Harbour

Wellington-Picton Ferry (Interislander Services)

Interislander

Cruise Ship
Passenger Terminal

Aotea Quay

Port of Wellington
Container Terminal

Westpac
Stadium

Waterloo Quay

Hutt Rd

Wellington Urban Mwy

Thorndon Quay

Hobson St

Murphy St

Molesworth St

Pipitea St

Aitken St

InterCity

Local Bus
Terminal

Wellington
Railway Station

Bunny St

Bluebridge
Ferries

Kate
Sheppard Pl

Naked
Bus

Thorndon
Quay

Lambton Quay

WADESTOWN

Park St

Wadestown Rd

Tinakori Rd

Hawkestone St

THORNDON

Hill St

Bowen St

Grant Rd

Te Ahumairangi
Hill

Town
Belt

Northern
Walkway

Sydney St W

Bolton St

WILTON

Wilton Rd

8

9

1

19

9

3

16

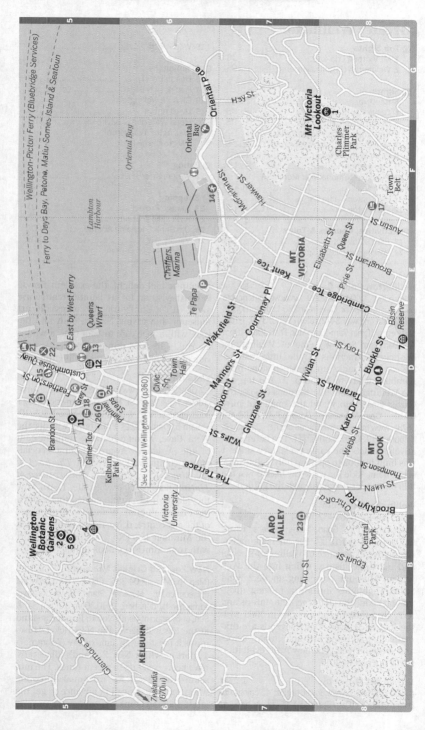

Greater Wellington

Wellington Cable Car   CABLE CAR

(Map p354; ☑04-472 2199; www.wellingtoncable
car.co.nz; Cable Car Lane, rear 280 Lambton Quay;
adult/child one way $4/2, return $7.50/3.50; ⊙de-
parts every 10min, 7am-10pm Mon-Fri, 8.30am-10pm
Sat, 9am-9pm Sun; ♠) One of Wellington's
big-ticket attractions is the little red cable car that clanks up the steep slope from
Lambton Quay to Kelburn. At the top are
the Wellington Botanic Gardens (p353), the
Carter Observatory and the small but nifty
Cable Car Museum (Map p354; ☑04-475
3578; www.museumswellington.org.nz; Upland St,
Kelburn; ⊙9.30am-5pm) **FREE**. The latter evocatively depicts the cable car's story since it
was built in 1902 to open up hilly Kelburn for
settlement. Ride the cable car back down the
hill, or wander down through the gardens.

Wellington Museum   MUSEUM

(Map p354; ☑04-472 8904; www.museums
wellington.org.nz; Bond Store, Queens Wharf;
⊙10am-5pm; ♠) **FREE** For an imaginative,
interactive experience of Wellington's social
and maritime history, swing into the Wellington Museum, occupying an 1892 Bond
Store. Highlights include a moving documentary on the *Wahine,* the interisland
ferry that sank in the harbour in 1968 with
the loss of 51 lives. Māori legends are dramatically told using tiny holographic actors
and special effects. The new 'Attic' exhibition
space opened in 2015.

Dowse Art Museum   GALLERY

(☑04-570 6500; www.dowse.org.nz; 45 Laings Rd,
Lower Hutt; ⊙10am-5pm; ♠) **FREE** A beacon
of culture and delight, the excellent Dowse
is worth visiting for its jaunty architecture
alone. It's a family-friendly, accessible art
museum showcasing NZ art, craft and design, with a nice cafe to boot (and a winter
ice rink!). It's a 15-minute drive or a short
ride on bus 83 from central Wellington.

Weta Cave   MUSEUM

(☑04-909 4100; www.wetanz.com; cnr Camp-
erdown Rd & Weka St, Miramar; admission & tour
adult/child $25/12, with return transport $65/40;
⊙9am-5.30pm) **FREE** Film buffs will dig the
Weta Cave, a mind-blowing minimuseum
of the Academy Award–winning special-
effects company that brought *The Lord of
the Rings, King Kong, The Adventures of
Tintin* and *The Hobbit* to life. Learn how
they do it on 45-minute guided tours, starting every half-hour. Weta Cave is 9km east
of the city centre: drive, ride your bike, catch
the Miramar bus (No 2) or book transport
with your admission. Book online.

New Zealand Cricket Museum   MUSEUM

(Map p354; ☑04-385 6602; www.nzcricket
museum.co.nz; Museum Stand, Basin Reserve;
admission by donation; ⊙10.30am-3.30pm Sat &
Sun, or by appointment) Nooked under a stand
at the Basin Reserve, the NZ Cricket Museum is a must-see for fans of the old game –
a sport at which New Zealand's 'Blackcaps'
have been excelling in recent times. The museum was closed for earthquake-proofing
when we visited – call in advance to get the
latest opening hours.

TREASURES OF TE PAPA

Te Papa (Map p360; 04-381 7000; www.tepapa.govt.nz; 55 Cable St; 10am-6pm;) FREE is Wellington's 'must-see attraction, for reasons well beyond the fact that it's New Zealand's national museum. It's highly interactive, fun, and full of surprises: aptly, 'Te Papa Tongarewa' loosely translates as 'treasure box'. The riches inside include an amazing collection of Māori artefacts and the museum's own colourful *marae* (meeting house); natural history and environment exhibitions; Pacific and NZ history galleries; the National Art Collection; and themed hands-on 'discovery centres' for children. Big-name temporary exhibitions incur an admission fee, although general admission is free.

You could spend a day exploring Te Papa's six floors and still not see it all. To cut to the chase, head to the information desk on level two and collect a map. For exhibition highlights and to get your bearings, the one-hour 'Introducing Te Papa' tour (adult/child $15/7) is a good idea; tours leave from the info desk at 10.15am, noon and 2pm daily, plus 7pm on Thursdays. 'Māori Highlights' tours ($20/10) run at 2pm daily. Two cafes and two gift shops complete the Te Papa experience, which could well consume a couple of rainy-day visits. The museum's current star attraction is the state-of-the-art exhibition 'Gallipoli: The Scale of Our War', charting the country's involvement in WWI's Gallipoli campaign through the experiences of eight ordinary New Zealanders; key to the exhibition's impact are the hyper-real models produced by Weta Workshop, which bring it all to life. Te Papa will host the exhibition until 2018.

Carter Observatory
OBSERVATORY

(Space Place; Map p354; 04-910 3140; www.carterobservatory.org; 40 Salamanca Rd, Kelburn; adult/child/family $12.50/8/39; 4-11pm Tue & Thu, 10am-11pm Sat, 10am-5.30pm Sun) At the top of the Botanic Gardens (p353), the Carter Observatory 'Space Place' features a full-dome planetarium offering regular space-themed multimedia shows (eg *We Are Aliens, Dynamic Earth, To Space and Back*) and stargazing sessions. Check the website for show times.

Otari-Wilton's Bush
PARK

(Map p354; 04-499 4444; www.wellington.govt.nz; 160 Wilton Rd, Wilton; daylight hours) FREE About 3km west of the city is Otari-Wilton's Bush, the only botanic gardens in NZ specialising in native flora. There are more than 1200 plant species sprouting forth here, including some of the city's oldest trees, as well as an 18m-high canopy walkway, 11km of walking trails and some beaut picnic areas. The Wilton bus (No 14) from the city passes the gates.

Wellington Zoo
ZOO

(04-381 6755; www.wellingtonzoo.com; 200 Daniell St, Newtown; adult/child/family $21/10.50/61; 9.30am-5pm, last entry 4.15pm) Committed to conservation, research and captive breeding programs, Wellington Zoo is home to a menagerie of native and exotic wildlife, including lions and tamarins. The nocturnal house has kiwi and tuatara. 'Close encounters' allow you to meet the big cats, red pandas, giraffes and mischievous meerkats (for a fee). The zoo is 4km south of the city; catch the Newtown bus (No 10).

Beehive
ARCHITECTURE

(Map p354; 04-817 9503; www.parliament.nz; Molesworth St; 10am-4pm) FREE Office workers swarm around the distinctive modernist Beehive (1980), which is exactly what it looks like, and which forms part of NZ's parliamentary complex. It was designed by British architect Sir Basil Spence. Controversy dogged its construction and, love it or loathe it, it's the architectural symbol of the country. Tours (including the adjacent **Parliament House** (Map p354;) depart from the foyer on the hour from 10am to 4pm – arrive 15 minutes early.

Katherine Mansfield Birthplace
HISTORIC BUILDING

(Map p354; 04-473 7268; www.katherinemansfield.com; 25 Tinakori Rd, Thorndon; adult/child $8/free, guided tours $10; 10am-4pm Tue-Sun) Often compared to Chekhov and Maupassant, Katherine Mansfield is one of NZ's most distinguished authors. Born in 1888, she died of tuberculosis in 1923 aged 34. This Tinakori Rd house is where she spent five years of her childhood. It's now a lovely heritage home with exhibitions in her honour, including a biographical film.

Pukeahu National War Memorial Park
PARK, LANDMARK

(Map p354; ☑04-385 2496; www.mch.govt.nz/pukeahu/park; SH1) You can see the art-deco National War Memorial tower (1932) from almost everywhere in Wellington, but what's new here is the park surrounding the tower – a sensitive and symbolic homage to NZ's servicemen and women. It's a sobering and oddly tranquil space – even the skaters stay away.

🏃 Activities

Wellington's harbour offers plenty of opportunities to get active: kayaking, paddle boarding, sailing, windsurfing... (Wellington is windy: might as well make the most of it!). Back on dry land there's rock climbing, cycling and high-wire walking to keep you entertained. Pick up the *Wellington City Cycle Map* for bike-trail info.

★ Ferg's Kayaks
KAYAKING, BICYCLE RENTAL

(Map p354; ☑04-499 8898; www.fergskayaks.co.nz; Shed 6, Queens Wharf; ◎10am-8pm Mon-Fri, 9am-6pm Sat & Sun) Stretch your tendons with indoor rock climbing (adult/child $15/10), cruise the waterfront wearing in-line skates ($20 for two hours) or go for a paddle in a kayak or on a stand-up paddle board (from $20 for one hour). There's also bike hire (one hour from $20) and guided kayaking trips.

Wellington Ocean Sports
SAILING

(Map p354; ☑04-939 6702; www.oceansports.org.nz; 115 Oriental Pde; harbour sails per person

$40; ◎booking office 9am-5pm) Harness Wellington's infamous wind on a one-hour harbour sailing trip, departing at 10.30am and 2pm on Fridays, Saturdays and Sundays – no experience required! Ask about stand-up paddle boarding, windsurfing and kayaking sessions.

Wild Winds
WINDSURFING, PADDLE BOARDING

(Map p354; ☑04-473 3458; www.wildwinds.co.nz; 36 Customhouse Quay; ◎10am-5.30pm Mon-Fri, to 3pm Sat) With all this wind and water, Wellington was made for windsurfing, kiteboading, and stand-up paddle boarding. Tackle one or all three with Wild Winds; lessons start from $110 for two hours.

Makara Peak Mountain Bike Park
MOUNTAIN BIKING

(www.makarapeak.org; 116 South Karori Rd, Karori; by donation; ◎daylight hours) In hilly Karori, 7km west of the city centre, this excellent 230-hectare park is laced with 45km of single-track, ranging from beginner to expert. The nearby **Mud Cycles** (☑04-476 4961; www.mudcycles.co.nz; 424 Karori Rd, Karori; half-day/full-day/weekend bike hire from $35/60/100; ◎9.30am-6.30pm Mon, Tue, Thu & Fri, to 7pm Wed, 9am-5pm Sat, 10am-5pm Sun) has mountain bikes for hire, and runs guided tours for riders of all abilities. Wellington is a true MTB mecca – visit www.tracks.org.nz for the evidence. Catch the Karori (No 3) bus.

On Yer Bike
BICYCLE RENTAL

(Map p360; ☑04-384 8480; www.onyerbikeavantiplus.co.nz; 181 Vivian St; city/mountain bike per day

---

WELLINGTON IN...

Two Days
To get a feel for the lie of the land, walk (or drive) up to the **Mt Victoria Lookout**, or ride the cable car up into the **Wellington Botanic Gardens**. After lunch on boho-hipster **Cuba St**, catch some Kiwi culture at **Te Papa** or the **Wellington Museum**. Top off the day by doing the rounds of the city's numerous craft-beer bars.

The next day, reconstitute with coffee and an eggy infusion at **Fidel's**, a real Wellington institution, then head to **Zealandia** to be with the birds and learn about New Zealand conservation. Alternatively, walk the halls with a different species of birdbrain on a tour of **Parliament House**. Raid **Moore Wilson** for cheese and wine for a picnic supper in Waitangi Park, before heading back into the night for some live music, or a movie at the gloriously restored **Embassy Theatre**.

Four Days
Shake and bake the two-day itinerary, then decorate with the following: hightail it out of Wellington for a seal-spotting safari to wild **Cape Palliser**, followed by a wine-tasting or two around **Martinborough** in the middle of Wairarapa Wine Country. The next day, head to **Paekakariki** on the Kapiti Coast for an ocean swim and ice cream before wandering through the dunes of **Queen Elizabeth Park** next door.

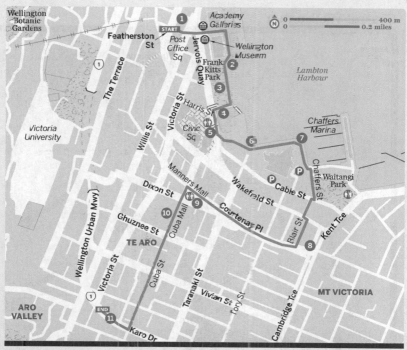

🏃 City Walk
City Sculpture

START POST OFFICE SQ
END KARO DR
LENGTH 3.5KM; TWO TO THREE HOURS

Get started in windswept Post Office Sq, where Bill Culbert's **1 SkyBlues** noodles into the air. Cross Jervois Quay and pass between the Academy Galleries and Wellington Museum. At the Queens Wharf waterfront, turn south, past the big shed to the **2 Water Whirler**, the largely lifeless needle of kooky kineticist Len Lye that whirrs crazily into life on the hour several times a day.

Continue along the promenade below the **3 mast of the Wahine**, which tragically sank in Wellington Harbour in 1968. Around the corner are the white, rather whale-like forms of the **4 Albatross Fountain**. Detour up onto the flotsamy **5 City to Sea Bridge** and check out the collection of weathered wooden sculptures here.

Back on the waterfront, continue past Te Raukura *whare waka* (canoe house), to the mooring of the **6 Hikitia**, the world's oldest working crane ship – something of a sculpture in itself. If you smell gelato on the breeze, follow your nose. Strip to your undies and jump off the diving platform, or perhaps just keep on trucking along wharf, past the bronze form of **7 Solace in the Wind** leaning over the harbour fringe.

Cross the footbridge to Waitangi Park to eyeball some roller action, before heading south to Courtenay Pl via Chaffers St, and Blair St with its century-old warehouses.

On Courtenay Pl, check out the leggy form of the industrial-cinematic **8 Tripod**, before heading west. Cross Taranaki St to wedge-shaped **9 Te Aro Park** with its canoe prow and trip hazards.

Turn south when you hit Cuba St, heading up the pedestrian mall. Watch out for the sly, sloshy **10 Bucket Fountain** – it lives to splash the leg of your jeans.

Change down to granny gear and wander through doorways, all the way to the top of Cuba St where a remnant heritage precinct is bisected by the controversial inner-city bypass. Book-end your sculpture walk with Regan Gentry's brilliant, ghostly **11 Subject to Change**. Alongside is the curious old 7.5m-deep Tonks' Well, dating from the mid-1800s.

Central Wellington

WELLINGTON REGION WELLINGTON

$30/40; ⊙ 8.30am-5.30pm Mon-Fri, 9am-5pm Sat)
Quality bike hire in the city centre.

Adrenalin Forest　ADVENTURE SPORTS
(☑ 04-237　8553；　www.adrenalin-forest.co.nz；
Okowai Rd, Porirua; adult/child 3hr $42/27;
⊙ 10am-2.30pm) Walk out on the high wire at
Adrenalin Forest – a web of cables, suspension bridges and platforms strung between
a copse of high pines. Bring your bravado!
Last admission 2.30pm. The Porirua (No
211) bus or Kapiti Line train will get you
within 2km – or go all the way with your
own transport.

☞ Tours

Walk Wellington　WALKING TOUR
(☑ 04-473 3145; www.walkwellington.org.nz; adult/
child $20/10) Informative and great-value
two-hour walking tours focusing on the city
and waterfront, departing the i-SITE. Book
online, by phone or just turn up. Tours 10am
daily, plus 5.30pm Monday, Wednesday and
Friday December to February.

Wellington Hop On Hop Off　BUS TOUR
(☑ 0800 246 877; www.hoponhopoff.co.nz; per person $45) Flexible two-hour scenic loop of the
city with 17 stops en route, leaving Welling-

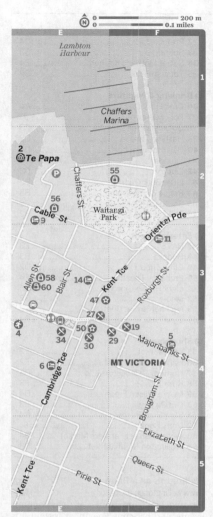

Middle-earth filming locations. Martinborough wine tours also available.

Zest Food Tours
FOOD

(☑04-801 9198; www.zestfoodtours.co.nz; tours from $179) Runs three- to 5½-hour small-group foodie tours around the city, plus day tours over the hills into Wairarapa Wine Country (p377).

Wellington Movie Tours
TOUR

(☑027 419 3077; www.adventuresafari.co.nz; adult/child tours from $45/30) Half- and full-day tours with more props, clips, and Middle-earth film locations than you can shake a staff at.

✷✷ Festivals & Events

Check at the Wellington i-SITE for comprehensive events listings. Most major ticketed events can be booked via Ticketek (www.ticketek.co.nz) and TicketDirect (www.ticketdirect.co.nz).

Summer City
CULTURAL

(www.wellington.govt.nz ⊙Jan-Mar) A summertime city-wide events bonanza – many free and outdoor happenings, including the lovely 'Gardens Magic' concerts. The Wellington Pasifika Festival and Waitangi Day celebrations also fall under the Summer City umbrella.

Wellington Sevens
SPORTS

(www.sevens.co.nz; ⊙late Jan-early Feb) The world's top seven-a-side rugby teams collide with Earth-shattering force. Book with lightning speed.

Fringe NZ
CULTURAL

(www.fringe.org.nz; ⊙Feb-Mar) Three weeks of way-out-there experimental visual arts, music, dance and theatre (...the fringe of society is where all the fun is).

New Zealand Festival
CULTURAL

(www.festival.co.nz; ⊙Feb-Mar) A month-long biennial (even years; around mid-February to mid-March) spectacular of theatre, dance, music, visual arts and literature. International acts aplenty. A real 'kick up the arts'!

NZ International Comedy Festival
COMEDY

(www.comedyfestival.co.nz; ⊙Apr-May) Three weeks of hysterics. World-famous-in-NZ comedians, and some truly world-famous ones too.

Wellington Jazz Festival
JAZZ

(www.jazzfestival.co.nz; ⊙mid-Jun) Five days of finger-snappin' bee-boppin' good times around the capital – a definite antidote for winter chills.

ton i-SITE hourly from 10am to 2pm. Tickets are valid for 24 hours.

Kiwi Coastal Tours
4WD TOUR

(☑027 252 0099, 021 464 957; www.kiwicoastaltours.co.nz; 3/5hr tours $150/250) Excellent 4WD exploration of the rugged south coast in the company of a local Māori guide with plenty of stories to tell.

Flat Earth
TOUR

(☑04-472 9635, 0800 775 805; www.flatearth.co.nz; half-/full-day tours $175/385) An array of themed small-group guided tours: city highlights, Māori treasures, arts, wilderness and

Central Wellington

Matariki   CULTURAL
(www.tepapa.govt.nz; ◷mid-Jun–mid-Jul) Celebrates the Māori New Year over four weeks, with a free festival of dance, music and other events at Te Papa (p357).

**New Zealand
International Film Festival**   FILM
(www.nzff.co.nz; ◷Jul-Aug) Roving (also in Auckland) two-week indie film fest screening the best of NZ and international cinema.

Beervana   BEER
(www.beervana.co.nz; ◷Aug) A barrel-load of craft-beer aficionados roll into town for a weekend of supping and beard-stroking. Join them at Westpac Stadium on the path to enlightened Beervana.

Wellington on a Plate   FOOD
(www.wellingtononaplate.com;   ◷Aug)
Lip-smacking program of gastronomic events, and bargains aplenty at restaurants around the city.

World of WearableArt Awards Show FASHION
(WOW;   www.worldofwearableart.com; ◷Sep)
A two-week run of spectacular garments (dresses or sculptures – it's a fine line). Tickets are hot property; hotel beds anywhere near the city sell out weeks in advance.

🛏 Sleeping

Accommodation in Wellington is more expensive than in regional areas, but there are plenty of options close to the city centre. Parking spots are a rarity – ask in advance about options.

Wellington's budget accommodation largely takes the form of multistorey hostel megaliths. Holiday park options lie beyond the outskirts of town; motels dot the city fringes. Self-contained apartments are popular, and often offer bargain weekend rates.

Book your bed well in advance in peak season (December to February) and during major events.

★ YHA Wellington City   HOSTEL $

(Map p360; ☑04-801 7280; www.yha.co.nz; cnr Cambridge Tce & Wakefield St; dm from $32, tw/d without bathroom $95/98, tw & d with bathroom $133; @🖧🛜) ✦ Wellington's best hostel wins points for fantastic communal areas including two big kitchens and dining areas, and separate rooms for games, reading and watching movies. Sustainable initiatives (recycling, composting and energy-efficient hot water) abound, and there's a comprehensive booking service and espresso machine at reception. New double-bed mattresses were being delivered when we visited (an excellent sign!).

Dwellington   HOSTEL $

(Map p354; ☑04-550 9373; www.thedwellington. co.nz; 8 Halswell St, Thorndon; dm/tw/d/tr incl breakfast from $25/90/90/100; 🅿🛜) Just a couple of years old, the Dwellington is a terrific conversion job: two conjoined heritage houses have been reinvented as a mod backpackers. Clean, bright and comfortable, it's handy to the ferry terminals and bus and rail hubs, but a fair hike from the after-dark fun around Cuba St. It all comes down to priorities… Free wi-fi and tennis!

Trek Global   HOSTEL $

(Map p360; ☑0800 868 735, 04-471 3480; www. trekglobal.net; 9 O'Reilly Ave; dm $22-29, s $59, tw with/without bathroom $89/69; 🅿@🛜) A highlight of this back-lane hostel is the funky and welcoming foyer hang-out and snug TV lounge. The sleeping quarters and kitchens are squeezed between rabbit-warren corridors. It's relatively quiet with clean rooms and laudable extras such as bike hire, parking ($20 per day) and a women-only dorm with a suntrap terrace.

Hotel Waterloo & Backpackers   HOSTEL $

(Map p354; ☑0800 225 725, 04-473 8482; www.hotelwaterloo.co.nz; dm/s/tw from $29/68/76, d with/without bathroom from $107/89; 🛜) Housed in a historic art-deco hotel (1937) at the railway end of town, the old Waterloo has tidy, bright rooms and plenty of capacious, character-filled communal areas (be sure to check out the bar). Budget meals in the mess hall morning and night.

Cambridge Hotel   HOSTEL, HOTEL $

(Map p360; ☑04-385 8829, 0800 375 021; www. cambridgehotel.co.nz; 28 Cambridge Tce; dm $25-30 with/without bathroom s from $90/65, d from $105/85; @🛜) City-centre accommodation in a heritage hotel with a ground-floor pub. En suite rooms have Sky TV and a fridge (try for a room at the back if you're a light sleeper). The backpacker wing has a snug kitchen-lounge, flash bathrooms and dorms with little natural light but sky-high timber-clad ceilings. Bonus $3 breakfast.

Nomads Capital   HOSTEL $

(Map p360; ☑04-978 7800, 050 866 6237; www.nomadsworld.com; 118 Wakefield St; dm/d incl breakfast & light dinner from $28/95; 🅿🛜) Smack bang in the middle of town, Nomads has good security, spick-and-span rooms and an on-site cafe-bar. Kitchen and lounge spaces are short on elbow room, but slick

---

WELLINGTON FOR CHILDREN

Let's cut to the chase: Welly's biggest hit for kids is **Te Papa** (p357), with the whole caboodle looking like it's curated by a team of five-year-old geniuses. It has interactive activities galore, more creepy, weird and wonderful things than you can shake a squid at, and heaps of special events for all ages. See the dedicated Kids page on the website for proof of Te Papa's prowess in this department.

Conveniently located either side of Te Papa are **Frank Kitts Park** and **Waitangi Park**, both with playgrounds and in close proximity to roller skates, ice creams, and life-saving espresso for the grown-ups.

A ride up the **cable car** (p356) and a lap around the **Wellington Botanic Gardens** (p353) will get the wee ones pumped up. When darkness descends head to the **Carter Observatory** (p357) to gaze at galaxies far, far away. On a more terrestrial plane, kids can check out some crazy New Zealand animals at the **Wellington Zoo** (p357) or **Zealandia** (p353).

service, heritage features and the hot location stop you from dwelling on the negatives. Parking $18.

Wellington

Top 10 Holiday Park HOLIDAY PARK $

(☑ 04-568 5913, 0800 948 686; www.wellingtontop10.co.nz; 95 Hutt Park Rd, Seaview; sites $50, cabins $70-112, units $120-185; P ☎) This park, 13km northeast of Wellington in Seaview, is reasonably convenient for the ferry and offers the closest camping to the city. Family-friendly facilities include communal kitchens, games room, jumping pillow and a playground, but the industrial back-block location detracts. Follow the signs off SH2 for Petone and Seaview, or take regular public transport (bus 83).

★ City Cottages RENTAL HOUSES $$

(Map p360; ☑ 021 073 9232; www.citybedandbreakfast.co.nz; 5 & 7 Tonks Gr; d/q $185/219; P ☎) These two tiny 1880 cottages squat amid a precious precinct of historic Cuba St buildings. Clever conversion has transformed them into all-mod-con, self-contained one-bedroom pads, comfortable for two but sleeping up to four (thanks to a sofa bed). Hip, convenient and totally Cuba. It's not the quietest location in the city, but it's the coolest.

★ Gourmet Stay BOUTIQUE HOTEL $$

(Map p360; ☑ 04-801 6800; www.gourmetstay.co.nz; 25 Frederick St; s/d/tr/f incl breakfast from $55/135/199/225; P ☎) This terrific new chocolate-coloured backstreet boutique hotel has 13 rooms over three floors, all with different configurations. Most have en suites; some have private bathrooms across the hall; all of them are tastefully designed, with nice linen and natty art. The blackboard in the breakfast room lists foodie tips around town. Nice one!

Booklovers B&B B&B $$

(Map p354; ☑ 04-384 2714; www.booklovers.co.nz; 123 Pirie St; s/d/tr from $160/200/295; P ☎) Author Jane Tolerton's gracious, book-filled B&B has three queen en suite guest rooms (one with an extra single bed). A bus service runs past the front gate to Courtenay Pl and the train station, and the city's 'green belt' begins right next door. Free wi-fi and parking.

Victoria Court Motor Lodge MOTEL $$

(Map p360; ☑ 0800 282 8502, 04-385 710; www.victoriacourt.co.nz; 201 Victoria St; d/q/f from $150/170/205; P ☎) Three-tier, lemon-yellow Victoria Court continues to deliver satisfaction in the city, with spacious studios and apartments with kitchenettes, quality joinery and furniture, and recently refreshed bathrooms. There are two disabled-access units, and larger units sleep up to six. It's just a short stumble to Cuba St. Free on-site parking.

CityLife Wellington APARTMENT $$

(Map p354; ☑ 04-922 2800, 0800 368 888; www.heritagehotels.co.nz; 300 Lambton Quay; d from $189, 1-/2-bedroom apt from $209/239; P @ ☎) Plush serviced apartments in the city centre, ranging from studios to multibedroom arrangements. Some have full kitchen and in-room laundry facilities, some offer harbour glimpses. Weekend rates are great bang for your buck. The vehicle entrance is off Gilmer Tce, itself off Boulcott St (parking $20 per night).

Apollo Lodge MOTEL, APARTMENT $$

(Map p360; ☑ 04-385 1849, 0800 361 645; www.apollolodge.co.nz; 49 Majoribanks St; d $145-165, 2-bedroom apt from $200, extra person $20; P ☎) Within staggering distance of Courtenay Pl, Apollo Lodge is a loose collation of a couple of dozen varied units (one or two bedrooms), ranging from studios to family-friendly units with full kitchen to long-stay apartments. Good value for this close to the city.

★ Ohtel BOUTIQUE HOTEL $$$

(Map p360; ☑ 04-803 0600; www.ohtel.com; 66 Oriental Pde; d $249-425; ☎) Ever feel like you've walked into a design magazine? This bijou hotel on Oriental Pde has individually decorated rooms. Suites feature stylish furniture, contemporary artwork and ceramics, avidly collected by the architect-owner. Mix yourself a cocktail, then soak it all up in a luxurious bathtub. The best rooms have harbour views. A truly slick product in a fab location.

Museum Art Hotel HOTEL $$$

(Map p360; ☑ 0800 994 335, 04-802 8900; www.museumhotel.co.nz; 90 Cable St; r/apt from $239/309; @ ☎ ☒) Formerly known as 'Museum Hotel de Wheels' (to make way for Te Papa, it was rolled here from its original location 120m away!), this art-filled hotel keeps the quirk-factor high. Bright-eyed staff, a terrific restaurant, flamboyant decor and groovy tunes piped into the lobby make a refreshing change from homogenised business hotels. Tasty weekend and weekly rates.

Bolton Hotel
HOTEL $$$

(Map p354; ☑04-472 9966; www.boltonhotel. co.nz; 12 Bolton St; d $199-354; P 🛜 🗟) Visiting diplomats and corporate types flock to the Bolton, filling 139 rooms spread over 19 floors. Rooms come in all shapes and sizes, but share a common theme of muted tones, fine linens and colourful artwork. Most have full kitchens; some come with park or city views. Independent and just a bit arty.

🍴 Eating

Wellington proffers a bewildering array of eating options: contemporary cafes, upmarket restaurants and oodles of noodle houses. Stiff competition keeps standards high and prices keen.

Three excellent inner-city food markets run from dawn till around 2pm on Sundays – the seriously fruit-and-veg **farmers market** (Map p360; cnr Victoria & Vivian Sts; ⊘6.30am-2.30pm Sun) and, next to Te Papa, the varied **Harbourside Market** (Map p360; ☑04-495 7895; www.harboursidemarket.co.nz; cnr Cable & Barnett Sts; ⊘7.30am-2pm Sun) and artisanal City Market (p370).

⭐ Fidel's
CAFE $

(Map p360; ☑04-801 6868; www.fidelscafe.com; 234 Cuba St; mains $10-24; ⊘7.30am-late Mon-Fri, 8am-late Sat, 9am-late Sun; 🍴) A Cuba St institution for caffeine-craving alternative types. Eggs any which way, pizza and super salads are cranked out of the itsy kitchen, along with Welly's best milkshakes. Revolutionary memorabilia adorns the walls of the deeply funky interior; there are chipper outdoor areas, too. A superbusy crew copes with the chaos admirably. Street-facing booth for takeaway coffees.

⭐ Mt Vic Chippery
FISH & CHIPS $

(Map p360; ☑04-382 8713; www.mtvicchippery. co.nz; 5 Majoribanks St; meals $8-16; ⊘noon-8.45pm; 🐟) At this backwater fish shack it's fish and chips by numbers: 1. Choose your fish (from at least three varieties). 2. Choose your coating (beer batter, panko crumb, tempura...). 3. Choose your chips (five varieties!). 4. Add aioli, coleslaw, salad or sauce, and a quality soft drink. 5. Chow down inside or takeaway. Burgers and battered sausages will placate the pescaphobes.

Midnight Espresso
CAFE $

(Map p360; ☑04-384 7014; www.facebook. com/midnightespresso; 178 Cuba St; mains $4-18; ⊘7.30am-3am Mon-Fri, 8am-3am Sat & Sun; 🍴) Let it all hang out after midnight at this devilishly good late-opener. Munch some

cheese lasagne, sticky date pudding or spinach-and-basil muffins if you must, but caffeine is really where it's at. Dig the little brass repair plates in the old floorboards and the Metallica pinball machine.

Havana Coffee Works
CAFE $

(Map p360; ☑04-384 7041; www.havana.co.nz; 163 Tory St; snacks $4-8; ⊘7am-5pm Mon-Fri) Continuing Wellington's unwavering obsession with all things Cuba, this fantastical roastery and 'First Class' coffee lounge offers a step backwards and forwards in time, with its invented history and contemporary attitude to service. Nibbles are limited to the likes of scones, cakes and pies from the warmer. Takeaway counter in the roastery; smiles and laughter all round.

Sweet Mother's Kitchen
AMERICAN $

(Map p360; ☑04-385 4444; www.sweetmothers kitchen.co.nz; 5 Courtenay Pl; mains $10-26; ⊘8am-10pm Sun-Thu, to late Fri & Sat; 🍴) Perpetually brimming with cool cats, Sweet Mother's serves dubious but darn tasty takes on the Deep South, such as burritos, nachos, pulled-pork po'boys, jambalaya, jerk chicken and key lime pie. It's cheap and cute, with craft beer and good sun.

Little Penang
MALAYSIAN $

(Map p360; ☑04-382 9818; www.facebook. com/littlepenang; Shop 16, Oaks Complex, Dixon St; mains $8-15; ⊘11am-3pm & 5pm-9pm Mon-Fri, 11am-9pm Sat) Among a troupe of great Malaysian diners, Little Penang steals the show with its fresh-flavoured, fiery street food. Order a *nasi lemak* with the good eggy, nutty, saucy stuff; or go for the bargain $8 roti bread with curry. And don't bypass the curry puffs. The lunchtime rush can border on the absurd.

Phoenician Falafel
LEBANESE $

(Map p360; ☑04-385 9997; www.phoenician. co.nz; 10 Kent Tce; mains $6-15; ⊘11.30am-9.30pm; 🍴) Authentic falafels, meat skewers and *shawarmas* (kebabs) served up by cheery Lebanese owners (who love a bit of reggae). The best kebabs in town, hands down. Also at 245 Cuba St.

Aunty Mena's
VEGETARIAN $

(Map p360; ☑04-382 8288; 167 Cuba St; meals $10-18; ⊘11.30am-9pm Mon-Wed, 11.30am-9.30pm Thu-Sat, 5-9pm Sun; 🍴) The lightest and healthiest of Welly's noodle houses is Aunty Mena's, a cheery cafe cranking out tasty vegie/vegan Malaysian and Chinese dishes to all comers. Easy-clean, overlit interior; kick-ass dumplings.

WORTH A TRIP

DAYS BAY & MATIU-SOMES ISLAND

The sweet little **East by West Ferry** (Map p354; ☏04-499 1282; www.eastbywest.co.nz) plies the waters between Queens Wharf and Days Bay in Eastbourne, via Matiu-Somes Island, and on fine weekends via Petone and Seatoun as well.

Locals have been jumping on a boat to Days Bay for decades. At the bay there's a beach, a park and a cafe, and a boatshed with kayaks and bikes for hire. A 10-minute walk from Days Bay leads to Eastbourne, a beachy township with cafes, a cute pub, a summer swimming pool and a playground.

Some ferries also stop at Matiu-Somes Island in the middle of the harbour, a DOC-managed reserve where you might see weta, tuatara, kakariki and little blue penguins, among other critters. The island is rich in history, having once been a prisoner-of-war camp and quarantine station. Take a picnic lunch, or even stay overnight in the campsite (adult/child $10/5) or at one of the DOC cottages here (sole-occupancy $200): book online at www.doc.govt.nz or at the **DOC Wellington Visitor Centre** (p371).

It's a 20- to 30-minute chug across the harbour. There are 16 sailings on weekdays, eight on Saturday and Sunday (return fare adult/child $22/12).

★ **Loretta** MODERN NZ **$$**
(Map p360; ☏04-384 2213; www.loretta.net.nz; 181 Cuba St; mains $10-28; ⊗7am-10pm Tue-Fri, 8am-10pm Sat, 8am-9pm Sun) From breakfast (waffles, crumpets, granola) through lunch (sandwiches, fritters, soup) and into dinner (pizzas, pastas, big salads), Loretta has been winning leagues of fans with her classy, well-proportioned offerings. Is this Wellington's ultimate risotto? Bright, airy and good-humoured. Bookings for lunch only.

Five Boroughs BURGERS **$$**
(Map p360; ☏04-384 9300; www.fiveboroughs. co.nz; 4 Roxburgh St; mains $10-36; ⊗3pm-late Mon, 10am-late Tue-Fri, 9am-late Sat & Sun) Get a dose of NYC Americana at Five Boroughs, a subway-tiled neighbourhood burger bar serving heart-stopping cheeseburgers, Reuben sandwiches, buttermilk fried chicken and hot pastrami sandwiches, plus astonishingly good milkshakes and bottomless filter coffee (also NYC style). Grab a beer or a cocktail at the bar, too, why don'tcha.

Prefab CAFE **$$**
(Map p360; ☏04-385 2263; www.pre-fab. co.nz; 14 Jessie St; mains $6-18; ⊗7am-4pm Mon-Fri, 8am-3.30pm Sat; 🖉) A big, industrial-minimalist space houses the city's slickest espresso bar and roastery, owned by long-time Wellington caffeine fiends. Beautiful house-baked bread features on a menu of flavourful, well-executed offerings – try the breakfast baguette with asparagus, poached eggs, Parmesan and hollandaise. Kids cavort on the sunny terrace.

Pizza Pomodoro PIZZA **$$**
(Map p360; ☏04-381 2929; www.pizza pomodoro.co.nz; 13 Leeds St; pizza $13-24; ⊗noon-2pm Wed-Fri, 5-9pm daily; 🖉) Pomodoro's Massimo is so serious about his wood-fired pizza he's a member of the Associazione Verace Pizza Napoletana, founded to protect and promote real pizza (his mozzarella is imported direct from Napoli). Dine in, take-away or eat at Golding's Free Dive (p368) across the courtyard, with a cold beer in hand. Yes, please.

Nikau Cafe CAFE **$$**
(Map p360; ☏04-801 4168; www.nikaucafe.co.nz; City Gallery, Civic Sq; mains $15-27; ⊗7am-4pm Mon-Fri, 8am-4pm Sat; 🖉) An airy affair at the sophisticated end of Wellington's cafe spectrum, Nikau consistently dishes up simple but sublime stuff (pan-fried halloumi, sage eggs, legendary kedgeree). Refreshing aperitifs, divine sweets and a sunny courtyard complete the package. The organic, seasonal menu changes daily. Good one!

Arthur's CAFE **$$**
(Map p360; ☏04-385 7227; www.arthursoncuba. co.nz; 272 Cuba St; mains lunch $10-19, dinner $20-26; ⊗noon-late Tue-Fri, 10am-late Sat, 10am-4pm Sun) A quiet little two-storey Cuba St joint where you can often find a seat when the rest of the street is full to capacity. The culinary vibe is mannish and meaty: lamb's fry, sirloin steak, savoury mince, lamb shanks, pork crackling, pot pies and Reuben sandwiches. Hearty and hale in equal measure. Fine wines to boot.

Scopa
ITALIAN $$

(Map p360; ☑04-384-6020; www.scopa.co.nz; cnr Cuba & Ghuznee Sts; pizza $12-25, mains $26-29; ⊙8am-late Mon-Fri, 9am-late Sat & Sun; ✐) Authentic pizza, pasta and gnocchi make dining at this modern *cucina* a pleasure. The *bianche* (white) pizzas change things up a bit, as does the *pizzaiolo* – pizza of the week. Watch the cavalcade of Cuba St from a seat in the window. Monday night meatballs; Peroni on tap.

Karaka Cafe
CAFE $$

(Map p360; ☑04-916 8369; www.karakacafe. co.nz; Wharewaka Function Centre, Odlins Sq, 109 Jervois Quay; mains $16-25; ⊙7.30am-dusk Mon-Fri, 8am-dusk Sat & Sun; ✐) Keen to try some Māori *kai* (food)? This fun, open-walled cafe is in a top spot by the harbour, fronted by sunny beanbag-strewn lawns. The *kai* mightn't be 100% authentic (pulled pork tacos?), but the happy atmosphere is infectious and the Monteith's flows freely.

Capitol
MODERN NZ $$

(Map p360; ☑04-384 2855; www.capitol restaurant.co.nz; 10 Kent Tce; mains lunch $15-26, dinner $25-38; ⊙noon-3pm Mon-Fri 9.30am-3pm Sat & Sun, 5.30-9.30pm daily) This consistent culinary star serves simple, seasonal fare using premium local ingredients, with a nod to classic Euro style (try the Parmesan-crusted lamb's liver). The dining room is a bit cramped and noisy, but elegant nonetheless – well worth a wait at the wee bar (no dinner bookings).

Wagamama
ASIAN $$

(Map p354; ☑04-473 7999; www.wagamama. co.nz; Meridian Bldg, 33 Customhouse Quay; mains $10-22; ⊙11.30am-10pm Sun-Thu, to 11pm Fri & Sat) Yeah, yeah, we know – Wagamama is a big international chain at the corporate end of culinary proceedings. But that doesn't mean it's bad! Especially not with these harbour views. Prop yourself at a blonde-wood communal table, guzzle some *gyoza* (dumplings) or a chilli beef ramen soup and watch the waves.

Tatsushi
JAPANESE $$

(Map p360; ☑04-472 3928; www.tatsushi.co.nz; 99 Victoria St; mains $8-19, set menus $29-39; ⊙11.30am-2.30pm Tue-Sat, 6-10pm Wed-Sat) A compact space reassuringly dominated by an open kitchen, from which authentic Japanese dishes such as super-fresh sashimi, homemade *agedashi* tofu, *chazuke* soup, squid *sunomono* (dressed salad) and more-

ish *karaage* chicken emerge. Tatsushi is the real deal. Sushi and bento boxes to go.

★ Ortega Fish Shack
SEAFOOD $$$

(Map p360; ☑04-382 9559; www.ortega.co.nz; 16 Marjoribanks St; mains $34-39; ⊙5.30pm-late Tue-Sat) Mounted trout, salty portraits, marine-blue walls and Egyptian floor tiles cast a Mediterranean spell over Ortega – a magical spot for a seafood dinner. Fish comes many ways (roasted with laksa sauce; with mango chutney and raita), while desserts continue the Med vibes with Catalan orange crêpes and one of Welly's best cheeseboards. Excellent stuff.

★ Logan Brown
MODERN NZ $$$

(Map p360; ☑04-801 5114; www.loganbrown. co.nz 192 Cuba St; mains $37-42; ⊙noon-2pm Tue-Sat, 5pm-late daily; ☎) Deservedly touted as Wellington's best restaurant, Logan Brown oozes class without being overly formal. Its 1920s banking-chamber dining room is a stunner as is the menu, which features such treats as Fiordland venison with black pudding, parsnip and sour cherries. The three-course bistro menu ($45) won't hurt your wallet too badly (but the epic wine list might force a blowout).

Duke Carvell's
MEDITERRANEAN $$$

(Map p360; ☑04-385 2240; www.dukecarvell. co.nz; 6 Swan Lane; small plates $6-19, large plates $30-80; ⊙noon-late Mon-Fri, 9am-late Sat & Sun) OK, so it's right on a car park...but that's just *sooo* Cuba (and check out the graffiti!). Inside, join the handsome Duke for an indulgent culinary romp: blood-sausage Scotch eggs, fried chicken sliders with white cabbage slaw, flaming ouzo cheese. Heirloom artwork adorns the walls; low-cut chandeliers cast sultry shadows. There's a spectacular-value three-course lunch ($38 including a glass of wine)

Jano Bistro
FRENCH $$$

(Map p360; ☑04-332 9892; www.janobistro. co.nz; 270 Willis St; mains $28-35, 7-course degustation with/without wine $145/95; ⊙10am-3pm Sat & Sun, 5.30pm-late Tue-Sun) Unexpected little Jano crops up on a bleak, windy stretch of Willis St – a small yellow 1880s cottage with a herb garden out the front and buckets of charm inside. Shuffle past the fireplace and up the stairs to the loft dining room for fine French: go for the lamb with chickpeas, aubergine, sweet peppers and black olives. *Magnifique!*

🍷 Drinking & Nightlife

Wellingtonians love a late night. The inner city is riddled with bars, with high concentrations around Courtenay Pl (short skirts, sexy shoes), Cuba St (beards and bohemia) and along the waterfront. A creative live-music scene keeps things thrumming, along with great NZ wines and even better craft beer. See www.craftbeercapital.com for beery propaganda. For gig listings see www.undertheradar.co.nz and www.eventfinder.co.nz.

★ Golding's Free Dive
CRAFT BEER

(Map p360; ☑04-381 3616; www.goldingsfreedive.co.nz; 14 Leeds St; ⊙noon-11pm; 🛜) Hidden down a busy little back alley near Cuba St, gloriously garish Golding's is a bijoux craft-beer bar with far too many merits to mention. We'll single out ex-casino swivel chairs, a nice wine list, a ravishing Reuben sandwich, and pizza from Pomodoro (p366) next door. Blues, Zappa and Bowie conspire across the airways.

★ Little Beer Quarter
CRAFT BEER

(LBQ; Map p360; ☑04-803 3304; www.littlebeerquarter.co.nz; 6 Edward St; ⊙3.30pm-late Mon, noon-late Tue-Sat, 3pm-late Sun) Buried in a back lane, lovely LBQ is warm, inviting and moodily lit in all the right places. Well-curated taps and a broad selection of bottled beer pack a hop-ish punch. Good cocktails, wines, and whiskies, too, plus zesty bar food. Pizza and a pint for $20 on Monday nights; Mark Knopfler on the stereo (never a bad thing).

Fork & Brewer
CRAFT BEER

(F&B; Map p360; ☑04-472 0033; www.forkandbrewer.co.nz; 14 Bond St; ⊙11.30am-late Mon-Sat) Aiming to improve on the 'kebab at 2am' experience, F&B offers 'excellent burgers, pizzas, pies, share plates and meaty mains to go along with its crafty brews (of which there are dozens – the Low Blow IPA comes highly recommended). Oh, and dark-beer doughnuts for dessert!

Thief
WINE BAR

(Map p360; ☑04-384 6400; www.thiefbar.co.nz; 19 Edward St; ⊙3pm-late) If your idea of a good time is fine wine, cocktails and conversation, steal away to Thief. It's a brick-lined, timbered, cellar-like space. Twinkly lighting plays across the faces of good-looking after-workers, and there's a rack of *Encyclopaedia Britannicas* behind the bar if you need to check any facts from 1986. One of the city's hidden gems.

Southern Cross
PUB

(Map p360; ☑04-384 9085; www.thecross.co.nz; 39 Abel Smith St; ⊙8am-late Mon-Fri, 9am-late Sat & Sun; 🛗) Welcoming to all – from frenetic five-year-olds to knitting nanas – the democratic Cross rambles through a series of colourful rooms, combining a respectable restaurant, a lively bar, a dance floor, a pool table and the best garden bar in town. There's good beer on tap, food for all budgets and regular events (bingo, gigs, quiz nights).

Library
BAR

(Map p360; ☑04-382 8593; www.thelibrary.co.nz; L1, 53 Courtenay Pl; ⊙5pm-late Mon-Thu, 4pm-late Fri-Sun) You'll find yourself in the right kind of bind at moody, bookish Library, with its velveteen booths, board games and swish cocktails. An excellent all-round drink selection is complemented by a highly shareable menu of sweet and savoury treats including tempura tuna, churros and cheese (not all together). Live music on occasion.

Laundry
BAR

(Map p360; ☑04-384 4280; www.laundry.net.nz; 240 Cuba St; ⊙4.30pm-late Mon-Fri, 9am-late Sat & Sun) Tumble into this lurid-green, junk-shop juke joint any time of the day or night for a tipple and a plate of jerk chicken, then hang with the hipsters in a wrinkle-free zone. Regular live music and DJs offset Southern-style bar food and carnivalesque decor pasted up with a very rough brush. Trailer-trash backyard complete with a caravan.

Rogue & Vagabond
CRAFT BEER

(Map p360; ☑04-381 2321; www.rogueandvagabond.co.nz; 18 Garrett St; ⊙11am-late) Fronting on to a precious pocket park in the dark heart of Cuba St, the Rogue is a lovably scruffy, colourful, kaleidoscopic craft-beer bar with heaps going on – via 18 taps and two hand-pulls. Voluminous, chewy-crust pizza ($15 to $22) and regular, rockin' gigs add further appeal. Swill around on the patio or slouch on the lawn.

Hawthorn Lounge
COCKTAIL BAR

(Map p360; ☑04-890 3724; www.hawthornlounge.co.nz; L1, 2 Tory St; ⊙5pm-late) This uppercut cocktail bar has a 1920s speakeasy feel, suited-up in waistcoats and wide-brimmed fedoras. Sip a whisky sour and play poker, or watch the behind-the-bar theatrics from the Hawthorn's mixologists, twisting and turning classics into modern-day masterpieces. Open 'til the wee small hours.

Hashigo Zake
CRAFT BEER

(Map p360; 04-384 7300; www.hashigozake. co.nz; 25 Taranaki St; noon-late;) This bricky bunker is the HQ for a zealous beer-import business, splicing big-flavoured international brews into a smartly selected NZ range. Hop-heads stand elbow-to-elbow around the bar, ogling the oft-changing taps and brimming fridges, and squeeze into the sweet little side-lounge on live-music nights (Saturdays 9.30pm). Neil Young rules.

Crafters & Co
CRAFT BEER

(Map p360; 04-891 2345; www.craftersand.co; 211 Victoria St; 10am-midnight Sun-Thu, to 3am Fri & Sat) Floating up on the NZ craft-beer tide, crafty Crafters have opened up this cool cafe-bar on the upper reaches of Victoria St. Stop by for a pint, a pie or a platter, or pick up a few takeaway bottles for the hotel-room fridge. Try the Cassels & Sons Best Bitter.

☆ Entertainment

Wellington's long-standing professional theatre, Circa (p370), runs a busy program, augmented by plenty of amateur companies, fringe performers, student shows and regular visiting tours. Peruse listings at www. eventfinder.co.nz. Many events are ticketed via Ticketek – box office at the Michael Fowler Centre (Map p360; 0800 842 538, 04-801 4231; www.ticketek.co.nz; 111 Wakefield St; box office 9am-5pm Mon-Fri, 10am-4pm Sat & Sun) – or TicketDirect (www.ticketdirect. co.nz). Discount same-day tickets for some productions are often available at the i-SITE.

Movie times are listed in the daily *Dominion Post* and at www.flicks.co.nz. There are some excellent indie cinemas here, plus the usual mainstream megaplexes.

★ Bodega
LIVE MUSIC

(Map p360; 04-384 8212; www.bodega.co.nz; 101 Ghuznee St; 4pm-late) Proudly displaying its 'since 1991' credentials, the good-old 'Bodge' has demonstrated admirable endurance and remains at the fore of Wellington's live-music scene. Expect a varied program of gigs – including frequent international acts – in a rock-vibed space with solid acoustics.

Light House Cinema
CINEMA

(Map p360; 04-385 3337; www.lighthousecinema. co.nz; 29 Wigan St; adult/child $17.50/12.50; 10am-late) Tucked away near the top end of Cuba St, this small, stylish cinema throws a range of mainstream, art-house and foreign films up onto the screens in three small theatres. High-quality snacks. Tuesday tickets $11.

San Fran
LIVE MUSIC

(Map p360; 04-801 6797; www.sanfran.co.nz; 171 Cuba St; 3pm-late Tue-Sat) This much-loved, midsize music venue is moving to a new beat; it's boarded the craft-beer bandwagon and rocks out smoky, meaty food along the way. Gigs still rule, dancing is de rigueur, and the balcony still gets good afternoon sun.

Meow
LIVE MUSIC

(Map p360; 04-385 8883; www.welovemeow. co.nz; 9 Edward St; 3am-late Tue, noon-late Wed-Fri, 6pm-late Sat) Truly the cat's pyjamas, Meow goes out on a limb to host a diverse range of gigs and performances: country, ragtime, DJs, acoustic rock, jazz, poetry... At the same time the kitchen plates up good-quality, inexpensive food at any tick of the clock (organic pork meatballs with goulash!). Mish-mashed retro decor; cool craft beers.

Embassy Theatre
CINEMA

(Map p360; 04-384 7657; www.embassy theatre.co.nz; 10 Kent Tce; adult/child from $19.50/15.50; 10am-late) Wellywood's cinema mother ship is an art-deco darling, built in the 1920s. Today she screens mainly mainstream films with state-of-the-art sound and vision. Bars and cafe on-site. Has the facade facelift been finished?

Circa Theatre
THEATRE

(Map p360; ☑ 04-801 7992; www.circa.co.nz; 1 Taranaki St; ⊙ box office 10am-2pm Mon, to 6.30pm Tue, to 4pm Wed, to 8pm Thu-Sat, 1-7pm Sun) Waterfront Circa houses two auditoriums in which it shows everything from edgy new works to Christmas panto. Standby tickets available an hour before the show. Dinner-and-show packages available.

BATS
THEATRE

(Map p360; ☑ 04-802 4175; www.bats.co.nz; 1 Kent Tce; tickets from $10; ⊙ box office 5pm-late Tue-Sat) Wildly alternative but accessible BATS presents cutting-edge and experimental NZ theatre – varied, cheap and intimate – in its freshly revamped theatre.

🛍 Shopping

Wellington supports a host of independent shops including scores of design stores and clothing boutiques. Despite cheap imports and online shopping, there's still plenty that's Kiwi-made here. Retailers fly their home-grown flags with pride.

★ Garage Project
DRINK

(Map p354; ☑ 04-384 3076; www.garageproject. co.nz; 68 Aro St, Aro Valley; ⊙ noon-6pm Mon, noon-8pm Tue-Thu, 10am-9pm Fri & Sat, 10am-7pm Sun) Put yourself in the pitcher at Garage Project microbrewery in bohemian Aro Valley, where you can buy craft beer by the litre, petrol-pump style. Try the Vesuvian Pale Ale or chance your arm on the Pernicious Weed. Free tastings.

Moore Wilson Fresh
FOOD & DRINK

(Map p360; ☑ 04-384 9906; www.moore wilsons.co.nz; 93 Tory St; ⊙ 7.30am-7pm Mon-Fri, to 6pm Sat, 9am-6pm Sun) A call-out to self-caterers: this positively swoon-inducing grocer is one of NZ's most committed supporters of independently produced and artisanal produce. If you want to chew on the best of Wellington and NZ, here's your chance. Wine, beer and cooking demonstrations as well.

Unity Books
BOOKS

(Map p360; ☑ 04-499 4245; www.unitybooks. co.nz; 57 Willis St; ⊙ 9am-6pm Mon-Thu, to 7pm Fri, 10am-6pm Sat, 11am-5pm Sun) Sets the standard for every bookshop in the land, with a dedicated NZ table piled high.

Wellington Night Market
MARKET

(Map p360; ☑ 022 074 2550; www.wellington nightmarket.co.nz; L1, 107 Cuba St; ⊙ 5-11pm Fri & Sat) Nocturnal fun and games on Cuba St, with international foods aplenty and more buskers and performers than you have eyes and ears.

Slow Boat Records
MUSIC

(Map p360; ☑ 04-385 1330; www.slowboat records.co.nz; 183 Cuba St; ⊙ 9.30am-5.30pm Mon-Thu, to 7.30pm Fri, 10am-5pm Sat & Sun) Country, folk, pop, indie, metal, blues, soul, rock, Hawaiian nose-flute music – it's all here at Slow Boat, Wellington's long-running music shop and Cuba St mainstay.

Hunters & Collectors
CLOTHING

(Map p360; ☑ 04-384 8948; www.facebook. com/huntersandcollectorswellington; 134 Cuba St; ⊙ 10am-6pm Mon-Sat, 11am-5pm Sun) Beyond the best-dressed window in NZ you'll find off-the-rack and vintage clothing (punk, skate, Western and mod), plus shoes and accessories. 'Nothing haunts us like the things we didn't buy', says the sign in the door. Sage advice.

City Market
MARKET

(Map p360; ☑ 04-801 8158; www.citymarket. co.nz; Chaffers Dock Bldg, 1 Herd St; ⊙ 8.30am-12.30pm Sun) Expect brilliant produce, baked goods, tastings, coffee, wine, book signings, entertainment and other weekend delights at this fab undercover market. The stately 1940 Chaffers Dock Building is worth the visit alone!

Ora Gallery
ARTS

(Map p360; ☑ 04-384 4157; 23 Allen St; ⊙ 9am-6pm Mon-Fri, to 5pm Sat, 10am-4pm Sun) Fresh, bold, bright contemporary art including sculpture, weaving, glass and jewellery: gifts for someone who's waiting for you back home. You can get a coffee here, too.

Vault
GIFTS

(Map p354; ☑ 04-4711 404; www.thevaultnz.com; 2 Plimmer Steps; ⊙ 9.30am-5.30pm Mon-Thu, 9.30am-7pm Fri, 10am-5pm Sat, 11am-4.30pm Sun) Exquisite jewellery, clothing, bags, ceramics, cosmetics – a lovely shop with lots of beautiful NZ-made things.

Old Bank Shopping Arcade
SHOPPING CENTRE

(Map p354; ☑ 04-922 0600; www.oldbank.co.nz; cnr Lambton Quay & Willis St; ⊙ 9am-6pm Mon-Thu, to 7pm Fri, 10am-4pm Sat, 11am-3pm Sun) This dear old building on a wedge-shaped city site is home to indulgent, high-end shops, predominantly jewellers and boutiques. Check out the fab mosaic floors and Corinthian columns.

Kirkcaldie & Stains DEPARTMENT STORE
(Map p354; 04-472 5899; www.kirkcaldies.
co.nz; 165-177 Lambton Quay; 9.30am-5.30pm
Mon-Thu, to 6pm Fri, 10am-5pm Sat & Sun) New
Zealand's answer to Bloomingdale's or Har-
rods, established in 1863. Bring your travel
documents with you for tax-free bargains.

ℹ Information

EMERGENCY & IMPORTANT NUMBERS

Ambulance, fire service & police	111
Lifeline Aotearoa	0800 543 354
Sexual Abuse Help Foundation	04-499 7532
Wellington Central Police Station	04-381 2000

INTERNET ACCESS

Free wi-fi is available throughout most of Wellington's CBD (www.cbdfree.co.nz); the i-SITE
also has internet access.

MEDICAL SERVICES

UFS Pharmacy (04-384 9499; www.ufs.
co.nz; 45 Courtenay Pl; 8.30am-6pm Mon,
8am-6pm Tue-Fri, 10am-2pm Sat) Handy
city-centre pharmacy.

Wellington Accident & Urgent Medical Centre
(0800 611 116, 04-384 4944; www.wamc.
co.nz; 17 Adelaide Rd, Newtown; 8am-11pm)
No appointment necessary; also home to an
after-hours pharmacy. It's close to the Basin Reserve around the northern end of Adelaide Rd.

Wellington Hospital (04-385 5999; www.
ccdhb.org.nz; Riddiford St, Newtown; 24hr)
One kilometre south of the city centre.

POST

Post Office (Map p360; 0800 501 501;
www.nzpost.co.nz; 2 Manners St; 8.30am-
5.30pm Mon-Fri, 9am-3pm Sat) This branch
has the longest opening hours of all the Wellington city post offices.

TOURIST INFORMATION

DOC Wellington Visitor Centre (Map p360;
04-384 7770; www.doc.govt.nz; 18 Manners
St; 9.30am-5pm Mon-Fri, 10am-3.30pm Sat)
Bookings, passes and information for local and
national walks (including Great Walks), parks,
huts and camping.

Wellington i-SITE (Map p360; 04-802
4860; www.wellingtonnz.com; Civic Sq, cnr
Wakefield & Victoria Sts; 8.30am-5pm Mon-
Fri, 9am-5pm Sat & Sun) Staff book almost
everything here, and cheerfully distribute
Wellington's *Official Visitor Guide*, along with
other maps and helpful pamphlets.

ℹ Getting There & Away

AIR

Wellington is an international gateway to NZ.
Wellington Airport (WLG; 04-385 5100;
www.wellingtonairport.co.nz; Stewart Duff Dr,
Rongotai) has the usual slew of airport accou-
trements: info kiosks, currency exchange, ATMs,
car-rental desks, shops, espresso... If you're in
transit or have an early flight, note that you can't
linger overnight inside the terminal.

Air New Zealand (04-474 8950; www.
airnewzealand.co.nz; 154 Fetherstone St;
9am-5pm Mon-Fri, 10am-1pm Sat) Offers
flights between Wellington and most domestic
centres, including Auckland, New Plymouth,
Napier, Nelson, Christchurch, Dunedin and
Queenstown. It also flies direct to/from Sydney,
Melbourne, Adelaide and Brisbane in Australia.

Jetstar (www.jetstar.com) Offers economical flights from Wellington to Auckland and
Christchurch, but takes no prisoners when it
comes to late check-in. It also flies direct to the
Gold Coast and Melbourne across the ditch.

Soundsair (www.soundsair.com) Flies between
Wellington and Picton up to eight times daily,
plus to Nelson, Blenheim and Westport down
south, and Taupo up north.

Qantas (www.qantas.com.au) Flies direct between Wellington and Auckland, and Wellington
and Christchurch. Also has direct connections
with Sydney, Melbourne and the Gold Coast in
Australia.

BOAT

On a clear day, sailing into Wellington Harbour or
into Picton in the Marlborough Sounds is magical. Cook Strait can cut up rough, but the big
ferries handle it well, and offer the distractions
of sport lounges, cafes, bars, information desks
and cinemas (but no pool tables).

Car-hire companies allow you to pick up and
drop off vehicles at ferry terminals. If you arrive
outside business hours, arrangements can be
made to collect your vehicle from the terminal
car park.

There are two ferry options:
Bluebridge Ferries (Map p354; 04-471
6188, 0800 844 844; www.bluebridge.co.nz;
50 Waterloo Quay) Crossing takes 3½ hours;
up to four sailings in each direction daily. Cars
and campervans from $120; motorbikes $51;
bicycles $10. Passenger fares from $53/27 per
adult/child.

Interislander (Map p354; 04-498 3302,
0800 802 802 www.interislander.co.nz; Aotea
Quay) Crossings take three hours 10 minutes;
up to five sailings in each direction daily. Cars
are priced from $119; campervans from $153;
motorbikes from $56; bicycles $15. Passenger
fares start from $55/28 per adult/child.

Bluebridge is based at Waterloo Quay, opposite Wellington train station. Interislander is about 2km northeast of the city centre at Aotea Quay (Map p354); a shuttle bus ($2) runs to/from platform 9 at Wellington train station (from where InterCity buses also depart). There's a taxi stand at the terminal, too.

BUS

Wellington is a major bus-travel hub, with **Inter City** (Map p354; ✆ 04-385 0520; www.intercity.co.nz) boasting the most extensive network. Services depart from platform 9 at Wellington train station. Destinations include the following:

DESTINATION	PRICE	DURATION (HR)
Auckland	$83	11
Napier	$45	5½
Palmerston North	$35	2¼
Rotorua	$65	7½

Naked Bus (Map p354; ✆ 0900 625 33; www.nakedbus.com) runs north from Wellington to all major North Island destinations, including an overnighter (with fold-down seats!) to Auckland. Buses depart from Bunny St opposite Wellington train station. Destinations include the following:

DESTINATION	PRICE	DURATION (HR)
Auckland	$35	10
Palmerston North	$24	2½
Rotorua	$30	6½
Taupo	$25	5

TRAIN

Wellington train station has six ticket windows (open 6.30am to 8pm Monday to Thursday, to 1.15am Friday and Saturday, to 7pm Sunday): two sell tickets for KiwiRail Scenic Journeys trains, Interislander ferries and InterCity coaches; the other four handle ticketing for local and regional **Tranz Metro** (✆ 0800 801 700; www.tranzmetro.co.nz) trains (Johnsonville, Melling, Hutt Valley, Kapiti and Wairarapa lines).

KiwiRail Scenic Journey (www.kiwirailscenic.co.nz) runs the just-hanging-in-there Northern Explorer service from Wellington to Auckland on Tuesday, Friday and Sunday, returning from Auckland on Monday, Thursday and Saturday (from $179, 12 hours). KiwiRail also runs the Capital Connection weekday commuter service from Palmerston North, leaving at 6.15am for Wellington, and returning to Palmerston North at 5.15pm ($35, two hours).

ⓘ Getting Around

Metlink (✆ 0800 801 700; www.metlink.org.nz) is the one-stop shop for Wellington's regional bus, train (linking to Tranz Metro) and harbour ferry networks.

TO/FROM THE AIRPORT

The airport is 8km southeast of the city. **Wellington Combined Shuttles** (✆ 04-387 8787; www.co-opshuttles.co.nz; 1/2 passengers $20/26) provides a door-to-door minibus service (15 minutes) between the city and airport. It's cheaper if two or more passengers are travelling to the same destination. Shuttles meet all arriving flights.

The **Airport Flyer** (✆ 0800 801 700; www.airportflyer.co.nz) bus runs between the airport, Wellington and the Hutt Valley, with a fare to the city centre costing around $8. Buses run from around 6am to 9pm and take roughly 20 minutes.

A taxi between the city centre and the airport costs takes around 15 minutes and costs about $30.

BICYCLE

If you're fit or keep to the flat, cycling is a viable option. City hirers include **On Yer Bike** (p358) near Cuba St, and **Ferg's Kayaks** (p358) on the waterfront. Another option is **Switched On Bikes** (Map p360; ✆ 0800 386 877, 022 075 8754; www.switchedonbikes.co.nz; Shed One, Queens Wharf; bike hire half-/full-day $45/75, guided tours from $65; ☺ 9am-5pm), offering electric-bike hire and guided tours.

Wellington's regional council shows great encouragement for cycling via maps and suggestions on its journey planner (www.journeyplanner.org.nz).

BUS

Frequent and efficient **Metlink** (p372) buses cover the whole Wellington region, running between approximately 6am and 11.30pm. Major bus terminals are at the **Wellington train station** (Map p354), and on **Courtenay Pl** (Map p360; Courtenay Pl) near the Cambridge Tce intersection. Pick up route maps and timetables from the i-SITE and convenience stores, or online. Fares are determined by zones: a trip across the city centre (Zone 1) costs $2, while all the way north to Masterton (Zone 14) costs $18.

Metlink also runs **After Midnight** buses, departing from two city stops (Courtenay Pl and Cuba St) between midnight and 4.30am Saturday and Sunday, following a number of routes to the outer suburbs. Fares range from $6.50 to $13, depending on how far away your bed is.

CAR & MOTORCYCLE

There are a lot of one-way streets in Wellington, and parking gets tight (and pricey) during the day. If you've got a car or a caravan, park on the outskirts and walk or take public transport into the city centre. Campervans can also park during the day at the **Wellington Waterfront Motorhome Park** (Map p354; www.wwmp. co.nz; 12 Waterloo Quay) and in the open-air car park outside Te Papa.

Aside from the major international rental companies, Wellington has several operators that will negotiate cheap deals, especially for rentals of two weeks or more. Rates generally aren't as competitive as in Auckland. Rack rates range from around $40 to $80 per day; cars are usually a few years old and in pretty good condition. Operators include the following:

Apex Car Rental (☑ 04-385 2163, 0800 300 110; www.apexrentals.co.nz)

Jucy Rentals (☑ 04-380 6211, 0800 399 736; www.jucy.co.nz)

Omega Rental Cars (☑ 04-472 8465, 0800 667 722; www.omegarentalcars.com)

If you plan on exploring both North and South Islands, most companies suggest you leave your car in Wellington and pick up another one in Picton after crossing Cook Strait. This is a common (and more affordable) practice, and car-hire companies make it a painless exercise.

There are often cheap deals on car relocation from Wellington to Auckland, as most renters travel in the opposite direction. The catch is that you may have only 24 or 48 hours to make the journey.

TAXI

Packed taxi ranks can be found on Courtenay Pl (Map p360), at the corner (Map p360) of Dixon and Victoria Sts, on Featherston St (Map p354), and outside the railway station (Map p354). Two of many operators:

Green Cabs (☑ 0508 447 336; www.green-cabs.co.nz)

Wellington Combined Taxis (☑ 04-384 4444; www.taxis.co.nz)

TRAIN

Tranz Metro (☑ 0800 801 700; www.tranz metro.co.nz) operates five train routes running through Wellington's suburbs to regional destinations. Trains run frequently from around 6am to 11pm, departing Wellington train station. The routes are as follows:

➡ Johnsonville via Ngaio and Khandallah

➡ Kapiti via Porirua, Plimmerton, Paekakariki and Paraparaumu

➡ Melling via Petone

➡ Hutt Valley via Waterloo to Upper Hutt

➡ Wairarapa service calling at Featherston, Carterton and Masterton

Timetables are available from convenience stores, the train station, Wellington i-SITE and

online. Standard fares from Wellington to the ends of the five lines range from $5 to $18. A Day Rover ticket ($14) allows unlimited off-peak and weekend travel on all lines except Wairarapa.

KAPITI COAST

With wide, crowd-free beaches, the Kapiti Coast acts as a summer playground and suburban extension for Wellingtonians. The region takes its name from Kapiti Island, a wildlife sanctuary 5km offshore from Paraparaumu.

The mountainous Tararua Forest Park forms a dramatic backdrop along the length of the coastline and has some accessible day walks and longer tramps.

The Kapiti Coast makes an easy day trip from Wellington, though if you're after a few restful days there's enough of interest to keep you entertained.

ℹ Information

The Kapiti Coast's official visitor centre is **Paraparaumu i-SITE** (p376), at the vile-looking roadside Coastlands shopping area (www. coastlands.co.nz; banks, ATMs, post office, supermarkets...)

ℹ Getting There & Around

AIR

The recently expanded **Kapiti Coast Airport** (www.kapitiairport.co.nz; Toru Rd) in Paraparaumu is a regular destination for Air2there (www.air2there.com), with daily flights to Blenheim and Nelson, and Air New Zealand (www.airnewzealand.co.nz), which flies direct to Auckland.

BUS

InterCity (www.intercity.co.nz) Stops at major Kapiti Coast towns on services from Wellington ($21, 45 minutes from Paraparaumu).

Naked Bus (www.nakedbus.com) Also Stops at major Kapiti Coast towns on its daily services.

Metlink (www.metlink.org.nz) Runs local bus services around Paraparaumu, and up to Waikanae ($3.50, 15 minutes) and Otaki ($6.50, 40 minutes), calling at highway and beach settlements along the way.

CAR & MOTORCYCLE

Getting here from Wellington is a breeze by car: just follow SH1 for 30 minutes to Paekakariki, or around 45 to Paraparaumu. It's motorway most of the way (the new flyover Kapiti Expressway is still a work in progress).

MĀORI NZ: WELLINGTON REGION

Referred to in legends as the 'mouth of Maui's fish' and traditionally called Te Whanga-nui-a-Tara, the Wellington area became known to Māori in the mid-19th century as 'Poneke' (a transliteration of Port Nicholas, its European name at the time).

The major *iwi* (tribes) of the region were Te Ati Awa and Ngāti Toa. Ngāti Toa was the *iwi* of Te Rauparaha, who composed the now famous *Ka Mate haka*. Like most urban areas the city is now home to Māori from many *iwi*, sometimes collectively known as Ngāti Poneke.

New Zealand's national museum, **Te Papa** (p357), presents excellent displays on Māori culture, traditional and modern, as well as a colourful *marae* (meeting house). In its gift shop you can see excellent carving and other crafts, as you can in both **Kura** (Map p360; 04-802 4934; www.kuragallery.co.nz; 19 Allen St; ⏱10am-6pm Mon-Fri, 11am-4pm Sat & Sun) and **Ora** (p370) galleries nearby.

Kapiti Island Nature Tours (p374) and **Kiwi Coastal Tours** (p361) offer intimate insights into the Māori culture of the rugged coast around Wellington.

TRAIN

Tranz Metro (www.tranzmetro.co.nz) commuter trains between Wellington and the coast are more convenient and more frequent than buses. Services run from Wellington to Paraparaumu ($11.50, generally half-hourly 6am to 11pm), stopping en route in Paeka-kariki ($10.50) and continuing to Waikanae ($12.50).

KiwiRail Scenic Journeys (www.kiwirailscenic.co.nz) has long-distance Northern Explorer trains from Auckland to Wellington stopping at Paraparaumu ($219). You can't stop at Paraparaumu when travelling north from Wellington on this service, but you can on the weekday-only, peak-hour Capital Connection, travelling from Palmerston North to Wellington in the morning stopping at Otaki ($14), Waikanae ($19) and Paraparaumu ($21), then returning to Palmerston North in the evening stopping at Paraparaumu ($10), Waikanae ($11) and Otaki ($14).

Kapiti Island

Kapiti Island is the coastline's dominant feature, a 10km by 2km slice that has been a protected reserve since 1897. Largely predator-free (22,500 possums were eradicated here in the 1980s), it's now home to a remarkable range of birds, including many species that are are or extinct on the mainland.

To visit the island, you must make your arrangements in advance with one of three licensed operators. Remember to reconfirm your arrangements on the morning of departure, as sailings are weather-dependent. All boats depart from Paraparaumu Beach, which can be reached by train.

🏃 Activities

The island is open to day walkers (there are some fab trails here), limited each day to 100 at **Rangatira**, where you can hike up to the 521m high point, Tuteremoana; and 60 visitors at the **northern end**, which has short, gentle walks to view points and around a lagoon.

☞ Tours

Kapiti Island Nature Tours TOUR
(06-362 6606, 021 126 7525; www.kapitiisland naturetours.co.nz; transport per person $75, day tours $165) The *whanau* (family) that runs these nature tours has a long-standing connection to the island. Tours look at the island's birds (incredible in range and number), seal colony, history and Māori traditions. Overnight stays include an after-dark walk in the bush to spot the cutest-ever bird, the rare little spotted kiwi (tour plus meals and camping/cabins $335/405).

ℹ Information

More information about Kapiti Island can be found in DOC's *Kapiti Island Nature Reserve* brochure (downloadable from www.doc.govt.nz), or in person at the **DOC Wellington Visitor Centre** (p371).

ℹ Getting There & Away

Kapiti Marine Charter (027 655 4739, 0800 433 779; www.kapitimarinecharter.co.nz; adult/child from $75/40), **Kapiti Tours** (04-237 7965, 0800 527 484; www.kapititours.co.nz; adult/child $75/40, with guided tour $95/50) and **Kapiti Island Nature Tours** (p374) provide boat transport to and from the island a couple of times a day. Book ahead.

Paekakariki

POP 1600

The first stop-worthy Kapiti Coast town you come to heading north from Wellington is cute little Paekakariki, 41km north of the capital. It's an arty seaside village stretched along a black-sand beach, serviced by a train station and passed by the highway.

Sights & Activities

★ **Queen Elizabeth Park** PARK
(☑04-292 8625; www.gw.govt.nz/qep; MacKay's Crossing, SH1; ☺8am-dusk; ⊕) ⌇ One of the last relatively unchanged areas of dune and wetland along the Kapiti Coast, this undulating 650-hectare beachside park offers swimming, walking, cycling and picnicking opportunities, as well as a tram museum (☑04-292 8361; www.wellingtontrams. org.nz; MacKay's Crossing, SH1; admission by donation, tram rides adult/child/family $10/5/24; ☺11am-4.30pm Sat & Sun, daily Jan), and horse riding outfit. There are three entrances: off Wellington Rd in Paekakariki, at MacKay's Crossing on SH1, and off the Esplanade in Raumati to the north.

Stables on the Park HORSE RIDING
(☑06-364 3336, 027 448 6764; www.stables onthepark.co.nz; MacKay's Crossing, SH1, Queen Elizabeth Park; 30/60/90min rides $55/80/120; ☺rides 11am & 2pm Sat & Sun, daily Dec-Feb, other times by arrangement) Mandy and friends run guided rides on well-mannered horses. The 90-minute trek will have you trotting along the beach with views of Kapiti Island before heading inland on park tracks. Beginners are welcome. Call for bookings.

Sleeping & Eating

Paekakariki Holiday Park HOLIDAY PARK $
(☑04-292 8292; www.paekakarikiholidaypark. co.nz; 180 Wellington Rd; sites per adult from $16, cabins & units from $70; @ᖴ) You couldn't say that this large, leafy park is fully engaged with NZ's contemporary holiday park zeitgeist, but it is well located, 1.5km north of the township at the southern entrance to Queen Elizabeth Park (good for tramping and biking).

Finn's HOTEL $$
(☑04-292 8081; www.finnshotel.co.nz; 2 Beach Rd; d/2-bedroom ste from $135/250; ᖴ) Finn's is a flashy beige suit in this low-key railway village, but redeems itself with spacious rooms, big bistro meals (mains $19 to $30), a cafe

area, craft beer on tap and an in-house 26-seat cinema (!). Double glazing keeps the highway at bay.

Beach Road Deli CAFE $
(☑04-902 9029; www.beach-road-deli.com; 5 Beach Rd; snacks $3-8, pizza $13-25; ☺7am-8pm Wed-Sat, to 4.30pm Sun; ☑) Bijou deli and wood-fired pizzeria, stocked with home-baked bread and patisserie, cheese, charcuterie and assorted imported goodies. Heaven-sent for the highway traveller, picnicker, or those looking for a sausage to fry and a bun to put it in. Ace coffee.

Paraparaumu

POP 25,270

Busy Paraparaumu is the Kapiti Coast's major commercial and residential hot spot. It's a tale of two towns: the main town on the highway, with its deeply unappealing shopping-mall sprawl; and Paraparaumu Beach, with its waterside park and walkway, decent swimming, and winning view out to Kapiti Island (island boat trips set sail from here). If you're into craft beer and cars (or both), you're in the right town!

The correct pronunciation is 'Pah-ra-pah-ra-oo-moo', meaning 'scraps from an oven', which is said to have originated when a Māori war party attacked the settlement and found only scraps of food remaining. It's a bit of a mouthful to pronounce; locals usually just corrupt it into 'Para-par-am'.

Sights

Tuatara Brewery BREWERY
(☑04-296 1953; www.tuatarabrewing.co.nz; 7 Sheffield St; ☺3-7pm Wed & Thu, noon-7pm Fri-Sun, tours 1.15pm & 3.15pm Sat) Visit the oldest and most famous of Wellington's craft breweries at its industrial-estate premises where you can slurp a pint or two and chew some bar snacks (biersticks, nachos, pizza). Book in advance for an enlightening Saturday tour of the brewery ($35, including tasting tray).

Southward Car Museum MUSEUM
(☑04-297 1221; www.southwardcarmuseum. co.nz; off Otaihanga Rd; adult/child $17/3; ☺9am-4.30pm; ⊕) This huge hangar-like museum has one of Australasia's largest collections of antique and unusual cars. Check out the DeLorean and the 1950 gangster Cadillac. It's a few kilometres north of the main Paraparaumu shops.

✖ Eating

Ambience Café　　　　　　CAFE $$
(✆04-298 9898; 10 Seaview Rd; mains $13-22;
⊘8am-3pm Mon-Sat, 8.30-3pm Sun; ✚) A very
'Wellington' cafe, with both light and sub-
stantial meals made with relish: fishcakes,
BLTs, salads, sandwiches, colourful vegie
options... Cake cabinet at full capacity, and
great coffee (of course).

❶ Information

Paraparaumu i-SITE (✆0800 486 486, 04-
298 8195; www.kapiticoast.govt.nz; Coastlands
Mall, Rimu Rd; ⊘8am-5pm Mon-Fri) Kapiti
Coast information, maps and brochures, includ-
ing the *Kapiti Coast Walking & Cycling* pamphlet
with the low-down on coastal trails and tracks.

Waikanae
POP 10,630

Around 20km north of Paraparaumu is
Waikanae, traditionally a retiree stamping
ground but in recent times a growing, go-
ahead town, bolstered by first-home-buyer
flight from unaffordable Wellington. It's a
cheery seaside enclave, good for some salt-
tinged R&R and natural-realm experiences.

As well as the beach (and a couple of
good cafes right next to it) the main attrac-
tion here is Nga Manu Nature Reserve. For
some killer coastal views, don't miss the
steep hike to the top of **Hemi Matenga Me-
morial Park Scenic Reserve** (✆04-296 1112;
www.doc.govt.nz; off Tui Cres, Waikanae; ⊘daylight
hours) **FREE**.

◉ Sights & Activities

Nga Manu Nature Reserve　WILDLIFE RESERVE
(✆04-293 4131; www.ngamanu.co.nz; 281 Nga-
rara Rd, Waikanae; adult/child/family $18/8/38;
⊘10am-5pm; ✚) ✎ Waikanae's main visi-
tor lure, Nga Manu Nature Reserve is a 15-
hectare bird sanctuary dotted with picnic
areas, bushwalks, aviaries and a nocturnal
house with kiwi, owls and tuatara. The eels
are fed at 2pm daily; guided bird-feeding
tours run at 11am daily (adult/child $25/12
including admission). To get here, turn sea-
wards from SH1 onto Te Moana Rd and then
right down Ngarara Rd and follow the signs.

Waikanae Estuary Bird Tours　BIRDWATCHING
(✆04-905 1001; www.kapitibirdtours.co.nz; 2hr
tours $25) ✎ The Waikanae Estuary is a hot
spot for birds, with around 66 species visit-
ing during the year. You can expect to see
around 20 of the little flappers on these per-
sonalised outings with a passionate guide.

⌑ Sleeping & Eating

Kapiti Gateway Motel　　　　MOTEL $$
(✆04-902 5876, 0800 429 360; www.kapiti
gateway.co.nz; 114 Main Rd, Waikanae; d $120-165;
🛜🆒) Tidy, airy motel on the highway –
old-fashioned on the outside, updated on
the inside – with solar-heated pool, great
hospitality and Polo the tabby cat. Holiday
hermits can make the most of the free wi-fi,
kitchen facilities and Sky TV.

Long Beach　　　　　　　　CAFE $$
(✆04-293 6760; www.longbeach.net.nz; 40 Tutere
St, Waikanae; mains $10-30; ⊘8.30am-10pm; ✚)
Neighbourly, family-friendly Long Beach
offers an extensive menu ranging from
manuka-smoked salmon and ratatouille,
through to pizza and fish and chips. It's
bright and beachy with a large conservatory
and herb garden, and you can get a cold Tu-
atara on tap. The slightly more formal **Front
Room** cafe next door is also very good.

THE WAIRARAPA

The Wairarapa is the large tract of land east
and northeast of Wellington, beyond the
Tararua and Rimutaka Ranges. It is named
after Wairarapa Moana – otherwise known
as Lake Wairarapa, translating as 'sea of glis-
tening waters'. This shallow 80-sq-km lake
and the surrounding wetland is the focus
of much-needed ecological restoration, re-
dressing generations of sheep farming in its
ambit. Fields of fluffy sheep still bound, as
do vineyards and the associated hospitality
which have turned the region into a deca-
dent weekend retreat.

Check out the Classic New Zealand Wine
Trail (www.classicwinetrail.co.nz) – a use-
ful tool for joining the dots throughout the
Wairarapa and the neighbouring wine re-
gions of Hawke's Bay and Marlborough.

Note that the telephone area code over
here is ✆06, not ✆04 like the rest of the
Wellington region.

❶ Getting There & Around

From Wellington, Tranz Metro (www.tranzmetro.
co.nz) commuter trains run to Masterton ($18,
five times daily on weekdays, twice daily on
weekends), calling at seven Wairarapa stations
including Featherston and Carterton (though
notably not Greytown or Martinborough). Tranzit
Coachlines (www.tranzit.co.nz) buses connect
the towns off the railway line, running between
Masterton and Featherston via Carterton, Grey-
town and Martinborough (fares $2 to $5).

Beyond the wineries, you'll need your own vehicle: most of this area's notable sights are out on the coast and along rural roads. As is often the case, getting there is half the fun: the drive up over the ranges from Wellington is super-scenic.

Martinborough

POP 1580

The sweetest visitor spot in the Wairarapa, Martinborough is a photogenic town with a leafy town square and some charming old buildings, surrounded by a patchwork of pasture and pinstripe grapevines. It is famed for its wineries, which draw in visitors to nose the pinot, pair it up with fine food and snooze it off at boutique accommodation.

Sights

★ **Martinborough Brewery** BREWERY
(☑06-306 6249; www.martinboroughbeer.com; 10 Ohio St; ⊙11am-7pm Thu-Mon) It's hard to go anywhere in NZ these days and not find a craft brewery bubbling away in the corner. Martinborough is no exception; the brewery counters the town's prevailing wine vibe with its range of meaty brews (dark beers a speciality). Sip a tasting paddle or a pint on the sunny terrace out the front. Brewery tours by arrangement.

🏃 Activities

The most ecofriendly way to explore the Wairarapa's wineries is by bicycle, as the flat landscape makes for puff-free cruising. Rental bikes are comfortable cruisers with saddle bags for your booty. Suffice to say, you ought to pay greater attention to your technique, and to the road, as the day wears on.

Rental outfitters include **Christina Estate Vineyard** (☑06-306 8920; www.wairarapanz.com/see-and-do/martinborough-bicycle-hire-christina-estate; 28 Puruatanga Rd; full-day bicycle/tandem $25/50; ⊙9.30am-5pm, extended summer hours), **Green Jersey Cycle Tours** (☑021 074 6640; www.greenjersey.co.nz; 3-4hr guided tours incl lunch $120, bike hire per half-/full day $30/40; 🖷). Martinborough Top 10 Holiday Park (p378) and Martinborough Wine Merchants (p379).

WAIRARAPA WINE COUNTRY

Wairarapa's world-renowned wine industry was nearly crushed in infancy. The region's first vines were planted in 1883, but in 1908 the prohibition movement put a cap on that corker of an idea. It wasn't until the 1980s that winemaking was revived, after Martinborough's *terroir* was discovered to be similar to that of Burgundy, France. A few vineyards sprang up, the number since ballooning to around 40 across the region. Martinborough is the undisputed hub of the action, but vineyards around Gladstone and Masterton are also on the up. Pinot noir is the region's grape of choice.

Wairarapa's wineries thrive on visitors: well-oiled cellar doors swing wide open for tastings. Some wineries charge a tasting fee; others are free. Some places feature a cafe or restaurant, while others will rustle up a picnic platter to be enjoyed in their gardens. Winter hours wind back to the minimum. The *Wairarapa Visitor Guide* (available from local i-SITEs and many other places) has maps to aid your navigations. Read all about it at www.winesfrommartinborough.com. A few of our favourites:

Ata Rangi (☑06-306 9570; www.atarangi.co.nz; 14 Puruatanga Rd ⊙noon-4pm) One of the region's pioneering winemakers. Great drops across the board and a cute cellar door.

Coney Wines (☑06-306 8345; www.coneywines.co.nz; Dry River Rd; ⊙11am-4pm Fri-Sun, closed Fri Jun-Aug) Fingers crossed that your tasting host will be the inimitable Tim Coney, an affable character who makes a mighty syrah and may sing at random. Also home to the excellent Trio Cafe (mains around $25); bookings recommended.

Haythornthwaite Wines (☑06-306 9889; www.ht3wines.co.nz; 45 Omarere Rd; ⊙1-5pm) Sustainable, hands-on winery producing complex drops including cherry-like pinot noir and gorgeous gewürztraminer. There's a cafe next door.

Poppies Martinborough (☑06-306 8473; www.poppiesmartinborough.co.nz; 91 Puruatanga Rd; ⊙11am-4pm) Delectable handcrafted wines served by the label's passionate winemaking and viticulturalist duo. Savour their wines alongside a well-matched platter in the stylishly simple cellar door.

CAPE PALLISER

The Wairarapa coast south of Martinborough around Palliser Bay and Cape Palliser is remote and sparsely populated. A trip to its landmark lighthouse is a must-do if you can spare the time and have your own wheels.

From Martinborough, the road wends through picturesque farmland before hitting the coast along **Cape Palliser Road**. This section of the drive is impossibly scenic, hugging the coast between wild ocean and black-sand beaches on one side and sheer cliffs on the other. Look for shadows of the South Island, visible on a clear day. Also in this neck of the woods is a significant wilderness area, **Aorangi (Haurangi) Forest Park** (☑06-377 0700; www.doc.govt.nz; via Cape Palliser Rd; ⊗24hr) **FREE**.

Further south along the coast is the wind-worn fishing village of **Ngawi**. The first things you'll notice here are the rusty bulldozers on the beach, used to drag fishing boats ashore. There's a grassy picnic spot from which to survey the scene.

Next stop is the malodorous **seal colony**, the North Island's largest breeding area for these fellers. Whatever you do in your quest for a photo, don't get between the seals and the sea: if you block their escape route they're likely to have a go at you!

Just beyond stands the **Cape Palliser Lighthouse**, where you can get a few puffs into the lungs on the 250-step climb to its base. It's a beaut view from up here, and a great place to linger if the wind isn't blowing your eyeballs into the back of your head.

On the way there or back, take a short detour to the crusty waterside settlement of **Lake Ferry**, overlooking Lake Onoke. There's the characterful old **Lake Ferry Hotel** (☑06-307 7831; www.lakeferryhotel.co.nz; 2 Lake Ferry Rd; mains $14-30; ⊗noon-3pm & 6-9pm) here, plus ranks of grey, shingled dunes at the river mouth where the water rushes and swirls and big black-backed gulls circle overhead. This is a classic coastal corner of New Zealand where nothing ever happens but there's plenty to see.

⛵ Tours

Zest Food & Wine Tours WINE, FOOD

(☑04-801 9198; www.zestfoodtours.co.nz; per person incl lunch $429) Exclusive small-group tours (two to four guests) around Martinborough and Greytown, with the focus squarely on quality wine and food. Pricey, but worth it if you want a really personalised experience.

Tranzit Tours WINE, FOOD

(☑06-370 6600, 0800 471 227; www.tranzit tours.co.nz; per person $199) Hop on the daily tasting tour run by Tranzit Tours, which features four vineyard tastings, lunch and late-afternoon cheese and coffee. Departs Wellington, with pick-ups also available in Wairarapa towns (knock $24 off the price).

🎉 Festivals & Events

Toast Martinborough WINE, FOOD

(www.toastmartinborough.co.nz; ⊗Nov) Martinborough plays host to Toast Martinborough, held annually on the third Sunday in November. Enjoyable on many levels (standing up and quite possibly lying on the grass), this is a hugely popular wine, food and music event – you'll have to be quick on the draw to get a ticket.

Wairarapa Wines Harvest Festival WINE, FOOD

(www.wairarapawines.co.nz; ⊗mid-Mar) The Wairarapa Wines Harvest Festival celebrates the beginning of the harvest with an extravaganza of wine, food and family fun. It's held at a remote riverbank setting 10 minutes from Carterton on a Saturday in mid-March. Tickets go on sale at the end of the preceding November – be quick!

🛌 Sleeping

⭐ Martinborough

Top 10 Holiday Park HOLIDAY PARK $

(☑0800 780 909, 06-306 8946; www.martinboroughholidaypark.com; cnr Princess & Dublin Sts; sites per person from $18, cabins from $70; 🐾) An appealing campsite with grapevine views, just five minutes' walk from town. Shady trees and the town pool over the back fence make it a cooling oasis on sticky days. Cabins are simple but great value, freeing up your dollars for the cellar door.

Good-quality bikes, including tandems and child seats, are available for hire from 9am to 6pm (full-day bicycle/tandem hire $35/70). Cheaper rates for park guests.

Claremont
MOTEL, APARTMENT **$$**

(☑0800 809 162, 06-306 9162; www.the claremont.co.nz; 38 Regent St; d/2-bedroom apt from $135/195; 🛜) A classy accommodation enclave 15 minutes' walk from town, the Claremont has two-storey, self-contained units in great nick, modern studios with spa baths, and sparkling two-bedroom apartments, all at reasonable rates (even cheaper in winter and/or midweek). Tidy gardens, barbecue areas and bike hire. Repent your cellar-door sins at the lovely old First Church nearby.

Lacoste Cottage
COTTAGE **$$**

(☑027 454 6959; www.lacostecottage.co.nz; 42 Dublin St; d $160, extra person $40; 🛜) While the decor may be a bit faux-Frenchy for some, this lovely early-1900s cottage is undeniably good-looking, with its powder-blue front door, rambling roses and wraparound veranda. Two double bedrooms, plus a single bed in the lounge (sleeps five total). Good for families.

Aylstone Retreat
BOUTIQUE HOTEL **$$$**

(☑06-306 9505; www.aylstone.co.nz; 19 Huangarua Rd; d incl breakfast $230-260; 🛜) Set among the vines on the edge of the village, this elegant retreat is a winning spot for the romantically inclined. Six en suite rooms exude flowery French-provincial charm and share a posh reading room. The whole shebang is surrounded by micro-mansion gardens sporting lawns, box hedges and chichi furniture.

✕ Eating

Village Cafe
CAFE **$**

(☑06-306 8814; www.facebook.com/thevillagecafe martinborough; 6 Kitchener St; mains $10-23; ⊙8am-4pm daily, 6-9pm Fri) 'The heart of Martinborough' might be overstating things just a little, but this busy central cafe is undoubtedly popular, serving eggy breakfasts, big salads, a mean Reuben sandwich, and pizzas on Friday nights. Lofty mess-hall vibes; mellow tunes and occasional live music.

Tirohana Estate
MODERN NZ **$$**

(☑06-306 9933; www.tirohanaestate.com; 42 Puruatanga Rd; lunch mains $12-22, 3-course dinners $59; ⊙11.30am-3pm & 6pm-late Mon-Sat, 6pm-late Sun) Enjoy a casual lunch over a glass or two on the terrace at this pretty vineyard, then come back for dinner in the elegant dining room (quite the occasion). Food (salmon fishcakes, lamb shanks, bread-and-butter pudding) is amply proportioned, proficiently prepared and impeccably served. Dinner bookings essential.

Pinocchio
CAFE **$$**

(☑06-306 6094; www.pinocchiomartinborough. co.nz; 3 Kitchener St; mains lunch $13-28, dinner $29-34; ⊙6pm-late Wed-Fri, 8.30am-late Sat & Sun) Pinocchio is a hip little cafe-bar wedged into a tight space behind the old Martinborough Hotel. It's hard to beat a weekend breakfast of eggs Benedict or smoked fishcakes with poached eggs at one of the forecourt tables. Burgers Wednesday nights, roasts on Sundays and West Coast whitebait fritters in season.

🍷 Drinking & Nightlife

★ Micro Wine Bar
WINE BAR

(☑06-306 9716; www.facebook.com/microwine bar; 14c Ohio St; ⊙4pm-late Mon, Thu & Fri, 3pm-late Sat & Sun) Moreish little Micro packs a punch with its excellent wine list (mostly local with some far-flung stars), notable craft-beer selection and yummy nibbles ranging from Asian dim sum to Mediterranean tapas. Catch the sun streetside or head to the courtyard where an evening might slip very easily away. Vinyl spins on the vintage '70s stereo.

☆ Entertainment

Circus
CINEMA

(☑movielne 06-306 9442; www.circus.net.nz; 34 Jellicoe St; adult/child $16/11; ⊙3pm-late Wed-Mon) Lucky old Martinborough has its own stylish art-house cinema. This mod, micro-size complex has two comfy studio theatres and a cafe opening out on to a sunny, somewhat Zen garden. Reasonably priced food (mains $22 to $34) includes bar snacks, pizzas and mains with seasonal vegies. Take your wine into the cinema with you.

🔒 Shopping

Martinborough Wine Merchants
WINE, FOOD

(☑06-306 9040; www.martinboroughwine merchants.co.nz; 6 Kitchener St; ⊙9.30am-5.30pm Sun-Thu, to 6pm Fri & Sat) An excellent spot to buy a couple of bottles or cases of local wine (and maybe taste a few). Also sells olive oils, books, clothing and art, and rents out bikes ($25/35 per half-/full day) for cellar-door adventures. The Village Cafe (p379) is here, too.

ℹ Information

Martinborough i-SITE (☑ 06-306 5010; www.wairarapanz.com; 18 Kitchener St; ⊘ 9am-5pm Tue-Sat, 10am-4pm Sun & Mon) Small, helpful and cheery, the local info centre stocks wine region maps and can point you in the right direction.

Greytown

POP 2320

The most polished of several small towns along SH2, Greytown has tarted itself up over recent years and is now home to a permanent population of urbane locals, and waves of Wellington weekenders. Greytown was the country's first planned inland town: intact Victorian architectural specimens line the main street (pick up the *Historic Greytown* brochure for some detail). Among the old buildings you'll find plenty of accommodation, decent eateries, three high-street pubs and some swanky shopping.

⊙ Sights

Cobblestones Museum   MUSEUM
(☑ 06-304 9687; www.cobblestonesmuseum.org.nz; 169 Main St; adult/child/family $7/5/15; ⊘ 10am-4pm; ♿) Sporting a spruce new exhibition space and shop, this endearing museum on the main street comprises an enclave of transplanted period buildings and donated old-time objects, dotted around pretty grounds just begging for a lie-down on a picnic blanket. There's a blacksmiths, a school, a fire station, a church, a wool shed... Wairarapa history in tangible form.

Stonehenge Aotearoa   MONUMENT
(☑ 06-377 1600; www.stonehenge-aotearoa.co.nz; 51 Ahiaruhe Rd; tours adult/child $16/8; ⊘ 10am-4pm) About 10km from Greytown in a farmer's backyard, this full-scale adaptation of the UK's Stonehenge is orientated for its southern hemisphere location on a grassy knoll overlooking the Wairarapa Plain. Its mission: to bring the night sky to life, even in daylight. The pretour talk and audiovisual presentation are excellent, and the henge itself a surreal (and delightfully eccentric) sight. Self-guided tours are also available for adult/child $8/4.

🛏 Sleeping & Eating

Oak Estate Motor Lodge   MOTEL $$
(☑ 06-304 8188, 0800 843 625; www.oakestate.co.nz; 2 Hospital Rd; r $135-190; 🐾) A stand of gracious roadside oaks and pretty gardens

shield this smart complex of red-roofed units at the southern end of town. Choose from studios, one- and two-bedroom options. Expect tasteful interiors and white doves strutting about on the lawns. Free wi-fi.

French Baker   BAKERY $
(☑ 06-304 8873; www.frenchbaker.co.nz; 81 Main St; light meals $7-13; ⊘ 8am-3pm Mon-Fri, to 4pm Sat & Sun; 🍴) Buttery croissants, tempting tarts and authentic breads – this artisan baking is le real McCoy. Grab and go from the cabinet, or tuck into a bacon butty or some broccoli and blue cheese soup, washed down with an espresso.

Schoc Chocolates   DELI $
(☑ 06-304 8960; www.schoc.co.nz; 177 Main St; bars $12-14; ⊘ 10am-4.30pm Mon-Fri, 10.30am-4.30pm Sat & Sun) No picnic? No worries. Visit Schoc in its 1920s cottage on the main street. Divine flavours (Earl Grey, tangerine, bitter chilli) are worth every penny. Truffles, rocky road and peanut brittle, too. Free tastings and sublime scents.

Masterton & Around

POP 24,400

Masterton is the Wairarapa's utilitarian hub, an unremarkable, unselfconscious town getting on with the business of life.

⊙ Sights

There are a few interesting sights in the surrounding area, one of which is **Castlepoint**, on the coast 68km east of Masterton. It's a truly awesome, end-of-the-world place, with a reef, the lofty 162m-high Castle Rock, some safe swimming and walking tracks. There's an easy (but sometimes ludicrously windy) 30-minute return walk across the reef to the lighthouse, where 70-plus shell species are fossilised in the cliffs. A one-hour return walk runs to a huge limestone cave (take a torch), or take the 1½-hour return track from Deliverance Cove to Castle Rock. Keep well away from the lower reef when there are heavy seas.

To the south is **Carterton**, one of a clutch of small rural towns punctuating SH2. It boasts by far the best hanging flower baskets of the lot, and adds a raft of good secondhand shops and some decent cafes to boot; don't pass through without stopping for a wander. There are also a couple of fine craft breweries in Carterton – ask at local i-SITEs for directions, or see the Wairarapa Visitor Guide.

★ Pukaha Mt Bruce National Wildlife Centre
WILDLIFE RESERVE

(06-375 8004; www.pukaha.org.nz; 85379 SH2, Masterton; adult/child/family $20/6/50, guided walks incl admission adult/child $45/22.50; 9am-4.30pm) About 30km north of Masterton, the 10-sq-km Pukaha Mt Bruce National Wildlife Centre is one of NZ's most successful wildlife and captive breeding centres. The scenic 1½-hour loop walk gives a good overview. There's also a kiwi house here and a series of aviaries for viewing other native birds. Tuatara are also on show, and the eels are fed daily at 1.30pm. Guided walks run daily and on Saturday nights – book in advance. Cafe and shop on-site.

Aratoi Wairarapa Museum of Art & History
MUSEUM

(06-370 0001; www.aratoi.co.nz; cnr Bruce & Dixon Sts, Masterton; admission by donation 10am-4.30pm) Hushed and refined, this small but splendid museum hosts an impressive program of exhibitions and events (and has a busy cafe and a shop).

Wool Shed
MUSEUM

(06-378 8008; www.thewoolshednz.com; 12 Dixon St, Masterton; adult/child/family $8/2/15; 10am-4pm) Occupying two historic woolsheds, this baaaa-loody marvellous little museum is dedicated to NZ's sheep-shearing and wool-production industries. Smell the lanolin! It's also a good spot to pick up a home-knitted hat.

🛏 Sleeping & Eating

Mawley Holiday Park
HOLIDAY PARK $

(06-378 6454; www.mawleypark.co.nz; 5 Oxford St, Masterton; unpowered/powered sites per 2 people $30/38, dm $25, cabins $60-70) An amenable, clean camping ground spread across the verdant banks of the Waipoua River just north of town. Shared backpacker cabins are BYO linen, or 'flashpacker'-style (linen supplied). And you can swim in the river!

★ Gladstone Inn
PUB FOOD $$

(06-372 7866; www.gladstoneinn.co.nz; 51 Gladstone Rd, Gladstone; pizza $16-18, mains $20-32; 11am-late) Gladstone, 18km south of Masterton, is less a town, more a state of mind. There's very little here except this classic old timber inn, haven to thirsty locals, bikers, Sunday drivers and lazy afternoon shandy sippers who hog the tables in the glorious garden bar. There's the odd crafty beer on tap, too. Ask for directions at Masterton i-SITE.

ⓘ Information

DOC Masterton Office (Department of Conservation; 06-377 0700; www.doc.govt.nz; 220 South Rd, Masterton; 9am-5pm Mon-Fri) Wairarapa-wide DOC information.

Masterton i-SITE (06-370 0900; www.wairarapanz.com; cnr Dixon & Bruce Sts, Masterton; 9am-5pm Mon-Fri, 10m-4pm Sat & Sun) Masterton i-SITE can sort you out with local information including a copy of the Wairarapa Visitor Guide, advice on accommodation, and directions to the Gladstone Inn.

WELLINGTON REGION MASTERTON & AROUND

Marlborough & Nelson

Best Places to Eat

➡ Arbour (p396)

➡ Hopgood's (p408)

➡ Green Dolphin (p402)

➡ Sans Souci Inn (p420)

➡ DeVille (p407)

Best Places to Sleep

➡ Hopewell (p392)

➡ Bay of Many Coves Resort (p391)

➡ Kaikoura Cottage Motels (p401)

➡ Adrift (p419)

➡ St Leonards (p395)

Why Go?

For many travellers, Marlborough and Nelson will be their introduction to what South Islanders refer to as the 'Mainland'. Having left windy Wellington, and made a white-knuckled crossing of Cook Strait, folk are often surprised to find the sun shining and the temperature 10°C warmer.

These top-of-the-South neighbours have much in common beyond an amenable climate: both boast renowned coastal holiday spots, particularly the Marlborough Sounds, Abel Tasman National Park and Kaikoura. There are two other national parks (Kahurangi and Nelson Lakes) amid more mountain ranges than you can poke a Leki-stick at.

And so it follows that these two regions have an abundance of produce, from game and seafood to summer fruits, and most famously the grapes that work their way into the wine glasses of the world's finest restaurants. Keep your penknife and picnic set at the ready.

When to Go

➡ The forecast is good: Marlborough and Nelson soak up some of New Zealand's sunniest weather, with January and February the warmest months when daytime temperatures average 22°C.

➡ July is the coldest, averaging 12°C. However, the top of the South sees some wonderful winter weather, with frosty mornings often giving way to sparklingly clear skies and T-shirt temperatures.

➡ The rumours are true: it *is* wetter and more windswept the closer you get to the West Coast.

➡ From around Christmas to mid-February, the top of the South teems with Kiwi holidaymakers, so plan ahead during this time and be prepared to jostle for position with a load of jandal-wearing families.

❶ Getting There & Away

Cook Strait can be crossed slowly and scenically on the ferries between Wellington and Picton, and swiftly on flights servicing key destinations.

InterCity is the major bus operator but there are also local shuttles. From October to May, KiwiRail's Coastal Pacific train takes the scenic route from Picton to Christchurch, via Blenheim and Kaikoura.

Renting a car is easy, with a slew of car-hire offices in Picton and depots throughout the region.

Popular coastal areas such as the Marlborough Sounds and Abel Tasman National Park are best navigated on foot or by kayak, with water-taxi services readily available to join the dots.

MARLBOROUGH REGION

Picton is the gateway to the South Island and the launching point for Marlborough Sounds exploration. A cork's pop south of Picton is Blenheim and its world-famous wineries, and further south still is Kaikoura, the whale-watching mecca.

History

Long before Abel Tasman sheltered on the east coast of D'Urville Island in 1642 (more than 100 years before James Cook blew through in 1770), Māori knew the Marlborough area as Te Tau Ihu o Te Waka a Māui (the prow of Māui's canoe). It was Cook who named Queen Charlotte Sound; his reports made the area the best-known sheltered anchorage in the southern hemisphere. In 1827 French navigator Jules Dumont d'Urville discovered the narrow strait now known as French Pass. His officers named the island just to the north in his honour. In the same year a whaling station was established at Te Awaiti in Tory Channel, which brought about the first permanent European settlement in the district.

❶ Getting There & Away

Air New Zealand (☑ 0800 747 000; www.airnewzealand.co.nz) has direct flights between Blenheim airport and Wellington, Auckland, and Christchurch, with onward connections. **Soundsair** (☑ 0800 505 005, 03-520 3080; www.soundsair.co.nz; 3 Auckland St) connects Blenheim with Wellington, Paraparaumu and Napier.

KiwiRail Scenic (☑ 0800 872 467; www.kiwirailscenic.co.nz) runs the Coastal Pacific service daily (October to May) each way between Picton and Christchurch via Blenheim and Kaikoura.

Buses serving Picton depart from the **Interislander terminal** (p387) or nearby **i-SITE** (p387).

InterCity (☑ 03-365 1113; www.intercity.co.nz) runs buses between Picton and Christchurch via Blenheim and Kaikoura, with connections to Dunedin, Queenstown and Invercargill. Services also run between Nelson and Picton, with connections to Motueka and the West Coast. At least one bus daily on each of these routes connects with a Wellington ferry service. **Naked Bus** (☑ 0900 625 33; www.nakedbus.com) runs south to Christchurch, Dunedin and Queenstown.

Picton

POP 2950

Half asleep in winter, but hyperactive in summer (with up to eight fully laden ferry arrivals per day), boaty Picton clusters around a deep gulch at the head of Queen Charlotte Sound. It's the main traveller port for the South Island, and the best base for tackling the Marlborough Sounds and Queen Charlotte Track. Over the last few years this little town has really bloomed, and offers visitors plenty of reason to linger even after the obvious attractions are knocked off the list.

⊙ Sights

Edwin Fox Maritime Museum MUSEUM
(www.edwinfoxsociety.co.nz; Dunbar Wharf; adult/child $15/5; ⊘9am-5pm) Purportedly the world's ninth-oldest surviving wooden ship, the *Edwin Fox* was built near Calcutta and

Marlborough & Nelson Highlights

1 **Kaikoura** (p398)
Getting up close to wildlife, including whale, seals, dolphins and albatrosses.

2 **Marlborough Wine Region** (p396) Nosing your way through the wineries.

3 **Queen Charlotte Track** (p390) Tramping or biking in the Marlborough Sounds.

4 **Great Taste Trail** (p409) Eating and drinking your way along this popular cycle trail.

5 **Abel Tasman National Park** (p414) Kayaking or tramping in this postcard-perfect park.

6 **Omaka Aviation Heritage Centre** (p393)

Getting blown away at one of NZ's best museums.

7 **Farewell Spit** (p421) Driving through a dunescape with gannets and godwits for company.

8 **Heaphy Track** (p422) Reaching the wild West Coast on foot, crossing through Kahurangi National Park.

launched in 1853. During its chequered career it carried troops to the Crimean War, convicts to Australia and immigrants to NZ. This museum has maritime exhibits, including the venerable old dear herself.

Picton Museum MUSEUM
(London Quay; adult/child $5/1; ⊙10am-4pm) If you dig local history – whaling, sailing and the 1964 Roller Skating Champs – this will float your boat. The photo displays are well worth a look, especially for five bucks.

🏃 Activities

The majority of activity happens around the Marlborough Sounds, but landlubbers will still find enough to occupy themselves.

The town has some very pleasant **walks**. A free i-SITE map details many of these, including an easy 1km track to **Bob's Bay**. The **Snout Track** (three hours return) continues along the ridge offering superb water views. Climbing a hill behind the town, the **Tirohanga Track** is a two-hour leg-stretching loop offering the best view in the house. For town explorations, hire bikes for the whole family from Wilderness Guides (388).

Nine Dives DIVING
(✆0800 934 837, 03-573 7199; www.ninedives. co.nz; trips $195-350) Offers dive trips around the Sounds taking in marine reserves and various wrecks including the *Mikhail Lermontov*, plus diver training. Snorkelling seal-swims also available ($150).

☞ Tours

Marlborough Tour Company TOUR
(✆0800 990 800, 03-577 9997; www.marlboroughtourcompany.co.nz; Town Wharf; adult/child $145/59; ⊙departs 1.30pm) Runs the 3½-hour 'Seafood Odyssea' cruise to a salmon farm, complete with an ocean bounty and sauvignon blanc tasting.

🛏 Sleeping

★ **Jugglers Rest** HOSTEL $
(✆03-573 5570; www.jugglersrest.com; 8 Canterbury St; sites from $20, dm $33, d $75-85; ⊙closed Jun-Sep; @🛜) ✐ Jocular hosts keep all their balls in the air at this well-run, ecofriendly, bunk-free backpackers. Peacefully located a 10-minute walk from town, or even less on a free bike. Cheery gardens are a good place to socialise with fellow travellers, especially during the occasional circus-skills shows.

Buccaneer Lodge LODGE $
(✆03-573 5002; www.buccaneerlodge.co.nz; 314 Waikawa Rd, Waikawa; s $90, d $99-124; 🛜) This Waikawa Bay lodge offers tidy, basic en suite rooms, many with expansive views of the Sounds from the 1st-floor balcony. Town transfers, bike hire and home-baked bread come courtesy of the kindly owners.

Tombstone Backpackers HOSTEL $
(✆C3-573 7116; www.tombstonebp.co.nz; 16 Gravesend Pl; dm $30-34, d with/without bathroom $87/30; @🛜) Rest in peace in a smart dorm, double room, or self-contained apartment ($118). Also on offer are a spa overlooking the harbour, free breakfast, a sunny reading room, table tennis, free internet, ferry pick-up and drop-off... The list goes on.

Sequoia Lodge Backpackers HOSTEL $
(✆C800 222 257, 03-573 8399; www.secuoialodge. co.nz; 3a Nelson Sq; dm $29-31, d with/without bathroom $84/74; 🛜) A well-managed backpackers in a colourful, high-ceilinged Victorian house. It's a little out of the centre, but has bonuses including free wi-fi, hammocks, barbecues, a hot tub and nightly chocolate pudding. Complimentary breakfast May to October.

Picton Top 10 Holiday Park HOLIDAY PARK $
(✆0800 277 444, 03-573 7212; www.pictontop10. co.nz; 70 Waikawa Rd; sites from $36, units $75-185; @🛜🏊) About 500m from town, this compact, well-kept park has plenty of lawn and picnic benches, plus crowd-pleasing facilities including a playground, barbecue area and swimming pool.

★ **Whatamonga Homestay** HOMESTAY $$
(✆03-573 7192; www.whsl.co.nz; 425 Port Underwood Rd; d incl breakfast $180; @🛜) Follow Waikawa Rd, which becomes Port Underwood Rd, for 8km and you'll bump into this classy waterside option – two self-contained units with king-sized beds and balconies with magic views. Two other rooms under the main house share a bathroom. Free kayaks, dinghies and fishing gear are available. Minimum two-night stay.

Harbour View Motel MOTEL $$
(✆03-573 6259, 0800 101 133; www.harbourviewpicton.co.nz; 30 Waikawa Rd; d $145-185; 🛜) Its elevated position means this motel commands good views of Picton's mast-filled harbour from its smart, self-contained studios with timber decks.

Picton

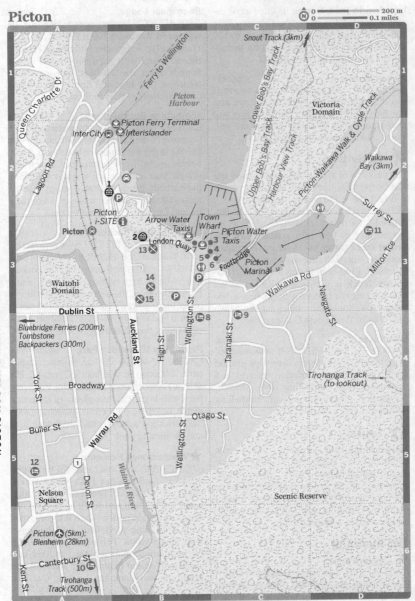

0 200 m
0 0.1 miles

MARLBOROUGH & NELSON PICTON

Snout Track (3km)

Picton
Harbour

Ferry to Wellington

Victoria
Domain

Lower Bob's Bay Track

Upper Bob's Bay Track

Harbour View Track

Picton-Waikawa Walk & Cycle Track

Waikawa
Bay (3km)

Surrey St

Picton Ferry Terminal
InterCity Interislander

1

Picton
i-SITE

Picton

Arrow Water
Taxis

Town
Wharf

Picton Water
Taxis

Footbridge

Picton
Marina

Milton Tce

11

2

London Quay

13

3
4
5
6
7

Waikawa Rd

Newgate St

Waitohi
Domain

14

15

Dublin St

Bluebridge Ferries (200m);
Tombstone
Backpackers (300m)

High St

Wellington St

8

Taranaki St

9

Auckland St

Tirohanga Track
(to lookout)

York St

Broadway

Buller St

Wairau Rd

Devon St

Otago St

Wellington St

Waitohi River

Scenic Reserve

12

Nelson
Square

Picton (5km);
Blenheim (28km)

Kent St

Canterbury St

10

Tirohanga
Track (500m)

Gables B&B B&B $$

(03-573 6772; www.thegables.co.nz; 20 Waikawa Rd; s $100, d $140-170, units $155-175; @) This historic B&B (once home to Picton's mayor) has three individually styled rooms in the main house and two homely self-contained units out the back. Lovely hosts show good humour (ask about the Muffin Club) and provide excellent local advice.

Picton

✖ Eating

Gusto CAFE $
(33 High St; meals $11-21; ⊙7.30am-2.30pm; ⊘)
This friendly and hard-working joint does
beaut breakfasts including first-class salmon-
scrambled eggs and a 'Morning Glory' fry-up
worth the calories. Lunch options may include local mussels or a steak sandwich.

Picton Village Bakkerij BAKERY $
(cnr Auckland & Dublin Sts; bakery items $2-8;
⊙6am-4pm Mon-Fri, to 3.30pm Sat; ⊘) Dutch
owners bake trays of European goodies here,
including interesting breads, filled rolls, cakes
and custardy, tarty treats. An excellent stop
before or after the ferry, or to stock a packed
lunch.

Café Cortado CAFE $$
(www.cortado.co.nz; cnr High St & London Quay;
mains $16-34; ⊙8am-late) A pleasant corner
cafe and bar with sneaky views of the har-
bour through the foreshore's pohutukawa
and palms. This consistent performer turns
out fish dishes, homemade cheeseburgers
and decent pizza.

ⓘ Information

Picton i-SITE (⌨03-520 3113; www.marlbor-
oughnz.com; Foreshore; ⊙8am-5pm Mon-Fri,
to 4pm Sat & Sun) All vital tourist guff includ-
ing maps, Queen Charlotte Track information,
lockers and transport bookings. Dedicated
Department of Conservation (DOC) counter.

ⓘ Getting There & Away

AIR

Soundsair (p383) flies between Picton and
Wellington (adult/child from $99/89); a shuttle
bus to/from the airstrip at Koromiko is available.

BOAT

There are two operators crossing Cook Strait
between Picton and Wellington, and although all
ferries leave from more or less the same place,
each has its own terminal. The main transport hub
(with car-rental depots) is at the Interislander Ter-
minal, which also has a cafe and internet facilities.

Bluebridge Ferries (⌨0800 844 844, 04-471
6188; www.bluebridge.co.nz; adult/child from
$51/26; ☎) Crossings take 3½ hours, and the
company runs up to four sailings in each di-
rection daily. Cars and campervans from $120,
motorbikes $51, bicycles $10. The sleeper
service arrives in Picton at 6am.

Interislander (⌨0800 802 802; www.inter
islander.co.nz; Interislander Ferry Terminal,
Auckland St; adult/child $55/28) Crossings
take at east three hours 10 minutes; up to four
sailings in each direction daily. Cars are priced
from $121, campervans (up to 5.5m) from $153,
motorbikes $56, bicycles $15.

BUS

Buses serving Picton depart from the Inter-
islander ferry terminal or the nearby i-SITE.

InterCity (⌨03-365 1113; www.intercity.co.nz;
outside Interislander Ferry Terminal, Auckland
St) runs south to Christchurch twice daily (5½
hours) via Blenheim (30 minutes) and Kaikoura
(2½ hours), with connections to Dunedin,
Queenstown and Invercargill. Services also run
to/from Nelson (2¼ hours), with connections to
Motueka and the West Coast. At least one bus
daily on each of these routes connects with a
Wellington ferry service.

Smaller shuttles running to Christchurch and
Nelson include **Atomic Shuttles** (⌨03-349
0697, 0508 108 359; www.atomictravel.co.nz).

TRAIN

KiwiRail Scenic (p383) runs the Coastal
Pacific service daily (October to May) each
way between Picton and Christchurch via
Blenheim and Kaikoura (and via 22 tunnels and
175 bridges), departing Picton at 1.15pm and
Christchurch at 7am. Adult one-way Picton–
Christchurch fares start at $79. The service
connects with the Interislander ferry (p387).

ⓘ Getting Around

Shuttle services around town and beyond are
offered by **A1 Picton Shuttles** (⌨022 018 8472;
www.a1pictonshuttles.co.nz).

Renting a car in Picton is easy and competitively
priced (as low as $40 per day), with numerous

MĀORI NZ: MARLBOROUGH & NELSON

While Māori culture on the South Island is much less evident than in the north, it can still be found in pockets, particularly around Kaikoura, which is rich in Māori history. **Maori Tours Kaikoura** (p399) provide an illuminating historical and contemporary insight into Māoridom.

rental companies based at the Interislander ferry terminal and many others within a short walk. **Ace** (☑ 03-573 8939; www.acerentalcars. co.nz; Interislander Ferry Terminal) and **Omega** (☑ 03-573 5580; www.omegarentalcars.com; 1 Lagoon Rd) are reliable local operators. Most agencies allow drop-offs in Christchurch; if you're planning to drive to the North Island, most companies suggest you leave your car at Picton and pick up another one in Wellington after crossing Cook Strait.

Marlborough Sounds

The Marlborough Sounds are a maze of peaks, bays, beaches and watery reaches, formed when the sea flooded deep river valleys after the last ice age. They are very convoluted: Pelorus Sound, for example, is 42km long but has 379km of shoreline.

Many spectacular locations can be reached by car. The wiggly 35km drive along **Queen Charlotte Drive** from Picton to Havelock is a great Sounds snapshot, but if you have a spare day, head out to **French Pass** (or even **D'Urville Island**) for some big-picture framing of the Outer Sounds. Roads are predominantly narrow and occasionally unsealed; allow plenty of driving time and keep your wits about you.

Sounds travel is invariably quicker by boat (for example, Punga Cove from Picton by car takes two to three hours, but just 45 minutes by boat). Fortunately, an armada of vessels offer scheduled and on-demand boat services, with the bulk operating out of Picton for the Queen Charlotte Sound, and some from Havelock for Kenepuru and Pelorus Sounds.

There are loads of walking, kayaking and biking opportunities, but there's diving as well – notably the wreck of the *Mikhail Lermontov*, a Russian cruise ship that sank in Port Gore in 1986.

◎ Sights

Motuara Island WILDLIFE RESERVE
(www.doc.govt.nz; Queen Charlotte Sound) 🍃
This DOC-managed, predator-free island reserve is chock-full of rare NZ birds including Okarito kiwi (rowi), native pigeons (kereru), saddleback (tieke) and King Shags. You can get here with water taxi and tour operators working out of Picton.

☞ Tours

From Picton

★**Wilderness Guides** TOUR
(☑ 0800 266 266, 03-573 5432; www.wilderness guidesnz.com; Town Wharf; 1-day guided trips from $130, kayak/bike hire per day $60) Host of the popular and flexible one- to three-day 'multisport' trips (kayak/walk/cycle) plus many other guided and independent biking, tramping and kayaking tours, including a remote Ship Cove paddle. Mountain bikes and kayaks for hire, too.

Cougar Line TOUR
(☑ 0800 504 090, 03-573 7925; www.cougarline. co.nz; Town Wharf; track round-trips $105, full-day tours from $85) Queen Charlotte Track transport, plus various half- and full-day cruise/ walk trips, including the rather special (and flexible) eco-cruise to Motuara Island and a day walk from Resolution Bay to Furneaux Lodge.

Beachcomber Cruises TOUR
(☑ 0800 624 526, 03-573 6175; www.beachcomber cruises.co.nz; Town Wharf, Picton; mail runs $97, cruises from $69, track round-trips $99) Two- to eight-hour cruise adventures, including the classic 'Magic Mail Run', plus walking, biking and resort lunch options and round-trip track transport.

Marlborough Sounds
Adventure Company TOUR
(☑ 0800 283 283, 03-573 6078; www.marlborough sounds.co.nz; Town Wharf; half- to 3-day guided packages $95-595, kayak hire per half-day from $40) Bike-walk-kayak trips, with options to suit every inclination and duration. A top day option is the kayak and hike ($175). Bikes, kayaks, stand-up paddle boards and camping equipment also available.

From Anakiwa

Sea Kayak Adventures KAYAKING, BIKING
(☑ 03-574 2765, 0800 262 5492; www.nzseakay aking.com; cnr Queen Charlotte Dr & Anakiwa Rd; half-/1-day guided paddles $85/125) Guided and

Marlborough Sounds

'guided then go' kayaking with bike/hike options around Queen Charlotte, Kenepuru and Pelorus Sounds. Also offers kayak and mountain-bike rental (half-/full-day $40/60).

From Havelock

Pelorus Mail Boat
CRUISE

(☑ 03-574 1088; www.themailboat.co.nz; Jetty 1, Havelock Marina; adult/child $128/free; ☺ departs 9.30am Tue, Thu & Fri) Popular full-day boat cruise through the far reaches of Pelorus Sound on a genuine NZ Post delivery run. Bookings essential; BYO lunch. Picton and Blenheim pick-up and drop-off available.

Waterways Boating Safaris
BOATING

(☑ 03-574 1372; www.waterways.co.nz; 745 Keneperu Rd; half-/full-day $110/150) Be guided around Kenepuru Sound while piloting your own zippy boat. A fun way to get out on the water, see the scenery and learn about the area's ecology and history. BYO lunch.

Greenshell Mussel Cruise
CRUISE

(☑ 03-577 9997, 0800 990 800; www.marlborough tourcompany.co.nz; Havelock Marina; adult/child $125/45; ☺ departs 1.30pm) Three-hour cruise to mussel in on Kenepuru's aquaculture. Includes a tasting of steamed mussels and a glass of wine. Bookings essential.

🛏 Sleeping

Some Sounds sleeping options are accessible only by boat and are deliciously isolated, but the most popular are those on (or just off) the Queen Charlotte Track. Some places close over winter; call ahead to check.

There are over 30 DOC camping grounds throughout the Sounds (many accessible only by boat), providing water and toilet facilities but not much else.

Ask at Picton i-SITE (p387) about local bachs for rent, of which there are many.

Marlborough Sounds

❶ Getting There & Away

The Marlborough Sounds are most commonly explored from Picton, where boat operators congregate at the centrally located Town Wharf. They offer everything from lodge transfers to cruises taking in sites such as **Ship Cove** and **Motuara Island** bird sanctuary, to round-trip **Queen Charlotte Track** transport and pack transfers that allow trampers to walk without a heavy burden. Bikes and kayaks can also be transported.

Arrow Water Taxis (☑ 027 444 4689, 03-573 8229; www.arrowwatertaxis.co.nz; Town Wharf, Picton) Pretty much anywhere, on demand, for groups of four or more.

Float Plane (☑ 021 704 248, 03-573 9012; www.nz-scenic-flights.co.nz; Ferry Terminal, Picton; flights from $110) Offers Queen Charlotte Track and Sounds accommodation transfers and scenic flights, plus flights and trips to Nelson, Abel Tasman National Park and across to Wellington.

Kenepuru Water Taxi (☑ 021 132 3261, 03-573 4344; www.kenepuru.co.nz; 7170 Kenepuru Rd, Raetihi) Taxi and sightseeing trips around Kenepuru Sound, on demand.

Pelorus Sound Water Taxi (☑ 0508 4283 5625, 027 444 2852; www.pelorussoundwatertaxis.co.nz; Pier C, Havelock Marina) Taxi and sightseeing trips from Havelock, around Pelorus and Kenepuru Sounds, on demand.

Picton Water Taxis (☑ 03-573 7853, 027 227 0284; www.pictonwatertaxis.co.nz; The Waterfront, cnr London Quay & Wellington St, Picton) Water taxi and sightseeing trips around Queen Charlotte, on demand.

Queen Charlotte Track

One of NZ's classic walks – and now one of its Great Rides, too – the meandering, 70km Queen Charlotte Track offers gorgeous coastal scenery on its way from historic Ship Cove to Anakiwa, passing through a mixture of privately owned land and DOC reserves. Access depends on the cooperation of local landowners; respect their property by utilising designated campsites and toilets, and carrying out your rubbish. Your purchase of the **Track Pass** ($10 to $18), available from the i-SITE and track-related businesses, provides the co-op with the means to maintain and enhance the experience for all.

Activities

Queen Charlotte is a well-defined track, suitable for people of average fitness. Numerous boat and tour operators service the track, allowing you to tramp the whole three- to five-day journey, or to start and finish where you like, on foot or by kayak or bike. We're talking mountain biking here, and a whole lot of fun for fit, competent off-roaders. Part of the track is off-limits to cyclists from 1 December to the end of February, but there is still good riding to be had during this time.

Ship Cove is the usual (and recommended) starting point – mainly because it's easier to arrange a boat from Picton to Ship Cove than vice versa – but the track can be started from Anakiwa. There's a public phone at Anakiwa but not at Ship Cove.

Estimated walk times:

TRACK SECTION	DISTANCE (KM)	DURATION (HR)
Ship Cove to Resolution Bay	4.5	1½-2
Resolution Bay to head of Endeavour Inlet	10.5	2½-3
Endeavour Inlet to Camp Bay/Punga Cove	12	3-4
Camp Bay/Punga Cove to Torea Saddle/Portage	24	6-8
Torea Saddle/Portage to Te Mahia Saddle	7.5	3-4
Te Mahia Saddle to Anakiwa	12.5	3-4

🛏 Sleeping

The beauty of the Queen Charlotte Track is that there are plenty of great day-trip options, allowing you to base yourself in Picton. However, there is also plenty of accommodation nicely spaced along the way, and boat operators will transport your luggage along the track for you.

At the self-sufficient end of the scale are six DOC campsites: **Schoolhouse Bay** (www.doc.govt.nz; adult/child $6/3), **Camp Bay** (www.doc.govt.nz; adult/child $6/3), **Bay of Many Coves** (www.doc.govt.nz; adult/child $6/3), **Black Rock** (www.doc.govt.nz; adult/child $6/3), **Cowshed Bay** (www.coc.govt.nz adult/child $10/5) and **Davies Bay** (www.doc.govt.nz; adult/child $6/3). All have toilets and a water supply but no cooking facilities. There's also a variety of resorts, lodges, backpackers and guesthouses. Unless you're camping, it pays to book your accommodation waaay in advance, especially in summer.

Smiths Farm Holiday Park   HOLIDAY PARK $
(☑ 03-574 2806; www.smithsfarm.co.nz; 1419 Queen Charlotte Dr, Linkwater; campsites from $16 per person, cabins $60, units $110-130; @ 🐾) 🐾 Located on the aptly named Linkwater flat between Queen Charlotte and Pelorus, friendly Smiths makes a handy base camp for the track and beyond. Well-kept cabins and motel units face out onto the bushy hillside, while livestock nibble around the lush camping lawns. Short walks extend to a waterfall and magical glowworm dell.

Mistletoe Bay   HOLIDAY PARK $
(☑ 03-573 4048; www.mistletoebay.co.nz; Onahau Bay; campsites adult/child $16/10, dm/d $30/70, linen $7.50; 🐾) 🐾 Surrounded by bushy hills, Mistletoe Bay offers attractive camping with no-frills facilities. There are eight modern cabins ($140) sleeping up to six, plus a bunkhouse. Environmental sustainability abounds, as does the opportunity to jump off the jetty, kayak in the bay, or tramp the Queen Charlotte Track.

⭐ Te Mahia Bay Resort   RESORT $$
(☑ 03-573 4089; www.temahia.co.nz; 63 Te Mahia Rd; d $160-258; 🐾) This lovely low-key resort is within cooee of the Queen Charlotte Track in a picturesque bay on Kenepuru Sound. It has a range of delightful rooms-with-a-view, our pick of which are the great-value heritage units. The on-site shop has precooked meals, pizza, cakes, coffee and camping supplies (wine!), plus there is kayak hire and massage.

Lochmara Lodge   RESORT $$
(☑ 0800 562 462, 03-573 4554; www.lochmara lodge.co.nz; Lochmara Bay; units $99-300; 🐾) 🐾 This arty, eco-retreat can be reached via the Queen Charlotte Track or direct from Picton aboard the lodge's water taxi ($30 one-way). There are en suite doubles, units and chalets, all set in lush surroundings, a fully licensed cafe and restaurant, plus a bathhouse where you can indulge in a spa or massage.

Anakiwa 401   HOSTEL $$
(☑ 03-574 1388; www.anakiwa401.co.nz; 401 Anakiwa Rd; s/q $75/180, d $100-140; 🐾) At the southern end of the track, this former schoolhouse is a soothing spot to rest and reflect. There are two doubles (one with en suite), one twin and a beachy self-contained unit. Jocular owners will have you jumping off the jetty for joy and imbibing espresso and ice cream (hallelujah) from their little green caravan (open summer afternoons). Free bikes and kayaks.

⭐ Bay of Many Coves Resort   RESORT $$$
(☑ 0800 579 9771, 03-579 9771; www.bayofmany coves.co.nz; Bay of Many Coves; 1-/2-/3-bedroom apt $710/930/1100; 🐾🏊) These schmick and secluded apartments feature all mod cons and private balconies overlooking the water. As well as upmarket cuisine, there are various indulgences such as massage, a spa and a hot tub. Kayaking and bush walks are also on the cards, as are adventures in the Sounds organised by the charming, hands-on owners and staff.

Mahana Lodge   LODGE $$$
(☑ 03-579 3373; www.mahanalodge.co.nz; Camp Bay, Endeavour Inlet; d $210; ⏰ closed Jun-Aug) This beautiful property features a pretty waterside lawn and purpose-built lodge with four en suite doubles. Ecofriendly initiatives include bush regeneration, pest trapping and an organic veggie garden. In fact, feel-good factors abound: free kayaks, home baking and a blooming conservatory where prearranged evening meals are served (three courses $55).

Punga Cove Resort   RESORT $$$
(☑ 03-579 8561; www.pungacove.co.nz; Endeavour Inlet; units $275-450; @ 🐾🏊) A rustic, charming resort offering self-contained studios, A-frame chalets and a lodge (sleeping up to seven), most with sweeping sea views. The backpackers is basic (single/double $58/116) but Punga's location atones. Ample activities (pool, spa, games and kayaks), plus a restaurant and boat-shed bar/cafe serving decent local beers and $26 pizza.

ℹ Information

The best place to get track information and advice is Picton **i-SITE** (p387), which also handles bookings for transport and accommodation. Also see the Queen Charlotte Track website (www.qctrack.co.nz).

ℹ Getting There & Away

Picton water taxis can drop you off and pick you up at numerous locations along the track.

Kenepuru & Pelorus Sounds

Kenepuru and Pelorus Sounds, to the west of Queen Charlotte Sound, are less populous and therefore offer fewer traveller services, including transport. There's some cracking scenery, however, and those with time to spare will be well rewarded by their explorations.

Havelock is the hub of this area, the western bookend of the 35km Queen Charlotte Drive (Picton being the eastern one) and the self-proclaimed 'Greenshell Mussel Capital of the World'. While hardly the most rock-and-roll of NZ towns, Havelock offers most necessities, including accommodation, fuel and food.

◉ Sights

If a stroll through the streets of Havelock leaves you thinking that there *must* be more to this area, you're right – and to get a taste of it you need go no further than the **Cullen Point Lookout**, a 10-minute drive from Havelock along the Queen Charlotte Drive. A short walk leads up and around a headland overlooking Havelock, the surrounding valleys and Pelorus Sound.

Information on local sites and activities can be found at the Havelock i-SITE (p393), which shares its home with the Eyes On Nature museum, chock-full of frighteningly lifelike, full-size replicas of birds, fish and other critters.

And of course, there's plenty to see and do exploring the Marlborough Sounds (p388) themselves.

🏃 Activities

Pelorus Eco Adventures   KAYAKING
(☑0800 252 663, 03-574 2212; www.kayak-newzealand.com; Blue Moon Lodge, 48 Main Rd, Havelock; per person $175) Float in an inflatable kayak on scenic Pelorus River, star of the barrel scene in *The Hobbit*. Wend your

way down exhilarating rapids, through crystal-clear pools and past native forest and waterfalls. No experience required. Minimum two people.

Nydia Track   TRAMPING
(www.doc.govt.nz) The Nydia Track (27km, 10 hours) starts at Kaiuma Bay and ends at Duncan Bay (or vice versa). You'll need water and road transport to complete the journey; Havelock's Blue Moon Lodge runs a shuttle to Duncan Bay.

Around halfway along is beautiful **Nydia Bay**, where there's a **DOC campsite** (www.doc.govt.nz; adult/child $6/3) and **Nydia Lodge** (☑03-520 3002; www.doc.govt.nz; Nydia Bay; dm $15, minimum charge $60), an unhosted 50-bed lodge. Also in Nydia Bay, **On the Track Lodge** (☑03-579 8411; www.nydiatrack.org.nz; Nydia Bay; dm $40, s $80-100, d $130-160) 🍃 is a tranquil, eco-focused affair offering everything from packed lunches to evening meals and a hot tub.

🛏 Sleeping

There's plenty of accommodation around Kenepuru and Pelorus, much of which is accessible off the Queen Charlotte Track. There are also some picturesque DOC campgrounds (most full to bursting in January), a few remote lodges and the very handy Smiths Farm (p391) holiday park at Linkwater, the crossroads for Queen Charlotte and Kenepuru, where you'll find a petrol station with snacks. Havelock also has a couple of decent offerings.

★**Hopewell**   LODGE $
(☑03-573 4341; www.hopewell.co.nz; 7204 Kenepuru Rd, Double Bay; dm/cottages from $40/195, d with/without bathroom from $140/105; @🐾🛜) Beloved of travellers from near and far, remote Hopewell sits waterside surrounded by native bush. Savour the long, winding drive to get there, or take a water taxi from Te Mahia ($20). Stay at least a couple of days, so you can chill out or enjoy the roll-call of activities: mountain biking, kayaking, sailing, fishing, eating gourmet pizza, soaking in the outdoor hot tub, and more.

Blue Moon Lodge   HOSTEL $
(☑03-574 2212, 0800 252 663; www.bluemoonhavelock.co.nz; 48 Main Rd, Havelock; dm $33, r with/without bathroom from $96/82; @🛜) 🍃 This pleasant and relaxed lodge has homely rooms in the main house, a spa family unit ($160), and cabins and a bunkhouse in the

yard. Notable features include a sunny barbecue deck, inflatable kayak trips on the Pelorus River, and Nydia Track transport.

Havelock Garden Motels
MOTEL $$

(03-574 2387; www.gardenmotels.com; 71 Main Rd, Havelock; d $125-160;) Set in a large, graceful garden complete with dear old trees and blooms galore, these 1960s units have been tastefully revamped to offer homely comforts. Local activities are happily booked for you.

ℹ Information

Havelock i-SITE (03-577 8080; www. pelorusnz.co.nz; 61 Main Rd, Havelock; ⊙9am-5pm summer only) This helpful wee visitor centre shares its home with the Eyes On Nature museum, chock-full of frighteningly lifelike, full-size replicas of birds, fish and other critters.

ℹ Getting There & Away

InterCity (p383) runs daily from Picton to Havelock via Blenheim (one hour), and from Havelock to Nelson (1¼ hours). **Atomic Shuttles** (p387) plies the same run. Buses depart from near the **Havelock i-SITE**.

Blenheim

POP 30,600

Blenheim is an agricultural town 29km south of Picton on the pretty Wairau Plains between the Wither Hills and the Richmond Ranges. The last decade or so has seen town beautification projects, the maturation of the wine industry and the addition of a landmark museum significantly increase the town's appeal to visitors.

◉ Sights

★**Omaka Aviation Heritage Centre**
MUSEUM

(03-579 1305; www.omaka.org.nz 79 Aerodrome Rd; adult/child $30/12, family from $45; ⊙9am-5pm Dec-Mar, 10am-4pm Apr-Nov) This exceptionally brilliant museum houses film-director Peter Jackson's collection of original and replica Great War aircraft, brought to life in a series of dioramas that depict dramatic wartime scenes, such as the death of the Red Baron. A new wing houses Dangerous Skies, a WW2 collection. Vintage biplane flights are available (20 minutes, $390 for two people).

A cafe and shop are on-site, and next door is **Omaka Classic Cars** (03-577 9419;

PELORUS BRIDGE

A peeky pocket of deep, green forest tucked between paddocks of bog-standard pasture, 18km west of Havelock, this scenic reserve contains one of the last stands of river-flat forest in Marlborough. It survived only because a town planned in 1865 didn't get off the ground by 1912, by which time obliterative logging made this little remnant look precious. Visitors can explore its many tracks, admire the historic bridge, take a dip in the limpid Pelorus River (alluring enough to star in Peter Jackson's *The Hobbit*), and partake in some home baking at the cafe. The fortunate few can stay overnight in DOC's small but perfectly formed **Pelorus Bridge Campground** (03-571 6019; www.doc.govt.nz; Pelorus Bridge, SH6; unpowered/powered sites per person $15/7.50), with its snazzy facilities building. Come sundown keep an eye out for long-tailed bats – the reserve is home to one of the last remaining populations in Marlborough.

---

www.omakaclassiccars.co.nz; adult/child $10/free; ⊙10am-4pm), which houses more than 100 vehicles dating from the '50s to the '80s.

Pollard Park
PARK

(Parker St) Ten minutes' walk from town, this 25-hectare park boasts beautiful blooming and scented gardens, a playground, tennis courts, croquet and a nine-hole golf course. It's pretty as a picture when lit up on summer evenings. Five minutes away, on the way to or from town, is the extensive **Taylor River Reserve**, a lovely place for a stroll.

Marlborough Museum
MUSEUM

(03-578 1712; www.marlboroughmuseum.org. nz; 26 Arthur Baker Pl, off New Renwick Rd; adult/child $10/5; ⊙10am-4pm) Besides a replica street-scene, vintage mechanicals and well-presented historical displays, there's the *Wine Exhibition*, for those looking to cap off their vineyard experiences.

🏃 Activities

★**Driftwood Eco-Tours**
KAYAKING, ECOTOUR

(03-577 7651; www.driftwoodecotours.co.nz; 749 Dillons Point Rd; kayak tours $70-180, 4WD tours for 2/3 people from $440/550) Go on a kayak or 4WD tour with passionate locals Will and

Rose for fascinating tours on and around the ecologically and historically significant Wairau Lagoon, just 10 minute' drive from Blenheim. Rare birds and the muppetty Royal Spoonbill may well be spotted. The self-contained 'retreat' offers accommodation for up to four people (double/quad $190/310; breakfast extra $15 per person) next to the Opawa River.

Wither Hills Farm Park WALKING
In a town as flat as a pancake, this hilly 11-sq-km park provides welcome relief, offering over 60km of walking and mountain-biking trails with grand views across the Wairau Valley and out to Cloudy Bay. Pick up a map from the i-SITE or check the information panels at the many entrances including Redwood St and Taylor Pass Rd.

High Country Horse Treks HORSE RIDING
(☑03-577 9424; www.high-horse.co.nz; 961 Taylor Pass Rd; 1-2hr treks $60-100) These animal-mad folks run horse treks for all abilities from their base 11km southwest of town (call for directions).

Tours

Wine tours are generally conducted in a minibus, last between four and seven hours, take in four to seven wineries and range in price from $65 to $95 (with a few grand tours up to around $200 for the day, including a winery lunch).

Highlight Wine Tours TOUR
(☑03-577 9046, 027 434 6451; www.highlightwine tours.co.nz) Visit a chocolate factory, too. Custom tours available.

Bubbly Grape Wine Tours TOUR
(☑027 672 2195, 0800 228 2253; www.bubbly grape.co.nz) Three different tours including a gourmet lunch option.

Sounds Connection TOUR
(☑03-573 8843, 0800 742 866; www.sounds connection.co.nz) This operator partners up with **Herzog Winery** (☑03-572 8770; www.herzog.co.nz; 81 Jefferies Rd; mains $24-36; ⊗12-3pm & 6-9pm Wed-Sun) for a wine-and-food-matched lunch.

Bike2Wine TOUR
(☑03-572 8458, 0800 653 262; www.bike2wine.co.nz; 9 Wilson St, Renwick; standard/tandem per day $30/60, pick ups from $10) An alternative to the usual minibus tours – get around the grapes on two wheels. This operator offers self-guided, fully geared and supported tours.

✦ Festivals & Events

Marlborough Wine Festival FOOD, WINE
(www.wine-marlborough-festival.co.nz; tickets $57; ⊗mid-Feb) Held at Brancott Vineyard (p396), this is an extravaganza of local wine, fine food and entertainment. Book accommodation well in advance.

Sleeping

Blenheim's budget beds fill with long-stay seasonal workers; hostels will help find work and offer weekly rates. Numerous midrange motels can be found on Middle Renwick Rd west of the town centre, and SH1 towards Christchurch.

Central Blenheim

Grapevine Backpackers HOSTEL $
(☑03-578 6062; www.thegrapevine.co.nz; 29 Park Tce; dm $25-26, d $60-70, tr $84-90; ⊛) Located inside an old maternity home a 10-minute walk from the town centre, Grapevine has respectable rooms set aside for travellers. The kitchen is tight, but offset by free canoes and a peaceful barbecue deck by the Opawa River. Bike hire is $25 per day.

Blenheim Top 10 Holiday Park HOLIDAY PARK $
(☑03-578 3667, 0800 268 666; www.blenheim top10.co.nz; 78 Grove Rd; sites $45, cabins $80-92, units & motel $135-145; @⊛⊜) Ten minutes' walk to town, this holiday park spreads out under and alongside the main road bridge over the Opawa River. Ask for the quietest spot available. Cabins and units are tidy but plain-Jane, set in a sea of asphalt. Funtime diversions include a spa, a pool, a playground and bike hire.

171 on High MOTEL $$
(☑0800 587 856, 03-579 5098; www.171onhighmotel.co.nz; 171 High St; d $145-185; ⊛) A welcoming option close to town, these tasteful, splash-o-colour studios and apartments are bright and breezy in the daytime, warm and shimmery in the evening. Expect a wide complement of facilities and 'extra mile' service.

Lugano Motorlodge MOTEL $$
(☑03-577 8808, 0800 584 266; www.lugano.co.nz; 91 High St; d $140-155; ⊛) In a prime location opposite pretty Seymour Sq and a two-minute walk to the centre of town, this is a beige but smart and upmarket motel complex with modern conveniences. Ask about the end unit with two balconies, or at least plump for upstairs. Hush glass mutes the main-road traffic noise.

Marlborough Wine Region

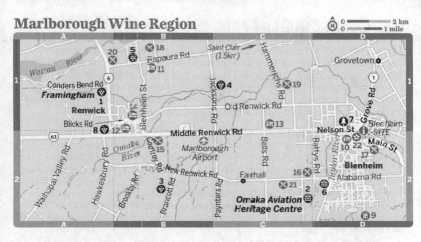

Marlborough Wine Region

MARLBOROUGH & NELSON BLENHEIM

Wine Region

Watson's Way Lodge LODGE $

(📞03-572 8228; www.watsonswaylodge.com; 56 High St, Renwick; campervans per person $18, d & tw $98; ⊗closed Aug-Sep; @🐾) This traveller-focused lodge has spick-and-span en suite rooms in a sweetly converted bungalow with a full kitchen and comfy lounge. There are also spacious leafy gardens dotted with fruit trees and hammocks, an outdoor claw-foot bath, bikes for hire (guest/public rate $18/28 per day) and local information aplenty.

★St Leonards COTTAGES $$

(📞03-577 8328; www.stleonards.co.nz; 18 St Leonards Rd, Blenheim; d incl breakfast $125-320; 🐾🐾🐾) Tucked into the 4.5-acre grounds of an 1886 homestead, these five stylish and rustic cottages offer privacy and a reason to stay put. Each is unique in its layout and perspective on the gardens and vines. Our pick is the capacious and cosy Woolshed, exuding agricultural chic. Resident sheep, chickens and deer await your attention.

Olde Mill House B&B $$

(📞03-572 8458; www.oldemillhouse.co.nz; 9 Wilson St, Renwick; d $160; 🐾) On an elevated section in otherwise flat Renwick, this charming old house is a treat. Dyed-in-the-wool local hosts run a welcoming B&B, with stately decor, and home-grown fruit and homemade goodies for breakfast. Free bikes, an outdoor spa and gardens make this a tiptop choice in the heart of the wine country.

MARLBOROUGH WINERIES

Marlborough is NZ's vinous colossus, producing around three-quarters of the country's wine. At last count, there were 229 sq km of vines planted – that's approximately 26,500 rugby pitches! Sunny days and cool nights create the perfect conditions for cool-climate grapes: world-famous sauvignon blanc, top-notch pinot noir, and notable chardonnay, riesling, gewürztraminer, pinot gris and bubbly. Drifting between tasting rooms and dining amongst the vines is a quintessential South Island experience.

A Taste of the Tastings

Around 35 wineries are open to the public. Our picks of the bunch provide a range of high-quality cellar-door experiences, with most being open from around 10.30am till 4.30pm (some scale back operations in winter). Wineries may charge a small fee for tasting, normally refunded if you purchase a bottle. Pick up a copy of the *Marlborough Wine Trail* map from **Blenheim i-SITE** (p397), also available online at www.wine-marlborough. co.nz. If your time is limited, pop into **Wino's** (www.winos.co.nz; 49 Grove Rd; ⊙10am-7pm Sun-Thu, to 8pm Fri & Sat) in Blenheim, a sterling one-stop shop for some of Marlborough's finer and less common drops.

Auntsfield Estate (☑03-578 0622; www.auntsfield.co.nz; 270 Paynters Rd; ⊙11am-4.30pm Mon-Fri summer only)

Bladen (www.bladen.co.nz; 83 Conders Bend Rd; ⊙11am-4.30pm)

Brancott Estate Heritage Centre (www.brancottestate.com; 180 Brancott Rd; ⊙10am-4.30pm)

Clos Henri Vineyard (www.clos-henri.com; 639 State Hwy 63, RD1; ⊙10am-4pm Mon-Fri summer only)

Cloudy Bay (www.cloudybay.co.nz; 230 Jacksons Rd, Blenheim; ⊙10am-4pm) 🌿

Forrest (www.forrest.co.nz; 19 Blicks Rd; ⊙10am-4.30pm)

Framingham (www.framingham.co.nz; 19 Conders Bend Rd, Renwick; ⊙10.30am-4.30pm) 🌿

Huia (www.huia.net.nz; 22 Boyces Rd, Blenheim; ⊙10am–5pm Oct-May) 🌿

Saint Clair Estate (www.saintclair.co.nz; 13 Selmes Rd, Rapaura; ⊙9am-5pm)

Marlborough Vintners Hotel　　HOTEL $$$
(☑0800 684 190, 03-572 5094; www.mvh.co.nz; 190 Rapaura Rd, Blenheim; d $190-325; 🛜) 🌿 Sixteen architecturally designed suites make the most of valley views and boast wet-room bathrooms and abstract art. The stylish reception building has a bar and restaurant opening out on to a cherry orchard and organic veggie garden.

✕ Eating & Drinking

★ Burleigh　　DELI $
(☑03-579 2531; 72 New Renwick Rd, Burleigh; pies $6; ⊙7.30am-3pm Mon-Fri, 9am-1pm Sat) The humble pie rises to stratospheric heights at this fabulous deli; try the sweet pork-belly or savoury steak and blue cheese, or perhaps both. Fresh-filled baguettes, local sausage, French cheeses and great coffee also make tempting appearances. Avoid the lunchtime rush.

Gramado's　　BRAZILIAN
(☑03-579 1192; www.gramadosrestaurant.com; 74 Main St, Blenheim; mains $26-38; ⊙4pm-late Tue-Sat) Injecting a little Latin American flair into the Blenheim dining scene, Gramado's is a fun place to tuck into unashamedly hearty meals such as lamb *assado*, feijoada (smoky pork and bean stew) and Brazilian-spiced fish. Kick things off with a caipirinha, of course.

Dodson Street　　CRAFT BEER
(☑03-577 8348; www.dodsonstreet.co.nz; 1 Dodson St, Mayfield; ⊙11am-11pm) Pub and garden with a beer-hall ambience and suitably Teutonic menu (mains $17 to $27) featuring pork knuckle, bratwurst and schnitzel. The stars of the show are the 24 taps pouring quality, ever-changing craft beer, including award-winning brewer and neighbour, Renaissance.

Spy Valley Wines (www.spyvalleywine.co.nz; 37 Lake Timara Rd, Waihopai Valley; ⊗10.30am-4.30pm daily summer, 10.30am-4.30pm Mon-Fri winter)

Te Whare Ra (www.twrwines.co.nz; 56 Anglesea St, Renwick; ⊗11am-4.30pm Mon-Fri, 12pm-4pm Sat & Sun Nov-Mar)

Vines Village (www.thevinesvillage.co.nz; 193 Rapaura Rd; ⊗10am-5pm)

Wairau River (www.wairauriverwines.com; 11 Rapaura Rd; ⊗10am-5pm)

Yealands Estate (☑03-575 7618; www.yealandsestate.co.nz; cnr Seaview & Reserve Rds, Seddon; ⊗10am-4.30pm)

Wining & Dining

Arbour (☑03-572 7989; www.arbour.co.nz; 36 Godfrey Rd, Renwick; mains $31-38; ⊗3pm-late Tue-Sat year-round, 6pm-late Mon-Jan-Mar; ☑) Located in the thick of Renwick wine country, this elegant restaurant offers 'a taste of Marlborough' by focusing on local produce fashioned into contemporary yet crowd-pleasing dishes. Settle in for a three-, four- or multiple-course à la carte offering ($73/85/98), or an end-of-the-day nibble and glass or two from the mesmerising wine list.

Wairau River Restaurant (☑03-572 9800; www.wairauriverwines.com; cnr Rapaura Rd & SH6, Renwick; mains $21-27; ⊗noon-3pm) Modishly modified mud-brick bistro with wide veranda and beautiful gardens with plenty of shade. Order the mussel chowder, or the double-baked blue-cheese soufflé. Relaxing and thoroughly enjoyable.

Rock Ferry (☑03-579 6431; www.rockferry.co.nz; 80 Hammerichs Rd, Blenheim; mains $23-27; ⊗11.30am-3pm) Pleasant environment inside and out, with a slightly groovy edge. The compact summery menu – think roasted salmon and peppers or organic open steak sandwich – is accompanied by wines from Marlborough and Otago.

Wither Hills (☑03-520 8284; www.witherhills.co.nz; 211 New Renwick Rd, Blenheim; mains $24-33, platters $38-68; ⊗11am-4pm) Simple, well-executed food in a stylish space. Pull up a beanbag on the Hockneyesque lawns and enjoy smoked lamb, Asian pork belly or a platter, before climbing the ziggurat for impressive views across the Wairau.

☆ Entertainment

Marlborough Civic Theatre THEATRE
(☑03-520 8558; www.mctt.co.nz; 42 Alfred St, Blenheim) Brand-spanking new theatre presenting a wide program of concerts and performances. Check out www.follow-me.co.nz to see what's on here and beyond.

❶ Information

Blenheim i-SITE (☑03-577 8080; www.marlboroughnz.com; 8 Sinclair St, Blenheim Railway Station; ⊗9am-5pm Mon-Fri, 9am-3pm Sat, 10am-3pm Sun) Information on Marlborough and beyond. Wine-trail maps and bookings for everything under the sun.

Wairau Hospital (☑03-520 9999; www.nmdhb.govt.nz; Hospital Rd, Blenheim)

Post Office (cnr Scott & Main Sts, Blenheim)

❶ Getting There & Away

AIR
Marlborough Airport (www.marlboroughairport.co.nz; Tancred Cres, Woodbourne) is 6km west of town on Middle Renwick Rd.

Air New Zealand (p383) has direct flights to/from Wellington, Auckland and Christchurch with onward connections. Soundsair (p383) connects Blenheim with Wellington, Paraparaumu and Napier.

BUS
InterCity (p383) Buses run daily from the Blenheim i-SITE to Picton (30 minutes) and Nelson (1¾ hours). Buses also head down south to Christchurch (two daily) via Kaikoura.

Naked Bus (p383) Tickets bargain seats on some of the same services, and on its own buses on major routes.

TRAIN
KiwiRail Scenic (p383) runs the daily Coastal Pacific service (October to May), stopping at

MARLBOROUGH & NELSON BLENHEIM

Blenheim en route to Picton (from $29) heading north, and Christchurch (from $79) via Kaikoura (from $59) heading south.

ℹ Getting Around

Avantiplus (☑ 03-578 0433; www.bike marlborough.co.nz; 61 Queen St; hire per half-/full day from $25/40) rents bikes; extended hire and delivery by arrangement.

Blenheim Shuttles (☑ 03-577 5277, 0800 577 527; www.blenheimshuttles.co.nz) Offer shuttles around Blenheim and the wider Marlborough region.

Marlborough Taxis (☑ 03-577 5511) Four-wheeled rescue is offered by Marlborough Taxis.

Kaikoura

POP 1971

Take SH1 129km southeast from Blenheim (or 180km north from Christchurch) and you'll encounter Kaikoura, a pretty peninsula town backed by the snow-capped Seaward Kaikoura Range. Few places in the world are home to such a variety of easily spottable wildlife: whale, dolphins, NZ fur seals, penguins, shearwaters, petrels and several species of albatross all live in or pass by the area.

Marine animals are abundant here due to ocean-current and continental-shelf conditions: the seabed gradually slopes away from the land before plunging to more than 800m where the southerly current hits the continental shelf. This creates an upwelling of nutrients from the ocean floor into the feeding zone.

◉ Sights

Point Kean Seal Colony   WILDLIFE RESERVE

At the end of the peninsula seals laze around in the grass and on the rocks, lapping up all the attention. Give them a wide berth (10m), and never get between them and the sea – they will attack if they feel cornered and can move surprisingly fast.

Kaikoura Museum   MUSEUM

(www.kaikoura.govt.nz; 14 Ludstone Rd; adult/child $5/1; ◎10am-4.30pm Mon-Fri, 2-4pm Sat & Sun) This provincial museum displays historical photographs, Māori and colonial artefacts, a huge sperm-whale jaw and the fossilised remains of a plesiosaur.

Fyffe House   HISTORIC BUILDING

(www.heritage.org.nz; 62 Avoca St; adult/child $10/ free; ◎10am-5pm daily Oct-Apr, to 4pm Thu-Mon

May-Sep) Kaikoura's oldest surviving building, Fyffe House's whale-bone foundations were laid in 1844. Proudly positioned and fronted with a colourful garden, the little two-storey cottage offers a fascinating insight into the lives of colonial settlers. Interpretive displays are complemented by historic objects, while peeling wallpaper and the odd cobweb lend authenticity. Cute maritime-themed shop.

🏃 Activities

There's a safe swimming **beach** in front of the Esplanade, alongside which is the **Lion's Swimming Pool** (191 Esplanade; adult/child $3/2; ◎10am-6pm Mon-Fri, 11am-5pm Sat & Sun) for those with a salt aversion.

Decent **surfing** can be found in the area, too, particularly at **Mangamaunu Beach** (15km north of town), where there's a 500m point break, which is fun in good conditions. Water-sports gear hire and advice are available from **Board Silly Surf & SUP Adventures** (☑ 027 418 8900, 0800 787 352; www.boardsilly.co.nz; 1 Kiwa Rd, Mangamaunu; 3hr lessons $80, board & suit from $40) and **Coastal Sports** (☑ 03-319 5028; www.coastalsports. co.nz; 24 West End; ◎9am-5.30pm Mon-Sat, 10am-5pm Sun, extended hours summer).

★**Kaikoura Peninsula Walkway**   WALKING

A foray along this walkway is a must-do. Starting from the town, the three- to four-hour loop heads out to Point Kean, along the cliffs to South Bay, then back to town over the isthmus (or in reverse, of course). En route you'll see fur seals and red-billed seagull and shearwater colonies. Lookouts and interesting interpretive panels abound. Collect a map at the i-SITE or follow your nose.

Kaikoura Coast Track   TRAMPING

(☑ 03-319 2715; www.kaikouratrack.co.nz; 356 Conway Flat Rd, Ngaroma; $190) This easy two-day, 26km, self-guided walk across private farmland combines coastal and alpine views. The price includes two nights' farm-cottage accommodation and pack transport; BYO sleeping bag and food. Starts 45km south of Kaikoura.

Clarence River Rafting   RAFTING

(☑ 03-319 6993; www.clarenceriverrafting.co.nz; 1/3802 SH1, at Clarence Bridge; half-day trips adult/child $120/80) Raft the bouncy Grade II rapids of the scenic Clarence River on a half-day trip (2½ hours on the water), or on longer journeys including a five-day adventure with wilderness camping (adult/child $1400/900). Based on SH1, 40km north of Kaikoura near Clarence Bridge.

☞ Tours

Marine Mammal-Watching

Whale Watch Kaikoura
ECOTOUR

(☎0800 655 121, 03-319 6767; www.whalewatch. co.nz; Railway Station; 3½hr tours adult/child $150/60) ⏺ With knowledgeable guides and fascinating 'world of whales' on-board animation, Kaikoura's biggest operator heads out on boat trips (with admirable frequency) to introduce you to some of the big fellas. It'll refund 80% of your fare if no whales are sighted (success rate: 95%). If this trip is a must for you, allow a few days flexibility in case the weather turns to custard.

Dolphin Encounter
ECOTOUR

(☎03-319 6777, 0800 733 365; www.encounter-kaikoura.co.nz; 96 Esplanade; swim adult/child $175/160, observation $95/50; ☺tours 8.30am & 12.30pm year-round, plus 5.30am Nov-Apr) ⏺ Claiming NZ's highest success rate (90%) for both locating and swimming with dolphins, this operator runs feel-good three-hour tours, which often encounter sizeable pods of sociable duskies – the classic Kaikoura treat.

Seal Swim Kaikoura
ECOTOUR

(☎0800 732 579, 03-319 6182; www.seal swimkaikoura.co.nz; 58 West End; tours $70-110, viewing adult/child $55/35; ☺Oct-May) Take a (warmly wet-suited) swim with Kaikoura's healthy population of playful seals – including very cute pups – on two-hour guided snorkelling tours (by boat) run by the Chambers family.

Birdwatching

★Albatross Encounter
BIRDWATCHING

(☎0800 733 365, 03-319 6777; www.encounter kaikoura.co.nz; 96 Esplanade; adult/child $125/60; ☺tours 9am & 1pm year-round, plus 6am Nov-Apr) ⏺ Even if you don't consider yourself a bird-nerd, you'll love this close encounter with pelagic species such as shearwaters, shags, mollymawks and petrels. It's the various albatross species, however, that steal the show. Just awesome.

Fishing

Kaikoura Fishing Charters
FISHING

(☎03-319 6888; www.kaikourafishing.co.nz) Dangle a line from the 12m *Takapu*, then take your filleted, bagged catch home to eat.

Fishing at Kaikoura
FISHING

(☎03-319 3003; gerard.diedrichs@xtra.co.nz) Fishing, crayfishing, scenic tours and water-skiing on the 6m *Sophie-Rose*.

Other Tours

Kaikoura Kayaks
KAYAKING

(☎0800 452 456, 03-319 7118; www.kaikourakay aks.nz; 19 Killarney St; 3hr tours adult/child $95/70; ☺tours 8.30am, 12.30pm & 4.30pm Nov-Apr, 9am & 1pm May-Oct) Excellent guided sea-kayak tours to view fur seals and explore the peninsula's coastline. Family-friendly; kayak fishing and other on-demand trips available; plus freedom kayak and paddle board hire.

Kaikoura Wilderness Walks
TRAMPING

(☎0800 945 337, 03-319 6966; www.kaikoura wilderness.co.nz; 2-night packages adult/child $1895/1595) ⏺ Three-day guided walks through the privately owned Puhi Peaks Nature Reserve high in the Seaward Kaikoura range. Packages include accommodation and sumptuous meals at the luxurious Shearwater Lodge.

Maori Tours Kaikoura
CULTURAL TOUR

(☎0800 366 267, 03-319 5567; www.maoritours. co.nz; 3½hr tours adult/child $134/74; ☺tours 9am & 1.30pm) ⏺ Fascinating half-day, small-group tours laced with Māori hospitality and local lore. Visit historic sites, hear legends and learn about indigenous use of trees and plants. Advance bookings required.

Kaikoura

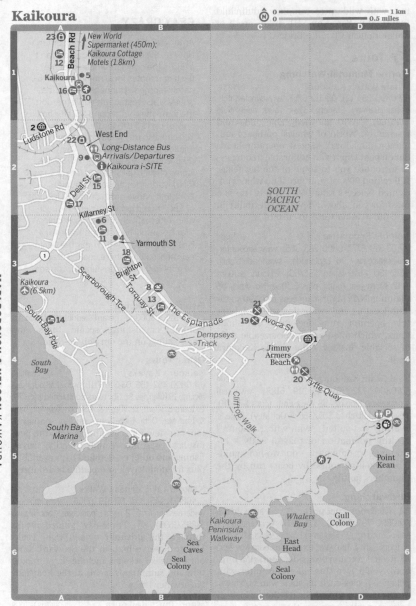

Kaikoura Helicopters   SCENIC FLIGHTS
(📞03-319 6609; www.worldofwhales.co.nz; Railway Station; 15-60min flights $100-490) Reliable whale-spotting flights (standard tour 30 minutes, $220 each for three or more people), plus jaunts around the peninsula, Mt Fyffe and peaks beyond.

Wings over Whales   SCENIC FLIGHTS
(📞03-319 6580, 0800 226 629; www.whales.co.nz; 30min flights adult/child $180/75) Light-plane

Kaikoura

flights departing from Kaikoura Airport, 8km south of town on SH1. Spotting success rate: 95%.

🛏 Sleeping

Albatross Backpacker Inn HOSTEL $
(☑0800 222 247, 03-319 6090; www.albatross-kaikoura.co.nz; 1 Torquay St; dm $29-32, tw/d $69/74; 🛜) ⊘ This arty backpackers resides in three sweet buildings, one a former post office. It's colourful and close to the beach but sheltered from the breeze. As well as a laid-back lounge with musical instruments for jamming, there are decks and verandas to chill out on.

Dolphin Lodge HOSTEL $
(☑03-319 5842; www.dolphinlodge.co.nz; 15 Deal St; dm $29, d with/without bathroom $74/66; @🛜) This small home-away-from-home has a lovely scented garden, sweet ocean views and a kindly owner. When the sun's shining most of the action is out or the fantastic deck, around the barbecue, or in the spa pool.

Alpine Pacific Holiday Park HOLIDAY PARK $
(☑0800 692 322, 03-319 6275; www.alpine-pacific.co.nz; 69 Beach Rd; sites from $46, cabins $78, units & motels $137-200; @🛜🏊) This compact and proudly trimmed park copes well with its many visitors and offers excellent facilities, including a pool, hot tubs and a barbecue pavilion. Rows of cabins and units are a tad more stylish than the average, and mountain views can be enjoyed from many angles.

Kaikoura Top 10 Holiday Park HOLIDAY PARK $
(☑0800 363 638, 03-319 5362; www.kaikouratop10.co.nz; 34 Beach Rd; sites $52, cabins $70-95, units & motels $110-185; @🛜🏊) Hiding from the highway behind a massive hedge, this busy, shipshape holiday park offers family-friendly facilities (heated pool, hot tub, jumping pillow) and cabins and units to the usual Top 10 standard.

⭐**Kaikoura Cottage Motels** MOTEL $$
(☑0800 526 882, 03-319 5599; www.kaikouracottagemotels.co.nz; cnr Old Beach & Mill Rds; d $140-160; 🛜) This enclave of eight modern tourist flats looks mighty fine, surrounded by attractive native plantings. Oriented for mountain views, spick-n-span self-contained units sleep four between an open plan studio-style living room and one private bedroom. Proud, lovely hosts seal the deal.

Bay Cottages MOTEL $$
(☑03-319 5506; www.baycottages.co.nz; 29 South Bay Pde; cottages/motel r $120/140; 🛜) Here's a great-value option on South Bay, a few kilometres south of town: five tourist cottages with kitchenette and bathroom that sleep up to four, and two slick motel rooms with stainless-steel benches, a warm feel and clean lines. The cheery owner may even take you crayfishing in good weather.

Sails Motel MOTEL $$
(☑03-319 6145; www.sailsmotel.co.nz; 134 Esplanade; d/apt $125/150; 🛜) There are no sea views (nor sails) at this motel, so the cherubic owner has to impress with quality. The four secluded, tastefully appointed

self-contained units are down a driveway in a garden setting (private outdoor areas abound).

Nikau Lodge
B&B $$$

(☑ 03-319 6973; www.nikaulodge.com; 53 Deal St; d $190-290; ☺☎) A waggly tailed welcome awaits at this beautiful B&B high on the hill with grand-scale vistas. Five en suite rooms are plush and comfy, with additional satisfaction arriving in the form of cafe-quality breakfasts accompanied by fresh local coffee. Good humour, home baking, free wi-fi, complimentary drinks, a hot tub and blooming gardens: you may want to move in.

Anchor Inn Motel
MOTEL $$$

(☑ 03-319 5426; www.anchorinn.co.nz; 208 Esplanade; d $185-255; ☎) The Aussie owners liked this Kaikoura motel so much they bought it and moved here. The sharp and spacious units are a pleasant 15-minute walk from town and about 10 seconds from the ocean.

✖ Eating

Reserve Hutt
CAFE $

(72 West End; meals $10-20; ☺8.30am-3pm; ☑) The best coffee in town, roasted on-site and espressoed by cheery baristas in Kaikoura's grooviest cafe. Puttin' out that rootsy retro-Kiwiana vibe we love so much, this is a neat place to linger over a couple of flatties and down a chocolate brownie, delicious ham croissant or the full eggy brunch.

Cafe Encounter
CAFE $

(96 Esplanade; meals $8-23; ☺7am-5pm; ☎☑) This cafe in the Encounter Kaikoura complex is more than just somewhere to wait for your tour. The cabinet houses respectable sandwiches, pastries and cakes, plus there's a tasteful range of daily specials such as homemade soup and pulled-pork rolls. A sunny patio provides sea views.

Kaikoura Seafood BBQ
SEAFOOD $

(Fyffe Quay; items from $5; ☺10.30am-6pm) Conveniently located on the way to the Point Kean seal colony, this long-standing roadside barbecue is a great spot to sample local seafood, including crayfish (half/full from $25/50) and scallops, at an affordable price.

Pier Hotel
PUB FOOD $$

(☑ 03-319 5037; www.thepierhotel.co.nz; 1 Avoca St; lunch $16-25, dinner $25-38; ☺11am-late) Situated in the town's primo seaside spot, with panoramic views, the historic Pier Hotel is a friendly and inviting place for a drink and respectable pub grub, including crayfish (half/whole $45/90). Great outside area for sundowners.

★ Green Dolphin
MODERN NZ $$$

(☑ 03-319 6666; www.greendolphinkaikoura.com; 12 Avoca St; mains $26-39; ☺5pm-late) Kaikoura's consistent top-ender dishes up high-quality local produce including seafood, beef, lamb and venison, as well as seasonal flavours such as fresh tomato soup. There are lovely homemade pasta dishes, too. The hefty drinks list demands attention, featuring exciting aperitifs, craft beer, interesting wines and more. Booking ahead is advisable, especially if you want to secure a table by the window and watch the daylight fade.

❶ Information

Kaikoura i-SITE (☑ 03-319 5641; www.kaikoura.co.nz; West End; ☺9am-5pm Mon-Fri, to 4pm Sat & Sun, extended hours Dec-Mar) Helpful staff make tour, accommodation and transport bookings, and help with DOC-related matters.

❶ Getting There & Away

BUS

InterCity (p383) buses run between Kaikoura and Nelson once daily (3¾ hours), and Picton (2¼ hours) and Christchurch (2¼ hours) twice daily. The **bus stop** is next to the i-SITE (tickets and info inside).

Atomic Shuttles (p387) also services Kaikoura on its Christchurch to Picton run, which links with destinations as far afield as Nelson, Queenstown and Invercargill.

Naked Bus (p383) tickets bargain seats on its own buses on major routes, and on other services depending on capacity.

TRAIN

KiwiRail Scenic (p383) runs the daily Coastal Pacific service (October to May), stopping at Kaikoura en route to Picton (from $59, 2¼ hours), and Christchurch (from $59, 2¾ hours). The northbound train departs Kaikoura at 9.59am; the southbound at 3.50pm.

❶ Getting Around

Kaikoura Shuttles (☑ 03-319 6166; www.kaikourashuttles.co.nz) will run you around the local sights as well as to and from the airport. For local car hire, contact **Kaikoura Rentals** (☑ 03-319 3311; www.kaikourarentals.co.nz; 94 Churchill St).

NELSON REGION

The Nelson region is centred upon Tasman Bay. It stretches north to Golden Bay and Farewell Spit, and south to Nelson Lakes. It's not hard to see why it's such a popular travel destination for international and domestic travellers alike: not only does it boast three national parks (Kahurangi, Nelson Lakes and Abel Tasman), it can also satisfy nearly every other whim, from food, wine and beer, art, craft and festivals, to that most precious of pastimes for which the region is well known: lazing about in the sunshine.

ℹ Getting There & Away

Nelson is the region's primary gateway, with competitive domestic airline connections, and comprehensive bus services linking it with all major South Island towns.

Abel Tasman Coachlines (☑03-548 0285; www.abeltasmantravel.co.nz)

Golden Bay Coachlines (☑03-525 8352; www.gbcoachlines.co.nz)

Trek Express (☑027 222 1872, 0800 128 735; www.trekexpress.co.nz)

Nelson

POP 46,440

Dishing up a winning combination of beautiful surroundings, sophisticated art and culinary scenes, and lashings of sunshine, Nelson is hailed as one of NZ's most 'liveable' cities. In summer it fills up with local and international visitors, who lap up its diverse offerings.

◉ Sights

Nelson has an inordinate number of galleries, most of which are listed in the *Art & Crafts Nelson City* brochure (with walking-trail map) available from the i-SITE (p408). A fruitful wander can be had by starting at the woolly **Fibre Spectrum** (☑03-548 1939; www.fibrespectrum.co.nz; 280 Trafalgar St), before moving on to *The Lord of the Rings* jeweller **Jens Hansen** (☑03-548 0640; www.jenshansen.com; 320 Trafalgar Sq), glass-blower **Flamedaisy** (☑03-548 4475; www.flamedaisy.co.nz; 324 Trafalgar Sq), then around the corner to the home of Nelson pottery, **South Street Gallery** (☑03-548 8117; www.nelsonpottery.co.nz; 10 Nile St W). Other interesting local creations can be found at the Nelson Market (p408) on Saturday.

★**Tahuna Beach** BEACH
Nelson's primo playground takes the form of an epic sandy beach (with lifeguards in summer) backed by dunes, and a large grassy parkland with a playground, an espresso cart, a hydroslide, bumper boats, a roller-skating rink, a model railway, and an adjacent restaurant strip. Weekends can get veerrrrry busy!

Suter Art Gallery GALLERY
(www.thesuter.org.nz; 208 Bridge St; ◉9.30am-4.30pm) FREE Adjacent to Queen's Gardens, Nelson's public art gallery presents changing exhibitions, floor talks, musical and theatrical performances, and films. The Suter's long-awaited reopening after a fabulous redevelopment is scheduled for late 2016. Check the website to confirm it's open, and to find out what's on.

NZ Classic Motorcycles MUSEUM
(☑03-545 7699; www.nzclassicmotorcycles.co.nz; 75 Haven Rd; adult/child $20/10; ◉9am-4pm Mon-Fri, 10am-3pm Sat & Sun) Motorcycle enthusiasts should race round to this exceptional 300+ collection of classic bikes, including a clutch of super-rare Brough Superiors and a tribe of Indians. Well-considered displays across two floors and a handy mobile app allow close inspection from multiple perspectives.

McCashin's Brewery BREWERY
(☑03-547 5357; www.mccashins.co.nz; 660 Main Rd, Stoke; ◉7am-6pm Mon & Tue, 7am-9.30pm Wed-Sat, 9am-6pm) A groundbreaker in the new era of craft brewing in NZ, which started way back in the 1980s. Visit the historic cider factory for a tasting, cafe meal or tour.

Nelson Provincial Museum MUSEUM
(☑03-548 9588; www.nelsonmuseum.co.nz; cnr Trafalgar St and Hardy St; adult/child $5/3; ◉10am-5pm Mon-Fri, to 4.30pm Sat & Sun) This modern museum space is filled with cultural heritage and natural history exhibits which have a regional bias, as well as regular touring exhibitions (for which admission fees vary). It also features a great rooftop garden.

Christ Church Cathedral CHURCH
(www.nelsoncathedral.org; Trafalgar Sq; ◉9am-6pm) FREE The enduring symbol of Nelson, the art-deco Christ Church Cathedral lords it over the city from the top of Trafalgar St. The best time to visit is during the 10am and 7pm Sunday services when you can hear the organist and the choir in song.

Central Nelson

Central Nelson

◎ Sights
1 Christ Church Cathedral B4
2 Jens Hansen B3
3 Nelson Provincial Museum B3
4 NZ Classic Motorcycles A1
5 Suter Art Gallery D2

◆ Activities, Courses & Tours
6 Trail Journeys B1

🛏 Sleeping
7 Cedar Grove Motor Lodge B1
8 Palazzo Motor Lodge A4
9 Prince Albert D4
10 Trampers Rest D4
11 YHA Nelson by Accents A2

✖ Eating
12 DeVille C2
13 Falafel Gourmet B3

14 Ford's B3
15 Hopgood's B3
16 Indian Café C2
17 Stefano's B2
18 Urban Oyster C3

🍷 Drinking & Nightlife
19 Free House C2
20 Rhythm and Brown C2
21 Sprig & Fern C3

✪ Entertainment
22 Theatre Royal A2

🛍 Shopping
23 Fibre Spectrum B3
24 Flamedaisy Glass Design B3
25 Nelson Farmers' Market C3
26 Nelson Market B2
27 South Street Gallery B4

Botanical Reserve · PARK
(Milton St) Walking tracks ascend Botanical Hill, where a spire proclaims the **Centre of New Zealand**. NZ's first-ever rugby match was played at the foot of the hill on 14 May 1870: Nelson Rugby Football Club trounced the lily-livered players from Nelson College 2-0.

Founders Heritage Park · MUSEUM
(☑03-548 2649; www.founderspark.co.nz; 87 Atawhai Dr; adult/child/family $7/5/15; ☉10am-4.30pm) Two kilometres from the city centre, this park comprises a replica historic village with a museum, gallery displays, and artisan products such as chocolate and clothing. It makes for a fascinating wander, which you can augment with a visit to the on-site **Founders Brewery & Café** (☑03-548 4638; www.foundersbrewery. co.nz; 87 Atawhai Dr; ☉9am-4.30pm, later in summer).

🏃 Activities

Walking & Cycling
There's plenty of walking and cycling to be enjoyed in and around the town, for which the i-SITE has maps. The classic walk from town is to the **Centre of NZ** atop the Botanical Reserve; if you enjoy that then ask about the **Grampians**.

Nelson has two of the New Zealand Cycle Trail's 23 Great Rides: **Dun Mountain Trail** (www.heartofbiking.org.nz), an awesome but challenging one-day ride ranging over the hills to the south of the city; and the **Great Taste Trail** (p409) offering a blissfully flat meander through beautiful countryside dotted with wine, food and art stops.

Gentle Cycling Company · BICYCLE TOUR
(☑0800 932 453, 03-929 5652; www.gentle cycling.co.nz; day tours $95-105) Self-guided cycle tours along the Great Taste Trail, with drop-ins (and tastings) at wineries, breweries, cafes and occasional galleries. Bike hire (per day $45) and shuttles also available.

Trail Journeys · BICYCLE TOUR
(☑0800 292 538, 03-540 3095; www.trailjourneys nelson.co.nz; MD Outdoors, 1/37 Halifax St; full-day tours from $89) Trail Journeys offers a range of self-guided cycle tours around Nelson city, and beyond along the Great Taste Trail, based at three conveniently located depots in central Nelson, Mapua Wharf and Kaiteriteri.

Nelson Cycle Hire & Tours · BICYCLE TOUR
(☑03-539 4193; www.nelsoncyclehire.co.nz; Nelson Airport; bike hire per day $45) Provides comfortable bikes for independent riding, plus guided or supported tours around the Great Taste Trail and beyond. Pick-up and delivery service, region-wide.

Paragliding, Hang Gliding & Kiteboarding
Nelson is a great place for adrenaline activities, with plenty of action in summer, particularly around the rather divine Tahuna Beach (p403). Tandem paragliding costs around $180, introductory kitesurfing starts at $150, and paddle board hire is around $20 per hour.

Nelson Paragliding · PARAGLIDING
(☑03-544 1182; www.nelsonparagliding.co.nz) Get high in the sky over Tahunanui with Nelson Paragliding.

Kite Surf Nelson · KITESURFING
(☑0800 548 363; www.kitesurfnelson.co.nz) Learn to kite surf at Tahunanui, or hire a stand-up paddle board.

Other Activities

Cable Bay Kayaks · KAYAKING
(☑03-545 0332; www.cablebaykayaks.co.nz; Cable Bay Rd, Hira; half-/full day guided trips $85/145) Fifteen minutes' drive from Nelson city, Nick and Jenny offer richly rewarding guided sea-kayaking trips exploring the local coastline, where you'll likely meet local marine life (snorkelling gear on board helps) and may even enter a cave.

Moana SUP · WATER SPORTS
(☑027 656 0268; www.moananzsup.co.nz) Learn what SUP with the guys at Moana, or hire a board if you're already enlightened.

Happy Valley Adventures · ADVENTURE SPORTS
(☑03-545 0304, 0800 157 300; www.happyvalley adventures.co.nz; 194 Cable Bay Rd; Skywire adult/child $85/55, quad-bike tours from $100, horse treks $75) Dangle 150m above the forest in the 'Skywire' (a chairlift/flying-fox hybrid), then soar through the air for its 1.65km length. If that ain't enough, take a quad-bike tour; or if it's too much, try a horse trek instead. Located a 15-minute drive northeast of Nelson along SH6; on-site cafe.

👉 Tours

Nelson Tours & Travel · TOUR
(☑027 237 5007, 0800 222 373; www.nelsontours andtravel.co.nz) CJ and crew run various

THE WONDROUS WORLD OF WEARABLE ART

Nelson is the birthplace of New Zealand's most inspiring fashion show, the annual World of WearableArt Awards Show. You can see 70 or so current and past entries in the sensory-overloading galleries of the **World of WearableArt & Classic Cars Museum** (WOW; ✆ 03-547 4573; www.wowcars.co.nz; 1 Cadillac Way; adult/child $24/10; ⊙10am-5pm), which include a glow-in-the-dark room. Look out for the 'Bizarre Bras'.

More car than bra? Under the same roof are more than 100 mint-condition classic cars and motorbikes. Exhibits change, but may include a 1959 pink Cadillac, a yellow 1950 Bullet Nose Studebaker convertible and a BMW bubble car.

The World of WearableArt Awards Show began humbly in 1987 when Suzie Moncrieff held an off-beat event featuring art that could be worn and modelled. Folks quickly cottoned on to the show's creative (and competitive) possibilities. You name it, they've shown that a garment can be made from it; wood, metal, shells, cable ties, dried leaves, ping-pong balls... The **festival** (p362) now has a new home in Wellington.

Between the galleries, cafe and art shop, allow a couple of hours if you can.

small-group, flexible tours honing in on Nelson's wine, craft beer, art and scenic highlights. The five-hour 'Best of Both Worlds' combines indulgence with your special interest, be it galleries or a trip to Rabbit Island ($105). Day tours of Marlborough wineries also available ($195).

✪ Festivals & Events

Nelson Jazz Festival　　　　　MUSIC
(www.nelsonjazzfest.co.nz; ⊙Jan) More scoo-bee-doo-bop events over a week in January than you can shake a leg at. Features local and national acts.

Nelson Arts Festival　　PERFORMING ARTS
(www.nelsonartsfestival.co.nz; ⊙Oct) Over two weeks in October; events include a street carnival, exhibitions, cabaret, writers, theatre and music.

🛌 Sleeping

Trampers Rest　　　　　　HOSTEL $
(✆ 03-545 7477; 31 Alton St; dm/s/d $30/52/64; ⊙closed Jun-Sep; @🛜) With just seven beds (no bunks), the tiny, much-loved Trampers is hard to beat for a homely environment. The enthusiastic owner is a keen tramper and cyclist, and provides comprehensive local information and free bikes. It has a small kitchen, a book exchange, and a piano for evening singalongs.

Shortbread Cottage　　　　HOSTEL $
(✆ 03-546 6681; www.shortbreadcottage.co.nz; 33 Trafalgar St; dm $29, s & d $65; @🛜) This renovated 102-year-old villa has room for only a dozen or so beds, but it's packed with charm and hospitality. It offers free internet, fresh-baked

bread, and shortbread on arrival. It's also only a stone's throw from the town centre.

Prince Albert　　　　　　HOSTEL $
(✆0800 867 3529, 03-548 8477; www.theprincealbert.co.nz; 113 Nile St; dm $29 s/tw/d $50/75/85; 🛜) A five-minute walk from the city centre, this lively, well-run backpackers has roomy en suite dorms surrounding a sunny courtyard. Private rooms are upstairs in the main building, which also houses an English-style pub where guests can meet the locals and refuel with a good-value meal.

Tasman Bay Backpackers　　HOSTEL $
(✆0800 222 572, 03-548 7950; www.tasmanbaybackpackers.co.nz; 10 Weka St; sites from $19, dm $27-30, d $74-87; @🛜) This well-designed, friendly hostel has airy communal spaces with a Kiwi soundtrack, hypercoloured rooms, a sunny outdoor deck and a well-used hammock. Good freebies: wi-fi, decent bikes, breakfast during winter, and chocolate pudding and ice cream year-round.

Tahuna Beach
Kiwi Holiday Park　　　HOLIDAY PARK $
(✆03-548 5159, 0800 500 501; www.tahunabeachholidaypark.co.nz; 70 Beach Rd, Tahunanui; sites/cabins/units from $20/65/120; @🛜) Close to Tahuna Beach, 5km from the city, this mammoth park is home to thousands in high summer, which you'll either find hellish or bloody brilliant, depending on your mood. Off season, you'll have the cafe and minigolf mostly to yourself.

YHA Nelson by Accents　　HOSTEL $
(✆03-545 9988, 0800 888 335; www.accentshostel.nz; 59 Rutherford St; dm/s $30/69, d with/

without bathroom $119/89; @🗢) A tidy, well-run, central hostel with spacious communal areas including well-equipped kitchens, a sunny terrace, a TV room and bike storage. Great local knowledge for tours and activities from new managers injecting some personality into this YHA-affiliated establishment.

Palazzo Motor Lodge MOTEL **$$**
(✏03-545 8171, 0800 472 5293; www.palazzomotorlodge.co.nz; 159 Rutherford St; studios $130-249, apt $230-390; 🗢) This modern, Italian-tinged motor lodge offers stylish studios and one- and two-room apartments featuring enviable kitchens with decent cooking equipment, classy glassware and a dishwasher. Its comfort and convenient location easily atone for the odd bit of dubious art.

Te Maunga House B&B **$$**
(✏03-548 8605; www.nelsoncityaccommodation.co.nz; 15 Dorothy Annie Way; s $90, d $125-145; 🗢) Aptly named ('the mountain'), this grand old family home has exceptional views and a well-travelled host. Two doubles and a twin have a homely feel with comfy beds and their own bathrooms. Your hearty breakfast can be walked off up and down *that* hill, a 10-minute climb with an extra five minutes to town. Closed May to October.

Sussex House B&B **$$**
(✏03-548 9972; www.sussex.co.nz; 238 Bridge St; d $170-190, tr $175; 🗢) In a relatively quiet riverside spot, only a five-minute walk to town, this creaky old lady dates back to around 1880. The five tastefully decorated rooms feature upmarket bedding, period-piece furniture and en suite bathrooms, except one room that has a private bathroom down the hall. Enjoy local fruit at breakfast in the grand dining room.

Cedar Grove Motor Lodge MOTEL **$$**
(✏03-545 1133; www.cedargrove.co.nz; cnr Trafalgar & Grove Sts; d $155-210; 🗢) A big old cedar landmark, this smart, modern block of spacious apartments is just a three-minute walk to town. Its range of studios and doubles are plush and elegant, with full cooking facilities.

✗ Eating

Falafel Gourmet MIDDLE EASTERN **$**
(✏03-545 6220; 195 Hardy St; meals $11-19; ⊙9.30am-5.30pm Mon-Sat, to 8pm Fr; ✗) A cranking joint dishing out the best kebabs for miles around. They're healthy, too!

Stefano's PIZZA **$**
(✏03-546 7530; www.pizzeria.co.nz; 91 Trafalgar St; pizzas $6-29; ⊙noon-2pm & 4.30pm-9pm; ✗) Located upstairs in the State Cinema complex, this Italian-run joint turns out the town's best pizza. Thin, crispy, authentic and delicious, with some variations a veritable bargain. Wash it down with a beer and chase it with a creamy dessert.

★ DeVille CAFE **$$**
(✏03-545 6911; www.devillecafe.co.nz; 22 New St; meals $12-21; ⊙8am-4pm Mon-Sat, 8.30am-2.30pm Sun; ✗) Most of DeVille's tables lie in its sweet walled courtyard, a hidden boho oasis in the inner city and the perfect place for a meal or morning tea. The food's good and local – from fresh baking to a chorizo-burrito brunch, Caesar salad and proper burgers, washed down with regional wines and beers. Open late for live music Fridays in summer.

Urban Oyster MODERN NZ **$$$**
(✏03-546 7861; www.urbaneatery.co.nz; 278 Hardy St; dishes $13-27; ⊙4pm-late Mon, 11am-late Tue-Sat) Slurp oysters from the shell, or revitalise with sashimi and ceviche, then sate your cravings with street-food dishes such as Korean fried chicken, or popcorn prawn tacos and a side of devilish poutine chips. Black butchery tiles, edgy artwork and fine drinks bolster this metropolitan experience.

Ford's MODERN NZ **$$**
(✏03-546 9400; www.fordsnelson.co.nz; 276 Trafalgar St; lunch $17-22; ⊙8am-late Mon-Fri, 9am-late Sat & Sun) Sunny pavement tables at the top of Trafalgar St make this a popular lunchtime spot, as does a menu of modern classics such as the excellent seafood chowder, steak sandwich, and house-smoked salmon niçoise. Pop in for coffee and a scone, or linger over dinner, for which prices leap up a tenner or so.

Indian Café INDIAN **$$**
(✏03-548 4089; www.theindiancafe.com; 94 Collingwood St; mains $13-23; ⊙12-2pm Mon-Fri, 5pm-late daily; ✗) This saffron-coloured Edwardian villa houses an Indian restaurant that keeps the bhajis raised with impressive interpretations of Anglo-Indian standards such as chicken tandoori, rogan josh and beef madras. Share the mixed platter to start, then mop up your mains with one of 10 different breads.

★**Hopgood's** MODERN NZ $$$
(📞03-545 7191; www.hopgoods.co.nz; 284 Trafalgar St; mains $27-40; ⏱5.30pm-late Mon-Sat) Tongue-and-groove-lined Hopgood's is perfect for a romantic dinner or holiday treat. The food is decadent and skilfully prepared but unfussy, allowing quality local ingredients to shine. Try confit duck with sour cherries, or pork belly and pine-nut butter. Desirable, predominantly Kiwi wine list. Bookings advisable.

🍷 Drinking & Nightlife

★**Free House** CRAFT BEER
(📞03-548 9391; www.freehouse.co.nz; 95 Collingwood St; ⏱3pm-late Mon-Fri, noon-late Sat, 10.30am-late Sun) Come rejoice at this church of ales. Tastefully converted from its original, more reverent purpose, it's now home to an excellent, oft-changing selection of NZ craft beers. You can imbibe inside, out, or even in a yurt, where there's regular entertainment. Hallelujah.

Rhythm and Brown BAR
(📞03-546 56319; www.facebook.com/rhythmandbrown; 19 New St; ⏱4pm-late Tue-Sat) Nelson's slinkiest late-night drinking den, where classy cocktails, fine wines and craft beer flow from behind the bar and sweet vinyl tunes drift from the speakers. Regular Saturday-night microgigs in a compact, groovy space.

Sprig & Fern CRAFT BEER
(📞03-548 1154; www.sprigandfern.co.nz; 280 Hardy St; ⏱11am-late) This outpost of Richmond's Sprig & Fern brewery offers 18 brews on tap, from lager through to doppelbock and berry

cider. No pokies, no TV, just decent beer, occasional live music and a pleasant outdoor area. Pizzas can be ordered in. Look for a second Sprig at 143 Milton St, handy to Founders Park.

☆ Entertainment

Theatre Royal THEATRE
(📞03-548 3840; www.theatreroyalnelson.co.nz; 78 Rutherford St) State-of-the-art theatre in a charmingly restored heritage building. This 'grand old lady of Nelson' (aged nearly 140) boasts a full program of local and touring drama, dance and musical productions. Visit the website for the current program and bookings, or visit the box office (10am to 4pm Monday to Friday). Also check out website (or www.itson.co.nz) for what's on and book online at www.ticketdirect.co.nz, or in the foyer.

🔒 Shopping

Nelson Farmers' Market MARKET
(📞022 010 2776; www.nelsonfarmersmarket.org.nz; Morrison Sq, cnr Morrison & Hardy Sts; ⏱11am-4pm Wed) Weekly market full to bursting with local produce to fill your picnic hamper.

Nelson Market MARKET
(📞03-546 6454; www.nelsonmarket.co.nz; Montgomery Sq; ⏱8am-1pm Sat) Don't miss Nelson Market, a big, busy weekly market featuring fresh produce, food stalls, fashion, local arts, crafts and buskers.

ℹ Information

After Hours & Duty Doctors (📞03-546 8881; 96 Waimea Rd; ⏱8am-10pm)
Nelson Hospital (📞03-546 1800; www.nmdhb.govt.nz; Waimea Rd)
Nelson i-SITE (📞03-548 2304; www.nelsonnz.com; cnr Trafalgar & Halifax Sts; ⏱8.30am-5pm Mon-Fri, 9am-4pm Sat & Sun) A slick centre complete with DOC information desk for the low-down on national parks and walks (including Abel Tasman and Heaphy tracks). Pick up a copy of the *Nelson Tasman Visitor Guide*.
Post Office (www.nzpost.co.nz; 209 Hardy St)

ℹ Getting There & Away

Book Abel Tasman Coachlines, InterCity, KiwiRail Scenic and Interisland ferry services at the **Nelson SBL Travel Centre** (📞03-548 1539; www.nelsoncoachlines.co.nz; 27 Bridge St) or the i-SITE.

AIR
Airline competition has hotted up in recent years: Nelson has never been so accessible.

MARLBOROUGH & NELSON NELSON

IN PURSUIT OF HOPPINESS

The Nelson region lays claim to the title of craft-brewing capital of New Zealand. World-class hops have been grown here since the 1840s, and a dozen breweries are spread between Nelson and Golden Bay.

Pick up a copy of the *Nelson Craft Beer Trail* map (available from the i-SITE and other outlets, and online at www.craftbrewingcapital.co.nz) and wind your way between brewers and pubs. Top picks for a tipple include the **Free House**, **McCashin's** (p403), the **Moutere Inn** (p411), **Golden Bear** (p410), and the **Mussel Inn** (p419).

WORTH A TRIP

GREAT TASTE TRAIL

In a stroke of genius inspired by great weather and easy topography, the Tasman region has developed one of NZ's most popular cycle trails. Why is it so popular? Because no other is so frequently punctuated by stops for food, wine, craft beer and art, as it passes through a range of landscapes from bucolic countryside to estuary boardwalk.

The 174km **Great Taste Trail** (www.heartofbiking.org.nz) stretches from Nelson to Kaiteriteri, with plans afoot to propel it further inland. While it can certainly be ridden in full in a few days, stopping at accommodation en route, it is even more easily ridden as day trips of various lengths. Mapua is a great place to set off from, with bike hire from **Wheelie Fantastic** (p410) and **Trail Journeys** (p405) at the wharf, and a ferry ride over to the trails of Rabbit Island. The trail also passes through thrilling **Kaiteriteri Mountain Bike Park** (p413).

Nelson's many other cycle-tour and bike-hire companies can get you out on the trail, with bike drops and pick-ups.

Nelson Airport is 5km southwest of town, near Tahunanui Beach. A taxi from there to town will cost around $25, or **Super Shuttle** (☑ 03-547 5782, 0800 748 885; www.supershuttle.co.nz) offers door-to-door service for around $20.

Air New Zealand (☑ 0800 737 000; www.airnewzealand.co.nz) Direct flights to/from Wellington, Auckland and Christchurch.

Air2There (☑ 04-904 5133, 0800 777 000; www.air2there.com) Flies/to from Paraparaumu.

Jetstar (☑ 09-975 9426, 0800 800 995; www.jetstar.com) Flies to/from Auckland and Wellington.

Kiwi Regional Airlines (☑ 07-444 5020; www.flykiwiair.co.nz) Flies to/from Dunedin and Hamilton.

Originair (☑ 0800 380 380; www.originair.co.nz) Based in Nelson; flies to/from Wellington and Palmerston North.

Soundsair (☑ 03-520 3080, 0800 505 005; www.soundsair.com) Loyal and long-standing provider; flies to/from Wellington and Paraparaumu.

BUS

Abel Tasman Coachlines (☑ 03-548 0285; www.abeltasmantravel.co.nz) operates bus services to Motueka (one hour), Takaka (two hours), Kaiteriteri and Marahau (both two hours). These services also connect with **Golden Bay Coachlines** (p403) services for Takaka and around. Transport to/from the three national parks is provided by **Trek Express** (p403).

Atomic Shuttles (☑ 0508 108 359, 03-349 0697; www.atomictravel.co.nz) runs from Nelson to Blenheim (2 hours), Picton (2½ hours), and Christchurch (7¾ hours) with a Greymouth connection, plus other southern destinations as far as Queenstown, Dunedin and Invercargill. Services can be booked at (and depart from) Nelson i-SITE.

InterCity (☑ 03-548 1538; www.intercity.co.nz; Bridge St, departs SLB Travel Centre) runs from Nelson to most key South Island destinations including Picton (two hours), Kaikoura (3½ hours), Christchurch (seven hours) and Greymouth (six hours).

ℹ Getting Around

BICYCLE

Bikes are available for hire from **Nelson Cycle Hire & Tours** (p405), among many other cycle tour companies.

BUS

Nelson Suburban Bus Lines (SBL; ☑ 03-548 3290; www.nbus.co.nz; 27 Bridge St) Nelson Suburban Bus Lines operates NBUS, the local service between Nelson, Richmond via Tahunanui and Stoke until about 7pm weekdays, 4.30pm on weekends. It also runs the Late Late Bus (www.nbus.co.nz; ⊙ hourly 10pm-3am Fri & Sat) from Nelson to Richmond via Tahunanui, departing the Westpac Bank on Trafalgar St. Maximum fare for these services is $4.

TAXI

Nelson City Taxis (☑ 03-548 8225; www.nelsontaxis.co.nz)

Sun City Taxis (☑ 03-548 2666; www.suncitytaxis.co.nz)

Ruby Coast & Moutere Hills

From Richmond, south of Nelson, there are two routes to Motueka: the quicker, busier route along the Ruby Coast, and the inland route through the Moutere Hills. If you're making a round-trip from Nelson, drive one route out, and the other on the way back.

The Ruby Coast route begins on SH60 and skirts around Waimea Inlet before diverting along the well signposted **Ruby Coast Scenic Route**. Although this is the quickest way to get from Nelson to Motueka (around a 45-minute drive), there are various distractions waiting to slow you down. Major attractions include Rabbit Island (p410) recreation reserve, and **Mapua**, near the mouth of the Waimea River, home to arty shops and eateries.

The inland **Moutere Highway** (signposted at Appleby on SH60) is a pleasant alternative traversing gently rolling countryside dotted with farms, orchards and lifestyle blocks. Visitor attractions are fewer and further between, but it's a scenic and fruitful drive, particularly in high summer when roadside stalls are laden with fresh produce. The main settlement along the way is **Upper Moutere**. First settled by German immigrants and originally named Sarau, today it's a sleepy hamlet with a couple of notable stops. Look for the *Moutere Artisans* trail guide (www.moutereartisans.co.nz).

The two highways aren't particularly far apart, and the whole area can be explored by bicycle on the Great Taste Trail (p409), so named for the many wineries and other culinary (and art) stops along the way. The *Nelson Wine Guide* pamphlet (www.winenelson.co.nz) will help you find them. Other useful resources for this area are the *Nelson Art Guide* or *Nelson's Creative Pathways* pamphlets.

◉ Sights

Golden Bear Brewing Company　　BREWERY
(www.goldenbearbrewing.com; Mapua Wharf, Mapua; meals $10-16) In Mapua village it won't be hard to sniff out the Golden Bear – a microbrewery with tons of stainless steel out back, and a dozen or so brews out front. Authentic Mexican food (burritos, quesadillas and huevos rancheros; meals $10 to $16) will stop you from getting a sore head, and there's regular live music on Friday nights and Sunday afternoons.

★**Waimea**　　WINERY
(☏03-544 6385; www.waimeaestates.co.nz; 59 Appleby Hwy, Richmond; ⊙10am-5pm Mon-Wed, to 9pm Thu-Sun) Just 2km from Richmond you'll hit Waimea winery, where a diverse range of interesting wines is available to taste. Onsite is the deservedly popular **Cellar Door** (www.thecellardoor.net.nz; mains $18-30; ⊙10am-5pm Mon-Wed, to 9pm Thu-Sun).

Rabbit Island/Moturoa　　BEACH, FOREST
Around 9km from Richmond on SH60 is the signposted turn-off to Rabbit Island/Moturoa, a recreation reserve offering estuary views from many angles, sandy beaches and quiet pine forest trails forming part of the Great Taste Trail (p409). The bridge to the island closes at sunset; overnight stays are not allowed.

Höglund Art Glass　　GALLERY
(☏03-544 6500; www.hoglundartglass.com; 52 Lansdowne Rd, Appleby; ⊙10am-5pm) Ola, Marie and their associates work the furnace to produce internationally acclaimed glass art. The process is amazing to watch, and the results beautiful to view in the gallery. Their jewellery and penguins make memorable souvenirs if their signature vases are too heavy to take home.

🏃 Activities

Wheelie Fantastic　　BICYCLE TOUR
(☏03-543 2245; www.wheeliefantastic.co.nz; Mapua Wharf, Mapua; self-guided tours from $95, bike hire per day from $30) Conveniently located at Mapua Wharf, this operator offers several different self-guided and fully guided day tours around the Great Taste Trail, with shuttle pick-ups available.

🍴 Eating & Drinking

★**Jester House**　　CAFE $
(☏03-526 6742; www.jesterhouse.co.nz; 320 Aporo Rd, Tasman; meals $15-22; ⊙9am-5pm) Long-standing Jester House is reason alone to take this coastal detour, as much for its tame eels as for the peaceful sculpture gardens that encourage you to linger over lunch. A short, simple menu puts a few twists into staples (venison burger, lavender shortbread), and there is local beer and wines. It's 8km to Mapua or Motueka.

Smokehouse　　FISH & CHIPS $
(www.smokehouse.co.nz; Mapua Wharf, Mapua; fish & chips $8-12; ⊙11am-8pm) Visit this Mapua institution to order fresh fish and chips and eat them on the wharf while the gulls eye up your crispy bits. Get some delicious wood-smoked fish and pâté to go.

Jellyfish　　MODERN NZ $$
(☏03-540 2028; www.jellyfishmapua.co.nz; Mapua Wharf, Mapua; lunch $16-24, dinner $24-34; ⊙9am-late; ☏) Between the waterside location, sunny patio and inspired East–West menu you've got an A-grade all-day cafe.

Local fish and other produce feature heavily as do fine wines and craft beer.

Moutere Inn
PUB

(☑ 03-543 2759; www.moutereinn.co.nz; 1406 Moutere Hwy, Upper Moutere) Reputedly NZ's oldest pub, complete with genuine retro interior, the Moutere Inn is a welcoming establishment serving thoughtful meals ($13 to $20; homemade burgers, falafel salad) and predominantly local craft beer. Sit in the sunshine with a beer-tasting platter, or settle in on music nights with a folksy bent. Rooms are on offer if you need to rest your head.

ℹ️ Getting There & Away

InterCity (p409) buses service Nelson and Motueka, but to access the Ruby Coast and Moutere Hills you'll need your own transport. Biking the **Great Taste Trail** (p409) is a good way of exploring.

Motueka

POP 7600

Motueka (pronounced mott-oo-ecka, meaning 'Island of Weka') is a bustling agricultural hub, and a great base from which to explore the region. It has vital amenities, ample accommodation, cafes and roadside fruit stalls, all in a beautiful river and estuary setting. Stock up here if you're en route to Golden Bay or the Abel Tasman and Kahurangi National Parks.

◎ Sights

While most of Mot's drawcards are out of town, there are a few attractions worth checking out, the buzziest of which is the active aerodrome, home to several air-raising activities. It's a good place to soak up some sun and views, and watch a few folks drop in.

While you might not realise it from the high street, Motueka is just a stone's throw from the sea. Eyeball the waters (with birds and saltwater baths) along the **estuary walkway** (which can also be cycled; hire bikes from the **Bike Shed** (☑ 03-929 8607; www.motuekabikeshed.co.nz; 145b High St; half-/full-day hire from $25/40)). Follow your nose or obtain a town map from the i-SITE (p413), where you can also get the *Motueka Art Walk* pamphlet detailing sculptures, murals and occasional peculiarities around town.

Hop Federation
BREWERY

(☑ 03-528 0486; www.hopfederation.co.nz; 483 Main Rd, Riwaka; ⊙ 11am-6pm) Pop in for tastings ($3) and fill a flagon to go at this teeny-weeny but terrific craft brewery 5km from Mot. Our pick of the ales is the Red IPA. (And note the cherry stall across the road.)

Motueka District Museum
MUSEUM

(☑ 03-528 7660; www.motuekadistrictmuseum.org.nz; 140 High St; admission by donation; ⊙ 10am-4pm Mon-Fri Dec-Mar, to 3pm Tue-Fri Apr-Nov) An interesting collection of regional artefacts, housed in a dear old school building.

🏃 Activities

⭐ Skydive Abel Tasman
ADVENTURE SPORTS

(☑ 03-528 4091, 0800 422 899; www.skydive.co.nz; Motueka Aerodrome, 60 College St; jumps 13,000ft/16,500ft $299/399) Move over, Taupo: we've jumped both and think Mot takes the cake. Presumably so do the many sports jumpers who favour this drop zone, some of whom you may see rocketing in. Photo and video packages are extra. Excellent spectating from the front lawn.

U-fly Extreme
ADVENTURE SPORTS

(☑ 03-528 8290, 0800 360 180; www.uflyextreme.co.nz; Motueka Aerodrome, 60 College St; 15min $395, 20min $495, plus flight lesson $200) You handle the controls in an open-cockpit Pitts Special stunt bi-plane. No experience necessary, just a stomach for loops and barrel rolls. Roger wilco!

Tasman Sky Adventures
SCENIC FLIGHTS

(☑ 0800 114 336, 027 223 3513; www.skyadventures.co.nz; Motueka Aerodrome, 60 College St; 15/30min flights $105/205) A rare opportunity to fly in a microlight. Keep your eyes open and blow your mind on a scenic flight above Abel Tasman National Park. Wow. And there's tandem hang gliding for the brave (15/30 minutes, 2500ft/5280ft $195/330).

🛏️ Sleeping

⭐ Motueka Top 10 Holiday Park
HOLIDAY PARK $

(☑ 03-528 7189; www.motuekatop10.co.nz; 10 Fearon St; sites from $48, cabins $69-160, units & motels $113-457; @ 🛜 ♨) 🏊 Close to town and the Great Taste Trail, this place is packed with grassy, green charm – check out those lofty kahikatea trees! Shipshape communal amenities include a swimming pool, spa and jumping pillow, and there are ample accommodation options from smart new cabins to an apartment sleeping up to 11. On-site bike hire, plus local advice and bookings freely offered.

Motueka

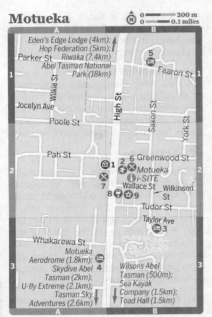

Motueka

◉ Sights
1 Motueka District Museum A2

◉ Activities, Courses & Tours
2 Bike Shed B2

◉ Sleeping
3 Equestrian Lodge Motel B3
4 Laughing Kiwi A3
5 Motueka Top 10 Holiday Park B1

◉ Eating
6 Motueka Sunday Market B2
7 Patisserie Royale A2

◉ Drinking & Nightlife
8 Sprig & Fern.. B2

◉ Entertainment
9 Gecko Theatre B2

Eden's Edge Lodge
HOSTEL $

(☎03-528 4242; www.edensedge.co.nz; 137 Lodder Lane, Riwaka; sites from $18, dm $31, d/tr with bathroom $99/86; ☎) ⌀ Surrounded by farmland, 4km from the bustle of Motueka, this purpose-built lodge comes pretty close to backpacker heaven. Well-designed facilities include a gleaming kitchen and inviting communal areas including a grassy garden. There's bike hire for tackling the Great Taste Trail, but it's also within walking distance of beer, ice cream and coffee.

Laughing Kiwi
HOSTEL $

(☎03-528 9229; www.laughingkiwi.co.nz; 310 High St; dm $29, d with/without bathroom $76/68; ☎) Compact, low-key YHA hostel with rooms spread between an old villa and a purpose-built backpacker lodge with a smart kitchen/lounge. The self-contained bach is a good option for groups of up to four ($180).

★ Equestrian Lodge Motel
MOTEL $$

(☎0800 668 782, 03-528 9369; www.equestrianlodge.co.nz; Avalon Ct; d $125-158, q $175-215; ☎☒) No horses, no lodge, but no matter. This excellent motel complex is close to town (off Tudor St) and features expansive lawns, rose gardens, and a heated pool and spa alongside a series of continually refreshed units. Cheerful owners will hook you up with local activities.

Resurgence
LODGE $$$

(☎03-528 4664; www.resurgence.co.nz; 574 Riwaka Valley Rd; d lodge from $695, chalets from $575; @☎☒) ⌀ Choose a luxurious en suite lodge room or a self-contained chalet at this magical green retreat. It's a 15-minute drive from Abel Tasman National Park, and a 30-minute walk from the picturesque source of the Riwaka River. Lodge rates include aperitifs and a four-course dinner as well as breakfast; chalet rates are for B&B, with dinner an extra $120.

✗ Eating

Patisserie Royale
BAKERY $

(152 High St; baked goods $2-8; ⊙5am-5pm Mon-Fri, to 3pm Sat & Sun; ☑) The best of several Mot bakeries and worth every delectable calorie. Lots of French fancies, delicious pies and bread with bite.

★ Toad Hall
CAFE $$

(☎03-528 6456; www.toadhallmotueka.co.nz; 502 High St; breakfast $10-20, lunch $10-23; ⊙8am-6pm, to 9pm summer) This fantastic cafe serves smashing breakfasts, such as smoked salmon rösti, and wholesome yet decadent lunches including pork-belly burgers. The sweet outdoor space is home to live music and pizza on Friday and Saturday nights in summer. Inside is a fine selection of smoothies, juices, baked goods, pies and selected groceries.

Motueka Sunday Market MARKET
(Wallace St; ☺8am-1pm Sun) On Sundays the
car park behind the i-SITE fills up with tres-
tle tables for the Motueka Sunday Market:
produce, jewellery, buskers, arts, crafts and
Doris' divine bratwurst.

Drinking & Nightlife

Sprig & Fern CRAFT BEER
(☏03-528 4684; www.sprigandfern.co.nz; Wallace
St; ☺2pm-late) A member of the local Sprig
& Fern brewery family, this backstreet tavern is the pick of Motueka's drinking holes.
Small and pleasant, with two courtyards, it
offers 20 hand-pulled brews, simple food
(pizza, platters and an awesome burger;
meals $15 to $23) and occasional live music.

☆ Entertainment

Gecko Theatre CINEMA
(☏03-528 9996; www.geckotheatre.co.nz; 23b
Wallace St; tickets $9-13) Pull up an easy chair
at this wee, independent theatre and see interesting art-house flicks.

ⓘ Information

Motueka i-SITE (☏03-528 6543; www.
motuekasite.co.nz; 20 Wallace St; ☺8.30am-
5pm Mon-Fri, 9am-4pm Sat & Sun) A endlessly
busy info centre with helpful staff handling
bookings from Kaitaia to Bluff and provide local
national-park expertise and necessaries.

ⓘ Getting There & Away

Bus services depart from Motueka i-SITE.
Abel Tasman Coachlines (☏03-548 0285;
www.abeltasmantravel.co.nz) runs daily from
Nelson (where you can connect to other South
Island Destinations via **InterCity** (p383)) to
Motueka (one hour), Kaiteriteri (25 minutes)
and Marahau (30 minutes). These services
connect with **Golden Bay Coachlines** (p403)
services to Takaka (1¼ hours) and other Golden
Bay destinations including Totaranui in Abel
Tasman National Park, Collingwood, and on to
the Heaphy Track trailhead. Note that from May
to September all buses run less frequently.

Kaiteriteri

POP 790
Known simply as 'Kaiteri', this seaside hamlet 13km from Motueka is the most popular
resort town in the area. During the summer
holidays its golden swimming beach feels
more like Noumea than NZ, with more tow-
els than sand. Consider yourself warned.

Kaiteri is also a major departure point for
Abel Tasman National Park transport, although Marahau is the main base.

Activities

Kaiteriteri
Mountain Bike Park MOUNTAIN BIKING
(www.kaiteriterimtbpark.org.nz) Extensive MTB
park with tracks to suit all levels of rider.

🛏 Sleeping & Eating

Kaiteri Lodge LODGE $
(☏03-527 8281; www.kaiterilodge.co.nz; Inlet Rd; dm $35, d $80-160; @☎) Modern,
purpose-built lodge with small, simple
dorms and en suite doubles. The nautical
decor adds some cheer to the somewhat lazily maintained communal areas. The sociable
Beached Whale (dinner $18-28; ☺4pm-late, re-
duced hours in winter) bar is on-site.

Torlesse Coastal Motels MOTEL $$
(☏03-527 8063; www.torlessemotels.co.nz; 8 Ko-
tare Pl, Little Kaiteriteri Beach; d $190-210, q $300-
350; ☎) Just 200m from Little Kaiteriteri
Beach (around the corner from the main
beach) is this congregation of roomy hill-
side units with pitched ceilings, full kitchens
and laundries. Most have water views, and
there's a ferny barbecue area and spa.

Bellbird Lodge B&B $$$
(☏03-527 8555; www.bellbirdlodge.co.nz; 160
Kaiteriteri-Sandy Bay Rd; d $275-350; @☎) An
upmarket B&B 1.5km up the hill from Kaiteri Beach, offering two en suite rooms, bush
and sea views, extensive gardens, spectacular breakfasts (featuring homemade muesli
and fruit compote), and gracious hosts. Dinner by arrangement in winter, when local
restaurant hours are irregular.

Shoreline RESTAURANT $$
(☏03-527 8507; www.shorelinekaiteriteri.co.nz;
cnr Inlet & Sandy Bay Rds; meals $18-22; ☺7.30am-
9pm, reduced hours Apr-Nov) A modern, beige
cafe-bar-restaurant right on the beach.
Punters chill out on the sunny deck, linger-
ing over sandwiches, pizzas, burgers and
other predictable fare, or pop in for coffee
and cake. Erratic winter hours; burger booth
out the back.

ⓘ Getting There & Away

Kaiteriteri is serviced by **Abel Tasman Coach-
lines** (☏03-548 0285; www.abeltasmantravel.
co.nz).

Marahau

POP 120

Just up the coast from Kaiteriteri and 18km north of Motueka, Marahau is the main gateway to Abel Tasman National Park. It's less of a town, more of a procession of holiday homes and tourist businesses.

🏃 Activities

Marahau Horse Treks　　　　HORSE RIDING

(📞03-527 8425; Marahau-Sandy Bay Rd; children's pony rides $35, 2hr horse rides $90) If you're in an equine state of mind, Marahau Horse Treks offers you a chance to belt along the beach on a horse, your hair streaming out behind you.

🛏 Sleeping

Barn　　　　HOSTEL $

(📞03-527 8043; www.barn.co.nz; 14 Harvey Rd; unpowered/powered sites per person $20/22, dm $32, d $68-85; @🛜) This backpackers has hit its straps with comfortable new dorms, a toilet block and a grassy camping field added to a mix of microcabins, alfresco kitchens and barbecue areas. The barn itself is the hub – the communal kitchen and lounge area are good for socialising, as is the central deck, which has a fireplace. Activity bookings and secure parking available.

Abel Tasman Marahau Lodge　　　　MOTEL $$

(📞03-527 8250; www.abeltasmanlodge.co.nz; 295 Sandy Bay-Marahau Rd; d $145-175, q $200-260; @🛜) 🅿 Enjoy halcyon days in this arc of 15 studios and self-contained units with groovy styling and cathedral ceilings, opening out on to landscaped gardens. There's also a fully equipped communal kitchen for self-caterers, plus spa and sauna. Cuckoos, tui and bellbirds squawk and warble in the bushy surrounds.

Ocean View Chalets　　　　CHALET $$

(📞03-527 8232; www.accommodationabeltasman. co.nz; 305 Sandy Bay-Marahau Rd; d $145-235, q $290; 🛜) On a leafy hillside affording plenty of privacy, these cheerful, cypress-lined chalets are 300m from the Coast Track with views out to Fisherman Island. All except the cheapest studios are self-contained; breakfast and packed lunches available.

🍴 Eating

Fat Tui　　　　BURGERS $

(cnr Marahau-Sandy Bay & Marahau Valley Rds; burgers $13-18; ⏱noon-8pm daily summer, Wed-Sun winter) Everyone's heard about this bird, based in a caravan that ain't rollin' anywhere fast. Thank goodness. Superlative burgers, such as the Cowpat (beef), the Ewe Beaut (lamb) and Roots, Shoots & Leaves (vege). Fish and chips, and coffee, too.

Hooked　　　　CAFE $$

(📞03-527 8576; www.hookedonmarahau.co.nz; 229 Marahau-Sandy Bay Rd; lunch $11-20, dinner $26-32; ⏱8am-10pm Dec-Mar, 8am-11am & 3pm-10pm Oct-Nov & Apr) This popular place certainly reels them in, so reservations are advisable for dinner. The art-bedecked interior opens on to an outdoor terrace with distracting views. Lunch centres on salads and seafood, while the dinner menu boasts fresh fish of the day, green-lipped mussels and NZ lamb shanks.

Park Cafe　　　　CAFE $$

(📞03-527 8270; www.parkcafe.co.nz; Harvey Rd; lunch $10-22, dinner $17-36; ⏱8am-late mid-Sep–May; 📶) Sitting at the Coast Track trailhead, this breezy cafe is perfectly placed for fuelling up or restoring the waistline. High-calorie options include the big breakfast, burgers and cakes, but there are also seafood and salad options plus wood-fired pizza Thursday through Saturday evenings. Enjoy in the room with a view or the sunny courtyard garden. Live music on occasion.

ℹ Getting There & Away

Marahau is serviced by **Abel Tasman Coach-lines** (📞03-548 0285; www.abeltasmantravel. co.nz).

Abel Tasman National Park

Coastal Abel Tasman National Park blankets the northern end of a range of marble and limestone hills that extend from Kahurangi National Park. Various tracks in the park include an inland route, although the Coast Track is what everyone is here for – it's NZ's most popular Great Walk.

🏃 Activities

Abel Tasman Coast Track

This is arguably NZ's most beautiful Great Walk – 60km of sparkling seas, golden sand, quintessential coastal forest, and hidden surprises such as Cleopatra's Pool. Such pulling power attracts around 30,000

Abel Tasman National Park

N
0 — 5 km
0 — 2.5 miles

Wharariki Bay

Taupo Point

Separation Point

Mutton Cove

Taupo Hill (205m)

Abel Tasman Point

Uarau Point

Whariwharangi Hut

Anapai Bay Track

Anapai Bay

Wainui Bay

Arapai Bay Campsite

Anapai Bay

Meshane Rd

Gibbs Hill (405m)

TASMAN SEA

Abel Tasman Dr

Pigeon Saddle

Totaranui Campsite

Totaranui

Goat Bay

Centre Peak (534m)

Awaroa Saddle

Skinner Point

Waiharakeke Bay

Totaranui Rd

Wainui Falls

Inland Track

Awaroa Rd

Awaroa Bay

Awaroa Head

Awapoto Hut

Waiharakeke Bay Campsite

Tonga Island Marine Reserve

Awapoto River

Awaroa Inlet

Awaroa Campsite

Tonga Saddle (260m)

Waterfall Creek

Wainui River

Camp Creek

Stony Hill (394m)

Onetahuti Bay Campsite

Onetahuti Beach

Tonga Island

Awaroa River

Tonga Quarry Campsite

Arch Point

Jenkins Falls

Foul Point

Table Creek

Tonga Hill (458m)

Mosquito Bay Campsite

Evans Creek

Bark Bay Campsite

Bark Bay Hut

Bark Bay

Medlands Beach Campsite

South Head

Sandfly Bay

Moa Park Shelter

Bare Knob (314m)

Cascade Falls

North Head

Falls River

Mt Evans (1156m)

Inland Track

Castle Rock Hut

Torrent River

Torrent Bay Village Campsite

Torrent Bay

Pitt Head

Te Pukatea Bay Campsite

Cleopatra's Pool

Aquapackers

Holyoake Clearing Shelter

Anchorage Campsite

Anchorage Hut

Watering Cove Campsite

Te Karetu Point

Marahau River

Observation Beach Campsite

Watering Cove

Akersten Bay Campsite

Yellow Point

Jules Point

Adele Island

Apple Tree Bay Campsite

Tinline Campsite

Appletree Bay

Day Shelter (Park Entrance)

Otuwheru River

Tinline Bay

Coquille Bay

Fisherman Island

Sandy Bay

Marahau

overnight trampers and kayakers per year, each of whom stay at least one night in the park. A major attraction is the terrain: well cut, well graded and well marked. It's almost impossible to get lost here and the track can be tramped in sneakers.

You will, however, probably get your feet wet, as this track features long stretches of beach and crazy tides. In fact the tidal differences in the park are among the greatest in the country, up to a staggering 6m. At Torrent and Bark Bays, it's much easier and more fun to doff the shoes and cross the soggy sands, rather than take the high-tide track. At Awaroa Bay you have no choice but to plan on crossing close to low tide. Tide tables are posted along the track and on the DOC website; regional i-SITEs also have them.

It's a commonly held belief that the Coast Track ends at Totaranui, but it actually extends to a car park near Wainui Bay. The entire tramp takes only three to five days, although with water taxi transport you can convert it into an almost endless array of options, particularly if you combine it with a kayak leg. If you can only spare a couple of days, a rewarding option is to loop around the northern end of the park, tramping the Coast Track from Totaranui, passing Anapai Bay and Mutton Cove, overnighting at Whariwharangi Hut, then returning to Totaranui via the Gibbs Hill Track. This will give you

PADDLING THE ABEL TASMAN

The Abel Tasman Coast Track has long been tramping territory, but its coastal beauty makes it an equally seductive spot for sea kayaking, which can easily be combined with walking and camping.

A variety of professional outfits are able to float you out on the water, and the possibilities and permutations for guided or freedom trips are vast. You can kayak from half a day up to three days, camping, or staying in DOC huts, bachs, even a floating backpackers, either fully catered or self-catering. You can kayak one day, camp overnight then walk back, or walk further into the park and catch a water taxi back.

Most operators offer similar trips at similar prices. Marahau is the main base, but trips also depart from Kaiteriteri. There are numerous day-trip options, including guided trips often departing Marahau and taking in bird-filled Adele Island (around $200). There are also various multiday guided trips, with three days a common option, costing anything from $260 to $750 depending on accommodation and other inclusions.

Freedom rentals (double-kayak and equipment hire) are around $70/110 per person for one/two days; all depart from Marahau with the exception of **Golden Bay Kayaks** (p420), which is based at Tata Beach in Golden Bay.

Instruction is given to everyone, and most tour companies have a minimum age of either eight or 14 depending on the trip. None allow solo hires. Camping gear is usually provided on overnight trips; if you're disappearing into the park for a few days, most operators provide free car parking.

November to Easter is the busiest time, with December to February the absolute peak. You can, however, paddle all year round, with winter offering its own rewards; the weather is surprisingly amenable, the seals are more playful, and there's more birdlife and less haze.

Following are the main players in this competitive market (shop around):

Abel Tasman Kayaks (☑ 0800 732 529, 03-527 8022; www.abeltasmankayaks.co.nz; Main Rd, Marahau)

Kahu Kayaks (☑ 0800 300 101, 03-527 8300; www.kahukayaks.co.nz; 11 Marahau Valley Rd)

Kaiteriteri Kayaks (☑ 0800 252 925, 03-527 8383; www.seakayak.co.nz; Kaiteriteri Beach)

Marahau Sea Kayaks (☑ 0800 529 257, 03-527 8176; www.msk.co.nz; Abel Tasman Centre, Franklin St, Marahau)

R&R Kayaks (☑ 0508 223 224; www.rrkayaks.co.nz; 279 Sandy Bay-Marahau Rd)

Sea Kayak Company (☑ 0508 252 925, 03-528 7251; www.seakayaknz.co.nz; 506 High St, Motueka)

Wilsons Abel Tasman (p417)

a slice of the park's best features (beaches seals, coastal scenery) while being far less crowded than other segments.

The track operates on DOC's Great Walks Pass. Children are free but bookings are still required. Book online (www.doc.govt.nz), contact the **Nelson Marlborough Bookings Helpdesk** (☑ 03-546 8210), or book in person at the Nelson, Motueka or Takaka i-SITES or DOC offices, where staff can offer suggestions to tailor the track to your needs and organise transport at each end. Book your trip well ahead of time, especially huts between December and March.

This track is so well trodden that a topographical map isn't essential for navigation. The map within DOC's *Abel Tasman Coast Track* brochure provides sufficient detail, and you can readily buy more illuminating maps at local visitor centres.

Other Activities

★ **Abel Tasman Canyons** ADVENTURE SPORTS
(☑ 0800 863 472, 03-528 9800; www.abeltasmancanyons.co.nz; full-day trips $259) Few Abel Tasman visitors see the Torrent River; here's your chance to journey down its staggeringly beautiful granite-lined canyon, via a fun-filled combination of swimming, sliding, abseiling and big leaps into jewel-like pools.

☞ Tours

Tour companies usually offer free Motueka pick-up/drop-off, with Nelson pick-up available at extra cost.

★ **Wilsons Abel Tasman** TOUR
(☑ 03-528 2027, 0800 223 582; www.abeltasman.co.nz; 409 High St, Motueka) This longstanding, family-owned operator offers an impressive array of cruises, walking, kayaking and combo tours, including a $36 daywalk special. Overnight stays are available at Wilsons' lodges in pretty Awaroa and Torrent Bay for guided-tour guests.

Offers an Explorer Pass for unlimited boat travel on three days over a seven-day period (adult/child $150/75).

Abel Tasman Eco Tours TOUR
(☑ 0800 223 538, 03-528 0946; www.abeltasmanecotours.co.nz; day tours adult/child $159/99) Take an ecology-focused day trip with marine scientist Stew Robertson, either cruising around the coast in a boat, or on a five-hour tramping trip in the Wainui Valley.

**Abel Tasman Tours
& Guided Walks** WALKING TOUR
(☑ 03-528 9602; www.abeltasmantours.co.nz; tours from $245) Small-group, day-long walking tours (minimum two people) that include a packed lunch and water taxis.

Abel Tasman Charters BOAT TOUR
(☑ 027 441 8588, 0800 223 522; www.abeltasmancharters.com; 6hr tours $265) Offers a six-hour trip combining walking, kayaking, swimming and cruising into the park from Stephens Bay (near Kaiteriteri).

Abel Tasman Sailing Adventures SAILING
(☑ 0800 467 245, 03-527 8375; www.sailingadventures.co.nz; Kaiteriteri; day trips $185) Scheduled and on-demand catamaran trips, with sail/walk/kayak combos available. The popular day trip includes lunch on Anchorage Beach.

🛏 Sleeping

Along the Abel Tasman Coast Track are four Great Walk huts ($32) with bunks, heating, flush toilets and limited lighting, but no cooking facilities. There are also 19 designated Great Walk campsites ($14). As the Coast Track is a Great Walk, all huts and campsites must be booked in advance year-round, either online through **Great Walks Bookings** (☑ 0800 694 732; www.doc.govt.nz) or at DOC visitor centres nationwide. Hut tickets and annual passes cannot be used on the track, and there is a two-night limit on stays in each hut or campsite, except for Totaranui campsite which has a one-night limit. Penalty fees apply to those who do not have a valid booking, and you may be required to leave the park if caught.

Aquapackers HOSTEL
(☑ 0800-30 744; www.aquapackers.co.nz; Anchorage; dm/r incl breakfast $75/225; ⊙ closed May-Sep) The specially converted 13m *Catarac* (catamaran), moored permanently in Anchorage Bay, provides unusual but buoyant backpacker accommodation for 22. Facilities are basic but decent; prices include bedding, dinner and breakfast. Bookings essential.

Totaranui Campsite CAMPGROUND
(☑ 03-528 3083; www.doc.govt.nz; summer/winter $15/10) An extremely popular facility with a whopping capacity (850 campers) and a splendid setting next to the beach backed by some of the best bush in the park. A staffed DOC office has interpretive displays, flush toilets, cold showers and a public phone.

ⓘ Getting There & Away

The closest big town to Abel Tasman is Motueka, with nearby Marahau the southern gateway. Although Wainui is the official northern trailhead, it is more common to finish in Totaranui, either skipping the northernmost section or looping back to Totaranui over Gibbs Hill Track. All gateways are serviced by either **Abel Tasman Coachlines** (p403) and **Golden Bay Coachlines** (p403).

ⓘ Getting Around

Once you hit the park, it is easy to get to/from any point on the track via numerous tour companies and water taxi operators offering scheduled and on-demand services, either from Kaiteriteri or Marahau. Typical one-way prices from either Marahau or Kaiteriteri: Anchorage and Torrent Bay ($35), Bark Bay ($40), Awaroa ($45) and Totaranui ($47).

Abel Tasman Aqua Taxi (☑ 0800 278 282, 03-527 8083; www.aquataxi.co.nz; Marahau-Sandy Bay Rd, Marahau) Scheduled and on-demand services as well as boat/walk options.

Marahau Water Taxis (☑ 0800 808 018, 03-527 8176; www.marahauwatertaxis.co.nz; Abel Tasman Centre, Franklin St, Marahau) Scheduled services plus boat/walk options.

Golden Bay

From Motueka, SH60 takes a stomach-churning meander over Takaka Hill to Golden Bay, a small region mixing rural charm, artistic endeavour, alternative lifestyles and a fair share of transient folk spending time off the grid.

For the visitor its main attractions are access to both the Abel Tasman and Kahurangi National Parks, along with other natural wonders including Farewell Spit and a swathe of beautiful beaches. Look out for (or download) DOC's *Walks in Golden Bay* brochure to kick-start your adventures.

ⓘ Getting There & Away

Golden Bay is well serviced by **Golden Bay Coachlines** (☑ 03-525 8352; www.gbcoachlines.co.nz), with daily runs between Nelson and the Heaphy Track via Motueka and Takaka, but to get to quiet corners you'll need to be wily or have your own wheels.

Takaka Hill

Takaka Hill (791m) butts in between Tasman Bay and Golden Bay. It looks pretty bushy but closer inspection reveals a remarkable marble landscape formed by millions of years of erosion. It's smooth beauty is revealed on the one-hour drive over the hill road (SH60), a steep, winding route punctuated by spectacular lookout points and a smattering of other interesting stops.

Just before the summit is the turn-off to **Canaan Downs Scenic Reserve**, reached at the end of an 11km gravel road. This area stars in both the *The Lord of the Rings* and *The Hobbit* movies, but **Harwoods Hole** is the most famous feature here. It's one of the largest *tomo* (caves) in the country at 357m deep and 70m wide, with a 176m vertical drop. It's a 30-minute walk from the car park. Allow us to state the obvious: the cave is off-limits to all but the most experienced cavers.

Mountain-bikers with intermediate-level skills can venture along a couple of loop tracks, or head all the way down to Takaka via the titillating **Rameka Track**. There's a basic DOC Campsite (adult/child $6/$3) here, too.

Also close to the top, the **Takaka Hill Walkway** is a three-hour loop through marble karst rock formations, native forest and farmland. Further along the road **Harwood Lookout** affords tantalising views down the Takaka River Valley to Takaka and Golden Bay. For more walks on the sunny side of the hill, see DOC's brochure *Walks in Golden Bay*.

◉ Sights

Ngarua Caves CAVES
(SH60; adult/child $17/7; ⊙45min tours hourly 10am-4pm Sep-May, open Sat & Sun only Jun-Aug) Just below the summit of Takaka Hill (literally) are the Ngarua Caves, a rock-solid attraction karst in stone, where you can see myriad subterranean delights including moa bones. Access is restricted to tours – you can't go solo spelunking.

Takaka

POP 1240

Boasting NZ's highest concentration of yoga pants, dreadlocks and bare feet in the high street, Takaka is a lovable little town and the last 'big' centre before the road west ends at Farewell Spit. You'll find most things you need here, and a few things you don't, but we all have an unworn tie-dyed tank top in our wardrobe, don't we?

◉ Sights

Many of Takaka's sights can readily be reached via bicycle, with hire and maps available from the time-warped **Quiet Rev-**

olution Cycle Shop (☑03-525 9555; www.
quietrevolution.co.nz; 11 Commercial St; bike hire
per day $25-65) on the main street. Shopping
is also a highlight if you enjoy festival chic
and homespun art and craft. To extend your
arty ambles, look for the free *Arts in Golden
Bay* and *Arts Trail* pamphlets.

Rawhiti Cave
CAVE

(www.doc.govt.nz) The ultimate in geological
eye-candy around these parts are the phyto-
karst features of Rawhiti Cave, a 15-minute
drive from Takaka (reached via Motupipi,
turning right into Glenview Rd, then left
into Packard Rd and following the signs).
The rugged two-hour-return walk (steep in
places; dangerous in the wet) may well leave
you speechless (although we managed 'monster', 'fangs', and even 'Sarlacc').

Grove Scenic Reserve
VIEWPOINT

(www.doc.govt.nz) Around a 10-minute drive
from Takaka (signposted down Clifton Rd),
you will find this crazy limestone maze
punctuated by gnarled old rata trees. The
walkway takes around 10 minutes and passes an impressive lookout.

Te Waikoropupū Springs
SPRING

(www.doc.govt.nz) The largest freshwater
springs in the southern hemisphere and
some of the clearest in the world, 'Pupū
Springs' is a colourful little lake refreshed
with around 14,000L of water per second
surging from underground vents. From
Takaka, head 4km northwest on SH60 and
follow the signs inland for 3km from Waita-
pu Bridge. There are illuminating information panels at the car park and a 30-minute
forest loop taking in the waters, which are
sacred and therefore off limits.

Activities

Pupu Hydro Walkway
TRAMPING

(www.doc.govt.nz; Pupu Valley Rd) This enjoyable two-hour circuit follows an old water
race through beech forest, past engineering
and gold-mining relics to the restored (and
operational) Pupu Hydro Powerhouse, built
in 1929. It's 9km from Takaka at the end of
Pupu Valley Rd; just follow the signs at the
Te Waikoropupū Springs junction.

Tours

Golden Bay Air
SCENIC FLIGHTS

(☑0800 588 385, 03-525 8725; www.goldenbayair.
co.nz; Takaka Airfield, SH60) Scenic and charter
flights around Golden Bay and surrounds;
from $35.

🛌 Sleeping

Kiwiana
HOSTEL $

(☑0800 805 494, 03-525 7676; www.kiwianaback
packers.co.nz; 73 Motupipi St; tent sites per person
$18, dm $29-31, s/d $54/68; @🛜) Beyond the
welcoming garden is a cute cottage where
rooms are named after classic Kiwiana (the
jandal, Buzzy Bee...). The garage has been
converted into a convivial lounge, with wood-
fired stove, table tennis, pool table, music,
books and games; free bikes for guest use.

Takaka Campground
CAMPGROUND $

(☑03-525 7300; www.takakacampingandcabins.
co.nz 53 Motupipi St; sites per person $18, cab-
ins s/d/tr $35/65/75; 🛜) This low-key and
convenient campground, within walking
distance of the Takaka high street, sports a
splendid rural outlook.

Golden Bay Kiwi Holiday Park
HOLIDAY PARK $

(☑03-525 9742; www.goldenbayholidaypark.co.nz;
99 Tukurua Rd, Tukurua; unpowered/powered sites
$43/47, cabins d $85; @🛜) Eighteen kilometres north of Takaka with a quiet beach
right out front, this gem of a park has acres
of grass, graceful shade trees and hedgerows, easily atoning for tight communal facilities. There are tidy, family-friendly cabins
for budget travellers, and luxury beach houses sleeping up to four (S180 to $270).

⭐ Adrift
COTTAGES $$$

(☑03-525 8353; www.adrift.co.nz; 53 Tukurua Rd,
Tukurua; d $250-540; 🛜) 🍴 Adrift on a heav-
enly bed of beachside bliss is what you'll be
in one of these five cottages dotted within
beautifully landscaped grounds, right on
the beach. Tuck into your breakfast hamper,
then self-cater in the fully equipped kitchen,
dine on the sunny deck, or soak in the spa
bath.

🍴 Eating & Drinking

Dangerous Kitchen
CAFE $$

(☑03-525 8586; 46a Commercial St; meals $13-
28; ⊙9am-8pm Mon-Sat; 🍴) 🍴 Dedicated
to Frank Zappa, DK serves largely healthy,
good-value fare such as falafel, pizza, bean
burritos, pasta, great baking and juices as
well as local wines and craft beer. It's mellow and musical, with a sunny courtyard out
back and people-watching out front.

⭐ Mussel Inn
PUB

(☑03-525 9241; www.musselinn.co.nz; 1259 SH60,
Onekaka; all-day snacks $5-17, dinner $13-30;
⊙11am-late, closed Jul-Aug) You will find one

of NZ's most beloved brewery-taverns half-way between Takaka and Collingwood. The Mussel Inn is rustic NZ at its most genuine, complete with creaking timbers, a rambling beer garden with a brazier, regular music and other events, and hearty, homemade food. Try the signature 'Captain Cooker', a brown beer brewed naturally with manuka.

☆ Entertainment

Village Theatre   CINEMA
(☑ 03-525 8453; www.villagetheatre.org.nz; 32 Commercial St; adult/child $14/8) Demonstrating, yet again, provincial NZ's commitment to quality viewing.

ℹ Information

Golden Bay Visitor Centre (☑ 03-525 9136; www.goldenbaynz.co.nz; Willow St; ⊙ 9am-4pm Mon-Fri, to 1pm Sat) A friendly little centre with all the necessary information, including the indispensable official tourist map. Bookings and DOC passes.

Golden Bay Area DOC Office (☑ 03-525 8026; www.doc.govt.nz; 62 Commercial St; ⊙ 1-3pm Mon-Fri) Information on Abel Tasman and Kahurangi National Parks, the Heaphy Track, Farewell Spit and Cobb Valley. Sells hut passes.

ℹ Getting There & Away

Golden Bay Air (p419) flies at least once and up to four times daily between Wellington and Takaka.

Golden Bay Coachlines (p403) departs from Takaka on Golden Bay and runs through to Collingwood (25 minutes), the Heaphy Track (one hour), Totaranui (one hour), and over the hill to Motueka (1¼ hours) and Nelson (2¼ hours).

Pohara

POP 550

About 10km northeast of Takaka is pint-sized Pohara, a beachy village with a population that quadruples over summer. It has more flash holiday homes than other parts of Golden Bay, but an agreeable air persists nonetheless, aided by decent food and lodging, and a beach that at low tide is as big as Heathrow's runway.

Pohara lies close to the northern gateway of Abel Tasman National Park. The largely unsealed road into the park passes **Tara-kohe Harbour** (Pohara's working port), followed by **Ligar Bay**. It's worth climbing to the Abel Tasman lookout as you pass by.

The next settlement along is **Tata Beach**, where **Golden Bay Kayaks** (☑ 03-525 9095;

www.goldenbaykayaks.co.nz; Tata Beach; half-day guided tours adult/child from $85/40, freedom hire half-/full day $90/120) offers freedom rental of kayaks and stand-up paddle boards, as well as guided trips (including multiday) into Abel Tasman National Park.

Signposted from the Totaranui Rd at **Wainui Bay** is a leafy walk to the best cascade in the bay: **Wainui Falls**. It's a one-hour return trip, but you could easily take longer by dipping a toe or two in the river.

🛏 Sleeping & Eating

Pohara Beach

Top 10 Holiday Park   HOLIDAY PARK $
(☑ 0800 764 272, 03-525 9500; www.poharabeach.com; 809 Abel Tasman Dr; sites per person from $22, cabins & units $65-169; @ ⚛) Lining grassy parkland between the dunes and the main road, this place is in prime position for some beach time. Sites are nice and there are some beaut cabins, but be warned – this is a favourite spot for NZ holidaymakers so it goes a bit mental in high summer. General store and takeaway on-site.

★ **Sans Souci Inn**   LODGE $$
(☑ 03-525 8663; www.sanssouciinn.co.nz; 11 Richmond Rd; s/d $95/120, units from $160; ⊙ closed Jul–mid-Sep; ⚛) 🌱 Sans Souci means 'no worries' in French, and this will be your mantra too after staying in one of the seven Mediterranean-flavoured, mud-brick rooms. Guests share a plant-filled, mosaic bathroom that has composting toilets, and an airy lounge and kitchen which open out on to the semitropical courtyard. Dinner in the on-site restaurant (bookings essential; mains $35 to $37) is highly recommended; breakfast by request.

Ratanui   LODGE $$$
(☑ 03-525 7998; www.ratanuilodge.com; 818 Abel Tasman Dr; d $155-359; @ ⚛ ⚛) A romantic haven close to the beach, this boutique lodge is styled with Victorian panache. It features myriad sensual stimulants such as perfumed rose gardens, a swimming pool, a spa, a massage service, cocktails, and a candelabra-lit restaurant showcasing local produce (open to the public; bookings required). Free bikes, too.

Penguin Café & Bar   PUB FOOD $$
(☑ 03-525 6126; www.penguincafe.co.nz; 822 Abel Tasman Dr; bar snacks $6-15, meals $16-31; ⊙ 11am-late Nov-Apr, 4pm-late Mon-Wed & 11am-late Thu-Sun May-Oct) A popular locals' hangout, this well-run spot sports a large garden suited to sundowners and thirst-quenchers

FAREWELL SPIT

Bleak, exposed and positively sci-fi, Farewell Spit is a wetland of international importance and a renowned bird sanctuary – the summer home of thousands of migratory waders, notably the godwit (which flies all the way from the Arctic tundra), Caspian tern and Australasian gannet. Walkers can explore the first 4km of the spit via a network of tracks (see DOC's *Farewell Spit & Puponga Farm Park* brochure $2 or downloadable from www.doc.govt.nz). Beyond that point access is limited to trips with the brilliant Farewell Spit Eco Tours, scheduled according to the tide.

The spit's 35km beach features colossal, crescent-shaped dunes, from where panoramic views extend across Golden Bay and a vast low-tide salt marsh.

At the foot of the spit is a hilltop visitor-centre-cum-cafe – a convenient spot to write a postcard over a coffee, especially on an inclement day.

Farewell Spit Eco Tours (⌀ 0800 808 257, 03-524 8257; www.farewellspit.com; 6 Tasman St, Collingwood; tours $125-165) has been operating for more than 70 years. Led by the inimitable Paddy and his expert guides, this company runs memorable tours ranging from two to 6½ hours. Departing from Collingwood tours take in the spit, the lighthouse, and up to 20 species of bird which may include gannets and godwits. Expect ripping yarns aplenty.

Befitting a frontier, this is the place to saddle up **Cape Farewell Horse Treks** (⌀ 03-524 8031; www.horsetreksnz.com; McGowan St, Puponga; treks from $80) is en route to Wharariki Beach. Treks in this wind-blown country range from 1½ hours (to Pillar Point) to three hours (to Wharariki Beach), with longer (including overnight) trips by arrangement.

on sunny days. There's an open fire inside for the odd inclement day. Chow down on belly-filling bar-snacks, and look out for local seafood specials come dinner time.

ⓘ Getting There & Away

Golden Bay Coachlines (⌀ 03-525 8352; www.gbcoachlines.co.nz) runs daily on the way to Totaranui.

Collingwood & Around

POP 240

Far-flung Collingwood (population 240) is the last town in Golden Bay, and has a real end-of-the-line vibe. It's busy in summer, though for most people it's simply a launch pad for the Heaphy Track or Farewell Spit.

ⓞ Sights

Wharariki Beach BEACH
Remote, desolate Wharariki Beach is along an unsealed road, then a 20-minute walk from the car park over farmland (part of the DOC-administered Puponga Farm Park). It's a wild introduction to the West Coast, with mighty dune formations, looming rock islets just offshore and a seal colony at its eastern end (keep an eye out for seals in the stream on the walk here). As inviting as a swim here may seem, there are strong undertows – what the sea wants, the sea shall have...

Collingwood Museum MUSEUM
(Tasman St, Collingwood; admission by donation; ⊙ 9am-6pm) The Collingwood Museum fills a tiny, unstaffed corridor with a quirky collection of saddlery, Māori artefacts, moa bones, shells and old typewriters.

Next door, the **Aorere Centre** has an on-rotation slide show featuring the works of the wonderful pioneer photographer, Fred Tyree.

🛏 Sleeping & Eating

⭐ **Innlet Backpackers & Cottages** HOSTEL $
(⌀ 03-524 3040, 027 970 8397; www.theinnlet.co.nz; 839 Collingwood-Puponga Rd, Pakawau; dm/d $34/80, cabins from $90; ⊙ closed Jun-Aug; 🛜) This flower-filled charmer is 10km from Collingwood on the way to Farewell Spit. The main house has elegant backpacker rooms, and there are self-contained options including a cottage sleeping six; campers can enquire about sites. Enjoy the garden, explore the local area on a bike or in a kayak, or venture out for a tramp on the property.

Somerset House HOSTEL $
(⌀ 03-524 8624; www.backpackerscollingwood.co.nz; 10 Gibbs Rd, Collingwood; dm/s/d incl breakfast $32/50/78; ⊙ closed May-Oct; 🅿🛜) A small, low-key hostel in a bright, historic building on a hill with views from the deck. Get tramping advice from the charming

owners, who offer track transport, free bikes and kayaks, freshly baked bread for breakfast, and your fourth night's stay free.

Old School Cafe CAFE $$

(1115 Collingwood-Puponga Rd, Pakawau; mains $14-31; ⊙4pm-late Thu-Fri, 11am-late Sat & Sun) These folks get an A for effort by providing honest food to an unpredictable flow of passing trade. What it lacks in imagination (steak, pizza and even a shrimp cocktail), it more than makes up for with arty ambience, a garden bar and a welcoming disposition.

🛈 Getting There & Away

Golden Bay Coachlines (☑03-525 8352; www.gbcoachlines.co.nz) runs twice daily from Takaka to Collingwood (25 minutes).

Kahurangi National Park

Kahurangi – 'blue skies' in one of several translations – is the second largest of NZ's national parks, and also one of its most diverse. Its most eye-catching features are geological, ranging from windswept beaches and sea cliffs to earthquake-shattered slopes and moraine-dammed lakes, and the smooth, strange karst forms of the interior tableland.

Around 85% of the 4520 sq km park is forested, with beech prevalent, along with rimu and other podocarps. In all, more than 50% of all NZ's plant species can be found in the park, including more than 80% of its alpine plant species. Among the park's 60 birds species are great spotted kiwi, kea, kaka and whio (blue duck). There are creepy cave weta, weird beetles and a huge, leggy spider, but there's also a majestic and ancient snail known as Powelliphanta – something of a (slow) flag bearer for the park's animal kingdom. If you like a field trip filled with plenty that's new and strange, Kahurangi National Park will certainly satisfy.

🏃 Activities

The best-known walk in Kahurangi is the Heaphy Track. The more challenging **Wangapeka** is not as well known as the Heaphy, but many consider it a more enjoyable walk. Taking about five days, the track starts 25km south of Karamea at Little Wanganui and runs 52km east to Rolling River near Tapawera. There's a chain of huts along the track.

The Heaphy and Wangapeka, however, are just part of a 650km network of tracks which includes excellent full-day and overnight walks such as those in the **Cobb Valley** and **Mt Arthur/Tablelands**. See www.doc.govt.nz for detailed information on all Kahurangi tracks.

Heaphy Track

The Heaphy Track is one of the most popular tracks in the country. A Great Walk in every sense, it traverses diverse terrain – dense native forest, the mystical Gouland Downs, secluded river valleys, and beaches dusted in salt spray and fringed by nikau palms.

Although quite long, the Heaphy is well cut and benched, making it easier than any other extended tramp found in Kahurangi National Park. That said, it may still be found arduous, particularly in unfavourable weather.

Walking from east to west most of the climbing is done on the first day, and the scenic beach walk is saved for the end, a fitting and invigorating grand finale.

The track is open to mountain bikers between May and October. Factoring in distance, remoteness and the possibility of bad weather, this epic journey is only suited to well-equipped cyclists with advanced riding skills. A good port of call for more information is the Quiet Revolution Cycle Shop (p418) in Takaka.

A strong tramper could walk the Heaphy in three days, but most people take four or five days. For a detailed track description, see DOC's *Heaphy Track* brochure. Estimated walking times:

ROUTE	TIME (HR)
Brown Hut to Perry Saddle Hut	5
Perry Saddle Hut to Gouland Downs Hut	2
Gouland Downs Hut to Saxon Hut	1½
Saxon Hut to James Mackay Hut	3
James Mackay Hut to Lewis Hut	3½
Lewis Hut to Heaphy Hut	2½
Heaphy Hut to Kohaihai River	5

👉 Tours

Kahurangi Guided Walks TRAMPING

(☑03-391 4120; www.kahurangiwalks.co.nz) Offers all-inclusive, week-long Heaphy hikes ($1750), plus one- to five-day trips in Abel Tasman National Park ($250 to $1400).

Bush & Beyond TRAMPING

(☑03-543 3742; www.bushandbeyond.co.nz)
Natural-history-orientated hikes around Kahurangi, ranging from Mt Arthur or Cobb
Valley day walks ($250) through to a guided
six-day Heaphy Track package ($1795).

🛏 Sleeping

Seven designated Great Walk huts ($32) lie
along the Heaphy Track, which have bunks
and a kitchen area, heating, flush toilets and
washbasins with cold water. Most but not
all have gas rings; a couple have lighting.
There are also nine Great Walk campsites
($14), plus the beachside **Kohaihai Camp-
site** (www.doc.govt.nz; $6) at the West Coast
trailhead. The two day shelters are just that;
overnight stays are not permitted.

As the Heaphy is a Great Walk, all huts
and campsites must be booked in advance
year-round. Bookings can be made online
through **Great Walks Bookings** (☑0800
694 732; www.doc.govt.nz) or at DOC visitor
centres nationwide.

❶ Getting There & Away

The two road ends of the Heaphy Track are an
almost unfathomable distance apart: 463km
to be precise. From Takaka, you can get to the
Heaphy Track (via Collingwood) with **Golden
Bay Coachlines** (p403) ($35, one hour).

The Kohaihai trailhead is 15km from the small
town of Karamea. **Karamea Express** (☑03-782
6757; info@karamea-express.co.nz) departs
from the shelter at 1pm and 2pm for Karamea
from October to the end of April ($15). **Karamea
Connections** (☑03-782 6767; www.karamea
connections.co.nz) offers on-demand pick-ups.
Heaphy Bus (☑0272 221 872, 0800 128 735;
www.theheaphybus.co.nz) offers a round-trip
shuttle service – drop off at Brown Hut and
pick up from Kohaihai ($150) – and other
on-demand local track transport.

Heaphy Track Help (☑03-525 9576; www.
heaphytrackhelp.co.nz) offers car relocations
(around $300, depending on the direction and
time), food crops, shuttles and advice

Adventure Flights Golden Bay (☑03-525
6167, 0800 150 338; www.adventureflights
goldenbay.co.nz; Takaka Airfield, SH60) will
fly you back to Takaka from Karamea (or vice
versa) for $185 to $200 per person (up to five
people). **Golden Bay Air** (☑0800 588 885;
www.goldenbayair.co.nz) flies the same route
for $149 to $169 per person, as does **Helicopter Charter Karamea** (p435), which will take
up to three/six passengers $750/1350.

Nelson Lakes National Park

Nelson Lakes National Park surrounds two
lakes – Rotoiti and Rotoroa – fringed by
sweet-smelling beech forest with a backdrop
of greywacke mountains. Located at the
northern end of the Southern Alps, and with
a dramatic glacier-carved landscape, it's an
awe-inspiring place to get up on high.

Part of the park, east of Lake Rotoiti, is
classed as a 'mainland island' where a conservation scheme aims to eradicate introduced pests (rats, possums and stoats), and
regenerate native flora and fauna. It offers
excellent tramping, including short walks,
lake scenery and one or two sandflies... The
park is flush with birdlife, and famous for
brown-trout fishing.

The human hub of the Nelson Lakes region
is the small, low-key village of **St Arnaud**.

🏃 Activities

Many spectacular walks allow you to appreciate this rugged landscape, but before you
tackle them, stop by the DOC Nelson Lakes
Visitor Centre (p424) for maps, track/
weather updates and to pay your hut or
camping fees.

There are two fantastic day hikes to be
had. The five-hour **Mt Robert Circuit Track**
starts at Mt Robert car park (a short drive
away from St Arnaud, serviced by Nelson
Lakes Shuttles, p424) and circumnavi-
gates the mountain. The optional side trip
along Robert Ridge offers staggering views
into the heart of the national park. Alternatively, the **St Arnaud Range Track** (five
hours return), on the east side of the lake,
climbs steadily to the ridgeline adjacent to
Parachute Rocks. Both tracks are strenuous,
but reward with jaw-dropping vistas of glaciated valleys, arête peaks and Lake Rotoiti.
Only attempt these tramps in fine weather.
At other times they are both pointless (no
views) and dangerous.

There are also plenty of shorter (and flatter) walks from Lake Rotoiti's Kerr Bay and
the road end at Lake Rotoroa. These and the
longer day tramps are described in DOC's
Walks in Nelson Lakes National Park
pamphlet ($2).

The fit and well-equipped can embark
upon longer hikes such as the **Lake Angelus Track**. This magnificent two-to-three day
tramp follows Robert Ridge to Lake Angelus,
where you can stay at the fine Angelus Hut

(adult/child $20/10, bookings essential late November to April; backcountry pass/tickets valid the rest of the year) for a night or two before returning to St Arnaud via one of three routes. Pick up or download DOC's *Angelus Hut Tracks & Routes* pamphlet ($2) for more details. And if you've heard about **Blue Lake**, seek advice from the visitor centre before you even so much as contemplate it.

Rainbow   SKIING, SNOWBOARDING
(☑03-521 1861, snow-phone 0832 226 05; www.skirainbow.co.nz; daily lift pass adult/child $75/35) The sunny Nelson region has a ski area, just 100km away (a similar distance from Blenheim). **Rainbow** borders the Nelson Lakes National Park, with varied terrain, minimal crowds and good cross-country skiing. Chains are often required. St Arnaud is the closest town (32km).

🛏 Sleeping

Kerr Bay DOC Campsite   CAMPGROUND $
(www.doc.govt.nz; unpowered/powered sites per person $10/15) Near the Lake Rotoiti shore, the hugely popular Kerr Bay campsite has powered sites, toilets, hot showers, a laundry and a kitchen shelter. It's an inspiring base for your adventures, but do book in advance. Overflow camping is available around at DOC's **West Bay Campsite** (☑03-521 1806; www.doc.govt.nz; $6; ☉summer), which is more basic.

Travers-Sabine Lodge   HOSTEL $
(☑03-521 1887; www.nelsonlakes.co.nz; Main Rd; dm/d $28/65; ☏) This hostel is a great base for outdoor adventure, being a short walk to Lake Rotoiti, inexpensive, clean and comfortable. It also has particularly cheerful Technicolor linen in the dorms, doubles and family room. The owners are experienced adventurers themselves, so tips come as standard; tramping equipment available for hire.

★ **Alpine Lodge**   LODGE $$
(☑03-521 1869; www.alpinelodge.co.nz; Main Rd, St Arnaud; d $155-210; @☏) Family owned and a consistent performer, this large lodge complex offers a range of accommodation,

the pick of which are the split-level doubles with mezzanine bedroom and spa. If nothing else, go for the inviting in-house restaurant – a snug affair sporting an open fire, mountain views, good food (meals $10 to $32; takeaway pizza $20) and local beer.

The restaurant serves lunch and dinner November to April; dinner only May and July through October; and closes for June.

The adjacent backpacker lodge (dorm/double $29/69) is spartan but warm and tidy. There's on-site bike hire, too.

Nelson Lakes Motels   MOTEL $$
(☑03-521 1887; www.nelsonlakes.co.nz; Main Rd, St Arnaud; d $125-140, q $135-180; ☏) These log cabins and newer board-and-batten units offer all the creature comforts, including kitchenettes and Sky TV. Bigger units have full kitchens and sleep up to six.

ℹ Information

DOC Nelson Lakes Visitor Centre (☑03-521 1806; www.doc.govt.nz; View Rd; ☉8am-4.30pm, to 5pm in summer) The Nelson Lakes Visitor Centre proffers park-wide information (weather, activities) and hut passes, plus displays on park ecology and history.

ℹ Getting There & Around

Nelson Lakes Shuttles (☑027 547 6896, 03-547 6896; www.nelsonlakesshuttles.co.nz) runs thrice-weekly scheduled services between Nelson and the national park from December to April (Monday, Wednesday and Friday; $45), and on-demand the rest of the year. It will also collect/drop off at Kawatiri Junction on SH63 to meet other bus services heading between Nelson and the West Coast, and offers services from St Arnaud through to Picton, Kaikoura, Hanmer Springs and other top-of-the-South destinations on demand. Try also **Trek Express** (p403), which regularly plies such routes.

Rotoiti Water Taxis (☑021 702 278; www.rotoitiwatertaxis.co.nz) Runs to/from Kerr Bay and West Bay to southern end of Lake Rotoiti (3/4 passengers $100/120). Kayaks, canoes and rowing boats can be hired from $50 per half-day; fishing trips and scenic lake cruises by arrangement.

The West Coast

Best Short Walks

➜ Scotts Beach (p433)

➜ Charming Creek Walkway (p431)

➜ Lake Matheson (p451)

➜ Ship Creek (p455)

Best Places to Sleep

➜ Old Slaughterhouse (p432)

➜ Breakers (p437)

➜ Drifting Sands (p444)

➜ Okarito Campground (p446)

Why Go?

Hemmed in by the wild Tasman Sea and the Southern Alps, the West Coast is like nowhere else in New Zealand.

The far extremities of the coast have a remote, end-of-the-road feel, from sleepy Karamea surrounded by farms butting up against Kahurangi National Park, to the southern end of State Hwy 6, gateway to NZ's World Heritage areas. In between is an alluring combination of wild coastline, rich wilderness, and history in spades.

Built on the wavering fortunes of gold, coal and timber, the stories of Coast settlers are hair-raising. A hardy and individual breed, they make up less than 1% of NZ's population, scattered around almost 9% of its land area.

Travellers tend to tick off the 'must see' sights of Punakaiki, and Franz Josef and Fox Glaciers, but sights such as Oparara Basin, Okarito Lagoon and the Coast's many lakes will amaze in equal measure.

When to Go

➜ December through February is peak season, so book accommodation ahead during this period.

➜ The shoulder months of October/November and March/April are increasingly busy, particularly around Punakaiki, Hokitika and the Glaciers.

➜ May to September can be warm and clear, with fewer crowds and cheaper accommodation.

➜ The West Coast has serious rainfall (around 5m annually) but still sees as much sunshine as Christchurch.

➜ No matter what time of year, backcountry trampers should check conditions with local DOC office staff. Rivers can prove seriously treacherous.

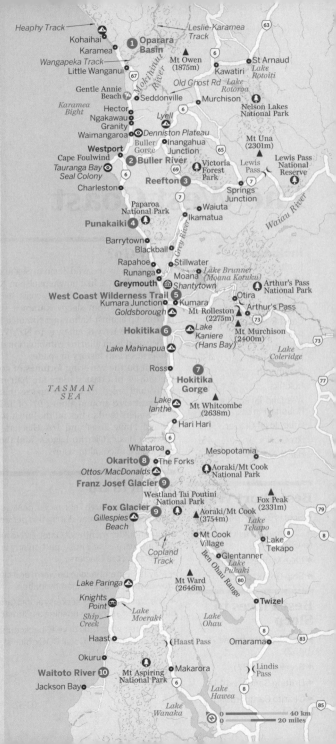

West Coast Highlights

1 **Oparara Basin** (p434) Exploring the limestone forms and forest.

2 **Buller River** (p427) Getting wet 'n' wild on this mighty river.

3 **Reefton** (p428) Delving into the West Coast's glittering past.

4 **Punakaiki** (p436) Marvelling at nature's beautiful fury at the 'Pancake Rocks'.

5 **West Coast Wilderness Trail** (p439) Getting back to nature by bike or on foot.

6 **Hokitika** (p441) Hunting out authentic local greenstone in working studios.

7 **Hokitika Gorge** (p442) Admiring surreal turquoise waters from a lofty swing bridge.

8 **Okarito** (p446) Kayaking through bird-filled, rainforest channels.

9 **Fox Glacier** (p451) & **Franz Josef Glacier** (p447) Flying high over the ice, up into the Southern Alps.

10 **Waiatoto River** (p456) Jetboating deep into Haast's World Heritage wilderness.

Heaphy Track
Leslie-Karamea Track
Kohaihai
Karamea
1 Oparara Basin
St Arnaud
Mt Owen (1875m)
Kawatiri
Lake Rotoiti
Wangapeka Track
Little Wanganui
Old Ghost Rd
Lake Rotoroa
Gentle Annie Beach
Murchison
Nelson Lakes National Park
Seddonville
Hector
Karamea Bight
Ngakawau
Lyell
Granity
Mt Una (2301m)
Waimangaroa
Denniston Plateau
Inangahua Junction
Westport
Buller Gorge
2 Buller River
Victoria Forest Park
Lewis Pass
Lewis Pass National Reserve
Cape Foulwind
Tauranga Bay
Seal Colony
Reefton 3
Lewis Pass
Springs Junction
Charleston
Waiau River
Paparoa National Park
Waiuta
Ikamatua
Punakaiki 4
Barrytown
Blackball
Rapahoe
Stillwater
Lake Brunner (Moana Kotuku)
Runanga
Moana
Arthur's Pass National Park
Greymouth
Shantytown
West Coast Wilderness Trail 5
Otira
Kumara Junction
Kumara
Arthur's Pass
Goldsborough
Mt Rolleston (2275m)
Hokitika 6
Lake Kaniere (Hans Bay)
Mt Murchison (2400m)
Lake Coleridge
Lake Mahinapua
TASMAN SEA
Ross
Hokitika Gorge 7
Lake Ianthe
Mt Whitcombe (2638m)
Hari Hari
Whataroa
Mesopotamia
Okarito 8
The Forks
Aoraki/Mt Cook National Park
Ottos/MacDonalds
Franz Josef Glacier 9
Westland Tai Poutini National Park
Fox Peak (2331m)
Fox Glacier 9
Aoraki/Mt Cook (3754m)
Gillespies Beach
Lake Tekapo
Mt Cook Village
Lake Tekapo
Copland Track
Glentanner
Lake Pukaki
Lake Paringa
Mt Ward (2646m)
Ben Ohau Range
Knights Point
Lake Moeraki
Twizel
Ship Creek
Lake Ohau
Haast
Haast Pass
Omarama
Okuru
Lindis Pass
Waitoto River 10
Mt Aspiring National Park
Makarora
Jackson Bay
Lake Hawea
Lake Wanaka
0   40 km
0   20 miles

ⓘ Getting There & Away

Air New Zealand (☑ 0800 737 000; www.airnz.co.nz) flies between Hokitika and Christchurch; **Sounds Air** (☑ 03-520 3080, 0800 505 005; www.soundsair.com) flies between Westport and Wellington.

Coaches and shuttle transport – while not exceptionally frequent – are at least reliable, and reach pretty much everywhere you might like to go including Nelson, Christchurch and Queenstown. Major and extensive networks are operated by **Atomic Travel** (p440), **InterCity** (☑ 03-365 1113; www.intercity.co.nz) and **Naked Bus** (www.nakedbus.com), while **West Coast Shuttle** (p440) runs a daily service between Greymouth and Christchurch. Local shuttle operators go here and there.

The **TranzAlpine** (p438), one of the world's great train journeys, links Greymouth and Christchurch.

BULLER REGION

Arriving from the east, Murchison is the gateway to the Buller region. Your big decision is which way to head when you reach the forks at Inangahua. Continuing west along SH6 through the Lower Buller Gorge will lead you to Westport, the gateway to the far north, and the northern end of the Great Coast Road leading to Punakaiki. Head south from Inangahua on SH69 and you skip Punakaiki but reach Reefton, where you can either head west to the coast at Greymouth, or east over the Lewis Pass to Hanmer Springs. You can also cut directly through to the Lewis Pass via SH65, 10km west of Murchison.

Murchison & Buller Gorge

POP 492

Murchison, 125km southwest of Nelson and 95km east of Westport, lies on the 'Four Rivers Plain'. In fact there aren't just four but multitudinous rivers, the mightiest being the Buller, which runs alongside the town. White-water sports and trout fishing are popular here, while the surrounding forested hills dish up adventure for intrepid adventurers.

From Murchison, SH6 snakes through Buller Gorge to the coast at Westport, a journey that could easily take a day or two by the time you've taken a rafting or jetboating trip and stopped at other interesting sites along the way.

⊙ Sights

Murchison Museum   MUSEUM

(60 Fairfax St; admission by donation; ☺10am-4pm) This museum showcases all sorts

---

ESSENTIAL WEST COAST

Eat Fish and chips, sitting near the beach at sunset.

Drink The only roast on the coast, organic and fair trade Kawatiri Coffee.

Read Eleanor Catton's 2013 Man Booker Prize–winning novel, *The Luminaries*, set around Hokitika.

Listen to Karamea's laid-back community radio station on 107.5FM; you can even spin your own tunes.

Watch *Denniston Incline* on YouTube, then imagine sitting in the wagon on the way down.

Festival Go bush-food crazy at Hokitika's Wildfoods Festival (p444).

Go Green At West Coast Wildlife Centre (p443) – fluffy kiwi chicks! Too cute!

Online www.westcoastnz.com, www.buller.co.nz, www.glaciercountry.co.nz

Area code ☑ 03

---

of local memorabilia, the most interesting of which relates to the 1929 and 1968 earthquakes.

🏃 Activities

Ask at the Murchison Information Centre (p428) for a copy of the *Murchison District Map*, which features local walks, such as the Skyline, Six Mile and Johnson Creek Tracks, plus mountain-bike rides. Staff can also hook you up with excellent trout-fishing guides.

★ Wild Rivers Rafting   RAFTING

(☑ 050 846 7233; www.wildriversrafting.co.nz; 2hr rafting adult/child $160/85) White-water rafting with Bruce and Marty on the particularly exciting Earthquake Rapids section of the beautiful Buller River (good luck with 'gunslinger' and the 'pop-up toaster'!).

Buller Canyon Jet   JETBOATING

(☑ 03-523 9883; www.bullercanyonjet.co.nz; SH6; adult/child $105/50; ☺Sep-Apr) Launching from Buller Gorge Swingbridge is one of NZ's most scenic and best-value jetboat trips – 40 minutes of ripping through the beautiful Buller with a good-humoured captain.

Ultimate Descents   RAFTING

(☑ 0800 748 377, 03 523 9899; www.rivers.co.nz; 38 Waller St) Offers white-water rafting and

MĀORI NZ: THE WEST COAST

Early Māori forged paths through to the alps' mountains and river valleys to the West Coast in search of highly prized *pounamu* (greenstone), carved into tools, weapons and adornments. View the *pounamu* exhibit at **Hokitika Museum** (p442) to polish your knowledge of the precious rock before admiring the classy carvings created by the town's artists.

kayaking trips on the Buller, including the classic grade III-IV gorge trip ($160), and gentler family excursions (adult/child $130/100); plus helirafting trips by arrangement. Based in Murchison.

Buller Gorge Swingbridge   ADVENTURE SPORTS
(☑0800 285 537; www.bullergorge.co.nz; SH6; bridge crossing adult/child $10/5; ⊙8am-7pm Dec-Apr, 9am-5.30pm May-Nov) About 15km west of Murchison is NZ's longest swingbridge (110m), across which lie short walks taking in the White Creek Faultline, epicentre of the 1929 earthquake. Coming back, ride the 160m Cometline Flying Fox, either seated (adult/child $30/15) or 'Supaman' ($60).

☞ Tours

Natural Flames Experience   TOUR
(☑0800 687 244; www.naturalflames.co.nz; adult/child $85/65) An enjoyable, informative half-day 4WD and bushwalking tour through remote valleys and beech forest to a hot spot among the trees and ferns, where natural gas seeping out of the ground has been burning since 1922. Boil a billy on the flames and cook pancakes before returning to civilisation.

🛏 Sleeping & Eating

Kiwi Park Motels & Holiday Park   MOTEL, HOLIDAY PARK $
(☑0800 228 080, 03-523 9248; www.kiwipark.co.nz; 170 Fairfax St; sites unpowered/powered from $20/25, cabins $65-85, motels $140-225; @🗟) This leafy park on the edge of town has plenty of accommodation options, from a campervan and tent area graced with mature trees, through to basic cabins, and roomy motel units nestled among the blooms. Cheery hosts and a menagerie of friendly farm animals make this one happy family.

Lazy Cow   HOSTEL $
(☑03-523 9451; www.lazycow.co.nz; 37 Waller St; dm $30-32, d $84-96; 🗟) It's easy to be a lazy cow here, with all the comforts of home, including cosy bedrooms and a sunny backyard. Guests are welcomed with free muffins or cake, and freshly cooked evening meals are sometimes available when the hosts aren't running their popular on-site Cow Shed restaurant.

Murchison Lodge   B&B $$
(☑0800 523 9196, 03-523 9196; www.murchisonlodge.co.nz; 15 Grey St; s $150-210, d $175-235; 🗟) This quality B&B surrounded by extensive gardens and paddocks is a short walk from the Buller River. Attractive timber features and charming hosts add to the comfortable feel. A hearty breakfast, home baking and plenty of local information are complimentary.

Cow Shed   PIZZA
(⊙5pm-9pm Wed-Sat) In the garage of the Lazy Cow backpackers, the cute Cow Shed restaurant is a deservedly popular option for its homey, good-value meals served in intimate surrounds. There's takeaway pizza for those who can't get a table.

❶ Information

Murchison has no ATM; the postal agency is on Fairfax St.

The **Murchison Information Centre** (☑03-523 9350; www.nelsonnz.com; 47 Waller St; ⊙10am-6pm Nov-Mar, to 4pm Apr & Oct, closed May-Sep) has info on local activities and transport.

❶ Getting There & Away

Buses passing through Murchison between the West Coast and Nelson/Picton are **InterCity** (☑03-365 1113; www.intercity.co.nz) and **Naked Bus** (www.nakedbus.com), both of which stop at Beechwoods Cafe on Waller St, as does **Trek Express** (p433), which runs frequently between Nelson and the Wangapeka/Heaphy Tracks during the peak tramping season.

Reefton

POP 1026

For generations, Reefton's claims to fame have been mining and its early adoption of the electricity grid and street lighting. Hence the tagline, 'the city of light'. Today, however, it's a different story, one which starts – improbably – with the building of the world-class Roller Park, which attracts stunt lovers from all corners of NZ. To quote a local, 'it's more than we deserve'. We disagree. If this many volunteers and sponsors are prepared to build such an edgy civic amenity in a town that still looks like the set of *Bonanza,* we suggest theres something a bit special about this crazy little town.

◉ Sights

With loads of crusty old buildings situated within a 200m radius, Reefton is a fascinating town for a stroll. To find out who lived where and why, undertake the short Heritage Walk outlined in the *Historic Reefton* leaflet ($1), available from the Reefton i-SITE (p430).

Waiuta   HISTORIC SITE
(www.waiuta.org.nz; off SH7) A once-burgeoning gold town abandoned in 1951 after the mineshaft collapsed, remote Waiuta is one of the West Coast's most famous ghost towns, complete with a big old rusty boiler, an overgrown swimming pool, stranded brick chimneys and the odd intact cottage, which face off against Mother Nature who has sent in the strangleweed. Spread over a square kilometre or so of plateau, surrounded by lowland forest and looking out towards the Southern Alps, Waiuta is a very satisfying place for an amble.

To get to there, drive 23km south of Reefton on SH7 to the signposted turn-off from where it's another 17km, the last half of which is unsealed, winding and narrow in places. Ask at local information centres for more information and maps.

Blacks Point Museum   MUSEUM
(203-732 8391; blksptmus@hotmail.co.nz; Franklyn St, Blacks Point, SH7; adult/child/family $5/3/15; 9am-noon & 1-4pm Wed-Fri & Sun, 1-4pm Sat Oct-Apr, plus school holidays during winter) Housed in an old church 2km east of Reefton on the Christchurch road, this museum is crammed with prospecting paraphernalia. Just up the driveway is the still-functional Golden Fleece Battery (203-732 8391; blksptmus@hotmail.co.nz; Franklyn St, Blacks Point, SH7; adult/child $1/free; 1pm-4pm Wed & Sun Oct-Apr), used for crushing gold-flecked quartz. The Blacks Point walks also start from here.

Bearded Mining Company   HISTORIC BUILDING
(203-732 8377; Broadway; admission by donation; 9am-2pm) Looking like a ZZ Top tribute band, the fellas hangin' at this high-street mining hut are champing at the bit to rollick your socks off with tales tall and true. If you're lucky, you'll get a cuppa from the billy.

🏃 Activities

Look out for a copy of the free *Reefton* leaflet detailing short walks, including the Bottled Lightning Powerhouse Walk (40 minutes) that has its own mobile app.

Surrounding Reefton is the 206,000-hectare Victoria Forest Park (NZ's largest forest park) which sports diverse flora and fauna as well as hidden historic sites, such as the old goldfields around Blacks Point. Starting at Blacks Point, the enjoyable Murray Creek Track is a five-hour return trip.

Other tramps in the Forest Park include the three-day Kirwans or two-day Big River Track, both of which can be traversed on a mountain bike. Pick up the free *Reefton Mountain Biking* ('the best riding in history') leaflet for more information; bikes can be hired from Reefton Sports Centre (203-732 8593; 56 Broadway; bike rental per day $30; 9am-5pm Mon-Sat), where you can also inquire about legendary trout fishing in the environs.

Inland Adventures   RAFTING
(20503 723 846; www.inlandadventures.co.nz) Runs day-long rafting trips on the grade III Upper Grey River (adult/child $190/160), and gentler half-day trips on the Arnold River, better suited to smaller children (adult/child $130/100. Based in Reefton.

🛏 Sleeping & Eating

Old Nurses Home Guesthouse   GUESTHOUSE $
(203-732 8881; www.reeftonaccommodation.co.nz; 104 Shiel St; s/d $60/80;) This stately old building is warm and comfortable, with noteworthy communal areas, including a pretty garden and patio. Bedrooms (shared bathrooms) are clean and airy with comfy beds.

Reef Cottage B&B   B&B $$
(203-732 8440; www.reefcottage.co.nz; 51-55 Broadway; d 135-170;) This converted 1887 barrister's office has compact rooms furnished in period style with modern touches, including swish bathrooms and a guest kitchen and lounge. Full breakfasts at the cafe next door are included in the price.

Broadway Tearooms & Bakery   BAKERY $$
(203-732 8497; 31 Broadway; snacks $3-8, meals $13-20; 8am-5pm) This joint gets by far the

most day-time traffic, being a civilised place for a spot of lunch, and to pick up a fresh loaf or a packet of shortbread. Middle-of-the-road meals range from egg breakfasts to a whitebait lunch. Survey Reefton's high-street bustle from tables out the front.

☆ Entertainment

Reefton Cinema   CINEMA
(📞 03-732 8391; www.reefton.co.nz; cnr Smith & Shiels Sts; adult/child $13.50/8.50) Reefton has gone digital and 3D at this cutesy cinema! Tickets and enquiries at the i-SITE.

ℹ Information

Reefton i-SITE (📞 03-732 8391; www.reefton. co.nz; 67 Broadway; ⊙ 9am-4.30pm Mon-Fri, 9.30am-2pm Sat, 9.30am-1pm Sun) This i-SITE has helpful staff, and a compact recreation of the Quartzopolis Mine (gold coin entry). There's internet at the library, which doubles as the postal agency.

ℹ Getting There & Away

East West Coaches (📞 03-789 6251; www. eastwestcoaches.co.nz) East West Coaches stops in Reefton every day except Saturday on the run between Westport (1¼ hours) and Christchurch (four hours).

Westport & Around

POP 4035

The 'capital' of the northern West Coast is Westport. The town's fortunes have waxed and waned on coal mining, but in the current climate it sits quietly stoked up on various industries, including dairy and, increasingly, tourism. It boasts respectable hospitality and visitor services, and makes a good base for exploring the fascinating coast north to Denniston, Charming Creek, Karamea and the Heaphy Track.

⊙ Sights

The most riveting sights are beyond Westport's city walls, particularly heading north on SH67, which passes **Granity**, **Ngakawau** (home to the utterly Charming Creek) and **Hector**, where stands a monument to Hector's dolphins, NZ's smallest, although you'll be lucky to see them unless your timing is impeccable. It's also worth poking around **Seddonville**, a small bush town on the Mokihinui River where **Seddonville Holiday Park** (📞 03-782 1314; 108 Gladstone St; sites per person $10) offers respectable camping in the grounds of the old school. This small dot on the map is about to get slightly bigger, being the northern trailhead for the spectacular new Old Ghost Road (p430).

Denniston Plateau   HISTORIC SITE
(www.doc.govt.nz) Six hundred metres above sea level, Denniston was once NZ's largest coal town, with 1500 residents in 1911. By 1981 there were eight. Its claim to fame was the fantastically steep Denniston Incline, which hurtled laden wagons down a 45-degree hillside.

Excellent interpretive displays bring the plateau's history to life. **Denniston Experience** (📞 0800 881 880; www.denniston.co.nz; Denniston) guided tours ride the 'gorge express' train into Banbury mine for an intriguing two-hour adventure (adult/child $99/40). A one-hour option (adult/child $45/20) rides the train to the mine entrance.

The *Denniston Rose Walking Tour* brochure ($2 from DOC and Westport Library; also available as an app) may lead the eager to read Jenny Pattrick's evocative novels set in these parts.The turn-off to Denniston is 16km north of Westport at Waimangaroa, with a shop worth a stop for a homemade pie and ice cream. Denniston is another nine winding kilometres inland from there.

Coaltown Museum   MUSEUM
(www.coaltown.co.nz; 123 Palmerston St; adult/child $10/2; ⊙ 9am-5pm Mon-Fri, 10am-4pm Sat & Sun) This modern museum retells the same old yarns of hard times, but with well-scripted display panels alongside an excellent selection of photographs, surrounding relics of local industries and general pioneer ephemera. The Denniston displays are a highlight.

🏃 Activities

Westport is good for a stroll – the i-SITE (p433) can direct you to the **Millennium Walkway** and **North Beach Reserve**. The most thrilling adventure in the area is cave rafting with Underworld Adventures (p431), although mountain biking is gaining momentum as a popular pastime among local and visiting backcountry adventurers. The folk at Habitat Sports (p433) offer bike rental, maps and advice.

Old Ghost Road   TRAMPING, CYCLING
(www.oldghostroad.org.nz) One of the gnarliest of NZ's new cycle trails, the 85km Old Ghost Road follows a historic miners' track that was started in the in the 1870s but never

finished as the gold rush petered out. Finally completed after an epic build, the spectacular track traverses native forests, tussock tops, river flats and valleys.

The southern trailhead is at Lyell, 50 minutes' drive (62km) east of Westport along the scenic Buller Gorge (SH6). The DOC campsite and day walks here have long been popular, with visitors drawn in by readily accessible historic sites, including a graveyard secreted in the bush. The northern trailhead is at Seddonville, 45 minutes' drive (50km) north of Westport off SH67, from where the track sidles along the steep-sided and utterly stunning Mokihinui River. Joining the two ends is a spectacular alpine section, with views from sunrise to sunset.

The track is dual use, but favours walkers (allow five days). For advanced mountain bikers, however, it is pretty much the Holy Grail, completed in two to four days, preferably from Lyell to Seddonville. The four huts along the way need to be booked in advance on the Old Ghost Road website, which also details a range of other ways to experience the track other than an end-to-end ride or hike. Day trips from either end are a rewarding, flexible way in, particularly from the West Coast end via the inimitable Rough & Tumble Lodge (p432).

Being a long and remote track through wild terrain, conditions can change quickly, so check the trail website for status. Westport's Buller Adventure Tours, Habitat Sports (p433) and **Hike n Bike Shuttle** (☑027 446 7876; www.hikenbikeshuttle.co.nz) provide bike and equipment hire, shuttles and other related services.

Cape Foulwind Walkway WALKING
(www.doc.govt.nz) On a good day, Cape Foulwind Walkway (1½ hours return) is a wonderful amble, traversing coastal hills between Omau and Tauranga Bay, south of Westport. Towards the southern end is the seal colony where – depending on the season – up to 200 NZ fur seals loll on the rocks. Further north the walkway passes a replica astrolabe (a navigational aid) and lighthouse.

Abel Tasman was the first European to sight the Cape, in 1642, naming it Clyppygen Hoek (Rocky Point). However, his name was eclipsed by James Cook in 1770, who clearly found it less than pleasing.

Cape Foulwind is well signposted from Westport. It's 13km to Lighthouse Rd at Omau, where the welcoming Star Tavern (p432) signals the walkway's northern end.

The southern end is 16km from town at Tauranga Bay, popular with surfers who dodge its rocky edges.

Charming Creek Walkway WALKING
(www.doc.govt.nz) Starting from either Ngakawau (30km north of Westport), or near Seddonville, a few kilometres further on, this is one of the best day walks on the coast, taking around six hours return. Following an old coal line through the Ngakawau River Gorge, it features rusty relics galore, tunnels, a suspension bridge and waterfall, and lots of interesting plants and geological formations.

Ask a local about transport if you don't want to walk it both ways.

Underworld Adventures CAVING
(☑03-788 8168, 0800 116 686; www.caverafting.com; SH6, Charleston) From its monolithic new base at Charleston, 26km south of Westport, this friendly bunch runs unforgettable 'Underworld' cave-rafting trips ($175, four hours) into the glowworm-filled Nile River Caves. Glow without the flow (no rafting) is $110 per person. Tours begin with a fun rainforest railway ride, available separately (adult/child $20/15, 1½ hours). The on-site cafe provides simple food during the day.

The Adventure Caving trip ($340, five hours) includes a 40m abseil into Te Tahi tomo (hole) with rock squeezes, waterfalls, prehistoric fossils and trippy cave formations.

Buller Adventure Tours JETBOATING, HORSE RIDING
(☑03-789 7286, 0800 697 286; www.adventuretours.co.nz; SH6) Located 5km from Westport, Barry and crew run jetboating trips through the lower Buller Gorge (adult/child $89/69); two-hour riverbank horse treks (adult/youth $89/69); and runs provides bike and transport packages for the Old Ghost Road.

🛏 Sleeping

★ Bazil's Hostel HOSTEL $
(☑03-789 6410; www.bazils.com; 54 Russell St, Westport; dm $30, d $100, without bathroom $72; 🛜) Mural-painted Bazil's is managed by worldly, sporty types who run their own surf school (three-hour lesson $70; board and suit hire per day $40) and rainforest SUP trips, as well as offering mountain-bike hire, free kayaks and hook-ups with other activities. Their tour-bus clientele are considerately corralled into a separate zone, leaving indy travellers in peace.

★**Old Slaughterhouse**   HOSTEL $

(☑027 529 7640, 03-782 8333; www.oldslaughter house.co.nz; SH67, Hector; dm $34-38, d $84; ☺sometimes closed Jun-Oct) 🅿 Around 1km north of Hector, this is a rather special hostel nestled high on the hill among native bush with epic views of the Tasman Sea. Built mainly from recycled timbers and dotted with interesting art and eclectic furniture, it also offers tranquil communal areas ideal for contemplation. The steep, 10-minute walk up the hill is well worth it and bolsters the off-the-grid charm.

Carters Beach

Top 10 Holiday Park   HOLIDAY PARK, MOTEL $

(☑03-789 8002, 050 893 7876; www.top10 westport.co.nz; 57 Marine Pde, Carters Beach; sites from $38, units $70-205; @🛜) Right on Carters Beach and conveniently located 4km from Westport and 12km to Tauranga Bay, this tidy complex has pleasant sites as well as comfortable cabins and motel units. It's a good option for tourers seeking a peaceful stop-off, and perhaps even a swim.

Trip Inn   HOSTEL $

(☑03-789 7367, 0800 737 773; www.tripinn.co.nz; 72 Queen St, Westport; dm $29-34, d & tw $96, without bathroom $75; 🛜) This stately option is a grand 150-year-old villa with mature gardens. There's a variety of tidy rooms within, plus more in an annexe, and voluminous communal areas.

★**Rough & Tumble Lodge**   LODGE $$

(☑03-782 1337; www.roughandtumble.co.nz; Mokihi-nui Rd, Seddonville; d incl continental breakfast $160, extra person $20; 🛜) This hidden treasure sits at the West Coast end of the Old Ghost Road at a bend in the Mokihinui River recently saved from decimation by hydro-dam. Invigorated and inspiring, it offers five atmospheric quad rooms in a virgin wilderness setting, with a homey lodge feel complete with honest meals (dinner $60) in the dining room.

Enquire about self-catering in the quieter low season.

Archer House   B&B $$

(☑0800 789 877, 03-789 8778; www.archerhouse. co.nz; 75 Queen St, Westport; d incl breakfast $190; @🛜) This beautiful 1890 heritage home sleeps up to eight in three rooms with private bathrooms, all sharing no fewer than three lounges, plus peaceful gardens. Lovely hosts, complimentary sherry and generous continental breakfast make this Westport's most refined accommodation option.

Omau Settlers Lodge   LODGE $$

(☑03-789 5200; www.omausettlerslodge.co.nz; 1054 Cape Rd, Cape Foulwind; r incl breakfast $165; 🛜) Close to Cape Foulwind and across the road from the excellent Star Tavern, these contemporary and stylish units offer rest, relaxation and satisfying continental breakfasts. Rooms have kitchenettes, but a shared kitchen and dining room offer a chance to socialise. A hot tub surrounded by bush maximises the take-it-easy quotient.

Charming Creek B&B   B&B $$

(☑03-782 8007; www.bullerbeachstay.co.nz; Ngakawau; d incl breakfast $149-179; 🛜) This lovely little B&B has homey rooms and a driftwood-fired hot tub right by the sea, where the self-contained 'Beach Nest' bach sleeps three to four people ($100 to $149, minimum two-night stay). Ask about the two-night walking package that includes dinners and a picnic lunch.

✖ Eating

Whanake Gallery & Espresso Bar   CAFE $

(☑03-789 5076; www.whanake.co.nz; 173 Palmerston St, Westport; snacks $3-8; ☺7.30am-5.30pm Mon-Fri, 8.30am-4.30pm Sat & Sun) Cranking out the town's best espresso and delicious biscuits, this neat little cafe was expanding to provide a greater range of food when last we visited. Pop in for a shot and check out the owners' inspiring photography and local souvenirs.

PR's Cafe   CAFE $

(☑03-789 7779; 124 Palmerston St, Westport; meals $10-20; ☺7am-4.30pm Mon-Fri, 7am-3pm Sat & Sun; 🛜) Westport's sharpest cafe has a cabinet full of sandwiches and pastries, and a counter groaning under the weight of cakes (Dutch apple, banoffee pie) and cookies. An all-day menu delivers carefully composed meals such as salmon omelette with dill aioli, spanakopita, and fish and chips.

Star Tavern   PUB FOOD $$

(☑03-789 6923; 6 Lighthouse Rd, Omau; meals $9-30; ☺4pm-late Mon-Fri, noon-late Sat & Sun) A motto of 'arrive as strangers, leave as friends' is backed up at this rural tavern handily positioned near Cape Foulwind. It dishes up generously proportioned grub in its old-fashioned dining room, a warm welcome, a pool table and a jukebox in its unprepossessing public bar, and relaxation in the garden. Proper hospitality, that's what this is.

ℹ️ Information

DOC Westport Office (☏03-788 8008; www. doc.govt.nz; 72 Russell St, Westport; ⏲8-11am & 2-4.30pm Mon-Fri) DOC bookings and information can be obtained from the i-SITE. For curly questions, visit this field office.

Westport i-SITE (☏03-789 6658; www. buller.co.nz; 123 Palmerston St, Westport; ⏲9am-5pm Mon-Fri, 10am-4pm Sat & Sun; 📶) Information on local tracks, walkways, tours, accommodation and transport. Self-help terminal for DOC information and hut and track bookings. See also www.westcoastnz.com.

ℹ️ Getting There & Away

AIR

Sounds Air (p427) has two to three flights daily to/from Wellington.

BUS

Westport is a stop on the daily Nelson to Fox Glacier runs of **InterCity** (☏03-365 1113; www. intercity.co.nz). Travel time to Nelson is 3½ hours, to Greymouth 2¼ hours, and to Franz Josef six hours. **Naked Bus** (www.nakedbus. com) runs the same route three times per week. Buses leave from the i-SITE.

East West Coaches (p430) Operates a service through to Christchurch, via Reefton and the Lewis Pass, every day except Saturday, departing from the Caltex petrol station.

Karamea Express (☏03-782 6757; info@ karamea-express.co.nz) Links Westport and Karamea (two hours) Monday to Friday May to September, plus Saturday from October to April, departing from the i-SITE.

Trek Express (☏0800 128 735, 027 221 872; www.trekexpress.co.nz) Passes through Westport on its frequent high-season tramper transport link between Nelson and the Wangapeka/Heaphy Tracks.

ℹ️ Getting Around

BICYCLE

Hire bikes and obtain advice from **Habitat Sports** (☏03-788 8002; www.habitatsports. co.nz; 234 Palmerston St, Westport; bike rental from $35; ⏲9am-5pm Mon-Fri, 9am-1pm Sat).

CAR

Hire some wheels at **Westport Hire** (☏03-789 5038; westporthire@xtra.co.nz; 294 Palmerston St, Westport).

TAXI

Buller Taxis (☏03-789 6900) can take you to/ from the airport (around $25).

Karamea & Around

POP 375

North from Westport, SH67 winds along the coast and over the view-filled Karamea Bluff to Karamea and the northern coast. If you're driving, fill your tank in Westport as it's 98km to the next petrol station. As you head over the bluff, it's worth stopping to do the **Lake Hanlon** walk (30 minutes return) on the Karamea side of the hill.

The relaxed town of Karamea (population 375) considers itself the West Coast's 'best kept secret', but those who've visited tend to boast about its merits far and wide. An end-of-the-road town it may well be, but it still has a bit of the 'hub' about it, servicing the end (or start) of the Heaphy and Wangapeka Tracks, and the magical Oparara Basin. With a friendly climate, and a take-it-easy mix of locals and chilled-out imports, the Karamea area is a great place to jump off the well-trodden tourist trail for a few lazy days.

👁 Sights

⭐ **Scotts Beach**   BEACH

It's a 45-minute walk each way from Kohaihai over the hill to Scotts Beach – a wild, empty shoreline shrouded in mist, awash in foamy waves, strewn with driftwood and backed by nikau palm forest. Watch and wander in wonder, but don't even think about dipping a toe in – there are dangerous currents at work here.

🏃 Activities

Hats off to the Karamea community who have established the very pleasant **Karamea Estuary Walkway**, a long-as-you-like stroll bordering the estuary and Karemea River. The adjacent beach can be reached via Flagstaff Rd, north of town. Both features plenty of birdlife and are best walked at sunset. The Karamea Information & Resource Centre (p435) has various maps, including the free *Karamea* brochure which details other walks such as **Big Rimu** (45 minutes return), **Flagstaff** (one hour return) and the **Zig Zag** (one hour return).

Longer walks around Karamea include the **Fenian Track** (four hours return) leading to **Cavern Creek Caves** and **Adams Flat**, where there's a replica gold-miner's hut; and the first leg of the **Wangapeka Track** to Belltown Hut. The Wangapeka Track is a four-to-six-day backcountry trip suitable for experienced trampers only.

OPARARA BASIN

To quote a local: 'if this were anywhere else, there'd be hordes streaming in'. Too true. Lying within Kahurangi National Park, the Oparara Basin is a natural spectacle of the highest order – a hidden valley concealing wonders such as limestone arches and strange caves within a thick forest of massive, moss-laden trees that tower over an undergrowth of Dr Seuss-esque form in every imaginable hue of green. Excellent information panels can be perused at the main car park and picnic area.

The valley's signature sight is the 200m-long, 37m-high **Oparara Arch**, spanning the picturesque Oparara River – home to the super-cute, rare blue duck (whio) – which wends alongside the easy walkway (45 minutes return). The smaller but no less stunning **Moria Gate Arch** (43m long, 19m high) is reached via a simply divine forest loop walk (1½ hours), which also passes the **Mirror Tarn**.

Just a 10-minute walk from the second car park are the **Crazy Paving and Box Canyon Caves**. Take your torch to enter a world of weird subterranean shapes and rare, leggy spiders. Spiders, caves, darkness...sound like fun?

Beyond this point are the superb **Honeycomb Hill Caves and Arch**, accessible only by guided tours (3-/5-/8-hour tours $95/150/240) run by the **Karamea Information & Resource Centre** (p435). Ask about other guided tours of the area, and also about transport for the **Oparara Valley Track**, a rewarding five-hour independent walk through ancient forest, along the river, popping out at the **Fenian Walk** car park.

To drive to the valley from Karamea, travel 10km along the main north road north and turn off at McCallum's Mill Rd, where signposts will direct you a further 14km up and over into the valley along a road that is winding, gravel, rough in places and sometimes steep.

Other local activities include swimming, fishing, whitebaiting, kayaking and mountain biking. Your best bet for advice on these is to ask a local and always use common sense – especially when it comes to the watery stuff. Flexible and friendly **Karamea Outdoor Adventures** (☑ 03-782 6181; www.karameaadventures.co.nz; Bridge St; guided kayak/riverbug trips from $80, kayak/bike hire per 2hr $40/30) offers guided and freedom kayaking and riverbug trips, plus mountain-bike hire and advice on other adventures, including horse treks.

Heaphy Track

The West Coast road ends 14km from Karamea at **Kohaihai**, the western trailhead (and most commonly, the finish point) of the Heaphy Track (p422), where there's also a **DOC campsite** (www.doc.govt.nz; sites per adult/child $6). A day walk or overnight stay can readily be had from here. Walk to Scotts Beach (p433) (1½ hours return), or go as far as the fabulous new **Heaphy Hut** (www.doc.govt.nz; huts/campsites $32/14) (five hours) and stay a night or two before returning.

This section can also be mountain-biked, as can the whole track (two to three days) from May to September; ask at Westport's Habitat Sports (p433) for bike hire and details.

Helicopter Charter Karamea (p435) offers flights through to the northern trailhead in Golden Bay: up to three/six passengers $750/1350; up to three/six passengers with mountain bikes $900/1550.

🛏 Sleeping

Rongo Backpackers   HOSTEL $
(☑ 03-782 6667; www.rongobackpackers.com; 130 Waverley St, Karamea; sites from $20, dm $32-35, s/tw/d $75/80/90; @ 🛜) 🌱 Part neo-hippie artists' haven and part organic vegie garden, this rainbow-coloured, carbon-negative hostel also runs the community radio station (107.5 FM, www.karamearadio.com). Popular with long-term guests who often end up tending the garden and spinning a few tunes. Every fourth night is free.

Karamea Farm Baches   CABIN $
(☑ 03-782 6838; www.karameafarmbaches.com; 17 Wharf Rd, Karamea; d/tr/q $95/120/145; 🛜) 🌱 Pushing reuse/recycle to the limit, these seven 1960s self-contained bachs are the real McCoy, right down to period wallpaper and grandma's carpet. If you dig organic gardening, friendly dogs and colourful hosts, this place will win you over.

Karamea Holiday Park   HOLIDAY PARK $
(☑ 03-782 6758; www.karamea.com; Maori Point Rd, Karamea; sites d powered/unpowered $33/30, units s $30-45, d $40-95; @ 🛜) A simple,

old-fashioned camp alongside the estuary in bush surrounds, 3km south of Karamea village. The retro weatherboard cabins are clean and well maintained.

Last Resort
LODGE $$

(☑03-782 6617, 0800 505 042; www.lastresort.co.nz; 71 Waverley St, Karamea; s $50 d $97-155, q $195; ☎) This iconic, rambling and rustic resort has entered an era of friendly welcomes and good management, and has had a general tidy up. Scope the joint with espresso and cake or a beer in the cafe or bar (meals $11 to $30) then consider the plunge into rooms ranging from simple doubles to family suites, all handcrafted using local timbers.

Karamea River Motels
MOTEL $$

(☑03-782 6955; www.karameamotel.co.nz; 31 Bridge St, Karamea; r $125-169; ☎) The smart rooms at this comfortable motel, five minutes' walk from Market Cross, range from studios to two-bedroom units. Features include relaxing blue hues, long-range views, a barbecue and lush gardens.

✖ Eating

Karamea Village Hotel
PUB FOOD $$

(☑03-782 6800; www.karameahotel.co.nz; cnr Waverley & Wharf Sts, Karamea; meals $11-34; ☺11am-11pm) Here lies simple pleasures and proper hospitality: a game of pool, a pint of ale, and a tasty roast dinner followed by old-fashioned pudding.

ℹ Information

Karamea Information & Resource Centre
(☑03-782 6652; www.karameainfo.co.nz; Market Cross; ☺9am-5pm Mon-Fri, 10am-1pm Sat & Sun, shorter hours May-Dec) This excellent, community-owned centre has the local low-down, internet access, maps and DOC hut tickets. It also doubles as the petrol station.

ℹ Getting There & Away

Karamea Express (p433) links Karamea and Westport ($35, two hours, Monday to Friday May to September, plus Saturdays from October to April). It also services Kohaihai twice daily during peak summer, and other times on demand. Wangapeka transport is also available.

Heaphy Bus (☑0800 128 735, 03-540 2042; www.theheaphybus.co.nz), based in Nelson services both ends of the Heaphy Track, as well as the Wangapeka.

Fly from Karamea to Takaka with **Helicopter Charter Karamea** (☑03-782 6111; www.karameahelicharter.co.nz; 79 Waverley St, Karamea), **Golden Bay Air** (☑0800 588 885;

www.goldenbayair.co.nz) or **Adventure Flights Golden Bay** (☑0800 150 338, 03-525 6167; www.adventureflightsgoldenbay.co.nz) starting from $150 per person, then walk back on the Heaphy Track; contact the Karamea Information & Resource Centre for details.

Based at Rongo Backpackers, **Karamea Connections** (☑03-782 6767; www.karameaconnections.co.nz) runs track and town transport, including services to Heaphy, Wangapeka, Oparara Basin and Westport on demand.

THE GREAT COAST ROAD

There are fine views all the way along this beautiful stretch of SH6, although its most famous attractions are the geologically fascinating Pancake Rocks at Punakaiki. Fill up in Westport if you're low on petrol and cash – there's no fuel until Runanga, 92km away, and the next ATM is in Greymouth.

Westport to Punakaiki

Set on 42 serene hectares, 17km south of Westport, the solar-powered, energy-efficient **Beaconstone Eco Lodge** (☑027 431 0491; www.beaconstoneecolodge.co.nz; Birds Ferry Rd; dm $34, d/tw $80-88; ☺Oct-May; ☎) ⊘ is a bushy retreat with touches of Americana cool. Inside are cosy beds and a laid-back communal area, while beyond the doorstep are bush walks leading to peaceful river swimming holes. There's only room for 14 people, so booking is recommended.

Jack's Gasthof (☑03-789 6501; www.jacksgasthof.co.nz; SH6; mains $12-28; ☺from 11am Oct-Apr) is 21km south of Westport on the Little Totara River, where Berliners Jack and Petra run their eternally popular pizzeria with an adjacent bar improbably bejewelled with a disco ball. Avail yourself of campsites (from $8) and a basic room ($50) if you require a sleepover.

For a true taste of the region's gold-mining past (with the odd trap-door widget), swing into **Mitchell's Gully Gold Mine** (☑03-789 6257; SH6; adult/child $10/free; ☺9am-5pm), 22km south of Westport, where you'll meet a pioneer's descendants and explore the family mine. There are interesting tales, tunnels, railway tracks, a waterwheel and the last working stamping battery in the village.

The next stop is **Charleston**, 26km south of Westport. It's hard to believe it now, but this place boomed during the 1860s gold rush, with 80 hotels, three breweries and hundreds of thirsty gold-diggers staking claims along the Nile River. There's not much left now except a motel, camping ground, a clutch of local houses, and the brilliant Underworld Adventures (p431), with which you can explore some utterly amazing hidden treasures.

From here to Punakaiki is a staggeringly beautiful panorama of lowland pakihi scrub and lush green forest alongside a series of bays dramatically sculpted by relentless ocean fury. Drive as slowly as the traffic behind you will allow.

Punakaiki & Paparoa National Park

POP 70

Located midway between Westport and Greymouth is Punakaiki, a small settlement beside the rugged 38,000-hectare Paparoa National Park. Most visitors come for a quick squiz at the Pancake Rocks, which is a shame because there's excellent tramping and other wild adventures, and plenty of accommodation.

◎ Sights

Paparoa National Park is blessed with high cliffs and empty beaches, a dramatic mountain range, crazy limestone river valleys, diverse flora, and a profusion of birdlife, including weka and the Westland petrel, a rare sea bird that nests only here.

★ **Pancake Rocks**   NATURAL FEATURE
(www.doc.govt.nz) Punakaiki's claim to fame is Dolomite Point, where a layering-weathering process called stylobedding has carved the limestone into what looks like piles of thick pancakes. Aim for high tide (tide timetables are posted in town; hope that it coincides with sunset) when the sea surges into caverns and booms menacingly through blowholes. See it on a wild day and be reminded that Mother Nature really is the boss. An easy 15-minute walk loops from the highway out to the rocks and blowholes.

⚡ Activities

Tramps around Punakaiki include the **Truman Track** (30 minutes return) and the **Punakaiki–Porari Loop** (3½ hours), which goes up the spectacular limestone Pororari River gorge before popping over a hill and coming down the bouldery Punakaiki River to rejoin the highway.

Surefooted types can embark on the **Fox River Cave Walk** (three hours return), 12km north of Punakaiki and open to amateur explorers. BYO torch and sturdy shoes.

Other tramps in the national park are detailed in the DOC *Paparoa National Park* pamphlet ($1). Note that many of Paparoa's inland walks are susceptible to river flooding so it is vital that you obtain updates from the Paparoa National Park Visitor Centre (p437) in Punakaiki before you depart.

Punakaiki Horse Treks   HORSE RIDING
(☑ 03-731 1839; www.pancake-rocks.co.nz; SH6; 2½hr ride $170; ⊙ Nov-May) Punakaiki Horse Treks, based at Hydrangea Cottages, conducts treks in the beautiful Punakaiki Valley, with river crossings, finishing at the beach.

Punakaiki Canoes   KAYAKING
(☑ 03-731 1870; www.riverkayaking.co.nz; SH6; canoe hire 2hr/full day $40/60, family rates available) This outfit rents canoes near the Pororari River bridge, for gentle, super-scenic paddling for all abilities.

🛏 Sleeping & Eating

★ **Punakaiki Beach Hostel**   HOSTEL $
(☑ 03-731 1852; www.punakaikibeachhostel.co.nz; 4 Webb St; sites per person $21, dm/s/d $29/65/77; @ 🖥) A laid-back hostel with a sea-view veranda, a short walk from Pancake Rocks, with savvy owners who know what makes a good hostel: good beds and great communal facilities, and staff who smile because they mean it. Cutesy Sunset Cottage ($130) and the en suite house bus ($115) are both well worth the splurge.

Te Nikau Retreat   HOSTEL $
(☑ 03-731 1111; www.tenikauretreat.co.nz; 19 Hartmount Pl; dm $28, d $75-90, cabins from $96; @ 🖥) ⦿ Relax, restore and explore at this clutch of accommodation offerings nestled into shady, rainforest nooks, just a short walk to the beach. There are rooms in the main building, several cute cabins, and the larger Nikau and Rata lodges sleeping up to five and 10 people respectively.

Punakaiki Beach Camp   HOLIDAY PARK $
(☑ 03-731 1894; www.punakaikibeachcamp.co.nz; 5 Owen St; sites per person powered/unpowered $20/17, d $68-98; 🖥) With a dramatic backdrop of sheer cliffs, this salty, beachside park with good grass is studded with clean, old-style cabins and amenities. A classic Kiwi coastal camping ground five to 10 minutes' walk from Pancake Rocks.

Hydrangea Cottages   COTTAGES $$
(☑ 03-731 1839; www.pancake-rocks.co.nz; SH6; d $165-320; 🛜) On a hillside overlooking the Tasman, these six standalone and mostly self-contained cottages (largest sleeping up to six) are built from salvaged timber and stone. It's a classy but relaxed enclave, with splashes of colourful mosaic tile, some outdoor baths, and pretty cottage gardens. The owners also run Punakaiki Horse Treks.

Punakaiki Tavern   PLB FOOD $$
(☑ 03-731 1188; www.punakaikitavern.co.nz; SH6; mains $20-40; ⊙8am-late; 🛜) Whether it's breakfast, lunch or dinner, this pub serves decent-size portions, and chips with pretty much everything, in comfortable surrounds featuring a pool table and out-of-tune piano. Beverage highlights include Benger nectarine juice.

ℹ️ Information

Paparoa National Park Visitor Centre (☑ 03-731 1895; www.doc.govt.nz; SH6; ⊙9am-5pm Oct-Nov, to 6pm Dec-Mar, to 4.30pm Apr-Sep) The Paparoa National Park Visitor Centre has information on the park and track conditions, and handles bookings for some local attractions and accommodation, including hut tickets.

ℹ️ Getting There & Away

InterCity (☑ 03-365 1113; www.intercity.co.nz) travels daily north to Westport (45 minutes), and south to Greymouth (45 minutes) and Fox Glacier (five hours). **Naked Bus** (www.nakedbus.com) runs to the same destinations three days a week. Both companies stop long enough for passengers to admire the Pancake Rocks.

Punakaiki to Greymouth

The highway between Punakaiki and Greymouth is flanked by white-capped waves and rocky bays on one side, and the steep, bushy Paparoa Ranges on the other.

At **Barrytown**, 17km south of Punakaiki, Steve and Robyn run **Barrytown Knifemaking** (☑ 0800 256 433, 03-731 1053; www.barrytownknifemaking.com; 2662 SH6, Barrytown; classes $150; ⊙closed Mon), where you can make your own knife – from hand-forging the blade to crafting a handle from native rimu timber. The day-long course features lunch, archery, axe-throwing and a stream of entertainingly bad jokes from Steve. Bookings essential, and transport from Punakaiki can be arranged.

With a rainforest backdrop and coastal views, **Ti Kouka House** (☑ 03-731 1460; www.tikoukahouse.co.nz; 2522 SH6, Barrytown; d incl breakfast $295; 🛜) boasts splendid architectural design, recycled building materials, and sculptural artwork both inside and out. You'll want to move in permanently, but you'll have to settle for a B&B stay in one of its three luxurious rooms.

Breakers (☑ 03-762 7743; www.breakers.co.nz; 1367 SH6, Nine Mile Creek; d incl breakfast $255-385; 🛜, 14km north of Greymouth, is one of the best-kept secrets on the coast. Beautifully appointed en suite rooms overlook the sea with fine surfing opportunities at hand for the intrepid. The hosts are sporty, friendly and have a nice dog.

Two kilometres south is **Rapahoe**, 12km shy of Greymouth. This tiny seaside settlement is the northern trailhead for the enjoyable Point Elizabeth Walkway (p439). Should you require refreshment before or after your walk, call in to the **Rapahoe Hotel** (☑ 03-762 7701; 1 Beach Rd, Rapahoe; mains $14-30), a simple country pub offering warm hospitality and a good feed of fish and chips in a picturesque location.

GREYMOUTH REGION

Bookending NZ's most famous alpine highway – Arthur's Pass – and sitting more or less halfway along the West Coast road, the Greymouth area provides easy access to the attractions north and south as well as offering a decent smattering of diversions within its boundaries.

Greymouth

POP 10,000

Welcome to the 'Big Smoke', crouched at the mouth of the imaginatively named Grey River. Known to Māori as Mawhera, the West Coast's largest town has gold in its veins, and today its fortunes still ebb and flow with the tide of mining. Tourism and dairy farming, however, are increasingly vital to the economy. The town is well geared for travellers, offering all the necessary services and the odd tourist attraction, the most famous of which is Shantytown.

◉ Sights

⭐ **Left Bank Art Gallery**   GALLERY
(www.leftbankarts.org.nz; 1 Tainui St; admission by donation; ⊙11am-4.30pm Tue-Fri, 11am-2pm Sat) This 95-year-old former bank houses

Greymouth

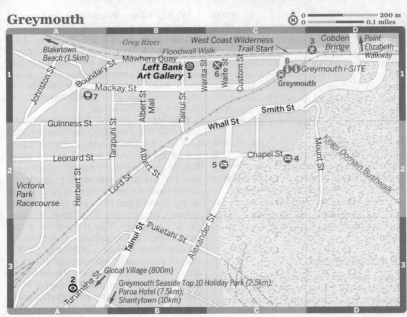

N
0 — 200 m
0 — 0.1 miles

Greymouth

contemporary NZ jade carvings, prints, paintings, photographs and ceramics. The gallery also fosters and supports a wide society of West Coast artists.

Monteith's Brewing Co   BREWERY
(☎03-768 4149; www.monteiths.co.nz; cnr Turumaha & Herbert Sts; guided tour $22; ☺11am-8pm)

The original Monteith's brewhouse may simply be brand HQ for mainstream product largely brewed elsewhere, but it still delivers heritage in spades through its excellent-value guided tour (25 minutes, includes generous samples; four tours daily). The flash tasting room-cum-bar is now Greymouth's most exciting watering hole (tasty snacks $9 to $22) – shame it shuts up shop so early.

Shantytown   MUSEUM
(www.shantytown.co.nz; Rutherglen Rd, Paroa; adult/child/family $33/16/78; ☺8.30am-5pm)
Eight kilometres south of Greymouth and 2km inland from SH6, Shantytown evocatively presents and preserves local history through a recreated 1860s gold-mining town, complete with steam-train rides, pub and Rosie's House of Ill Repute. There's also gold panning, a sawmill, a gory hospital, and short holographic movies in the Princess Theatre.

🏃 Activities

TranzAlpine   TRAIN TOUR
(☎0800 872 467, 03-341 2588; www.kiwirailscenic.co.nz; one way adult/child from $99/69; ☺departs Christchurch 8.15am, Greymouth 1.45pm) The TranzAlpine is one of the world's great train journeys, traversing the Southern Alps be-

WORTH A TRIP

WEST COAST WILDERNESS TRAIL

The 136km **West Coast Wilderness Trail** (www.westcoastwildernesstrail.co.nz) is one of 23 NZ Cycle Trails (www.nzcycletrail.com). Stretching from Greymouth to Ross, the mostly gently graded track follows gold-rush trails, water races, logging tramways and old railway lines, as well as forging new routes cross-country. Along the way it reveals outstanding landscapes of dense rainforest, glacial rivers, lakes and wetlands, with views all the way from the snow-capped mountains of the Southern Alps to the wild Tasman Sea. It's a great way to immerse yourself in this special place.

The full shebang is a good four days of riding but can easily be sliced up into sections of various lengths, catering to every ability and area of interest. Ask about the 'Big Day Out' from Kawhaka to Kaniere, which takes in major highlights, or a ride taking in the track's historic pubs at Paroa, Kumara and Ross.

Bike hire, transport and advice is available from the major setting-off points. In Hokitika, contact **Wilderness Trail Shuttle** ([phone] 03-755 5042, 021 263 3299; www.wildernesstrail shuttle.co.nz) and in Greymouth **Trail Transport** ([phone] 03-768 6618; www.trailtransport.co.nz).

tween Christchurch and Greymouth, from the Pacific Ocean to the Tasman Sea, passing through Arthur's Pass National Park. En route is a sequence of dramatic landscapes, from the flat, alluvial Canterbury Plains, through narrow alpine gorges, an 8.5km tunnel, beech-forested river valleys and alongside a lake fringed with cabbage trees.

The 4½-hour journey is unforgettable, even in bad weather (if it's raining on one coast, it's probably fine on the other).

Point Elizabeth Walkway
WALKING

(www.doc.govt.nz) Accessible from Dommett Esplanade in Cobden, 6km north of Greymouth, this enjoyable walkway (three hours return) skirts around a richly forested headland in the shadow of the Rapahoe Range to an impressive ocean lookout, before continuing on to the northern trailhead at Rapahoe (11km from Greymouth) – small town, big beach, friendly local pub.

Floodwall Walk
WALKING

Take a 10-minute riverside stroll along Mawhera Quay (the start of the West Coast Wilderness Trail (p439)), or keep going for an hour or so, taking in the fishing boat harbour, Blaketown Beach and breakwater – a great place to experience the power of the ocean and savour a famous West Coast sunset.

🛏 Sleeping

★ Global Village
HOSTEL **$**

([phone] 03-768 7272; www.globalvillagebackpackers. co.nz; 42 Cowper St; sites per person $18, dm/d/tr $30/76/102; [icons]) A collage of African and Asian art is infused with a passionate trav-

ellers' vibe here. Free kayaks – the Lake Karoro wetlands reserve is just metres away – and mountain bikes are on tap, and relaxation comes easy with a spa, sauna, barbecue and fire pit.

Ardwyn House
B&B **$**

([phone] 03-768 6107; ardwynhouse@hotmail.com; 48 Chapel St; s/d incl breakfast from $65/100; [icon]) This old-fashioned, homey B&B nestles amid steep gardens on a quiet dead-end street. Mary, the well-travelled host, cooks a splendid breakfast.

Greymouth Seaside
Top 10 Holiday Park
HOLIDAY PARK, MOTEL **$**

([phone] 03-768 6618, 0800 867 104; www.top10 greymouth.co.nz; 2 Chesterfield St; sites $40-46, cabins $60-125, motel r $110-374; [icons]) Well positioned for sunset walks on the adjacent beach and 2.5km south of the town centre, this large park has various tent and campervan sites as well as accommodation ranging from simple cabins to deluxe sea-view motels – arguably the flashest units in town. A shipshape stop for every budget.

Noah's Ark Backpackers
HOSTEL **$**

([phone] 0800 662 472, 03-768 4868; www.noahs. co.nz; 16 Chapel St; sites per person $18, dm/s/d $30/74/74; [icons]) Originally a monastery, colourful Noah's has eccentric animal-themed rooms, a sunset-worthy balcony and a pretty back garden with a spa pool. Bikes and fishing rods are provided free of charge.

Paroa Hotel
HOTEL **$$**

([phone] 0800 762 6860, 03-762 6860; www.paroa. co.nz; 508 Main South Rd, Paroa; d $128-140; [icon]) Opposite the Shantytown turn-off, this family-owned hotel (62 years and counting) has spacious units sharing a large lawned garden next to the beach. The notable bar and restaurant (mains $18 to $35) dishes up warm hospitality in the form of roast dinners, whitebait, pavlova and beer, amid local clientele.

✕ Eating & Drinking

DP1 Cafe CAFE **$**
(104 Mawhera Quay; meals $7-23; ☺8am-5pm Mon-Fri, 9am-5pm Sat & Sun; ☎) A stalwart of the Greymouth cafe scene, this hip joint serves great espresso, along with good-value grub. Groovy tunes, wi-fi, local art and quayside tables make this a welcoming spot to linger. Swing in for the $6 morning muffin and coffee special.

Ferrari's BAR
(☑03-768 4008; www.ferraris.co.nz; 6 Mackay St; ☺5pm-late Thur-Sat, 12-6pm Sun) Valiantly trying to capture the sophistication and glamour of golden-era Hollywood in good old Greymouth, this bar inside the Regent Cinema is an atmospheric and comfortable place to plonk yourself down in a leather sofa for a drink or two.

❶ Information

Grey Base Hospital (☑03-768 0499; High St)
Greymouth i-SITE (☑03-768 5101, 0800 473 966; www.westcoasttravel.co.nz; 164 Mackay St, Greymouth Train Station; ☺9am-5pm Mon-Fri, 9.30am-4pm Sat & Sun; ☎) The helpful crew at the train station can assist with all manner of advice and bookings, including those for DOC huts and walks. See also www.westcoastnz.com.

❶ Getting There & Away

Combined with the i-SITE in the train station, the **West Coast Travel Centre** (☑03-768 7080; www.westcoasttravel.co.nz; 164 Mackay St, Greymouth Train Station; ☺9am-5pm Mon-Fri, 10am-4pm Sat & Sun; ☎) books local and national transport, and offers luggage storage.

BUS
All buses stop outside the train station.
InterCity (p427) has daily buses north to Westport (two hours) and Nelson (six hours), and south to Franz Josef Glacier (3½ hours).
Naked Bus (p427) runs the same route three days a week. Both companies offer connections to destinations further afield.
Atomic Travel (☑03-349 0697, 0508 108 359; www.atomictravel.co.nz) runs daily between Greymouth and Christchurch, as does **West Coast Shuttle** (☑03-768 0028, 0274 927 000; www.westcoastshuttle.co.nz).

TRAIN
KiwiRail Scenic (☑0800 872 467; www.kiwirailscenic.co.nz)

❶ Getting Around

Several car-hire company desks are located within the train station. Local companies include **Alpine West** (☑0800 257 736, 03-768 4002; www.alpinerentals.co.nz; 11 Shelley St) and **NZ Rent-a-Car** (☑03-768 0379; www.nzrentacar.co.nz; 170 Tainui St).
Greymouth Taxis (☑03-768 7078)

Blackball

POP 291
Around 25km upriver of Greymouth sits the ramshackle town of Blackball – established in 1866 to service gold diggers; coal mining kicked in between 1890 and 1964. The National Federation of Labour (a trade union) was conceived here, born from influential strikes in 1908 and 1931. This story is retold in historical displays on the main road.

Alongside you will find the hub of the town, **Formerly the Blackball Hilton** (☑03-732 4705, 0800 425 225; www.blackballhilton.co.nz; 26 Hart St; s/d incl breakfast $55/110; ☎), where you can collect a copy of the helpful 'Historic Blackball' map. This official historic place has memorabilia galore, hot meals ($15 to $34), cold beer, heaps of afternoon sun and a host of rooms oozing the charm of yesteryear; it was named so after a certain global hotel chain got antsy when its name was appropriated.

Competing with the Hilton in the fame stakes is the **Blackball Salami Co** (☑03-732 4111; www.blackballsalami.co.nz; 11 Hilton St; ☺8am-4pm Mon-Fri, 9am-2pm Sat), manufacturer of tasty salami and sausages ranging from chorizo to black pudding.

Blackball's other claim to fame is as the southern end of the historic **Croesus Track** (www.doc.govt.nz), a one- to two-day hike (or bike ride) clambering over to Barrytown. In the next few years it will form part of the new **Pike River Great Walk**. Watch this space.

❶ Getting There & Away

From the West Coast Hwy it's half an hour's drive or so to Blackball; you'll need your own wheels.

Lake Brunner

POP 270

Lying inland from Greymouth, Lake Brunner (www.golakebrunner.co.nz) can be reached via the SH7 turn-off at Stillwater, a journey of 39km. It can also be reached from the south via Kumara Junction.

One of many lakes in the area, Brunner is a tranquil spot for bushwalks, bird-spotting and various watersports, including boating and fishing. Indeed, the local boast is that the lake and Arnold River are 'where the trout die of old age', which implies that the local fish are particularly clever or the fisherfolk are somewhat hopeless. Greymouth i-SITE can hook you up with a guide. Head to the marina to undertake one or all of several pretty short walks.

Moana is the main settlement, home to numerous accommodation options of which the best is **Lake Brunner Country Motel** (☑ 03-738 0144; www.lakebrunnermotel.co.nz; 2014 Arnold Valley Rd; sites from $34, cabins $62-72, cottages d $135-150; ☜), 2km from the lake. It features cabins, cottages and campervan sites tucked into native plantings through extensive parklike grounds, while tenters can enjoy the lush grassy camping field. This is proper peace and quiet, unless you count birdsong and the bubbling of the spa pool.

Moana also has a couple of places to eat, including a cafe opposite the train station where the *TranzAlpine* pulls in. There's also food at the local pub, which is trending upward, and groceries at the petrol station.

❶ Getting There & Away

The *TranzAlpine* pulls into Moana train station twice daily on its way between Christchurch and Greymouth. **Atomic Travel** (p440) shuttles also pass through on on the same journey.

Kumara

POP 309

Thirty kilometres south of Greymouth, near the western end of Arthur's Pass (SH73), Kumara was yet another busy gold-rush town that ground to a halt, leaving behind a thin posse of flinty citizens. In recent times its claim to fame has been as stellar supporter of the Coast to Coast (www.coasttocoast. co.nz), NZ's most famous multisport race. Held each February, the strong, the brave and the totally knackered run, cycle and kayak a total of 243km all the way across the mountains to Christchurch, with top competitors dusting it off in just under 11 hours.

Nowadays Kumarians extend their hospitality to highway travellers and an increasing number of cyclists following the West Coast Wilderness Trail (p439), which passes through the town. Anticipating their arrival is the show-stopping **Theatre Royal Hotel** (☑ 03-736 9277; www.theatreroyalhotel. co.nz; 81 Seddon St, SH73, Kumara; d $100-290; ☺ 10am-late; ☜), a fully restored beauty that has kicked Kumara well and truly into the 21st century with its classy restaurant and sumptuous accommodation options styled with full historic honours. The attention to detail in furnishings and heritage displays is simply wonderful. Stop in to enjoy some of the best food on the coast (fish and chips, game, pizza and cakes) or just pull in for a drink and a yarn with the locals.

Should you be to-ing or fro-ing over Arthur's Pass, consider staying at **Jacksons Retreat** (☑ 03-738 0474; www.jacksonsretreat. co.nz; Jacksons, SH73, Kumara; sites from $40; ❀ ☜ ☞, 33km west of Arthur's Pass Village. Set upon 15 sloping acres with exceptional views over the Taramakau River, it offers stacks of excellent amenities for campervanner and tenter alike.

❶ Getting There & Away

West Coast Shuttle (p440) passes through Kumara (not to be confused with Kumara Junction, close to the coast) on its daily service between Greymouth and Christchurch.

WESTLAND

The bottom third or so of the West Coast is known as Westland, a mix of farmland and rainforest backed by the Southern Alps, which pop straight up in a neck-cricking fashion. This region is most famous for its glaciers, currently in retreat but fortunately surrounded by equally spectacular sights ready to steal the show.

Hokitika

POP 3078

Popular with history buffs and the setting for numerous NZ novels, including the 2013 Man Booker Prize-winning *The Luminaries* by Eleanor Catton, Hokitika's riches come in many forms. Founded on gold, today

Hokitika

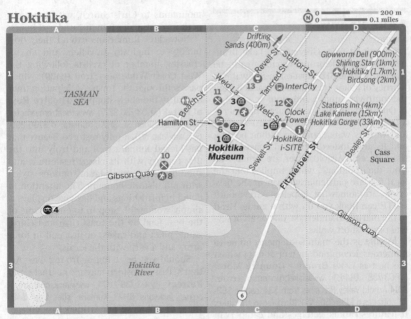

Hokitika

THE WEST COAST HOKITIKA

the town is the stronghold of indigenous *pounamu* (greenstone), which jostles for attention amid many other arts and crafts, drawing rafts of visitors to its wide open streets.

◉ Sights

★**Hokitika Museum**   MUSEUM
(www.hokitikamuseum.co.nz; 17 Hamilton St; adult/
child $6/3; ◷ 10am-5pm Nov-Mar, 10am-2pm Apr-
Oct) Housed in the imposing Carnegie Building (1908), this is an exemplary provincial
museum, with intelligently curated exhibitions presented in a clear, modern style.
Highlights include the fascinating *Whitebait!* exhibition, and the Pounamu room –
the ideal primer before you hit the galleries
looking for greenstone treasures.

★**Lake Kaniere**   LAKE
(www.doc.govt.nz) Lying at the heart of a
7000-hectare scenic reserve, beautiful Lake
Kaniere is 8km long, 2km wide, 195m deep,
and freezing cold as you'll discover if you
swim. You may, however, prefer simply to
camp or picnic at Hans Bay (p444), or undertake one of numerous walks in the surrounds,
ranging from the 15-minute Canoe Cove Walk
to the seven-hour return gut-buster up Mt Tuhua. The historic **Kaniere Water Race Walkway** (3½ hours one way) forms part of the
West Coast Wilderness Trail (p439).

Hokitika Gorge   GORGE
(www.doc.govt.nz) A picturesque 35km drive
leads to Hokitika Gorge, a ravishing ravine

with unbelievably turquoise waters coloured by glacial 'flour'. Photograph the scene from every angle via the short forest walkway and swingbridge. The gorge is well signposted from Stafford St (past the dairy factory). En route, you will pass **Kowhitirangi**, the site of one of NZ's deadliest mass murders (immortalised in the 1982 classic film *Bad Blood*). A poignant roadside monument lines up the farmstead site through a stone shaft.

Sunset Point   VIEWPOINT
(Gibson Quay) A spectacular vantage point at any time of day, this is – as the name suggests – the primo place to watch the day's light fade away. Surfers, seagulls, longshore drift, and fish and chips: *this* is New Zealand.

Glowworm Dell   NATURAL FEATURE
On the northern edge of town, a short stroll from SH6 leads to this glowworm dell, an easy opportunity to enter the other-worldly home of NZ's native fungus gnat larvae (so not even a worm at all). An information panel at the entrance will further illuminate your way.

Galleries
Art and craft galleries are a strong spoke in Hoki's wheel, and you could easily spend a day spinning around the lot. There are plenty of opportunities to meet the artists, and in some studios you can watch them at work. Be aware that some galleries sell jade imported from Europe and Asia, as precious local *pounamu* (greenstone) is not surrendered lightly by the wilds.

Hokitika Craft Gallery   GALLERY
(www.hokitikacraftgallery.co.nz; 25 Tancred St; ⊙8.30am-5pm) The town's best one-stop shop, this co-op showcases a wide range of local work, including *pounamu*, jewellery, textiles, ceramics and woodwork.

Waewae Pounamu   GALLERY
(www.waewaepounamu.co.nz; 39 Weld St; 8am-5pm) This stronghold of NZ *pounamu* displays traditional and contemporary designs in its main-road gallery.

Hokitika Glass Studio   GALLERY
(www.hokitikaglass.co.nz; 9 Weld St; ⊙8.30am-5pm) Glass art covering a continuum from garish to glorious; watch the blowers at the furnace on weekdays.

 Activities

Hokitika is a great base for walking and cycling. Download or collect a copy of DOC's

brochure *Walks in the Hokitika Area* ($1), and visit **Hokitika Cycles & Sports World** (☑03-755 8662; www.hokitikasportsworld.co.nz; 33 Tancred St; bike rental per day $55) for bike rental and advice on tracks, including the West Coast Wilderness Trail (p439).

Bonz 'N' Stonz   CARVING
(www.bonz-n-stonz.co.nz; 16 Hamilton St; full-day workshop $85-180) Design, carve and polish your own *pounamu*, bone or paua (shellfish) masterpiece, with tutelage from Steve. Prices vary with materials and design complexity. Bookings recommended.

Hokitika Heritage Walk   WALKING
Ask staff at the i-SITE for the worthy 50c leaflet before wandering the old wharf precinct, or ask them about a guided walk with Mr Verrall. Another map details the **Hokitika Heritage Trail**, an 11km (two- to three-hour) loop taking in historic sites and interesting town views.

Wilderness Wings   SCENIC FLIGHTS
(☑0800 755 8118; www.wildernesswings.co.nz; Hokitika Airport; flights from $285) A highly regarded operator running scenic flights over Hokitika and further afield to Aoraki/Mt Cook and the glaciers.

✪ Festivals & Events

Driftwood & Sand ART
(www.driftwoodandsand.co.nz; ☉ Jan) During three days in January, flotsam and jetsam is fashioned into a surprising array of arty, crafty and daft sculpture on Hokitika beach.

Wildfoods Festival FOOD
(www.wildfoods.co.nz; ☉ Mar) Held in early March, this fun festival attracts swarms of curious and brave gourmands who eat a whole lot of things they would usually flee from or flick from their hair. Book early.

🛏 Sleeping

★ Drifting Sands HOSTEL $
(📞 03-755 7654; www.driftingsands.co.nz; 197 Revell St; dm $36, d & tr $109; 🖥) If only all hostels were this stylish. Natural tones and textures, upcycled furniture, chic furnishings and hip vibes make this beachside pad a winner, as does quality bedding, a cosy lounge and hot bread in the morning. Fab!

Hans Bay DOC Campground CAMPGROUND $
(www.doc.govt.nz; sites per adult/child $6/3) This basic DOC campsite occupies a prime site on grassy terraces with grandstand views of the lake and bushy surrounding hills.

Birdsong HOSTEL $
(📞 03-755 7179; www.birdsong.co.nz; SH6; dm/s $34/67, d $119, without bathroom $85; 🖥) Located 2.5km north of town, this bird-themed hostel has sea views and a homey atmosphere. Free bikes, handy beach access and hidden extras will entice you into extending your stay.

Shining Star HOLIDAY PARK, MOTEL $$
(📞 03-755 8921; 16 Richards Dr; sites unpowered/powered $32/40, d $115-199; 🖥) Attractive and versatile beachside spot with everything from camping to classy self-contained seafront units. Kids will love the menagerie, including pigs and alpacas straight from Dr Doolittle's appointment book. Parents might prefer the spa or sauna.

Stations Inn MOTEL $$
(📞 03-755 5499; www.stationsinnhokitika.co.nz; Blue Spur Rd; d $170-300; 🖥) Five minutes' drive from town on rolling hills overlooking the distant ocean, this smart, modern motel complex has plush units featuring king-sized beds and spa bath. With a patio, pond and waterwheel out the front, the on-site restaurant (mains are $30 to $45; open from 5pm Tuesday to Saturday) specialises in meaty fare.

Teichelmann's B&B B&B $$$
(📞 03-755 8232; www.teichelmanns.co.nz; 20 Hamilton St; d $235-260; 🖥) Once home to surgeon, mountaineer and professional beard-cultivator Ebenezer Teichelmann, this old gem is now a charming B&B with amicable hosts. All rooms have an airy, restorative ambience along with their own bathrooms, including the more private Teichy's Cottage in the garden.

🍴 Eating & Drinking

Dulcie's Takeaways FISH & CHIPS $
(cnr Gibson Quay & Wharf St; fish & chips $6-12; ☉ 11am-9pm Tue-Sun) Net yourself some excellent fish and chips (try the turbot or blue cod), then scoff them down the road at Sunset Point for an extra sprinkle of sea salt.

★ Fat Pipi Pizza PIZZA $$
(89 Revell St; pizzas $20-30; ☉ 12-2.30pm Wed-Sun, 5-9pm daily; 🖉) Vegetarians, carnivores and everyone in between will be salivating for the pizza (including a whitebait version) made with love right before your eyes. Lovely cakes, honey buns and Benger juices, too. Best enjoyed in the garden bar – one of the town's (in fact the West Coast's) best dining spots.

Ramble + Ritual CAFE
(📞 03-755 6347; 51 Sewell St; snacks $3-8, meals $8-15; ☉ 8am-4pm Mon-Fri, 9am-1pm Sat; 🖉) Tucked away near the Clock Tower, this gallery-cum-cafe is a stylish little spot to linger over great espresso, delicious fresh baking and simple, healthy salads made to order. The ginger oaty may well be the best in the land.

West Coast Wine Bar WINE BAR
(www.westcoastwine.co.nz; 108 Revell St; ☉ 8am-late Tue-Sat, 8am-2pm Mon) Upping Hoki's sophistication factor, this weeny joint with a cute garden bar packs a fridge full of fine wine and craft beer, with the option of ordering up pizza from Fat Pipi Pizza, down the road.

ℹ Information

Hokitika i-SITE (📞 03-755 6166; www.hokitika.org; 36 Weld St; ☉ 8.30am-6pm Mon-Fri, 9am-5pm Sat & Sun) One of NZ's best i-SITEs offers extensive bookings, including all bus services. Also holds DOC info, although you'll need to book online or at DOC visitor centres further afield. See also www.westcoastnz.com.

Westland Medical Centre (📞 03-755 8180; 54a Sewell St; ☉ 8am-4.45pm Mon-Fri) Ring after hours.

ⓘ Getting There & Away

AIR

Hokitika Airport (www.hokitikaairport.co.nz; Airport Dr, off Tudor St) is 1.5km east of the town centre. **Air New Zealand** (p427) has three flights most days to/from Christchurch.

BUS

InterCity (☑ 03-365 1113; www.intercity.co.nz) buses leave from the Kiwi Centre on Tancred St, then outside the i-SITE, daily for Greymouth (45 minutes), Nelson (seven hours) and Franz Josef Glacier (two hours). **Naked Bus** (www.nakedbus.com) services the same destinations three times a week, with both companies offering connections to destinations further afield.

ⓘ Getting Around

Car hire is available from **NZ Rent A Car** (☑ 027 294 8986, 03-755 6353; www.nzrentacar.co.nz) in town; there are a couple of other options at Hokitika Airport.
Hokitika Taxis (☑ 03-755 5075)

Hokitika to Westland Tai Poutini National Park

From Hokitika it's 140km south to Franz Josef Glacier. Most travellers fast-forward without stopping, but there are some satisfying stopping points for those inclined. Bus services with InterCity and Naked Bus stops along this stretch of SH6.

Lake Mahinapua

Mahinapua Walkway follows an old logging tramway with relics and a diverse range of forest. It's a lovely four-hour return walk and now part of the West Coast Wilderness Trail (p439). The walkway car park is located 8km south of Hokitika on SH6.

Two kilometres south of the Mahinapua Walkway car park is the entrance to tranquil **Lake Mahinapua Scenic Reserve**, with a picnic area, DOC campsite and several short walks.

Five kilometres further on is a signposted turn-off to the **West Coast Treetops Walkway** (☑ 03-755 5052, 050 887 3386; www.treetopsnz.com; 1128 Woodstock-Rimu Rd; adult/child $38/15; ◷ 9am-5pm), a further 2km away. This steel walkway – 450m long and 20m off the ground – offers an unusual perspective on the rainforest canopy, featuring many old rimu and kamahi. The highlight is the 40m-high tower, from where there are extensive views

across Lake Mahinapua, the Southern Alps and Tasman Sea. There's a cafe and souvenir shop in the information centre.

Ross

POP 297

Ross, 30km south of Hokitika, is where the unearthing of NZ's largest gold nugget (the 2.772kg 'Honourable Roddy') caused a kerfuffle in 1907. The **Ross Goldfields Heritage Centre** (www.ross.org.nz; 4 Aylmer St; ◷ 9am-4pm Dec-Mar, to 2pm Apr-Nov) displays a replica Roddy, along with a scale model ($2) of the town in its shiny years. The town now bookends the new West Coast Wilderness Trail (p439).

The **Water Race Walk** (one hour return) starts near the museum, passing old gold-diggings, caves, tunnels and a cemetery. Try **gold panning** by hiring a pan from the information centre ($10) and head to Jones Creek to look for Roddy's great, great grandnuggets.

Established in 1866, the **Empire Hotel** (☑ 03-755 4005; 19 Aylmer St) is one of the West Coast's hidden gems, the bar (and many of its patrons) are testament to a bygone era. Breathe in the authenticity, along with a whiff of woodsmoke, over a pint and an honest meal.

Hari Hari

POP 330

About 22km south of Lake Ianthe, Hari Hari is where swashbuckling Australian aviator Guy Menzies crash-landed his trusty biplane into a swamp after completing the first solo trans-Tasman flight from Sydney, in 1931. Read all about it and view a replica of his plane at a commemorative park at the southern end of town.

The 2¾-hour **Hari Hari Coastal Walk** (www.doc.govt.nz) is a low-tide loop along the Poerua and Wanganui Rivers through bogs, estuaries and a swamp forest. The walk starts 20km from SH6, the last 8km unsealed; follow the signs from Wanganui Flats Rd. Tide times are posted at the Pukeko Store, which serves tearoom food and coffee.

Should you need a sleepover, **Flaxbush Motels** (☑ 03-753 3116; www.flaxbushmotels.co.nz; SH6; d $65-120; ☎) has characterful cabins and units covering a wide range of budgets. It also has a friendly disposition towards birds (ducks and peacocks in particular), and a willingness to negotiate room rates for longer stays. Ask about glowworms.

Whataroa

POP 288

A dot of a town strung out along SH6, Whataroa is the departure point for tours to the **Kotuku Sanctuary**, NZ's only nesting site for the kotuku (white heron), which roosts here between November and February. The only way to visit the nesting site is with **White Heron Sanctuary Tours** (📞0800 523 456, 03-753 4120; www.whiteheron tours.co.nz; SH6, Whataroa; adult/child $120/55; ☺4 tours daily late Aug-Mar) on an enjoyable 2½-hour tour involving a gentle jetboat ride and short boardwalk to a viewing hide. Seeing the scores of birds perched in the bushes is a magical experience. A scenic rainforest tour without the herons is available year-round for the same price.

White Heron Sanctuary Tours also runs the **Sanctuary Tours Motel** (📞0800 523 456, 03-753 4120; www.whiteherontours.co.nz; SH6; cabins $65-75, d $110-135), with basic cabins with shared bathrooms ($10 extra for bedlinen), and enthusiastically painted motel units.

Glacier Country Scenic Flights (📞03-753 4096, 0800 423 463; www.glacieradventures.co.nz; SH6, Whataroa; flights $195-435) offers a range of scenic flights and helihikes, lifting off from Whataroa Valley. These guys give you more mountain-gawping for your buck than many of the operators flying from the glacier townships.

If it's open, call in to the **Peter Hlavacek Gallery** (📞03-753 4199; www.nzicescapes.com; SH6, Whataroa; ☺9am-5pm Mon-Fri) on the highway. Many regard him as one of NZ's finest landscape photographers.

Okarito

POP 30

The magical seaside hamlet of Okarito sits alongside **Okarito Lagoon**, the largest unmodified wetland in NZ and a superb place for spotting birds, including rare kiwi and the majestic kotuku. Okarito has no shops and limited visitor facilities, so stock up and book before you arrive. Travelling by car, 15km south of Whataroa is the turn-off to the Forks, which branches west for 13km to Okarito.

🏃 Activities

From a car park on the Strand you can begin the easy **Wetland Walk** (20 minutes), a longer mission along the **Three Mile Pack Track** (three hours, with the coastal return route tide dependent, so check in with the locals for tide times), and a jolly good puff up to **Okarito Trig** (1½ hours return), which rewards the effort with spectacular Southern Alps and Okarito Lagoon views (weather contingent).

★**Okarito Nature Tours**   KAYAKING
(📞03-753 4014, 0800 652 748; www.okarito.co.nz; kayaking half-/full day $65/75) Hires out kayaks for paddles across the lagoon into luxuriant rainforest channels where all sorts of birds hang out. Guided tours are available (from $100), while overnight rentals ($100) allow experienced paddlers to explore further afield. There's espresso, smoothies, snacks and wi-fi in the office-lounge.

Okarito Boat Tours   WILDLIFE TOUR
(📞03-753 4223; www.okaritoboattours.co.nz) Okarito Boat Tours runs bird-spotting lagoon tours, the most fruitful of which is the 'early bird' ($80, 1½ hrs, 7.30am). The popular two-hour 'ecotour' offers deeper insight into this remarkable natural area ($90, 9am and 11.30am). Cheery, long-time Okaritians Paula and Swade can also fix you up with accommodation in the village.

Okarito Kiwi Tours   WILDLIFE TOUR
(📞03-753 4330; www.okaritokiwitours.co.nz; 3hr tours $75) Runs nightly expeditions to spot the rare bird (95% success rate) with an interesting education along the way. Numbers are limited to eight, so booking is recommended.

🛏 Sleeping

Okarito Campground   CAMPGROUND $
(off Russell St; sites adult/child $12.50/free) Okarito Campground is a breezy patch of community-managed greenery complete with kitchen, barbecue area and hot showers ($1). Gather driftwood from the beach for the firepit, or build your bonfire on the beach while the sun goes down. No reservations necessary.

Okarito Beach House   LODGE $
(📞03-753 4080; www.okaritobeachhouse.com; The Strand; d & tw $85-105; 🐾) The Okarito Beach House has a variety of accommodation. The weathered, self-contained 'Hutel' ($120, sleeping two people) is worth every cent. The Summit Lodge has commanding views and the best dining-room table you've ever seen.

ℹ Getting There & Away

To reach Okarito you'll need your own wheels.

WESTLAND TAI POUTINI NATIONAL PARK

The biggest drawcards of Westland Tai Poutini National Park are the Franz Josef and Fox Glaciers. Nowhere else at this latitude do glaciers come so close to the ocean. The glaciers' existence is largely due to the West Coast's ample rain, with snow falling in the glaciers' broad accumulation zones that fuses into clear ice at 20m depth, and then creeps down the steep valleys.

During the last ice age (15,000 to 20,000 years ago) Westland's twin glaciers reached the sea. In the ensuing thaw they may have crawled back even further than their current positions, but in the 14th century a mini ice age caused them to advance to their greatest modern-era extent around 1750, and the terminal moraines from this time are still visible.

Climate change, however, has seen a consistent retreat over recent years, reducing opportunities for viewing these glaciers on foot. Both glacier terminal faces are roped off to prevent people being caught in icefalls and river surges, and the only way to get close to or on to the ice safely is with a guided tour. Check in with DOC and the locals to get the latest information on the best viewpoints.

Beyond the glaciers, the park's lower reaches harbour deserted Tasman Sea beaches, rising up through rich podocarp forests to NZ's highest peaks. Diverse and often unique habitats huddle next to each other in interdependent ecological sequence. Seals frolic in the surf as deer sneak through the forests. The resident endangered bird species include kakariki, kaka and rowi (the Okarito brown kiwi), as well as kea, the South Island's native parrot. Kea are inquisitive and endearing, but feeding them can kill them.

Heavy tourist traffic often swamps the twin towns of Franz and Fox, 23km apart. Franz is the more action-packed of the two, while Fox has a subdued alpine charm. From November through March visitor numbers can get a little crazy in both towns, so consider visiting in either April or October.

Franz Josef Glacier

POP 444

The early Māori knew Franz Josef as Ka Roimata o Hine Hukatere (Tears of the Avalanche Girl). Legend tells of a girl losing her lover who fell from the local peaks, and her

---

GLACIERS FOR DUMMIES

Hashtag a few of these suckers into your social media posts and make yourself look like a #geologist #geek.

Ablation zone Where the glacier melts.

Accumulation zone Where the ice and snow collects.

Bergschrund A large *crevasse* in the ice near the glacier's starting point.

Blue ice As the accumulation zone (*névé*) snow is compressed by subsequent snowfalls, it becomes *firn* and then blue ice.

Calving The process of ice breaking away from the glacier terminal face.

Crevasse A crack in the glacial ice formed as it crosses obstacles while descending.

Firn Partly compressed snow en route to becoming *blue ice*.

Glacial flour Finely ground rock particles in the milky rivers flowing off glaciers.

Icefall When a glacier descends so steeply that the upper ice breaks into a jumble of ice blocks.

Kettle lake A lake formed by the melt of an area of isolated dead ice.

Moraine Walls of debris formed at the glacier's sides (lateral moraine) or end (terminal moraine).

Névé Snowfield area where *firn* is formed

Seracs Ice pinnacles formed, like *crevasses*, by the glacier rolling over obstacles.

Terminal The final ice face at the bottom of the glacier.

Franz Josef Glacier & Village

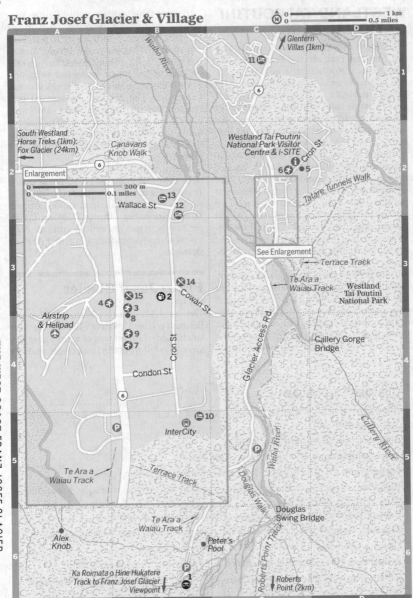

See Enlargement

THE WEST COAST FRANZ JOSEF GLACIER

flood of tears freezing into the glacier. The glacier was first explored by Europeans in 1865, with Austrian Julius Haast naming it after the Austrian emperor. The car park for various glacier valley walks is 5km from Franz Josef Village.

◉ Sights

West Coast Wildlife Centre   WILDLIFE
(www.wildkiwi.co.nz; cnr Cron & Cowan Sts; day pass adult/child/family $35/20/85, incl backstage pass $55/35/145) 🖉 The purpose of this feel-good attraction is breeding two of the

Franz Josef Glacier & Village

world's rarest kiwi – the rowi and the Haast tokoeka. The entry fee is well worthwhile by the time you've viewed the conservation, glacier and heritage displays, and hung out with real, live kiwi in their ferny enclosure. The additional backstage pass into the incubating and rearing area is a rare opportunity to learn how a species can be brought back from the brink of extinction.

Cafe and shop on-site.

Activities

Independent Walks

A series of walks start from the glacier car park, all rewarding way beyond a view of the ice. A nice, short option is **Sentinel Rock** (20 minutes return), while **Ka Roimata o Hine Hukatere Track** (1½ hours return), the main glacier valley walk, leads you to the best permissible view of the terminal face.

Other walks include the **Douglas Walk** (one hour return), off the Glacier Access Rd, which passes moraine piled up by the glacier's advance in 1750, and **Peter's Pool**, a small kettle lake. The **Terrace Track** (30 minutes return) is an easy amble over bushy terraces behind the village, with Waiho River views. Two good rainforest walks, **Tatare Tunnels** and **Callery Gorge Walk** (both around 1½ hours return), start from Cowan St.

Much more challenging walks, such as the five-hour **Roberts Point Track** and eight-hour **Alex Knob Track**, are detailed, along with all the others, in DOC's excellent *Glacier Region Walks* booklet ($2), which provides maps and illuminating background reading.

A rewarding alternative to driving to the glacier car park is the richly rainforested **Te Ara a Waiau Walkway/Cycleway**, starting from near the fire station at the south end of town. It's a one-hour walk (each way) or half that by bicycle (available for hire from

Across Country Quad Bikes (☑ 0800 234 288, 03-752 0123; www.acrosscountryquadbikes. co.nz; Air Safaris Bldg, Main Rd) or the YHA; p450). Leave your bikes at the car park – you can't cycle on the glacier walkways.

Guided Walks & Helihikes

Small group walks with experienced guides (boots, jackets and equipment supplied) are offered by **Franz Josef Glacier Guides** (☑ 0800 484 337, 03-752 0763; www.franzjosefglacier.com; 63 Cron St). Both standard tours require helicopter transfers on to the ice: the 'Ice Explorer' ($339) is bookended by a four-minute flight, with around three hours on the ice; the easier 'Heli Hike' ($435) explores higher reaches of the glacier, requiring a 10-minute flight with around two hours on the ice. Taking around three hours, the 'Glacier Valley Walk' ($75) follows the Waiho River up to the moraine, offering a chance to get beyond the public barriers for close-up views of the ice. All trips are $10 to $30 cheaper for children.

Glacier Valley Eco Tours   GUIDED TOUR (☑ 0800 999 739, 03-752 0699; www.glaciervalley. co.nz) Offers leisurely three- to eight-hour walking tours around local sights ($75 to $170), packed with local knowledge; plus regular shuttle services to the glacier car park ($12.50 return).

Skydiving & Aerial Sightseeing

Forget sandflies and mozzies. The buzzing you're hearing is a swarm of aircraft in the skies around the glaciers and just beyond in the realm of Aoraki/Mt Cook. A common heliflight ($220 to $240) is 20 minutes' long, and goes to the head of Franz Josef Glacier with a snow landing up top. A 'twin glacier' flight – taking in Fox as well as Franz in around 30 minutes – costs in the region of $300, with a 40-minute trip (swooping

THE WEST COAST FRANZ JOSEF GLACIER

around Aoraki/Mt Cook) from $420. Fares for children under 12 years cost between 50% and 70% of the adult price. Shop around: most operators are situated on the main road in Franz Josef Village.

Skydive Franz   SKYDIVING
(☑03-752 0714, 0800 458 677; www.skydivefranz. co.nz; Main Rd) Claiming NZ's highest jump (19,000ft, 80 to 90 seconds freefall; $559), this company also offers 16,000ft for $419, and 13,000ft for $319. With Aoraki/Mt Cook in your sights, this could be the most scenic jump you ever do.

Air Safaris   SCENIC FLIGHTS
(☑0800 723 274, 03-752 0716; www.airsafaris. co.nz; Main Rd) Franz' only fixed-wing flyer offers 30-minute 'twin glacier' ($270) and 50-minute 'grand traverse' ($360) flights.

Fox & Franz Josef Heliservices SCENIC FLIGHTS
(☑03-752 0793, 0800 800 793; www.scenic-flights. co.nz; Main Rd; 20-40min flights $210-420) Operator based in Franz Josef with over 30 years' experience zipping sightseers up and down the glaciers, and around Aoraki/Mt Cook on longer flights. It also has an office in Fox Glacier (p453).

Glacier Country Helicopters   SCENIC FLIGHTS
(☑0800 359 37269, 03-752 0203; www.glacier countryhelicopters.co.nz; 25-45min flights $235-440) Based in Franz Josef, this family-owned and operated company offers five different scenic options, including an affordable 12-minute flight ($165).

Glacier Helicopters   SCENIC FLIGHTS
(☑0800 800 732, 03-752 0755; www.glacier helicopters.co.nz; 20-40min flights $235-450) Scenic flights around the glaciers and Aoraki/ Mt Cook, all with a snow landing. The helihike option ($399) gets you out on the ice for at least a couple of hours.

Helicopter Line   SCENIC FLIGHTS
(☑03-752 0767, 0800 807 767; www.helicop ter.co.nz; Main Rd; 20-40min flights $235-450) Long-standing operator offering multiple scenic flight options, including a majestic 40-minute flight taking in Aoraki/Mt Cook and Tasman Glacier – NZ's longest glacier.

Mountain Helicopters   SCENIC FLIGHTS
(☑0800 369 423, 03 -751 0045; www.mountainheli copters.co.nz; Main Rd; 20-40min flights $220-420) Privately owned company offering flights over Fox and Franz Josef Glaciers, including a short but affordable 10-minute trip ($99 to $119).

Other Activities

⭐**Glacier Hot Pools**   HOT SPRING
(☑03-752 0099; www.glacierhotpools.co.nz; 63 Cron St; adult/child $26/22; ☉1-9pm, last entry 8pm) Cleverly set into a pretty rainforest setting on the edge of town, this stylish and well-maintained outdoor hot-pool complex is perfect après-hike or on a rainy day. Massage and private pools also available.

Glacier Country Kayaks   KAYAKING
(☑0800 423 262, 03-752 0230; www.glacier kayaks.com; 64 Cron St; 3hr kayak $115) Take a guided kayak trip on Lake Mapourika (7km north of Franz), with fascinating commentary, birdlife, mountain views, a serene channel detour and an additional bushwalk on offer. Go in the morning for better conditions. Ask about family trips and the new small-boat cruises.

Eco-Rafting   RAFTING
(☑03-755 4254, 021 523 426; www.ecorafting. co.nz; family trip adult/child $135/110, 7hr trip $450) Rafting adventures throughout the coast, from gentle, family trips, to the seven-hour 'Grand Canyon' trip on the Whataroa River with its towering granite walls, which includes a 15-minute helicopter ride.

South Westland Horse Treks   HORSE RIDING
(☑0800 187 357, 03-752 0223; www.horsetreknz. com; Waiho Flats Rd; 1/2/3hr trek $70/110/165) Located 5km west of town, this trekking company runs equine excursions across farmland and remote beaches, with spectacular views aplenty.

🛏 Sleeping

Franz Josef

Top 10 Holiday Park   HOLIDAY PARK $
(☑0800 467 8975, 03-752 073; www.franzjosef top10.co.nz; 2902 Franz Josef Hwy; sites $42-48, d $65-165; @☎) This spacious holiday park, 1.5km from the township, has more sleeping options than you can shake a stick at. Tenters are well catered for with sunny, free-draining grassy sites away from the road, looking out over farm paddocks.

Franz Josef Glacier YHA   HOSTEL $
(☑03-752 0754; www.yha.co.nz; 2-4 Cron St; dm $26-33, s $85, d $107-135; ☎) This tidy hostel has warm, spacious communal areas, family rooms, free sauna, on-site bike hire, and a booking desk for transport and activities. It has 87 beds, but you'll still need to book ahead.

Rainforest Retreat
HOSTEL, HOLIDAY PARK $$

(☑0800 873 346, 03-752 0220; www.rainforest
retreat.co.nz; 46 Cron St; sites $39-44, dm $30-34,
d $69-220; @⋒) This capacious enterprise
packs plenty of options into its forested
grounds. The pick are the tree huts and
self-contained options nestled in the bush.
Campervans enjoy similar privacy but lose
out on tight, manky facilities, while the back-
packer lodge brims with tour-bus custom.
The on-site Monsoon Bar has a low top shelf,
lively atmosphere and decent meals ($20
to $32).

★ Glenfern Villas
APARTMENT $$$

(☑0800 453 633, 03-752 0054; www.glenfern.
co.nz; SH6; d $217-239; ⋒) A desirable 3km
from the tourist hubbub these delightful one- and two-bedroom villas sit amid
groomed grounds with private decks survey-
ing mountain scenery. Top-notch beds, full
kitchens, bike hire and family-friendly facilities strongly suggest 'holiday', not 'stop-off'.

Te Waonui Forest Retreat
HOTEL $$$

(☑0800 696 963, 03-752 0555; www.tewaonui.
co.nz; 3 Wallace St; s/d from $579/699; @⋒) 🏊
Franz' top-end hotel appears earthy and un-
flashy, with the inside following suit in natu-
ral, textured tones brightened by bold, zippy
carpet. It offers a classy package of porter
service, degustation dinners (included, with
breakfast, in the price) and a snazzy bar,
along with luxurious rooms in which you'll
sleep like a log. All have a deck facing into
the forest.

✗ Eating

Alice May
MODERN NZ $$

(☑03-752 0740; www.alicemay.co.nz; cnr Cowan &
Cron Sts; mains $20-32; ⊗4pm-late) A faux Tu-
dor corner pub with pastoral chic, mellow
vibe and family-friendly attitude, Alice May
serves up meaty meals with $20 options,
including a daily roast, pasta, and venison
burger, with sirloin steak and fish at the upper end. Sticky toffee pudding also features,
as does happy hour and mountain views
from outdoor tables.

Landing Bar & Restaurant
PUB FOOD $$

(☑03-752 0229; www.thelandingbar.co.nz; Main
Rd; mains $20-42; ⊗7.30am-late; ⋒) This busy
but well-run pub offers an inordinately huge
menu of crowd-pleasing food such as burg-
ers, steaks and pizza. The patio – complete
with sunshine and gas heaters – is a good
place to warm up after a day on the ice.

ℹ Information

Franz Josef Health Centre (☑03-752 0700,
0800 7943 2584; 97 Cron St; ⊗9am-4pm Mon-
Fri) South Westland's main medical centre.

Franz Josef i-SITE (www.glaciercountry.co.nz;
63 Cron St) Helpful local centre offering advice
and booking service for activities, accommoda-
tion and transport in the local area and beyond.

**Westland Tai Poutini National Park Visitor
Centre** (☑03-752 0360; www.doc.govt.nz; 69
Cron St; ⊗8.30am-6pm summer, to 5pm win-
ter) Housed in its flash new quarters, the na-
tional park visitor centre has insightful exhibits,
weather information, maps, and all-important
track updates and weather forecasts.

ℹ Getting There & Away

The bus stop is opposite the Fern Grove Four
Square supermarket.

InterCity (☑03-365 1113; www.intercity.co.nz)
has daily buses south to Fox Glacier (35 min-
utes) and Queenstown (eight hours); and north
to Nelson (10 hours). Book at the DOC office or
YHA. **Naked Bus** (www.nakedbus.com) services
the same routes three times a week. Both pro-
vide connections to destinations further afield.

ℹ Getting Around

Glacier Valley Eco Tours (p449) runs sched-
uled shuttle services to the glacier car park
(return trip $12.50).

Fox Glacier
POP 305

Fox Glacier is relatively small and quiet,
with a farmy feel and open aspect. Beautiful
Lake Matheson is a highlight, as are the salty
walks down at Gillespies Beach.

⊙ Sights

Fox Glacier Lookout
LOOKOUT

This is one of the best land-based positions
from which to see Fox Glacier, although its
retreat may mean you see just a snippet.

⚶ Activities

Independent Walks

★ Lake Matheson
TRAMPING

(www.doc.govt.nz) The famous 'mirror lake'
can be found about 6km down Cook Flat
Rd. Wandering slowly (as you should), it will
take 1½ hours to complete the circuit. The
best time to visit is early morning, or when
the sun is low in the late afternoon, although
the presence of the Matheson Cafe (p454)
means that any time is a good time.

Fox Glacier & Village

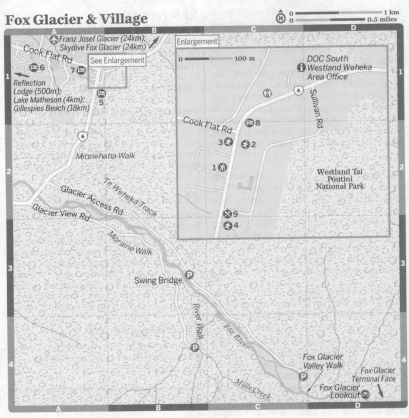

Fox Glacier & Village

🟠 Activities, Courses & Tours

Fox & Franz Josef Heliservices	(see 1)
1 Fox Glacier Guiding	C2
2 Glacier Helicopters	C2
3 Helicopter Line	C2
4 Mountain Helicopters	C3

🟢 Sleeping

5 Fox Glacier Lodge	A1
6 Fox Glacier Top 10 Holiday Park	A1
7 Rainforest Motel	A1
8 Westhaven	C2

🟠 Eating

9 Last Kitchen	C2

At the far end of the circuit – on a clear day – you may, just may, get the money shot, but failing that you can buy a postcard at the excellent gift store by the car park.

Copland Track TRAMPING
(www.doc.govt.nz) About 26km south of Fox Glacier, along SH6, is the trailhead for the Copland Track, a six-to-seven-hour tramp to legendary Welcome Flat, where thermal springs bubble up next to DOC's **Welcome Flat Hut** (www.doc.govt.nz; adult/child $15/7.50). Unsurprisingly, the hut and adjacent camping ground are extremely popular, with wardens in attendance, so book in advance either online or in person at DOC visitor centres.

Gillespies Beach TRAMPING
(www.doc.govt.nz) Follow Cook Flat Rd for its full 21km (unsealed for the final 12km) to the remote black-sand Gillespies Beach, site of an old mining settlement (and basic campsite). Interesting walks from here include a five-minute zip to the old miners' cemetery, and the 3½-hour return walk to **Galway Beach**, a seal haul-out. Don't disturb them.

Along the road to Gillespie's Beach is **Peak View Picnic Area**, which offers a faraway but fine perspective of Fox Glacier. You can also spin the dial to identify which mountain you're looking at.

Glacier Walks & Helihikes

The only way on to the ice is by taking a helihiking trip, run by Fox Glacier Guiding (p453). Independent walks, however, offer a chance to explore the valley – raw and staggeringly beautiful even in its ice-less lower reaches – and get as close to the glacier's terminal face as safety allows.

It's 1.5km from Fox Village to the glacier turn-off, and a further 2km to the car park, which you can reach under your own steam via **Te Weheka Walkway/Cycleway**, a pleasant rainforest trail starting just south of the Bella Vista motel. It's just over an hour each way to walk, or 30 minutes to cycle (leave your bikes at the car park – you can't cycle on the glacier walkways). Hire bikes from Westhaven (p453).

From the car park, the terminal-face viewpoint is around 40 minutes' walk, depending on current conditions. Obey all signs: this place is dangerously dynamic.

Short walks near the glacier include the **Moraine Walk** (over a major 18th-century advance) and **Minnehaha Walk**. The fully accessible **River Walk Lookout Track** (20 minutes return) starts from the Glacier View Rd car park and allows people of all abilities the chance to view the glacier.

Pick up a copy of DOC's excellent *Glacier Region Walks* booklet ($2), which provides maps and illuminating background reading.

Fox Glacier Guiding　　　　GUIDED WALK
(☑ 03-751 0825, 0800 111 600; www.foxguides. co.nz; 44 Main Rd) Guided helihikes (equipment provided) are organised by Fox Glacier Guiding. The standard trip (up to three hours on the ice) is $399/369 per adult/child, but there are other options, including an easygoing two-hour interpretive walk to the glacier (adult/child $59/45). Note that age restrictions vary depending on the trip.

Skydiving & Aerial Sightseeing

A common heliflight ($220 to $240) is 20 minutes' long, and goes to the head of Fox Glacier with a snow landing up top. A 'twin glacier' flight – taking in Franz as well as Fox in around 30 minutes – costs in the region of $300, with a 40-minute trip (swooping around Aoraki/Mt Cook) from $420. Fares for children under 12 years cost between 50% and 70% of the adult price. Shop around: most operators are situated on the main road in Fox Glacier Village.

Skydive Fox Glacier　　　　SKYDIVING
(☑ 0800 751 0080, 03-751 0080; www.skydivefox. co.nz; Fox Glacier Airfield, SH6) Eye-popping scenery abounds on leaps from 16,500ft ($399) or 13,000ft ($299). The airfield is conveniently located three minutes' walk from village centre.

Fox & Franz Josef Heliservices　SCENIC FLIGHTS
(☑ 03-751 0866, 0800 800 793; www.scenic-flights. co.nz; 44 Main Rd; 20-40min flights $210-420) Operator with over 30 years' experience zipping sightseers up and down the glaciers, and around Aoraki/Mt Cook on longer flights. It also has an office in Franz Josef (p450).

Glacier Helicopters　　　　SCENIC FLIGHTS
(☑ 0800 800 732, 03-751 0803; www.glacier helicopters.co.nz; SH6; 20-40min flights $235-450) Scenic flights around the glaciers and Aoraki/Mt Cook, all with a snow landing. The helihike option ($399) gets you out on the ice for at least a couple of hours.

Helicopter Line　　　　SCENIC FLIGHTS
(☑ 0800 807 767, 03-752 0767; www.helicopter. co.nz; SH6; 20-40min flights $235-450) Long-standing operator offering multiple scenic flight options, including a majestic 40-minute flight taking in Aoraki/Mt Cook and Tasman Glacier – NZ's longest glacier.

Mountain Helicopters　　　SCENIC FLIGHTS
(☑ 03-751 0045, 0800 369 423; www.mountain helicopters.co.nz; 43 Main Rd; 20-40min flights $220-420) Privately owned company offering flights over Fox and Franz Josef Glaciers, including a short but affordable 10-minute trip ($99 to $119).

🛏 Sleeping

★ Fox Glacier

Top 10 Holiday Park　　　　HOLIDAY PARK $
(☑ 0800 154 366, 03-751 0821; www.fghp.co.nz; Kerrs Rd; sites $42-45, cabins & units $73-255; @ 🛜) This park has options to suit all budgets, from grassy and hard campervan sites, to lodge rooms and upscale motel units. Excellent amenities include a modern communal kitchen and dining room, playground and spa pool, but it's the mountain views that give it the X-factor.

Westhaven　　　　MOTEL $$
(☑ 0800 369 452, 03-751 0084; www.thewest haven.co.nz; SH6 d $145-185; 🛜) These smart suites are a classy combo of corrugated steel and local stone amid burnt-red and ivory walls. The deluxe king rooms have spa baths, and there are bikes to hire for the energetic (half-/full day $20/40).

Rainforest Motel
MOTEL $$

(📞 0800 724 636, 03-751 0140; www.rainforest motel.co.nz; 15 Cook Flat Rd; d $125-160; 🛜) Rustic log cabins on the outside with neutral decor on the inside. Epic lawns for running around on or simply enjoying the mountain views. A tidy, good-value option.

Reflection Lodge
B&B $$$

(📞 03-751 0707; www.reflectionlodge.co.nz; 141 Cook Flat Rd; d $210; 🛜) The gregarious hosts of this ski-lodge-style B&B go the extra mile to make your stay a memorable one. Blooming gardens complete with alpine views and a Monet-like pond seal the deal.

Fox Glacier Lodge
B&B, MOTEL $$$

(📞 0800 369 800, 03-751 0888; www.foxglacier lodge.com; 41 Sullivan Rd; d $175-225; 🛜) Beautiful timber adorns the exterior and interior of this attractive property, imparting a mountain-chalet vibe. Similarly woody self-contained mezzanine units with spa baths and gas fires are also available.

✖ Eating

★ Matheson Cafe
MODERN NZ $$

(📞 03-751 0878; www.lakematheson.com; Lake Matheson Rd; breakfast & lunch $10-21, dinner $17-33; ⊙ 8am-late Nov-Mar, to 4pm Apr-Oct) Next to Lake Matheson, this cafe does everything right: sharp architecture that maximises inspiring mountain views, strong coffee, craft beers and upmarket fare from a smoked-salmon breakfast bagel, to slow-cooked lamb followed by berry crumble. Part of the complex is the ReflectioNZ Gallery next door, stocking quality, primarily NZ-made art and souvenirs.

Last Kitchen
CAFE $$

(📞 03-751 0058; cnr Sullivan Rd & SH6; lunch $10-20, dinner $24-32; ⊙ 11.30am-late) Making the most of its sunny corner location with outside tables, the Last Kitchen is a good option, serving contemporary fare, such as haloumi salad, pistachio-crusted lamb and genuinely gourmet burgers. It also satisfies for coffee and a wine later in the day.

ℹ Information

Activity operators and accommodation providers are well-oiled at providing information on local services (and usually a booking service, too), but you can also find info online at www.glaciercountry.co.nz. Note that there's no ATM in Fox (which means no cash out south until Wanaka), and that **Fox Glacier Motors** (📞 03-751 0823; SH6) is your last chance for fuel before Haast, 120km away.

DOC South Westland Weheka Area Office

(📞 03-751 0807; SH6; ⊙ 10am-2pm Mon-Fri) This is no longer a general visitor-information centre, but has the usual DOC information, hut tickets, and weather and track updates.

Fox Glacier Health Centre (📞 0800 7943 2584, 03-751 0836; SH6) Clinic opening hours are displayed at the centre, or ring the 0800 number for assistance from the **Franz Josef Health Centre** (p451).

ℹ Getting There & Away

Most buses stop outside the Fox Glacier Guiding building.

InterCity (📞 03-365 1113; www.intercity.co.nz) runs two buses a day north to Franz Josef (40 minutes), the morning bus continuing to Nelson (11 hours). Daily southbound services run to Queenstown (7½ hours).

Naked Bus (www.nakedbus.com) runs three times a week north along the coast all way through to Nelson, and south to Queenstown.

ℹ Getting Around

Fox Glacier Shuttles, staffed by the inimitable Murray, will drive you around the area from Franz Josef to the Copland Valley, and including Lake Matheson, Gillespies Beach and the glaciers. Look for him parked opposite **Fox Glacier Motors** (p454).

HAAST REGION

Between Fox Glacier and Haast it's a 120km (two-hour) drive along a scenic stretch of highway chopped through lowland forest and occasional pasture, with views inland to sheer-sided valleys and intermittent but grand views seaward. This section of highway only opened in 1965, as commemorated in the roadside monument at Knights Point (p455), 5km south of Lake Moeraki. Stop there if humanly possible – it's an utterly cracking viewpoint.

The Haast region bookends the West Coast road. It's a vast and rich wilderness of kahikatea and rata forests, wetlands, sand dunes, seal and penguin colonies, birdlife and sweeping beaches, hence its inclusion in the Southwest New Zealand (Te Wahipounamu) World Heritage Area.

Haast

POP 240

Haast crouches around the mouth of the wide Haast River in three distinct pockets: Haast Junction, Haast Village and Haast Beach. As well as being a handy stop for filling the tank and tummy, it's also the gateway to some spectacular scenery along the road to the end of the line at Jackson Bay. Explore with the help of the free Haast Visitor Map (www. haastnz.com) or DOC's brochure *Walks and Activities in the Haast Area* ($2, or downloadable online), but also seriously consider a trip with Waiatoto River Safaris (p456) – it's up there with NZ's best jetboat adventures.

If you're heading north, check your fuel gauge as Haast petrol station is the last one before Fox Glacier.

Sights & Activities

Knights Point
LOOKOUT

A monument at this spectacular roadside lookout commemorates the opening of this section of coastal highway, in 1965. It's an easy pull-over off the highway, 5km south of Lake Moeraki.

Lake Moeraki
LAKE

Alongside the highway and within the bounds of the World Heritage wilderness, Lake Moeraki is an undeveloped and tranquil spot to contemplate the forested, mountainous surroundings. There's a car park at the southeastern end.

★ Ship Creek
WALKING

(www.doc.govt.nz) Ship Creek, 15km north of Haast, is a terrific place to stretch the legs, boasting two fascinating walks with interesting interpretive panels: the Dune Lake Walk (30 minutes return), which is all sand dunes and stunted forest, leading to a surprising view, and the unsurprisingly swampy Kahikatea Swamp Forest Walk (20 minutes return).

Sleeping & Eating

Haast Beach Holiday Park
HOLIDAY PARK $

(☑ 0800 843 226, 03-750 0860; www.haastpark.com; 1348 Jackson Bay Rd, Haast Beach; sites from $34, dm $25, d $50-110) Well worth the 14km drive south of Haast Junction, this old dear dishes up just enough charm, with its clean and tidy facilities that range from basic cabins to self-contained units, and a pleasant campers' block with a comfortable lounge and views from the deck. The Hapuka Estuary Walk is across the road, and it's 20 minutes' walk to an epic beach.

Haast Lodge
LODGE $

(☑ 03-750 0703, 0800 500 703; www.haastlodge. com; Marks Rd, Haast Village; sites from $16, dm $25, d & tw $55-65, units d $98-130; ☎) Covering all accommodation bases, Haast Lodge offers clean, well-maintained facilities that include a pleasant communal area for lodge

users and campervanners, and tidy motel units at the Aspiring Court next door.

Collyer House
B&B $$

(☑ 03-750 0022; www.collyerhouse.co.nz; Cuttance Rd, Okuru; d $180-250; @☎) This gem of a B&B has thick bathrobes, quality linen, beach views and a sparkling host who cooks a terrific breakfast. This all adds up to make Collyer House a comfortable, upmarket choice. Follow the signs off SH6 for 12km down Jackson Bay Rd.

Wilderness Lodge Lake Moeraki
LODGE $$$

(☑ 03-750 0881; www.wildernesslodge.co.nz; SH6; d inc breakfast & dinner $790-1150; ☎) ✦ At the southern end of Lake Moeraki, 31km north of Haast, you will find one of NZ's best nature lodges. Set in a verdant setting on the edge of the Moeraki River, it offers comfortable rooms and four-course dinners, but the real delights here are the outdoor activities, such as kayak trips and coastal walks, guided by people with conservation in their blood.

Hard Antler
PUB FOOD $$

(☑ 03-750 0034; Marks Rd, Haast Village; dinner mains $20-30; �lmam-late, dinner 5-9pm) This display of deer antlers confirms that you're in manly territory, as does the general ambience of this bold but welcoming and well-run pub. Plain, meaty food on offer with bain-marie action on the side.

ℹ Information

DOC Haast Visitor Centre (☑ 03-750 0809; www.doc.govt.nz; cnr SH6 & Jackson Bay Rd; �9am-6pm Nov-Mar, to 4.30pm Apr-Oct) Located near Haast Junction, the Visitor Centre has wall-to-wall regional information and screens the all-too-brief but free Haast landscape film *Edge of Wilderness*.

Haast Promotions (www.haastnz.com)

ℹ Transport

InterCity (☑ 03 365 1113; www.intercity.co.nz) buses stop on Marks Rd (opposite Wilderness Backpackers) on their daily runs between the West Coast and Queenstown. **Naked Bus** (www.nakedbus.com) also passes through three times a week.

Haast Pass Highway

Early Māori travelled this route between Central Otago and the West Coast in their quest for *pounamu*, naming it Tioripatea, meaning 'Clear Path'. The first party of Europeans to

JACKSON BAY ROAD

From Haast Junction, the road most travelled is SH6, upwards or across. But there is another option, heading south to the end of the line along the quiet and intensely scenic Jackson Bay Rd.

Towered over by the Southern Alps, the farms on the flat and the settlements dotted between them stand testament to some of the hardiest souls who ever attempted settlement in New Zealand. Up until the 1950s, the only way to reach Haast overland was via bush tracks from Hokitika and Wanaka. Supplies came by a coastal shipping service that called every couple of months or so.

Besides the ghosts and former glories, which make an appearance here and there, there's plenty to warrant a foray down to Jackson Bay.

Near Okuru is the **Hapuka Estuary Walk** (www.doc.govt.nz) (20 minutes return), a winding boardwalk that loops through a sleepy wildlife sanctuary with good interpretation panels en route.

Five kilometres further south (19km south of Haast Junction) is where you'll find the base for **Waiatoto River Safaris** (☏03-750 0780, 0800 538 723; www.riversafaris.co.nz; 1975 Haast-Jackson Bay Rd, Hannahs Clearing; adult/child $199/139; ☺trips 10am, 1pm & 4pm), which offers a memorable two-hour jetboat trip up river and down, through distinct landscapes from deep-mountain World Heritage forest to the salt-misted river mouth. Operators Wayne and Ruth, and the Waiatoto's remote wilderness atmosphere make this one of NZ's best boat tours.

The road continues west to **Arawhata Bridge**, where a turn-off leads to the **Lake Ellery Track** (www.doc.govt.nz), 3.5km away. This pleasant amble through mossy beech forest (1½ hours return) leads to **Ellery Lake**, where a picnic bench encourages lunch with perhaps a skinny dip for afters.

It's less than an hour's drive from Haast town to the fishing hamlet of **Jackson Bay**, the only natural harbour on the West Coast. Migrants arrived here in 1875 under a doomed settlement scheme, their farming and timber-milling aspirations mercilessly shattered by never-ending rain and the lack of a wharf, not built until 1938. Those families who stayed turned their hands to largely subsistence living.

With good timing you will arrive when the **Cray Pot** (fish & chips $17-29; ☺12-4pm, hours may vary) is open. This place is just as much about the dining room (a caravan) and location (looking out over the bay) as it is about the honest seafood, including a good feed of fish and chips, crayfish, chowder or whitebait. Ask a local to confirm current opening times.

Walk off your fries on the **Wharekai Te Kou Walk** (www.doc.govt.nz), 40 minutes return, to Ocean Beach, a tiny bay that hosts pounding waves and some interesting rock formations, or the longer, three- to four-hour **Smoothwater Bay Track**, nearby.

make the crossing may well have been led by the German geologist Julius von Haast, in 1863 – hence the name of the pass, river and township – but evidence suggests that Scottish prospector Charles Cameron may have pipped Haast at the post. It was clearly no mean feat, for such is the terrain that the Haast Pass Hwy wasn't opened until 1965.

Heading inland from Haast towards Wanaka (145km, 2½ hours), the highway (SH6) snakes alongside the Haast River, crossing the boundary into Mt Aspiring National Park shortly after you hit fourth gear. The further you go, the narrower the river valley becomes, until the road clambers around sheer-sided valley walls streaked with waterfalls and scarred by rock slips. Princely sums are involved in keeping this

highway clear, and even so it sets plenty of traps for unwary drivers.

Stop to admire the scenery, availing yourself of the many signposted lookouts and short walkways, such as those to **Fantail** and **Thunder Creek** falls. These are detailed in DOC's booklet *Walks along the Haast Highway* ($2), but sufficient detail is provided at the trailheads.

The highway tops out at the 563m pass mark, shortly after which you will reach food and fuel at Makarora. Oh, hello Otago!

❶ Getting There & Away

InterCity (p455) (daily) and **Naked Bus** (p455) (thrice weekly) travel over Haast Pass between the West Coast and Wanaka/ Queenstown.

Christchurch & Canterbury

Best Places to Eat

➡ Pegasus Bay (p487)

➡ Twenty Seven Steps (p473)

➡ Supreme Supreme (p472)

➡ Bodhi Tree (p474)

➡ Oxford (p496)

Best Places to Sleep

➡ Onuku Farm Hostel (p480)

➡ Halfmoon Cottage (p480)

➡ Peel Forest (p493)

➡ Lake Ohau Lodge (p501)

➡ Lake Tekapo Lodge (p500)

Why Go?

Nowhere in New Zealand is changing and developing as fast as post-2016-earthquake Christchurch. Visiting the country's second-largest city as it's being rebuilt and reborn is both interesting and inspiring.

A short drive from Christchurch's dynamic re-emergence, Banks Peninsula conceals hidden bays and beaches – a backdrop for wildlife cruises with a sunset return to the attractions of Akaroa. To the north are the vineyards of the Waipara Valley and the family-holiday ambience of Hanmer Springs. Westwards, the chequerboard farms of the Canterbury Plains morph quickly into the dramatic wilderness of the Southern Alps.

Canterbury's summertime attractions include tramping along alpine valleys and over passes around Arthur's Pass, and mountain biking around the turquoise lakes of Mackenzie Country. During winter, the attention switches to the ski fields. Throughout the seasons, Aoraki/Mt Cook, the country's tallest peak, stands sentinel over this diverse region.

When to Go

➡ Canterbury is one of NZ's driest regions, as moisture-laden westerlies from the Tasman Sea dump their rainfall on the West Coast before hitting the eastern side of the South Island. Visit from January to March for hot and settled summer weather, and plenty of opportunities to get active amid the region's spectacular landscapes.

➡ The shoulder seasons of October to November and March to May can be cool and dry, and blissfully uncrowded.

➡ Hit the winter slopes from July to October at Mt Hutt or on one of Canterbury's smaller club ski fields.

Christchurch & Canterbury Highlights

1 Christchurch
(p457) Experiencing the dynamic rebuilding and re-emergence of the city post-earthquake.

2 Christchurch Botanic Gardens
(p462) Meandering through the city's beautiful green heart.

3 Mt John (p498)
Marvelling at the otherworldly views of Mackenzie Country and the surreal azure blue of Lake Tekapo from the top.

4 Hanmer Springs Thermal Pools
(p484) Taking a soothing soak at this famous hot spring.

5 Banks Peninsula
(p478) Admiring the surf-bitten edges from Summit Rd before descending to the quaint and Francophilic

SOUTH PACIFIC OCEAN

50 km
25 miles

village of Akaroa
(p480).

6 Aoraki/Mt Cook
(p503) Ogling
the cloud-piercing
silhouette of NZ's
highest peak.

**7 Alps 2 Ocean
Trail** (p501) Cycling
the best bits of the trail
from unspoiled Twizel.

ℹ Getting There & Away

AIR

Christchurch's international airport is the South Island's main hub. Air New Zealand flies here from 15 domestic destinations, while Jetstar has flights from Auckland and Wellington. Air New Zealand also flies between Timaru and Wellington.

BUS

Christchurch is the hub for coaches and shuttles heading up the coast as far as Picton, down the coast to Dunedin (and on to Te Anau), over the Alps to Greymouth and inland down to Queenstown.

TRAIN

The TranzAlpine service connects Christchurch and Greymouth, and the Coastal Pacific chugs north to Picton, with ferry connections across Cook Strait to the North Island.

CHRISTCHURCH

POP 342,000

Welcome to a vibrant city in transition, coping creatively with the aftermath of NZ's second-worst natural disaster. Traditionally the most English of NZ cities, Christchurch's heritage heart was all but hollowed out following the 2010 and 2011 earthquakes that left 186 people dead.

Today Christchurch boasts more road cones and repurposed shipping containers

---

ESSENTIAL CHRISTCHURCH & CANTERBURY

Eat Salmon spawned in the shadow of NZ's tallest mountains.

Drink Some of NZ's finest pinot noir and riesling from the Waipara Valley.

Read *Old Bucky & Me*, a poignant account of the 2011 earthquake by Christchurch journalist Jane Bowron.

Listen To the soulful tones and uplifting beats of Christchurch's Ladi6.

Watch Accounts of bravery and resilience at Christchurch's Quake City (p463).

Go green At the ecofriendly Okuti Garden (p480) on Banks Peninsula.

Online www.christchurchnz.com, www.mtcooknz.com, www.midcanterburynz.com, www.visithurunui.co.nz

Area code ☏03

---

than anywhere else in the world, waypoints in an epic rebuild that sees construction sites throughout the CBD. There is dust, noise, and heavy traffic at times. But don't be deterred. The city centre is graced by numerous notable arts institutions, the stunning Botanic Gardens and Hagley Park. Inner-city streets conceal art projects and pocket gardens, dotted among a thinned-out cityscape featuring remnant stone buildings and the sharp, shiny architecture of the new.

Curious travellers will revel in this chaotic, crazy and colourful mix, full of surprises and inspiring in ways you can't even imagine. And despite all the hard work and heartache, the locals will be only too pleased to see you.

History

The first people to live in what is now Christchurch were moa hunters, who arrived around 1250. Immediately prior to colonisation, the Ngāi Tahu tribe had a small seasonal village on the banks of the Avon called Otautahi.

When British settlers arrived in 1880 it was an ordered Church of England project; the passengers on the 'First Four Ships' were dubbed 'the Canterbury Pilgrims' by the British press. Christchurch was meant to be a model of class-structured England in the South Pacific, not just another scruffy colonial outpost. Churches were built rather than pubs, the fertile farming land was deliberately placed in the hands of the gentry, and wool made the elite of Christchurch wealthy.

In 1856 Christchurch officially became NZ's first city, and a very English one at that. Town planning and architecture assumed a close affinity with the 'Mother Country' and English-style gardens were planted, earning it the nickname, the 'Garden City'. To this day, Christchurch in spring is a glorious place to be.

◎ Sights

Starting from the ground up after the earthquakes, the Gap Filler folks fill the city's empty spaces with creativity and colour. Projects range from temporary art installations, performance spaces and gardens, to a minigolf course scattered through empty building sites and the 'Grandstandium' – a mobile grandstand that's a total fun-magnet. Gaps open up and get filled, so check out the Gap Map on the website (www.gapfiller.org.nz), or simply wander the streets and see what you can find.

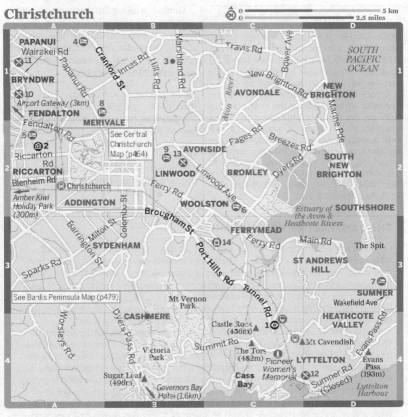

Christchurch

◉ City Centre

★ **Christchurch Botanic Gardens** GARDENS
(Map p464; www.ccc.govt.nz; Rolleston Ave;
⊘7am-8.30pm Oct-Mar, to 6.30pm Apr-Sep) **FREE**
Strolling through these blissful 30 riverside
hectares of arboreal and floral splendour
is a consummate Christchurch experience.
Gorgeous at any time of the year, the gardens are particularly impressive in spring
when the rhododendrons, azaleas and daf-
fodil woodland are in riotous bloom. There
are thematic gardens to explore, lawns to
sprawl on, and a playground adjacent to
the **Botanic Gardens Information Centre**
(Map p464; ☑03-941 8999; ⊘9am-4pm Mon-
Fri, 10.15am-4pm Sat & Sun).

Guided walks ($10) depart at 1.30pm
(mid-September to mid-May) from the Canterbury Museum (p463), or you can chug
around the gardens on the **Caterpillar train**
(☑0800 88 22 23; www.welcomeaboard.co.nz;
adult/child $20/9; ⊘11am-3pm).

★ **Christchurch Art Gallery** GALLERY
(Map p464; ☑03-941 7300; www.christchur-
chartgallery.org.nz; cnr Montreal St & Worcester
Blvd; ⊘10am-5pm Thu-Tue, to 9pm Wed) **FREE**
Damaged in the earthquakes, Christchurch's
fantastic art gallery has reopened brighter
and bolder, presenting a stimulating mix of
primarily NZ exhibitions.

THE CANTERBURY EARTHQUAKES

Christchurch's seismic nightmare began at 4.35am on 4 September 2010. Centred
40km west of the city, a 40-second, 7.1-magnitude earthquake jolted Cantabrians from
their sleep, and caused widespread damage to older buildings in the central city. Close to
the quake's epicentre in rural Darfield, huge gashes erupted amid grassy pastures, and
the South Island's main railway line was bent and buckled. Because the tremor struck in
the early hours of the morning when most people were home in bed, there were no fatalities, and many Christchurch residents felt that the city had dodged a bullet.

Fast forward to 12.51pm on 22 February 2011, when central Christchurch was busy with
shoppers and workers enjoying their lunch break. This time the 6.3-magnitude quake was
much closer, centred just 10km southeast of the city and only 5km deep. The tremor was
significantly greater, and many locals report being flung violently and almost vertically into
the air. The peak ground acceleration exceeded 1.8, almost twice the acceleration of gravity.

When the dust settled after 24 traumatic seconds, NZ's second-largest city had
changed forever. The towering spire of the iconic ChristChurch Cathedral lay in ruins;
walls and verandas had cascaded down on shopping strips; and two multistorey buildings had pancaked. Of the 185 deaths (across 20 nationalities), 115 occurred in the
six-storey Canterbury TV building, where many international students at a language
school were killed. Elsewhere, the historic port town of Lyttelton was badly damaged;
roads and bridges were crumpled; and residential suburbs in the east were inundated as
a process of rapid liquefaction saw tons of oozy silt rise from the ground.

In the months that followed literally hundreds of aftershocks rattled the city's trauma-
tised residents (and claimed one more life), but the resilience and bravery of Cantabrians
quickly became evident. From the region's rural heartland, the 'Farmy Army' descended
on the city, armed with shovels and food hampers. Social media mobilised 10,000 students, and the Student Volunteer Army became a vital force for residential clean-ups in
the city's beleaguered eastern suburbs. Heartfelt aid and support arrived from across NZ,
and seven other nations sent specialised urban-search-and-rescue teams.

The impact of the events of a warm summer's day in early 2011 will take longer than
a generation to resolve. Entire streets and neighbourhoods in the eastern suburbs have
had to be abandoned, and Christchurch's heritage architecture is irrevocably damaged.
Families in some parts of the city have been forced to live in substandard accommodation, waiting for insurance claims to be settled. Around 80% of the buildings within the
city centre's famed four avenues have been or are still due to be demolished. Amid the
doomed, the saved, and the shiny new builds are countless construction sites and empty
plots still strewn with rubble.

Plans for the next 20 years of the city's rebuild include a compact, low-rise city centre,
large green spaces, and parks and cycleways along the Avon River. It's estimated that the
total rebuild and repair bill could reach $40 or even $50 billion.

Hagley Park
PARK

(Map p464; Riccarton Ave) Wrapping itself around the Botanic Gardens, Hagley Park is Christchurch's biggest green space, stretching for 165 hectares. Riccarton Ave splits it in two and the Avon River snakes through the north half. It's a great place to stroll, whether on a foggy autumn morning, or a warm spring day when the cherry trees lining Harper Ave are in flower. Joggers make the most of the tree-lined avenues, year-round.

Canterbury Museum
MUSEUM

(Map p464; ☎03-366 5000; www.canterbury museum.com; Rolleston Ave; ⊙9am-5pm) **FREE** Yes, there's a mummy and dinosaur bones, but the highlights of this museum are more local and more recent. The Māori galleries contain some beautiful *pounamu* (greenstone) pieces, while Christchurch Street is an atmospheric walk through the colonial past. The reproduction of Fred & Myrtle's gloriously kitsch Paua Shell House embraces Kiwiana at its best, and kids will enjoy the interactive displays in the Discovery Centre (admission $2). Hour-long guided tours commence at 3.30pm on Tuesday and Thursday.

Quake City
MUSEUM

(Map p464; www.quakecity.co.nz; 99 Cashel St; adult/child $20/free; ⊙10am-5pm) A must-visit for anyone interested in the Canterbury earthquakes and conveniently located in the Re:START Mall, this compact museum tells stories through photography, video footage and various artefacts, including bits that have fallen off the Cathedral. Most affecting of all is the film featuring locals recounting their own experiences.

Transitional Cathedral
CHURCH

(Map p464; www.cardboardcathedral.org.nz; 234 Hereford St; entry by donation; ⊙9am-5pm to 7pm summer) Universally known as the Cardboard Cathedral due to the 98 cardboard tubes used in its construction, this interesting structure serves as both the city's temporary Anglican cathedral and as a concert venue. Designed by Japanese 'disaster architect' Shigeru Ban, the entire building was up in 11 months.

Gondola
CABLE CAR

(Map p461; www.gondola.co.nz; 10 Bridle Path Rd; return adult/child $28/12; ⊙10am-5pm) Take a ride to the top of Mt Cavendish (500m) on this 945m cable car for wonderful views over the city, Lyttelton, Banks Peninsula and the Canterbury Plains. At the top there's a cafe and the child-focused *Time Tunnel* ride through historical scenes. You can also walk

to Cavendish Bluff Lookout (30 minutes return) or the **Pioneer Women's Memorial** (Map p461) (one hour return).

Arts Centre
HISTORIC BUILDING

(Map p464; www.artscentre.org.nz; 2 Worcester Blvd) Dating from 1877, this enclave of Gothic Revival buildings was originally Canterbury College, the forerunner of Canterbury University. The college's most famous alumnus was the father of nuclear physics Lord Ernest Rutherford, the NZ physicist who first split the atom in 1917 (that's him on the $100 bill).

You'll have to be content to admire the architecture from the street, as the complex was badly damaged in the earthquakes. Some parts are due to reopen during 2016, with the whole project due for completion in 2019.

Cathedral Square
SQUARE

(Map p464) Christchurch's city square stands largely flattened and forlorn amid the surrounding rebuild, with the remains of ChristChurch Cathedral emblematic of the loss. The February 2011 earthquake brought down the 63m-high spire, while subsequent earthquakes in June 2011 and December 2011 destroyed the prized stained-glass rose window. Other heritage buildings around the square were also badly damaged, but one modern landmark left unscathed is the 18m-high metal sculpture *Chalice*, designed by Neil Dawson. It was erected in 2001 to commemorate the new millennium.

The much-loved Gothic ChristChurch Cathedral lies at the centre of a battle between those who seek to preserve what remains of Christchurch's heritage, the fiscal pragmatists, and those ideologically inclined to things new. Despite the nave remaining

Central Christchurch

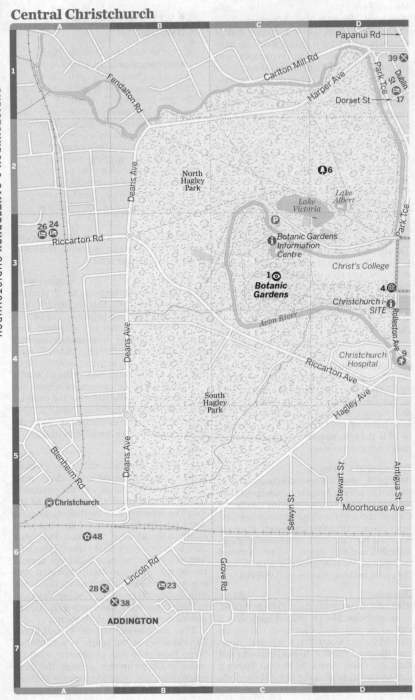

Papanui Rd

Carlton Mill Rd

Harper Ave

Park Tce

Dublin St

39

Dorset St

17

Fendalton Rd

North Hagley Park

6

Lake Albert

Lake Victoria

P

Botanic Gardens Information Centre

Deans Ave

26 24

Riccarton Rd

Christ's College

1

Botanic Gardens

4

Christchurch i-SITE

Avon River

9

Riccarton Ave

Christchurch Hospital

Rolleston Ave

Park Tce

South Hagley Park

Hagley Ave

Deans Ave

Stewart St

Antigua St

Moorhouse Ave

Selwyn St

Christchurch

Blenheim Rd

48

Lincoln Rd

23

Grove Rd

28

38

ADDINGTON

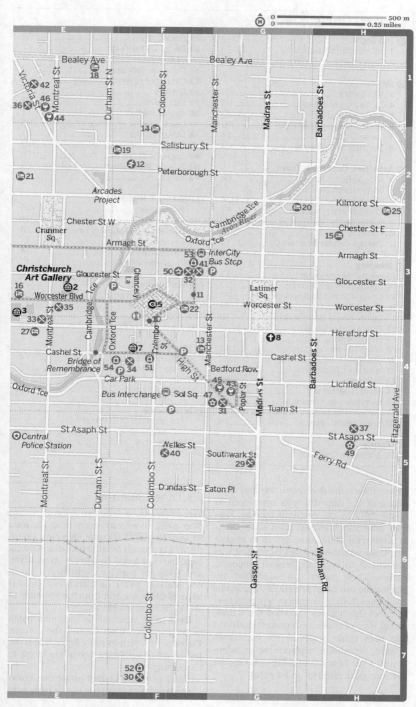

largely intact, the deconstruction and demolition of the cathedral was announced in March 2012 by the Anglican Diocese. Heritage advocates launched court proceedings to prevent the demolition, and an independent, Government-appointed consultant was brought in to negotiate between opposing parties. Their report concluded that 'replacing the cathedral presents no particular challenges from an engineering perspective'. In effect this has just muddied the waters, and at time of writing no concrete decisions had been made regarding the cathedral's rebuild, demolition, replacement or 'adaptation'. A plethora of opposing views means the wrangling could go on for years.

◉ Other Suburbs

Riccarton House & Bush   HISTORIC BUILDING
(Map p461; www.riccartonhouse.co.nz; 16 Kahu Rd, Riccarton) **FREE** Historic Riccarton House (1856) sits proudly amid 12 hectares of pretty parkland and forest beside the Avon River, and hosts the popular Christchurch Farmers' Market (p473) on Saturdays. Guided tours of the house run from 2pm Sunday to Friday (adult/child $18/5).

Even more venerable is the small patch of predator-free bush behind the cottage. Enclosed by a vermin-proof fence, this is the last stand of kahikatea floodplain forest in Canterbury.

Kahikatea is NZ's tallest native tree, growing to heights of 60m; the tallest trees here are a mere 30m and around 300 to 600 years old. A short loop track heads through the heart of the forest.

Orana Wildlife Park ZOO
(☑03-359 7109; www.oranawildlifepark.co.nz; McLeans Island Rd, McLeans Island; adult/child $34.50/9.50; ◷10am-5pm) Orana describes itself as an 'open range zoo' and you'll know what they mean if you opt to jump in the cage for the lion encounter (an additional $45). There's an excellent, walk-through native-bird aviary, a nocturnal kiwi house, and a reptile exhibit featuring tuatara. Most of the 80-hectare grounds are devoted to Africana, including rhino, giraffe, zebras, cheetahs and even gorillas.

Willowbank Wildlife Reserve ZOO
(☑03-359 6226; www.willowbank.co.nz; 60 Hussey Rd, Northwood; adult/child $28/11; ◷9.30am-7pm Oct-Apr, to 5pm May-Sep) ◢ About 10km north of the central city, Willowbank focuses on native NZ critters (including kiwi), heritage farmyard animals and hands-on enclosures with wallabies, deer and lemurs. There's also a recreated Māori village, the setting for the evening Ko Tane (p469).

International Antarctic Centre MUSEUM
(☑0508 736 4846; www.iceberg.co.nz; 38 Orchard Rd, Christchurch Airport; adult/child $39/19; ◷9am-5.30pm) Part of a huge complex built for the administration of the NZ, US and Italian Antarctic programs, this centre gives visitors the opportunity to see penguins and learn about the icy continent. Attractions include the Antarctic Storm chamber, where you can get a taste of -18°C wind chill.

A free shuttle departs from outside the Canterbury Museum (p463) on the hour from 10am to 4pm, and from the Antarctic Centre on the half-hour.

The 'Xtreme Pass' (adult/child $59/29) includes the '4D theatre' (a 3D film with moving seats and a water spray) and rides on a Hägglund all-terrain amphibious Antarctic vehicle. An optional extra is the Penguin Backstage Pass (adult/child $25/15), which allows visitors behind the scenes of the Penguin Encounter.

🏃 Activities
Boating
Antigua Boat Sheds BOATING, KAYAKING
(Map p464; ☑03-366 6768; www.boatsheds.co.nz; 2 Cambridge Tce; ◷9am-5pm) Dating from 1882, the photogenic green-and-white Antigua Boat Sheds hires out rowing boats ($35), kayaks ($12), Canadian canoes ($35) and bikes (adult/child $10/5); all prices are per hour. There's also a good cafe.

Punting on the Avon BOATING
(Map p464; www.punting.co.nz; 2 Cambridge Tce; adult/child $28/20; ◷9am-6pm Oct-Mar, 10am-4pm Apr-Sep) ◢ The Antigua Boat Sheds are the starting point for half-hour punting trips through the Botanic Gardens. Relax in a flat-bottomed boat while a strapping lad in Edwardian clobber with a long pole does all the work. An alternative trip departs from the Worcester St Bridge and punts through the city's regenerating centre.

CHRISTCHURCH IN...

Two Days
After breakfast at **Supreme Supreme** (p472), take some time to walk around the ruined and regenerating city centre, visit **Quake City** (p463) and wander through **Cathedral Square** (p463). Make your way to **Christchurch Art Gallery** (p462) then gather picnic supplies at **Canterbury Cheesemongers** (p473). After lunch, visit the excellent **Canterbury Museum** (p463) and take a walk through the lovely **Botanic Gardens** (p462). That evening, explore the Victoria St restaurant strip or head to **Smash Palace** (p474) for beer and a burger amid the hipster-bogans.

Start day two at the **Addington Coffee Co-op** (p473) and then head up Mt Cavendish on the gondola for views and a walk at the top. Continue on to Lyttelton for lunch before returning through the tunnel and around to Sumner for a late-afternoon swim or stroll, then stop for dinner and catch a flick at the **Hollywood Cinema** (Map p461; www.hollywoodcinema.co.nz; 28 Marriner St; adult/child $17/12).

Four Days
Follow the two-day itinerary, then head to Akaroa to explore its wildlife-rich harbour and walk its pretty streets, enjoying stupendous views on the way there and back again. On day four, visit **Orana Wildlife Park** (p467) and finish the day with shopping, beer and pizza at the **Tannery** (p475) in Woolston.

Swimming & Surfing

Despite having separate names for different sections, it's one solid stretch of sandy beach that spreads north from the estuary of the Avon and Heathcote rivers. Closest to the city centre is **New Brighton**, with a distinctive pier reaching 300m out to sea. On either side, **South New Brighton** and **North Beach** are quieter options. **Waimairi**, a little further north, is our personal pick.

The superstar is **Sumner**, 12km from the city centre on the south side of the estuary. Its beachy vibe, eateries and art-house cinema make it a satisfying place for a day trip.

Further east around the headland, isolated **Taylors Mistake** has the cleanest water of any Christchurch beach and some good surf breaks. Beginners should stick to Sumner or New Brighton.

Walking

The i-SITE provides information on walking tours as well as independent town and country options including the rewarding **Avon River Walk**, which takes in major city sights. At the time of writing a new map was due out detailing the popular **Port Hills** trails; you can also search www.ccc.govt.nz with the keywords 'Port Hills'.

For long-range city views, take the walkway from the **Sign of the Takahe** on Dyers Pass Rd. The various 'Sign of the...' places in this area were originally roadhouses built during the Depression as rest stops. This walk leads up to the **Sign of the Kiwi**, through Victoria Park and then along the view-filled Summit Rd to Scotts Reserve.

You can walk to Lyttelton on the **Bridle Path** (1½ hours), which starts at Heathcote Valley (take bus 28). The **Godley Head Walkway** (two hours return) begins at Taylors Mistake, crossing and recrossing Summit Rd, and offers beautiful views on a clear day.

Walks in Christchurch and throughout Canterbury are well detailed at www.christchurchnz.com.

Cycling

Being mostly flat and boasting more than 300km of cycle trails, Christchurch is a brilliant place to explore on two wheels. For evidence, look no further than the free *Christchurch City Cycle Guide* pamphlet or the city council's website (www.ccc.govt.nz). The i-SITE can advise on bicycle hire and guided tours.

There's some great off-road riding around the Port Hills; look out for the new trails map. Towards Banks Peninsula you'll find the best section of the Little River Trail (p479), one of New Zealand's Great Rides.

Vintage Peddler Bike Hire Co BICYCLE RENTAL (Map p464; ☏03-365 6530; www.thevintagepeddler.co.nz; 7/75 Peterborough St; per hour/day from $15/30) Take to two retro wheels on these funky vintage bicycles. Helmets, locks and local knowledge are all supplied.

City Cycle Hire BICYCLE RENTAL (☏03-377 5952; www.cyclehire-tours.co.nz; bike hire half-/full day from $25/35) Offers door-to-door delivery of on- and off-road city bikes and touring bikes. Will also meet you with a bike at the top of the gondola if you fancy a 16km descent ($70 including gondola ride; 1½ hours).

 Courses

Bone Dude COURSE (Map p461; ☏03-385 4509; www.thebonedude.co.nz; 153 Marshland Rd, Shirley; from $60; ⊗1-4pm Fri, 10am-1pm Sat) Creative types should consider booking a session with the Bone Dude, who'll show you how to carve your own bone pendant (allow three hours). Sessions are limited to eight participants, so book ahead.

CHRISTCHURCH FOR CHILDREN

There's no shortage of kid-friendly sights and activities in Christchurch. If family fun is a priority, consider planning your travels around NZ's biggest children's festival, **KidsFest** (p470). It's held every July and is chock-full of shows, workshops and parties. The annual **World Buskers Festival** (p470) is also bound to be a hit.

For picnics and open-air frolicking, visit the **Botanic Gardens** (p462); there's a playground beside the cafe, and little kids will love riding on the Caterpillar train. Extend your nature-based experience with a wildlife encounter at **Orana Wildlife Park** (p467) or the **Willowbank Wildlife Reserve** (p467), or get them burning off excess energy in a rowing boat or kayak from the **Antigua Boat Sheds** (p467). Fun can be stealthily combined with education at the **International Antarctic Centre** (p467) and the Discovery Centre at **Canterbury Museum** (p463).

If the weather's good, hit the beaches at Sumner or New Brighton.

MĀORI NZ: CHRISTCHURCH & CANTERBURY

Only 14% of NZ's Māori live on the South Island: of those, half live in Canterbury. The first major tribe to become established here were Waitaha who were subsequently conquered and assimilated into the Ngāti Māmoe tribe in the 16th century. In the following century, they in turn were conquered and subsumed by Ngāi Tahu (www.ngaitahu.iwi. nz) a tribe that has its origins in the East Coast of the North Island.

In 1848 most of Canterbury was sold to the crown under an agreement which stipulated that an area of 10 acres per person would be reserved for the tribe; less than half of that actually was. With so little land left to them, Ngāi Tahu were no longer able to be self-sufficient and suffered great financial hardship. It wasn't until 1997 that this injustice was addressed, with the tribe receiving an apology from the crown and a settlement valued at $170 million. Part of the deal was the official inclusion of the Māori name for the most spiritually significant part of the tribe's ancestral land: Aoraki/Mt Cook.

Today, Ngāi Tahu is considered to be one of Māoridom's great success stories, with a reputation for good financial management, sound cultural advice and a portfolio including property, forestry, fisheries and many high-profile tourism operations.

There are many ways to engage in Māori culture in Canterbury. Artefacts can be seen at **Canterbury Museum** (p463), **Akaroa Museum** (p481), **Okains Bay Māori & Colonial Museum** (p478) and **South Canterbury Museum** (p494). **Willowbank Wildlife Reserve** (p467) has a replica Māori village and an evening cultural show. Further south in Timaru, the **Te Ana Māori Rock Art Centre** (p494) has interactive displays and arranges tours to see centuries-old work in situ.

Tours

★ Tram
TRAM

(Map p464; 03-377 4790; www.tram.co.nz; adult/child $20/free; 9am-6pm Oct-Mar, 10am-5pm Apr-Sep) Excellent driver commentary makes this so much more than a tram ride. The beautifully restored old dears trundle around a 17-stop loop, leaving every 15 minutes, taking in a host of city highlights including Cathedral Sq and New Regent St. The full circuit takes just under an hour, and you can hop-on and hop-off all day.

TranzAlpine
TRAIN TOUR

(0800 872 467, 03-341 2588; www.kiwirailscenic.co.nz) The TranzAlpine is one of the world's great train journeys, traversing the Southern Alps between Christchurch and Greymouth, from the Pacific Ocean to the Tasman Sea, passing through Arthur's Pass National Park. En route is a sequence of dramatic landscapes, from the flat, alluvial Canterbury Plains to narrow alpine gorges, an 8.5km tunnel, beech-forested river valleys, and a lake fringed with cabbage trees.

The 4½-hour journey is unforgettable, even in bad weather (if it's raining on one coast, it's probably fine on the other). Departs Christchurch at 8.15am, Greymouth at 1.45pm.

Christchurch Free Tours
WALKING TOUR

(Map p464; www.freetours.co.nz; Cathedral Sq; 11am) FREE Yes, a free tour. Just turn up at the *Chalice* sculpture in Cathedral Sq and look for the red-T-shirted person. If you enjoy your two-hour amble, tip your guide. Nice!

Red Bus Rebuild Tour
BUS TOUR

(0800 500 929; www.redbus.co.nz; adult/child $35/17) Commentaries focus on the past, present and future of earthquake-damaged sites in the city centre. Tours take 90 minutes and include video footage of the old streetscapes.

Hassle Free Tours
BUS TOUR

(03-385 5775; www.hasslefree.co.nz) Explore Christchurch on an open-top double-decker bus (adult/child $35/19). Regional options include a 4WD alpine safari, Kaikoura whale-watching, and visiting the location of Edoras from the *Lord of the Rings* trilogy.

Christchurch Bike & Walking Tours
CYCLING, WALKING

(Map p464; 0800 733 257; www.chchbiketours.co.nz; 2 Cambridge Tce) See the city's highlights on an informative, two-hour bicycle tour (adult/child $50/30) or two-hour walking tour (adult/child $35/20). Tours leave from the Antigua Boat Sheds at 10am and 2pm daily; bookings are essential.

Ko Tane
CULTURAL TOUR

(www.kotane.co.nz; 60 Hussey Rd, Northwood; adult/child $135/68; 5.30pm) Rousing Māori cultural performance by members of the

Ngāi Tahu tribe comprising a *powhiri* (welcome), the famous *haka*, a buffet *hangi* (earth-oven) meal, and plenty of *waiata ā ringa* (singing and dancing). At Willowbank Wildlife Reserve (p467).

Christchurch Sightseeing Tours BUS TOUR
(☏ 03-377 5300; www.christchurchtours.co.nz; tours from $75) City tours, plus further-afield options to Akaroa, Hanmer Springs and the Waipara wine region.

Garden City Helicopters SCENIC FLIGHT
(☏ 03-358 4360; www.helicopters.net.nz; 515 Memorial Ave; 20min $199) Flights above the city and Lyttelton let you observe the impact of the earthquake and the rebuilding efforts.

Discovery Tours BUS TOUR
(☏ 0800 372 879; www.discoverytravel.co.nz; tours from $155) Excursions to Akaroa, Aoraki/Mt Cook, Hanmer Springs, Kaikoura and the Waipara Valley wine region. The Arthur's Pass tour ($315) packs the *TranzAlpine* train, jetboating and a farm tour into one action-packed day.

🎭 Festivals & Events

World Buskers Festival PERFORMING ARTS
(www.worldbuskersfestival.com; ◷ Jan) National and international talent entertains passers-by for 10 days in mid-January. Check the website for locations – and don't forget to throw money in the hat.

Festival of Flowers FLORAL
(www.festivalofflowers.co.nz; ◷ Feb) A three-week blooming spectacle around Christchurch's heritage gardens.

KidsFest CHILDREN
(www.kidsfest.org.nz; ◷ Jul) If family fun is a priority, consider planning your travels around NZ's biggest children's festival, KidsFest. It's chock-full of shows, workshops and parties.

Christchurch Arts Festival PERFORMING ARTS
(www.artsfestival.co.nz; ◷ mid-Aug–mid-Sep) Month-long biennial (2017, 2019 etc) arts extravaganza, celebrating music, theatre and dance.

NZ Cup & Show Week SPORTS
(www.nzcupandshow.co.nz; ◷ Nov) Various horse races, fashion shows, fireworks and the centrepiece A&P Show, where the country comes to town. Held over a week.

Garden City SummerTimes MUSIC
(www.summertimes.co.nz; ◷ Dec-Mar) Say g'day to summer at a huge array of outdoor events.

🛏 Sleeping

City Centre

Chester Street Backpackers HOSTEL $
(Map p464; ☏ 03-377 1897; www.chesterst.co.nz; 148 Chester St E; dm/d $34/74; @ 🕏) This relaxed wooden villa is painted in bright colours and has a sunny front room for reading. Vinnie the house cat is a regular guest at hostel barbecues in the peaceful wee garden.

YHA Christchurch HOSTEL $
(Map p464; ☏ 03-379 9536; www.yha.co.nz; 36 Hereford St; dm/d from $40/100; @ 🕏) Smart, well-run 100-plus-bed hostel conveniently located near the museum and botanical gardens. Dorms and doubles include many with en suite bathrooms. If it's full here, Christchurch's other YHA is one street away (5 Worcester Blvd).

Dorset House Backpackers HOSTEL $
(Map p464; ☏ 03-366 8268; www.dorset.co.nz; 1 Dorset St; dm $38, d $99-119; P @ 🕏) 🍃 Built in 1871, this tranquil wooden villa has a sunny deck, a large regal lounge with a pool table, and beds instead of bunks. It's a short stroll to Hagley Park.

Foley Towers HOSTEL $
(Map p464; ☏ 03-366 9720; www.backpack.co.nz/foley.html; 208 Kilmore St; dm $31-34, d with/without bathroom $80/74; P @ 🕏) Sheltered by well-established trees, Foley Towers provides a wide range of well-maintained rooms and dorms encircling quiet garden-trimmed courtyards. Friendly, helpful staff will provide the latest local info.

Pomeroy's on Kilmore B&B $$
(Map p464; ☏ 03-374 3532; www.pomeroysonkilmore.co.nz; 282 Kilmore St; r $145-195; P 🕏) Even if this cute wooden house wasn't the sister and neighbour of Christchurch's best craft-beer pub, it would still be one of our favourites. Three of the five elegantly furnished, en suite rooms open on to a sunny garden. Rates include breakfast at Little Pom's (p474) cafe.

Focus Motel MOTEL $$
(Map p464; ☏ 03-943 0800; www.focusmotel.com; 344 Durham St N; r $160-250; P 🕏) Sleek and centrally located, this friendly motel offers studio and one-bedroom units with big-screen TVs, iPod docks, kitchenettes and super-modern decor. There's a guest barbecue and laundry, and pillow-top chocolates sweeten the deal.

BreakFree on Cashel HOTEL $$
(Map p464; ☑03-360 1064; www.breakfreeon-cashel.co.nz; 165 Cashel St; d $90-220; P🗗) ✈ This new, large hotel in the heart of the city's rejuvenating CBD has options to suit all budgets. Rooms are compact and sharply designed, with high-tech features such as smart TVs and sci-fi pod bathrooms.

CentrePoint on Colombo MOTEL $$
(Map p464; ☑03-377 0859; www.centrepointon colombo.co.nz; 859 Colombo St; r/apt from $165/195; P🗗) The friendly Kiwi-Japanese management has imbued this centrally located motel with style and comfort. Little extras such as stereos, blackout curtains and spa baths (in the deluxe rooms) take it to the next level.

⭐**George** HOTEL $$$
(Map p464; ☑03-379 4560; www.thegeorge.com; 50 Park Tce; r $356-379, ste $574-761; P@🗗) ✈ The George has 53 handsomely decorated rooms within a defiantly 1970s-looking building on the fringe of Hagley Park. Discreet staff attend to every whim, and ritzy features include huge TVs, luxury toiletries, glossy magazines and two highly rated in-house restaurants – Pescatore and 50 Bistro.

Classic Villa B&B $$$
(Map p464; ☑03-377 7905; www.theclassicvilla.co.nz; 17 Worcester Blvd; s $199, d $299-409, ste $499; P🗗) ✈ Pretty in pink, this 1897 house is one of Christchurch's most elegant accommodation options. Rooms are trimmed with antiques and Turkish rugs, and the Mediterranean-style breakfast is a shared social occasion.

Eliza's Manor HOTEL $$$
(Map p464; ☑03-366 8584, 0800 366 859; www.elizas.co.nz; 82 Bealey Ave; r $245-345; P🗗) ✈ An infestation of teddy bears has done little to dint the heritage appeal of this large 1861 mansion. Wisteria curls around weatherboards, while inside the rooms are spacious and frilly.

Heritage Christchurch HOTEL $$$
(Map p464; ☑03-983 4800; www.heritagehotels.co.nz; 28-30 Cathedral Sq; ste $235-440 🗗) ✈ Standing grandly on Cathedral Sq while all around it is in ruins, the 1909 Old Government Building owes its survival to a thorough strengthening when it was converted to a hotel in the 1990s. After a three-year postearthquake restoration its spacious suites are more elegant than ever. All have full kitchens.

Merivale

Merivale Manor MOTEL $$
(Map p461; ☑03-355 7731; www.merivalemanor.co.nz; 122 Papanui Rd; d $165-229; P🗗) A gracious 19th-century Victorian mansion is the hub of this elegant motel, with units both in the main house and in the more typically motel-style blocks lining the drive. Accommodation ranges from studios to two-bedroom apartments, and there's a bonus complimentary continental breakfast.

Fendalton

Fendalton House B&B $$
(Map p461; ☑03-343 1661; www.fendaltonhouse.co.nz; 28a Kotare St; r $185; P🗗) There's only one guest room available at this friendly, homestay-style B&B amid the pleasant streets of leafy Fendalton. Rates include a cooked breakfast and free wi-fi.

Riccarton

Amber Kiwi Holiday Park HOLIDAY PARK $
(☑03-348 3327, 0800 348 308; www.amberpark.co.nz; 308 Blenheim Rd, Riccarton; sites $42-50, units $82-200; @🗗) Blooming lovely gardens and close proximity to the city centre make this urban holiday park a great option for campervaners and tenters. Tidy cabins and more-spacious motel units are also available.

Lorenzo Motor Inn MOTEL $$
(Map p464; ☑03-348 8074; www.lorenzomotor lodge.co.nz; 36 Riccarton Rd; units $169-239; P🗗) There's a Mediterranean vibe to this trim two-storey motel – the best of many on the busy Riccarton Rd strip. Units range from studio to two-bedroom apartments; some have spa baths and little balconies.

Roma on Riccarton MOTEL $$
(Map p464; ☑03-341 2100; www.romaon riccarton.co.nz; 38 Riccarton Rd; d $158-235; P🗗) It may be the mirror image of neighbouring Lorenzo Motor Inn, but they are completely separate businesses. Like its twin, the units are all thoroughly modern, ranging from studios to two-bedroom apartments.

Addington

⭐**Jailhouse** HOSTEL $
(Map p464; ☑03-982 7777, 0800 524 546; www.jail.co.nz; 338 Lincoln Rd, Addington; dm $35-38, tw/d $90/95; @🗗) From 1874 to 1999 this was Addington Prison; it's now one of

Christchurch's most appealing and friendly hostels. Private rooms are a bit on the small side – they don't call them cells for nothing. Bikes for hire (half-day/full day $10/15).

Sumner

Le Petit Hotel
B&B $$
(Map p461; ☑03-326 6675; www.lepetithotel. co.nz; 16 Marriner St, Sumner; d $159-175; P@ ⊛) Relaxed coffee-and-croissant breakfasts, friendly owners, Francophilic furnishings and close proximity to Sumner beach make this a definite *'oui'* from us. Get in early and request an upstairs room with a view.

Other Suburbs

Haka Lodge
HOSTEL $
(Map p461; ☑03-980 4252; www.hakalodge.com; 518 Linwood Ave, Woolston; dm/d/apt $33/84/170; ⊛) ⬢ Sprawled across three floors of a modern suburban house, Haka Lodge is one of Christchurch's newest hostels. Bunk-free dorms and rooms are clean and colourful. Bonuses include a comfy lounge and bird-filled garden with barbecue.

Old Countryhouse
HOSTEL $
(Map p461; ☑03-381 5504; www.oldcountry housenz.com; 437 Gloucester St, Linwood; dm $42-45, d with/without bathroom $145/120; P@⊛) Spread between three separate villas, 2km east of Cathedral Sq, this chilled-out hostel has handmade wooden furniture, a reading lounge and a lovely garden with native ferns and lavender. A spa pool and sauna heat things up.

Christchurch Top 10
HOLIDAY PARK $
(Map p461; ☑03-352 9176; www.christchurch top10.co.nz; 39 Meadow St, Papanui; sites $35-52, units with/without bathroom from $94/76; P@⊛⬡) ⬢ Family owned and operated for nearly 50 years, this large holiday park has a wide range of accommodation along with various campervan nooks and grassy tent sites. It has a raft of facilities and bike hire, too. Of particular interest is travel advice and bookings provided by enthusiastic staff.

Airport Gateway
MOTEL $$
(☑03-358 7093; www.airportgateway.co.nz; 45 Roydvale Ave, Burnside; d $140-199; P@⊛) Handy for those early flights, this large motel has a variety of rooms with good facilities. Airport transfer is available 24-hours a day, at no extra charge. The newer block is very comfortable and good value.

✖ Eating

While many cafes and restaurants still occupy the suburban premises they were forced into after the earthquakes – particularly around Addington, Riccarton, Merivale and Sumner – many new places are springing up in the midst of the CBD rebuild. Expect plenty of high-quality, exciting surprises.

✖ City Centre

★ Supreme Supreme
CAFE $
(Map p464; ☑03-365 0445; www.supreme supreme.co.nz; 10 Welles St; breakfast $7-18, lunch $10-20; ⊙7am-4pm Mon-Fri, 8am-4pm Sat & Sun; ⬢) With so much to love, where to start? Perhaps with a kimchi Bloody Mary, a chocolate-fish milkshake, or maybe just an exceptional espresso alongside ancient-grain muesli or pulled corn-beef hash. One of NZ's original and best coffee roasters comes to the party with a right-now cafe of splendid style, form and function.

Caffeine Laboratory
CAFE $
(Map p464; www.caffeinelab.co.nz; 1 New Regent St; snacks $4-12, meals $14-26; ⊙8am-late Wed-Sat, to 4pm Tue & Sun; ⬢) The small-scale, corner C-lab is hooked on coffee, but also cooks up addictive deliciousness such as house-smoked salmon, smashed broad beans, and burgers with homemade patties. In the evening, eschew the espresso for craft beer and tapas.

Dimitris
GREEK $
(Map p464; ☑03-377 7110; Re:START Mall, Cashel St; souvlaki $11-16; ⊙11am-4pm; ⬢) Amid a cluster of food trucks in the Re:START Mall, Dimitris rules the roost with souvlaki full of tasty chicken, lamb or falafel, wrapped up with heaps of fresh salad in a light, puffy bread. Sooooo good.

Vic's Cafe
CAFE $
(Map p464; www.vics.co.nz; 132 Victoria St; mains $10-22; ⊙7.30am-4.30pm; ⬢) Pop in for a robust breakfast on the big shared tables or linger over lunch on the front terrace. Otherwise grab baked goodies and still-warm artisanal bread for a DIY riverside picnic.

Black Betty
CAFE $
(Map p464; ☑03-365 8522; www.blackbetty. co.nz; 165 Madras St; mains $9-20; ⊙8am-4pm; ⬢) Infused with aromas from Switch Espresso's roastery, Black Betty's industrial-chic warehouse is a popular destination for students from the nearby college. Attractions include avocado smash on the all-day breakfast menu, excellent counter food, fine wine and craft beer.

C1 Espresso
CAFE $

(Map p464; www.c1espresso.co.nz; 135 High St; mains $10-21; ⊙7am-10pm; 🛜) 🍴 C1 sits pretty in a grand former post office that somehow escaped the cataclysm. Recycled materials fill the interior (Victorian oak panelling, bulbous 1970s light fixtures) and tables spill onto a little square. Eggy brekkies and bagels are available all day, while sliders slip onto the afternoon/evening menu.

Canterbury Cheesemongers
DELI $

(Map p464; 📞03-379 0075; www.cheesemongers. co.nz; rear, 301 Montreal St; ⊙9am-5pm Tue-Fri, to 4pm Sat) Pop in to gather up artisanal cheese, bread and accompaniments such as pickles and smoked salmon, then get your espresso to go and head down the road to the Botanic Gardens for your picnic.

Fiddlesticks
MODERN NZ $$

(Map p464; 📞03-365 0533; www.fiddlesticksbar. co.nz; 48 Worcester Blvd; lunch $25-40, dinner $24-48; ⊙8am-late Mon-Fri, 9am-late Sat & Sun) Sidle into slick Fiddlesticks and seat yourself in either the more formal dining room or the glassed-in patio attached to the curvy cocktail bar. Food ranges from soups and beautifully presented salads to fluffy gnocchi and Angus steaks.

Lotus Heart
VEGETARIAN $$

(Map p464; 📞03-377 2727; www.thelotusheart. co.nz; 363 St Asaph St; mains $13-25; ⊙7.30am-3pm Tue-Sun & 5-9pm Fri & Sat; 🖋) 🍴 Run by students of Sri Chinmoy, this vegetarian eatery serves curry, pizza, wraps, burgers and freshly squeezed organic juices. Organic, vegan and gluten-free options abound, and there's an interesting gift and music shop on-site.

★ Twenty Seven Steps
MODERN NZ $$$

(Map p464; 📞03-366 2727; www.twentyseven steps.co.nz; 16 New Regent St; mains $30-40; ⊙5pm-late Tue-Sat) Upstairs on the Edwardian New Regent St strip, the pared-back interior of this elegant restaurant puts the focus firmly on a menu showcasing local produce. Mainstays include modern renditions of lamb, beef, venison and seafood, but there's also outstanding risotto and desserts such as caramelised lemon tart.

Saggio di Vino
EUROPEAN $$$

(Map p464; 📞03-379 4006; www.saggiodivino. co.nz; 179 Victoria St; mains $40-43; ⊙5pm-late) Elegant Italo-French restaurant that's up there with Christchurch's best. Expect delicious, modern takes on terrine, rack of lamb and *Café de Paris* steak, plus a well-laden cheese trolley to finish you off. The wine list makes long, interesting reading.

King of Snake
ASIAN $$$

(Map p464; 📞03-365 7363; www.kingofsnake. co.nz; 145 Victoria St; mains $27-43; ⊙11am-late Mon-Fri, 4pm-late Sat & Sun) Dark wood, gold tiles and purple skull-patterned wallpaper fill this hip restaurant and cocktail bar with just the right amount of sinister opulence. The exciting menu gainfully plunders the cuisines of Asia – from India to Korea – to delicious, if pricey, effect.

✕ Riccarton

Christchurch Farmers Market
MARKET $

(Map p461; www.christchurchfarmersmarket. co.nz; 16 Kahu Rd, Riccarton; ⊙9am-1pm Sat) Held in the pretty grounds of Riccarton House (p466), this excellent farmers market offers a tasty array of organic fruit and vegies, South Island cheeses and salmon, local craft beer and ethnic treats.

✕ Addington

Addington Coffee Co-op
CAFE $

(Map p464; 📞03-943 1662; www.addingtoncoffee. org.nz; 297 Lincoln Rd; meals $8-21; ⊙7.30am-4pm Mon-Fri, 9am-4pm Sat & Sun; 🛜🖋) You will find one of Christchurch's biggest and best cafes packed to the rafters most days. A compact shop selling fair-trade gifts jostles for attention with delicious cakes, gourmet pies and the legendary house breakfasts (until 2pm). An on-site launderette completes the deal for busy travellers.

Mosaic by Simo
MOROCCAN $

(Map p464; www.mosaicbysimo.co.nz; 300 Lincoln Rd, Addington; tapas & mains $8-20; ⊙9am-9pm Mon-Sat; 🖋) This deli-cafe is popular for its takeaway *bocadillos* (grilled wraps filled with a huge selection of Middle Eastern– and African-inspired fillings, sauces and toppings). Other tasty offerings include super-generous platters, merguez sausages and tagines.

✕ Sumner

Cornershop Bistro
FRENCH $$

(Map p461; 📞03-326 6720; www.cornershop bistro.co.nz; 32 Nayland St, Sumner; lunch $17-35, dinner $29-38; ⊙10am-3pm Fri-Sun, 5.30pm-10pm Wed-Sun) Classic dishes such as *coq au vin* are expertly executed at this superior French-style bistro which never forgets it's in a relaxed beachside suburb. Spend longer than you planned to lingering over brunch.

✕ Other Suburbs

★ Bodhi Tree
BURMESE $$

(Map p461; ☑03-377 6808; www.bodhitree.co.nz; 399 Ilam Rd, Bryndwr; dishes $13-21; ☻6-10pm Tue-Sat; ☑) Bodhi Tree has been wowing locals with the nuanced flavours of Burmese cuisine for more than a decade. Its feel-good food comes in sharing-sized dishes and sings with zing. Standouts include *le pet thoke* (pickled tea-leaf salad) and *ameyda nut* (slow-cooked beef curry).

Kinji
JAPANESE $$

(Map p461; ☑03-359 4697; www.kinjirestaurant.com; 279b Greers Rd, Bishopdale; mains $16-24; ☻5.30-10pm Mon-Sat) Despite being hidden away in suburbia this acclaimed Japanese restaurant has a loyal following, so it's wise to book. Tuck into the likes of sashimi, grilled ginger squid and venison tataki, but save room for the green tea tiramisu, a surprising highlight.

Under the Red Verandah
CAFE $$

(Map p461; www.utrv.co.nz; 29 Tancred St, Linwood; mains $14-25; ☻7.30am-4pm Mon-Fri, 8.30am-4pm Sat & Sun; ☑) This lucky suburban backstreet boasts a cafe beloved by locals and travellers alike. Take a seat under said veranda and tuck into baked goodies, oaty pancakes, homemade pies and eggs multiple ways.

Burgers & Beers Inc
BURGERS $$

(Map p464; www.burgersandbeersinc.co.nz; 355 Colombo St, Sydenham; burgers $14-18; ☻11am-late) Quirkily named gourmet burgers – try the Woolly Sahara Sand Hopper (Moroccan-spiced lamb with lemon yogurt) or the Shagged Stag (venison with tamarillo and plum chutney) – and an ever-changing selection of Kiwi craft beers give you reason to head south.

🍸 Drinking & Nightlife

🍷 City Centre

★ Smash Palace
BAR

(Map p464; ☑03-366 5369; www.thesmashpalace.co.nz; 172 High St; ☻4pm-late Mon-Fri, 12pm-late Sat & Sun) Epitomising the spirit of transience, tenacity and number-eight wire that Christchurch is now known for, this deliberately downcycled and ramshackle beer garden is an intoxicating mix of grease-monkey garage, trailer-trash park, and proto-hipster hang-out complete with a psychedelic school bus, edible garden and blooming roses. There's craft beer, chips and cereal, and burgers made from scratch ($11 to $15).

★ Pomeroy's Old Brewery Inn
PUB

(Map p464; ☑03-365 1523; www.pomspub.co.nz; 292 Kilmore St; ☻3-11pm Tue-Thu, noon-11pm Fri-Sun) For fans of great beer, there's no better place than Pomeroy's for supping a drop or two alongside a plate of proper pork crackling. Among this British-style pub's many other endearing features are regular live music, a snug, sunny courtyard and Victoria's Kitchen, serving comforting pub food (mains $24 to $30). The newest addition, pretty Little Pom's cafe, serves super-fine fare (meals $14 to $22) until mid-afternoon.

Dux Central
BAR

(Map p464; ☑03-943 7830; www.duxcentral.co.nz; 6 Poplar St; ☻11am-late) Pumping a whole lot of heart back into the flattened High St precinct, the epic new Dux comprises a brew bar serving its own and other crafty drops, the Emerald Room wine bar, Upper Dux restaurant and the Poplar Social Club cocktail bar, all within the confines of a lovingly restored old building.

Boo Radley's
BAR

(Map p464; ☑03-366 9906; www.booradleys.co.nz; 98 Victoria St; ☻4pm-late) Above Tequila Mockingbird, this companion bar is decked out in fine fashion: Southern style with bourbons galore and dude food such as sliders, fried chicken and mac-and-cheese croquettes (snacks $8 to $20). An intimate, speakeasy vibe makes Boo's an alluring late-night hang-out.

Tequila Mockingbird
BAR

(Map p464; www.tequilamockingbird.co.nz; 98 Victoria St; shared plates $8-30; ☻5pm-late Mon-Fri, 9.30am-late Sat & Sun) If the awesome name's not enough to lure you through the door of this upmarket Latin bar-restaurant, then perhaps the Caribbean-inflected cocktails, nifty decor and late-night DJs will. The food's excellent, too.

Revival
BAR

(Map p464; ☑03-379 9559; www.revivalbar.co.nz; 92-96 Victoria St; ☻3pm-late Mon-Thu, 12pm-late Fri-Sun) Revival is the hippest of Christchurch's shipping container bars. Expect regular DJs and a funky lounge area dotted with a quirky collection of automotive rear ends and vintage steamer trunks.

🍷 Other Suburbs

The Brewery
CRAFT BEER

(Map p461; www.casselsbrewery.co.nz; 3 Garlands Rd, Woolston; ☻7am-late) An essential destination for beer-loving travellers, the

Cassels & Sons' brewery crafts beers using a wood-fired brew kettle, resulting in big, bold ales. Tasting trays are available for the curious and the indecisive, live bands perform regularly, and the food – including wood-fired pizzas ($20 to $24) – is top-notch, too.

☆ Entertainment

For live music and club listings, see www.undertheradar.co.nz, www.muk.na.co.nz and www.christchurchmusic.org.nz. Also look out for the *Groove Guide* magazine in cafes.

Isaac Theatre Royal THEATRE
(Map p464; ☑03-366 6326; www.isaactheatreroyal.co.nz; 145 Gloucester St) This century-old dear survived the quakes and emerged restored to full glory in 2014. Its heritage features are a decided bonus for those venturing in for shows ranging from opera and ballet to concerts of virtually every persuasion.

Alice Cinematheque CINEMA
(Map p464; ☑03-365 0615; www.aliceinvideoland.co.nz; 209 Tuam St; adult/child $17/12) This small Egyptian-themed art-house cinema can be found within the long-standing and excellent Alice In Videoland speciality video and DVD shop.

darkroom LIVE MUSIC
(Map p464; www.darkroom.bar; 336 St Asaph St; ⊙7pm-late Wed-Sun) A hip combination of live-music venue and bar, darkroom has lots of Kiwi beers and great cocktails. Live gigs are frequent – and frequently free.

Court Theatre THEATRE
(Map p464; ☑03-963 0870; www.courttheatre.org.nz; Bernard St, Addington) Christchurch's original Court Theatre was an integral part of the city's Arts Centre, but it was forced to relocate to this warehouse after the earthquakes. The new premises are much more spacious; it's a great venue to see popular international plays and works by NZ playwrights.

🛍 Shopping

★Tannery SHOPPING CENTRE
(Map p461; www.thetannery.co.nz; 3 Garlands Rd, Woolston; ⊙10am-5pm Mon-Wed, Fri & Sat, to 8pm Thu) In a city mourning the loss of its heritage, this postearthquake conversion of a 19th-century tannery couldn't be more welcome. The Victorian buildings have been jooshed up in period style, and filled with boutique shops selling everything from books to fashion to surfboards. Don't miss the woolly hats. Nonshoppers can slink off

to The Brewery (p474) or catch a movie in the brand-new cinemas.

Re:START Mall MALL
(Map p464; www.restart.org.nz; Cashel St; ⊙10am-5pm; 🛜) This labyrinth of shipping containers was the first retail 'mall' to reopen in the CBD postquakes. With cafes, food trucks, shops and people-watching opportunities, it remains a pleasant place to hang out, particularly on a sunny day. At the time of writing, there were no plans for the Re:START to disappear any time soon.

New Regent St MALL
(Map p464; www.newregentstreet.co.nz) A forerunner to the modern mall, this pretty little stretch of pastel Spanish Mission–style shops was described as NZ's most beautiful street when it was completed in 1932. Fully restored postearthquake, it's once again a delightful place to stroll and peruse the tiny galleries, gift shops and cafes.

Ballantynes DEPARTMENT STORE
(Map p464; www.ballantynes.com; cnr Colombo & Cashel Sts; ⊙9am-5pm) A venerable Christchurch department store selling men's and women's fashions, cosmetics, travel goods and speciality NZ gifts. Fashionistas should check out the Contemporary Lounge upstairs.

Colombo Mall MALL
(Map p464; www.thecolombo.co.nz; 363 Colombo St; ⊙9am-5.30pm Mon-Sat, 10am-5pm Sun) Within walking distance of the CBD, this neat little mall sports interesting, independent shops with an emphasis on gorgeous and groovy, plus respectable food outlets proffering dumplings, French fancies and picnic supplies.

ⓘ Information

EMERGENCY & IMPORTANT NUMBERS
Ambulance, fire service & police (111)
CERA (www.cera.govt.nz) The Canterbury Earthquake Recovery Authority has the lowdown on rebuild plans and status updates.
Christchurch City Council (www.ccc.govt.nz) The city council's official website.

MEDICAL SERVICES
24-Hour Surgery (☑03-365 7777; www.24hoursurgery.co.nz; cnr Bealey Ave & Colombo St) No appointment necessary.
Christchurch Hospital (☑03-364 0640, emergency dept 03-364 0270; www.cdhb.govt.nz; 2 Riccarton Ave) Has a 24-hour emergency department.
Urgent Pharmacy (☑03-366 4439; cnr Bealey Ave & Colombo St; ⊙6-11pm Mon-Fri, 9am-11pm Sat & Sun) Located beside the 24 Hour Surgery.

TOURIST INFORMATION

Christchurch Airport i-SITE (☑03-353 7774; www.christchurchnz.com; ☺8am-6pm)

Christchurch DOC Visitor Centre (Map p464; ☑03-379 4082; www.doc.govt.nz; Cashel St, Re:START Mall; ☺10am-5pm) Offers country-wide information and Great Walk bookings. A change in premises was on the cards at the time of writing; ring or check the website for updates.

Christchurch i-SITE (Map p464; ☑03-379 9629; www.christchurchnz.com; Botanic Gardens, Rolleston Ave; ☺8.30am-5pm, extended hours summer) This ever-helpful and eternally busy i-SITE also now has an outpost in the Re:START Mall, open daily from November to March.

Visitor Kiosk (Map p464; ☑03-379 9629; www.christchurchnz.com; Cashel Mall, Re:START Mall; ☺8.30am-5pm Nov-Apr) Outpost of the ever-helpful and eternally busy **i-SITE** (p476) located in the Botanic Gardens.

Getting There & Away

AIR

Christchurch Airport (CHC; ☑03-358 5029; www.christchurchairport.co.nz; 30 Durey Rd) is the South Island's main international gateway, with excellent facilities including baggage storage, hire-car counters, ATMs, foreign-exchange offices and an i-SITE visitor information centre.

Air New Zealand (☑0800 737 000; www.airnewzealand.co.nz) Flies to/from Auckland, Wellington, Dunedin and Queenstown. Code-share flights with smaller regional airlines head to/from Blenheim, Hamilton, Hokitika, Invercargill, Napier, Nelson, New Plymouth, Palmerston North, Paraparaumu, Rotorua and Tauranga.

Jetstar (☑0800 800 995; www.jetstar.com) Flies to/from Auckland and Wellington.

BUS

The following services stop outside the Canterbury Museum on Rolleston Ave, unless otherwise stated. Enquire at the i-SITE about seasonal ski shuttles.

Akaroa French Connection (☑0800 800 575; www.akaroabus.co.nz; one way/return $25/45) Daily service to Akaroa.

Akaroa Shuttle (☑0800 500 929; www.akaroashuttle.co.nz; one way/return $35/50) Heads to Akaroa daily, increasing to twice daily from November to April.

Atomic Shuttles (☑03-349 0697; www.atomictravel.co.nz) Destinations include Picton ($35, 5¼ hours), Greymouth ($45, 3¾ hours), Timaru ($25, 2½ hours), Dunedin ($30 to $35, 5¾ hours) and Queenstown ($50, 7 hours).

Budget Buses & Shuttles (☑03-615 5119; www.budgetshuttles.co.nz; ☺Mon-Sat) Offers a door-to-door shuttle to Geraldine ($57) and

Timaru ($50), along with cheaper scheduled runs (from $27).

Hanmer Connection (☑0800 242 663; www.hanmerconnection.co.nz; one way/return $30/50) Daily bus to/from Hanmer Springs via Amberley and Waipara.

InterCity (☑03-365 1113; www.intercity.co.nz) New Zealand's widest and most reliable coach network. The **main bus stop** (Map p464; www.intercity.co.nz) is on Armagh St, between New Regent and Manchester Sts. Coaches head to Picton (from $26, 5¼ hours), Timaru (from $28, 2½ hours), Dunedin (from $40, six hours) and Queenstown (from $55, eight to 11 hours) twice daily; and to Te Anau (from $61, 10¾ hours) daily.

Naked Bus (www.nakedbus.com) Destinations include Picton (4½ to 5¾ hours), Kaikoura (1½ hours), Dunedin (six hours), Wanaka (7½ hours) and Queenstown (eight hours).

West Coast Shuttle (☑03-768 0028; www.westcoastshuttle.co.nz) Bus stop is at the **Bus Interchange** (Map p464) on Lichfield St, heading to/from Springfield ($32, 1¼ hours), Arthur's Pass ($42, 2¾ hours) and Greymouth ($55, four hours).

TRAIN

Christchurch Railway Station (www.kiwirailscenic.co.nz; Troup Dr, Addington; ☺ticket office 6.30am-3pm) is the terminus for two highly scenic train journeys, the hero of which is the **TranzAlpine** (p469). The other, the *Coastal Pacific*, runs daily from September to April, departing from Christchurch at 7am and arriving at Picton at 12.20pm ($79 to $179). Other stops include Waipara ($59, 56 minutes), Kaikoura ($49 to $69, three hours) and Blenheim ($79 to $159, 4¾ hours). It then departs Picton at 1.15pm, returning to Christchurch at 6.23pm.

Getting Around

TO/FROM THE AIRPORT

Christchurch Airport is only 10km from the city centre but a **taxi** between the two can cost a hefty $45 to $65. Alternatively, the airport is well served by **public buses** (www.metroinfo.co.nz). The purple line bus heads through Riccarton (25 minutes) to the central bus station (35 minutes) and on to Sumner (80 minutes). Bus 29 heads through Fendalton (10 minutes) to the bus station (30 minutes). Both services cost $8 and run every half-hour from roughly 7am to 11pm.

Shuttle services include the following:

Steve's Shuttle (☑0800 101 021; www.steveshuttle.co.nz; city centre fares $23, each additional passenger $5; ☺3.30am-6pm)

Super Shuttle (☑0800 748 885; www.supershuttle.co.nz; city centre fares $24, each additional passenger $5; ☺24hr)

CAR & MOTORCYCLE

Most major car- and campervan-rental companies have offices in Christchurch, as do numerous smaller local companies. Operators with national networks often want cars from Christchurch to be returned to Auckland because most renters travel in the opposite direction, so you may find a cheaper price on a northbound route.

Local options include the following:

Ace Rental Cars (✆ 03-360 3270; www.ace rentalcars.co.nz; 20 Abros Pl, Burnside)

First Choice (www.firstchoice.co.nz)

New Zealand Motorcycle Rentals & Tours (✆ 09-486 2472; www.nzbike.com)

Omega Rental Cars (✆ 03-377 4558; www. omegarentalcars.com; 252 Lichfield St)

Pegasus Rental Cars (✆ 03-358 5890; www. rentalcars.co.nz; 34b Sheffield Cres, Burnside)

PUBLIC TRANSPORT

Christchurch's **Metro** (✆ 03-366 8855; www. metroinfo.co.nz) bus network is inexpensive and efficient. Most buses run from the **Bus Interchange** (p476). Get timetables from the i-SITE or the station's information kiosk. Tickets (adult/child $3.50/1.80) can be purchased on board and include one free transfer within two hours. Metrocards allow unlimited two-hour/full-day travel for $2.50/5; cards cost $10 and must be loaded up with a minimum of $10 additional credit.

TAXI

Blue Star (✆ 03-379 9799; www.bluestartaxis. org.nz)

First Direct (✆ 03-377 5555; www.firstdirect. net.nz)

Gold Band (✆ 03-379 5795; www.goldband taxis.co.nz)

AROUND CHRISTCHURCH

Lyttelton

POP 2859

Southeast of Christchurch are the prominent Port Hills, which slope down to the city's port on Lyttelton Harbour. Christchurch's first European settlers landed here in 1850 to embark on their historic trek over the hills. Nowadays a 2km road tunnel makes the journey considerably quicker.

Lyttelton was badly damaged during the 2010 and 2011 earthquakes, and many of the town's heritage buildings along London St were subsequently demolished. However, Lyttelton has re-emerged as one of Christchurch's most interesting communi-

ties. The town's arty, independent and bohemian vibe is stronger than ever, and it's once again a hub for good bars, cafes and restaurants. It's well worth catching the bus from Christchurch and getting immersed in the local scene, especially on a Saturday morning when the market's buzzing.

 Eating

Lyttelton Farmers' Market MARKET $
(Map p461; www.lyttelton.net.nz; London St; ⊙1am-1pm Sat) Every Saturday morning, food stalls take the place of cars on Lyttelton's main street. As well as being a great place to stock up on local produce, there's always plenty of excellent baked goods and hot food to snack on at the market.

Lyttelton Coffee Company CAFE $$
(Map p461; ✆ 03-328 8096; www.lytteltoncoffee. co.nz; 29 London St; meals $11-23; ⊙7am-4pm Mon-Fri, 8am-4pm Sat & Sun; 🖋🚻) Local institution Lyttelton Coffee Company has risen from the rubble and continued its role as a supergroovy, family-friendly cafe serving wholesome food, including great salads and soothing smoothies. Cool artwork, occasional music and harbour views from the back deck further its appeal.

Freemans ITALIAN $$
(Map p461; ✆ 03-328 7517; www.freemansdining room.co.nz; 47 London St; breakfast $16-18, lunch $20-27, dinner $22-38; ⊙3pm-late Wed & Thu, 11.30am-late Fri, 10am-late Sat & Sun; 🖋) Freemans consistently pleases with fresh pasta, top-notch pizzas and craft beers from Christchurch's Three Boys. Grab a spot on the deck for great harbour views and Sunday afternoon jazz from 3pm.

★ Roots MODERN NZ $$$
(Map p461; ✆ 03-328 7658; www.rootsrestaurant. co.nz; 8 London St; 5-/8-/12-course degustation excl wine $90/125/185; ⊙11.30am-2pm Fri & Sat, 5.30pm-late Tue-Sat) 🖋 Let chef/owner Giulio Sturla take you on a magical mystery tour via degustation menus championing all things local and seasonal. Individual dishes are revealed and described as they arrive at the table, and can be accompanied by carefully curated wine matches, should you choose to splurge.

🍷 **Drinking & Nightlife**

Wunderbar BAR
(Map p461; ✆ 03-328 8818; www.wunderbar. co.nz; 19 London St; ⊙5pm-late Mon-Fri, 1pm-late Sat & Sun) Wunderbar is a top spot to get

down, with regular live music covering all spectra, and clientele to match. The kooky decor and decapitated dolls' heads alone are worth the trip to Lyttelton. Enter via the rear car park.

Civil and Naval BAR

(Map p461; ☑03-328 7206; www.civilandnaval. co.nz; 16 London St; ☺10am-11pm Mon-Thu & Sun, to 1am Fri & Sat) Steadfast staff at this compact, bijou bar serve up a quality selection of cocktails, fine wines and craft beers, while the kitchen keeps patrons civil with an eclectic range of tapas ($6 to $18).

Governors Bay Hotel PUB

(☑03-329 9433; www.governorsbayhotel.co.nz; 52 Main Rd, Governors Bay; ☺11am-late; ☝) Take a scenic 9km drive from Lyttelton to one of NZ's oldest still-operating pubs (1870). You couldn't want for a more inviting deck and garden in which to quaff an afternoon tipple. The food is good, too, covering all of the classic pub-grub bases (mains $23 to $35).

Upstairs is accommodation in chicly renovated rooms with shared bathrooms (double rooms $119 to $169).

❶ Information

Lyttelton Visitor Information Centre (Map p461; ☑03-328 9093; www.lytteltonharbour. info; 20 Oxford St; ☺10am-4pm)

❶ Getting There & Away

Buses 28 and 535 run from Christchurch to Lyttelton (adult/child $3.50/1.80, 25 minutes). At the time of writing, Summit Rd between Christchurch and Lyttelton (via Sumner) was still closed.

From Lyttelton, **Black Cat** (Map p461; ☑03-328 9078; www.blackcat.co.nz; 5 Norwich Quay) provides ferries to sheltered Quail Island (adult/child return $30/15, October to April only), as well as to sleepy Diamond Harbour (adult/child one way $6.20/3.10).

Banks Peninsula

POP 3050

Gorgeous Banks Peninsula (Horomaka) was formed by two giant volcanic eruptions about eight million years ago. Harbours and bays radiate out from the peninsula's centre, giving it an unusual cogwheel shape. The historic town of Akaroa, 80km from Christchurch, is a highlight, as is the absurdly beautiful drive along Summit Rd around the edge of one of the original craters. It's also worth exploring the little bays that dot the peninsula's perimeter.

The waters around Banks Peninsula are home to the smallest and one of the rarest dolphin species, the Hector's dolphin, found only in NZ waters. A range of tours depart from Akaroa to spot these and other critters, including white-flippered penguins, orcas and seals.

History

James Cook sighted the peninsula in 1770. Thinking it was an island, he named it after the naturalist Sir Joseph Banks.

In 1831 Onawe *pa* (fortified village) was attacked by the Ngāti Toa chief Te Rauparaha and in the massacres that followed, the local Ngāi Tahu population was dramatically reduced. Seven years later, whaling captain Jean Langlois negotiated the purchase of Banks Peninsula from the survivors and returned to France to form a trading company. With French government backing, 63 settlers headed for the peninsula in 1840, but only days before they arrived, panicked British officials sent their own warship to raise the flag at Akaroa, claiming British sovereignty under the Treaty of Waitangi. Had the settlers arrived two years earlier, the entire South Island could have become a French colony, and NZ's future might have been quite different.

The French did settle at Akaroa, but in 1849 their land claim was sold to the New Zealand Company, and in 1850 a large group of British settlers arrived. The heavily forested land was cleared and soon farming became the peninsula's main industry.

◉ Sights

Hinewai Reserve FOREST

(Long Bay Rd) ✚ FREE Get a glimpse of what the peninsula once looked like in this privately owned 1050-hectare nature reserve which has been replanted with native forest. Pick up a map outlining the walking tracks at the visitor centre.

Okains Bay
Māori & Colonial Museum MUSEUM

(www.okainsbaymuseum.co.nz; 1146 Okains Bay Rd; adult/child $10/2; ☺10am-5pm) Northeast of Akaroa, this museum has a respectable array of European pioneer artefacts, but it is the nationally significant Māori collection, featuring a replica *wharenui* (meeting house), *waka* (canoes), stone tools and personal adornments, that makes this a must-see. Note the cute shop down the road.

Banks Peninsula

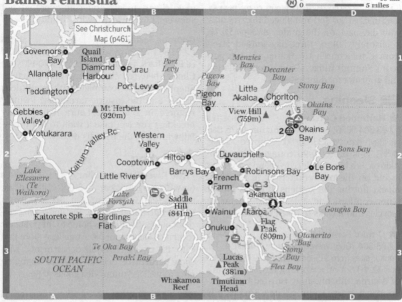

🏃 Activities

Tramping

Banks Peninsula Track TRAMPING
(☏06-304 7612; www.bankstrack.co.nz; 2-/4-days from $185/295; ⏰Oct-Apr) This privately owned and maintained 35km four-day walk traverses farmland and forest along the dramatic coast east of Akaroa. Fees include transport from Akaroa and hut accommodation. The two-day option covers the same ground at twice the pace.

Cycling

One of the new Great Rides of the NZ Cycle Trail, this easy-graded, 49-km cycle trail (www.littleriverrailtrail.co.nz) runs from Hornby, on the outskirts of Christchurch, to Little River at the base of the Banks Peninsula. Along the way it rolls across rural plains, past weathered peaks, and along the shores of Lake Ellesmere, home to NZ's most diverse bird population, and its smaller twin Lake Forsyth. The best section of track can be enjoyed as a return-ride from Little River where there is a cafe and bike hire.

👉 Tours

Pohatu Plunge WILDLIFE TOUR
(☏03-304 8542; www.pohatu.co.nz) Runs evening tours from Akaroa to the Pohatu

Banks Peninsula

○ **Sights**
1 Hinewai Reserve C3
2 Okains Bay Māori & Colonial
  Museum C2

🛏 **Sleeping**
3 Coombe Farm C2
4 Double Dutch C2
5 Okains Bay Camping Ground C2
6 Okuti Garden B2
7 Onuku Farm Hostel C3

white-flippered penguin colony (adult/child $75/55), with a self-drive option available (adult /child $25/12). Viewing is best during breeding season, August to January, but is possible throughout the year. Sea kayaking and 4WD nature tours are also available, as is the option of staying overnight in a secluded cottage.

Akaroa Farm Tours TOUR
(☏03-304 8511; www.akaroafarmtours.com; adult/child $80/50) Tours depart from Akaroa iSITE and head to a hill-country farm near Paua Bay for shearing demonstrations, sheepdog shenanigans, garden strolls and homemade scones; allow 2¾ hours.

Tuatara Tours WALKING TOUR
(📞 03-962 3280; www.tuataratours.co.nz; per person $1695; ⊙ Nov-Apr) You'll need to carry only your day-pack on the guided *Akaroa Walk,* a leisurely 39km, three-day guided stroll from Christchurch to Akaroa via the gorgeous Summit Ridge. Good accommodation and gourmet food included.

🛏 Sleeping

★ Halfmoon Cottage HOSTEL $
(📞 03-304 5050; www.halfmoon.co.nz; SH75, Barrys Bay; dm/s/d $33/55/80; ⊙ closed Jul-Aug; @ 🛜) This pretty 1896 cottage, 12km from Akaroa, is a blissful place to spend a few days lazing on the big verandas or in the hammocks dotting the gardens. It offers proper home comforts and style, with the bonus of bicycles and kayaks to take exploring.

★ Onuku Farm Hostel HOSTEL $
(📞 03-304 7066; www.onuku.co.nz; Hamiltons Rd, Onuku; sites from $15, dm/d from $29/68; ⊙ Oct-Apr; @ 🛜) Set on a working farm 6km south of Akaroa, this blissfully isolated backpackers has a grassy camping area, simple, tidy rooms in a farmhouse and 'stargazer' cabins ($40 for two, BYO linen). Tonga Hut affords more privacy and breathtaking sea views ($80). Ask about the swimming-with-dolphins tours (from $100), kayaking trips (from $50) and the Skytrack walk.

Okuti Garden HOSTEL $
(📞 03-325 1913; www.okuti.co.nz; 216 Okuti Valley Rd; per adult/child $50/25; ⊙ closed May-Sep; @ 🛜) 🍃 Ecologically sound creds are just part of this delightfully eccentric package which features a house truck and a series of romantic yurts dotted throughout colourful potager gardens. Freshly picked herbs, a pizza oven, a fire-warmed bath, hammocks and free-roaming chickens give this place some serious *Good Life* vibe.

Double Dutch HOSTEL $
(📞 03-304 7229; www.doubledutch.co.nz; 32 Chorlton Rd; dm/s $32/64, d with/without bathroom $86/78; @ 🛜) Posh enough to be a B&B, yet budget-friendly, this relaxed hostel is perched in 20 acres of farmland on a secluded river estuary. There's a general store (and a beach) just a short walk away, but it's best to bring your own ingredients for the flash kitchen.

Okains Bay Camping Ground CAMPGROUND $
(📞 03-304 8789; www.okainsbaycamp.co.nz; 1357 Okains Bay Rd; sites adult/child $12/6) This up-and-coming camp sits on a pine-tree-peppered swathe of land right by a lovely beach and estuary. Tidy facilities are limited to kitchens, toilets and coin-operated hot showers, but the locale wins the day.

Coombe Farm B&B $$
(📞 03-304 7239; www.coombefarm.co.nz; 18 Old Le Bons Track, Takamatua Valley; d $170-190; 🛜) Choose between the private and romantic Shepherd's Hut – complete with an outdoor bath – and the historic farmhouse lovingly restored in shades of Laura Ashley. After breakfast you can take a walk to the waterfall with Ned, the friendly dog.

🍴 Eating

Little River Cafe & Gallery CAFE $
(www.littlerivergallery.com; SH75, Little River; mains $9-20; ⊙ 9am-5pm) On SH75 between Christchurch and Akaroa, the flourishing settlement of Little River is home to this fantastic combo of contemporary art gallery, store and cafe. It's top-notch in all departments, with some particularly delectable home-baking on offer as well as yummy deli goods to go.

★ Hilltop Tavern PUB FOOD $$
(📞 03-325 1005; www.thehilltop.co.nz; 5207 Christchurch-Akaroa Rd; pizzas $24-26, mains $23-30; ⊙ 10am-late, reduced hours in winter) Killer views, craft beer, proper wood-fired pizzas and a pool table. Occasional live music seals the deal for locals and visitors alike at this historic pub. Enjoy grandstand views of Akaroa harbour backdropped by the peninsula.

ℹ Getting There & Away

From November to April the **Akaroa Shuttle** (📞 0800 500 929; www.akaroashuttle.co.nz; one way/return $35/50) runs daily services from Christchurch to Akaroa (departs 8.30am), returning to Christchurch at 3.45pm. Check the website for Christchurch pick-up options. Scenic tours from Christchurch exploring Banks Peninsula are also available.

French Connection (📞 0800 800 575; www. akaroabus.co.nz; return $45) has a year-round daily departure from Christchurch at 9am, returning from Akaroa at 4pm.

Akaroa

POP 624

Akaroa ('Long Harbour' in Māori) was the site of the country's first French settlement and descendants of the original French pioneers still reside here. It's a charming town that strives to recreate the feel of a French provincial village, down to the names of its streets and houses. Generally it's a sleepy place, but the peace is periodically shattered by hordes descending from gargantuan cruise ships. The ships used to dock in Lyttelton Harbour but since the earthquakes Akaroa has been a popular substitute. Even when Lyttelton's back on its feet, the ships will be reluctant to leave.

◉ Sights

★ Giant's House
GARDENS
(www.thegiantshouse.co.nz; 68 Rue Balguerie; adult/child $20/10; ⊙12-5pm Jan-Apr, 2-4pm May-Dec) An ongoing labour of love by local artist Josie Martin, this playful and whimsical combination of sculpture and mosaics cascades down a hillside garden above Akaroa. Echoes of Gaudí and Miró can be found in the intricate collages of mirrors, tiles and broken china, and there are many surprising nooks and crannies to discover. Martin also exhibits her paintings and sculpture in the lovely 1880 house, the former residence of Akaroa's first bank manager.

★ Akaroa Museum
MUSEUM
(www.akaroamuseum.org.nz; cnr Rues Lavaud & Balguerie; ⊙10.30am-4.30pm) FREE An arduous postquake revamp has rewarded Akaroa with one of the smartest regional museums in the land. Learn about the various phases of the peninsula's settlement and its fascinating natural and industrial history, and hear stories of old characters including Pompey the penguin. A 20-minute film fills in some gaps while several adjacent historic buildings keep it real. Note the donation box.

St Peter's Anglican Church
CHURCH
(46 Rue Balguerie) Graciously restored in 2015, this 1864 Anglican gem features extensive exposed timbers, stained glass and an historic organ, and it has a few stories to tell. Well worth a look whether you're godly or not.

Old French Cemetery
CEMETERY
The first consecrated burial ground in Canterbury, this hillside cemetery makes for a poignant wander. Follow the trail off Rue Brittan.

🏃 Activities

Akaroa Guided Sea Kayaking Safari
KAYAKING
(021 156 4591; www.akaroakayaks.com; 3hr/half-day $125/159) Paddle out at 7.30am on a three-hour guided Sunrise Nature Safari, or if early starts aren't your thing, try the 11.30am Bays & Nature Paddle. The half-day Try Sea Kayaking Experience is a more challenging option.

Akaroa Sailing Cruises
SAILING
(0800 724 528; www.aclasssailing.co.nz; Main Wharf; adult/child $75/37.50) Set sail for a 2½-hour hands-on cruise on a gorgeous 1946 A-Class yacht.

Akaroa Adventure Centre
OUTDOORS
(03-304 7784; www.akarca.com; 74a Rue Lavaud; ⊙9am-6pm) Rents out sea kayaks and stand-up paddle boards (per hour/day $20/60), paddle boats (per hour $30), bikes (per hour/day $15/65), and fishing rods (per day $10). Based at the i-SITE.

👉 Tours

Black Cat Cruises
BOAT TOUR
(03-304 7641; www.blackcat.co.nz; Main Wharf; nature cruises adult/child $74/30, dolphin swims adult/child $155/120) As well as a two-hour nature cruise Black Cat offers a three-hour swimming with dolphins' experience. Wet suits and snorkelling gear are provided, plus hot showers back on dry land. Observers can tag along (adult/child $80/40) but only 12 people can swim per trip, so book ahead.

Cruises have a 98% success rate in seeing dolphins, and an 81% success rate in actually swimming with them (there's a $50 refund if there's no swim).

Akaroa Dolphins
BOAT TOUR
(03-304 7866; www.akaroadolphins.co.nz; 65 Beach Rd; adult/child $75/35; ⊙12.45pm year-round, plus 10.15am & 3.15pm Oct-Apr) Two-hour wildlife cruises on a comfortable 50ft catamaran, complete with a complimentary drink, home baking and, most importantly, the company of Sydney, wildlife-spotting dog extraordinaire.

Coast Up Close
BOAT TOUR
(0800 126 278; www.coastupclose.co.nz; Main Wharf; adult/child from $75/25; ⊙departs 10.15am & 1.45pm Oct-Apr) Scenic boat trips with an emphasis on wildlife watching. Fishing trips can be arranged.

Eastern Bays Scenic Mail Run
DRIVING TOUR
(03-304 8526; tours $80; ⊙9am Mon-Fri) Travel along with the ex-conservation-ranger postie to visit isolated communities and bays on this 120km, five-hour mail delivery service. Departs from the i-SITE (p484); bookings are essential as there are only eight seats available.

🎉 Festivals & Events

French Fest
FOOD
(www.ccc.govt.nz; ⊙Oct) This Gallic-inspired, two-day get together has an emphasis on

Akaroa

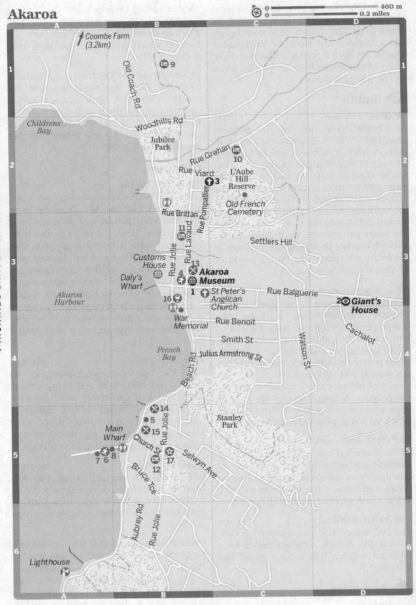

food, wine, music and art. Don't miss (or stand on) *Le Race D'Escargots,* where sleek, highly trained snails negotiate a compact course. It's held biennially (odd-numbered years).

🛏 Sleeping

Chez la Mer   HOSTEL **$**
(📞 03-304 7024; www.chezlamer.co.nz; 50 Rue Lavaud; dm $30, d with/without bathroom $86/76; 🛜) Pretty in pink, this historic building is home to a friendly backpackers with well-

Akaroa

kept rooms and a shaded garden, complete with fish pond, hammocks and barbecue. It's a TV-free zone but free bikes and fishing rods are available.

Akaroa Top 10 Holiday Park HOLIDAY PARK $
(☎0800 727 525, 03-304 7471; www.akaroaholidaypark.co.nz; 96 Morgans Rd; sites from $40-44, units $72-135; @ 🐾 ☀️) Grandstand views of the harbour and peninsula hills are the main drawcard for this holiday park. Cabins and motels are basic but tidy, while the facilities blocks could do with an overhaul.

Tresori Motor Lodge MOTEL $$
(☎03-304 7500; www.tresori.co.nz; cnr Rue Jolie & Church St; d $160-205; 🐾) There are 12 clean and smart units at this modern motel. All have kitchenettes, but given its proximity to Akaroa's waterfront cafe and restaurant strip, you needn't worry about using them. Blooming flower boxes are a nice touch.

★ **Beaufort House** B&B $$$
(☎03-304 7517; www.beauforthouse.co.nz; 42 Rue Grehan; r $375; ☉closed Jun-Aug; 🐾) Tucked away along a quiet street and behind gorgeous gardens, this lovely 1878 house is adorned with covetable artwork and antiques, and even has its own boutique vineyard. The only one of the five rooms without an en suite compensates with a large private bathroom with a claw-foot tub just across the hall.

✗ **Eating & Drinking**

Akaroa Butchery & Deli DELI $
(67 Rue Lavaud; ☉10am-5.30pm Mon-Fri, 9am-4pm Sat) A dream scenario for picnickers and self-caterers, this sharp butchery champions all manner of local produce from bread,

salmon, cheese and pickles, to delicious pies, smallgoods and meat for the barbecue.

Bully Hayes CAFE $$
(www.bullyhayes.co.nz; 57 Beach Rd; breakfast $14-23, lunch $11-30, dinner $22-43; ☉8am-9pm; 🐾) Named after a well-travelled American buccaneer, Bully Hayes is Akaroa's best breakfast option. A sunny spot overlooking the harbour draws the brunch-time crowd for the likes of eggs, burgers and fresh seafood, while a bar vibe keeps them lingering over a few cold ones later in the day.

Trading Rooms FRENCH $$$
(☎03-304 7656; www.thetradingrooms.co.nz; 71 Beach Rd; lunch $18-35, dinner $28-43; ☉10am-3pm Thu-Mon, 5-10pm Fri-Mon) Housed in Akaroa's most impressive waterside shopfront, decked out period-style in dark timbers and burgundy, this is an atmospheric spot to linger over a refined meal. French cuisine such as snails and cassoulet dominate, although at lunch its Gallic guard drops a little to reveal burgers and gourmet club sandwiches.

Harbar BAR
(83 Rue Jolie; ☉5pm-9.30pm) Sporadic opening hours, dictated by weather and demand, should not deter you from attempting a sundowner at Akaroa's favourite waterside bar. A crowd may gather, and a guitar may get strummed.

☆ **Entertainment**

Akaroa Cinema & Café CINEMA
(☎03-304 8898; www.cinecafe.co.nz; cnr Rue Jolie & Selwyn Ave; adult/child $15/13; 🐾) Grab a beer and settle in to watch an art-house, classic or foreign flick with high-quality sound and projection.

ℹ️ Information

Akaroa i-SITE & Adventure Centre (📞 03-304 8600; www.akaroa.com; 74a Rue Lavaud; ⏰ 9am-5pm) A helpful little hub offering info and bookings for local activities, transport, et al. Doubles as the post office.

NORTH CANTERBURY

Heading south from Kaikoura, SH1 crosses the Hundalee Hills and heads into Hurunui District, an area known for its wine and the thermal resort of Hanmer Springs. It's also the start of the Canterbury Plains, a vast, flat, richly agricultural area partitioned by distinctive braided rivers. The region is bounded to the west by the Southern Alps. If you're crossing into Canterbury from either Westport or Nelson, the most direct route cuts through the Alps on the beautiful Lewis Pass Hwy (SH7).

Lewis Pass

The northernmost of the three main mountain passes connecting the West Coast to the east, 864m-high Lewis Pass is not as steep as the others (Arthur's and Haast) and the forest isn't as dense either. However, the drive is arguably just as scenic. Vegetation comprises mainly beech (red and silver) and kowhai trees growing along river terraces.

From Lewis Pass the highway wiggles east for 62km before reaching the turn-off to Hanmer Springs.

🏃 Activities

The area has some interesting **tramps**, passing through beech forest with a backdrop of snow-capped mountains, lakes, and alpine tarns and rivers. Popular tracks include the **St James Walkway** (66km; four to five days) and those through **Lake Sumner Forest Park**; see the Department of Conservation (DOC) pamphlet *Lake Sumner & Lewis Pass* ($2). Subalpine conditions apply, so make sure you sign the intentions books at the huts.

Maruia Springs   SPA, HOT SPRING
(📞 03-523 8840; www.maruiasprings.co.nz; SH7; adult/child $22/12, guests free; ⏰ pools 8am-7.30pm) Maruia Springs is a small Japanese-style hot spring resort on the banks of the Maruia River, 6km west of Lewis Pass, with fairly spartan accommodation (doubles $159 to $199), a cafe-bar and a Japanese restaurant (dinner only). Water with black mineral flakes, known as 'hot spring flowers', is pumped into outdoor rock pools. It's a magical setting during a winter snowfall, but mind the sandflies in summer.

At the time of writing, new owners were about to take over. Changes (and hopefully upgrades) are afoot, but the hot water should keep flowing.

ℹ️ Transport

East West Coaches (📞 03-789 6251; www.eastwestcoaches.co.nz) East West Coaches stop at Maruia Springs and the St James Walkway on their way between Westport and Christchurch, and back again.

Hanmer Springs

POP 843

Ringed by sculpted mountains, Hanmer Springs is the main thermal resort on the South Island. It's a pleasantly low-key spot to indulge yourself, whether by soaking in hot pools, dining out or being pampered in the spa complex. If that all sounds too soporific, fear not; there are plenty of family-friendly activities on offer, including a few to get the adrenaline pumping.

🎯 Sights

Hanmer Springs Animal Park   FARM
(📞 03-315 7772; www.hanmer-animal-park.nz; 108 Rippingale Rd; adult/child/family $12/6/35; ⏰ 10am-5pm Wed-Sun, daily during school holidays; 🚼) With more animals than Dr Dolittle's Facebook page, this farm park is great for kids. Llamas, Tibetan yak, deer, goats, guinea pigs and chinchillas all feature, and many of the critters can be hand-fed; pony rides are also available. For mum and dad there's a licensed cafe and a craft gallery.

🏃 Activities

⭐**Hanmer Springs Thermal Pools**   HOT SPRING
(📞 03-315 0000; www.hanmersprings.co.nz; 42 Amuri Ave; adult/child $22/11, locker $2; ⏰ 10am-9pm; 🚼) ❦ Māori legend has it that these hot springs are the result of embers from Mt Ngauruhoe in the North Island falling from the sky. The main complex consists of a series of large pools of various temperatures, along with smaller, adult-only landscaped rock pools, a freshwater 25m lap pool, private thermal pools ($30 per 30 minutes) and a cafe.

Kids of all ages will love the water slides and the whirl-down-the-plughole-thrill of the Superbowl ($10). There's also an adjacent spa (p485).

Hanmer Forest Park TRAMPING, MOUNTAIN BIKING
(www.visithurunui.co.nz) Trampers and mountain bikers will find plenty of room to move within the 130 sq km expanse of forest abutting the town. The easy Woodland Walk starts 1km up Jollies Pass Rd and goes through Douglas fir, poplar and redwood stands before joining Majuba Walk, which leads to Conical Hill Lookout and then back towards town (1½ hours). The Waterfall Track is an excellent half-day tramp starting at the end of McIntyre Rd. The i-SITE (p487) stocks a *Forest Park Walks* booklet and a mountain-biking map (both $3).

Hanmer Springs Spa SPA
(☑03-315 0029, 0800 873 529; www.hanmer-springs.co.nz; 42 Amuri Ave; ☺10am-7pm) Hanmer Springs Spa has massage and beauty treatments from $85. Recent refurbishments have lifted the spa to international standards.

Entry to the adjacent Hanmer Springs Thermal Pools (p484) is discounted to $15 if you partake of the spa's facilities.

Mt Lyford Alpine Resort SKIING
(☑0274 710 717, snow-phone 03-366 1220; www.mtlyford.co.nz; day passes $75/35) Around 60km from both Hanmer Springs and Kaikoura, and 4km from Mt Lyford Village, this is more of a 'resort' than most NZ ski fields, with accommodation and eating options. There's a good mix of runs and a terrain park.

Hanmer Springs Ski Area SKIING
(☑027 434 1806; www.skihanmer.co.nz; day passes adult/child/family $60/30/130) Only 17km from town via an unsealed road, this small complex has runs to suit all levels of ability. The **Adventure Centre** (☑0800 358 7386, 03-315 7233; www.hanmeradventure.co.nz; 20 Conical Hill Rd; ☺8.30am-5pm) provides shuttles during the season.

Thrillseekers Adventures ADVENTURE SPORTS
(☑03-315 7046, 0800 661 538; www.thrillseekers.co.nz; 839 Hanmer Springs Rd) Bungy off a 35m-high bridge ($169), jetboat the Waiau Gorge (adult/child $115/60), explore the Grade II Waiau River in a raft (adult/child $149/79) or inflatable kayak (five hours, adult/child $299/189), or get dirty on a quad bike (adult/child $149/99). The Thrillseekers Adventure centre is next to the bridge near the turn-off from SH7, and there's a **booking office** (☑03-315 7346, 0800 661 538; www.thrillseekers.co.nz; Conical Hill Rd; ☺9am-5pm) in town.

Hanmer Springs

Hanmer Springs

○ **Activities, Courses & Tours**
1 Hanmer Springs Adventure
   Centre..A2
   Hanmer Springs Spa..................(see 2)
2 Hanmer Springs Thermal Pools.........A2
3 Thrillseekers Adventures
   Booking Office......................................A2

○ **Sleeping**
4 Chalets Motel..A2
5 Cheltenham House...............................B2
6 Hanmer Springs Top 10.....................A3
7 Kakapo Lodge......................................A3
8 Rose's..A2
9 Scenic Views.......................................A3
10 St James...A2

○ **Eating**
11 Coriander's..A2
12 Hanmer Springs Bakery...................A2
13 No. 31...A3
14 Powerhouse Cafe...............................A2

○ **Drinking & Nightlife**
15 Monteith's Brewery Bar...................A2

🛏 Sleeping

Jack in the Green HOSTEL $
(☑03-315 5111; www.jackinthegreen.co.nz; 3 Devon St; site per person $20, dm $32, d with/without bathroom $52/76; @🛜) This charming

MOLESWORTH STATION

Filling up 1807 mountainous sq km between Hanmer Springs and Blenheim, Molesworth Station is NZ's largest farm, with the country's largest cattle herd (up to 10,000). It's also an area of national ecological significance and the entire farm is now administered by DOC (☎03-572 9100; www.doc.govt.nz).

Visits are usually only possible when the Acheron Rd through the station is open from November to early April (weather permitting; check with DOC or at the Hanmer Springs i-SITE). The 207km drive from Hanmer Springs north to Blenheim on this narrow, un-sealed backcountry road takes around six hours. Note that the gates are only open from 7am to 7pm, and overnight camping (adult/child $6/3) is permitted in certain areas (no open fires allowed). Pick up DOC's *Molesworth Station* brochure from the i-SITE (p487) or download it from the website.

Molesworth Heritage Tours (☎027 201 4536, 03-315 7401; www.molesworth.co.nz; tours $198-750; ☉Oct-May) leads 4WD coach trips to the station from Hanmer Springs. Day tours include a picnic lunch, but there's also a five-hour 'no frills' option. From the Blenheim side, **Molesworth Tours** (☎03-572 8025; www.molesworthtours.co.nz) offers one- to four-day all-inclusive heritage and 4WD trips ($220 to $1487), as well as four-day fully supported (and catered) mountain-bike adventures ($1460).

converted old home is a 10-minute walk from the centre. Large rooms (no bunks), relaxing gardens and a lovely lounge area are the main drawcards. For extra privacy, book an en suite garden 'chalet'.

Kakapo Lodge HOSTEL $
(☎03-315 7472; www.kakapolodge.co.nz; 14 Amuri Ave; dm $28, d with/without bathroom $90/66; ☎) The YHA-affiliated Kakapo has a cheery owner, a roomy kitchen and lounge, chill-busting underfloor heating and a 1st-floor deck. Bunk-free dorms (some with bathrooms) are joined by two motel-style units ($95 to $100).

Hanmer Springs Top 10 HOLIDAY PARK $
(☎0800 904 545, 03-315 7113; www.hanmerspringstop10.co.nz; 5 Hanmer Springs Rd; sites $34-50, units with/without bathroom from $95/78; @☎) This family-friendly park is just a few minutes' walk from the town's eponymous pools. Kids will love the playground and jumping pillow. Take your pick from basic cabins (BYO everything) to attractive motel units with everything supplied.

★**Woodbank Park Cottages** COTTAGE $$
(☎03-315 5075; www.woodbankcottages.co.nz; 381 Woodbank Rd; d $190-210) These two plush cottages in a woodland setting are a six-minute drive from Hanmer, but feel a million miles away. Decor is crisp and modern, bathrooms and kitchens are well appointed, and wooden decks come equipped with gas barbecues and rural views. Log burners, and complimentary fresh juices and cheese platters, seal the deal.

Chalets Motel MOTEL $$
(☎03-315 7097; www.chaletsmotel.co.nz; 56 Jacks Pass Rd; d $140-180; ☎) Soak up the mountain views from these tidy, reasonably priced, free-standing wooden chalets, set on the slopes behind the town centre. All chalets have full kitchens, and one unit has a spa bath.

Scenic Views MOTEL $$
(☎03-315 7419, 0800 843 974; www.hanmerscenicviews.co.nz; 2 Amuri Ave; d $140-240; ☎) An attractive timber-and-stone complex with modern studios (one with an outdoor spa pool) and two- and three-bedroom apartments. Mountain views come standard, as do free wi-fi and plunger coffee.

Rosie's B&B $$
(☎03-315 7095; www.rosiesbandbhanmer.co.nz; 9 Cheltenham St; d $95-145; ☎) Rosie has left the building but the hospitality continues at this homely, good-value B&B. Half the rooms are en suite, and rates include a continental breakfast and scrummy toasted croissants.

St James APARTMENTS $$$
(☎03-315 5225; www.thestjames.co.nz; 20 Chisholm Cres; apt $190-365; ☎) Luxuriate in a schmick modern apartment with all mod cons, including iPod dock and fully equipped kitchen. Sizes range from studios to two-bedroom apartments, with balconies or patios. Most have mountain views.

Cheltenham House B&B $$$
(☎03-315 7545; www.cheltenham.co.nz; 13 Cheltenham St; r $235-280; ☎) This large 1930's house has room for both a billiard table

and a grand piano. There are four art-filled suites in the main house and two in cosy garden cottages. Cooked gourmet breakfasts are delivered to the rooms and wine is served in the evening.

✕ Eating

Hanmer Springs Bakery   BAKERY $
(☑ 03-315 7714; www.hanmerbakery.co.nz; 16 Conical Hill Rd; ⊙ 6am-4pm) In peak season queues stretch out the door for this humble bakery's meat pies and salmon bagels.

Coriander's   INDIAN $$
(☑ 03-315 7616; www.corianders.co.nz; Chisholm Cres; mains $14-22; ⊙ 11.30am-2pm Mon-Fri, 5-10pm daily; ☑) Spice up your life at this brightly painted North Indian restaurant complete with bhangra-beats soundtrack. It's a beef-free zone, but there are plenty of tasty lamb, chicken and seafood dishes to choose from, plus a fine vegetarian selection.

Powerhouse Cafe   CAFE $$
(☑ 03-315 5252; www.powerhousecafe.co.nz; 8 Jacks Pass Rd; brunch $15-24; ⊙ 730am-3pm; ☑) Power up with a huge High Country breakfast, or a Highland Fling caramelised whisky-sodden porridge. Return for a burger, laksa or salmon salad for lunch, then finish with one of the lavishly iced friands.

No. 31   MODERN NZ $$$
(☑ 03-315 7031; www.restaurant-no31.nz; 31 Amuri Ave; mains $36-39; ⊙ 5.30-11pm Tue-Sun) Substantial servings of good-quality, albeit conservative, cuisine are on offer in this pretty wooden cottage. The upmarket ambience befits the prices; the paper napkins and chunky glasses don't. Good beer list, and solid wine selection.

🍷 Drinking & Nightlife

Monteith's Brewery Bar   PUB
(☑ 03-315 5133; www.mbbh.co.nz; 47 Amuri Ave; ⊙ 9am-11pm) This large, overlit and slightly worn brand-pub is the town's busiest. It serves food all day (breakfast $15 to $21, bar snacks $9 to $16, dinner $24 to $35). Live musicians kick off from 4pm Sundays.

ℹ Information

Hanmer Springs i-SITE (☑ 03-315 0020, 0800 442 663; www.visithanmersprings.co.nz; 40 Amuri Ave; ⊙ 10am-5pm) Books transport, accommodation and activities.

ℹ Getting There & Away

The **main bus stop** is near the corner of Amuri Ave and Jacks Pass Rd.

Hanmer Connection (☑ 03-382 2952, 0800 242 663; www.hanmerconnection.co.nz; one way/return $30/50) Runs daily bus to/from Christchurch via Waipara and Amberley.

Hanmer Tours & Shuttle (☑ 03-315 7418; www.hanmertours.co.nz) Runs shuttles to/from Waipara ($20), Amberley ($20) Christchurch city centre ($30) and Christchurch airport ($40).

Waipara Valley

Conveniently stretched along SH1 near the Hanmer Springs turn-off, this resolutely rural area makes for a tasty pit stop en route to Christchurch. The valley's warm dry summers followed by cool autumn nights have proved a winning formula for growing grapes, olives, hazelnuts and lavender. While it accounts for less than 3% of NZ's grapes, it produces some of the country's finest cool-climate wines including riesling, pinot noir and gewürztraminer.

Of the region's 30 or so wineries, around a dozen have cellar doors to visit, four with restaurants. To explore the valley's bounty fully, pick up a copy of the *Waipara Valley Map* (or download it from www.waiparavalleynz.com). Otherwise, you'll spot several of the big players from the highway. The area's two main towns are tiny Waipara and slightly larger Amberley, although the latter is just outside the main wine-growing area.

◉ Sights

★**Pegasus Bay**   WINERY
(☑ 03-314 6869; www.pegasusbay.com; Stockgrove Rd; ⊙ tastings 10am-5pm) It's fitting that Waipara Valley's premier winery should have the loveliest setting and one of Canterbury's best restaurants (mains $36 to $44, serving noon to 4pm Thursday to Monday). Beautiful gardens set the scene but it's the contemporary NZ menu and luscious wines that steal the show. Pétanque available upon request.

Black Estate   WINERY
(☑ 03-314 6085; www.blackestate.co.nz; 614 Omihi Rd/SH1; ⊙ 10am-5pm Wed-Sun, daily Dec-Jan) The sharpest of Waipara's wineries architecturally, this striking black barn overlooking the valley is home to some excellent wine, and food that champions local producers (mains $25 to $40). As well as the region's common cool-climate wines, look out for its interesting pinot/chardonnay rosé and seductive chenin blanc.

Brew Moon   BREWERY
(☑ 03-314 8036; www.brewmoon.co.nz; 12 Markham St, Amberley; ⊙ 3cm-late Wed-Fri, noon-late

Sat & Sun) The variety of craft beers available to taste at this wee brewery never wanes. Stop in to fill a rigger (flagon) to take away, or sup an ale with a platter or a pizza (food from 3pm).

🛏 Sleeping & Eating

Old Glenmark Vicarage   B&B $$$
(📞 03-314 6775; www.glenmarkvicarage.co.nz; 161 Church Rd, Waipara; d $230, barn d $210; 🛜 ☕) There are two divine options in this beautifully restored century-old vicarage: cosy up with bed and breakfast in the main house, or lounge around in the character-filled, converted barn that sleeps up to five. The beautiful gardens and swimming pool are a blessed bonus.

★ Little Vintage Espresso   CAFE $
(20 Markham St, Amberley; brunch $8-18; ⊘ 7.30am-4.30pm Mon-Sat) This little cracker of a cafe just off SH1 serves up the best coffee in town with food to match. High-quality, contemporary sandwiches, slices and cakes are gobbled up by locals and tourists alike.

Pukeko Junction   CAFE, DELI $$
(📞 03-314 8834; www.pukekojunction.co.nz; 458 Ashworths Rd/SH1, Leithfield; mains $15-21; ⊘ 9am-4.30pm; 🍴) A deservedly popular roadside pit stop, this cafe in Leithfield (south of Amberley) serves delicious baked goods including gourmet sausage rolls and lamb shank pies. As well as arts and crafts, the shop next door stocks an excellent selection of local wine.

Waipara Springs   CAFE $$
(www.waiparasprings.co.nz; SH1; mains $24-28; ⊘ 11am-5pm; 🚹) Slightly north of Waipara township, one of the valley's oldest vineyards has a fine line in righteous rieslings. The casual cafe serves platters and bistro fare in the lovely family-friendly garden.

ℹ Getting There & Away

The *Coastal Pacific* train (October to May) from Christchurch to Picton stops at Waipara. Wine tours are available from a few Christchurch-based companies.

Hanmer Connection (📞 0800 242 663; www. hanmerconnection.co.nz) Heads to Hanmer Springs ($20, 50 minutes) and Christchurch ($20, 1¼ hours).

Hanmer Tours & Shuttle (📞 03-315 7418; www.hanmertours.co.nz) Runs shuttles to/from Hanmer Springs ($20), Christchurch city centre ($15) and Christchurch airport ($25).

InterCity (📞 03-365 1113; www.intercity.co.nz) Coaches head to/from Picton (from $29, 4½

hours), Blenheim (from $27, four hours), Kaikoura (from $16, 1¾ hours) and Christchurch (from $12, one hour) at least twice daily.

CENTRAL CANTERBURY

While the dead-flat agricultural heartland of the Canterbury Plains blankets the majority of the region, there's plenty of interest for travellers in the west, where the Southern Alps soar to snowy peaks. Here you'll find numerous ski fields and some brilliant wilderness walks.

Unusually for NZ, the most scenic routes avoid the coast, and most items of interest can be accessed from one of two spectacular roads: the Great Alpine Highway (SH73), which wends from the Canterbury Plains deep into the mountains and over to the West Coat, and the Inland Scenic Route (SH72), which skirts the mountains foothills on its way south towards Tekapo.

Selwyn District

Named after NZ's first Anglican bishop, this largely rural district has swallowed an English map book and regurgitated place names such as Lincoln, Darfield and Sheffield to punctuate this green and pleasant land. Yet any illusions of Albion are quickly dispelled by the looming presence of the snow-capped Southern Alps, providing a rugged retort to 'England's mountains green'.

Selwyn's numerous ski fields may not be the country's most glamorous but they provide plenty of thrills for ski bunnies. **Porters** (📞 03-318 4002, snow-phone 03-379 9931; www.skiporters.co.nz; daily lift passes adult/child $84/44) is the main commercial field; club fields include **Mt Olympus** (📞 03-318 5840; www.mtolympus.co.nz; daily lift passes adult/child $70/35), **Cheeseman** (📞 03-344 3247, snow-phone 03-318 8794; www.mtcheeseman.co.nz; daily lift passes adult/child $79/39), **Broken River** (📞 03-318 8713; www.brokenriver.co.nz; daily lift passes adult/child $75/35), **Craigieburn Valley** (📞 03-318 8711; www.craigieburn.co.nz; daily lift passes adult/child $75/35) and **Temple Basin** (📞 03-377 7788; www.templebasin.co.nz; daily lift passes adult/child $70/39).

The highly scenic Great Alpine Hwy pierces the heart of the district on its journey between Christchurch and the West Coast. Before it leaves the Canterbury Plains, it passes through the little settlement of **Springfield** (population 300), which is distinguished by a monument to notable local Rewi Alley

(1897–1987) who became a great hero of the Chinese Communist Party. His life story is a tale indeed, retold well in the roadside information panels.

The town's other major monument is a giant pink-iced doughnut, originally erected to promote *The Simpsons Movie* but now a permanent feature. Is that an #InstaDonut I feel coming on?

The Southern Alps loom larger as SH73 heads west from Springfield into Arthur's Pass.

🏃 Activities

Rubicon Horse Treks　　　HORSE RIDING
(☑03-318 8886; www.rubiconvalley.co.nz; 534 Rubicon Rd) Operating from a sheep farm 6km from Springfield, Rubicon offers hour-long farm treks ($55), two-hour river or valley rides ($98), two-hour sunset rides ($120), and six-hour mountain trail rides ($285).

🛏 Sleeping & Eating

Smylies Accommodation　　HOSTEL $
(☑03-318 4740; www.smylies.co.nz; 5653 West Coast Rd, Springfield; dm/s/d $30/50/80; 🛜) 🍃 This well-seasoned, welcoming, YHA-associated hostel has a piano, manga comics galore, and a DVD library. There's also a handful of self-contained motel units ($85 to $160) and a three-bedroom cottage ($220). Winter packages including ski-equipment rental and ski-field transport available.

Famous Sheffield Pie Shop　　BAKERY $
(www.sheffieldpieshop.co.nz; 51 Main West Rd, Sheffield; pies $5-6; ⊙7.30am-4pm) Heaven forbid you should blink and miss this roadside bakery, a stellar purveyor of meat pies produced here in more than 20 varieties. While you're at it, snaffle a bag of its exemplary afghan biscuits – such cornflakey, chocolatey goodness!

❶ Getting There & Away

Public transport is limited in the Selwyn District, so it's best to organise your own vehicle.

Arthur's Pass

POP 300

Having left the Canterbury Plains at Springfield, the Great Alpine Hwy heads over Porter's Pass into the mountainous folds of the Torlesse and **Craigieburn** Ranges and into Arthur's Pass.

Māori used this pass to cross the Southern Alps long before its 'discovery' by Arthur Dobson in 1864. The Westland gold rush created the need for a dependable crossing over the Alps from Christchurch, and the coach road was completed within a year. Later, the coal and timber trade demanded a railway, duly completed in 1923.

Today it's an amazing journey. Successive valleys display their own character and special sights, not least the spectacular braided Waimakariri River Valley, encountered as you enter **Arthur's Pass National Park**.

Arthur's Pass village (population 62) is 4km from the actual pass. At 900m, it's NZ's highest-altitude settlement and a handy base for tramps, climbs and skiing. The weather, however, is a bit of a shocker. Come prepared for rain.

◉ Sights

★**Castle Hill/Kura Tawhiti**　　LANDMARK
Scattered across lush paddocks around 33km from Springfield, these limestone formations are so odd they were named 'treasure from a distant land' by early Māori. A car park (with toilets) provides easy access on foot into the strange rock garden, favoured by rock climbers and photographers.

Arthur's Pass National Park　NATIONAL PARK
(www.doc.govt.nz) Straddling the Southern Alps and known to Māori as Ka Tiriti o Te Moana (steep peak of glistening white), this vast alpine wilderness became the South Island's first national park in 1923. Of its 1148 sq km, two-thirds lies on the Canterbury side of the main divide; the rest is in Westland. It is a rugged, mountainous area, cut by deep valleys, and ranging in altitude from 245m at the Taramakau River to 2408m at Mt Murchison. There are plenty of well-marked day walks, especially around Arthur's Pass village.

Pick up a copy of DOC's *Discover Arthur's Pass* booklet to read about popular walks including: **Arthur's Pass Walkway**, a reasonably easy track from the village to the Dobson Memorial at the summit of the pass (2½ hours return); the one-hour return walk to **Devils Punchbowl** falls; and the steep walk to beautiful views at **Temple Basin** (three hours return). More challenging, full-day options include **Bealey Spur** track and the classic summit hike to **Avalanche Peak**.

The park's many multiday trails are mostly valley routes with saddle climbs in between, such as **Goat Pass** and **Cass-Lagoon Saddles Tracks**, both two-day options. These and the park's longer tracks require previous tramping experience as flooding can make the rivers dangerous and the weather is extremely changeable. Always seek advice from DOC before setting out.

Cave Stream Scenic Reserve CAVE
(www.doc.govt.nz) Near Broken River Bridge, 2km northeast of Castle Hill, a car park signals access to this 594m-long cave. As indicated by the information panels, the walk through it is an achievable adventure, even for beginners, but only with a foolproof torch and warm clothing, and definitely only if the water level is less than waist-deep where indicated. Heed all notices, take necessary precautions and revel in the spookiness. Failing that, just wander around the 10-minute loop track for a gander at the surrounds.

🛏 Sleeping

Camping is possible near the basic **Avalanche Creek Shelter** (adult/child $6/3) opposite the DOC centre, where there's running water, a sink, tables and a toilet. You can also camp for free at **Klondyke Corner** or **Hawdon Shelter**, 8km and 24km south of Arthur's Pass respectively, where facilities are limited to toilets and stream water for boiling.

Mountain House YHA HOSTEL $
(☑ 03-318 9258; www.trampers.co.nz; 83 Main Rd; dm $31-34, s/d/unit $74/86/155; 🖥) Spread around the village, this excellent suite of accommodation includes a well-kept hostel, two upmarket motel units and two three-bedroom cottages with log fires ($340, for up to eight people). The enthusiastic manager runs a tight ship and can provide extensive local tramping information.

Arthur's Pass Village B&B B&B $$
(☑ 021 394 776; www.arthurspass.org.nz; 72 School Tce; d $140-160; 🖥) This lovingly restored former railway cottage is now a cosy B&B, complete with two guest bedrooms (share bathroom), free-range bacon and eggs, and freshly baked bread for breakfast, and the company of interesting owners. Home-cooked dinners are also available ($35). Ask about the scorched floorboard.

Arthur's Pass Alpine Motel MOTEL $$
(☑ 03-318 9233; www.apam.co.nz; 52 Main Rd; d $125-150; 🖥) On the southern approach to the village, this cabin-style motel complex combines the homely charms of yesteryear with the beauty of double-glazing and the advice of active, enthusiastic hosts.

Wilderness Lodge LODGE $$$
(☑ 03-318 9246; www.wildernesslodge.co.nz; Cora Lynn Rd, Bealey; s $499-749, d $778-1178; 🖥) 🌿 For tranquillity and natural grandeur, this mid-size alpine lodge tucked into beech forest just off the highway takes some beating. It's a class act with a focus on immersive, nature-based experiences. Two daily guided activities (such as tramping and kayaking) are included in the tariff along with dinner and breakfast.

🍴 Eating

Arthur's Pass Store & Cafe CAFE $
(85 Main Rd; breakfast & lunch $7-24; ⊙ 8am-5pm; 🖥) You want it, this is your best chance, with odds-on for egg sandwiches, hot chips, good coffee, petrol and basic groceries.

ℹ Information

DOC Arthur's Pass Visitor Centre (☑ 03-318 9211; www.doc.govt.nz; 80 Main Rd; ⊙ 8.30pm-4.30pm) Displays include ecological information and the history of Arthur's Pass. Helpful staff provide advice on suitable tramps and the all-important weather forecast. Detailed route guides and topographical maps will further aid your safety, as will hire of a locator beacon and logging your trip details on AdventureSmart (www.adventuresmart.org.nz) via the on-site computer.

ℹ Getting There & Away

Fill your fuel tank before you leave Springfield (or Hokitika or Greymouth, if you're travelling in the other direction). There's a pump at Arthur's Pass Store but it's expensive and only operates from 8am until 5pm.

Atomic Shuttles (☑ 03-349 0697; www.atomictravel.co.nz) From Arthur's Pass a bus heads to/from Christchurch ($35, 2½ hours), Springfield ($35, one hour), Lake Brunner ($30, 50 minutes) and Greymouth ($35, 1¼ hours).

TranzAlpine (☑ 04-495 0775, 0800 872 467; www.kiwirailscenic.co.nz; all fares $89) One train daily in each direction stops in Arthur's Pass, heading to/from Springfield (1½ hours) and Christchurch (2½ hours), or Lake Brunner (one hour) and Greymouth (two hours).

West Coast Shuttle (☑ 03-768 0028; www.westcoastshuttle.co.nz) Buses stopping at Arthur's Pass head to/from Christchurch ($42, 2¾ hours) and Greymouth ($32, 1¾ hours).

Methven

POP 1707

Methven is busiest in winter, when it fills up with snow bunnies heading to nearby Mt Hutt. At other times tumbleweeds don't quite blow down the main street – much to the disappointment of the wannabe gunslingers arriving for the raucous October rodeo. Over summer it's a low-key and affordable base for fisherfolk, and for trampers and mountain bikers heading into the spectacular mountain foothills.

Activities

Ask at the i-SITE (p492) about local walks (including the town heritage trail and Methven Walk/Cycleway) and longer tramps, horse riding, mountain biking, fishing, clay-shooting, archery, golfing, scenic helicopter flights, and jetboating through the nearby Rakaia Gorge.

Black Diamond Safaris
SKIING

(☑ 027 450 8283; www.blackdiamondsafaris.co.nz) Provides access to uncrowded club ski fields by 4WD. Prices start at $150 for transport, safety equipment and familiarisation, while $275 includes a lift pass, guiding and lunch.

Methven Heliski
SKIING

(☑ 03-302 8108; www.methvenheli.co.nz; Main St; 5-run day trips $1045) Epic guided, all-inclusive backcountry ski trips, featuring five runs averaging drops of 750 to 1000 vertical metres.

Aoraki Balloon Safaris
BALLOONING

(☑ 03-302 8172; www.nzballooning.com; flights $385) Early-morning combo of snow-capped peaks and a breakfast with bubbly.

Skydiving Kiwis
SKYDIVING

(☑ 0800 359 549; www.skydivingkiwis.com; Ashburton Airport, Seafield Rd) Offers tandem jumps from 6,000ft ($235), 9,000ft ($285) and 12,000ft ($335), departing Ashburton airport.

Sleeping

Some accommodation is closed in summer; others open year-round. During the ski season, it pays to book well ahead, especially for budget accommodation. We've listed summer prices; expect them to rise in winter.

Alpenhorn Chalet
HOSTEL $

(☑ 03-302 8779; www.alpenhorn.co.nz; 44 Allen St; dm $30, d $65-85; @ ⊚) This small, inviting home has a leafy conservatory housing an indoor spa pool, a log fire, and complimentary espresso coffee. Bedrooms are spacious and brightly coloured, with lots of warm, natural wood; one double room has an en suite bathroom.

Rakaia Gorge Camping Ground
CAMPGROUND $

(☑ 03-302 9353; 6686 Arundel-Rakaia Gorge Rd; sites per adult/child under 12 $8.50/free) There are no powered sites and only toilets, showers and a small kitchen shelter, but don't let that put you off. This is the best camping ground for miles, perched handsomely above the ultrablue Rakaia River, and a good base for exploring the area. Amenities closed May to October.

MT HUTT

Mt Hutt (☑ 03-302 8811; www.nzski.com; day lift passes adult/child $98/56; ⊙ 9am-4pm) One of the highest ski areas in the southern hemisphere, and one of NZ's best, Mt Hutt has the largest skiable area of any of NZ's commercial fields (365 hectares). The ski field is only 26km from Methven but in wintry conditions the drive takes about 40 minutes; allow two hours from Christchurch. Road access is steep: be extremely cautious in lousy weather. **Methven Travel** (p492) runs shuttle buses from both towns in season ($20).

Half of the terrain is suitable for intermediate skiers, with a quarter each for beginning and advanced skiers. The longest run stretches for 2km. Other attractions include chairlifts, heliskiing and wide-open faces that are good for learning to snowboard. The season usually runs from mid-June to mid-October.

Mt Hutt Bunkhouse
HOSTEL $

(☑ 03-302 8894; www.mthuttbunkhouse.co.nz; 8 Lampard St; dm $31, d $68-80, cottage $280-350; ⊚) Enthusiastic on-site owners run this basic, well-equipped, bright and breezy hostel. There's a comfy lounge, and a large garden sporting a barbecue and a volleyball court. The cottage (sleeps up to 18) is economical for large groups.

Big Tree Lodge
HOSTEL $

(☑ 03-302 9575; www.bigtreelodge.co.nz; 25 South Belt; dm $35-40, r $75-80, apt $110-160; ⊚) Once a vicarage, this relaxed hostel has bunk-free dorms and wood-trimmed bathrooms. Tucked just behind is Little Tree Studio, a self-contained unit sleeping up to four people.

Redwood Lodge
HOSTEL, LODGE $$

(☑ 03-302 8964; www.redwoodlodge.co.nz; 3 Wayne Pl; s $55-65, d $104-149; @ ⊚) Expect a warm, woolly welcome and no dorms at this charming and peaceful family-friendly lodge. Most rooms are en suite, and bigger rooms can be reconfigured to accommodate families. The large shared lounge is ideal for resting ski-weary limbs.

Whitestone Cottages
RENTAL HOUSE $$$

(☑ 03-928 8C50; www.whitestonecottages.co.nz; 3016 Methven Hwy; cottages $175-255) When you just want to spread out, cook a meal, do your laundry and have your own space, these four large free-standing houses in leafy grounds are just the ticket. Each sleeps six in two en suite bedrooms. Base rates are for two; each extra person is $35.

 Eating

Cafe 131   CAFE $
(131 Main St; meals $10-20; ⊙7.30am-5pm; ⊛) Polished timber and lead-light windows lend atmosphere to this conservative but reliable local favourite. Highlights include good coffee, tasty all-day breakfasts and admirable home-baking, with a tipple on offer should you fancy it. Free wi-fi makes this the town's de facto internet cafe.

★ **Dubliner**   RESTAURANT $$
(www.dubliner.co.nz; 116 Main St; meals $26-34; ⊙4pm-late) This authentically Irish bar and restaurant is housed in Methven's lovingly restored old post office. Great food includes pizza, Irish stew and other hearty fare suitable for washing down with a pint of craft beer.

Aqua   JAPANESE $$
(☑03-302 8335; 112 Main St; mains $13-21; ⊙5-9pm, closed Nov) A ski-season stalwart with unpredictable summer hours (so ring ahead), this tiny restaurant sports kimono-clad waitresses and traditional Japanese cuisine including yakisoba (fried noodles), ramen (noodle soup) and izakaya-style small plates to share with ice-cold beer or warming sake.

☆ **Entertainment**

Cinema Paradiso   CINEMA
(☑03-302 1975; www.cinemaparadiso.co.nz; Main St; adult/child $17/12; ⊙Wed-Mon) Quirky cinema with an art-house slant.

ℹ **Information**

Methven i-SITE (☑03-302 8955; www.methvenmthutt.co.nz; 160 Main St; ⊙9.30am-5pm daily Jul-Sep, 9am-5pm Mon-Fri, 10am-3pm Sat & Sun Oct-Jun; ⊛) Ask staff here about local walks and other activities, then enjoy the free art gallery and the hands-on NZ Alpine & Agriculture Encounter (adult/child $12.70/7.50).

Medical Centre (☑03-302 8105; The Square, Main St; ⊙8.30am-5.30pm)

ℹ **Getting There & Away**

Methven Travel (☑0800 684 888, 03-302 8106; www.methventravel.co.nz; 160 Main St) Runs shuttles between Methven and Christchurch airport ($45) three to four times a week October to June, increasing to three times daily during the ski season. Also runs shuttles up to Mt Hutt ski field in winter ($20 return).

Mt Somers

The small settlement of Mt Somers sits on the edge of the Southern Alps, beneath the mountain of the same name. The biggest drawcard to the area is the **Mt Somers track** (26km), a two-day tramp circling the mountain, linking the popular picnic spots of Sharplin Falls and Woolshed Creek. Trail highlights include volcanic formations, Māori rock drawings, deep river canyons and botanical diversity. The route is subject to sudden weather changes, so precautions should be taken.

There are two DOC huts on the track: **Pinnacles Hut** and **Woolshed Creek Hut** (adult/child $15/7.50). Hut tickets and information are available at the Mt Somers General Store and Staveley Store.

🛏 **Sleeping & Eating**

Mt Somers Holiday Park   HOLIDAY PARK $
(☑03-303 9719; www.mountsomers.co.nz; 87 Hoods Rd; sites $18-32, cabin with/without bathroom $80/55) This small, friendly park offers pleasant sites in leafy grounds along with en suite, fully made-up cabins. You'll need to bring your own linen (or hire it) for the standard cabins. There's wi-fi at the tavern across the road.

Stronechrubie   MOTEL $$
(☑03-303 9814; www.stronechrubie.co.nz; cnr Hoods Rd & SH72; d $120-160; ⊛) Comfortable chalets overlooking bird-filled gardens range in size from studio to two-bedroom, but it's the up-and-coming culinary hub that's the draw here. Enjoy a more formal meal in the lauded, long-standing restaurant (mains $34 to $38; serves dinner Wednesday through Sunday and lunch Sunday). Or head to the flash new bar and bistro (open 5.30pm to late Thursday to Saturday) for modern, tapas-style fare alongside lovely wines and craft beer.

Staveley Store   CAFE
(☑03-303 0859; 2 Burgess Rd, Staveley; ⊙9am-4.30pm) Call into this cute little country store for a cheese roll, a sausage roll, a salad roll, ice cream or basic groceries. Also sells hut tickets for the Mt Somers track.

ℹ **Information**

Mt Somers General Store (☑03-303 9831; 61 Pattons Rd; ⊙8am-6pm) Hut tickets for the Mt Somers track, plus information.

SOUTH CANTERBURY

After crossing the Rangitata River into South Canterbury, SH1 and the Inland Scenic Route (SH72) narrow to within 8km of each other at the quaint town of Geraldine. Here you can choose to take the busy coastal highway through the port city of Timaru (and on to Oamaru and Dunedin), or continue inland on SH79 into Mackenzie Country, the expansive high ground from which NZ's tallest peaks rise above powder blue lakes. Most travellers pick the latter.

The Mackenzie Basin is a wild, tussock-strewn bowl at the foot of the Southern Alps, carved out by ancient glaciers. It takes its name from the legendary James 'Jock' McKenzie, who ran his stolen flocks in this then-uninhabited region in the 1840s. When he was finally caught, other settlers realised the potential for grazing in this seemingly inhospitable land and followed in his footsteps.

Director Sir Peter Jackson made the most of this rugged and untamed landscape while filming the *Lord of the Rings* films, choosing Mt Cook Village as the setting for Minas Tirith and a sheep station near Twizel as Gondor's Pelennor Fields.

ⓘ Getting There & Away

Atomic Shuttles (☏03-349 0697; www.atomictravel.co.nz) and **InterCity** (☏03-548 1538; www.intercity.co.nz) are the main transport players in South Canterbury, while **Cook Connection** (☏0800 266 526; www.cookconnect.co.nz) will get you up close to NZ's highest mountain.

Peel Forest

POP 180

Tucked away between the foothills of the Southern Alps and the Rangitata River (well signposted from SH72), Peel Forest is a small but important remnant of indigenous podocarp (conifer) forest. Many of the totara, kahikatea and matai trees here are hundreds of years old and are home to an abundance of birdlife including riflemen, kereru (wood pigeons), bellbirds, fantails and grey warblers.

A road from nearby Mt Peel sheep station leads to Mesopotamia, the run of English writer Samuel Butler in the 1860s. His experiences here partly inspired his famous satire *Erewhon* ('nowhere' backwards, almost; 1872).

◉ Sights

St Stephen's Church CHURCH
(1200 Peel Forest Rd) Sitting in a pretty glade right next to the general store, this gor-

geous little Anglican church (1885) has a warm wooden interior and some interesting stained glass. Look for St Francis of Assisi surrounded by NZ flora and fauna (get the kids to play spot-the-tuatara).

🏃 Activities

The magnificent podocarp forest consists of totara, kahikatea and matai. One fine example of totara on the **Big Tree Walk** (30 minutes return) is 31m tall, has a circumference of 9m and is over 1000 years old. There are also trails to **Emily Falls** (1½ hours return), **Rata Falls** (two hours return) and **Acland Falls** (one hour return); pick up the *Peel Forest Area* brochure from Peel Forest Store or download it from the DOC website (www.doc.govt.nz).

★ Rangitata Rafts RAFTING
(☏0800 251 251; www.rafts.co.nz; Rangitata Gorge Rd ⊙Sep-May) Three-hour trips start in the stupendously beautiful braided Rangitata River valley before heading on an exhilarating ride through the gorge's Grade V rapids ($210, minimum age 15). The gentler two-hour journey downstream encounters only Grade II rapids ($170, minimum age six).

Peel Forest Horse Trekking HORSE RIDING
(☏03-696 3703; www.peelforesthorsetrekking.co.nz; 1hr/2hr/half-day/full day $55/110/180/360) Ride through lush forest on short stints or multiday treks ($950 to $1600, minimum four people). Accommodation packages are available in conjunction with Peel Forest Lodge.

🛏 Sleeping & Eating

★ Peel Forest DOC Campsite CAMPGROUND $
(☏03-696 3567; www.peelforest.co.nz; sites per adult/child $17/7.50, cabins $50-80) Near the Rangitata River, around 3km beyond Peel Forest Store (p493), this lovely campground is equipped with basic two- to four-berth cabins (bring your own sleeping bag), hot showers and a kitchen. Check in at the store.

Peel Forest Lodge LODGE $$$
(☏03-696 3703; www.peelforestlodge.co.nz; 96 Brake Rd; d $330 additional adult/child $40/20; 🐾) This beautiful log cabin hidden in the forest has four rooms sleeping eight people. It only takes one booking at a time, so you and your posse will have the place to yourself. It's fully self-contained, but meals can be arranged, as can horse treks, rafting trips and other explorations of this fascinating area.

Peel Forest Store CAFE $$
(☏03-696 3567; www.peelforest.co.nz; 1202 Peel Forest Rd; lunch $13-19, dinner $20-29;

⊘ 9.30am-5.30pm Sun-Thu, to 9pm Fri & Sat; 🛜) Your one-stop-shop for groceries, hut tickets, internet access and DOC campsite (p493) bookings. The attached cafe-bar offers espresso and takeaways as well as burgers, pizza and suchlike to eat in.

❶ Getting There & Away

Atomic Shuttles (p497) and **InterCity** (p498) buses will get you as close as Geraldine, but you'll need your own transport or a lift to get to Peel Forest itself.

Timaru

POP 31,000

Trucking on along the SH1 through Timaru, travellers could be forgiven for thinking that this small port city is merely a handy place for food and fuel halfway between Christchurch and Dunedin. Drop the anchors, people! Straying into the CBD reveals a remarkably intact Edwardian precinct boasting some good dining and interesting shopping, not to mention a clutch of cultural attractions and lovely parks, all of which sustain at least a day's stopover.

The town's name comes from the Māori name Te Maru, meaning 'The Place of Shelter'. No permanent settlement existed here until 1839, when the Weller brothers set up a whaling station. The *Caroline,* a sailing ship that transported whale oil, gave the picturesque bay its name.

⊙ Sights

⭐ **Aigantighe Art Gallery**   GALLERY
(www.timaru.govt.nz/art-gallery; 49 Wai-iti Rd; ⊘ 10am-4pm Tue-Fri, noon-4pm Sat & Sun) FREE One of the South Island's largest public galleries, this 1908 mansion houses a notable collection of NZ and European art across various eras, alongside changing exhibitions staged by the gallery's ardent supporters. The Gaelic name means 'at home' and is pronounced 'egg-and-tie'. Should the gallery be closed, take a wander in the sculpture garden.

Caroline Bay Park   PARK, BEACH
(Marine Pde) Fronting the town, this expansive park ranges over an Edwardian-style garden under the Bay Hill cliff, then across broad lawns to low sand dunes and the beach itself. It has something for everyone between its playground, skate park, soundshell, ice cream kiosk, and myriad other attractions. Don't miss the Trevor Griffiths Rose Garden, a triumphant collection of heritage varieties, and consider an evening picnic making the most of the late sun. If you're lucky enough

to spot a seal or penguin on the beach, do keep your distance.

Te Ana Māori Rock Art Centre   MUSEUM
(📞 03-684 9141; www.teana.co.nz; 2 George St; adult/child admission \$22/11, tours \$130/65; ⊘ 10am-3pm) Passionate Ngāi Tahu guides bring this innovative multimedia exhibition about Māori rock paintings to life. You can also take a three-hour excursion (departing 2pm, November to April) to see isolated rock art in situ; prior booking is essential.

South Canterbury Museum   MUSEUM
(www.timaru.govt.nz/museum; Perth St; admission by donation; ⊘ 10am-4.30pm Tue-Fri, 1.30-4.30pm Sat & Sun) Historic and natural artefacts of the region are displayed here. Highlights include the Māori section and a replica of the aeroplane designed and flown by local pioneer aviator and inventor Richard Pearse. It's speculated that his mildly successful attempts at flight came before the Wright brothers' famous achievement in 1903.

Sacred Heart Basilica   CHURCH
(7 Craigie Ave, Parkside) Roman Catholic with a definite emphasis on the Roman, this beautiful neoclassical church (1911) impresses with multiple domes, Ionian columns and richly coloured stained glass. Its architect, Francis Petre, also designed the large basilicas in Christchurch (now in ruins) and Oamaru. Inside, there's an art-nouveau feel to the plasterwork, which includes intertwined floral and sacred-heart motifs. There are no set opening hours; try the side door.

Timaru Botanic Gardens   GARDENS
(cnr King & Queen Sts; ⊘ 8am-dusk) FREE Established in 1864, these gardens are a restful place to while away an hour or two, with a pond, lush lawns, shady trees, a playground and vibrant plant collections. With luck you'll arrive during rhododendron or rose bloom-time. Enter from Queen St, south of the city centre.

Trevor Griffiths Rose Garden   GARDENS
(Caroline Bay Park, Marine Pde) FREE Rose fans should visit the Trevor Griffiths Rose Garden, with almost 1200 romantic blooms set around arbours and water features. The finest displays are from December to February. It's a fragrant place to sit and contemplate on a balmy afternoon.

🎉 Festivals & Events

Timaru Festival of Roses   CULTURAL
(www.festivalofroses.co.nz; ⊘ Nov) Featuring a market day, concerts and family fun, this week-long celebration capitalises on Tima-

Timaru

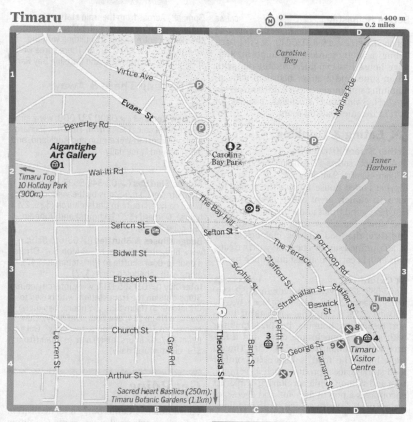

ru's obsession with all things rose-y. The festival is held annually for one week at the end of November.

🛏 Sleeping

Timaru Top 10 Holiday Park HOLIDAY PARK **$**
(☑ 03-684 7690; www.timaruholidaypark.co.nz; 154a Selwyn St, Marchwiel; sites $39-44, units with/without bathroom from $97/65; 🛜) 🅿 Tucked away in the suburbs, this excellent holiday park has clean, colourful amenities and a host of accommodation options throughout mature, leafy grounds. Helpful staff go out of their way to assist with local advice and bookings.

Glendeer Lodge B&B **$$**
(☑ 03-686 9274; www.glendeer.co.nz; 51 Scarborough Rd, Scarborough; d $170-260; 🛜) 🅿 Set on five acres, 4km from downtown, this purpose-built lodge is a peaceful option away from busy SH1. Walk to the lighthouse, relax in the garden watching fallow deer nibbling the paddock, then retire to the plush,

Timaru

self-contained lodge offering three en suite rooms. The owners' fly-fishing guiding business lends a wilderness vibe.

Sefton Homestay
B&B $$

(☑03-688 0017; www.seftonhomestay.co.nz; 32 Sefton St, Seaview; s & d $130-140; 🐾) Set back behind a pretty garden, this imposing heritage house has two guest rooms: one with an en suite, and a larger bedroom with an adjoining sun lounge and a bathroom across the hall. Swap travel stories over a glass of port in the guest sitting room.

✖ Eating & Drinking

Arthur Street Kitchen
CAFE $

(8 Arthur St; snacks $2-8, mains $9-19; ⏱7am-5.30pm Mon-Fri, 9am-3pm Sat; 🖋) Timaru's hippest coffee house follows the recipe for success: namely great coffee, contemporary cafe fare, good tunes and a mix of arty inside and sunny outside seating. Made with flair and care, the food offering includes grainy salads, refined sandwiches and pastry treats, plus an à la carte breakfast and lunch menu.

★ Oxford
MODERN NZ $$

(☑03-688 3297; www.theoxford.co.nz; 152 Stafford St; mains $26-32; ⏱11am-late Mon & Wed-Fri, 9.30am-late Sat & Sun) This sophisticated corner restaurant honours its 1925 building with stylish monochrome decor and a feature wall commemorating the day Timaru went bust. The food is high-class comfort food starring local produce such as venison, beef and salmon, while an alluring drinks list encourages a pop in for wine and cheese, or a glass of sticky with golden syrup pudding.

Koji
JAPANESE $$

(☑03-686 9166; 7 George St; snacks $5-15, mains $23-36; ⏱11am-2pm & 5-9pm Tue-Fri, 5pm-10pm Sat & Sun) Unassuming it may be from the exterior, but this split-level restaurant makes a jolly good job of creating a Japanese vibe. Sit in the downstairs dining room or at the cute bar, or better still head up to the upper level and watch flames rise from the teppanyaki grill. Delicious dishes include sashimi, tempura, gyoza and *takoyaki* complete with dancing bonito flakes.

Speight's Ale House
PUB

(www.timarualehouse.co.nz; 2 George St; ⏱11.30am-late; 🐾) The pub most likely to be registering a pulse of an evening, this enterprise redeems its dubious decor and over-branding with a sunny courtyard and the historic features of the 1870s stone warehouse it occupies.

ℹ Information

Timaru Visitor Centre (☑03-687 9997; www. southcanterbury.org.nz; 2 George St; ⏱10am-3pm; 🐾) Across from the train station (trains in this area only carry freight, not passengers), the visitor centre shares its building with the Te Ana Māori Rock Art Centre. There's free wi-fi throughout Timaru's CBD and Caroline Bay Park.

ℹ Getting There & Away

AIR

Air New Zealand (☑0800 737 000; www.air newzealand.co.nz) Flies from Timaru's Richard Pearse Airport to Wellington and Auckland, and back, around twice daily.

BUS

Atomic Shuttles (☑03-349 0697; www. atomictravel.co.nz) Stops by the visitor centre twice daily, en route to Christchurch ($25, 2½ hours), Oamaru ($20,1¼ hours) and Dunedin ($25, 2¾ hours).

Budget Buses & Shuttles (☑03-615 5119; www.budgetshuttles.co.nz; ⏱Mon-Sat) Offers a door-to-door shuttle to Christchurch ($47), along with scheduled runs ($27).

InterCity (☑03-365 1113; www.intercity.co.nz) Stops outside the train station, with buses to Christchurch (from $28, 2½ hours, two daily), Oamaru (from $14, one hour, two daily), Dunedin (from $32, three hours, two daily), Gore (from $47, six hours, daily) and Te Anau (from $51, eight hours, daily).

Geraldine

POP 2420

Consummately Canterbury in its dedication to English-style gardening, pretty Geraldine has a village vibe and an active arts scene. In spring, duck behind the war memorial on Talbot St to the River Garden Walk, where green-fingered locals have gone completely bonkers planting azaleas and rhododendrons. Ask visitor centre staff about the trails in Talbot Forest on the town fringe.

◉ Sights & Activities

Geraldine Museum
MUSEUM

(5 Cox St; ⏱10am-3pm Mon-Sat, 12.30-3pm Sun) FREE Occupying the photogenic Town Board Office building (1885), and sporting a new side wing, this cute little museum tells the town's story with an eclectic mix of exhibits, including an extensive collection of photographs.

Vintage Car & Machinery Museum
MUSEUM

(☑03-693 8756; 178 Talbot St; adult/child $10/ free; ⏱9.30am-4pm Oct-May, 10am-4pm Sat & Sun Jun-Sep) You don't have to be a rev-head to enjoy this vintage car collection featuring a 1907 De Dion-Bouton and a gleaming 1926

Bentley. There's also a purpose-built Daimler used for the 1954 royal tour, plus some very nice Jags, 1970s muscle cars and all sorts of farm machinery.

Big Rock Canyons ADVENTURE SPORTS
(☑0800 244 762; www.bigrockcanyons.co.nz ☺Oct-Apr) Offers slippy, slidey day-long adventures in the Kaumira Canyon ($360) near Geraldine, as well as in five other canyons with varying degrees of difficulty.

🛏 Sleeping

Rawhiti Backpackers HOSTEL $
(☑03-693 8252; www.rawhitibackpackers.co.nz; 27 Hewlings St; dm/s/d $34/50/78; ☎) On a hillside on the edge of town, this former maternity hospital is now a sunny and spacious hostel with good communal areas, comfortable rooms, a lemon tree and two cute cats. Bikes are available to borrow.

**Geraldine Kiwi
Holiday Park** HOLIDAY PARK, MOTEL $
(☑03-693 8147; www.geraldineholidaypark.co.nz; 39 Hislop St; sites $34-39, d $52-135; @☎) 🐾
This top-notch holiday park is set amid well-established parkland, two minutes' walk from the high street. Tidy accommodation ranges from budget cabins to plusher motel units, plus there's a TV room and playground.

Scenic Route Motor Lodge MOTEL $$
(☑03-693 9700; www.motelsceniroute.co.nz; 28 Waihi Tce; d $135-155; ☎) There's a vaguely heritage feel to this stone and timber motel, but the modern units have double-glazing, flat-screen TVs and even stylish wallpaper. Larger studios have spa baths.

🍴 Eating

Long overdue to be lauded 'Cheese & Pickle Capital of NZ', Geraldine is excellent for self-caterers. It boasts a terrific butchery and numerous artisan producers in the Four Peaks Plaza; seek out a bag of Heartland potato chips here, made down the road. Every Saturday during summer the town kicks into foodie gear with a **farmers' market** (St Mary's Church car park; ☺9am-12.30pm Sat Oct-Apr) 🐾.

★Talbot Forest Cheese DELI $
(www.talbotforestcheese.co.nz; Four Peaks Plaza, Talbot Rd; cheeses $5-10; ☺9am-5pm; 🐾) This little shop not only showcases the cheeses made on-site (including fine Parmesan and Gruyère), it doubles as a deli with all you need for a tasty picnic.

MACKENZIE COUNTRY

Heading to Queenstown and the southern lakes from Christchurch means a turn off SH1 onto SH79, a scenic route towards the high country and the Aoraki/Mt Cook National Park's eastern foothills. The road passes through Geraldine and Fairlie before joining SH8, which heads over Burkes Pass to the blue intensity of Lake Tekapo.

The expansive high ground from which the scenic peaks of Aoraki/Mt Cook National Park escalate is known as Mackenzie Country, after the legendary James 'Jock' McKenzie, who ran his stolen flocks in this then-uninhabited region in the 1840s. When he was finally caught, other settlers realised the potential of the land and followed in his footsteps. The first people to traverse the Mackenzie were the Māori, trekking from Banks Peninsula to Otago hundreds of years ago.

Verde CAFE $
(☑03-693 9616; 45 Talbot St; mains $11-18; ☺9am-4pm; 🐾) Down the lane beside the old post office and set in beautiful gardens, this excellent cafe is easily the best of Geraldine's eateries. It's just a shame that it's not open for dinner.

☆ Entertainment

Geraldine Cinema CINEMA
(☑03-693 8118; www.geraldinecinema.co.nz; Talbot St; adult/child $12/8) Snuggle into an old sofa to watch a Hollywood favourite or an art-house surprise. There's also occasional live music, usually with a folk, blues or country spin.

ℹ Information

Geraldine Visitor Information Centre (☑03-693 1101; www.southcanterbury.org.nz; 38 Waihi Tce; ☺8am-5.30pm) The information centre is located inside the Kiwi Country visitor complex. See also www.gogeraldine.co.nz.

ℹ Getting There & Away

Atomic Shuttles (☑03-349 0697; www.atomictravel.co.nz) Daily buses to/from Christchurch ($30, two hours), Lake Tekapo (from $20, 1¼ hours), Twizel ($30, two hours), Cromwell (from $30, 4¼ hours) and Queenstown ($35, five hours).

Budget Buses & Shuttles (☑03-615 5119; www.budgetshuttles.co.nz; ☺Mon-Sat) Offers a door-to-door shuttle to Christchurch ($57), along with a cheaper scheduled run ($47).

InterCity (☑ 03-365 1113; www.intercity.co.nz) Daily coaches head to/from Christchurch (from $32, 2¼ hours), Lake Tekapo (from $21, 1¼ hours), Cromwell (from $40, 4¾ hours) and Queenstown (from $42, 5¾ hours).

Fairlie

POP 693

Leafy Fairlie describes itself as 'the gateway to the Mackenzie', but in reality this wee, rural town feels a world away from tussocky Mackenzie Country over Burkes Pass, to the west. The bakery and picnic area make it a good lunchtime stop.

◎ Sights

Fairlie Heritage Museum   MUSEUM
(www.fairlieheritagemuseum.co.nz; 49 Mt Cook Rd; adult/child $6/free; ⊙ 9.30am-5pm) A somewhat dusty window on to rural NZ of old, this museum endears with its farm machinery, model aeroplanes, dodgy dioramas and the generally random. Highlights include the home-spun gyrocopter, historic cottage, and new automotive wing featuring mint-condition tractors. The little cafe attached bakes a good biscuit.

✻ Activities

The information centre can provide information on nearby **tramping and mountain biking** tracks. The main ski resort, **Mt Dobson** (☑ 03-685 8039; www.mtdobson.co.nz; daily lift passes adult/child $78/44), lies in a 3km-wide treeless basin 26km northwest of Fairlie. There's also a club ski field 29km northwest at **Fox Peak** (☑ 03-685 8539, snow-phone 03-688 0044; www.foxpeak.co.nz; daily lift passes adult/child $60/10) in the Two Thumb Range.

⛏ Sleeping & Eating

Musterer's   MOTEL $$
(☑ 03-685 8284; www.musterers.co.nz; 9 Gordon St; d $150, extra adult/child $25/15; ⊛) On the western edge of Fairlie, these stylish self-contained cottages afford all mod cons with the bonus of a shared barbecue area and woolshed 'lounge', plus donkeys, goats and a pony. Plush, with tiled bathrooms, the three family units (sleeping up to six) and one double studio each have their own wood-fired hot tub ($40 extra) for a stargazing soak.

★**Fairlie Bakehouse**   BAKERY $
(www.liebers.co.nz; 74 Main St; pies $5-7; ⊙ 7.30am-4.30pm; ☑) Famous for miles around and probably the top-ranking reason to stop in

Fairlie, this terrific little bakery turns out exceptional pies including the legendary salmon and bacon. American doughnuts and raspberry cheesecake elbow their way in among Kiwi classics such as custard squares and cream buns. Yum.

ⓘ Information

Fairlie Heartland Resource & Information Centre (☑ 03-685 8496; www.fairlienz.com; 67 Main St; ⊙ 10am-4pm Mon-Fri) This helpful centre stocks the well-produced *Fairlie* brochure (free).

ⓘ Getting There & Away

Atomic Shuttles (☑ 03-349 0697; www.atomictravel.co.nz) Daily buses to/from Christchurch ($30, 2½ hours), Geraldine ($20, 35 minutes), Lake Tekapo ($20, 40 minutes), Cromwell ($35, 3¾ hours) and Queenstown ($35, 4½ hours).
InterCity (☑ 03-365 1113; www.intercity.co.nz) Daily coaches head to/from Christchurch (from $34, 3¼ hours), Lake Tekapo (from $13, 35 minutes), Mt Cook (from $30, 2½ hours), Cromwell (from $39, four hours) and Queenstown (from $40, five hours).

Lake Tekapo

POP 369

Born of a hydropower scheme completed in 1953, today Tekapo is booming off the back of a holiday home explosion and tourism, although it has long been a popular tour-bus stop on the route between Christchurch and Queenstown. Its popularity is well deserved: the town faces out across the turquoise lake to a backdrop of snow-capped mountains.

Such splendid Mackenzie Country and Southern Alps views are reason enough to linger, but there's infinitely more to see if you wait till dark. In 2012 the Aoraki Mackenzie area was declared an International Dark Sky Reserve, one of only ten in the world, and Tekapo's Mt John – under pollution-free skies – is the ultimate place to experience the region's glorious night sky.

◎ Sights

Church of the Good Shepherd   CHURCH
(Pioneer Dr; ⊙ 9am-5pm) The prime disgorging point for tour buses, this interdenominational lakeside church was built of stone and oak in 1935. A picture window behind the altar gives churchgoers a distractingly divine view of lake and mountain majesty; needless to say, it's a firm favourite for weddings. Come early in the morning or late afternoon to avoid the peace-shattering masses.

Nearby is a statue of a collie, a tribute to the sheepdogs that helped develop Mackenzie Country.

🏃 Activities

When the Mackenzie Basin was scoured out by glaciers, **Mt John** (1029m) remained as an island of tough bedrock in the centre of a vast river of ice. A road leads to the summit, or you can walk via a circuit track (2½ hours return). To extend it to an all-day tramp, continue on to Alexandrina and McGregor Lakes.

The free town map details this and other walks in the area, along with cycling tracks including **Cowan's Hill** and those in **Lake Tekapo Regional Park**. Mountain bikes (per hour/half-day $10/25) and kayaks (per hour $25) can be hired from the Lake Tekapo YHA (p500).

In winter, Lake Tekapo is a base for downhill skiing at Mt Dobson (p498) and **Roundhill** (📞021 680 694, snow-phone 03-680 6977; www.roundhill.co.nz; daily lift passes adult/child $78/39), and cross-country skiing on the Two Thumb Range.

Mackenzie Alpine Horse Trekking   HORSE RIDING
(📞0800 628 269; www.maht.co.nz; Godley Peaks Rd; 1hr/2hr/day $70/110/310) Located on the road to Mt John, these folks run various treks taking in the area's amazing scenery.

Tekapo Springs   SPA
(📞03-680 6550; www.tekaposprings.co.nz; 6 Lakeside Dr; adult/child pools $22/13, ice-skating $16/12; ⏰10am-9pm) Turn up the heat from the 36°C pool, to the 38°C and 40°C pools, soaking in the thermal goodness in landscaped surrounds overlooking the lake. There's a steam room and sauna ($6 extra), along with a day spa offering various indulgences including massage (from $80). Cold pools and an 'aqua play' park were under development on our last visit.

Attached to the complex is a winter ice-skating rink and snow-tubing slide, while in summer there's the world's largest inflatable slide and slippery-slope tubing.

👉 Tours

Earth & Sky   TOUR
(📞03-680 6960; www.earthandsky.co.nz; SH8) 🚩 If you've ever wanted to tour an observatory and survey the night sky, this is the place to do it. Nightly tours head up to the University of Canterbury's observatory on Mt John (adult/child $145/80). Day tours of the facility are given on demand in winter, while in summer there's usually a guide available at

LAKE PUKAKI LOOKOUT

The largest of the Mackenzie's three alpine lakes, Pukaki is a vast jewel of totally surreal colour. On its shore, just off SH8 between Twizel and Lake Tekapo, is a well-signed and perennially popular lookout affording picture-perfect views across the lake's waters all the way up to Aoraki/Mt Cook and its surrounding peaks.

Beside the lookout, the **Lake Pukaki Visitor Centre** (www.mtcookalpinesalmon.com; SH8; ⏰8.30am-6pm) is actually an outpost of Mt Cook Alpine Salmon, the highest salmon farm on the planet, which operates in a hydroelectric canal system some distance away. The visitor centre offers the opportunity to pick up some sashimi ($10) or a smoked morsel for supper.

the observatory from around midday to 3pm (adult/child $20/10).

For those on a tighter budget or with small children in tow (the minimum age for Mt John tours is eight), there are hour-long night tours to the smaller Cowan Observatory (adult/child $90/50).

Air Safaris   SCENIC FLIGHTS
(📞03-680 6880; www.airsafaris.co.nz; SH8) Awe-inspiring views of Aoraki/Mt Cook National Park's peaks and glaciers are offered on the 'Grand Traverse' fixed-wing flight (adult/child $360/230), and there are various other options including similar trips in a helicopter.

Tekapo Helicopters   SCENIC FLIGHTS
(📞03-680 6229; www.tekapohelicopters.co.nz; SH8) Offers five options, from a 20-minute flight ($199) to an hour-long trip taking in Aoraki/Mt Cook, and Fox and Franz Josef Glaciers ($500). All flights include an alpine landing.

🛏 Sleeping

Tailor-Made-Tekapo Backpackers   HOSTEL $
(📞03-680 6700; www.tailor-made-backpackers.co.nz; 11 Aorangi Cres; dm/s $32/62, d with/without bathroom $95/85; 📶) Favouring beds rather than bunks, this sociable hostel is spread over three well-tended houses on a peaceful street 300m from town. There's also a large garden complete with barbecue, hammock, chickens and bunnies, plus tennis and basketball courts next door for the energetic.

Tekapo Motels & Holiday Park
HOLIDAY PARK, MOTEL **$**

(☑03-680 6825; www.laketekapo-accommodation.co.nz; 2 Lakeside Dr; sites $34-44, dm $30-32, d $90-110; ☜) Supremely situated on terraced, lakefront grounds, this place has something for everyone. Backpackers get the cosy, log-cabin-style lodge, while others can enjoy cute Kiwi 'bachs', basic cabins, and smart en suite units with particularly good views. Camper-vaners and tenters are spoilt for choice, and share the fantastic new amenities block.

YHA Lake Tekapo
HOSTEL **$**

(☑03-680 6857; www.yha.co.nz; 3 Simpson Lane; sites per person $20, dm $33-38, d $99-104; @☜) ✎ Older-style, tidy, and well-maintained hostel with million-dollar views of Lake Tekapo. Snuggle around the fire in winter, or chill out by the lake in summer. Make the most of the local cycle trails with bikes for hire.

★ Lake Tekapo Lodge
B&B **$$$**

(☑03-680 6566; www.laketekapolodge.co.nz; 24 Aorangi Cres; r $300-450; ☜) This fabulously designed, luxurious B&B is filled to the brim with covetable contemporary Kiwi art, and boasts painterly views of the lake and mountains from the sumptuous rooms and lounge. Fine-dining evening meals by arrangement.

Chalet Boutique Motel
APARTMENTS **$$$**

(☑03-680 6774; www.thechalet.co.nz; 14 Pioneer Dr; units $190-310; ☜) The 'boutique motel' tag doesn't do justice to this collection of attractive accommodation options in three adjacent properties beside the lake. The wonderfully private 'Henkel hut' is a stylish option for lovebirds. Charming hosts will happily provide all the local information you need.

✖ Eating & Drinking

★ Astro Café
CAFE **$**

(Mt John University Observatory; mains $7-12; ☺9am-5pm) This glass-walled pavilion atop Mt John has spectacular 360-degree views across the entire Mackenzie Basin – quite possibly one of the planet's best locations for a cafe. Tuck into bagels with local salmon, or fresh ham-off-the-bone sandwiches; the coffee and cake are good, too.

Kohan
JAPANESE **$$**

(☑03-680 6688; www.kohannz.com; SH8; dishes $8-20, mains $19-30; ☺11am-2pm daily, 6-9pm Mon-Sat) With all the aesthetic charm of an office cafeteria, this is still one of Tekapo's best dining options, both for its distracting lake views, and its authentic Japanese food including fresh-as-a-daisy salmon sashimi. Leave room for the handmade green-tea ice cream.

Mackenzie's Bar & Grill
BAR

(SH8; ☺11.30am-late Mon-Fri, 10am-late Sat & Sun) While full immersion on the menu front is not necessarily advisable, this tidy gastro-pub-style establishment is a safe bet for a few cold ones and some bar snacks. The views are grand, particularly outside from the patio and garden in front.

❶ Information

Kiwi Treasures & Information Centre (☑03-680 6686; SH8; ☺8am-5.30pm Mon-Fri, to 6pm Sat & Sun) This little gift shop doubles as the post office and info centre with local maps and advice, plus bookings for local activities and national bus services. See also www.tekapotourism.co.nz.

❶ Getting There & Away

Atomic Shuttles (☑03-349 0697; www.atomictravel.co.nz) Daily buses to/from Christchurch ($30, 3¼ hours), Geraldine ($20, 1¼ hours), Twizel ($20, 40 minutes), Cromwell ($30, three hours) and Queenstown ($30, 3¾ hours).

Cook Connection (☑0800 266 526; www.cookconnect.co.nz) Shuttle service to Mt Cook ($35, 1½ hours).

InterCity (☑03-365 1113; www.intercity.co.nz) Daily coaches head to/from Christchurch (from $36, 3¾ hours), Geraldine (from $21, 1¼ hours), Mt Cook (from $30, 1½ hours), Cromwell (from $36, 2¾ hours) and Queenstown (from $36, 4¾ hours).

Twizel
POP 1300

Pronounced 'twy-zel' but teased with 'Twizzel' and even 'Twizzelsticks' by outsiders, Twizel gets the last laugh. The town was built in 1968 to service construction of the nearby hydro-electric power station, and was due for obliteration in 1984 when the project was completed. But there was no way the locals were upping their twizzlesticks and relinquishing their relaxed, mountain country lifestyle.

Today the town is thriving with a modest boom in holiday home subdivisions and recognition from travellers that – as plain-Jane as it is – it's actually in the middle of everything and has almost everything one might need (within reason).

✦ Activities

Twizel sits in the midst of some spectacular country offering all sorts of adventure. On

DON'T MISS

ALPS 2 OCEAN CYCLE TRAIL

One of the best Great Rides within the New Zealand Cycle Trail (www.nzcycletrail.com), the 'A2O' serves up epic vistas on its way from the foot of the Southern Alps all the way to the Pacific Ocean at Oamaru.

New Zealand's highest mountain – Aoraki/Mt Cook – is just one of many stunning sights. Others include braided rivers, glacier-carved valleys, turquoise hydro-lakes, tussock-covered highlands and lush farmland. Off-the-bike activities include wine tasting, penguin spotting, glider flights and soaking in alfresco hot tubs. Country hospitality, including food and accommodation, along with shuttles and other services, make the whole trip easy to organise and enjoy.

The trail is divided into nine easy-to-intermediate sections across terrain varying from canal paths, quiet country roads, old railway lines and expertly cut cross-country track, to some rougher, hilly stuff for the eager. The whole journey takes around four to six days, but it can easily be sliced into short sections.

Twizel is an excellent base for day rides. Options include taking a shuttle to Lake Tekapo for a five- to six-hour, big-sky ride back to Twizel, or riding from Twizel out to Lake Ohau Lodge for lunch or dinner. Both rides, sections of the Alps 2 Ocean, serve up the sublime lake and mountain scenery for which the Mackenzie is famous.

The trail is well supported by tour companies offering bike hire, shuttles, luggage transfers and accommodation. These include Twizel-based **Cycle Journeys** (☑ 03-435 0578, 0800 224 475; www.cyclejourneys.co.nz; 2a Wairepo Rd) and **Jollie Biker** (☑ 027 223 1761, 03-435 0517; www.thejolliebiker.co.nz; 193 Glen Lyon Rd). The Alps 2 Ocean website (www.alps2ocean.com) has comprehensive details.

the edge of town, **Lake Ruataniwha** is popular for rowing, boating and windsurfing. Pick up the excellent town map to find it, along with walking and cycle trails including a nice ramble along the river. Twizel is also the best hub for day rides on the Alps 2 Ocean Cycle Trail.

Fishing in local rivers, canals and lakes is also big business; ask at the information centre about local guides, and ask them about swimming in **Loch Cameron** while you're at it (but don't tell them we tipped you off).

Ohau   SKIING, SNOWBOARDING
(☑ 03-438 9885; www.ohau.co.nz; daily lift passes adult/child $83/34) This commercial ski area lines the flanks of Mt Sutton, 42km from Twizel. Expect a high percentage of intermediate and advanced runs, excellent terrain for snowboarding, two terrain parks, and Lake Ohau Lodge for après-ski.

☞ Tours

Helicopter Line   SCENIC FLIGHTS
(☑ 03-435 0370; www.helicopter.co.nz; Pukaki Airport, Harry Wigley Dr) Flight options include the hour-long Aoraki/Mt Cook Discovery ($750), the 45-minute Southern Alps Experience ($540), the 35-minute Alpine Scenic Flight ($355) and the 25-minute Alpine Express ($295). All but the shortest guarantee snow landings.

OneRing Tours   TOUR
(☑ 03-435 0073, 0800 213 868; www.lordoftheringstour.com; cnr Ostler & Wairepo Sts) How often do you get the opportunity to charge around like a mad thing wielding replica *LOTR* gear? Not often enough! Tours head onto the sheep station used for the location of the Battle of the Pelennor Fields and include lots of information about the filming. Choose between a two-hour version (adult/child $84/45) and a truncated one-hour option (adult/child $64/35).

There's also an adults-only twilight tour; enjoy beer, wine and nibbles as the sun sets over Gondor ($115).

🛏 Sleeping

Twizel Holiday Park   HOLIDAY PARK $
(☑ 03-435 0507; www.twizelholidaypark.co.nz; 122 Mackenzie Dr; sites from $36, dm $32, units $95-215; 🛜) Offers green, flower-filled grounds, and accommodation in a refurbished maternity hospital. There are a few en suite cabins and a bunk room along with grassed sites and tight communal facilities. The modern, self-contained cottages are particularly good value. Bike hire is available for $35 per day.

★ Lake Ohau Lodge   LODGE $$
(☑ 03-438 9885; www.ohau.co.nz; Lake Ohau Rd; s $144-200, d $159-220 🌿) Idyllically sited

RUATANIWHA CONSERVATION PARK

Taking in a large chunk of the space between Lake Pukaki and Lake Ohau, the 368-sq-km protected area of **Ruataniwha Conservation Park** (www.doc.govt.nz) includes the rugged Ben Ohau Range along with the Dobson, Hopkins, Huxley, Temple and Maitland valleys. It offers plenty of tramping and mountain-biking opportunities, as detailed in DOC's *Ruataniwha Conservation Park* pamphlet (available online), with several day options close to Twizel.

DOC huts and camping areas are scattered throughout the park, and a more comfortable stay is available at Lake Ohau Lodge (p501). Passing through these parts is the Alps 2 Ocean Cycle Trail (p501), a great way to survey these grand surroundings.

on the western shore of remote Lake Ohau, 42km west of Twizel. Accommodation includes everything from budget rooms with shared facilities to upmarket rooms with decks and mountain views.

The lodge is the buzzy wintertime hub of the Ohau Ski Field; in summer it's a quieter retreat. DB&B packages are available.

Omahau Downs   LODGE, COTTAGE **$$**
(☑ 03-435 0199; www.omahau.co.nz; SH8; s $115, d $135-165, cottages $125-225; ⊙ closed Jun-Aug; 🅿) This farmstead, 2km north of Twizel, has two cosy, self-contained cottages (one sleeping up to six), and a lodge with sparkling, modern rooms and a deck looking out at the Ben Ohau Range.

Heartland Lodge   B&B, APARTMENT **$$$**
(☑ 03-435 0008; www.heartland-lodge.co.nz; 19 North West Arch; apt $170, s $240-280, d $280-320; 🅿) Built on the leafy outskirts of town, this elegant modern house offers spacious, en suite rooms upstairs and comfortable, convivial communal space on the ground floor. Friendly hosts prepare a cooked breakfast using organic, local produce where possible. The adjacent 'retreat' apartment (sleeping up to six) has its own kitchenette; breakfast not provided.

✗ Eating

★ Shawty's   CAFE **$$**
(☑ 03-435 3155; www.shawtys.co.nz; 4 Market Pl; brunch $12-20, dinner $29-34; ⊙ 8.30am-3pm Mon & Tue, to late Wed-Sun Apr-Oct, to late daily Nov-Mar; 🅿 🅿) The town centre's social hub and hottest meal ticket serves up big breakfasts, gourmet pizzas ($18 to $20) and fancy lamb racks as the sun goes down. A considerate kids' menu, cocktails, alfresco dining and live music make it all the more endearing.

High Country Salmon   FISH **$$**
(☑ 0800 400 385; www.highcountrysalmonfarm.co.nz; SH8; ⊙ 8.30am-6pm) The glacial waters of this floating fish farm, 3km from Twizel, produce mighty delicious fish, available as fresh whole fillets and smoked portions. Our pick is the hot-smoked, flaked into hot pasta, perhaps with a dash of cream. (The Lonely Planet Cookbook, coming to a bookshop near you...)

ℹ Information

Twizel Information Centre (☑ 03-435 3124; www.twizel.info; Market Pl; ⊙ 8.30am-5pm Mon-Fri, 11am-3pm Sat & Sun)

ℹ Getting There & Away

Atomic Shuttles (☑ 03-349 0697; www.atomictravel.co.nz) Runs daily services to the following:

DESTINATION	FARE	DURATION
Christchurch	$35	3¾hr
Cromwell	$30	2¼hr
Geraldine	$25	2hr
Lake Tekapo	$20	40min
Queenstown	$30	3¼hr

Cook Connection (☑ 0800 266 526; www.cookconnect.co.nz) runs daily shuttle services to Mt Cook Village (one way/return $27/49, one hour).

InterCity (☑ 03-365 1113; www.intercity.co.nz) Runs daily services to the following:

DESTINATION	FARES FROM	DURATION
Christchurch	$40	5¼hr
Cromwell	$29	2hr
Lake Tekapo	$13	50mins
Mt Cook Village	$32	1hr
Queenstown	$35	3hr

Naked Bus (www.nakedbus.com) services Christchurch and Queenstown/Wanaka.

Aoraki/Mt Cook National Park

POP 120

The spectacular 700-sq-km Aoraki/Mt Cook National Park, along with Fiordland, Aspiring and Westland National Parks, is part of the Southwest New Zealand (Te Wahipounamu) World Heritage Area, which extends from Westland's Cook River down to Fiordland. Fenced in by the Southern Alps and the Two Thumb, Liebig and Ben Ohau Ranges, more than one-third of the park has a blanket of permanent snow and glacial ice.

Of the 23 NZ mountains over 3000m, 19 are in this park. The highest is mighty Aoraki/Mt Cook – at 3754m it's the tallest peak in Australasia. Among the region's other many great peaks are Sefton, Tasman, Silberhorn, Malte Brun, La Perouse, Hicks, De la Beche, Douglas and the Minarets. Many can be ascended from Westland National Park, and there are climbers' huts on both sides of the divide.

Aoraki/Mt Cook is a wonderful sight, assuming there's no cloud in the way. Most visitors arrive on tour buses, stop at the Hermitage hotel for photos, and then zoom off back down SH80. Hang around to soak up this awesome peak and the surrounding landscape, and to try the excellent short walks. On the trails, look for the thar, a Himalayan goat; the chamois, smaller and of lighter build than the thar, and originally hailing from Europe; and red deer, also European. Summertime brings into bloom the Mt Cook lily, a large mountain buttercup, and mountain daisies, gentians and edelweiss.

History

Known to Māori as Aoraki (Cloud Piercer), after an ancestral deity in Māori mythology the mountain was given its English name in 1851, in honour of explorer Captain James Cook.

This region has always been the focus of climbing in NZ. On 2 March 1882 William Spotswood Green and two Swiss alpinists failed to reach the summit of Cook after an epic 62-hour ascent. Two years later a trio of local climbers – Tom Fyfe, George Graham and Jack Clarke – were spurred into action by the news that two well-known European alpinists were coming to attempt Cook, and set off to climb it before the visitors. On Christmas Day 1894 they ascended the Hooker Glacier and north ridge, a brilliant climb in those days, and stood on the summit.

In 1913 Australian climber Freda du Faur became the first woman to reach the summit. In 1948 Edmund Hillary's party climbed the south ridge; Hillary went on to become the first to reach the summit of Mt Everest. Since then, most of the daunting face routes have been climbed.

⊙ Sights

★ **Aoraki/Mt Cook National Park Visitor Centre** MUSEUM
(☏ 03-435 1186; www.doc.govt.nz; 1 Larch Grove; ⊗ 8.30am-4.30pm, to 5pm Oct-Apr) FREE Arguably the best DOC visitor centre in NZ. It not only dispatches all necessary information and advice on tramping routes and weather conditions, it also houses excellent displays on the park's natural and human history. It's a fabulous place to commune with the wilderness, even on a rainy day. Most activities can be booked here.

Sir Edmund Hillary Alpine Centre MUSEUM
(www.hermitage.co.nz; The Hermitage, Terrace Rd; adult/child $20/10; ⊗ 7am-8.30pm Oct-Mar, 8am-7pm Apr-Sep) This multimedia museum opened just three weeks before the January 2008 death of the man widely regarded as the greatest New Zealander of all time. Sir Ed's commentary tracks were recorded only a few months before he died. As well as memorabilia and displays about mountaineering, there's a domed digital planetarium (showing four different digital presentations) and a cinema (screening four documentaries, including the *Mt Cook Magic* 3D movie and a fascinating 75-minute film about Sir Ed's conquest of Mt Everest).

🏃 Activities

Tramping & Climbing

Various easy walks from the Hermitage area are outlined in the (multilingual) *Walking & Cycling Tracks* pamphlet available from the visitor centre (p503) and online. Longer tramps are only recommended for those with mountaineering experience, as tracks and conditions at higher altitudes become dangerous. Highly changeable weather is typical around here: Aoraki/Mt Cook is only 44km from the coast and weather conditions rolling in from the Tasman Sea can mean sudden storms.

As for climbing, there's unlimited scope for the experienced, but those without experience must go with a guide. Regardless of your skills, take every precaution – more than 200 people have died in climbing accidents in the park. The bleak *In Memoriam* book in the visitor information centre begins with the first death on Aoraki/Mt Cook

Aoraki/Mt Cook National Park

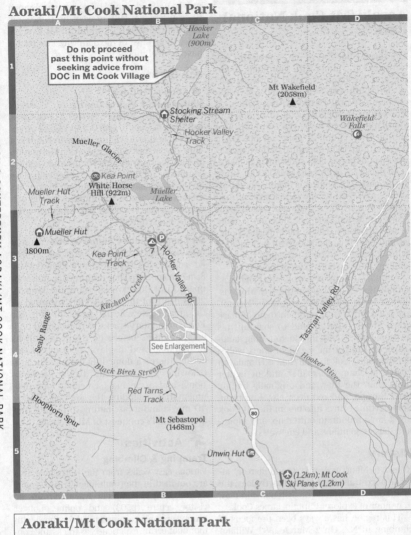

Aoraki/Mt Cook National Park

◎ Sights
1 Aoraki/Mt Cook National Park Visitor Centre	E4
2 Public Shelter	E5
3 Sir Edmund Hillary Alpine Centre	E4

✪ Activities, Courses & Tours
4 Alpine Guides	E4
Big Sky	(see 8)
Glacier Explorers	(see 8)
Glacier Kayaking	(see 10)
Southern Alps Guiding	(see 10)

🛏 Sleeping
5 Aoraki Court Motel	F5
6 Aoraki/Mt Cook Alpine Lodge	E5
7 DOC White Horse Hill Campground	B3
8 Hermitage	E4
9 Mt Cook YHA	F5

✕ Eating
10 Old Mountaineers' Cafe	E4

⊖ Drinking & Nightlife
11 Chamois Bar & Grill	F5

village, which has running water, toilets and coin-operated showers. Note that this shelter cannot be used for overnight stays.

★ Sealy Tarns Track
TRAMPING

The walk to Sealy Tarns (three to four hours return) branches off the Kea Point Track and continues up the ridge to Mueller Hut (dorm $36), a comfortable 28-bunk hut with gas, cooking facilities and long-drop toilets.

Hooker Valley Track
TRAMPING

Perhaps the best of the area's day walks, this track (three hours return from Mt Cook Village) heads up the Hooker Valley and crosses three swing bridges to the Stocking Stream and the terminus of the Hooker Glacier. After the second swing bridge, Aoraki/Mt Cook totally dominates the valley, and you may see icebergs floating in Hooker Lake.

Kea Point Track
TRAMPING

The trail to Kea Point (two hours return from Mt Cook Village) is lined with native plants and ends at a platform with excellent views of Aoraki/Mt Cook, the Hooker Valley and the ice faces of Mt Sefton and the Footstool. Despite the name, you're no more likely to see a kea here than in other parts of the park. If you do, don't feed it.

Snow Sports

Southern Alps
Guiding
ROCK CLIMBING, SNOW SPORTS

(☑ 03-435 1890; www.mtcook.com; Old Mountaineers' Cafe, 3 Larch Grove Rd) Offers mountaineering instruction and guiding, plus three- to four-hour helihiking trips on Tasman Glacier year-round ($495). From June to October heliskiers can head up Tasman Glacier for a 10km to 12km downhill run (three runs, from $895). There's also a ski-plane option (two runs, from $895).

Alpine Guides
ROCK CLIMBING

(☑ 03-435 1834; www.alpineguides.co.nz; 98 Bowen Dr, Mt Cook Village) Guided climbs and mountaineering courses, along with ski-touring including heli options. Its Hermitage shop stocks outdoor clothing and mountaineering gear, and rents ice axes, crampons, day-packs and sleeping bags.

Other Activities

Glacier Kayaking
KAYAKING

(☑ 03-435 1890; www.mtcook.com; Old Mountaineers' Cafe, Bowen Dr; per person $155; ⊘ Oct-Apr) Suitable for paddlers with just an ounce of experience, these guided trips head out on the terminal lake of the Tasman or Mueller

in 1907; since then more than 80 climbers have died on the peak.

Check with the park rangers before attempting any climb and always heed their advice. If you're climbing, or even going on a longer walk, fill out an intentions card before starting out so rangers can check on you if you're overdue coming back. Sign out again when you return. The visitor centre also hires locator beacons (per three days/week $30/40).

If you intend to stay at any of the park's huts, it's essential to register your intentions at the visitor centre and pay hut fees. Walkers can use the public shelter in Mt Cook

Glaciers. With luck there will be icebergs to negotiate, but regardless this is a cool adventure in a crazy place with a fascinating geology lesson thrown in. Expect to spend about two hours on the water; book at the Old Mountaineers' Cafe (p507).

Big Sky
STARGAZING

(🖉 0800 686 800; www.hermitage.co.nz; The Hermitage, Terrace Rd; adult/child $65/32.50; ⊙ 9.30pm Oct-Apr, 8.30pm May-Sep) NZ's southern sky is introduced with a 45-minute presentation in the Alpine Centre's digital planetarium. Afterwards participants venture outside to study the real deal with telescopes, binoculars and an astronomy guide.

Glentanner Horse Trekking
HORSE RIDING

(🖉 03-435 1855; www.glentanner.co.nz; Glentanner Park Centre, SH80; 1/2/3hr rides $70/90/150; ⊙ Nov-Apr) Leads guided treks on a high-country sheep station with options suited to all levels of experience.

🖙 Tours

Mount Cook Ski Planes
SCENIC FLIGHTS

(🖉 03-430 8026; www.mtcookskiplanes.com; Mt Cook Airport) Based at Mt Cook Airport, this outfit offers 45-minute (adult/child $425/310) and 55-minute (adult/child $560/425) flights, both with snow landings. Flight-seeing without a landing is a cheaper option; try the 25-minute Mini Tasman trip (adult/child $245/200) or 45-minute Alpine Wonderland (adult/child $310/250).

Glacier Explorers
BOAT TOUR

(🖉 03-435 1641; www.glacierexplorers.com; The Hermitage, Terrace Rd; adult/child $155/77.50; ⊙ Sep-May) Head out on the terminal lake of the Tasman Glacier for this small-boat tour, which gets up close and personal with old icebergs and crazy moraines. Includes a short walk. Book at the activities desk at the Hermitage.

Tasman Valley 4WD & Argo Tours
TOUR

(🖉 0800 686 800; www.mountcooktours.co.nz; adult/child $79/39.50) Offers year-round, 90-minute Argo (8WD all-terrain vehicle) tours checking out the Tasman Glacier and its terminal lake, with alpine flora and an interesting commentary along the way. Book online or at the Hermitage activities desk.

Helicopter Line
SCENIC FLIGHTS

(🖉 03-435 1801; www.helicopter.co.nz; Glentanner Park, Mt Cook Rd) From Glentanner Park, the Helicopter Line offers 20-minute Alpine Vista flights ($235), an exhilarating 35-minute flight over the Ben Ohau Range ($355) and

a 40-minute Mountains High flight over the Tasman Glacier and alongside Aoraki/Mt Cook ($450). All feature snow landings.

🛏 Sleeping

Mt Cook YHA
HOSTEL $

(🖉 03-435 1820; www.yha.co.nz; 4 Bowen Dr; dm/d $38/137; 🛜) 🧖 Handsomely decked out in pine, this excellent hostel has a free sauna, a drying room, log fires and DVDs. Rooms are clean and warm, although some are a tight squeeze (particularly the twin bunk rooms).

DOC White Horse Hill Campground
CAMPGROUND $

(🖉 03-435 1186; www.doc.govt.nz; Hooker Valley Rd; sites per adult/child $10/5) Located 2km up the Hooker Valley from Mt Cook Village, this self-registration camping ground has a basic shelter with (cold-water) sinks, tables and toilets, along with blissful views and close proximity to various walking tracks.

Glentanner Park Centre
HOLIDAY PARK $

(🖉 03-435 1855; www.glentanner.co.nz; Mt Cook Rd; sites $22-25, dm $32, units with/without bathroom $180/100; @🛜) 🧖 On the northern shore of Lake Pukaki, 22km south of the Mt Cook Village, this is the nearest fully equipped campground to the national park. Features include cabins and motel units, a bunk room, a cafe and free-roaming rabbits.

★ Aoraki/Mt Cook Alpine Lodge
LODGE $$

(🖉 03-435 1860; www.aorakialpinelodge.co.nz; Bowen Dr; d $169-240; 🛜) This lovely modern lodge has en suite rooms, including some suitable for families and two with kitchenettes; most have views. The huge lounge and kitchen area also has a superb mountain outlook, as does the barbecue area – a rather inspiring spot to sizzle your dinner.

Hermitage
HOTEL $$$

(🖉 03-435 1809; www.hermitage.co.nz; Terrace Rd; r $215-510; @🛜) Completely dominating Mt Cook Village, this famous hotel offers awesome mountain views. While the corridors in some of the older wings can seem a little hospital-like, all of the rooms have been renovated to a reasonable standard. In addition to the on-site shop and Sir Ed Alpine Centre, there are three dining options of low to middling standard.

Aoraki Court Motel
MOTEL $$$

(🖉 03-435 1111; www.aorakicourt.co.nz; 26 Bowen Dr; d $185-265) While it wouldn't command these prices elsewhere, this clump of modern motel units is sharp, with good views.

DON'T MISS

TASMAN GLACIER

At 29km long and up to 4km wide, the **Tasman Glacier** (www.doc.govt.nz) is the largest of NZ's glaciers, but it's melting fast, losing hundreds of metres from its length each year. It is also melting from the surface down, shrinking around 150m in depth since it was first surveyed in 1891. In its lower section the melts have exposed rocks, stones and boulders, which form a solid unsightly mass on top of the ice. Despite this considerable shrinkage, at its thickest point the ice is still estimated to be over 600m deep.

Tasman Lake, at the foot of the glacier, started to form only in the early 1970s and now stretches to 4km. The ongoing effects of climate change are expected to extend it to 8km within the next 20 years. The lake is covered by a maze of huge icebergs which are continuously being sheared off the glacier's terminal face. On 22 February 2011 the Christchurch earthquake caused a 1.3km long, 300m high, 30-million-ton chunk of ice to break off, causing 3.5m waves to roll into the tourist boats on the lake at the time (no one was injured). You can kayak on Tasman Lake with Glacier Kayaking (p505).

In the glacier's last major advance (17,000 years ago), the glacier crept south far enough to carve out Lake Pukaki. A later advance did not reach out to the valley sides, so there's a gap between the outer valley walls and the lateral moraines of this later advance. The unsealed Tasman Valley Rd, which branches off Mt Cook Rd 800m south of Mt Cook Village, travels through this gap. From the Blue Lakes shelter, 8km along the road, the **Tasman Glacier View Track** (30 minutes return) climbs interminable steps to an aptly rewarding viewpoint on the moraine wall, with a side trip to Blue Lakes on the way.

Feature wallpaper sharpens up the decor, and the tiled bathrooms have designery touches. Some units even have spa baths, and there are bikes for hire.

Eating & Drinking

Old Mountaineers' Cafe　　　CAFE $$
(www.mtcook.com; Bowen Dr; breakfast $10-15, lunch $14-26 dinner $18-35; ⊙10am-9pm daily Nov-Apr, Tue-Sun May & Jul-Oct; 🖘) 🍴 Encouraging lingering with books, memorabilia and mountain views through picture windows, the village's best eatery also supports local and organic suppliers through a menu sporting salmon and bacon pies, cooked breakfasts, burgers and pizza.

Chamois Bar & Grill　　　PUB
(www.mountcookbackpackers.co.nz; Bowen Dr; ⊙4pm-late) Upstairs in Mt Cook Backpacker Lodge, this large bar offers pub grub (meals $15 to $30), a pool table, a big-screen TV and the occasional live gig, but the views are its best feature.

ⓘ Information

The **DOC Visitor Centre** (p503) is the best source of local information. The nearest ATM and supermarket are in Twizel.

ⓘ Getting There & Away

Mt Cook Village's small airport only serves aerial sightseeing companies. Some of these may be willing to combine transport to the West Coast (ie Franz Josef) with a scenic flight, but flights are heavily dependent on weather.

If you're driving, fill up at Lake Tekapo or Twizel. There is petrol at Mt Cook, but it's expensive and involves summoning an attendant from the Hermitage (for a fee).

Cook Connection (🕿0800 266 526; www.cookconnect.co.nz) runs shuttle services to Lake Tekapo ($38, 1½ hours) and Twizel ($27, one hour).

Daily InterCity coaches (see table below stop at the YHA and the Hermitage, both of which handle bookings.

DESTINATION	FARES FROM	DURATION (HR)
Christchurch	$67	5¼
Cromwell	$59	2¾
Geraldine	$38	3
Lake Tekapo	$30	1½
Queenstown	$64	4

Dunedin & Otago

Best Places to Eat

→ Riverstone Kitchen (p517)

→ Fleur's Place (p518)

→ No 7 Balmac (p525)

→ Bracken (p525)

→ Otago Farmers Market (p524)

Best Places to Sleep

→ Pen-y-bryn Lodge (p516)

→ Oliver's (p537)

→ Pitches Store (p534)

→ Old Bones Backpackers (p515)

→ Kiwi's Nest (p523)

Why Go?

Otago has attractions both urban and rural, ranging from quirky towns to world-class wineries and some of the country's most accessible wildlife. Its historic heart is Dunedin, home to a vibrant student culture and arts scene. From the town's stately Edwardian train station it's possible to catch the famous Taieri Gorge Railway inland, and continue on two wheels along the craggily scenic Otago Central Rail Trail.

Those seeking colonial New Zealand can soak up the frontier atmosphere of gold-rush towns such as Clyde, St Bathans, Naseby and cute-as-a-button Ophir. For wildlife, head to the Otago Peninsula, where penguins, albatross, sea lions and seals are easily sighted. Seaside Oamaru has a wonderful historic precinct, resident penguin colonies and a quirky devotion to steampunk culture.

Unhurried and overflowing with picturesque scenery, Otago is generous to explorers who are after a more leisurely style of holiday.

When to Go

→ February and March have settled, sunny weather (usually...), and the juicy appeal of fresh apricots, peaches and cherries.

→ At Easter, hook yourself a 'Southern Man' at the Middlemarch Singles Ball, or drown your sorrows at the Clyde Wine & Food Festival.

→ Take to two wheels on the Otago Central Rail Trail during the quieter month of September.

→ In November, watch the pros battle it out on the Highlands Motorsport Park, then ride graciously into the past on a penny farthing bicycle at Oamaru's Victorian Heritage Celebrations.

ⓘ Getting There & Away

Air New Zealand (☑ 0800 737 000; www.
airnewzealand.co.nz) flies from Dunedin to
Christchurch, Wellington and Auckland, and
Jetstar (☑ 0800 800 995; www.jetstar.com)
flies to Wellington and Auckland.

The only train services are **heritage trips**
(p522) from Dunedin to Middlemarch and
Dunedin to Palmerston.

The main bus routes follow SH1 or SH8.

WAITAKI DISTRICT

The broad, braided Waitaki River provides
a clear dividing line between Otago and
Canterbury to the region's north. The Waitaki Valley is a direct but less-travelled route
from the Southern Alps to the sea, featuring
freaky limestone formations, Māori rock
paintings and ancient fossils. The area is
also one of NZ's newest winemaking regions,
and a major component of the new Alps 2
Ocean Cycle Trail (p501), which links Aora-
ki/Mt Cook National Park to Oamaru on the
coast. The district's main town, Oamaru, is
a place of penguins and glorious heritage
architecture.

ⓘ Getting There & Away

Buses stop in Oamaru and Moeraki, en route
from Christchurch to Dunedin and Te Anau. Other
services pass through Omarama on their journey
between Queenstown/Wanaka and Christchurch.
No buses traverse the Waitaki Valley.

The only rail service is the Seasider tourist
train that heads between Dunedin and Oamaru.

Omarama

POP 267

At the head of the Waitaki Valley, Omarama
is surrounded by mountain ranges and fabulous landscapes. Busy times in this sleepy
place include the rodeo (28 December) and
the sheepdog trials (March).

◉ Sights & Activities

Clay Cliffs Paritea   LANDMARK
(Henburn Rd; vehicles $5) This bizarre moon-
scape is the result of two million years of
erosion on layers of silt and gravel that were
exposed along the active Ostler fault line.
The cliffs are on private land; before setting
out, pay the vehicle admission fee at Omarama Hot Tubs. To get to the area, head north
from town for 3km on SH8, turn left onto

Quailburn Rd, and then turn left after 3km
onto unsealed Henburn Rd.

Wrinkly Rams   FARM
(☑ 03-438 9751; www.thewrinklyrams.co.nz; 24-
30 Omarama Ave/SH8; adult/child $20/10) A
regular stop for tour buses, Wrinkly Rams
stages 30-minute shearing and sheepdog
shows, including lamb-feeding in season.
Phone ahead to tag along with a tour group,
or book your own one-off show. Attached is
one of Omarama's better **cafes** (mains $10-25;
☉ 7am-4.30pm; 🖥).

Omarama Hot Tubs   SPA
(☑ 03-438 9703; www.hottubsomarama.co.nz;
29 Omarama Ave/SH8; per 1/2/3/4-person tub
$52/90/114/136, pod $75/140/180/200; ☉ 11am-
late) If your legs are weary after mountain
biking or tramping, or you just want to cosy
up with your significant other, these private,
wood-fired hot tubs could be just the ticket. Choose between a 90-minute soak in a
tub (each has its own dressing room) or a
two-hour session in a 'wellness pod', which
includes a sauna.

The chemical-free glacier and snow-melt
water is changed after each booking, and the
used water is recycled for irrigation.

The concept is Japanese, but with the
surrounding mountain ranges, the lakeside
setting and a pristine night sky, you could

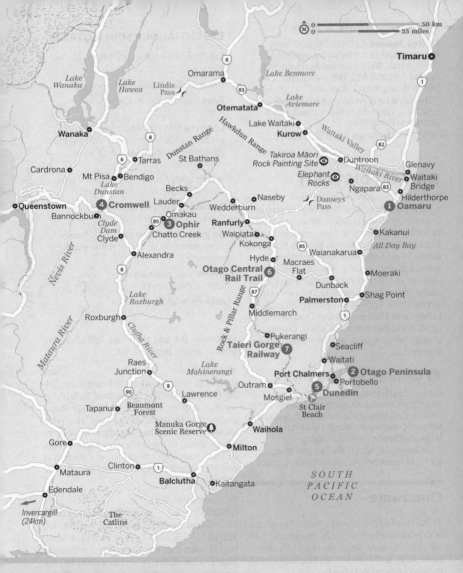

Dunedin & Otago Highlights

1 **Oamaru** (p512)
Experiencing a heritage past and a possible steampunk future.

2 **Otago Peninsula** (p528)
Peering at penguins, admiring albatross and staring at seals.

3 **Ophir** (p534) Exploring New Zealand's gold-mining heritage in a quaint backcountry village.

4 **Cromwell** (p538) Taste-testing some of the planet's best pinot noir in the wineries scattered around the fruit bowl of the south.

5 **Dunedin** (p518)
Sampling local beers and listening out for local bands in the city's bars and cafes.

6 **Otago Central Rail Trail** (p536) Cycling through lonely vistas of brown and gold on the route of a defunct train line.

7 **Taieri Gorge Railway** (p522) Winding through gorges, alongside canyons and across tall viaducts on this snaking railway.

only be on the South Island of NZ. Therapeutic massages (30/60 minutes $60/100) are also available.

Glide Omarama

GLIDING

(☑03-438 9555; www.glideomarama.com) The area's westerlies and warm summer thermals allow for world-class gliding over the hills and spectacular Southern Alps, and a national gliding meet is held here in December or January. This crew offers lessons and scenic flights ranging from 30 minutes ($345) to 2½ hours ($745).

🛌 Sleeping & Eating

Buscot Station

FARMSTAY, HOSTEL $

(☑027 222 1754; SH8; site/dm/s/d $10/25/40/60) For a completely different and uniquely Kiwi experience, grab a room in the home-style farmhouse attached to a huge sheep and cattle station, or a bed in the large dormitory out the back. The sunset views are terrific and there's plenty of acreage for quiet explorations. Look for it on SH8, 10km north of Omarama.

Omarama Top 10 Holiday Park

HOLIDAY PARK $

(☑03-438 9875; www.omaramatop10.co.nz; 1 Omarama Ave (SH8); sites $35-40, units with/without bathroom $115/58; @ ☎) ✔ Facilities are good at this holiday park, squeezed between the highway and a stream. Standard cabins are compact, but larger en suite cabins and self-contained motel units are also available.

Ladybird Hill

MODERN NZ $$

(☑03-438 9550; www.ladybirdhill.co.nz; 1 Pinot Noir Ct; mains lunch $16-24, dinner $28-33; ⊙10am-4pm Wed, 10am-10pm Thu-Sun Aug-May) Sure, you can do it the easy way and simply order a leisurely lunch from the menu. Or you can grab a rod, catch a salmon from the well-stocked ponds (around $49) and wait until it's prepared and either smoked or sliced into sashimi ($55, feeding several people). Other attractions include a kids playground and walking tracks through the vineyard.

ⓘ Information

Omarama Hot Tubs (p509) doubles as the information office, and can assist with accommodation and transport information. See www.discoveromarama.co.nz for more details.

MĀORI NZ: DUNEDIN & OTAGO

The early Māori history of Otago echoes that of Canterbury (p469), with Ngāi Tahu the dominant tribe at the time the British arrived. One of the first parcels of land that Ngāi Tahu sold was called the Otago block, a 1618-sq-km parcel of land which changed hands in 1844 for £2400. The name Otago reflects the Ngāi Tahu pronunciation of Ōtākou, a small village on the far reaches of the Otago Peninsula, where there's still a *marae* (meeting place).

Dunedin's **Otago Museum** (p519) has the finest Māori exhibition on the South Island, including an ornately carved *waka taua* (war canoe) and finely crafted *pounamu* (greenstone). Māori rock art can still be seen in situ in the Waitaki Valley.

ⓘ Getting There & Away

Atomic Shuttles (☑03-349 0697; www.atomictravel.co.nz) Services stop in Omarama for a break before continuing on to Christchurch ($35, four hours), Lake Tekapo ($20, one hour), Twizel ($20, 20 minutes), Cromwell ($25, 1½ hours) and Queenstown ($30, 2¼ hours).

InterCity (☑03-471 7143; www.intercity.co.nz) Two coaches a day head to/from Christchurch (from $42, 5¾ hours), Twizel (from $13, 19 minutes), Cromwell (from $23, 1½ hours) and Queenstown (from $32, 2½ hours), and one heads to/from Mt Cook Village ($70, 1¼ hours).

Naked Bus (www.nakedbus.com; prices vary) Two daily services to/from Christchurch (5¾ hours), Lake Tekapo (1½ hours) and Cromwell (2½ hours), with one terminating in Queenstown (3¼ hours) and the other in Wanaka (1¾ hours).

Waitaki Valley

Wine, waterskiing and salmon-fishing are just some of the treats on offer along this little-travelled route. Coming from Omarama, SH83 passes an array of arrestingly blue lakes, each abutted by a hydroelectric power station. For a scenic detour along the north bank, leave the highway at Otematata and cross over the huge Benmore Dam, then cross over Aviemore Dam to rejoin the highway.

A succession of sleepy little heartland towns line the highway, peppered with rustic old bank buildings and pubs. One of the most appealing is tiny lost-in-time **Kurow** (population 302), the hometown of World Cup–winning retired All Blacks captain Richie McCaw. From almost-as-cute **Duntroon** (population 90), adventurous (and appropriately insured) drivers can take the unsealed road over Danseys Pass to Naseby.

Although they've got a long way to go to attain the global reputation enjoyed by their colleagues on the other side of the mountains in Central Otago, a few winemaking pioneers in Waitaki Valley are producing wine of which international experts are taking notice.

⊙ Sights

⊙ Kurow

**Kurow Heritage
& Information Centre**   MUSEUM
(☑ 03-436 0950; www.kurow.org.nz; 57 Bledisloe St; ⊘ 9.30am-4pm Mon-Fri) **FREE** While Richie McCaw might get all the attention these days, Kurow's other famous son was Arnold Nordmeyer (1901–89), a Labour Party leader who was one of the key architects of NZ's welfare and public health system. His memory is honoured in this interesting community museum, which jokingly refers to itself as the National Museum of Social Security.

Pasquale Kurow Winery   WINERY
(☑ 03-436 0443; www.pasquale.co.nz; 5292 Kurow-Duntroon Rd/SH83; ⊘ 10am-4pm Nov-Mar) The valley's most impressive winery, Pasquale produces killer pinot noir, pinot gris and riesling, as well as less common varietals such as gewürztraminer, arneis and viognier. Drop in for a wine-tasting session ($10, refundable upon purchase) and an antipasto and cheese platter.

⊙ Duntroon & Around

**Takiroa Māori
Rock Painting Site**   ARCHAEOLOGICAL SITE
FREE Hidden within the honeycomb cliffs lining the highway, this well-signposted site, 3km west of Duntroon, features centuries-old drawings of mystical creatures, animals and even a sailing ship.

**Maerewhenua Māori
Rock Painting Site**   ARCHAEOLOGICAL SITE
(Livingstone-Duntroon Rd) **FREE** Sheltered by an impressive limestone overhang, this site

contains charcoal-and-ochre paintings dating to before the arrival of Europeans in NZ. Head east from Duntroon and take the first right after crossing the Maerewhenua River; the site is on the left after about 400m.

Vanished World Centre   MUSEUM
(www.vanishedworld.co.nz; 7 Campbell St, Duntroon; adult/child $10/free; ⊘ 10am-4.30pm daily Nov-Mar, 10.30am-4pm Fri-Mon Apr-Oct) Perhaps there wouldn't be quite so many bad dolphin tattoos and dancing penguin films if more people stopped in Duntroon to check out this small but interesting volunteer-run centre. Once you see the 25-million-year-old fossils of shark-toothed dolphins and giant penguins, they suddenly don't seem so cute.

Pick up a copy of the *Vanished World Trail* map ($6.50) outlining 20 different interesting geological locations around the Waitaki Valley and North Otago coast.

🏃 Activities

Awakino Skifield   SKIING
(☑ 021 890 584; www.skiawakino.com; Awakino Skifield Rd; daily lift pass adult/child $50/25) Situated high above Kurow, Awakino is a small player on the NZ ski scene, but worth a visit for intermediate skiers who fancy some peace and quiet. Weekend lodge-and-ski packages are available.

Oamaru

POP 12,900

Nothing moves very fast in Oamaru. Tourists saunter, locals linger and penguins waddle. Even its recently resurrected heritage modes of transport – penny farthings and steam trains – reflect an unhurried pace. Most travellers come here for the penguins, but hang around and you'll sense the wellspring of eccentricity bubbling under the surface. Put simply, this is NZ's coolest town.

Down by the water, a neighbourhood of once-neglected Victorian buildings now swarms with oddballs, antiquarians and bohemians of all stripes, who run offbeat galleries, fascinating shops, hip venues and even an 'urban winery'. Most visible are the steampunks, whose aesthetic boldly celebrating the past and the future with an ethos of 'tomorrow as it used to be'.

What Oamaru used to be was rich and ambitious. In its 1880s heyday, Oamaru was about the same size as Los Angeles was at the time. Refrigerated meat-shipping had its origins nearby and the town became wealthy enough to erect the imposing buildings that grace Thames St today. However, the town overreached itself and spent the end of the 19th century teetering on the verge of bankruptcy.

Economic decline in the 20th century meant that there wasn't the impetus to swing the wrecking ball with the same reckless abandon that wiped out much of the built heritage of NZ's main centres. It's only in recent decades that canny creative types have cottoned on to the uniqueness of Oamaru's surviving Victorian streetscapes and have started to unlock this otherwise unremarkable town's potential for extreme kookiness.

Sights

★ Blue Penguin Colony
BIRD SANCTUARY

(☑ 03-433 1195; www.penguins.co.nz; 2 Waterfront Rd; ⊙ 10am until 2hr after sunset) ∅ Every evening the little tykes from the Oamaru little-penguin colony surf in and wade ashore, heading to their nests in an old stone quarry near the waterfront. Stands are set up on either side of the waddle route. General admission (adult/child $28/14) will give you a good view of the action but the premium stand ($40/20), accessed by a boardwalk through the nesting area, will get you closer.

You'll see the most penguins (up to 250) in November and December. From March to August there may be only 10 to 50 birds. They arrive in clumps called rafts just before dark (around 5.30pm in midwinter and 9.30pm midsummer), and it takes them about an hour to all come ashore; nightly viewing times are posted at the i-SITE. Use of cameras is prohibited and you're advised to dress warmly.

To understand the centre's conservation work and its success in increasing the penguin population, take the daytime, behind-the-scenes tour (adult/child self-guided $10/5 or guided $16/8); packages that combine night viewing and the daytime tour are available.

Do not under any circumstances wander around the rocks beside the sea here at night looking for penguins. It's damaging to their environment and spoils studies into the human effects on the birds.

★ Victorian Precinct
NEIGHBOURHOOD

Consisting of only a couple of blocks centred on Harbour and Tyne Sts, this atmospheric enclave has some of NZ's best-preserved Victorian commercial buildings. Descend on a dark and foggy night and it's downright Dickensian. It's also ground zero for all that is hip, cool and freaky in Oamaru, and one of the most fun places to window-shop in the entire South Island.

Wander around during the day and you'll discover antiquarian bookshops, antique stores, galleries, vintage-clothing shops, kooky gift stores, artist studios, old-fashioned lolly shops and craft bookbinders. At night there are some cute little bars, and you might even see a penguin swaggering along the street – we did!

The precinct is at its liveliest on Sundays when the excellent Oamaru farmers market is in full swing. Note that some shops and attractions are closed on Mondays. There's also a brand new heritage centre in the works; enquire about its progress at the i-SITE.

Yellow-Eyed Penguin Colony
BIRD SANCTUARY

(Bushy Beach Rd) FREE Larger and much rarer than their little blue cousins, yellow-eyed penguins waddle ashore at Bushy Beach in the late afternoon to feed their young. In order to protect these endangered birds, the beach is closed to people at 3pm, but there are hides set up on the cliffs (you'll need binoculars for a decent view). The best time to see them is two hours before sunset.

Despite their Māori name, hoiho, meaning 'noisy shouter', they're extremely shy critters; if they see or hear you they'll head back into the water and the chicks will go hungry.

Thames St
AREA

Oamaru's main drag owes its expansive girth to the need to accommodate the minimum turning circle of a bullock cart. Oamaru's grand pretensions reached their peak in a series of gorgeous buildings constructed from the milky local limestone (known as Oamaru stone or whitestone), with their forms reflecting the fashion of the times; there's a particular emphasis on the neoclassical.

Impressive examples include the Forrester Gallery (at No 9, built 1883), the ANZ Bank (No 11, 1871), the Waitaki District Council building (No 20, 1883), the North Otago Museum (No 60, 1882), the Courthouse (No 88, 1883) and the Opera House (No 92, 1907).

Steampunk HQ
GALLERY

(☑ 027 778 6547; www.steampunkoamaru.co.nz; 1 Itchen St; adult/child $10/2; ⊙ 10am-5pm)

Oamaru

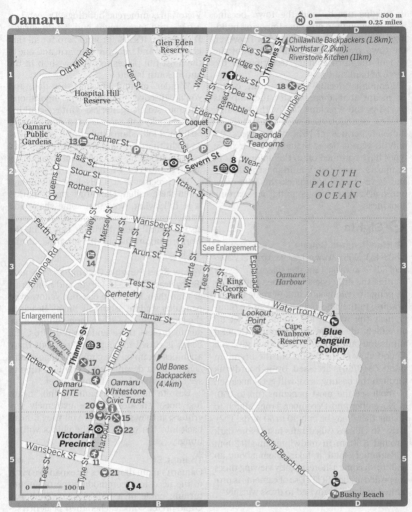

Discover an alternative past – or maybe a quirky version of the future – in this fascinating art project celebrating steampunk culture. Ancient machines wheeze and splutter, and the industrial detritus of the last century or so is repurposed and reimagined to creepy effect. Bring a $2 coin to fire up the sparking, space-age locomotive out the front.

St Patrick's Basilica CHURCH
(☎03-434 8543; www.cdd.org.nz/st-patrick-oamaru; 64 Reed St) If you've ever fantasised about being transported back to Ancient Rome, stroll through the Corinthian col-

umns and into this gorgeous Catholic church (built in 1873). Renowned architect Francis Petre went for the full time warp with this one, right down to a coffered ceiling and a cupola above the altar.

Forrester Gallery GALLERY
(☎03-433 0853; www.culturewaitaki.org.nz; 9 Thames St; ⊗10.30am-4.30pm) **FREE** Housed in a temple-like former bank building, the Forrester Gallery has an excellent collection of regional and NZ art. It's a good place to see works by Colin McCahon, one of NZ's most significant modern artists.

Oamaru

Oamaru Public Gardens GARDENS
(Severn St; ⊙ dawn-dusk) Opened in 1876, these beautiful gardens are a lovely place to chill out on a hot day, with expansive lawns, waterways, bridges and a children's playground.

North Otago Museum MUSEUM
(☑ 03-433 0852; www.culturewaitaki.org.nz; 58-60 Thames St; ⊙ 10.30am-4.30pm Mon-Fri, 1-4.30pm Sat & Sun) FREE Behind its classical facade, the North Otago Museum has exhibits on Māori and Pākehā history, local writer Janet Frame, architecture and geology.

🏃 Activities

Vertical Ventures CYCLING, ROCK CLIMBING
(☑ 03-434 5010; www.alps2oceancycletours.co.nz; 4 Wansbeck St) Rent a mountain bike (from $45 per day), or join guided mountainbiking trips, including the Alps 2 Ocean Cycle Trail (seven days including transport, food and accommodation for $2695) and helibiking day trips (from $415). The 'vertical' part comes in the form of rock climbing (from $140 per person).

Oamaru Steam & Rail TOURIST TRAIN
(www.oamaru-steam.org.nz; adult/child/family one-way $5/2/12, return $8/3/20; ⊙ 11am-4.30pm Sun Oct-Apr, to 3pm Sun May-Sep) On Sundays, take a half-hour ride on a vintage steam train from the Victorian Precinct to the waterfront.

👉 Tours

Penguins Crossing WILDLIFE WATCHING
(☑ 03-477 9083; www.travelheadfirst.com; 4 Wansbeck St; adult/child from $65/25) Door-to-door tour taking in the blue- and yellow-eyed-penguin colonies. Prices include admission to the blue-penguin colony.

🎉 Festivals & Events

Victorian Heritage Celebrations CULTURAL
(www.vhc.co.nz; ⊙ mid-Nov) Five days of costumed hijinks, culminating in a grand fete.

🛏 Sleeping

★ **Old Bones Backpackers** HOSTEL $
(☑ 03-434 8115; www.oldbones.co.nz; Beach Rd; r $95, campervans per person $20; @ 🛜) About 5km south of Oamaru on the coast road, this top-notch dorm-free hostel has tidy rooms off a huge, sunny, central space. Relax in this isolated setting listening to the surf crashing over the road. Or book one of the hot tubs (from $50) and drift into ecstasy while gazing at the stars.

Chillawhile Backpackers HOSTEL $
(☑ 03-437 0168; www.chillawhile.co.nz; 1 Frome St; dm $28-32, s/c without bathroom $56/72; 🛜) Unleash your creative spirit at this funky and colourful hostel in a two-storey Victorian residence. Guests are encouraged to draw and paint, or create sweet soul music on the hostel's varied instruments.

Oamaru Top 10 Holiday Park HOLIDAY PARK $
(☑ 03-434 7666; www.oamarutop10.co.nz; 30 Chelmer St; sites $36-44, units with/without bathroom from $105/73; @ 🛜) Grassy and well maintained, this Top 10 has trees out the back and the public gardens next door. Standard cabins are basic, but the other units (with varying levels of self-contained comfort) are much nicer.

Highfield Mews

MOTEL $$

(☑ 03-434 3437; www.highfieldmews.co.nz; 244 Thames St; units from $170; @ 🤶) 𝒫 Motels have come a long away from the gloomy concrete-block constructions of the 1960s and '70s, as this new build attests. The units are basically smart apartments, with kitchens, desks, stereos, tiled bathrooms and outdoor furniture.

★ Pen-y-bryn Lodge

B&B $$$

(☑ 03-434 7939; www.penybryn.co.nz; 41 Towey St; r $625-750; 🤶) Well-travelled foodie owners have thoroughly revitalised this beautiful 1889 residence. There are two rooms in the main house but we prefer the three recently and luxuriously refurbished ones in the rear annexe. Predinner drinks and canapés are served in the antique-studded drawing room, and you can arrange a four-course dinner in the fabulous dining room ($125 per person).

✖️ Eating

Steam

CAFE $

(www.facebook.com/steamoamaru; 7 Thames St; mains $10-13; ⊘ 7.30am-4.30pm Mon-Fri, 8am-3pm Sat & Sun; 🤶) Steam specialises in coffees and fruit juices, and it's a good spot to stock up on freshly ground beans for your own travels. Aside from crêpes, the food is mainly limited to what you see on the counter: freshly baked muffins, croissants and the like.

Whitestone Cheese Factory

DELI, CAFE $

(☑ 03-434 8098; www.whitestonecheese.com; 3 Torridge St; platters $7.50-15; ⊘ 9am-5pm) The home of award-winning artisan cheeses, Whitestone is a local culinary institution and the little factory-door cafe is a fine place to challenge one's arteries. Food is limited to the likes of cheese scones, cheese-only platters and large platters with crackers and quince paste.

Harbour St Bakery

BAKERY $

(☑ 03-434 0444; www.harbourstreetbakery.com; 4 Harbour St; pies $5.50; ⊘ 10am-4pm Tue-Sun) Selling both European-style bread and pastries and Kiwi meat pies, this Dutch bakery covers its bases well. Grab an outdoor seat and watch Oamaru's heritage streetlife scroll past like an old-time movie.

Midori

JAPANESE $$

(☑ 03-434 9045; www.facebook.com/MidoriJapaneseSushiBarAndRestaurant; 1 Ribble St; sushi $5-11, mains $13-20; ⊘ 10.30am-8.30pm Mon-Sat, noon-8.30pm Sun) Midori, housed in a heritage stone building, serves sashimi and sushi that makes the most of fresh local seafood. Other carefully prepared dishes include teriyaki salmon and blue cod, udon soup and a variety of bento boxes. If you just want to grab and go, it also runs the Sushi Espresso takeaway next door.

Northstar

MODERN NZ $$

(☑ 03-437 1190; www.northstarmotel.co.nz; 495a Thames Hwy; mains lunch $19-23, dinner $30-34; ⊘ noon-3pm & 6-9pm) Surprisingly upmarket for a restaurant attached to an SH1 motel, Northstar is the first choice for Oamaruvians with something to celebrate. Expect robust bistro fare with a touch of contemporary flair. The bar is popular, too.

🍺 Drinking & Entertainment

Criterion Hotel

PUB

(☑ 03-434 6247; www.criterionhotel.co.nz; 3 Tyne St; ⊘ 11.30am-late Tue-Sun) The most Victorian of the Victorian Precinct's watering holes, this corner beauty has a good beer selection and plenty of local wines. There's usually live music on Fridays.

Scott's Brewing Co.

BREWERY

(☑ 03-434 2244; www.scottsbrewing.co.nz; 1 Wansbeck St; ⊘ 11am-7.30pm) Drop into this old waterfront warehouse to sample the output of Oamaru's premier craft brewers. Slouch against the counter for a tasting or head out onto the sunny deck for a pint and a pizza.

★ Penguin Club

LIVE MUSIC

(www.thepenguinclub.co.nz; Emulsion Lane, off Harbour St; admission varies) Tucked down an atmospheric alley off a 19th-century street, the Penguin's unusual location matches its acts: everything from touring Kiwi bands to punky/grungy/rocky/country locals.

ℹ️ Information

Oamaru i-SITE (☑ 03-434 1656; www.visitoamaru.co.nz; 1 Thames St; ⊘ 9am-5pm; 🤶) Mountains of information including details on local walking trips and wildlife, plus daily penguin-viewing times are posted here. There's also bike hire ($28/40 per half-/full day) and an interesting 10-minute DVD on the history of the town.

Oamaru Whitestone Civic Trust (☑ 03-434 5385; www.victorianoamaru.co.nz; 2 Harbour St; ⊘ 10am-4pm) Vintage B&W photos of Oamaru's heritage, information and walking-tour brochures covering the historic precinct.

RIVERSTONE

It's well worth taking the 14km trip from Oamaru to this idiosyncratic complex, hidden along the unassuming short stretch of SH1 between the braided mouth of the Waitaki River and SH83 turn-off.

First and foremost it's the home of **Riverstone Kitchen** (☑ 03-431 3505; www.river stonekitchen.co.nz; 1431 SH1, Waitaki Bridge; breakfast $16-18, lunch $20-32, dinner $32-35; ☺ 9am-5pm Thu-Mon, 6pm-late Thu-Sun), a sophisticated cafe-restaurant that outshines any in Oamaru itself. A riverstone fireplace and polished concrete floors set the scene for a menu that's modern without being overworked. Much of the produce is from the extensive on-site kitchen gardens (take a look, they're impressive), topped up with locally sourced venison, pork, salmon and beef. It's a smashing brunch option, with excellent coffee and legendary truffled scrambled eggs.

Next door, behind a set of fake heritage shopfronts, **Riverstone Country** (☑ 03-431 3872; 1431 SH1, Waitaki Bridge; ☺ 9am-5pm) is literally packed to the rafters with gifts, crafts, homewares, fake flowers, garden ornaments and Christmas decorations. Outside, there's an aviary stocked with canaries, lorikeets and guinea pigs.

If this all points to an eccentric mind at the helm, take a look at the moated castle being constructed at the rear of the complex. Once the finishing touches are added to the six towers, moat and drawbridge, that's where the owners will reside.

If you're looking for a good place to stay nearby, **Waitaki Waters** (☑ 03-431 3880; www.campingoamaru.co.nz; 305 Kaik Rd, Waitaki Bridge; sites/cabins from $15/40; ☎) is a holiday park with sparkling facilities, manicured hedges and an enthusiastic young owner, 3km off SH1. Cabins are simple but well maintained; bring your own bedding.

Post Office (☑ 03-433 1190; www.nzpost. co.nz; 2 Severn St; ☺ 9am-5pm Mon-Fri, to 1pm Sat)

ⓘ Getting There & Away

Most buses and shuttles depart from the **Lagonda Tearooms** (☑ 03-434 8716; www.facebook. com/LagondaTeaRooms; 191 Thames St; ☺ 9am-4.30pm; ☎). Both the tearooms and the i-SITE take bookings.

Atomic Shuttles (☑ 03-349 0697; www.atomic travel.co.nz) Buses to/from Christchurch ($30, four hours), Timaru ($20,1½ hours) and Dunedin ($20, 1½ hours), twice daily.

Coast Line Tours (☑ 03-434 7744; www. coastline-tours.co.nz; one-way/return $30/55) Shuttles to/from Dunedin; detours to Moeraki and Dunedin Airport can be arranged.

InterCity (☑ 03-471 7143; www.intercity.co.nz) Two daily coaches to/from Christchurch (from $33, four hours), Timaru (from $22, one hour), the Moeraki turn-off (from $17, 28 minutes) and Dunedin (from $22, 1½ hours), and one to Te Anau (from $45, 6½ hours).

Naked Bus (www.nakedbus.com; prices vary) Daily buses head to/from Christchurch (3¾ hours), Timaru (1¼ hours), Moeraki (35 minutes) and Dunedin (1¾ hours).

The Seasider tourist train, operated by **Dunedin Railways** (p522), is a scenic way to travel to Dunedin.

Moeraki

The name Moeraki means 'a place to sleep by day', which should give you some clue as to the pace of life in this little fishing village. You might be surprised to learn that this was one of the first European settlements in NZ, with a whaling station established here in 1836. Since then, Moeraki has nurtured the creation of several national treasures, from Frances Hodgkins' paintings to author Keri Hulme's *The Bone People*, and Fleur Sullivan's cooking.

Apart from Fleur's eponymous restaurant, the main attraction is the collection of large spherical boulders scattered along a beautiful stretch of beach like a giant kid's discarded marbles. The famed **Moeraki Boulders** (Te Kaihinaki) lie just off SH1, a kilometre north of the Moeraki turn-off. Try to time your visit with low tide.

It's a pleasant 45-minute walk along the beach from the village to the boulders. Head in the other direction on the Kaiks Wildlife Trail and you'll reach a cute old wooden lighthouse. You might even spot yellow-eyed penguins and fur seals (be sure to keep your distance).

🛏 Sleeping & Eating

Riverside Haven Lodge
& Holiday Park
HOSTEL $

(☑03-439 5830; www.riversidehaven.nz; 2328 Herbert Hampden Rd/SH1, Waianakarua; sites/dm $12/31, s/d without bathroom $50/75, d with bathroom $85; 🛜) 🅿 Nestled in a loop of the Waianakarua River, 12km north of the Moeraki turn-off, this pretty farm offers both bucolic camping sites and a colourful lodge with a sunny communal lounge. Kids will love the playground and highland cattle; parents will love the spa and peaceful vibe.

Moeraki Beach Motel
MOTEL $

(☑03-439 4862; www.moerakibeachmotels.co.nz; cnr Cleddy & Haven Sts; units from $115; 🛜) The four split-level units at this wood-lined motel are spacious and comfortable. Each has two bedrooms, a full kitchen and a balcony.

⭐Fleur's Place
SEAFOOD $$$

(☑03-439 4480; www.fleursplace.com; Old Jetty, 169 Haven St; mains $35-44; ⏰10.30am-late Wed-Sun) There's a rumble-tumble look about it, but this much graffitied timber hut houses one of the South Island's best seafood restaurants. Head for the upstairs deck and tuck into fresh shellfish, tender muttonbird and other recently landed ocean bounty. Bookings are strongly recommended.

ℹ Getting There & Around

All of the buses on the Oamaru–Dunedin run stop on SH1 by the Moeraki turn-off. From here it's about a 2km walk to both the centre of the village and to the boulders.

DUNEDIN

POP 121,000

Two words immediately spring to mind when Kiwis think of their seventh-largest city: 'Scotland' and 'students'. The 'Edinburgh of the South' is immensely proud of its Scottish heritage, never missing an opportunity to break out the haggis and bagpipes on civic occasions.

In fact, the very name Dunedin is derived from the Scottish Gaelic name for Edinburgh: *Dùn Èideann*. The first permanent European settlers, two shiploads of pious, hard-working Scots, arrived at Port Chalmers in 1848, including the nephew of Scotland's favourite son, Robbie Burns. A statue of the poet dominates the Octagon, the city's civic heart, and the city even has its own tartan.

If there were a tenuous link between the Scottish and the students that dominate Dunedin in term time, it would probably be whisky. The country's oldest university provides plenty of student energy to sustain the local bars, and in the 1980s it even spawned its own internationally influential indie music scene, with Flying Nun Records and the 'Dunedin sound'.

Dunedin is an easy place in which to while away a few days. Weatherboard houses ranging from stately to ramshackle pepper its hilly suburbs, and bluestone Victorian buildings punctuate the compact city centre. It's a great base for exploring the wildlife-rich Otago Peninsula, which officially lies within the city limits.

◉ Sights

○ City Centre

⭐Toitū Otago Settlers Museum
MUSEUM

(Map p520; ☑03-477 5052; www.toituosm.com; 31 Queens Gardens; ⏰10am-5pm) FREE Storytelling is the focus of this excellent interactive museum. The engrossing Māori section is followed by a large gallery where floor-to-ceiling portraits of Victorian-era settlers stare out from behind their whiskers and lace; click on a terminal to learn more about the individuals that catch your eye. Other displays include a recreated passenger-ship cabin, an awesome car collection and a room devoted to the underground stars of Flying Nun Records.

Dunedin Railway Station
HISTORIC BUILDING

(Map p520; 22 Anzac Ave) Featuring mosaic-tile floors and glorious stained-glass windows, Dunedin's striking bluestone railway station (built between 1903 and 1906) claims to be NZ's most photographed building. Head upstairs for the **New Zealand Sports Hall of Fame** (Map p520; ☑03-477 7775; www.nzhalloffame.co.nz; Dunedin Railway Station; adult/child $6/2; ⏰10am-4pm), a small museum devoted to the nation's obsession, and the **Art Station** (Map p520; ☑03-477 9465; www.otagoartsociety.co.nz; ⏰10am-4pm) FREE, the local Art Society's gallery and shop.

Dunedin Public Art Gallery
GALLERY

(Map p520; ☑03-474 3240; www.dunedin.art.museum; 30 The Octagon; ⏰10am-5pm) FREE Explore NZ's art scene at this expansive and airy gallery. Only a fraction of the collection is displayed at any given time, with most of the space given over to often-edgy temporary shows.

St Paul's Cathedral
CHURCH

(Map p520; www.stpauls.net.nz; Moray Pl; ⊙10am-3pm) Even in Presbyterian Dunedin, the 'established church' (aka the Church of England) gets the prime spot on the Octagon. A Romanesque portal leads into the Gothic interior of this beautiful Anglican cathedral, where soaring white Oamaru-stone pillars spread into a vaulted ceiling. The main part of the church dates from 1919 although the sanctuary was left unfinished until 1971; hence the jarring modern extension. The massive organ (3500 pipes) is said to be one of the finest in the southern hemisphere.

Dunedin Chinese Garden
GARDENS

(Map p520; ☑03-477 3248; www.dunedin chinesegarden.com; cnr Rattray & Cumberland Sts; adult/child $9/free; ⊙10am-5pm) Built to recognise the contribution of Chinese people to Dunedin since its earliest days, this walled garden was prefabricated in Shanghai before being dismantled then reassembled here. Its tranquil confines contain all of the elements of a classical Chinese garden, including ponds, pavilions, rockeries, stone bridges and a tea house. There's also a small display on the history of the local Chinese community.

Speight's Brewery
BREWERY

(Map p520; ☑03-477 7697; www.speights. co.nz; 200 Rattray St; adult/child $28/12; ⊙tours noon, 2pm, 4pm & 6pm Jun-Sep, plus 5pm & 7pm Oct-May) Speight's has been churning out beer on this site since the late 1800s. The 90-minute tour offers samples of six different brews, and there's an option to combine a tour with a meal at the neighbouring Ale House (lunch/dinner $58/65).

◉ North Dunedin

Otago Museum
MUSEUM

(Map p520; ☑03-474 7474; www.otagomuseum. nz; 419 Great King St; ⊙10am-5pm) **FREE** The centrepiece of this august institution is *Southern Land, Southern People,* showcasing Otago's cultural and physical past and present, from geology and dinosaurs to the modern day. The *Tangata Whenua* Māori gallery houses an impressive *waka taua* (war canoe), wonderfully worn old carvings, and some lovely *pounamu* (greenstone) weapons, tools and jewellery. Other major

galleries include *Pacific Cultures*, *People of the World* (including the requisite mummy), *Nature, Maritime* and the *Animal Attic*.

The hands-on *Discovery World* science centre (adult/child $10/5) is mainly aimed at kids, although the adjoining tropical forest, filled with colourful live butterflies, is an all-ages treat.

Guided highlights tours depart at 2pm daily (gold coin admission).

Knox Church
CHURCH

(Map p520; www.knoxchurch.net; 449 George St) Dunedin's second grand Presbyterian church sprung up in 1876, only three years after the equally imposing First Church, and quickly became an emblem of the city. Built in the Gothic Revival style out of bluestone edged in white Oamaru stone, its most striking feature is its soaring 50m steeple. Inside there's a beautiful wooden ceiling and such good acoustics that the church is regularly used for concerts and other events.

Dunedin Botanic Garden
GARDENS

(Map p530; www.dunedinbotanicgarden.co.nz; cnr Great King St & Opoho Rd; ⊙dawn-dusk) **FREE** Dating from 1863, these 22 peaceful, grassy and shady hectares include rose gardens, rare natives, a four-hectare rhododendron dell, glasshouses, a playground and a cafe. Kids love tootling about on the Community Express 'train' (adult/child $3/1).

◉ Other Suburbs

★ Olveston
HOUSE

(Map p520; ☑03-477 3320; www.olveston.co.nz; 42 Royal Tce, Roslyn; adult/child $20/11; ⊙tours 9.30am, 10.45am, noon, 1.30pm, 2.45pm & 4pm) Although it's a youngster by European standards, this spectacular 1906 mansion provides a wonderful window into Dunedin's past. Entry is via fascinating guided tours; it pays to book ahead. There's also a pretty little garden to explore.

Until 1966 Olveston was the family home of the wealthy Theomin family, notable patrons of the arts who were heavily involved with endowing the Public Art Gallery. This artistic bent is evident in Olveston's grand interiors, which include works by Charles Goldie and Frances Hodgkins (a family friend). A particular passion was Japanese art, and the home is liberally peppered with exquisite examples. The family was Jewish, and the grand dining table is set up as if for Shabbat dinner.

Central Dunedin

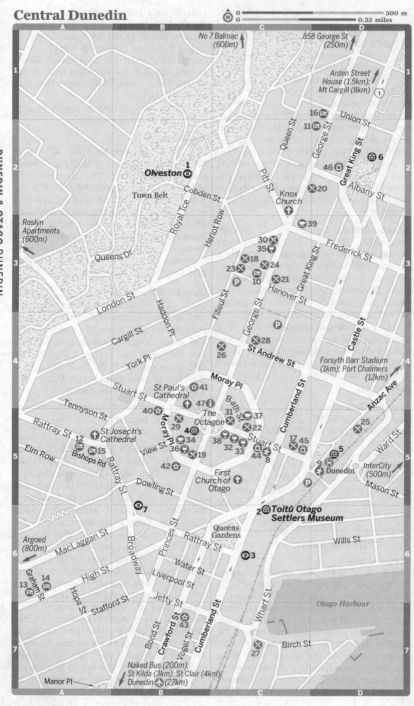

N

0 — 500 m
0 — 0.25 miles

No 7 Balmac (600m)

858 George St (250m)

Arden Street House (1.5km); Mt Cargill (8km)

Olveston **1**

Town Belt

Roslyn Apartments (600m)

Queens Dr

London St

Cargill St

York Pl

Stuart St

Tennyson St

Rattray St

Elm Row

MacLaggan St

High St

Graham St

Argoed (800m)

Cobden St

Royal Tce

Heriot Row

Haddon Pl

Moray Pl

St Paul's Cathedral

The Octagon

Moray Pl

St Joseph's Cathedral

Bishops Rd

Dowling St

First Church of Otago

Queens Gardens

Water St

Liverpool St

Jetty St

Stafford St

Manor Pl

Queen St

George St

Union St

Great King St

Albany St

Knox Church

Pitt St

Filleul St

George St

Hanover St

St Andrew St

Great King St

Frederick St

Castle St

Cumberland St

Forsyth Barr Stadium (1km); Port Chalmers (12km)

Anzac Ave

Ward St

Mason St

InterCity (500m)

Dunedin

Toitū Otago Settlers Museum **2**

Wills St

Otago Harbour

Birch St

Wharf St

Cumberland St

Crawford St

Vogel St

Bond St

Broadway

Princes St

Rattray St

View St

Stuart St

Bath St

Naked Bus (200m); St Kilda (3km); St Clair (4km); Dunedin (27km)

1
6
16
11
46
20
39
30
35
18
24
23
10
21
28
26
41
47
40
31
37
29
4
34
36
38
32
33
19
42
17
45
44
8
9
5
25
7
3
13
14
43
27
12
15
22

Central Dunedin

Baldwin St
LANDMARK

(Map p530; North East Valley) The world's steepest residential street (or so says the *Guinness Book of World Records*), at its peak Baldwin St has a gradient of 1 in 2.86 (19°). From the city centre, head 2km north up Great King St to where the road branches sharp left to Timaru. Get in the right-hand lane and continue straight ahead. This becomes North Rd, and Baldwin St is on the right after 1km.

✻ Activities

Swimming & Surfing
St Clair and St Kilda are both popular swimming beaches (though you need to watch for rips at St Clair). Both have consistently good left-hand breaks, and you'll also find good surfing at Blackhead further south, and at Aramoana on Otago Harbour's North Shore.

St Clair Hot Salt Water Pool
SWIMMING

(Map p530; www.dunedin.govt.nz; Esplanade, St Clair; adult/child $6.20/3.10; ⊗ 8.30am-6pm daily Oct-Apr, 9am-5pm Wed-Mon May-Sep) This heated, outdoor pool sits on the western headland of St Clair Beach.

Esplanade Surf School
SURFING

(Map p530; ☏ 0800 484 141; www.espsurfschool. co.nz; 1 Esplanade, St Clair; 90min group lesson $60, private instruction $120) Operating from a van parked at St Clair Beach in summer (call at other times), this experienced crew provides equipment and lessons.

Hiking/Tramping
The Otago Tramping & Mountaineering Club (www.otmc.co.nz) organises day and overnight tramps on weekends, often to the Silver Peaks Reserve north of Dunedin. Nonmembers are welcome, but must contact trip leaders beforehand.

Tunnel Beach Walkway
WALKING

(Tunnel Beach Rd, Blackhead) This short but extremely steep track (15 minutes down, 30 back up) accesses a dramatic stretch of coast where the wild Pacific has carved sea stacks, arches and unusual formations out of the limestone. Strong currents make swimming here dangerous.

It takes its name from a hand-hewn stone tunnel at the bottom of the track, which civic father John Cargill had built to give his family access to secluded beachside picnics.

The track is 7km southwest of central Dunedin. Head south on Princes St and continue as it crosses under the motorway and then a railway bridge. Turn right at the next traffic lights onto Hillside Rd and follow it until the end, then make a quick left then right onto Easther Cres. Stay on this road for 3.5km (it changes name several times) and then look for Tunnel Beach Rd on the left.

Mt Cargill-Bethunes Gully Walkway
WALKING

(Map p530; Norwood St, Normanby) Yes, it's possible to drive up 676m Mt Cargill, but that's not the point. The track (3½ hours return) starts from Norwood St, which is accessed from North Rd. From Mt Cargill, a trail continues to the 10-million-year-old, lava-formed Organ Pipes and, after another half-hour, to Mt Cargill Rd on the other side of the mountain.

Other Activities

Dunedin Railways
TOURIST TRAIN

(Map p520; ☑03-477 4449; www.dunedin railways.co.nz; Dunedin Railway Station; ⊙office 8am-5pm Mon-Fri, 8.30am-3pm Sat & Sun) Two interesting heritage train journeys start at Dunedin's railway station. The best is the scenic **Taieri Gorge Railway**, with narrow tunnels, deep gorges, winding tracks, rugged canyons and viaduct crossings. The four-hour return trip aboard 1920s heritage coaches travels to Pukerangi (one-way/return $63/91), 58km away. Some trains carry on to Middlemarch ($75/113, six hours return) – handy for the Otago Central Rail Trail.

The **Seasider** heads north, partly along the coast, as far as Oamaru ($72/109, seven hours return), although it's possible to get off the train at Moeraki ($66/99) for a two-hour stop before hopping on the return train. Shorter trips head as far as Palmerston ($59/89, four hours return). Aim for a seat on the right-hand side of the train for better sea views.

Cycle World
BICYCLE RENTAL

(Map p520; ☑03-477 7473; www.cycleworld. co.nz; 67 Stuart St; per day $40; ⊙8.30am-6pm Mon-Fri, 10am-3pm Sat & Sun) Rents out bikes, performs repairs and has mountain-biking information.

🛏 Sleeping

🛏 City Centre

Hogwartz
HOSTEL $

(Map p520; ☑03-474 1487; www.hogwartz.co.nz; 277 Rattray St; dm $31, with/without bathroom s $82/65, d $90/74, apt from $106; P@🕸) The Catholic bishop's residence from 1872 to 1999, this beautiful building is now a fascinating warren of comfortable and sunny rooms, many with harbour views. The old coach house and stables have recently been converted into swankier en suite rooms and apartments.

Chalet Backpackers
HOSTEL $

(Map p520; ☑03-479 2075; www.chaletback packers.co.nz; 296 High St; dm/s/d $31/50/68; P@🕸) The kitchen of this rambling old building is big, sunny and festooned with flowers, and there's also a compact garden, pool table, piano and rumours of a ghost. There are no en suite rooms but some have handbasins.

315 Euro
MOTEL $$

(Map p520; ☑03-477 9929; www.eurodunedin. co.nz; 315 George St; apt from $175; P🕸) This sleek complex is accessed by an unlikely looking alley off Dunedin's main retail strip. Choose from modern studios or larger one-bedroom apartments with full kitchens and laundries. Double glazing keeps George St's irresistible buzz at bay.

Brothers Boutique Hotel
HOTEL $$$

(Map p520; ☑03-477 0043; www.brothershotel. co.nz; 295 Rattray St; r $170-395; P🕸) Rooms in this 1920s Christian Brothers residence have been refurbished beyond any monk's dreams, while still retaining many unique features. The chapel room even has its original arched stained-glass windows. There are great views from the rooftop units. Rates include a continental breakfast and an evening drink.

Fletcher Lodge
B&B $$$

(Map p520; ☑03-477 5552; www.fletcherlodge. co.nz; 276 High St; s/d/apt from $295/355/650; P@🕸) 🖉 Originally home to one of NZ's wealthiest industrialists, this gorgeous redbrick mansion is just minutes from the city, but the secluded gardens feel wonderfully remote. Rooms are elegantly trimmed with antique furniture and ornate plaster ceilings.

North Dunedin

★Kiwi's Nest   HOSTEL $
(Map p520; ☑03-471 9540; www.kiwisnest.co.nz; 597 George St; dm $28, with/without bathroom s $68/48, d $88/68, apt $105; P@⊚) This wonderfully homely two-storey house has a range of tidy centrally heated rooms, some with en suites, fridges and kettles. Plus it's a flat walk to the Octagon – something few Dunedin hostels can boast.

★858 George St   MOTEL $$
(☑03-474 0047; www.858georgestreetmotel. co.nz; 858 George St; units from $150; P⊚) ✦ Cleverly designed to blend harmoniously with the neighbourhood's two-storey Victorian houses, this top-quality motel complex has units ranging in size from studios to two bedrooms. Studios are fitted with microwaves, fridges, toasters and kettles, while the larger units also have stove tops or full ovens.

★Bluestone on George   APARTMENT $$$
(Map p520; ☑03-477 9201; www.bluestone dunedin.co.nz; 571 George St; apt from $225; P@⊚) ✦ If you're expecting an imposing old bluestone building, think again: this four-storey block couldn't be more contemporary. The elegant studio units are decked out in muted tones, with kitchenettes, laundry facilities and decks or tiny balconies. There's also a small gym and a guest lounge.

St Clair

Majestic Mansions   APARTMENT $$
(Map p530; ☑03-456 5000; www.st-clair. co.nz; 15 Bedford St; apt from $140; P⊚) One street back from St Clair beach, this venerable 1920s apartment block has been thoroughly renovated, keeping the layout of the original little flats but sprucing them up with feature wallpaper and smart furnishings. Each has kitchen and laundry facilities.

Hotel St Clair   HOTEL $$$
(Map p530; ☑03-456 0555; www.hotelstclair.com; 24 Esplanade; r $205-255, ste $370; P⊚) Soak up St Clair's surfy vibe from the balcony of your chic room in this contemporary medium-rise hotel. All but the cheapest have ocean views, and the beach is only metres from the front door.

Other Suburbs

Leith Valley Touring Park   HOLIDAY PARK $
(Map p530; ☑03-467 9936; www.leithvalley touringpark.co.nz; 103 Malvern St, Woodhaugh; sites per person $19, units with/without bathroom from $92/59; P@⊚) ✦ This holiday park is surrounded by native bush studded with walks, glowworm caves and a creek. Self-contained modern motel units are spacious, and tourist flats are smaller but have a more rustic feel (linen required).

Argoed   B&B $$
(☑03-474 1639; www.argoed.co.nz; 504 Queens Dr, Belleknowes; s/d from $150/190; P⊚) Roses and rhododendrons encircle this gracious two-storey wooden villa, built in the 1880s. Each of the three charmingly old-fashioned bedrooms has its own bathroom but only one is en suite. Guests can relax in the conservatory or tinkle the ivories of the grand piano in the lounge.

Arden Street House   B&B $$
(Map p530; ☑03-473 8860; www.ardenstreet house.co.nz; 36 Arden St, North East Valley; s $75, d with/without bathroom $130/120; P@⊚) With crazy artworks, an organic garden, charming hosts and a lived-in feeling, this 1930s hill-top house makes a wonderfully eccentric base. Some of the rooms have great views and one, in a converted garage, has a kitchenette. To get here from the city, drive up North Rd, turn right into Glendining Ave and then left into Arden St.

Roslyn Apartments   APARTMENT $$$
(☑03-477 6777; www.roslynapartments.co.nz; 23 City Rd, Roslyn; apt from $215; P⊚) Modern decor and brilliant city and harbour views are on tap at these apartments, just a short walk from Roslyn's eating strip. Each has full kitchen and laundry facilities.

✗ Eating

Cafes and inexpensive Asian restaurants are clustered along George St. Uphill from the Octagon, Roslyn has good restaurants and cafes, and the beachy ambience of St Clair is great for a lazy brunch.

✗ City Centre

★ Otago Farmers Market
MARKET $

(Map p520; www.otagofarmersmarket.org.nz; Dunedin Railway Station; ⊗8am-12.30pm Sat) This thriving market is all local, all edible (or drinkable) and mostly organic. Grab felafels or an espresso to sustain you while you browse, and stock up on fresh meat, seafood, vegies and cheese for your journey. Sorted.

Good Oil
CAFE $

(Map p520; ☑03-479 9900; www.thegoodoilcafe. com; 314 George St; mains $9-18; ⊗7.30am-4pm) This sleek little cafe is a great spot for coffee and cake or fresh salads. If you're still waking up, kickstart the day with imaginative brunches such as kumara hash with hot smoked salmon.

Modaks Espresso
CAFE $

(Map p520; ☑03-477 6563; 337-339 George St; mains $9-17; ⊗7.30am-3.30pm; ☑) This funky little place with brick walls, mismatched formica tables, plastic animal heads and bean bags for slouching in is popular with students and those who appreciate sweet indie pop while they nurse a pot of tea. Plump, toasted bagels warm the insides in winter.

JUST GIVE ME THE COFFEE & NO ONE WILL GET HURT

Dunedin has some excellent coffee bars in which you can refuel and recharge:

The Fix (Map p520; www.thefixcoffee. co.nz; 15 Frederick St; ⊗7am-4pm Mon-Fri, 8am-noon Sat) Wage slaves queue at the pavement window every morning, while students and others with time on their hands relax in the courtyard.

Mazagran Espresso Bar (Map p520; 36 Moray Pl; ⊗8am-6pm Mon-Fri, 10am-2pm Sat) The godfather of Dunedin's coffee scene, this compact wood-and-brick coffee house is the source of the magic bean for many of the city's restaurants and cafes.

Strictly Coffee Company (Map p520; ☑03-479 0017; www.strictlycoffee. co.nz; 23 Bath St; ⊗7.30am-4pm Mon-Fri) This stylish retro coffee bar is hidden down grungy Bath St. Different rooms provide varying views and artworks to enjoy while you sip and sup.

Best Cafe
FISH & CHIPS $

(Map p520; www.facebook.com/bestcafedunedin; 30 Stuart St; takeaways $6-10, mains $10-23; ⊗11am-2.30pm & 5-8pm Mon-Sat) Serving up fish and chips since 1932, this local stalwart has its winning formula down pat, complete with vinyl tablecloths, hand-cut chips and curls of butter on white bread.

Velvet Burger
BURGERS $

(Map p520; ☑03-477 7089; www.velvetburger. co.nz; 150 Stuart St; mains $9-16; ⊗11.30am-late) Well positioned for the post-beer crowd, Velvet Burger has gourmet offerings that are an excellent alcohol sop, especially the mammoth Goneburger (beef, chicken *and* bacon). There's another branch at **375 George St** (Map p520; ☑03-477 0124; mains $9-16; ⊗11.30am-late).

Miga
KOREAN $$

(Map p520; ☑03-477 4770; www.migadunedin. co.nz; 4 Hanover St; mains lunch $9.50-13, dinner $16-39; ⊗11.30am-2pm & 5-10pm Mon-Sat) Settle into a booth at this attractive brick-lined eatery, and order claypot rice or noodle dishes from the extensive menu. Japanese dishes include tempura, katsu and incredible ramen soups, made with fresh noodles that are specially made for them. Otherwise go for broke and cook a Korean barbecue right at your table.

Etrusco at the Savoy
ITALIAN $$

(Map p520; ☑03-477 3737; www.etrusco.co.nz; 8a Moray Pl; mains $17-21; ⊗5.30pm-late) New Zealand has very few dining rooms to match the Edwardian elegance of the Savoy, with its moulded ceilings, stained-glass crests, brass chandeliers, green Ionian columns and fabulously over-the-top lamps. Pizza and pasta might seem like an odd fit, but Etrusco's deliciously rustic dishes absolutely hold their own.

Paasha
TURKISH $$

(Map p520; ☑03-477 7181; www.paasha.co.nz; 31 St Andrew St; mains lunch $12-21, dinner $21-36; ⊗11.30am-3pm & 5-9pm Mon-Wed, 11.30am-late Thu-Sun; ☑) Authentic Turkish kebabs, dips and salads are faithfully created at this long-running Dunedin favourite. It's a top place for takeaways, and most nights the spacious and warm interior is filled with groups drinking Efes beer and sharing heaving platters of tasty Ottoman goodness.

Saigon Van VIETNAMESE $$

(Map p520; ✆03-474 1445; 66a St Andrew St; mains $11-23; ⏱11.30am-2pm & 5-9pm Tue-Sun; ✍) The decor looks high-end Asian, but the prices are more moderate than you'd imagine. Try the combination spring rolls and a bottle of Vietnamese beer to recreate lazy nights in Saigon. The bean-sprout-laden *pho* (noodle soup) and salads are also good.

Izakaya Yuki JAPANESE $$

(Map p520; ✆03-477 9539; 29 Bath St; dishes $4-12; ⏱noon-2pm Mon-Fri, 5pm-late daily; ✎) Cute and cosy, with a huge array of small dishes on which to graze, Yuki is a lovely spot for supper or a relaxed, drawn-out Japanese meal. Make a night of it with sake or Asahi beer, sashimi, teppanyaki and multiple plates of *kushiyaki* (grilled skewers).

★Bracken MODERN NZ $$$

(Map p520; ✆03-477 9779; www.brackenrestaurant.co.nz; 95 Filleul St; 5/7/9-course menu $79/99/120; ⏱5.30-11pm Tue-Sat) Bracken's tasting menus offer a succession of pretty little plates bursting with flavour. While the dishes are intricate, nothing's overly gimmicky, and the setting, in an old wooden house, is classy without being too formal.

Plato MODERN NZ $$$

(Map p520; ✆03-477 4235; www.platocafe.co.nz; 2 Birch St; mains lunch $19-24, dinner $34-36; ⏱noon-2pm Wed-Sun, 6pm-late daily) The kooky decor (including collections of toys and beer tankards) gives little indication of the seriously good food on offer at this relaxed eatery by the harbour. Fresh fish and shellfish feature prominently in a lengthy menu full of international flavours and subtle smoky elements. Servings are enormous.

Scotia SCOTTISH $$$

(Map p520; ✆03-477 7704; www.scotiadunedin.co.nz; 199 Stuart St; mains $32-38; ⏱5pm-late Tue-Sat) Occupying a cosy heritage townhouse, Scotia toasts all things Scottish with a wall full of single-malt whisky and hearty fare such as smoked salmon and Otago hare. The two Scottish Robbies – Burns and Coltrane – look down approvingly on a menu that also includes haggis and whisky-laced pâté.

North Dunedin

Everyday Gourmet CAFE, DELI $

(Map p520; www.everydaygourmet.net.nz; 466 George St; mains $9-19; ⏱8am-4pm Mon-Sat) Apart from cooked breakfasts and pasta, most of the good stuff beckons from the counter of this excellent bakery-style cafe and deli. It's light, bright and extremely popular, with a good selection of magazines and newspapers.

St Clair

Starfish CAFE $$

(Map p530; ✆03-455 5940; www.starfishcafe.co.nz; 7/240 Forbury Rd; mains brunch $14-20, dinner $20-30; ⏱7am-5pm Sun-Tue, to late Wed-Sat) Starfish is the coolest creature in the growing restaurant scene at St Clair Beach. Pop out on a weekday to score an outside table, and tuck into gourmet pizza and wine. Evening meals are big and robust (steak, fish and chips, pulled-pork sliders), and there's a good selection of craft beer.

Other Suburbs

★No 7 Balmac CAFE $$

(✆03-464 0064; www.no7balmac.co.nz; 7 Balmacewen Rd, Maori Hill; mains brunch $14-25, dinner $29-37; ⏱7am-late Mon-Fri, 8.30am-late Sat, 8.30am-5pm Sun; ✎) We wouldn't recommend walking to this sophisticated cafe at the top of Maori Hill, but luckily it's well worth the price of a cab. The fancy cafe fare stretches to the likes of venison loin and dry-aged beef. If you're on a diet, avoid eye contact with the sweets cabinet.

Drinking & Nightlife

★Mou Very BAR

(Map p520; ✆03-477 2180; www.facebook.com/MouVeryBar; 357 George St; ⏱7am-5pm Mon & Tue, 7am-12.30am Wed-Fri, 9am-12.30pm Sat, 9am-5pm Sun) Welcome to one of the world's smallest bars – it's only 1.8m wide, but is still big enough to host regular DJs, live bands and poetry readings. There are just six bar stools, so patrons spill out into an adjacent laneway. By day, it's a handy caffeine-refuelling spot.

Carousel COCKTAIL BAR

(Map p520; ✆03-477 4141; www.carouselbar.co.nz; upstairs, 141 Stuart St; ⏱5pm-late Tue-Sat) Tartan wallpaper, a roof deck and great cocktails leave the dressed-up clientele looking pleased to be seen somewhere so deadly cool. DJs spin deep house until late from Thursday through to Saturday, and there's live jazz on Friday evenings from 8.30pm.

Inch Bar
BAR

(Map p530; ☑03-473 6496; 8 Bank St, North East Valley; ☺3-11.30pm) Make the short trek from town to this cavelike little bar for its selection of Kiwi craft beers and tasty tapas, and the cute little indoor-outdoor beer garden. Despite its diminutive dimensions, it oftens hosts live music.

Albar
BAR

(Map p520; 135 Stuart St; ☺11am-late) This former butcher is now a bohemian little bar attracting maybe the widest age range in Dunedin. Most punters are drawn by the many single-malt whiskies, interesting tap beers and cheap-as-chips bar snacks ($6 to $9).

Pequeno
COCKTAIL BAR

(Map p520; ☑03-477 7830; www.pequeno.co.nz; behind 12 Moray Pl; ☺5pm-late Mon-Fri, 7pm-late Sat) Down the alley opposite the Rialto Cinema, Pequeno attracts a sophisticated crowd with leather couches, a cosy fireplace and an excellent wine and tapas menu. Music is generally laid-back, with regular live acts.

Di Lusso
COCKTAIL BAR

(Map p520; ☑03-477 3885; www.dilusso.co.nz; 117 Stuart St; ☺3pm-3am Mon-Sat) Upmarket and designery with wood panelling, chandeliers and a backlit drinks display, Di Lusso serves seriously good cocktails. DJs play from Thursday to Saturday.

Stuart St Brew Bar
BAR

(Map p520; ☑03-477 3776; www.stuartst.co.nz; 12 The Octagon; ☺11am-late) Nelson's Mac's brewery is making a strike deep into Speight's territory in the form of this funky bar right on the Octagon. It's the sunniest spot for an afternoon drink, and after the sun sets there's often live music or DJs.

Speight's Ale House
PUB

(Map p520; ☑03-471 9050; www.thealehouse. co.nz; 200 Rattray St; ☺11.30am-late) Busy even in the non-university months, the Ale House is a favourite of strapping young lads in their cleanest dirty shirts. It's a good spot to watch the rugby on TV and to try the full range of Speight's beers.

☆ Entertainment

Metro Cinema
CINEMA

(Map p520; ☑03-471 9635; www.metrocinema. co.nz; Moray Pl) Within the town hall, Metro shows art-house and foreign flicks.

Rialto Cinemas
CINEMA

(Map p520; ☑03-474 2200; www.rialto.co.nz; 11 Moray Pl) Blockbusters and art-house flicks. Rates cheaper on Tuesdays.

Fortune Theatre
THEATRE

(Map p520; ☑03-477 8323; www.fortunetheatre. co.nz; 231 Stuart St) The world's southernmost professional theatre company has been staging dramas, comedies, pantomimes, classics and contemporary NZ productions for over 40 years. Shows are performed – watched over by the obligatory theatre ghost – in an old Gothic-style Wesleyan church.

Sammy's
LIVE MUSIC

(Map p520; ☑03-477 2185; 65 Crawford St) Dunedin's premier live-music venue draws an eclectic mix of genres from noisy-as-hell punk to chilled reggae and gritty dubstep. It's the venue of choice for visiting Kiwi bands and up-and-coming international acts.

🔒 Shopping

Gallery De Novo
ARTS

(Map p520; ☑03-474 9200; www.gallerydenovo. co.nz; 101 Stuart St; ☺9.30am-5.30pm Mon-Fri, 10am-3pm Sat & Sun) This interesting, contemporary fine art gallery is worth a look whether you're likely to invest in a substantial piece of Kiwi art or not.

University Book Shop
BOOKS

(Map p520; ☑03-477 6976; www.unibooks. co.nz; 378 Great King St, North Dunedin; ☺8.30am-5.30pm Mon-Fri, 11am-3pm Sat & Sun) Dunedin's best bookshop, with lots of Māori, Pacific and NZ titles.

Stuart Street Potters Cooperative
CRAFTS

(Map p520; ☑03-471 8484; 14 Stuart St; ☺10am-5pm Mon-Fri, 9am-3pm Sat) Locally designed and made pottery and ceramic art.

ℹ Information

DOC Visitors Centre (Department of Conservation; Map p520; ☑03-474 3300; www. doc.govt.nz; 50 The Octagon; ☺8.30am-5pm Mon-Fri) Housed within the Dunedin i-SITE, this office provides information and maps on regional walking tracks, Great Walks bookings and hut tickets. When the DOC desk isn't staffed, the i-SITE workers fill in the gaps.

Dunedin Hospital (☑03-474 0999; www. southerndhb.govt.nz; 201 Great King St)

Dunedin i-SITE (Map p520; ☑03-474 3300; www.isitedunedin.co.nz; 50 The Octagon; ☺8.30am-5pm) Dunedin's tourist office incorporates the DOC Visitors Centre.

Urgent Doctors (☏03-479 2900; www.dunedinurgentdoctors.com; 95 Hanover St; ☉8am-10pm) There's also a late-night pharmacy next door.

ⓘ Getting There & Away

AIR

Air New Zealand (☏0800 737 000; www.airnewzealand.co.nz) Flies to/from Auckland, Wellington and Christchurch.

Jetstar (☏0800 800 995; www.jetstar.com) Flies to/from Auckland and Wellington.

Kiwi Regional Airlines (☏07-444 5020; www.flykiwiair.co.nz) Flies to Nelson from Dunedin, with connections to Tauranga and Hamilton.

Virgin Australia (☏0800 670 000; www.virginaustralia.com) Flies to/from Brisbane.

BUS

Buses and shuttles leave from the Dunedin Railway Station, except where we've noted otherwise.

Alpine Connexions (☏03-443 9120; www.alpineconnexions.co.nz) Shuttles head to/from Alexandra ($40, 2½ hours), Clyde ($40, three hours), Cromwell ($45, 3¼ hours) Wanaka ($45, four hours) and Queenstown ($45, 4½ hours), as well as key stops on the Otago Central Rail Trail.

Atomic Shuttles (☏03-349 0697; www.atomictravel.co.nz) Buses to/from Christchurch ($35, 5¾ hours), Timaru ($25,1¾ hours) and Oamaru ($20, 1½ hours), twice daily.

Catch-a-Bus (☏03-449-2024; www.trailjourneys.co.nz) Bike-friendly shuttles to/from key Rail Trail towns, including Middlemarch ($45, one hour), Ranfurly ($49, two hours), Alexandra ($56, 3¼ hours), Clyde ($56, 3½ hours) and Cromwell ($60, 3¾ hours).

Coast Line Tours (☏03-434 7744; www.coastline-tours.co.nz) Shuttles to Oamaru depart from the Octagon; detours to Dunedin Airport and Moeraki can be arranged.

InterCity (Map p530; ☏03-471 7143; www.intercity.co.nz; departs 7 Halsey St) Coaches to/from Christchurch (from $40, six hours) and Oamaru (from $22, 1½ hours) twice daily, and Cromwell (from $22, 3¾ hours), Queenstown (from $36, 4¼ hours) and Te Anau (from $37, 4½ hours) daily.

Naked Bus (www.nakedbus.com; departs 630 Princes St; prices vary) Daily buses head to/from Christchurch (six hours), Timaru (3½ hours), Dunedin Airport (45 minutes), Gore (2½ hours) and Invercargill (3¼ hours).

TRAIN

The tourist trains operated by **Dunedin Railways** (p522) can be used as a transport connection. The Taieri Gorge Railway heads to Middlemarch twice a week, while the Seasider is an option for Moeraki and Oamaru.

ⓘ Getting Around

TO/FROM THE AIRPORT

Dunedin Airport (DUD; ☏03-486 2879; www.dnairport.co.nz; 25 Miller Rd, Momona) is 27km southwest of the city. A standard taxi ride between the city and the airport costs around $90. There is no public bus service. For door-to-door shuttles, try **Kiwi Shuttles** (☏03-487 9790; www.kiwishuttles.co.nz; per 1/2/3/4 passengers $20/36/48/60) or **Super Shuttle** (☏0800 748 885; www.supershuttle.co.nz; per 1/2/3/4 passengers $30/40/50/60).

BUS

Dunedin's **GoBus** (☏03-474 0287; www.orc.govt.nz; adult fare $2.20-6.70) network extends across the city. It's particularly handy for getting to St Clair, St Kilda, Port Chalmers and as far afield as Portobello on the Otago Peninsula. Buses run regularly during the week, but services are greatly reduced (or nonexistent) on weekends and holidays.

CAR

The big rental companies all have offices in Dunedin, and inexpensive local outfits include **Mainland Rental Vehicles** (☏0800 284 284; www.mainlandcarrentals.co.nz) and **Hanson Rental Vehicles** (☏03-453 6576; www.hanson.net.nz).

TAXI

Dunedin Taxis (☏03-477 7777; www.dunedintaxis.co.nz)

Southern Taxis (☏03-476 6300; www.southerntaxis.co.nz)

AROUND DUNEDIN

Port Chalmers

POP 137C

Little Port Chalmers is only 13km out of central Dunedin but it feels a world away. Somewhere between working class and bohemian, Port Chalmers has a history as a port town but has long attracted Dunedin's arty types. Dunedin's best rock-and-roll pub, **Chick's Hotel** (Map p530; ☏022 672 4578; www.facebook.com/ChicksHotel; 2 Mount St; ☉4pm-1am Wed-Sun), is an essential after-dark destination, and daytime attractions include a few raffish cafes, design stores and galleries.

◎ Sights

Orokonui Ecosanctuary WILDLIFE RESERVE
(Map p530; ☏03-482 1755; www.orokonui.org.
nz; 600 Blueskin Rd; adult/child $16/8; ⊙9.30am-
4.30pm) ✦ From the impressive visitors
centre there are great views over this 307-
hectare predator-free nature reserve, which
encloses cloud forest on the mountainous
ridge above Port Chalmers and stretches to
the estuary on the opposite side. Its mission
is to provide a mainland refuge for species
usually exiled to offshore islands for their
own protection. Visiting options include
self-guided explorations, hour-long guided
tours (adult/child $30/15; 11am and 1.30pm
daily) and two-hour guided tours (adult/
child $45/22; 11am daily).

Rare bird species finding sanctuary here
include kiwi, takahe and kaka, while reptiles
include tuatara and Otago skinks.

Orokonui is a well-signposted 6km drive
from the main road into Port Chalmers.

🏃 Activities

Traditional rock climbing (nonbolted) is
popular at Long Beach and the cliffs at Mihiwaka, both accessed via Blueskin Rd north
of Port Chalmers.

Hare Hill HORSE RIDING
(Map p530; ☏03-472 8496; www.horseriding-
dunedin.co.nz; 207 Aramoana Rd, Deborah Bay;
treks $85-160) Horse treks include thrilling
beach rides and farm trips.

🛏 Sleeping

Billy Brown's HOSTEL $
(Map p530; ☏03-472 8323; www.billybrowns.
co.nz; 423 Aramoana Rd, Hamilton Bay; dm/d
$30/75; ⊙Sep-May) On a farm 5km fur-
ther along the road from Port Chalmers,
this hostel has magnificent views across
the harbour to the peninsula. There's a
lovely rustic shared lounge with a cosy
wood-burner and plenty of retro vinyl to
spin. If you're not comfortable with big
dogs, look elsewhere.

❶ Getting There & Away

On weekdays, 17 buses travel between Dunedin
and Port Chalmers, with two additional services
on Friday nights (adult/child $5.20/3). On
Saturdays this reduces to 11, and on Sundays
to three.

Otago Peninsula

POP 4220

The Otago Peninsula is home to the South
Island's most accessible diversity of wildlife.
Albatross, penguins, fur seals and sea lions
are some of the highlights, as well as rugged countryside, wild walks, beaches and
interesting historical sites. Despite a host of
tours exploring the peninsula, it maintains
its quiet rural air.

◎ Sights

**★Nature's Wonders
Naturally** WILDLIFE RESERVE
(Map p530; ☏03-478 1150; www.natureswonders.
co.nz; Taiaroa Head; adult/child $59/45; ⊙tours
from 10.15am) What makes the improbably
beautiful beaches of this coastal sheep farm
different from other important wildlife habitats is that (apart from pest eradication and
the like) they're left completely alone. Many
of the multiple private beaches haven't suffered a human footprint in years. The result
is that yellow-eyed penguins can often be
spotted (through binoculars) at any time of
the day, and NZ fur seals laze around rocky
swimming holes, blissfully unfazed by tour
groups passing by.

Depending on the time of year, you might
also see whales and little penguin chicks.

The tour is conducted in 'go-anywhere'
Argo vehicles by enthusiastic guides, at
least some of whom double as true-blue
Kiwi farmers. If you don't believe it, ask
about the sheep-shed experience (price on
application).

**Royal Albatross Centre
& Fort Taiaroa** BIRD SANCTUARY
(Map p530; ☏03-478 0499; www.albatross.
org.nz; Taiaroa Head; ⊙11.30am-dusk Oct-Apr,
10.15am-dusk May-Sep) Taiaroa Head, at the
peninsula's northern tip, has the world's
only mainland royal albatross colony, along
with a late 19th-century military fort. The
only public access to the area is by guided
tour. The hour-long Classic tour (adult/child
$50/15) focuses on the albatross, or there's
a 30-minute Fort tour ($25/10); the two can
be combined on the Unique tour ($55/20).
Otherwise you can just call into the centre
to look at the displays and have a bite in the
cafe.

Albatross are present on Taiaroa Head
throughout the year, but the best time to
see them is from December to March, when

one parent is constantly guarding the young while the other delivers food throughout the day. Sightings are most common in the afternoon when the winds pick up; calm days don't see as many birds in flight.

Little penguins swim ashore at Pilots Beach (just below the car park) around dusk to head to their nests in the dunes. For their protection, the beach is closed to the public every evening, but viewing is possible from a specially constructed wooden platform (adult/child $30/10). Depending on the time of year, 50 to 300 penguins might waddle past.

Fort Taiaroa was built in 1885 in response to a perceived threat of Russian invasion. Its Armstrong Disappearing Gun was designed to be loaded and aimed underground, then popped up like the world's slowest jack-in-the-box to be fired.

Larnach Castle CASTLE
(Map p530; ☏03-476 1616; www.larnachcastle. co.nz; 145 Camp Rd; adult/child castle & grounds $30/10, grounds only $15/4; ☉9am-7pm Oct-Mar, 9am-5pm Apr-Sep) ☝ Standing proudly on top of a hill, this gorgeous Gothic Revival mansion was built in 1871 by Dunedin banker, merchant and Member of Parliament William Larnach to impress his wife, who was descended from French nobility. It's filled with intricate woodwork and exquisite antique furnishings, and the crenellated tower offers expansive views of the peninsula. A self-guided tour brochure is provided with admission, or you can buy an iPhone tour app ($5) that digitally peoples the rooms with costumed actors.

The castle didn't end up bringing Larnach much happiness. After his first two wives died and his third was rumoured to be having an affair with his son, he shot himself in a committee room in Parliament in 1898. His son later followed suit.

After lording it about in the mansion, take a stroll through the pretty gardens or settle in for high tea in the ballroom café.

Penguin Place BIRD SANCTUARY
(Map p530; ☏03-478 0286; www.penguinplace. co.nz; 45 Pakihau Rd, Harington Point; adult/child $52/15) On private farmland, this reserve protects nesting sites of the yellow-eyed penguin. The 90-minute tours focus on penguin conservation and close-up viewing from a system of hides. The 2½-hour Ultimate Combo includes the penguins and a guided trek through forest and wetlands. Bookings are essential.

Glenfalloch Woodland Garden GARDENS
(Map p530; ☏03-476 1006; www.glenfalloch. co.nz; 430 Portobello Rd, Macandrew Bay; ☉8am-dusk) FREE Expect spectacular harbour views at this 12-hectare garden, filled with flowers, walking tracks and swaying, mature trees, including a 1000-year-old matai. There's also a good restaurant on-site. The Portobello bus stops out the front.

🏃 Activities

The peninsula's coastal and farmland walkways offer blissful views and the chance of spotting some wildlife; pick up or download the DOC *Dunedin Walks* brochure. A popular walking destination is beautiful **Sandfly Bay**, reached from Seal Point Rd (moderate, one hour return). You can also follow a trail from the end of Sandymount Rd to the Sandymount summit and on to the impressive Chasm and Lovers Leap (one hour return). Note that this track is closed from September to mid-October for lambing.

Wild Earth Adventures KAYAKING
(☏03-489 1951; www.wildearth.co.nz; trips $115-235) Offers trips in double sea kayaks, with wildlife often sighted en route. Trips take between three hours and a full day, with pickups from the Octagon in Dunedin.

👉 Tours

Back to Nature Tours BUS TOUR
(☏0800 286 000; www.backtonaturetours.co.nz) ☝ The full-day Royal Peninsula tour (adult/child $189/125) heads to points of interest around Dunedin before hitting the Otago Peninsula. Stops include Larnach Castle's gardens (castle entry is extra), Penguin Place and the Royal Albatross Centre. There's also a half-day option that visits various bays and beaches ($79/55) and another tackling the Lovers Leap and Chasm tracks ($89/55).

Elm Wildlife Tours WILDLIFE WATCHING
(☏03-454 4121; www.elmwildlifetours.co.nz; tours from $99) ☝ Well-regarded, small-group, wildlife-focused tours, with options to add the Royal Albatross Centre or a Monarch Cruise. Pick-up and drop-off from Dunedin is included

Monarch Wildlife Cruises & Tours BOAT TOUR
(Map p530; ☏03-477 4276; www.wildlife.co.nz) ☝ One-hour boat trips from Wellers Rock (adult/child $52/22), and half-day ($90/33) and full-day ($240/124) tours cruising right along the harbour from Dunedin. You may

Dunedin & the Otago Peninsula

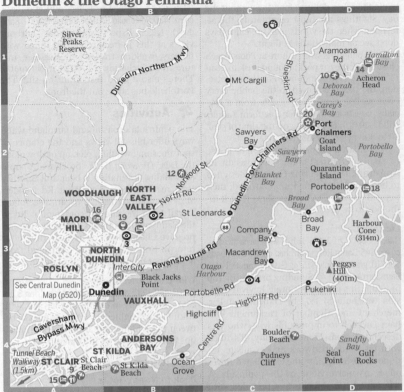

Dunedin & the Otago Peninsula

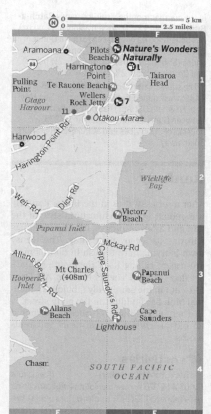

spot sea lions, penguins, albatross and seals. The full-day option includes admission to the Royal Albatross Centre and Penguin Place.

🛏 Sleeping & Eating

McFarmers Backpackers HOSTEL $
(Map p530; ☑03-478 0389; mcfarmers@xtra. co.nz; 774 Fortobello Rd, Broad Bay; s/d without bathroom $55/66, cottage $120-150) On a working sheep farm with harbour views, the rustic timber lodge and self-contained cottage here are steeped in character and feel instantly like home. The Portobello bus goes past the gate.

★ Portobello Motel MOTEL $$
(Map p530; ☑03-478 0155; www.portobello motels.com; 10 Harington Point Rd, Portobello; units from $160; 🕿) These sunny, modern, self-contained units are just off the main road in Portobello. Studio units have small decks

overlooking the bay. Spacious one- and two-bedroom versions are also available, but lack the views.

Larnach Castle B&B $$$
(Map p530; ☑03-476 1616; www.larnachcastle. co.nz; 145 Camp Rd; r stable/lodge/estate $160/290/460; @🕿) 🍃 Pricey Larnach Castle's back-garden lodge has 12 individually whimsically decorated rooms with views. Less frivolous are the atmospheric rooms in the 140-year-old stables (bathrooms are shared). A few hundred metres from the castle, Camp Estate has luxury suites worthy of a romantic splurge. The rates for each option include breakfast and castle entry; dinner in the castle is extra ($70).

1908 Cafe CAFE, BISTRO $$
(Map p530; ☑03-478 0801; www.1908cafe.co.nz; 7 Harington Point Rd, Portobello; mains lunch $13-24, dinner $3-34; ⊙noon-2pm & 6-10pm, closed Mon & Tue Apr-Oct) Salmon, venison and steak are joined by fresh fish and blackboard specials at this casual, friendly eatery. Cafe fare, such as soup and toasted sandwiches, is served at lunch. The venerable interiors are cheerfully embellished with local art.

Portobello Hotel & Bistro PUB FOOD $$
(Map p530; www.portobellohotelandbistro.co.nz; 2 Harington Point Rd, Portobello; mains lunch $15-17, dinner $25-29; ⊙11.30am-11.30pm) Refreshing thirsty travellers since 1874, the Portobello pub is still a popular pit stop. Grab a table in the sun and tuck into seafood chowder, a burger or a lamb pie.

ⓘ Getting There & Around

On weekdays, 13 buses (adult/child $6/3.60) travel between Dunedin's Cumberland St and Portobello Village, two of which continue on to Harington Point at the tip of the peninsula. On Saturdays this reduces to 10, and on Sundays to four. Once on the peninsula, it's tough to get around without your own transport. Most tours will pick you up from your Dunedin accommodation.

There's no petrol available on the peninsula.

CENTRAL OTAGO

Rolling hills that turn from green to gold in the relentless summer sun provide a backdrop to a succession of tiny, charming goldrush towns where rugged, laconic 'Southern Man' types can be seen propping up the bar in lost-in-time pubs. As well as being one of the country's top wine regions, the area

DUNEDIN & OTAGO OTAGO PENINSULA

provides fantastic opportunities for those on two wheels, whether mountain biking along old gold-mining trails or traversing the district on the Otago Central Rail Trail.

Middlemarch

POP 156

With the Rock & Pillar Range as an impressive backdrop, the small town of Middlemarch is the terminus of both the Taieri Gorge Railway and the Otago Central Rail Trail. It's famous in NZ for the Middlemarch Singles Ball (held across Easter in odd-numbered years), where southern men gather to entice city gals to the country life.

🏃 Activities

Cycle Surgery   BICYCLE RENTAL
(📞03-464 3630; www.cyclesurgery.co.nz; Swansea St; rental per day from $35; ⊙depot mid-Sep–mid-May) Rents bikes and serves coffee to Rail Trailers from its main office in Middlemarch. Also has a drop-off depot at the Clyde trailhead.

Trail Journeys   BICYCLE RENTAL
(📞03-464 3213; www.trailjourneys.co.nz; Swansea St; rental per day from $42; ⊙depot Oct-Apr) Provides bike rental and logistical support to riders on the Otago Central Rail Trail. This includes shuttles, bag transfers and an accommodation booking service. Also has a depot in Clyde, at the other end of the trail.

🛏 Sleeping & Eating

Otago Central Hotel   HOTEL $$
(📞03-444 4800; www.hydehotel.co.nz; SH87, Hyde; with/without bathroom s $120/100, d $170/120) Most of the tidy rooms in this cool old hotel, 27km along the trail from Middlemarch, have private bathrooms, but only some are en suite. It's no longer a working pub and the licensed cafe on the sunny terrace shuts at 4pm, leaving the $40 set dinner the only meal option for many miles around.

Kissing Gate Cafe   CAFE $
(📞03-464 3224; 2 Swansea St; mains $7-18; ⊙8.30am-4pm; 🛜) Sit out under the fruit trees in the pretty garden of this cute little wooden cottage and tuck into a cooked breakfast, fancy meat pie, zingy salad or some home baking. Nana-chic at its best.

ℹ Getting There & Away

Both of the main cycle companies offer shuttles to Dunedin, Pukerangi and the Rail Trail towns.

In the warmer months, Trail Journey's **Catch-a-Bus** (📞03-449 2150; www.trailjourneys.co.nz) has scheduled daily services to/from Dunedin ($45, one hour), Ranfurly ($27, one hour), Alexandra ($55, two hours), Clyde ($55, 2½ hours) and Cromwell ($59, 2¾ hours).

The scenic **Taieri Gorge Railway** (📞03-477 4449; www.dunedinrailways.co.nz; ⊙Sun May-Sep, Fri & Sun Oct-Apr) has only limited runs between Dunedin and Middlemarch ($75, 2½ hours); most services end at Pukerangi Station, 20km away.

Ranfurly

POP 663

After a series of fires in the 1930s, Ranfurly was rebuilt in the architectural style of the day, and a few attractive art-deco buildings still line its sleepy main drag. The teensy town is trying hard to cash in on this meagre legacy, calling itself the 'South Island's art deco capital'. There's even an Art Deco Museum in the admittedly fabulous Centennial Milk Bar building on the main street.

There are a couple of cafes in town and an old pub which serves meals and rents rooms.

🏃 Activities

Maniototo 4WD Safaris   DRIVING TOUR
(📞03-444 9703; www.maniototo4wdsafaris.co.nz; half-/full day $130/190) Explore the rugged terrain made famous by noted Central Otago landscape artist Grahame Sydney.

🛏 Sleeping

Peter's Farm Lodge   LODGE $
(📞03-444 9811; www.petersfarm.co.nz; 113 Tregonning Rd, Waipiata; per person $55) Set on a sheep farm 13km south of Ranfurly, this rustic 1882 farmhouse offers comfy beds, hearty barbecue dinners ($25) and free pick-ups from the Rail Trail. Kayaks, fishing rods and gold pans are all available, so it's worth staying a couple of nights. Further beds are available in neighbouring Tregonnings Cottage (1882).

Hawkdun Lodge   MOTEL $$
(📞03-444 9750; www.hawkdunlodge.co.nz; 1 Bute St; s/d from $113/150; 🛜) 🅟 This smart boutique motel is the best option in the town centre by far. Each unit has a kitchenette with a microwave, but travelling chefs can flex their skills in the guest kitchen and on the barbecue. Rates include a continental breakfast.

Kokonga Lodge B&B $$$

(☑ 03-444 9774; www.kokongalodge.co.nz; 33 Kokonga-Waipiata Rd; s/d $235/285; @ 🗢) Just off SH87 between Ranfurly and Hyde, this upmarket rural property offers six contemporary en suite rooms, one of which was occupied by Sir Peter Jackson when he was filming *The Hobbit* in the area. The Rail Trail passes nearby.

❶ Information

Ranfurly i-SITE (☑ 03-444 1005; www.centralotagonz.com; 3 Charlemont St; ◷ 9am-5pm; 🗢) Located in the old train station. Grab a copy of *Rural Art Deco – Ranfurly Walk* for a self-guided tour.

❶ Getting There & Away

In the warmer months, Trail Journey's **Catch-a-Bus** (☑ 03-449 2150; www.trailjourneys.co.nz; ◷ Nov-Apr) passes through Ranfurly on its way between Cromwell ($52, 1¾ hours) and Dunedin ($49, two hours).

Naseby

POP 120

Cute as a button, surrounded by forest and dotted with 19th-century stone buildings, Naseby is the kind of small settlement where life moves slowly. That the town is pleasantly obsessed with the fairly insignificant world of NZ curling indicates there's not much else going on. It's that lazy small-town vibe, along with good mountain-biking and walking trails through the surrounding forest, that makes Naseby an interesting place to stay for a couple of days.

🏃 Activities

**Maniototo Curling
International** SNOW SPORTS

(☑ 03-444 9878; www.curling.co.nz; 1057 Channel Rd; per 90min adult/child $30/12; ◷ 10am-5pm May-Oct, 9am-7.30pm Nov-Apr) All year-round you can shimmy after curling stones at the indoor ice rink; tuition is available. In winter there's also an outdoor ice rink to skate around.

🛏 Sleeping

Royal Hotel PUB $

(☑ 03-444 9990; www.naseby.co.nz; 1 Earne St; dm $40, r with/without bathroom $110/80; 🗢) The better of the town's historic pubs, the 1863 Royal Hotel sports the royal coat of arms and what just might be NZ's most rustic garden bar. Rooms are simple but spotless.

Naseby Lodge APARTMENT $$

(☑ 03-444 8222; www.nasebylodge.co.nz; cnr Derwent & Oughter Sts; 1-/2-bedroom apt $170/260) Constructed of environmentally friendly straw-bale walls sheathed in rustic corrugated iron, these free-standing modern apartments are smart and spacious, with fully equipped kitchens and underfloor heating in the bathrooms. There's also a good restaurant on-site.

Old Doctor's Residence B&B $$$

(☑ 03-444 9775; www.olddoctorsresidence.co.nz; 58 Derwent St; r/ste $295/345; 🗢) ◆ Old doctors take note: this is how to reside! Sitting behind a pretty garden, this gorgeous 1870s house offers two luxurious guest rooms and a lounge where wine and nibbles are served of an evening. The suite has a sitting room and an en suite bathroom (with a fabulous make-up desk). The smaller room's bathroom is accessed from the corridor.

❶ Information

Ernslaw One Forestry Office (☑ 03-444 9995; www.ernslaw.co.nz/naseby-recreational-area; 16 Oughter St; ◷ 9am-4pm Mon-Fri) Administers the 500-hectare recreation reserve within the privately owned Naseby Forest. Call in for maps of walking tracks and mountain-bike trails.

Naseby Information Centre (☑ 03-444 9961; www.nasebyinfo.org.nz; Old Post Office, Derwent St; ◷ 9am-1pm Tue-Thu, 10am-4pm Fri-Mon, reduced hours in winter)

❶ Getting There & Away

The Ranfurly–Naseby Rd leaves SH85, 4km north of Ranfurly. There's no public transport and cyclists should factor in a 12km detour from the Rail Trail. From Naseby, you can wind your way on unsealed roads northeast through spectacular scenery to Danseys Pass and through to Duntroon in the Waitaki Valley.

St Bathans

POP 6

A worthwhile 17km detour north from SH85 heads into the foothills of the imposing Dunstan Mountains and on to diminutive St Bathans. This once-thriving gold-mining town of 2000 people is now home to only half a dozen permanent residents living amid a cluster of cutesy 19th-century buildings, almost all of which have 'For Sale' signs in front of them.

The **Blue Lake** is an accidental attraction: a large hollow filled with blue water that has run off abandoned gold workings. Walk along the sculpted cliffs to the lookout for a better view of the alien landscape (one hour return).

Sleeping

Vulcan Hotel PUB $$
(☏03-447 3629; stbathans.vulcanhotel@xtra. co.nz; Main St; r per person $60) The Vulcan Hotel is an atmospheric (and famously haunted) spot to drink, eat or stay in, even if the reception isn't always entirely welcoming. Considering St Bathans' tiny population, you'll find the bar here pretty busy on a Friday night as thirsty farmers from around the valley descend en masse.

St Bathans Jail & Constable's Cottage RENTAL HOUSE $$
(☏0800 555 016; www.stbathansnz.co.nz; 1648 Loop Rd; house $145-340) Built in 1884, these neighbouring buildings are an atmospheric option. The cottage has three bedrooms (sleeping six) and is fully self-contained, with a barbecue in the garden. The jail has been converted into a bedroom with an en suite bathroom in the old cell and a kitchen in the entrance lobby.

Lauder, Omakau & Ophir

Separated by 8km of SH85, tiny **Lauder** (population 12) and larger **Omakau** (population 250) are good stops if you're a hungry Rail Trailer with a sore bum and in need of a feed and a bed. However, the area's real gem is adorable **Ophir** (population 58), 2km from Omakau across the Manuherikia River.

Gold was discovered here in 1863 and the town swiftly formed, adopting the name of the biblical place where King Solomon sourced his gold. By 1875, the population hit over 1000 but when the gold disappeared, so did the people. Ophir's fate was sealed when the railway bypassed it in 1904, leaving its main street trapped in time.

The most photogenic of Ophir's many heritage buildings is the still-functioning 1886 **post office** (www.historic.org.nz; 53 Swindon St; ⊙9am-noon Mon-Fri). At the far end of the town, the sealed road ends at the 1870s wooden-planked **Dan O'Connell Bridge**, a bumpy but scenic crossing that continues via a gravel road to SH85.

Ophir lays claim to the country's widest range of temperatures: from -21.6°C to 35°C.

Sleeping & Eating

Muddy Creek Cutting B&B $$
(☏03-447 3682; www.muddycreekcutting.co.nz; SH85, Lauder; per person $80) Art fills the walls of this charmingly restored 1930s mudbrick farmhouse, with five bedrooms that share two bathrooms. Dinners with a local, organic spin are also available ($60 per person).

Chatto Creek Tavern HERITAGE HOTEL $$
(☏03-447 3710; www.chattocreektavern.co.nz; 1544 SH85, Chatto Creek; dm/s/d without bathroom $60/100/130; ☎) Dating from 1886, this attractive stone hotel sits right beside the Rail Trail and highway, 10km southwest of Omakau. Pop in for a whitebait fritter (in season) or lamb shanks, or rest your weary calf muscles in a dorm bed or double room. Rates include breakfast. Free, informal camping is also possible, with a $5 charge for a shower.

★**Pitches Store** B&B $$$
(☏03-447 3240; www.pitches-store.co.nz; 45 Swindon St, Ophir; r $280; ⊙restaurant 10am-late daily Nov-Apr, 10am-3pm Mon, Sun & Thu, 10am-late Fri & Sat May & Aug-Oct) Formerly a general store and butcher, this heritage building has been sensitively transformed into six elegant guest rooms and a humdinger of a cafe-restaurant (brunch mains $13 to $19, dinner mains $33 to $37). Exposed stone walls may speak of the past but the menu offers contemporary country cooking.

Muddy Creek Cafe CAFE $
(2 Harvey St, Omakau; mains $8-16; ⊙8.30am-7pm Mon-Sat, 10am-7pm Sun) Take a break from the Rail Trail at this friendly spot festooned with old radios. Cafe treats include all-day breakfasts, paninis, pies and ice cream, or you can grab a burger or fish and chips from the takeaway counter.

Stationside Cafe CAFE $
(Lauder-Matakanui Rd, Lauder; mains $8-18; ⊙8am-5pm Oct-Apr) Home baking and country cooking are showcased at this great little trailside place with a wonderfully charming hostess. Options include healthy salads, sandwiches, soups and pasta. Sadly, the coffee's not up to much.

Alexandra

POP 4800

Unless you've come especially for the Easter Bunny Hunt or the springtime Blossom Festival and NZ Merino Shearing Championships, the main reason to visit unassum-

ROXBURGH

Heading south from Alexandra, SH8 winds along rugged rock-strewn hills above the Clutha River as it passes Central Otago's famous orchards. In season, roadside fruit stalls sell just-picked stone fruit, cherries and berries. En route are a scattering of small towns, many dating from gold-rush days.

Thirteen kilometres south of Alexandra, the historic **Speargrass Inn** (☑ 03-449 2192; www.speargrassinn.co.nz; 1300 Fruitlands-Roxburgh Rd/SH8, Fruitlands; r $180; ☺ cafe 8.30am-4pm Mon-Thu, 8.30am-9pm Fri-Sun, closed Tue & Wed May-Sep; ☏) has three handsome rooms in a block out the back, set in attractive gardens. The original 1869 building houses a charming cafe (mains $13 to $26). It's a good place to stop for coffee and cake or a more substantial meal.

Further south, the Clutha broadens into **Lake Roxburgh** with a large hydroelectric power station at its terminus, before rushing past Roxburgh itself (population 522). Call into the friendly **i-SITE** (☑ 03-446 8920; www.centralotago.com; 120 Scotland St; ☺ 9am-5pm daily Nov-Mar, 9am-5pm Mon-Fri Apr-Oct) for information on mountain biking, water sports and seasonal fruit-picking work in the surrounding apple and stone-fruit orchards.

Another source of fruit-picking contacts is **Villa Rose Backpackers** (☑ 03-446 8761; www.villarose.co.nz; 79 Scotland St; dm $35, d with/without bathroom from $120/100; ☏). This lovely old bungalow has spacious dorm rooms, comfortable self-contained units and a huge modern kitchen.

Before you leave Roxburgh, drop into **Jimmy's Pies** (☑ 03-446 9012; www.jimmyspies.co.nz; 143 Scotland St; pies $4-6.50; ☺ 7.30am-5pm Mon-Fri), renowned across the South Island since 1959. If you're at a loss as to which meaty pastry to choose, try the apricot chicken – you're in orchard country after all.

Continuing south from Roxburgh, the road passes through Lawrence and the Manuka Gorge Scenic Reserve, a picturesque route through wooded hills and gullies. SH8 joins SH1 near Milton.

ing Alexandra is mountain biking. It's the biggest Central Otago Rail Trail settlement by far, offering more eating and sleeping options than the rest of the one-horse (or fewer) towns on the route. It's also the start of the new Roxburgh Gorge Trail.

Alex, as it's known to the locals, marks the southeastern corner of the acclaimed Central Otago wine region. Of the dozen wineries in the immediate vicinity, only a handful are open for tastings. These are detailed on the *Central Otago Wine Map*, available from the i-SITE (p536).

◎ Sights

Central Stories   MUSEUM
(☑ 03-448 6230; www.centralstories.com; 21 Centennial Ave; admission by donation; ☺ 10am-4pm) Central Otago's history of gold-mining, winemaking, orcharding and sheep farming is covered in this excellent regional museum and gallery, which shares a building with the i-SITE.

🏃 Activities

Walkers and mountain bikers will love the old gold trails weaving through the hills; collect maps from the i-SITE. The **Alexandra–Clyde**

150th Anniversary Walk (12.8km, three hours one way) is a riverside trail that's fairly flat, with ample resting spots and shade.

Roxburgh Gorge Trail   MOUNTAIN BIKING
(www.cluthagold.co.nz) Opened to considerable fanfare in 2013, this well-constructed cycling and walking track was intended to connect Alexandra to Roxburgh Dam. As access through some of the farmland in the middle section wasn't successfully negotiated, riding the 'full trail' requires prearranging a scenic 13km jet-boat ride (adult/child $95/55) through the local information centres or directly with Clutha River Cruises (p536).

Once you add on the noncompulsory track maintenance donation ($25/50 per adult/family), it's an expensive ride.

An alternative is to make a return trip from each end: Alexandra–Doctors Point (20km return) or Roxburgh Dam–Shingle Creek (22km return).

From Roxburgh Dam you can continue on the Clutha Gold Trail, an easier 73km track that follows the Clutha through Roxburgh to Beaumont and then heads to Lawrence. The same maintenance fee covers both tracks.

Clutha River Cruises BOAT TOUR

(☑0800 258 842; www.clutharivercruises.co.nz; boat ramp, Dunorling St; adult/child $95/45; ☺2pm Oct-May) Explore the scenery and history of the region on a 2½-hour heritage cruise. They also run the jetboat transfer for cyclists on the Roxburgh Gorge Trail.

Altitude Bikes BICYCLE RENTAL

(☑03-448 8917; www.altitudeadventures.co.nz; 88 Centennial Ave; per day from $25; ☺8.30am-5.30pm Mon-Fri, 9am-1pm Sat) Rents bikes in conjunction with Henderson Cycles and organises logistics for riders on the Otago Central, Clutha Gold and Roxburgh Gorge Trails.

🛏 Sleeping & Eating

Marj's Place HOSTEL $

(☑03-448 7098; www.marjsplace.co.nz; 5 Theyers St; dm/s/d without bathroom $30/40/80; 🛜) The standard varies widely between the three neighbouring houses that comprise Marj's sprawling 'place'. The 'homestay' has private rooms, a Finnish sauna and a spa bath. It's much nicer than the 'backpackers', which is let mainly to seasonal workers.

★ Courthouse Cafe & Larder CAFE $

(☑03-448 7818; www.packingshedcompany.com; 8 Centennial Ave; mains $10-20; ☺8am-4pm) Floral wallpaper and bright vinyl tablecloths help to dispel any lingering austerity from this stone courthouse building, dating from 1878 and surrounded by lawns. The counter groans under the weight of an extraordinary array of baked goods (macadamia custard croissants, gooey doughnuts, slices, cakes), which compete with a menu full of interesting dishes (beef-cheek burgers, pulled-pork sliders, eggy breakfasts).

ℹ Information

Alexandra i-SITE (☑03-262 7999; www.centralotagonz.com; 21 Centennial Ave; ☺9am-5pm; 🛜) Pick up a free map of this very spread-out town.

ℹ Getting There & Away

Atomic Shuttles (☑03-349 0697; www.atomictravel.co.nz) A daily bus heads to/from Dunedin ($30, 2¼ hours), Roxburgh ($15, 30 minutes), Cromwell ($15, 30 minutes) and Wanaka ($25, 1¾ hours).

Catch-a-Bus (☑03-449 2024; www.trailjourneys.co.nz) Shuttles to Cromwell ($25, 30 minutes), Clyde ($15, 10 minutes), Ranfurly ($43, one hour), Middlemarch ($55, two hours) and Dunedin ($56, 3¼ hours).

InterCity (☑03-471 7143; www.intercity.co.nz) A daily coach heads to/from Dunedin (from $21, three hours), Roxburgh (from $14, 34 minutes), Clyde (from $10, nine minutes), Cromwell (from $12, 24 minutes) and Queenstown (from $15, 1½ hours).

OTAGO CENTRAL RAIL TRAIL

Stretching from Dunedin to Clyde, the Central Otago rail branch linked small, inland goldfield towns with the big city from the early 20th century through to the 1990s. After the 150km stretch from Middlemarch to Clyde was permanently closed, the rails were ripped up and the trail resurfaced. The result is a year-round mainly gravel trail that takes bikers, walkers and horse riders along a historic route containing old rail bridges, viaducts and tunnels.

With excellent trailside facilities (toilets, shelters and information), few hills, gob-smacking scenery and profound remoteness, the trail attracts well over 25,000 visitors annually. March is the busiest time, when there are so many city slickers on the track that you might have to wait 30 minutes at cafes en route for a panini. Consider September for a quieter ride.

The trail can be followed in either direction. The entire trail takes approximately four to five days to complete by bike (or a week on foot), but you can obviously choose to do as short or as long a stretch as suits your plans. There are also easy detours to towns such as Naseby and St Bathans.

Mountain bikes can be rented in Dunedin, Middlemarch, Alexandra and Clyde. Any of the area's i-SITEs can provide detailed information. See www.otagocentralrailtrail.co.nz and www.otagorailtrail.co.nz for track information, recommended timings, accommodation options and tour companies.

Due to the popularity of the trail, a whole raft of sleeping and eating options have sprung up in remote locales en route, although some stops are still poorly served.

Clyde

POP 1020

Much more charming than his buddy Alex, 8km down the road, Clyde looks more like a 19th-century gold-rush film set than a real town. Set on the banks of the emerald-green Clutha River, Clyde retains a friendly, small-town feel, even when holidaymakers arrive in numbers over summer. It's also at one end of the Otago Central Rail Trail.

◉ Sights

Clyde Historical Museums MUSEUM
(5 Blyth St; admission by donation; ☺3-5pm Tue-Sun Nov-Apr) The main building showcases Māori and Victorian exhibits and provides information about the Clyde Dam. Larger exhibits (machinery, horse-drawn carts etc) are housed in the Herb Factory complex at 12 Fraser St.

🏃 Activities

Pick up a copy of *Walk Around Historic Clyde* from the Alexandra i-SITE (p536). The **Alexandra–Clyde 150th Anniversary Walk** (three hours one way) is a riverside trail that's fairly flat, with ample resting spots and shade.

Trail Journeys BICYCLE RENTAL
(☏03-449 2150; www.trailjourneys.co.nz; 16 Springvale Rd; ☺tours Sep-Apr) 🚲 Right by the Rail Trailhead, Trail Journeys rents bikes (from $42 per day) and arranges cycling tours, baggage transfers and shuttles. It also has a depot in Middlemarch.

🎉 Festivals & Events

Clyde Wine & Food Festival WINE, FOOD
(www.promotedunstan.org.nz; ☺10.30am-4.30pm Easter Sun) Showcases the region's produce and wines.

🛏 Sleeping & Eating

Dunstan House B&B $$
(☏03-449 2295; www.dunstanhouse.co.nz; 29 Sunderland St; s/d without bathroom from $110/130, d/ste with bathroom from $170/240; ☺Oct-Apr; 🛜) This restored late-Victorian balconied inn has lovely bar and lounge areas, and rooms decorated in period style. The less expensive rooms share bathrooms but are just as comfortable and atmospheric.

★Oliver's B&B $$$
(☏03-449 2600; www.oliverscentralotago.co.nz; Holloway Rd; r/ste from $225/495; 🛜) 🚲 Oliver's fills an 1860s merchant's house and stone stables with luxurious rooms decked out with old maps, heritage furniture and claw-foot baths. Most of the rooms open onto a secluded garden courtyard.

Bank Cafe CAFE $
(www.bankcafe.co.nz; 31 Sunderland St; mains $10-15; ☺9am-4pm) Grab a table inside or out and tuck into cakes, slices, waffles and delicious burgers. The robust takeaway sandwiches are perfect for lunch on two wheels.

★Oliver's MODERN NZ $$
(☏03-449 2805; www.oliverscentralotago.co.nz; 34 Sunderland St; mains lunch $18-26, dinner $30-39; ☺11.30am-2.30pm & 5.30-9.30pm) Housed in a gold-rush-era general store, this wonderful complex incorporates a craft brewery (the Victoria Store Brewery), bar and deli-cafe within its venerable stone walls. The restaurant shifts gears from on-trend cafe fare at lunchtime (tuna sliders, pulled pork belly etc) to a bistro showcasing the best local, seasonal produce in the evenings (venison noisette, lamb rump, salmon etc).

🛍 Shopping

Central Gourmet Galleria FOOD
(☏03-449 3331; www.centralgourmetgalleria. co.nz; 27 Sunderland St; ☺10am-4pm Tue-Sun) This former butcher's stocks a selection of award-winning local wines, many of which you won't find anywhere else. There are also plenty of Central Otago foodie treats such as jams and chutneys.

ℹ Getting There & Away

Alpine Connexions (☏03-443 9120; www. alpineconnexions.co.nz) Shuttles head to/from Dunedin ($40, three hours), Alexandra ($15, 15 minutes), Cromwell ($24, 20 minutes), Queenstown ($35, 1½ hours) and Wanaka ($35, one hour), as well as key stops on the Otago Central Rail Trail.

Catch-a-Bus (☏03-449 2024; www.trail journeys.co.nz; ☺Nov-Apr) Shuttles to Cromwell ($25, 20 minutes), Alexandra ($15, 10 minutes), Ranfurly ($43, 1½ hours), Middlemarch ($55, 2½ hours) and Dunedin ($56, 3½ hours) during the main cycling season.

InterCity (☏03-471 7143; www.intercity. co.nz) A daily coach heads to/from Dunedin (from $32, 3½ hours), Roxburgh (from $21, 44 minutes), Alexandra (from $10, nine minutes), Cromwell (from $16, 14 minutes) and Queenstown (from $22, 1½ hours).

Cromwell

POP 4150

Cromwell has a charming lakeside historic precinct, a great weekly farmers market and perhaps the South Island's most over-the-top 'big thing' – a selection of giant fruit by the highway.

It's also at the very heart of the prestigious Central Otago wine region (www.cowa.org.nz), known for its extraordinarily good pinot noir and, to a lesser extent, riesling, pinot gris and chardonnay. The Cromwell Basin – which stretches from Bannockburn, 5km southwest of Cromwell, to north of Lake Dunstan – accounts for over 70% of Central Otago's total wine production. Pick up the *Central Otago Wine Map* for details of upwards of 50 local wineries.

◎ Sights

Cromwell Heritage Precinct   HISTORIC BUILDINGS

(www.cromwellheritageprecinct.co.nz; Melmore Tce) When the Clyde Dam was completed in 1992 it flooded Cromwell's historic town centre, 280 homes, six farms and 17 orchards. Many historic buildings were disassembled before the flooding and have since been rebuilt in a pedestrianised precinct beside Lake Dunstan. While some have been set up as period pieces (stables and the like), others house some good cafes, galleries and interesting shops. In summer it plays host to an excellent weekly **farmers market** (◎9am-1pm Sun Nov-Feb).

🏃 Activities

Highlands Motorsport Park   ADVENTURE SPORTS

(☑03-445 4052; www.highlands.co.nz; cnr SH6 & Sandflat Rd; ◎10am-5pm) Transformed from a paddock into a top-notch 4km racing circuit in just 18 months, this revheads' paradise hosted its first major event in 2013. The action isn't reserved just for the professionals, with various high-octane experiences on offer, along with an excellent museum.

Budding speed freaks can start out on the go-karts ($39 per 10 minutes) before taking a 200km/h ride in the **Highlands Taxi** ($75/120 for two/four people), completing three laps of the circuit as a passenger in a **Porsche GT3** ($295), or having a go at the wheel of a **V8 muscle car** ($395).

If you'd prefer a less racy experience, the **National Motorsport Museum** (adult/child $25/10) showcases racing cars and displays about Kiwi legends such as Bruce McLaren, Possum Bourne, Emma Gilmour and Scott Dixon. Family groups can opt for the **Jurassic Safari Adventure**, a trip in a safari van through a forest inhabited by dinosaurs ($79 including museum entry). Plus there's free **mini-golf** and, across the car park, the **Nose cafe**, which offers wine tastings.

☞ Tours

Central Otago Motorcycle Hire   TOUR

(☑03-445 4487; www.comotorcyclehire.co.nz; 271 Bannockburn Rd; per day from $165) The sinuous and hilly roads of Central Otago are perfect for negotiating on two wheels. This crew hires out bikes and advises on improbably scenic routes. Is also offers guided trail-bike tours (from $195) and extended road tours (from $575).

Goldfields Jet   ADVENTURE TOUR

(☑03-445 1038; www.goldfieldsjet.co.nz; SH6; adult/child $109/49) Zip through the Kawarau Gorge on a 40-minute jetboat ride.

🎉 Festivals & Events

Highlands 101   SPORTS

(◎Nov) A three-day motor-racing festival at Highlands Park, including the final round of the Australian GT Championship.

🛏 Sleeping

Cromwell Top 10 Holiday Park   HOLIDAY PARK $

(☑03-445 0164; www.cromwellholidaypark.co.nz; 1 Alpha St; sites $40-44, units with/without bathroom from $110/75; @ 🛜) The size of a small European nation and packed with cabins and self-contained units of various descriptions, all set in tree-lined grounds.

Carrick Lodge   MOTEL $$

(☑03-445 4519; www.carricklodge.co.nz; 10 Barry Ave; units $140-180; 🛜) One of Cromwell's more stylish motels, Carrick has spacious, modern units and is just a short stroll from the main shopping complex. Executive units have spa baths and views over the golf course.

★ Burn Cottage Retreat   B&B, COTTAGE $$$

(☑03-445 3050; www.burncottageretreat.co.nz; 168 Burn Cottage Rd; r/cottages $200/225; 🛜) Set among walnut trees and gardens 3km northwest of Cromwell, this peaceful retreat has three luxurious, self-contained cottages with classy decor, spacious kitchens and modern bathrooms. B&B accommodation is available in the main house.

Eating

⭐ Armando's Kitchen
CAFE $$

(☑ 03-445 0303; 71 Melmore Tce; mains $10-22; ◷ 10am-3pm Sat-Thu, to 9pm Fri, extended hours in summer) Cromwell's heritage precinct is best enjoyed from the veranda of Armando's Kitchen, with an espresso or gourmet ice cream in hand. The homemade pasta, pizza and cakes are all excellent, and the breakfasts are legendary. On Friday nights it opens late for pizza and drinks

Mt Difficulty
MODERN NZ $$

(☑ 03-445 3445; www.mtdifficulty.co.nz; 73 Felton Rd, Bannockburn; mains $30-35; ◷ tastings 10.30am-4.30pm, restaurant noon-4pm) As well as making our favourite NZ pinot noir, Mt Difficulty is a lovely spot for a leisurely lunch looking down over the valley. There are large wine-friendly platters to share, but save room for the decadent desserts. Wines can be tasted for a gold coin donation.

Bannockburn Hotel
PUB FOOD $$

(☑ 03-445 0615; www.bannockburnhotel.com; 420 Bannockburn Rd, Bannockburn; mains $24-30; ◷ 11am-9pm) Head out to the historic Bannockburn watering hole for massive serves of pub grub (ribs, steaks, fish and chips) and even bigger skies from the front terrace. It's 5km out of town, but they operate a free courtesy bus.

ℹ Information

Cromwell i-SITE (☑ 03-445 0212; www.central otagonz.com; 2d The Mall; ◷ 9am-7pm Jan-Mar to 5pm Apr-Dec) Stocks the *Walk Cromwell* brochure, covering local mountain-bike and walking trails, including the nearby gold-rush ghost-town of Bendigo.

ℹ Getting There & Away

Alpine Connexions (☑ 03-443 9120; www.alpineconnexions.co.nz) Scheduled shuttles to/from Dunedin ($45, 3¼ hours), Alexandra ($24, 25 minutes), Clyde ($24, 20 minutes), Wanaka ($25, 45 minutes) and Queenstown ($25, one hour).

Atomic Shuttles (☑ 03-349 0697; www.atomictravel.co.nz) Daily buses head to/from Queenstown ($15, 55 minutes), Alexandra ($15, 50 minutes), Roxburgh ($25, 1¼ hours), Dunedin ($30, 3¾ hours) and Christchurch ($40, 5¼ hours).

Catch-a-Bus (☑ 03-449 2024; www.trailjourneys.co.nz; ◷ Nov-Apr) Bike-friendly shuttles to Clyde ($25, 20 minutes), Alexandra ($25, 30 minutes), Ranfurly ($52, 1¾ hours), Middlemarch ($59, 2¾ hours) and Dunedin ($60, 3¾ hours).

InterCity (☑ 03-471 7143; www.intercity.co.nz) There are four daily coaches to Queenstown (from $11, one hour), and one to Fox Glacier (from $44, 6½ hours), Christchurch (from $51, 7¼ hours), Alexandra (from $12, 24 minutes) and Dunedin (from $22, 3¾ hours).

Naked Bus (www.nakedbus.com; prices vary) One bus per day from Queenstown (one hour) and one from Wanaka (55 minutes) stop in Cromwell before continuing on to Omarama (2½ hours), Lake Tekapo (3¾ hours) and Christchurch (8¼ hours).

Queenstown & Wanaka

Best Places to Eat

➜ Blue Kanu (p555)

➜ Chop Shop (p565)

➜ La Rumbla (p565)

➜ Fergbaker (p554)

➜ Saffron (p565)

Best Places to Sleep

➜ Adventure Queenstown (p551)

➜ The Dairy (p553)

➜ Wanaka Bakpaka (p569)

➜ Lakeside (p570)

➜ Criffel Peak View (p570)

Why Go?

With a cinematic background of mountains and lakes, and a 'what can we think of next?' array of adventure activities, it's little wonder Queenstown tops the itineraries of many travellers.

Slow down slightly in Wanaka – Queenstown's less flashy cousin – which also has good restaurants, bars and outdoor adventures on tap. With Mt Aspiring National Park nearby, you're only a short drive from true NZ wilderness.

Slow down even more in Glenorchy, an improbably scenic reminder of what Queenstown and Wanaka were like before the adventure groupies moved in. Negotiate the Greenstone and Routeburn Tracks for extended outdoor thrills, or kayak the upper reaches of Lake Wakatipu.

Across in historic Arrowtown, consider the town's gold-mining past over a chilled wine or dinner in a cosy bistro. The following day there'll be plenty more opportunities to dive back into Queenstown's action-packed whirlwind.

When to Go

➜ The fine and settled summer weather from January to March is the perfect backdrop to Queenstown's active menu of adventure sports and outdoor exploration. March also brings the Gibbston Wine & Food Festival to Queenstown Gardens.

➜ Mid- to late March sees an inundation of mountain bikers for the Queenstown Bike Festival.

➜ In late June the Queenstown Winter Festival celebrates the coming of the ski season. From June to August, the slopes surrounding Queenstown and Wanaka are flush with an international crew of ski and snowboard fans.

➜ The Wanaka Fest heralds the spring thaw in October.

ⓘ Getting There & Away

Domestic flights head to Queenstown from Auckland, Wellington and Christchurch, with smaller planes servicing Dunedin, Nelson and Hamilton. International flights head to Queenstown from Australian destinations including Brisbane, the Gold Coast, Sydney and Melbourne. Queenstown is the main bus hub for the region, with services radiating out to the West Coast (via Wanaka and Haast Pass), Christchurch, Dunedin (via Central Otago), Invercargill and Te Anau. Wanaka also has services to Christchurch and Dunedin.

QUEENSTOWN

POP 12,500

Surrounded by the soaring indigo heights of the Remarkables and framed by the meandering coves of Lake Wakatipu, Queenstown is a right show-off. Looking like a small town, but displaying the energy of a small city, it wears its 'Global Adventure Capital' badge proudly, and most visitors take the time to do crazy things that they've never done before. No-one's ever visited and said, 'I'm bored'.

Then there's the other Queenstown. The one with the cosmopolitan restaurant and arts scene, excellent vineyards and five international-standard golf courses. Go ahead and jump off a bridge or out of a plane, but take time to slow down and experience Queenstown without the adrenaline. At the very least, find a lakeside bench at dusk and immerse yourself in one of NZ's most beautiful views.

Queenstown is well used to visitors with international accents, so expect great tourist facilities but also big crowds, especially in summer and winter. Autumn (March to May) and spring (October to November) are slightly quieter, but Queenstown is a true year-round destination.

The town's bars are regularly packed with a mainly young crowd that really know how to holiday. If you're a more private soul, drop in to see what all the fuss is about, but then get out and explore the sublime wilderness further up the lake at Glenorchy.

History

The region was deserted when the first British people arrived in the mid-1850s, although there is evidence of previous Māori settlement. Sheep farmers came first, but after two shearers discovered gold on the banks of the Shotover River in 1862, a deluge of prospectors followed.

QUEENSTOWN & WANAKA QUEENSTOWN

Queenstown & Wanaka Highlights

❶ **Queenstown** (p541) Doing things you've only dreamed about in the adrenaline-rush capital of NZ.

❷ **Wanaka** (p566) Soaking up the sophisticated small-town vibe and sublime lake views.

❸ **Arrowtown** (p562) Relaxing and dining after a day's mountain biking and gold panning.

❹ **Routeburn Track** (p559) Walking this peaceful and diverse alpine trail, arguably the best of NZ's Great Walks.

❺ **Glenorchy** (p559) Exploring the upper reaches of Lake Wakatipu by horseback, kayak or jetboat.

❻ **Roy Roy Glacier Track** (p569) Restraining the urge to yodel as you stroll through the sublime Matukituki Valley before climbing to the glacier.

❼ **Queenstown bar-hopping** (p556) Partying until the early hours among a multitude of accents in cosmopolitan Queenstown.

Within a year Queenstown was a mining town with streets, permanent buildings and a population of several thousand. It was declared 'fit for a queen' by the NZ government, hence Queenstown was born. Lake Wakatipu was the principal means of transport, and at the height of the boom there were four paddle steamers and 30 other craft plying the waters.

By 1900 the gold had petered out and the population was a mere 190. It wasn't until the 1950s that Queenstown became a popular holiday destination.

◉ Sights

Lake Wakatipu
LAKE

(Map p546) Shaped like a perfect cartoon thunderbolt, this gorgeous lake has a 212km shoreline and reaches a depth of 379m (the average depth is over 320m). Five rivers flow into it but only one (the Kawarau) flows out, making it prone to sometimes quite dramatic floods.

If the water looks clean, that's because it is. Scientists have rated it as 99.9% pure – making it the second-purest lake water in the world. In fact, you're better off dipping your glass in the lake than buying bottled water. It's also very cold. That beach by Marine Parade may look tempting on a scorching day, but trust us – you won't want to splash about in water that hovers at around 10°C year-round. Because cold water increases the risk of drowning, local bylaws require the wearing of lifejackets in all boats

ESSENTIAL QUEENSTOWN & WANAKA

Eat A leisurely lunch at a vineyard restaurant.

Drink One of the surprising seasonal brews by Wanaka Beerworks (p566).

Read *Walking the Routeburn Track* by Philip Holden for a wander through the history, flora and fauna of this tramp.

Listen to The silence as you kayak blissfully around Glenorchy and Kinloch.

Watch *Top of the Lake*, the Jane Campion–directed TV series set around the top of Wakatipu.

Online www.queenstownnz.co.nz, www.lakewanaka.co.nz

Area code ☎03

under 6m, including kayaks, on all of the district's lakes.

Māori tradition sees the lake's shape as the burnt outline of the evil giant Matau sleeping with his knees drawn up. Local lad Matakauri set fire to the bed of bracken on which the giant slept in order to rescue his beloved Manata, a chief's daughter who was kidnapped by the giant. The fat from Matau's body created a fire so intense that it burnt a hole deep into the ground.

Queenstown Gardens
PARK

(Map p546; Park St) Set on its own little tongue of land framing Queenstown Bay, this pretty park was laid out in 1876 by those garden-loving Victorians as a place to promenade. The clothes may have changed (they've certainly shrunk), but people still flock to this leafy peninsula to stroll, picnic and laze about. Less genteel types head straight for the frisbee golf course (p548).

Other attractions include an ice-skating rink, skate park, lawn-bowling club, tennis courts, mature exotic trees (including large sequoias and some fab monkey puzzles by the rotunda) and a rose garden. There's also a memorial to Captain Robert Scott (1868–1912), leader of the doomed South Pole expedition, which includes an engraving of his moving final message.

Kiwi Birdlife Park
ZOO

(Map p546; ☎03-442 8059; www.kiwibird.co.nz; Brecon St; adult/child $45/23; ☺9am-5pm, shows 11am & 3pm) These five acres are home to 10,000 native plants, tuatara and scores of birds, including kiwi, kea, moreporks, parakeets and extremely rare black stilts. Stroll around the aviaries, watch the conservation show, and tiptoe quietly into the darkened kiwi houses.

Skyline Gondola
CABLE CAR

(Map p546; ☎03-441 0101; www.skyline.co.nz; Brecon St; adult/child return $32/20; ☺9am-late) 🏆 Hop aboard for fantastic views. At the top there's the inevitable cafe, restaurant, souvenir shop and observation deck, as well as the Queenstown Bike Park (p547), Skyline Luge (p548), **Ledge Bungy** (Map p546; ☎0800 286 4958; www.bungy.co.nz; adult/child $195/145), **Ledge Swing** (Map p546; ☎0800 286 4958; www.bungy.co.nz; adult/child $160/110) and Ziptrek Ecotours (p548). At night there are Māori culture shows from Kiwi Haka (p557) and stargazing tours (including gondola adult/child $85/45).

Walking trails include a loop track through the Douglas firs (30 minutes return). The energetic (or frugal) can forgo the gondola and hike to the top on the **Tiki Trail** (Map p546) and then continue on the **Ben Lomond Track** (Map p546; www.doc.govt.nz).

Underwater Observatory
VIEWPOINT

(Map p552; ☑ 03-409 0000; www.kjet.co.nz; main jetty; adult/child $10/5; ☺ 9am-7pm Nov-Mar, to 5pm Apr-Oct) Six windows showcase life under the lake in this reverse aquarium (the people are behind glass). Large brown trout abound, and look out for freshwater eels and scaup (diving ducks), which cruise right past the windows – especially when the coin-operated food-release box is triggered.

🏃 Activities

A baffling array of activities is offered by a baffling number of shops in the town centre. It's even more confusing due to the fact that some shops change their name from winter to summer, some run multiple activities from the same shop, and some activities are branded differently but are actually the same thing. Several places call themselves information centres, but only the i-SITE (p558) is the true, independent, official information centre.

If you're planning on tackling several activities, various combination tickets are available, including those offered by **Queenstown Combos** (Map p552; ☑ 03-442 7318; www.combos.co.nz; The Station, cnr Shotover & Camp Sts).

Hiking/Tramping & Climbing

Pick up the *Wakatipu Walks* brochure ($5) from DOC and the i-SITE for local tramping tracks ranging from easy one-hour strolls to tough eight-hour slogs.

Ultimate Hikes
TRAMPING

(Map p552; ☑ 03-450 1940; www.ultimatehikes. co.nz; 9 Duke St; ☺ Nov-Apr) 🔗 Offers day walks on the Routeburn Track (from $179) and the Milford Track (from $299), departing from Queenstown. Or you can do these multiday tracks in their entirety, staying in Ultimate Hike's own staffed lodges rather than DOC huts, where hot meals and en suite bathrooms await. In the winter the office is rebranded as Snowbiz and rents skis and snowboards.

Guided Walks New Zealand
WALKING, TRAMPING

(☑ 03-442 3000; www.nzwalks.com; adult/child from $107/67) Excellent walks in the Queen-

stown area, ranging from half-day nature walks to the full three-day Hollyford Track. Also offers snowshoeing in winter.

Climbing Queenstown
ROCK CLIMBING

(Map p552; ☑ 027 477 9393; www.climbingqueenstown.com; 23 Brecon St; from $149) Rock climbing via ferrata (climbing with fixed metal rungs, rails, pegs and cables), mountaineering and alpine trekking lead by qualified guides.

Bungy & Swings

Shotover Canyon Swing
ADVENTURE SPORTS

(Map p552; ☑ 03-442 6990; www.canyonswing. co.nz; 35 Shotover St; per person $219, additional swings $45) 🔗 Be released loads of different ways – backwards, in a chair, upside down. From there it's a 60m free fall and a wild swing across the canyon at 150km/h. The price includes the transfer from the Queenstown booking office.

AJ Hackett Bungy
ADVENTURE SPORTS

(Map p552; ☑ 03-450 1300; www.bungy.co.nz; The Station, cnr Camp & Shotover Sts) The bungy originators now offer jumps from three sites in the Queenstown area, with giant swings available at two of them. It all started at the historic 1880 **Kawarau Bridge** (Map p544; ☑ 0800 286 4958; www.bungy.co.nz; Gibbston Hwy; adult/child $190/145; 23km from Queenstown (transport included). In 1988 it became the world's first commercial bungy site, offering a 43m leap over the river. It's also the only bungy site in the region to offer tandem jumps.

New to the Kawarau Bridge site is the **Kawarau Zipride** (Map p544; ☑ 0800 286

Queenstown Region

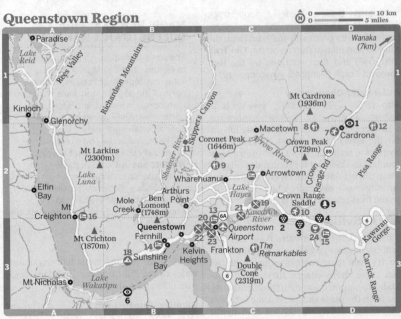

Queenstown Region

4958; www.bungy.co.nz; Gibbston Hwy; adult/child $50/40, 3-/5-ride pack $105/150), three 130m ziplines mainly targeted to kids – but also a thrill for adults not keen to take a giant leap of faith. Multi-ride packs can be split between groups, making it a far cheaper alternative to the bungy.

The closest options to Queenstown are the Ledge Bungy (p542) and Ledge Swing (p542) at the top of the Skyline Gondola; the drop is only 47m, but it's 400m above town. In winter you can even leap into the dark.

Last but most pant-wetting is the **Nevis Bungy** (☑0800 286 4958; www.bungy.co.nz; per

QUEENSTOWN IN...

Two Days

Start your day at **Bespoke Kitchen** before either hitting the slopes or heading to Shotover St to book your adrenal ne-charged activities. Ride the **Skyline Gondola** to get the lay of the land and have a go on the **luge**. Head out on the **Shotover Jet** and then wind down with a walk through **Queenstown Gardens** to capture dramatic views of the **Remarkables** at dusk. Have a sunset drink at **Atlas Beer Cafe** before dinner at **Rata** and an evening of bar hopping.

The next day fuel up at **Fergbaker** before devoting the morning to snowboarding, bungy jumping, skydiving or white-water rafting. Spend the afternoon on two wheels, either at the **Queenstown Bike Park** or touring around the **Gibbston** wineries. Have dinner at **Blue Kanu** before hitting the bars.

Four Days

Follow the two-day itinerary, then head to **Arrowtown** to wander the **Chinese settlement**, have lunch at **Chop Shop** and browse the stores. The following day, drive along the shores of Lake Wakatipu to tiny **Glenorchy**. Have lunch at the **Glenorchy Cafe** and then drive to the trailhead of the **Routeburn Track** for a short tramp.

---

person \$275) – the highest bungy in Australasia. 4WD buses will transport you onto private farmland where you can jump from a specially constructed pod, 134m above the Nevis River. The **Nevis Swing** (☑ 0800 286 4958; www.bungy.co.nz; solo/tandem \$195/350) starts 160m above the river and cuts a 300m arc across the canyon on a rope longer than a rugby field – yes, it's the world's biggest swing.

If you're keen to try more than one AJ Hackett experience, enquire about combo tickets.

White-Water Rafting

Queenstown Rafting RAFTING
(Map p552; ☑ 03-442 9792; www.rafting.co.nz; 35 Shotover St; rafting/helirafting \$209/309) 🌿 Rafts year-round on the choppy Shotover River (Grades III to V) and calmer Kawarau River (Grades II to III). Trips take four to five hours with two to three hours on the water. Helirafting trips are an exciting alternative. Participants must be at least 13 years old and weigh more than 40kg.

If you book through other rafting companies such as **Extreme Green** (☑ 03-442 8517; www.extremegreenrafting.co.nz; rafting/helirafting \$209/309) and **Challenge** (Map p552; ☑ 03-442 7318, 0800 423 836; www.raft.co.nz; The Station, cnr Shotover & Camp Sts; rafting/helirafting \$219/319) you'll end up on the same trips.

It's possible to drive in to the rafting launch sites on the Kawarau River all year, but in winter, access to the Shotover River requires a helicopter.

Family Adventures RAFTING
(☑ 03-442 8836; www.familyadventures.co.nz; adult/child \$179/120; �❚) Gentler (Grades I to II) trips on the Shotover suitable for children three years and older. Operates in summer only.

Jetboating

Shotover Jet BOAT TOUR
(☑ 03-442 8570; www.shotoverjet.com; Gorge Rd, Arthurs Point; adult/child \$135/75) 🌿 Half-hour jetboat trips through the rocky Shotover Canyon, with lots of thrilling 360-degree spins

Skippers Canyon Jet BOAT TOUR
(Map p544; ☑ 03-442 9434; www.skipperscanyonjet.co.nz; Skippers Rd; adult/child \$139/79) 🌿 Incorporates a 30-minute blast through the narrow gorges of the remote Skippers Canyon, on the upper reaches of the Shotover River. The three-hour return trips (picking up from Queenstown) also cover the region's gold-mining history.

Hydro Attack BOAT TOUR
(Map p552; ☑ 0508 493 762; www.hydroattack.co.nz; Lapsley Butson Wharf; 15min \$149; ⊙9am-6pm Nov-Mar, 10am-4.30pm Apr-Oct) Did you see that 5.5m shark leaping out of the lake? Well jump inside, strap yourself in and take a ride. This 'Seabreacher X Watercraft' can travel at 80km/h on the water, dive 2m underneath and then launch itself nearly 6m into the air. It's almost as much fun to watch as it is to ride.

Queenstown

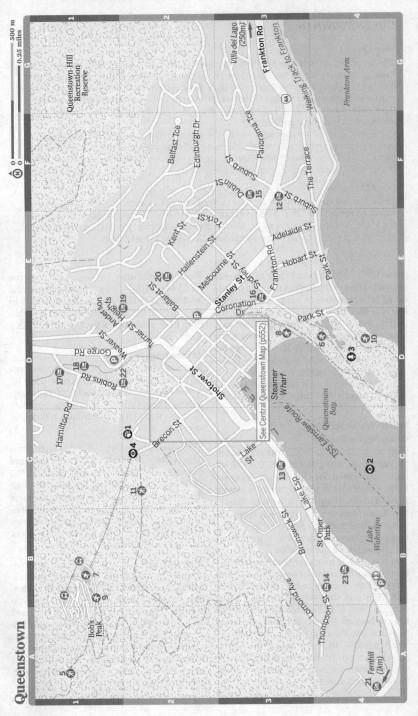

Queenstown

Skydiving, Gliding & Parasailing

NZone ADVENTURE SPORTS
(Map p552; ☑03-442 5867; www.nzonesky dive.co.nz; 35 Shotover St; from $299) ✈ Jump out of a perfectly good airplane – with a tandem-skydiving expert.

GForce Paragliding PARAGLIDING
(Map p546; ☑03-441 8581; www.nzgforce.com; incl gondola $219) Tandem paragliding from the top of the gondola (9am departures are $30 cheaper).

Queenstown Paraflights ADVENTURE SPORTS
(Map p552; ☑0800 225 520; www.paraflights. co.nz; solo/tandem/triple $159/258/297) Paraglide 200m above the lake as you're pulled behind a boat. Departs from the town pier.

Mountain Biking

With the opening of the Queenstown Bike Park, the region is now firmly established as an international destination for mountain bikers. If you're in town for a while, consider joining the Queenstown Mountain Bike Club (www.queenstownmtb.co.nz).

The **Queenstown Trail** – more than 100km in total – links five scenic smaller cycling routes showcasing Queenstown, Arrowtown, Gibbston, Lake Wakatipu, Jack's Point and Lake Hayes. The trail is suitable for cyclists of all levels.

Queenstown Bike Park MOUNTAIN BIKING
(Map p546; ☑03-441 0101; www.skyline. co.nz; Skyline; half-/full day incl gondola $60/85; ◷10am-6pm, extended to 8pm as light permits Oct-Apr) Over 20 different trails – from easy (green) to extreme (double black) – traverse Bob's Peak high above the lake. Once you've descended on two wheels, simply jump on the gondola and do it all over again. The best trail for novice riders is the 6km-long **Hammy's Track**, which is studded with lake views and picnic spots. BYO bike.

Vertigo Bikes MOUNTAIN BIKING
(Map p552; ☑03-442 8378; www.vertigobikes. co.nz; 4 Brecon St; rental half-/full day from $39/59) If you're serious about getting into mountain biking QT-style, Vertigo is an essential first stop. Options include skills-training clinics (from $149), guided sessions in the Queenstown Bike Park (from $159) and Remarkables helibiking ($399).

Fat Tyre Adventures MOUNTAIN BIKING
(☑0800 328 897; www.fat-tyre.co.nz; from $209) Tours cater to different abilities with backcountry day tours, multiday tours, high-country helibiking and single-track riding. Bike hire and trail snacks are included.

Skiing & Snowboarding

Queenstowners have two excellent ski fields to chose between in **the Remarkables** (Map p544; ☑03-442 4615; www.nzski.com; Remarkables Skifield Rd; daily lift pass adult/child $104/59) and **Coronet Peak** (Map p45; ☑03-442 4620; www.nzski.com; Coronet Peak Rd; daily lift pass adult/child $104/59), and when they fancy a change of scenery, there's always Cardrona Alpine Resort (p573) and **Treble Cone** (☑03-443 1406, snow-phone 03-443 7444; www. treblecone.com; daily lift pass adult/child $106/52) ✈ near Wanaka. Coronet Peak is the only field to offer night skiing, which on a star-filled night is an experience not to be missed.

QUEENSTOWN FOR CHILDREN

While Queenstown is brimming with activities, some of them have age restrictions that may exclude the youngest in your group. Nevertheless, you shouldn't have any trouble keeping the littlies busy.

All-age attractions include the **Kiwi Birdlife Park** (p542), lake cruises on the **TSS Earnslaw** (p549) and 4WD tours of narrow, snaking Skippers Canyon. **Queenstown Gardens** (p542) has a good beachside **playground** (Map p546) near the entrance on Marine Pde. Also in the park, **Queenstown Ice Arena** (Map p546; ☎03-441 8000; www.queenstownicearena.co.nz; 29 Park St; entry incl skate hire adult/child $19/15; ⊙10am-5pm Sat-Thu, to 9.30pm Fri Apr-Oct) is great for a rainy day, and there's **Frisbee Golf**. The **Skyline Gondola** (p542) offers a slow-moving activity from dizzying heights. Small children can also ride the **luge** with an adult, but need to be at least six years old and taller than 110cm to go it alone.

For a high that will make sugar rushes seem passé, a surprising number of activities cater to little daredevils. Children as young as two can take a tandem ride with **Queenstown Paraflights** (p547), provided the smallest harness fits them. **Family Adventures** (p545) runs gentler rafting trips suitable for three-year-olds. Under-fives can ride on the **Shotover Jet** (p545) for free, provided they're over a metre tall, and six-year-olds can tackle the ziplines with **Ziptrek Ecotours**. Fearless 10-year-olds can bungy or swing at any of **AJ Hackett's jumps** (p543), except the Nevis Bungy (minimum age 13). Eight- and nine-year-olds can, however, tackle the **Kawarau Zipride** (p543).

Several places in town hire out tandem bicycles and child-sized bikes.

For more ideas and information – including details of local babysitters – visit the **i-SITE** (p558) or www.kidzgo.co.nz.

The ski season generally lasts from around June to September. In winter, the shops are full of ski gear for purchase and hire; **Outside Sports** (Map p552; ☎03-441 0074; www.outsidesports.co.nz; 9 Shotover St; ⊙8.30am-8pm) is a reliable option.

Even outside of the main season, heliskiing is an option for cashed-up serious skiers; try Over The Top (p549), **Harris Mountains Heli-Ski** (Map p552; ☎03-442 6722; www.heliski.co.nz; The Station, cnr Shotover & Camp Sts; from $940), **Alpine Heliski** (Map p552; ☎03-441 2300; www.alpineheliski.com; 37 Shotover St; 3-8 runs $875-1275; ⊙Jul-Sep) or **Southern Lakes Heliski** (Map p552; ☎03-442 6222; www.heliskinz.com; Torpedo 7 building, 20 Athol St; from $895).

Other Activities

It would be impractical to list absolutely every activity on offer in Queenstown. If you're interested in golf, minigolf, sailing or diving, enquire at the i-SITE (p558).

Frisbee Golf　　　　　　OUTDOORS
(Map p546; www.queenstowndiscgolf.co.nz; Queenstown Gardens) **FREE** A series of 18 tree-mounted chain baskets set among the trees; local sports stores sell frisbees and scorecards.

Ziptrek Ecotours　　　　ADVENTURE SPORTS
(Map p546; ☎03-441 2102; www.ziptrek.co.nz; Skyline) ✈ Incorporating a series of ziplines (flying foxes), this harness-clad thrill-ride takes you from treetop to treetop high above Queenstown. Ingenious design and eco-friendly values are a bonus. Choose from the two-hour four-line 'Moa' tour (adult/child $135/85) or the gnarlier three-hour six-line 'Kea' option ($185/135).

Skyline Luge　　　　　　ADVENTURE SPORTS
(Map p546; ☎03-441 0101; www.skyline.co.nz; Skyline; 2/3/4/5 rides incl gondola $45/48/49/55; ⊙10am-8pm Oct-Mar, to 5pm Apr-Sep) ✈ Ride the gondola to the top, then hop on a three-wheeled cart to ride the 800m track. Nail the Blue Track once and you're allowed on the more advanced Red Track, with its banked corners and tunnel.

☞ Tours

Lake Cruises

Million Dollar Cruise　　　BOAT TOUR
(Map p552; ☎03-442 9770; www.milliondollarcruise.co.nz; cruise $35; ⊙11am, 2pm & 4pm) Good-value, informative, 90-minute cruises heading up the Frankton end of the lake, past the multi-million-dollar real estate of Kelvin Heights.

TSS Earnslaw
BOAT TOUR

(Map p552; ☑ 0800 656 501; www.realjourneys. co.nz; Steamer Wharf, Beach St; adult/child $57/22) The stately, steam-powered TSS *Earnslaw* celebrated a centenary of continuous service in 2012. Once the lake's major means of transport, now its ever-present cloud of black soot seems a little incongruous in such a pristine setting. Climb aboard for the standard 1½-hour Lake Wakatipu tour or take a 3½-hour excursion to the high-country **Walter Peak Farm** (Map p544; 1 Mount Nicholas-Beach Bay Rd; sheep show incl cruise adult/child $77/22) for sheepdog and shearing demonstrations.

Scenic Flights

Air Milford
SCENIC FLIGHTS

(☑ 03-442 2351; www.airmilford.co.nz; 1 Tex Smith Lane, Frankton) Options include a Milford Sound flyover (adult/child $420/255), a fly-cruise-fly combo ($499/300), and longer flights to Doubtful Sound and Aoraki/Mt Cook.

Glenorchy Air
SCENIC FLIGHTS

(☑ 03-442 2207; www.glenorchyair.co.nz; Queenstown Airport, Frankton) Scenic trips from Queenstown or Glenorchy include a Milford Sound fly-cruise-fly option (adult/child $485/295) and an Aoraki/Mt Cook flyover (adult/child $645/365).

Over The Top
SCENIC FLIGHTS

(☑ 03-442 2233; www.flynz.co.nz; Tex Smith Lane, Frankton) Offers helicopter flights to the Sounds, secluded fishing spots and a high-country sheep station. From July to October it offers heliskiing.

Sunrise Balloons
BALLOONING

(☑ 03-442 0781; www.ballooningnz.com; adult/child $495/295) One-hour sunrise rides including a champagne breakfast; allow four hours for the entire experience.

Winery Tours

Most tours include wineries in the Gibbston, Bannockburn and Cromwell Basin subregions.

Appellation Central Wine Tours
TOUR

(☑ 03-442 0246; www.appellationcentral.co.nz; tours $185-230) 🖋 Tours visit wineries in Gibbston, Bannockburn and Cromwell, and include platter lunches at a winery restaurant.

New Zealand Wine Tours
TOUR

(☑ 027 305 2004; www.nzwinetours.co.nz; from $185) Small-group or private winery tours, including lunch, snacks and an 'aroma room' experience.

Milford Sound Tours

Day trips from Queenstown to Milford Sound via Te Anau take 12 to 13 hours, including a two-hour cruise on the sound. Bus-cruise-flight options are also available, as is pick-up from the Routeburn Track trailhead. To save on travel time and cost, consider visiting Milford from Te Anau.

REMEMBER, YOU'RE ON HOLIDAY

Here's our pick of the best experiences to slow down, recharge, and remind your body that there's more to the travelling life than scaring yourself silly.

➡ **Onsen Hot Pools** (☑ 03-442 5707; www.onsen.co.nz; 160 Arthurs Point Rd, Arthurs Point; 1/2/3/4 people $46/88/120/140; ⊘ 11am-10pm) has private Japanese-style hot tubs with mountain views. Book ahead and one will be warmed up for you.

➡ To reboot your system after a few days of skiing, biking and jetboating, ease into in-room massage and spa treatments with the **Mobile Massage Company** (Map p552; ☑ 0800 426 161; www.queenstownmassage.co.nz; 2c Shotover St; 1hr from $120; ⊘ 9am-9pm).

➡ Slow down even more by checking into **Hush Spa** (Map p552; ☑ 03-442 9656; www. hushspa.co.nz; 1st fl, 32 Rees St 30/60min massage from $70/128; ⊘ 9am-6pm Fri-Mon, to 9pm Tue-Thu) for a massage or a pedicure.

➡ For truly world-class spa treatments, make the short trek to Millbrook near Arrowtown, where the **Spa at Millbrook** (Map p544; ☑ 03-441 7017; www.millbrook.co.nz; Malaghans Rd; treatments from $79) has been rated one of NZ's best.

➡ Catch a water taxi across the lake to **Eforea Spa at Hilton** (Map p544; ☑ 03-450 9416; www.queenstownhilton.com; 79 Peninsula Rd, Kelvin Heights; treatments from $70; ⊘ 9am-late).

BBQ Bus
TOUR

(☎03-442 1045; www.milford.net.nz; adult/child $199/100) Smaller group tours to Milford Sound (up to 22 people), including a cruise and a barbecue lunch. Te Anau drop offs and pick-ups are $30 cheaper.

Real Journeys
TOUR

(Map p552; ☎0800 656 501; www.realjourneys. co.nz; Steamer Wharf, Beach St; adult/child from $230/115) 🖉 Day or overnight tours to Milford and Doubtful Sounds, along with a host of other experiences.

Other Tours

Off Road Adventures
DRIVING TOUR

(Map p552; ☎03-442 7858; www.offroad.co.nz; 61a Shotover St) Exciting offroad tours by 4WD (from $109), or you can drive yourself on a quad-bike (from $199), dirt-bike (from $289) or 4WD buggy ($248, seats two).

Nomad Safaris
DRIVING TOUR

(Map p552; ☎03-442 6699; www.nomadsafaris. co.nz; 37 Shotover St; adult/child from $175/89) 🖉 Take in spectacular scenery and hard-to-get-to backcountry vistas around Skippers Canyon and Macetown, or head on a 'Safari of the Scenes' through Middle-earth locations around Glenorchy and the Wakatipu Basin. You can also quad-bike through a sheep station on Queenstown Hill ($245).

🎊 Festivals & Events

Gibbston Wine & Food Festival
WINE, FOOD

(www.gibbstonwineandfood.co.nz) Gibbston comes to Queenstown Gardens for a day in mid-March.

Queenstown Bike Festival
SPORTS

(www.queenstownbikefestival.co.nz) Ten days of two-wheeled action in mid- to late March.

THE GIBBSTON VALLEY

Gung-ho visitors to Queenstown might be happiest dangling off a giant rubber band, but as they're plunging towards the Kawarau River, they might not realise they're in the heart of Gibbston, one of Central Otago's main wine subregions, accounting for around 20% of plantings.

Almost opposite the Kawarau Bridge, a precipitous 2km gravel road leads to **Chard Farm** (Map p544; ☎03-441 8452; www.chardfarm.co.nz; Chard Rd, Gibbston; ⊙11am-5pm) **FREE**, the most picturesque of the Gibbston wineries. A further 800m along the Gibbston Hwy (SH6) is **Gibbston Valley** (Map p544; ☎03-442 6910; www.gibbstonvalley.com; 1820 Gibbston Hwy (SH6), Gibbston; tastings $5-12, tour incl tastings $15; ⊙10am-5pm), a large complex with a 'cheesery' and a restaurant. Tours of its impressive wine cave leave on the hour from 10am to 4pm.

A further 3km along SH6, **Peregrine** (Map p544; ☎03-442 4000; www.peregrinewines. co.nz; 2127 Gibbston Hwy (SH6), Gibbston; ⊙10am-5pm) is one of Gibbston's top wineries, producing excellent sauvignon blanc, pinot gris, riesling and, of course, pinot noir. Also impressive is the winery's architecture – a bunker-like building with a roof reminiscent of a falcon's wing in flight.

The **Gibbston River Trail** is a scenic walking and mountain-biking track that follows the Kawarau River from the Kawarau Bridge to Peregrine winery (one to two hours, 5km). From Peregrine, walkers (but not cyclists) can continue on the **Wentworth Bridge Loop** (one hour, 2.7km), which crosses over old mining works on various timber and steel bridges.

While you're in the area, be sure to call into the impossibly rustic **Gibbston Tavern** (Map p544; ☎03-409 0508; www.gibbstontavern.co.nz; Coal Pit Rd, Gibbston; ⊙11.30am-7pm Sun-Thu, to 10.30pm Fri & Sat Oct-Apr, closed Mon May-Sep), just off the highway past Peregrine. Ask to try the tavern's own Moonshine Wines, as you won't find them anywhere else.

If you're keen to explore the valley's wines without needing to contemplate a drive afterwards, considering staying among the vines in **Kinross Cottages** (Map p544; ☎021 0881 6595; www.kinrosscottages.co.nz; 2300 Gibbston Hwy (SH6), Gibbston; r $225; 🛜). Each heritage-looking but brand-new cottage is split into two luxurious studio rooms. Plus it has its own tasting room, representing several of Gibbston's smaller producers (tastings are $15 for five wines).

Ask at the **Queenstown i-SITE** (p558) or **DOC visitor centre** (p558) for maps and information about touring the area.

Queenstown Winter Festival SPORTS
(www.winterfestival.co.nz) Ten days of wacky ski and snowboard activities, live music, comedy, fireworks, a community carnival, parade, ball and plenty of frigid frivolity in late June and early July.

Gay Ski Week GAY & LESBIAN
(www.gayskiweekqt.com) The South Island's biggest and best gay-and-lesbian event, held in late August/early September.

🛏 Sleeping

Queenstown has endless accommodation options, but midpriced rooms are hard to come by. The hostels, however, are extremely competitive, offering ever-more extras to win custom – they're worth considering even if it's not usually your thing. Places book out and prices rocket during the peak summer (Christmas to February) and ski (June to September) seasons; book well in advance.

Goodstays (Map p552; ☑03-409 0537; www.goodstays.co.nz; 1st fl, 19 Camp St) has a huge variety of holiday homes and apartments on its website, with prices ranging from around $190 to $2000 per night; a minimum stay of between two and five nights usually applies.

🏘 Central Queenstown

Haka Lodge HOSTEL $
(Map p552; ☑03-442 4970; www.hakalodge.com; 6 Henry St; dm/r without bathroom from $31/89, apt $180; P🛜) Slap your thighs and kick up your heels, this *haka* is well worth participating in. In response to traveller research, the brightly painted dorms have custom-built bunks including large lockable storage chests, privacy curtains, personal lights and electrical sockets. There's also a two-bedroom apartment attached, with its own kitchen, spacious lounge and laundry facilities.

Butterfli Lodge HOSTEL $
(Map p546; ☑03-442 6367; www.butterfli.co.nz; 62 Thompson St; dm/s/d $30/66/69; P🛜) This little hostel sits on a quiet hillside west of the town centre, ruled over by Jimmy the cat. There are no bunks but no en suite bathrooms either. You won't believe the views from the deck.

Nomads HOSTEL $
(Map p552; ☑03-441 3922; www.nomadsworld.com; 5 Church St; dm with/without bathroom $32/30, r $110-140; @🛜) 🅿 With a prime location in the heart of Queenstown's nightlife, this massive hostel has facilities galore, including its own mini-cinema, en suite rooms, large kitchens, a free sauna and an on-site travel agency. It even sweetens the deal with free breakfast and dinner.

Hippo Lodge HOSTEL $
(Map p546; ☑03-442 5785; www.hippolodge.co.nz; 4 Anderson Heights; site $25, dm $30-36, s $50, d with/without bathroom from $96/76; P@🛜) Homely and slightly shabby but well kept, this relaxed hostel has a student-flat vibe, although it's a lot cleaner than that implies. The terrific views come with a correspondingly high number of stairs.

Flaming Kiwi Backpackers HOSTEL $
(Map p546; ☑03-442 5494; www.flamingkiwi.co.nz; 39 Robins Rd; dm/s/d without bathroom $35/72/82; P@🛜) Close to the town centre but on a quiet and mercifully hill-free street, this friendly hostel offers tidy dorms with a locker for every bed, three kitchens, unlimited wi-fi and a bottle of sunblock at reception. An excellent choice, then.

Bumbles HOSTEL $
(Map p546; ☑03-442 6298; www.bumblesbackpackers.co.nz; cnr Lake Esplanade & Brunswick St; site/dm/r $30/33/72; P@🛜) Enjoying a prime lakeside location, this popular wee hive has colourful decor and a supremely laid-back vibe. All of the rooms share bathrooms and there's limited space for tents out the back.

Sir Cedric's Southern Laughter HOSTEL $
(Map p552; ☑03-441 8828; www.sircedrics.co.nz; 4 Isle St; dm $27-32, r with/without bathroom $85/75; P🛜) Lame jokes cover the walls of this sprawling old-school hostel, but don't let that put you off as it's perfectly pleasant otherwise. The friendly staff, free vegie soup and spa pool should at least put a smile on your face.

YHA Queenstown Lakefront HOSTEL $
(Map p546; ☑03-442 8413; www.yha.co.nz; 88-90 Lake Esplanade; dm/s/d without bathroom from $32/70/89; @) 🅿 This large lakefront hostel has recently been renovated. Queenstown's nightlife is a 10- to 15-minute lakeside stroll away.

Adventure Queenstown HOSTEL $$
(Map p552; ☑03-409 0862; www.aqhostel.co.nz; 36 Camp St; dm with/without $33/31, d/tr $130/150; @🛜) Run by experienced travellers (as evidenced by the photos displayed

Central Queenstown

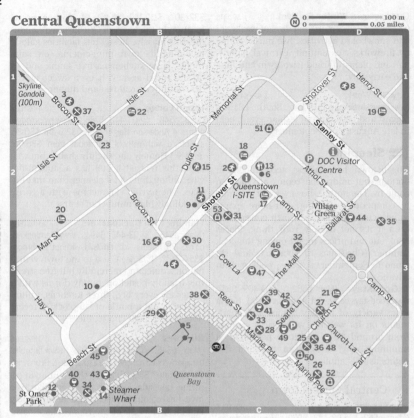

throughout), this central hostel has spotless dorms, a modern kitchen and envy-inducing balconies. Free stuff includes unlimited internet, international calling to 30 countries, bicycles and frisbees. Private rooms have en suite bathrooms, as do some of the dorms.

Creeksyde Queenstown
Holiday Park & Motels HOLIDAY PARK $$
(Map p546; ☑ 03-442 9447; www.camp.co.nz; 54 Robins Rd; site $55, d without bathroom $81, unit from $138; ⓟ@�☎) ✐ In a garden setting, this pretty and extremely well-kept holiday park has accommodation ranging from small tent sites to fully self-contained motel units. Quirky touches include oddball sculptures and an ablutions block disguised as a medieval oast house (hop kiln).

Coronation Lodge LODGE $$
(Map p546; ☑ 03-441 0860; www.coronation lodge.co.nz; 10 Coronation Dr; d $170-210; ⓟ☎) Right beside Queenstown Gardens, this tidy

block has basement parking, plush bed linen, wooden floors and Turkish rugs. Larger rooms have kitchenettes. The attractive little wood-lined breakfast room at the front serves both cooked and continental options (costs extra).

Alexis MOTEL $$
(Map p546; ☑ 03-409 0052; www.alexis queenstown.co.nz; 69 Frankton Rd; unit from $165; ⓟ☎) This modern hillside motel is an easy 10-minute walk from town along the lakefront. The pleasant self-contained units have thoughtful extras such as stereos and robes, along with beaut lake views.

Lomond Lodge MOTEL $$
(Map p552; ☑ 03-442 7375; www.lomondlodge.com; 33 Man St; d $145-169; ⓟ☎) A makeover has modernised this midrange motel's decor. Share your on-the-road stories with fellow travellers around the garden barbecue or in the guest kitchen, although all rooms also

Central Queenstown

Sights

1 Underwater Observatory C4

Activities, Courses & Tours

2 AJ Hackett Bungy C2
Alpine Heliski .... (see 9)
Challenge Rafting .... (see 2)
3 Climbing Queenstown A1
Harris Mountains Heli-Ski .... (see 2)
4 Hush Spa B3
5 Hydro Attack B4
6 Kiwi Discovery C2
7 Million Dollar Cruise B4
8 Mobile Massage Company D1
9 Nomad Safaris B2
NZone .... (see 11)
10 Off Road Adventures A3
Queenstown Combos .... (see 2)
Queenstown Paraflights .... (see 1)
11 Queenstown Rafting B2
12 Real Journeys A4
Shotover Canyon Swing .... (see 11)
13 Southern Lakes Heliski C2
14 TSS Earnslaw A4
15 Ultimate Hikes B2
16 Vertigo Bikes B3

Sleeping

17 Adventure Queenstown C2
18 Goodstays C2
19 Haka Lodge D1
20 Lomond Lodge A2
21 Nomads D3
22 Sir Cedric's Southern Laughter B1
23 The Dairy A2

Eating

24 Bespoke Kitchen A2
25 Blue Kanu C4
26 Botswana Butchery D4
27 Devil Burger D3
28 Eichardt's Bar C4
29 Empanada Kitchen B3
Fergbaker .... (see 30)
30 Fergburger B3
31 Habebe's C2
32 Kappa C3
33 Madame Woo C4
34 Public Kitchen & Bar A4
35 Rata D3
36 Sasso D4
37 Taco Medic A1
38 Vudu Cafe & Larder B3
39 Winnie's C3

Drinking & Nightlife

40 Atlas Beer Cafe A4
41 Ballarat Trading Company C3
42 Bardeaux C3
43 Little Blackwood A4
44 Pig & Whistle D2
45 Pub on Wharf A4
46 Rhino's Ski Shack C3
47 The Bunker C3
48 Vinyl Underground D4
49 Zephyr C4

Shopping

50 Artbay Gallery C4
51 Outside Sports C2
52 Vesta D4
53 Walk In Wardrobe C2

have their own fridges and microwaves. It's worth paying extra for a lake view.

★Dairy BOUTIQUE HOTEL $$$

(Map p552; ☎03-442 5164; www.thedairy.co.nz; 10 Isle St; s/d from $435/465; P 📶) Once a corner store, the Dairy is now a luxury B&B with 13 rooms packed with classy touches such as designer bed linen, silk cushions and luxurious mohair rugs. Rates include cooked breakfasts and freshly baked afternoon teas.

Queenstown Park BOUTIQUE HOTEL $$$

(Map p546; ☎03-441 8441; www.queenstownpark.co.nz; 21 Robins Rd; r from $360; P 📶) 🍃 White curtains billow over beds decked out in luxurious linen at this very chic 19-room hotel. The 'Remarkables rooms' have balconies facing over a park to the mountain range (there aren't any lake views). The gondola-facing rooms are smaller but have courtyards or balconies. All have kitchenettes, and guests can avail themselves of free wine and nibbles during 'canapé hour'.

Historic Stone House APARTMENT $$$

(Map p546; ☎03-442 9812; www.historicstonehouse.co.nz; 47 Hallenstein St; apt from $245; P 📶) Formerly the mayor's digs, this lovely stone building (1874) has been converted into a three-bedroom apartment, with an additional one-bedroom unit in a wooden extension and another in an elevated building behind it. Inside, modern kitchens and bathrooms meld with antique furniture, while outside there are pretty gardens and a spa pool.

Platinum Villas RENTAL HOUSE $$$

(Map p546; ☎03-746 7700; www.platinumqueenstown.co.nz; 96 Fernhill Rd, Fernhill; house from $383; P 📶) Nab one of these 32 identical, luxurious, three-bedroom townhouses and make yourself at home. Each has a large open-plan living area with a big stone fireplace, laundry facilities and a proper garage. The 'lakeside' villas aren't actually on the lake, but they do have unimpeded watery views, while the 'alpine' villas catch silvery glimpses.

Chalet Queenstown
B&B **$$$**

(Map p546; ☑03-442 7117; www.chaletqueens town.co.nz; 1 Dublin St; r $245; P🌐) The seven perfectly appointed rooms at this stylish B&B are decked out with flat-screen TVs, interesting original artworks and quality bed linen. All have bathrooms, although some of them are tiny. Most also have balconies with views; get in early and request one looking over the lake.

🛏 Surrounds

Queenstown Top 10 Holiday Park
HOLIDAY PARK **$**

(☑03-442 9306; www.qtowntop10.co.nz; 70 Arthurs Point Rd, Arthurs Point; sites $48, units with/without bathroom from $95/85; P🌐) 🥾 High above the Shotover River, this relatively small, family-friendly park with excellent motel units is 10 minutes' drive from the hustle and bustle of Queenstown. Fall out of your campervan straight onto the famous Shotover Jet.

Twelve Mile Delta Campsite
CAMPGROUND **$**

(Map p544; www.doc.govt.nz; Glenorchy Rd, Mt Creighton; adult/child $10/5) Right by the lake, 12km west of Queenstown, this DOC campsite offers little more than a flat space to pitch a tent or park a campervan, and toilets of the nonflushing variety. The scenery's gorgeous and you can even pan for gold flakes on the lakefront.

Little Paradise Lodge
LODGE **$$**

(Map p544; ☑03-442 6196; www.littleparadise. co.nz; Glenorchy-Queenstown Rd, Mt Creighton; dm $45, r with/without bathroom $160/140; P) Wonderfully eclectic, this slice of arty paradise is the singular vision of the Swiss/Filipina owners. Each rustic room features wooden floors, quirky artwork and handmade furniture. Outside the fun continues with well-crafted walkways through beautiful gardens.

Asure Queenstown Gateway Apartments
MOTEL **$$**

(Map p544; ☑03-442 3599; www.gateway.net. nz; 1066 Frankton Rd, Frankton; s/d from $148/175; P🌐) On the highway near the airport (and hence cheaper than its equivalents in the town proper), this motel complex has two-bedroom split-level apartments with private courtyards. Request a rear unit for a quieter stay.

Villa del Lago
APARTMENT **$$$**

(☑03-442 5727; www.villadellago.co.nz; 249 Frankton Rd, Queenstown East; apt from $360; P🌐) 🥾 Clinging to the cliffs between the highway and the lake, these spacious one- to three-bedroom apartments have lake-facing terraces, incredible views and all the mod-cons including full kitchens, laundries and gas fires. The water taxi stops at the private jetty, or you can walk along the lake to Queenstown in 20 minutes.

Evergreen Lodge
B&B **$$$**

(Map p544; ☑03-442 6636; www.evergreen lodge.co.nz; 28 Evergreen Pl, Sunshine Bay; r $695; P@🌐) Tucked away above Sunshine Bay, this luxurious American-run B&B offers bigger-than-Texas rooms in a supremely private location with unfettered lake and mountain views. Add complimentary beer and wine, and a sauna and gym, and you've got a very relaxing escape from Queenstown's bustle.

🍴 Eating

🍴 Central Queenstown

⭐Fergbaker
BAKERY **$**

(Map p552; 42 Shotover St; items $5-9; ⏰6.30am-4.30am) Fergburger's sweeter sister bakes all manner of tempting treats – and although most things look tasty with 3am beer goggles on, it withstands the daylight test admirably. Goodies include meat pies, filled rolls, danish pastries and banoffee tarts. If you're after gelato, call into Mrs Ferg next door.

Taco Medic
FAST FOOD **$**

(Map p552; www.tacomedic.co.nz; 11 Brecon St; tacos $7; ⏰11am-9pm Nov-Apr, 10am-6.30pm May-Oct) Operating out of a food truck by the bike-hire place on Brecon St, these convivial lads dispense tacos of tasty fish, beef, pork belly and black bean to a devoted group of fans. One's a snack and two's a meal. During the ski season they move to an empty lot on the corner of Gorge Rd and Bowen St.

Empanada Kitchen
FAST FOOD **$**

(Map p552; ☑021 0279 2109; www.the empanadakitchen.com; 60 Beach St; empanadas $5.50; ⏰10am-5.30pm) This little hole-in-the-wall kiosk (attached to a public toilet, would you believe) serves only empanadas accompanied by a variety of sauces, and they're absolutely delicious. The flavours change daily and include savoury and sweet options.

Habebe's   MIDDLE EASTERN $
(Map p552; ✆ 03-442 9861; www.habebes.co.nz; Plaza Arcade, 30 Shotover St; meals $8-18; ☺ 8am-5pm; ✐) Middle Eastern-inspired kebabs, salads and wraps are the go. Soups and yummy pies (try the chicken, kumara and mushroom one) break the mould.

Blue Kanu   MODERN NZ $$
(Map p552; ✆ 03-442 6060; www.bluekanu. co.nz; 16 Church St; mains $27-39; ☺ 4pm-late) Disproving the rule that all tiki houses are inherently tacky, Blue Kanu somehow manages to be not just tasteful but stylish. The menu meshes robust Māori, Pasifika and Asian flavours with local ingredients to come up with an exotic blend of delicious dishes, designed to be shared. The service is excellent, too.

Public Kitchen & Bar   MODERN NZ $$
(Map p552; ✆ 03-442 5969; www.publickitchen. co.nz; Steamer Wharf, Beach St; dishes $15-45; ☺ 9am-11pm) The trend towards informal, shared dining has come to Queenstown in the form of this excellent waterfront eatery. Grab a posse and order a selection of plates of varying sizes from the menu; the meaty dishes, in particular, are excellent.

Fergburger   BURGERS $$
(Map p552; ✆ 03-441 1232; www.fergburger.com; 42 Shotover St; burgers $11-19; ☺ 8.30am-5am) Queenstown's famous Fergburger has now become a tourist attraction in itself, forcing many locals to look elsewhere for their big-as-your-head gourmet burger fix. The burgers are as tasty and satisfying as ever, but is any burger worth a 30-minute wait? You decide.

Vudu Cafe & Larder   CAFE $$
(Map p552; ✆ 03-441 8370; www.vucu.co.nz; 16 Rees St; mains $14-20; ☺ 7.30am-6pm) Excellent home-style baking combines with great coffee and tasty cooked breakfasts at this cosmopolitan cafe. Admire the huge photo of a much less populated Queenstown from an inside table, or head through to the rear garden for lake and mountain views.

Devil Burger   BURGERS $$
(Map p552; www.devilburger.com; 5-11 Church St; mains $10-20; ☺ 10am-4am; ✐) Look out Ferg –

you've got competition in the Queenstown burger wars. This diabolical new kid on the block also does tasty wraps. Try the hangover-busting 'Walk of Shame' wrap, stuffed with what's basically a full cooked breakfast.

Eichardt's Bar   TAPAS $$
(Map p552; www.eichardtshotel.co.nz; 1-3 Marine Pde; breakfast $16-18, lunch $25-26, tapas $7.50-12; ☺ 7.30am-late) Elegant without being stuffy, the small bar attached to Eichardt's Private Hotel is a wonderful refuge from the buzz of the streets. Foodwise, tapas is the main focus – and although the selection isn't particularly Spanish, it is particularly delicious.

Bespoke Kitchen   CAFE $$
(Map p552; ✆ 03-409 0552; www.facebook.com/ Bespokekitchenqueenstown; 9 Isle St; mains $11-19; ☺ 7.30am-5pm; ☎) Occupying a light-filled corner site between the town centre and the gondola, Bespoke delivers everything you'd expect of a smart Kiwi cafe. There's a good selection of counter food, beautifully presented cooked options, free wi-fi and, of course, great coffee.

Madam Woo   MALAYSIAN $$
(Map p552; ✆ 03-442 9200; www.madamwoo. co.nz; 5 The Mall; mains $16-32; ☺ noon-late; ✐) Wooing customers with a playful take on Chinese and Malay hawker food, the Madame serves up lots of tasty snacks for sharing (wontons, steamed dumplings, greasy filled-roti rolls), alongside larger dishes (beef rendang, duck salad, sambal prawns). Kids and distracted adults alike can have fun colouring in the menu.

Sasso   ITALIAN $$
(Map p552; ✆ 03-409 0994; www.sasso.co.nz; 14 Church St; mains $26-36; ☺ 4-11pm) Whether you're snuggled by one of the fireplaces inside the stone cottage (1882) or you've landed a table under the summer stars on the front terrace, this upmarket Italian eatery isn't short on atmosphere. Thankfully the food is also excellent.

Winnie's   PIZZA $$
(Map p552; www.winnies.co.nz; L1, 7 The Mall; mains $18-29; ☺ noon-late; ☎) Part-bar and part-restaurant, Winnie's always seems busy. Pizzas with a Thai, Mexican or Moroccan accent and massive burgers, pasta and steaks soak up the alcohol and keep energy levels high. On balmy nights the whole roof opens up and the party continues into the wee smalls.

Kappa
JAPANESE $$

(Map p552; ☑03-441 1423; L1, 36a The Mall; lunch $11-17, dinner $16-20; ☺noon-2.30pm & 5.30pm-late Mon-Sat) See if you can grab a spot on the tiny balcony so you can watch the passing parade on the Mall as you down a sake or Japanese beer and graze your way through *izakaya*-style dishes (food to snack on while you're drinking). The menu is short, sharp and very tasty.

Rata
MODERN NZ $$$

(Map p552; ☑03-442 9393; www.ratadining. co.nz; 43 Ballarat St; mains $36-42, 2-/3-course lunch $28/38; ☺noon-11pm) After gaining Michelin stars for restaurants in London, New York and LA, chef-owner Josh Emett has brought his exceptional but surprisingly unflashy cooking back home in the form of this upmarket but informal back-lane eatery. Native bush, edging the windows and in a large-scale photographic mural, sets the scene for a short menu showcasing the best seasonal NZ produce.

Botswana Butchery
MODERN NZ $$$

(Map p552; ☑03-442 6994; www.botswana butchery.co.nz; 17 Marine Pde; mains $38-53; ☺noon-11pm) Lake views and schmick interiors set the scene for a scintillating menu that's predominantly but not exclusively meaty, and a wine list of telephone directory dimensions. The $15 Express Lunch is a great deal.

✖ Surrounds

Boat Shed
CAFE $$

(Map p544; ☑03-441 4146; www.boatshed queenstown.com; Sugar Lane, Frankton; mains $12-25; ☺8am-5pm) Occupying a historic NZ Railways shipping office right by the lake, this great little cafe serves excellent, artfully arranged breakfasts and the likes of venison-and-bacon burgers for lunch. It's the perfect pit stop if you're cycling or walking the lakeside trail.

Sherwood
MODERN NZ $$

(Map p544; ☑03-450 1090; www.sherwood queenstown.nz; 554 Frankton Rd, Queenstown East; brunch $9-16, dinner $20-30; ☺7am-late) Despite being located at the heart of a faux-Tudor resort and having a ludicrously complicated wine list, this oasis of cool is well worth the 3km schlep from the town centre. Dishes are relatively simple but beautifully cooked (chicken, salmon, slow-cooked lamb, skirt steak) and are designed to be mixed and matched with vegetable dishes and shared.

Wakatipu Grill
EUROPEAN $$$

(Map p544; ☑03-450 9400; www.queenstown hilton.com; Hilton Queenstown, Peninsula Rd, Kelvin Heights; mains $34-40; ☺6-11pm) The Hilton sprawls along the lakeside by the Kawarau River outlet, and part of the fun of visiting its signature restaurant is the 8km water-taxi ride. As the name implies, there's always a decent selection of steak on the menu, but much more besides, including locally sourced fish and lamb.

Gantley's
MODERN NZ $$$

(☑03-442 8999; www.gantleys.co.nz; 172 Arthurs Point Rd, Arthurs Point; mains $40-44; ☺6-10pm) Gantley's French-influenced menu and highly regarded wine list justify the 7km journey from Queenstown. The atmospheric dining experience is showcased in a stone-and-timber building, built in 1863 as a wayside inn. If you feel like splurging, try the six-course degustation ($90).

🍷 Drinking & Nightlife

Queenstown offers a good range of options for after-dark carousing, even on Monday and Tuesday nights. However, in a bid to curb drunkenness and unruly behaviour, many venues enforce a one-way door policy after 2am, meaning you can leave but not enter.

A couple of outfits run organised pub crawls, where a wristband buys you a riotous night of discounted drinks, giveaways and games along the way; look for the ads in hostels and bars around town.

Zephyr
BAR

(Map p552; ☑03-409 0852; www.facebook.com/ zephyrqt; 1 Searle Lane; ☺8pm-4am) Queenstown's coolest indie rock bar is located – as all such places should be – in a grungy basement off a back lane. There's a popular pool table and regular live bands.

Atlas Beer Cafe
BAR

(Map p552; ☑03-442 5995; www.atlasbeer cafe.com; Steamer Wharf, Beach St; ☺10am-late) Perched at the end of Steamer Wharf, this pint-sized bar specialises in beers from Dunedin's Emerson's Brewery, Queenstown's Altitude and regular guest brews from further afield. It's also one of the best places in Queenstown for a good-value meal, serving excellent cooked breakfasts and simple hearty fare such as steaks, burgers and chicken parmigiana (mains $10 to $20).

Ballarat Trading Company
PUB

(Map p552; ☑03-442 4222; www.ballarat.co.nz; 7-9 The Mall; ☺11am-4am) Beyond the eclectic decor (stuffed bear, rampant wall-mounted ducks), Ballarat is quite a traditional spot, with gleaming beer taps, cover bands, sports on TV, quiz nights, occasional lapses into 1980s music and robust meals.

Pub on Wharf
PUB

(Map p552; ☑03-441 2155; www.pubonwharf. co.nz; 88 Beach St; ☺10am-late; 🛜) Ubercool interior design combines with handsome woodwork and lighting fit for a hipster hideaway, with fake sheep heads to remind you that you're still in NZ. Mac's beers on tap, scrummy nibbles and a decent wine list make this a great place to settle in for the evening. There's live music nightly and comedy occasionally.

Vinyl Underground
BAR

(Map p552; www.facebook.com/Vinylunder groundqt; 12 Church St; ☺6pm-2am) Enter the underworld, or at least the space under the World Bar, for a devilishly appealing venue lined with band posters, album covers and a large Ron Burgundy (*Anchorman*) portrait. There are live bands on Sundays, open-mic night on Mondays and DJs most other times. Plus it's fun to play 'count the Bowie pictures' – we stopped at five.

Bunker
COCKTAIL BAR

(Map p552; ☑03-441 8030; www.thebunker. co.nz; 14 Cow Lane; ☺5pm-4am) Perversely located upstairs rather than down, this chi-chi little bar clearly fancies itself the kind of place that Sean Connery's James Bond might frequent, if the photos on the wall are anything to go by. Best of all is the roof terrace, with couches, a big TV screening classic movies, and a fire in winter.

Little Blackwood
COCKTAIL BAR

(Map p552; ☑03-441 8066; www.littleblackwood. com; Steamer Wharf; ☺3pm-1am) With subway tiles on the walls, interesting art and barmen dressed in stripy shirts looking like old-fashioned sailor boys or perhaps extras from '*Allo 'Allo!*, Little Blackwood is an appealingly quirky addition to the Steamer Wharf complex. It's much more stylish than it sounds, and the cocktails are good, too.

Pig & Whistle
PUB

(Map p552; ☑03-442 9055; www.pigandwhistle pub.co.nz; 41 Ballarat St; ☺11am-midnight; 🛜) With 17 beers on tap, eight large TV screens and big sloppy serves of ribs to chew on, this British-style pub is a great place to watch the rugger, catch a covers band or to test your mettle in the highly competitive Tuesday night quiz.

Rhino's Ski Shack
BAR

(Map p552; ☑03-441 3329; www.rhinosskishack. com; 8 Cow Lane; ☺3pm-late Jun-Sep, 5pm-2am Oct-May) Queenstown's number-one spot for hip-hop loving, hipster, ski bunnies, Rhino's is a vibey basement bar serving a scattering of craft beers, $5 Rhino's lager on tap and pizza. Animal pelts and skis line the recycled wood-lined walls, giving it an appropriately rustic après-ski feel.

Bardeaux
WINE BAR

(Map p552; ☑03-442 8284; www.goodgroup. co.nz; Eureka Arcade, Searle Lane; ☺3pm-4am) This small, low-key, cavelike wine bar is all class. Under a low ceiling are plush leather armchairs and a fireplace made from Central Otago schist. The wine list is extraordinary, with the price of several bottles reaching four digits.

☆ Entertainment

Pick up *The Source* (www.facebook.com/ SourceNZ), a free monthly flyer with a gig guide and events listings.

Sherwood
LIVE MUSIC

(Map p544; ☑03-450 1090; www.sherwood queenstown.nz; 554 Frankton Rd, Queenstown East) As well as being a brilliant spot for a meal or a drink, the Sherwood has quickly become Queenstown's go-to spot for visiting musos. Many of NZ's bigger names have performed here; check the website for coming gigs.

Kiwi Haka
TRADITIONAL MUSIC

(Map p546; ☑03-441 0101; www.skyline.co.nz; Skyline; adult/child excl gondola $39/26) For a traditional Māori cultural experience, head to the top of the gondola for one of the 30-minute shows. There are usually three shows per night; bookings are essential.

🛍 Shopping

★ Vesta
ARTS, CRAFTS

(Map p552; ☑03-442 5687; www.vestadesign. co.nz; 19 Marine Pde; ☺10am-6pm) Showcasing really cool NZ-made art and craft, Vesta is full of interesting prints, paintings, glass art and gifts. It's housed in Williams Cottage (1864), Queenstown's oldest home. It's worth visiting just to check out the 1930s wallpaper and 1920s garden.

Artbay Gallery
ARTS

(Map p552; ☑03-442 9090; www.artbay.co.nz; 13 Marine Pde; ☺11am-6pm Mon-Wed, to 9pm Thu-Sun) Occupying an attractive 1863-built

Freemason's Hall on the lakefront, Artbay is always an interesting place to peruse, even if you don't have thousands to spend on a delicately carved ram's skull. It showcases the work of contemporary NZ artists, most of whom have a connection to the region.

Walk In Wardrobe CLOTHING
(Map p552; ☑ 03-409 0190; www.thewalkin wardrobe.co.nz; Beech Tree Arcade, 34 Shotover St; ☺ 10am-6pm Tue & Wed, to 8.30pm Thu-Mon) Benefitting from wealthy travellers lightening their suitcases before jetting out, this 'preloved fashion boutique' is a great place to hunt for bargain designer duds. Womenswear fills most of the racks.

ℹ Information

DOC Visitor Centre (Map p552; ☑ 03-442 7935; www.doc.govt.nz; 50 Stanley St; ☺ 8.30am-5pm) Head here to pick up confirmed bookings for the Routeburn Track and backcountry hut passes, and to get the latest weather and track updates. It can also advise on walks to suit your level of ability.

Post Office (Map p552; ☑ 0800 501 501; www.nzpost.co.nz; 13 Camp St; ☺ 9am-5pm Mon-Fri, 10am-2pm Sat)

Queenstown i-SITE (Map p552; ☑ 03-442 4100; www.queenstowninformation.com; cnr Shotover & Camp Sts; ☺ 8.30am-7pm) Friendly and informative despite being perpetually frantic, the saintly staff here can help with bookings and information on Queenstown, Gibbston, Lake Hayes, Arrowtown and Glenorchy.

ℹ Getting There & Away

AIR

Air New Zealand (☑ 0800 737 000; www.airnewzealand.co.nz) flies to Queenstown from Auckland, Wellington and Christchurch. **Jetstar** (☑ 0800 800 995; www.jetstar.com) also flies the Auckland route.

Various airlines offer direct flights to Queenstown from Australian destinations including Brisbane, the Gold Coast, Sydney and Melbourne.

BUS

Alpine Connexions (☑ 03-443 9120; www.alpineconnexions.co.nz) Shuttles head to/from Cardrona ($35, 55 minutes, two daily), Wanaka ($35, 1¼ hours, four daily), Cromwell ($25, one hour, four daily), Alexandra ($35, 1¾ hours, two daily) and Dunedin ($45, 4½ hours, daily).

Atomic Shuttles (☑ 03-349 0697; www.atomic travel.co.nz) Daily bus to and from Cromwell ($15, 55 minutes), Omarama ($30, 2¼ hours), Twizel ($30, 3¼ hours), Lake Tekapo ($30, 3¾ hours) and Christchurch ($50, seven hours).

Catch-a-Bus South (☑ 03-479 9960; www.catchabussouth.co.nz) Runs shuttles from Invercargill ($55, 2¾ hours) and Bluff ($70, 3¼ hours) most days, heading via Gore ($56, 2¾ hours) twice a week.

Connect Wanaka (☑ 0800 405 066; www.connectabus.com) Heads to/from Wanaka twice daily ($35, 1½ hours).

InterCity (☑ 03-442 4922; www.intercity.co.nz) Daily coaches to/from Wanaka (from $17, 1½ hours), Franz Josef (from $62, eight hours), Dunedin (from $24, 4¾ hours) and Invercargill ($48, three hours), and twice daily to Christchurch (from $55, 8½ to 11½ hours).

Naked Bus (www.nakedbus.com; prices vary) Two buses to Wanaka (1¼ hours) daily; one to Cromwell (one hour), Te Anau (2¾ hours), Franz Josef (5½ hours) and Christchurch (nine hours).

HIKERS' & SKIERS' TRANSPORT

Buckley Track Transport (☑ 03-442 8215; www.buckleytracktransport.nz) Transport between Queenstown and the trailheads of the Routeburn and Greenstone tracks.

Info & Track (☑ 03-442 9708; www.infotrack.co.nz; 37 Shotover St; ☺ 7.30am-9pm) During the Great Walks season, this agency provides transfers to the trailheads of the Routeburn and Greenstone & Caples tracks. In winter it morphs into Info & Snow and heads to the Cardrona and Treble Cone ski fields instead.

NZSki Snowline Express (www.nzski.com; return $20) During the ski season shuttles depart from outside the Snow Centre on Duke St every 20 minutes from 8am until 11.30am, heading to both Coronet Peak and the Remarkables. Buses return as they fill up, from 1.30pm onwards. They also leave on the hour from 4pm to 7pm for night skiing at Coronet Peak, returning on the half-hour from 5.30pm to 9.30pm.

Trackhopper (☑ 021-187 7732; www.trackhopper.co.nz; from $230, plus fuel) Offers a handy car-relocation service from either end of the Routeburn, Greenstone & Caples and Milford tracks.

Tracknet (☑ 03-249 7777; www.tracknet.net) This Te Anau–based outfit offers Queenstown connections to the Routeburn, Greenstone & Caples, Kepler, Hollyford and Milford tracks throughout the Great Walks season.

ℹ Getting Around

TO/FROM THE AIRPORT

The **Queenstown Airport** (ZQN; Map p544; ☑ 03-450 9031; www.queenstownairport.co.nz; Sir Henry Wrigley Dr, Frankton) is 7km east of the town centre. **Queenstown Taxis** (☑ 03-450 3000; www.queenstown.bluebubbletaxi.co.nz) and **Green Cabs** (☑ 0508 447 336; www.green-cabs.co.nz) charge around $40 to $45 for a trip into town from the airport, but only $35 to $40 for the return leg.

Alpine Connexions (p558) Has scheduled shuttles to/from Queenstown ($5, 15 minutes, four daily), Cromwell ($25, 50 minutes, daily) and Wanaka (from $25, one hour, four daily).

Connectabus (☑03-441 4471; www.connectabus.com) Route 11 runs between the airport and Camp St in Queenstown every 15 minutes from 6.50am to 11pm (adult/child $13/8). There's also a twice daily service to Wanaka ($35/20).

Super Shuttle (☑0800 748 885; www.supershuttle.co.nz; fare $20) Picks up and drops off in Queenstown.

PUBLIC TRANSPORT

Connectabus has various colour-coded routes, reaching as far as Sunshine Bay, Ferrhill, Arthurs Point, Frankton and Arrowtown. A day pass (adult/child $33/17) allows travel on the entire network. Pick up a route map and timetable from the i-SITE. Buses leave from Camp St.

AROUND QUEENSTOWN

Glenorchy & Around

POP 360

Set in achingly beautiful surroundings, postage-stamp-sized Glenorchy is the perfect low-key antidote to Queenstown. An expanding range of adventure operators will get you active on the lake and in nearby mountain valleys by kayak, horse or jetboat, and if you prefer to strike out on two legs, the mountainous region at the northern end of Lake Wakatipu is the setting for some of the South Island's finest tramps.

Those with sturdy wheels can explore the superb valleys north of Glenorchy. **Paradise** lies 15km northwest of town, just before the start of the Dart Track. Keep your expectations low: Paradise is just a paddock, but the gravel road there runs through beautiful farmland fringed by majestic mountains. You might recognise it from *The Lord of the Rings* movies as the approach to both Isengard and Lothlórien.

🏃 Activities

Almost all operators offer shuttles to and from Queenstown for a small surcharge. Other activities on offer include farm tours, fly fishing, guided photography tours and cookery classes; enquire at the Queenstown i-SITE (p558).

Hiking/Tramping

DOC's *Head of Lake Wakatipu* and *Wakatipu Walks* brochures (both $5, or download for free) detail day walks taking in the Routeburn Valley, Lake Sylvan, Dart River and Lake Rere. Two of the best short tracks are the **Routeburn Nature Walk** (one hour), at the trailhead of the Routeburn Track, and the **Lake Sylvan tramp** (one hour 40 minutes).

Another goody is the **Glenorchy Walkway**, which starts in the town centre and loops around Glenorchy lagoon, switching to boardwalks for the swampy bits. It's split into the Southern Circuit (30 minutes) and the Northern Circuit (one hour), and there are plenty of seats along the way, well positioned for views over the water to the mountains.

Before setting out on any of the longer tramps, call into the DOC in Queenstown (p558) or Te Anau (p580) for the latest track conditions and to purchase detailed maps. Another good resource is Lonely Planet's *Hiking & Tramping in New Zealand*.

For track snacks or meals, stock up on groceries in Queenstown. Track transport is at a premium during the Great Walks season (late October to March); try to book in advance. Many of the local accommodation providers offer trailhead transport.

★ Routeburn Track TRAMPING

(www.doc.govt.nz) Passing through a huge variety of landscapes with fantastic views all along the way, the 32km-long, two- to four-day Routeburn Track is one of the most popular rainforest/subalpine tracks in NZ. It's one of NZ's nine designated 'Great Walks', and many trampers rate it as the very best of them all.

Along the way you'll encounter mirror-like tarns, gurgling streams, fairy glades lined with plush moss, craggy mountain vistas and gnarled trees with long, straggly, lichen beards.

The track can be started from either end but we think the views are marginally better if you start from the Divide. Not far from the Divide, a highly recommended one-hour detour heads up to the **Key Summit**, where there are panoramic views of the Hollyford Valley and the Eglinton and Greenstone River Valleys. The hardest part of the Routeburn is the climb up to the **Harris Saddle**. From here, if you have any energy left you can expend it on a steep 1½- to two-hour

Routeburn, Greenstone & Caples Tracks

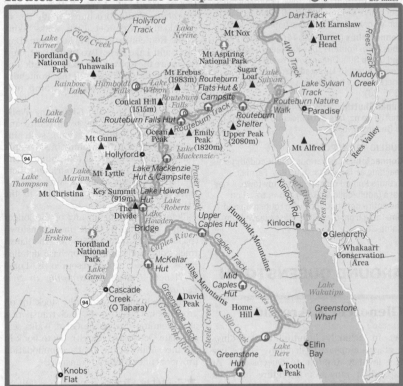

QUEENSTOWN & WANAKA GLENORCHY & AROUND

detour up **Conical Hill**. On a clear day you can see waves breaking at Martins Bay, far away on the West Coast, but it's not worth doing on a cloudy or windy day.

Increased pressure on the track has necessitated the introduction of an online booking system in the Great Walks season, which covers all huts and campsites on the route. You'll then need to call into the DOC Visitor Centre in either Queenstown or Te Anau to collect actual tickets, either the day before or on the day of departure. Outside of the season, bookings aren't required but you'll still need to visit one of the DOC centres to purchase your hut and campsite tickets. There are four basic huts along the track: Lake Howden, Lake Mackenzie, Routeburn Falls and Routeburn Flats. Both the Lake Mackenzie and Routeburn Flats huts have campsites nearby. The other option is to take a guided walk staying at luxury lodges along the way, operated by Ultimate Hikes (p561).

The Routeburn track remains open in winter. However, to traverse the alpine section after the snow falls is not recommended for casual hikers, as winter mountaineering skills are required. There are 32 avalanche paths across the section between the Lake Howden and Routeburn Falls huts, and the avalanche risk continues through to spring. Always check conditions with DOC.

There are car parks at both ends of the track, but they're unattended, so don't leave any valuables in your vehicle. Various track shuttles are available, and many people arrange to get dropped at the Divide to start their walk after a Milford Sound tour, or alternatively they time the end of their walk to catch one of the Milford Sound buses.

ROUTE	ESTIMATED WALKING TIME (HR)
Routeburn Shelter to Flats Hut	1½-2½
Flats Hut to Falls Hut	1-1½
Falls Hut to Lake Mackenzie Hut	4½-6
Lake Mackenzie Hut to Howden Hut	3-4
Howden Hut to the Divide	1-1½

Greenstone & Caples Tracks   TRAMPING
(www.doc.govt.nz; Greenstone Station Rd) Following meandering rivers through lush, peaceful valleys, these two tracks form a loop that many trampers stretch out into a moderate four- or five-day tramp. En route are the basic DOC-run Mid Caples Hut, McKellar Hut and Greenstone Hut; backcountry hut passes must be purchased in advance.

The tracks connect to the Routeburn Track; you can either follow the Routeburn's tail end to the Divide or (if you've prebooked) pursue it back towards the Glenorchy side of the mountains. From the McKellar Hut you can tramp two or three hours to the Howden Hut on the Routeburn Track, which is an hour from the Divide.

Access to the Greenstone & Caples Tracks is from Greenstone Wharf; you'll find unattended parking nearby.

ROUTE	ESTIMATED WALKING TIME (HR)
Greenstone Wharf to Mid Caples Hut	2-3
Mid Caples Hut to McKellar Hut	6-7
McKellar Hut to Greenstone Hut	4½-6½
Greenstone Hut to Greenstone Wharf	3-5

Other Activities

Dart Stables   HORSE RIDING
(☑03-442 5688; www.dartstables.com; Coll St) Guided treks traverse many locations familiar from Sir Peter Jackson's Tolkien adaptations, including a two-hour 'River Wild' ride ($145), a 1½-hour 'Ride of the Rings' ($165) and an hour-long 'Hobbits' Hack' ($85). If you're really keen and a fit, advanced rider, consider the three-hour 'Trilogy Loop' ($185).

Skydive Paradise   ADVENTURE SPORTS
(☑03-442 8333; www.skydiveparadise.co.nz; Glenorchy Airfield, Glenorchy-Queenstown Rd;

12,000-15,000ft jump $335-409) Tandem skydiving above some of the planet's most spectacular scenery.

Heli Glenorchy   SCENIC FLIGHTS
(☑0800 435 449; www.heliglenorchy.co.nz; Mull St) You'd be driving for the best part of a day to get from Glenorchy to Milford Sound, but it's only 15 minutes by helicopter. This crew offers a three-hour Milford Sound heli-cruise-heli package ($795) and a wilderness drop-off so that you can walk the last 11km of the famous Milford Track before being whisked back over the mountains ($850).

☞ Tours

Ultimate Hikes   WALKING TOUR
(☑03-450 1940; www.ultimatehikes.co.nz; ⊙Nov-Apr) If you value comfort as much as adventure, Ultimate Hikes offers three-day guided tramps on the Routeburn (from $1325); a six-day Grand Traverse, combining walks on the Routeburn and Greenstone tracks (from $1760); and the Classic, an eight-day tour combining the Routeburn and Milford tracks (from $3355). Prices include transfers from Queenstown, meals and accommodation in Ultimate's own well-appointed lodges.

Also offers a one-day Routeburn Encounter ($179).

Dart River Wilderness Jet   BOAT TOUR
(☑03-442 9992; www.dartriver.co.nz; 45 Mull St; adult/child $229/129; ⊙departs 9am & 1pm) Journeys into the heart of spectacular wilderness, including a short walk through beech forest and a backroad excursion. The round trip from Glenorchy takes three hours. Also offers jetboat rides combined with a river descent in an inflatable three-seater 'funyak' (departs 8.30am, adult/child $329/229). Prices include Queenstown pick-ups, which depart an hour prior to each trip.

Private Discovery Tours   DRIVING TOUR
(☑03-442 2299; www.privatediscoverytours.co.nz; half-/full day $185/395) Tours head by 4WD through a high-country sheep station in a remote valley between Mts Earnslaw and Alfred and include Middle-earth movie locations. Prices include pick-up from Queenstown.

🛏 Sleeping & Eating

Kinloch Lodge   LODGE $$
(☑03-442 4900; www.kinlochlodge.co.nz; Kinloch Rd; dm $35, d with/without bathroom from $159/95; @🔊) Across Lake Wakatipu from Glenorchy (26km by road; five minutes

by boat), this wonderfully remote 1868 lodge rents mountain bikes, offers guided kayaking and provides transfers to tramping trailheads. The Heritage Rooms are small but stylish, with shared bathrooms. Rooms in the YHA-associated hostel are comfy and colourful, and there's a post-tramp hot tub.

The cafe-bar is open for lunch year-round, for à la carte dinners in summer, and for set dinners in winter.

Glenorchy Lake House   B&B $$$

(☑03-442 4900; www.glenorchylakehouse. co.nz; Mull St, Glenorchy; r/house $295/495; 🛜) 🏊 After a day's tramping, recharge in the spa pool of this boutique B&B, attached to the excellent Trading Post cafe. The two guest bedrooms are decked out with Egyptian cotton sheets, flat-screen TVs and nice toiletries. Packages including transfers to the Routeburn and Greenstone Tracks are available.

Glenorchy Cafe   CAFE $$

(GYC; ☑03-442 9978; 25-27 Mull St, Glenorchy; mains $10-20, pizza $25; ☺9am-5pm Sun-Thu, to 9pm Fri & Sat Jan-Apr, 10am-4.30pm Sun-Fri, to 9pm Sat May-Dec) Grab a sunny table out the back of this cute little cottage and tuck into cooked breakfasts, sandwiches and soup. Head inside at night to partake in pizza and beer underneath the oddball light fixtures.

ℹ Information

Glenorchy Information Centre & Store

(☑03-409 2049; www.glenorchy-nz.co.nz; 42-50 Mull St, Glenorchy; ☺8.30am-6pm) Attached to the Glenorchy Hotel, this little shop is a good source of updated weather and track information. Fishing rods and mountain bikes can be hired. Ask about trail maps for walking or mountain biking in the nearby Whakaari Conservation Area.

ℹ Getting There & Away

Glenorchy lies at the head of Lake Wakatipu, a scenic 40-minute (46km) drive northwest from Queenstown. With sweeping vistas and gem-coloured waters, the sealed road is wonderfully scenic, although its constant hills are a killer for cyclists. There are no bus services but there are **trampers' shuttles** (p558) during the Great Walks season (late October to March).

There is a petrol station in Glenorchy, but fill up with cheaper fuel before you leave Queenstown.

Arrowtown

POP 2450

Beloved by day-trippers from Queenstown, exceedingly quaint Arrowtown sprang up in the 1860s following the discovery of gold in the Arrow River. Today its pretty, tree-lined avenues retain more than 60 of their original gold-rush buildings, but the only gold flaunted these days are the credit cards being waved in the expanding array of fashionable shops.

Instead of joining the bonanza of daytime tourists, consider using Arrowtown as a base for exploring Queenstown and the wider region. That way you can enjoy its history, charm and excellent restaurants when the tour buses have decamped back to Queenstown.

Exciting things are afoot in the high country surrounding Arrowtown. Record producer Mutt Lange (famous for his work with AC/DC, the Cars and Shania Twain, to whom he was once married) owns a vast chunk of the land between Arrowtown and Wanaka, having purchased four huge sheep stations covering 555 sq km. In 2014 Lange placed a covenant over the land through the QEII National Trust, protecting it for future generations, and embarked on a massive campaign of pest eradication and environmental restoration. There are moves afoot to build an interpretation centre and to improve public access through the construction of walking tracks – creating something akin to a private national park. Watch this space.

⊙ Sights

Lakes District Museum & Gallery   MUSEUM

(www.museumqueenstown.com; 49 Buckingham St; adult/child $10/3; ☺8.30am-5pm) Exhibits cover the gold-rush era and the early days of Chinese settlement around Arrowtown. Younger travellers will enjoy the Museum Fun Pack ($5), which includes activity sheets, museum treasure hunts, greenstone and a few flecks of gold. You can also rent pans here to try your luck panning for gold on the Arrow River ($3); you're more likely to find some traces if you head away from the town centre.

Chinese Settlement   HISTORIC SITE

(Buckingham St; ☺24hr) FREE Arrowtown has NZ's best example of an early Chinese settlement. Interpretive signs explain the lives of Chinese diggers during and after the gold rush (the last resident died in 1932), while

Arrowtown

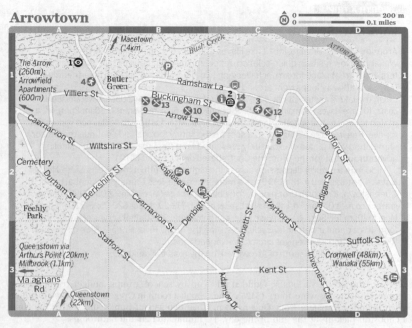

Arrowtown

restored huts and shops make the story more tangible. Subjected to significant racism, the Chinese often had little choice but to rework old tailings rather than seek new claims.

🏃 Activities

The information centre stocks a *Cycling & Walking Trail* brochure ($1) outlining some excellent tracks in the area. One particularly good new cycling route is the **Arrow River Bridges Ride** (12km, 90 minutes each way) from Arrowtown to the Kawarau Bridge, which traverses various new suspension bridges and a tunnel cut under the highway.

Arrowtown Bike Hire   MOUNTAIN BIKING
(☏ 0800 224 473; www.arrowtownbikehire.co.nz; 59 Buckingham St; half-/full-day rental $38/55) Hires bikes and provides great advice about local trails. If you fancy tackling the Arrow River Bridges Ride and then indulging in tastings at some of the Gibbston wineries, staff will collect you, your mates and your bikes for $60. Multiday rentals are also available.

Queenstown Bike Tours   MOUNTAIN BIKING
(☏ 03-442 0339; www.queenstownbiketours.co.nz; Dudley's Cottage, 4 Buckingham St; per half-/full day $45/55; ⊙ Sep-May) Rents bikes and

WORTH A TRIP

LAKE HAYES

Around 14,000 years ago, little Lake Hayes was joined to the Frankton Arm of Lake Wakatipu. Now it sits in quiet isolation, reflecting the neighbouring hills in its placid waters. It's a great place for an unchallenging two-hour walk, as the 8km bike-friendly **Lake Hayes Walkway** loops right around it.

On the lake's eastern flank is **Amisfield** (Map p544; ☑ 03-442 0556; www.amisfield. co.nz; 10 Lake Hayes Rd; mains $38-45; ☺ tasting 10am-6pm, restaurant 11.30am-8pm) 🍴 , a match for any of the wineries in nearby Gibbston. After tasting its acclaimed wines ($10 for five, free if you're dining), grab a spot on the sunny terrace and continue the sensory stimulation with plates of exquisitely presented food from the bistro. If you're feeling adventurous, opt for the 'Trust the Chef' shared dining menu ($70).

Hidden in a natural depression across the highway, south of the lake, is **Lake Hayes Estate**, established in the 1990s as a more affordable, less touristy residential option to Queenstown. It's worth dropping by for a bite at **Graze** (Map p544; ☑ 03-441 4074; www. grazenz.co.nz; 1 Onslow Rd, Lake Hayes Estate; brunch $12-20, dinner $20-25; ☺ 7.30am-5pm Mon, to 10pm Tue-Sun; ☜), a stylish cafe-bar delivering substantial serves of good, honest food. It's a popular detour for cyclists tackling the Arrow River Bridges Ride or the Twin Rivers Ride, and it's even got a microbrewery attached.

Lake Hayes is 4km south of Arrowtown, on the road to Frankton.

gets you started on various self-guided adventures, including wine tours ($125). The price includes transfers from Queenstown, a Gibbston pick-up at the end of the day, a cheese board at Gibbston Valley Cheese and, of course, the bike.

Dudley's Cottage   GOLD PANNING
(☑ 03-409 8162; www.dudleyscottagenz.com; 4 Buckingham St; ☺ 9am-5pm) Call into this historical cottage for a gold-panning lesson ($10, plus an extra $5 if you're keen to rent a pan and give it go). If you've already got the skills, rent a pan and shovel ($6) or sluice box ($25) and head out on your own. The cottage also houses an interesting gift shop and a cafe.

👉 Tours

Arrowtown Time Walks   WALKING TOUR
(☑ 021 782 278; www.arrowtowntimewalks.com; adult/child $20/12; ☺ 1.30pm Oct-Apr) Guided walks (90 minutes) depart from the museum daily, tracing a path through the township, pointing out places of interest along the way and delving into Arrowtown's goldrush history.

🛏 Sleeping

Arrowtown Born Of Gold   HOLIDAY PARK $
(☑ 03-442 1876; www.arrowtownholidaypark. co.nz; 12 Centennial Ave; sites/units from $38/130, r without bathroom $75; @ ☜) Close to the centre, this small holiday park offers a lane of en suite cabins trimmed with roses and a newish amenities block with coin-operated showers for campers. When it's not booked up by school groups, budget travellers can book a room in Oregon Lodge, each of which has two sets of bunks and shares the communal kitchen and bathrooms.

Arrowtown Lodge   B&B $$
(☑ 03-442 1101; www.arrowtownlodge.co.nz; 7 Anglesea St; r/cottage $195/395; ☜) From the outside, the guest rooms look like heritage cottages, but inside they're cosy and modern, with en suite bathrooms. Each has a private entrance from the pretty gardens. A continental breakfast is provided.

Old Villa   B&B $$
(☑ 03-442 1682; www.arrowtownoldvilla.co.nz; 13 Anglesea St; s $110, d $140-160; ☜) Freshly baked bread and homemade preserves welcome visitors to this heritage-style villa with a garden just made for summer barbecues. The two en suite double rooms come trimmed with fresh flowers and antique-style furnishings. One of the rooms has an additional single bed.

Shades of Arrowtown   MOTEL $$
(☑ 03-442 1613; www.shadesofarrowtown.co.nz; cnr Buckingham & Merioneth Sts; unit from $150; ☜) Tall shady trees and a garden setting give these stylish bungalow-style cottages a relaxed air. Some have full kitchens and spa baths. The two-storey family unit is good value if you're travelling with the whole clan.

Arrow   BOUTIQUE HOTEL $$$
(☑ 03-409 8600; www.thearrow.co.nz; 63 Manse Rd; ste from $385; ☜) Five understated but luxurious suites feature at this modern property

on the outskirts of Arrowtown. Accommodation is chic and contemporary with huge picture windows showcasing the surrounding countryside. Breakfast is included.

Arrowfield Apartments RENTAL HOUSES $$$
(☑03-442 0012; www.arrowfield.co.nz; 115 Essex Ave, Butel Park; houses from $250; 🖃🌊) Lining a quiet crescent in a new development on the edge of Arrowtown, these 13 identical spacious townhouses all have internal garages, full kitchens, gas fires and three bedrooms. Bedroom doors can be locked off for a smaller, cheaper rental.

Millbrook RESORT $$$
(Map p544; ☑03-441 7000; www.millbrook. co.nz; Malaghans Rd; r from $212; @🖃🌊) 🖋 Just outside Arrowtown, this enormous resort is a town unto itself. Cosy private villas have every luxury and there's a top-class golf course right at your front door. At the end of the day, take your pick from four restaurants, or relax at the spa (p549).

✕ Eating

Arrowtown Bakery BAKERY, CAFE $
(☑03-442 1587; www.arrowtownbakery.co.nz; Buckingham St; mains $5.50-13; ⊗8am-5pm) Equal parts bakery and cafe, this little eatery serves a wide selection of gourmet savoury pies, including exotic flavours such as venison and Thai chicken. Also on the menu are cooked breakfasts and fish and chips, or you can just settle in for coffee and a slice.

La Rumbla TAPAS $$
(☑03-442 0509; www.facebook.com/larumbla. arrowtown; 54 Buckingham St; tapas $11-22; ⊗4pm-midnight Tue-Sun) Tucked behind the post office, this little gem does a brilliant job of bringing the bold flavours and late-dining habits of Spain to sleepy little Arrowtown. Local produce is showcased in tasty bites such as lamb meatballs and Southland suede croquettes. The decor is a little uninspired but there's some serious NZ art on the walls.

Chop Shop CAFE $$
(☑03-442 1116; 7 Arrow Lane; mains $18-27; ⊗8am-3.30pm) Perhaps the tables are a little tightly packed and the staff a tad too chirpy, but we're splitting hairs. This place is uniformly fabulous – from the internationally inspired menu (pork dumplings, Turkish eggs, smoked pork-hock hash) to the interesting decor (pressed-tin bar, cool wallpaper, bevel-edged mirrors). Great coffee, too.

Provisions CAFE $$
(☑03-445 4048; www.provisions.co.nz; 65 Buckingham St; mains $8.50-24; ⊗8.30am-5pm; 🖃) One of Arrowtown's oldest cottages is now a cute cafe surrounded by fragrant gardens. Pop in for breakfast or a coffee and don't leave town without trying one of its deservedly famous sticky buns. Everything is baked on-site, including bread and bagels.

Saffron MODERN NZ $$$
(☑03-442 0131; www.saffronrestaurant.co.nz; 18 Buckingham St; lunch $22-29, dinner $39-40; ⊗noon-3pm & 6pm-late) Saffron offers hefty and delicious serves of grown-up food in a formal setting. The ever-changing trio of curries effortlessly traverses Asia, while other dishes jet to Europe and back. Fans can purchase *The Taste of Central Otago* cookbook, showcasing the restaurant's best recipes.

🍷 Drinking & Nightlife

Blue Door BAR
(☑03-442 0131; www.saffronrestaurant.co.nz; 18 Buckingham St; ⊗5pm-late; 🖃) Hidden away behind a tricky-to-find blue door, this cool little bar has a formidable wine list and enough rustic ambience to keep you entertained for the evening. Low ceilings, an open fire and abundant candles create an intimate quaffing location. On Wednesdays there's an open mic jam night.

Fork & Tap PUB
(☑03-442 1860; www.theforkandtap.co.nz; 51 Buckingham St; ⊗11am-11pm) Craft beers, great food and a sunny, kid-friendly back garden make this the pick of Arrowtown's pubs. Built in 1870 as a bank, it now hosts Irish bands on Wednesdays and other acts on Sundays in summer. Brew aficionados can sample four 150ml craft beers for $14.

☆ Entertainment

Dorothy Browns CINEMA
(☑03-442 1964; www.dorothybrowns.com; Ballarat Arcade 18 Buckingham St; adult/child $19/10) This is what a cinema should be like: ultra-comfortable seating with the option to cuddle with your neighbour. Fine wine and cheese boards are available to accompany the mostly art-house films on offer. Most screenings in the main theatre have an intermission – the perfect opportunity to tuck into a tub of gourmet ice cream.

WORTH A TRIP

MACETOWN

Macetown, 14km north of Arrowtown, is a gold-rush ghost town reached via a rugged, flood-prone road (the original miners' wagon track), which crosses the Arrow River more than 25 times.

Don't even think about taking the rental car here. A much more sensible option is the 4WD tour offered by **Nomad Safaris** (p550), which also includes gold panning. You can also hike there from Arrowtown (16km each way, 7½ hours return), but it's particularly tricky in winter and spring; check with the information centre about conditions before heading out.

ℹ️ Information

Arrowtown Visitor Information Centre (☑ 03-442 1824; www.arrowtown.com; 49 Buckingham St; ⊙ 8.30am-5pm) Shares premises with the Lake District Museum & Gallery.

ℹ️ Getting There & Away

Connectabus (☑ 03-441 4471; www.connectabus.com) Runs regular services (roughly hourly from 7.45am to 11pm) on its No 10 route from Frankton to Arrowtown. From Queenstown, you'll need to catch a No 11 bus to Frankton and change there.

WANAKA

POP 6480

Which is better, Queenstown or Wanaka? That's the perennial question around these parts and one which doesn't have an easy answer. It's hard to say which is more beautiful – both have blissful lake and mountain settings. Ditto, the jury's out as to which offers better skiing and tramping opportunities.

The main difference is in size, scale and buzz. Unlike its amped-up sibling across the Crown Range, Wanaka retains a laid-back, small-town feel. It's definitely not a sleepy hamlet anymore, though, and new restaurants and bars are adding a veneer of sophistication. And while it doesn't have quite the same range of adrenaline-inducing activities on offer, Wanaka is no slacker on the outdoor adventure front. Importantly, it's also cheaper.

⊙ Sights

National Transport & Toy Museum MUSEUM
(☑ 03-443 8765; www.nttmuseumwanaka.co.nz; 891 Wanaka Luggate Hwy/SH6; adult/child $17/5; ⊙ 8.30am-5pm; ☷) Small armies of Smurfs, Star Wars figurines and Barbie dolls share billing with dozens of classic cars and a mysteriously acquired MiG jet fighter in this vast collection, which fills four giant hangers near the airport. There are around 30,000 items in total, including plenty of toys that you're bound to remember from rainy childhood afternoons.

Puzzling World AMUSEMENT PARK
(☑ 03-443 7489; www.puzzlingworld.com; 188 Wanaka Luggate Hwy/SH84; adult/child $20/14; ⊙ 8.30am-5.30pm; ☷) A 3D Great Maze and lots of fascinating brain-bending visual illusions to keep people of all ages bemused, bothered and bewildered. It's en route to Cromwell, 2km from town.

Warbirds & Wheels MUSEUM
(www.warbirdsandwheels.com; Wanaka Airport, 11 Lloyd Dunn Av; adult/child $20/5; ⊙ 9am-4pm) Dedicated to NZ combat pilots, the aircraft they flew and the sacrifices they made, this museum features Hawker Hurricanes, a de Havilland Vampire and lots of shiny, beautifully restored classic cars. There's also an art gallery and retro diner attached.

Rippon WINERY
(☑ 03-443 8084; www.rippon.co.nz; 246 Mt Aspiring Rd; ⊙ noon-5pm Jul-Apr) **FREE** Along with just about the best view of any NZ winery, Rippon has great wine, too. To save fights over who's going to be the designated driver, take a 2km stroll along the lakeside and look out for the track up the hill from the end of Sargood Dr.

Wanaka Beerworks BREWERY
(☑ 03-443 1865; www.wanakabeerworks.co.nz; 891 Wanaka Luggate Hwy/SH6; tour incl tasting $15; ⊙ tours 2pm Sun-Thu) Somewhat incongruously attached to the toy museum, this small brewery's main beers (Cardrona Gold lager, Brewski pilsner, Treble Cone wheat beer and Black Peak coffee stout) are complemented by those of its sister label Jabberwocky, along with various seasonal brews.

🏃 Activities

Wanaka is the gateway to Mt Aspiring National Park and to the Treble Cone (p547), Cardrona (p573), Harris Mountains and Pisa Range Ski Areas.

Hiking/Tramping

For walks close to town, including various lakeside walks, pick up the DOC brochure *Wanaka Outdoor Pursuits* ($3.50). The

Wanaka

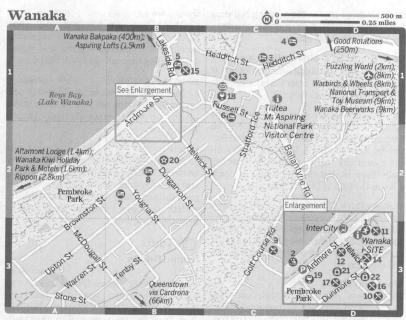

Wanaka

short climb to the top of **Mt Iron** (527m, 1½ hours return) reveals panoramic views.

To the north of Wanaka, the usually unpeopled **Minaret Burn Track** (six to seven hours) in the Mt Alta Conservation Area is suitable for walking and mountain biking. After about two to three hours, a track heads down to **Colquhouns Beach**, a great swimming spot.

Aspiring Guides ADVENTURE SPORTS
(☏ 03-443 9422; www.aspiringguides.com; L1, 99 Ardmore St) This crew offers a multitude of options, including guided wilderness tramping (from two to eight days); mountaineering and ice-climbing courses; guided ascents of Tititea/Mt Aspiring, Aoraki/Mt Cook, Mt Brewster and Mt Tasman; and off-piste skiing (one- to five-day backcountry expeditions).

Adventure Consultants ADVENTURE SPORTS
(☏ 03-443 8711; www.adventureconsultants.com) Offers two-days guided excursions on Brewster Glacier (from $890), three-day trips in the Gillespie Pass ($1250) and four-day

'Alpine Adventures' in Mt Aspiring National Park (from $1390). Also runs mountaineering and ice-climbing courses.

Rock Climbing & Mountaineering

Excellent rock climbing can be found at Hospital Flat – 25km from Wanaka towards Mt Aspiring National Park.

Basecamp Wanaka ROCK CLIMBING
(☑03-443 1110; www.basecampwanaka.co.nz; 50 Cardrona Valley Rd; day pass $23-30; ⊙noon-8pm Mon-Fri, 10am-6pm Sat & Sun) Before you hit the mountains, learn the ropes on climbing walls. Even fearless three-year-olds can have a go on the Clip 'n Climb (from $10).

Wanaka Rock Climbing ROCK CLIMBING
(☑03-443 6411; www.wanakarock.co.nz) Introductory rock-climbing course (half-/full day $140/210), a half-day abseiling intro ($140), and bouldering and multipitch climbs for the experienced.

Mountain Biking

Hundreds of kilometres of tracks and trails in the region are open to mountain bikers. Pick up the DOC brochure *Wanaka Outdoor Pursuits* ($3.50), describing mountain-bike rides ranging from 2km to 24km, including the **Deans Bank Loop Track** (12km).

One particularly scenic new route is the **Newcastle Track** (12km), which follows the raging blue waters of the Clutha River from the Albert Town Bridge to Red Bridge. You can make it a 30km loop by joining the **Upper Clutha River Track** at Luggate.

Good Rotations BICYCLE RENTAL
(☑027 874 7377; www.goodrotations.co; 34 Anderson Rd; half-/full day $59/89) Hires bicycles including electric bikes and all-terrain 'fat bikes' with superwide tyres (great for the pebbles on the lakefront). Drop by the neighbouring coffee-and-food cart for a pre-ride rev-up.

Other Activities

Wanaka Kayaks KAYAKING
(☑0800 926 925; www.wanakakayaks.co.nz; Ardmore St; ⊙9am-6pm Oct-Easter) Rents kayaks ($20 per hour) and stand-up paddle boards ($20 per hour), and offers guided paddle-powered tours of the lake (half-/full day $95/189) and the 'Mighty Clutha' River (half-day $189). You'll find them on the lakefront, opposite the Lake Bar.

Skydive Lake Wanaka ADVENTURE SPORTS
(☑03-443 7207; www.skydivewanaka.com; from $329) Jump from 12,000ft, or go the whole hog with a 15,000ft leap and 60 seconds of freefall.

Deep Canyon ADVENTURE SPORTS
(☑03-443 7922; www.deepcanyon.co.nz; from $230; ⊙Oct-Apr) Specialises in canyoning expeditions: climbing, walking and waterfall-abseiling through confined, wild gorges.

Wanaka Paragliding PARAGLIDING
(☑0800 359 754; www.wanakaparagliding.co.nz; tandem $199) Count on around 20 minutes soaring on the summer thermals around Treble Cone.

Hatch FISHING
(☑03-443 8446; www.hatchfishing.co.nz; half-/full day $450/750) Lakes Wanaka and Hawea and the surrounding rivers are excellent for trout fishing. Hatch offers guided fly-fishing, with the option of accessing remote spots by helicopter or jetboat.

👉 Tours

Scenic Flights

U-Fly SCENIC FLIGHTS
(☑03-445 4005; www.u-flywanaka.co.nz; from $199) Scratch 'flying a plane' off the bucket list on a scenic flight over Mt Aspiring National Park. Don't fret, there are dual controls ready for the pilots to take over at a moment's notice – they're not completely insane.

Classic Flights SCENIC FLIGHTS
(☑03-443 4043; www.classicflights.co.nz; from $249) Runs sightseeing flights in a vintage Tiger Moth or Waco biplane. 'Biggles' goggles and flowing silk scarf provided.

Wanaka Helicopters SCENIC FLIGHTS
(☑03-443 1085; www.wanakahelicopters.co.nz) Options range from 10-minute tasters ($99) to two-hour-plus trips to Milford Sound (from $995).

Wanaka Flightseeing SCENIC FLIGHTS
(☑03-443 8787; www.flightseeing.co.nz) Spectacular flyovers of Tititea/Mt Aspiring (adult/child $248/165), Aoraki/Mt Cook ($445/285) and Milford Sound ($498/315).

Other Tours

Wanaka Bike Tours MOUNTAIN BIKING
(☑03-443 6363; www.wanakabiketours.co.nz; from $199) Guided trips including helibiking options.

Eco Wanaka Adventures TRAMPING, CRUISE
(☑03-443 2869; www.ecowanaka.co.nz) 🖉 Guided tours include a full-day trek to the Rob Roy Glacier ($275), a four-hour cruise and walk on Mou Waho island ($225), and a full-day cruise-4WD combo ($450). Also offers helihikes.

MT ASPIRING NATIONAL PARK

Verdant valleys, alpine meadows, unspoiled rivers, craggy mountains and more than 100 glaciers make Mt Aspiring National Park an outdoor enthusiast's paradise. Protected as a national park in 1964, and later included in the Te Wahipounamu (Southwest New Zealand) World Heritage Area, the park now blankets 3555 sq km along the Southern Alps, from the Haast River in the north to its border with Fiordland National Park in the south. Lording it over all is colossal Tititea/Mt Aspiring (3033m), the highest peak outside the Aoraki/Mt Cook area.

While the southern end of the national park near Glenorchy includes better known tramps such as the **Routeburn** (p559) and **Greenstone & Caples** (p561) tracks, there are plenty of blissful short walks and more demanding multiday tramps in the Matukituki Valley, close to Wanaka; see the DOC brochure *Matukituki Valley Tracks* ($2).

The dramatic **Rob Roy Glacier Track** (9km, three to four hours return) takes in glaciers, waterfalls and a swing bridge. It's a moderate walk, but some parts are quite steep. The **West Matukituki Valley Track** goes on to the Aspiring Hut (four to five hours return; peak/off-peak $30/25 per night), a scenic walk over mostly grassy flats. For overnight or multiday tramps offering great views of Mt Aspiring, continue up the valley to the Liverpool Hut (at an elevation of 1000m; $15 per night) and French Ridge Hut (at 1465m; $25 per night).

Many of these tramps are prone to snow and avalanches and can be treacherous. It is extremely important to consult with the DOC staff at the **Tititea Mt Aspiring National Park Visitor Centre** (p572) in Wanaka and to purchase hut tickets before heading off. You should also register your intentions on www.adventuresmart.org.nz.

Tracks are reached from Raspberry Creek at the end of Mt Aspiring Rd, 50km from Wanaka. The road is unsealed for 30km and involves nine ford crossings; it's usually fine in a 2WD, except in very wet conditions (check at the visitor centre).

Wanaka River Journeys   TOUR
(☑ 03-443 4416; www.wanakariverjourneys.co.nz; adult/child $229/139) ☞ Combination bush walk (50 minutes) and jetboat ride in the gorgeous Matukituki Valley.

Ridgeline Adventures   DRIVING TOUR
(☑ 0800 234 000; www.ridgelinenz.com; from $165) ☞ Explore the wilderness surrounding Wanaka on a 4WD nature safari.

★☆ Festivals & Events

Rippon Festival   MUSIC
(www.ripponfestival.co.nz) Big-name Kiwi bands and musicians headline at the lakeside Rippon Vineyard. It's held in even-numbered years on Waitangi weekend (around 6 February).

Warbirds over Wanaka   AIR SHOW
(☑ 0800 496 920, 03-443 8619; www.warbirds overwanaka.com; Wanaka Airport; 3-day adult/child $190/25) Held every second Easter (in even-numbered years), this incredibly popular international airshow attracts upwards of 50,000 people. Individual day tickets can be purchased separately.

Wanaka Fest   CARNIVAL
(www.wanakafest.co.nz) This mid-October event has the feel of a small-town fair. Street parades, live music, wacky competitions and fine regional produce get the locals saying 'g'day' to the warmth of spring.

🛏 Sleeping

★ Wanaka Bakpaka   HOSTEL $
(☑ 03-443 7837; www.wanakabakpaka.co.nz; 117 Lakeside Rd; dm $30-31, d with/without bathroom $92/74; @ 🛜) An energetic husband-and-wife team run this friendly hostel above the lake with just about the best views in town. Amenities are top-shelf and the onto-it staff consistently offer a red-carpet welcome to weary travellers. It's worth considering paying a bit extra for the en suite double with the gorgeous views.

YHA Wanaka Purple Cow   HOSTEL $
(☑ 03-443 1880; www.yha.co.nz; 94 Brownston St; dm $30-35, d with/without bathroom from $100/89; @ 🛜) ☞ In the top echelons of NZ YHAs, the Purple Cow offers a range of shared and private rooms, including some with en suites in a newer building out the back. Best of all are the large lounge, with commanding lake and mountain views, and a wood stove.

Altamont Lodge
LODGE $

(☎03-443 8864; www.altamontlodge.co.nz; 121 Mt Aspiring Rd; s/d $55/89; ☎) At the quiet end of town, Altamont is like a hostel for grown-ups. There are no dorms but the tidy little rooms share bathrooms and a spacious, well-equipped kitchen. Pine-lined walls give it a ski-lodge ambience, while the spa pool and roaring fire in the lounge will warm you up post-slopes.

Wanaka Kiwi Holiday Park & Motels
HOLIDAY PARK $

(☎03-443 7766; www.wanakakiwiholidaypark. nz; 263 Studholme Rd North; campsites $25-27, unit with/without bathroom from $100/85; @☎) Grassy sites for tents and campervans, lots of trees, and pretty views add up to a charming and relaxing campground. Facilities include a barbecue area with gas heaters, and free wi-fi, spa pool and sauna. Older-style motel units have all been renovated, and the newest budget cabins are warm and cosy with wooden floors.

Mountain View Backpackers
HOSTEL $

(☎03-443 9010; www.wanakabackpackers.co.nz; 7 Russell St; dm $28-29, d without bathroom $68; P@☎) This colourful and characterful house features a manicured lawn and warm, comfortable rooms. Fire up the barbecue after a busy day's exploring. Handy features include a drying room and off-street parking.

★ Alpine View Lodge
B&B $$

(☎03-443 7111; www.alpineviewlodge.co.nz; 23 Studholme Rd South; d from $180, cottage $285; ☎) In a peaceful, rural setting on the edge of town, this excellent lodge has three B&B rooms, one of which has its own, private, bush-lined deck. Little extras include homemade shortbread in the rooms and a hot tub. Alternatively, you can opt for the fully self-contained two-bedroom cottage, which opens onto the garden.

★ Criffel Peak View
B&B $$

(☎03-443 5511; www.criffelpeakview.co.nz; 98 Hedditch St; s/d/apt from $135/160/270; ☎) Situated in a quiet cul-de-sac, this excellent B&B has three rooms sharing a large lounge with a log fire and a sunny wisteria-draped deck. The charming hostesses live in a separate house behind, which also has a self-contained two-bedroom apartment attached.

Wanaka View Motel
MOTEL $$

(☎03-443 7480; www.wanakaviewmotel.co.nz; 122 Brownston St; unit $120-195; ☎) The refurbished Wanaka View has five apartments with Sky TV, spa baths and full kitchens. The largest has three bedrooms and most of them have lake views. There's also a comfortable studio unit tucked around the back, which is cheaper but doesn't have a kitchen or view.

Archway Motels
MOTEL $$

(☎03-443 7698; www.archwaymotels.co.nz; 64 Hedditch St; unit from $125; ☎) This older motel with clean and spacious units and chalets is a short uphill walk from the town centre. Cedar hot tubs with mountain views give this place an extra edge. Book directly for good off-peak discounts.

★ Lakeside
APARTMENTS $$$

(☎03-443 0188; www.lakesidewanaka.co.nz; 7 Lakeside Rd; apt from $295; ☎☀) ✿ Luxuriate in a modern apartment in a prime position overlooking the lake, right by the town centre. All have three bedrooms but can be rented with only one or two bedrooms open. The swimming pool is a rarity in these parts and an appealing alternative to the frigid lake on a sweltering day.

Aspiring Lofts
B&B $$$

(☎03-443 7856; www.aspiringlofts.co.nz; 42 Manuka Cres; s/d $180/220; ☎) Perched on a ridge overlooking the lake, this modern house has a beautiful garden and two upmarket B&B rooms in the loft above the garage. Each has its own private balcony to make the most of the views.

Riverview Terrace
B&B $$$

(☎03-443 7377; www.riverviewterrace.co.nz; 31 Matheson Cres, Albert Town; r $350; ☎) ✿ Part of a new development on a hill overlooking the Clutha River, this swish, modern house has three well-appointed guest rooms. Rates include a cooked breakfast, bikes to borrow and a natural-water hot tub under the stars.

✘ Eating

Florence's Foodstore & Cafe
CAFE $

(☎03-443 7078; www.florencesfoodstore.co.nz; 71 Cardrona Valley Rd; mains $9.50-18; ⊙8.30am-3pm) Wood, corrugated iron and jute-cladding create a rustic feel for this edge-of-town gourmet provedore. Call in for the region's prettiest smoked salmon benedict, as well as French-style pastries and delicious filled bagels.

Red Star
BURGERS $

(www.facebook.com/redstarwanaka; 26 Ardmore St; burgers $10-17; ⊙11.30am-late) Red Star spoils diners with a menu featuring inventive ingredients and 19 different burgers made Kiwi-style, with crunchy toasted buns. Grab a seat on the terrace and sup on a craft beer while you wait.

Soulfood
CAFE $

(☑ 03-443 7885; www.soulfoodwanaka.co.nz; 74 Ardmore St; mains $10-18; ☺ 8am-6pm Mon-Fri, to 4pm Sat & Sun; ☑) ∅ It's not soul food in the African American sense, rather this little organics store offers a healthy range of id-affirming soups, pizzas, pastas and muffins. Not everything's strictly vegetarian, with wild venison and free-range pork sausages breaking the spell. Juices and smoothies are suitably virtuous, but coffee's limited to the plunger variety.

Yohei
JAPANESE $

(☑ 03-443 4222; Spencer House Mall, 23 Dunmore St; mains $9-14; ☺ 9am-5.30pm; ☎☑) Tucked away in a shopping arcade, this relaxed eatery does interesting local spins on sushi (how about venison?), Japanese curries, noodles and superlative juices and smoothies.

★ Francesca's Italian Kitchen
ITALIAN $$

(☑ 03-443 5599; www.fransitalian.co.nz 93 Ardmore St; mains $20-26; ☺ noon-3pm & 5pm-late) Ebullient expat Francesca has brought the big flavours and easy conviviality of an authentic Italian family trattoria to Wanaka in the form of this stylish and perennially busy eatery. Even simple things such as pizza, pasta and polenta chips are exceptional. She also runs a pizza cart on Brownston St, opposite Cinema Paradiso.

Ritual
CAFE $$

(☑ 03-443 6662; 18 Helwick St; mains $11-20; ☺ 9am-5pm) A classic 21st-century Kiwi cafe, Ritual is smart but not too trendy, gay-friendly but family-friendly, too, and filled to the gills with delicious food. The counter positively groans under the weight of tasty salads, slices and scones.

Spice Room
INDIAN $$

(☑ 03-443 1133; www.spiceroom.co.nz; 43 Helwick St; mains $21-27; ☺ 5-10pm; ☑) The combination of authentic curry, crispy garlic naan and cold beer is a great way to recharge after a day's snowboarding or tramping. Beyond the spot-on renditions of all your subcontinental favourites, the Spice Room springs a few surprises, with starters including a zingy scallop masala salad.

Federal Diner
CAFE $$

(☑ 03-443 5152; www.federaldiner.co.nz; 47 Helwick St brunch $12-20, mains $18-35; ☺ 7am-4pm Mon & Tue, to 9pm Wed-Sun; ☎) Tucked away in a back lane, this cosmopolitan cafe delivers robust breakfasts, excellent coffee, legendary scones and chunky gourmet sandwiches. In the evenings, the menu shifts to substantial dishes meant for sharing.

Kai Whakapai
CAFE $$

(☑ 03-443 7795; cnr Helwick & Ardmore Sts; brunch $13-19, dinner $19-23; ☺ 7am-11pm; ☎) An absolute Wanaka institution, Kai (the Māori word for 'food') is the place to be for a liquid sundowner accompanied by a massive filled baguette or pizza. Locally brewed craft beers are on tap and there are Central Otago wines as well.

Bistro Gentil
FRENCH $$$

(☑ 03-443 2299; www.bistrogentil.co.nz; 76a Golf Course Rd; mains $38-44; ☺ 11.30am-late) Lake views, fabulous NZ art and delicious modern French cuisine – Gentil ticks plenty of boxes for a memorable night out. There's oodles of wines by the glass, but at these prices we would prefer it was poured for us, rather than having to contend with the gimmicky digital self-pour system. On a balmy night, request an outside table.

🍷 Drinking & Nightlife

Gin & Raspberry
COCKTAIL BAR

(☑ 03-443 4216; www.ginandraspberry.co.nz; L1, 155 Ardmore St; ☺ 3pm-late) If you're in the swing for bling, this lush bar offers gilded mirrors, sparking chandeliers, a piano and a central fireplace. Classic movies provide a backdrop to classic cocktails (including various martinis), and the occasional live band fires things up.

Lalaland
COCKTAIL BAR

(☑ 03-443 4911; www.lalalandwanaka.co.nz; L1, 99 Ardmore St; ☺ 6pm-2.30am) Keep a watchful eye on the lake or sink into a comfy chair at this little, low-lit, completely over-the-top cocktail palace/bordello. The young barmeister-owner truly knows his stuff, concocting elixirs to suit every mood. Entry is via the rear stairs.

Barluga & Woody's
BAR

(☑ 03-443 5400 Post Office Lane, 33 Ardmore St; ☺ 4pm-2.30am) Sharing both a courtyard and owners, these neighbouring bars operate more or less in tandem, especially when there's a DJ event on. Barluga's leather armchairs and retro wallpaper bring to mind a refined gentlemen's club. Wicked cocktails and killer back-to-back beats soon smash that illusion. Woody's plays the role of the younger, sportier brother, with pool tables and indie sounds.

☆ Entertainment

Ruby's CINEMA
(☑ 03-443 6901; www.rubyscinema.co.nz; 50 Cardrona Valley Rd; adult/child $19/15) Channelling a lush New York or Shanghai vibe, this hip-art-house-cinema-meets-chic-cocktail-bar is a real surprise in outdoorsy Wanaka. Luxuriate in the huge cinema seats, or chill out in the red-velvet lounge with craft beers, classic cocktails and sophisticated bar snacks. You'll find Ruby's concealed within the Basecamp Wanaka building on the outskirts of town.

Cinema Paradiso CINEMA
(☑ 03-443 1505; www.paradiso.net.nz; 72 Brownston St; adult/child $15/9.50) Stretch out on a comfy couch, a dentist's chair or in an old Morris Minor at this Wanaka institution, screening the best of Hollywood and art-house flicks. At intermission the smell of freshly baked cookies and pizza wafts through the theatre, although the homemade ice cream is just as alluring.

🛍 Shopping

Chop Shop CLOTHING
(☑ 03-443 8297; www.chopshopwanaka.co.nz; 3 Pembroke Mall; ⊙ 10am-6pm) The best coffee in town and a natty range of locally designed beanies and cool T-shirts for the discerning snowboarder.

Gallery Thirty Three ARTS, CRAFTS
(☑ 03-443 4330; www.gallery33.co.nz; 33 Helwick St; ⊙ 10am-5pm) Pottery, glass and jewellery from local artists.

ℹ Information

Post Office (☑ 03-443 8211; www.nzpost.co.nz; 39 Ardmore St; ⊙ 9am-5pm Mon-Fri, to noon Sat)
Tititea Mt Aspiring National Park Visitor Centre (☑ 03-443 7660; www.doc.govt.nz; cnr Ardmore & Ballantyne Sts; ⊙ 8.30am-5pm daily Nov-Apr, Mon-Sat May-Oct) In an A-framed building on the edge of the town centre, this DOC centre takes hut bookings and offers advice on tracks and conditions. Be sure to call in before undertaking any wilderness tramps. There's also a small display on Wanaka geology, flora and fauna.
Wanaka i-SITE (☑ 03-443 1233; www.lake-wanaka.co.nz; 103 Ardmore St; ⊙ 8.30am-5.30pm) Extremely helpful but always busy.

Wanaka Medical Centre (☑ 03-443 0710; www.wanakamedical.co.nz; 23 Cardrona Valley Rd; ⊙ 9am-5pm Mon-Fri) Patches up adventure-sports mishaps.

ℹ Getting There & Away

Alpine Connexions (☑ 03-443 9120; www.alpinecoachlines.co.nz) Links Wanaka with Queenstown, Cromwell, Alexandra, Dunedin and the Rail Trail towns of Central Otago. Also have shuttles to Wanaka Airport, the Mt Aspiring trailheads and Lake Hawea in summer, and Cardrona and Treble Cone in winter.
Atomic Shuttles (☑ 03-349 0697; www.atomictravel.co.nz) Daily bus to/from Dunedin ($35, 4½ hours) via Cromwell ($15, 50 minutes), Alexandra ($25, 1¾ hours) and Roxburgh ($30, 2¼ hours).
Connectabus (☑ 0800 405 066; www.connectabus.com; one way/return $35/65) Handy twice-daily service linking Wanaka with Queenstown Airport (1¼ hours) and Queenstown (1½ hours). Free pick-up from most accommodation.
InterCity (☑ 03-442 4922; www.intercity.co.nz) Coaches depart from outside the Log Cabin on the lakefront, with daily services to Cromwell (from $10, 44 minutes), Queenstown (from $17, 1½ hours), Lake Hawea (from $10, 20 minutes), Makarora (from $12, 1¾ hours) and Franz Josef (from $43, 6½ hours).
Naked Bus (www.nakedbus.com; prices vary) Services to Queenstown (1¼ hours), Cromwell (40 minutes), Franz Josef (4¼ hours), Lake Tekapo (three hours) and Christchurch (7¼ hours).

ℹ Getting Around

Adventure Rentals (☑ 03-443 6050; www.adventurerentals.co.nz; 51 Brownston St) Rents out cars and 4WDs.
Yello (☑ 03-443 5555; www.yello.co.nz) Operates taxis and shuttles to the ski fields.

AROUND WANAKA

Cardrona

The cute hamlet of Cardrona reached its zenith in the 1870s at the height of the gold rush when its population numbered over a thousand. Now it's a sleepy little place that wakes up with a jolt for the ski season.

With views of foothills and countless snowy peaks, the **Crown Range Road** from Cardrona to Queenstown is one of the South Island's most scenic drives. At 1076m, it's the highest sealed road in NZ. It passes through tall, swaying tussock grass in the **Pisa Conservation Area** (Map p544), which has several short walking trails. There are some great places to stop and drink in the view, particularly at the Queenstown end of the road before you start the switchback down towards Lake Hayes. However, the road is narrow and winding, and needs to be tackled with care in poor weather. In winter it's sometimes closed after heavy snows, and you'll often need snow chains for your wheels.

◉ Sights

Cardrona Distillery & Museum DISTILLERY
(Map p544; ☑03-443 1393; www.cardrona distillery.com; 2125 Cardrona Valley Rd; tours from $45; ◷9.30am-5pm) An interesting diversion for those travelling along the valley, this brand-new distillery produces single-malt whisky, vodka, gin and an orange liqueur. Book ahead for tours, which leave on the hour from 10am to 3pm.

🏃 Activities

Cardrona Alpine Resort SKIING
(Map p544; ☑03-443 8880, snow phone 03-443 7007; www.cardrona.com; Cardrona Skifield Access Rd; day pass adult/child $101/52; ◷9am-4pm Jul-Sep) Well organised and professional, this 345-hectare ski field offers runs to suit all abilities (25% beginners, 50% intermediate, 25% advanced) at elevations ranging from 1670m to 1860m. Cardrona has several high-capacity chairlifts, beginners' tows and extreme snowboard terrain. Buses run from Wanaka and Queenstown during ski season. In summer, the mountain bikers take over.

**Backcountry
Saddle Expeditions** HORSE RIDING
(Map p544; ☑03-443 8151; www.backcountry saddles.co.nz; 2416 Cardrona Valley Rd; adult/child $90/70) Runs horse treks through the Cardrona Valley on Appaloosa horses.

Snow Farm SKIING
(Map p45; ☑03-443 7542; www.snowfarmnz. com; Snow Farm Access Rd; day pass adult/child $40/20; ♿) In winter this is home to fantastic cross-country skiing and snow-shoeing, with 55km of groomed trails. Lessons and ski hire are available.

🛏 Sleeping

Cardrona Hotel PUB $$
(☑03-443 8153; www.cardronahotel.co.nz; 2310 Cardrona Valley Rd; r $185; 🛜) Such an icon of the region that it was featured in Speight's Brewery's 'Southern Man' beer commercials, this 1863 hotel really comes into its own

après-ski. There's a good restaurant (breakfast $14 to $20, mains $26 to $34) and in summer you can relax in the garden bar at the rear. The lovingly restored rooms have snug, country-style furnishings and patios opening onto the garden (expect some noise on summer nights).

Waiorau Homestead B&B $$$
(Map p544; ☑03-443 2225; www.waiorau homestead.co.nz; 2127 Cardrona Valley Rd; r $270; @🛜♿) Tucked away in a private, bucolic nook near the Snow Farm, this lovely stone house has deep verandas and three luxurious guest bedrooms, each with their own bathroom. Rates include a full cooked breakfast and afternoon tea. Enquire about the cheaper 'pool room' ($140); the owners usually rent it on Airbnb.

ⓘ Getting There & Away

Ski shuttles are offered by Alpine Connexions (p572) Yello (p572) and Ridgeline Adventures (p569) in Wanaka, and Kiwi Discovery (Map p552; ☑03-442 7340; www.kiwidiscovery.com; 37 Camp St) in Queenstown.

Lake Hawea
POP 2180

The small town of Lake Hawea, 15km north of Wanaka, sits near the dam at the southern end of its 141-sq-km namesake. Separated from Lake Wanaka by a narrow isthmus called the Neck, blue-grey Lake Hawea is 35km long and 410m deep. It's particularly popular with fisherfolk looking to do battle with its trout and landlocked salmon. The lake was raised 20m in 1958 to facilitate the power stations downriver.

🛏 Sleeping

Lake Hawea Holiday Park HOLIDAY PARK $
(☑03-443 1767; www.haweaholidaypark.co.nz; SH6; sites from $16, unit with/without bathroom $130/60; @🛜) On the lakeshore, this spacious and peaceful old-fashioned holiday park is a favourite of fishing and boating enthusiasts. Units range from a block of basic cabins with brightly painted doors to motel units and cottages.

Lake Hawea Hotel HOTEL $$$
(☑03-443 1224; www.lakehawea.co.nz; 1 Capell Ave; r $240; 🛜) The rooms have been refurbished and have unbeatable views across the lake, but they're rather pricey for what's basically an upmarket motel. The complex

includes a large bar and restaurant (mains $18 to $25) with equally stellar vistas.

ℹ Getting There & Away

InterCity (☎03-442 4922; www.intercity. co.nz) Coaches stop at the dam (SH6) daily, heading to/from Queenstown (from $20, two hours), Cromwell (from $14, 1¼ hours), Wanaka (from $10, 20 minutes), Makarora (from $10, 1¼ hours) and Franz Josef (from $40, six hours).

Makarora

POP 40

Remote Makarora is the last frontier before you cross Haast Pass and enter the wild West Coast – and it certainly feels that way. Aside from the tour buses passing through, it feels wonderfully remote.

🏃 Activities

The best short walk in this secluded area is the **Haast Pass Lookout Track** (one hour return, 3.5km), which offers great views from above the bush line. Other options include the **Bridle Track** (1½ hours one way, 3.5km), from the top of Haast Pass to Davis Flat, and the **Blue Pools Walk** (30 minutes return), where you may see huge rainbow and brown trout.

Longer tramps go through magnificent countryside but shouldn't be undertaken lightly. Changeable alpine and river conditions mean you must be well prepared; consult with DOC before heading off. Its *Tramping in the Makarora Region* brochure ($2) is a worthwhile investment. Call in to the Tititea Mt Aspiring National Park Visitor Centre (p572) in Wanaka to check conditions and routes before undertaking any wilderness tramps.

Gillespie Pass   TRAMPING

The three-day Gillespie Pass loop tramp goes via the Young, Siberia and Wilkin Valleys. This is a high pass with avalanche danger in winter and spring. With a jetboat ride down the Wilkin to complete it, this rates as one of NZ's most memorable tramps. Jetboats go to Kerin Forks, and a service goes across the Young River mouth when the Makarora floods.

Wilkin Valley Track   TRAMPING

The Wilkin Valley Track starts from the Makarora River and heads along the Wilkin River to the Kerin Forks Hut (four to five hours, 15km). After another day's walk up the valley you'll reach the Top Forks Huts (six to eight hours, 15km), from which the picturesque Lakes Diana, Lucidus and Castalia (one hour, 1½ hours, and three to four hours respectively) can be reached.

Wilkin River Jets   BOATING

(☎03-443 8351; www.wilkinriverjets.co.nz; adult/child $119/69) A superb 50km, one-hour jetboating trip into Mt Aspiring National Park, following the Makarora and Wilkin Rivers. Trips can be combined with a helicopter ride.

☞ Tours

Siberia Experience   ADVENTURE TOUR

(☎03-443 4385; www.siberiaexperience.co.nz; adult/child $355/287) 🖉 This thrill-seeking extravaganza combines a 25-minute scenic small-plane flight, a three-hour bush walk through a remote mountain valley and a half-hour jetboat trip down the Wilkin and Makarora Rivers in Mt Aspiring National Park.

Southern Alps Air   SCENIC FLIGHTS

(☎03-443 4385, 0800 345 666; www.southernalpsair.co.nz) 🖉 Flies to Aoraki/Mt Cook and the glaciers (adult/child $445/285), along with Milford Sound flyovers ($415/265) and Milford fly-cruise combos ($498/315).

ℹ Information

Makarora Tourist Centre (☎03-443 8372; www.makarora.co.nz; 5944 Haast Pass-Makarora Rd/SH6; ⊙8am-8pm) A large complex incorporating a cafe, bar, shop, information centre, campground, bunk house and self-contained units.

ℹ Getting There & Away

InterCity (☎03-442 4922; www.intercity. co.nz) Daily coaches to/from Queenstown (from $24, 3½ hours), Cromwell (from $19, 2½ hours), Wanaka (from $12, 1¾ hours), Lake Hawea (from $10, 1¼ hours) and Franz Josef (from $36, 4¾ hours).

Fiordland & Southland

Best Places to Eat

➜ Batch (p593)

➜ Redcliff Cafe (p579)

➜ Louie's (p593)

➜ Elegance at 148 on Elles (p593)

➜ Miles Better Pies (p579)

Best Places to Sleep

➜ Newhaven Holiday Park (p598)

➜ Observation Rock Lodge (p604)

➜ Bushy Point Fernbirds (p592)

➜ Mohua Park (p598)

➜ Slope Point Backpackers (p596)

Why Go?

Welcome to scenery that travellers dream of and cameras fail to do justice to.

To the west is Fiordland National Park, with jagged misty peaks, glistening lakes and fiords, and a remarkable surfeit of stillness. Enter this beautiful isolation via the world-famous Milford Track, just one of many trails that meander through densely forested, glacier-sculptured valleys confined by mighty mountain ranges. Fiordland is also home to Milford and Doubtful Sounds, where verdant cliffs soar almost vertically from deep, indigo waters.

In Southland's east, a sharp turn off the beaten track leads through the peaceful Catlins, where waterfalls cascade through lush forest and diverse wildlife congregates around a rugged and beautiful coastline.

And then there's the end of the line – Stewart Island/Rakiura, an isolated isle home to friendly seafarers and a flock of beautiful rare birds, including New Zealand's beloved icon, the kiwi.

When to Go

➜ Visit from December to April for the best chance of settled weather amid Fiordland's notoriously fickle climate (although chances are, you'll still see rain!).

➜ Late October to late April is the Great Walks season for the Milford, Kepler, Routeburn and Rakiura Tracks, so you'll need to book in advance if you want to hike these popular routes.

➜ Stewart Island/Rakiura's changeable weather can bring four seasons in one day, at any time of year, although the temperature is milder than you'd expect, with winter averaging around 10°C and summer 16.5°C.

Fiordland & Southland Highlights

1 **Milford Sound** (p585)
Being overwhelmed by your first glimpse of the sheer majesty of Mitre Peak rising from the inky waters of the fiord.

2 **Milford Track** (p582)
Tramping through a World Heritage wilderness.

3 **Doubtful Sound** (p587)
Soaking up sunset and sunrise in glorious surrounds on an overnight cruise.

4 **Te Waewae Bay** (p589)
Marvelling at the wild power of nature on this surf-battered stretch of coast.

5 **Rakiura Track** (p602)
Savouring the solitude on NZ's southernmost Great Walk.

6 **Ulva Island** (p601)
Immersing yourself in a bird-filled paradise.

7 **The Catlins** (p595)
Exploring side roads, forest waterfalls and lonely southern beaches in this peaceful, windswept corner of the country.

8 **Curio Bay** (p595)
Spotting rare wildlife such as Hector's dolphins and yellow-eyed penguins.

ℹ Getting There & Away

Invercargill is the main transport hub, welcoming flights from Wellington and Christchurch, and buses from as far afield as Queenstown and Dunedin. Te Anau has direct bus connections with Queenstown, Dunedin and Christchurch.

FIORDLAND

Formidable Fiordland is NZ's largest and most impenetrable wilderness, a jagged, mountainous, densely forested landmass ribbed with deeply recessed sounds (technically fiords) reaching inland like crooked fingers from the Tasman Sea.

Fiordland National Park forms part of the Te Wāhipounamu Southwest New Zealand World Heritage Area, a combination of four national parks in the bottom left corner of NZ (the others being Aoraki/Mt Cook, Westland Tai Poutini and Mt Aspiring). This vast wilderness covers 2.6 million hectares and is recognised internationally for its unique geological features and ecosystems. It's also of great cultural significance to the local Ngāi Tahu people, who revered it as Te Wāhipounamu, 'The Place of Greenstone'.

Popular boat trips head out on the sounds, but it's walkers who can delve the deepest into this remote and magical area, not only on the famous, multiday Milford, Kepler and Hollyford Tracks, but even on short day walks, easily accessible from the highway.

Te Anau

POP 1910

Peaceful, lakeside Te Anau township is the main gateway to Fiordland National Park tramps and the ever-popular Milford Sound, as well as a pleasant place to while away a few days. It's large enough to have a smattering of good eateries and places to stay, but it's much easier on the liver and the wallet than attention-grabbing Queenstown.

To the east are the pastoral areas of central Southland, while west across Lake Te Anau lie the rugged mountains of Fiordland. The lake, NZ's second-largest, was gouged out by a huge glacier and has several arms that extend into the mountainous, forested western shore. Its deepest point is 417m, about twice the depth of Loch Ness.

◎ Sights

Punanga Manu o Te Anau   BIRD SANCTUARY
(www.doc.govt.nz; Te Anau–Manapouri Rd; ☉ dawn–dusk) FREE By the lake, this set of

outdoor aviaries offers a chance to see native bird species difficult to spot in the wild, including the precious icon of Fiordland, the extremely rare takahe.

Te Anau Glowworm Caves   CAVE
(✆ 0800 656 501; www.realjourneys.co.nz; adult/child $79/22) Once present only in Māori legends, these impressive caves were rediscovered in 1948. Accessible only by boat, the 200m-long system of caves is a magical place with sculpted rocks, waterfalls small and large, whirlpools and a glittering glowworm grotto in its inner reaches. Real Journeys runs 2¼-hour guided tours, reaching the heart of the caves via a lake cruise, walkway and a short underground boat ride. Journeys depart from its office on Lakefront Dr.

🏃 Activities

Te Anau's **Lakeside Track** makes for a very pleasant stroll or cycle in either direction – north to the marina and around to the Upukerora River (around an hour return), or south past the Fiordland National Park Visitor Centre and on to the control gates and start of the Kepler Track (50 minutes).

Day tramps in the national park are readily accessible from Te Anau. Kepler Water Taxi (p581) will scoot you over to Brod Bay, from where you can walk to Mt

Te Anau

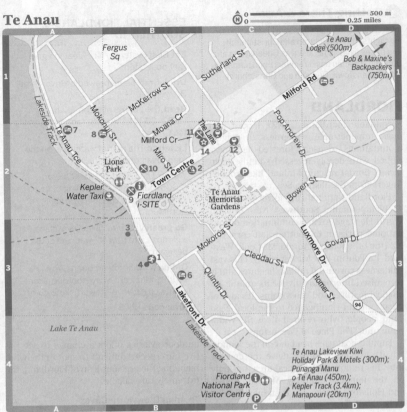

FIORDLAND & SOUTHLAND TE ANAU

Te Anau

Luxmore (seven to eight hours) or back along the Lakeside Track to Te Anau (two to three hours). During summer, Trips & Tramps (p584) offers small-group, guided day hikes on the Kepler and Routeburn, among other tracks. Real Journeys (p588) runs guided day hikes (adult/child $195/127, November to mid-April) along an 11km stretch of the Milford Track. Various day walks can also be completed by linking with regular bus services run by Tracknet (p580).

For self-guided adventures, pick up DOC's *Fiordland National Park Day Walks* brochure ($2) from the Fiordland i-SITE or Fiordland National Park Visitor Centre, or download it at www.doc.govt.nz.

☞ Tours

Fiordland Tours
TOUR

(☑ 0800 247 249; www.fiordlandtours.co.nz; adult/child from $139/59) Runs small-group bus and Milford Sound cruise tours, departing from Te Anau and stopping at some interesting sights on the way. It also provides track transport and guided day walks on the Kepler Track.

Luxmore Jet
JETBOATING

(☑ 0800 253 826; www.luxmorejet.com; Lakefront Dr; adult/child $99/49) One-hour trips on the Upper Waiau River (aka the River Anduin).

Southern Lakes Helicopters
SCENIC FLIGHTS

(☑ 03-249 7167; www.southernlakeshelicopters.co.nz; Lakefront Dr) Flights over Te Anau for 30 minutes ($240), longer trips over Doubtful, Dusky and Milford Sounds (from $685), and various helihike, helibike and heliski options.

🛏 Sleeping

Te Anau Top 10
HOLIDAY PARK $

(☑ 0800 249 746, 03-249 7462; www.teanautop10.co.nz; 128 Te Anau Tce; sites from $44, unit from $129, without bathroom from $77; @ 🛜) Near the town and lake, this excellent, compact holiday park has private sites, a playground, lake-facing hot tubs, bike hire, a barbecue area and modern kitchen facilities. The motels units are very good indeed and there are well-priced cabins for those not bothered by communal bathrooms.

Bob & Maxine's Backpackers
HOSTEL $

(☑ 03-249 7429; www.bbh.co.nz; 20 Paton Pl, off Oraka St; dm $36, s/tw $70/90; 🛜) Only 2.5km out of town, off the Te Anau–Milford Hwy, this relaxed and modern hostel gets rave reviews for the big mountain vistas from the communal lounge. Warm up beside the woodburner, cook up a storm in the well-equipped kitchen, or just chill out in a private en suite room. Free bikes and wi-fi.

Te Anau YHA
HOSTEL $

(☑ 03-249 7847; www.yha.co.nz; 29 Mokonui St; dm $34-39, s without bathroom $80-100, d with/without bathroom $105/96; @ 🛜) This centrally located, modern hostel has great facilities and comfortable, colourful rooms. Play volleyball in the grassy backyard, crank up the barbecue or get cosy by the fire in the lounge.

Keiko's Cottages
B&B $$

(☑ 03-249 9248; www.keikos.cc.nz; 228 Milford Rd; d from $175; ⊙ closed Jun-Aug; 🛜) Surrounded by Japanese-style gardens, Keiko's self-contained cottages are private, comfortable and quite lovely. Breakfast poses a difficult choice: Kiwi- or Japanese-style? The spa and sauna are worthy extras.

Radfords on the Lake
MOTEL $$$

(☑ 03-249 9186; www.radfordsonthelake.co.nz; 56 Lakefront Dr; units from $285; 🛜) ✏ Radfords isn't your bog-standard motel, as you've probably already guessed by the grand-sounding name and commensurate prices. Set on manicured lawns across from the lake, this angular complex offers 14 luxurious units over two levels, all angled towards the view. They all have kitchens and five of them have spa baths.

Te Anau Lodge
B&B $$$

(☑ 03-249 7477; www.teanaulodge.com; 52 Howden St; s/c from $210/240; 🛜) The former 1930s-built Sisters of Mercy Convent, relocated to just north of town, offers an old-fashioned ambience with decor to match. Sip your complimentary wine in a chesterfield in front of the fire, retire to your spa bath before collapsing on a king-size bed, then awaken to a fresh, delicious breakfast in the old chapel.

🍴 Eating

★ Miles Better Pies
FAST FOOD $

(☑ 03-249 9044; www.milesbetterpies.co.nz; 19 Town Centre; pies $5-6.50; ⊙ 6am-3pm) The bumper selection includes venison, lamb and mint, and fruit pies. There are a few pavement tables, but sitting and munching beside the lake is nicer.

Sandfly Cafe
CAFE $

(☑ 03-249 9529; 9 The Lane; mains $7-20; ⊙ 7am-4.30pm; 🛜) Clocking the most local votes for the town's best espresso, simple but satisfying Sandfly is a top spot to enjoy an all-day breakfast, soup, sandwich or sweet treat, while listening to cruisy music or sunning yourself on the lawn.

★ Redcliff Cafe
MODERN NZ $$$

(☑ 03-249 7431; www.theredcliff.co.nz; 12 Mokonui St; mains $38-42; ⊙ 4-10pm) Housed in a replica settler's cottage, relaxed Redcliff offers generous fine-dining in a convivial atmosphere backed by sharp service. The predominantly locally sourced food is truly terrific: try the wild venison or hare. Kick off or wind it up with a drink in the rustic front bar, which often hosts live music.

Drinking & Entertainment

Ranch Bar & Grill
PUB

(☑03-249 8801; www.theranchbar.co.nz; 111 Town Centre; ◉noon-late) Popular with locals for its generous pub meals, head to the Ranch for a quality Sunday roast dinner ($15). Thursday jam night or a big sports match.

Fat Duck
BAR

(☑03-249 8480; 124 Town Centre; ◉noon-late Tue-Sun; ◈) This corner bar with pavement seating is a sound choice for supping a pint or two of Mac's beer. The kitchen dishes up marginally trendy gastropub and cafe fare, opening for breakfast daily in summer.

Fiordland Cinema
CINEMA

(☑03-249 8812; www.fiordlandcinema.co.nz; 7 The Lane; ◈) In between back-to-back showings of the excellent *Ata Whenua/Fiordland on Film* (adult/child $10/5), essentially a 32-minute advertisement for Fiordland scenery, Fiordland Cinema serves as the local movie house. The **Black Dog Bar** (☑03-249 8844; www.blackdogbar.co.nz; ◉10am-late; ◈) downstairs is the town's most sophisticated watering hole.

ℹ Information

Fiordland i-SITE (☑03-249 8900; www.fiordland.org.nz; 19 Town Centre; ◉8.30am-7pm Dec-Mar, to 5.30pm Apr-Nov) Activity, accommodation and transport bookings.

Fiordland Medical Centre (☑03-249 7007; 25 Luxmore Dr; ◉8am-5.30pm Mon-Fri, 9am-noon Sat)

Fiordland National Park Visitor Centre (DOC; ☑03-249 7924; www.doc.govt.nz; cnr Lakefront Dr & Te Anau–Manapouri Rd; ◉8.30am-4.30pm) Can assist with Great Walks bookings, general hut tickets and information, with the bonus of a natural history display, and a shop stocking tramping supplies and essential topographical maps for backcountry trips.

ℹ Getting There & Away

InterCity (☑03-442 4922; www.intercity.co.nz) Twice daily services to Milford Sound (from $28, 1½ hours) and Queenstown (from $28, 3¼ hours), and daily buses to Gore (from $30, 1¾ hours), Dunedin (from $37, 4½ hours) and Christchurch (from $61, 11 hours). Buses depart outside Kiwi Country on Miro St.

Naked Bus (www.nakedbus.com; prices vary) Has a daily bus to Queenstown (2¾ hours) and Milford Sound (2¼ hours).

Topline Tours (☑03-249 8059; www.toplinetours.co.nz) Offers year-round shuttles between Te Anau and Manapouri ($20), and transfers from Te Anau to the Kepler Track trailheads at the control gates ($5) and the Rainbow Reach swing bridge ($8) from November to March.

Tracknet (☑0800 483 262; www.tracknet.net) From November to April Te Anau–based Tracknet has three scheduled buses to/from Te Anau Downs ($25, 30 minutes), the Divide ($39, 1¼ hours) and Milford Sound ($49, 2¼ hours), and two buses to/from Manapouri ($25, 30 minutes) and Queenstown ($45, 2¾ hours). In winter, services are on demand.

Around Te Anau

Te Anau is the gateway to three Great Walks – the Kepler, Milford and Routeburn – and the less visited but equally worthy Hollyford. Detailed information can be found in Lonely Planet's *Hiking & Tramping New Zealand* guide, and from the helpful folk at the Fiordland National Park Visitor Centre, where you can also register your intentions via the Adventuresmart website (www.adventuresmart.org.nz).

Kepler Track

Opened in 1988 to relieve pressure on the Milford and Routeburn, the Kepler is one of NZ's best-planned tracks and now one of its most popular. The route takes the form of a moderately strenuous 60km loop beginning and ending at the Waiau River control gates at the southern end of Lake Te Anau. It features an all-day tramp across the mountain tops taking in incredible panoramas of the lake, the Jackson Peaks and the Kepler Mountains. Along the way it traverses rocky ridges, tussock lands and peaceful beech forest.

The route can be covered in four days, staying in the three huts, although it is possible to reduce the tramp to three days by continuing past Moturau Hut and leaving the track at the Rainbow Reach swing bridge. However, spending a night at Moturau Hut on the shore of Lake Manapouri is an ideal way to end this tramp. The track can be walked in either direction, although the most popular is Luxmore–Iris Burn–Moturau.

The alpine sections require a good level of fitness and may be impassible in winter, although this is a heavily weather-dependent track at any time of year.

Kepler Track

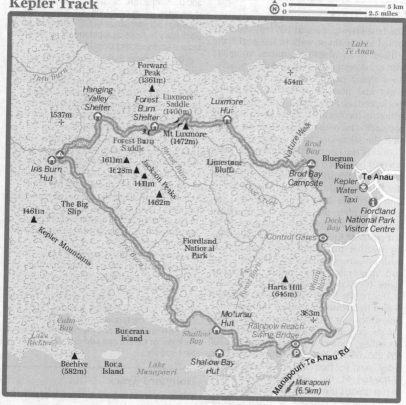

Estimated walking times:

DAY	ROUTE	TIME
1	Fiordland National Park Visitor Centre to control gates	45min
1	Control gates to Brod Bay	1½hr
1	Brod Bay to Luxmore Hut	3½–4½hr
2	Luxmore Hut to Iris Burn Hut	5–6hr
3	Iris Burn Hut to Moturau Hut	5–6hr
3	Moturau Hut to Rainbow Reach	1½–2hr
4	Rainbow Reach to control gates	2½–3½hr

ⓘ Bookings & Transport

The Kepler is officially a Great Walk. Between late October and mid-April you must obtain a Great Walk pass for the **Luxmore Hut, Iris Burn Hut** and **Moturau Hut**. Passes must be obtained in advance, and it pays to book well in advance, either online via DOC's **Great Walks Bookings** (☑ 0800 694 732; www.greatwalks.co.nz) or in person at a DOC visitor centre. In the low season the huts revert to the Serviced category. There are campsites at **Brod Bay** and **Iris Burn**.

The recommended map for this tramp is 1:60,000 Parkmap 335-09 (Kepler Track).

Conveniently, the track begins under an hour's walk from the Fiordland National Park Visitor Centre, via the lakeside track alongside the Manapouri–Te Anau Rd (SH95). There's a car park and shelter near the control gates. **Tracknet** (p530) and **Topline Tours** (p580) both run shuttles to and from both the control gates and the Rainbow Reach trailheads.

Kepler Water Taxi (☑ 027 249 8365; www. facebook.com/keplerwatertaxi; each way $25) offers morning boat services across Lake Te Anau to Brod Bay, slicing 1½ hours off the first day's tramp.

Milford Track

The best-known track in NZ and routinely touted as 'the finest walk in the world', the Milford is an absolute stunner, complete with rainforest, deep glaciated valleys, a glorious alpine pass surrounded by towering peaks and powerful waterfalls, including the legendary Sutherland Falls, one of the loftiest in the world. All these account for its popularity: more than 14,000 trampers complete the 54km-long track each year.

During the Great Walks season, the track can only be walked in one direction, starting from Glade Wharf. You must stay at Clinton Hut the first night, despite it being only one hour from the start of the track, and you must complete the trip in the prescribed three nights and four days. This is perfectly acceptable if the weather is kind, but when the weather turns sour you'll still have to push on across the alpine Mackinnon Pass and may miss some rather spectacular views. It's all down to the luck of the draw.

During the Great Walk season, the track is also frequented by guided tramping parties, which stay at cosy, carpeted lodges with hot showers and proper food. If that sounds appealing, contact **Ultimate Hikes** (📞0800 659 255, 03-450 1940; www.ultimatehikes.co.nz; 5-day tramp incl food dm/s/d $2195/3085/5210; ☉Nov-Apr) 🍴, the only operator permitted to run guided tramps on the Milford.

The track is covered by 1:70,000 *Parkmap 335-01 (Milford Track)*.

Estimated walking times:

DAY	ROUTE	TIME
1	Glade Wharf to Glade House	20min
1	Glade House to Clinton Hut	1hr
2	Clinton Hut to Mintaro Hut	5-6hr
3	Mintaro Hut to Dumpling Hut	6-7hr
3	Side trip to Sutherland Falls	1½hr return
4	Dumpling Hut to Sandfly Point	5½-6hr

🛈 Bookings & Transport

The Milford Track is officially a Great Walk. Between late October and mid-April, you need a Great Walk pass ($162) to cover your three nights in the huts: **Clinton Hut**, **Mintaro Hut** and **Dumpling Hut**. Passes must be obtained in advance, either online via DOC's Great Walks Bookings or in person at a DOC visitor centre. Book early to avoid disappointment as the entire season books up very quickly.

In the low season the huts revert to the Serviced category ($15), and the track can be walked in any time frame you like. This makes late April and early May a great time to tramp, weather dependent. The same can't be said of the month prior to the season starting, as there's a very real danger of avalanches in spring.

The track starts at Glade Wharf, at the head of Lake Te Anau, accessible by a 1½-hour boat trip from Te Anau Downs, itself 29km from Te Anau on the road to Milford Sound. The track finishes at Sandfly Point, a 15-minute boat trip from Milford Sound village, from where you can return by road to Te Anau, around two hours away. You will be given options to book this connecting transport online, at the same time as you book your hut tickets.

Tracknet (p580) offers transport from Queenstown and Te Anau to meet the boats at Te Anau Downs and Milford Sound. There are other options for transport to and from the track, including a float-plane hop from Te Anau to Glade Wharf with **Wings & Water** (📞03-249 7405; www.wingsandwater.co.nz; Lakefront Dr). Fiordland i-SITE and the Fiordland National Park Visitor Centre can advise on options to best suit you.

Hollyford Track

The four- to five-day (each way), 58km Hollyford Track is an easy to moderate tramp through the lower Hollyford – the longest valley in Fiordland National Park – to remote Martin's Bay. Track upgrades and improved transport services, combined with the fact that it's a low-level hike achievable year-round, have resulted in more trampers discovering the splendid mountain and lake vistas, beautiful forest, extensive bird life and magical coast that make the Hollyford so special. Even so, the track averages only 4000 trampers a year, making it a good option for those in search of solitude.

The track is basically one way (unless combined with the super-challenging Pyke–Big Bay Route), with the majority of trampers turning tail and retracing their steps, or flying out from the airstrip at Martins Bay. If possible, spend an extra day in the bay, where you can view a seal colony and get a sneaky peak at a penguin, if you're lucky. This will more than make up for the misdeeds of the most demonic sandflies in NZ.

Milford Track

0 ____ 5 km
0 ____ 2.5 miles

Travsit River

Mt Phillips
(1446m)

Milford
Sound

Milford

Sound Hwy

Terror
Peak
(1786m)

Camp Oven Creek

Sandfly
Point

Cleddau
River

Danger
Mountain
(1825m)

Devils
Armchair
(1627m)

Milford
Sound
Lodge

Sheerdown
Peak
(1878m)

Shoulder
Hill
(1729m)

Giant Gate
Falls

Lake
Ada

Sheerdown Hills

Giant Gate
Falls Shelter

North Branch

The
Chasm

Steep
Hill
(1631m)

Mackay
Creek

Mackay
Falls

Odyssey
Peak
(1821m)

Mt Ada
(1881m)

Mt Isolation
(1620m)

Mt Edgar
(1673m)

Bell Rock

Swing
Bridge

Lake
Brown

Access
Peak
(1865m)

West
Branch

Te Anau-Milford Hwy

South Branch

Poseidon Creek

Joes River

Boatshed
Shelter
(Private)

Arthur River

1655m

Homer
Tunnel

Dumpling
Hill
(575m)

Mt Kepka
(1781m)

Talbot River

Lloyd
Peak
(1952m)

Gulliver
Peak
(1776m)

Dumpling
Hut

Mt Elliot
(1990m)

Basin
Peak
(1865m)

Buttercup
Lake

Cirque
Peak
(1902m)

Sutherland
Falls

Jervois
Glacier

Mt Wilmur
(1710m)

Surprise Creek

Mt Gendarme
(1931m)

Lake
Thompson

Dudleigh
Falls

Robert Allen Shelter

Mt Balloon
(1847m)

1350m

Mt Mitchelson
(1936m)

Wick Mountains

Mackinnon Pass Shelter

Lake Mintaro

Mt
Hart
(1769m)

Mackinnon
Pass
(1069m)

Mintaro Hut

Mirror Lake

Marshall
Pass

Lake
Iceberg

Clinton
Canyon

St Quintin
Falls

Epidote Cataract

North Branch

Swing Bridge

Pompolona Hut
(Private)

Bus Stop
Shelter

Castle Mtn
(2122m)

Prairie
Shelter

1920m

Milford Track

Mt Fisher
(1869m)

Hidden
Lake

Hirere
Falls

Mt Anau
(1956m)

Fiordland
National
Park

Hirere
Shelter
(MTGW)

Lookout

Neale Burn

Castle River

Clinton
Forks

Clinton River
(West Branch)

Lake
Ross

Worsley Stream

McQueen Creek

Inglession Creek

1713m

Clinton
Hut

Wetland Walk

Clinton River

Glade Burn

Lookout

Glade House
(Private)

1483m

Glade
Wharf

Te Anau Downs
(by launch) (45km)

Lake
Te Anau

The best maps for this tramp are *CA09 (Alabaster)* and *CA08 (Milford Sound)*. DOC produces a *Hollyford Track* brochure.

❶ Bookings & Transport

Trampers have the use of six DOC huts on the track, ranging from Serviced ($15) to Standard ($5). Camping ($5) is permitted next to the huts, although sandflies will prevent this from being remotely enjoyable. Tickets should be obtained in advance online from DOC Visitor Centres.

Tracknet (p580) and **Trips & Tramps** (☎03-249 7081, 0800 305 807; www.tripsandtramps. com) both run shuttles to the Hollyford trailhead. Nine kilometres (two hours' walk) shy of the trailhead is **Gunn's Camp** (www.gunnscamp. org.nz; sites per person $15, dm $25, cabins $65, bed linen extra $5), a good bolthole before or after the feat with car storage available.

Fly Fiordland (☎0800 359 346; www.flyfiord land.com; up to 4 people $620) flies between Te Anau and the Martins Bay airstrip, usually as a charter but with a per-person rate of $175 at busy times.

Ngāi Tahu-owned **Hollyford Track** (☎03-442 3000; www.hollyfordtrack.com; adult/child from $1795/1395; ☺ late Oct-late Apr) runs excellent three-day guided trips on the Hollyford staying at private lodges. The journey is shortened with a jetboat trip down the river and Lake McKerrow on day two, and ends with a scenic flight to Milford Sound.

Te Anau–Milford Highway

Sometimes the road is the destination in itself and that's certainly true of the superlative 119km stretch from Te Anau to Milford Sound (SH94). It offers the most easily accessible experience of Fiordland in all its diversity, taking in stretches of beautiful beech forest, gentle river valleys, mirror-like lakes, exquisite alpine scenery and ending at arguably NZ's most breathtaking vista.

Head out from Te Anau early (by 8am) or later in the morning (11am) to avoid the tour buses heading for midday sound cruises. Fill up with petrol in Te Anau before setting off, and note that chains must be carried on icy or avalanche-risk days from May to November (there will be signs on the road); these can be hired from most service stations in Te Anau.

The trip takes two to 2½ hours if you drive straight through, but take time to stop and experience the majestic landscape. Pull off the road and explore the many viewpoints and nature walks en route. Pick up DOC'S *Fiordland National Park Day Walks* brochure ($2) from Fiordland i-SITE or

Fiordland National Park Visitor Centre, or download it at www.doc.govt.nz.

The first part of the road meanders through rolling farmland atop the lateral moraine of the glacier that once gouged out Lake Te Anau. At the 29km mark it passes **Te Anau Downs**, where the boats for the Milford Track depart. From here, an easy 45-minute return walk leads through forest to **Lake Mistletoe**, a small glacier-formed lake.

The road then heads into the Eglinton Valley, at first pocketed with sheepy pasture, then reaching deeper wilderness immersion as it crosses the boundary into Fiordland National Park. The knobby peaks, thick beech forest, lupin-lined river banks and grassy meadows are a grand sight indeed.

Just past the **Mackay Creek** campsite (at 51km) are great views to Pyramid Peak (2295m) and Ngatimamoe Peak (2164m) ahead. The boardwalk at **Mirror Lakes** (at 58km) takes you through beech forest and wetlands, and on a calm day the lakes reflect the mountains across the valley.

At the 77km mark is **Cascade Creek** and **Lake Gunn**. This area was known to Māori as O Tapara, and a stopover for parties heading to Anita Bay in search of *pounamu* (greenstone). The **Lake Gunn Nature Walk** (45 minutes return) loops through tall red beech forest ringing with bird calls, with side trails leading to quiet lakeside beaches.

At 84km the vegetation changes as you pass across the **Divide**, the lowest east–west pass in the Southern Alps. The roadside shelter here is used by trampers either finishing or starting the Routeburn or Greenstone and Caples Tracks. From here you can embark on a marvellous two-hour return walk along the the start of the Routeburn, climbing up through beech forest to the alpine tussockland of **Key Summit**. On a good day the views of the Humboldt and Darran Mountains are sure to knock your socks off, and the nature walk around the boggy tops and stunted beech is a great excuse to linger.

From the Divide, the road falls into the beech forest of the **Hollyford Valley** (stop at Pop's View for a great outlook) and there's a worthwhile detour off SH94 down the Lower Hollyford to Gunn's Camp, 8km along the unsealed road leading to the Hollyford Track. The track starts a further 9km away, where you will also find the track to **Humboldt Falls** (30 minutes return).

Back on the main road to Milford, the road climbs through a cascade-tastic valley to the **Homer Tunnel**, 101km from Te Anau and framed by a spectacular, high-walled, ice-carved amphitheatre. Begun as a relief project in the 1930s and finally opened to motor traffic in 1954, the tunnel is one way, with the world's most alpine set of traffic lights to direct vehicle flow. Dark, magnificently rough-hewn and dripping with water, the 1270m-long tunnel emerges at the other end at the head of the spectacular **Cleddau Valley**. Any spare 'wows' might pop out about now. Kea (alpine parrots) hang around the tunnel entrance looking for food from tourists, but don't feed them as it's bad for their health.

About 10km before Milford Sound, the wheelchair- and pram-friendly **Chasm Walk** (20 minutes return) is well worth a stop. The forest-cloaked Cleddau River plunges through scooped-out boulders in a narrow chasm, creating deep falls and a natural rock bridge. From here, watch for glimpses of **Mt Tutoko** (2746m), Fiordland's highest peak, above the beech forest.

🛌 Sleeping

There are nine basic DOC campsites (per adult/child $6/3) along the highway. All are scenic but also popular with sandflies.

Knob's Flat   MOTEL $$

(☑️03-249 9122; www.knobsflat.co.nz; sites per adult/child $15/8, d $130-150) In the Eglinton Valley, 63km from Te Anau. Knob's Flat has six self-contained units that are perfect for those who appreciate the simple things in life, such a cosy room with a view. And boy, do these units have views. Unpowered sites cater to those who want back-to-nature camping with the relative luxuries of hot showers (S5) and a kitchen.

ℹ️ Getting There & Away

Tracknet (☑️0800 483 262 www.tracknet. net) From November to April, Tracknet has three scheduled buses on the Milford Sound–Te Anau route that stop at the Divice and Te Anau Downs; two continue on to Queenstown ($90, five hours). In winter, services are on demand.

Milford Sound

POP 114

Sydney Opera House, Big Ben, the Eiffel Tower – one's first glimpse of the world's most famous sights can stop you in your tracks and immediately insert a lump in your throat. So it is with Mitre Peak (Rahotu), the spectacular, 1692m-high mountain rising from the

dark waters of Milford Sound (Piopiotahi). This image has dominated NZ tourism brochures since Maui was a lad and is one of very few such vistas that is truly worthy of the word 'iconic'.

From the road's end it sits dead centre of an exceedingly beautiful landscape of sheer rocky cliffs anchored in inky waters. From time to time the precarious forests clinging to the slopes relinquish their hold, causing a 'tree avalanche' into the fiord.

Milford Sound receives about half a million visitors each year, many of them crammed into the peak months (January and February). Some 14,000 arrive by foot, via the Milford Track, which ends at the sound. Some buzz through in helicopters. Many more drive from Te Anau, but most arrive via the multitude of bus tours. But don't worry: out on the water all this humanity seems tiny compared to nature's vastness.

🏃 Activities

The clue is in the name: Milford Sound is all about the water, and the landforms that envelop it. It's enough to make you go misty-eyed, as an average annual rainfall of 7m fuels innumerable cascading waterfalls. The unique ocean environment – caused by freshwater sitting atop warmer seawater – replicates deep-ocean conditions, encouraging the activity of marine life such as dolphins, seals and penguins. Getting out on the water is a must.

Rosco's Milford Kayaks   KAYAKING

(☑️03-249 8500, 0800 476 726; www.roscosmilfordkayaks.com; 72 Town Centre, Te Anau; trips $99-199; ⏱️Nov-Apr) Guided, tandem-kayak trips including the 'Morning Glory' ($199), a challenging paddle the full length of the fiord to Anita Bay, and the easier 'Stirling Sunriser' (S195), which ventures beneath the 151m-high Stirling Falls. Among many other options are trips 'your grandmother could do', and kayak-walk combos on the Milford Track.

Descend Scubadiving   DIVING

(www.descend.co.nz; 2 dives incl gear $299) Descend runs day trips with four hours of cruising on Milford Sound in a 7m catamaran and two dives along the way. The marine reserve is home to unique marine life, including a multitude of corals. Transport, equipment, hot drinks and snacks are supplied.

👉 Tours

A cruise on Milford Sound is Fiordland's most accessible experience, as evident from the slew of companies located in the flash cruise terminal, which is a 10-minute walk from the main car park.

Each cruise company claims to be quieter, smaller, bigger, cheaper, or in some way preferable to the rest. What really makes a difference is the timing of the cruise. Most bus tours aim for 1pm sailings, so if you avoid that time of day there will be less people on the boat, less boats on the water and less buses on the road. With some companies you get a better price on cruises outside rush hour, too.

If you're particularly keen on wildlife, ask whether there will be a nature guide on board. It's wise to book ahead regardless. You generally need to arrive 20 minutes before departure. Most companies offer coach transfers from Te Anau for an additional cost. Day trips from Queenstown make for a very long 13-hour day.

All the cruises visit the mouth of the sound, just 15km from the wharf, poking their prow into the choppy waves of the Tasman Sea. The shorter cruises visit less of the en route 'highlights', which include Bowen Falls, Mitre Peak, Anita Bay and Stirling Falls.

Only visitable on trips run by Southern Discoveries and Mitre Peak Cruises, **Milford Discovery Centre** (www.southerndiscoveries. co.nz; Harrison Cove; adult/child $36/18; ⊙9am-4pm) is a floating underwater observatory offering a chance to view deep-water corals, tube anemones and bottom-dwelling sea perch from 10m below the waterline.

Cruise Milford   BOAT TOUR
(☑0800 645 367; www.cruisemilfordnz.com; adult/child from $80/18; ⊙10.45am. 12.45pm & 2.45pm) A small boat heads out three times a day on a 1¾-hour cruise.

Go Orange   BOAT TOUR
(☑0800 246 672, 03-249 8585; www.goorange. co.nz; adult/child from $55/15; ⊙9am, 12.30pm & 3pm) Real Journeys' low-cost two-hour cruises along the full length of Milford Sound, with the added bonus of a complimentary breakfast, lunch or snack.

Real Journeys   BOAT TOUR
(☑0800 656 501, 03-249 7416; www.realjourneys. co.nz) ⬦ Milford's biggest operator runs various trips, including the popular 1¾-hour scenic cruise (adult/child from $76/22). The 2½-hour nature cruise (adult/child from $88/22) hones in on wildlife with a specialist nature guide providing commen-

tary. Overnight cruises are also available, on which you can kayak and take nature tours in small boats en route.

Overnight trips depart from the cruise terminal in the mid-afternoon and return around 9.30am the following day. The *Milford Wanderer*, modelled on an old trading scow, accommodates 36 passengers in two- and four-bunk cabins with shared bathrooms (dorm/single/double $305/621/710). The *Milford Mariner* sleeps 60 in more-up-market single ($744) or double ($850) en suite cabins. Cheaper prices apply from April through to September; coach transport from Te Anau is extra.

🛏 Sleeping

Milford Sound Lodge   LODGE $$$
(☑03-249 8071; www.milfordlodge.com; SH94; sites from $25, dm/d without bathroom $35/99, chalets $345-395; 🖵) Alongside the Cleddau River, 1.5km from the Milford hub, this simple but comfortable lodge has a down-to-earth, active vibe. Travellers and trampers commune in the lounge or on-site Pio Pio Cafe, which provides meals, wine and espresso. Luxurious chalets enjoy an absolute riverside location. Booking ahead is strongly recommended.

❶ Information

Discover Milford Sound Information Centre
(☑03-249 7931; www.southerndiscoveries. co.nz; ⊙8am-4pm) Although it's run by Southern Discoveries, this centre near the main car park sells tickets for most of the tour and cruise companies, as well as for scenic flights and InterCity buses. There's also a cafe attached.

❶ Getting There & Away

BUS

InterCity (☑03-442 4922; www.intercity. co.nz) Runs twice daily bus services to Milford Sound from Te Anau (from $28, 1½ hours) and Queenstown (from $47, 4¼ hours), on to which you can add a cruise or scenic flight when you book.

Naked Bus (www.nakedbus.com; prices vary) Daily buses between Te Anau and Milford Sound (2¼ hours).

Tracknet (☑03-249 7777; www.tracknet.net) From November to April Tracknet has three scheduled buses to/from the Divide ($35, 45 minutes), Te Anau Downs ($47, 1¾ hours) and Te Anau ($49, 2¼ hours), and two buses to/from Queenstown ($90, five hours). In winter, services are on demand.

CAR

Fill up with petrol in Te Anau before setting off. Snow chains must be carried on ice- and avalanche-risk days from May to November (there will be signs on the road), and can be hired from service stations in Te Anau.

Manapouri

POP 228

Manapouri is the jumping-off point for cruises to Doubtful Sound, with most visitors heading straight to the boat harbour for the ferry to West Arm. This leaves it sleepy and somewhat underrated, for not only is Lake Manapouri one of NZ's most beautiful towns, with a backdrop bettering Te Anau, there are ample interesting things to do and local people to do them with.

In 1969 Manapouri was the site of NZ's first major environmental campaign. The original plan for the West Arm hydroelectric power station, built to supply electricity for the aluminium smelter near Invercargill, required raising the level of the lake by 30m. A petition gathered a staggering 265,000 signatures (17% of voting-age New Zealanders at the time) and the issue contributed to the downfall of the government at the following election. The win proved big for environmentalists, for not only was the power station built without the lake levels being changed, it also spawned more nationwide environmental action through the 1970s and '80s.

Activities

By crossing the Waiau River at Pearl Harbour you can embark on day walks as detailed in DOC's *Fiordland National Park Day Walks* brochure. The classic outing is the **Circle Track** (three hours return), which can be extended to **Hope Arm** (five to six hours return). You can cross the river aboard a hired rowboat or water taxi from **Adventure Manapouri** (03-249 8070; www.adventuremanapouri.co.nz; rowboat hire per day $40, water taxi return $20), which also offers guided walks and fishing tours.

Running between the northern entrance to Manapouri township and Pearl Harbour, the one-hour **Frasers Beach** walk offers picnic and swimming spots as well as fantastic views across the lake.

The Kepler Track (p580) is accessible from the northern end of Lake Manapouri at Rainbow Reach, 10km north of town.

Manapouri is also a staging point for the remote **Dusky Track**, a highly challenging 84km tramp taking eight to 10 days. For more information contact DOC.

🛏 Sleeping

Manapouri Motels & Holiday Park HOLIDAY PARK $
(03-249 6624; www.manapourimotels.co.nz; 86 Cathedral Dr; sites from $36, units from $95, without bathroom from $60; 🐾) This eccentric but ultimately charming old-style camping ground features inexpensive cabins (from mock-Swiss Alpine to sweet little weatherboard), quiet campsites, and a homey amenities block. But wait, there's more...including a fleet of old Morris Minors and a collection of vintage pinball machines.

Freestone Backpackers HOSTEL $
(03-249 6893; www.freestone.co.nz; 270 Hillside Rd; dm $22-33, d $86, without bathroom $66; 🐾) These rustic cabins nestle on a hillside about 3km east of town, each with a gas hob, potbelly stove and veranda. Bathrooms are basic and communal. A converted family home offers another eight beds for singles doubles and twins, with communal facilities including a full kitchen. Ask about boat cruises.

❶ Getting There & Away

Topline Tours (p580) Offers year-round shuttles between Te Anau and Manapouri ($20).

Tracknet (03-249 7777; www.tracknet.net; adult/child $25/18) Runs between Te Anau and Manapouri twice daily from November to April, and on demand at other times of the year.

Doubtful Sound

Magnificent Doubtful Sound is a wilderness area of fractured and gouged mountains, dense forest and thundering waterfalls. Technically a fiord, having being carved by glaciers, Doubtful is one of NZ's largest sounds – three times the length and 10 times the area of Milford. It is also much, *much* less visited. If you have the time and the money and the weather's behaving, it's an essential experience.

Until relatively recently, only the most intrepid tramper or sailor ever explored Doubtful Sound. Even Captain Cook only observed it from off the coast in 1770, because he was 'doubtful' whether the winds in the sound would be sufficient to blow the ship back out to sea. The sound became more accessible when the road over Wilmot Pass opened in 1959 to facilitate construction of the West Arm power station.

☞ Tours

Your major considerations here are overnight (pricey but preferable) or day trip, and size of boat. Another consideration is whether you want to tour the power station. Overnight cruises include meals plus the option of fishing and kayaking.

Real Journeys   BOAT TOUR
(☎0800 656 501; www.realjourneys.co.nz) ✎ The day-long 'wilderness cruise' (adult/child from $250/65) includes a three-hour journey aboard a modern catamaran with a specialist nature guide. The overnight cruise, which runs from September to May, is aboard the *Fiordland Navigator*, which sleeps 70 in en suite cabins (quad-share per adult/child $385/193, single/double $1076/1230). Some trips include a visit to the West Arm power station.

Adventure Kayak & Cruise   KAYAKING
(☎0800 324 966; www.fiordlandadventure.co.nz; day/overnight tour $249/295; ☺Oct-Apr) Runs day trips to Doubtful Sound, or two-day trips with a night camping on a beach.

Fiordland Cruises   BOAT TOUR
(☎0800 368 283; www.fiordlandcruises.co.nz; tour from $1650; ☺Oct-May) Overnight cruise on the *Southern Secret* (maximum 12 passengers); cabins are en suite doubles.

Go Orange Kayaks   KAYAKING
(☎03-249 8585; www.goorangekayaks.co.nz; 1/2/3/5 days $245/399/550/775; ☺Oct-Apr) Two- to five-day kayaking and camping trips around Doubtful Sound, or single day 'tasters'. The price includes transfers from Te Anau and hot drinks, but not food.

❶ Getting There & Away

Getting to Doubtful Sound involves boarding a boat at Pearl Harbour in Manapouri for a one-hour trip to West Arm power station, followed by a 22km (40-minute) drive over Wilmot Pass to Deep Cove (permanent population: two), where you hop aboard a boat for your cruise on the sound. Manapouri is the easiest place to base yourself, although Te Anau and Queenstown pick-ups are readily organised through the cruise-boat operators.

CENTRAL SOUTHLAND

New Zealand's 'deep south' is a starkly contrasting mix of raw coastlines, untouched wilderness and great swaths of farmland. Laid-back and lightly populated, it's a region where getting off the beaten path goes with the territory.

Tuatapere

POP 558

Formerly a timber-milling town, sleepy Tuatapere is now largely a farming centre that for no easily explainable reason likes to refer to itself as the 'sausage capital of the world'. Those early woodcutters were very efficient, so only a remnant of a once-large tract of native podocarp (conifer) forest remains.

Wilderness, however, is not far away. Tuatapere is the base for the **Hump Ridge Track**, conceived and built by the local community, and opened in 2001. The three-day, 58km track makes relatively easy work of a tramp across craggy heights. Rich in natural and cultural history – from spectacular coastal and alpine scenery to the intriguing relics of a historic timber town – there's bird life aplenty, and the chance to see Hector's dolphins on the lonely windswept coast. En route the path crosses a number of towering historic wooden viaducts, including NZ's highest.

To hike the track you need to book through the Tuatapere Hump Ridge Track Information Centre (p589). Packages include transport to the trailhead (at Rarakau, 19km from Tuatapere) and comfortable lodge accommodation. The tramp is possible year-round and operates in three seasonal bands, priced accordingly (from $175), with guided tramps also available. Advance bookings are essential.

Another outstanding slice of wilderness surrounds **Lake Hauroko**, west of Tuatapere, reached by a mostly unsealed 32km road. Lined with dark, brooding, steeply forested slopes, it's the deepest lake in NZ, reaching a depth of 462m. The **Dusky Track** ends (or begins) on its northern shores; book a boat with Tuatapere-based **Lake Hauroko Tours** (☎03-225 5677; www.duskytrack.co.nz; track transport $99) ✎ to access the trailhead.

Lake Hauroko drains into the Tasman Sea from its southern end via the Wairaurahiri River. Two local jetboat operators – **W-Jet** (☎0800 376 174; www.wjet. co.nz; tour from $225) ✎ and **Hump Ridge**

Jet (📞 0800 270 556; www.wildernessjet.co.nz; day tour $225) – offer thrill-seeking rides along the forest-shrouded river.

◉ Sights

Clifden Suspension Bridge   BRIDGE
Spanning the Waiau River about 12km north of Tuatapere, this elegant wooden suspension bridge is the longest of its kind in NZ. Information panels, a picnic table and toilets encourage a pit stop.

✖ Eating

Yesteryears Museum Cafe   CAFE $
(📞 03-226 6682; 3a Orawia Rd; light meals $5-10; ⊙ 8am-5pm, reduced hours in winter) Rip into Aunt Daisy's sugar buns and a quintessentially Kiwi milkshake, and buy homemade jams for on-the-road breakfasts. There's an interesting jumble of quirky household items from a bygone era to peruse while you're at it.

ⓘ Information

Tuatapere Hump Ridge Track Information Centre (📞 03-226 6739, 0800 486 774; www.humpridgetrack.co.nz; 31 Orawia Rd; ⊙ 7.30am-5pm, limited hours in winter) Assists with local information, Hump Ridge hut passes and transport.

ⓘ Getting There & Away

Trips and Tramps (📞 03-249 7081, 0800 305 807; www.tripsandtramps.co.nz) Offers transport from Te Anau to the launching point of the boats to the Dusky Track trailhead.

Te Waewae & Colac Bays

Te Waewae – why wouldn't you! Arguably the most dramatically beautiful spot on the entire Scenic Southern Route, this long, moody, windswept stretch of beach sets a steely glare towards Antarctica. It's particularly impressive if you're travelling from the east, as it provides a first glimpse of the snowcapped Southern Alps descending into the sea, framing the western end of the bay.

Stop at the spectacular lookout at Mc-Cracken's Rest and keep an eye out for the Hector's dolphins and southern right whales that are occasionally sighted here. Just past Orepuki is the turn-off for Monkey Island, a grassy islet just metres off shore and accessible at low tide. Linger at the beach until dusk to watch the sun sink below the distant snowy peaks.

SOUTHERN SCENIC ROUTE

The quiet but gorgeous Southern Scenic Route cuts a meandering, lazy arc from Queenstown to Te Anau, Manapouri, Tuatapere, Riverton and Invercargill. From Invercargill it continues east and then north through the Catlins to Dunedin. See www.southernscenicroute.co.nz or pick up the free *Southern Scenic Route* map to join all the dots.

Colac Bay, 15km to the east, is a popular holiday place and a good surfing spot. Southerlies provide the best swells here, but it's pretty consistent year-round and never crowded. **Colac Bay Tavern** (📞 03-234 8399; jilly.wazza@xtra.co.nz; 15 Colac Bay Rd; sites from $15, cabins s/d $30/65; ⊙ 11am-9.30pm; 🛜) is a welcoming spot for a meal of wood-fired pizza or fish and chips, with the convenience of a camping ground with basic rooms out the back.

Riverton

POP 1430

Quiet little Riverton (in Māori, Aparima), only 38km short of Invercargill, is worth a lunch stop. If near-Antarctic swimming takes your fancy, the long, broad sands of Taramea Bay are good for a dip.

◉ Sights

Te Hikoi Southern Journey   MUSEUM
(📞 03-234 8260; www.tehikoi.co.nz; 172 Palmerston St; adult/child $6/free; ⊙ 10am-4pm) This cracker little museum relates local stories in clever and inspiring ways, starting off with an interesting 16-minute film. Oh, that all small-town museums could be this good! Inside you will also find the Riverton Visitor Information Centre, which can assist with maps and heritage trail brochures, as well as accommodation.

✖ Eating

Mrs Clark's Cafe   CAFE $$
(📞 03-234 8600; 108 Palmerston St; meals $12-24; ⊙ 8am-3pm Sun-Thu, to 8pm Fri & Sat; 🛜) Housed in an insanely turquoise building that has been various forms of eatery since 1891, Mrs Clark's serves thoroughly contemporary and delicious day-time food (beaut baking!), ace espresso, craft beer, and pizza on Friday and Saturday evenings.

Invercargill

POP 51,700

This flat and somewhat featureless town tends to inspire ambivalence in its visitors (except for Keith Richards, who famously dubbed it the 'arsehole of the world' during the Rolling Stones' 1965 visit), yet it satisfies all key requirements as a pit-stop between the Catlins, Stewart Island/Rakiura and Fiordland. Moreover, it sports some handsome buildings, a notable craft brewery, a handful of good eateries, beautiful parks and significant sites of interest for the devoted rev-head.

⊙ Sights

The streets of Invercargill boast a slew of historic buildings and other features that can be discovered with the *Invercargill Heritage Trail* brochure. The *Short Walks* brochure details various walks in and around the town, including several around **Sandy Point** butting out on to the Oreti River. **Oreti Beach**, 10km to the southwest of town, is a nice spot for a walk or swim.

Southland Museum & Art Gallery   MUSEUM
(☑ 03-219 9069; www.southlandmuseum.com; Queens Park, 108 Gala St; ⊙ 9am-5pm Mon-Fri, 10am-5pm Sat & Sun) FREE Housed in a big white pyramid (a low-rent Louvre?), Invercargill's cultural hub has permanent displays on Southland's natural and human history, recounting plenty of fascinating tales around maritime exploits, in particular. The museum's rock stars are undoubtedly the tuatara, NZ's unique lizard-like reptiles, unchanged for 220 million years. If the slow-moving 115-years-old-and-counting patriarch Henry is any example, they're not planning to do much for the next 220 million years either. Feeding time is 4pm on Fridays.

Outside of opening hours the tuatara can be viewed through windows at the rear of the pyramid.

Queens Park   PARK
(Gala St) Half-wild, half-tamed Queens Park encompasses a whopping 80 hectares of trees, plant collections, playing fields, ponds, playgrounds, farm animals, aviaries and even a Wonderland castle.

E Hayes & Sons   MUSEUM
(☑ 03-218 2059; www.ehayes.co.nz; 168 Dee St; ⊙ 7.30am-5.30pm Mon-Fri, 10am-4pm Sat & Sun) FREE We can't think of another hardware shop to have made it into a Lonely Planet guidebook, but in among the aisles of bolts, barbecues and brooms in this classic art-deco building are over 100 items of motoring memorabilia, including the actual motorbike on which the late Burt Munro broke the world speed record (as immortalised in the 2005 film *The World's Fastest Indian*, starring Sir Anthony Hopkins). There's also a replica of Burt's Indian, which you can be photographed in.

Other highlights include a 1910 Buick 8, a Ford Thunderbolt and some shiny Chevies. Admission is free, but you're invited to leave a donation for the local hospice – that is unless you're just calling by to stock up on nails and turpentine.

Anderson Park   PARK
(☑ 03-215 7432; www.andersonparkgallery.co.nz; 91 McIvor Rd, Waikiwi; ⊙ gardens 8am-dusk) Stretching over 24 hectares, this beautiful park includes landscaped gardens surrounding an elegant 1925 Georgian-style mansion, fringed with an expanse of native bush. The children's playground is extremely popular with local families and there's also an interesting carved *wharepuni* (traditional Māori sleeping house) to discover.

Sadly the house itself is off limits at present due to a potential earthquake risk. When (and if) a solution is found, you'll be able to visit the excellent gallery within, which features works from many prominent NZ artists.

Bill Richardson Transport World   MUSEUM
(☑ 03-217 1600; www.transportworld.co.nz; 26 Dart St, Hawthorndale) At the time of writing, the doors were soon expected to be flung open to this vast private museum, housing what is reputed to be the world's biggest collection of vintage trucks (over 300, including a significant number of rare Fords) and petrol bowsers (over 150). If for any reason it hasn't opened, enquire directly about a private viewing.

Invercargill Brewery   BREWERY
(☑ 03-214 5070; www.invercargillbrewery.co.nz; 72 Leet St; tour $25; ⊙ 10am-6pm Mon-Sat) New Zealand's great southern brewery has 20 taps for flagon-fills plus a bottled section of its own brews and guests. Pop in for a tasting, or the 45-minute daily tour at 1pm. Our favourites are the crisp B.man Pilsner and the chocolatey Pitch Black stout.

Invercargill

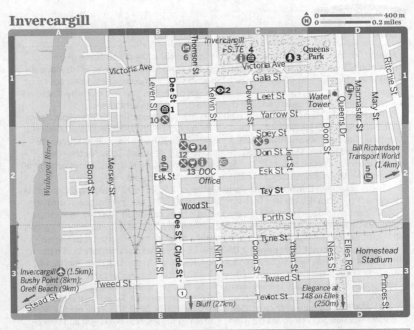

Invercargill

◎ Sights
1 E Hayes & Sons B1
2 Invercargill Brewery C1
3 Queens Park C1
4 Southland Museum & Art Gallery C1

🛏 Sleeping
5 Bella Vista D2
6 Southern Comfort Backpackers B1
7 Tower Lodge Motel D1
8 Victoria Railway Hotel B2

⊗ Eating
9 Batch C2
10 Louie's B1
11 Rocks B2
12 Three Bean Café B2

⊜ Drinking & Nightlife
13 The Kiln B2
14 Tillermans Music Lounge B2

🛏 Sleeping

Many places will store luggage for guests heading to Stewart Island/Rakiura. Motels cluster along Hwy 1 East (Tay St) and Hwy 6 North (North Rd).

Southern Comfort Backpackers HOSTEL $
(📱 03-218 3838; www.southerncomfortbackpackers.com; 30 Thomson St, Avenal; dm/s/d from $30/54/68; 📶) This large, lovely Victorian house offers a well-equipped kitchen and a TV-free lounge (hooray!) as well as colourful rooms, including spacious doubles. Pick herbs from the peaceful gardens; you'd hardly know you were five minutes' walk from town.

Lorneville Lodge HOLIDAY PARK $
(📱 0800 234 600, 03-235 8031; www.lornevillelodge.nz; 352 Lorne-Dacre Rd, Lorneville; sites per person $19, units $120, without bathroom $60; 📶🚲) Plenty of personality is packed into this well-set-out holiday park surrounded by farmland. Homey units feature lovingly preserved and enhanced retro style. Rural relaxation, grassy sites, a playground and friendly animals – what a charmer. It's located around 10km north of central Invercargill, east of the Lorneville roundabout.

Invercargill Top 10 HOLIDAY PARK $
(📱 0800 486 873, 03-218 9032; www.invercargilltop10.co.nz; 77 McIvor Rd, Waikiwi; sites from $40, unit $102, without bathroom $80; 📶) A particularly attractive option for motel- and

WORTH A TRIP

GORE

Around 66km northeast of Invercargill, Gore (pop 9910) is the proud 'home of country music' in NZ, with the annual **Gold Guitar Week** (www.goldguitars.co.nz; ☉ late May-early Jun) in late May and early June ensuring the town's accommodation is booked out for at least 10 days per year. For the other 355 days, good reasons to stop include a notable art gallery, a neat little museum, and the chance to fly in vintage aeroplanes.

The **Hokonui Heritage Centre** (☑ 03-208 7032; 16 Hokonui Dr; ☉ 8.30am-5pm Mon-Sat, 1-4pm Sun) **FREE** incorporates the Gore Visitor Centre, the Gore Historical Museum and the **Hokonui Moonshine Museum** (☑ 03-208 9907; www.hokonuiwhiskey.com; 16 Hokonui Dr; adult/child $5/free; ☉ 8.30am-5pm Mon-Sat, 1-4pm Sun). Together they celebrate the town's proud history of fishing, farming and illegal distilleries. Admission to the Moonshine Museum includes a wee dram of the local liquid gold.

The outstanding **Eastern Southland Gallery** (☑ 03-208 9907; www.esgallery.co.nz; 14 Hokonui Dr; ☉ 10am-4.30pm Mon-Fri, 1-4pm Sat & Sun) **FREE** – aka the 'Goreggenheim' – in Gore's century-old former public library houses a hefty collection of NZ art, including a large Ralph Hotere collection. The amazing John Money Collection combines indigenous folk art from West Africa and Australia with works by esteemed NZ artist Rita Angus.

Croydon Aircraft Company (☑ 03-208 9755; www.croydonaircraft.com; 1558 Waimea Hwy, SH94; 10/30min flight $95/220; ☉ 9.30am-4.30pm Mon-Fri Nov-Mar, 11am-3pm Mon-Fri Apr-Oct), 16km along SH94 towards Queenstown, restores vintage aircraft. Inside a viewing hangar (admission $10) several gems can be seen, including a rare Dragonfly. Flights are offered in a 1930s Tiger Moth biplane and other wee aircraft. Adjacent, the **Moth** (☑ 03-208 9662; www.themoth.co.nz; 1558 Waimea Hwy, SH94; lunch $12-26, dinner $27-34; ☉ 10am-late Wed-Sun year-round, plus 10am-4pm Mon & Tue Dec-Feb) is a bright and breezy place for a meal.

cabin-dwellers, this leafy park 6.5km north of town also has pleasant tent and campervan sites and smart communal facilities.

⭐ **Bushy Point Fernbirds**　　B&B **$$**
(☑ 03-213 1302; www.fernbirds.co.nz; 197 Grant Rd, Otatara; s/d $150/170) Two friendly corgis are among the hosts at this eco-aware homestay set on the edge of 4.5 hectares of private forest reserve and wetlands. Fernbirds is very popular with birding types, so booking ahead is essential. It's five minutes' drive from central Invercargill, and rates include a guided walk in the reserve.

Bella Vista　　MOTEL **$$**
(☑ 03-217 9799; www.bellavista.co.nz; 240 Tay St; unit from $120; 🛜) Friendly hosts, reasonable prices and tidy, well-equipped units put this modern, two-level place near the top of Invercargill's competitive motel pack. Units range from cosy studios with tea- and toast-making facilities, to proper apartments with full kitchens.

Tower Lodge Motel　　MOTEL **$$**
(☑ 03-217 6729; www.towerlodgemotel.co.nz; 119 Queens Dr; unit from $130; 🛜) Right opposite Invercargill's oddly ornate Victorian water tower, this older motel has been made over with new carpets, fresh decor and a mushroom colour scheme. Even the studio units are spacious and some of the one-bedrooms have spa baths.

Victoria Railway Hotel　　HOTEL **$$**
(☑ 03-218 1281, 0800 777 557; www.hotelinvercargill.com; cnr Leven & Esk Sts; s/d from $130/145; @🛜) For a hit of 19th-century heritage, this grand old refurbished hotel fits the bill – although the dated, generic decor doesn't really live up to its potential. Partake of breakfast or dinner in the dining room, or a locally brewed ale in the cosy house bar.

✗ Eating

Three Bean Café　　CAFE **$**
(☑ 03-214 1914; 73 Dee St; meals $11-18; ☉ 7am-4pm Mon-Fri, 8am-2.30pm Sat; 🛜) This borderline old-fashioned main-street cafe prides itself on good coffee then matches the promise with carefully prepared snacks, such as savoury pies and delightful lemon cake, and more substantial meals such as soup, salad and burgers. Helpful staff get our thumbs up, too.

★**Batch**   CAFE $$
(☑ 03-214 6357; 173 Spey St; meals $13-20;
⊙7am-4.30pm; 🛜) Large, shared tables, a
relaxed beachy ambience, and top-notch
coffee and smoothies add up to this cafe
being widely regarded as Southland's best.
Delicious counter food includes bagels,
sumptuously filled rolls, bancffee brioches,
brownies and cakes that are little works of
art. A smallish wine and beer list partners
healthy lunch options. In summer, it stays
open until 8pm on Fridays.

★**Louie's**   TAPAS $$
(☑ 03-214 2913; 142 Dee St; tapas $13-16, mains
$29-32; ⊙5pm-late Wed-Sat) Proving that cool
Invercargill isn't quite an oxymoron, this
cosy tapas bar is a great place to while away
an evening, snuggled into a sofa or a fireside
nook. The menu veers from creative tapas
(venison tacos, muttonbird, mussels with
lime and chilli) to more substantial mains.
You really can't go wrong with the locally
sourced blue cod.

Rocks   CAFE $$
(☑ 03-218 7597; www.shop5rocks.com Court-
ville Pl, 101 Dee St; lunch $18-23, dinner $28-41;
⊙10am-2pm & 5pm-late Tue-Sat) Tucked away
in a shopping arcade, this family-style eat-
ery offers a relaxed and fairly unchallenging
dining experience. Lunch highlights include
pork-belly open sandwiches, pastas and
salads, while stars of the extended evening
menu are venison in blueberry sauce and a
particularly delicious Sicilian fish bowl.

★**Elegance at
148 on Elles**   FRENCH, BRITISH $$$
(☑ 03-216 1000; 148 Elles Rd, Georgetown; mains
$26-38; ⊙6-11pm Mon-Sat) Welcome to 1984,
and we mean that in a completely affec-
tionate way. Elegance is the sort of old-fashioned, upmarket, regional restaurant where
the menu is vaguely French, vaguely British,
and you can be guaranteed of a perfectly
cooked piece of venison served on a bed of
creamy mash. And there's an awful lot to be
said for that.

🍷 Drinking & Nightlife

Tillermans Music Lounge   BAR, CLUB
(☑ 03-218 9240; 16 Don St; ⊙11pm-3.30am Fri
& Sat) The saviour of Southland's live-music scene, Mr Tillerman's venue hosts
everything from thrash to flash, with a battered old dance floor to show for it. Visit
the fun downstairs Vinyl Bar, which is open

from 8pm, to find out what's coming up and
to put in your request for whichever battered old LP takes your fancy.

Kiln   BAR
(☑ 03-218 2258; www.thekiln.co.nz; 7 Don St;
⊙11am-late 🛜) Invercargill's best gastropub
is also its most appealing, with trendy wallpaper and muted lighting from oversized
lampshades. Food comes in epic portions
(mains $30 to $37) and runs a well-honed
gamut between mussels and Caesar salad, to
fish and chips, to a joint of meat to share between friends. There's live music on Fridays
and Saturdays.

ℹ️ Information

DOC Office (☑ 03-211 2400; www.doc.govt.nz;
7th fl, 33 Don St; ⊙8.30am-4.30pm Mon-Fri)
An office rather than a visitor centre, you're
best to make the i-SITE your first port of call.
However, it can sort you out with maps and
advice if you draw a blank elsewhere.

Invercargill i-SITE (☑ 03-211 0895; www.
invercargillnz.com; Queens Park, 108 Gala St;
⊙8am-5pm) Sharing the Southland Museum
pyramid, the i-SITE can help with general
enquiries and is a godsend if you're stuck for
Stewart Island/Rakiura or Catlins accommodation options .

Post Office (☑ 03-214 7700; www.nzpost.
co.nz; 51 Don St; ⊙9am-5.30pm Mon-Fri, to
1pm Sat)

ℹ️ Getting There & Away

AIR

Air New Zealand (☑ 0800 737 000; www.
airnz.co.nz) Flights link Invercargill to
Christchurch and Wellington.

Stewart Island Flights (☑ 03-218 9129; www.
stewartislandflights.com) Regular connections
to Stewart Island/Rakiura.

BUS

Catch-a-Bus South (☑ 03-479 9960; www.
catchabussouth.co.nz) Offers scheduled
shuttle services at least daily to Bluff ($22,
30 minutes), Queenstown Airport ($55, three
hours), Queenstown ($55, 3¼ hours), Gore
($27, 1½ hours) and Dunedin ($55, 3½ hours).

InterCity (☑ 03-471 7143; www.intercity.co.nz)
Direct coaches to/from Gore (from $12, one
hour, two daily), Queenstown Airport ($48, 3½
hours, daily) and Queenstown ($48, 3¾ hours,
daily).

Naked Bus (www.nakedbus.com) Daily buses
to and from Gore (50 minutes), Dunedin (3½
hours) and Queenstown (3¾ hours).

ⓘ Getting Around

Invercargill Airport (☏ 03-218 6367; www.invercargillairport.co.nz; 106 Airport Ave) is 3km west of central Invercargill. The door-to-door **Airport Shuttle** (☏ 03-214 3434; exec.car. service@xtra.co.nz) costs around $14 from the city centre; more for residential pick-up. By taxi it's around $20; try **Blue Star Taxis** (☏ 03-217 7777; www.bluestartaxis.co.nz).

Bluff

POP 1800

Windswept and more than a little bleak, Bluff is Invercargill's port, located at the end of a protruding strip of land, 27km south of the city. It's also home to NZ's only aluminium smelter.

The main reason folk come here is to catch the ferry to Stewart Island/Rakiura or to pose for photos beside the **Stirling Point signpost**, which signifies that you've reached the furthest southern reaches of NZ. Sorry to disappoint you, but you haven't. Despite the oft-quoted phrase 'from Cape Reinga to Bluff' and the fact that SH1 terminates at Stirling Point, the South Island's southernmost point is Slope Point in the Catlins, with Stewart Island/Rakiura and remote dots of rock lying even further south. But let's not let the facts get in the way of a good story...

Mention Bluff to any New Zealander and what's the bet that they'll be thinking of oysters. Bluff's bulging bivalves are in huge demand from the minute they come into season (late March to late August). Top restaurants from as far away as Auckland compete to be the first to add them to their menus. As oysters go, they're whoppers. Don't expect to be able to slurp one down in a dainty gulp – these beasts take some chewing. If you want to know what all the fuss is about, you can buy fresh Bluff oysters when they're in season from Fowlers Oysters on the way into town on the left. Otherwise, time your visit for the annual Bluff Oyster & Food Festival in May.

⊙ Sights

Bluff Hill   HILL
(Flagstaff Rd) A steep sealed road leads up to the top of 265m Bluff Hill (Motupōhue), where a path spirals up to a lookout. If the wind isn't threatening to sweep you off your feet, stop to read the information panels along the way. Various walking tracks head up here, including the Foveaux Walkway to Stirling Point and Ocean Beach.

Bluff Maritime Museum   MUSEUM
(☏ 03-212 7534; 241 Foreshore Rd; adult/child $3/1; ⊙10am-4.30pm Mon-Fri year-round, 12.30-4.30pm Sat & Sun Oct-Apr) Salty tales abound round these parts, and many are preserved in this small museum, alongside a century-old oyster boat and a big old steam engine. It also houses interesting displays on Bluff history and on the annual muttonbird (tītī) harvest, an important tradition for local Māori.

⁂ Festivals & Events

Bluff Oyster & Food Festival   FOOD
(www.bluffoysterfest.co.nz; ⊙May) Celebrate Bluff's most famous export.

✖ Eating

Oyster Cove   SEAFOOD $$
(☏ 03-212 8855; www.oystercove.co.nz; 8 Ward Pde; mains $18-33; ⊙11am-4pm Mon-Thu, to 7pm Fri-Sun; 🕾) Right by the famous signpost at Stirling Point, this restaurant gazes out to sea through large curvy glass windows. In reality the view trumps the food, but it's not a bad place to try local delicacies such as muttonbird, paua, Stewart Island mussels, blue cod and, of course, the renowned oysters.

🔒 Shopping

Fowlers Oysters   FOOD
(☏ 03-212 8792; Ocean Beach Rd; ⊙9am-5pm Mar-Aug) To buy fresh Bluff oysters, visit Fowlers Oysters on the way into town on the left.

ⓘ Getting There & Away

Catch-a-Bus South (☏ 03-479 9960; www.catchabussouth.co.nz) Offers scheduled shuttle services at least daily to Invercargill ($22, 30 minutes), Queenstown Airport ($70, 3½ hours), Queenstown ($70, 3¾ hours), Gore ($40, two hours) and Dunedin ($70, four hours).

Stewart Island Experience (☏ 03-212 7660; www.stewartislandexperience.co.nz) Runs a shuttle between Bluff and Invercargill connecting with its Stewart Island ferry. It also offers secure vehicle storage by the ferry terminal ($8 per day). Transfers from Te Anau and Queenstown to Bluff are available from late October to late April.

THE CATLINS

Bypassed entirely by SH1, the often-overlooked Catlins coast is tucked away at the southeastern corner of the South Island, straddling Southland and Otago. Named after a 19th-century whaling captain, it's an enchanting region, combining fecund farmland, native forest, lonely lighthouses, empty beaches, bushwalks and wildlife-spotting opportunities. On a clear summer's day it is a beauty to behold. In the face of an Antarctic southerly it's an entirely different kettle of fish. Good luck.

The only way to properly explore the area is with your own wheels. It's a slow-going route, with plenty of winding bits, narrows, gravel sections and optional detours, but this is *all* about the journey, rather than the destination.

From Invercargill, the Southern Scenic Route (p589) cuts an arc through the Catlins. However we suggest you leave it at Fortrose in order to visit Waipapa Point, Slope Point, Curio Bay and Waikawa before rejoining it north of Niagara. Note, the section between Haldane and Curio Bay involves 9km of unsealed road.

Flora & Fauna

The Catlins is a wonderful place for independent wildlife-watching. Fur seals and sea lions laze along the coast, while in spring migratory southern right whales are occasionally spotted. Dolphins are also frequent visitors.

Unlike much of Southland, tall kahikatea, totara and rimu forests still exist in the Catlins. Prolific bird life includes tui, bellbird, kereru (wood pigeon), the endangered yellow-eyed penguin and the rare mohua (yellowhead).

ℹ️ Information

The i-SITEs in Invercargill and Balclutha have lots of Catlins information. On the road you'll pass two information centres: the small **Owaka Museum & Catlins Information Centre** (p598) and the even smaller **Waikawa Museum & Information Centre** (p596). For further information, see www.catlins.org.nz and www.catlins-nz.com.

The Catlins has no banks and limited options for eating out and grocery shopping. There's an ATM at the Four Square supermarket in Owaka, and petrol stations (hours can be irregular) in Fortrose, Papatowai and Owaka.

ℹ️ Getting There & Away

There is no public transport in the Catlins area.

Curio Bay & Around

The beachy settlement of Curio Bay attracts a deluge of sunseekers in the summer months but it's a sleepy hamlet at other times. Most of the holiday houses are lined up along Porpoise Bay, a glorious long stretch of sand that's arguably the best swimming beach in the Catlins. Blue penguins nest in the dunes and in summer Hector's dolphins come here to rear their young. Whales are occasional visitors, and fur seals and sea lions may also be spotted.

Curio Bay itself lies just around the southern headland on a much less inviting stretch of coast. It's famous for its fossilised Jurassic-age trees, which are visible for four hours either side of low tide. Yellow-eyed penguins waddle ashore here an hour or so before sunset. Do the right thing and keep your distance.

◉ Sights & Activities

Waipapā Lighthouse   LIGHTHOUSE
(Waipapa Lighthouse Rd) Standing on a desolate but beautiful point surrounded by farmland, this lighthouse dates from 1884, three years after 131 people lost their lives in the wreck of SS *Tararua*. Information panels recount the terrible tale. Tip-toe through the sea lions to survey the beach. The turn-off to Waipapa Point is at Otara, 12km southeast of Fortrose.

Slope Point   LANDMARK
(Slope Point Rd) A 20-minute walk across farmland leads to a signpost designating the South Island's true southerly point in underwhelming fashion. The views more than make up for it, not only of the ocean but of the chunky rocks tumbling down to meet it. The track is closed in September and October for lambing. To get here, follow the signs from Haldane

Catlins Surf   SURFING
(📞 03-246 8552; www.catlins-surf.co.nz; 601 Curio Bay Rd; 2hr lesson $60, hire per 3hr/day $50/65) Based at the Curio Bay Holiday Park, this surf school offers lessons on Porpoise Bay, much to the amusement of any passing dolphins. If you're already confident on the waves, you can hire a board, wetsuit (very necessary) and flippers. Owner Nick also offers stand-up paddleboarding tuition ($75, 2½ hours).

The Catlins

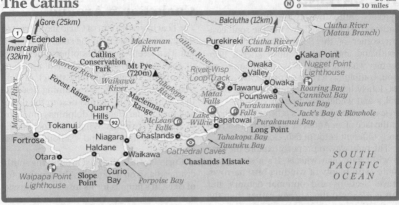

🛏 Sleeping

Lazy Dolphin Lodge
HOSTEL $

(☑ 03-246 8579; www.lazydolphinlodge.co.nz; 529 Curio Bay Rd; dm/r without bathroom $38/80; @🛜) This perfect hybrid of seaside holiday home and hostel has light-filled bedrooms sporting cheerful linen. There are two kitchens and lounges, but you'll want to hang out upstairs on the deck overlooking Porpoise Bay. A path at the rear of the property leads directly to the beach.

Slope Point Backpackers
HOSTEL $

(☑ 03-246 8420; www.slopepoint.co.nz; 164 Slope Point Rd; sites from $15, dm $25-30, d with/without bathroom $90/50; 🛜) This rural property has modern dorms and rooms, along with a great-value self-contained unit and a whole three-bedroom house a little further up the road. There are grassy tent pitches and gravel sites for campervans, and the owners' children are always keen to show off the working farm. Board games, puzzles and loads of magazines take the place of TV.

Curio Bay Boutique Studios
APARTMENT $$

(☑ 03-246 8797; www.curiobay.co.nz; 521a Curio Bay Rd; apt from $180) Three plush units are on offer here – one apartment attached to the hosts' house, and two similar units down the road. All are self-contained, decorated in rustic, beachy style, with big windows and sun-drenched decks right next to the beach. There's also an old-fashioned Kiwi bach, sleeping up to six people.

Waikawa & Around

Waikawa occupies a pretty spot on an estuary, 5km north of Curio Bay. It was once a major timber port but now it's most famous for its fish-and-chip truck, which does a roaring trade in summer.

👁 Sights

Waikawa Museum & Information Centre
MUSEUM

(☑ 03-246 8464; waikawamuseum@hyper.net. nz; 604 Niagara–Waikawa Rd; gold coin donation; ☺10am-5pm) Something of a one-stop shop in a one-horse town, this little museum features the usual array of dusty agricultural artefacts and photographs of mainly local interest. However, it also incorporates the information centre, acts as the reception for some local holiday rentals, and sells important stuff like newspapers and stamps.

🛏 Sleeping & Eating

Penguin Paradise Holiday Lodge
HOSTEL $

(☑ 03-246 8552; www.catlins-surf.co.nz; 612 Niagara–Waikawa Rd; dm/r without bathroom $30/68) This laid-back backpackers occupies a heritage cottage in the heart of Waikawa village, near the estuary. Special deals combine one night's accommodation and a 90-minute surf lesson ($85).

Waikava Harbour View
RENTAL HOUSE $$

(☑ 03-246 8866; www.southcatlins.co.nz; 14 Larne St; house from $120) Right on the estuary, Harbour View is a modern four-bedroom house that's an excellent option for families or a group; up to 12 people can be accommodated. The newer one-bedroom Harakeke and Toi Tois units are also good value, sleeping up to four.

Niagara Falls CAFE $$

(☑ 03-246 8577; www.niagarafallscafe.co.nz; 256 Niagara–Waikawa Rd, Niagara; mains $14-22; ☺ 11am-late Dec-Mar, 11am-4pm Thu-Mon Apr-Nov; ☎) Located in a Victorian schoolhouse, this is a decent spot to linger over coffee and a scone, or to tuck into homemade meals. Tasty lamb burgers are sandwiched into freshly baked bread, and there's blue cod, chowder and decadent chocolate brownies. Relax in the grassy garden with a local craft beer or a glass of wine.

Papatowai & Around

Nestled near the mouth of the Tahakopa River, the leafy village of Papatowai has perhaps a few dozen regular inhabitants but swells with holidaymakers in summer, mainly drawn by the languid vibe and the potential for some good bushwalks. There are a couple of short walks in the immediate vicinity, as well as a picnic spot at the river mouth, but further places of interest are spread along the highway in both directions.

Twelve kilometres to the west is the turn-off to **McLean Falls**. The car park is 4km off the highway, with the falls themselves a 40-minute return walk through tree ferns and rimu. Around 5km west of Papatowai, an easy forest walk leads to the dark peaty waters of **Lake Wilkie** (20 minutes return). Bellbirds may ring. Another 1km east of here, a short gravel road leads to sweeping **Tautuku Bay**, which can also be viewed from on high at the **Florence Hill Lookout** just before the descent into Papatowai.

Heading north you can follow the highway to **Matai Falls** (a 30-minute return walk) on the Maclennan River, then head southeast on the signposted road to the tiered **Purakaunui Falls** (20 minutes return). Both falls are reached via cool, dark forest walks through totara and tree fern.

Continue along the gravel road from Purakaunui through Tarara, Ratanui and Hinahina to Jacks Bay, where a track leads through farmland to the 55m-deep **Jack's Blowhole**. In the middle of a paddock 200m from the sea but connected by a subterrane-

an cavern, this huge cauldron was named after Chief Tuhawaiki, nicknamed Bloody Jack for his cussin'. It's a fairly brisk 30-minute walk each way.

◎ Sights & Activities

Lost Gypsy Gallery GALLERY

(☑ 03-415 8908; www.thelostgypsy.com; 2532 Papatowai Hwy; admission $5; ☺ 10am-5pm Thu-Tue, closed May-Sep) Fashioned from remaindered bits and bobs, artist Blair Sommerville's intricately crafted automata are wonderfully irreverent. The bamboozling collection in the bus (free entry) is a teaser for the carnival of creations through the gate (young children not allowed, sorry...). The buzz, bong and bright lights of the organ are bound to tickle your ribs. Espresso caravan and wi-fi on-site.

Cathedral Caves CAVE

(www.cathedralcaves.co.nz; 1069 Chaslands Hwy; adult/child $5/1; ☺ Nov-May) Cutting back into cliffs right on the beach, the huge, arched Cathedral Caves are only accessible for two hours either side of low tide (tide timetables are posted on the website, at the highway turn-off and at visitor information centres) – and even then they can be closed at short notice if the conditions are deemed too dangerous. If you're happy to wade, you can walk in one entrance and out the other.

From SH92 it's 2km to the car park, then a peaceful 15-minute forest walk down to the beach and a further 25 minutes to the caves.

Catlins Wildlife Trackers WILDLIFE

(☑ 03-415 8613, 0800 228 5467; www.catlins-ecotours.co.nz) ✦ Running since 1990, Catlins Wildlife Trackers offers customised guided walks and tours with a focus on ecology. If you want to see the beloved mohua, penguins, sea lions or other wildlife, Mary and Fergus will track them down for you. The fully guided three-night/two-day package costs $1200, including all food, accommodation and transport.

🛏 Sleeping & Eating

Hilltop LODGE $

(☑ 03-415 8028; www.hilltopcatlins.co.nz; 77 Tahakopa Valley Rd; dm $38, d $110, without bathroom $100) High on a hill 1.5km out of town with native forest at the back door and surrounded by a sheep farm, these two ship-shape cottages command spectacular views of the Tahakopa Valley and coast. Rent by the room or the whole house; the en suite double is the pick of a very nice bunch.

Catlins Kiwi Holiday Park   HOLIDAY PARK $
(📞03-415 8338; www.catlinskiwiholidaypark.com; 9 Rewcastle Rd, Chaslands; sites from $46, units from $145, without bathroom from $189; @🛜) This modern holiday park offers personality-packed accommodation ranging from cute cabins to smart family motels. Tenters share good communal amenities with the cute 'Kiwiana' cabins. Hop along to the on-site Whistling Frog Cafe for the Catlins' best food.

★ Mohua Park   COTTAGE $$
(📞03-415 8613; www.catlinsmohuapark.co.nz; 744 Catlins Valley Rd; cottage $190) 🍃 Situated on the edge of a peaceful 14-hectare nature reserve (7km off the highway), these four spacious self-contained cottages offer peace, quiet and privacy with an interesting mixed forest on the doorstep and a Disney movie worth of feathery companions. The owners also have beachfront accommodation at Papatowai.

Whistling Frog Cafe & Bar   CAFE $$
(📞03-415 8338; www.whistlingfrogcafe.com; 9 Rewcastle Rd, Chaslands; mains $18-23; ⏰8.30am-9.30pm Nov-Mar, 9.30am-6.30pm Apr-Oct; 🛜) Colourful and fun, the Frog is the best dining option in the Catlins, offering craft beer on tap and a crowd-pleasing menu. We're talking seafood chowder, gourmet burgers and a seriously rich steak, lager and aged-cheddar pie. Ribbit! It's located at the Catlins Kiwi Holiday Park, near McLean Falls.

Owaka & Around

Owaka is the Catlins' main town (population a hefty 303), and it's well worth calling in to visit the excellent museum and to stock up on petrol and groceries before continuing on.

Pounawea, a beautiful hamlet on the edge of the Catlins River Estuary, 4km to the east, is a much more appealing place to put down roots. Just across the inlet is **Surat Bay**, notable for the sea lions that lie around the beach between here and **Cannibal Bay**, an hour's beach-walk away.

⊙ Sights & Activities

Owaka Museum & Catlins Information Centre   MUSEUM
(📞03-415 8323; www.owakamuseum.org.nz; 10 Campbell St, Owaka; adult/child $5/free; ⏰10am-4pm) More interesting than most local history museums, this whizz-bang modern establishment supports Māori and settler stories with an interesting array of artefacts. The Catlins' reputation as a shipwreck coast is explained in short video presentations. It also doubles as the main information centre for the Catlins.

Catlins River–Wisp Loop Track   TRAMPING
(www.doc.govt.nz) This 24km loop comprises two 12km sections: the low-level, well-formed Catlins River Walk (five to six hours), and the Wisp Loop Walk (four to five hours), a higher-altitude tramp with a side trip to Rocky Knoll boasting great views and sub-alpine vegetation.

The routes can be walked in either direction as one long day, divided over two days, or split into shorter sections accessed via various entry/exit points. The main access is via Catlins Valley Road, south of Owaka.

Catlins Horse Riding   HORSE RIDING
(📞03-415 8368; www.catlinshorseriding.co.nz; 41 Newhaven Rd, Owaka; 1/2/3hr rides $60/105/145) Explore the idiosyncratic coastline and landscapes on four legs. Both learners' treks and the full gallop available.

🛏 Sleeping & Eating

★ Newhaven Holiday Park   HOLIDAY PARK $
(📞03-415 8834; www.newhavenholiday.com; 324 Newhaven Rd, Owaka; sites from $32, units from $100, without bathroom from $66; 🛜) Sitting on the estuary edge at the gateway to the Surat Bay beach walk, this excellent little holiday park has good communal facilities, cheerful cabins and three self-contained units. When we last sneaked around, not only were we serenaded by a bellbird but we swear the toilets smelt of cinnamon.

Split Level   HOSTEL $
(📞03-415 8868; www.thesplitlevel.co.nz; 9 Waikawa Rd, Owaka; dm $33, r from $82, without bathroom from $74; 🛜) Very much like staying at a mate's house, this tidy two-level home has a comfortable lounge with a large TV and leather couches, and a very well-equipped kitchen. Upstairs rooms open onto decks, while downstairs there's a little en suite unit with its own fridge and microwave.

Pounaewa Grove Motel   MOTEL **$$**

(☑03-415 8339; www.pounaweagrove.co.nz; 5 Ocean Grove; r $140; 🖪) If you're looking for modern units with big, comfy beds, plush textiles, art on the walls, flat-screen TVs and sharp bathrooms, this four-unit studio complex will tick all the boxes.

Catlins Cafe   CAFE **$$**

(☑03-415 8040; www.catlinscafe.co.nz; 3 Main Rd, Owaka; brunch $15-22, dinner $23-30; ☺9am-8.30pm; 🖪) The best of the Owaka bunch starts the day with cooked breakfasts and continues into the evening with fish and chips, burgers, a roast-of-the-day and, in season, whitebait fritters served with a truck-load of salad.

Kaka Point & Around

With a permanent population nudging just over the 200 mark, Kaka Point is a lethargic coastal community set back from a surfy swimming beach.

The biggest attraction in the vicinity is **Nugget Point** (Tokatā), 8km further down the coast. This is the king of the Catlins viewpoints, made all the more interesting by the wave-thrashed cliffs and the toothy islets known as the Nuggets protruding from the surf. Seals and sea lions can often be spotted lolling about below and there's also plenty of bird life, such as soaring shearwaters and spoonbills huddling in the lee of the breeze. A 900m walk leads from the car park to the lighthouse on the point itself.

Just shy of the Nugget Point car park is the car park for **Roaring Bay**, where a well-placed hide allows you to see yellow-eyed penguins (hōiho) coming ashore (best two hours before sunset). Obey all signs: as you can see, this is a pretty precarious existence.

🛌 Sleeping

Kaka Point Camping Ground   HOLIDAY PARK **$**

(☑03-412 8801; www.kakapointcamping.co.nz; 39 Tarata St, Kaka Point; sites unpowered/powered from $129/32, cabins s/d $30/56; 🖪) Cabins are basic but functional, and there are grassy, hedged areas for campers. Bushwalks delve into the surrounding forest, and it's a short, though steep, stroll downhill to the beach and village.

Nugget Lodge   RENTAL HOUSE **$$**

(☑03-412 8783; www.nuggetlodge.co.nz; 367 The Nuggets Rd, Kaka Point; unit $190; 🖪) Sitting on a seaside knoll on the road to the lighthouse are two modern bach-style self-contained units – one with balcony, one with private garden. It's worth opting for the huge continental breakfast ($15 per person) with freshly baked bread and homemade muesli. If you're lucky, you might spy a couple of resident sea lions lolling on the beach below you.

Drinking & Nightlife

Point Cafe & Bar   PUB

(☑03-412 3800; 58 Esplanade, Kaka Point; ☺8.30am-7.30pm) Prop yourself at the driftwood bar for a cool beer, hit the pool table or grab a window seat for a sea view. Takeaways and ice creams are available at the attached store, or you can tuck into blue cod and chips or a seafood chowder in the cafe (mains $26 to $29).

STEWART ISLAND

POP 378

If you make the short but extremely rewarding trip to Stewart Island/Rakiura you'll have one up on most New Zealanders, many of whom maintain an active curiosity about the country's 'third island' without ever actually going there.

Travellers who make the effort are rewarded with a warm welcome from both the local kiwi and the local Kiwis. This is arguably the best place to spy the country's shy, feathered icon in the wild, and the close-knit community of Stewart Islanders are relaxed hosts. If you're staying on the island for just a few days, don't be too surprised if most people quickly know who you are and where you came from – especially if you mix and mingle over a beer at NZ's southernmost pub in Oban, the island's only settlement.

Stewart Island offers plenty of active adventure opportunities including kayaking, and tramping the Great Walk or other tracks in Rakiura National Park, which makes up 85% of the land area. As well as beautiful coastal and inland scenery, a major impetus for such excursions is bird life. Stewart Island/Rakiura is a bird sanctuary of international repute, and even the most amateur of spotters are likely to be distracted by the constant – and utterly glorious – squawking, singing and flitting of feathery flocks.

History

Stewart Island's Māori name is Rakiura (Glowing Skies), and you only need to catch a glimpse of a spectacular blood-red sunset or the aurora australis to see why. According

Stewart Island (North)

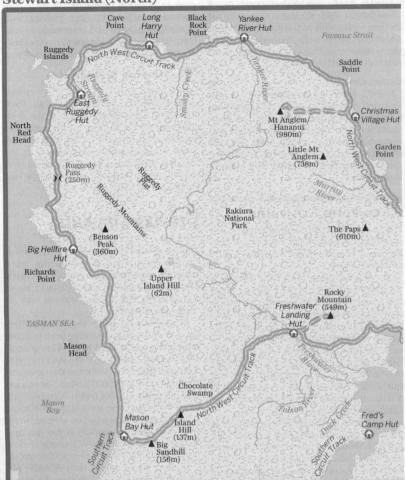

to myth, New Zealand was hauled up from the ocean by Māui, who said, 'Let us go out of sight of land, far out in the open sea, and when we have quite lost sight of land, then let the anchor be dropped'. The North Island was the fish that Māui caught, the South Island his canoe and Rakiura was the anchor – Te Punga o te Waka o Māui.

There is evidence that parts of Rakiura were occupied by moa hunters as early as the 13th century. The titi (muttonbird or sooty shearwater) on adjacent islands were an important seasonal food source for the southern Māori.

The first European visitor was Captain Cook. Sailing around the eastern, southern and western coasts in 1770 he mistook it for the bottom end of the South Island and promptly named it South Cape. In 1809 the sealing vessel *Pegasus* circumnavigated Rakiura and named it after its first officer, William Stewart.

In June 1864 Stewart and the adjacent islets were bought from local Māori for £6000. Early industries were sealing, timber-milling, fish-curing and shipbuilding, with a short-lived gold rush towards the end of the 19th century. Today the island's economy is dependent on tourism and fishing.

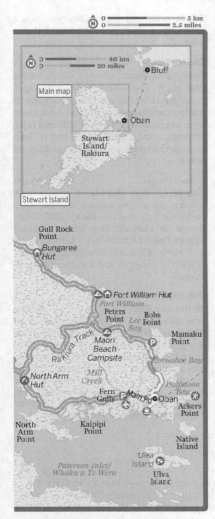

Flora & Fauna

With an absence of mustelids (ferrets, stoats and weasels) and large areas of intact forest, Stewart Island/Rakiura has one of the largest and most diverse bird populations of anywhere in NZ. Even in the streets of Oban the air resonates with birds such as tui, bellbirds and kaka, which share their island home with weka, kakariki, fernbirds, robins and Rakiura tokoeka/kiwi. There are also plenty of shore- and seabirds, including dotterels, shags, mollymawks, prions, petrels and albatross, as well as the sooty shearwater, which is seen in large numbers during breeding season. Ask locals about the evening parade of penguins on cliffs near the wharf; and *please* – don't feed the birds. It's bad for them.

Exotic animals include two species of deer, the red and the Virginia (whitetail), introduced in the early 20th century, as were brush-tailed possums, which are now numerous throughout the island and destructive to the native bush. Stewart Island/Rakiura also has NZ fur seals, NZ sea lions, elephant seals and occasionally leopard seals that visit the beaches and rocky shores.

Beech, the tree that dominates much of NZ is absent from Stewart Island/Rakiura. The predominant lowland bush is podocarp forest, with exceptionally tall rimu, miro and totara forming the canopy. Because of mild winters, frequent rainfall and porous soil, most of the island is a lush forest, thick with vines and carpeted in deep green ferns and mosses.

◉ Sights

★ Ulva Island BIRD SANCTUARY

(Map p600) A tiny paradise covering only 250 hectares, Ulva Island/Te Wharawhara is a great place to see lots of native NZ birds. Established as a bird sanctuary in 1922, it remains one of Stewart Island/Rakiura's wildest corners – 'a rare taste of how NZ once was and perhaps could be again', according to DOC. The island was declared rat-free in 1997 and three years later was chosen as the site to release endangered South Island saddlebacks.

Today the air is bristling with birdsong, which can be appreciated on walking tracks in the island's northwest as detailed in *Ulva: Self-Guided Tour* ($2), available from the Rakiura National Park Visitor Centre. Many paths intersect amid beautiful stands of rimu, miro, totara and rata. Any water-taxi company will run you to the island from Golden Bay wharf, with scheduled services offered by **Ulva Island Ferry** (Map p600; ☑03-219 1013; return adult/child $20/10; ☺departs 9am, noon, 4pm, returns noon, 4pm, 6pm). To get the most out of Ulva Island, go on a tour with Ulva's Guided Walks (p603).

Rakiura Museum MUSEUM

(Map p603; ☑03-219 1221; www.rakiuramuseum. co.nz; 9 Ayr St, Halfmoon Bay; adult/child $2/50c; ☺10am-1.30pm Mon-Sat, noon-2pm Sun Oct-Apr, 10am-noon Mon-Fri, 10am-1.30pm Sat, noon-2pm Sun May-Sep) Historic photographs are stars of this small museum focused on local natural and human history, and featuring Māori artefacts, whaling gear and household items.

 Activities

Rakiura National Park protects 85% of the island, making it a mecca for trampers and birdwatchers. There are plenty of tracks on which to explore the wilderness, ranging from short, easy trails, readily accessible on foot from Oban, to the epic North West Circuit, one of NZ's most isolated backcountry tramps.

Numerous operators offer guided tours: walking, driving, boating and by air, most focusing on wildlife with history slotted in. Independent walkers have plenty to choose from; visit Rakiura National Park Visitor Centre for details on local tramps, long and short, and huts along the way. The trails in DOC's *Stewart Island/Rakiura Short Walks* pamphlet ($2) would keep you busy for several days, and a bit less if you hire a bike from the Red Shed to fast-track the road sections. Longer tramps can also be shortened and indeed enhanced via an air hop with Stewart Island Flights (p606), which works with Seaview Water Taxis to offer the fulfilling day-long **Coast to Coast** cross-island hike.

If you haven't ever sea-fished, or just fancy it, this is the place for NZ boasts no better fishermen. Oh, and the answer to the question of swimming is definitely 'yes': yes, it is possible, and yes, you will probably freeze solid.

Short Walks

Observation Rock   WALKING
(Map p603) This short but quite sharp 15-minute climb through Oban's back streets reaches the Observation Rock lookout where there are panoramic views of Paterson Inlet, Mt Anglem and Rakeahua. The trail is clearly marked from the end of Leonard Rd, off Ayr St.

Ackers Point   WALKING
(Map p600) This three-hour return walk features an amble around the bay to a bushy track passing the historic 1835 **Stone House** at **Harrald Bay** before reaching **Ackers Point Lighthouse**, where there are wide views of Foveaux Strait and the chance to see blue penguins and a muttonbird (titi) colony.

Overnight Hikes

★ Rakiura Track   TRAMPING
(www.doc.govt.nz) One of NZ's nine Great Walks, the 39km, three-day Rakiura Track is a peaceful and leisurely loop that sidles around beautiful beaches before climbing over a 250m-high forested ridge and traversing the sheltered shores of Paterson Inlet/ Whaka ā Te Wera. It passes sites of historical interest and introduces many of the common sea and forest birds of the island.

SPOTTING A KIWI

Stewart Island/Rakiura is one of the few places on earth where you can spot a kiwi in the wild – and certainly the only place you're likely to see them in daylight. The bird has been around for 70 million years and is related to the now-extinct moa. Brown feathers camouflage the kiwi against its bush surroundings and a largely nocturnal lifestyle means spying one in the wild is a challenge.

As big as a barnyard chicken and estimated to number around 15,000 birds, the Stewart Island/Rakiura brown kiwi (*Apteryx australis lawryi,* also known as the tokoeka) is larger in size, longer in the beak and thicker in the legs than its northern cousins. They are also the only kiwi active during daylight hours, and birds may be seen around sunrise and sunset foraging for food in grassed areas and on beaches, where they mine sand-hoppers under washed-up kelp. If you spot one, keep silent, and stay still and well away. The birds' poor eyesight and single-mindedness in searching for food will often lead them to bump right into you.

Organised tours are your best bet for a sighting. Given the island's fickle weather – with tours sometimes cancelled – allow a few nights on the island if you're desperate for an encounter. Otherwise, it's sometimes possible to spot the birds in and around Oban itself. Head to the bushy fringes of the rugby field after sundown and you might get lucky. And let's face it, it's the most perfectly apposite place for such an occurrence.

Oban

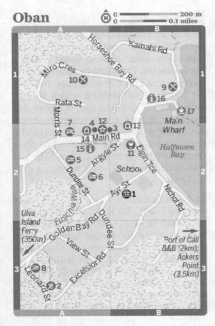

N 0 ——— 200 m
0 ——— 0.1 miles

Rakiura Track is actually only 32km long, but adding in the road sections at either end bumps it up to 39km, conveniently forming a circuit from Oban. It's a well-defined loop requiring a moderate level of fitness, suitable for tramping year-round. Being a Great Walk, it has been gravelled to eliminate most of the mud for which the island is infamous.

There are two Great Walk huts ($22) en route, which need to be booked in advance, either via the DOC website or in person at the Rakiura National Park Visitor Centre. There is a limit of two consecutive nights in any one hut. Camping ($6) is permitted at the Standard campsites near the huts, and also at Māori Beach.

North West Circuit Track   TRAMPING
(www.doc.govt.nz) The North West Circuit Track is Stewart Island/Rakiura's legendary tramp, a demanding coastal epic around a remote and natural coastline featuring isolated beaches, sand dunes, birds galore and miles of mud. It's 125km, and takes nine to 11 days, although there are several options for shortening it involving boats and planes.

The track begins and ends in Oban. There are well-spaced huts along the way, all of which are Standard ($5) except for two Great Walk Huts ($22), which must be booked in advance. A North West Circuit Pass ($35) provides for a night in each of the Standard huts.

Locator beacons are advised and be sure to call into DOC for up-to-date information and to purchase the essential topographical maps. You should also register your intentions at Adventuresmart (www.adventuresmart.org.nz) as this is no easy walk in the park.

☞ Tours

Ulva's Guided Walks   WALKING TOUR
(☎ 03-219 1216; www.ulva.co.nz) Focused firmly on birding and guided by expert naturalists, these excellent half-day tours ($125; transport included) explore Ulva Island. Book at the **Stewart Island Gift Shop** (Map p603;

📞 03-219 1453; www.stewartislandgiftshop.co.nz; 20 Main Rd, Oban; ⏱ 10.30am-5pm, reduced hours in winter). If you're a mad-keen twitcher, look for the Birding Bonanza trip ($395) on Ulva's website.

Bravo Adventure Cruises　　BIRDWATCHING
(📞 03-219 1144; www.kiwispotting.co.nz) Departing around sunset, Bravo runs small-group kiwi-spotting tours ($140) on a scenic reserve reached by a 30-minute boat trip and involving gentle walking through forest and on a beach.

Rakiura Charters & Water Taxi　　BOAT TOUR
(Map p603; 📞 0800 725 487, 03-219 1487; www.rakiuracharters.co.nz; 10 Main Rd, Oban; adult/child from $100/70) The most popular outing on the *Rakiura Suzy* is the half-day fishing cruise that stops in at the historic Whalers' Base. Trips can be tailored to suit timing and interests, such as wildlife-spotting and tramping.

Ruggedy Range
Wilderness Experience　　ECOTOUR
(Map p603; 📞 0274 784 433, 03-219 1066; www.ruggedyrange.com; 14 Main Rd, Oban) 🚶 Nature-guide Furhana runs small-group guided walks, including 'bird and forest' trips to Ulva Island (half-/full day $135/205); overnight trips to see kiwi in the wild (from $680); and a three-day guided wilderness walk where your packs are ferried to huts along the route ($970).

Lo-Loma Fishing Charters　　FISHING
(📞 03-219 1141, 027 393 8362; www.loloma.co.nz) Join Squizzy Squires on the *Lo-Loma* for a fun, hand-lining fishing trip.

Phil's Sea Kayak　　KAYAKING
(📞 027 444 2323; www.observationrocklodge.co.nz; trips from $90) Stewart Island/Rakiura's only kayaking guide, Phil runs trips on Paterson Inlet tailored for all abilities, with sightings of wildlife along the way.

Stewart Island Experience　　TOUR
(Map p603; 📞 0800 000 511, 03-219 0056; www.stewartislandexperience.co.nz; 12 Elgin Tce) 🚶 Runs 2½-hour Paterson Inlet cruises (adult/child $95/22), including an hour's guided walk on Ulva Island; and 1½-hour minibus tours of Oban and the surrounding bays ($45/22).

🛏 Sleeping

Finding accommodation can be difficult, especially in the low season when many places shut down. Booking ahead is highly recommended. The island has many holiday homes, which are often good value and offer the benefit of self-catering, which is especially handy if you do a spot of fishing (although many impose a two-night minimum stay or charge a surcharge for one night). Invercargill i-SITE (p593) and the Red Shed Oban Visitor Centre (p605) can help you book such rentals. See also www.stewartisland.co.nz.

Jo & Andy's B&B　　B&B $
(Map p603; 📞 03-219 1230; jariksem@clear.net.nz; 22 Main Rd, Oban; s $60, d & tw $90; @ 🛜) A great option for budget travellers, this cosy blue home squeezes in twin, double and single rooms that share bathroom facilities. A big breakfast of muesli, fruit and homemade bread prepares you for the most active of days. Jo is splendid company and there's hundreds of books if the weather packs up.

Bunkers Backpackers　　HOSTEL $
(Map p603; 📞 027 738 1796; www.bunkersbackpackers.co.nz; 15 Argyle St, Oban; dm/s/d $34/56/80; ⏱ closed mid-Apr–mid-Oct; 🛜) A converted wooden villa houses Stewart Island/Rakiura's best hostel option, which is somewhat squeezed but offers the benefits of a cosy lounge, sunny garden, inner village location and friendly vibe.

Bay Motel　　MOTEL $$
(Map p603; 📞 03-219 1119; www.baymotel.co.nz; 9 Dundee St, Oban; unit from $175; 🛜) 🚶 This hillside motel offers spacious, comfortable units with lots of light and views over the harbour. Some rooms have spa baths, all have kitchens and two are wheelchair-accessible. When you've exhausted the island's bustling after-dark scene, Sky TV's on hand for on-tap entertainment.

★ Observation Rock Lodge　　B&B $$$
(Map p603; 📞 03-219 1444; www.observationrocklodge.co.nz; 7 Leonard St, Oban; r $395; 🛜) Secluded in bird-filled bush and angled for sea, sunset and aurora views, Annett and Phil's lodge has three stylish, luxurious rooms with private decks and a shared lounge. Guided activities, a sauna, a hot tub

and Annett's gourmet dinners are included in the deluxe package ($780) or by arrangement as additions to the standard B&B rate.

Port of Call B&B B&B $$$
(☑ 03-219 1394, 027 2244 4722; www.portofcall.co.nz; Leask Bay Rd; s/d incl breakfast $320/385, cottages $175-250) Take in ocean views, relax before an open fire, or explore an isolated beach. Two cosy self-contained options are also available – The Bach, near the B&B (which is 2km southwest of Oban, near Acker's Point), and Turner Cottage in Oban. All have a two-night minimum stay, and guided walks and water-taxi trips can be arranged.

✖ Eating & Drinking

Stewart Island Smoked Salmon SEAFOOD $
(Map p603; ☑ 03-219 1323; www.siss.co.nz; 11 Miro Cres, Oban; 200g salmon $15) If you're a fan of freshly smoked salmon, pop up to the smokehouse to see if anyone's in. This sweet, hot-smoked fish is a tasty treat for a picnic or pasta.

Church Hill
Restaurant & Oyster Bar MODERN NZ $$$
(Map p603; ☑ 03-219 1123; www.churchhill.co.nz; 36 Kamahi Rd, Oban; lunch $14-28, dinner $37-39; ☺ noon-2.30pm Sun, 5.30pm-late daily) During summer this heritage villa's sunny deck provides hilltop views, and in cooler months you can get cosy inside beside the open fire. Big on local seafood, highlights include oysters, crayfish and salmon, prepared in refined modern style, followed by excellent desserts. Dinner bookings advisable.

South Sea Hotel PUB
(Map p603; ☑ 03-219 1059; www.stewart-island.co.nz; 26 Elgin Tce, Oban; ☺ 7am-9pm; ☎) Welcome to one of NZ's classic pubs, complete with stellar cod and chips, beer by the quart, a reliable cafe (mains $15 to $33) and plenty of friendly banter in the public bar. Great at any time of day (or night), try to wash up for the Sunday night quiz – an unforgettable slice of island life. Basic rooms are available, too.

☆ Entertainment

Bunkhouse Theatre CINEMA
(Map p603; ☑ 027 867 9381; www.bunkhousetheatre.co.nz; 10 Main Rd, Oban; tickets $10; ☺ screenings 11am, 2pm & 4pm) Oban's comfy little theatre screens the quirky, cute 40-minute film *A Local's Tail*, which provides an entertaining overview of Stewart Island/Rakiura history and culture. Jaffas and DIY popcorn.

🛍 Shopping

Glowing Sky CLOTHING
(Map p603; ☑ 03-219 1518; www.glowingsky.co.nz; Elgin Tce, Oban; ☺ 10.30am-3.30pm Mon-Thu, 10am-5pm Fri-Sun) Founded on the island but now produced on the mainland, Glowing Sky sells T-shirts with Māori designs and merino clothing.

ℹ Information

The best place for information is the **Invercargill i-SITE** (p593) back on the mainland.
Rakiura National Park Visitor Centre (Map p603; ☑ 03-219 0009; www.doc.govt.nz; 15 Main Rd, Oban; ☺ 8am-5pm Dec-Apr, 8.30am-4.30pm Mon-Fri, 10am-3pm Sat & Sun May-Nov) Stop in to obtain information on walking tracks, as well as hut bookings and passes, topographical maps, locator beacons, books and a few tramping essentials, such as insect repellent and wool socks. Information displays introduce Stewart Island/Rakiura's flora and fauna, while a video library provides entertainment and education (a good rainy day Plan B). Register your intentions here via Adventuresmart (www.adventuresmart.org.nz).

Red Shed Oban Visitor Centre (Map p603; ☑ 0800 000 511, 03-219 0056; www.stewart islandexperience.co.nz; 12 Elgin Tce, Oban; ☺ 7.30am-6.30pm Oct-Apr, 8am-5pm May-Sep) Conveniently located next to the wharf, this Stewart Island Experience booking office can hook you up with nearly everything on and around the island, including accommodation, guided tours, boat trips, bikes, scooters and rental cars.

Stewart Island/Rakiura has no banks. In the Four Square supermarket there's an ATM, which has a mind of its own; credit cards are accepted for most activities.

ℹ Getting There & Away

Stewart Island Experience (Map p603; ☑ 0800 000 511, 03-212 7660; www.stewart islandexperience.co.nz; Main Wharf, Oban; adult/child one way $175/38, return $130/65) The passenger-only ferry runs between Bluff and Oban up to four times daily (reduced in winter). Book a few days ahead in summer. The crossing takes one hour and can be a rough ride. The company also runs a shuttle between Bluff and Invercargill (adult/child $24/12) with pick-ups and drop-offs in Invercargill at the i-SITE, Tuatara Backpackers and Invercargill Airport.

Vehicles can be stored in a secure car park at Bluff for an additional cost.

Stewart Island Flights (☑ 03-218 9129; www. stewartislandflights.com; Elgin Tce, Oban; adult/child one way $123/80, return $213/128) Flies between the island and Invercargill three times daily, with good standby and over-60s discounts. The price includes transfers between the island airport and its office on the Oban waterfront.

ℹ Getting Around

Roads on the island are limited to Oban and the bays surrounding it. Stewart Island Experience rents cars and scooters from the **Red Shed** (p605).

Water taxis offer pick-ups and drop-offs to Ulva Island and to remote parts of the main island – a handy service for trampers. Operators include **Aihe Eco Charters & Water Taxi** (☑ 03-219 1066; www.aihe.co.nz), **Rakiura Charters & Water Taxi** (p604) and **Stewart Island Water Taxi & Eco Guiding** (☑ 0800 469 283, 03-219 1394; www.stewartislandwatertaxi.co.nz).

Understand New Zealand

New Zealand Today

New Zealand has had a bad run on the disaster front in recent years, with devastating earth-quakes and mining and helicopter tragedies rattling the national psyche. But things are looking up: tourism is booming, the arts and local craft-beer scenes are effervescing, and the Kiwi rugby and cricket teams are in awesome form – there's plenty to put a smile on the country's collective dial.

Best on Film

Lord of the Rings trilogy (Sir Peter Jackson; 2001–03) Hobbits, dragons and magical rings – Tolkien's vision comes to life.

The Hobbit trilogy (Sir Peter Jackson; 2012–14) Hairy feet on the move – more eye-popping Tolkienism.

The Piano (Jane Campion; 1993) A piano and its owners arrive on a mid-19th century West Coast beach.

Whale Rider (Niki Caro; 2002) Magical tale of family and heritage on the East Coast.

Once Were Warriors (Lee Tamahori; 1994) Brutal relationship dysfunction in South Auckland.

Best in Print

The Luminaries (Eleanor Catton; 2013) Man Booker Prize winner: crime and intrigue on the West Coast goldfields.

Mister Pip (Lloyd Jones; 2007) Tumult on Bougainville, mirroring Dickens' *Great Expectations*.

Live Bodies (Maurice Gee; 1998) Post-WWII loss and redemption in New Zealand.

The 10pm Question (Kate de Goldi; 2009) Twelve-year-old Frankie grapples with life's big anxieties.

The Collected Stories of Katherine Mansfield (2006) Kathy's greatest hits.

Reasons to be Cheerful

Christchurch's recovery from the 2010 and 2011 earth-quakes is ongoing, producing as much good news and bad. On one hand it is testing relationships between the citizens and government agencies, as tough decisions are made about fix-ups and pay-outs. On the other, Christchurch's recovery reinforces Kiwis' perceptions of themselves as 'battlers' with strong communities and civic pride.

Speaking of pride, New Zealanders have been flush with it of late. Following the All Blacks' success at the 2011 Rugby World Cup at home, the beloved national team beat arch-rivals Australia 34-17 in the 2015 final in London. In doing so, NZ became the first country ever to win back-to-back Rugby World Cups, capping off a remarkable four-year period in which the All Blacks lost just three (and drew one) of their 53 matches between World Cup wins.

But the depth of Kiwi sporting talent ranges beyond the rugby pitch. In 2015 the national men's cricket team, the Black Caps, made the final of the Cricket World Cup for the first time, stringing together an impressive series of test cricket results both before and afterwards. Other Kiwi sporting stars making their mark include golfing sensation Lydia Ko, who became world No 1 in 2015, aged just 17; NBA seven-footer Steven Adams (from Rotorua), currently playing with the Oklahoma City Thunder; quadruple US IndyCar champion Scott Dixon; and Valerie Adams, the greatest female shot-putter the world has ever seen (also from Rotorua – something in the water?).

On the arts front, Canadian director James Cameron has set up a rural home base near Wellington, and will create three *Avatar* sequels in the capital from 2016, bringing substantial investment and cementing NZ's reputation as a world-class film-making destination.

And at the end of a long day, Kiwi craft beer is consolidating itself at the top of the global scene. You can't go anywhere in NZ these days without stumbling across these microbrewed delights: local, flavoursome, potent and passionately marketed. The NZ wine industry is looking nervously over its shoulder, wondering where all its sav blanc drinkers have gone.

A New Flag?

At the time of writing, New Zealanders were in the throes of deciding whether or not to adopt a new national flag. What was wrong with the old one? Nothing, really, it was just fine. Except that it had a big British Union Jack in the corner, harking back to the days when NZ was a British colony.

In a post-colonial age – and in keeping with NZ's progressive way of viewing itself and its place on the planet – the suggestion was that perhaps the time had come to cut this last remaining tie with Mother England and unite, free and independent, beneath a new national flag. Of course, NZ has been united, free and independent for many decades, but changing the flag seemed to be the last symbolic gesture. Canada pulled off this manoeuvre with aplomb back in 1965 – why not New Zealand?

A public referendum to decide which of five proposed designs Kiwis preferred happened in late 2015. The winner was the 'Silver Fern Flag', replacing the Union Jack with a black-backed silver fern. Yet the second referendum, held in 2016, determined that New Zealanders preferred the old flag to the challenger. Was it a waste of time and taxpayers' money, or an important step in furthering New Zealand's independence? Time will tell.

The Trans-Pacific Partnership

In October 2015 after seven long years of negotiations, the Trans-Pacific Partnership was ratified by 12 nations with Pacific interests – Australia, Brunei, Canada, Chile, Japan, Malaysia, Mexico, New Zealand, Peru, Singapore, the United States and Vietnam – bringing into effect a broad raft of initiatives aimed at boosting relationships and economies within the region. For New Zealand, the new agreement will cut taxes and tariffs on NZ exports, which it's hoped will have a beneficial effect on exports, particularly in the dairy sector.

Critics of the TPP suggest that it will lead to increased costs of basic medicines in NZ, and that it grants too much freedom to large corporations to sidestep international and internal labour, environmental, health, financial and food-safety laws, angling for profit rather than social benefit. It remains to be seen whether the TPP will sink or swim – watch this space.

POPULATION: **4.64 MILLION**

AREA: **268,021 SQ KM**

GDP GROWTH: **2.4% (2015)**

INFLATION: **0.4% (2015)**

UNEMPLOYMENT: **6% (2015)**

if New Zealand were 100 people

65 would be European
15 would be Māori
12 would be Asian
7 would be Pacific Islanders
1 would be Other

where they live
(% of New Zealanders)

63 North Island
20 South Island
10 Australia
5 Rest of the World
2 Travelling

population per sq km

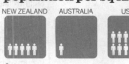

NEW ZEALAND   AUSTRALIA   USA

🧍 = 3 people

History

by James Belich

New Zealand's history is not long, but it is fast. In less than a thousand years these islands have produced two new peoples: the Polynesian Māori and European New Zealanders. The latter are often known by their Māori name, 'Pākehā' (though not all like the term). NZ shares some of its history with the rest of Polynesia, and with other European settler societies, but has unique features as well. It is the similarities that make the differences so interesting, and vice versa.

Making Māori

One of New Zealand's foremost modern historians, James Belich has written a number of books on NZ history and hosted the TV documentary series *The New Zealand Wars*.

Despite persistent myths, there is no doubt that the first settlers of NZ were the Polynesian forebears of today's Māori. Beyond that, there are a lot of question marks. Exactly where in east Polynesia did they come from – the Cook Islands, Tahiti...maybe the Marquesas? When did they arrive? Did the first settlers come in one group or several? Some evidence, such as the diverse DNA of the Polynesian rats that accompanied the first settlers, suggests multiple founding voyages. On the other hand, only rats and dogs brought by the founders have survived, not the more valuable pigs and chickens. The survival of these cherished animals would have had high priority, and their failure to be successfully introduced suggests fewer voyages.

For a thorough overview of NZ history from Gondwanaland to today, visit www.history-nz.org.

NZ seems small compared with Australia, but is bigger than Britain, and very much bigger than other Polynesian islands. Its regions vary wildly in environment and climate. Prime sites for first settlement were warm coastal gardens for the food plants brought from Polynesia (kumara or sweet potato, gourd, yam and taro); sources of workable stone for knives and adzes; and areas with abundant big game. NZ has no native land mammals apart from a few species of bat, but 'big game' is no exaggeration: the islands were home to a dozen species of moa (a large flightless bird), the largest of which weighed up to 240kg, about twice the size of an ostrich. There were also other species of flightless birds and large sea mammals such as fur seals, all unaccustomed to being hunted. For people from small Pacific islands, this was like hitting the jackpot. The

TIMELINE	AD 1000–1200	1642	1769
	Possible date of the arrival of Māori in NZ. Solid archaeological evidence points to about AD 1200, but much earlier dates have been suggested for the first human impact on the environment.	First European contact: Abel Tasman arrives on an expedition from the Dutch East Indies (Indonesia) to find the 'Great South Land'. His party leaves without landing, after a sea skirmish with Māori.	European contact recommences with visits by James Cook and Jean de Surville. Despite some violence, both manage to communicate with Māori. This time NZ's link with the outside world proves permanent.

THE MYTHICAL MORIORI

One of NZ's most persistent legends is that Māori found mainland NZ already occupied by a more peaceful and racially distinct Melanesian people, known as the Moriori, whom they exterminated. This myth has been regularly debunked by scholars since the 1920s, but somehow hangs on.

To complicate matters, there were real 'Moriori', and Māori did treat them badly. The real Moriori were the people of the Chatham Islands, a windswept group about 900km east of the mainland. They were, however, fully Polynesian, and descended from Māori – 'Moriori' was their version of the same word. Mainland Māori arrived in the Chathams in 1835, as a spin-off of the Musket Wars, killing some Moriori and enslaving the rest, but they did not exterminate them.

first settlers spread far and fast, from the top of the North Island to the bottom of the South Island within the first 100 years High-protein diets are likely to have boosted population growth.

By about 1400, however, with big-game supply dwindling, Māori economics turned from big game to small game – forest birds and rats – and from hunting to gardening and fishing. A good living could still be made, but it required detailed local knowledge, steady effort and complex communal organisation, hence the rise of the Māori tribes. Competition for resources increased, conflict did likewise, and this led to the building of increasingly sophisticated fortifications, known as *pa*. Vestiges of *pa* earthworks can still be seen around the country (on the hilltops of Auckland, for example).

Māori had no metals and no written language (and no alcoholic drinks or drugs). But their culture and spiritual life was rich and distinctive. Below Ranginui (sky father) and Papatuanuku (earth mother) were various gods of land, forest and sea, joined by deified ancestors over time. The mischievous demigod Māui was particularly important. In legend, he vanquished the sun and fished up the North Island before meeting his death between the thighs of the goddess Hine-nui-te-pō in an attempt to conquer the human mortality embodied in her. Traditional Māori performance art, the group singing and dancing known as *kapa haka*, has mesmerising power, even for modern audiences. Visual art, notably woodcarving, is something special – 'like nothing but itself', in the words of 18th-century explorer-scientist, Sir Joseph Banks.

Rumours of late survivals of the giant moa bird abound, but none have been authenticated. So if you see a moa on your travels, photograph it – you have just made the greatest zoological discovery of the last 100 years.

Enter Europe

NZ became an official British colony in 1840, but the first authenticated contact between Māori and the outside world took place almost two centuries earlier in 1642, in Golden Bay at the top of the South Island.

1772	1790s	1818–36	1837
Marion du Fresne's French expedition arrives; it stays for some weeks at the Bay of Islands. Relations with Māori start well, but a breach of Māori *tapu* (sacred law) leads to violence.	Whaling ships and sealing gangs arrive in the country. Relations are established with Māori, with Europeans depending on the contact for essentials such as food, water and protection.	Intertribal Māori 'Musket Wars' take place: tribes acquire muskets and win bloody victories against tribes without them. The war tapers off in 1836, probably due to the equal distribution of weapons.	Possums are introduced to NZ from Australia. Brilliant.

CAPTAIN JAMES COOK

If aliens ever visit earth, they may wonder what to make of the countless obelisks, faded plaques and graffiti-covered statues of a stiff, wigged figure gazing out to sea from Alaska to Australia, from NZ to North Yorkshire, from Siberia to the South Pacific. James Cook (1728–79) explored more of the Earth's surface than anyone in history, and it's impossible to travel the Pacific without encountering the captain's image and his controversial legacy in the lands he opened to the West.

For a man who travelled so widely, and rose to such fame, Cook came from an extremely pinched and provincial background. The son of a day labourer in rural Yorkshire, he was born in a mud cottage, had little schooling, and seemed destined for farm work – and for his family's grave plot in a village churchyard. Instead, Cook went to sea as a teenager, worked his way up from coal-ship servant to naval officer, and attracted notice for his exceptional charts of Canada. But Cook remained a little-known second lieutenant until, in 1768, the Royal Navy chose him to command a daring voyage to the South Seas.

In a converted coal ship called *Endeavour*, Cook sailed to Tahiti, and then became the first European to land in New Zealand and the east coast of Australia. Though the ship almost sank after striking the Great Barrier Reef, and 40% of the crew died from disease and accidents, the *Endeavour* limped home in 1771. On a return voyage (1772–75), Cook became the first navigator to pierce the Antarctic Circle and circled the globe near its southernmost latitude, demolishing the ancient myth that a vast, populous and fertile continent surrounded the South Pole. Cook also criss-crossed the Pacific from Easter Island to Melanesia, charting dozens of islands between. Though islanders killed and cooked 10 of his sailors, the captain remained strikingly sympathetic to islanders. 'Notwithstanding they are cannibals,' he wrote, 'they are naturally of a good disposition.'

On Cook's final voyage (1776–79), in search of a northwest passage between the Atlantic and Pacific, he became the first European to visit Hawaii, and coasted America from Oregon to Alaska. Forced back by Arctic pack ice, Cook returned to Hawaii, where he was killed during a skirmish with islanders who had initially greeted him as a Polynesian god. In a single decade of discovery, Cook had filled in the map of the Pacific and, as one French navigator put it, 'left his successors with little to do but admire his exploits'.

But Cook's travels also spurred colonisation of the Pacific, and within a few decades of his death, missionaries, whalers, traders and settlers began transforming (and often devastating) island cultures. As a result, many indigenous people now revile Cook as an imperialist villain who introduced disease, dispossession and other ills to the region (hence the frequent vandalising of Cook monuments). However, as islanders revive traditional crafts and practices, from tattooing to *tapa* (traditional barkcloth), they have turned to the art and writing of Cook and his men as a resource for cultural renewal. For good and ill, a Yorkshire farm boy remains the single most significant figure in the shaping of the modern Pacific.

Tony Horwitz is a Pulitzer-winning reporter and nonfiction author. In researching Blue Latitudes *(or* Into the Blue*), Tony travelled the Pacific – 'boldly going where Captain Cook has gone before'.*

1840	1844	1858	1860–69
Starting at Waitangi in the Bay of Islands on 6 February, around 500 chiefs countrywide sign the Treaty of Waitangi to 'settle' sovereignty once and for all. NZ becomes a nominal British colony.	Young Ngāpuhi chief Hone Heke challenges British sovereignty, first by cutting down the British flag at Kororareka (now Russell), then by sacking the town itself. The ensuing Northland war continues until 1846.	The Waikato chief Te Wherowhero is installed as the first Māori King.	First and Second Taranaki wars, starting with the controversial swindling of Māori land by the government at Waitara, and continuing with outrage over the confiscation of more land as a result.

Two Dutch ships sailed from Indonesia, to search for southern land and anything valuable it might contain. The commander, Abel Tasman, was instructed to pretend to any natives he might meet 'that you are by no means eager for precious metals, so as to leave them ignorant of the value of the same'.

When Tasman's ships anchored in the bay, local Māori came out in their canoes to make the traditional challenge: friends or foes? Misunderstanding this, the Dutch challenged back, by blowing trumpets. When a boat was lowered to take a party between the two ships, it was attacked. Four crewmen were killed. Tasman sailed away and did not come back; nor did any other European for 127 years. But the Dutch did leave a name: initially 'Statenland', which was then changed to 'Nieuw Zeeland' or 'New Sealand'.

Contact between Māori and Europeans was renewed in 1769, when English and French explorers arrived, under James Cook and Jean de Surville. Relations were more sympathetic, and exploration continued, motivated by science, profit and political rivalry. Cook made two more visits between 1773 and 1777, and there were further French expeditions.

Unofficial visits, by whaling ships in the north and sealing gangs in the south, began in the 1790s. The first mission station was founded in 1814, in the Bay of Islands, and was followed by dozens of others: Anglican, Methodist and Catholic. Trade in flax and timber generated small European–Māori settlements by the 1820s. Surprisingly, the most numerous category of European visitor was probably American. New England whaling ships favoured the Bay of Islands for rest and recreation; 271 called there between 1833 and 1839 alone. To whalers, 'rest and recreation' meant sex and drink. Their favourite haunt, the little town of Kororareka (now Russell), was known to the missionaries as 'the hellhole of the Pacific'. New England visitors today might well have distant relatives among the local Māori.

One or two dozen bloody clashes dot the history of Māori–European contact before 1840 but, given the number of visits, inter-racial conflict was modest. Europeans needed Māori protection, food and labour, and Māori came to need European articles, especially muskets. Whaling stations and mission stations were linked to local Māori groups by intermarriage, which helped keep the peace. Most warfare was between Māori and Māori: the terrible intertribal 'Musket Wars' of 1818–36. Because Northland had the majority of early contact with Europe, its Ngāpuhi tribe acquired muskets first. Under their great general Hongi Hika, Ngāpuhi then raided south, winning bloody victories against tribes without muskets. Once they acquired muskets, these tribes then saw off Ngāpuhi, but also raided further south in their turn. The domino effect continued to the far south of the South Island in 1836. The missionaries

Abel Tasman named NZ 'Statenland', assuming it was connected to Staten Island near Argentina. It was subsequently named after the province of Zeeland in Tasman's native Holland.

Similarities in language between Māori and Tahitian indicate close contact in historical times. Māori is about as similar to Tahitian as Spanish is to French, despite the 4294km separating these island groups.

1861	1863–64	1868–72	1886–87
Gold discovered in Otago by Gabriel Read, an Australian prospector. As a result, the population of Otago climbs from less than 13,000 to over 30,000 in six months.	Waikato Land War. Up to 5000 Māori resist an invasion mounted by 20,000 imperial, colonial and 'friendly' Māori troops. Despite surprising successes, Māori are defeated and much land is confiscated.	East Coast war. Te Kooti, having led an escape from his prison on the Chatham Islands, leads a holy guerrilla war in the Urewera region. He finally retreats to establish the Ringatu Church.	Tuwharetoa tribe gifts the mountains of Ruapehu, Ngauruhoe and Tongariro to the government to establish what is only the world's fourth national park.

claimed that the Musket Wars then tapered off through their influence, but the restoration of the balance of power through the equal distribution of muskets was probably more important.

Europe brought such things as pigs (at last) and potatoes, which benefited Māori, while muskets and diseases had the opposite effect. The negative effects have been exaggerated, however. Europeans expected peoples like the Māori to simply fade away at contact, and some early estimates of Māori population were overly high – up to one million. Current estimates are between 85,000 and 110,000 for 1769. The Musket Wars killed perhaps 20,000, and new diseases did considerable damage, too (although NZ had the natural quarantine of distance: infected Europeans usually recovered or died during the long voyage, and smallpox, for example, which devastated indigenous North Americans, did not make it here). By 1840, Māori had been reduced to about 70,000, a decline of at least 20%. Māori bent under the weight of European contact, but they certainly did not break.

Making Pākehā

By 1840, Māori tribes described local Europeans as 'their Pākehā', and valued the profit and prestige they brought. Māori wanted more of both, and concluded that accepting nominal British authority was the way to get them. At the same time, the British government was overcoming its reluctance to undertake potentially expensive intervention in NZ. It too was influenced by profit and prestige, but also by humanitarian considerations. It believed, wrongly but sincerely, that Māori could not handle the increasing scale of unofficial European contact. In 1840, the two peoples struck a deal, symbolised by the treaty first signed at Waitangi on 6 February that year. The Treaty of Waitangi now has a standing not dissimilar to that of the Constitution in the US, but is even more contested. The original problem was a discrepancy between British and Māori understandings of it. The English version promised Māori full equality as British subjects in return for complete rights of government. The Māori version also promised that Māori would retain their chieftainship, which implied local rights of government. The problem was not great at first, because the Māori version applied outside the small European settlements. But as those settlements grew, conflict brewed.

In 1840 there were only about 2000 Europeans in NZ, with the shanty town of Kororareka as the capital and biggest settlement. By 1850 six new settlements had been formed with 22,000 settlers between them. About half of these had arrived under the auspices of the New Zealand Company and its associates. The company was the brainchild of Edward Gibbon Wakefield, who also influenced the settlement of South Australia. Wakefield hoped to short-circuit the barbarous frontier phase of set-

The Waitangi Treaty Grounds, where the Treaty of Waitangi was first signed in 1840, is now a tourist attraction for Kiwis and non-Kiwis alike. Each year on 6 February, Waitangi hosts treaty commemorations and protests.

'Kaore e mau te rongo – ake, ake!' (Peace never shall be made – never, never!) War chief Rewi Maniapoto in response to government troops at the battle of Orakau, 1864

1893	1901	1908	1914–18
NZ becomes the first country in the world to grant the vote to women, following a campaign led by Kate Sheppard, who petitioned the government for years.	New Zealand politely declines the invitation to join the new Commonwealth of Australia, but thanks for asking.	NZ physicist Ernest Rutherford is awarded the Nobel Prize in chemistry for 'splitting the atom', investigating the disintegration of elements and the chemistry of radioactive substances.	NZ's contribution to WWI is staggering: for a country of just over one million people, about 100,000 NZ men serve overseas. Some 60,000 become casualties, mostly on the Western Front in France.

tlement with 'instant civilisation', but his success was limited. From the 1850s his settlers, who included a high proportion of upper-middle-class gentlefolk, were swamped by succeeding waves of immigrants that continued to wash in until the 1880s. These people were part of the great British and Irish diaspora that also populated Australia and much of North America, but the NZ mix was distinctive. Lowland Scots settlers were more prominent in NZ than elsewhere, for example, with the possible exception of parts of Canada. NZ's Irish, even the Catholics, tended to come from the north of Ireland. NZ's English tended to come from the counties close to London. Small groups of Germans, Scandinavians and Chinese made their way in, though the last faced increasing racial prejudice from the 1880s, when the Pākehā population reached half a million.

The Ministry for Culture & Heritage's history website (www. nzhistory.net.nz) is an excellent source of info on NZ history.

LAND WARS

Five separate major conflicts made up what are now collectively known as the New Zealand Wars (also referred to as the Land Wars or Māori Wars). Starting in Northland and moving throughout the North Island, the wars had many complex causes, but *whenua* (land) was the one common factor. In all five wars, Māori fought both for and against the NZ government, on whose side stood the Imperial British Army, Australians and NZ's own Armed Constabulary. Land confiscations imposed on the Māori as punishment for involvement in these wars are still the source of conflict today, with the government struggling to finance compensation for what are now acknowledged to have been illegal seizures.

Northland War (1844–45) 'Hone Heke's War' began with the famous chopping of the flagpole at Kororareka (now Russell) and 'ended' at Ruapekapeka (south of Kawakawa). In many ways, this was almost a civil war between rival Ngāpuhi factions, with the government taking one side against the other.

First Taranaki War (1860–61) Starting in Waitara, the first Taranaki War inflamed the passions of Māori across the North Island.

Waikato War (1863–64) The largest of the five wars. Predominantly involving Kingitanga, the Waikato War was caused in part by what the government saw as a challenge to sovereignty. However, it was land, again, that was the real reason for friction. Following defeats such as Rangiriri, the Waikato people were pushed entirely from their own lands, south into what became known as the King Country.

Second Taranaki War (1865–69) Caused by Māori resistance to land confiscations stemming from the first Taranaki War, this was perhaps the war in which the Māori came closest to victory, under the brilliant, one-eyed prophet-general Titokowaru. However, once he lost the respect of his warriors (probably through an indiscretion with the wife of one of his warriors), the war, too, was lost.

East Coast War (1868–72) Te Kooti's holy guerilla war.

1931	1935–49	1936	1939–45
A massive earthquake in Napier and Hastings kills 131 people.	First Labour government in power, under Michael Savage. This government creates NZ's pioneering version of the welfare state, and also takes some independent initiatives in foreign policy.	NZ aviatrix Jean Batten becomes the first aviator to fly solo from Britain to NZ.	NZ troops back Britain and the Allied war effort during WWII; from 1942 around 100,000 Americans arrive to protect NZ from the Japanese.

Much of the mass immigration from the 1850s to the 1870s was assisted by the provincial and central governments, which also mounted large-scale public works schemes, especially in the 1870s under Julius Vogel. In 1876 Vogel abolished the provinces on the grounds that they were hampering his development efforts. The last imperial governor with substantial power was the talented but Machiavellian George Grey, who ended his second governorship in 1868. Thereafter, the governors (governors-general from 1917) were largely just nominal heads of state; the head of government, the premier or prime minister, had more power. The central government, originally weaker than the provincial governments, the imperial governor and the Māori tribes, eventually exceeded the power of all three.

The Māori tribes did not go down without a fight, however. Indeed, their resistance was one of the most formidable ever mounted against European expansion, comparable to that of the Sioux and Seminole in the US. The first clash took place in 1843 in the Wairau Valley, now a wine-growing district. A posse of settlers set out to enforce the myth of British control, but encountered the reality of Māori control. Twenty-two settlers were killed, including Wakefield's brother, Arthur, along with about six Māori. In 1845 more serious fighting broke out in the Bay of Islands, when Hone Heke sacked a British settlement. Heke and his ally Kawiti baffled three British punitive expeditions, using a modern variant of the traditional *pa* fortification. Vestiges of these innovative earthworks can still be seen at Ruapekapeka (south of Kawakawa). Governor Grey claimed victory in the north, but few were convinced at the time. Grey had more success in the south, where he arrested the formidable Ngāti Toa chief Te Rauparaha, who until then wielded great influence on both sides of Cook Strait. Pākehā were able to swamp the few Māori living in the South Island, but the fighting of the 1840s confirmed that the North Island at that time comprised a European fringe around an independent Māori heartland.

In the 1850s settler population and aspirations grew, and fighting broke out again in 1860. The wars burned on sporadically until 1872 over much of the North Island. In the early years a Māori nationalist organisation, the King Movement, was the backbone of resistance. In later years some remarkable prophet-generals, notably Titokowaru and Te Kooti, took over. Most wars were small-scale, but the Waikato war of 1863–64 was not. This conflict, fought at the same time as the American Civil War, involved armoured steamships, ultramodern heavy artillery, telegraph and 10 proud British regular regiments. Despite the odds, Māori forces won several battles, such as that at Gate Pa, near Tauranga, in 1864. But in the end they were ground down by European numbers and resources. Māori political, though not cultural, independence ebbed away in the last decades of the 19th century. It finally expired when police invaded its last sanctuary, the Urewera Mountains, in 1916.

'I believe we were all glad to leave New Zealand. It is not a pleasant place. Amongst the natives there is absent that charming simplicity...and the greater part of the English are the very refuse of society.' Charles Darwin, referring to Kororareka (Russell), in 1860.

Maurice Shadbolt's *Season of the Jew* (1987) is a semifictionalised story of bloody campaigns led by warrior Te Kooti against the British in Poverty Bay in the 1860s. Te Kooti and his followers compared themselves to the Israelites cast out of Egypt. To find out more about the New Zealand Wars, visit www.newzealandwars.co.nz.

1948	1953	1973	1974
Maurice Scheslinger invents the Buzzy Bee, NZ's most famous children's toy.	New Zealander Edmund Hillary, with Tenzing Norgay, 'knocks the bastard off'; the pair become the first men to reach the summit of Mt Everest.	Fledgling Kiwi prog-rockers Split Enz enter a TV talent quest...finishing second to last.	Pacific Island migrants who have outstayed visas are subjected to Dawn Raids (crackdowns by immigration police) under Robert Muldoon and the National government. These raids continue until the early 1980s.

Welfare & Warfare

From the 1850s to the 1880s, despite conflict with Māori, the Pākehā economy boomed on the back of wool exports, gold rushes and massive overseas borrowing for development. The crash came in the 1880s, when NZ experienced its Long Depression. In 1890 the Liberals came to power, and stayed there until 1912, helped by a recovering economy. The Liberals were NZ's first organised political party, and the first of several governments to give NZ a reputation as 'the world's social laboratory'. NZ became the first country in the world to give women the vote in 1893, and introduced old-age pensions in 1898. The Liberals also introduced a long-lasting system of industrial arbitration, but this was not enough to prevent bitter industrial unrest in 1912-13. This happened under the conservative 'Reform' government, which had replaced the Liberals in 1912. Reform remained in power until 1928, and later transformed itself into the National Party. Renewed depression struck in 1929, and the NZ experience of it was as grim as any. The derelict little farmhouses still seen in rural areas often date from this era.

In 1935 a second reforming government took office: the First Labour government, led by Michael Joseph Savage, easily NZ's favourite Australian. For a time the Labour government was considered the most socialist government outside Soviet Russia. But, when the chips were down in Europe in 1939, Labour had little hesitation in backing Britain.

NZ had also backed Britain in the Boer War (1899-1902) and WWI (1914-18), with dramatic losses in WWI in particular. You can count the cost in almost any little NZ town: a central square or park will contain a memorial lined with names - more for WWI than WWII. Even in WWII, however, NZ did its share of fighting: 100,000 or so New Zealanders fought in Europe and the Middle East. New Zealand, a peaceful-seeming country, has spent much of its history at war. In the 19th century it fought at home; in the 20th, overseas.

Better Britons?

British visitors have long found NZ hauntingly familiar. This is not simply a matter of the British and Irish origin of most Pākehā. It also stems from the tightening of NZ links with Britain from 1882, when refrigerated cargoes of food were first shipped to London. By the 1930s, giant ships carried frozen meat, cheese and butter, as well as wool, on regular voyages taking about five weeks one way. The NZ economy adapted to the feeding of London, and cultural links were also enhanced. NZ children studied British history and literature, not their own. NZ's leading scientists and writers, such as Ernest Rutherford and Katherine Mansfield, gravitated to Britain. This tight relationship has been described as

'God's own country, but the devil's own mess.' NZ Prime Minister (1893-1906) Richard 'King Dick' Seddon, explaining the source of the country's self-proclaimed nickname 'Godzone'.

Wellington-born Nancy Wake (codenamed 'The White Mouse') led a guerrilla attack against the Nazis with a 7000-strong army. She had the multiple honours of being the Gestapo's most wanted person and the most decorated Allied servicewoman of WWII.

1981	1985	1992	1995
Springbok rugby tour divides the nation. Many New Zealanders show a strong anti-apartheid stance by protesting the games. Other Kiwis feel that sport and politics should not mix, and support the South African tour going ahead.	*Rainbow Warrior* sunk in Auckland Harbour by French government agents to prevent the Greenpeace protest ship from making its intended voyage to Moruroa, where the French government is conducting a nuclear-testing program.	Government begins reparations for land confiscated in the Land Wars, and confirms Māori fishing rights in the 'Sealord deal'. Major settlements follow, including, in 1995, reparations for the Waikato land confiscations.	Peter Blake and Russell Coutts win the Americas Cup for NZ, sailing *Black Magic*; red socks become a matter of national pride.

'recolonial', but it is a mistake to see NZ as an exploited colony. Average living standards in NZ were normally better than in Britain, as were the welfare and lower-level education systems. New Zealanders had access to British markets and culture, and they contributed their share to the latter as equals. The list of 'British' writers, academics, scientists, military leaders, publishers and the like who were actually New Zealanders is long. Indeed, New Zealanders, especially in war and sport, sometimes saw themselves as a superior version of the British – the Better Britons of the south. The NZ–London relationship was rather like that of the American Midwest and New York.

'Recolonial' NZ prided itself, with some justice, on its affluence, equality and social harmony. But it was also conformist, even puritanical. Until the 1950s it was technically illegal for farmers to allow their cattle to mate in fields fronting public roads, for moral reasons. The 1953 Marlon Brando movie, *The Wild One,* was banned until 1977. Sunday newspapers were illegal until 1969, and full Sunday trading was not allowed until 1989. Licensed restaurants hardly existed in 1960, nor did supermarkets or TV. Notoriously, from 1917 to 1967, pubs were obliged to shut at 6pm. Yet the puritanical society of Better Britons was never the whole story. Opposition to Sunday trading stemmed, not so much from belief in the sanctity of the Sabbath, but from the belief that workers should have weekends, too. Six o'clock closing was a standing joke in rural areas, notably the marvellously idiosyncratic region of the South Island's West Coast. There was always something of a Kiwi counterculture, even before imported countercultures took root from the 1960s onward.

There were also developments in cultural nationalism, beginning in the 1930s but really flowering in the 1970s. Writers, artists and film-makers were by no means the only people who 'came out' in that era.

Coming In, Coming Out

The 'recolonial' system was shaken several times after 1935, but managed to survive until 1973, when Mother England ran off and joined the Franco–German commune now known as the EU. NZ was beginning to develop alternative markets to Britain, and alternative exports to wool, meat and dairy products. Wide-bodied jet aircraft were allowing the world and NZ to visit each other on an increasing scale. NZ had only 36,000 tourists in 1960, compared with more than two million a year now. Women were beginning to penetrate first the upper reaches of the workforce and then the political sphere. Gay people came out of the closet, despite vigorous efforts by moral conservatives to push them back in. University-educated youths were becoming more numerous and more assertive.

Scottish influence can still be felt in NZ, particularly in the south of the South Island. NZ has more Scottish pipe bands per capita than Scotland itself.

The Six o'clock Swill referred to the frantic after-work drinking at pubs when men tried to drink as much as possible from 5.05pm until the 6pm strict closing time.

2004	2010	2011	2011
Māori TV begins broadcasting – for the first time a channel committed to NZ content and the revitalisation of Māori language and culture hits the small screen.	A cave-in at Pike River coalmine on the South Island's West Coast kills 29 miners.	A severe earthquake strikes Christchurch, killing 185 people and badly damaging the central business district.	NZ hosts and wins the Rugby World Cup for just the second time; brave France succumbs 8-7 in the final.

From 1945, Māori experienced both a population explosion and massive urbanisation. In 1936, Māori were 17% urban and 83% rural. Fifty years later, these proportions had reversed. The immigration gates, which until 1960 were pretty much labelled 'whites only', widened, first to allow in Pacific Islanders for their labour, and then to allow in (East) Asians for their money. These transitions would have generated major socioeconomic change whatever happened in politics. But most New Zealanders associate the country's recent 'Big Shift' with the politics of 1984.

That year, NZ's third great reforming government was elected – the Fourth Labour government, led nominally by David Lange, and in fact by Roger Douglas, the Minister of Finance. This government adopted an antinuclear foreign policy, delighting the left, and a more-market economic policy, delighting the right. NZ's numerous economic controls were dismantled with breakneck speed. Middle NZ was uneasy about the antinuclear policy, which threatened NZ's ANZUS alliance with Australia and the US. But in 1985 French spies sank the antinuclear protest ship *Rainbow Warrior* in Auckland Harbour, killing one crewman. The lukewarm American condemnation of the French act brought middle NZ in behind the antinuclear policy, which became associated with national independence. Other New Zealanders were uneasy about the more-market economic policy, but failed to come up with a convincing alternative. Revelling in their new freedom, NZ investors engaged in a frenzy of speculation, and suffered even more than the rest of the world from the economic crash of 1987.

The early 21st century is an interesting time for NZ. Like NZ food and wine, film and literature are flowering as never before, and the new ethnic mix is creating something very special in popular music. There are continuities, however – the pub, the sportsground, the quarter-acre section, the bush, the beach and the bach – and they too are part of the reason people like to come here. Understanding that New Zealand has a rich culture and an intriguing history, as well as a superb natural environment, will double the bang for your buck.

New Zealand's staunch anti-nuclear stance earned it the nickname 'The Mouse that Roared'.

2013	2013	2015	2015
New Zealand becomes one of just 15 countries in the world to legally recognise same-sex marriage.	Auckland teenager Ella Yelich-O'Connor, aka Lorde, hits No 1 on the US music charts with her mesmeric, chant-like tune 'Royals'.	New Zealand's beloved All Blacks win back-to-back Rugby World Cups in England, defeating arch-rivals Australia 34-17 in the final.	Having watched NZ win its third Rugby World Cup, legendary former All Black Jonah Lomu dies aged 40 after a long battle with kidney disease.

Environment

by Vaughan Yarwood

New Zealand is a young country – its present shape is less than 10,000 years old. Having broken away from the supercontinent of Gondwanaland (which included Africa, Australia, Antarctica and South America) in a stately geological dance some 85 million years ago, it endured continual uplift and erosion, buckling and tearing, and the slow fall and rise of the sea as ice ages came and went.

The Land

Straddling the boundary of two great colliding slabs of the earth's crust – the Pacific plate and the Indian/Australian plate – to this day NZ remains the plaything of nature's strongest forces.

Vaughan Yarwood is a historian and travel writer who is widely published in New Zealand and internationally. Get a hold of his book *The History Makers: Adventures in New Zealand Biography*.

The result is one of the most varied and spectacular landscapes in the world, ranging from snow-dusted mountains and drowned glacial valleys to rainforests, dunelands and an otherworldly volcanic plateau. It is a diversity of landforms you would expect to find across an entire continent rather than a small archipelago in the South Pacific.

Evidence of NZ's tumultuous past is everywhere. The South Island's mountainous spine – the 650km-long ranges of the Southern Alps – is a product of the clash of the two plates; the result of a process of rapid lifting that, if anything, is accelerating today. Despite NZ's highest peak, Aoraki/Mt Cook, losing 10m from its summit overnight in a 1991 landslide, the Alps are on an express elevator that, without erosion and landslides, would see them reach 10 times their present height within a few million years.

On the North Island, the most impressive changes have been wrought by volcanoes. Auckland is built on an isthmus peppered by scoria cones, on many of which you can still see the earthworks of *pa* (fortified villages) built by early Māori. The city's biggest and most recent volcano, 600-year-old Rangitoto Island, is just a short ferry ride from the downtown wharves. Some 300km further south, the classically shaped cone of snowcapped Mt Taranaki overlooks tranquil dairy pastures.

But the real volcanic heartland runs through the centre of the North Island, from the restless bulk of Mt Ruapehu in Tongariro National Park, northeast through the Rotorua lake district out to NZ's most active volcano, White Island, in the Bay of Plenty. Called the Taupo Volcanic Zone, this great 250km-long rift valley – part of a volcano chain known as the 'Pacific Ring of Fire' – has been the seat of massive eruptions that have left their mark on the country physically and culturally.

Most spectacular were the eruptions from the volcano that created Lake Taupo. Considered the world's most productive volcano in terms of the amount of material ejected, Taupo last erupted 1800 years ago in a display that was the most violent anywhere on the planet within the past 5000 years.

You can experience the aftermath of volcanic destruction on a smaller scale at Te Wairoa (the Buried Village (p297)), near Rotorua on the shores of Lake Tarawera. Here, partly excavated and open to the public, lie the remains of a 19th-century Māori village overwhelmed when nearby Mt Tarawera erupted without warning. The famous Pink and White Terraces (one of several claimants to the popular title 'eighth wonder of the world') were destroyed overnight by the same upheaval.

But when nature sweeps the board clean with one hand she often rebuilds with the other: Waimangu Volcanic Valley (p294), born of all that geothermal violence, is the place to go to experience the hot earth up close and personal amid geysers, silica pans, bubbling mud pools, and the world's biggest hot spring; or you can wander around Rotorua's Whakarewarewa Village (p282), where descendants of Māori displaced by the eruption live in the middle of steaming vents and prepare food for visitors in boiling pools.

A second by-product of movement along the tectonic plate boundary is seismic activity – earthquakes. Not for nothing has New Zealand been called 'the Shaky Isles'. Most quakes only rattle the glassware, but one was indirectly responsible for creating an internationally celebrated tourist attraction: in 1931, an earthquake measuring 7.9 on the Richter scale levelled the Hawke's Bay city of Napier, causing huge damage and loss of life. Napier was rebuilt almost entirely in the then-fashionable art-deco architectural style, and walking its streets today you can relive its brash exuberance in this mecca for lovers of art deco.

However, the North Island doesn't have a monopoly on earthquakes. In September 2010 Christchurch was rocked by a magnitude 7.1 earthquake. Less than six months later, in February 2011, a magnitude 6.3 quake destroyed much of the city's historic heart and claimed 185 lives, making it the country's second-deadliest natural disaster. NZ's second city continues to be jostled by aftershocks as it builds anew.

The South Island can also see some evidence of volcanism – if the remains of the old volcanoes of Banks Peninsula weren't there to repel the sea, the vast Canterbury Plains, built from alpine sediment washed down the rivers from the Alps, would have eroded long ago.

But in the south it is the Southern Alps themselves that dominate, dictating settlement patterns, throwing down engineering challenges and offering outstanding recreational opportunities. The island's mountainous backbone also helps shape the weather, as it stands in the path of the prevailing westerly winds that roll in, moisture-laden, from the Tasman Sea. As a result, bush-clad lower slopes of the western Southern Alps are among the wettest places on earth, with an annual precipitation of some 15,000mm. Having lost its moisture, the wind then blows dry across the eastern plains towards the Pacific coast.

The North Island has a more even rainfall and is spared the temperature extremes of the South, which can plunge when a wind blows in from Antarctica. The important thing to remember, especially if you are tramping at high altitude, is that NZ has a maritime climate. This means weather can change with lightning speed, catching out the unprepared.

Native Fauna

New Zealand may be relatively young, geologically speaking, but its plants and animals go back a long way. The tuatara, for instance, an ancient reptile unique to these islands, is a Gondwanaland survivor closely related to the dinosaurs, while many of the distinctive flightless birds here (ratites) have distant African and South American cousins.

Due to its long isolation, the country became a veritable warehouse of unique and varied plants, most of which are found nowhere else. And with separation of the landmass occurring before mammals appeared on the scene, birds and insects have evolved in spectacular ways to fill the gaps.

NZ is one of the most spectacular places in the world to see geysers. Rotorua's short-lived Waimangu geyser, formed after the Mt Tarawera eruption, was once the world's largest, often gushing to a dizzying height of 400m.

Nature Guide to the New Zealand Forest by J Dawson and R Lucas is a beautifully photographed foray into the world of NZ's forests. These lush treasure houses are home to ancient species dating from the time of the dinosaurs.

ENVIRONMENT NATIVE FAUNA

The now-extinct flightless moa, the largest of which grew to 3.5m tall and weighed over 200kg, browsed open grasslands much as cattle do today (skeletons can be seen at Auckland Museum), while the smaller kiwi still ekes out a nocturnal living rummaging among forest leaf litter for insects and worms, much as small mammals do elsewhere. One of the country's most ferocious-looking insects, the mouse-sized giant weta, meanwhile, has taken on a scavenging role elsewhere filled by rodents.

As one of the last places on Earth to be colonised by humans, NZ was for millennia a safe laboratory for such risky evolutionary strategies, but with the arrival of Māori, and Europeans soon after, things went downhill fast.

ENVIRONMENTAL ISSUES IN NEW ZEALAND

Employing images of untouched landscapes, Tourism New Zealand's 100% Pure marketing campaign has been critically acclaimed, and is the envy of tourism organisations worldwide. Such portrayals of a pristine environment have, however, been repeatedly rumbled in recent years as environmentalists – and the media – place NZ's 'clean green' credentials under the microscope. Mining, offshore oil and gas exploration, pollution, biodiversity loss, conservation funding cuts, and questionable urban planning – there have been endless hooks for bad-news stories, and numerous reasons to protest.

A 2013 university study found that New Zealanders rate water quality as the country's most serious environmental issue. Their concern is well founded, with one-third of the country's 425 lakes, rivers and beaches deemed unsafe for swimming; research from diverse quarters confirms that the health of NZ's waterways is in serious decline. The primary culprit is 'dirty dairying' – cow effluent leaching into freshwater ecosystems, carrying with it high levels of nitrates, as well as bacteria and parasites such as E. coli and giardia.

The dairy industry is NZ's biggest export earner, and it continues to boom with more land being converted to dairy farming, despite clear evidence of its detrimental effects, which include the generation of half of NZ's greenhouse gas emissions. Present Parliamentary Commissioner for the Environment, Jan Wright, has referred to the matter as a 'classic economy versus environment dilemma'. NZ's dominant dairy cooperative – Fonterra – has expressed a commitment to upping its game to ensure farm management practices 'preserve New Zealand's clean green image'; some farmers are indeed cleaning up their act.

There are many other threats to water and land ecosystems, including proliferation of invasive weeds and pests, with biodiversity loss continuing in parallel. The worst offenders are possums, stoats and rats, which chomp through swaths of forest and kill wildlife, particularly birds. Controversy rages at the Department of Conservation (DOC) use of 1080 poison (sodium fluoroacetate) to control these pests, despite it being sanctioned by prominent environmental groups such as Forest & Bird and the Parliamentary Commissioner for the Environment. Vehement opposition to 1080 is expressed by such diverse camps as hunters and animal-rights activists, who cite detriments such as by-kill and the poison's transmittal into waterways.

This is just one of DOC's increasing range of duties, which includes processing applications for mining within the conservation estate. Public feeling runs high on this issue, too, as demonstrated by recent ructions over opencast coalmining on the West Coast's Denniston Plateau. DOC has increasingly found itself in the thick of it; at the same time, budget cuts and major internal restructuring have left it appearing thinner on the ground.

Meanwhile, the principle legislation governing the NZ environment – the 1991 Resource Management Act – has been undergoing controversial reforms suspected of opening the door to further exploitation of the environment. NGOs and community groups – ever-vigilant and already making major contributions to the welfare of NZ's environment – will find plenty to keep them occupied in the years to come.

Sarah Bennett & Lee Slater

Many endemic creatures, including moa and the huia, an exquisite songbird, were driven to extinction, and the vast forests were cleared for their timber and to make way for agriculture. Destruction of habitat and the introduction of exotic animals and plants have taken a terrible environmental toll and New Zealanders are now fighting a rearguard battle to save what remains.

Bird-Watching

The first Polynesian settlers found little in the way of land mammals – just two species of bat – but forests, plains and coasts alive with birds. Largely lacking the bright plumage found elsewhere, NZ's birds – like its endemic plants – have an understated beauty that does not shout for attention.

Among the most musical is the bellbird, common in both native and exotic forests everywhere except Northland, though like many birds it is more likely to be heard than seen. Its call is a series of liquid bell notes, most often sounded at dawn or dusk.

The tui, another nectar eater and the country's most beautiful songbird, is a great mimic, with an inventive repertoire that includes clicks, grunts and chuckles. Notable for the white throat feathers that stand out against its dark plumage, the tui often feeds on flax flowers in suburban gardens but is most at home in densely tangled forest ('bush' to New Zealanders).

Fantails are commonly encountered on forest trails, swooping and jinking to catch insects stirred up by passing hikers; while pukeko, elegant swamp-hens with blue plumage and bright-red beaks, are readily seen along wetland margins and even on the sides of roads nearby – be warned, they have little road sense.

If you spend any time in the South Island high country, you are likely to come up against the fearless and inquisitive kea – an uncharacteristically drab green parrot with bright-red underwings. Kea are common in the car parks of the Fox and Franz Josef Glaciers, where they hang out for food scraps or tear rubber from car windscreens.

Then there is the takahe, a rare flightless bird thought extinct until a small colony was discovered in 1948; and the equally flightless kiwi, NZ's national emblem and the nickname for New Zealanders themselves. The kiwi has a round body covered in coarse feathers, strong legs and a long, distinctive bill with nostrils at the tip for sniffing out food. It is not easy to find them in the wild, but they can be seen in simulated environments. One of the best is the Otorohanga Kiwi House & Native Bird Park (p187), which also has native falcons, moreporks (owls) and weka.

To get a feel for what the bush used to be like, take a trip to Tiritiri Matangi Island just north of Auckland. This regenerating island is an open sanctuary and one of the country's most successful exercises in community-assisted conservation.

Marine Mammal-Watching

Kaikoura, on the northeast coast of the South Island, is NZ's nexus of marine mammal-watching. The main attraction here is whale-watching. The sperm whale, the largest toothed whale, is pretty much a year-round resident here, and depending on the season you may also see migrating humpback whales, pilot whales, blue whales and southern right whales. Other mammals – including fur seals and dusky dolphins – are seen year-round.

Kaikoura is also a hot-spot for swimming with dolphins, with pods of up to 500 dusky dolphins commonly seen. Dolphin swimming is common elsewhere in NZ, with the animals gathering off the North Island near Whakatane, Paihia, Tauranga and in the Hauraki Gulf, and off Akaroa on the South Island's Banks Peninsula. Seal swimming also happens in Kaikoura and in Abel Tasman National Park.

B Heather and H Robertson's *Field Guide to the Birds of New Zealand* is a comprehensive guide for bird-watchers and a model of helpfulness for anyone even casually interested in the country's remarkable bird life. Another good guide is *Birds of New Zealand: Locality Guide* by Stuart Chambers.

Travellers seeking sustainable tourism operators should look for businesses accredited with Qualmark Green (www.qualmark. co.nz) or those listed at Organic Explorer (www. organicexplorer. co.nz).

But these kinds of wildlife encounters are controversial. Whale populations around the world have declined rapidly over the past 200 years: the same predictable migration habits that once made the giants easy prey for whalers nowadays make them easy targets for whale-watchers. As NZ's whale-watching industry has grown, so has concern over its impact. At the centre of the debate is the practice of swimming with whales and dolphins. While it's undoubtedly one of the more unusual experienc-

National Parks & Forest Parks

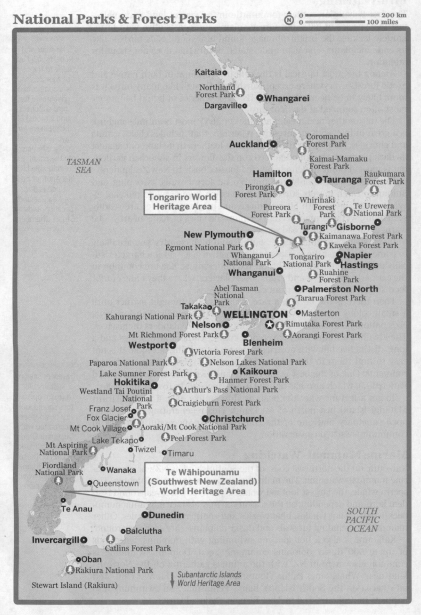

es you can have on the planet, some suggest that human interaction with these marine mammals – especially with mothers and calves, when they are at their most vulnerable – has a disruptive effect on behaviours and breeding patterns. Taking a longer view, others say that given humanity's historic propensity for slaughtering whales by the tens of thousands, it's time we gave them a little peace and quiet.

That said, if whale-watching is a bucket-list essential for you, there are few better places to do it than New Zealand. The Department of Conservation's strict guidelines and protocols ensure that all operators are licensed and monitored. Still – give yourself a few days to do it so that there is no pressure on the operator to 'chase' whales in order to keep you happy. And if you feel your whale-, dolphin- or seal-swim operator has breached the boundaries and 'hassled' the animals in any way, report them to DOC immediately.

National Parks

A third of the country – more than 50,000 sq km – is protected in environmentally important parks and reserves that embrace almost every conceivable landscape: from mangrove-fringed inlets in the north to the snow-topped volcanoes of the Central Plateau, and from the forested fastness of the Ureweras in the east to the Southern Alps' majestic mountains, glaciers and fiords. The 14 national parks and more than 25 marine reserves and parks, along with numerous forest parks, offer huge scope for wilderness experiences, ranging from climbing, snow skiing and mountain biking to tramping, kayaking and trout fishing.

Three places are World Heritage Areas: NZ's Subantarctic Islands, Tongariro National Park, and Te Wāhipounamu (Southwest New Zealand), an amalgam of several national parks in southwest NZ that boast the world's finest surviving Gondwanaland plants and animals in their natural habitats.

Access to the country's wild places is relatively straightforward, though huts on walking tracks require passes and may need to be booked in advance. In practical terms, there is little difference for travellers between a national park and a forest park, though dogs are not allowed in national parks without a permit. Camping is possible in all parks, but may be restricted to dedicated camping grounds – check with DOC first.

The Department of Conservation website (www. doc.govt.nz) has useful information on the country's national parks, tracks and walkways. It also lists backcountry huts and campsites.

Māori Culture

by John Huria

'Māori' once just meant 'common' or 'everyday', but now it means...let's just begin by saying that there is a lot of 'then' and a lot of 'now' in the Māori world. Sometimes the cultural present follows on from the past quite seamlessly; sometimes things have changed hugely; sometimes we just want to look to the future.

John Huria (Ngāi Tahu, Muaūpoko) has an editorial, research and writing background with a focus on Māori writing and culture. He was senior editor for Māori publishing company Huia (NZ) and now runs an editorial and publishing services company, Ahi Text Solutions Ltd (www.ahitext solutions.co.nz).

Māori today are a diverse people. Some are engaged with traditional cultural networks and pursuits; others are occupied with adapting tradition and placing it into a dialogue with globalising culture. The Māori concept of *whanaungatanga* – family relationships – is central to the culture: families spread out from the *whānau* (extended family) to the *hapū* (subtribe) and *iwi* (tribe) and even, in a sense, beyond the human world and into the natural and spiritual worlds.

Māori are New Zealand's *tangata whenua* (people of the land), and the Māori relationship with the land has developed over hundreds of years of occupation. Once a predominantly rural people, many Māori now live in urban centres, away from their traditional home base. But it's still common practice in formal settings to introduce oneself by referring to home: an ancestral mountain, river, sea or lake, or an ancestor. There's no place like home, but it's good to be away as well.

If you're looking for a Māori experience in NZ you'll find it – in performance, in conversation, in an art gallery, on a tour...

Māori Then

Some three millennia ago people began moving eastward into the Pacific, sailing against the prevailing winds and currents (hard to go out, easier to return safely). Some stopped at Tonga and Samoa, and others settled the small central East Polynesian tropical islands.

Kupe's passage is marked around NZ: he left his sails (Nga Ra o Kupe) near Cape Palliser as triangular land-forms; he named the two islands in Wellington Harbour Matiu and Makoro after his daughters; his blood stains the red rocks of Wellington's south coast.

The Māori colonisation of Aotearoa began from an original homeland known to Māori as Hawaiki. Skilled navigators and sailors travelled across the Pacific, using many navigational tools – currents, winds, stars, birds and wave patterns – to guide their large, double-hulled ocean-going craft to a new land. The first of many was the great navigator Kupe, who arrived, the story goes, chasing an octopus named Muturangi. But the distinction of giving NZ its well-known Māori name – Aotearoa – goes to his wife, Kuramarotini, who cried out, '*He ao, he ao tea, he ao tea roa!*' (A cloud, a white cloud, a long white cloud!).

Kupe and his crew journeyed around the land, and many places around Cook Strait (between the North and South Islands) and the Hokianga in Northland still bear the names that the crew gave them and the marks of their passage. Kupe returned to Hawaiki, leaving from (and naming) Northland's Hokianga. He gave other seafarers valuable navigational information. And then the great *waka* (ocean-going craft) began to arrive.

HOW THE WORLD BEGAN

In the Māori story of creation, first there was the void, then the night, then Ranginui (sky father) and Papatuanuku (earth mother) came into being, embracing with their children nurtured between them. But nurturing became something else. Their children were stifled in the darkness of their embrace. Unable to stretch out to their full dimensions and struggling to see clearly in the darkness, their children tried to separate them. Tāwhirimātea, the god of winds, raged against them; Tūmatauenga, the god of war, assaulted them. Each god child in turn tried to separate them, but still Rangi and Papa pressed against each other. And then Tāne Mahuta, god of the great forests and of humanity, placed his feet against his father and his back against his mother and slowly, inexorably, began to move them apart. Then came the world of light, of demigods and humanity.

In this world of light Māui, the demigod ancestor, was cast out to sea at birth and was found floating in his mother's topknot. He was a shape-shifter, becoming a pigeon or a dog or an eel if it suited his purposes. He stole fire from the gods. Using his grandmother's jawbone, he bashed the sun so that it could only limp slowly across the sky, so that people would have enough time during the day to get things done (if only he would do it again!). Using the South Island as a canoe, he used the jawbone as a hook to fish up Te Ika-a-Māui (the fish of Māui) – the North Island. And, finally, he met his end trying to defeat death itself. The goddess of death, Hine-nui-te-pō, had obsidian teeth in her vagina (obsidian is a volcanic glass that takes a razor edge when chipped). Māui attempted to reverse birth (and hence defeat death) by crawling into her birth canal to reach her heart as she slept. A small bird – a fantail – laughed at the absurd sight. Hine-nui-te-pō awoke, and crushed Māui between her thighs. Death one, humanity nil.

The *waka* that the first settlers arrived on, and their landing places, are immortalised in tribal histories. Well-known *waka* include *Tākitimu, Kurahaupō, Te Arawa, Mataatua, Tainui, Aotea* and *Tokomaru*. There are many others. Māori trace their genealogies back to those who arrived on the *waka* (and further back as well).

What would it have been like making the transition from small tropical islands to a much larger, cooler land mass? Goodbye breadfruit, coconuts, paper mulberry; hello moa, fernroot, flax – and immense space (relatively speaking). NZ has over 15,000km of coastline. Rarotonga, by way of contrast, has a little over 30km. There was land, lots of it, and a flora and fauna that had developed more or less separately from the rest of the world for 80 million years. There was an untouched, massive fishery. There were great seaside mammalian convenience stores – seals and sea lions – as well as a fabulous array of birds.

The early settlers went on the move, pulled by love, by trade opportunities and greater resources; pushed by disputes and threats to security. When they settled, Māori established *mana whenua* (regional authority), whether by military campaigns, or by the peaceful methods of intermarriage and diplomacy. Looking over tribal history it's possible to see the many alliances, absorptions and extinctions that went on.

Histories were carried by the voice, in stories, songs and chants. Great stress was placed on accurate learning – after all, in an oral culture where people are the libraries, the past is always a generation or two away from oblivion.

Māori lived in *kainga* (small villages), which often had associated gardens. Housing was quite cosy by modern standards – often it was

Māori legends are all around you as you tour NZ: Māui's *waka* became today's Southern Alps; a *taniwha* formed Lake Waikaremoana in its death throes; and a rejected Mt Taranaki walked into exile from the central North Island mountain group, carving the Whanganui River.

hard to stand upright while inside. From time to time people would leave their home base and go to harvest seasonal foods. When peaceful life was interrupted by conflict, the people would withdraw to *pa* (fortified dwelling places).

And then Europeans began to arrive.

Māori Today

Today's culture is marked by new developments in the arts, business, sport and politics. Many historical grievances still stand, but some *iwi* (Ngāi Tahu and Tainui, for example) have settled historical grievances and are major forces in the NZ economy. Māori have also addressed the decline in Māori language use by establishing *kohanga reo, kura kaupapa Māori* and *wananga* (Māori-medium preschools, schools and universities). There is now a generation of people who speak Māori as a first language. There is a network of Māori radio stations, and Māori TV attracts a committed viewership. A recently revived Māori event is becoming more and more prominent – Matariki, or Māori New Year. The constellation Matariki is also known as the Pleiades. It begins to rise above the horizon in late May or early June and its appearance traditionally signals a time for learning, planning and preparing as well as singing, dancing and celebrating. Watch out for talks and lectures, concerts, dinners, and even formal balls.

The best way to learn about the relationship between the land and the *tangata whenua* (people of the land) is to get out there and start talking with Māori.

Religion

Christian churches and denominations are important in the Māori world: televangelists, mainstream churches for regular and occasional worship, and two major Māori churches (Ringatu and Ratana) – we've got it all.

But in the (non-Judeo-Christian) beginning there were the *atua Māori,* the Māori gods, and for many Māori the gods are a vital and relevant force still. It is common to greet the earth mother and sky father when speaking formally at a *marae* (meeting-house complex). The gods are represented in art and carving, sung of in *waiata* (songs), invoked through *karakia* (prayer and incantation) when a meeting house is opened, when a *waka* is launched, even (more simply) when a meal is served. They are spoken of on the *marae* and in wider Māori contexts. The traditional Māori creation story is well known and widely celebrated.

You can check out a map that shows *iwi* distribution and a good list of *iwi* websites on Wikipedia (www.wikipedia.org/wiki/list_of_iwi).

The Arts

There are many collections of Māori *taonga* (treasures) around the country. Some of the largest and most comprehensive are at Wellington's Te Papa Museum (p357) and the Auckland Museum (p68). Canterbury Museum (p463) in Christchurch also has a good collection, and Hokitika Museum (p442) has an exhibition showing the story of *pounamu* (nephrite jade, or greenstone).

You can stay up to date with what's happening in the Māori arts by reading *Mana* magazine (available from most newsagents), listening to *iwi* stations (www.irirangi.net) or weekly podcasts from Radio New Zealand (www.radionz.co.nz). Māori TV also has regular features on the Māori arts – check out www.maoritelevision.com.

Māori TV went to air in 2004, an emotional time for many Māori who could at last see their culture, their concerns and their language in a mass medium. Over 90% of content is NZ made, and programs are in both Māori and English: they're subtitled and accessible to everyone. If you want to really get a feel for the rhythm and meter of spoken Māori from the comfort of your own chair, switch to Te Reo (www.maori television.com/tv/te-reo-channel), a Māori-language-only channel.

Ta Moko

Ta Moko is the Māori art of tattoo, traditionally worn by men on their faces, thighs and buttocks, and by women on their chins and lips. *Moko* were permanent grooves tapped into the skin using pigment (made from burnt caterpillar or kauri gum soot) and bone chisels (fine, sharp combs for broad work, and straight blades for detailed work). Museums in the major centres – Auckland Museum (p68), Te Papa (Wellington) (p357) and Canterbury Museum (Christchurch) (p463) – all display traditional implements for *ta moko*.

The modern tattooist's gun is common now, but bone chisels are coming back into use for Māori who want to reconnect with tradition. Since the general renaissance in Māori culture in the 1960s, many artists have taken up *ta moko* and now many Māori wear *moko* with quiet pride and humility.

Can visitors get involved, or even get some work done? The term *kirituhi* (skin inscriptions) has arisen to describe Māori-motif-inspired modern tattoos that non-Māori can wear.

> See Ngahuia Te Awekotuku's book *Mau Moko: The World of Maori Tattoo* (2007) for the big picture, with powerful, beautiful images and an incisive commentary.

Carving

Traditional Māori carving, with its intricate detailing and curved lines, can transport the viewer. It's quite amazing to consider that it was done with stone tools, themselves painstakingly made, until the advent of iron (nails suddenly became very popular).

Some major traditional forms are *waka* (canoes), *pataka* (storage buildings), and *wharenui* (meeting houses). You can see sublime examples of traditional carving at Te Papa (p357) in Wellington, and at the following:

Auckland Museum (p68) Māori Court

Hells Gate (p295) Carver in action every day; near Rotorua

Otago Museum (p519) Nice old *waka* and *whare runanga* (meeting house) carvings; Dunedin

Putiki Church (p233) Interior covered in carvings and *tukutuku* (wall panels); Whanganui

Taupo Museum (p253) Carved meeting house

Te Manawa (p245) Museum with a Māori focus; Palmerston North

Waikato Museum (p169) Beautifully carved *waka taua* (war canoe); Hamilton

Wairakei Terraces (p253) Carved meeting house; Taupo

Waitangi Treaty Grounds (p142) *Whare runanga* and *waka taua*

Whakarewarewa Thermal Village (p282) The 'living village' – carving, other arts, meeting house and performance; Rotorua

Whanganui Regional Museum (p233) Wonderful carved *waka*

The apex of carving today is the *whare whakairo* (carved meeting house). A commissioning group relates its history and ancestral stories to a carver, who then draws (sometimes quite loosely) on traditional motifs to interpret or embody the stories and ancestors in wood or composite fibreboard.

Rongomaraeroa Marae by artist Cliff Whiting, at Te Papa in Wellington, is a colourful example of a contemporary re-imagining of a traditional art form. The biggest change in carving (as with most traditional

VISITING MARAE

As you travel around NZ, you will see many *marae* complexes. Often *marae* are owned by a descent group. They are also owned by urban Māori groups, schools, universities and church groups, and they should only be visited by arrangement with the owners. Some *marae* that may be visited include: **Huria Marae** (☏07-578 7838; www.ngaitamarawaho. co.nz/marae; Te Kaponga St, Judea) **FREE** in Tauranga; **Koriniti Marae** (Map p240; ☏06-345 0303, 021 0292 4785; Koriniti Pa Rd; ⏰9am-5pm) **FREE** on the Whanganui River Rd; **Te Manuka Tutahi Marae** (p311) in Whakatane; and the *marae* at **Te Papa museum** (p357) in Wellington.

Marae complexes include a *wharenui* (meeting house), which often embodies an ancestor. Its ridge is the backbone, the rafters are ribs, and it shelters the descendants. There is a clear space in front of the *wharenui* (ie the *marae atea*). Sometimes there are other buildings: a *wharekai* (dining hall); a toilet and shower block; perhaps even classrooms, play equipment and the like.

Hui (gatherings) are held at *marae*. Issues are discussed, classes conducted, milestones celebrated and the dead farewelled. Te reo Māori (the Māori language) is prominent, and sometimes the only language used.

Visitors sleep in the meeting house if a *hui* goes on for longer than a day. Mattresses are placed on the floor, someone may bring a guitar, and stories and jokes always go down well as the evening stretches out...

The Powhiri

If you visit a *marae* as part of an organised group, you'll be welcomed in a *powhiri*. The more common ones are outlined here.

There may be a *wero* (challenge). Using *taiaha* (quarter-staff) moves a warrior will approach the visitors and place a baton on the ground for a visitor to pick up.

There is a *karanga* (ceremonial call). A woman from the host group calls to the visitors and a woman from the visitors responds. Their long, high, falling calls begin to overlap and interweave and the visiting group walks on to the *marae atea*. It is then time for *whaikōrero* (speechmaking). The hosts welcome the visitors, the visitors respond. Speeches are capped off by a *waiata* (song), and the visitors' speaker places a *koha* (gift, usually an envelope of cash) on the *marae*. The hosts then invite the visitors to *hariru* (shake hands) and *hongi*. Visitors and hosts are now united and will share light refreshments or a meal.

The Hongi

Press forehead and nose together firmly, shake hands, and perhaps offer a greeting such as '*Kia ora*' or '*Tēnā koe*'. Some prefer one press (for two or three seconds, or longer), others prefer two shorter (press, release, press). Men and women sometimes kiss on one cheek. Some people mistakenly think the *hongi* is a pressing of noses only (awkward to aim!) or the rubbing of noses (even more awkward).

Tapu

Tapu (spiritual restrictions) and *mana* (power and prestige) are taken seriously in the Māori world. Sit on chairs or seating provided (never on tables), and walk around people, not over them. The *powhiri* is *tapu,* and mixing food and *tapu* is right up there on the offence-o-meter. Do eat and drink when invited to do so by your hosts. You needn't worry about starvation: an important Māori value is *manaakitanga* (kindness).

Depending on area, the *powhiri* has gender roles: women *karanga* (call), men *whaikōrero* (orate); women lead the way on to the *marae,* men sit on the *paepae* (speakers' bench at the front). In a modern context, the debate around these roles continues.

arts) has been in the use of new mediums and tools. Rangi Kipa uses a synthetic polymer called Corian to make his *hei tiki*, the same stuff that is used to make kitchen benchtops. You can check out his gallery at www.rangikipa.com.

Weaving

Weaving was an essential art that provided clothing, nets and cordage, footwear for rough country travel, mats to cover earthen floors, and *kete* (bags) to carry stuff in. Many woven items are beautiful as well as practical. Some were major works – *korowai* (cloaks) could take years to finish. Woven predominantly with flax and bird feathers, they are worn now on ceremonial occasions – a stunning sight.

Working with natural materials for the greater good of the people involved getting things right by maintaining the supply of raw material and ensuring that it worked as it was meant to. Protocols were necessary, and women were dedicated to weaving under the aegis of the gods. Today, tradition is greatly respected, but not all traditions are necessarily followed.

Flax was (and still is) the preferred medium for weaving. To get a strong fibre from flax leaves, weavers scraped away the leaves' flesh with a mussel shell, then pounded until it was soft, dyed it, then dried it. But contemporary weavers are using everything in their work: raffia, copper wire, rubber – even polar fleece and garden hoses!

The best way to experience weaving is to contact one of the many weavers running workshops. By learning the art you'll appreciate the examples of weaving in museums even more. And if you want your own? Woven *kete* and backpacks have become fashion accessories and are on sale in most cities. Weaving is also found in dealer art galleries around the country.

Haka

Experiencing *haka* can get the adrenaline flowing, as it did for one Pākehā observer in 1929 who thought of dark Satanic mills: 'They looked like fiends from hell wound up by machinery'. *Haka* can be awe-inspiring; they can also be uplifting. The *haka* is not only a war dance – it is used to welcome visitors, honour achievement, express identity or to put forth very strong opinions.

Haka involve chanted words, vigorous body movements, and *pukana* (when performers distort their faces, eyes bulging with the whites showing, perhaps with tongue extended).

The well-known *haka* 'Ka Mate', performed by the All Blacks before rugby test matches, is credited to the cunning fighting chief Te Rauparaha. It celebrates his escape from death. Chased by enemies, he hid himself in a food pit. After they had left, a friendly chief named Te Whareangi (the 'hairy man' referred to in the *haka*), let him out; he climbed out into the sunshine and performed 'Ka Mate'.

You can experience *haka* at various cultural performances, including at Mitai Maori Village (p293), Tamaki Maori Village (p293), Te Puia (p282) and Whakarewarewa Thermal Village (p282) in Rotorua; Ko Tane (p469) at Willowbank in Christchurch; and Maori Tours (p399) in Kaikoura.

But the best displays of *haka* are at the national Te Matatini National Kapa Haka Festival (www.tematatini.co.nz), when NZ's top groups compete. It's held every two years (in odd-numbered years).

Read Hirini Moko Mead's *Tikanga Māori*, Pat and Hiwi Tauroa's *Visiting a Marae*, and Anne Salmond's *Hui* for detailed information on Māori customs.

Contemporary Theatre

The 1970s saw the emergence of many Māori playwrights and plays, and theatre is a strong area of the Māori arts today. Māori theatre drew heavily on the traditions of the *marae*. Instead of dimming the lights and immediately beginning the performance, many Māori theatre groups began with a stylised *powhiri,* had space for audience members to respond to the play, and ended with a *karakia* or a farewell.

Taki Rua is an independent producer of Māori work for both children and adults and has been in existence for over 25 years. As well as staging its shows in the major centres, it tours most of its work – check out its website (www.takirua.co.nz) for the current offerings. Māori drama is also often showcased at the professional theatres in the main centres as well as the biennial New Zealand Festival (p361). Hone Kouka and Briar Grace-Smith (both have published playscripts available) have toured their works around NZ and to festivals in the UK.

For information on Māori arts today, check out Toi Māori at www.maoriart.org.nz.

Contemporary Dance

Contemporary Māori dance often takes its inspiration from *kapa haka* (cultural dance) and traditional Māori imagery. The exploration of pre-European life also provides inspiration. For example, a Māori choreographer, Moss Patterson, used *kokowai* (a body-adorning paste made from reddish clay and shark oil) as the basis of his most recent piece of the same name.

NZ's leading specifically Māori dance company is the Atamira Dance Collective (www.atamiradance.co.nz), which has been producing critically acclaimed, beautiful and challenging work since 2000. If that sounds too earnest, another choreographer to watch out for is Mika Torotoro, who happily blends *kapa haka*, drag, opera, ballet and disco. You can check out clips of his work at www.mika.co.nz.

Māori Film-Making

Although there had already been successful Māori documentaries (*Patu!* and the *Tangata Whenua* series are brilliant, and available from some urban video stores), it wasn't until 1987 that NZ had its first fictional feature-length movie by a Māori director, with Barry Barclay's *Ngati*. Mereta Mita was the first Māori woman to direct a fiction feature, with *Mauri* (1988). Both Mita and Barclay had highly political aims and ways of working, which involved a lengthy pre-production phase, during which they would consult with and seek direction from their *kaumātua* (elders). Films with significant Māori participation or control include the harrowing *Once Were Warriors* and the uplifting *Whale Rider*. Oscar-shortlisted Taika Waititi, of Te Whanau-a-Apanui descent, wrote and directed *Eagle vs Shark* and *Boy*.

The New Zealand Film Archive (www.filmarchive.org.nz) is a great place to experience Māori film, with most showings being either free or relatively inexpensive. It has offices in Auckland and Wellington.

Māori Writing

There are many novels and collections of short stories by Māori writers, and personal taste will govern your choices. How about approaching Māori writing regionally? Read Patricia Grace *(Potiki, Cousins, Dogside Story, Tu)* around Wellington, and maybe Witi Ihimaera *(Pounamu, Pounamu; The Matriarch; Bulibasha; The Whale Rider)* on the North Island's East Coast. Keri Hulme *(The Bone People, Stonefish)* and the South Island go together like a mass of whitebait bound in a frying pan by a single egg (ie very well). Read Alan Duff *(Once Were*

Warriors) anywhere, but only if you want to be saddened, even shocked. Definitely take James George *(Hummingbird, Ocean Roads)* with you to Auckland's West Coast beaches and Northland's Ninety Mile Beach. Paula Morris *(Queen of Beauty, Hibiscus Coast, Trendy but Casual)* and Kelly Ana Morey *(Bloom, Grace Is Gone)* – hmm, Auckland and beyond? If poetry appeals you can't go past the giant of Māori poetry in English, the late, lamented Hone Tuwhare *(Deep River Talk: Collected Poems)*. Famously sounding like he's at church and in the pub at the same time, you *can* take him anywhere.

Arts & Music

It took a hundred years for post-colonial New Zealand to develop its own distinctive artistic identity. In the first half of the 20th century it was writers and visual artists who led the charge. By the 1970s NZ pub rockers had conquered Australia, while in the 1980s, indie-music obsessives the world over hooked into Dunedin's weird and wonderful alternative scene. However, it took the success of the film industry in the 1990s to catapult the nation's creativity into the global consciousness.

Literature

In 2013 New Zealanders rejoiced to hear that 28-year-old Eleanor Catton had become only the second NZ writer to ever win the Man Booker Prize, arguably the world's most prestigious award for literature. Lloyd Jones had come close in 2007 when his novel *Mister Pip* was shortlisted, but it had been a long wait between drinks since Keri Hulme took the prize in 1985. Interestingly, both Catton's epic historical novel *The Luminaries* and Hulme's haunting *The Bone People* were set on the numinous West Coast of the South Island – both books capturing something of the raw and mysterious essence of the landscape.

Catton and Hulme continue in a proud line of NZ women writers, starting in the early 20th century with Katherine Mansfield. Mansfield's work began a Kiwi tradition in short fiction, and for years the standard was carried by novelist Janet Frame, whose dramatic life was depicted in Jane Campion's film of her autobiography, *An Angel at My Table*. Frame's novel *The Carpathians* won the Commonwealth Writers' Prize in 1989.

Less recognised internationally, Maurice Gee has gained the nation's annual top fiction gong six times, most recently with *Blindsight* (2005). His much-loved children's novel *Under the Mountain* (1979) was made into a seminal NZ TV series in 1981, and then a major motion picture in 2009. In 2004 the adaptation of another of his novels, *In My Father's Den* (1972), won major awards at international film festivals and is one of the country's highest-grossing films.

Maurice is an auspicious name for NZ writers, with the late Maurice Shadbolt achieving much acclaim for his many novels, particularly those set during the NZ Wars. Try *Season of the Jew* (1987) or *The House of Strife* (1993).

MĀORI VOICES IN PRINT

Some of the most interesting and enjoyable NZ fiction voices belong to Māori writers, with Booker winner Keri Hulme leading the way. Witi Ihimaera's novels give a wonderful insight into small-town Māori life on the East Coast – especially *Bulibasha* (1994) and *The Whale Rider* (1987), which was made into an acclaimed film. Patricia Grace's work is similarly filled with exquisitely told stories of rural *marae*-centred life: try *Mutuwhenua* (1978), *Potiki* (1986), *Dogside Story* (2001) or *Tu* (2004). *Chappy* (2015) is Grace's expansive tale of a prodigal son returning to NZ to untangle his cross-cultural heritage.

MIDDLE-EARTH TOURISM

If you are one of those travellers inspired to come to Aotearoa by the scenery of the *Lord of the Rings (LOTR)* movies, you won't be disappointed. Jackson's decision to film in NZ wasn't mere patriotism. Nowhere else on earth will you find such wildly varied, unspoiled landscapes – not to mention poorly paid actors.

You will doubtless recognise some places from the films: for example, Hobbiton (near Matamata), Mt Doom (instantly recognisable as towering Ngauruhoe) and the Misty Mountains (the South Island's Southern Alps). The visitor information centres in Wellington, Twizel or Queenstown should be able to direct you to local *LOTR* sites of interest. If you're serious about finding the exact spots where scenes were filmed, buy a copy of Ian Brodie's nerdtastic *The Lord of the Rings: Location Guidebook*, which includes instructions, and even GPS coordinates, for finding all the important places.

Cinema & TV

If you first got interested in New Zealand by watching it on the silver screen, you're in good company. Sir Peter Jackson's NZ-made *The Lord of the Rings* and *The Hobbit* trilogies were the best thing to happen to NZ tourism since Captain Cook.

Yet NZ cinema is hardly ever easygoing. In his BBC-funded documentary, *Cinema of Unease*, NZ actor Sam Neill described the country's film industry as producing bleak, haunted work. One need only watch Lee Tamahori's harrowing *Once Were Warriors* (1994) to see what he means.

The Listener's former film critic, Philip Matthews, made a slightly more upbeat observation: Between (Niki Caro's) *Whale Rider*, (Christine Jeffs') *Rain* and *The Lord of the Rings*, you can extract the qualities that our best films possess. Beyond slick technical accomplishment, all share a kind of land-mysticism, an innately supernatural sensibility'.

You could add to this list Jane Campion's *The Piano* (1993) and *Top of the Lake* (2013), Brad McGann's *In My Father's Den* (2004) and Jackson's *Heavenly Creatures* (1994) – all of which use magically lush scenery to couch disturbing violence. It's a land-mysticism constantly bordering on the creepy.

Even when Kiwis do humour it's as resolutely black as their rugby jerseys; check out Jackson's early splatter-fests and Taika Waititi's *Boy* (2010). Exporting NZ comedy hasn't been easy, yet the HBO-produced TV musical parody *Flight of the Conchords* – featuring a mumbling, bumbling Kiwi folk-singing duo trying to get a break in New York – found surprising international success.

It's the Polynesian giggle-factor that seems likeliest to break down the bleak house of NZ cinema, with feel-good-through-and-through *Sione's Wedding* (2006) netting the second-biggest local takings of any NZ film.

New Zealanders have gone from never seeing themselves in international cinema to having whole cloned armies of Temuera Morrisons invading the universe in *Star Wars*. Familiar faces such as Cliff Curtis and Karl Urban seem to constantly pop up playing Mexican or Russian gangsters in action movies. Many of them got their start in long-running soap opera *Shortland St* (7pm weekdays, TV2).

Visual Arts

The NZ 'can do' attitude extends to the visual arts. If you're visiting a local's home don't be surprised to find one of the owner's paintings on the wall or one of their mate's sculptures in the back garden, pieced together out of bits of shell, driftwood and a length of the magical 'number 8 wire'.

This is symptomatic of a flourishing local art and crafts scene cultivated by lively tertiary courses churning out traditional carvers and

Other than 2003's winner *The Return of the King, The Piano* is the only NZ movie to be nominated for a Best Picture Oscar. Jane Campion was the first Kiwi nominated as Best Director and Peter Jackson the first to win it.

The only Kiwi actors to have won an Oscar are Anna Paquin (for *The Piano*) and Russell Crowe (for *Gladiator*). Paquin was born in Canada but moved to NZ when she was four, while Crowe moved from NZ to Australia at the same age.

weavers, jewellery-makers, multimedia boffins, and moulders of metal and glass. The larger cities have excellent dealer galleries representing interesting local artists working across all media.

Not all the best galleries are in Auckland or Wellington. The amazing new Len Lye Centre (p217) – home to the legacy of sculptor and film-maker Len Lye – is worth a visit to New Plymouth in itself, and Gore's Eastern Southland Gallery (p592) has an important and growing collection.

Traditional Māori art has a distinctive visual style with well-developed motifs that have been embraced by NZ artists of every race. In the painting medium, these include the cool modernism of the work of Gordon Walters and the more controversial pop-art approach of Dick Frizzell's *Tiki* series. Likewise, Pacific Island themes are common, particularly in Auckland. An example is the work of Niuean-born, Auckland-raised John Pule.

It should not be surprising that in a nation so defined by its natural environment, landscape painting constituted the first post-European body of art. John Gully and Petrus van der Velden were among those to arrive and paint memorable (if sometimes overdramatised) depictions of the land.

A little later, Charles Frederick Goldie painted a series of compelling, realist portraits of Māori, who were feared to be a dying race. Debate over the political propriety of Goldie's work raged for years, but its value is widely accepted now: not least because Māori themselves generally acknowledge and value them as ancestral representations.

From the 1930s NZ art took a more modern direction and produced some of the country's most celebrated artists, including Rita Angus, Toss Woollaston and Colin McCahon. McCahon is widely regarded to have been the country's most important artist. His paintings might seem inscrutable, even forbidding, but even where McCahon lurched into Catholic mysticism or quoted screeds from the Bible, his spirituality was rooted in geography. His bleak, brooding landscapes evoke the sheer power of New Zealand's terrain.

> Gareth Shute wrote the Music section. He is the author of four books, including *Hip Hop Music in Aotearoa* and *NZ Rock 1987–2007*. He is also a musician and has toured the UK, Europe and Australia as a member of the Ruby Suns and the Brunettes. He now plays in garage rock group, The Conjurors.

Music

NZ music began with the *waiata* (singing) developed by Māori following their arrival in the country. The main musical instruments were wind instruments made of bone or wood, the most well known of which is the *nguru* (also known as the 'nose flute'), while percussion was provided by chest- and thigh-slapping. These days, the liveliest place to see Māori music being performed is at *kapa haka* competitions in which groups compete with their own routines of traditional song and dance: track down the Te Matatini National Kapa Haka Festival (p631), which happens in March in odd-numbered years at different venues (it's at Kahungunu in Hawke's Bay in 2017). In a similar vein, Auckland's Pasifika Festival (p79) represents each of the Pacific Islands. It's a great place to see both traditional and modern forms of Polynesian music: modern hip-hop, throbbing Cook Island drums, or island-style guitar, ukulele and slide guitar.

> For indie-rock fans, a great source of local info is www.cheeseontoast.co.nz, which lists gigs and has band interviews and photos. For more on local hip-hop, pop and rock, check out www.thecorner.co.nz and the long-running www.muzic.net.nz.

Classical & Opera

Early European immigrants brought their own styles of music and gave birth to local variants during the early 1900s. In the 1950s Douglas Lilburn became one of the first internationally recognised NZ classical composers. More recently the country has produced a number of world-renowned musicians in this field, including opera singer Dame Kiri Te Kanawa, million-selling pop diva Hayley Westenra, composer John Psathas (who created music for the 2004 Olympic Games) and composer/percussionist Gareth Farr (who also performs in drag under the name Lilith).

> An up-to-date list of gigs in the main centres is listed at www.ripitup.co.nz. Tickets for most events can be bought at www.ticketek.co.nz, www.ticketmaster.co.nz, or, for smaller gigs, www.undertheradar.co.nz.

Rock

New Zealand has a strong rock scene, its most acclaimed exports being the revered indie label Flying Nun and the music of the Finn Brothers.

In 1981 Flying Nun was started by Christchurch record-store owner Roger Shepherd. Many of the early groups came from Dunedin, where local musicians took the DIY attitude of punk but used it to produce a lo-fi indie-pop that received rave reviews from the likes of *NME* in the UK and *Rolling Stone* in the US. *Billboard* even claimed in 1989 'There doesn't seem to be anything on Flying Nun Records that is less than excellent.'

Many of the musicians from the Flying Nun scene still perform live to this day, including David Kilgour (from the Clean) and Shayne Carter (from the Straitjacket Fits, and subsequently Dimmer and the Adults). The Bats are still releasing albums, and Martin Phillipps' band the Chills released a comeback album *Silver Bullets* in 2015.

Reggae, Hip-Hop & Dance

The genres of music that have been adopted most enthusiastically by Māori and Polynesian New Zealanders have been reggae (in the 1970s) and hip-hop (in the 1980s), which has led to distinct local forms. In Wellington, a thriving jazz scene took on a reggae influence to create a host of groups that blended dub, roots, and funky jazz – most notably Fat Freddy's Drop. The national public holiday, Waitangi Day, on 6 February, also happens to fall on the birthday of Bob Marley, and annual reggae concerts are held on this day in Auckland and Wellington.

The local hip-hop scene has its heart in the suburbs of South Auckland, which have a high concentration of Māori and Pacific Island residents. This area is home to one of New Zealand's foremost hip-hop labels, Dawn Raid, which takes its name from the infamous 1970s early-morning house raids that police performed on Pacific Islanders suspected of outstaying their visas. Dawn Raid's most successful artist is Savage, who

THE BROTHERS FINN

There are certain tunes that all Kiwis can sing along to, given a beer and the opportunity. A surprising proportion of these were written by Tim and Neil Finn, many of which have been international hits. Tim and Neil were both born in the small town of Te Awamutu: the local museum has a collection documenting their work.

Tim Finn first came to prominence in the 1970s group Split Enz. When the original guitarist quit, Neil flew over to join the band in the UK, despite being only 15 at the time. Split Enz amassed a solid following in Australia, NZ and Canada before disbanding in 1985.

Neil then formed Crowded House with two Australian musicians (Paul Hester and Nick Seymour) and one of their early singles, 'Don't Dream It's Over', hit number two on the US charts. Tim later did a brief spell in the band, during which the brothers wrote 'Weather With You' – a song that reached number seven on the UK charts, pushing their album *Woodface* to gold sales. The original line-up of Crowded House played their final show in 1996 in front of 100,000 people on the steps of the Sydney Opera House (though Finn and Seymour reformed the group in 2007 and continue to tour and record occasionally). Tim and Neil have both released a number of solo albums, as well as releasing material together as the Finn Brothers.

More recently, Neil has also remained busy, organising a set of shows/releases under the name 7 Worlds Collide – a collaboration with well-known overseas musicians including Jeff Tweedy (Wilco), Johnny Marr (The Smiths) and members of Radiohead. His latest band is the Pajama Club, a collaboration with wife Sharon and Auckland musicians Sean Donnelly and Alana Skyring.

Neil's son Liam also has a burgeoning solo career, touring the US with Eddie Vedder and the Black Keys and appearing on the *Late Show with David Letterman*.

GOOD LORDE!

Of course, the big news in Kiwi music recently has been the success of Lorde, a singer-songwriter from Devonport on Auckland's North Shore. Known less regally to her friends as Ella Yelich-O'Connor, Lorde was 16 years old when she cracked the number-one spot on the US Billboard charts in 2013 with her magical, school-yard-chant-evoking hit 'Royals' – the first NZ solo artist to top the American charts. 'Royals' then went on to win the Song of the Year Grammy in 2014. Her debut album *Pure Heroine* has spawned a string of hits and is selling millions of copies worldwide.

sold a million copies of his single 'Swing' after it was featured in the movie *Knocked Up*. Within New Zealand, the most well-known hip-hop acts are Scribe, Che Fu, and Smashproof (whose song 'Brother' held number one on the NZ singles charts longer than any other local act).

Dance music gained a foothold in Christchurch in the 1990s, spawning dub/electronica outfit Salmonella Dub and its offshoot act, Tiki Taane. Drum 'n' bass remains popular locally and has spawned internationally renowned acts such as Concord Dawn and Shapeshifter.

A wide range of cultural events are listed on www.eventfinda.co.nz. This is a good place to find out about concerts, classical music recitals and *kapa haka* performances. For more specific information on the NZ classical music scene, see www.sounz.org.nz.

New Music

Since 2000, the NZ music scene has developed new vitality after the government convinced commercial radio stations to adopt a voluntary quota of 20% local music. This enabled commercially oriented musicians to develop solid careers. Rock groups such as Shihad, the Feelers and Op-shop have thrived in this environment, as have a set of soulful female solo artists (who all happen to have Māori heritage): Bic Runga, Anika Moa, and Brooke Fraser (daughter of All Black Bernie Fraser). NZ also produced two internationally acclaimed garage rock acts over this time: the Datsuns and the D4.

Current Kiwis garnering international recognition include the incredibly gifted songstress Kimbra (who sang on Gotye's global smash 'Somebody That I Used To Know'); indie anthem alt-rockers the Naked & Famous; multitalented singer-songwriter Ladyhawke; the arty Lawrence Arabia; and the semi-psychedelic Unknown Mortal Orchestra. Aaradhna is a much-touted R&B singer who made a splash with her album *Treble & Reverb,* which won Album of the Year at the 2013 New Zealand Music Awards. The 2015 awards were dominated by Broods, a brother-sister alt-pop duo from Nelson, and Marlon Williams, a Christchurch singer with Jeff Buckley–like gravitas.

Survival Guide

Directory A–Z

Accommodation

Book your beds well in advance during peak tourist times: summer holidays from Christmas to late January, at Easter, and during winter in snowy resort towns like Queenstown and Wanaka.

Motels Most towns have decent, low-rise, midrange motels on their outskirts.

Holiday Parks A top choice if you're camping or touring in a campervan, with myriad options from unpowered tent sites to family en suite cabins.

Hostels Backpacker hostels range from beery, party-prone joints to classy family-friendly 'flashpackers'.

Hotels NZ hotels range from small-town pubs to slick global-chain operations – with commensurate price ranges.

B&Bs

Bed and breakfast (B&B) accommodation in NZ pops up in the middle of cities, in rural hamlets and on stretches of isolated coastline, with rooms on offer in everything from suburban bungalows to stately manors.

Breakfast may be 'continental' (cereal, toast and tea or coffee), 'hearty continental' (add yoghurt, fruit, home-baked bread or muffins), or a stomach-loading cooked meal (eggs, bacon, sausages...). Some B&B hosts may also cook dinner for guests and advertise dinner, bed and breakfast (DB&B) packages.

B&B tariffs are typically in the $120 to $200 bracket (per double), though some places cost upwards of $300 per double. Some hosts cheekily charge hefty prices for what is, in essence, a bedroom in their home. Off-street parking is often a bonus in the big cities.

Resources include the following:

New Zealand Bed & Breakfast www.bnb.co.nz

Bed and Breakfast New Zealand www.bed-and-breakfast.co.nz

Booking Services

Local visitor information centres around NZ provide reams of local accommodation information, sometimes in the form of folders detailing facilities and up-to-date prices; many can also make bookings on your behalf.

Online, check out the following:

Lonely Planet (www.lonelyplanet.com/new-zealand/hotels) The full range of NZ accommodation, from hostels to hotels.

Automobile Association (www.aa.co.nz) Online accommodation bookings (especially good for motels, B&Bs and holiday parks).

Jasons (www.jasons.com) Long-running travel service with myriad online booking options.

New Zealand Bed & Breakfast (www.bnb.co.nz) The name says it all.

Bed & Breakfast New Zealand (www.bed-and-breakfast.co.nz) B&B and self-contained accommodation listings.

Rural Holidays NZ (www.ruralholidays.co.nz) Farm and homestay listings across NZ.

SLEEPING PRICE RANGES

The following price ranges refer to a double room with bathroom during high season:

CATEGORY	COST
$	less than $120
$$	$120–200
$$$	more than $200

Price ranges generally increase by 20% to 25% in Auckland, Wellington and Christchurch. Here you can still find budget accommodation at up to $120 per double, but midrange stretches from $120 to $250, with top-end rooms more than $250.

Book a Bach (www.bookabach. co.nz) Apartment and holiday-house bookings (and maybe even a bach or two!).

Holiday Houses (www.holiday houses.co.nz) Holiday-house rentals NZ-wide.

New Zealand Apartments (www.nzapartments.co.nz) Rental listings for upmarket apartments of all sizes.

Camping & Holiday Parks

Campers and campervan drivers alike converge on NZ's hugely popular 'holiday parks', slumbering peacefully in powered and unpowered sites, cheap bunk rooms (dorm rooms), cabins and self-contained units (often called motels or tourist flats). Well-equipped communal kitchens, dining areas, and games and TV rooms often feature. In cities, holiday parks are usually a fair way from the action, but in smaller towns they can be impressively central or near lakes, beaches, rivers and forests.

The nightly cost of holiday-park camping is usually between $15 and $20 per adult, with children charged half price; powered sites are a couple of dollars more. Cabin/unit accommodation normally ranges from $70 to $120 per double. Unless noted otherwise, Lonely Planet lists campsite, campervan site, hut and cabin prices for two people.

DOC & FREEDOM CAMPING

A fantastic option for those in campervans is the 250-plus vehicle-accessible 'Conservation Campsites' run by the Department of Conservation (DOC; www.doc.govt.nz), with fees ranging from free (basic toilets and fresh water) to $15 per adult (flush toilets and showers). DOC publishes free brochures with detailed descriptions and instructions to find every campsite (even GPS coordinates). Pick up copies from DOC offices before you hit the road, or visit the website.

DOC also looks after hundreds of 'Backcountry Huts' and 'Backcountry Campsites', which can only be reached on foot. See the website for details. 'Great Walk' huts and campsites are also managed by DOC.

New Zealand is so photogenic, it's tempting to just pull off the road at a gorgeous viewpoint and camp the night. But never just assume it's OK to camp somewhere: always ask a local or check with the local i-SITE, DOC office or commercial campground. If you are 'freedom camping', treat the area with respect. Note that if your chosen campsite doesn't have toilet facilities and neither does your campervan, it's illegal for you to sleep there (your campervan must also have an on-board grey-water storage system). Legislation allows for $200 instant fines for camping in prohibited areas or improper disposal of waste (in cases where dumping waste could damage the environment, fees are up to $10,000) See www.camping.org.nz for more freedom-camping tips.

Farmstays

Farmstays open the door to the agricultural side of NZ life, with visitors encouraged to get some dirt beneath their fingernails at orchards, and dairy, sheep and cattle farms. Costs can vary widely, with bed-and-breakfast generally ranging from $80 to $140. Some farms have separate cottages where you can fix your own food; others offer low-cost, shared, backpacker-style accommodation.

Farm Helpers in NZ (www.fhinz. co.nz) Produces a booklet ($25) that lists around 350 NZ farms providing lodging in exchange for four to six hours' work per day.

Rural Holidays NZ (www.rural holidays.co.nz) Lists farmstays and homestays throughout the country.

Hostels

NZ is packed to the rafters with backpacker hostels, both independent and part of large chains, ranging from small, homestay-style affairs with a handful of beds, to refurbished hotels and towering modern structures in the big cities. Hostel bed prices listed by Lonely Planet are nonmember rates, usually between $25 and $35 per night.

HOSTEL ORGANISATIONS

Budget Backpacker Hostels (www.bbh.co.nz) NZ's biggest hostel group with around 220 hostels. Membership costs $45 for 12 months and entitles you to stay at member hostels at rates listed in the annual (free) BBH Backpacker Accommodation booklet. Nonmembers pay an extra $3 per night. Pick up a membership card from any member hostel or order one online ($50); see the website for details.

YHA New Zealand (www.yha. co.nz) Around 40 hostels in prime NZ locations. The YHA is part of the Hostelling International network (www.hihostels. com), so if you're already an HI member in your own country, membership entitles you to use NZ hostels. If you don't already have a home membership, you can join at major NZ YHA hostels or online for $25, valid for 12 months. Nonmembers pay an extra $3 per night.

Base Backpackers (www.stayat base.com) Chain with 10 hostels around NZ: Bay of Islands, Auckland, Rotorua, Taupo, Wellington, Wanaka, Queenstown, Nelson, Dunedin and Christchurch. Expect clean dorms, girls-only areas, and party opportunities aplenty. Offers a 10-night 'Base Jumping' accommodation card for $259, bookable online.

VIP Backpackers (www.vip backpackers.com) International organisation affiliated with around 20 NZ hostels (not BBH or YHA), mainly in the cities and tourist hot-spots. For around $61 (including postage) you'll receive a 12-month membership entitling you to a $1 discount off nightly accommodation. Join online or at VIP hostels.

Nomads Backpackers (www. nomadsworld.com) Aussie outfit with seven franchises in NZ, plus affilations with Base Backpackers: Auckland, Bay of Islands, Rotorua, Taupo, Wellington, Abel Tasman National Park, Wanaka, Dunedin and Queenstown. Membership costs AUD$19.50 for 12 months and offers a 5% discount off the cost of nightly accommodation. Join at participating hostels or online.

Haka Lodge (www.hakalodge. com) A local chain on the way up, with snazzy hostels in Auckland, Queenstown, Christchurch, Taupo and Paihia. Rates are comparable to other hostels

around NZ, and quality is high. Tours are also available.

Pubs, Hotels & Motels

The least expensive form of NZ hotel accommodation is the humble pub. Some are full of character (and characters); others are grotty, ramshackle places that are best avoided (especially by women travelling solo). Check whether there's a band playing the night you're staying – you could be in for a sleepless night. In the cheapest pubs, singles/doubles might cost as little as $30/60 (with a shared bathroom down the hall); $50/80 is more common.

At the top end of the hotel scale are five-star international chains, resort complexes and architecturally splendorous boutique hotels, all of which charge a hefty premium for their mod cons, snappy service and/or historic opulence. We quote 'rack rates' (official advertised rates) for such places, but discounts and special deals often apply.

NZ's towns have a glut of nondescript, low-rise motels and 'motor lodges', charging between $80 and $180 for double rooms. These tend to be squat structures skulking by highways on the edges of towns. Most are modernish

(though decor is often mired in the early 2000s) and have similar facilities, namely tea- and coffee-making equipment, fridge and TV. Prices vary with standard.

Rental Accommodation

The basic Kiwi holiday home is called a 'bach' (short for 'bachelor', as they were historically used by single men as hunting and fishing hideouts); in Otago and Southland they're known as 'cribs'. These are simple self-contained cottages that can be rented in rural and coastal locations. Prices are typically $80 to $150 per night, which isn't bad for a whole house or self-contained bungalow. For more upmarket holiday houses, expect to pay anything from $150 to $400 per double.

Online resources:

➡ www.holidayhomes.co.nz

➡ www.bookabach.co.nz

➡ www.holidayhouses.co.nz

➡ www.nzapartments.co.nz

Customs Regulations

For the low-down on what you can and can't bring into NZ, see the New Zealand Customs Service website (www.customs.govt.nz). Per-person duty-free allowances:

➡ Three 1125mL (max) bottles of spirits or liqueur

➡ 4.5L of wine or beer

➡ 50 cigarettes, or 50g of tobacco or cigars

➡ dutiable goods up to the value of $700

It's a good idea to declare any unusual medicines. Tramping gear (boots, tents etc) will be checked and may need to be cleaned before being allowed in. You must declare any plant or animal products (including anything made of wood), and food of

---

WWOOFING

If you don't mind getting your hands dirty, an economical way of travelling around NZ involves doing some voluntary work as a member of the international **Willing Workers On Organic Farms** (WWOOF; ☑03-544 9890; www.wwoof.co.nz) scheme. Down on the farm, in exchange for a hard day's work, owners provide food, accommodation and some hands-on organic farming experience. Contact farm owners a week or two beforehand to arrange your stay, as you would for a hotel or hostel – don't turn up unannounced!

A one-year online membership costs $40. A farm-listing book, which is mailed to you, costs an extra $10 to $30, depending on where in the world your mailbox is. You should have a Working Holiday Visa when you visit NZ, as the immigration department considers wwoofers to be working.

Climate

Auckland

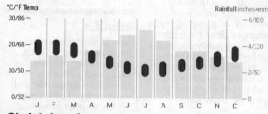

Christchurch

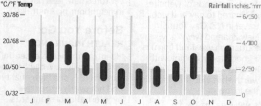

Queenstown

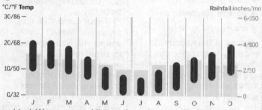

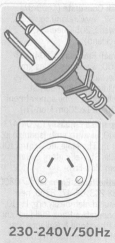

230-240V/50Hz

any kind. Weapons and firearms are either prohibited or require a permit and safety testing. Don't take these rules lightly – non-compliance penalties will really hurt your hip pocket.

Discount Cards

The internationally recognised **International Student Identity Card** is produced by the ISIC Association (www.isic.org), and issued to full-time students aged 12 and over. It provides discounts on accommodation, transport and admission to attractions. The same folks also produce the **International Youth Travel Card**, available to travellers under 30 who are not full-time students, with equivalent benefits to the ISIC. Also similar is the **International Teacher Identity Card**, available to teaching professionals. All three cards ($30 each) are available online at www.isiccard.co.nz, or from student travel companies like STA Travel.

The **New Zealand Card** (www.newzealandcard.com) is a $35 discount pass that score you between 5% and 50% off a range of accommodation, tours, sights and activities.

Travellers over 60 with some form of identification (eg an official seniors card from your home country) are often eligible for concession prices.

Electricity

To plug yourself into the electricity supply (230V AC, 50Hz), use a three-pin adaptor (the same as in Australia; different to British three-pin adaptors).

Embassies & Consulates

Most principal diplomatic representations to NZ are in Wellington, with a few in Auckland.

Australian High Commission (☎04-473 6411; www.newzealand.highcommission.gov.au; 72-76 Hobson St, Thorndon, Wellington; ☺9am-4pm Mon-Fri)

Canadian High Commission (☎04-473 9577; www.canadainternational.gc.ca; L11, 125 The Terrace, Wellington; ☺8.30am-noon Mon-Fri)

Chinese Embassy (☎04-473 3514; www.chinaembassy.org.nz; 4 Halswell St, Thorndon, Wellington; ☺9-11.30am Mon-Fri, 2-4pm Mon, Wed & Fri)

Fijian High Commission (☎04-473 5401; www.fiji.org.nz; 31 Pipitea St, Thorndon, Wellington; ☺9am-5pm Mon-Fri)

French Embassy (☎04-473 2555; www.ambafrance-nz.org; 34-42 Manners St, Wellington; ☺9am-noon & 2-5pm Mon-Thu, 9am-noon & 2-4pm Fri)

German Embassy (☎04-473 6063; www.wellington.diplo.de; 90-92 Hobson St, Thorndon, Wellington; ☺10.45am-noon Mon-Fri)

Irish Consulate (☏09-977 2252; www.ireland.co.nz; L3, Tower 1, 205 Queen St, Auckland)

Israeli Embassy (☏04-439 9500; www.embassies.gov. il/wellington; Lvl 13, Bayleys Building, 36 Brandon St, Wellington; ⊙by appointment 9.30am-12.30pm Mon-Fri)

Japanese Embassy (☏04-473 1540; www.nz.emb-japan.go.jp; Lvl 18, The Majestic Centre, 100 Willis St, Wellington; ⊙9am-5pm Mon-Fri)

Netherlands Embassy (☏0800 388 243, 04-471 6395; new zealand.nlembassy.org; Lvl 10, Cooperative Bank Building, cnr Featherstone & Ballance Sts; ⊙by appointment 9.30am-12.30pm & 1-3.30pm Mon-Fri)

UK High Commission (☏04-924 2888; www.gov.uk; 44 Hill St, Thorndon, Wellington; ⊙9am-5pm Mon-Fri)

US Embassy (☏04-462 6000; newzealand.usembassy.gov; 29 Fitzherbert Tce, Thorndon, Wellington; ⊙9am-5pm Mon-Fri)

Food & Drink

New Zealand is a mighty fine place to wine and dine. For the low-down, see **Food & Drink** (p52).

LGBTI Travellers

The gay tourism industry in NZ isn't as high profile as it is in other developed nations, but LGBT communities are prominent in Auckland and Wellington, with myriad support organisations across both islands. NZ has progressive laws protecting human rights: same-sex marriage was legalised here in 2013, while the legal minimum age for sex between consenting persons is 16. Generally speaking, Kiwis are fairly relaxed and accepting about gender fluidity, but that's not to say that homophobia doesn't exist. Rural communities tend to be more conservative; here public displays of affection should probably be avoided.

Resources

There are loads of websites dedicated to gay and lesbian travel in NZ. Gay Tourism New Zealand (www.gay-tourismnewzealand.com) is a good starting point, with links to various sites. Other worthwhile websites include the following:

➡ www.gaynz.com
➡ www.gaynz.net.nz
➡ www.lesbian.net.nz
➡ www.gaystay.co.nz

Check out the nationwide monthly magazine *express* (www.gayexpress.co.nz) for the latest happenings, reviews and listings on the NZ gay scene.

Festivals & Events

Auckland Pride Festival (www. aucklandpridefestival.org. nz) Two-and-a-bit weeks of rainbow-hued celebrations in February.

Big Gay Out (www.biggayout. co.nz) Free festival (food, drink, entertainment) held every February in Auckland.

Gay Ski Week (www. gayskiweekqt.com) Annual Queenstown snow-fest in August/September.

Out Takes (www.outtakes.org. nz) G&L film festival staged in Auckland and Wellington in May/June. Didn't happen in 2015, but will return in 2016.

Health

New Zealand is one of the healthiest countries in the world in which to travel. Diseases such as malaria and typhoid are unheard of, and the absence of poisonous snakes or other dangerous animals makes outdoor adventures here less risky than in neighbouring Australia.

Before You Go
HEALTH INSURANCE

Health insurance is essential for all travellers. While health care in NZ is of a high quality and not overly expensive by international standards, considerable costs can be built up and repatriation can be pricey.

If your current health insurance doesn't cover you for medical expenses incurred overseas, consider extra insurance – see www.lonelyplanet.com/travel-insurance for more information. Find out in advance if your insurance plan will make payments directly to providers or reimburse you later for overseas health expenditures.

MEDICATIONS

Bring any prescribed medications for your trip in their original, clearly labelled containers. A signed and dated letter from your physician describing your medical conditions and medications (including generic names) and any requisite syringes or needles, is also wise.

VACCINATIONS

NZ has no vaccination requirements for any traveller, but the World Health Organization recommends that all travellers should be covered for diphtheria, tetanus, measles, mumps, rubella, chickenpox and polio, as well as hepatitis B, regardless of their destination. Ask your

---

EATING PRICE RANGES

The following price ranges refer to the average price of a main course:

$ less than $15

$$ $15–32

$$$ more than $32

doctor for an *International Certificate of Vaccination* (or 'the yellow booklet') in which they will list all the vaccinations you've received.

In New Zealand
AVAILABILITY & COST OF HEALTH CARE

NZ's public hospitals offer a high standard of care (free for residents). All travellers are covered for medical care resulting from accidents that occur while in NZ (eg motor-vehicle accidents, adventure-activity accidents) by the Accident Compensation Corporation (www.acc. co.nz). Costs incurred due to treatment of a medical illness that occurs while in NZ will only be covered by travel insurance. For more details, see www.health.govt.nz.

The 24-hour, free-call **Healthline** (📞0800 611 116) offers health advice throughout NZ.

ENVIRONMENTAL HAZARDS

There's very little that can bite, sting or eat you in NZ, but hypothermia and drowning are genuine threats.

HYPOTHERMIA

Hypothermia is a significant risk, especially during winter and year-round at altitude. Mountain ranges and/or strong winds produce a high chill factor, which can cause hypothermia even in moderate temperatures. Early signs include the inability to perform fine movements (such as doing up buttons), shivering and a bad case of the 'umbles' (fumbles, mumbles, grumbles, stumbles).

To treat, minimise heat loss: remove wet clothing, add dry clothes with wind- and waterproof layers, and consume water and carbohydrates to allow shivering to build the internal temperature. In severe hypothermia cases, shivering actually stops; this is a medical emergency requiring rapid evacuation in addition to the above measures.

PRACTICALITIES

DVDs Kiwi DVDs are encoded for Region 4, which includes Australia, the Pacific, Mexico, Central America, the Caribbean and South America.

Newspapers Check out Auckland's *New Zealand Herald* (www.nzherald.co.nz), Wellington's *Dominion Post* (www.stuff.co.nz/dominion-post) or Christchurch's *The Press* (www.stuff.co.nz/the-press).

Radio Tune in to Radio New Zealand (www.radionz. co.nz) for news, current affairs, classical and jazz. Radio Hauraki (www.hauraki.co.nz) cranks out the rock.

TV Watch one of the national government-owned TV stations – including TV One, TV2, Māori TV or the 100% Māori language Te Reo – or subscriber-only Sky TV (www.skytv.co.nz)

Weights & measures NZ uses the metric system.

SURF BEACHES

NZ has exceptional surf beaches. The power of the surf can fluctuate as a result of the varying slope of the seabed: rips and undertows are common, and drownings do happen. Check with local surf-lifesaving organisations before jumping in the sea and be aware of your own limitations and expertise.

INFECTIOUS DISEASES

Aside from the usual sexually transferred discomforts (take normal precautions), giardiasis does occur in NZ.

GIARDASIS

The giardia parasite is widespread in NZ waterways: drinking untreated water from streams and lakes is not recommended. Using water filters and boiling or treating water with iodine are effective ways of preventing the disease. Symptoms consist of intermittent diarrhoea, abdominal bloating and wind. Effective treatment is available (tinidazole or metronidazole).

PHARMACEUTICALS

Over-the-counter medications are widely available in NZ through private chemists (pharmacies). These include painkillers, antihistamines, skin-care products and sun-

screen. Some medications, such as antibiotics and the contraceptive pill, are only available via a prescription obtained from a general practitioner. If you take regular medications, bring an adequate supply and details of the generic name, as brand names differ country-to-country.

TAP WATER

Tap water throughout New Zealand is generally safe to drink. NZ has strict standards about drinking water, applicable across the country.

Insurance

➡ A watertight travel-insurance policy covering theft, loss and medical problems is essential. Some policies specifically exclude designated 'dangerous activities' such as scuba diving, bungy jumping, whitewater rafting, skiing and even tramping. If you plan on doing any of these things (a distinct possibility in NZ!), make sure your policy covers you fully.

➡ It's worth mentioning that under NZ law, you cannot sue for personal injury (other than exemplary damages). Instead, the country's

Accident Compensation Corporation (www.acc.co.nz) administers an accident compensation scheme that provides accident insurance for NZ residents and visitors to the country, regardless of fault. This scheme, however, does not negate the necessity for your own comprehensive travel-insurance policy, as it doesn't cover you for such things as income loss, treatment at home or ongoing illness.

➡ Consider a policy that pays doctors or hospitals directly, rather than you paying on the spot and claiming later. If you have to claim later, keep all documentation. Some policies ask you to call (reverse charges) to a centre in your home country where an immediate assessment of your problem is made. Check that the policy covers ambulances and emergency medical evacuations by air.

➡ Worldwide travel insurance is available at www.lonelyplanet.com/travel-insurance. You can buy, extend and claim online anytime – even if you're already on the road.

Internet Access

Getting online in NZ is easy in all but the most remote locales. In Lonely Planet's New Zealand reviews, we use the wi-fi (🛜) and internet (@) icons to indicate the availability of wireless access or actual computers on which you can get online.

Wi-fi & Internet Service Providers

Wi-fi You'll be able to find wi-fi access around the country, from hotel rooms to pub beer gardens to hostel dorms. Usually you have to be a guest or customer to log in; you'll be issued with an access code. Sometimes it's free, sometimes there's a charge.

Hot-spots The country's main telecommunications company is Spark New Zealand (www.spark.co.nz), which has wireless hot-spots around the country where you can purchase prepaid access cards. Alternatively, purchase a prepaid number from the login page at any wireless hot-spot using your credit card. See Spark's website for hot-spot listings.

Equipment & ISPs If you've brought your palmtop or laptop, consider buying a prepay USB modem (aka a 'dongle') with a local SIM card: both Spark and Vodafone (www.vodafone.co.nz) sell these from around $100. If you want to get connected via a local internet service provider (ISP), options include the following:

Clearnet (☎0508 888 800; www.clearnet.co.nz) Affiliated with Vodafone.

Earthlight (☎03-479 0303; www.earthlight.co.nz)

Slingshot (☎0800 892 000; www.slingshot.co.nz)

Internet Cafes

There are fewer internet cafes around these days than there were five years ago, but you'll still find them in the bigger cities. Access costs anywhere from $4 to $6 per hour.

Similarly, most youth hostels have done away with actual computers in favour of wi-fi. Most hotels, motels, B&Bs and holiday parks also offer wi-fi, sometimes for free, but usually for a small charge.

Legal Matters

Marijuana is widely indulged in but illegal: anyone caught carrying this or other illicit drugs will have the book thrown at them.

Drink-driving is a serious offence and remains a significant problem in NZ. The legal blood alcohol limit is 0.05% for drivers over 20, and zero for those under 20.

If you are arrested, it's your right to consult a lawyer before any formal questioning begins.

Maps

New Zealand's **Automobile Association** (AA; ☎0800 500 444; www.aa.co.nz/travel) produces excellent city, town, regional, island and highway maps, available from its local offices. The AA also produces a detailed *New Zealand Road Atlas*. Other reliable country-wide atlases, available from visitor information centres and bookshops, are published by Hema, KiwiMaps and Wises.

Land Information New Zealand (www.linz.govt.nz) publishes several exhaustive map series, including street, country and holiday maps, national park and forest park maps, and topographical trampers' maps. Scan the larger bookshops, or try the nearest DOC office or visitor information centre for topo maps.

Online, log onto AA Maps (www.aamaps.co.nz) or Wises (www.wises.co.nz) to pinpoint exact NZ addresses.

Money

ATMs are widely available in cities and larger towns. Credit cards accepted in most hotels and restaurants.

ATMs & Eftpos

Branches of the country's major banks across both islands have ATMs, but you won't find them everywhere (eg not in small towns).

Many NZ businesses use Eftpos (electronic funds transfer at point of sale), allowing you to use your bank card (credit or debit) to make direct purchases and often withdraw cash as well. Eftpos is available practically everywhere: just like at an ATM, you'll need a personal identification number (PIN).

Bank Accounts

We've heard mixed reports on the subject of travellers opening bank accounts in NZ, and bank websites are vague. Some sources say opening an account is as simple as flashing a few pieces of ID; others say banks won't allow visitors to open an account unless the application is accompanied by proof of employment. Either way, you'll need to open an account if you want to work in NZ in any capacity (including working holiday scenarios). Do your homework before you arrive.

Credit & Debit Cards

CREDIT CARDS

Credit cards (Visa, MasterCard) are widely accepted for everything from a hostel bed to a bungy jump, and are pretty much essential for car hire. They can also be used for over-the-counter cash advances at banks and from ATMs, but be aware that such transactions incur charges. Diners Club and American Express cards are not as widely accepted.

DEBIT CARDS

Debit cards enable you to draw money directly from your home bank account using ATMs, banks or Eftpos facilities. Any card connected to the international banking network (Cirrus, Maestro, Visa Plus and Eurocard) should work with your PIN. Fees will vary depending on your home bank; check before you leave. Alternatively, companies such as Travelex offer debit cards with set withdrawal fees and a balance you can top up from your personal bank account while on the road.

Currency

NZ's currency is the NZ dollar, comprising 100 cents. There are 10c, 20c, 50c, $1 and $2 coins, and $5, $10, $20, $50 and $100 notes. Prices are often still marked in single cents and then rounded to the nearest 10c when you hand over your money.

Money Changers

Changing foreign currency (and to a lesser extent old-fashioned travellers cheques) is usually no problem at NZ banks or at licensed money changers (eg Travelex) in major tourist areas, cities and airports.

Taxes & Refunds

The Goods and Services Tax (GST) is a flat 15% tax on all domestic goods and services. NZ prices listed by Lonely Planet include GST. There's no GST refund available when you leave NZ.

Tipping

Tipping is completely optional in NZ – the total at the bottom of a restaurant bill is all you need to pay (note that sometimes there's an additional service charge). That said, it's totally acceptable to reward good service – between 5% and 10% of the bill is fine.

Travellers Cheques

Amex, Travelex and other international brands of travellers cheques are a bit old-hat these days, but they're still easily exchanged at banks and money changers. Present your passport for identification when cashing them; shop around for the best rates.

Opening Hours

Opening hours vary seasonally (eg Dunedin is quiet during winter), but use the following as a general guide. Note that most places close on Christmas Day and Good Friday.

Banks 9.30am–4.30pm Monday to Friday, some also 9am–noon Saturday

Cafes 7am–4pm

Post Offices 8.30am–5pm Monday to Friday; larger branches also 9.30am–1pm Saturday

Pubs & Bars noon–late ('late' varies by region, and by day)

Restaurants noon–2.30pm and 6.30–9pm

Shops & Businesses 9am–5.30pm Monday to Friday and 9am to noon or 5pm Saturday

Supermarkets 8am–7pm, often 9pm or later in cities

Post

The services offered by **New Zealand Post** (☎0800 501 501; www.nzpost.co.nz) are reliable and reasonably inexpensive. See the website for info on national and international zones and rates, plus post office (or 'post shop') locations.

Public Holidays

NZ's main public holidays:

New Year 1 and 2 January

Waitangi Day 6 February

Easter Good Friday and Easter Monday; March/April

Anzac Day 25 April

Queen's Birthday First Monday in June

Labour Day Fourth Monday in October

Christmas Day 25 December

Boxing Day 26 December

In addition, each NZ province has its own anniversary-day holiday. The dates of these provincial holidays vary: when they fall on Friday to Sunday, they're usually observed the following Monday; if they fall on Tuesday to Thursday, they're held on the preceding Monday.

Provincial anniversary holidays:

Southland 17 January

Wellington 22 January

Auckland 29 January

Northland 29 January

Nelson 1 February

Otago 23 March

Taranaki 31 March

South Canterbury 25 September

Hawke's Bay 1 November

Marlborough 1 November

Chatham Islands 30 November

Westland 1 December

Canterbury 16 December

School Holidays

The Christmas holiday season, from mid-December to late January, is part of the summer school vacation: expect transport and accommodation to book out in advance, and queues at tourist attractions. There are three shorter school-holiday periods during the year: from mid- to late April, early to mid-July, and mid-September to early October. For exact dates see the Ministry of Education website (www. education.govt.nz).

Safe Travel

It's no more dangerous than any other developed country, but violent crime does happen in NZ. Play it safe on the streets after dark and in remote areas.

➡ Avoid leaving valuables in vehicles: theft from cars is a problem.

➡ NZ's climate is unpredictable: hypothermia is a risk in high-altitude areas.

➡ At the beach, beware of rips and undertows, which can drag swimmers out to sea.

➡ Kiwi roads are often made hazardous by map-distracted tourists, wide-cornering campervans and traffic-ignorant sheep.

➡ In the annoyances category, NZ's sandflies are a royal (and intensely itchy) pain. Lather yourself with insect repellent in coastal areas.

Telephone

Key phone service providers include the following:

Spark New Zealand (www.spark. co.nz) The country's key domestic player, also with a stake in the local mobile (cell) market.

Skinny Mobile (www.skinny. co.nz) Mobile-network option.

Vodafone (www.vodafone.co.nz) Mobile-network option.

2 Degrees (www.2degrees-mobile.co.nz) Mobile-network option.

Mobile Phones

Most NZ mobile phone numbers are preceded by the prefix ☏021, ☏022 or ☏027. Mobile phone coverage is good in cities and towns and most parts of the North Island, but can be a bit patchy away from urban centres on the South Island.

If you want to bring your own phone and use a prepaid service with a local SIM card (rather than pay for expensive global roaming on your home network), Vodafone (www.vodafone.co.nz) is a practical option. Any Vodafone shop (in most major towns) will set you up with a NZ Travel SIM and a phone number (from around $30; valid for 30, 60 or 90 days). Top-ups can be purchased at newsagencies, post offices and petrol stations all over the country.

Alternatively, you can rent a phone from Vodafone, with pick-up and drop-off outlets at Auckland, Christchurch and Queenstown international airports. Phone Hire New Zealand (www.phonehirenz. com) also rents out mobiles, SIM cards, modems and GPS systems.

Local Calls

Local calls from private phones are free! Local calls from payphones cost $1 for the first 15 minutes, and $0.20 per minute thereafter, though coin-operated payphones are scarce (and if you do find one, chances are the coin slot will be gummed up); you'll generally need a phonecard. Calls to mobile phones attract higher rates.

International Calls

To make international calls from NZ (which is possible on payphones), you need to dial the international access code ☏00, then the country code and the area code (without the initial '0'). So for a London number, for example, you'd dial ☏00-44-20, then the number.

If dialling NZ from overseas, the country code is ☏64, followed by the appropriate area code minus the initial '0'.

Long Distance Calls & Area Codes

NZ uses regional two-digit area codes for long-distance calls, which can be made from any payphone. If you're making a local call (ie to someone else in the same town), you don't need to dial the area code. But if you're dialling within a region (even if it's to a nearby town with the same area code), you do have to dial the area code.

Information & Toll-Free Calls

Numbers starting with ☎0900 are usually recorded information services, charging upwards of $1 per minute (more from mobiles). These numbers cannot be dialled from payphones, and sometimes not from prepay mobile phones.

Toll-free numbers in NZ have the prefix ☎0800 or ☎0508 and can be called from anywhere in the country, though they may not be accessible from certain areas or from mobile phones. Numbers beginning with ☎0508, ☎0800 or ☎0900 cannot be dialled from outside NZ.

Phonecards

NZ has a wide range of phonecards available, which can be bought at hostels, newsagencies and post offices for a fixed-dollar value (usually $5, $10, $20 and $50). These can be used with any public or private phone by dialling a toll-free access number and then the PIN number on the card. Shop around – rates vary from company to company.

Time

NZ is 12 hours ahead of GMT/UTC and two hours ahead of Australian Eastern Standard Time. The Chathams are 45 minutes ahead of NZ's main islands.

In summer, NZ observes daylight saving time, where clocks are wound forward by one hour on the last Sunday in September; clocks are wound back on the first Sunday of the following April.

Toilets

Toilets in NZ are sit-down Western style. Public toilets are plentiful, and are usually reasonably clean with working locks and plenty of toilet paper.

See www.toiletmap.co.nz for public toilet locations around the country.

Tourist Information

The website for the official national tourism body, **Tourism New Zealand** (www.newzealand.com), is the best place for pretrip research. Emblazoned with the hugely successful 100% Pure New Zealand branding, the site has information in several languages, including German, Spanish, French, Chinese and Japanese.

Local Tourist Offices

Almost every Kiwi city or town seems to have a visitor information centre. The bigger centres stand united within the outstanding **i-SITE network** (www.newzealand. com/travel/i-sites) – around 80 info centres affiliated with Tourism New Zealand. i-SITEs have trained staff, information on local activities and attractions, and free brochures and maps. Staff can also book activities, transport and accommodation.

Bear in mind that some information centres only promote accommodation and tour operators who are paying members of the local tourist association, and that sometimes staff aren't supposed to recommend one activity or accommodation provider over another.

There's also a network of **Department of Conservation** (DOC; www.doc. govt.nz) visitor centres to help you plan activities and make bookings. DOC visitor centres – in national parks, regional centres and major cities – usually also have displays on local lore, flora, fauna and biodiversity.

Travellers with Disabilities

Kiwi accommodation generally caters fairly well for travellers with disabilities, with many hostels, hotels, motels and B&Bs equipped with wheelchair-accessible rooms. Many tourist attractions similarly provide wheelchair access, with wheelchairs often available.

Tour operators with accessible vehicles operate from most major centres. Key cities are also serviced by 'kneeling' buses (buses that hydraulically stoop down to kerb level to allow easy access), and taxi companies offer wheelchair-accessible vans. Large car-hire firms (Avis, Hertz etc) provide cars with hand controls at no extra charge (but advance notice is required). Air New Zealand is also very well equipped to accommodate travellers in wheelchairs.

Activities

Out and about, the Department of Conservation maintains plenty of tracks that are wheelchair accessible, categorised as 'easy access short walks': the Cape Reinga Lighthouse Walk and Milford Foreshore Walk are two prime examples.

If cold-weather activity is more your thing, see the Disabled Snowsports NZ website (www.disabledsnowsports.org.nz).

Resources

Weka (www.weka.net.nz) Good general information, with categories including Transport and Travel.

Blind Foundation (www.blind foundation.org.nz)

National Foundation for the Deaf (www.nfd.org.nz)

Mobility Parking (www.mobilityparking.org.nz) Info on mobility parking permits and online applications.

Visas

Visa application forms are available from NZ diplomatic missions overseas, travel agents and **Immigration New Zealand** (☑0508 558 855, 09-914 4100; www.immigration.govt.nz). Immigration New Zealand has over a dozen offices overseas; consult the website.

Visitor Visa

Citizens of Australia don't need a visa to visit NZ and can stay indefinitely (provided they have no criminal convictions). UK citizens don't need a visa either and can stay in the country for up to six months.

Citizens of another 58 countries that have visa-waiver agreements with NZ don't need a visa for stays of up to three months per visit, for no more than six months within any 12-month period, provided they have an onward ticket and sufficient funds to support their stay: see the website for details. Nations in this group include Canada, France, Germany, Ireland, Japan, the Netherlands, South Africa and the USA.

Citizens of other countries must obtain a visa before entering NZ. Visitor visas allow stays of up to nine months within an 18-month period, and cost between NZ$170 and $220, depending on where in the world the application is processed.

A visitor's visa can be extended from nine to 12 months, but if you get this extension you'll have to leave NZ after your 12-month stay has expired and wait another 12 months before you can come back. Applications are assessed on a case-by-case basis; you may need to provide proof of adequate funds

to sustain you during your visit (NZ$1000 per month) plus an onward ticket establishing your intent to leave. Apply for extensions at any Immigration New Zealand office – see the website for locations.

Work Visa

It's illegal for foreign nationals to work in NZ on a visitor visa, except for Australians who can legally gain work without a visa or permit. If you're visiting NZ to find work, or you already have an employment offer, you'll need to apply for a work visa, which can be valid for up to three years, depending on your circumstance. You can apply for a work permit after you're in NZ, but its validity will be backdated to when you entered the country. The fee for a work visa can be anything upwards of NZ$190, depending on where and how it's processed (paper or online) and the type of application.

Working Holiday Scheme

Eligible travellers who are only interested in short-term employment to supplement their travels can take part in one of NZ's working holiday schemes (WHS). Under these schemes citizens aged 18 to 30 years from 42 countries – including Canada, France, Germany, Ireland, Japan, Malaysia, the Netherlands, Scandinavian countries, the UK and the USA – can apply for a visa. For most nationalities the visa is valid for 12 months. It's only issued to those seeking a genuine working holiday, not permanent work, so you're not supposed to work for one employer for more than three months.

WHS-eligible nationals must apply online for this visa from within their own country. Applicants must have an onward ticket, a passport valid for at least three months from the date they will leave NZ and evi-

dence of at least NZ$4200 in accessible funds. The application fee is NZ$165 regardless of where you apply, and isn't refunded if your application is declined.

The rules vary for different nationalities, so make sure you read up on the specifics of your country's agreement with NZ at www.immigration.govt.nz/migrant/stream/work/workingholiday.

Volunteering

NZ presents a swath of active, outdoorsy volunteer opportunities for travellers to get some dirt under their fingernails and participate in conservation programs. Programs can include anything from tree-planting and weed removal to track construction, habitat conservation and fencing. Ask about local opportunities at any regional i-SITE visitor information centre, join one of the programs run by DOC (www.doc.govt.nz/getting-involved), or check out these online resources:

➜ www.conservation volunteers.org.nz

➜ www.helpx.net

➜ www.nature.org.nz

➜ www.volunteeringnz.org.nz

➜ www.wwf.org.nz

Women Travellers

NZ is generally a very safe place for female travellers, although the usual sensible precautions apply (for both sexes): avoid walking alone at night; never hitchhike alone; if you're out on the town have a plan on how to get back to your accommodation safely. Sexual harassment is not a widely reported problem in NZ, but of course that doesn't mean it doesn't happen. See www.womentravel.co.nz for tours aimed at solo women.

Work

If you arrive in NZ on a visitor visa, you're not allowed to work for pay. If you're caught breaching this (or any other) visa condition, you could be booted back to where you came from.

If you have been approved for a working holiday scheme (WHS) visa, there are a number of possibilities for temporary employment in NZ. Pay rates are around $14 to $20 an hour (ie, not very high). There's plenty of casual work around, mainly in agriculture (fruit picking, farming, wineries), hospitality (bar work, waiting tables) or at ski resorts. Office-based work can be found in IT, banking, finance and telemarketing. Register with a local office-work agency to get started.

Seasonal fruit picking, pruning and harvesting is prime short-term work for visitors. More than 30,000 hectares of apples, kiwifruit and other fruit and veg are harvested from December to May. It is physically taxing toil, working in the dirt under the hot sun – turnover of workers is high. You're usually paid by how much you pick (per bin, bucket or kilogram): if you stick with it for a while, you'll get faster and fitter and can actually make some reasonable cash. Prime North Island picking locations include the Bay of Islands (Kerikeri and Paihia), rural Auckland, Tauranga and the Bay of Plenty, Gisborne and Hawke's Bay (Napier and Hastings); on the South Island try Nelson (Tapawera and Golden Bay), Marlborough (around Blenheim) and Central Otago (Alexandra and Roxburgh).

Winter work at ski resorts and their service towns includes bartending, waiting, cleaning, ski-tow operation and, if you're properly qualified, ski or snowboard instructing.

Resources

Backpacker publications, hostel managers and other travellers are the best sources of info on local work possibilities. Base Backpackers (www.stayatbase.com/work) runs an employment service via its website, while the Notice Boards page on the Budget Backpacker Hostels website (www.bbh.co.nz) lists job vacancies in BEH hostels and a few other possibilities.

Kiwi Careers (www.careers.govt.nz) lists professional opportunities in various fields (agriculture, creative, health, teaching, volunteer work and recruitment), while Seek (www.seek.co.nz) is one of the biggest NZ job-search networks, with thousands of jobs listed.

Check ski-resort websites for work opportunities in the snow. In the fruit-picking/horticultural realm, try the following websites:

→ www.seasonalwork.co.nz
→ www.seasonaljobs.co.nz
→ www.picknz.co.nz
→ www.pickingjobs.com

Income Tax

Death and taxes – no escape! For most travellers, Kiwi dollars earned in NZ will be subject to income tax, deducted from payments by employers – a process called Pay As You Earn (PAYE).

PAYE income tax rates are 11.95% for annual salaries up to $14,000, then 18.95% up to $48,000, 31.45% up to $70,000, then 34.45% for higher incomes. A NZ Accident Compensation Corporation (ACC) scheme levy (around 1.5%) will also be deducted from your pay packet. Note that these rates tend to change slightly year-to-year.

If you visit NZ and work for a short time (eg on a working holiday scheme) you may qualify for a tax refund when you leave. Lodging a tax return before you leave NZ is the best way of securing a refund. For more info, see the Inland Revenue Department website (www.ird.govt.nz), or call 03-951 2020.

IRD Number

Travellers undertaking paid work in NZ (including working holiday scenarios) must first open a New Zealand bank account, then obtain an IRD (Inland Revenue Department) number. Download the *IRD number application - non-resident/offshore individual IR742* form from the Inland Revenue Department website (www.ird.govt.nz). IRD numbers normally take eight to 10 working days to be issued.

Transport

GETTING THERE & AWAY

New Zealand is a long way from almost everywhere – most travellers jet in from afar. Flights, cars and tours can be booked online at lonelyplanet.com/bookings.

Entering the Country

Disembarkation in New Zealand is generally a straightforward affair, with only the usual customs declarations and the luggage-carousel scramble to endure. Under the the Orwellian title of 'Advance Passenger Screening', documents that used to be checked after you touched down in NZ (passport, visa etc) are now checked before you board your flight – make sure all your documentation is in order so that your check-in is stress-free.

Passport

There are no restrictions when it comes to foreign citizens entering NZ. If you have a current passport and visa (or don't require one), you should be fine.

Air

NZ's abundance of year-round activities means that airports here are busy most of the time: if you want to fly at a particularly popular time of year (eg over the Christmas period), book well in advance.

The high season for flights into NZ is during summer (December to February), with slightly less of a premium on fares over the shoulder months (October/November and March/April). The low season generally tallies with the winter months (June to August), though this is still a busy time for airlines ferrying ski bunnies and powder hounds.

Airports & Airlines

INTERNATIONAL AIRPORTS

A number of NZ airports handle international flights, with Auckland receiving the most traffic:

Auckland Airport (AKL; Map p66; ☑09-275 0789; www.aucklandairport.co.nz; Ray Emery Dr, Mangere)

Christchurch Airport (CHC; ☑03-358 5029; www.christchurchairport.co.nz; 30 Durey Rd)

Dunedin Airport (DUD; ☑03-486 2879; www.dnairport.co.nz; 25 Miller Rd, Momona)

Queenstown Airport (ZQN; Map p544; ☑03-450 9031; www.queenstownairport.co.nz; Sir Henry Wrigley Dr, Frankton)

Wellington Airport (WLG; ☑04-385 5100; www.wellingtonairport.co.nz; Stewart Duff Dr, Rongotai)

Note that Hamilton, Rotorua and Palmerston North airports are capable of handling direct international arrivals

---

CLIMATE CHANGE & TRAVEL

Every form of transport that relies on carbon-based fuel generates CO_2, the main cause of human-induced climate change. Modern travel is dependent on aeroplanes, which might use less fuel per kilometre per person than most cars but travel much greater distances. The altitude at which aircraft emit gases (including CO_2) and particles also contributes to their climate change impact. Many websites offer 'carbon calculators' that allow people to estimate the carbon emissions generated by their journey and, for those who wish to do so, to offset the impact of the greenhouse gases emitted with contributions to portfolios of climate-friendly initiatives throughout the world. Lonely Planet offsets the carbon footprint of all staff and author travel.

TRAVEL TAXES

An international 'passenger service charge' of up to NZ$25 applies when leaving New Zealand's various international airports, which is built into your ticket price. Other charges also apply ($1.50 civil aviation fee. $12 aviation security service fee. $6 departure fee, $16 arrival fee), which are also added to your ticket price.

and departures, but are not currently doing so.

AIRLINES FLYING TO & FROM NEW ZEALAND

New Zealand's international carrier is Air New Zealand (www.airnewzealand.co.nz), which flies to runways across Europe, North America, eastern Asia, Australia and the Pacific, and has an extensive network across NZ.

Winging in from Australia, Virgin Australia (www.virginaustralia.com), Qantas (www.qantas.com.au), Jetstar (www.jetstar.com) and Air New Zealand are the key players.

Joining Air New Zealand from North America, other operators include Air Canada (www.aircanada.com) and American Airlines (www.aa.com).

From Europe, the options are a little broader, with British Airways (www.britishairways.com), Lufthansa (www.lufthansa.com) and Virgin Atlantic (www.virginatlantic.com) entering the fray, and plenty of others stopping in NZ on broader round-the-world routes.

From Asia and the Pacific there are myriad options, with direct flights from China, Japan, Singapore, Malaysia, Thailand and Pacific Island nations.

Sea

Yacht It is possible (though by no means straightforward) to make your way between NZ, Australia and the Pacific islands by crewing on a yacht. Try asking around at harbours, marinas, and yacht and sailing clubs. Popular yachting harbours in NZ include the Bay of Islands and Whangarei

(both in Northland), Auckland and Wellington. March and April are the best months to look for boats heading to Australia. From Fiji, October to November is a peak departure season to beat the cyclones that soon follow in that neck of the woods.

Cruise Ship If you're looking for something with a slower pace plenty of passenger cruise liners stop in NZ on the South Pacific legs of their respective schedules: try P&O Cruises (www.pocruises.com.au) for starters.

Cargo Ship Alternatively, a berth on a cargo ship or freighter to/ from New Zealand is a quirky way to go: check out websites such as www.freightercruises.com and www.freighterexpeditions.com.au for more info.

GETTING AROUND

Air

Those who have limited time to get between NZ's attractions can make the most of a widespread (and very reliable and safe) network of intra- and inter-island flights.

Airlines in New Zealand

The country's major domestic carrier, Air New Zealand, has an aerial network covering most of the country, often operating under the Air New Zealand Link moniker on less popular routes. Australia-based Jetstar also flies between main urban areas. Between them, these two airlines carry the vast majority of domestic passengers in NZ. Beyond this, several small-scale regional operators

provide essential transport services to outlying islands such as Great Barrier Island in the Hauraki Gulf, to Stewart Island and the Chathams. There are also plenty of scenic- and charter-flight operators around NZ, not listed here. Operators include the following:

Air Chathams (03-305 0209; www.airchathams.co.nz) Services to the remote Chatham Islands from Wellington, Christchurch and Auckland. Auckland–Whakatane flights also available.

Air New Zealand (0800 737 000; www.airnewzealand.co.nz) Offers flights between 20-plus domestic destinations, plus myriad overseas hubs.

Air2there.com (0800 777 000; www.air2there.com) Connects destinations across Cook Strait, including including Paraparaumu, Wellington, Nelson and Blenheim.

FlyMySky (0800 222 123; www.flymysky.co.nz) At least three flights daily from Auckland to Great Barrier Island.

Golden Bay Air (0800 588 885; www.goldenbayair.co.nz) Flies regularly between Wellington and Takaka in Golden Bay. Also connects to Karamea for Heaphy Track trampers.

Barrier Air (0800 900 600; www.barrierair.kiwi) Plies the skies over Great Barrier Island, Auckland, Tauranga, Whitianga, Kaitaia and Whangarei.

Jetstar (0800 800 995; www.jetstar.com) Joins the dots between key tourism centres: Auckland, Wellington, Christchurch, Dunedin, Queenstown, Nelson, Napier, New Plymouth and Palmerston North.

Kiwi Regional Airlines (07-444 5020; www.flykiwi.co.nz) New operator with services linking Nelson with Dunedin, Hamilton and Tauranga.

Soundsair (0800 505 005; www.soundsair.co.nz) Numerous flights each day between Picton and Wellington, plus flights from Wellington to Blenheim, Nelson, Westport and Taupo. Also flies Blenheim to Paraparaumu and Napier, and Nelson to Paraparaumu.

Stewart Island Flights (03-218 9129; www.stewartislandflights. com) Flies between Invercargill and Stewart Island.

Sunair (0800 786 247; www. sunair.co.nz) Flies to Whitianga from Ardmore (near Auckland), Great Barrier Island and Tauranga, plus numerous other North Island connections between Hamilton, Rotorua, Gisborne and Whakatane.

Air Passes

Available exclusively to travellers from the USA or Canada who have bought an Air New Zealand fare to NZ from the USA or Canada, Australia or the Pacific Islands, Air New Zealand offers the good-value **New Zealand Explorer Pass** (www.airnewzealand.com/ explorer-pass). The pass lets you fly between up to 27 destinations in New Zealand, Australia and the South Pacific islands (including Norfolk Island, Tonga, New Caledonia, Samoa, Vanuatu, Tahiti, Fiji, Niue and the Cook Islands). Fares are broken down into four discounted, distance-based zones: zone one flights start at US$99 (eg Auckland to Christchurch); zone two from US$129 (eg Auckland to Queenstown); zone three from US$214 (eg Wellington to Sydney); and zone four from US$295 (eg Tahiti to Auckland). You can buy the pass before you travel, or after you arrive in NZ.

Bicycle

Touring cyclists proliferate in NZ, particularly over summer. The country is clean, green and relatively uncrowded, and has lots of cheap accommodation (including camping) and abundant fresh water. The roads are generally in good nick, and the climate is usually not too hot or cold. Road traffic is the biggest danger: trucks overtaking too close to cyclists are a particular threat. Bikes and cycling gear are readily available to rent or buy in the main centres, and bicycle-repair shops are common.

By law all cyclists must wear an approved safety helmet (or risk a fine); it's also vital to have good reflective safety clothing. Cyclists who use public transport will find that major bus lines and trains only take bicycles on a 'space available' basis and charge up to $10. Some of the smaller shuttle bus companies, on the other hand, make sure they have storage space for bikes, which they carry for a surcharge.

If importing your own bike or transporting it by plane within NZ, check with the relevant airline for costs and the degree of dismantling and packing required.

See www.nzta.govt.nz/ traffic/ways/bike for more bike safety and legal tips, and the New Zealand Cycle Trail (Nga Haerenga; p50) – a network of 23 'Great Rides' across NZ.

Hire

Rates offered by most outfits for renting road or mountain bikes are usually around $20 per hour to $60 per day. Longer-term rentals may be available by negotiation. You can often hire bikes from your accommodation (hostels, holiday parks, etc), or rent more reputable machines from bike shops in the larger towns.

Buying a Bike

Bicycles can be readily bought in NZ's larger cities, but prices for newer models are high. For a decent hybrid bike or rigid mountain bike you'll pay anywhere from $800 to $1800, though you can get a cheap one for around $500 (but you still then need to buy panniers, helmet, lock etc, and the cost quickly climbs). Other options include the post-Christmas sales and midyear stocktakes, when newish cycles can be heavily discounted.

Boat

NZ may be an island nation but there's virtually no long-distance water transport around the country.

Obvious exceptions include the boat services between Auckland and various islands in the Hauraki Gulf, the interisland ferries that cross the Cook Strait between Wellington and Picton, and the passenger ferry that negotiates Foveaux Strait between Bluff and the town of Oban on Stewart Island.

If you're cashed-up, consider the cruise liners that chug around the NZ coastline as part of broader South Pacific itineraries: P&O Cruises (www.pocruises.com.au) is a major player.

Bus

Bus travel in NZ is easygoing and well organised, with services transporting you to the far reaches of both islands (including the start/end of various walking tracks)...but it can be expensive, tedious and time-consuming.

NZ's main bus company is **InterCity** (www.intercity. co.nz), which can drive you to just about anywhere on the North and South Islands. **Naked Bus** (www.nakedbus. com) has similar routes and remains the main competition. Both bus lines offer fares as low as $1(!).

InterCity also has a South Island sightseeing arm called **Newmans Coach Lines** (www.newmanscoach.co.nz), travelling between Queenstown, Christchurch and the West Coast glaciers.

Seat Classes & Smoking

There are no allocated economy or luxury classes on NZ buses (very democratic), and smoking on the bus is a definite no-no.

Naked Bus has, however, introduced a **sleeper class** on overnight services between Auckland and Wellington (stopping at Hamilton and Palmerston North) where you can lie flat in a 1.8m-long bed (bring earplugs). See www.naked-bus.com/nz/bus/naked-bus-sleeper for details.

Reservations

Over summer, school holidays and public holidays, book well in advance on popular routes (a week or two if possible). At other times a day or two ahead is usually fine. The best prices are generally available online, booked a few weeks in advance.

Bus Passes

If you're covering a lot of ground, both InterCity and Naked Bus offer bus passes that can be cheaper than paying as you go, but they do of course lock you into using their respective networks. Passes are usually valid for 12 months.

On fares other than bus passes, InterCity offers a discount of around 10% for YHA, ISIC, Nomads, BBH or VIP backpacker card holders.

NATIONWIDE PASSES

Flexipass A hop-on/hop-off InterCity pass, allowing travel to pretty much anywhere in NZ, in any direction, including the Interislander ferry across Cook Strait. The pass is purchased in blocks of travel time: minimum 15 hours ($119), maximum 60 hours ($449). The average cost of each block becomes cheaper the more hours you buy. You can top up the pass if you need more time.

Aotearoa Explorer, Tiki Tour & Island Loop Hop-on/hop-off, fixed-itinerary nationwide passes offered by InterCity. These passes link up tourist hot-spots and range in price from $738 to $995. See www.intercity.co.nz/bus-pass/travelpass for details.

Naked Passport (www.naked-passport.com) A Naked Bus pass that allows you to buy trips in blocks of five, which you can add to any time, and book each trip as needed. Five/15/30 trips cost $151/318/491. An unlimited pass costs $597 – great value if you're travelling NZ for many moons.

NORTH ISLAND PASSES

InterCity offers six hop-on/hop-off, fixed-itinerary North Island bus passes, ranging from short $119 runs between Auckland and Paihia to $384 trips from Auckland

to Wellington via the big sights in between. See www.intercity.co.nz/bus-pass/travelpass for details.

SOUTH ISLAND PASSES

On the South Island, InterCity offers six hop-on/hop-off, fixed-itinerary passes, ranging from $119 runs along the West Coast between Picton and Queenstown, to a $509 loop around the whole island. See www.intercity.co.nz/bus-pass/travelpass for details.

Shuttle Buses

As well as InterCity and Naked Bus, regional shuttle buses fill in the gaps between the smaller towns. Operators include the following (see www.tourism.net.nz/transport/bus-and-coach-services for a complete list), offering regular scheduled services and/or bus tours and charters:

Abel Tasman Travel (www.abeltasmantravel.co.nz) Traverses the roads between Nelson, Motueka, Golden Bay and Abel Tasman National Park.

Alpine Scenic Tours (www.alpinescenictours.co.nz) Runs tours around Taupo and into Tongariro National Park, plus the ski fields around Mt Ruapehu and Mt Tongariro.

Atomic Shuttles (www.atomictravel.co.nz) Has services throughout the South Island, including to Christchurch, Dunedin, Invercargill, Picton, Nelson, Greymouth, Hokitika, Queenstown and Wanaka.

Catch-a-Bus South (www.catchabussouth.co.nz) Invercargill and Bluff to Dunedin and Queenstown.

Cook Connection (www.cookconnect.co.nz) Triangulates between Mt Cook, Twizel and Lake Tekapo.

East West Coaches (www.eastwestcoaches.co.nz) Offers a service between Christchurch and Westport via Lewis Pass.

Go Kiwi Shuttles (www.go-kiwi.co.nz) Links Auckland with Whitianga on the Coromandel Peninsula daily.

Hanmer Connection (www.hanmerconnection.co.nz) Daily services between Hanmer Springs and Christchurch.

Manabus (www.manabus.com) Runs in both directions daily between Auckland and Wellington via Hamilton, Rotorua, Taupo and Palmerston North. Also runs to Tauranga, Paihia and Napier. Some services operated by Naked Bus.

Tracknet (www.tracknet.net) Summer track transport (Milford, Routeburn, Kepler) with Queenstown, Te Anau and Invercargill connections.

Trek Express (www.trekexpress.co.nz) Shuttle services to all tramping tracks in the top half of the South Island.

Waitomo Wanderer (www.travelheadfirst.com) Does a loop from Rotorua or Taupo to Waitomo.

West Coast Shuttle (www.westcoastshuttle.co.nz) Daily bus from Greymouth to Christchurch and back.

Backpacker Buses

If you feel like clocking up some kilometres (and often some hangovers) with like-minded fellow travellers, the following operators run fixed-itinerary bus tours, nationwide or on the North or South Islands. Accommodation, meals and hop-on/hop-off flexibility are often included.

Adventure Tours New Zealand (www.adventuretours.com.au) Five 11- to 22-day NZ tours, either South Island, North Island or both.

Bottom Bus (www.travelheadfirst.com/local-legends/bottom-bus) South Island nether-region tours ex-Dunedin, Invercargill and Queenstown.

Flying Kiwi (www.flyingkiwi.com) Good-fun, activity-based trips around NZ (four to 28 days) with camping and cabin accommodation.

Haka Tours (www.hakatours.com) Three- to 16-day tours with adventure, snow or mountain-biking themes.

Kiwi Experience (www.kiwiexperience.com) The major

hop-on/hop-off player, with myriad tours available.

Stray Travel (www.straytravel. com) A wide range of flexible hop-on/hop-off passes and tours.

Car & Motorcycle

The best way to explore NZ in depth is to have your own wheels. It's easy to hire cars and campervans at good rates. Alternatively, if you're in NZ for a few months, you might consider buying your own vehicle.

Automobile Association (AA)

New Zealand's **Automobile Association** (AA; ☑0800 500 444; www.aa.co.nz/ travel) provides emergency breakdown services, maps and accommodation guides (from holiday parks to motels and B&Bs).

Members of overseas automobile associations should bring their membership cards – many of these bodies have reciprocal agreements with the AA.

Driving Licences

International visitors to NZ can use their home country driving licence – if your licence isn't in English, it's a good idea to carry a certified translation with you. Alternatively, use an International Driving Permit (IDP), which will usually be issued on the spot (valid for 12 months) by your home country's automobile association.

Fuel

Fuel (petrol, aka gasoline) is available from service stations across NZ: unless you're cruising around in something from the '70s, you'll be filling up with 'unleaded', or LPG (gas). LPG is not always stocked by rural suppliers; if you're on gas, it's safer to have dual-fuel capability. Aside from remote locations like Milford Sound and Mt Cook, petrol prices don't vary

much from place to place: per-litre costs at the time of research were around $2.

Hire

CAMPERVAN

Check your rear-view mirror on any far-flung NZ road and you'll probably see a shiny white campervan (aka mobile home, motor home, RV) packed with liberated travellers, mountain bikes and portable barbecues cruising along behind you.

Most towns of any size have a campground or holiday park with powered sites (where you can plug your vehicle in) for around $35 per night. There are also 250-plus vehicle-accessible Department of Conservation (DOC; www.doc.govt.nz) campsites around NZ, ranging in price from free to $15 per adult: check the website for info.

You can hire campervans from dozens of companies. Prices vary with season, vehicle size and length of rental.

A small van for two people typically has a minikitchen and foldout dining table, the latter transforming into a double bed when dinner is done and dusted. Larger 'superior' two-berth vans include shower and toilet. Four- to six-berth campervans are the size of trucks (and similarly sluggish) and, besides the extra space, usually contain a toilet and shower.

Over summer, rates offered by the main rental firms for two-/four-/six-berth vans booked six months in advance start at around $110/150/210 per day for a month-long rental, dropping to as low as $50/70/100 per day during winter.

Major operators include the following:

Apollo (☑09-889 2976, 0800 113 131; www.apollocamper. co.nz)

Britz (☑09-255 3910, 08 00 081 032; www.britz.co.nz) Also does 'Britz Bikes' (add a mountain or city bike from $12 per day).

Kea (☑09-448 8800, 0800 464 613; www.keacampers. com)

Maui (☑09-255 3910, 0800 688 558; www.maui.co.nz)

Wilderness Motorhomes (☑09-282 3606; www.wilderness.co.nz)

BACKPACKER VAN

Budget players in the campervan industry offer slick deals and funky (often gregariously spray-painted), well-kitted-out vehicles for backpackers. Rates are competitive (from $25/50 per day for a two-/four-berth van from May to September; from $90/150 per day from December to February). Operators include the following:

Backpacker Sleeper Vans (☑0800 321 939, 03-359 4731; www.sleepervans.co.nz)

Escape Campervans (☑0800 216 171; www.escaperentals. co.nz)

Hippie Camper (☑0800 113 131; www.hippiecamper.co.nz)

Jucy (☑09-929 2462, 0800 399 736; www.jucy.co.nz)

Mighty Cars & Campers (☑0800 422 505; www. mightycampers.co.nz)

Spaceships (☑0800 772 237, 09-526 2130; www.spaceshipsrentals.co.nz)

CAR

Competition between car-rental companies in NZ is torrid, particularly in the big cities and Picton. Remember that if you want to travel far, you need unlimited kilometres. Some (but not all) companies require drivers to be at least 21 years old – ask around.

Most car-hire firms suggest (or insist) that you don't take their vehicles between islands on the Cook Strait ferries. Instead, you leave your car at either Wellington or Picton terminal and pick up another car once you've crossed the strait. This saves you paying to transport a vehicle on the ferries, and is a pain-free exercise.

INTERNATIONAL RENTAL COMPANIES

The big multinational companies have offices in most major cities, towns and airports. Firms sometimes offer one-way rentals (eg collect a car in Auckland, leave it in Wellington), but there are often restrictions and fees. On the other hand, an operator in Christchurch may need to get a vehicle back to Auckland and will offer an amazing one-way car relocation deal (sometimes free!).

The major companies offer a choice of either unlimited kilometres, or 100km (or so) per day free, plus so many cents per subsequent kilometre. Daily rates in main cities typically start at around $40 per day for a compact, late-model, Japanese car, and around $75 for medium-sized cars (including GST, unlimited kilometres and insurance).

Avis (☑09-526 2847, 0800 655 111; www.avis.co.nz)

Budget (☑09-529 7784, 0800 283 438; www.budget.co.nz)

Europcar (☑0800 800 115; www.europcar.co.nz)

Hertz (☑03-358 6789, 0800 654 321; www.hertz.co.nz)

Thrifty (☑03-359 2720, 0800 737 070; www.thrifty.co.nz)

LOCAL RENTAL COMPANIES

Local rental firms proliferate. These are almost always cheaper than the big boys – sometimes half the price – but the cheap rates may come with serious restrictions: vehicles are often older, depots might be further away from airports/city centres, and with less formality sometimes comes a less protective legal structure for renters.

Rentals from local firms start at around $30 per day for the smallest option. It's obviously cheaper if you rent for a week or more, and there are often low-season and weekend discounts.

Affordable, independent operators with national networks include the following:

a2b Car Rentals (☑09-254 4397, 0800 545 000; www.a2b-car-rental.co.nz)

Ace Rental Cars (☑09-303 3112, 0800 502 277; www.acerentalcars.co.nz)

Apex Rentals (☑03-363 3000, 0800 500 660; www.apexrentals.co.nz)

Ezi Car Rental (☑09-254 4397, 0800 545 000; www.ezicarrental.co.nz)

Go Rentals (☑09-974 1598, 0800 467 368; www.gorentals.co.nz)

Omega Rental Cars (☑09-377 5573, 0800 525 210; www.omegarentalcars.com)

Pegasus Rental Cars (☑09-275 3222, 0800 803 580; www.rentalcars.co.nz)

Transfercar (☑09-630 7533; www.transfercar.co.nz) One-way relocation specialists.

MOTORCYCLE

Born to be wild? NZ has great terrain for motorcycle touring, despite the fickle weather in some regions. Most of the country's motorcycle-hire shops are in Auckland and Christchurch, where you can hire anything from a little 50cc moped (aka nifty-fifty) to a throbbing 750cc touring motorcycle and beyond. Recommended operators (who also run guided tours) offer rates of anywhere from $50 per day:

New Zealand Motorcycle Rentals & Tours (☑09-486 2472; www.nzbike.com)

Te Waipounamu Motorcycle Tours (☑03-372-3537; www.motorcycle-hire.co.nz)

Insurance

Rather than risk paying out wads of cash if you have an accident, you can take out your own comprehensive insurance policy, or (the usual option) pay an additional fee per day to the rental company to reduce your excess. This brings the amount you must pay in the event of an accident down from around $1500 or $2000 to around $200 or $300. Smaller operators offering cheap rates often have a compulsory insurance excess, taken as a credit-card bond, of around $900.

Most insurance agreements won't cover the cost of damage to glass (including the windscreen) or tyres, and insurance coverage is often invalidated on beaches and certain rough (4WD) unsealed roads – read the fine print.

See www.acc.co.nz for info on NZ's Accident Compensation Corporation insurance scheme (fault-free personal injury insurance).

Purchase

Buying a car then selling it at the end of your travels can be one of the cheapest and best ways to see NZ. Auckland is the easiest place to buy a car, followed by Christchurch: scour the hostel noticeboards. Turners Auctions (www.turners.co.nz) is NZ's biggest car-auction operator, with 10 locations.

LEGALITIES

Make sure your prospective vehicle has a Warrant of Fitness (WoF) and registration valid for a reasonable period: see the New Zealand Transport Agency website (www.nzta.govt.nz) for details.

Buyers should also take out third-party insurance, covering the cost of repairs to another vehicle in an accident that is your fault: try the **Automobile Association** (AA; ☑0800 500 444; www.aa.co.nz/travel). NZ's no-fault Accident Compensation Corporation (www.acc.co.nz) scheme covers personal injury, but make sure you have travel insurance, too.

If you're considering buying a car and want someone to check it out for you, various car-inspection companies inspect cars for around $150; find them at car auctions, or they will come to you. Try **Vehicle Inspection New Zealand** (VINZ; ☑09-

573 3230, 0800 468 469; www.vinz.co.nz) or the AA.

Before you buy it's wise to confirm ownership of the vehicle, and find out if there's anything dodgy about the car (eg stolen, or outstanding debts). The AA's **LemonCheck** (☎09-420 3090, 0800 536 662; www.lemoncheck.co.nz) offers this service.

BUY-BACK DEALS

You can avoid the hassle of buying/selling a vehicle privately by entering into a buy-back arrangement with a dealer. Predictably, dealers often find sneaky ways of knocking down the return-sale price, which may be 50% less than what you paid, so hiring or buying and selling a vehicle yourself (if you have the time) is usually a better bet.

Road Hazards

There's an unusually high percentage of international drivers involved in road accidents in NZ – something like 30% of accidents involve a non-local driver. Kiwi traffic is usually pretty light, but it's easy to get stuck behind a slow-moving truck or campervan – pack plenty of patience, and know your road rules before you get behind the wheel. There are also lots of slow wiggly roads, one-way bridges and plenty of gravel roads, all of which require a more cautious driving approach. And watch out for sheep!

To check road conditions call 0800 444 449 or see www.nzta.govt.nz/traffic.

Road Rules

➡ Kiwis drive on the left-hand side of the road; cars are right-hand drive. Give way to the right at intersections.

➡ At single-lane bridges (of which there are a surprisingly large number), a smaller red arrow pointing in your direction of travel means that *you* give way.

➡ Speed limits on the open road are generally 100km/h; in built-up areas the limit is usually 50km/h. Speed cameras and radars are used extensively.

➡ All vehicle occupants must wear a seatbelt or risk a fine. Small children must be belted into approved safety seats.

➡ Always carry your licence when driving. Drink-driving is a serious offence and remains a significant problem in NZ, despite widespread campaigns and severe penalties. The legal blood alcohol limit is 0.05% for drivers over 20, and 0% (zero) for those under 20.

Hitching & Ride-Sharing

Hitching is never entirely safe, and we don't recommend it. Travellers who hitch should understand that they are taking a small but potentially serious risk. That said, it's not unusual to see hitchhikers along NZ country roads.

Alternatively, check hostel noticeboards for ride-share opportunities.

Local Transport
Bus, Train & Tram

NZ's larger cities have extensive bus services but, with a few honourable exceptions, they are mainly daytime, weekday operations; weekend services can be infrequent or nonexistent. Negotiating inner-city Auckland is made easier by Link buses; Hamilton has a free city-centre loop bus; Christchurch has a free city-shuttle service and the historic tramway. Most main cities have late-night buses for boozy Friday and Saturday nights.

The only cities with decent local train services are Auckland and Wellington, with four and five suburban routes respectively.

Taxi

The main cities have plenty of taxis and even small towns may have a local service. Taxis are metred, and generally reliable and trustworthy.

Train

NZ train travel is all about the journey, not about getting anywhere in a hurry. **KiwiRail Scenic Journeys** (☎0800 872 467, 04-495 0775; www.kiwirailscenic.co.nz) operates four routes, listed below; reservations can be made through KiwiRail Scenic Journeys directly, or at most train stations (notably not at Palmerston North or Hamilton), travel agents and visitor information centres. All services are for day travel (no sleeper services).

Capital Connection Weekday commuter service between Palmerston North and Wellington.

Coastal Pacific Between Christchurch and Picton along the South Island's east coast.

Northern Explorer Between Auckland and Wellington: southbound on Mondays, Thursdays and Saturdays; northbound on Tuesdays, Fridays and Sundays.

TranzAlpine Over the Southern Alps between Christchurch and Greymouth – one of the world's most famous train rides.

Train Passes

A KiwiRail Scenic Journeys Scenic Journey Rail Pass (www.kiwirailscenic.co.nz/scenic-rail-pass) allows unlimited travel on all of its rail services, including passage on the Wellington–Picton Interislander ferry. There are two types of pass, both requiring you to book your seats a minimum of 24 hours before you want to travel:

Fixed Pass Limited duration fares for one/two/three weeks, costing $599/699/799 per adult (a little bit less for kids).

Freedom Pass Affords you travel on a certain number of days over a 12-month period; a three-/seven-/10-day pass costs $417/903/1290.

Behind the Scenes

SEND US YOUR FEEDBACK

We love to hear from travellers – your comments keep us on our toes and help make our books better. Our well-travelled team reads every word on what you loved or loathed about this book. Although we cannot reply individually to your submissions, we always guarantee that your feedback goes straight to the appropriate authors, in time for the next edition. Each person who sends us information is thanked in the next edition – the most useful submissions are rewarded with a selection of digital PDF chapters.

Visit **lonelyplanet.com/contact** to submit your updates and suggestions or to ask for help. Our award-winning website also features inspirational travel stories, news and discussions.

Note: We may edit, reproduce and incorporate your comments in Lonely Planet products such as guidebooks, websites and digital products, so let us know if you don't want your comments reproduced or your name acknowledged. For a copy of our privacy policy visit lonelyplanet.com/privacy.

OUR READERS

Many thanks to the travellers who used the last edition and wrote to us with helpful hints, useful advice and interesting anecdotes:

Sain Alizada, Ian Baker, Sal Bolton, Iain Cook, Erin Crampton, Alkistis Danilatou, Gary Dickman, Hans Elander, Jack & Deidre Evans, Nadine Haas, Rüdiger Heß, Jinghan Di, Shona Leisk, Jeroen Loopstra, Kathy Manville, Kelly McFaden, Thomas Michel, Yu Morikawa, Chuck Perso, Phillip Roullard, Olivia Rowland, Gary Salloum, Kerstin Stiegler, Lukas Toma, Jean Tuck, Lisa Wilkie

AUTHOR THANKS

Charles Rawlings-Way

Thanks to the many generous, knowledgeable and quietly self-assured Kiwis I met on the road, especially the staff at the Hastings, Whanganui and New Plymouth i-SITEs who flew through my questions with the greatest of ease. Huge thanks to Tasmin Waby for signing me up, and the in-house LP content deities who electrified this CMS Frankenstein. Humongous gratitude to my tireless, witty and professional co-authors – Lee, Sarah, Peter and Brett – who always bring the humour and the class. Most of all, thanks to Meg, Ione and Remy for holding the fort while I was away.

Brett Atkinson

Thanks to all of the i-SITE, DOC and information centre staff who patiently answered all my questions. Cheers to the innovative chefs and inspired craft brewers of New Zealand for sustenance on the road, and to Carol for support on occasional beach, island, capital city and Hobbit-inspired getaways. Thanks to my fellow authors, the wittiest crew one could aspire to work with, and my appreciation to Tasmin Waby at Lonely Planet for the opportunity to again explore my Kiwi backyard.

Sarah Bennett & Lee Slater

Thanks to everyone who helped us on the road, including tourism organisations, DOC and visitor centre staff, business operators and travellers. Thanks also to friends and family who provided a park for the campervan, a fridge for the flagon, and company on vital research missions. Finally, thanks to our fellow NZ authors for the camaraderie, as always, and Tasmin Waby for leading the team.

Peter Dragicevich

I owe a great deal of thanks to Hamish, Jill and John Blennerhassett in Wanaka, Scott and Sophie Kennedy in Queenstown, Michael

Wilson in Invercargill, and Joanne and Phil Cole on Waiheke Island. Special thanks to Michael Woodhouse for his comradeship on the road in Otago. And to all of my Auckland friends and family who enthusiastically supped and gorged with me in the city's bars and restaurants, good work!

ACKNOWLEDGMENTS

Climate map data adapted from Peel MC, Finlayson BL & McMahon TA (2007) 'Updated World Map of the Köppen-Geiger Climate Classification', *Hydrology and Earth System Sciences*, 11, 1633–44.

Cover photograph: Crater Lake, Mt Ruapehu, Tongariro National Park, North Island, Danita Delimont Stock / AWL ©

THIS BOOK

This 18th edition of Lonely Planet's *New Zealand* guidebook was researched and written by Charles Rawlings-Way, Brett Atkinson, Sarah Bennett, Peter Dragicevich and Lee Slater. The 17th and 16th editions were researched by the same writers. This guidebook was produced by the following:

Destination Editor
Tasmin Waby

Product Editors
Elizabeth Jones, Tracy Whitmey

Senior Cartographer
Diana Von Holdt

Book Designer
Michael Buick

Assisting Editors
Imogen Bannister, Michelle Bennett, Nigel Chin, Gabrielle Innes, Jodie Martire, Kristin Odijk, Gabrielle Stefanos, Saralinda Turner

Assisting Cartographers
Hunor Csutoros, Corey Hutchison, Rachel Imeson

Cover Researcher
Naomi Parker

Thanks to Anita Banh, Jennifer Carey, David Carroll, Daniel Corbett, Ryan Evans, Andi Jones, Lauren Keith, Karyn Noble, Darren O'Connell, Mazzy Prinsep, Kirsten Rawlings, Diana Saengkham, Dianne Schallmeiner, Eleanor Simpson, Angela Tinson, Anna Tyler, Dora Whitaker

Index

Map Legend

Sights

- Beach
- Bird Sanctuary
- Buddhist
- Castle/Palace
- Christian
- Confucian
- Hindu
- Islamic
- Jain
- Jewish
- Monument
- Museum/Gallery/Historic Building
- Ruin
- Shinto
- Sikh
- Taoist
- Winery/Vineyard
- Zoo/Wildlife Sanctuary
- Other Sight

Activities, Courses & Tours

- Bodysurfing
- Diving
- Canoeing/Kayaking
- Course/Tour
- Sento Hot Baths/Onsen
- Skiing
- Snorkelling
- Surfing
- Swimming/Pool
- Walking
- Windsurfing
- Other Activity

Sleeping

- Sleeping
- Camping

Eating

- Eating

Drinking & Nightlife

- Drinking & Nightlife
- Cafe

Entertainment

- Entertainment

Shopping

- Shopping

Information

- Bank
- Embassy/Consulate
- Hospital/Medical
- Internet
- Police
- Post Office
- Telephone
- Toilet
- Tourist Information
- Other Information

Geographic

- Beach
- Gate
- Hut/Shelter
- Lighthouse
- Lookout
- Mountain/Volcano
- Oasis
- Park
- Pass
- Picnic Area
- Waterfall

Population

- Capital (National)
- Capital (State/Province)
- City/Large Town
- Town/Village

Transport

- Airport
- Border crossing
- Bus
- Cable car/Funicular
- Cycling
- Ferry
- Metro station
- Monorail
- Parking
- Petrol station
- Subway station
- Taxi
- Train station/Railway
- Tram
- Underground station
- Other Transport

Note: Not all symbols displayed above appear on the maps in this book

Routes

- Tollway
- Freeway
- Primary
- Secondary
- Tertiary
- Lane
- Unsealed road
- Road under construction
- Plaza/Mall
- Steps
- Tunnel
- Pedestrian overpass
- Walking Tour
- Walking Tour detour
- Path/Walking Trail

Boundaries

- International
- State/Province
- Disputed
- Regional/Suburb
- Marine Park
- Cliff
- Wall

Hydrography

- River, Creek
- Intermittent River
- Canal
- Water
- Dry/Salt/Intermittent Lake
- Reef

Areas

- Airport/Runway
- Beach/Desert
- Cemetery (Christian)
- Cemetery (Other)
- Glacier
- Mudflat
- Park/Forest
- Sight (Building)
- Sportsground
- Swamp/Mangrove

Peter Dragicevich

Auckland, Dunedin & Otago, Queenstown & Wanaka, Fiordland & Southland After nearly a decade working for off-shore publishing companies, Peter's life has come full circle, returning to his home city of Auckland. As Managing Editor of *Express* newspaper he spent much of the nineties writing about the local arts, club and bar scene. This is the 5th edition of the *New Zealand* guidebook to which he has contributed and, after dozens of Lonely Planet assignments, it remains his favourite gig.

Read more about Peter at:
http://auth.lonelyplanet.com/profiles/peterdragicevich

Contributing Writers

Professor James Belich wrote the History chapter. James is one of NZ's pre-eminent historians and the award-winning author of *The New Zealand Wars, Making Peoples* and *Paradise Reforged*. He has also worked in TV – *New Zealand Wars* was screened in NZ in 1998.

Tony Horwitz wrote the Captain James Cook boxed text in the History chapter. Tony is a Pulitzer-winning reporter and nonfiction author. His fascination with James Cook, and with travel, took him around NZ, Australia and the Pacific while researching *Blue Latitudes* (alternatively titled *Into the Blue*), part biography of Cook and part travelogue

John Huria (Ngai Tahu, Muaupoko) wrote the Māori Culture chapter. John has an editorial, research and writing background with a focus on Māori writing and culture. He was senior editor for Māori publishing company Huia and now runs an editorial and publishing services company Ahi Text Solutions Ltd (www.ahitextsolutions.co.nz).

Josh Kronfeld wrote the Surfing in New Zealand boxed text in the Extreme New Zealand chapter. Josh is an ex–All Black flanker, whose passion for surfing NZ's beaches is legendary and who found travelling for rugby a way to surf other great breaks around the world.

Gareth Shute wrote the Music section in the Arts & Music chapter. Gareth is the author of four books, including *Hip Hop Music in Aotearoa* and *NZ Rock 1987–2007*. He is also a musician and has toured the UK, Europe and Australia as a member of the Ruby Suns and the Brunettes. He now plays in indie soul group The Cosbys.

Vaughan Yarwood wrote the Environment chapter. Vaughan is an Auckland-based writer whose books include *The History Makers: Adventures in New Zealand Biography, The Best of New Zealand: A Collection of Essays on NZ Life and Culture by Prominent Kiwis*, which he edited, and the regional history *Between Coasts: From Kaipara to Kawau* He has written widely for NZ and international publications and is the former associate editor of *New Zealand Geographic*, for which he has also written for many years.

OUR STORY

A beat-up old car, a few dollars in the pocket and a sense of adventure. In 1972 that's all Tony and Maureen Wheeler needed for the trip of a lifetime – across Europe and Asia overland to Australia. It took several months, and at the end – broke but inspired – they sat at their kitchen table writing and stapling together their first travel guide, *Across Asia on the Cheap*. Within a week they'd sold 1500 copies. Lonely Planet was born.

Today, Lonely Planet has offices in Dublin, Franklin, London, Melbourne, Oakland, Beijing and Delhi, with more than 600 staff and writers. We share Tony's belief that 'a great guidebook should do three things: inform, educate and amuse'.

OUR WRITERS

Charles Rawlings-Way

Taranaki & Whanganui, East Coast (North Island), Wellington English by birth, Australian by chance, All Blacks fan by choice: Charles's early understanding of Aotearoa was less than comprehensive (sheep, mountains, sheep on mountains...). He realised there was more to it when a wandering uncle returned with a faux-jade tiki in 1981. He wore it with pride until he saw the NZ cricket team's beige uniforms in 1982... Mt Taranaki's snowy summit, Napier's art deco deliverance and Whanganui's raffish charm have helped him forgive: he's once again smitten with the country's phantasmal landscapes, disarming locals, and determination to sculpt its own political and indigenous destiny. Charles also wrote the Planning, Understand and Survival Guide chapters.

Brett Atkinson

Bay of Islands & Northland, Waikato & Coromandel Peninsula, Taupo & the Central Plateau, Rotorua & the Bay of Plenty Born in Rotorua, but now a proud resident of Auckland, Brett explored the top half of New Zealand's North Island for this edition. Excursions to Northland, the Coromandel Peninsula and Tongariro National Park echoed family holidays from an earlier century, and rediscovering his home town also evoked great memories. Brett's contributed to Lonely Planet guidebooks spanning Europe, Asia and the Pacific, and covered around 50 countries as a food and travel writer. See www.brett-atkinson.net for his latest adventures.

Sarah Bennett & Lee Slater

Marlborough & Nelson, West Coast (South Island), Christchurch & Canterbury Sarah and Lee specialise in NZ travel, with a particular focus on outdoor adventure including hiking, mountain biking and camping. In addition to five editions of the *New Zealand* guidebook, they are also co-authors of Lonely Planet's *Hiking & Tramping in New Zealand* and *New Zealand's Best Trips*. Read more at www.bennettandslater.co.nz. Sarah and Lee also wrote the Skiing & Snowboarding, Hiking and Extreme New Zealand chapters.

OVER PAGE MORE WRITERS

Published by Lonely Planet Global Limited
CRN 554153
18th edition – Sep 2016
ISBN 978 1 78657 024 6
© Lonely Planet 2016   Photographs © as indicated 2016
10 9 8 7 6 5 4 3 2 1
Printed in China